American Casebook Series
Hornbook Series and Basic Legal Texts
Black Letter Series and Nutshell Series

of

WEST PUBLISHING COMPANY
P.O. Box 64526
St. Paul, Minnesota 55164–0526

Accounting

FARIS' ACCOUNTING AND LAW IN A NUT-SHELL, 377 pages, 1984. Softcover. (Text)

FIFLIS' ACCOUNTING ISSUES FOR LAWYERS, TEACHING MATERIALS, , 706 pages, 1991. Teacher's Manual available. (Casebook)

SIEGEL AND SIEGEL'S ACCOUNTING AND FINANCIAL DISCLOSURE: A GUIDE TO BASIC CONCEPTS, 259 pages, 1983. Softcover. (Text)

Administrative Law

BONFIELD AND ASIMOW'S STATE AND FEDERAL ADMINISTRATIVE LAW, 826 pages, 1989. Teacher's Manual available. (Casebook)

GELLHORN AND LEVIN'S ADMINISTRATIVE LAW AND PROCESS IN A NUTSHELL, Third Edition, 479 pages, 1990. Softcover. (Text)

MASHAW AND MERRILL'S CASES AND MATERIALS ON ADMINISTRATIVE LAW—THE AMERICAN PUBLIC LAW SYSTEM, Second Edition, 976 pages, 1985. (Casebook) 1989 Supplement.

ROBINSON, GELLHORN AND BRUFF'S THE ADMINISTRATIVE PROCESS, Third Edition, 978 pages, 1986. (Casebook)

Admiralty

HEALY AND SHARPE'S CASES AND MATERIALS ON ADMIRALTY, Second Edition, 876 pages, 1986. (Casebook)

MARAIST'S ADMIRALTY IN A NUTSHELL, Second Edition, 379 pages, 1988. Softcover. (Text)

SCHOENBAUM'S HORNBOOK ON ADMIRALTY

AND MARITIME LAW, Student Edition, 692 pages, 1987 with 1989 pocket part. (Text)

Agency—Partnership

DEMOTT'S FIDUCIARY OBLIGATION, AGENCY AND PARTNERSHIP: DUTIES IN ONGOING BUSINESS RELATIONSHIPS, 740 pages, 1991. Teacher's Manual available. (Casebook)

FESSLER'S ALTERNATIVES TO INCORPORATION FOR PERSONS IN QUEST OF PROFIT, Third Edition, 339 pages, 1991. Softcover. (Casebook)

HENN'S CASES AND MATERIALS ON AGENCY, PARTNERSHIP AND OTHER UNINCORPORATED BUSINESS ENTERPRISES, Second Edition, 733 pages, 1985. Teacher's Manual available. (Casebook)

REUSCHLEIN AND GREGORY'S HORNBOOK ON THE LAW OF AGENCY AND PARTNERSHIP, Second Edition, 683 pages, 1990. (Text)

SELECTED CORPORATION AND PARTNERSHIP STATUTES, RULES AND FORMS. Softcover. 937 pages, 1991.

STEFFEN AND KERR'S CASES ON AGENCY-PARTNERSHIP, Fourth Edition, 859 pages, 1980. (Casebook)

STEFFEN'S AGENCY-PARTNERSHIP IN A NUTSHELL, 364 pages, 1977. Softcover. (Text)

Agricultural Law

MEYER, PEDERSEN, THORSON AND DAVIDSON'S AGRICULTURAL LAW: CASES AND MATERIALS, 931 pages, 1985. Teacher's Manual available. (Casebook)

Alternative Dispute Resolution

KANOWITZ' CASES AND MATERIALS ON ALTER-

Alternative Dispute Resolution—Cont'd

NATIVE DISPUTE RESOLUTION, 1024 pages, 1986. Teacher's Manual available. (Casebook) 1990 Supplement.

RISKIN AND WESTBROOK'S DISPUTE RESOLUTION AND LAWYERS, 468 pages, 1987. Teacher's Manual available. (Casebook)

RISKIN AND WESTBROOK'S DISPUTE RESOLUTION AND LAWYERS, Abridged Edition, 223 pages, 1987. Softcover. Teacher's Manual available. (Casebook)

American Indian Law

CANBY'S AMERICAN INDIAN LAW IN A NUTSHELL, Second Edition, 336 pages, 1988. Softcover. (Text)

GETCHES AND WILKINSON'S CASES AND MATERIALS ON FEDERAL INDIAN LAW, Second Edition, 880 pages, 1986. (Casebook)

Antitrust—see also Regulated Industries, Trade Regulation

FOX AND SULLIVAN'S CASES AND MATERIALS ON ANTITRUST, 935 pages, 1989. Teacher's Manual available. (Casebook)

GELLHORN'S ANTITRUST LAW AND ECONOMICS IN A NUTSHELL, Third Edition, 472 pages, 1986. Softcover. (Text)

HOVENKAMP'S BLACK LETTER ON ANTITRUST, 323 pages, 1986. Softcover. (Review)

HOVENKAMP'S HORNBOOK ON ECONOMICS AND FEDERAL ANTITRUST LAW, Student Edition, 414 pages, 1985. (Text)

POSNER AND EASTERBROOK'S CASES AND ECONOMIC NOTES ON ANTITRUST, Second Edition, 1077 pages, 1981. (Casebook) 1984–85 Supplement.

SULLIVAN'S HORNBOOK OF THE LAW OF ANTITRUST, 886 pages, 1977. (Text)

Appellate Advocacy—see Trial and Appellate Advocacy

Architecture and Engineering Law

SWEET'S LEGAL ASPECTS OF ARCHITECTURE, ENGINEERING AND THE CONSTRUCTION PROCESS, Fourth Edition, 889 pages, 1989. Teacher's Manual available. (Casebook)

Art Law

DUBOFF'S ART LAW IN A NUTSHELL, 335 pages, 1984. Softcover. (Text)

Banking Law

BANKING LAW: SELECTED STATUTES AND REGULATIONS. Softcover. 263 pages, 1991.

LOVETT'S BANKING AND FINANCIAL INSTITUTIONS LAW IN A NUTSHELL, Second Edition, 464 pages, 1988. Softcover. (Text)

SYMONS AND WHITE'S BANKING LAW: TEACHING MATERIALS, Third Edition, 818 pages, 1991. Teacher's Manual available. (Casebook)

Statutory Supplement. *See Banking Law: Selected Statutes*

Business Planning—see also Corporate Finance

PAINTER'S PROBLEMS AND MATERIALS IN BUSINESS PLANNING, Second Edition, 1008 pages, 1984. (Casebook) 1990 Supplement.

Statutory Supplement. *See Selected Corporation and Partnership*

Civil Procedure—see also Federal Jurisdiction and Procedure

AMERICAN BAR ASSOCIATION SECTION OF LITIGATION—READINGS ON ADVERSARIAL JUSTICE: THE AMERICAN APPROACH TO ADJUDICATION, 217 pages, 1988. Softcover. (Coursebook)

CLERMONT'S BLACK LETTER ON CIVIL PROCEDURE, Second Edition, 332 pages, 1988. Softcover. (Review)

COUND, FRIEDENTHAL, MILLER AND SEXTON'S CASES AND MATERIALS ON CIVIL PROCEDURE, Fifth Edition, 1284 pages, 1989. Teacher's Manual available. (Casebook)

COUND, FRIEDENTHAL, MILLER AND SEXTON'S CIVIL PROCEDURE SUPPLEMENT. 476 pages, 1991. Softcover. (Casebook Supplement)

FEDERAL RULES OF CIVIL PROCEDURE—EDUCATIONAL EDITION. Softcover. 816 pages, 1991.

FRIEDENTHAL, KANE AND MILLER'S HORNBOOK ON CIVIL PROCEDURE, 876 pages, 1985. (Text)

KANE AND LEVINE'S CIVIL PROCEDURE IN CALIFORNIA: STATE AND FEDERAL 543 pages, 1991. Softcover. (Casebook Supplement)

KANE'S CIVIL PROCEDURE IN A NUTSHELL, Third Edition, 303 pages, 1991. Softcover. (Text)

KOFFLER AND REPPY'S HORNBOOK ON COM-

Civil Procedure—Cont'd

MON LAW PLEADING, 663 pages, 1969. (Text)

LEVINE, SLOMANSON AND WINGATE'S CALIFORNIA CIVIL PROCEDURE, CASES AND MATERIALS, . 546 pages, 1991. (Casebook)

MARCUS, REDISH AND SHERMAN'S CIVIL PROCEDURE: A MODERN APPROACH, 1027 pages, 1989. Teacher's Manual available. (Casebook) 1991 Supplement.

MARCUS AND SHERMAN'S COMPLEX LITIGATION–CASES AND MATERIALS ON ADVANCED CIVIL PROCEDURE, 846 pages, 1985. Teacher's Manual available. (Casebook) 1989 Supplement.

PARK AND MCFARLAND'S COMPUTER-AIDED EXERCISES ON CIVIL PROCEDURE, Third Edition, 210 pages, 1991. Softcover. (Coursebook)

SIEGEL'S HORNBOOK ON NEW YORK PRACTICE, Second Edition, Student Edition, 1068 pages, 1991. Softcover. (Text)

Commercial Law

BAILEY AND HAGEDORN'S SECURED TRANSACTIONS IN A NUTSHELL, Third Edition, 390 pages, 1988. Softcover. (Text)

EPSTEIN, MARTIN, HENNING AND NICKLES' BASIC UNIFORM COMMERCIAL CODE TEACHING MATERIALS, Third Edition, 704 pages, 1988. Teacher's Manual available. (Casebook)

HENSON'S HORNBOOK ON SECURED TRANSACTIONS UNDER THE U.C.C., Second Edition, 504 pages, 1979, with 1979 pocket part. (Text)

MURRAY'S COMMERCIAL LAW, PROBLEMS AND MATERIALS, 366 pages, 1975. Teacher's Manual available. Softcover. (Coursebook)

NICKLES' BLACK LETTER ON COMMERCIAL PAPER, 450 pages, 1988. Softcover. (Review)

NICKLES, MATHESON AND DOLAN'S MATERIALS FOR UNDERSTANDING CREDIT AND PAYMENT SYSTEMS, 923 pages, 1987. Teacher's Manual available. (Casebook)

NORDSTROM, MURRAY AND CLOVIS' PROBLEMS AND MATERIALS ON SALES, 515 pages, 1982. (Casebook)

NORDSTROM, MURRAY AND CLOVIS' PROBLEMS AND MATERIALS ON SECURED TRANSACTIONS,

594 pages, 1987. (Casebook)

RUBIN AND COOTER'S THE PAYMENT SYSTEM: CASES, MATERIALS AND ISSUES, 885 pages, 1989. Teacher's Manual Available. (Casebook)

SELECTED COMMERCIAL STATUTES. Softcover. 1851 pages, 1991.

SPEIDEL'S BLACK LETTER ON SALES AND SALES FINANCING, 363 pages, 1984. Softcover. (Review)

SPEIDEL, SUMMERS AND WHITE'S COMMERCIAL LAW: TEACHING MATERIALS, Fourth Edition, 1448 pages, 1987. Teacher's Manual available. (Casebook)

SPEIDEL, SUMMERS AND WHITE'S COMMERCIAL PAPER: TEACHING MATERIALS, Fourth Edition, 578 pages, 1987. Reprint from Speidel et al., Commercial Law, Fourth Edition. Teacher's Manual available. (Casebook)

SPEIDEL, SUMMERS AND WHITE'S SALES: TEACHING MATERIALS, Fourth Edition, 804 pages, 1987. Reprint from Speidel et al., Commercial Law, Fourth Edition. Teacher's Manual available. (Casebook)

SPEIDEL, SUMMERS AND WHITE'S SECURED TRANSACTIONS: TEACHING MATERIALS, Fourth Edition, 485 pages, 1987. Reprint from Speidel et al., Commercial Law, Fourth Edition. Teacher's Manual available. (Casebook)

STOCKTON'S SALES IN A NUTSHELL, Second Edition, 370 pages, 1981. Softcover. (Text)

STONE'S UNIFORM COMMERCIAL CODE IN A NUTSHELL, Third Edition, 580 pages, 1989. Softcover. (Text)

WEBER AND SPEIDEL'S COMMERCIAL PAPER IN A NUTSHELL, Third Edition, 404 pages, 1982. Softcover. (Text)

WHITE AND SUMMERS' HORNBOOK ON THE UNIFORM COMMERCIAL CODE, Third Edition, Student Edition, 1386 pages, 1988. (Text)

Community Property

MENNELL AND BOYKOFF'S COMMUNITY PROPERTY IN A NUTSHELL, Second Edition, 432 pages, 1988. Softcover. (Text)

VERRALL AND BIRD'S CASES AND MATERIALS ON CALIFORNIA COMMUNITY PROPERTY, Fifth

Community Property—Cont'd

Edition, 604 pages, 1988. (Casebook)

Comparative Law

BARTON, GIBBS, LI AND MERRYMAN'S LAW IN RADICALLY DIFFERENT CULTURES, 960 pages, 1983. (Casebook)

GLENDON, GORDON AND OSAKWE'S COMPARATIVE LEGAL TRADITIONS: TEXT, MATERIALS AND CASES ON THE CIVIL LAW, COMMON LAW AND SOCIALIST LAW TRADITIONS, 1091 pages, 1985. (Casebook)

GLENDON, GORDON AND OSAKWE'S COMPARATIVE LEGAL TRADITIONS IN A NUTSHELL. 402 pages, 1982. Softcover. (Text)

Computers and Law

MAGGS, SOMA AND SPROWL'S COMPUTER LAW—CASES, COMMENTS, AND QUESTIONS, Approximately 725 pages, 1992. Teacher's Manual available. (Casebook)

MAGGS AND SPROWL'S COMPUTER APPLICATIONS IN THE LAW, 316 pages, 1987. (Coursebook)

MASON'S USING COMPUTERS IN THE LAW: AN INTRODUCTION AND PRACTICAL GUIDE, Second Edition, 288 pages, 1988. Softcover. (Coursebook)

Conflict of Laws

CRAMTON, CURRIE AND KAY'S CASES–COMMENTS–QUESTIONS ON CONFLICT OF LAWS, Fourth Edition, 876 pages, 1987. (Casebook)

HAY'S BLACK LETTER ON CONFLICT OF LAWS, 330 pages, 1989. Softcover. (Review)

SCOLES AND HAY'S HORNBOOK ON CONFLICT OF LAWS, Student Edition, approximately 1025 pages, 1992. (Text)

SIEGEL'S CONFLICTS IN A NUTSHELL, 470 pages, 1982. Softcover. (Text)

Constitutional Law—Civil Rights—see also First Amendment and Foreign Relations and National Security Law

ABERNATHY'S CIVIL RIGHTS AND CONSTITUTIONAL LITIGATION, CASES AND MATERIALS, Second Edition, approximately 750 pages, 1992. (Casebook)

BARRON AND DIENES' BLACK LETTER ON CONSTITUTIONAL LAW, Third Edition, 440 pages, 1991. Softcover. (Review)

BARRON AND DIENES' CONSTITUTIONAL LAW IN A NUTSHELL, Second Edition, 483 pages, 1991. Softcover. (Text)

ENGDAHL'S CONSTITUTIONAL FEDERALISM IN A NUTSHELL, Second Edition, 411 pages, 1987. Softcover. (Text)

FARBER AND SHERRY'S HISTORY OF THE AMERICAN CONSTITUTION, 458 pages, 1990. Softcover. Teacher's Manual available. (Text)

GARVEY AND ALEINIKOFF'S MODERN CONSTITUTIONAL THEORY: A READER, Second Edition, 559 pages, 1991. Softcover. (Reader)

LOCKHART, KAMISAR, CHOPER AND SHIFFRIN'S CONSTITUTIONAL LAW: CASES–COMMENTS–QUESTIONS, Seventh Edition, 1643 pages, 1991. (Casebook) 1991 Supplement.

LOCKHART, KAMISAR, CHOPER AND SHIFFRIN'S THE AMERICAN CONSTITUTION: CASES AND MATERIALS, Seventh Edition, approximately 1200 pages, 1991. Abridged version of Lockhart, et al., Constitutional Law: Cases–Comments–Questions, Seventh Edition. (Casebook) 1991 Supplement.

LOCKHART, KAMISAR, CHOPER AND SHIFFRIN'S CONSTITUTIONAL RIGHTS AND LIBERTIES: CASES AND MATERIALS, Seventh Edition, approximately 1375 pages, 1991. Reprint from Lockhart, et al., Constitutional Law: Cases–Comments–Questions, Seventh Edition. (Casebook) 1991 Supplement.

MARKS AND COOPER'S STATE CONSTITUTIONAL LAW IN A NUTSHELL, 329 pages, 1988. Softcover. (Text)

NOWAK AND ROTUNDA'S HORNBOOK ON CONSTITUTIONAL LAW, Fourth Edition, 1357 pages, 1991. (Text)

ROTUNDA'S MODERN CONSTITUTIONAL LAW: CASES AND NOTES, Third Edition, 1085 pages, 1989. (Casebook) 1991 Supplement.

VIEIRA'S CONSTITUTIONAL CIVIL RIGHTS IN A NUTSHELL, Second Edition, 322 pages, 1990. Softcover. (Text)

WILLIAMS' CONSTITUTIONAL ANALYSIS IN A NUTSHELL, 388 pages, 1979. Softcover. (Text)

Consumer Law—see also Commercial Law

EPSTEIN AND NICKLES' CONSUMER LAW IN A NUTSHELL, Second Edition, 418 pages, 1981. Softcover. (Text)

Consumer Law—Cont'd

SELECTED COMMERCIAL STATUTES. Softcover. 1851 pages, 1991.

SPANOGLE, ROHNER, PRIDGEN AND RASOR'S CASES AND MATERIALS ON CONSUMER LAW, Second Edition, 916 pages, 1991. Teacher's Manual available. (Casebook)

Contracts

CALAMARI AND PERILLO'S BLACK LETTER ON CONTRACTS, Second Edition, 462 pages, 1990. Softcover. (Review)

CALAMARI AND PERILLO'S HORNBOOK ON CONTRACTS, Third Edition, 1049 pages, 1987. (Text)

CALAMARI, PERILLO AND BENDER'S CASES AND PROBLEMS ON CONTRACTS, Second Edition, 905 pages, 1989. Teacher's Manual Available. (Casebook)

CORBIN'S TEXT ON CONTRACTS, One Volume Student Edition, 1224 pages, 1952. (Text)

FESSLER AND LOISEAUX'S CASES AND MATERIALS ON CONTRACTS—MORALITY, ECONOMICS AND THE MARKET PLACE, 837 pages, 1982. Teacher's Manual available. (Casebook)

FRIEDMAN'S CONTRACT REMEDIES IN A NUTSHELL, 323 pages, 1981. Softcover. (Text)

FULLER AND EISENBERG'S CASES ON BASIC CONTRACT LAW, Fifth Edition, 1037 pages, 1990. (Casebook)

HAMILTON, RAU AND WEINTRAUB'S CASES AND MATERIALS ON CONTRACTS, Second Edition, approximately 850 pages, May, 1992 Pub. (Casebook)

KEYES' GOVERNMENT CONTRACTS IN A NUTSHELL, Second Edition, 557 pages, 1990. Softcover. (Text)

SCHABER AND ROHWER'S CONTRACTS IN A NUTSHELL, Third Edition, 457 pages, 1990. Softcover. (Text)

SUMMERS AND HILLMAN'S CONTRACT AND RELATED OBLIGATION: THEORY, DOCTRINE AND PRACTICE, Second Edition, approximately 1100, March, 1992 Pub. Teacher's Manual available. (Casebook)

Copyright—see Patent and Copyright Law

Corporate Finance—see also Business Planning

HAMILTON'S CASES AND MATERIALS ON COR-PORATION FINANCE, Second Edition, 1221 pages, 1989. (Casebook)

OESTERLE'S THE LAW OF MERGERS, ACQUISITIONS AND REORGANIZATIONS, 1096 pages, 1991. (Casebook)

Corporations

HAMILTON'S BLACK LETTER ON CORPORATIONS, Second Edition, 513 pages, 1986. Softcover. (Review)

HAMILTON'S CASES AND MATERIALS ON CORPORATIONS—INCLUDING PARTNERSHIPS AND LIMITED PARTNERSHIPS, Fourth Edition, 1248 pages, 1990. Teacher's Manual available. (Casebook) 1990 Statutory Supplement.

HAMILTON'S THE LAW OF CORPORATIONS IN A NUTSHELL, Third Edition, 518 pages, 1991. Softcover. (Text)

HENN'S TEACHING MATERIALS ON THE LAW OF CORPORATIONS, Second Edition, 1204 pages, 1986. Teacher's Manual available. (Casebook)

Statutory Supplement. *See Selected Corporation and Partnership*

HENN AND ALEXANDER'S HORNBOOK ON LAWS OF CORPORATIONS, Third Edition, Student Edition, 1371 pages, 1983, with 1986 pocket part. (Text)

SELECTED CORPORATION AND PARTNERSHIP STATUTES, RULES AND FORMS. Softcover. 937 pages, 1991.

SOLOMON, SCHWARTZ AND BAUMAN'S MATERIALS AND PROBLEMS ON CORPORATIONS: LAW AND POLICY, Second Edition, 1391 pages, 1988. Teacher's Manual available. (Casebook) 1990 Supplement.

Statutory Supplement. *See Selected Corporation and Partnership*

Corrections

KRANTZ' THE LAW OF CORRECTIONS AND PRISONERS' RIGHTS IN A NUTSHELL, Third Edition, 407 pages, 1988. Softcover. (Text)

KRANTZ AND BRANHAM'S CASES AND MATERIALS ON THE LAW OF SENTENCING, CORRECTIONS AND PRISONERS' RIGHTS, Fourth Edition, 619 pages, 1991. Teacher's Manual available. (Casebook)

ROBBINS' CASES AND MATERIALS ON POST-CONVICTION REMEDIES, 506 pages, 1982.

Corrections—Cont'd
(Casebook)

Creditors' Rights

BANKRUPTCY CODE, RULES AND OFFICIAL FORMS, LAW SCHOOL EDITION. 909 pages, 1991. Softcover.

EPSTEIN'S DEBTOR-CREDITOR LAW IN A NUT-SHELL, Fourth Edition, 401 pages, 1991. Softcover. (Text)

EPSTEIN, LANDERS AND NICKLES' CASES AND MATERIALS ON DEBTORS AND CREDITORS, Third Edition, 1059 pages, 1987. Teacher's Manual available. (Casebook)

LOPUCKI'S PLAYER'S MANUAL FOR THE DEBTOR-CREDITOR GAME, 123 pages, 1985. Softcover. (Coursebook)

NICKLES AND EPSTEIN'S BLACK LETTER ON CREDITORS' RIGHTS AND BANKRUPTCY, 576 pages, 1989. (Review)

RIESENFELD'S CASES AND MATERIALS ON CREDITORS' REMEDIES AND DEBTORS' PROTECTION, Fourth Edition, 914 pages, 1987. (Casebook) 1990 Supplement.

WHITE'S CASES AND MATERIALS ON BANKRUPTCY AND CREDITORS' RIGHTS, 812 pages, 1985. Teacher's Manual available. (Casebook) 1987 Supplement.

Criminal Law and Criminal Procedure—see also Corrections, Juvenile Justice

ABRAMS' FEDERAL CRIMINAL LAW AND ITS ENFORCEMENT, 866 pages, 1986. (Casebook) 1988 Supplement.

AMERICAN CRIMINAL JUSTICE PROCESS: SELECTED RULES, STATUTES AND GUIDELINES. 723 pages, 1989. Softcover.

DIX AND SHARLOT'S CASES AND MATERIALS ON CRIMINAL LAW, Third Edition, 846 pages, 1987. (Casebook)

GRANO'S PROBLEMS IN CRIMINAL PROCEDURE, Second Edition, 176 pages, 1981. Teacher's Manual available. Softcover. (Coursebook)

HEYMANN AND KENETY'S THE MURDER TRIAL OF WILBUR JACKSON: A HOMICIDE IN THE FAMILY, Second Edition, 347 pages, 1985. (Coursebook)

ISRAEL, KAMISAR AND LaFAVE'S CRIMINAL PROCEDURE AND THE CONSTITUTION: LEADING SUPREME COURT CASES AND INTRODUCTORY TEXT. 767 pages, 1991 Edition. Softcover. (Casebook)

ISRAEL AND LaFAVE'S CRIMINAL PROCEDURE—CONSTITUTIONAL LIMITATIONS IN A NUTSHELL, Fourth Edition, 461 pages, 1988. Softcover. (Text)

JOHNSON'S CASES, MATERIALS AND TEXT ON CRIMINAL LAW, Fourth Edition, 759 pages, 1990. Teacher's Manual available. (Casebook)

JOHNSON'S CASES AND MATERIALS ON CRIMINAL PROCEDURE, 859 pages, 1988. (Casebook) 1991 Supplement.

KAMISAR, LaFAVE AND ISRAEL'S MODERN CRIMINAL PROCEDURE: CASES, COMMENTS AND QUESTIONS, Seventh Edition, 1593 pages, 1990. (Casebook) 1991 Supplement.

KAMISAR, LaFAVE AND ISRAEL'S BASIC CRIMINAL PROCEDURE: CASES, COMMENTS AND QUESTIONS, Seventh Edition, 792 pages, 1990. Softcover reprint from Kamisar, et al., Modern Criminal Procedure: Cases, Comments and Questions, Seventh Edition. (Casebook) 1991 Supplement.

LaFAVE'S MODERN CRIMINAL LAW: CASES, COMMENTS AND QUESTIONS, Second Edition, 903 pages, 1988. (Casebook)

LaFAVE AND ISRAEL'S HORNBOOK ON CRIMINAL PROCEDURE, Second Edition, approximately 1350 pages, 1992. (Text)

LaFAVE AND SCOTT'S HORNBOOK ON CRIMINAL LAW, Second Edition, 918 pages, 1986. (Text)

LOEWY'S CRIMINAL LAW IN A NUTSHELL, Second Edition, 321 pages, 1987. Softcover. (Text)

LOW'S BLACK LETTER ON CRIMINAL LAW, Revised First Edition, 443 pages, 1990. Softcover. (Review)

SALTZBURG AND CAPRA'S CASES AND COMMENTARY ON AMERICAN CRIMINAL PROCEDURE, Fourth Edition, approximately 1300 pages, May, 1992 Pub. Teacher's Manual available. (Casebook)

VORENBERG'S CASES ON CRIMINAL LAW AND PROCEDURE, Second Edition, 1088 pages, 1981. Teacher's Manual available. (Casebook) 1990 Supplement.

Domestic Relations

CLARK'S HORNBOOK ON DOMESTIC RELATIONS, Second Edition, Student Edition, 1050 pages, 1988. (Text)

CLARK AND GLOWINSKY'S CASES AND PROBLEMS ON DOMESTIC RELATIONS, Fourth Edition. 1150 pages, 1990. Teacher's Manual available. (Casebook)

KRAUSE'S BLACK LETTER ON FAMILY LAW, 314 pages, 1988. Softcover. (Review)

KRAUSE'S CASES, COMMENTS AND QUESTIONS ON FAMILY LAW, Third Edition, 1433 pages, 1990. (Casebook)

KRAUSE'S FAMILY LAW IN A NUTSHELL, Second Edition, 444 pages, 1986. Softcover. (Text)

KRAUSKOPF'S CASES ON PROPERTY DIVISION AT MARRIAGE DISSOLUTION, 250 pages, 1984. Softcover. (Casebook)

Economics, Law and—see also Antitrust, Regulated Industries

BARNES AND STOUT'S CASES AND MATERIALS ON LAW AND ECONOMICS, Approximately 550 pages, March, 1992 Pub. (Casebook)

GOETZ' CASES AND MATERIALS ON LAW AND ECONOMICS, 547 pages, 1984. (Casebook)

MALLOY'S LAW AND ECONOMICS: A COMPARATIVE APPROACH TO THEORY AND PRACTICE, 166 pages, 1990. Softcover. (Text)

Education Law

ALEXANDER AND ALEXANDER'S THE LAW OF SCHOOLS, STUDENTS AND TEACHERS IN A NUTSHELL, 409 pages, 1984. Softcover. (Text)

YUDOF, KIRP AND LEVIN'S EDUCATIONAL POLICY AND THE LAW, Third Edition, 860 pages, 1992. (Casebook)

Employment Discrimination—see also Gender Discrimination

ESTREICHER AND HARPER'S CASES AND MATERIALS ON THE LAW GOVERNING THE EMPLOYMENT RELATIONSHIP, 962 pages, 1990. Teacher's Manual available. (Casebook) Statutory Supplement. 1991 Supplement.

JONES, MURPHY AND BELTON'S CASES AND MATERIALS ON DISCRIMINATION IN EMPLOYMENT, (The Labor Law Group). Fifth Edition, 1116 pages, 1987. (Casebook) 1990 Supplement.

PLAYER'S FEDERAL LAW OF EMPLOYMENT DISCRIMINATION IN A NUTSHELL, Third Edition, approximately 270 pages, 1992. Softcover. (Text)

PLAYER'S HORNBOOK ON EMPLOYMENT DISCRIMINATION LAW, Student Edition, 708 pages, 1988. (Text)

PLAYER, SHOBEN AND LIEBERWITZ' CASES AND MATERIALS ON EMPLOYMENT DISCRIMINATION LAW, 827 pages, 1990. Teacher's Manual available. (Casebook)

Energy and Natural Resources Law—see also Oil and Gas

LAITOS' CASES AND MATERIALS ON NATURAL RESOURCES LAW, 938 pages, 1985. Teacher's Manual available. (Casebook)

LAITOS AND TOMAIN'S ENERGY AND NATURAL RESOURCES LAW IN A NUTSHELL, Approximately 525 pages, 1992. Softcover. (Text)

SELECTED ENVIRONMENTAL LAW STATUTES—EDUCATIONAL EDITION. Softcover. 1256 pages, 1991.

Environmental Law—see also Energy and Natural Resources Law; Sea, Law of

BONINE AND MCGARITY'S THE LAW OF ENVIRONMENTAL PROTECTION: CASES—LEGISLATION—POLICIES, Second Edition, approximately 1050 pages, 1992. (Casebook)

FINDLEY AND FARBER'S CASES AND MATERIALS ON ENVIRONMENTAL LAW, Third Edition, 763 pages, 1991. (Casebook)

FINDLEY AND FARBER'S ENVIRONMENTAL LAW IN A NUTSHELL, Third Edition, approximately 375 pages, February, 1992 Pub. Softcover. (Text)

PLATER, ABRAMS AND GOLDFARB'S ENVIRONMENTAL LAW AND POLICY: NATURE, LAW AND SOCIETY, Approximately 950 pages, 1992. Teacher's Manual available. (Casebook)

RODGERS' HORNBOOK ON ENVIRONMENTAL LAW, 956 pages, 1977, with 1984 pocket part. (Text)

SELECTED ENVIRONMENTAL LAW STATUTES—EDUCATIONAL EDITION. Softcover. 1256 pages, 1991.

Equity—see Remedies

Estate Planning—see also Trusts and Estates; Taxation—Estate and Gift

LYNN'S AN INTRODUCTION TO ESTATE PLANNING IN A NUTSHELL, Third Edition, 370 pages, 1983. Softcover. (Text)

Evidence

BROUN AND BLAKEY'S BLACK LETTER ON EVIDENCE, 269 pages, 1984. Softcover. (Review)

BROUN, MEISENHOLDER, STRONG AND MOSTELLER'S PROBLEMS IN EVIDENCE, Third Edition, 238 pages, 1988. Teacher's Manual available. Softcover. (Coursebook)

CLEARY, STRONG, BROUN AND MOSTELLER'S CASES AND MATERIALS ON EVIDENCE, Fourth Edition, 1060 pages, 1988. (Casebook)

FEDERAL RULES OF EVIDENCE FOR UNITED STATES COURTS AND MAGISTRATES. Softcover. 381 pages, 1990.

FRIEDMAN'S THE ELEMENTS OF EVIDENCE, 315 pages, 1991. Teacher's Manual available. (Coursebook)

GRAHAM'S FEDERAL RULES OF EVIDENCE IN A NUTSHELL, Third Edition, approximately 475 pages, 1992. Softcover. (Text)

LEMPERT AND SALTZBURG'S A MODERN APPROACH TO EVIDENCE: TEXT, PROBLEMS, TRANSCRIPTS AND CASES, Second Edition, 1232 pages, 1983. Teacher's Manual available. (Casebook)

LILLY'S AN INTRODUCTION TO THE LAW OF EVIDENCE, Second Edition, 585 pages, 1987. (Text)

McCORMICK, SUTTON AND WELLBORN'S CASES AND MATERIALS ON EVIDENCE, Sixth Edition, 1067 pages, 1987. (Casebook)

McCORMICK'S HORNBOOK ON EVIDENCE, Fourth Edition, Student Edition, approximately 1150 pages, March, 1992 Pub. (Text)

ROTHSTEIN'S EVIDENCE IN A NUTSHELL: STATE AND FEDERAL RULES, Second Edition, 514 pages, 1981. Softcover. (Text)

Federal Jurisdiction and Procedure

CURRIE'S CASES AND MATERIALS ON FEDERAL COURTS, Fourth Edition, 783 pages, 1990. (Casebook)

CURRIE'S FEDERAL JURISDICTION IN A NUTSHELL, Third Edition, 242 pages, 1990.

Softcover. (Text)

FEDERAL RULES OF CIVIL PROCEDURE—EDUCATIONAL EDITION. Softcover. 816 pages, 1991.

REDISH'S BLACK LETTER ON FEDERAL JURISDICTION, Second Edition, 234 pages, 1991. Softcover. (Review)

REDISH'S CASES, COMMENTS AND QUESTIONS ON FEDERAL COURTS, Second Edition, 1122 pages, 1989. (Casebook) 1990 Supplement.

VETRI AND MERRILL'S FEDERAL COURTS PROBLEMS AND MATERIALS, Second Edition, 232 pages, 1984. Softcover. (Coursebook)

WRIGHT'S HORNBOOK ON FEDERAL COURTS, Fourth Edition, Student Edition, 870 pages, 1983. (Text)

First Amendment

SHIFFRIN AND CHOPER'S FIRST AMENDMENT, CASES—COMMENTS—QUESTIONS, 759 pages, 1991. Softcover. (Casebook) 1991 Supplement.

Foreign Relations and National Security Law

FRANCK AND GLENNON'S FOREIGN RELATIONS AND NATIONAL SECURITY LAW, 941 pages, 1987. (Casebook)

Future Interests—see Trusts and Estates

Gender Discrimination—see also Employment Discrimination

KAY'S TEXT, CASES AND MATERIALS ON SEX-BASED DISCRIMINATION, Third Edition, 1001 pages, 1988. (Casebook) 1990 Supplement.

THOMAS' SEX DISCRIMINATION IN A NUTSHELL, Second Edition, 395 pages, 1991. Softcover. (Text)

Health Law—see Medicine, Law and

Human Rights—see International Law

Immigration Law

ALEINIKOFF AND MARTIN'S IMMIGRATION: PROCESS AND POLICY, Second Edition, 1056 pages, 1991. (Casebook)

    Statutory Supplement. *See Immigration and Nationality Laws*

IMMIGRATION AND NATIONALITY LAWS OF THE UNITED STATES: SELECTED STATUTES, REGULATIONS AND FORMS. Softcover. 477 pages,

Immigration Law—Cont'd
1991.

WEISSBRODT'S IMMIGRATION LAW AND PROCE-DURE IN A NUTSHELL, Second Edition, 438 pages, 1989, Softcover. (Text)

Indian Law—see American Indian Law

Insurance Law
DEVINE AND TERRY'S PROBLEMS IN INSUR-ANCE LAW, 240 pages, 1989. Softcover. Teacher's Manual available. (Coursebook)

DOBBYN'S INSURANCE LAW IN A NUTSHELL, Second Edition, 316 pages, 1989. Soft-cover. (Text)

KEETON'S CASES ON BASIC INSURANCE LAW, Second Edition, 1086 pages, 1977. Teach-er's Manual available. (Casebook)

KEETON'S COMPUTER-AIDED AND WORKBOOK EXERCISES ON INSURANCE LAW, 255 pages, 1990. Softcover. (Coursebook)

KEETON AND WIDISS' INSURANCE LAW, Stu-dent Edition, 1359 pages, 1988. (Text)

WIDISS AND KEETON'S COURSE SUPPLEMENT TO KEETON AND WIDISS' INSURANCE LAW, 502 pages, 1988. Softcover. Teacher's Manual available. (Casebook)

WIDISS' INSURANCE: MATERIALS ON FUNDA-MENTAL PRINCIPLES, LEGAL DOCTRINES AND REGULATORY ACTS, 1186 pages, 1989. Teacher's Manual available. (Casebook)

YORK AND WHELAN'S CASES, MATERIALS AND PROBLEMS ON GENERAL PRACTICE INSURANCE LAW, Second Edition, 787 pages, 1988. Teacher's Manual available. (Casebook)

International Law—see also Sea, Law of
BUERGENTHAL'S INTERNATIONAL HUMAN RIGHTS IN A NUTSHELL, 283 pages, 1988. Softcover. (Text)

BUERGENTHAL AND MAIER'S PUBLIC INTERNA-TIONAL LAW IN A NUTSHELL, Second Edition, 275 pages, 1990. Softcover. (Text)

FOLSOM'S EUROPEAN COMMUNITY LAW IN A NUTSHELL, Approximately 425 pages, 1992. Softcover. (Text)

FOLSOM, GORDON AND SPANOGLE'S INTERNA-TIONAL BUSINESS TRANSACTIONS—A PROB-LEM-ORIENTED COURSEBOOK, Second Edition, 1237 pages, 1991. Teacher's Manual available. (Casebook) 1991 Documents Supplement.

FOLSOM, GORDON AND SPANOGLE'S INTERNA-TIONAL BUSINESS TRANSACTIONS IN A NUT-SHELL, Third Edition, 509 pages, 1988. Softcover. (Text)

HENKIN, PUGH, SCHACHTER AND SMIT'S CASES AND MATERIALS ON INTERNATIONAL LAW, Second Edition, 1517 pages, 1987. (Casebook) Documents Supplement.

JACKSON AND DAVEY'S CASES, MATERIALS AND TEXT ON LEGAL PROBLEMS OF INTERNA-TIONAL ECONOMIC RELATIONS, Second Edi-tion, 1269 pages, 1986. (Casebook) 1989 Documents Supplement.

KIRGIS' INTERNATIONAL ORGANIZATIONS IN THEIR LEGAL SETTING, 1016 pages, 1977. Teacher's Manual available. (Casebook) 1981 Supplement.

WESTON, FALK AND D'AMATO'S INTERNATION-AL LAW AND WORLD ORDER—A PROBLEM-ORIENTED COURSEBOOK, Second Edition, 1335 pages, 1990. Teacher's Manual available. (Casebook) Documents Supple-ment.

Interviewing and Counseling
BINDER AND PRICE'S LEGAL INTERVIEWING AND COUNSELING, 232 pages, 1977. Softcover. Teacher's Manual available. (Coursebook)

BINDER, BERGMAN AND PRICE'S LAWYERS AS COUNSELORS: A CLIENT–CENTERED AP-PROACH, 427 pages, 1991. Softcover. (Coursebook)

SHAFFER AND ELKINS' LEGAL INTERVIEWING AND COUNSELING IN A NUTSHELL, Second Edition, 487 pages, 1987. Softcover. (Text)

Introduction to Law—see Legal Method and Legal System

Introduction to Law Study
HEGLAND'S INTRODUCTION TO THE STUDY AND PRACTICE OF LAW IN A NUTSHELL, 418 pages, 1983. Softcover. (Text)

KINYON'S INTRODUCTION TO LAW STUDY AND LAW EXAMINATIONS IN A NUTSHELL, 389 pages, 1971. Softcover. (Text)

Judicial Process—see Legal Method and Legal System

Jurisprudence

CHRISTIE'S JURISPRUDENCE—TEXT AND READINGS ON THE PHILOSOPHY OF LAW, 1056 pages, 1973. (Casebook)

Juvenile Justice

FOX'S JUVENILE COURTS IN A NUTSHELL, Third Edition, 291 pages, 1984. Softcover. (Text)

Labor and Employment Law—see also Employment Discrimination, Workers' Compensation

FINKIN, GOLDMAN AND SUMMERS' LEGAL PROTECTION OF INDIVIDUAL EMPLOYEES, (The Labor Law Group). 1164 pages, 1989. (Casebook)

GORMAN'S BASIC TEXT ON LABOR LAW—UNIONIZATION AND COLLECTIVE BARGAINING, 914 pages, 1976. (Text)

LESLIE'S LABOR LAW IN A NUTSHELL, Third Edition, approximately 400 pages, 1992. Softcover. (Text)

NOLAN'S LABOR ARBITRATION LAW AND PRACTICE IN A NUTSHELL, 358 pages, 1979. Softcover. (Text)

OBERER, HANSLOWE, ANDERSEN AND HEINSZ' CASES AND MATERIALS ON LABOR LAW—COLLECTIVE BARGAINING IN A FREE SOCIETY, Third Edition, 1163 pages, 1986. Teacher's Manual available. (Casebook) Statutory Supplement. 1991 Case Supplement.

RABIN, SILVERSTEIN AND SCHATZKI'S LABOR AND EMPLOYMENT LAW: PROBLEMS, CASES AND MATERIALS IN THE LAW OF WORK, (The Labor Law Group). 1014 pages, 1988. Teacher's Manual available. (Casebook) 1988 Statutory Supplement.

Land Finance—Property Security—see Real Estate Transactions

Land Use

CALLIES AND FREILICH'S CASES AND MATERIALS ON LAND USE, 1233 pages, 1986. (Casebook) 1991 Supplement.

HAGMAN AND JUERGENSMEYER'S HORNBOOK ON URBAN PLANNING AND LAND DEVELOPMENT CONTROL LAW, Second Edition, Student Edition, 680 pages, 1986. (Text)

WRIGHT AND GITELMAN'S CASES AND MATERIALS ON LAND USE, Fourth Edition, 1255 pages, 1991. Teacher's Manual available.

(Casebook)

WRIGHT AND WRIGHT'S LAND USE IN A NUTSHELL, Second Edition, 356 pages, 1985. Softcover. (Text)

Legal History—see also Legal Method and Legal System

PRESSER AND ZAINALDIN'S CASES AND MATERIALS ON LAW AND JURISPRUDENCE IN AMERICAN HISTORY, Second Edition, 1092 pages, 1989. Teacher's Manual available. (Casebook)

Legal Method and Legal System—see also Legal Research, Legal Writing

ALDISERT'S READINGS, MATERIALS AND CASES IN THE JUDICIAL PROCESS, 948 pages, 1976. (Casebook)

BERCH AND BERCH'S INTRODUCTION TO LEGAL METHOD AND PROCESS, 550 pages, 1985. Teacher's Manual available. (Casebook)

BODENHEIMER, OAKLEY AND LOVE'S READINGS AND CASES ON AN INTRODUCTION TO THE ANGLO-AMERICAN LEGAL SYSTEM, Second Edition, 166 pages, 1988. Softcover. (Casebook)

DAVIES AND LAWRY'S INSTITUTIONS AND METHODS OF THE LAW—INTRODUCTORY TEACHING MATERIALS, 547 pages, 1982. Teacher's Manual available. (Casebook)

DVORKIN, HIMMELSTEIN AND LESNICK'S BECOMING A LAWYER: A HUMANISTIC PERSPECTIVE ON LEGAL EDUCATION AND PROFESSIONALISM, 211 pages, 1981. Softcover. (Text)

KEETON'S JUDGING, 842 pages, 1990. Softcover. (Coursebook)

KELSO AND KELSO'S STUDYING LAW: AN INTRODUCTION, 587 pages, 1984. (Coursebook)

KEMPIN'S HISTORICAL INTRODUCTION TO ANGLO-AMERICAN LAW IN A NUTSHELL, Third Edition, 323 pages, 1990. Softcover. (Text)

MEADOR'S AMERICAN COURTS, 113 pages, 1991. Softcover. (Text)

REYNOLDS' JUDICIAL PROCESS IN A NUTSHELL, Second Edition, 308 pages, 1991. Softcover. (Text)

Legal Research

COHEN'S LEGAL RESEARCH IN A NUTSHELL, Fourth Edition, 452 pages, 1985. Soft-

Legal Research—Cont'd

cover. (Text)

COHEN, BERRING AND OLSON'S HOW TO FIND THE LAW, Ninth Edition, 716 pages, 1989. (Text)

COHEN, BERRING AND OLSON'S FINDING THE LAW, 570 pages, 1989. Softcover reprint from Cohen, Berring and Olson's How to Find the Law, Ninth Edition. (Coursebook)

Legal Research Exercises, 3rd Ed., for use with Cohen, Berring and Olson, 229 pages, 1989. Teacher's Manual available.

ROMBAUER'S LEGAL PROBLEM SOLVING—ANALYSIS, RESEARCH AND WRITING, Fifth Edition, 524 pages, 1991. Softcover. Teacher's Manual with problems available. (Coursebook)

STATSKY'S LEGAL RESEARCH AND WRITING, Third Edition, 257 pages, 1986. Softcover. (Coursebook)

TEPLY'S LEGAL RESEARCH AND CITATION, Third Edition, 472 pages, 1989. Softcover. (Coursebook)

Student Library Exercises, 3rd ed., 391 pages, 1989. Answer Key available.

Legal Writing and Drafting

CHILD'S DRAFTING LEGAL DOCUMENTS: PRINCIPLES AND PRACTICES, Second Edition, approximately 300 pages, April, 1992 Pub. Softcover. Teacher's Manual available. (Coursebook)

DICKERSON'S MATERIALS ON LEGAL DRAFTING, 425 pages, 1981. Teacher's Manual available. (Coursebook)

FELSENFELD AND SIEGEL'S WRITING CONTRACTS IN PLAIN ENGLISH, 290 pages, 1981. Softcover. (Text)

GOPEN'S WRITING FROM A LEGAL PERSPECTIVE, 225 pages, 1981. (Text)

MARTINEAU'S DRAFTING LEGISLATION AND RULES IN PLAIN ENGLISH, 155 pages, 1991. Softcover. Teacher's Manual available. (Text)

MELLINKOFF'S DICTIONARY OF AMERICAN LEGAL USAGE, Approximately 900 pages, March, 1992 Pub. (Text)

MELLINKOFF'S LEGAL WRITING—SENSE AND NONSENSE, 242 pages, 1982. Softcover. Teacher's Manual available. (Text)

PRATT'S LEGAL WRITING: A SYSTEMATIC APPROACH, 468 pages, 1990. Teacher's Manual available. (Coursebook)

RAY AND COX'S BEYOND THE BASICS: A TEXT FOR ADVANCED LEGAL WRITING, 427 pages, 1991. Softcover. Teacher's Manual available. (Text)

RAY AND RAMSFIELD'S LEGAL WRITING: GETTING IT RIGHT AND GETTING IT WRITTEN, 250 pages, 1987. Softcover. (Text)

SQUIRES AND ROMBAUER'S LEGAL WRITING IN A NUTSHELL, 294 pages, 1982. Softcover. (Text)

STATSKY AND WERNET'S CASE ANALYSIS AND FUNDAMENTALS OF LEGAL WRITING, Third Edition, 424 pages, 1989. Teacher's Manual available. (Text)

TEPLY'S LEGAL WRITING, ANALYSIS AND ORAL ARGUMENT, 576 pages, 1990. Softcover. Teacher's Manual available. (Coursebook)

WEIHOFEN'S LEGAL WRITING STYLE, Second Edition, 332 pages, 1980. (Text)

Legislation—see also Legal Writing and Drafting

DAVIES' LEGISLATIVE LAW AND PROCESS IN A NUTSHELL, Second Edition, 346 pages, 1986. Softcover. (Text)

ESKRIDGE AND FRICKEY'S CASES AND MATERIALS ON LEGISLATION: STATUTES AND THE CREATION OF PUBLIC POLICY, 937 pages, 1988. Teacher's Manual available. (Casebook) 1990 Supplement.

NUTTING AND DICKERSON'S CASES AND MATERIALS ON LEGISLATION, Fifth Edition, 744 pages, 1978. (Casebook)

STATSKY'S LEGISLATIVE ANALYSIS AND DRAFTING, Second Edition, 217 pages, 1984. Teacher's Manual available. (Text)

Local Government

FRUG'S CASES AND MATERIALS ON LOCAL GOVERNMENT LAW, 1005 pages, 1988. (Casebook) 1991 Supplement.

MCCARTHY'S LOCAL GOVERNMENT LAW IN A NUTSHELL, Third Edition, 435 pages, 1990. Softcover. (Text)

REYNOLDS' HORNBOOK ON LOCAL GOVERN-

Local Government—Cont'd

MENT LAW, 860 pages, 1982, with 1990 pocket part. (Text)

VALENTE AND MCCARTHY'S CASES AND MATERIALS ON LOCAL GOVERNMENT LAW, Fourth Edition, approximately 1150 pages, 1992. Teacher's Manual available. (Casebook)

Mass Communication Law

GILLMOR, BARRON, SIMON AND TERRY'S CASES AND COMMENT ON MASS COMMUNICATION LAW, Fifth Edition, 947 pages, 1990. (Casebook)

GINSBURG, BOTEIN AND DIRECTOR'S REGULATION OF THE ELECTRONIC MASS MEDIA: LAW AND POLICY FOR RADIO, TELEVISION, CABLE AND THE NEW VIDEO TECHNOLOGIES, Second Edition, 657 pages, 1991. (Casebook) Statutory Supplement.

ZUCKMAN, GAYNES, CARTER AND DEE'S MASS COMMUNICATIONS LAW IN A NUTSHELL, Third Edition, 538 pages, 1988. Softcover. (Text)

Medicine, Law and

FISCINA, BOUMIL, SHARPE AND HEAD'S MEDICAL LIABILITY, 487 pages, 1991. Teacher's Manual available. (Casebook)

FURROW, JOHNSON, JOST AND SCHWARTZ' HEALTH LAW: CASES, MATERIALS AND PROBLEMS, Second Edition, 1236 pages, 1991. Teacher's Manual available. (Casebook)

FURROW, JOHNSON, JOST AND SCHWARTZ' BIOETHICS: HEALTH CARE LAW AND ETHICS, Reprint from Furrow et al., Health Law, Second Edition. Softcover. Teacher's Manual available. (Casebook)

FURROW, JOHNSON, JOST AND SCHWARTZ' THE LAW OF HEALTH CARE ORGANIZATION AND FINANCE,Reprint from Furrow et al., Health Law, Second Edition. Softcover. Teacher's Manual available.

FURROW, JOHNSON, JOST AND SCHWARTZ' LIABILITY AND QUALITY ISSUES IN HEALTH CARE, Reprint from Furrow et al., Health Law, Second Edition. Softcover. Teacher's Manual available. (Casebook)

HALL AND ELLMAN'S HEALTH CARE LAW AND ETHICS IN A NUTSHELL, 401 pages, 1990. Softcover (Text)

JARVIS, CLOSEN, HERMANN AND LEONARD'S AIDS LAW IN A NUTSHELL, 349 pages, 1991. Softcover. (Text)

KING'S THE LAW OF MEDICAL MALPRACTICE IN A NUTSHELL, Second Edition, 342 pages, 1986. Softcover. (Text)

SHAPIRO AND SPECE'S CASES, MATERIALS AND PROBLEMS ON BIOETHICS AND LAW, 892 pages, 1981. (Casebook) 1991 Supplement.

Military Law

SHANOR AND TERRELL'S MILITARY LAW IN A NUTSHELL, 378 pages, 1980. Softcover. (Text)

Mortgages—see Real Estate Transactions

Natural Resources Law—see Energy and Natural Resources Law, Environmental Law

Negotiation

GIFFORD'S LEGAL NEGOTIATION: THEORY AND APPLICATIONS, 225 pages, 1989. Softcover. (Text)

TEPLY'S LEGAL NEGOTIATION IN A NUTSHELL, Approximately 250 pages, 1992. Softcover. (Text)

WILLIAMS' LEGAL NEGOTIATION AND SETTLEMENT, 207 pages, 1983. Softcover. Teacher's Manual available. (Coursebook)

Office Practice—see also Computers and Law, Interviewing and Counseling, Negotiation

HEGLAND'S TRIAL AND PRACTICE SKILLS IN A NUTSHELL, 346 pages, 1978. Softcover (Text)

MUNNEKE'S LAW PRACTICE MANAGEMENT: MATERIALS AND CASES, 634 pages, 1991. Teacher's Manual available. (Casebook)

Oil and Gas—see also Energy and Natural Resources Law

HEMINGWAY'S HORNBOOK ON THE LAW OF OIL AND GAS, Third Edition, Student Edition, approximately 700 pages, 1992. (Text)

KUNTZ, LOWE, ANDERSON AND SMITH'S CASES AND MATERIALS ON OIL AND GAS LAW, 857 pages, 1986. Teacher's Manual available. (Casebook) Forms Manual. Revised.

LOWE'S OIL AND GAS LAW IN A NUTSHELL,

Oil and Gas—Cont'd

Second Edition, 465 pages, 1988. Softcover. (Text)

Partnership—see Agency—Partnership

Patent and Copyright Law

CHOATE, FRANCIS AND COLLINS' CASES AND MATERIALS ON PATENT LAW, INCLUDING TRADE SECRETS, COPYRIGHTS, TRADEMARKS, Third Edition, 1009 pages, 1987. (Casebook)

HALPERN, SHIPLEY AND ABRAMS' CASES AND MATERIALS ON COPYRIGHT, Approximately 700 pages, April, 1992 Pub. (Casebook)

MILLER AND DAVIS' INTELLECTUAL PROPERTY—PATENTS, TRADEMARKS AND COPYRIGHT IN A NUTSHELL, Second Edition, 437 pages, 1990. Softcover. (Text)

NIMMER, MARCUS, MYERS AND NIMMER'S CASES AND MATERIALS ON COPYRIGHT AND OTHER ASPECTS OF ENTERTAINMENT LITIGATION—INCLUDING UNFAIR COMPETITION, DEFAMATION, PRIVACY, ILLUSTRATED, Fourth Edition, 1177 pages, 1991. (Casebook) Statutory Supplement. See *Selected Intellectual Property Statutes*

SELECTED INTELLECTUAL PROPERTY AND UNFAIR COMPETITION STATUTES, REGULATIONS AND TREATIES. Softcover.

Products Liability

FISCHER AND POWERS' CASES AND MATERIALS ON PRODUCTS LIABILITY, 685 pages, 1988. Teacher's Manual available. (Casebook)

PHILLIPS' PRODUCTS LIABILITY IN A NUTSHELL, Third Edition, 307 pages, 1988. Softcover. (Text)

Professional Responsibility

ARONSON, DEVINE AND FISCH'S PROBLEMS, CASES AND MATERIALS IN PROFESSIONAL RESPONSIBILITY, 745 pages, 1985. Teacher's Manual available. (Casebook)

ARONSON AND WECKSTEIN'S PROFESSIONAL RESPONSIBILITY IN A NUTSHELL, Second Edition, 514 pages, 1991. Softcover. (Text)

MELLINKOFF'S THE CONSCIENCE OF A LAWYER, 304 pages, 1973. (Text)

PIRSIG AND KIRWIN'S CASES AND MATERIALS ON PROFESSIONAL RESPONSIBILITY, Fourth Edition, 603 pages, 1984. Teacher's Manual available. (Casebook)

ROTUNDA'S BLACK LETTER ON PROFESSIONAL RESPONSIBILITY, Third Edition, approximately 400 pages, 1992. Softcover. (Review)

SCHWARTZ AND WYDICK'S PROBLEMS IN LEGAL ETHICS, Second Edition, 341 pages, 1988. (Coursebook)

SELECTED STATUTES, RULES AND STANDARDS ON THE LEGAL PROFESSION. Softcover. 844 pages, 1991.

SMITH AND MALLEN'S PREVENTING LEGAL MALPRACTICE, 264 pages, 1989. Reprint from Mallen and Smith's Legal Malpractice, Third Edition. (Text)

SUTTON AND DZIENKOWSKI'S CASES AND MATERIALS ON PROFESSIONAL RESPONSIBILITY FOR LAWYERS, 839 pages, 1989. Teacher's Manual available. (Casebook)

WOLFRAM'S HORNBOOK ON MODERN LEGAL ETHICS, Student Edition, 1120 pages, 1986. (Text)

Property—see also Real Estate Transactions, Land Use, Trusts and Estates

BERNHARDT'S BLACK LETTER ON PROPERTY, Second Edition, 388 pages, 1991. Softcover. (Review)

BERNHARDT'S REAL PROPERTY IN A NUTSHELL, Second Edition, 448 pages, 1981. Softcover. (Text)

BOYER, HOVENKAMP AND KURTZ' THE LAW OF PROPERTY, AN INTRODUCTORY SURVEY, Fourth Edition, 696 pages, 1991. (Text)

BROWDER, CUNNINGHAM, NELSON, STOEBUCK AND WHITMAN'S CASES ON BASIC PROPERTY LAW, Fifth Edition, 1386 pages, 1989. Teacher's Manual available. (Casebook)

BRUCE, ELY AND BOSTICK'S CASES AND MATERIALS ON MODERN PROPERTY LAW, Second Edition, 953 pages, 1989. Teacher's Manual available. (Casebook)

BURKE'S PERSONAL PROPERTY IN A NUTSHELL, 322 pages, 1983. Softcover. (Text)

CUNNINGHAM, STOEBUCK AND WHITMAN'S HORNBOOK ON THE LAW OF PROPERTY, Student Edition, 916 pages, 1984, with 1987 pocket part. (Text)

DONAHUE, KAUPER AND MARTIN'S CASES ON PROPERTY, Second Edition, 1362 pages,

Property—Cont'd

1983. Teacher's Manual available. (Casebook)

HILL'S LANDLORD AND TENANT LAW IN A NUTSHELL, Second Edition, 311 pages, 1986. Softcover. (Text)

JOHNSON, JOST, SALSICH AND SHAFFER'S PROPERTY LAW, CASES, MATERIALS AND PROBLEMS, Approximately 925 pages, April, 1992 Pub. (Casebook)

KURTZ AND HOVENKAMP'S CASES AND MATERIALS ON AMERICAN PROPERTY LAW, 1296 pages, 1987. Teacher's Manual available. (Casebook) 1991 Supplement.

MOYNIHAN'S INTRODUCTION TO REAL PROPERTY, Second Edition, 239 pages, 1988. (Text)

Psychiatry, Law and

REISNER AND SLOBOGIN'S LAW AND THE MENTAL HEALTH SYSTEM, CIVIL AND CRIMINAL ASPECTS, Second Edition, 1117 pages, 1990. (Casebook)

Real Estate Transactions

BRUCE'S REAL ESTATE FINANCE IN A NUTSHELL, Third Edition, 287 pages, 1991. Softcover. (Text)

MAXWELL, RIESENFELD, HETLAND AND WARREN'S CASES ON CALIFORNIA SECURITY TRANSACTIONS IN LAND, Fourth Edition, approximately 775 pages, 1992. (Casebook)

NELSON AND WHITMAN'S BLACK LETTER ON LAND TRANSACTIONS AND FINANCE, Second Edition, 466 pages, 1988. Softcover. (Review)

NELSON AND WHITMAN'S CASES ON REAL ESTATE TRANSFER, FINANCE AND DEVELOPMENT, Third Edition, 1184 pages, 1987. (Casebook)

NELSON AND WHITMAN'S HORNBOOK ON REAL ESTATE FINANCE LAW, Second Edition, 941 pages, 1985 with 1989 pocket part. (Text)

Regulated Industries—see also Mass Communication Law, Banking Law

GELLHORN AND PIERCE'S REGULATED INDUSTRIES IN A NUTSHELL, Second Edition, 389 pages, 1987. Softcover. (Text)

MORGAN, HARRISON AND VERKUIL'S CASES AND MATERIALS ON ECONOMIC REGULATION OF BUSINESS, Second Edition, 666 pages,

1985. (Casebook)

Remedies

DOBBS' HORNBOOK ON REMEDIES, 1067 pages, 1973. (Text)

DOBBS' PROBLEMS IN REMEDIES. 137 pages, 1974. Teacher's Manual available. Softcover. (Coursebook)

DOBBYN'S INJUNCTIONS IN A NUTSHELL, 264 pages, 1974. Softcover. (Text)

FRIEDMAN'S CONTRACT REMEDIES IN A NUTSHELL, 323 pages, 1981. Softcover. (Text)

LEAVELL, LOVE AND NELSON'S CASES AND MATERIALS ON EQUITABLE REMEDIES, RESTITUTION AND DAMAGES, Fourth Edition, 1111 pages, 1986. Teacher's Manual available. (Casebook)

O'CONNELL'S REMEDIES IN A NUTSHELL, Second Edition, 320 pages, 1985. Softcover. (Text)

SCHOENBROD, MACBETH, LEVINE AND JUNG'S CASES AND MATERIALS ON REMEDIES: PUBLIC AND PRIVATE, 848 pages, 1990. Teacher's Manual available. (Casebook)

YORK, BAUMAN AND RENDLEMAN'S CASES AND MATERIALS ON REMEDIES, Fifth Edition, approximately 1275 pages, 1992. (Casebook)

Sea, Law of

SOHN AND GUSTAFSON'S THE LAW OF THE SEA IN A NUTSHELL, 264 pages, 1984. Softcover. (Text)

Securities Regulation

HAZEN'S HORNBOOK ON THE LAW OF SECURITIES REGULATION, Second Edition, Student Edition, 1082 pages, 1990. (Text)

RATNER'S SECURITIES REGULATION IN A NUTSHELL, Third Edition, 316 pages, 1988. Softcover. (Text)

RATNER AND HAZEN'S SECURITIES REGULATION: CASES AND MATERIALS, Fourth Edition, 1062 pages, 1991. Teacher's Manual available. (Casebook) Problems and Sample Documents Supplement.

   Statutory Supplement. *See Securities Regulation, Selected Statutes*

SECURITIES REGULATION, SELECTED STATUTES, RULES, AND FORMS. Softcover. Approximately 1375 pages, 1992.

Sports Law

SCHUBERT, SMITH AND TRENTADUE'S SPORTS LAW, 395 pages, 1986. (Text)

Tax Practice and Procedure

GARBIS, RUBIN AND MORGAN'S CASES AND MATERIALS ON TAX PROCEDURE AND TAX FRAUD, Third Edition, approximately 925 pages, 1992. Teacher's Manual available. (Casebook)

MORGAN'S TAX PROCEDURE AND TAX FRAUD IN A NUTSHELL, 400 pages, 1990. Softcover. (Text)

Taxation—Corporate

KAHN AND GANN'S CORPORATE TAXATION, Third Edition, 980 pages, 1989. Teacher's Manual available. (Casebook) 1991 Supplement.

SCHWARZ AND LATHROPE'S BLACK LETTER ON CORPORATE AND PARTNERSHIP TAXATION, 537 pages, 1991. Softcover. (Review)

WEIDENBRUCH AND BURKE'S FEDERAL INCOME TAXATION OF CORPORATIONS AND STOCKHOLDERS IN A NUTSHELL, Third Edition, 309 pages, 1989. Softcover. (Text)

Taxation—Estate & Gift—see also Estate Planning, Trusts and Estates

MCNULTY'S FEDERAL ESTATE AND GIFT TAXATION IN A NUTSHELL, Fourth Edition, 496 pages, 1989. Softcover. (Text)

PEAT AND WILLBANKS' FEDERAL ESTATE AND GIFT TAXATION: AN ANALYSIS AND CRITIQUE, 265 pages, 1991. Softcover. (Text)

PENNELL'S CASES AND MATERIALS ON INCOME TAXATION OF TRUSTS, ESTATES, GRANTORS AND BENEFICIARIES, 460 pages, 1987. Teacher's Manual available. (Casebook)

Taxation—Individual

DODGE'S THE LOGIC OF TAX, 343 pages, 1989. Softcover. (Text)

GUNN AND WARD'S CASES, TEXT AND PROBLEMS ON FEDERAL INCOME TAXATION, Third Edition, approximately 850 pages, May, 1992 Pub. Teacher's Manual available. (Casebook)

HUDSON AND LIND'S BLACK LETTER ON FEDERAL INCOME TAXATION, Third Edition, 406 pages, 1990. Softcover. (Review)

KRAGEN AND MCNULTY'S CASES AND MATERIALS ON FEDERAL INCOME TAXATION—INDIVIDUALS, CORPORATIONS, PARTNERSHIPS, Fourth Edition, 1287 pages, 1985. (Casebook)

MCNULTY'S FEDERAL INCOME TAXATION OF INDIVIDUALS IN A NUTSHELL, Fourth Edition, 503 pages, 1988. Softcover. (Text)

POSIN'S HORNBOOK ON FEDERAL INCOME TAXATION, Student Edition, 491 pages, 1983, with 1989 pocket part. (Text)

ROSE AND CHOMMIE'S HORNBOOK ON FEDERAL INCOME TAXATION, Third Edition, 923 pages, 1988, with 1991 pocket part. (Text)

SELECTED FEDERAL TAXATION STATUTES AND REGULATIONS. Softcover. 1690 pages, 1992.

Taxation—International

DOERNBERG'S INTERNATIONAL TAXATION IN A NUTSHELL, 325 pages, 1989. Softcover. (Text)

KAPLAN'S FEDERAL TAXATION OF INTERNATIONAL TRANSACTIONS: PRINCIPLES, PLANNING AND POLICY, 635 pages, 1988. (Casebook)

Taxation—Partnership

BERGER AND WIEDENBECK'S CASES AND MATERIALS ON PARTNERSHIP TAXATION, 788 pages, 1989. Teacher's Manual available. (Casebook) 1991 Supplement.

BISHOP AND BROOKS' FEDERAL PARTNERSHIP TAXATION: A GUIDE TO THE LEADING CASES, STATUTES, AND REGULATIONS, 545 pages, 1990. Softcover. (Text)

BURKE'S FEDERAL INCOME TAXATION OF PARTNERSHIPS IN A NUTSHELL, Approximately 400 pages, February, 1992 Pub. Softcover. (Text)

SCHWARZ AND LATHROPE'S BLACK LETTER ON CORPORATE AND PARTNERSHIP TAXATION, 537 pages, 1991. Softcover. (Review)

Taxation—State & Local

GELFAND AND SALSICH'S STATE AND LOCAL TAXATION AND FINANCE IN A NUTSHELL, 309 pages, 1986. Softcover. (Text)

HELLERSTEIN AND HELLERSTEIN'S CASES AND MATERIALS ON STATE AND LOCAL TAXATION, Fifth Edition, 1071 pages, 1988. (Casebook)

Torts—see also Products Liability

CHRISTIE AND MEEKS' CASES AND MATERIALS ON THE LAW OF TORTS, Second Edition, 1264 pages, 1990. (Casebook)

DOBBS' TORTS AND COMPENSATION—PERSONAL ACCOUNTABILITY AND SOCIAL RESPONSIBILITY FOR INJURY, 955 pages, 1985. Teacher's Manual available. (Casebook) 1990 Supplement.

KEETON, KEETON, SARGENTICH AND STEINER'S CASES AND MATERIALS ON TORT AND ACCIDENT LAW, Second Edition, 1318 pages, 1989. (Casebook)

KIONKA'S BLACK LETTER ON TORTS, 339 pages, 1988. Softcover. (Review)

KIONKA'S TORTS IN A NUTSHELL, Second Edition, approximately 500 pages, March, 1992 Pub. Softcover. (Text)

MALONE'S TORTS IN A NUTSHELL: INJURIES TO FAMILY, SOCIAL AND TRADE RELATIONS, 358 pages, 1979. Softcover. (Text)

PROSSER AND KEETON'S HORNBOOK ON TORTS, Fifth Edition, Student Edition, 1286 pages, 1984 with 1988 pocket part. (Text)

ROBERTSON, POWERS AND ANDERSON'S CASES AND MATERIALS ON TORTS, 932 pages, 1989. Teacher's Manual available. (Casebook)

Trade Regulation—see also Antitrust, Regulated Industries

MCMANIS' UNFAIR TRADE PRACTICES IN A NUTSHELL, Second Edition, 464 pages, 1988. Softcover. (Text)

SCHECHTER'S BLACK LETTER ON UNFAIR TRADE PRACTICES, 272 pages, 1986. Softcover. (Review)

WESTON, MAGGS AND SCHECHTER'S UNFAIR TRADE PRACTICES AND CONSUMER PROTECTION, CASES AND COMMENTS, Fifth Edition, approximately 975 pages, 1992. Teacher's Manual available. (Casebook)

Trial and Appellate Advocacy—see also Civil Procedure

APPELLATE ADVOCACY, HANDBOOK OF, Second Edition, 182 pages, 1986. Softcover. (Text)

BERGMAN'S TRIAL ADVOCACY IN A NUTSHELL, Second Edition, 354 pages, 1989. Softcover. (Text)

BINDER AND BERGMAN'S FACT INVESTIGATION:

FROM HYPOTHESIS TO PROOF, 354 pages, 1984. Teacher's Manual available. (Coursebook)

CARLSON'S ADJUDICATION OF CRIMINAL JUSTICE: PROBLEMS AND REFERENCES, 130 pages, 1986. Softcover. (Casebook)

CARLSON AND IMWINKELRIED'S DYNAMICS OF TRIAL PRACTICE: PROBLEMS AND MATERIALS, 414 pages, 1989. Teacher's Manual available. (Coursebook) 1990 Supplement.

DESSEM'S PRETRIAL LITIGATION: LAW, POLICY AND PRACTICE, 608 pages, 1991. Softcover. Teacher's Manual available. (Coursebook)

DEVINE'S NON-JURY CASE FILES FOR TRIAL ADVOCACY, 258 pages, 1991. (Coursebook)

GOLDBERG'S THE FIRST TRIAL (WHERE DO I SIT? WHAT DO I SAY?) IN A NUTSHELL, 396 pages, 1982. Softcover. (Text)

HAYDOCK, HERR, AND STEMPEL'S FUNDAMENTALS OF PRE-TRIAL LITIGATION, Second Edition, approximately 700 pages, 1992. Softcover. Teacher's Manual available. (Coursebook)

HAYDOCK AND SONSTENG'S TRIAL: THEORIES, TACTICS, TECHNIQUES, 711 pages, 1991. Softcover. (Text)

HEGLAND'S TRIAL AND PRACTICE SKILLS IN A NUTSHELL, 346 pages, 1978. Softcover. (Text)

HORNSTEIN'S APPELLATE ADVOCACY IN A NUTSHELL, 325 pages, 1984. Softcover. (Text)

JEANS' HANDBOOK ON TRIAL ADVOCACY, Student Edition, 473 pages, 1975. Softcover. (Text)

LISNEK AND KAUFMAN'S DEPOSITIONS: PROCEDURE, STRATEGY AND TECHNIQUE, Law School and CLE Edition. 250 pages, 1990. Softcover. (Text)

MARTINEAU'S CASES AND MATERIALS ON APPELLATE PRACTICE AND PROCEDURE, 565 pages, 1987. (Casebook)

NOLAN'S CASES AND MATERIALS ON TRIAL PRACTICE, 518 pages, 1981. (Casebook)

SONSTENG, HAYDOCK AND BOYD'S THE TRIALBOOK: A TOTAL SYSTEM FOR PREPARATION AND PRESENTATION OF A CASE, 404 pages, 1984. Softcover. (Coursebook)

WHARTON, HAYDOCK AND SONSTENG'S CALI-

Trial and Appellate Advocacy—Cont'd

FORNIA CIVIL TRIALBOOK, Law School and CLE Edition. 148 pages, 1990. Softcover. (Text)

Trusts and Estates

ATKINSON'S HORNBOOK ON WILLS, Second Edition, 975 pages, 1953. (Text)

AVERILL'S UNIFORM PROBATE CODE IN A NUTSHELL, Second Edition, 454 pages, 1987. Softcover. (Text)

BOGERT'S HORNBOOK ON TRUSTS, Sixth Edition, Student Edition, 794 pages, 1987. (Text)

CLARK, LUSKY AND MURPHY'S CASES AND MATERIALS ON GRATUITOUS TRANSFERS, Third Edition, 970 pages, 1985. (Casebook)

DODGE'S WILLS, TRUSTS AND ESTATE PLANNING—LAW AND TAXATION, CASES AND MATERIALS, 665 pages, 1988. (Casebook)

MCGOVERN'S CASES AND MATERIALS ON WILLS, TRUSTS AND FUTURE INTERESTS: AN INTRODUCTION TO ESTATE PLANNING, 750 pages, 1983. (Casebook)

MCGOVERN, KURTZ AND REIN'S HORNBOOK ON WILLS, TRUSTS AND ESTATES—INCLUDING TAXATION AND FUTURE INTERESTS, 996 pages, 1988. (Text)

MENNELL'S WILLS AND TRUSTS IN A NUTSHELL, 392 pages, 1979. Softcover. (Text)

SIMES' HORNBOOK ON FUTURE INTERESTS, Second Edition, 355 pages, 1966. (Text)

TURANO AND RADIGAN'S HORNBOOK ON NEW YORK ESTATE ADMINISTRATION, 676 pages, 1986 with 1991 pocket part. (Text)

UNIFORM PROBATE CODE, OFFICIAL TEXT WITH COMMENTS. 839 pages, 1990. Softcover.

WAGGONER'S FUTURE INTERESTS IN A NUTSHELL, 361 pages, 1981. Softcover. (Text)

WATERBURY'S MATERIALS ON TRUSTS AND ESTATES, 1039 pages, 1986. Teacher's Manual available. (Casebook)

Water Law—see also Energy and Natural Resources Law, Environmental Law

GETCHES' WATER LAW IN A NUTSHELL, Second Edition, 459 pages, 1990. Softcover. (Text)

SAX, ABRAMS AND THOMPSON'S LEGAL CONTROL OF WATER RESOURCES: CASES AND MATERIALS, Second Edition, 987 pages, 1991. Teacher's Manual available. (Casebook)

TRELEASE AND GOULD'S CASES AND MATERIALS ON WATER LAW, Fourth Edition, 816 pages, 1986. (Casebook)

Wills—see Trusts and Estates

Workers' Compensation

HOOD, HARDY AND LEWIS' WORKERS' COMPENSATION AND EMPLOYEE PROTECTION LAWS IN A NUTSHELL, Second Edition, 361 pages, 1990. Softcover. (Text)

MALONE, PLANT AND LITTLE'S CASES ON WORKERS' COMPENSATION AND EMPLOYMENT RIGHTS, Second Edition, 951 pages, 1980. Teacher's Manual available. (Casebook)

[xviii]

PROPERTY LAW
CASES, MATERIALS AND PROBLEMS

By

Sandra H. Johnson
Professor of Law
Saint Louis University, School of Law

Timothy S. Jost
Professor of Law
Ohio State University, School of Law

Peter W. Salsich, Jr.
McDonnell Professor of Justice in American Society
Saint Louis University, School of Law

Thomas L. Shaffer
Robert E. & Marion D. Short Professor of Law
Notre Dame Law School

AMERICAN CASEBOOK SERIES ®

WEST PUBLISHING CO.
ST. PAUL, MINN., 1992

American Casebook Series, the key symbol appearing on the front cover and the WP symbol are registered trademarks of West Publishing Co. Registered in the U.S. Patent and Trademark Office.

COPYRIGHT © 1992 By WEST PUBLISHING CO.
610 Opperman Drive
P.O. Box 64526
St. Paul, MN 55164–0526

Library of Congress Cataloging-in-Publication Data

Property law : cases, materials, and problems / by Sandra H. Johnson
... [et al.].
      p.   cm. — (American casebook series)
   Includes index.
   ISBN 0–314–00340–1
   1. Property—United States—Cases. I. Johnson, Sandra H.
II. Series.
KF560.P74   1992
346.7304—dc20
[347.3064]   92–282
                                                        CIP

ISBN 0–314–00340–1

(J.J.S.& S.) Prop.Law ACB

To

Dean Rudolph C. Hasl

Arthur and Esther Jost

In memory of Professor William Dewey Rollison

In memory of Peter W. Salsich, Sr.

*

Preface

This book is designed for regular first year property law courses, whether they be one-semester, four-hour courses, or two-semester five-or-six hour courses. Basic doctrinal and policy issues respecting property are covered, although some topics are treated in greater detail than others. The topics are arranged in a rather standard order, reflecting the general consensus that possessory and ownership concepts should be mastered before exposure to the common law system of estates in land, the property transfer system, and the rules respecting private and public restrictions on use.

The major innovation of the book is an extensive integration of three related topics, not normally covered in "substantive" first year courses: 1) counseling and planning, 2) legal ethics, and 3) non-adversarial, as well as adversarial, approaches to dispute resolution.

Background material and exercises are provided to introduce students to the planning aspect of property law, including the counseling skill of evaluating the strengths and weaknesses of a range of alternative courses of action for acquiring and disposing of property, and the procedure for planning the process for resolving disputes, e.g., through leases, arrangements for homeowners' associations, co-operative and condominium boards, and collective approaches to land use covenants.

The first year property course provides an ideal vehicle for the introduction of students to ethical and moral issues facing lawyers. Decisions regarding acquisition or disposition of property have lasting consequences for a variety of reasons, including the long term nature of most property transactions, the fact that property transactions, particularly the purchase of a home, often represent the largest investment by a family, and the emphasis on private ownership of property in our legal system. Lawyers have struggled to describe their place in the process, but have had difficulty in doing so. Property transactions tend to produce the largest number of lawyer malpractice complaints, as well as potential for conflicts of interest because of dual representation of buyer and seller or parents and children. Such issues are explored throughout the book as the relevant legal doctrine is covered.

The inclusion of dispute resolution serves a number of purposes. It acquaints students, during their first year of law study, both with techniques of dispute resolution not ordinarily presented in the case-book method of law teaching, and with an expanded, more realistic view of the role of the lawyer outside of litigation. In addition, the students' consideration of dispute avoidance and dispute resolution can lead them to a more sophisticated tolerance for ambiguity in the law as they see the limits of rules in resolving disputes.

In many areas of property law, particularly the acquisition, development, and transfer of land, the lawyer's role is to guide individuals so that their goals can be achieved. In a system that relies so heavily on voluntary transactions, resort to litigation usually is an admission of failure to accomplish a desired result.

Property law presents few legal theories that allow for compromise of claims by the courts. There is no comparative negligence concept, no contributory negligence theory. In part, this is due to the subject matter of the dispute. Rarely are judges or juries in property cases allowed to play Solomon and divide the *res* between the parties. Ownership of property must be clear and undiluted in order to enhance its transferability and productivity. Physical division of property often destroys its value.

In considering how to resolve property disputes, students are exposed to the limits of rules on property relationships. Perhaps because of the doctrinal or rule-oriented nature of property law, students tend to believe that "punching the right buttons" will produce an answer to every property dispute. Problems and questions following the cases are designed to contradict this perception. For example, litigating adverse possession disputes over boundary lines in a residential neighborhood may produce a property winner, but destroy the neighborly relationship in the process.

Exercises in dispute resolution are included to introduce students to skills and methods of dispute resolution and also to reinforce property doctrine by application of that doctrine to the solution of particular problems. For example, landlord-tenant problems provide excellent vehicles for comparing adversarial (arbitration, litigation) techniques for resolving disputes with non-adversarial techniques (mediation, negotiation). Students generally have some familiarity with the emotional and physical settings of landlord-tenant disputes. Parties to a landlord-tenant dispute often desire to maintain their relationship of landlord and tenant after the dispute is resolved. The revolution in landlord-tenant law has changed dramatically the relative bargaining positions of landlord and tenant. Comparative exercises in arbitration and mediation can illustrate these points, as well as provide a useful means of reinforcing the process of learning the law.

The attorney-client relationship is explored in a number of settings, particularly in the acquisition and disposition of property. Questions concerning the lawyer's obligation to be loyal to her clients and to serve the public are raised. Opportunities are presented to discuss the relationship of morality to law, and the concept of law practice as a profession.

The book is shorter than many first year law books for a reason. We wanted the book to serve as a teaching resource rather than as a research tool or a law treatise. Our experience with first year classes persuades us that 10 to 15 pages per 50 minute class is about all that can realistically be covered because of the emphasis placed in the first year on the development of analytical skills. We have edited cases as much as possible and have oriented the notes toward teaching rather than research.

Brackets indicate that only a citation has been omitted. Deletions are noted by ellipses at the point of deletion and by centered ellipses where a paragraph or more has been omitted. Most footnotes have been omitted. Those that are retained have been renumbered consecutively by chapter.

Many people helped in the preparation of this book. A special note of appreciation is extended to the hundreds of students at Notre Dame, Ohio State and Saint Louis University who wrestled with earlier drafts of these chapters. They told us, in a forthright but caring manner, which cases and notes worked and which did not.

We would also like to thank the following colleagues and friends who offered suggestions, contributed problems and note ideas, and critiqued our efforts: Dean Frank Beytagh, Michael Braunstein, Jane C. Clarke, Patrice Cushman, Miranda Duncan, Barbara Fick, Barbara Glesner, Dean Rudolph Hasl, Dean David Link, Leonard Riskin, and Florence Roisman. Student research assistants Karen Biagi, Karen Coriell, Bruce Crowe, Thomas Dixon, Judith Fox, Elizabeth Healy, Kathleen Ives, Myron Maher, Philip Rothermich, Daniel Semmens, and Angela Standish made valuable contributions. Julie Hake, Stephanie Haley, Linda Harrington, Mary Ann Jauer, Jo Ann Mattler, Kathy Nachtweih, and Edward Shaffer responded to our many requests for help in the preparation of manuscript drafts.

We hope you will enjoy the study of Property law as much as we do. Property law is a fascinating blend of economics, history, philosophy, and politics. It mirrors society and the tensions between individuals and groups as we struggle to allocate fairly the resources of our planet and to provide opportunities for people to develop their individual talents and interests. Property law is about things, but more importantly, it is about people—with all their accomplishments, foibles, quirks, energy, and spirit.

S.H.J.
T.S.J.
P.W.S.
T.L.S.

March, 1992

*

Acknowledgements

Permission to reprint from the following material is gratefully acknowledged.

American Bar Association, Model Rules of Professional Conduct. Copyright © 1983 by the American Bar Association. All rights reserved. Permission to reprint granted by the American Bar Association.

American Land Title Association, Owner's Policy Form from the Understanding the ALTA Title Insurance Policy Forms Handbook. Reprinted with the permission of the American Land Title Association.

BAMSL Residential Real Estate Sale Contract. Reprinted with permission of The Bar Association of Metropolitan St. Louis. Copyright © 1990 Bar Association of Metropolitan St. Louis—All Rights Reserved.

Berger, Hard Leases Made Bad Law, Colum.L.Rev. Vol. 74 pp. 814–815 (1974). Copyright © 1974 by the Directors of the Columbia Law Review Association. All Rights Reserved. This article originally appeared at 74 Colum.L.Rev. 791 (1974). Reprinted by permission.

Blanchard and Meehan, Mediation from a Law Student Perspective. Reprinted by permission of the authors.

Boatmen's Residential Note and Mortgage Forms. Reprinted with permission of Boatman's National Bank.

Alexander A. Bove, Jr., The Boston Globe, May 19, 1988. Reprinted with permission of Mr. Bove.

Boyer, Hovenkamp and Kurtz, The Law of Property, Problem 4.8 (1991). Reprinted with permission of West Publishing Co.

Brokerage Listing Agreement. Reprinted by permission of the Columbus, Ohio, Board of Realtors.

Brown and Shaffer, Toward a Jurisprudence for the Law Office, 17 American Journal of Jurisprudence 125 (1972).

Clark, Condominium: A Reconciliation of Competing Interests? 18 Vanderbilt Law Review 1773 (1965). Reprinted with permission of the Vanderbilt Law Review.

R. Cunningham, W. Stoebuck & D. Whitman, The Law of Property, 357–359, 395–397 (1984). Reprinted by permission of West Publishing Company.

Dobris, Medicaid Asset Planning by the Elderly: A Policy View of Expectations, Entitlement and Inheritance, 24 Real Property, Probate and Trust Journal 1 (1989). Reprinted with permission of the American Bar Association.

Ellickson, Suburban Growth Controls: An Economic and Legal Analysis. Reprinted from The Yale Law Journal, Vol. 86, pp. 385, 490 (1977) by permission of the Yale Law Journal Company, Fred B. Rothman & Company and the author.

Epstein, Notice and Freedom of Contract in the Law of Servitudes, 55 S.Cal.L.Rev. 1353–1368 (1982), reprinted with the permission of the Southern California Law Review and the author.

Fletcher, "Courthouse Heirs," Va. Lawyers Weekly, July 25, 1988. Reprinted with permission of Paul E. Fletcher and Virginia Lawyers Weekly.

Frank, The Legal Ethics of Louis D. Brandeis, 17 Stanford Law Review 683 (1965). Copyright © 1965 by the Board of Trustees of the Leland Stanford Junior University. Reprinted with permission of Stanford Law Review and Fred B. Rothman & Co.

French, Servitudes Reform and the New Restatement of Property, 73 Cornell L.Rev. 928 (1988). Copyright © 1988 by Cornell University. All Rights Reserved. Reprinted by permission of the Cornell Law Review, Fred B. Rothman & Co. and the author.

L. Glantz, Mike Ahab problem. Reprinted with permission of Professor Leonard Glantz, Boston University.

Halper, Can You Find a Fair Lease? 14 Real Est.L.J. 99, 100–101, 121 (1985). Reprinted by permission of the Publisher from the Real Estate Law Journal, volume number 14, "Can You Find a Fair Lease?" © Warren, Gorham & Lamont 1985.

Johnstone, Land Transfers: Process and Processors, 22 Valparaiso University Law Review 493 (1988). Reprinted with the permission of Valparaiso University Law Review and the author.

Morgan, "The Evolving Concept of Professional Responsibility", 90 Harvard Law Review 702. Copyright © (1977) by the Harvard Law Review Association. Reprinted by permission of the Harvard Law Review Association and the author.

Moynihan, Introduction to the Law of Real Property 58–60, 65–71 (2d Ed.1988). Reprinted by permission of West Publishing Company.

G. Nelson & D. Whitman, Real Estate Finance Law 505–506, 534–538, 776–780 (2d Ed.1985). Reprinted by permission of West Publishing Company.

North Shore Woods Lease. Reprinted with permission of Joel Bullard, General Partner.

Note, Executive Right in a Mineral Estate is a Separate Interest in Real Property Subject to Property Law Principles: Day & Co. v. Texland Petroleum, Inc., 786 S.W.2d 667 (Tex.1990), 22 Texas Tech Law Review 281 (1991). Reprinted with permission of Kevin J. Croy and Texas Tech Law Review.

Off Campus Rental Agreement, University of Notre Dame (1988). Reprinted with permission of the University of Notre Dame.

O. Phipps, Titles in a Nutshell 216 (1968). Reprinted with permission of West Publishing Co.

Preble & Cartwright, Convertible and Shared Appreciation Loans: Unclogging The Equity of Redemption, originally published in: 20 Real Prop., Prob. & T.J. 821, 823–824 (1985). Reprinted by permission of the American Bar Association and the authors.

Probate, Trust and Real Property Section, Indiana State Bar, "Uniform Marital Property Act," Res Gestae, November, 1984, p. 237. Reprinted with permission of the Indiana State Bar Association.

Rait, Lollipop Condominiums: Air Rights, The Takings Clause, and Disclosure Under New York's New Guidelines, 17 Real Estate Law Journal 335, 337–340 (1989). Reprinted with permission of Warren, Gorham, & Lamont, Inc.

Reichman, Toward a Unified Concept of Servitudes, 55 S.Cal.L.Rev. 1177–1260 (1982), reprinted with the permission of the Southern California Law Review, and the author.

Restatement (Second) of Property §§ 5.4, 6.1 Comment (d), 450, 476, 535, 547. Copyright by the American Law Institute. Reprinted with the permission of the American Law Institute.

Restatement (Third) of Property (tentative drafts No. 1 & No. 2) §§ 2.4 Comment b, 2.6, Comment 4, 3.4, 3.5. Copyright by The American Law Institute. Reprinted with the permission of The American Law Institute.

Restatement (Second) of Torts, §§ 4.6, 821B Comment d, 821D, 826, 827, 828a. Copyright by The American Law Institute. Reprinted with the permission of The American Law Institute.

Riskin, Mediation and Lawyers, 43 Ohio State L.J. 29–30, 34–36 (1982). Originally published at 43 Ohio St.L.J. 29 (1982). Reprinted by permission of the Ohio State Law Journal and the author.

L. Riskin & J. Westbrook, Instructor's Manual, Dispute Resolution and Lawyers, 277–286, 398, 402–404, 544–556 (1987). Reprinted by permission of West Publishing Company.

L. Riskin & J. Westbrook, Dispute Resolution and Lawyers, 231–233 (1987). Reprinted by permission of West Publishing Company.

Salsich, Keystone Bituminous Coal, First English and Nollan: A Framework for Accommodation? 34 J.Urb. & Contemp.L. 173, 187–190 (1988).

Salsich and Fitzgerald, Mediation of Landlord-Tenant Disputes, 19 Creighton L.Rev. 791–95, 809–15 (1986). Reprinted from Creighton Law Review by permission. Copyright © 1986 by Creighton University School of Law.

Salsich, Land Use Regulation, 414–416, 541–543. Reprinted by permission of Shepard's/McGraw-Hill, Inc. (1991).

Shaffer, The Ethics of Estate Planning, Probate Notes, American College of Probate Counsel, Spring, 1979, p. 19. Reprinted with permission of The American College of Probate Counsel.

T. Shaffer, American Legal Ethics 453–455 (1985). Copyright © 1985 by Matthew Bender & Company, Inc. Reprinted with permission.

T. Shaffer and C. Mooney, The Planning and Drafting of Wills and Trusts 173–179 (3d ed. 1991). Reprinted with permission of the Foundation Press, Inc.

Sterk, "Freedom from Freedom of Contract," 70 Iowa L.Rev. 615 (1985) (reprinted with permission).

Marvin B. Sussman, Judith N. Cates, and David T. Smith, The Family and Inheritance, Ch. 6, "Conceptions of Justice: The Heirs" 121–145 (1970). Reprinted with permission of the Russell Sage Foundation.

Thompson, Crisis in Rural America: The Genesis of Farmer-Lender Mediation, Nat. Inst. for Dispute Rev., FORUM, p. 4 (Fall 1990).

Uniform Residential Landlord and Tenant Act, 7B Uniform Laws Annotated 460–461, 474–477 (1985). Reprinted by permission of West Publishing Company. This Act has been reprinted through the permission of the National Conference of Commissioners on Uniform State Laws, and copies of the Act may be ordered from them at a nominal cost at 676 North St. Clair Street, Suite 1700, Chicago, Illinois 60611, (312) 915–0195.

Uniform Vendor and Purchaser Risk Act. This Act has been reprinted through the permission of the National Conference of Commissioners on Uniform State Laws, and copies of the Act may be ordered from them at a nominal cost at 676 North St. Clair Street, Suite 1700, Chicago, Illinois 60611, (312) 915–0195.

Summary of Contents

Table of Contents

*

Table of Cases

The principal cases are in bold type. Cases cited or discussed in the text are roman type. References are to pages. Cases cited in principal cases and within other quoted materials are not included.

*

PROPERTY LAW
CASES, MATERIALS AND PROBLEMS

*

Chapter One

BASIC PROPERTY CONCEPTS: POSSESSION AND OWNERSHIP

I. WHO IS THE OWNER?

"How do things come to be owned? This is a fundamental puzzle for anyone who thinks about property. One buys things from other owners, to be sure, but how did the other owners get those things? Any chain of ownership or title must have a first link." Rose, Possession as the Origin of Property, 52 U.Chi.L.Rev. 73 (1985).

If you have been around children, you know that they often have an intense awareness of "ownership." They may be quite possessive of their belongings. It is not uncommon to overhear wails of "It's mine!" "No. It's mine!" How have you as a parent, a teacher, or simply as an adult desiring some peace and quiet resolved such disputes? If you believe the story of the child who is displeased with your decision, you simply chose the child you liked best. You may have chosen on the basis of merit, whatever that meant in the particular situation. Or you may have chosen the oldest or the youngest; or the most verbal; or the one who needed it the most; or the one who could make the best use of the desired object. You simply may have supervised the children in negotiating their own resolution.

Of course, questions over who owns a particular item of property frequently arise in the "grown up" world as well. University faculty members fight intensely over parking spaces. Two neighbors claim the same strip of land running between their homes or farms. Two people claim the same piece of jewelry, one because it was hers only until it was stolen, and the other because she paid good money for the jewelry from someone who seemed to own it. Someone finds a roll of $20 bills on the floor of a department store and now both he and the store claim the money. In this first section of materials, we examine cases in which courts have resolved disputes between two or more persons claiming the same thing using some form of the theory that "possession" is a legally recognized method of acquiring property.

1

"[The maxim of the common law is that] possession is the root of title. Merely to state the proposition is to raise two critical questions: what counts as possession, and why is it the basis for a claim to title. In exploring the quaint old cases' answers to these questions, we hit on some fundamental views about the nature and purposes of a property regime." *Rose,* supra.

A. DISCOVERY AND OCCUPANCY

JOHNSON AND GRAHAM'S LESSEE v. McINTOSH

United States Supreme Court, 1823.
21 U.S. (8 Wheat.) 543, 5 L.Ed. 681.

Mr. Chief Justice Marshall delivered the opinion of the Court.

[This was an action in ejectment, by which the plaintiff sought to recover possession of a large tract of the land north of the Ohio river in southern Illinois and Indiana. The plaintiff claimed the land through grants to predecessors in title from the Illinois and Piankeshaw (Wabash) Indians in 1773, several years after the conclusion of the French and Indian Wars. Because of the hostilities of the Revolutionary War and the War of 1812, plaintiff's predecessors never took possession of the land. The defendant received title to the land through a patent (grant) issued by the United States in 1818 as part of a program to reward veterans for their service in the military and to encourage settlement of the Northwest territory.]

* * * The facts, as stated in the case agreed, show the authority of the chiefs who executed this conveyance, so far as it could be given by their own people; and likewise show, that the particular tribes for whom these chiefs acted were in rightful possession of the land they sold. The inquiry, therefore, is, in a great measure, confined to the power of Indians to give, and of private individuals to receive, a title, which can be sustained in the courts of this country.

As the right of society to prescribe those rules by which property may be acquired and preserved is not, and cannot, be drawn into question; as the title to lands, especially, is, and must be, admitted, to depend entirely on the law of the nation in which they lie; it will be necessary, in pursuing this inquiry, to examine, not simply those principles of abstract justice, which the Creator of all things has impressed on the mind of his creature man, and which are admitted to regulate, in a great degree, the rights of civilized nations, whose perfect independence is acknowledged; but those principles also which our own government has adopted in the particular case, and given us as the rule for our decision.

On the discovery of this immense continent, the great nations of Europe were eager to appropriate to themselves so much of it as they could respectively acquire. Its vast extent offered an ample field to the ambition and enterprise of all; and the character and religion of its inhabitants afforded an apology for considering them as a people over whom the superior genius of Europe might claim an ascendency. The potentates of the old world found no difficulty in convincing themselves, that they made ample compensation to the inhabitants of the new, by bestowing on them civilization and Christianity, in exchange for unlimited independence. But as they were all in pursuit of nearly the same object, it was necessary, in order to avoid conflicting settlements, and consequent war with each other, to establish a principle, which all should acknowledge as the law by which the right of acquisition, which they all asserted, should be regulated, as between themselves. This principle was, that discovery gave title to the government by whose subjects, or by whose authority, it was made, against all other European governments, which title might be consummated by possession. The exclusion of all other Europeans, necessarily gave to the nation making the discovery the sole right of acquiring the soil from the natives, and establishing settlements upon it. It was a right with which no Europeans could interfere. It was a right which all asserted for themselves, and to the assertion of which, by others, all assented. Those relations which were to exist between the discoverer and the natives, were to be regulated by themselves. The rights thus acquired being exclusive, no other power could interpose between them.

In the establishment of these relations, the rights of the original inhabitants were, in no instance, entirely disregarded; but were, necessarily, to a considerable extent, impaired. They were admitted to be the rightful occupants of the soil, with a legal as well as just claim to retain possession of it, and to use it according to their own discretion; but their rights to complete sovereignty, as independent nations, were necessarily diminished, and their power to dispose of the soil, at their own will, to whomsoever they pleased, was denied by the original fundamental principle, that discovery gave exclusive title to those who made it. While the different nations of Europe respected the right of the natives, as occupants, they asserted the ultimate dominion to be in themselves; and claimed and exercised, as a consequence of this ultimate dominion, a power to grant the soil, while yet in possession of the natives. These grants have been understood by all, to convey a title to the grantees, subject only to the Indian right of occupancy.

The history of America, from its discovery to the present day, proves, we think, the universal recognition of these principles. Spain did not rest her title solely on the grant of the Pope. Her discussions respecting boundary, with France, with Great Britain, and with the United States, all show that she placed it on the rights given by discovery. Portugal sustained her claim to the Brazils by the same title. France, also, founded her title to the vast territories she claimed in America on discovery. However conciliatory her conduct to the natives may have been, she still asserted her right of dominion over a great extent of country, not actually settled by Frenchmen, and her exclusive right to acquire and dispose of the soil which remained in the occupation of Indians. Her monarch claimed all Canada and Acadie, as colonies of France, at a time when the French population was very inconsiderable, and the Indians occupied almost the whole country. He also claimed Louisiana, comprehending the immense territories watered by the Mississippi, and the rivers which empty into it, by the title of discovery. The letters-patent granted to the Sieur Demonts, in 1603, constitute him Lieutenant-General, and the representative of the king, in Acadie, which is described as stretching from the 40th to the 46th degree of north latitude; with authority to extend the power of the French over that country, and its inhabitants, to give laws to the people, to treat with the natives, and enforce the observance of treaties, and to parcel out, and give title to lands, according to his own judgment. The States of Holland also made acquisitions in America, and sustained their right on the common principle adopted by all Europe. * * * The claim of the Dutch was always contested by the English; not because they questioned the title given by discovery, but because they insisted on being themselves the rightful claimants under that title. Their pretensions were finally decided by the sword.

* * * Thus, all the nations of Europe, who have acquired territory on this continent, have asserted in themselves, and have recognised in others, the exclusive right of the discoverer to appropriate the lands occupied by the Indians. Have the American states rejected or adopted this principle?

By the treaty which concluded the war of our revolution, Great Britain relinquished all claim, not only to the government, but to the "propriety and territorial rights of the United States," whose boundaries were fixed in the second article. By this treaty, the powers of government, and the right to soil, which had previously been in Great Britain, passed definitively to these states. We had before taken possession of them, by declaring independence; but neither the declaration of independence, nor the treaty confirming it, could give us more than that which we before possessed, or to which Great Britain was before entitled. It has never been doubted, that either the United States, or the several states, had a clear title to all the lands within the boundary lines described in the treaty, subject only to the Indian right of occupancy, and that the exclusive power to extinguish that right, was vested in that government which might constitutionally exercise it.

* * *

The states, having within their chartered limits different portions of territory covered by Indians, ceded that territory, generally, to the United States, on conditions expressed in their deeds of cession, which demonstrate the opinion, that they ceded the soil as well as jurisdiction, and that in doing so, they granted a productive fund to the government of the Union. The lands in controversy lay within the chartered limits of Virginia, and were ceded with the whole country north-west of the river Ohio. This grant contained reservations and stipulations, which could only be made by the owners of the soil; and concluded with a stipulation, that "all the lands in the ceded territory, not reserved, should be considered as a common fund, for the use and benefit of such of the United States as have become, or shall become, members of the confederation," &c., "according to their usual respective proportions in the general charge and expenditure, and shall be faithfully and *bonâ fide* disposed of for that purpose, and for no other use or purpose whatsoever." The ceded territory was occupied by numerous and warlike tribes of Indians; but the exclusive right of the United States to extinguish their title, and to grant the soil, has never, we believe, been doubted.

* * *

The United States, then, have unequivocally acceded to that great and broad rule by which its civilized inhabitants now hold this country. They hold, and assert in themselves, the title by which it was acquired. They maintain, as all others have maintained, that discovery gave an exclusive right to extinguish the Indian title of occupancy, either by purchase or by conquest; and gave also a right to such a degree of sovereignty, as the circumstances of the people would allow them to exercise. The power now possessed by the government of the United States to grant lands, resided, while we were colonies, in the crown or its grantees. The validity of the titles given by either has never been questioned in our courts. It has been exercised uniformly over territory in possession of the Indians. The existence of this power must negative the existence of any right which may conflict with and control it. An absolute title to lands cannot exist, at the same time, in different persons, or in different governments. An absolute must be an exclusive title, or at least a title which excludes all others not compatible with it. All our institutions recognise the absolute title of the crown, subject only to the Indian right of occupancy, and recognise the absolute title of the crown to extinguish that right. This is incompatible with an absolute and complete title in the Indians.

We will not enter into the controversy, whether agriculturists, merchants and manufacturers, have a right, on abstract principles, to expel hunters from the territory they possess, or to contract their limits. Conquest gives a title which the courts of the conqueror cannot deny, whatever the private and speculative opinions of individuals may be, respecting the original justice of the claim which has been successfully asserted. * * *

Although we do not mean to engage in the defence of those principles which Europeans have applied to Indian title, they may, we think, find some excuse, if not justification, in the character and habits of the people whose rights have been wrested from them. The title by conquest is acquired and maintained by force. The conqueror prescribes its limits. Humanity, however, acting on public opinion, has established, as a general rule, that the conquered shall not be wantonly oppressed, and that their condition shall remain as eligible as is compatible with the objects of the conquest. Most usually, they are incorporated with the victorious nation, and become subjects or citizens of the government with which they are connected. The new and old members of the society mingle with each other; the distinction between them is gradually lost, and they make one people. Where this incorporation is practicable, humanity demands, and a wise policy requires, that the rights of the conquered to property should remain unimpaired; that the new subjects should be governed as equitably as the old, and that confidence in their security should gradually banish the painful sense of being separated from their ancient connections, and united by force to strangers. When the conquest is complete, and the conquered inhabitants can be blended with the conquerors, or safely governed as a distinct people, public opinion, which not even the conqueror can disregard, imposes these restraints upon him; and he cannot neglect them, without injury to his fame, and hazard to his power.

But the tribes of Indians inhabiting this country were fierce savages, whose occupation was war, and whose subsistence was drawn chiefly from the forest. To leave them in possession of their country, was to leave the country a wilderness; to govern them as a distinct people, was impossible, because they were as brave and as high-spirited as they were fierce, and were ready to repel by arms every attempt on their independence. What was the inevitable consequence of this state of things? The Europeans were under the necessity either of abandoning the country, and relinquishing their pompous claims to it, or of enforcing those claims by the sword, and by the adoption of principles adapted to the condition of a people with whom it was impossible to mix, and who could not be governed as a distinct society, or of remaining in their neighborhood, and exposing themselves and their families to the perpetual hazard of being massacred. Frequent and bloody wars, in which the whites were not always the aggressors, unavoidably ensued. European policy, numbers and skill prevailed; as the white population advanced, that of the Indians necessarily receded; the country in the immediate neighborhood of agriculturists became unfit for them; the game fled into thicker and more unbroken forests, and the Indians followed. The soil, to which the crown originally claimed title, being no longer occupied by its ancient inhabitants, was parcelled out according to the will of the sovereign power, and taken possession of by persons who claimed immediately from the crown, or mediately, through its grantees or deputies.

That law which regulates, and ought to regulate in general, the relations between the conqueror and conquered, was incapable of application to a people under such circumstances. The resort to some new and different rule, better adapted to the actual state of things, was unavoidable. Every rule which can be suggested will be found to be attended with great difficulty. However extravagant the pretension of converting the discovery of an inhabited country into conquest may appear; if the principle has been asserted in the first instance, and afterwards sustained; if a country has been acquired and held under it; if the property of the great mass of the community originates in it, it becomes the law of the land, and cannot be questioned. So too, with respect to the concomitant principle, that the Indian inhabitants are to be considered merely as occupants, to be protected, indeed, while in peace, in the possession of their lands, but to be deemed incapable of transferring the absolute title to others. However this restriction may be opposed to natural right, and to the usages of civilized nations, yet, if it be indispensable to that system under which the country has been settled, and be adapted to the actual condition of the two people, it may, perhaps, be supported by reason, and certainly cannot be rejected by courts of justice.

* * *

Another view has been taken of this question, which deserves to be considered. The title of the crown, whatever it might be, could be acquired only by a conveyance from the crown. If an individual might extinguish the Indian title, for his own benefit, or, in other words, might purchase it, still he could acquire only that title. Admitting their power to change their laws or usages, so far as to allow an individual to separate a portion of their lands from the common stock, and hold it in severalty, still it is a part of their territory, and is held under them, by a title dependent on their laws. The grant derives its efficacy from their will; and, if they choose to resume it, and make a different disposition of the land, the court of the United States cannot interpose for the protection of the title. The person who purchases lands from the Indians, within their territory, incorporates himself with them, so far as respects the property purchased; holds their title under their protection, and subject to their laws. If they annul the grant, we know of no tribunal which can revise and set aside the proceeding. We know of no principle which can distinguish this case from a grant made to a native Indian, authorizing him to hold a particular tract of land in severalty. As such a grant could not separate the Indian from his nation, nor give a title which our courts could distinguish from the title of his tribe, as it might still be conquered from, or ceded by his tribe, we can perceive no legal principle which will authorize a court to say, that different consequences are attached to this purchase, because it was made by a stranger. By the treaties concluded between the United States and the Indian nations, whose title the plaintiffs claim, the country comprehending the lands in controversy has been ceded to the United States, without any reservation of their title. These nations had been at war with the United States, and had an unquestionable right to annul any grant they had made to American citizens. Their cession of the country, without a reservation of this land, affords a fair presumption, that they considered it as of no validity. They ceded to the United States this very property, after having used it in common with other lands, as their own, from the date of their deeds to the time of cession; and the attempt now made, is to set up their title against that of the United States.

The proclamation issued by the king of Great Britain, in 1763, has been considered, and we think, with reason, as constituting an additional objection to the title of the plaintiffs. By that proclamation, the crown reserved under its own dominion and protection, for the use of the Indians, "all the land and territories lying to the westward of the sources of the rivers which fall into the sea from the west and north-west," and strictly forbade all British subjects from making any pur-chases or settlements whatever, or taking possession of the reserved lands. * * * It is supposed to be a principle of universal law, that, if an uninhabited country be discovered by a number of individuals, who acknowledge no connection with, and owe no allegiance to, any govern-ment whatever, the country becomes the property of the discoverers, so far at least as they can use it. They acquire a title in common. The title of the whole land is in the whole society. It is to be divided and parcelled out according to the will of the society, expressed by the whole body, or by that organ which is authorized by the whole to express it. If the discovery be made, and possession of the country be taken, under the authority of an existing government, which is ac-knowledged by the emigrants, it is supposed to be equally well settled, that the discovery is made for the whole nation, that the country becomes a part of the nation, and that the vacant soil is to be disposed of by that organ of the government which has the constitutional power to dispose of the national domains, by that organ in which all vacant territory is vested by law.

* * * So far as respected the authority of the crown, no distinction was taken between vacant lands and lands occupied by the Indians. The title, subject only to the right of occupancy by the Indians, was admitted to be in the king, as was his right to grant that title. The lands, then, to which this proclamation referred, were lands which the king had a right to grant, or to reserve for the Indians.

* * *

Much reliance is also placed on the fact, that many tracts are now held in the United States, under the Indian title, the validity of which is not questioned. Before the importance attached to this fact is conceded, the circumstances under which such grants were obtained, and such titles are supported, ought to be considered. These lands lie chiefly in the eastern states. It is known that the Plymouth Company made many extensive grants, which, from their ignorance of the coun-try, interfered with each other. It is also known, that Mason, to whom New Hampshire, and Gorges, to whom Maine was granted, found great difficulty in managing such unwieldy property. The country was settled by emigrants, some from Europe, but chiefly from Massachu-setts, who took possession of lands they found unoccupied, and secured themselves in that possession by the best means in their power. The disturbances in England, and the civil war and revolution which fol-lowed those disturbances, prevented any interference on the part of the mother country, and the proprietors were unable to maintain their title. In the meantime, Massachusetts claimed the country and gov-erned it. As her claim was adversary to that of the proprietors, she encouraged the settlement of persons made under her authority, and encouraged, likewise, their securing themselves in possession, by purchasing the acquiescence and forbearance of the Indians.

After the restoration of Charles II., Gorges and Mason, when they attempted to establish their title, found themselves opposed by men, who held under Massachusetts, and under the Indians. The title of the proprietors was resisted; and though, in some cases compromises were made, and in some, the opinion of a court was given ultimately in their favor, the juries found uniformly against them. They became wearied with the struggle, and sold their property. The titles held under the Indians, were sanctioned by length of possession; but there is no case, so far as we are informed, of a judicial decision in their favor.

* * *

It has never been contended, that the Indian title amounted to nothing. Their right of possession has never been questioned. The claim of government extends to the complete ultimate title, charged with this right of possession, and to the exclusive power of acquiring that right. The object of the crown was, to settle the sea-coast of America; and when a portion of it was settled, without violating the rights of others, by persons professing their loyalty, and soliciting the royal sanction of an act, the consequences of which were ascertained to be beneficial, it would have been as unwise as ungracious, to expel them from their habitations, because they had obtained the Indian title, otherwise than through the agency of government. The very grant of a charter is an assertion of the title of the crown, and its words convey the same idea. * * *

[The] charter, and [the] letter [to Rhode Island], certainly sanction a previous unauthorized purchase from Indians, under the circumstances attending that particular purchase, but are far from supporting the general proposition, that a title acquired from the Indians would be valid against a title acquired from the crown, or without the confirmation of the crown.

The acts of the several colonial assemblies, prohibiting purchases from the Indians, have also been relied on, as proving, that, independent of such prohibitions, Indian deeds would be valid. But, we think, this fact, at most, equivocal. While the existence of such purchases would justify their prohibition, even by colonies which considered Indian deeds as previously invalid, the fact that such acts have been generally passed, is strong evidence of the general opinion, that such purchases are opposed by the soundest principles of wisdom and national policy.

After bestowing on this subject a degree of attention which was more required by the magnitude of the interest in litigation, and the able and elaborate arguments of the bar, than by its intrinsic difficulty, the court is decidedly of opinion, that the plaintiffs do not exhibit a title which can be sustained in the courts of the United States; and that there is no error in the judgment which was rendered against them in the district court of Illinois.

Judgment affirmed, with costs.

Notes and Questions

1. The plaintiffs Joshua Johnson and Thomas Graham claimed the disputed land as devisees under the will of Thomas Johnson, one of the original grantees in a 1775 conveyance from the Indian tribes. Thomas Johnson died in 1819. Why was the Indians' right to transfer relevant nearly fifty years after the original conveyance?

2. How did Justice Marshall frame the issue of the case? What alternatives exist? Can this case be reconciled with Rose's statement at the beginning of the case that "possession is the root of title" in our common-law system? Is this a case about what "counts" as possession?

3. According to Marshall, what acts of the European settlers gained for them property rights in the land claimed by the Indians? What did the property rights gained by the Europeans entitle them to do in relation to the land? Did the Indians have any property rights remaining? What was the source and nature of those rights?

Can it be said that two or more people can hold property interests in the same piece of land at the same time? One of the characteristics of the modern Anglo–American concept of property is that property can be divided into numerous separate interests on several levels of abstraction, including space, time, and function. The trust concept, discussed in greater detail in Chapter Two, is one example of this conceptualization. In a trust, the managerial rights and responsibilities associated with property are separated from the rights to enjoy the fruits of the property. The manager (trustee) has strict obligations (a fiduciary responsibility) to account to the beneficiary of the trust.

4. Note the name of the procedural approach to this dispute—an action in ejectment. Note also the reference to a landlord-tenant relationship in the title of the case, i.e., Graham's Lessee. Ejectment is one of the old common-law forms of action that was used to determine who had the right to possess land. It developed from the early days of landlord-tenant law and was borrowed from that branch of property law by lawyers who represented clients that were asserting ownership interests to land. Because of its origin in landlord-tenant law and a peculiar tendency of common-law judges and lawyers to reform the law through indirect methods such as legal fictions, the ejectment action came to require an allegation that a landlord-tenant relationship existed and that the tenant (lessee) wrongfully had been deprived of possession. Ejectment is still available, but it is a cumbersome procedure that is not used very often. It has been replaced in most jurisdictions by summary-possession actions such as unlawful detainer, discussed in Chapter Four.

5. *Johnson v. McIntosh* may illustrate competing views of the nature and source of property ownership. The following excerpts elaborate on that question.

John Quincy Adams, Oration at the Anniversary of the Sons of the Pilgrims (December 22, 1802):

There are moralists who have questioned the right of Europeans to intrude upon the possessions of the aborigines in any case and under any limitations whatsoever. But have they maturely considered the whole subject? The Indian right of possession itself stands, with regard to the greatest part of the country, upon a questionable foundation. Their cultivated fields, their constructed habitations, a space of ample sufficiency for their subsistence, and whatever they had annexed to themselves by personal labor, was undoubtedly by the laws of nature theirs. But what is the right of a huntsman to the forest of a thousand miles over which he has accidentally ranged in quest of prey? Shall the liberal bounties of Providence to the race of man be monopolized by one of ten thousand for whom they were created? * * * Shall he forbid the wilderness to blossom like the rose? Shall he forbid the oaks of the forest to fall before the ax of industry and rise again transformed into the habitations of ease and elegance? * * * Shall the mighty rivers, poured out by the hands of nature as channels of communication between numerous nations, roll their waters in sullen silence and eternal solitude to the deep? Have hundreds of commodious harbors, a thousand leagues of coast, and a boundless ocean been spread in the front of this land, and shall every purpose of utility to which they could be applied be prohibited by the tenant of the woods? No, generous philanthropists!

Chief Sealth of the Duwanish Indians in Washington State in a letter to President Franklin Pierce responding to the President's expression of interest in buying the tribe's land:

The Great Chief in Washington sends word that he wishes to buy our land. How can you buy or sell the sky—the warmth of the land? The idea is strange to us. Yet we do not own the freshness of the air or the sparkle of the water. How can you buy them from us? Every part of this earth is sacred to my people. * * *

We know that white man does not understand our ways. One portion of the land is the same to him as the next, for he is a stranger who comes in the night and takes from the land whatever he needs. The earth is not his brother but his enemy, and when he has conquered it he moves on. * * *

There is no quiet place in the white man's cities. No place to hear the leaves of spring or the rustle of insect wings. But perhaps because I am savage and do not understand—the clatter only seems to insult the ears.

How would you describe the concept of possession that Adams holds? How does it differ from the concept held by Chief Sealth? Or does Chief Sealth have no concept of possession?

6. One way to analyze legal reasoning in an area of law is to examine the cultural myths that underlie the analysis. According to William Bassett, the property law of sixteenth and seventeenth-century England, which formed the foundation of the property relationships of the colonists with the Native Americans, was informed by the "myth of the nomad." The characterization of Native Americans as nomadic people is quite clear in John Quincy Adams' oration, as is the proposed relation of this charac-

terization to the allocation of property rights. Bassett argues that the roots of the nomad myth in North America had been set in the justifications of the dispossession of the Irish by the English "colonization" of Ireland in the sixteenth century. Bassett distinguishes this colonization from earlier invasions of Ireland in that this effort included dispossessing the majority of the inhabitants of their property rather than ousting only the ruling class. Because the English viewed the Gaelic Irish as barbarians, according to Bassett, they were able to justify war and expropriation of the Irish lands. Quoting a variety of sources, Bassett finds that the English viewed the Irish as pagans ["They are all Papists by their profession, but in the same so blindly and brutishly informed for the most part as that you would rather think them atheists or infidels."] The Gaelic Irish were viewed as barbarians because they "neither possessed any grounds, nor had any seats or houses to dwell in, but wandered through wilderness and desert places driving their flocks and herds of beasts before them." The mission of the English was "to inhabit and reforme so barbarous a nation."

The relationship of the nomadic myth and the allocation of property rights emerged from the work of natural-law theorists and social theorists of the eighteenth century who, according to Bassett, viewed economic and social development as occurring in stages. Adam Smith, for example, identified four stages: "first, the Age of Hunters; second, the Age of Shepherds; third, the Age of Agriculture; and fourth, the Age of Commerce." Private property does not arise until agriculture takes hold. Bassett, The Myth of the Nomad in Property Law, 4 J. of Law and Religion 133 (1986).

Susan Williams, in a response to Bassett, argues that "it is not possible, nor would it be desirable, to 'demythologize' the law. * * * The effort to eliminate those myths would produce legal concepts that were far less human, and probably no more humane." Williams, The Uses of Myth: A Response to Professor Bassett, 4 J. of Law and Religion 153 (1986).

One contemporary area of property law in which one might say a "myth" has operated is landlord-tenant law. Margaret Radin, in her article, Property and Personhood, 34 Stanford Law Review 957 (1982), observes that "[c]ourts frequently picture the residential lease transaction as taking place between a poor or middle-class tenant acquiring a home and a business enterprise owning and leasing residential property. This is one basis for the revolution in tenants' rights. Courts began to view the rights in question as more closely related to the personhood of the tenant than to that of the landlord, and accordingly moved to protect the leasehold as the tenant's home." Radin does not call these characterizations mythology. She uses them, instead, to illustrate a sense of the interrelationship of certain types of property and one's personhood. (Bassett lists the landlord-tenant law reform cases among cases revealing a mythology in property law.)

Does identifying an assumption or generalization or observation as a "myth" add anything to the critique of a case or a specific set of legal norms? On what basis would you find a myth useful? Destructive?

7. Discussing the mythology adopted in an opinion resolving a legal question of property ownership, and analyzing the costs and benefits of a

particular allocation are different ways of raising the question of who *ought* to be called "owner," using "ought" in a moral, political or economic context rather than simply as a way of asking who the rules determine should be the owner. These issues are neatly raised in questions concerning "original owners" or "first owners." A nearly endless variety of answers have been proposed for the question of who ought to be the owner. The labor theory argues that the one who applies labor to a thing and *transforms* it deserves to be the owner; the social contract theory argues that the owner is the one who received title through the consent of humanity or society; the natural law theory argues that the identification of the owner is to be found in natural principles of human ordering; utilitarianism argues that ownership is placed where it achieves the greatest aggregate good (i.e., the greatest good for the greatest number). Which of these theories, if any, are evident in *Johnson v. McIntosh?* Recall these theories as you read the cases in the following sections as well.

8. In policymaking, decisions concerning conflicting claims or positions are often examined through a cost-benefit analysis. In this analysis, the costs (disadvantages quantified and weighted by severity and probability) are identified and compared to the benefits (similarly quantified and weighted) of the proposed result. Describe the cost-benefit analysis that might be performed by Adams and Sealth in considering a potential dispute resolution in *Johnson.*

A cost-benefit analysis may be used in disputes concerning the government's exercise of its power of eminent domain, by which the government has the power to purchase the property of an individual, despite the individual's refusal to sell, when that purchase is for a public purpose and supported by the general welfare of the community. For example, a St. Louis law firm recently asked the local government to give the law firm the authority to condemn and take possession of their next-door neighbor's building. (Missouri has a statute that authorizes local governments to award the power of eminent domain to private parties incorporated as urban redevelopment corporations under certain conditions. Mo.Rev.Stat. § 353.130.) The law firm claimed that its expanded payroll would produce $100,000 in additional taxes for the city. See also, the Poletown case reproduced in Chapter Seven, in the section on public land-use control, in which the Michigan Supreme Court held that it was constitutional for the city of Detroit to condemn the Poletown neighborhood and force the owners to sell their property to the city, which then sold it to General Motors. The purpose of the condemnation and razing of the homes was the alleviation of unemployment promised by GM's building a new factory. If you were on the city council for each of these decisions, how would you go about deciding?

Do these cases and *Johnson v. McIntosh* indicate that we have a legal norm that the most productive user gets title?

9. Chief Justice Marshall pronounced a rule of law governing the relationship between the United States and Native Americans that is the basis for current federal policy with respect to Native Americans. What was that rule? For 150 years after the case was decided, the rule tended to be ignored in property transactions as the country was settled. In the

1970s, a young attorney from St. Louis, Mo., Thomas N. Tureen, accepted a case on behalf of the Passamaquoddy Tribe and sued the federal government seeking return of the lands comprising the state of Maine and half the state of Massachusetts. Over the years, those two states had purchased and otherwise acquired land from the Passamaquoddy Tribe and reconveyed the land to private citizens.

In the lawsuit, the Tribe argued that a statute enacted in 1790, the Indian Nonintercourse Act, 25 U.S.C. § 177, forbidding the conveyance of Indian land without the consent of the United States, established a trust relationship between the United States and the Passamaquoddy Tribe, and rendered invalid all of the land transfers that had taken place between the Tribe and the states. The United States District Court for the District of Maine agreed with the plaintiff's argument that Justice Marshall's opinion in *Johnson v. McIntosh,* as well as later opinions involving the Cherokee Nation; e.g., Worcester v. Georgia, 31 U.S. (6 Pet.) 515, 8 L.Ed. 483 (1832); Cherokee Nation v. Georgia, 30 U.S. (5 Pet.) 1, 8 L.Ed. 25 (1831), established that Native Americans had property rights of occupancy in land. While those rights could not be transferred except to the sovereign (United States), and could be destroyed by the sovereign, the sovereign was required to protect those rights against interference from third parties. Joint Tribal Council of Passamaquoddy Tribe v. Morton, 388 F.Supp. 649, 657 (D.Maine 1975), aff'd., 528 F.2d 370 (1st Cir.1975).

The court also agreed that the Nonintercourse Act established a trust relationship and that plaintiffs should be permitted to litigate the question whether subsequent transfers of property without the consent of the federal government constituted breaches of the trust obligations. The Passamaquoddy case was finally settled by Congress in 1980 by an appropriation of $81.5 million to two tribes in Maine ($27 million for a permanent trust fund and $54.4 million to enable the tribes to purchase 300,000 acres of land between two reservations the tribes occupied).

B. CAPTURE

PIERSON v. POST

Supreme Court of New York, 1805.
3 Caines 175.

TOMPKINS, J. delivered the opinion of the court.

This was an action of trespass on the case commenced in a justice's court, by the present defendant against the now plaintiff.

The declaration stated that Post, being in possession of certain dogs and hounds under his command, did, "upon a certain wild and uninhabited, unpossessed and waste land, called the beach, find and start one of those noxious beasts called a fox," and whilst there hunting, chasing and pursuing the same with his dogs and hounds, and when in view thereof, Pierson, well knowing the fox was so hunted and pursued, did, in the sight of Post, to prevent his catching the same, kill and carry it off. A verdict having been rendered for the plaintiff below, the defendant there sued out a *certiorari,* and now assigned for error, that the declaration and the matters therein contained were not sufficient in law to maintain an action.

* * *

The question submitted by the counsel in this cause for our determination is, whether Lodowick Post, by the pursuit with his hounds in the manner alleged in his declaration, acquired such a right to, or property in, the fox as will sustain an action against Pierson for killing and taking him away?

The cause was argued with much ability by the counsel on both sides, and presents for our decision a novel and nice question. It is admitted that a fox is an animal *feræ naturæ*, and that property in such animals is acquired by occupancy only. These admissions narrow the discussion to the simple question of what acts amount to occupancy, applied to acquiring right to wild animals.

If we have recourse to the ancient writers upon general principles of law, the judgment below is obviously erroneous. Justinian's Institutes (lib. 2, tit. 1, sec. 13), and Fleta (lib. 3, ch. 2, p. 175), adopt the principle, that pursuit alone vests no property or right in the huntsman; and that even pursuit, accompanied with wounding, is equally ineffectual for that purpose, unless the animal be actually taken. The same principle is recognized by Breton (lib. 2, ch. 1, p. 8).

Puffendorf (lib. 4, ch. 6, sec. 2 and 10) defines occupancy of beasts *feræ naturæ*, to be the actual corporeal possession of them, and Bynkershock is cited as coinciding in this definition. It is indeed with hesitation that Puffendorf affirms that a wild beast mortally wounded or greatly maimed, cannot be fairly intercepted by another, whilst the pursuit of the person inflicting the wound continues. The foregoing authorities are decisive to show that mere pursuit gave Post no legal right to the fox, but that he became the property of Pierson, who intercepted and killed him.

It, therefore, only remains to inquire whether there are any contrary principles or authorities, to be found in other books, which ought to induce a different decision. Most of the cases which have occurred in England, relating to property in wild animals, have either been discussed and decided upon the principles of their positive statute regulations, or have arisen between the huntsman and the owner of the land upon which beasts *feræ naturæ* have been apprehended; the former claiming them by title of occupancy, and the latter *ratione soli*. Little satisfactory aid can, therefore, be derived from the English reporters.

Barbeyrac, in his notes on Puffendorf, does not accede to the definition of occupancy by the latter, but, on the contrary, affirms that actual bodily seizure is not, in all cases, necessary to constitute possession of wild animals. He does not, however, describe the acts which, according to his ideas, will amount to an appropriation of such animals to private use, so as to exclude the claims of all other persons, by title of occupancy, to the same animals; and he is far from averring that pursuit alone is sufficient for that purpose. To a certain extent, and as far as Barbeyrac appears to me to go, his objections to Puffendorf's definition of occupancy are reasonable and correct. That is to say, that actual bodily seizure is not indispensable to acquire right to, or possession of, wild beasts; but that, on the contrary, the mortal wounding of such beasts, by one not abandoning his pursuit, may, with the utmost propriety, be deemed possession of him; since thereby the pursuer manifests an unequivocal intention of appropriating the animal to his individual use, has deprived him of his natural liberty, and brought him within his certain control. So, also, encompassing and securing such animals with nets and toils, or otherwise intercepting them in such a manner as to deprive them of their natural liberty, and render escape impossible, may justly be deemed to give possession of them to those persons who, by their industry and labor, have used such means of apprehending them. * * *

We are the more readily inclined to confine possession or occupancy of beasts *feræ naturæ*, within the limits prescribed by the learned authors above cited, for the sake of certainty, and preserving peace and order in society. If the first seeing, starting or pursuing such animals, without having so wounded, circumvented or ensnared them, so as to deprive them of their natural liberty, and subject them to the control of their pursuer, should afford the basis of actions against others for intercepting and killing them, it would prove a fertile source of quarrels and litigation.

However uncourteous or unkind the conduct of Pierson towards Post, in this instance, may have been, yet this act was productive of no injury or damage for which a legal remedy can be applied. We are of opinion the judgment below was erroneous, and ought to be reversed.

LIVINGSTON, J. My opinion differs from that of the court.

[The question of this case is:] Whether a person who, with his own hounds, starts and hunts a fox on waste and uninhabited ground, and is on the point of seizing his prey, acquires such an interest in the animal as to have a right of action against another, who in view of the huntsman and his dogs in full pursuit, and with knowledge of the chase, shall kill and carry him away.

This is a knotty point, and should have been submitted to the arbitration of sportsmen, without poring over Justinian, Fleta, Bracton, Puffendorf, Locke, Barbeyrac, or Blackstone, all of whom have been cited; they would have had no difficulty in coming to a prompt and correct conclusion. In a court thus constituted, the skin and carcass of poor Reynard would have been properly disposed of, and a precedent set, interfering with no usage or custom which the experience of ages has sanctioned, and which must be so well known to every votary of Diana. But the parties have referred the question to our judgment, and we must dispose of it as well as we can, from the partial lights we possess, leaving to a higher tribunal the correction of any mistake which we may be so unfortunate as to make. By the pleadings it is admitted that a fox is a "wild and noxious beast." Both parties have regarded him, as the law of nations does a pirate, "*hostem humani generis,*" and although "*de mortuis nil nisi bonum*" be a maxim of our profession, the memory of the deceased has not been spared. His depredations on farmers and on barnyards, have not been forgotten; and to put him to death wherever found, is allowed to be meritorious, and of public benefit. Hence it follows, that our decision should have in view the greatest possible encouragement to the destruction of an animal, so cunning and ruthless in his career. But who would keep a pack of hounds; or what gentleman, at the sound of the horn, and at peep of day, would mount his steed, and for hours together, "*sub jove frigido,*" or a vertical sun, pursue the windings of this wily quadruped, if, just as night came on, and his stratagems and strength were nearly exhausted, a saucy intruder, who had not shared in the honors or labors of the chase, were permitted to come in at the death, and bear away in triumph the object of pursuit? Whatever Justinian may have thought of the matter, it must be recollected that his code was compiled many hundred years ago, and it would be very hard indeed, at the distance of so many centuries, not to have a right to establish a rule for ourselves. In his day, we read of no order of men who made it a business, in the language of the declaration in this cause, "with hounds and dogs to find, start, pursue, hunt, and chase," these animals, and that, too, without any other motive than the preservation of Roman poultry; if this diversion had been then in fashion, the lawyers who composed his institutes, would have taken care not to pass it by, without suitable encouragement. If anything, therefore, in the digests or pandects shall appear to militate against the defendant in error, who, on this occasion, was the fox hunter, we have only to say *tempora mutantur;* and if men themselves change with the times, why should not laws also undergo an alteration?

It may be expected, however, by the learned counsel, that more particular notice be taken of their authorities. I have examined them all, and feel great difficulty in determining, whether to acquire dominion over a thing, before in common, it be sufficient that we barely see it, or know where it is, or wish for it, or make a declaration of our will respecting it; or whether, in the case of wild beasts, setting a trap, or lying in wait, or starting, or pursuing, be enough; or if an actual wounding, or killing, or bodily tact and occupation be necessary. Writers on general law, who have favored us with their speculations on these points, differ on them all; but, great as is the diversity of sentiment among them, some conclusion must be adopted on the question immediately before us. After mature deliberation, I embrace that of Barbeyrac as the most rational and least liable to objection. If at liberty, we might imitate the courtesy of a certain emperor, who, to avoid giving offense to the advocates of any of these different doctrines, adopted a middle course, and by ingenious distinctions, rendered it difficult to say (as often happens after a fierce and angry contest) to whom the palm of victory belonged. He ordained, that if a beast be followed with large dogs and hounds, he shall belong to the hunter, not to the chance occupant; and in like manner, if he be killed or wounded with a lance or sword; but if chased with beagles only, then he passed to the captor, not to the first pursuer. If slain with a dart, a sling, or a bow, he fell to the hunter, if still in chase, and not to him who might afterwards find and seize him.

Now, as we are without any municipal regulations of our own, and the pursuit here, for aught that appears on the case, being with dogs and hounds of imperial stature, we are at liberty to adopt one of the provisions just cited, which comports also with the learned conclusion of Barbeyrac, that property in animals *feræ naturæ* may be acquired without bodily touch or manucaption, provided the pursuer be within reach, or have a reasonable prospect (which certainly existed here) of taking what he has thus discovered an intention of converting to his own use.

When we reflect also that the interest of our husbandmen, the most useful of men in any community, will be advanced by the destruction of a beast so pernicious and incorrigible, we cannot greatly err in saying that a pursuit like the present, through waste and unoccupied lands, and which must inevitably and speedily have terminated in corporeal possession, or bodily seisin, confers such a right to the object of it, as to make any one a wrong-doer who shall interfere and shoulder the spoil. The justice's judgment ought, therefore, in my opinion, to be affirmed.

Judgment of reversal.

Notes and Questions

1. The rule governing the case before the Supreme Court of New York in *Pierson* was clear to the majority: "a fox is an animal *feræ naturæ,* and * * * property in such animals is acquired by occupancy only." In deciding the case before them, did the court simply follow the rule or did it do something else? On what basis did the majority find that mere pursuit was not sufficient to establish a property right? With what policies was the court concerned? The majority opinion discusses situations of "mortal wounding." What relevance did that have to this case?

2. Relying only on *Pierson,* how would you resolve the following problem?

Mike "Captain" Ahab, a whaler, located a whale and harpooned it. His harpoon was attached to his boat by a super strong rope. However, following a long and exhausting struggle, the rope broke and the whale swam free. Ahab was somewhat upset, but comforted himself in the knowledge that his harpoon had been engraved with the following words:

IF FOUND, PLEASE NOTIFY MIKE AHAB OF ROCKPORT, MAINE, WHO IS THE OWNER OF THIS HARPOON AND ANY WHALE THAT IT MAY BE FOUND IN.

The following day Olive Holmes, a law student, found the whale on the beach in front of her summer home. She thought to herself, "I read the case of *Pierson v. Post,* and it is clear to me that Ahab does not own this whale." She accordingly sold the whale to a whale processor and used the money to pay part of her tuition.

Olive returned the harpoon to Ahab but refused to turn over the proceeds of the sale. You are a lawyer. Ahab comes to you with this story and is extremely upset. He thinks the whale is his and that the money Olive Holmes got for the whale should be returned to him. He wants to know if he can win a lawsuit against Ms. Holmes for the value of the whale. On the basis of *Pierson v. Post* alone, what would you tell him and why? (This problem was developed by Professor Leonard Glantz, Boston University.)

3. An article in Wisconsin Natural Resources (Nov./Dec. 1986) describes a conflict among sportsmen. A hunter named Preuss writes to the magazine: "I have had an experience that is giving me mixed feelings on deer hunting, human nature and doing what is right." Preuss reports that he was standing in the middle of his woodlot, heard five shots to the west, and then saw deer running down a wooded hill. Preuss shot the deer, which dropped immediately, though the bullet hit the deer only in the back. Preuss administered the "killing shot" to the neck and then went back to his stand for a cup of coffee before dressing the deer. When he returned to the deer, another hunter was there and claimed that he had "gutshot" the buck only 75 yards from that spot. This second hunter claimed ownership under an "unwritten law" that the "first hunter to put a killing shot into a deer owns a deer." Preuss, who had reluctantly let the second hunter have the deer, asked readers of the magazine: "Whose deer was it?" Many readers responded. One wrote: "Hunter ethics and common sense dictate that the person who administers the killing shot should be the legal claimant. Since it is common knowledge, among those who know, that a gutshot deer does not die for at least a couple of days or longer, the stranger's argument is totally ridiculous." Another hunter wrote that he had shot an eight-point buck, trailed it, "but didn't find it until the next morning—dead from a gutshot, bloated and spoiled. How I wish another hunter had 'finished off' that fine deer. He could have had the venison, and the animal wouldn't have suffered a slow death." Another hunter disagrees: "A gutshot deer is a dead deer." And another says, "[I]t belongs to the hunter who first wounded the animal and was sportsman enough to follow up his shot. Only greed * * * would make a hunter tag another person's cripple. The owner of the deer is the one who drew first blood."

The article reports that, according to an attorney with the state's Department of Natural Resources, the Wisconsin Supreme Court in 1914 ruled that a wounded animal belongs to the person who brings it under control in a way to make actual possession practically inevitable. This gives the hunter a property right that cannot be divested by someone who intervenes and kills the animal. The attorney also reported that under Wisconsin statute, however, "a deer must be tagged immediately upon taking it. Failure to tag a deer as required by statute relieves the hunter of any vested property right in the animal. Therefore, it appears that in this instance, the hunter who ultimately tagged the deer has ownership."

What is the purpose of the statute requiring that deer be tagged in order to preserve the ownership of the hunter?

4. Was the result in *Pierson* a just result? Did Post suffer harm from Pierson? If you conclude that Pierson harmed Post, would you have a better chance of success by focusing the attention of the court on Pierson's wrongful acts rather than on property rights that Post may have acquired? Is the engagement in a lawful activity enough to give Post the right to continue that lawful activity without interference? See, e.g., Keeble v. Hickeringill, 103 Eng.Rep. (Q.B. 1707) (shots fired at flying ducks to scare them away from decoys that plaintiff put on his duck pond held to be an unlawful interference with plaintiff's right to use his property in a lawful manner). Suppose that instead of firing shots, the defendant had used a mechanical duck that was a more effective attraction than the plaintiff's decoys? Suppose that Pierson used a mechanical rabbit to entice the fox to him and away from Post?

———

Argument by analogy is a common tool of legal analysis. The rule of *feræ naturæ* used in *Pierson* has been extended by analogy beyond property rights in wild animals to property rights in "migratory resources" such as oil and gas. In the principal case below, the Supreme Court of Kentucky modifies case law that relied on the rule of capture for oil and gas and that had stated the law of Kentucky for the past fifty years.

TEXAS AMERICAN ENERGY CORPORATION v. CITIZENS FIDELITY BANK & TRUST COMPANY

Supreme Court of Kentucky, 1987.
736 S.W.2d 25.

OPINION OF THE COURT

This court having granted discretionary review from an opinion of the Court of Appeals and being of the opinion that the Amended Opinion of the Hopkins Circuit Court by Honorable Thomas B. Spain, judge of said court, is correct, hereby adopts that opinion as the opinion of this court, as follows:

> [Texas American purchased Western Kentucky Gas Company (Western), a natural gas retailer. Western purchases gas from fields in Texas and Louisiana, and pipes the gas through its distribution pipeline and into underground storage fields in Kentucky. The natural gas is retrieved during peak demand mid-winter months for distribution to customers. In order for Western to purchase these gas reserves, Texas American entered into a loan agreement with Citizens Fidelity. This dispute arose when Texas American sought to use these gas reserves as security for the loan. Texas American considered the reserves to be personal property; therefore, only a "security interest" was required. Citizens Fidelity, however, considered the gas to be part of the real estate since it had been injected back into the land. If the natural gas

is considered part of the real estate, a "mortgage interest" is required to secure the loan. The differences between a security and mortgage interest are not important for our discussion. Consider how the principles in *Pierson v. Post* are used to resolve the property status of natural gas.]

"With these facts in mind, we now move to the first question to be answered, namely whether natural gas, removed from its original 'home' and injected into a foreign location with confinement integrity, remains personal property as it is uniformly held to be upon its original production, or whether it reverts to an interest in real estate.

"The parties agree that until now the case law in Kentucky has considered such injected or extraneous gas not to be personal property when it is not confined. This is because of an opinion of the late revered Commissioner Osso Stanley of the former Court of Appeals in the now fifty-year-old case of *Hammonds v. Central Kentucky Natural Gas Co.*, 255 Ky. 685, 75 S.W.2d 204 (1934).

"In that case Della Hammonds owned 54 unleased acres located within the boundary of the gas company's 15,000 acre gas storage field. It was undisputed that the reservoir underlay her tract. She sued alleging trespass because the gas company's injected gas had 'invaded' the formation under her land without her consent. The trial Court found against her [and] Kentucky's highest Court [affirmed], holding that once the foreign gas was injected back into the earth, (into an uncontrolled gas storage formation), it ceased being the property of the gas company, and would only become personal property again when and if it was produced or reduced to actual possession by extraction a second time.

"In reaching this conclusion, Commissioner Stanley traced the evolution of judicial thought with regard to oil and gas as distinguished from the 'solid minerals.' He adopted the then popular theory that because of their fugacious nature, oil and gas were 'wild and migratory in nature,' and hence similar to animals *feræ naturæ* (i.e. wild by nature). This being so, he reasoned, the law as applied to wild animals ought to be applicable by analogy to oil and gas—minerals *feræ naturæ*. Consequently, since a fox until his capture in the forest belonged to all mankind, and if trapped and released in another forest reverted to common property, shouldn't the same logic apply to 'captured' and injected natural gas? Commissioner Stanley also quoted from Thornton's Work on Oil and Gas, Sect. 1264, wherein Judge Willis equated injected gas in storage with timber. 'Standing in the woods, timber is a part of the land. When severed it becomes personal property. If made into lumber and used to construct a building it becomes again a part of the land to which it is attached. When gas is stored in the natural reservoir it is subject to all the properties that inhered in it originally. A neighbor could take it with impunity through adjacent wells, if he owned land within the radius of the reservoir. Hence it should be taxed only as part of the land in which it is placed, and in such circumstances could not be treated as personal property.'

"Texas American calls this Court's attention to the cases of *White v. New York State Natural Gas Corporation,* 190 F.Supp. 342 (W.D.Pa. 1960) and *Lone Star Gas Company v. Murchison,* 353 S.W.2d 870; 94 A.L.R.2d 529 (Tex.1962). In both these cases *Hammonds* is referred to and rejected, along with the 'wild animal' analogy as applied to injected stored gas. The following portion of the opinion in *White* is particularly succinct:

> Generally stated, the law relating to ownership of wild animals is based on possessory concepts, with title being acquired only by reduction of the animal *feræ naturæ* to possession and being divested by loss of possession through escape and return of the animal to its natural and ferocious state. [   ]

> It becomes readily apparent, however, that a strict application of this analogy to the present facts is of no benefit to the plaintiff's cause. To begin with, the storage gas in question has not escaped from its owners. On the contrary, it is yet very much in the possession of the storage companies, being within a well-defined storage field, the Hebron–Ellisburg Field, and being subject to the control of the storage companies through the same wells by which the gas originally had been injected into the storage pool. [   ]

> Moreover, there has been no return of storage gas to its 'natural habitat' since Southwest gas, differing materially in chemical and physical properties from native Oriskany gas, is not native to the Oriskany Sands underlying the Hebron–Ellisburg Field. Deferring to the analogy of animals *feræ naturæ* under the circumstances of this case would no more divest a storage company of title to stored gas than a zookeeper in Pittsburgh to title to an escaped elephant. [   ]

"In *Lone Star* the Court comments that our *Hammonds* case 'in its application of *feræ naturæ* doctrine, has been the subject of violent adverse criticism by many authors and law review writers' [   ] The Opinion then continues:

> * * * The analogy of wild animals upon which Hammonds is founded fails to undergird the ultimate decision of that case. Gas has no similarity to wild animals. Gas is an inanimate, diminishing nonreproductive substance lacking any will of its own, and instead of running wild and roaming at large as animals do, is subject to be moved solely by pressure or mechanical means. It cannot be logically regarded as personal property of the human race as are wild animals, instead of being turned loose in the woods as the fanciful fox or placed in the streams as the fictitious fish, gas, a privately owned commodity, has been stored for use, as required by the consuming public being, as alleged by appellant, subject to its control and withdrawal at any time. Logic and reason dictates the application of the White decision rather than Hammonds, to the end, that in Texas, the owner of gas does not lose title thereof by storing the same in a well-defined underground reservoir.

"For the same 'sound and logical reason, especially in the light of advanced knowledge and scientific achievement in the oil and gas industry * * * ' this Court is of the opinion that it is time to limit *Hammonds* and to now hold that natural gas once converted to personal property by extraction remains personal property notwithstanding its subsequent storage in underground reservoirs with confinement integrity.

"*Hammonds* should be narrowly construed or limited as it applies to the instant case, for the reason that the fact situations in the two are distinguishable. In *Hammonds* there was a known 'leak' in the gas storage reservoir inasmuch as Mrs. Hammonds' land was, in fact, a part of the natural reservoir, though not controlled by the storage company. In the case at hand, however, it has been stipulated that the gas reservoir has total integrity, and the gas cannot escape nor can it be extracted by anyone except Western. Using the *feræ naturæ* analogy, Western has captured the wild fox, hence reducing it to personal property. The fox has not been released in another forest, permitting it to revert to the common property of mankind; but rather, the fox has only been released in a private confinement zoo. The fox is no less under the control of Western than if it were on a leash.

"Accordingly, the Court is of the opinion that *Hammonds* does not control in the instant case and that under the stipulated facts, the injected gas remains the personal property of Western.

"This being so, there is no more reason to require that it can only be hypothecated or encumbered by a real estate mortgage than there would be to require such of a recreational vehicle temporarily parked at a campground or of coal stockpiled at a tipple."

End of opinion of lower court.

It is therefore the opinion of this court that, in those instances when previously extracted oil or gas is subsequently stored in underground reservoirs capable of being defined with certainty and the integrity of said reservoirs is capable of being maintained, title to such oil or gas is not lost and said minerals do not become subject to the rights of the owners of the surface above the storage fields. * * *

STEPHENS, C.J., and GANT, LAMBERT, LEIBSON, VANCE and WINTERSHEIMER, JJ., concur.

STEPHENSON, J., dissents and files a separate dissenting opinion.

Notes and Questions

1. What is left of *Hammonds* after the *Texas American* case? Which case states the law of Kentucky?

2. How do you assess whether an analogy is persuasive? The *Hammonds* case, quoted in *Texas American,* found that gas was like a wild animal and so applied rules that were developed for resolving ownership claims to wild animals to the issue before them. How is the wild animal analogy a good analogy for gas? A bad analogy? Why would lawyers argue legal questions by using analogies?

3. When the valuable commercial potential of oil and gas was discovered in the United States, considerable litigation ensued over ownership rights in these natural resources. Courts established ownership interests in oil and gas by analogizing these substances to other forms of property, and applying the property rules associated with those forms of property. In *Texas American*, for example, you saw an application of the rule of capture. Other alternatives also existed.

Under traditional common law, *cujus est solum, ejus est usque ad coelum et ad inferos*—To whomever the soil belongs, he owns also to the sky and to the depths. In other words, the surface owner was also considered the owner of the column of air directly above his surface, extending to the heavens, and a column of dirt directly below his surface, extending to the center of the earth. This ownership included any thing that might be found within this column of air and dirt.

Courts analogized oil and gas to other solid minerals that were part of the land. Thus, whoever owned the surface over an oil or gas reservoir, also owned the oil and gas. However, unlike solid minerals, oil and gas have physical properties that allow these substances to migrate within connected underground caverns. This migration is caused by changes in pressure that result from extracting the oil and gas. Thus, if oil is extracted from reservoir 1, oil from reservoir 2 may migrate into reservoir 1, replacing the oil that has been extracted. If oil from your reservoir migrates into your neighbor's reservoir because he has been drilling, do you have a cause of action against your neighbor? Does this allocation rule further the goal of productive use of property? Is productivity an appropriate goal?

The doctrine of correlative rights was created to allocate rights to underground water. Under this system, all surface owners above a common aquifer had a right to take water from the reservoir. Along with this right, however, were corresponding duties not to injure the reservoir, take an undue portion or waste the water that was taken. Similarly, under the doctrine of riparian rights, all surface owners adjacent to a flowing stream had a right to use the water. This right also carried with it a duty not to use the water in a way that would diminish the quantity or quality of water reaching downstream riparian owners. Since oil and gas had physical properties similar to water, courts used these rules to allocate oil and gas rights.

Unlike water, oil and gas are not necessary for sustaining life, for the productive use of the surface, or for physical support of the surface. Also, oil and gas do not arise from a continuous source; therefore, when these substances are taken, the entire source is diminished. Do these differences justify modifying application of the water doctrines? What changes could be made? How does one determine what is a "due portion"—is it in proportion to the surface area, based on need, or the social value attached to the particular use? What other factors might be taken into consideration? For a thorough discussion of rights to oil and gas, see W.L. Summers, The Law of Oil and Gas § 11, 61–63 (1954) and R.W. Hemingway, The Law of Oil and Gas § 1.3 (1983).

4. One way to analyze property rules is to examine the consequences a rule would have for human behavior. The "law and economics" school of thought is one form of analysis that focuses attention on the consequences of legal rules. See Ackerman, Economic Foundations of Property Law (1975), for a good collection of some of the classic articles using a "law and economics" approach to analyze property law issues. The rule of capture established in *Pierson* illustrates one of the paradigms of the economic analysis of property law.

You will recall that Livingston's opinion in *Pierson* based its result in part on its view that killing of foxes was to be encouraged and that the court's holding would encourage that behavior. The rule of capture establishes a race for first possession of the resource itself, whether it be foxes, oil and gas, or fish. Several economists have described the impact of this race on the "overconsumption" of the resource itself. For example: "The blade of grass that the manorial cow herd leaves behind is valueless to him, for tomorrow it may be eaten by another's animal; the oil left under the earth is valueless to the driller, for another may legally take it; the fish left in the sea are valueless to the fisherman, because there is no assurance that they will be there for him tomorrow if they are left behind today." Gordon, The Economic Theory of a Common Property Resource: The Fishery, Journal of Political Economy (1954) at 124. Other consequences include the "overinvestment" in the means of production, for example, better and more lobster traps to maximize the catch during a legally-limited season. See also, Haddock, First Possession versus Optimal Timing: Limiting the Dissipation of Economic Value, 64 Wash.U.L.Q. 775 (1986). The illustration of the inefficiencies of the rule of capture is also used by Garrett Hardin in his leading article, The Tragedy of the Commons, 162 Science 1243 (1968), to justify private ownership of property.

As with all property theories, the law and economics approach has its critics. For example, Carol Rose questions its assumptions about human behavior:

> "If there were no property rights in the berry patch, all of us would have to fight all the time for the berries. Instead, a property regime allocates this part of the patch to X and that part to Y; and this (or any other) allocation gives each owner a sense of security. Besides that, exclusive property rights identify who has what and allow all of us owners to trade instead of fighting. As a result, everything gets more valuable, because the property regime encourages us to work and then to trade the results of our work, instead of wasting time and effort in fighting.

* * *

"This is the standard version of property.

"[A]cquisitiveness, the desire to have property, is 'just there' * * * universal and omnipresent. Thus one can always predict a human desire to have things for one's self, or as they say more lately, the human propensity to be a self-interested rational utility maximizer.

"If we take these preferences for life and acquisition as given, then economics can make a bid to be a kind of logical science in politics and law. With these preferences understood, we can sensibly talk about how the law gives people incentives to do this thing and that, and we can manipulate future welfare by institutionalizing the proper ex ante approaches.

"In the real world, rational self-interest has to be explained * * *; it is not 'just there'; it has a history. [T]he 'self-interested utility maximizer' is just another story; it is the endless repetition of the 'naturalness' of self-interest that has made us think no further explanation or narration is needed.

Rose, Property and Story–Telling, 2 Yale J.L. and Humanities 37 (1990).

Laura Underkuffler also argues against an "absolute" notion of property that emphasizes individual control over all other interests:

The contemporary impulse toward equating the sphere of absolute individual autonomy with the concept of property is, in fact, a radical narrowing of the historical understanding of property. * * * I argue that property, in the historical view, did not represent the autonomous sphere of the individual to be asserted against the collective; rather, it embodied and reflected the inherent tension between the individual and the collective. This tension—now seen as something external to the concept of property—was in fact internal to it.

* * *

The concept of property has powerful, rhetorical force. It is not incidental to our lives or to our legal system; it is of central, almost emotional importance. Contemporary approaches proceed from a vision of property as that which protects and separates the individual from the collective sphere. By viewing the collective context as necessary for the definition and exercise of individual rights, the comprehensive approach forces us to rethink our image of the relationships between individuals and the collectives of which they are parts. It can lead us to a different concept of individual well-being and autonomy: one that recognizes the individual's need for freedom as well as the need for the development and expression of that freedom in the context of relatedness to others.

Underkuffler, On Property, 100 Yale L.J. 127 (1990).

How might Underkuffler's approach alter the analysis of the rule of capture?

C. FINDERS (AND, INCIDENTALLY, "CONSTRUCTIVE" POSSESSION)

Every so often you read in the newspaper of some lucky person who has found a significant sum of money or jewels. Most states have statutes governing the law of finders. Some of these statutes codify common-law rules that distinguished among "lost" items, "mislaid" items, "abandoned" items and treasure trove. It is interesting to examine the historical roots of such distinctions and their current utility, if any; but that is not the purpose of including finders cases here. The cases on finders illustrate some important points concerning the legal concept of possession, building on possession as capture in *Pierson* and including the flexible concept of "constructive possession." Many of the property rules that you will study later, especially adverse possession of land, rely on possession as a determining factor. In addition to developing a sense of the legal definition of possession, you should focus on what has been called the "relativity of title."

ARMORY v. DELAMIRIE
King's Bench, 1722.
1 Strange 525.

The plaintiff being a chimney sweeper's boy found a jewel and carried it to the defendant's shop (who was a goldsmith) to know what it was, and delivered it into the hands of the apprentice, who under pretence of weighing it, took out the stones, and calling to the master to let him know it came to three halfpence, the master offered the boy the money, who refused to take it, and insisted to have the thing again; whereupon the apprentice delivered him back the socket without the stones. And now in trover against the master these points were ruled:

1. That the finder of a jewel, though he does not by such finding acquire an absolute property or ownership, yet he has such a property as will enable him to keep it against all but the rightful owner, and consequently may maintain trover.

* * *

3. As to the value of the jewel several of the trade were examined to prove what a jewel of the finest water that would fit the socket would be worth; and the Chief Justice directed the jury, that unless the defendant did produce the jewel, and shew it not to be of the finest water, they should presume the strongest against him, and make the value of the best jewels the measure of their damages: which they accordingly did.

Notes and Questions

1. How does *Armory* illustrate the proposition that possession is the root of title if the possessor (the jeweler's apprentice) is not held to have title?

2. If the chimney sweep's boy had lost the jewel on the way to the jeweler and the jeweler's apprentice had simply found it on the street, would the chimney sweep's boy still win in a suit to recover the jewel? Your answer to that question will illustrate the relativity of title. The concept of relativity of title contributes to the modern legal notion that property is not a thing—a car, land, a book—but the legal relationships of persons as to a thing. This definition of property as relationship will be further explored in the discussion of property rights in body parts and the right to exclude later in this chapter.

A Note on Bailments

The legal relationship between the chimney sweep's boy and the jeweler in *Armory* is called a bailment. Bailments are common relationships in commerce and in friendships. Bailments occur frequently and are very familiar to anyone who has released possession of a chattel to another with the understanding, either express or implied, that the thing is to be returned to his or her possession at some time in the future. For example, you take in your shoes for repair or your clothes for cleaning. Or you lend a book or your notes to a classmate. Or at semester's end, you store furniture with a storage company. In each of these situations you have released possession of a chattel to another with the understanding, either expressed or implied, that this thing is to be returned to you at some time in the future.

In analyzing a claim based on bailment, the first question to consider is whether a bailment exists. A bailment requires that the bailee: (a) "take possession" of the thing; and (b) have the intent to possess or control the item.

The bailment can be either expressed or implied. In an expressed bailment, the bailor and bailee have discussed the critical terms of the bailment. For example, the bailor and bailee explicitly agree that the bailor's furniture will be deposited in the bailee's warehouse for a period of six months and that the bailee will then return the furniture. In an implied bailment, the parties may have failed to discuss the terms of the bailment. Your friend says "May I have your car?" and you toss her the keys. This can be an implied bailment in which the law fills in the missing terms. A second type of implied bailment occurs when the parties had not specifically intended a bailment, but the law places their relationship in that legal framework nonetheless. An example of this type of implied bailment is the relationship between the finder and the loser of a thing. (Did you wonder whether the chimney sweep's boy received a windfall in *Armory* by getting the full value of the jewel rather than the value of the jewel adjusted by the odds that the "true owner" would return and demand the jewel from the boy? Part of the rationale for awarding the finder the full value is that he is a bailee to the loser and has the general duty to return the thing found.)

Once the relationship is characterized as a bailment, the second issue is to identify the type of bailment. There are three choices at this point: (i) bailment for the sole benefit of the bailee (e.g., as when A borrows B's car); (ii) bailment for the sole benefit of the bailor (e.g., in a situation in which A stores B's stereo during summer vacation as a favor to B); and (iii) bailment for the mutual benefit of bailor and bailee (e.g., the deposit of an item with a shop for repair).

The characterization of the bailment purportedly defines the liability of the bailee for bailed goods that are lost, damaged or stolen due to the bailee's negligence. The bailment for the sole benefit of the bailee results in the bailee's liability for even slight negligence; the bailment for the sole benefit of bailor results in the bailee's liability for only gross negligence; and the bailment for mutual benefit results in the bailee's liability for ordinary negligence. Whether a particular failing of a bailee is grossly negligent, slightly negligent, or simply negligent is determined in light of the particular circumstances.

Develop arguments for *both* the bailee and bailor in the following case:

(A) Diana Lewis and Irene Preston both work for the same company downtown and have offices in the same building. In August, Diana, who has all her personal mail delivered to her office, took a two-week vacation to the Rocky Mountains. Before she left, she asked Irene to take all her mail to Irene's house for the duration of her vacation. Diana had done the same for Irene earlier in the summer.

The mail at the company was distributed by a company letter carrier who simply placed the day's mail on each person's desk. Each day, Irene picked up Diana's mail at Diana's desk.

When Diana arrived home from her vacation, she went to Irene's house and retrieved her mail. She then noticed that two items that she had expected to receive were missing.

(1) First, a small box containing a necklace valued at approximately $200 was not among the mail. Upon investigation, Diana discovered that the box had been delivered to the company and had been placed by the company letter carrier on Diana's desk. Evidently, a fellow office worker had picked up Diana's mail that day and placed it, including the box, on Irene's desk while Irene was out to lunch. The box apparently was quickly stolen by a still-unknown thief who thus had quite a successful day at the office.

(2) Second, Diana was missing a $1,000 negotiable bond sent to her by her father. Irene did recall Diana's receiving a "certified-return receipt requested" letter from her father; however, Irene can't find it now. Irene had left the mail on her desk while she briefly left her office. Although she made every effort to recover the letter, she was unsuccessful.

(B) Would your arguments be different if Diana had paid Irene for her services? What if she had brought her a gift?

HANNAH v. PEEL

King's Bench, 1945.
1 K.B. 509.

Action tried by BIRKETT J.

On December 13, 1938, the freehold of Gwernhaylod House, Overton-on-Dee, Shropshire, was conveyed to the defendant, Major Hugh

Edward Ethelston Peel, who from that time to the end of 1940 never himself occupied the house and it remained unoccupied until October 5, 1939, when it was requisitioned, but after some months was released from requisition. Thereafter it remained unoccupied until July 18, 1940, when it was again requisitioned, the defendant being compensated by a payment at the rate of 250*l.* a year. In August, 1940, the plaintiff, Duncan Hannah, a lance-corporal, serving in a battery of the Royal Artillery, was stationed at the house and on the 21st of that month, when in a bedroom, used as a sick-bay, he was adjusting the black-out curtains when his hand touched something on the top of a window-frame, loose in a crevice, which he thought was a piece of dirt or plaster. The plaintiff grasped it and dropped it on the outside window ledge. On the following morning he saw that it was a brooch covered with cobwebs and dirt. Later, he took it with him when he went home on leave and his wife having told him it might be of value, at the end of October, 1940, he informed his commanding officer of his find and, on his advice, handed it over to the police, receiving a receipt for it. In August, 1942, the owner not having been found the police handed the brooch to the defendant, who sold it in October, 1942, for 66*l.*, to Messrs. Spink & Son, Ltd., of London, who resold it in the following month for 88*l.* There was no evidence that the defendant had any knowledge of the existence of the brooch before it was found by the plaintiff. The defendant had offered the plaintiff a reward for the brooch, but the plaintiff refused to accept this and maintained throughout his right to the possession of the brooch as against all persons other than the owner, who was unknown. By a letter, dated October 5, 1942, the plaintiff's solicitors demanded the return of the brooch from the defendant, but it was not returned and on October 21, 1943, the plaintiff issued his writ claiming the return of the brooch, or its value, and damages for its detention. By his defence, the defendant claimed the brooch on the ground that he was the owner of Gwernhaylod House and in possession thereof.

BIRKETT J. There is no issue of fact in this case between the parties. As to the issue in law, the rival claims of the parties can be stated in this way: The plaintiff says: "I claim the brooch as its finder and I have a good title against all the world, save only the true owner." The defendant says: "My claim is superior to yours inasmuch as I am the freeholder. The brooch was found on my property, although I was never in occupation, and my title, therefore, ousts yours and in the absence of the true owner I am entitled to the brooch or its value." Unhappily the law on this issue is in a very uncertain state and there is need of an authoritative decision of a higher court. Obviously if it could be said with certainty that this is the law, that the finder of a lost article, wherever found, has a good title against all the world save the true owner, then, of course, all my difficulties would be resolved; or again, if it could be said with equal certainty that this is the law, that the possessor of land is entitled as against the finder to all chattels found on the land, again my difficulties would be resolved. But, unfortunately, the authorities give some support to each of these conflicting propositions.

In the famous case of *Armory v. Delamirie,* the plaintiff, who was a chimney sweeper's boy, found a jewel and carried it to the defendant's shop, who was a goldsmith, in order to know what it was, and he delivered it into the hands of the apprentice in the goldsmith's shop, who made a pretence of weighing it and took out the stones and called to the master to let him know that it came to three-halfpence. The master offered the boy the money who refused to take it and insisted on having the jewel again. Whereupon the apprentice handed him back the socket of the jewel without the stones, and an action was brought in trover against the master, and it was ruled "that the finder of a jewel, though he does not by such finding acquire an absolute property or ownership, yet he has such a property as will enable him to keep it against all but the rightful owner, and consequently may maintain trover." The case of *Bridges v. Hawkesworth* is in process of becoming almost equally as famous because of the disputation which has raged around it. The headnote in the Jurist is as follows: "The place in which a lost article is found does not constitute any exception to the general rule of law, that the finder is entitled to it as against all persons except the owner." The case was in fact an appeal against a decision of the county court judge at Westminster. The facts appear to have been that in the year 1847 the plaintiff, who was a commercial traveller, called on a firm named Byfield & Hawkesworth on business, as he was in the habit of doing, and as he was leaving the shop he picked up a small parcel which was lying on the floor. He immediately showed it to the shopman, and opened it in his presence, when it was found to consist of a quantity of Bank of England notes, to the amount of 65*l.* The defendant, who was a partner in the firm of Byfield & Hawkesworth, was then called, and the plaintiff told him he had found the notes, and asked the defendant to keep them until the owner appeared to claim them. Then various advertisements were put in the papers asking for the owner, but the true owner was never found. No person having appeared to claim them, and three years having elapsed since they were found, the plaintiff applied to the defendant to have the notes returned to him, and offered to pay the expenses of the advertisements, and to give an indemnity. The defendant refused to deliver them up to the plaintiff, and an action was brought in the county court of Westminster in consequence of that refusal. The county court judge decided that the defendant, the shopkeeper, was entitled to the custody of the notes as against the plaintiff, and gave judgment for the defendant. Thereupon the appeal was brought which came before the court composed of Patteson J. and Wightman J. Patteson J. said: "The notes which are the subject of this action were incidentally dropped, by mere accident, in the shop of the defendant, by the owner of them. The facts do not warrant the supposition that they had been deposited there intentionally, nor has the case been put at all upon that ground. The plaintiff found them on the floor, they being manifestly lost by someone. The general right of the finder to any article which has been lost, as against all the world, except the true owner, was established in the case of *Armory v. Delamirie* which has never been disputed. This right would clearly have accrued to the plaintiff had the notes been picked up by him outside the shop of the defendant and if he once had the right, the case finds that he did not intend, by delivering the notes to the defendant, to waive the title (if any) which he had to them, but they were handed to the defendant merely for the purpose of delivering them to the owner should he appear." Then a little later: "The case, therefore, resolves itself into the single point on which it appears that the learned judge decided it, namely, whether the circumstance of the notes being found inside the defendant's shop gives him, the defendant, the right to have them as against the plaintiff, who found them." After discussing the cases, and the argument, the learned judge said: "If the discovery had never been communicated to the defendant, could the real owner have had any cause of action against him because they were found in his house? Certainly not. The notes never were in the custody of the defendant, nor within the protection of his house, before they were found, as they would have been had they been intentionally deposited there; and the defendant has come under no responsibility, except from the communication made to him by the plaintiff, the finder, and the steps taken by way of advertisement. * * * We find, therefore, no circumstances in this case to take it out of the general rule of law, that the finder of a lost article is entitled to it as against all persons except the real owner, and we think that that rule must prevail, and that the learned judge was mistaken in holding that the place in which they were found makes any legal difference. Our judgment, therefore, is that the plaintiff is entitled to these notes as against the defendant."

It is to be observed that in *Bridges v. Hawkesworth* which has been the subject of immense disputation, neither counsel put forward any argument on the fact that the notes were found in a shop. Counsel for the appellant assumed throughout that the position was the same as if the parcel had been found in a private house, and the learned judge spoke of "the protection of his (the shopkeeper's) house." The case for the appellant was that the shopkeeper never knew of the notes. Again, what is curious is that there was no suggestion that the place where the notes were found was in any way material; indeed, the judge in giving the judgment of the court expressly repudiates this * * *. It is, therefore, a little remarkable that in *South Staffordshire Water Co. v. Sharman*, Lord Russell of Killowen C.J. said: "The case of *Bridges v. Hawkesworth* stands by itself, and on special grounds; and on those grounds it seems to me that the decision in that case was right. Someone had accidentally dropped a bundle of banknotes in a public shop. The shopkeeper did not know they had been dropped, and did not in any sense exercise control over them. The shop was open to the public, and they were invited to come there." That might be a matter of some doubt. Customers were invited there, but whether the public at large was, might be open to some question. * * * Patteson J. [in *Bridges*] never made any reference to the public part of the shop and, indeed, went out of his way to say that the learned county court judge was wrong in holding that the place where they were found made any legal difference.

Bridges v. Hawkesworth has been the subject of considerable comment by text-book writers and, amongst others, by Mr. Justice Oliver Wendell Holmes, Sir Frederick Pollock and Sir John Salmond.... Mr. Justice Oliver Wendell Holmes wrote: "Common law judges and civilians would agree that the finder got possession first and so could keep it as against the shopkeeper. For the shopkeeper, not knowing of the thing, could not have the intent to appropriate it, and, having invited the public to his shop, he could not have the intent to exclude them from it." So he introduces the matter of two intents which are not referred to by the judges who heard the case. [The court describes the positions of other commentators on *Bridges* who all agree that the premises owner did not have custody of the notes because he did not know they were there and could not, therefore, claim title.]

* * * The facts [in *South Staffordshire*] were that the defendant Sharman, while cleaning out, under the orders of the plaintiffs, the South Staffordshire Water Company, a pool of water on their land, found two rings embedded in the mud at the bottom of the pool. He declined to deliver them to the plaintiffs, but failed to discover the real owner. In an action brought by the company against Sharman in detinue it was held that the company were entitled to the rings. Lord Russell of Killowen C.J. said: "The plaintiffs are the freeholders of the locus in quo, and as such they have the right to forbid anybody coming on their land or in any way interfering with it. They had the right to say that their pool should be cleaned out in any way that they thought fit, and to direct what should be done with anything found in the pool in the course of such cleaning out. It is no doubt right, as the counsel for the defendant contended, to say that the plaintiffs must show that they had actual control over the locus in quo and the things in it; but under the circumstances, can it be said that the Minster Pool and whatever might be in that pool were not under the control of the plaintiffs? In my opinion they were. * * * The principle on which this case must be decided, and the distinction which must be drawn between this case and that of *Bridges v. Hawkesworth,* is to be found in a passage in Pollock and Wright's 'Essay on Possession in the Common Law,' p. 41: 'The possession of land carries with it in general, by our law, possession of everything which is attached to or under that land, and, in the absence of a better title elsewhere, the right to possess it also'." If that is right, it would clearly cover the case of the rings embedded in the mud of the pool * * *. Lord Russell continued: "And it makes no difference that the possessor is not aware of the thing's existence * * *. [W]here a person has possession of house or land, with

a manifest intention to exercise control over it and the things which may be upon or in it, then, if something is found on that land, whether by an employee of the owner or by a stranger, the presumption is that the possession of that thing is in the owner of the locus in quo." *South Staffordshire Water Co. v. Sharman* which was relied on by counsel for the defendant, has also been the subject of some discussion. It has been said that it establishes that if a man finds a thing as the servant or agent of another, he finds it not for himself, but for that other, and indeed that seems to afford a sufficient explanation of the case. The rings found at the bottom of the pool were not in the possession of the company, but it seems that though Sharman was the first to obtain possession of them, he obtained them for his employers and could claim no title for himself.

* * *

* * * It is fairly clear from the authorities that a man possesses everything which is attached to or under his land. Secondly, it would appear to be the law from the authorities I have cited, and particularly from *Bridges v. Hawkesworth* that a man does not necessarily possess a thing which is lying unattached on the surface of his land even though the thing is not possessed by someone else. A difficulty however, arises, because the rule which governs things an occupier possesses as against those which he does not, has never been very clearly formulated in our law. * * *

There is no doubt that in this case the brooch was lost in the ordinary meaning of that term, and I should imagine it had been lost for a very considerable time. Indeed, from this correspondence it appears that at one time the predecessors in title of the defendant were considering making some claim. But the moment the plaintiff discovered that the brooch might be of some value, he took the advice of his commanding officer and handed it to the police. His conduct was commendable and meritorious. The defendant was never physically in possession of these premises at any time. It is clear that the brooch was never his, in the ordinary acceptation of the term, in that he had the prior possession. He had no knowledge of it, until it was brought to his notice by the finder. * * * In those circumstances I propose to follow the decision in *Bridges v. Hawkesworth,* and to give judgment in this case for the plaintiff for 66*l*.

Judgment for plaintiff.

Notes and Questions

1. Major Peel lost, but why? Do you think the result would have been different had Peel actually lived in the house himself? Why or why not? The Gospel written by St. Matthew includes the following advice to finders:

> [T]he kingdom of heaven is like a treasure hid in a field; which when a man has found it, he hides it, and for joy thereof goes and sells all that he has, and buys the field.

Good advice?

2. How does the court handle the *South Staffordshire* case? Do you think that the holdings in *Bridges* and *South Staffordshire* are reconcilable? Contradictory? The court deciding *Bridges* relied on bailment law to support its holding against the shopowner. How?

3. After having read *Hannah,* and the facts and results of *Bridges* and *South Staffordshire* as discussed in *Hannah, Armory v. Delamirie,* appears to be a very simple case. Assume now that in addition to the chimney sweep's boy and the jeweler's apprentice, the owner of a tavern, where the chimney sweep's boy found the jewel lying on a brick in the fireplace, also claimed the jewel. If this dispute were in court, what should the arguments be and who should win? If instead, both the chimney sweep's boy and the tavern owner show up at the jeweler's claiming the jewel, what should the jeweler do?

4. As evidenced in *Armory v. Delamirie* and *Hannah v. Peel,* courts sometimes base the ownership of "found" property on whether the property is characterized as "lost," "mislaid," "abandoned" or "treasure trove." When the true owner has been unintentionally dispossessed of the property, it is considered lost. At common law, the finder of lost property is entitled to possess the lost property against everyone but the true owner. Mislaid property is that which is intentionally put in a certain place, to be retrieved at a later date, but which is subsequently forgotten. The finder of mislaid property acquires no rights in the property, and the owner of the site where the property is found has a right against all but the true owner. When an owner intends to relinquish all rights in the property and leaves it so that it may be appropriated by another, the property is deemed abandoned. The finder of abandoned property has an unqualified right to the property. Treasure trove is money, coins, gold or silver hidden either under or above the ground, which has been hidden for a length of time so that it is not reasonably possible to determine the true owner. Treasure trove is usually awarded to the finder, so long as the finder is not trespassing. However, some states do not recognize the category of treasure trove, and classify the property under lost or mislaid, depending upon all the circumstances.

The courts use these categories to resolve conflicting claims. See, for example, the following cases. $6325 found on seat of chair in safe deposit vault, finder claiming cash was lost and bank claiming it was mislaid: Paset v. Old Orchard Bank and Trust Co., 62 Ill.App.3d 534, 19 Ill.Dec. 389, 378 N.E.2d 1264 (1978), (holding that cash was lost); family donated bags of old clothing to thrift shop where employee discovered a wallet and sterling silver in the bags, purchased the bags, and claimed the property was "abandoned": Kahr v. Markland, 187 Ill.App.3d 603, 135 Ill.Dec. 196, 543 N.E.2d 579 (1989) (holding that items were lost and must be returned to true owner).

4. Major Peel argued that he was entitled to the brooch because it was in his house. Major Peel's claim would not satisfy the requirements of actual possession; however, it may fit within a claim of constructive possession. Black's Law Dictionary defines the word "constructive" as "that which is established by the mind of the law in its act of construing

facts, conduct, circumstances, or instruments; that which has not the character assigned to it in its own essential nature, but acquires such character in consequence of the way in which it is regarded by a rule or policy of law; * * * inferred, implied, made out of legal interpretation." In defining "constructive possession," Black's states that constructive possession is "not actual but [is] assumed to exist."

In State v. Schmidt, 110 N.J. 258, 540 A.2d 1256, 1260–1262 (1988), the Supreme Court of New Jersey reversed the conviction of the defendant for a drug offense. Justice O'Hern presented his theory of constructive possession:

We recognize that possession has different meanings in different contexts. Like the elusive fox in *Pierson v. Post*, the seemingly simple concept of possession has escaped containment. Generations of law students have wondered whether it was Pierson or Post who had gained legal possession of the fox the later chased and the former found exhausted. * * *

[O]bviously, as Holmes explains, possession means more than its most literal connotations, else "one could only possess what was under his hand." Holmes, The Common Law 236 (1881). The jurist gives the example of a man who has left a purse of gold at his distant and isolated country estate; could anyone doubt that a burglar would deprive the absent owner of possession of the purse? Could anyone doubt that the original owner's possession would not end "until the burglar, by an overt act, had manifested his power and intent to exclude others from the purse"?

What must be distinguished are the possession of an object and the possession of rights with respect to that object. Holmes contends that it is the "ambiguity of language which has led to much confusion of thought. We use the word 'possession' indifferently, to signify [both] the presence of all the facts needful to gain it, and also the condition of him who, although some of the[se facts] no longer exist, is still protected as if they did." Thus do the concepts of possession and ownership diverge: the absent squire without present power over his purse is nonetheless viewed in the law as continuing to possess it. The question is always "whether we cannot dispense with even more" of the facts apparently necessary for possession under law.

In recent decades, courts have dispensed with many "facts needful to gain" possession of narcotics. To achieve the ends of justice, they have deemed it necessary to expand the legal concept of possession. As has been explained:

Quite frequently, the ringleaders or overlords of the narcotics business do not stultify themselves by possession when handlers can be so cheaply hired. Therefore, in an effort to bring a modicum of reality into the picture, the courts in the absence of Congressional action have had to create the doctrine of constructive possession or control.

[United States v. Bentvena, 319 F.2d 916, 950 (2nd Cir.1963), cert. denied sub nom., 375 U.S. 940, 84 S.Ct. 354, 11 L.Ed.2d 271 (1963).]

* * * Some individuals to whom the constructive possession theory clearly applies are: the owner of luggage checked with an airline, the owner of a footlocker checked on a train, the street peddler who uses his female courier to carry drugs for delivery to his customers, and the doctor who arranges to have drugs, ostensibly for a patient, delivered by a pharmacist to his office * * *.

* * * From this we may infer that there is a considerable degree of latitude within which courts may seek to expand the legal fiction of constructive possession in order to achieve the ends of justice. * * *

Are there any limits to constructive possession? Or is it simply a method for courts to reach the result that they want? How did you use constructive possession in your arguments on Diana's and Irene's bailment problem? You will come back to constructive possession when you study adverse possession.

5. Arguments concerning discovery and constructive possession come into play in resolving disputes concerning sunken treasure. Consider the following problem.

The Sunken Treasure Problem

The Columbus–America Discovery Group (based in Columbus, Ohio) won exclusive salvage rights in 1987 by successfully arguing "tele-possession" of the wreck of the Central America (and its gold cargo worth up to $1 billion) which lay under 8,000 feet of water. Columbus–America based their claim on retrieving one piece of coal using a deep-water robot they named Nemo. The judge allowed the salvage claim despite the failure to meet the customary standard requiring a diver to physically visit the site. Yet to be decided is the ownership of the cargo itself.

Columbus–America's president Thomas Thompson claims ownership. They spent 13 years and $12 million in finding the ship. Which, incidentally, was not located on the spot identified in an earlier court case concerning the wreck. Some competitors of Columbus–America claim that it misrepresented the location of the wreck in order to decoy the real site. Columbus–America claims it discovered the wreck as it was heading toward the earlier identified location. According to Thompson, "no one was there" and his team "exercised exclusive control over the shipwreck site." They now have recovered about one ton of the approximately three tons of cargo.

Contenders for the gold also include ten insurance companies that claim they paid off on the loss when the ship was sunk in 1857. Columbus–America claims that the insurance companies cannot prove they paid; and even if they can, they abandoned the wreck and made no effort to recover it. The insurance companies respond that they don't abandon property and, furthermore, the gold was simply "in storage."

Columbia University has also made a claim. The University says that Columbus–America relied on sonar studies it had produced. It also claimed that a vessel it owned discovered the shipwreck in 1984 but had not realized it at the time.

Finally, preservationists are upset that Columbus–America is destroying the wreck by retrieving the cargo in this way. The gold already recovered was on display briefly before it was moved to an undisclosed location. Preservationists claim that the wreck could be a valuable resource to historians, oceanographers and archaeologists. (Taken from a series of news articles reported April 3–6, 1990.)

What do you think of the judge's creation of a rule of tele-possession in granting salvage rights? How would you resolve this dispute? Would any of the theories of property ownership we discussed earlier influence your result?

D. ADVERSE POSSESSION

Adverse possession is a combination of statutory and common law. The statutory foundation for adverse possession is the statute of limitations on an action for ejectment of trespassers. Statutes of limitations limit the amount of time an aggrieved party has to bring suit against a wrongdoer. The statutes govern all common-law actions including actions for breach of contract, negligence, and professional malpractice, as well as ejectment of trespassers. The Missouri statute of limitations, which governs the case that follows, provides:

516.010 Actions for recovery of lands commenced, when.—No action for the recovery of any lands, tenements or hereditaments, or for the recovery of the possession thereof, shall be commenced, had or maintained by any person, whether citizen, denizen, alien, resident or non-resident of this state, unless it appear that the plaintiff, his ancestor, predecessor, grantor or other person under whom he claims was seized or possessed of the premises in question, within ten years before the commencement of such action.

The primary purpose of a statute of limitations is to assure that lawsuits are brought within a reasonable amount of time. Trespass can be a continuous injury; for example, in a situation in which a trespasser remains on the land over a period of time. In this type of case, the statute of limitations would never bar a lawsuit by the owner of the property, and the trespasser would always be at risk of ejectment. The doctrine of adverse possession avoids this result. Under this doctrine, a trespasser who meets the requirements of adverse possession over the required period of time (usually the statutory limit for an action in ejectment) may not only bar a suit by the owner, but actually may take title to the property himself.

Trespass is not ordinarily viewed as a good thing. Then why is it rewarded in adverse possession? Part of the answer to this question may be that there are "good" trespassers and there are "bad" trespassers, and there are "diligent" landowners and "irresponsible" landowners. In most adverse-possession cases, however, the relative goodness or badness of the claimants is not directly addressed. Instead, possession is rewarded for some of the same reasons discussed in the material following *Johnson v. McIntosh*. As you might expect, however, good and bad are not totally ignored. The extent to which concerns over "good" and "bad" trespassers enter court opinions on adverse possession is discussed after the principal case.

By the way, a recent computer search of state appellate court decisions involving adverse possession revealed more than 350 cases over a period of 18 months.

TESON v. VASQUEZ

Court of Appeals of Missouri, 1977.
561 S.W.2d 119.

GUNN, PRESIDING JUDGE.

This is a consolidated cross appeal from judgments of the circuit court, sitting without a jury, quieting title to certain tracts of land located in St. Louis County in claimants, Teson, Sommers, Keeven and Behle, by adverse possession and quieting title to other tracts in defendants Vasquez under their quitclaim deed. Defendants argue on appeal that the elements of adverse possession were not established by the claimants in whom title was quieted. Claimants, Klaus and Teson, who were found not to have established title by adverse possession, appeal from the court's finding, arguing that they proved their title under that theory.

We affirm in part and reverse in part.

Claimant, Lawrence Teson, commenced this suit on August 25, 1969, by filing a petition in the circuit court seeking to have title to certain lands near his home quieted in favor of himself and his wife. Defendants, Leo and Velma Vasquez, then filed a motion to make more definite and certain. No further action was taken until December 8, 1972, when Teson, with leave of court, filed a first amended petition seeking to quiet title to the same tract of land by adverse possession. Claimants, Keeven, Behle, Klaus and Sommers, who claimed title to nearby and adjoining lands by adverse possession, were added as parties plaintiff. Defendant's answer, filed March 30, 1973, was a general denial. In their counterclaim, defendants alleged that they were conveyed good title to the entire property in question by a quitclaim deed from Hugo and Alvina Essen on October 2, 1950 and prayed that title be quieted in them on the basis of this recorded deed.[1] Prior to trial defendants' motion to separate was sustained, and each claimant's suit was ordered to be tried separately but seriatim. The Teson and Sommers cases were so tried. Because of the confusion and repetition

---

1. In their counterclaim, defendants disclaimed ownership to certain property lying between Aubuchon Road and Cowmire Creek, even though it was within the tract described by the deed from the Essens because it was found to have been erroneously included.

of evidence encountered in those cases, the Keeven–Behle and Klaus cases were tried together.

The property in controversy consists of approximately 208 acres of rich river bottom land in northeast St. Louis County. It is bounded on the north by the Missouri River and on the south by Aubuchon Road. The eastern and western boundaries are not marked by any distinct landmarks but are merely prolongations of United States survey lines from their endpoint at Aubuchon Road extending to the Missouri River. The four parcels claimed by adverse possession are shaped roughly as rectangles, and each is bounded by Aubuchon Road, the river and the prolongations of the United States survey lines. Title to a 92 acre parcel situated between the Teson and Klaus tracts was quieted in defendants in *Baxter v. Vasquez,* 501 S.W.2d 201 (Mo.App.1973). This suit concerns the title to the remaining 208 acres purportedly conveyed to defendants by the Essens under the 1950 quitclaim deed. The following generally depicts the location of the property involved:

[See following illustration.]

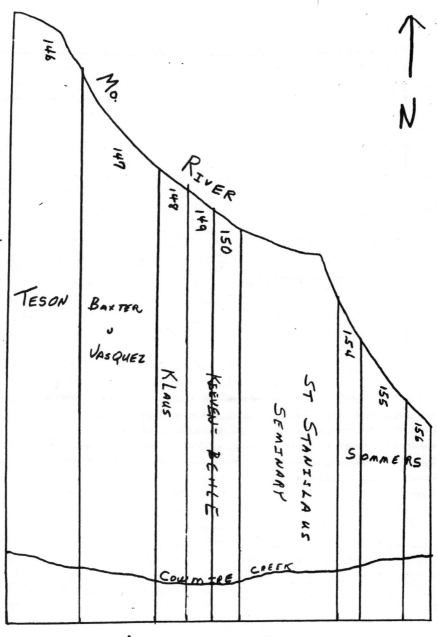

The land in controversy, though it is rich farmland today, was not always so. In the mid 1800's when the area was first surveyed and platted this land was an island in the middle of the Missouri River. The St. Louis County bank of the river was located at what is now called Cowmire Creek near Aubuchon Road. Over the last century and one half, the river channel slowly shifted northward until the former island became attached to the St. Louis County riverbank. Even after it became part of the mainland early in this century, almost none of the land was suitable for farming because of the low-lying swampy character of the land, the dense growth of timber, brush and vines and the frequent flooding. In 1950 when the Essens conveyed this property to defendants, it remained largely a vast wasteland of little value. Since that time many improvements have taken place increasing the worth of the land. One or more levees have been constructed which have lessened, though not eliminated, the flooding problems, and which have decreased the acreage covered by swamps. Additionally, the land was cleared of floodplain vegetation. This clearing occurred slowly and sporadically in the 1950's, but its pace quickened appreciably in the early 1960's and has continued until the present. Today the vast majority of the land is suitable for farming. There remain, however, a number of low-lying sloughs crisscrossing the property as well as the free-flowing Cowmire Creek.

Before detailing and examining claimant's acts of possession which allegedly vested title in them to the land in controversy, we indite the well settled precepts of the law of adverse possession. The claimant has the burden of proving by the preponderance of the evidence the existence for the entire statutory period of each and every element of adverse possession. He must show actual, hostile, i.e., under a claim of right, open and notorious, exclusive and continuous possession of the property for ten years. [The statutory period in Missouri.] Failure to prove any one element prevents the ripening of title by adverse possession. [ ]

In dealing with a case of adverse possession, it must be remembered that we are presented with mixed questions of law and fact in which the application of the facts to the law presents the major issues of controversy. Moreover, our task is further complicated by the fact that every piece of property is unique. Thus, in determining whether the facts in evidence authorize a finding that the elements of adverse possession have been satisfied, each case must be decided in light of its own unique circumstances. Much depends on the location, the character and the use to which the land in question may reasonably be put. [ ] Those specific manifestations of possession and ownership exhibited by a claimant which would support a finding of title by adverse possession in a populous and highly developed area are not the same as those which would support such a finding where, as here, the property is sparsely populated farm and waste land. * * *

The first element is actual possession. Two concepts are relevant in determining whether a claimant has established his actual possession of the land claimed. They are his present ability to control the land and his intent to exclude others from such control. Where the claimant occupies land without color of title, in order to prevail, he must show physical possession of the entire area claimed. A mere mental enclosure of land does not constitute the requisite actual possession. Rather, there must be continual acts of occupying, clearing, cultivating, pasturing, erecting fences or other improvements and paying taxes on the land. The performance of all or any combination of these acts of occupancy serves as evidence of actual possession but is not conclusive. [ ] Each case must be decided on its own peculiar facts.

Where the claimant occupies land under color of title the requirement of actual possession of the entire area claimed is relaxed. By statute, one who occupies land under color of title is required only to physically possess a part of the tract claimed in the name of the whole, if during the period of possession he exercises the usual acts of ownership over the whole. Thus, color of title is not an element of adverse possession, but it serves to extend actual possession of some portion of the land claimed to constructive possession of the whole tract described in the instrument providing the basis for color of title.[2] [ ] The instrument relied upon as color of title must be bona fide and must purport on its face to convey title to the land. [ ] It need not actually convey legal title so long as it pretends to make the claimant the apparent owner. Even a void deed is sufficient to constitute color of title if it includes within its description the land claimed. [ ]

In addition to describing the land claimed, it is also required that the true owner have actual or constructive notice of the instrument and its contents. Thus, he must be advised not only of the claimant's actual possession, which must be open and notorious to satisfy the requirements of adverse possession, but also the constructive extent and boundary of the land claimed. [ ] This can only be known by being actually apprised of the contents or having the opportunity to be so apprised by the fact of recordation of the instrument bestowing color of title. Once color of title is established, less weight of evidence is required to support an adverse entry under its apparent authority than for a bare entry by one without a claim of right. [ ]

The second element which must be proved to establish adverse possession is that the possession be hostile or under a claim of right. Naked possession asserted for any period of time, no matter now lengthy, is insufficient to ripen into adverse possession. For possession to be hostile it is neither required that the true owner have knowledge of the hostile claim of right or that the claimant intend to deprive him

2. There has been some confusion over the distinction between color of title and claim of right. The former relates to the existence of a deed or proceeding which apparently vests the title to the land in question in the claimant. The latter is part of the element of hostile possession and requires that claimant enter and remain on the land with a belief that his right to do so is superior to that of the alleged owner. [ ]

of title. The possession must be opposed and antagonistic to the claims of all others, i.e., the claimant must occupy the land with the intent to possess it as his own and not in subservience to a recognized, superior claim of another. Furthermore, the claim of right or ownership must be unequivocal.

The third element of adverse possession is that the possession be open and notorious. To satisfy this element it is necessary to prove that the claimant's occupancy was conspicuous, widely recognized and commonly known. One may not acquire title by adverse possession if his occupancy has been so covert that it is unknown to the persons who deal regularly with and around the land claimed. The reason the law requires open and notorious possession for title to ripen by adverse possession is to give the owner cause to know of the adverse claim of ownership by another. Thus, if the true owner has actual knowledge that another claims in defiance of and in opposition to his title, the openness and notoriety requirement is satisfied. It is not the mere knowledge of occupation of his land by another which will prejudice the true owner's rights under his title. Rather, it is the adverse and hostile character of the occupation which must be known. If actual knowledge is not proved then the claimant must show an occupancy so obvious and well recognized as to be inconsistent with and injurious to the real owner's rights that the law will authorize a presumption from the facts that he had such knowledge.

The fourth element of adverse possession, that of exclusivity of possession, only requires that the claimant occupy the land for his own use and not for that of another. Generally, one may not be vicariously vested with title by adverse possession as a result of possession by another, though where there is the requisite relationship between the parties, tacking of possession is allowed. [Tacking is discussed later in this case.] . . .

The final element of adverse possession is that the occupancy be continuous, i.e., without lapse, for the entire statutory period. Temporary absence from the land without an intention to abandon possession will not break the continuity of possession; intermittent and sporadic occupancy will. In judging the continuity of possession, the character and use to which the land is adaptable must be taken into account. For instance, under the facts of this case, the periodic flooding which made access to and use of the property impossible for entire growing seasons would not interrupt the continuity of possession unless there was an intent to abandon possession after the waters receded.

One overriding requirement to establish adverse possession to a particular piece of property is that the precise location of the land claimed be identified in such a way that the boundaries may be ascertained and recognized. Absent proof by claimant of the exact location of lands claimed, any judgment would be void, because it would rest entirely on speculation and conjecture. * * *

[W]e review both the law and the evidence giving due recognition to the superior position of the trial court to judge the credibility of the witnesses. The judgment must be sustained unless it is without substantial evidentiary support, unless it is against the weight of the evidence or unless it erroneously declares or applies the law.

The land claimed by Lawrence Teson is a fertile 75 acre strip contained within the prolongation of the United States survey 146 extending north of Aubuchon Road to the Missouri River. It lies within the river's floodplain with the result that the low-lying areas are often covered by back water from the several sloughs which traverse the land. In 1950 when the Essens conveyed this land to defendants, it was almost totally overgrown with timber, brush and vines. Only a negligible portion was suitable for farming. The only commercial activity on the land at that time was intermittent timber and pulp wood removal by various persons.

In 1925, Teson was conveyed title by quit-claim deed to $23^{11}/_{100}$ acres lying within United States survey 146 immediately adjacent to Aubuchon Road. There was no mention in this deed of land lying north of Aubuchon Road or of any right to accretions. Nevertheless, Teson testified that it was his understanding that the deed conveyed not only the land lying south of Aubuchon Road but also accretions on the north to the river. It is uncontested that Teson did in fact farm a parcel of the land claimed immediately north of Aubuchon Road continuously since 1941 when the elements permitted. So much of this parcel as lies between Aubuchon Road and Cowmire Creek is not in controversy, because defendant has disclaimed any rights of ownership to land south of Cowmire Creek. Whether the parcel farmed by Teson near Aubuchon Road included land north of Cowmire Creek was in dispute.

In addition to farming the southern parcel Teson claims that he and his sons began clearing and farming small "spots" (4–5 acres each) on the north near the river sometime in the late 1950's. Exactly where these "spots" were located and whether they were kept continuously cleared in the wake of the periodic floods which inundated the land is not clear from the evidence. These early instances of clearing were accomplished by man and horse power alone, without the aid of modern equipment. In the early 1960's the pace of clearing was accelerated and larger sections of land within the strip claimed by Teson were made tillable and were farmed. By 1962 twelve acres, 1500–2000 feet south of the river's bank, were suitable for farming. In 1964, Teson hired a heavy equipment operator for a few days to help clear more land. This clearing activity has continued so that at the time of trial approximately 50 acres were cleared and used as farmland. Though Teson, who was 81 years of age at the time of trial, testified that he continuously farmed lands on the northern end of the property near the river prior to 1960, he admitted in his deposition that he only began farming this tract a few years prior to trial, because before that time it was all timber.

Teson testified that the boundary of the land he claimed was marked by cedar and iron posts from Aubuchon Road back to the river. He admitted that the iron posts were implanted after a survey he had conducted five to seven years prior to the trial. Teson claimed that at one time fences existed in places along his claimed boundary but that they were washed out by floods. At the time of trial no fences existed marking any boundaries on this property.

In addition to cutting timber, clearing brush and farming the reclaimed areas, Teson claimed to have paid taxes on the property from 1925 to 1965. He introduced receipts for those years showing that he paid taxes on 75 acres of accretions, but the receipts did not specify where those 75 acres were located. Further, in 1968, Teson paid over $1400 for repair to a levee crossing the parcel claimed. He also claims to have ejected various hunters and other intruders from the land over the years. He contends that at one time in the 1950's, he personally warned defendant not to intrude on the property he claimed.

Defendant relies solely on the 1950 quit-claim deed from the Essens as the basis for his claim of title. Defendant rarely visited this property. He averaged only ten visits per year over the entire 300 acre tract, and these were primarily for recreational purposes. 1953 was the only year defendant farmed any part of the land claimed, and he planted only a few acres near the river. Defendant, who owned an excavating business, directed his employees to enter the property with heavy equipment in 1964 to clear approximately ten acres to be used for farming by his relatives. Also, defendant paid real estate taxes on the property from 1948 to the time of trial. He carried liability insurance on the property from 1959.

Defendant testified that he never saw Teson on the contested property prior to 1964. Several witnesses, adjoining landowners and former farm laborers, testified that they observed no farm activity on the tract claimed by Teson prior to the early 1960's when small patches of land near the river were cleared of underbrush.

The trial court held that Teson's 1925 deed did not constitute color of title. Nevertheless, it held that Teson had established the elements of adverse possession to a tract of approximately twenty acres adjacent to Aubuchon Road extending north of Cowmire Creek to a small tarn known as "Round Pond." Title to a second parcel of almost forty acres near the river was also vested in Teson. Title to the land between these two parcels was quieted in defendant.

Under the foregoing facts we affirm the trial court's judgment as to the parcel near Aubuchon Road and reverse as to the parcel near the river. The trial court correctly concluded that Teson could claim no color of title to the property north of Aubuchon Road under his 1925 deed. As such, he could acquire title by adverse possession only to the lands he had actually physically possessed for the statutory period. Teson's proof failed to establish that he had continuously and actually possessed any specific portion of the property near the river. There was testimony of sporadic clearing and cultivation of land somewhere near the river over the years by various persons, including defendant and his relatives. There was little credible evidence of any sustained and permanent clearing until the mid 1960's. Teson admitted in his deposition that he had not farmed the northern portion of the land claimed until the last few years before the trial, because it was covered with timber. Though there is sufficient proof that Teson and his sons did engage in some farming activities on the land near the river, the evidence completely failed to establish the precise boundaries of any tract Teson used for the statutory period. As such, the trial court had no basis to conclude that Teson actually and continuously possessed the 40 acre tract it awarded him.

Furthermore, title by adverse possession to land near the river could not vest in Teson, because his possession was not open and notorious for the entire statutory period. There is no evidence that defendant had actual knowledge of Teson's possession. Nor does the record reveal sufficient facts from which we could presume constructive knowledge on the part of defendant. Teson's presence on the land was only sporadic and until the mid 1960's was confined to small areas which he could clear with hand equipment. The land was densely thicketed with trees, brush and vines which served to obscure any progress made. Moreover, there were no fences or other readily observable boundaries. Thus, the trial court's finding of title by adverse possession to the northern 40 acres in Teson was in error, because actual, open and notorious possession was not proved. Nor were exact boundaries established to any smaller parcel for which the elements of adverse possession may have been satisfied. Therefore, the trial court's designation of title to the northern 40 acres in Teson was speculative and conjectural and cannot stand.

As to the southern portion near Aubuchon Road, it cannot be said that the trial court erred in finding title by adverse possession in Teson. It is clear that Teson had acquired title to the tract between Aubuchon Road and Cowmire Creek by adverse possession. Defendant disclaimed any interest in this property, and its ownership was not in controversy. The land in question is only that which lies between Cowmire Creek and Round Pond.

The testimony was conflicting, but there was competent evidence that Teson had farmed the 20 acres between Aubuchon Road and Round Pond continuously for a time well beyond the statutory period. This parcel, unlike that near the river, was in plain sight from Aubuchon Road. The cultivation must have been clearly visible from the public thoroughfare and open and notorious.

The trial court's finding of title in defendant to the center portion of the tract claimed by Teson was correct. Defendant introduced a recorded quitclaim deed clearly encompassing this area. For the purpose of conveying title, a quitclaim is as effective as any other deed. Teson, on the other hand, relied entirely on an adverse possession theory which he failed to prove. He had no basis on which to claim this center portion as the trial court correctly concluded.

The land claimed by Sommers is that included within the prolongation of United States survey 154 lying north of Old Charbonnier Road to the Missouri River. Sommers contends that the land was conveyed to him and his wife on October 3, 1952, by a warranty deed from John Little and wife. The deed described the land as consisting of 3½ acres in the western portion of survey 154 but further recited that the land was bounded by the Missouri River with all accretions.

Defendant Vasquez claims title to the property in question north of Cowmire Creek under the 1950 quitclaim deed from the Essens. He disclaims any title to land within the prolongation of survey 154 lying south of Cowmire Creek.

Shortly after Mr. Sommers took possession of the property in 1952, he erected fences along the entire prolongation of survey 154 to the Missouri River. He maintained those fences until the early 1960's. During this period he also constructed a barn just north of Cowmire Creek. His agricultural activities included raising a small number of Brahman cattle and up to 80 horses on the property. Although about 80% of the property was already cleared in 1952, Sommers continued the clearing operations so that almost the entire area was cleared by the time of the trial.

Sometime between 1960 and 1967 Sommers traded the use of land claimed by him north of Cowmire Creek to St. Stanislaus Seminary, an adjacent landowner, for the use of other seminary property. The seminary then removed the fences north of the creek and farmed the land as its own until 1971 when another party purchased the seminary property. Sommers testified, however, that he continued to use the barn north of Cowmire Creek until 1965. Both Vasquez and Sommers claimed to have paid real estate taxes on the property.

Defendant testified that at the time he was conveyed the property in 1950 it was used for crop and pasture land and that fences were on the eastern and western boundaries. He acknowledged that he never made use of the property but stated that it was he who gave permission to St. Stanislaus Seminary to use the land in 1960 or 1961. Defendant admitted that as early as 1954 he was aware that a barn had been constructed and that livestock was being raised on the property.

The trial court correctly concluded that the recorded deed from the previous owners, the Littles, to the Sommers gave the latter color of title to the land claimed. Though ambiguous because of the reference to the 3½ acre plot, the deed clearly purports on its face to convey title in Sommers to land bounded on the north by the Missouri River with all accretions. The only real challenge to the court's finding that Sommers established title by adverse possession relates to whether his possession was continuous for the requisite period. The evidence shows that Sommers entered into possession of the property in 1952 and exercised sufficient dominion over it until the trade so that title could be vested in him by adverse possession. The evidence does not clearly and unambiguously establish the date of the trade with the seminary. Sommers, an elderly gentleman who had suffered a stroke just prior to trial, testified as to various dates between 1960 and 1964. Other witnesses, who lived or worked nearby stated that the trade occurred in 1967. No one from the seminary testified as to the date of the trade.

No question of law is presented under these facts. We are faced squarely with a question of the credibility and accuracy of the various witnesses. We defer to the superior opportunity of the trial court to judge the credibility of the witnesses and to resolve the inconsistencies in testimony. The judgment quieting title in claimant Sommers must be affirmed.

The property claimed by Keeven and Behle consists of 76 acres lying within the prolongations of United States surveys 149 and 150 between Cowmire Creek and the Missouri River. They rest their claim of ownership on adverse possession but argue they have at least color of title by virtue of a 1963 warranty deed from Mary Hagen. The Hagens were purportedly conveyed title to this property in 1954. At that time, little of the property had been cleared for farming. But Hagen initiated clearing operations so that by 1962, 20 acres near the river and 15–20 acres near Cowmire Creek were cleared and farmed. Hagen used the uncleared middle section to raise hogs. Hagen's farming operations continued until the fall of 1961 when he failed to harvest his soybean crop. He died in early 1962.

After Mrs. Hagen gave Keeven and Behle the deed in April of 1963, they immediately began to fence the eastern and western boundaries of the land from Cowmire Creek to the river. Once the fencing project was completed in October, 1963, cattle were placed on the property. Simultaneously with the fencing, claimants began clearing the land of its dense overgrowth of floodplain vegetation. By 1965 they had cleared over 30 acres for farming. They planted this acreage in bluegrass for use in their commercial sod business and installed a portable irrigation system. After a few years the cattle were removed and about 500 head of hogs were placed on the property. From 1963 until the time of trial claimants paid taxes on this property.

Defendant claims the property under the 1950 Essen deed. He rarely visited this property, though he admitted seeing some small areas farmed and noticed a few stray hogs on the property in the mid 1950's. Defendant first learned that Keeven and Behle claimed the land in the prolongation of surveys 149 and 150 at a wedding the parties attended in 1963. At that time defendant told them that he had prior deed to the same property and that Keeven and Behle had better check their title. Defendant maintains that he told them that they could go ahead and use the property until "the deeds were straightened out." Obviously, the disputed claims of ownership were not reconciled though defendant, and Keeven had several telephone conversations on the subject subsequent to their meeting at the wedding. In addition to Keeven and Behle, defendant maintained that he had given permission to Donald Teson, Louis Tebeau and the priests at St. Stanislaus Seminary to farm his bottom land including the surveys 149 and 150 parcels. He neither charged nor received rent from any of the parties. The trial court held that Keeven and Behle had established their title by adverse possession to the entire parcel claimed.

* * *

Defendant's challenge to Keeven and Behle's claim of title by adverse possession goes solely to the continuity of possession. In order to prevail, claimants must be able to tack their possession to that of their grantors, the Hagens. When the Hagens took possession of this property in 1954, they were presented with a deed from the prior owner which set the northern boundary of their property at the Missouri River. Therefore, they occupied the land under color of title. As such, the Hagens needed only to have actual possession of a part of the property with the intent to possess the whole. This they did. Mr. Hagen cleared and farmed sections near the river and Cowmire Creek in addition to raising hogs on the property. It is true that Mr. Hagen failed to harvest his soybean crop in the fall of 1961, but in light of the fact that he died in early 1962 the trial court could reasonably conclude that he had not abandoned the property. The finding of continuous possession for the statutory period by tacking the possessions of the Hagens and Keeven and Behle has support in the record. The trial court's judgment quieting title by adverse possession in them is supported by substantial evidence and is affirmed.

* * *

* * * The judgment of the trial court quieting title in defendant to the tract claimed by Klaus and the tract claimed by Teson north of Round Pond must be affirmed.

KELLY and WEIER, JJ., concur.

Notes and Questions

1. The court states that one claiming title through adverse possession must satisfy all of the requirements for the required period of time. When do you begin counting for each of the claimants in this case? For successful claims, the adverse possessors actually become the owners of the property on the date on which the ten-year period is satisfied. When was this for each of the successful claimants in this case? In order for the adverse claimant to succeed, the elements of adverse possession must exist throughout the entire statutory period. Thus, any significant interruption in the claimant's possession will defeat the continuous requirement. After such a break in possession, reentry by the claimant begins the statutory period anew. Interruptions may occur due to the claimant's voluntary absence, conditions of the property, or ouster by the true owner or another. But what constitutes a significant interruption? The same considerations used to determine actual possession are also used to determine whether a given interruption is substantial enough to break the chain of continuity,

e.g. the nature of the property and its suitability for the use, and the totality of circumstances. For example, in Weiss v. Meyer, 208 Neb. 429, 303 N.W.2d 765 (1981), several years of drought which prevented the cultivation of hay did not create a disruption in the continuity of possession.

The title holder can interrupt the statutory period by filing suit for ejectment. The time stops on the date of the filing. In *Teson*, Vasquez claimed that he learned of Keeven's and Behle's claim at a wedding reception in 1963. Vasquez claimed that he told Keeven and Behle to "go ahead and use the property" until things were resolved. How could Vazquez have argued that this conversation interrupted Keeven's and Behle's claim?

2. All state statutes of limitations contain provisions to toll or extend the period for persons under specific disabilities when the cause of action accrues. Insanity, minority of age, imprisonment and absences due to military duty are typical disabilities. See, e.g., Mings v. Mings, 782 S.W.2d 165 (Mo.App.1990); Barstow v. State of Texas, 742 S.W.2d 495 (Tex.App. 1987); Hillman v. Stults, 263 Cal.App.2d 848, 70 Cal.Rptr. 295 (1968). Disabilities that arise after the statute of limitations begins to run will not stop the running of the clock.

The Arkansas statute of limitations for ejectment includes the following provision on disabilities:

> If any person who is, or shall be, entitled to commence and prosecute a suit or action in law or equity is, or shall be, at the time the right or title first accrued come or fallen within the age of twenty-one (21) years or non compos mentis, the person or his heirs, shall and may, notwithstanding the seven (7) years may have expired, bring his suit or action if the infant or non compos mentis, or his heirs, shall bring it within three (3) years next after full age or coming of sound mind.

Ark.Code.Ann. § 18–61–101(b). Assume that O owned land currently possessed by P and that O wants to bring an action for ejectment under Arkansas law where the statute of limitations for this action is seven years. You find that P has been in possession for ten years. Is the action barred if (1) O was 10 years old when P took possession? (2) O was 15 years old when P took possession? (3) O was mentally ill and incompetent when P took possession?

3. When an individual adverse possessor cannot meet the statutory period for possession, he may still acquire title by tacking periods of a prior possessor who has met the requirements of adverse possession. Thus, a series of adverse possessors may sequentially tack their possessory times, until the statutory period is fulfilled. The combined possessions, however, must create a continuous chain of adverse possession. Tacking is only allowed where privity exists between the prior and current adverse possessor. Any voluntary transfer or surrender of the property is sufficient to establish privity. Similarly, when the true owner transfers his title to the property, the statutory time that has run against him is tacked to the new owner of record title. Thus, the new owner has only the remaining statutory time to seek ejectment of the adverse possessor. For example,

assuming a ten-year statutory period, if the possessor has established the elements for adverse possession for seven years, and the true owner transfers his title, the subsequent title holder only has three years in which to seek ejectment of the possessor.

The following problem to test the requirements of tacking is provided in Boyer, Hovenkamp and Kurtz, The Law of Property (1991):

> O owned Blackacre. In a jurisdiction where the statutory period to recover the possession of real property was 20 years, A went into adverse possession of Blackacre and remained in possession for 5 years. A then died intestate. H was A's sole heir. H took possession of Blackacre, remained in possession for the next 3 years and then conveyed Blackacre to M. M remained in possession of Blackacre for 2 years and then died. Under M's will Blackacre was bequeathed to P who took possession of Blackacre for 5 years and then orally conveyed the premises to X. X possessed the premises for 3 years and leased it to L for one year. When the lease was terminated X re-possessed Blackacre. Two weeks later X joined the United States Army. Before leaving for military service, X called D and advised him to take over Blackacre and make the most of it and that X would make no further claim to it. D took possession at X's suggestion and remained in possession for 2 months when D was called to another state on account of her father's serious illness. She stayed with her father for 3 months and then returned to Blackacre and remained in possession for more than 3 years. D then called O and said to him: "O, I have decided to abandon Blackacre. It is yours if you want it." D then moved off Blackacre with no intent to return. Who owns Blackacre?

4. Both Teson and Sommers claimed to have color of title. Why did Teson's claim of color of title fail and Sommers' claim succeed?

5. The common law requirements for adverse possession can be modified by legislation. States may establish varying statutory times for acquiring title by adverse possession dependent upon the wild or uncultivated nature of the land. See, e.g., N.J.Rev.Stat. § 2A:14–30 (1987). Other states adjust the statutory period where the claim is under a "color of title," diminishing the period necessary to acquire valid title. Payment of taxes may create a presumption of "color of title." See, e.g., Ark.Stat.Ann. § 18–11–102, 103 (1989); Ala.Code § 6–5–200 (1989). Frequently, adverse claims require payment of taxes during the statutory period before title can be vested in the possessor. See, e.g., Ind.Code Ann. § 32–1–20–1 (Burns 1989). Also, some states have specified what acts are considered possessory, such as establishing boundaries by a substantial enclosure, or cultivating the land. See, e.g., Fla.Stat. § 95.16 (1988). Finally, some states limit the amount of land that may be claimed and how frequently any person may make adverse possession claims. See, e.g., Haw.Rev.Stat. § 669–1(c).

6. You may have noticed in reading the case and notes in this section on adverse possession that there is great significance attached to whether the person claiming adverse possession fenced in the area. Why do you suppose that is? You might consider that fencing is the most common way of exerting control over land. Or you might conclude that fencing land that is not your own is the most visible way of giving notice to the owner

that you are exerting control. Some of the discussion in *Teson* concerning activities that constitute actual possession is reminiscent of the discussion of acquisition in *Johnson v. McIntosh.*

Not surprisingly, some scholars have attributed other broader meanings to the significance of fencing. Professor Ball argues that the legal significance of fencing reveals our view of law in general, i.e., that law is a bulwark that operates as a device for dividing and protecting holdings: "Bounded land and fences came to have an added and eventually dominant connotation; they describe a commodity." Ball, Law Natural: Its Family of Metaphors and Its Theology, 3 J. of Law and Religion 141 (1985). Professor Alexander identifies four unspoken premises of "Fortress America" signified by the importance of fences: "insecurity of our own existence and hunger for order; the sense that self is protected from ambiguity by boundaries and distance from others; an insistence that freedom lies in personal choice; and frustration that accompanies a sense of incompleteness." Alexander, Demythologizing Law, 3 J. of Law and Religion 167 (1985). Professor Shaffer responds to these views by arguing that the metaphor of bulwark adopted by both Ball and Alexander is at least premature and a perversion of ownership. Shaffer argues that the metaphor for private property is not bulwark, "it is home * * * a place to be." Shaffer believes that good fences make good neighbors. He describes a strip of land between his yard and that of his neighbor: "I do not know where people in the county court house would say my side lawn ends and my neighbor's begins; my neighbor doesn't know either. We each fertilize and cut two or three mower widths past where the line probably is; the broad strip of lawn over which we communicate—over which we do justice—is the best nourished and best cut part of either lawn." He notes that if they have to someday find a boundary, they are both at risk, but states that "lawyers provide moral leadership in such enterprises, more often than we think." Shaffer, Slippered Feet Aboard the African Queen, 3 J. of Law and Religion 193 (1985). What do you think "moral leadership" requires in such a case? Does it describe your duty to your client?

7. The doctrine of agreed boundaries has developed to lend stability to agreements, which are made by neighboring landowners, to fix a disputed or uncertain boundary. An actual transfer of land does not take place; rather, the boundary is redefined by an expressed agreement of the parties. The agreement does not need to be in writing in order to be binding, but the subsequent conduct of the parties must demonstrate that the agreement exists. Boundaries by agreement require: (a) uncertainty or dispute as to the true boundary; (b) an express or implied agreement that designates what the parties will consider to be the boundary; and (c) acceptance of, or acquiescence to, the agreed upon boundary for a period of time, frequently equal to the statute of limitations for adverse possession. See Annot. 7 A.L.R. 4th 53 (1981). Would this resolve Professor Shaffer's situation with his neighbor? A threshold determination is whether there is an unknown, uncertain or disputed boundary. See, Gameson v. Remer, 96 Idaho 789, 537 P.2d 631 (1975), holding that since the subdivision plat was recorded, the true boundaries were known and the doctrine of agreed boundaries was inapplicable. A common source of disputes is whether there has been an agreement to set a boundary. It is generally stated that

mere acquiescence to a barrier or monument is not sufficient to establish title. See Townsend v. Koukol, 148 Mont. 1, 416 P.2d 532 (1966), holding that there was no evidence of an agreement and that mere acquiescence to a fence as a barrier did not establish boundary by acquiescence. See also, Mesnick v. Caton, 183 Cal.App.3d 1248, 228 Cal.Rptr. 779 (1986), in which the court held that there was no evidence of an express agreement, and an implied agreement was negated by the unkempt condition, irregular shape and contour of a grapestick fence. An implied agreement was found in Herrmann v. Woodell, 107 Idaho 916, 693 P.2d 1118 (App.1985). The plaintiffs sought title up to a fence, which was erected within the legal description of the defendant's land. The court held that where there is no proof of an express agreement, erection of a fence and long-term acquiescence to the fence as a boundary establishes a *rebuttable* presumption of an implied agreement. Finally, the agreement must establish a certain and defined boundary. See, Declerk v. Johnson, 268 Ark. 868, 596 S.W.2d 359 (App.1980), where the court held that when the evidence only indicated that the agreement was to an approximate boundary, and not to a definite and certain line, there was no boundary by agreement.

8. The standard statement of the law of adverse possession identifies the hostile or adverse nature of the claimant's possession as a critical element of the law. Hostility does not require a wrongful intent to dispossess another. Any possession which is non-permissive and inconsistent with the possessory rights of the true owner is considered hostile. Permissive possession, either express or implicit in the true owner's conduct, will defeat the claim to adverse possession. Determining if and when possession holds the requisite hostility is crucial to an adverse possession claim, because the statute of limitations does not begin to run until this requirement is met. The court in *Teson v. Vasquez* did not see any problem with the claimants' satisfaction of the hostility element. Why not? The element of hostility is a major issue in the following case.

CHARLTON v. CROCKER

Court of Appeals of Missouri, 1984.
665 S.W.2d 56.

TITUS, JUDGE.

This is a suit involving ownership and possessory rights to three contiguous lots in a platted subdivision situate in Camden County, Missouri. The case was tried to the court sitting without a jury and judgment was rendered for defendants. From this judgment, vesting title to the property in defendants, plaintiffs have appealed.

Plaintiffs, husband and wife, base their claim to the disputed land on three warranty deeds executed on July 31, 1981, each of which conveyed one of the three constituent lots. Defendants, husband and wife, base their claim upon title acquired by adverse possession of the land for the ten-year period prescribed. * * *

The land in question consists of lots 9, 10, and 11 in Revelation Subdivision, dedicated and developed by Frank and Bertha Heise. In April of 1971 defendants Tommie and Ruth Crocker purchased and moved onto adjacent lots 7 and 8, where they established their residence in a two-bedroom house. Within that month a number of fires broke out in the subdivision, posing a threat to but never actually harming the Crocker home.[3] As their trial testimony reflects, defendants considered the brush-covered condition of lots 9, 10, and 11 a danger to their property and desired that the neighboring lots be cleared sufficiently to minimize the risk of fire.[4]

To that end they contacted Mrs. Heise as well as the attorney for the subdivision and the Camden County prosecutor. According to Mr. Crocker, both Mrs. Heise and the subdivision's attorney acknowledged that the condition of lots 9, 10, and 11 presented a fire hazard and opined that it would be all right if defendant cleared them himself. The prosecutor was said to have advised that defendant could not get into any trouble for clearing the lots and that, "if [the record owners] don't pay you for your labor, after ten years you could claim [the property]." The prosecutor also informed Mr. Crocker of the availability of the mechanic's lien as a device to secure payment for labor done on the lots. Before commencing work on the property defendants again consulted Mrs. Heise, who reiterated her previous "authorization" to do so.

Defendants initiated clearing in April, 1971, with what Mr. Crocker described as "a chopping axe and a grubbing hoe." Sometime later that year—the rather underdeveloped record does not indicate specifically when—Mr. Crocker began to remove vegetation with the aid of a "brush hog" and a tractor. He testified that his son, grandson, sister-in-law, and brother-in-law assisted in the clearing effort at various times (not subject to specific recollection by defendant) by removing brush, raking leaves, picking up rocks, etc. Further, defendant hired one Carl Coffee to "brush hog" the lots on a number of occasions. The record is not as complete as it might be with respect to this activity but it appears that brush-hogging was done "every year" over the six years next preceding trial.[5] Mr. Crocker testified to having done some brush-hogging himself—"three or four times"—over the years. Additional acts of clearing by defendants included the extraction of tree stumps, the removal in 1972 of seven pick-up truckloads of trash, and the removal of what defendant estimated to be 35 to 40 tons of rock. Defendants also installed a water line across the property sometime in 1974 or 1975; seeded, fertilized, and limed the property in the fall of 1980; and constructed a fence along the north and south sides of the property in early 1981.

3. On one occasion some neighbors of defendants fought a fire to keep it from defendants' house and that of another resident of the vicinity.

4. Mr. Crocker testified that at the time he and his wife moved onto their lots the vegetation on lots 9, 10, and 11 ranged in height from one and a half to eleven feet.

The lots were also covered with debris, including piled brush and leaves, discarded beverage cans and bottles, and assorted other refuse.

5. The date of trial, which served as a reference point for much of the testimony, was September 27, 1982.

Aside from defendants' clearing activity, their ostensible exercise of dominion over the property included the placement thereon of certain items of personalty. Among these were a flat-bed trailer, left on the property for approximately one year (the year immediately prior to trial); a bulldozer used to remove stumps, left for a time during 1981; axles and wheels, left somewhere on the lots for three months in 1981; and three 55-gallon drums used as trash barrels, placed on the property at the inception of defendants' "occupancy" and still there as of the time of trial.

The foregoing catalog of acts performed on the property by defendants does not include such evidence as would indicate what defendants regarded to be the legal significance of those acts. Inasmuch as this issue is the focal point of our discussion, infra, testimony adduced in regard thereto is here presented at some length.

Mr. Crocker testified that since 1971 whenever he had been asked about ownership of the disputed lots and whether they were for sale he had responded by saying they were his and were not for sale. He did not, however, allude to any specific occasions on which such communications took place. He further testified to having once told Carl Coffee that plaintiff Mr. Charlton tried to buy the lots "out from under me" and to having told Mr. Charlton that he, defendant, was claiming the lots and would build a house on them someday.

As mentioned, supra, the record indicates that the *sine qua non* to defendants' commencement of activity on the property was that it presented a fire hazard to their lots 7 and 8. On four disparate occasions during trial defendants testified to this effect, stating that their original purpose in clearing the disputed property was to protect their home from fire.

Also relevant to Mr. Crocker's "attitude" toward his performance of work on the property is the following exchange, excerpted from his testimony on cross-examination:

Q: [by Mr. Foster]: And you expected to get paid for that [the work on lots 9–11], didn't you? You mowed someone else—

A: To claim title to the land.

Q: Answer my question.—You expected to get paid for it?

A: Paid for it by title to the land.

* * *

Q: And you expected to get paid for that, didn't you? For the work that you did on that property?

A: From someone, or the title.

Mr. Crocker testified that he tried to get the Adamses, the record owners until July 31, 1981, to clean up the lots, to "let somebody else do it, hire them or let me do it or sell me the lots" and that he sent a letter to them—the record is silent as to whom specifically—requesting as much. Asked when he sent this letter defendant responded, "It started in April of '71."

On or about April 19, 1982, Mr. Crocker filed a mechanic's lien against lots 9–11 which stated as the basis for the $4275 "debt" secured the various items of labor performed by defendants on the property since 1971. The lien also recited the following:

> This [i.e., the assertion of a lien] is the result of the advice of the prosecuting attorney's office in April, 1971 when I could not get an answer from the Adams's (sic) on the condition of the property or what they would do about cleaning it up. Wilbur Adams promised to come and talk to me and he never did.

Mr. Crocker could not recall exactly when Adams made this promise, only that he did so "before five years ago," i.e., before September of 1977. Sometime prior to filing the lien, Mr. Crocker sent the Adamses a handwritten statement dated September 23, 1981, which set forth the specific acts of labor performed by defendants on lots 9–11 and requested payment of $4275. Plaintiffs received such a bill on or about April 19, 1982.

On redirect examination defendants' attorney sought to clarify what Mr. Crocker's intention had been in filing the lien. Defendant stated his aim had been "[t]o get paid for the work that I had done on the lots or get title to it (sic)." When asked on cross-examination why for the five years between the date the letter was sent to Adams and the date the lien was filed he had done nothing to obtain payment for his work, Mr. Crocker responded: "because [Adams] said he would come and see me and he never did."

Mr. Crocker testified that he paid no taxes on lots 9–11 for any of the ten years during which he purports to have asserted his claim. He stated that instead of paying the taxes he "went to see if they were paid." Mr. Charlton testified that he paid taxes on the lots for 1981, the first year of his record ownership.

Defendant Ruth Crocker's testimony also includes statements which reflect upon the nature of defendants' claim to the lots. It appears therefrom that in 1971 defendants bought a mobile home which they placed on their lots 7 and 8 and which they used as a residence. When asked on direct examination why defendants sold this mobile home in the fall of 1978, Mrs. Crocker responded, "we had to delete [it] because it was sitting so close to the property line that we could not build or add onto the back of it because it was only about six feet from the property line of lot 9." Twice during cross-examination of Mrs. Crocker inquiry was made as to defendants' reason for selling their mobile home and on both occasions she stated that they could not build onto the back of it because it was too close to the property line.

* * *

Plaintiffs contend, * * *, that the trial court's finding of adverse possession was against the weight of the evidence in that it included a determination that defendants in fact asserted the requisite claim of right to lots 9–11. Specifically, plaintiffs point to three distinct and affirmative actions of defendants, each of which is said to have evinced a recognition on their part that, despite their dominion over and "affected" claim to the property, title thereto was actually held by others. * * *

The first of the three actions alluded to, supra, occurred in April of 1971 at the inception of the relevant ten-year period, when defendants requested permission from the subdivision owner to work on lots 9–11. We recount that such a request was made on more than one occasion, the most recent immediately prior to defendants' commencement of activity on the property. That defendants sought permission to work on the lots—even from someone arguably without such interest in them as would confer upon her authority to grant permission—strongly suggests that, as of that time, defendants were not asserting the unequivocal claim of ownership required in order for title by adverse possession to ripen. * * *

Inasmuch as defendants' request for permission to work on the lots was made of someone other than the record owner, we feel obliged to explain that it is not necessary, in order for an adverse possession claim to fail for want of hostility, that the claimant believe title to be held by the record owner as such. It is enough that he be doubtful as to his own right to the property. This much is evident from those cases holding that possession of land in recognition of a lack of title is insufficient to ripen into title by adverse possession, [ ]: "It is not necessary that [the claimant] intend to take away from the true owner something which he knows belongs to another, or even that he be indifferent as to the facts of the legal title. It is the intent to possess, and not the intent to take irrespective of his right, which governs."

One other observation must be made concerning defendants' requests for permission to clear the lots. While it is true that such requests, as evidence of an absence of hostility, may be rendered irrelevant by a subsequent categorical assertion of right on the part of the adverse claimant,[6] such a situation did not obtain in this case. Defendants had the burden of establishing the existence for the statutory period of all the elements of adverse possession. The evidence allows for no other conclusion than that such period extended from 1971 to 1981. There appears no evidence, save defendants' references at trial to their subjective claim to the property as of 1971, of such a positive, unequivocal act as would counter the inference to be drawn

---

6. "An adverse claim must be hostile at its inception. The phrase 'hostile in its inception' does not relate to the original entry of the disseisor, but to the act by which the possession became adverse; in other words, the possession must have been hostile for the statutory period. Thus the original entry need not always be of a hostile character * * *. [W]here the original entry is not adverse, it does not become so and the statute does not begin to run as against the rightful owner until the adverse claimant disavows the idea of holding for, or in subserviency to, another and actually sets up an exclusive right in himself by some clear, positive, and unequivocal act brought home to the owner." 3 Am. Jur.2d, Adverse Possession § 33, pp. 117–118.

from their requests for permission that they did not actually believe themselves to have a right to the property.

The second significant intent-probative action of defendants was the sale of their mobile home in the fall of 1978. Mrs. Crocker thrice testified that she and her husband sold their mobile home when it became apparent that they could not build or otherwise add onto it because it was positioned too close to the property line of lot 9. Defendants' fear of encroachment upon that property presupposed a belief on their part that they were without right to do so. Such is the essence of the kind of equivocal claim that courts of this state have refused to recognize as sufficient for purposes of adverse possession. * * *

That Mrs. Crocker's candid revelation * * * may very well have been inadvertent only lends strength to its character as a window on the minds of defendants, as claimants. * * *

The last of defendants' three displays of tergiversation occurred in April of 1982 when Mr. Crocker filed a mechanic's lien against the disputed property to secure payment for the work he and his wife had done thereon. The trial court determined that the assertion of this lien was not prejudicial to defendants' adverse possession claim inasmuch as such action is within the ambit of the following principle, enunciated in *Mather v. Walsh*, 107 Mo. 121, 131, 17 S.W. 755, 757 (1891), and relied upon more recently in *Feinstein v. McGuire*, 297 S.W.2d 513, 517[7] (Mo.1957), and *Jurgensmeyer v. Yoest*, 647 S.W.2d 808, 810[3] (Mo.App. 1982): "A direct purchase of any ostensible *title* by one in possession has no * * * force as an admission. A party in possession of land may *fortify* his right *thereto* by acquiring any outstanding interest *therein,* without thereby weakening the force or effect of his possession." (Emphasis supplied.)

With due respect to the court below, we think that *Mather* is inapposite. The assertion of a lien against property does not constitute the acquisition of an outstanding interest in that property. On the contrary, the effectiveness of a lien as a security device depends upon its nature as a *charge upon* property *of another,* i.e., the debtor. [ ] That defendants may have filed the lien merely to "cover themselves" in the event their adverse possession claim failed simply underscores the provisional and contingent nature of their posture vis-a-vis the property in question. The numerous cases requiring an *unequivocal* claim of right on the part of an adverse possessor make it clear that such mugwumpery is fatal to an adverse possession claim.

It may be urged that, as defendants did not file the mechanic's lien until after the ten-year period in question, hence, after title to the property would have ripened, such action is irrelevant to the issue of whether defendants' possession was of a hostile character. The answer to this contention may be found in *Bridle Trail Assoc. v. O'Shanick*, 290 S.W.2d 401, 407[10] (Mo.App.1956), wherein the court noted that "a request [for permission to use the property of another], made even after the expiration of the period of limitation, has been characterized as 'important,' 'strong,' 'very powerful' evidence tending to show that the prior possession was not adverse."   * * *

Our review of this case has left us with the suspicion that defendants, informed of a wonderful land acquisition device called "adverse possession", were purposely attempting to establish its elements with respect to the disputed property.   While it is true, owing to the absence of a good faith requirement, that one may acquire property of another by means of a knowing and deliberate satisfaction of all the requirements of adverse possession, one of those requirements is that the adverse possession be under an *unequivocal* claim of right.   In that connection, the three actions discussed, supra, are collectively something of a Pinocchio's nose on the otherwise ingenuous countenance of defendants' claim.   * * *   The judgment is reversed and the cause remanded with directions to the trial court to enter judgment for plaintiffs, awarding them possession of the property in question and quieting in them title to same.

FLANIGAN, P.J., GREENE, C.J., and CROW, J., concur.

Notes and Questions

1.   Why did the Crockers lose?   Do you think that the court simply viewed them as bad actors?   Why do you think the trial court judge awarded the land to the Crockers?

2.   The Crockers apparently relied on the advice of the prosecuting attorney.   Was the attorney representing Mr. and Mrs. Crocker?   Was the advice sound legally?   How will you handle similar requests for information or your opinion?

3.   What should be the result in circumstances where the true owner has actual knowledge of the claimant's possession and use?   Is his acquiescence implied permission?   For example, in Deatherage v. Lewis, 131 Ill.App.3d 685, 86 Ill.Dec. 797, 475 N.E.2d 1364 (1985), the claimant attempted to tack his father's prior possession of the land onto his possession. The father, however, had been a good friend of the true owner, leading the court to believe that the father's possession was not hostile.   What criteria should the courts use to determine hostility in such cases?   Should the courts require more possessory acts than might otherwise be required? What purpose would such a requirement serve?

4.   If adverse possession requires proof of the state of mind of the claimant, how would you, as an attorney, handle the preparation for trial of a client claiming adverse possession?   Assume, for example, that the Crockers have come to you for help in gaining title to the disputed land. Would you tell them that adverse possession requires an unequivocal intent to claim the land as their own?   Or would you ask them first what they had intended over the years; i.e., to claim title or not?   What would you have advised if they came to you ten years or so earlier?   (Recall that the court in *Charlton v. Crocker* specifically quoted several passages from the testimony of the Crockers.)

Ethical Consideration 7–6 of the ABA Model Code of Professional Responsibility provides:

Whether the proposed action of a lawyer is within the bounds of the law may be a perplexing question when his client is contemplating a course of conduct having legal consequences that vary according to the client's intent, motive, or desires at the time of the action. Often a lawyer is asked to assist his client in developing evidence relevant to the state of mind of the client at a particular time. He may properly assist his client in the development and preservation of evidence of existing motive, intent, or desire; obviously he may not do anything furthering the creation or preservation of false evidence. In many cases a lawyer may not be certain as to the state of mind of his client, and in those situations he should resolve reasonable doubts in favor of his client.

The more recent ABA Model Rules of Professional Conduct provide in Rule 3.4 that a lawyer shall not "falsify evidence, counsel or assist a witness to testify falsely."

The ABA Model Code Ethical Consideration 7–3 addresses the role of the lawyer as counselor: "In asserting a position on behalf of his client, an advocate for the most part deals with past conduct and must take the facts as he finds them. By contrast, a lawyer serving as adviser primarily assists his client in determining the course of future conduct and relationships. While serving as advocate, a lawyer should resolve in favor of his client doubts as to the bounds of the law. In serving a client as adviser, a lawyer in appropriate circumstances should give his professional opinion as to what the ultimate decisions of the courts would likely be as to the applicable law."

A commentator on the role of standards governing the lawyer as adviser stated that "such standards should require a greater recognition and protection for the interest of the public generally than is presently expressed in the canons. Also, the counselor's obligation should extend to requiring him to inform and to impress upon the client a just solution of the problem, considering all the interests involved." Thode, The Ethical Standard for the Advocate, 39 Texas L.Rev. 575, 578–579 (1961). What implications would this approach have for advising clients concerning adverse possession claims? Recall Shaffer's comment that lawyers provide "moral leadership" in such circumstances more often than thought. What would that mean here? Is adverse possession legalized theft?

5. Traditional hornbook presentation of the law of adverse possession holds that the doctrine does not require the claimant to prove his subjective intent, but rather, examines only the claimant's acts of possession. Under this view, the "good faith" or "bad faith" of the claimant is irrelevant.

There has been an ongoing scholarly debate over whether or not recent judicial decisions in adverse possession cases have favored claimants who occupied property with a subjective good faith belief, though mistaken, that they actually owned the property they claim, and disfavored claimants who occupied property in bad faith, that is, occupied land that they knew belonged to someone else. See Helmholz, Adverse Possession and Subjective Intent, 61 Wash.U.L.Q. 331 (1983); Cunningham, Adverse Possession and Subjective Intent: A Reply to Professor Helmholz, 64 Wash.U.L.Q. 65 (1986); Cunningham, More On Adverse Possession: A Rejoinder to Professor Helmholz, 64 Wash.U.L.Q. 1167 (1986).

Professor Helmholz argues that while recent judicial decisions have not explicitly said so, the subjective good faith and bad faith of the claimants have influenced the courts' application of the doctrinal requirements of adverse possession, especially in relation to the requirement of hostility. On the other hand, Professor Cunningham believes that the existence of good faith or bad faith has not influenced judicial opinions, and that the decisions that Helmholz categorizes as turning on good faith or bad faith actually are based purely on an application of the requirements of adverse possession. Cunningham questions why courts would not openly state that ethical considerations are a factor if in fact these concerns are important in their decisions. Do you think that courts are influenced by factors that are not specifically relevant to the applicable rules in a case? If so, is this appropriate?

6. Two recent cases directly addressed the issue of a "good faith" requirement for adverse possession, reaching opposing conclusions. In Halpern v. Lacy Investment Corporation, 259 Ga. 264, 379 S.E.2d 519, 521 (1989), the court held that only a good faith trespass could ripen into title by adverse possession: "To enter upon the land without any honest claim of right to do so is but a trespass." In contrast, the Washington Supreme Court affirmed an appellate court decision denying title to the claimant for his failure to prove exclusivity, but discussed the issue of intentional trespass: "The doctrine of adverse possession * * * protect[s] both those who knowingly appropriated the land of others and those who honestly held the property in the belief that it was their own." ITT Rayonier v. Bell, 112 Wash.2d 754, 774 P.2d 6, 9 (1989). Which do you think is the better result?

THE GOOD NEIGHBOR PROBLEM

The Andersons and Sullivans both purchased their homes in 1978, when the Woodlands subdivision was first developed. The Andersons live on a corner lot; their house faces Briarwood Lane; and their backyard abuts the Sullivans' side yard. The Sullivans' home faces Clovercrest Lane. A drainage ditch borders these two lots, but veers inward into the Andersons' yard, as it approaches Clovercrest Lane. This creates a triangular-shaped, partially-wooded area that is included in the Andersons' deed. Although the two families have been friends for the past 11 years, they have never discussed who owns this area.

Mr. Sullivan has always mowed the cleared area of the triangle. Both the Anderson and Sullivan children have played together in the triangle, setting up a lemonade stand in the summers, and using the cleared area as part of a playing field for football and soccer games. In 1982, Mr. Sullivan helped the children build a tree house on the area, but it has since been dismantled. In 1987, Mr. Anderson built a bridge over the ditch, leading to the triangle, and since then Mrs. Anderson has cultivated various wild flowers and plants in the wooded areas.

Since the bridge has been built, Mr. Anderson has also mowed the cleared areas of the triangle.

The Andersons have planned to build a gazebo in this triangle, and a 1989 survey confirmed that it was part of their property. Recently, at the annual Woodlands picnic, the Sullivans learned of the gazebo plans and are outraged. They think the gazebo will be unsightly, and in plain view from their living room window. Furthermore, the triangle looks like it belongs to them and they have been caring for it since they moved into their home. Can the Sullivans prevent the Andersons from building the gazebo? What claims can they make? What defenses will the Andersons raise? (Assume a ten-year statute of limitations.) Would you advise the Sullivans to sue the Andersons?

MEDIATION: THE PATIO PROBLEM

This problem is based on a case handled by a dispute resolution center in St. Louis. In reviewing this case, assume that you are an attorney employed by a neighborhood dispute-resolution center that offers non-adversarial dispute-resolution services, including mediation. You have been asked to help the parties attempt to reach a resolution of this dispute.

This case concerns two adjacent property owners, Mr. and Mrs. Miller and Mr. and Mrs. Aimes. The parties live in a 20–year–old subdivision. Eight months ago, Mr. and Mrs. Aimes had a concrete patio poured in their backyard. About a week after the work was completed, Mr. and Mrs. Miller, who had been on vacation while the work was done, advised Mr. and Mrs. Aimes of the fact that the new patio was one foot over the property line and so extended onto the Miller property.

Fifteen years ago, a fence had been erected by the predecessor in title to Mrs. and Mr. Aimes on what was mistakenly believed to be the boundary line. The fence was actually placed three feet beyond the property line so that it rested on the Miller property. Mrs. and Mr. Miller purchased the property five years ago; and Mrs. and Mr. Aimes purchased their property eight years ago. Mrs. and Mr. Aimes have always mowed the lawn up to the fence and had planted two trees near the fence. Mr. and Mrs. Miller first discovered that the fence was actually on their property rather than on the boundary line when a survey was taken recently as part of an application for a home equity loan.

What would your strategy be in helping these parties to resolve their dispute? What do you think the chances are that some resolution can be worked out? If Mr. and Mrs. Miller had come to you for legal advice and raised the possibility of working through the dispute resolution center, how would you have advised them? How would you have advised Mrs. and Mr. Aimes?

II. WHAT DOES IT MEAN TO BE THE OWNER?

"In a developed society a man's property is not merely something which he controls and enjoys, which he can make the basis of his labour and the scene of his ordered activities but something whereby he can control another man and make it the basis of that man's labour and the scene of activities ordered by himself. * * * Now these two functions of property, the control of things, which gives freedom and security, and the control of persons through things, which gives power to the owner, are very different. In some respects they are radically opposed." Hobhouse, The Historical Evolution of Property, in Fact and in Idea, in Property: Its Duties and Rights 3, 9–11 (ed ed. 1922).

"God the Lord and Father of all, has given no one of his Children such a Property, in his peculiar Portion of the things of this World, but that he has given his needy Brother a Right to the Surplusage of his Goods; so that it cannot justly be denied him, when his pressing Wants call for it. And therefore no Man could ever have a just Power over the Life of another, by Right of property in Land or Possessions." John Locke, Two Treatises on Government at 205 (P. Laslett rev. ed. 1963) (3d ed. 1698).

"To achieve proper self-development—to be a person—an individual needs some control over resources in the external environment. The necessary assurances of control take the form of property rights." Radin, Property and Personhood, 34 Stan.L.Rev. 957 (1982).

This section on what it means to be the owner is organized around the three major rights that describe property ownership—the right to exclude, the right to use, and the right to transfer. Viewing property in terms of these rights represents the "bundle of sticks" theory of property ownership. This concept was introduced in the notes following *Johnson v. McIntosh* when you were asked to consider what property rights remained in the Native Americans, if any, and what property rights lodged in the European discoverers and later conquerors. This section also explores the legal concept that property is certainly not an object, but is rather "the relationship of persons as to a thing." (We leave to another day the question of whether "thing" is rightfully in the definition at all when property has been used to build a framework for patent, copyright, trademark, and entitlements to public benefits or employment.)

This concept of property as divisible by rights or functions is as "real" *legally* as the concept that property is divisible geographically or by time. But it remains a metaphor, though a powerful one.

Richard Epstein, criticizes the "modern discussion of property rights" as a "bundle of sticks," while arguing that the rights making up the concept of property are integral to the common law: "By using that metaphor [the bundle of sticks], you get the impression that these sticks have been hastily thrown together, that they are not all quite the same length, and that it is almost a matter of random chance that they stand next to one another. I suggest that the bundle of rights normally associated with the concept of property, far from being randomly and fortuitously put together, actually coheres and forms the basis of huge portions of the terrain of the ordinary common law. * * *

"The first stick says, in effect, that you can <u>exclude</u> everybody else in the world from doing something with your property. * * * If we stopped with possession, we would have a system of property rights that worked up to a grand blockade. The world would remain a tundra, in which I could keep my own place on the barren square of the checkerboard. To fill in the gaps, a system of <u>use rights</u> is associated with property. Now more than a <u>blockade</u> is at stake; you get <u>production</u> as well—a vast improvement.

"If you just stop with a system that contains only the right to exclude and the right to use, then you have to ask the following question: What happens if its value in use to somebody else is greater than its value in use to you? * * * Generally speaking, gains from trade are made possible in both a social and an economic sense only if we include in our property definition the right of disposition [or transfer]."

Epstein goes on to describe how common-law <u>doctrines of trespass</u> and <u>nuisance</u>, among others, protect these property rights. He criticizes, however, the "modern" approach to property in which the Supreme Court, and others, "eviscerate the common-law institution of property incident by incident, so that the right to exclusive possession can be easily overridden in many cases on fairly feeble justifications. The idea that you may use your property to the limit, save only the live-and-let-live exceptions, is now replaced by a law of zoning. * * * If you look at various kinds of cases having to do with rights of disposition, whether you are talking about prohibitions against the sale of eagle feathers, rent control, price controls, wage controls and so forth, you will discover that the right of disposition is constantly and systematically compromised." Espstein, Property and Necessity, 13 Harv.J. of Law & Publ.Pol. 2 (1990).

Thomas Grey goes even further than Epstein and attributes the disintegration of property as a concept to the metaphor of a "bundle of sticks." According to Grey, the "bundle of sticks" concept abstracts property and is responsible for shifting the focus from the relationship between a person and a thing to a relationship among persons with respect to a thing. With that shift, the concept of property became largely irrelevant in legal and economic analysis of the allocation of resources. Grey, The Disintegration of Property, 22 Nomos: Property (1980).

Despite these caveats, you will see the right to exclude, the right to use, and the right to transfer treated throughout this course as separable attributes of property ownership because the "bundle of sticks" concept dominates modern thought about what property is. The following cases introduce two of the major "sticks in the bundle"—the right to exclude and the right to transfer—and highlight the relationship aspect of property ownership.

A. THE RIGHT TO EXCLUDE

STATE v. SHACK

Supreme Court of New Jersey, 1971.
58 N.J. 297, 277 A.2d 369.

WEINTRAUB, C.J.

Defendants entered upon private property to aid migrant farm-workers employed and housed there. Having refused to depart upon the demand of the owner, defendants were charged with violating N.J.S.A. 2A:170–31 which provides that "[a]ny person who trespasses on any lands * * * after being forbidden so to trespass by the owner * * * is a disorderly person and shall be punished by a fine of not more than $50." Defendants were convicted in the Municipal Court of Deerfield Township and again on appeal in the County Court of Cumberland County on a trial *de novo*. We certified their further appeal before argument in the Appellate Division.

Before us, no one seeks to sustain these convictions. The complaints were prosecuted in the Municipal Court and in the County Court by counsel engaged by the complaining landowner, Tedesco. However Tedesco did not respond to this appeal, and the county prosecutor, while defending abstractly the constitutionality of the trespass statute, expressly disclaimed any position as to whether the statute reached the activity of these defendants.

Complainant, Tedesco, a farmer, employs migrant workers for his seasonal needs. As part of their compensation, these workers are housed at a camp on his property.

Defendant Tejeras is a field worker for the Farm Workers Division of the Southwest Citizens Organization for Poverty Elimination, known by the acronym SCOPE, a nonprofit corporation funded by the Office of Economic Opportunity pursuant to an act of Congress, 42 U.S.C.A. §§ 2861–2864. The role of SCOPE includes providing for the "health services of the migrant farm worker."

Defendant Shack is a staff attorney with the Farm Workers Division of Camden Regional Legal Services, Inc., known as "CRLS," also a nonprofit corporation funded by the Office of Economic Opportunity pursuant to an act of Congress, 42 U.S.C.A. § 2809(a)(3). The mission of CRLS includes legal advice and representation for these workers.

Differences had developed between Tedesco and these defendants prior to the events which led to the trespass charges now before us. Hence when defendant Tejeras wanted to go upon Tedesco's farm to find a migrant worker who needed medical aid for the removal of 28 sutures, he called upon defendant Shack for his help with respect to the legalities involved. Shack, too, had a mission to perform on Tedesco's farm; he wanted to discuss a legal problem with another migrant worker there employed and housed. Defendants arranged to go to the farm together. Shack carried literature to inform the migrant farm-workers of the assistance available to them under federal statutes, but no mention seems to have been made of that literature when Shack was later confronted by Tedesco.

Defendants entered upon Tedesco's property and as they neared the camp site where the farmworkers were housed, they were confront-ed by Tedesco who inquired of their purpose. Tejeras and Shack stated their missions. In response, Tedesco offered to find the injured worker, and as to the worker who needed legal advice, Tedesco also offered to locate the man but insisted that the consultation would have to take place in Tedesco's office and in his presence. Defendants declined, saying they had the right to see the men in the privacy of their living quarters and without Tedesco's supervision. Tedesco thereupon sum-moned a State Trooper who, however, refused to remove defendants except upon Tedesco's written complaint. Tedesco then executed the formal complaints charging violations of the trespass statute.

I.

The constitutionality of the trespass statute, as applied here, is challenged on several scores. * * *

These constitutional claims are not established by any definitive holding. We think it unnecessary to explore their validity. The reason is that we are satisfied that under our State law the ownership of real property does not include the right to bar access to governmental services available to migrant workers and hence there was no trespass within the meaning of the penal statute. The policy considerations which underlie that conclusion may be much the same as those which would be weighed with respect to one or more of the constitutional challenges, but a decision in nonconstitutional terms is more satisfac-tory, because the interests of migrant workers are more expansively served in that way than they would be if they had no more freedom than these constitutional concepts could be found to mandate if indeed they apply at all.

II.

Property rights serve human values. They are recognized to that end, and are limited by it. Title to real property cannot include dominion over the destiny of persons the owner permits to come upon the premises. Their well-being must remain the paramount concern of a system of law. Indeed the needs of the occupants may be so imperative and their strength so weak, that the law will deny the occupants the power to contract away what is deemed essential to their health, welfare, or dignity.

Here we are concerned with a highly disadvantaged segment of our society. We are told that every year farmworkers and their families numbering more than one million leave their home areas to fill the seasonal demand for farm labor in the United States. The Migratory Farm Labor Problem in the United States (1969 Report of Subcommittee on Migratory Labor of the United States Senate Committee on Labor and Public Welfare), p. 1. The migrant farmworkers come to New Jersey in substantial numbers. The report just cited places at 55,700 the number of man-months of such employment in our State in 1968 (p. 7). The numbers of workers so employed here in that year are estimated at 1,300 in April; 6,500 in May; 9,800 in June; 10,600 in July; 12,100 in August; 9,600 in September; and 5,500 in October (p. 9).

The migrant farmworkers are a community within but apart from the local scene. They are rootless and isolated. Although the need for their labors is evident, they are unorganized and without economic or political power. It is their plight alone that summoned government to their aid. In response, Congress provided under Title III–B of the Economic Opportunity Act of 1964 (42 U.S.C.A. § 2701 et seq.) for "assistance for migrant and other seasonally employed farmworkers and their families." Section 2861 states "the purpose of this part is to assist migrant and seasonal farmworkers and their families to improve their living conditions and develop skills necessary for a productive and self-sufficient life in an increasingly complex and technological society." Section 2862(b)(1) provides for funding of programs "to meet the immediate needs of migrant and seasonal farmworkers and their families, such as day care for children, education, health services, improved housing and sanitation (including the provision and maintenance of emergency and temporary housing and sanitation facilities), legal advice and representation, and consumer training and counseling." As we have said, SCOPE is engaged in a program funded under this section, and CRLS also pursues the objectives of this section although, we gather, it is funded under § 2809(a)(3), which is not limited in its concern to the migrant and other seasonally employed farmworkers and seeks "to further the cause of justice among persons living in poverty by mobilizing the assistance of lawyers and legal institutions and by providing legal advice, legal representation, counseling, education, and other appropriate services."

These ends would not be gained if the intended beneficiaries could be insulated from efforts to reach them. It is in this framework that we must decide whether the camp operator's rights in his lands may stand between the migrant workers and those who would aid them. The key to that aid is communication. Since the migrant workers are outside the mainstream of the communities in which they are housed and are unaware of their rights and opportunities and of the services available to them, they can be reached only by positive efforts tailored to that end. The Report of the Governor's Task Force on Migrant Farm Labor (1968) noted that "One of the major problems related to seasonal farm labor is the lack of adequate direct information with regard to the availability of public services," and that "there is a dire need to provide the workers with basic educational and informational material in a language and style that can be readily understood by the migrant" (pp. 101–102). The report stressed the problem of access and deplored the notion that property rights may stand as a barrier, saying "In our judgment, 'no trespass' signs represent the last dying remnants of paternalistic behavior" (p. 63).

A man's right in his real property of course is not absolute. It was a maxim of the common law that one should so use his property as not to injure the rights of others. Broom, Legal Maxims (10th ed. Kersley 1939), p. 238; 39 Words and Phrases, "Sic Utere Tuo ut Alienum Non Laedas," p. 335. Although hardly a precise solvent of actual controversies, the maxim does express the inevitable proposition that rights are relative and there must be an accommodation when they meet. Hence it has long been true that necessity, private or public, may justify entry upon the lands of another.

The subject is not static. As pointed out in 5 Powell, Real Property (Rohan 1970) § 745, pp. 493–494, while society will protect the owner in his permissible interests in land, yet

" * * * [S]uch an owner must expect to find the absoluteness of his property rights curtailed by the organs of society, for the promotion of the best interests of others for whom these organs also operate as protective agencies. The necessity for such curtailments is greater in a modern industrialized and urbanized society than it was in the relatively simple American society of fifty, 100, or 200 years ago. The current balance between individualism and dominance of the social interest depends not only upon political and social ideologies, but also upon the physical and social facts of the time and place under discussion."

Professor Powell added in § 746, pp. 494–496:

"As one looks back along the historic road traversed by the law of land in England and in America, one sees a change from the viewpoint that he who owns may do as he pleases with what he owns, to a position which hesitatingly embodies an ingredient of stewardship; which grudgingly, but steadily, broadens the recognized scope of social interests in the utilization of things.   * * *

To one seeing history through the glasses of religion, these changes may seem to evidence increasing embodiments of the golden rule. To one thinking in terms of political and economic ideologies, they are likely to be labeled evidences of 'social enlightenment,' or of 'creeping socialism' or even of 'communistic infiltration,' according to the individual's assumed definitions and retained or acquired prejudices. With slight attention to words or labels, time marches on toward new adjustments between individualism and the social interests."

This process involves not only the accommodation between the right of the owner and the interests of the general public in his use of his property, but involves also an accommodation between the right of the owner and the right of individuals who are parties with him in consensual transactions relating to the use of the property. * * *

The argument in this case understandably included the question whether the migrant worker should be deemed to be a tenant and thus entitled to the tenant's right to receive visitors, [ ], or whether his residence on the employer's property should be deemed to be merely incidental and in aid of his employment, and hence to involve no possessory interest in the realty. [ ] These cases did not reach employment situations at all comparable with the one before us. Nor did they involve the question whether an employee who is not a tenant may have visitors notwithstanding the employer's prohibition. Rather they were concerned with whether notice must be given to end the employee's right to remain upon the premises, with whether the employer may remove the discharged employee without court order, and with the availability of a particular judicial remedy to achieve his removal by process. We of course are not concerned here with the right of a migrant worker to remain on the employer's property after the employment is ended.

We see no profit in trying to decide upon a conventional category and then forcing the present subject into it. That approach would be artificial and distorting. The quest is for a fair adjustment of the competing needs of the parties, in the light of the realities of the relationship between the migrant worker and the operator of the housing facility.

Thus approaching the case, we find it unthinkable that the farmer-employer can assert a right to isolate the migrant worker in any respect significant for the worker's well-being. The farmer, of course, is entitled to pursue his farming activities without interference, and this defendants readily concede. But we see no legitimate need for a right in the farmer to deny the worker the opportunity for aid available from federal, State, or local services, or from recognized charitable groups seeking to assist him. Hence representatives of these agencies and organizations may enter upon the premises to seek out the worker at his living quarters. So, too, the migrant worker must be allowed to receive visitors there of his own choice, so long as there is no behavior hurtful to others, and members of the press may not be denied reasonable access to workers who do not object to seeing them.

It is not our purpose to open the employer's premises to the general public if in fact the employer himself has not done so. We do not say, for example, that solicitors or peddlers of all kinds may enter on their own; we may assume for the present that the employer may regulate their entry or bar them, at least if the employer's purpose is not to gain a commercial advantage for himself or if the regulation does not deprive the migrant worker of practical access to things he needs.

And we are mindful of the employer's interest in his own and in his employees' security. Hence he may reasonably require a visitor to identify himself, and also to state his general purpose if the migrant worker has not already informed him that the visitor is expected. But the employer may not deny the worker his privacy or interfere with his opportunity to live with dignity and to enjoy associations customary among our citizens. These rights are too fundamental to be denied on the basis of an interest in real property and too fragile to be left to the unequal bargaining strength of the parties. [ ]

It follows that defendants here invaded no possessory right of the farmer-employer. Their conduct was therefore beyond the reach of the trespass statute. The judgments are accordingly reversed and the matters remanded to the County Court with directions to enter judgments of acquittal.

For reversal and remandment: CHIEF JUSTICE WEINTRAUB and Justices JACOBS, FRANCIS, PROCTOR, HALL and SCHETTINO—6.

For affirmance: None.

WESTERN PENNSYLVANIA SOCIALIST WORKERS 1982 CAMPAIGN v. CONNECTICUT GENERAL LIFE INSURANCE COMPANY

Supreme Court of Pennsylvania, 1986.
512 Pa. 23, 515 A.2d 1331.

HUTCHINSON, JUSTICE.

Appellants are a political committee, its chairman, gubernatorial candidate and a campaign worker. They appeal by allowance a Superior Court order, 335 Pa.Super. 493, 485 A.2d 1, affirming Allegheny County Common Pleas. Common Pleas had dismissed their suit for a mandatory injunction directing appellee, owner of a shopping mall, to cease interfering with appellants' political activities on appellee's premises. Appellants claim that they have the right, under the Pennsylvania Constitution's guarantees of free speech and petition, to collect signatures on the gubernatorial candidate's nominating petition in privately-owned shopping malls and that appellee cannot deny them access to its mall for that purpose.

We believe that the Pennsylvania Constitution does not guarantee access to private property for the exercise of such rights where, as here, the owner uniformly and effectively prohibits all political activities and similarly precludes the use of its property as a forum for discussion of matters of public controversy. We would therefore affirm Superior Court.

In the spring of 1982, appellants began a drive to collect signatures on nominating papers in an effort to place a candidate on that November's gubernatorial ballot. They sought permission to solicit signatures and educate the public about their cause in a shopping mall known as South Hills Village. South Hills Village is a large enclosed shopping mall in suburban Pittsburgh. The mall contains approximately one million square feet of enclosed space, hosts some 126 stores and is circumscribed by a 5000–vehicle parking lot. It was opened in 1964;

appellee has owned it since 1982. The mall has a uniform policy of forbidding all political solicitation and appellants' request was denied. Rather than risk criminal prosecution by soliciting signatures in the face of this policy, appellants filed a complaint in equity in the Court of Common Pleas of Allegheny County. They sought to enjoin appellee from enforcing its no political solicitation policy on the ground that it violated their speech and petition rights under the Pennsylvania Constitution. Pa. Const., art. I, §§ 2, 7, 20.

* * *

The social and economic development with which we are concerned here is the ongoing substitution of enclosed shopping malls for individual retail stores clustered in downtown shopping areas. These stores were themselves substitutes for the open sheds of the colonial market which was generally located on public ground. Despite these developments in the past two hundred years, common law has not yet given an individual the general right to enter upon the private property of another. [ ] Moreover, even if invited for one purpose, the invitee has no recognized right to engage in another activity against the landowner's wishes. [ ] Here, the public at large, including appellants, were invited to South Hills Village for commercial purposes: shopping, dining and entertainment. Political solicitation was uniformly forbidden.

Appellants' argument that shopping malls have usurped the function of "Main Street, U.S.A." and town business districts is not lost on us. Both statistics and common experience show that business districts, particularly in small and medium sized towns, have suffered a marked decline. At the same time, shopping malls, replete with creature comforts, have boomed. These malls have begun to serve as social as well as commercial outlets for the communities they serve. Young people often come to a mall to socialize with their peers. Older people come to enjoy the parklike atmosphere offered in many malls or to view displays erected in the corridors. Members of the community have an opportunity by chance or design to mix, meet and converse. However, these social benefits are ancillary to the commercial purpose of shopping malls and do not involve organized campaigns on particular issues by political or special interest groups. Law and sociology are not coextensive. Though shopping malls may fulfill some of the societal functions of the traditional main street or town market place, we do not believe that this makes them their legal equivalent. Nor does it yet require them to provide a political forum for persons or groups with views on public issues, so long as the owner does not grant unfair advantage to particular interests or groups by making his premises arbitrarily available to those he favors while excluding all others.[7]

Appellants argue that our decision in *Commonwealth v. Tate*, [432 A.2d 1382 (1981)] controls this case. We agree that it controls. How-

7. This caveat does not apply to non-political, charitable groups. A mall owner may pick and choose among them because political solicitation is not involved.

ever, it does not help these appellants. In our view, it demonstrates a limiting rationale for applying our constitution's rights of speech and assembly to property private in name but used in fact as a forum for public debate. In *Tate,* a private institution of higher learning sponsored a community anti-crime symposium which included a speech by then FBI Director Clarence Kelley. The symposium was open to the public; in fact, the public was encouraged to attend. Appellants, the Lehigh–Pocono Committee of Concern (LEPOCO), sought to peacefully protest against Director Kelley because of his refusal to supply them with information they had requested under the Freedom of Information Act, and to protest generally against FBI policies. The College summarily denied LEPOCO's request for a permit; apparently no criteria for granting or denying permits existed. On the day of Director Kelley's speech, members of LEPOCO entered the campus and peacefully distributed leaflets near the auditorium. Twice college officials and the police asked them to leave; they refused. The protesters were arrested for defiant trespass. We held that LEPOCO members had a right to speak freely without fear of criminal conviction under art. I, § 7 of the Pennsylvania Constitution, because the college had made itself into a public forum and [the Pennsylvania trespass statute] provided a defense to a charge of defiant trespass in those circumstances.

South Hills Village, on the other hand, has not made itself a public forum in this manner. Appellee has invited the public at large into the mall only for commercial purposes. By adhering to a strict no political solicitation policy, appellee has uniformly and generally prevented the mall from becoming a public forum. South Hills Village is operated as a market place for the exchange of goods and services but not as a market place for the exchange of ideas. * * *

A shopping mall is not equivalent to a town. Though it duplicates the commercial function traditionally associated with a town's business district or marketplace, the similarity ends there. People do not live in shopping malls. Malls do not provide essential public services such as water, sewers, roads, sanitation or vital records, nor are they responsible for education, recreation or transportation. * * *

* * *

The highest courts of other jurisdictions are divided on this issue. * * *

The order of Superior Court is affirmed.

Notes and Questions

1. Why did Justice Weintraub believe that the interests of the migrants would receive greater protection under common-law property rules than under the constitutional rights asserted?

2. Did Justice Weintraub decide that migrant farm workers and their lawyers and caseworkers had property rights in Tedesco's land? If not, what was the basis of his decision?

3. Was Justice Weintraub saying that there was no good reason not to permit the lawyer and the caseworker to talk to the migrant farm workers in private on the owner's property? What does this do to the power to exclude? Would Justice Weintraub permit the landowner to exclude the lawyer and the caseworker under other circumstances? If so, what might those circumstances be?

4. How does the Pennsylvania Supreme Court in *Western Pennsylvania* reconcile the constitutional interest asserted under the Pennsylvania Constitution with the common law of property? What approach does the court believe should be taken to resolve disputes between individuals regarding access to or use of private property? Is the role of the common law to allow the parties to resolve such disputes without interference from the government? If so, what law controls when they are unsuccessful in resolving such disputes and resort to courts?

5. Suppose a privately-owned shopping mall with a "no solicitation" policy is the beneficiary of considerable financial assistance from public authorities, including the purchase by the city of $2 million of improvements that the mall owner made to adjacent streets and drainage systems. The mall also provides rent-free space in the mall to the city for a police substation from which police respond to complaints throughout the city as well as in the mall. In addition, the Army, Navy and Marine Corps have recruiting stations in the mall, and the county clerk maintains a temporary office for voter registration in the mall. Would these facts tip the balance in favor of the "public forum" characterization? See Bock v. Westminster Mall Co., 819 P.2d 55, 60 U.S.L.W. 2239 (Colo.1991) (mall "effectively functions as a latter-day public forum" and thus may not prohibit distribution of political pamphlets and solicitation of signatures for petitions regarding governmental policies).

6. To what extent should the state be able to regulate access to private property? May, for example, public officials seeking evidence of drug use be able to search without a warrant trash placed in covered containers on private property under circumstances in which: (a) municipal trash regulations require the trash containers to be kept out of sight; and (b) trash haulers customarily go onto private property in order to remove the trash? See California v. Greenwood, 486 U.S. 35, 108 S.Ct. 1625, 100 L.Ed.2d 30 (1988) (Yes, with respect to trash left at the curb for pick up).

May a city bar picketing on public streets in front of individual residences when the picketing is designed to call attention to the activities of the owner or resident of the property? See Frisby v. Schultz, 487 U.S. 474, 108 S.Ct. 2495, 101 L.Ed.2d 420 (1988) (Yes, so long as picketing is not prohibited on public streets generally and the picketers keep moving).

Problems: Bruce Wayne and Westgate

Both *Shack* and *Western Pennsylvania* may be viewed as cases in which the owner's use of the property had an impact on the scope of the owner's right to exclude. What were the pivotal facts in these cases? What do you think the result would be if these two courts were faced with the following situations?

(a) Bruce Wayne owns an estate that is coveted by not-for-profit and political organizations for fundraising events. Mr. Wayne frequently lends his estate to organizations such as the Arts Council, the local chapter of the United Nations Association, state and local political campaigns and a number of other organizations. There is at least one event each month on his grounds. Many of these fundraisers include speeches by nationally prominent individuals associated with the particular cause. Most often these events are open to the general public who pay the suggested or required contribution for admission. Mr. Wayne rarely attends these events as he is frequently out of town.

This weekend an organization called Freedom for the Arts is holding a fundraiser. This event has been listed in the calendar section of the newspaper and in its society column. Admission requires that you reserve a ticket in advance by calling Freedom for the Arts. The tickets are free. They intend to raise money through pledges and an auction during the event. Mr. Wayne's personal assistant has heard that a number of persons who have reserved tickets intend to circulate leaflets opposing government funding of several performance artists, including the person who will perform as the major attraction for the fundraiser. They also intend to stand with their backs turned to the stage during the performance and all speeches. Does Mr. Wayne have a right to prevent these people from attending?

(b) Westgate Manor is a private assisted-living center for elderly individuals who are too physically or mentally impaired to live alone, but who do not need skilled nursing care. Residents rent their own apartment at Westgate and pay a monthly service fee. Westgate provides a full range of services including a dining hall, doctors' house calls, recreation, housekeeping, and seasonal shopping. It also provides transportation to shopping areas and entertainment for those able to take advantage of the service. The management of Westgate has established a set of rules that govern the usual concerns. Some of these rules govern access to Westgate by visitors. Children are allowed to visit only between 9:00 a.m. and 5:00 p.m., for example. All guests must check in at the front gate, and only guests who have an invitation by a resident and whose names are recorded at the gate are allowed access. Certain groups are welcomed for particular purposes. For example, a choir attends Sunday services, and groups of school children visit to perform on certain holidays.

Several groups have asked permission to talk with the residents of Westgate. Some of these groups are political. (Like most groups of older citizens, a very large percentage of residents of Westgate vote.) Other groups want to inform residents of services available from local hospitals, support groups and other sources. All of these requests have been denied. Does the owner-operator of Westgate have a right to exclude these groups?

COMPLEX NEGOTIATION PROBLEM: THE SCHOOL AND THE SHELTER

One of the questions raised by the "power to exclude" cases is whether litigation is the ideal way to resolve such disputes. In fact, property lawyers spend a small fraction of their time in courts and use other techniques, particularly negotiation, in helping clients work through a process of accommodation similar to the process of analysis used in *State v. Shack*.

Property lawyers who work on land-use and -development problems resort to negotiation in two different types of situations: (1) "deal making"—where the client is seeking to develop property in some particular manner and needs to acquire sufficient control over the property, or seeks to raise money for the project; and (2) "dispute resolution"—where the client is seeking to resolve a dispute concerning the use of the property with neighbors, public officials, or partners. In both situations, the client's interests may require a greater degree of flexibility in approaching the matter than the "winner take all" outcome with which litigation may be concerned. This is particularly true if the client has a relationship with her potential adversaries that she wishes to maintain after the matter at hand is resolved.

Property rights questions, such as those raised in *Shack* and *Western Pennsylvania*, may be amenable to negotiated or mediated settlements outside of court. Offered the opportunity to negotiate a resolution of issues with Tejeras in *State v. Shack*, should the attorneys for the farm workers negotiate or litigate? If offered terms that would satisfy the needs of the farm workers on Tejeras' farm, should the attorneys recommend that their clients accept the offer or litigate? Under the holding of *Western Pennsylvania*, is it advisable for the shopping mall to make some arrangements to accommodate greater access to the mall?

Representatives of Vo-tech University have come to your city to offer the homeless the opportunity to enroll in vocational training courses. The courses can be financed with federally-subsidized loans. University recruiters offer to help applicants complete the necessary paperwork for the loans as part of the application process. Typical courses meet for three hours one night a week for 12 weeks. Tuition for most courses is $750. Students can enroll in as many as three courses at a time.

The Shining Light Shelter is a private, not-for-profit, church-affiliated corporation that provides beds for 85 homeless individuals each night, and a day center, at which homeless individuals can receive a meal, take a shower, and get some medical care. The Shelter has refused to give school recruiters access to the shelter to talk to the residents each night.   Officials of the shelter have said that they refused access because "homeless people are being set up for failure"; job prospects are uncertain; and homeless people have no realistic possibility of being able to repay the loans.   Also, the visits might be disruptive, and persons who are "psychiatrically impaired" might be exploited.   A negotiation session has been scheduled for two hours from now.   Representatives of the shelter, the school, and the homeless will participate.   A press conference is scheduled for later that day.

What would be the interests of each group?   You might try a simulated negotiation of this problem.

B.   THE RIGHT TO TRANSFER

The common law generally favors the transferability, or alienability, of property.   As you will see in Chapter Two, broad "restraints on alienation" of property, even when those restrictions are included in a voluntary transaction, are void.   Yet, there are objects that would have value "in the market" but remain legally inalienable.   In this section, we look at property claims to human body parts for two purposes. First, we want to look at the "stick" of transferability.   Does it make sense to call something "property" if it is inalienable?   Second, we want to examine a final question for this introductory section: What does it mean to be property?

MOORE v. REGENTS OF THE UNIVERSITY OF CALIFORNIA

Supreme Court of California, In Bank, 1990.
51 Cal.3d 120, 271 Cal.Rptr. 146, 793 P.2d 479.

* * *

The plaintiff is John Moore (Moore), who underwent treatment for hairy-cell leukemia at the Medical Center of the University of California at Los Angeles (UCLA Medical Center).   The five defendants are: (1) Dr. David W. Golde (Golde), a physician who attended Moore at UCLA Medical Center;   (2) the Regents of the University of California (Regents), who own and operate the university;   (3) Shirley G. Quan, a researcher employed by the Regents;   (4) Genetics Institute, Inc. (Genetics Institute);   and (5) Sandoz Pharmaceuticals Corporation and related entities (collectively Sandoz).

Moore first visited UCLA Medical Center on October 5, 1976, shortly after he learned that he had hairy-cell leukemia.   After hospitalizing Moore and "withdr[awing] extensive amounts of blood, bone marrow aspirate, and other bodily substances," Golde confirmed that diagnosis.   At this time all defendants, including Golde, were aware that "certain blood products and blood components were of great value in a number of commercial and scientific efforts" and that access to a patient whose blood contained these substances would provide "competitive, commercial, and scientific advantages."

On October 8, 1976, Golde recommended that Moore's spleen be removed. Golde informed Moore "that he had reason to fear for his life, and that the proposed splenectomy operation * * * was necessary to slow down the progress of his disease." Based upon Golde's representations, Moore signed a written consent form authorizing the splenectomy.

Before the operation, Golde and Quan "formed the intent and made arrangements to obtain portions of [Moore's] spleen following its removal" and to take them to a separate research unit. Golde gave written instructions to this effect on October 18 and 19, 1976. These research activities "were not intended to have * * * any relation to [Moore's] medical * * * care." However, neither Golde nor Quan informed Moore of their plans to conduct this research or requested his permission. Surgeons at UCLA Medical Center, whom the complaint does not name as defendants, removed Moore's spleen on October 20, 1976.

Moore returned to the UCLA Medical Center several times between November 1976 and September 1983. He did so at Golde's direction and based upon representations "that such visits were necessary and required for his health and well-being, and based upon the trust inherent in and by virtue of the physician-patient relationship. * * * " On each of these visits Golde withdrew additional samples of "blood, blood serum, skin, bone marrow aspirate, and sperm." On each occasion Moore travelled to the UCLA Medical Center from his home in Seattle because he had been told that the procedures were to be performed only there and only under Golde's direction.

"In fact, [however,] throughout the period of time that [Moore] was under [Golde's] care and treatment, * * * the defendants were actively involved in a number of activities which they concealed from [Moore] * * *." Specifically, defendants were conducting research on Moore's cells and planned to "benefit financially and competitively * * * [by exploiting the cells] and [their] exclusive access to [the cells] by virtue of [Golde's] on-going physician-patient relationship. * * * "

Sometime before August 1979, Golde established a cell line from Moore's T-lymphocytes. On January 30, 1981, the Regents applied for a patent on the cell line, listing Golde and Quan as inventors. "[B]y virtue of an established policy * * *, [the] Regents, Golde, and Quan would share in any royalties or profits * * * arising out of [the] patent." The patent issued on March 20, 1984, naming Golde and Quan as the inventors of the cell line and the Regents as the assignee of the patent. * * *

Moore admits in his complaint that "the true clinical potential of each of the lymphokines * * * [is] difficult to predict, [but] * * * competing commercial firms in these relevant fields have published reports in biotechnology industry periodicals predicting a potential market of approximately $3.01 Billion Dollars by the year 1990 for a whole range of [such lymphokines] * * *."

With the Regents' assistance, Golde negotiated agreements for commercial development of the cell line and products to be derived from it. Under an agreement with Genetics Institute, Golde "became a paid consultant" and "acquired the rights to 75,000 shares of common stock." Genetics Institute also agreed to pay Golde and the Regents "at least $330,000 over three years, including a pro-rata share of [Golde's] salary and fringe benefits, in exchange for * * * exclusive access to the materials and research performed" on the cell line and products derived from it. On June 4, 1982, Sandoz "was added to the agreement," and compensation payable to Golde and the Regents was increased by $110,000. * * *

Based upon these allegations, Moore attempted to state 13 causes of action. * * *

[**Editor's note:** The trial court considered only the cause of action for conversion and held that Moore had failed to state a claim. The Court of Appeal reversed and held that Moore could claim conversion. The California Supreme Court in this decision reverses the Court of Appeal on the claim of conversion. The Supreme Court held that Moore did state a claim for breach of fiduciary duty and lack of informed consent based on the defendant physicians' failure to disclose their intended use of his body fluids and tissue. Only the portion of the opinion that concerns conversion is reproduced here.]

1. MOORE'S CLAIM UNDER EXISTING LAW

"To establish a conversion, plaintiff must establish an actual interference with his *ownership or right of possession* * * * Where plaintiff neither has title to the property alleged to have been converted, nor possession thereof, he cannot maintain an action for conversion." [ ]

Since Moore clearly did not expect to retain possession of his cells following their removal, to sue for their conversion he must have retained an ownership interest in them. But there are several reasons to doubt that he did retain any such interest. First, no reported judicial decision supports Moore's claim, either directly or by close analogy. Second, California statutory law drastically limits any continuing interest of a patient in excised cells. Third, the subject matters of the Regents' patent—the patented cell line and the products derived from it—cannot be Moore's property.

Neither the Court of Appeal's opinion, the parties' briefs, nor our research discloses a case holding that a person retains a sufficient interest in excised cells to support a cause of action for conversion. We do not find this surprising, since the laws governing such things as human tissues, transplantable organs, blood, fetuses, pituitary glands, corneal tissue, and dead bodies deal with human biological materials as objects sui generis, regulating their disposition to achieve policy goals rather than abandoning them to the general law of personal property.

It is these specialized statutes, not the law of conversion, to which courts ordinarily should and do look for guidance on the disposition of human biological materials.

* * *

The next consideration that makes Moore's claim of ownership problematic is California statutory law, which drastically limits a patient's control over excised cells. Pursuant to Health and Safety Code section 7054.4, "[n]otwithstanding any other provision of law, recognizable anatomical parts, human tissues, anatomical human remains, or infectious waste following conclusion of scientific use shall be disposed of by interment, incineration, or any other method determined by the state department [of health services] to protect the public health and safety." Clearly the Legislature did not specifically intend this statute to resolve the question of whether a patient is entitled to compensation for the nonconsensual use of excised cells. A primary object of the statute is to ensure the safe handling of potentially hazardous biological waste materials. Yet one cannot escape the conclusion that the statute's practical effect is to limit, drastically, a patient's control over excised cells. By restricting how excised cells may be used and requiring their eventual destruction, the statute eliminates so many of the rights ordinarily attached to property that one cannot simply assume that what is left amounts to "property" or "ownership" for purposes of conversion law.

It may be that some limited right to control the use of excised cells does survive the operation of this statute. There is, for example, no need to read the statute to permit "scientific use" contrary to the patient's expressed wish. A fully informed patient may always withhold consent to treatment by a physician whose research plans the patient does not approve. That right, however, * * *, is protected by the fiduciary-duty and informed-consent theories.

Finally, the subject matter of the Regents' patent—the patented cell line and the products derived from it—cannot be Moore's property. This is because the patented cell line is both factually and legally distinct from the cells taken from Moore's body.[8] Federal law permits the patenting of organisms that represent the product of "human ingenuity," but not naturally occurring organisms. [ ] * * * It is this *inventive effort* that patent law rewards, not the discovery of naturally

---

8. The distinction between primary cells (cells taken directly from the body) and patented cell lines is not purely a legal one. Cells change while being developed into a cell line and continue to change over time. (OTA Rep., supra, p. 34.) * * *

The cell line in this case, for example, after many replications began to generate defective and rearranged forms of the HTLV–II virus. A published research paper to which defendants contributed suggests that "the defective forms of virus were probably generated during the passage [or replication] of the cells rather than being present in the original tumor cells of the patient." Possibly because of these changes in the virus, the cell line has developed new abilities to grow in different media. (Chen, McLaughlin, Gasson, Clark & Golde, Molecular Characterization of Genome of a Novel Human T-cell Leukaemia Virus, Nature (Oct. 6, 1983) vol. 305, p. 505.)

* * *

occurring raw materials. Thus, Moore's allegations that he owns the cell line and the products derived from it are inconsistent with the patent, which constitutes an authoritative determination that the cell line is the product of invention. * * *

2. SHOULD CONVERSION LIABILITY BE EXTENDED?

* * *

There are three reasons why it is inappropriate to impose liability for conversion based upon the allegations of Moore's complaint. First, a fair balancing of the relevant policy considerations counsels against extending the tort. Second, problems in this area are better suited to legislative resolution. Third, the tort of conversion is not necessary to protect patients' rights. For these reasons, we conclude that the use of excised human cells in medical research does not amount to a conversion.

Of the relevant policy considerations, two are of overriding importance. The first is protection of a competent patient's right to make autonomous medical decisions. That right, * * *, is grounded in well-recognized and long-standing principles of fiduciary duty and informed consent. [ ] This policy weighs in favor of providing a remedy to patients when physicians act with undisclosed motives that may affect their professional judgment. The second important policy consideration is that we not threaten with disabling civil liability innocent parties who are engaged in socially useful activities, such as researchers who have no reason to believe that their use of a particular cell sample is, or may be, against a donor's wishes.

* * *

[A]n examination of the relevant policy considerations suggests an appropriate balance: Liability based upon existing disclosure obligations, rather than an unprecedented extension of the conversion theory protects patients' rights of privacy and autonomy without unnecessarily hindering research.

To be sure, the threat of liability for conversion might help to enforce patients' rights indirectly. This is because physicians might be able to avoid liability by obtaining patients' consent, in the broadest possible terms, to any conceivable subsequent research use of excised cells. Unfortunately, to extend the conversion theory would utterly sacrifice the other goal of protecting innocent parties. Since conversion is a strict liability tort, it would impose liability on all those into whose hands the cells come, whether or not the particular defendant participated in, or knew of, the inadequate disclosures that violated the patient's right to make an informed decision. In contrast to the conversion theory, the fiduciary-duty and informed-consent theories protect the patient directly, without punishing innocent parties or creating disincentives to the conduct of socially beneficial research.

* * *

* * * Since the patent office requires the holders of patents on cell lines to make samples available to anyone, many patent holders place their cell lines in repositories to avoid the administrative burden of responding to requests.   At present, human cell lines are routinely copied and distributed to other researchers for experimental purposes, usually free of charge.   This exchange of scientific materials, which still is relatively free and efficient, will surely be compromised if each cell sample becomes the potential subject matter of a lawsuit.   [   ][9]

* * * So long as a physician discloses research and economic interests that may affect his judgment, the patient is protected from conflicts of interest.   Aware of any conflicts, the patient can make an informed decision to consent to treatment, or to withhold consent and look elsewhere for medical assistance.   As already discussed, enforcement of physicians' disclosure obligations protects patients directly, without hindering the socially useful activities of innocent researchers.

For these reasons, we hold that the allegations of Moore's third amended complaint state a cause of action for breach of fiduciary duty or lack of informed consent, but not conversion.

* * *

ARABIAN, JUSTICE, concurring.

Plaintiff has asked us to recognize and enforce a right to sell one's own body tissue *for profit*.   He entreats us to regard the human vessel—the single most venerated and protected subject in any civilized society—as equal with the basest commercial commodity.   He urges us to commingle the sacred with the profane.   He asks much.

* * *

Whether, as plaintiff urges, his cells should be treated as property susceptible to conversion is not, in my view, ours to decide.   The question implicates choices which not only reflect, but which ultimately define our essence.   A mark of wisdom for us as expositors of the law is the recognition that we cannot cure every ill, mediate every dispute, resolve every conundrum.   Sometimes, as Justice Brandeis said, "the most important thing we do, is not doing."

Where then shall a complete resolution be found?   Clearly the Legislature, as the majority opinion suggests, is the proper deliberative forum.   Indeed, a legislative response creating a licensing scheme, which establishes a fixed rate of profit sharing between researcher and subject, has already been suggested.   [   ] Such an arrangement would not only avoid the moral and philosophical objections to a free market

9.   * * * The availability of patent protection for cell lines actually *increases* the availability of research materials, since the Patent Office requires patent holders to make patented microorganisms available to researchers immediately after a patent issues.   [   ] Generally available cell lines are of substantial importance not just to academic research, but to commercial research as well.   Indeed, some biotechnology companies "do not use any original human tissue in research, concentrating their efforts on established cell lines instead. These companies obtain and manipulate generally available cell lines, resulting in new, unique, or improved cell lines."   [   ]

operation in body tissue, but would also address stated concerns by eliminating the inherently coercive effect of a waiver system and by compensating donors regardless of temporal circumstances.

* * *

MOSK, JUSTICE, dissenting.

* * *

1.

The majority's first reason [to reject a claim of conversion] is that "no reported judicial decision supports Moore's claim, either directly or by close analogy." Neither, however, is there any reported decision rejecting such a claim. The issue is as new as its source—the recent explosive growth in the commercialization of biotechnology.

The majority next cite several statutes regulating aspects of the commerce in or disposition of certain parts of the human body, and conclude in effect that in the present case we should also "look for guidance" to the Legislature rather than to the law of conversion. Surely this argument is out of place in an opinion of the highest court of this state. As the majority acknowledge, the law of conversion is a creature of the common law. " 'The inherent capacity of the common law for growth and change is its most significant feature. Its development has been determined by the social needs of the community which it serves. It is constantly expanding and developing in keeping with advancing civilization and the new conditions and progress of society, and adapting itself to the gradual change of trade, commerce, arts, inventions, and the needs of the country.' [ ] In short, as the United States Supreme Court has aptly said, 'This flexibility and capacity for growth and adaptation is the peculiar boast and excellence of the common law.' [ ] * * * Although the Legislature may of course speak to the subject, in the common law system the primary instruments of this evolution are the courts, adjudicating on a regular basis the rich variety of individual cases brought before them." (*Rodriguez v. Bethlehem Steel Corp.* (1974) 12 Cal.3d 382, 394, 115 Cal.Rptr. 765, 525 P.2d 669.)

* * *

2.

The majority's second reason for doubting that Moore retained an ownership interest in his cells after their excision is that "California statutory law * * * drastically limits a patient's control over excised cells." * * *

[I]n my view the statute does not authorize the principal use that defendants claim the right to make of Moore's tissue, i.e., its commercial exploitation. * * *

* * * I would agree that "scientific use" at least includes routine postoperative examination of excised tissue conducted by a pathologist for diagnostic or prognostic reasons (e.g., to verify preoperative diagnosis or to assist in determining postoperative treatment). I might further agree that "scientific use" could be extended to include purely scientific study of the tissue by a disinterested researcher for the purpose of advancing medical knowledge—provided of course that the patient gave timely and informed consent to that use. It would stretch the English language beyond recognition, however, to say that commercial exploitation of the kind and degree alleged here is also a usual and ordinary meaning of the phrase "scientific use."

* * * I do not stress the concept of profit, but the concept of *science:* the distinction I draw is not between nonprofit scientific use and scientific use that happens to lead to a marketable by-product; it is between a truly *scientific* use and the blatant *commercial* exploitation of Moore's tissue that the present complaint alleges. Under those allegations, defendants Dr. David W. Golde and Shirley G. Quan were not only scientists, they were also full-fledged entrepreneurs * * *.

Secondly, even if section 7054.4 does permit defendants' commercial exploitation of Moore's tissue under the guise of "scientific use," it does not follow that—as the majority conclude—the statute "eliminates so many of the rights ordinarily attached to property" that what remains does not amount to "property" or "ownership" for purposes of the law of conversion. [ ]

The concepts of property and ownership in our law are extremely broad. [ ] A leading decision of this court approved the following definition: " 'The term "property" is sufficiently comprehensive to include every species of estate, real and personal, and everything which one person can own and transfer to another. It extends to every species of right and interest capable of being enjoyed as such upon which it is practicable to place a money value.' " (*Yuba River Power Co. v. Nevada Irr. Dist.* (1929) 207 Cal. 521, 523, 279 P. 128.)

Being broad, the concept of property is also abstract: rather than referring directly to a material object such as a parcel of land or the tractor that cultivates it, the concept of property is often said to refer to a "bundle of rights" that may be exercised with respect to that object— principally the rights to possess the property, to use the property, to exclude others from the property, and to dispose of the property by sale or by gift. * * * But the same bundle of rights does not attach to all forms of property. For a variety of policy reasons, the law limits or even forbids the exercise of certain rights over certain forms of property. For example, both law and contract may limit the right of an owner of real property to use his parcel as he sees fit. [citing zoning, nuisance and real covenants]. Owners of various forms of personal property may likewise be subject to restrictions on the time, place, and manner of their use [citing public health and safety regulations]. Limitations on the disposition of real property, while less common, may also be imposed [citing condominium agreements]. Finally, some types of personal property may be sold but not given away, [citing property in bankruptcy] while others may be given away but not sold, [citing wild fish and game captured by sports people] and still others may neither be given away nor sold [citing professional licenses].

In each of the foregoing instances, the limitation or prohibition diminishes the bundle of rights that would otherwise attach to the property, yet what remains is still deemed in law to be a protectible property interest.   * * * The same rule applies to Moore's interest in his own body tissue: even if we assume that section 7054.4 limited the use and disposition of his excised tissue in the manner claimed by the majority, Moore nevertheless retained valuable rights in that tissue. Above all, at the time of its excision he at least had *the right to do with his own tissue whatever the defendants did with it:* i.e., he could have contracted with researchers and pharmaceutical companies to develop and exploit the vast commercial potential of his tissue and its products. Defendants certainly believe that *their* right to do the foregoing is not barred by section 7054.4 and is a significant property right, as they have demonstrated by their deliberate concealment from Moore of the true value of his tissue, their efforts to obtain a patent on the Mo cell line, their contractual agreements to exploit this material, their exclusion of Moore from any participation in the profits, and their vigorous defense of this lawsuit. The Court of Appeal summed up the point by observing that "Defendants' position that plaintiff cannot own his tissue, but that they can, is fraught with irony." It is also legally untenable. As noted above, the majority cite no case holding that an individual's right to develop and exploit the commercial potential of his own tissue is *not* a right of sufficient worth or dignity to be deemed a protectible property interest. In the absence of such authority—or of legislation to the same effect—the right falls within the traditionally broad concept of property in our law.

3.

The majority's third and last reason for their conclusion that Moore has no cause of action for conversion under existing law is that "the subject matter of the Regents' patent—the patented cell line and the products derived from it—cannot be Moore's property." [   ] The majority then offer a dual explanation: "This is because the patented cell line is *factually* and *legally* distinct from the cells taken from Moore's body." [   ] Neither branch of the explanation withstands analysis.

First, in support of their statement that the Mo cell line is "factually distinct" from Moore's cells, the majority assert that "Cells change while being developed into a cell line and continue to change over time," and in particular may acquire an abnormal number of chromosomes. No one disputes these assertions, but they are nonetheless irrelevant. For present purposes no distinction can be drawn between Moore's cells and the Mo cell line. It appears that the principal reason for establishing a cell line is not to "improve" the quality of the parent cells but simply to extend their life indefinitely, in order to permit long-term study and/or exploitation of the qualities already present in such cells. The complaint alleges that Moore's cells naturally produced certain valuable proteins in larger than normal quantities; indeed, that was why defendants were eager to culture them in the first place. Defendants do not claim that the cells of the Mo cell line are in any degree more productive of such proteins than were Moore's own cells. Even if the cells of the Mo cell line in fact have an abnormal number of chromosomes, at the present stage of this case we do not know if that fact has any bearing whatever on their capacity to produce proteins; yet it is in the commercial exploitation of that capacity—not simply in their number of chromosomes—that Moore seeks to assert an interest. For all that appears, therefore, the emphasized fact is a distinction without a difference.

Second, the majority assert in effect that Moore cannot have an ownership interest in the Mo cell line because defendants patented it. The majority's point wholly fails to meet Moore's claim that he is entitled to compensation for defendants' unauthorized use of his bodily tissues *before* defendants patented the Mo cell line: defendants undertook such use immediately after the splenectomy on October 20, 1976, and continued to extract and use Moore's cells and tissue at least until September 20, 1983; the patent, however, did not issue until March 20, 1984, more than seven years after the unauthorized use began. Whatever the legal consequences of that event, it did not operate retroactively to immunize defendants from accountability for conduct occurring long before the patent was granted.

Nor did the issuance of the patent in 1984 necessarily have the drastic effect that the majority contend. To be sure, the patent granted defendants the exclusive right to make, use, or sell the invention for a period of 17 years. [ ] But Moore does not assert any such right for himself. Rather, he seeks to show that he is entitled, in fairness and equity, to some share in the profits that defendants have made and will make from their commercial exploitation of the Mo cell line. I do not question that the cell line is primarily the product of defendants' inventive effort. Yet likewise no one can question Moore's crucial contribution to the invention—an invention named, ironically, after him: but for the cells of Moore's body taken by defendants, *there would have been no Mo cell line.* Thus the complaint alleges that Moore's "Blood and Bodily Substances were absolutely essential to defendants' research and commercial activities with regard to his cells, cell lines, [and] the Mo cell-line, * * * and that defendants could not have applied for and had issued to them the Mo cell-line patent and other patents described herein without obtaining and culturing specimens of plaintiff's Blood and Bodily Substances." Defendants admit this allegation by their demurrers, as well they should: for all their expertise, defendants do not claim they could have extracted the Mo cell line out of thin air.

* * *

4.

Having concluded—mistakenly, in my view—that Moore has no cause of action for conversion under existing law, the majority next consider whether to "extend" the conversion cause of action to this context. Again the majority find three reasons not to do so, and again I respectfully disagree with each.

* * *

* * * The majority observe that many researchers obtain their tissue samples, routinely and at little or no cost, from cell-culture repositories. The majority then speculate that "This exchange of scientific materials which still is relatively free and efficient will surely be compromised if each cell sample becomes the potential subject matter of a lawsuit." [   ]. There are two grounds to doubt that this prophecy will be fulfilled.

To begin with, if the relevant exchange of scientific materials was ever "free and efficient," it is much less so today. Since biological products of genetic engineering became patentable in 1980 [   ], human cell lines have been amenable to patent protection and, as the Court of Appeal observed in its opinion below, "The rush to patent for exclusive use has been rampant." Among those who have taken advantage of this development, of course, are the defendants herein: as we have seen, defendants Golde and Quan obtained a patent on the Mo cell line in 1984 and assigned it to defendant Regents. With such patentability has come a drastic reduction in the formerly free access of researchers to new cell lines and their products: the "novelty" requirement for patentability prohibits public disclosure of the invention at all times up to one year before the filing of the patent application. [   ] Thus defendants herein recited in their patent specification, "At no time has the Mo cell line been available to other than the investigators involved with its initial discovery and only the conditioned medium from the cell line has been made available to a limited number of investigators for collaborative work with the original discoverers of the Mo cell line."

An even greater force for restricting the free exchange of new cell lines and their products has been the rise of the biotechnology industry and the increasing involvement of academic researchers in that industry. When scientists became entrepreneurs and negotiated with biotechnological and pharmaceutical companies to develop and exploit the commercial potential of their discoveries—as did defendants in the case at bar—layers of contractual restrictions were added to the protections of the patent law.

In their turn, the biotechnological and pharmaceutical companies demanded and received exclusive rights in the scientists' discoveries, and frequently placed those discoveries under trade secret protection. Trade secret protection is popular among biotechnology companies because, among other reasons, the invention need not meet the strict standards of patentability and the protection is both quickly acquired and unlimited in duration.   * * *

Secondly, to the extent that cell cultures and cell lines may still be "freely exchanged," e.g., for purely research purposes, it does not follow that the researcher who obtains such material must necessarily remain ignorant of any limitations on its use: by means of appropriate record-keeping, the researcher can be assured that the source of the material has consented to his proposed use of it, and hence that such use is not a conversion.   * * *

* * *

In any event, in my view whatever merit the majority's single policy consideration may have is outweighed by two contrary considerations, i.e., policies that are promoted by recognizing that every individual has a legally protectible property interest in his own body and its products.   First, our society acknowledges a profound ethical imperative to respect the human body as the physical and temporal expression of the unique human persona.   One manifestation of that respect is our prohibition against direct abuse of the body by torture or other forms of cruel or unusual punishment.   Another is our prohibition against indirect abuse of the body by its economic exploitation for the sole benefit of another person.   The most abhorrent form of such exploitation, of course, was the institution of slavery.   Lesser forms, such as indentured servitude or even debtor's prison, have also disappeared. Yet their specter haunts the laboratories and boardrooms of today's biotechnological research-industrial complex.   It arises wherever scientists or industrialists claim, as defendants claim here, the right to appropriate and exploit a patient's tissue for their sole economic benefit.

* * * In short, as the Court of Appeal succinctly put it, "If this science has become science for profit, then we fail to see any justification for excluding the patient from participation in those profits."

5.

* * *

The inference I draw from the current statutory regulation of human biological materials, moreover, is the opposite of that drawn by the majority.   By selective quotation of the statutes the majority seem to suggest that human organs and blood cannot legally be sold on the open market—thereby implying that if the Legislature were to act here it would impose a similar ban on monetary compensation for the use of human tissue in biotechnological research and development.   But if that is the argument, the premise is unsound: contrary to popular misconception, it is not true that human organs and blood cannot legally be sold.

As to organs, the majority rely on the Uniform Anatomical Gift Act [   ] for the proposition that a competent adult may make a post mortem gift of any part of his body but may not receive "valuable consideration" for the transfer.   But the prohibition of the UAGA against the sale of a body part is much more limited than the majority recognize: by its terms [   ] the prohibition applies only to sales for "transplantation" or "therapy."   Yet a different section of the UAGA authorizes the transfer and receipt of body parts for such additional purposes as "medical or dental education, research, or advancement of medical or dental science."   [ ] No section of the UAGA prohibits anyone from selling body parts for any of those additional purposes; by clear implication, therefore, such sales are legal.   Indeed, the fact that the UAGA prohibits *no* sales of organs other than sales for "transplantation" or "therapy" raises a further implication that it is also legal for anyone to sell human tissue to a biotechnology company for research and development purposes.

With respect to the sale of human blood the matter is much simpler: there is in fact no prohibition against such sales.   * * * [B]ecause such statutes treat both organs and blood as property that can legally be sold in a variety of circumstances, they impliedly support Moore's contention that his blood cells are likewise property for which he can and should receive compensation, and hence are protected by the law of conversion.

6.

* * *

I disagree, * * * with the majority's further conclusion that in the present context a nondisclosure cause of action is an adequate—in fact, a superior—substitute for a conversion cause of action.   In my view the nondisclosure cause of action falls short on at least three grounds.

* * *

[**Editor's note:** The dissent argues that a claim of nondisclosure or failure of informed consent requires that plaintiff prove that a reasonably prudent person in plaintiff's position would not have consented to removal of tissue if he had had the information the physician withheld.   The dissent believes that this presents an impossible task for someone in Moore's position.]

* * *

The second reason why the nondisclosure cause of action is inadequate for the task that the majority assign to it is that it fails to solve half the problem before us: it gives the patient only the right to *refuse* consent, i.e., the right to prohibit the commercialization of his tissue; it does not give him the right to *grant* consent to that commercialization on the condition that he share in its proceeds.   * * *

Reversing the words of the old song, the nondisclosure cause of action thus accentuates the negative and eliminates the positive: the patient can say no, but he cannot say yes and expect to share in the proceeds of his contribution.   Yet as explained above, there are sound reasons of ethics and equity to recognize the patient's right to participate in such benefits.   The nondisclosure cause of action does not protect that right; to that extent, it is therefore not an adequate substitute for the conversion remedy, which does protect the right.

Third, the nondisclosure cause of action fails to reach a major class of potential defendants: all those who are outside the strict physician-patient relationship with the plaintiff. Thus the majority concede that here only defendant Golde, the treating physician, can be directly liable to Moore on a nondisclosure cause of action * * * As to [the Regents, Quan, Genetics Institute, and Sandoz], the majority can offer Moore only a slim hope of recovery: if they are to be liable on a nondisclosure cause of action, say the majority, "it can only be on account of Golde's acts and on the basis of a recognized theory of secondary liability, such as respondeat superior." Although the majority decline to decide the question whether the secondary-liability allegations of the complaint are sufficient, they strongly imply disapproval of those allegations. * * *

* * *

In sum, the nondisclosure cause of action (1) is unlikely to be successful in most cases, (2) fails to protect patients' rights to share in the proceeds of the commercial exploitation of their tissue, and (3) may allow the true exploiters to escape liability. It is thus not an adequate substitute, in my view, for the conversion cause of action.

7.

My respect for this court as an institution compels me to make one last point: I dissociate myself completely from the amateur biology lecture that the majority impose on us throughout their opinion.

[**Editor's note:** The dissent argues that the "uniqueness" of Moore's cells is legally irrelevant—both ordinary property and unique property is protected from conversion. He further argues that the scientific material was written in "highly technical scientific jargon" and was not supported by expert testimony that might have explained the material, and that the court does not have the resources to perform a search of medical literature and must rely on articles submitted by the parties.]

Notes and Questions

1. Did John Moore win or lose? What about the defendants?

2. What is the holding of this case? Does Moore have any right to transfer his cell lines?

(a) Assume that John Moore, David Golde, and UCLA had actually entered into an agreement concerning the use of Moore's body fluids and tissues that provided that John Moore was to get a small percentage of payments received by Golde or UCLA for products developed from his cells. If UCLA and Golde had refused to pay the amount agreed upon, do you think that the California Supreme Court would enforce the agreement?

(b) Assume that David Golde and UCLA meet another patient with the potential of John Moore. How should they handle the situation? The majority opinion in *Moore* holds that they must disclose to the patient Dr. Golde's participation in research. If university counsel drafts a disclosure document that is accurate and understandable and the patient understands the situation and signs the document, both the treatment and the research can proceed. What if the patient refuses to consent unless he is compensated? Can the university pay him? Would you treat this situation any differently than the previous one?

3. Ellen Frankel Paul takes a turn at analyzing the property question in *Moore* from the perspective of three different theories concerning the allocation of property rights:

> Surely, if the decision had been written 200 years ago, the court would have explicitly articulated a natural rights or natural law approach, and the matter would have been settled with little fuss. [A]fter a good half-century of "bundles of sticks" thinking about property rights, no such explicit approach would have been conceivable. Instead, the court [would ponder] whether it should "give the patient that right." A natural law jurist would have sought to "find" the law. The difference is subtle but important.

> For a utilitarian, Moore would be easily dispatched. Great public benefit arises from scientific research derived from the discarded body parts. Thus, Mr. Moore has no claim on conversion; because he has no property right, there was no illegitimate taking of property and, hence, no damages. It is perfectly conceivable that an analyst using utilitarian principles might reach an opposite conclusion. The argument would assert that the social benefit lies in protecting property in one's own person as a general rule * * * or even that in this case the harm to Mr. Moore might outweigh the social benefit (although it is difficult to see how this might be made out) * * *.

> Where might a Paretian stand on the issue raised by Moore? * * * A rearrangement of resources is considered Pareto-superior to the status quo if no one is harmed by the change and at least one person is better off * * *.

> * * * Mr. Moore would fare rather poorly [under a Paretian analysis]. To begin with, many people will be better off as a result of the pharmaceuticals developed from Mr. Moore's cell line, including the researchers themselves, the university, and the drug companies, to say nothing of patients whose lives will be enhanced or even saved. Was anyone harmed? Even if he had been harmed * * * he could have been compensated for any slight harm. * * *

Paul, Natural Rights and Property Rights, 13 Harv.J. of Law & Public Policy 10 (1990). Did this case use any of these theories? For additional comments on *Moore* see also, Note, Moore v. Regents of the University of California: Patients, Property Rights and Public Policy, 35 St. Louis U.L.J. 433 (1991).

4. The majority opinion invites legislative action. Assume that you are a legal advisor to a federal or state commission considering whether to recommend a statute that would recognize property rights in human tissue, including functioning organs. In addition to the situation reviewed in *Moore,* consider the issues involved in the inadequate supply of human organs for transplantation. How would you advise such a commission?

Can you frame your analysis in terms of some of the theories we saw in this chapter? Does the "bundle of sticks" metaphor help? Are you persuaded by the theories that focus on the consequences of the rule, such as utilitarianism and the law and economics approach? Would you argue from a "natural rights" starting point? Is there any other approach you would find attractive?

5. The majority opinion in *Moore* discusses the protection of invention through patent law and relies on the patentability of the cell line as part of its framework for denying property rights to Moore. Intellectual property, such as inventions and designs, artistic and literary products and commercial symbols, is protected by a web of federal patent, copyright and trademark laws. The concept of ownership of "ideas" is not entirely uncontroversial. See for example, Symposium on Law and Philosophy, 13 Harvard Journal of Law & Public Policy 757–948 (1990).

6. Because the supply of transplantable human organs still falls far short of the numbers required, there have been some proposals that human organs should be viewed as transferable on the market. Federal law currently prohibits the sale of organs for transplant. 42 U.S.C. § 274(e). Should that continue to be the case? For discussion see, Annas, Life, Liberty and the Pursuit of Organ Sales, 14 Hastings Center Report 22 (Feb.1984); Cohen, Increasing the Supply of Transplant Organs: The Virtues of a Futures Market, 58 George Washington L.Rev. 1 (1989).

Under the statutes of many states, the removal of the corneas from a dead body is authorized without the consent of the deceased. The claim that human tissue is property has been used in cases in which families have discovered that the corneas have been removed. These families have claimed that the statutes authorizing nonconsensual removal of this body tissue violate the Constitution's prohibition of the taking of property without due process and just compensation. The purpose of this property claim is to protect the integrity of the body. Should it be treated differently from other claims that the human body is property? For discussion see, Note, "She's Got Bette Davis['s] Eyes: Assessing the Nonconsensual Removal of Cadaver Organs under the Takings and Due Process Clauses, 90 Colum.L.Rev. 528 (1990).

7. Sometimes there is disagreement over what is being sold. It is clearly illegal to sell babies. But does a contract governing a surrogacy arrangement involve the sale of a baby or the sale of services by the woman providing the ovum and carrying the pregnancy? In the most notorious case, the Supreme Court of New Jersey invalidated a surrogacy contract involving Baby M, In the Matter of Baby M, 109 N.J. 396, 537 A.2d 1227 (1988), holding that "this is the sale of a child, or, at the very least, the sale of a mother's right to her child." Does it matter which it is? Arguments against surrogacy generally claim that legalized commercial surrogacy will result in the exploitation of poor women; will cause emotional harm to the

children who learn of their origin; or will weaken the values of society overall. Arguments favoring commercial surrogacy claim that surrogacy is voluntary and that it allows infertile couples to have a child. If you remove money from the transaction, do the issues change?

8. The questions of What is Property?; and What is For Sale? inevitably must reflect on the fearsome time in our history when human beings were property and human beings were for sale. Derrick Bell writes of this in one of his chronicles where he speaks as the character "Geneva Crenshaw," an African–American woman of the twentieth century, addressing the Constitutional Convention of 1787:

> "Gentlemen, it was * * * Thomas Jefferson who, considering the evil of slavery, wrote: 'I tremble for my country when I reflect that God is just; that his justice cannot sleep forever.' "

> "It grieves me," [a delegate said.] "* * * But what alternative do we have? Unless we here frame a constitution that can first gain our signatures and then win ratification by the states, we shall soon have no nation. For better or worse, slavery has been the backbone of our economy, the source of much of our wealth. It was condoned in the colonies and recognized in the Articles of Confederation. The majority of the delegates to this convention own slaves and must have that right protected if they and their states are to be included in the new government."

> [Crenshaw responds:] "What is lacking here is not legislative skill but the courage to recognize the evil of holding blacks in slavery—an evil that would be quickly and universally condemned were the subjects of bondage members of the Caucasian race. You fear that unless the slavery of blacks is recognized and given protection, the nation will not survive. And my message is that the compromises you are making here mean that the nation's survival will always be in doubt. For now in my own day, after two hundred years and despite bloody wars and the earnest efforts of committed people, the racial contradiction you sanction in this document remains and threatens to tear this country apart."

Bell, And We Are Not Saved: The Elusive Quest for Racial Justice (1987).

9. A final note: In this first chapter we considered the question of the acquisition of property in the absence of a voluntary sale, gift, lease, or bequest. It is likely that transfer of property by these voluntary methods is much more common than those methods we examine in this chapter. Nearly all property casebooks begin with an examination of the law of discovery/conquest, capture, finders, and adverse possession, however. In part, these cases introduce you to the legal concept of possession (which is, after all, "nine-tenths of the law") and to the modern legal concept of property as a bundle of rights, which gives you the tools for many modern property transactions that separate the rights to possess, use, exclude, transfer, and allocate these rights, usually for a price, among several

individuals. But these cases also provide an opportunity for examining the role of "property" in our system and the variety of competing ideas concerning property and the allocation of property. And, although not treated in the majority of property cases, issues concerning whether "new property", such as mineral nodules in the deep sea, human tissue and organs, and new life forms, can be owned, and how its ownership is to be decided, are not all that rare.

You may have a sense from this chapter that property law is infinitely elastic. But reserve judgment. You may, or you may not, find the same elasticity in the rules applying to voluntary transfers. In the following chapters you will see some strong counterweights to flexibility and change in property law. These opposing forces are stability and predictability, and they tend to take a stronger hand in some areas of property law.

Chapter Two

COMMON LAW ESTATES

Common law estates is about the practice of property law, for clients who are buyers, sellers, owners, donors, donees, and users of property. It is—unlike torts, criminal law, or civil procedure—a law-office subject.

A PRELUDE ON LAW IN THE LAW OFFICE

Law-office law, including most of the practice of property law, is a green-eyeshade subject. The green eyeshade, in case you haven't seen one lately, looks like the visor-without-a-cap that golfers wear, except that a lawyer's green eyeshade is transparent and tinted—and it is worn indoors. It is worn to protect eyes from the glare of the lamp on the white paper over which the lawyer labors, as modern ophthalmological devices on computer screens protect us from losing our eyesight when we interface.

The practitioner of property law is a lawyer in a garment that has long sleeves, maybe even with garters holding the cuffs away from the dust on the top of the desk, putting down on paper the words that will do what his or her client wants done. He practices his art in ordinary, civilized times, on Wednesday afternoons, say, when court has adjourned early and the physicians are on the golf course. She practices in the law office, in the county-seat town, near the courthouse—not because that is where *court* is, but because that is where the land records are—the official records that give the world notice of ownership.

In our quaint, old-fashioned imagination, the law office is across the street from the courthouse, on the second floor of a commercial building, reached by outside stairs, and heated by a pot-bellied, coal-burning stove. It is like the office of Gavin Stevens, in Jefferson, Mississippi, in William Faulkner's lawyer stories; or like Atticus Finch's office in Maycomb, Alabama (*To Kill a Mockingbird*), where Atticus docked the entail for Mr. Cunningham and drafted a will for

Mrs. Dubose. It is the law office of Abraham Lincoln, now preserved as a museum in Springfield, Illinois.

You can vary the image a bit, without affecting the notion of practice we want to suggest with it, by thinking of the family solicitor in Victorian English novels: In Britain, the legal profession has two branches, the trial lawyers—barristers—and office lawyers—attorneys and solicitors. If the novel involves a trial in London (as Anthony Trollope's novels often did), the barrister, in gown and wig, functions eloquently in court. But the usual and more potent legal power in the Victorian stories is the solicitor, writing in a special way, on paper of a special size, in his office; or talking to the young squire in the library of the manor house; or talking to the old squire, upstairs at the bedside, so that the old squire can make a few last-minute revisions in his will before he slips into eternity.

The family solicitor was an important minor character in the novels of Trollope or of Charles Dickens; his work was in place to define the comfort and even the destiny of Jane Austen's characters, or William Thackeray's, or those of the Bronte sisters and George Eliot. The family solicitor was above all else a *property lawyer*. He was the arbiter of ownership among siblings, between generations, in widowhood, among in-laws, in the country and in town, in a nation-state that pursued its destiny on an island. In Trollope's novel *The Eustace Diamonds,* a thousand pages of plot turn on what the family lawyer will say about the ownership of a necklace that Lizzie Eustace's husband gave her before he died. The lawyer takes his time; he even seeks advice from another lawyer; but when he finally speaks the matter is settled.

Property lawyers *do* go to court. Books of materials for the study of property law, including this one, teem with the opinions of appellate judges. Each of these opinions stands for the fact that a property lawyer went to one court and then another and then another until she either won the case or could go no further. But property lawyers are not in business to litigate; they are in business to avoid litigation. Their trips to court are rare, and they are almost always tragic; they are memorials to failure at the fundamental arts of property law. And they should always be read with this question in mind: *What went wrong?*

Litigation is a small, small part of a property lawyer's work (and a bit of an adventure that is given more prominence in lawyers' memories than it deserves to have). Litigation is a rare outcome for the papers a lawyer prepares, with green eyeshade on, on Wednesday afternoon. Judicial opinions in property matters are not so much a source of law as they are evidence of wreckage in the law. The office lawyer fails—*loses the case*—when a judge, rather than clients and their families and their colleagues in business, decide what the lawyer's papers mean, what law is to govern relations within the family and business, and how law will fashion the face the family will show to its neighbors.

Here are some excerpts from a conversation about law-office jurisprudence. The participants are Professor Louis M. Brown, a great teacher of preventive law, and founder of the national client-counseling competition, and one of your authors.[1]

"Shaffer: Legal counseling develops much of its jurisprudence from modern humanistic psychology. The counselor relates at a person-to-person level in which feelings (his own and his client's) are relevant *as facts*. And he operates within a set of concerns in which counselor behavior is more useful than conflict (advocacy) behavior. * * *

"But the helping-person model in law-office jurisprudence narrows and professionalizes this humanistic [psychological] view of clients. * * * [V]iewing the law office product as a *legal* decision suggests the qualities of foresight and comprehension. The optimistic view of [people] is specialized into a prudent view of [people]; because of his counselor, the [lawyer's] client understands the consequences of his actions. * * * Law office jurisprudence is like conflict jurisprudence, but different because it is also a helping-person jurisprudence. It is like the helping-person philosophy prominent in non-legal counseling, but different because the law-office process is a process of decision-making.

"The decision in the law office is assented to by at least two people, but, like 'justice' writ large, it depends for its validity on a consensus that reaches beyond the law office. Litigated decisions must be 'just'— that is, they must satisfy most of the people most of the time. A law office decision must be preventive; it must satisfy the people who live with its consequences. Non-legal counseling can afford to pay less attention to consequences and consensus. It aims at information and at the facilitation of decision-making by the client. But legal counseling is always done in the shadow of external, even institutional, validation. The legal counselor has to make up her mind; other counselors often do not.

"Brown: We assume that some alternatives are legally safer than others. There is a jurisprudential foundation for this premise. It lies within a formula which can be diagrammed as FACT→LAW (or legal consequence). There can be no legal consequence save that which rests upon some factual occurrence(s). Change or alter facts and you may modify legal consequences. It does make a difference in legal consequences whether a person does or does not sign on the dotted line. One set of words, rather than another set of words, can make a legal difference in the rights and duties of the parties. Because legal consequences are constructed on facts, preventive law guidance is possible. The helping lawyer seeks to guide the client so as to maximize his rights and minimize his risks * * *."

1.　Louis M. Brown and Thomas L. Shaffer, "Toward a Jurisprudence for the Law Office," 17 American Journal of Jurisprudence 125 (1972).

This is to say that, in court law, what Professor Brown calls "curative law," the law follows from facts of the case. The facts are established before the law is provided or even discussed. The facts are a premise for the law; they are like the statement of facts in an appellate opinion. They are, to use a word Professor Brown uses in teaching preventive law, *cold*. In law-office law, the sequence is reversed. The law is the cold premise; the facts follow from the law. *Office lawyers choose the facts* in order to locate and specify the law that will do for the client what the client wants done. Office facts are, to use Professor Brown's word, *hot*.

In another distinction about facts, Professor Brown notes that "curative" law, because of circumstantial limits on what the judges in the courthouse can do, takes account only of limited sets of facts. It limits the facts it will consider, as, for example, through concepts of relevance or reliability that are embodied in the law of evidence. In that sense, the facts in litigation law are often said to be *hard* facts. Office law takes account of context, nuance, and emotion more carefully and more advertently. Office law considers *soft* facts. Professor Brown continues:

> "In curative law we seek to determine and manage past facts, and attach the desired legal consequences to them. At this level legal consequences can be attached without any consideration of the client's emotional involvement. In general, the client's total emotional equipment is not usually part of the word formula in codes of law. I believe, though, that the total environment does become involved in the lawyering process. That process includes, but is not limited to, the LAW→ FACT formula. An elemental translation of that formula leads to the question—what is the applicable law or legal result? But * * * the answer to that question is often insufficient for lawyering. In earthy terms, the client's questions are: What do I do? What course of action? What decisions must I make, or [what decisions] do you, as my lawyer, make?

> "In preventive-law practice the LAW→FACT formula provides the legal consequences to a proposed course of action, but does not provide the answer to the ultimate decision, that is, for example, Should the client sign? In litigation practice the lawyer may make or decline to make a prediction of an attainable legal result if his client, or potential client, brings a lawsuit, but the lawyering (and client) decision is whether and when to bring the suit. * * *

> "Shaffer: The irrational facts—the emotional and feeling facts— may well be the greatest distinction between office lawyering and what you call 'curative law.' In this connection, I find useful your recognition that law-office decision-making is a vastly more complex (and * * * more openly emotional) environment. Three preliminary points should be made about that distinction, though:

> "First, litigation decisions, especially those we in retrospect regard as historic, have never been confined in conception or consequences to the facts in the record. They have always reflected what Holmes

called 'the felt necessity of the time.' And, I think, good legal counselors take the emotional climate of a case into account when they act or advise in reference to probable judicial (or, for that matter, legislative) decisions in the case. * * *

"Second, litigation law (law which comes from the FACT→LAW continuum) is not very useful, and is rarely dispositive, in legal counseling. Part of the reason is that good law-office decision-making comes from a preventive-law stance in the lawyer; and that 'lawyering' stance always takes broader account of human factors than [predicting what courts or legislators may do]. Another part of the reason is that the client who is making a law-office decision is being counseled toward an ability to choose as well as toward choice itself. The legal counselor is in what our friend Robert S. Redmount calls a *facilitative* posture.[2]

"Finally, the law-office decision depends for its soundness and survival on acceptance and validation in people and in places where factors relevant to litigation either don't count, or don't count enough. An example is a dead [person's] will which depends in its operative phase on the largely emotional consent of family members who take or fail to take under it. The factors relating to judges' law in both of these examples are usually, literally, irrelevant. * * *

"Brown: In the practice of preventive law, the lawyering process can be * * * complex. Elementary preventive-law practice appears relatively simple; that is, the lawyer describes (predicts) for a client the legal consequences of a proposed course of action. The lawyer informs a client, about to sign an apartment lease already signed by the landlord, that his client's signature creates, in the usual situation, a legal obligation (to pay rent, etc.) and some legal rights (to occupy the premises, etc.). But a more extended preventive-law practice might be addressed to predictions in a different realm. The preventive-law issues can become predictions as to whether a dispute will likely arise in the future, and if a dispute arises, then a prediction as to the behavior of the parties during that dispute, and a prediction of the legal consequences of that dispute. When we think in terms of potential disputes, we are concerned with only the 'minimizing risks' aspect of preventive-law practice. The practice of 'maximizing rights' complicates the process. It is at this point that the lawyering creativity stretches one's imagination. The issue is not confined to determining which alternative course of action presented by the client for the lawyer's consideration is best calculated to maximize the client's position; but, in addition, whether there is or might be another (as yet unstated) course of action even more appropriate, and which may further improve the client's legal (and practical) position. * * * [L]itigation law is not dispositive in preventive-law counseling."

For example, my corporate business client is buying, from a shopping-center owner, a piece of land on which it proposes to build a warehouse. There is a river on one side of this land; the shopping

2. R. Redmount, "Humanistic Law Through Legal Counseling," 2 Connecticut Law Review 98 (1969).

center is on the opposite side. The land my client is buying is on a gentle slope between the shopping center and the river. The shopping center is paved; rain and snow that at one time fell on and was absorbed by that land is now discharged on the land my client wants to buy. I notice, or one of my client's managers does, or an engineering expert employed by my client does, that there is a potential "surface water" problem in this case; in fact there is already evidence of erosion on the land my client wants to buy. The water that comes from the shopping center may harm my client's warehouse, or the area around it that my client proposes to landscape, or both. There are hundreds of surface-water disputes in the reports of appellate courts in the United States.

In the narrow sense Professor Brown first mentioned, to notice the possibility of this dispute is to resolve it. The scars of two days of surface-water law in my property course in law school, coupled with the evidence of erosion that is in front of me as I walk down the hill toward the river, combine to give me an occasion for the use of the LAW→ FACT continuum. One way to prevent the dispute would be to include in the land-purchase agreement an undertaking by the shopping center to provide drainage for surface water from the shopping center. It will make a difference whether this is in form a promise between the parties or what we will come to call a "restrictive covenant." Another way would be to put the drainage obligation on my client, with an appropriate adjustment in the purchase price. There are several forms for the expression of that obligation, too.

Litigation law bears on the bargaining between the parties, the suggestions lawyers propose, and the form the resolution takes. Surface-water law in the jurisdiction deals with obligations to prevent surface-water drainage, or to endure it. The probable outcome of a potential dispute between this buyer and this seller is probably resolved, or at least indicated, in statutes and judicial opinions in the jurisdiction. The state of that law may affect the substance and form of the agreement I propose, or the price of the land, but it does not limit what the parties can do. The possibilities are routine on Wednesday afternoons in a property lawyer's work.

This buyer and seller may do something more creative, and less routine, than is indicated in curative law; they may, for example, enter upon a joint drainage project. They may, in view of their mutual concern for water to irrigate my client's warehouse landscaping, decide upon a collection system for the surface water. They may even want to—or be obliged to—take into account the possible "non-point" water pollution that results from rain and snow falling on a shopping-center parking lot. Their choice of a device for these two purposes may bear on other legal relations they have—even on such things as the property and income taxes each of them will pay. Each of these "creative" alternatives is an instance of what Professor Brown meant when he spoke of a "course of action even more appropriate ... which may further improve the client's legal (and practical) position." Litigation law is, as he said, not dispositive. It may not even be a place to begin.

INTRODUCTION TO COMMON LAW ESTATES

The English statute, *Quia Emptores,* 1290, is where modern, green-eyeshade, Wednesday-afternoon, real-property law practice begins. That statute, which is American common law, made it possible for lawyers in England to choose between feudal, hierarchical forms of land ownership and what we Anglo–Americans came to call free alienability. It made it possible to choose between:

> (i) a form of ownership that carried with it a legal interpersonal relationship (the old example was the vassal who "held" land "of" his lord; a modern example is the tenant of an apartment who "holds" the apartment "of" his landlord); and

> (ii) a form of ownership that stood on its own, somewhat independent of the hierarchical feudal system ("substitution," rather than "sub-infeudation," to use the medieval legal terms).

This gave property lawyers a choice between: (1) feudal, tenurial ownership (under which, in form, every land owner is a tenant who pays rent to a landlord); and (2) free-standing ownership. The choice was available for use for clients; lawyers began to be able to look at the system of land ownership as if it were a complex machine and to invent an array of levers, handles, gears, and valves they could use to make the machine do what clients wanted it to do.

The metaphor is both the *use* and the *invention* of tools. These lawyers' tools were not all laid out in a natural or divinely decreed [3] tool box. The lawyers who used some tools invented others. That is as true of the practice of property law today as it was in the twelfth century. Our forebears and our elders arranged the tools they invented and the tools they inherited from their professional forebears and elders as if they were dentists or automobile mechanics. The rules of property law were gimmicks and devices that could be used to obtain for clients what clients wanted.

Of course, as is the case with dentistry and auto mechanics, tools proliferate. Some are improved upon, some become obsolete, and some are neglected by the current generation even though older practitioners know that they are perfectly good tools. One way and another, as time goes by, there are more and more tools for students of the subject to learn how to use. Students are even told it is necessary for them to learn about tools that are not used any more, in order to understand how to use the tools that replaced them. Workshop history parallels

---

3. Which is not to scoff at divine decrees, but is, rather, to notice, with one of the greatest of medieval lawyers, Sir Thomas More, that God made us to serve Him in the tangle of the mind.

political and cultural history. Time creates sources of complexity for students of the subject. It is perhaps some comfort amid the pain of learning complexity to remember that complexity has been the means to better service for the clients of lawyers.

Thus the study of common-law estates in property is learning about the tools we property lawyers use to serve our clients. The best service will provide flexibility for clients, as their situations and their personalities differ. We are going to oversimplify history a bit in this Chapter and look at the property lawyer's tools in terms of four sources of flexibility: (1) time; (2) differing present interests; (3) conditions; and (4) choice of law.

(1) Ownership on the Plane of Time

Property ownership can be *spread on the plane of time.* (The phrase is Baron Pollock's.) It is possible to divide ownership chronologically—to create, for example, a present possession in property that will end at a future date (as an apartment lease does) or on the happening of an event (as possession for the owner's life does). The most common use of this tool, over the centuries, has been to provide ownership (and therefore material support) for a relative until that relative dies, and then to provide ultimate and full ownership in someone else: "to my husband for life and then to my daughter," for example.

The tools in the plane-of-time part of our property-lawyer's tool box have other uses, most of them consistent with provision for relatives: Most tools in property planning can be used for multiple purposes—to maximize rights and minimize risks, in Professor Brown's phrase—but most of them are used most of the time for families and businesses. Suppose, for example, that a widowed modern American landowner of substantial wealth tells her lawyer that she wants her vast country estate to go to her only child, a son, after she dies. She and her son foresee that, when her son dies, the estate will go to his youngest daughter. The tools that seem most evidently called for by what the client indicates are two wills: Mother's will gives the estate to the client's son. Son's will gives it to his daughter. We have had the will tool in our box since 1540. Our forebears had ways to accomplish much the same thing, with other tools, tools we no longer use but need to understand, for a long time before that. The will tool does not necessarily involve spreading ownership on the plane of time. Before she dies, our client will own, in the present, all the law allows. After our client dies, if she doesn't change her will, her son will own what she owned—all of it. Her son will then make a will favoring his youngest daughter.

Clients may know what they want, but clients do not always know what is in our property-lawyers' tool boxes. Here, for example, it is possible to combine the will tool with one of the plane-of-time tools and gain advantages for our client that she may not at first have thought about. If we use the will tool and our client gives the estate, at her death, to her son, as sole owner, state and federal death taxation will be imposed on the estate at the client's death. If the same will tool is used again by Son, as the client hopes, death taxes will be imposed a second time when Son dies and gives the estate, by will, to Granddaughter. If the plane-of-time tool were used here, in addition to the will tool (to Son for life, then to Granddaughter):

— What the client wanted would be achieved;

— The result would be more certain, since it would not depend on Son's making the will the client wants Son to make, or risk his revoking the will the client wants him to make; and

— Death taxes would be imposed only once, at the client's death. At Son's death there would be nothing to tax. His ownership would end when his life ended. Granddaughter would be the donee of her grandmother, not of her father.

This use of the plane-of-time tool, to avoid death taxes, is one of the oldest instances of its usefulness and one of the most perennially contentious. It accounts for half a dozen of the most arcane medieval rules of property. It remains close to the top on anybody's list of death-tax reform issues. At present in the United States, for example, there is a federal "generation-skipping" transfer tax that will be imposed if a life estate is used to carry property ownership past a generation. It will reach our transaction unless we can find an exception to fit our case. The generation-skipping transfer tax was invented recently. It does not raise much revenue and it is remarkably complex. When tax reform is discussed in Congress, someone usually suggests that the generation-skipping transfer tax be repealed. A 15th century English family solicitor no doubt looks down from Glory on his professional descendants in America and says to himself, "The more things change the more they remain the same."

(2) Ownership Divided Into Different Present Interests

Our client who owns the vast country estate has what property scholars call a bundle of property "rights." The image is what we referred to in Chapter One as a bundle of sticks, which is to say that our client's estate is many different things, each of which she owns, and that the legal notion "property" is not so much a notion about things, as a notion about relationships among people. What she owns is a farm; it has water on and under it, in streams, "freshets" in flood time, wells, and hidden aquifers; it has minerals on and under the surface (coal, maybe, or oil or uranium or even gold and silver). It has air above the land and views to the mountains, valleys, and seashore. It is possible, by using tools in our Wednesday-afternoon property-lawyer's tool box, to divide those interests among people: give some to one person, sell some to another, reserve some for our client. Property lawyers who know how to do this have made possible—with varying consequences in terms of distributive justice—coal mining in Appalachia; the development of the petroleum industry in Texas and Oklahoma; orderly irrigation in the arid West; and tiered condominia by the ocean in Florida.

An example: Our client would like to find some way to assure that her country estate will not be turned into a computer factory or a shopping center. She would like it to remain as it is—agricultural. Among the many tools we can use to try to achieve that result for our client is to divide from her bundle of rights the one that gives her power over the use of the surface of her land. If favorable statutes and local ordinances are in effect, it might be possible for her to give her power over surface development to a local government or non-profit association—only that one "stick," and none of the others—which would mean that someone (or some agency) with an interest in preserving the land for agricultural use would have the legal power to prevent its being used for some other purpose—only that and nothing more. It may even be possible to do this and get our client a current income-tax deduction (for a gift to charity). After we remove this one stick from the bundle, our client will still be able to spread her remaining ownership on the plane of time and to apply other tools to it. She can still make the will in favor of her son and granddaughter, still gain for her family the death-tax advantages we suggested in that connection.

(3) Choice of Law on Ownership

Anglo–American governments have had, since before *Quia Emptores,* two systems of judges, following two systems of law. One is the common law, which traces to King Henry II's dispatching royal judges to roam the twelfth-century English countryside and impose decisions according to the customs and practices of the people; we have been talking so far in this Chapter about that system. It gets modified from time to time by statutes. Most of the English property statutes that were enacted by Parliament before our revolution are regarded as American common law.

The other system of law is equity, which obtained closer to home, in the King's conscience at first, perhaps, or, more likely, in the learning and judgment of a priest who was probably at first the King's confessor and who became his chancellor. The distinction that is useful for property lawyers is the distinction between the law that obtains in courts that apply the common law of property ownership, and the law that obtains in chancery courts that seek to apply the more clearly moralistic principles of equity.

During all of the most formative period of Anglo–American property law, these two systems of courts competed with one another for judicial business. Each offered advantages and disadvantages to property owners. Their sources of law were different; equity tended to look to moral impulses and to continental or canon (church) law. The judges in the two systems were different people, with different educations and different political and professional loyalties. (Until the 16th century, the chancellor, who was the chief judge of the equity courts, was a clergyman.) The lawyers who practiced in the two systems of courts were also different people, and they competed for law-office business.

We modern property lawyers practice in both systems. This is confusing for beginning students in property law, but it has provided a wonderful set of tools for Wednesday-afternoon law practice, because it has held out the possibility that, when your client was blocked by one kind of law, the other kind might provide a detour.

An example property teachers are fond of (and it is probably over-simplified history) involved the Franciscan friars who came to England in the 13th century. The friars were forbidden by the rules of their religious order from owning property; but, of course, they came rather quickly to accept the innocent advantages of comfort and security. They were able to reconcile comfort and security with the Gospel, but not with the stern, specific demands of St. Francis of Assisi, their Italian founder. They could not own the property, but they wanted to have the benefit (comfort and security) of it. They went to a law office and (the simplified history goes) their lawyer found a charitable layman who was willing to take ownership of the property *for the use of* the friars. Those words—"for the use of the friars"—were part of the conveyance of ownership of the property to the charitable layman. The charitable layman of course never went near the place.

The arrangement was informal and extra-legal at first. It worked well until the charitable layman turned out not to be so charitable after all, and the friars needed governmental coercion to remind him that the land was for the use of the friars, not for his use. When the friars went to the common-law courts, they were turned away with the observation that Charitable Layman, not the friars, owned the land. They had better luck with the chancellor, who eventually came to decree that Layman had to use the land for the benefit of the friars. At that point, as property lawyers saw it, one system of law provided a form of ownership—and thereby a lawyer's tool—the other system did not offer.

The chancellor decided that he could not decree *legal* ownership, though; the determination of legal ownership was in the law courts. But he had the power of the Crown, after all; he could pile rocks on people, or stretch them on the rack, or lock them up in dismal places. He could see to it that Layman held and used the land for the benefit of the friars; he did this through decrees that ordered Layman to use the property in certain ways. The theory he used is the theory on which the modern law of trusts rests: that one person can hold property for the benefit of another. A modern lawyer invokes the theory by invoking the rules of equity. The important point for present purposes is that a planning lawyer can choose between those rules of *equitable* ownership, and common-law rules on *legal* ownership.[4] It is possible to do in one system what you cannot do in the other.

(4) Ownership Subject to Condition

You never know what's going to happen. Ownership on the plane of time is one way—one of the principal ways, in our property-owning culture—to provide against the manageable risks of the melancholy fact that the future is hidden. But the choice of who is to own in the future would be a dim choice if lawyers had to inflict on their clients the risk of being wrong when they guess who will survive, who will be poor or rich, who will behave himself and who won't. The tool that is needed here is one that will let our client say: "to my husband for life, but not if he remarries; then to my children, but only to those who are living when my husband dies; and, as to them, only to those who remain Republicans and do not marry outside the Roman Catholic faith; and if nobody behaves as herein provided, to my parish church but only so long as the pastor is an Italian."

We green-eyeshade lawyers can do all of that. And more besides. Doing it will involve the use of old tools that have to do with conditions and shifts in ownership. It will involve spreading ownership on the plane of time and may involve separating interests among people. We will have to use some law and some equity and some curious mixtures of the two. This sort of job got to be about as complicated as any job our forebears had to do in the law office. It is usually less complicated now, but is still tricky—enough so that property students have to learn a lot about the past in order to know when the past is not dead (not even past, as William Faulkner's county-seat lawyer said).

(5) A Short Vocabulary Lesson

Precise use of words of conveyance was important to the old common-law judges (less so to judges in equity, and a little less so to modern common-law judges). The most memorable example was no doubt the creation of the greatest estate in land, the fee simple absolute. This estate is the most the law allows a person to own; it is useful to think of it as the *whole thing,* from which (depending on your metaphor for the moment) the stick is taken from the bundle, or the interests are spread on the plane of time. It is the complete bundle of sticks, and ownership forever. The fee simple is like one of those wooden Russian dolls that come apart in the middle and have half a dozen smaller dolls inside, each one of which (except the smallest) comes apart in the middle and has a smaller doll inside. The fee simple is the big one, the one you start with. Since *Quia Emptores* (except as to tenurial ownership), it has not come out of an even bigger doll.

---

4. Equitable ownership is just as legal   is a specialized use.
as legal ownership is. This use of "legal"

The present little lesson is about vocabulary. The old common-law judges insisted that formal words be used to create a fee simple; the words were: "to the grantee and his heirs." The grantee's heir didn't get anything in this form of conveyance; the grantee got the big doll, all of it.[5] But "and his heirs" signified that the property was his and would be his through his successors. The common-law lawyers said that "to" and the grantee's name were words of *purchase,* indicating the new owner, and that "and his heirs" were words of *limitation,* indicating the "quality" of estate the new owner took. In fact, it became customary to add "forever" to the formula, although that was not required: "to the grantee and his heirs forever." If the property lawyer failed to add the magic words, a fee simple was not created. This was true of future interests as well as of present possessory interests, so that a conveyance to one's wife for life, then to one's son in fee simple, had to contain magic words in the description of the remainder: "to W for life, then to S and his heirs." In default of words sufficient to create a fee simple, the grant was a grant for life. So: "to A" created a life estate. So did: "to A in fee simple." If the grantor conveyed less than she owned, what she retained was a *reversion.* If she owned a fee simple and conveyed less than a fee simple (a life estate for example) to one person, and in the same transaction conveyed some of the rest of her fee simple (a future, succeeding life estate, for example), she would, usually, have created a *remainder* in the second grantee. If she conveyed so that she retained a reversion, she could then, later and in a separate conveyance, give her reversion to a grantee; in that case the grantee had a reversion rather than a remainder.

Describe in legal language the interests of Alice, Emily, Rosa, and Sam, after the following conveyances:

1. Alice conveys to Emily for life and then to Rosa.

2. Alice conveys to Emily for life and then to Rosa and her heirs.

3. Alice conveys to Emily for life and then to Rosa in fee simple absolute, forever, and Alice really means it.

4. Alice conveys to Emily for life. Alice then dies, leaving a valid will in which she gives all of her property to Rosa and her heirs.

5. Alice conveys to Emily for life. Alice then dies, leaving a valid will in which she gives all of her property to Rosa for life. Alice's heir is Sam.

---

5. "Heirs" at common law (before the 17th century) was usually a plural only if you took succeeding generations into account. In any one generation it typically meant only one person—the oldest and closest male descendant. (The system is still used to determine succession to the throne in Britain.) And it did not necessarily mean a son or grandson. The owner's younger brother, or even a cousin, could be the heir if there were no male descendants available.

There are two kinds of remainders in the common-law system. (And here we are being precise. There are also future interests in the *equitable* system; we are talking here only about the common-law system.) Some remainders are *vested* and some are *contingent*. The distinction made an immense difference in medieval property practice and in nineteenth-century American practice. It still makes a difference, although the difference is less immense than it was. Telling the difference is simple in clear cases, arcane in close cases, an engine of confusion for students, and an engine of flexibility for modern judges who will strain a good bit to protect a penniless widow from her husband's rapacious brother.

A vested remainder is one in which (i) there are no conditions precedent,[6] other than the (natural) termination of the preceding estate, and (ii) the owner is ascertained: "to Alice for life, then to Bruce and his heirs" (life estate in Alice, vested remainder in fee simple in Bruce, who is ascertained).

A contingent remainder is one that is subject to a condition precedent, or is owned by an unascertained person, or both:

> (i) "to A for life, then to B and her heirs if B marries C";
>
> (ii) "to A for life, then to the heirs of B and their heirs," and B is living (no one is heir to the living; or, in Latin, *nemo est haeres viventis*; the heirs of B are therefore unascertained);
>
> (iii) "to A for life, then to the heirs of B who survive A and their heirs."[7]

A remainder could vest even though not all of the people it described were in being. "To A for life, then to the children of B" creates a vested remainder in any children of B who are in being at the time of the conveyance. But if B is living then, there may be more children of B. This remainder is *vested subject to open*.[8]

Future interests retained by a grantor (reversions) are always treated as vested, whether they fit the definition or not, and whether they are held by the grantor, by the grantor's heir, or by someone to whom the grantor conveyed his reversion.

6. "To Henry when he marries," for example; or "to Susan when she reaches the age of 21."

7. A remainder can be vested subject to divestment: "To A for life, then to B and his heirs but if B does not survive C to C and her heirs." The remainder is no less vested in B than if the remainder were unqualified, and it is vested even though it seems to be designed to work the same as a contingent remainder would ("to A for life, then, if B survives C, to B and his heirs and, if not, to C and her heirs"). We take this up, infra, in our discussion of property interests subject to conditions. It makes a difference which classification is used, and the order of the words is not always a sure guide to what the classification will be.

8. A remainder may be both vested subject to divestment *and* vested subject to open. Consider: "To A for life and then to the children of B, but if any child of B becomes a Unitarian. * * *"

Which of the following future interests are vested and which contingent? (Some of these conveyances result in more than one future interest.)

6. Alice conveys to Emily for life and then to Rosa and her heirs if Rosa is living at Emily's death. Alice, Emily, and Rosa are living.

7. Alice conveys to Emily for life and then to Rosa and her heirs.

8. Alice conveys to Emily for life.

9. Alice conveys to Emily for life. Alice then dies; her heir is Rosa.

10. Alice conveys to Emily for life and then to those of Rosa's children who are living at Emily's death and their heirs. Alice, Rosa and Emily are living.

11. Alice conveys to Emily for life and then to those of Rosa's children who are living at Rosa's death and their heirs. Rosa dies; Alice and Emily live on.

The grantor was and is regarded as having a reversion after a contingent remainder. And—to repeat—grantor interests are always treated as vested. Both of these rules were (and are) fictions:

12. Alice conveys to Emily for life and then to Rosa and her heirs if Rosa marries Henry before Emily's death, and to Henry and his heirs if Rosa does not marry Henry before Emily's death. (There are *three* future interests here.)

The logic of that conveyance is that no interest is left in Alice: Rosa and Henry will either get married before Emily dies, or won't. If they do marry in time, Rosa will get the fee simple; if not, Henry will get it. Alice, having accomplished this much, probably walks away thinking the matter is settled. But the common-law judges held that there was a reversion in Alice so long as Rosa and Henry were unmarried. (Of course, when they marry, even if Emily is living, the remainder will no longer be contingent, and the reversion in Alice will disappear.)

A consequence of the rule that there is always a reversion after a contingent remainder—and, probably, the political and economic reason for the long survival of the rule—was that contingent remainders were *destructible*. There was a way for Alice and Emily to get together and destroy Rosa's and Henry's future interests, to come up with a possessory fee simple and thereby to make the property alienable, and more attractive to the government. The destructibility rule is no longer the law, but, in the way property law has of keeping the past in the present, it is still the rule that there is always a reversion after a contingent remainder. More about this later.

And it is still the rule that grantor future interests, including reversions, are treated as vested, whether they are or not—so that Alice's fictional future interest in Example 13 is not destructible. (There are other advantages to being vested, if you are a future interest; one that endures in modern law, as we will see, has to do with the rule against perpetuities.)

(6) Another Look at Historical Context

The English and American legal history we have summarized and simplified in family-practice terms was also a political history that had to do with the fact that England was a small island trying through much pain and bloodshed to become first a nation and then the seat of an empire. Considering the subject from a more political perspective:

The law of estates in land evolved over centuries, beginning with William the Conqueror's success in the Battle of Hastings (1066) and culminating in the great landed estates in England in the seventeenth and eighteenth centuries. The law of estates in land came to America with the English colonists. It developed here as a species of state rather than federal law, being received as part of the common law by the several states at the time statehood was achieved. While the common law principles remain, they have been modified considerably by the states to accommodate our egalitarian politics of property ownership.

The estates-in-land system began as a management technique for William as he consolidated his control of the English countryside in the years after the Battle of Hastings. As a reward for loyalty and in return for services, William put individuals in charge of large tracts of land and gave them titles (tenants-in-chief or "lords"). He ordered a detailed accounting of all the land in his new domain, as well as the "things" on the land (cows, pigs, trees, etc.). This accounting was memorialized in the Domesday Book of 1086.

As a result of this rudimentary system of management, individuals were said to "hold" the land of the King (only the King "owned" the land). But individuals holding the land were given possession and control of it in return for providing services to the King, such as military service, economic service, or religious service (singing mass or praying for grantor's soul). This exchange of land for services gave rise to the tenurial or land tenure system that *Quia Emptores* rendered optional.

The history of the development of the law of estates in land is the history of a continuing conflict between two extremely powerful social forces, the desire to control/organize the lives of others, and the desire to be free from such control. Down through the centuries, common-law lawyers and judges, in the process of resolving specific disputes, some of which have been immortalized in song and story, fashioned a set of rules to give content to William's original managerial plan and to encourage the resolution of future disputes by establishing a logical predictability to the process.

The estates-in-land system developed so that it could, by the seventeenth century, when it moved to America, be characterized by maximum flexibility within a limited number of choices. It became, in other words, less political and more a matter of lawyers' tools.

The common law recognized four types of present freehold interests:

(1) Fee simple (O → A and her heirs);

(2) Fee tail (O → A and the heirs of her body);

(3) Life estate (O → A for life); and

(4) Fee simple defeasible (O → A so long as, or upon condition that).

No other interests could be created, so, for example, a conveyance that attempted to limit the takers to a particular class of heirs, such as those on the father's side or the mother's side, would be construed as a fee simple, inheritable by heirs on the mother's side as well as the father's side.

Fee Simple: The common law fee simple was the estate with the greatest status. It represented the "entire bundle" of property rights and was potentially infinite in duration. Upon the death of the holder of a fee simple, the estate was inherited by the heirs of the holder under the laws of intestate succession. The heirs did not take present ownership of a future interest, though, because they were not ascertained until the death of the holder. Prior to that time, they were merely "heirs apparent." The words "and her heirs" in the conveyance are words of limitation that identify the duration of the interest as potentially infinite. Today, the common-law requirement that these "magic words" be used to create a fee simple has been abolished in favor of a presumption that a grantor intends to transfer her entire interest unless the contrary intent is expressed in the conveyance. Thus, a conveyance from O to A is sufficient to create a fee simple in American jurisdictions.

Early conflicts over the transferability of land interests produced the most important piece of property legislation on the fee simple: The statute *Quia Emptores* ("Forasmuch as purchasers of lands and tenements") (1290) introduced the concept of free transfer of land by permitting *substitution* of persons responsible for providing the feudal incidents to the tenant-in-chief of the grantor, while prohibiting the process of diffusing the accountability for the feudal incidents called *subinfeudation.*

Fee Tail: Another early property statute, enacted five years earlier in 1285, the statute *De Donis,* recognized the fee tail, which became the principal device for landholders to keep their lands "in the family" for generations. The magic words for a fee-tail conveyance are "to A and the heirs of his body." The holder of a fee tail has an interest of potentially infinite duration, but only if he has an unbroken line of descendants ("issue"). The interest may be transferred, subject to the right of the issue to take upon the death of the holder. Thus, the only interest capable of being transferred is in effect a life interest. The fee tail is not as extensive as the fee simple. When O transfers "to A and the heirs of his body," O retains a reversion that will become possessory if and when A's line of descendants runs out. The fee tail is thus a way to spread ownership on the plane of time: "To A and the heirs of his body and then to B and her heirs" (or "remainder to B and her heirs"). Today, only a handful of American states give effect to the common-law fee tail. Most states have abolished the fee tail.

Life Estate: The life estate is a present possessory freehold interest that lasts only as long as the life of the grantee. The holder of a life estate has rights of possession and use, with a corresponding power to exclude others who have interests in the land, but must respect the interests of the holders of the balance of the fee simple. This requirement, which is governed by the law of waste, has the effect of limiting the developmental potential of property held in life tenancy. In addition, the holder of a life estate has limited ability to transfer the land. The life estate is not devisable or descendible, because the interest dies with the holder. It is transferable *inter vivos,* but only to the extent of what the transferor holds—a life estate. The transferee would get a life estate for the duration of the *transferor's* life. The common-law lawyers, who affected a lawyer's sort of French, called this an estate *pur autre vie.*

The life estate can be used to keep property in the family, but the limitations on development and transfer noted above severely limit the effectiveness of the life estate as a means of providing economic security for persons believed to be incapable of providing for themselves (e.g., young children, developmentally disabled, elderly, etc.).

Describe in legal language the interests of Alice, Emily, Rosa, and Sam, after the following conveyances:

13. Alice conveys, in 1400, to Emily and the heirs of her body.

14. Alice conveys, in 1400, to Emily and the heirs of her body and then to Sam.

15. Alice conveys, in 1400, to Emily and the heirs of her body and then to Sam and his heirs.

16. In 1800, Alice conveys to Emily for life and then to Rosa and the heirs of her body and then to Sam.

17. In 1800, Alice conveys to Emily for life and then to Rosa and the heirs of her body and then to Sam and his heirs.

18. Alice conveys to Emily for life and then to Sam and his heirs. Emily then conveys all that she owns to Rosa and her heirs, and enters a convent.

I. OWNERSHIP ON THE PLANE OF TIME

A. OWNERSHIP FOR LIFE AND THE PRESENT CREATION OF OWNERSHIP OF WHAT'S LEFT OVER

SUMMERS v. SUMMERS

Appeals Court of Massachusetts, 1988.
26 Mass.App.Ct. 592, 530 N.E.2d 370.

ARMSTRONG, JUSTICE.

In 1980, the plaintiff's [James's] wife by will left him a life estate in her North Falmouth residence with the remainder to [their son] the defendant [Thomas] and the plaintiff's other son in equal shares. The plaintiff was authorized, however, at any time to sell the property, in which event "there shall be paid to my said husband from the proceeds of sale an amount representing the then current value of his life interest therein, and the balance of the net proceeds shall be distributed, in equal shares, to my sons. * * * " The plaintiff sold the property in 1986; the parties are in dispute as to the value of his life estate.

The parties agree that the "then current value" of the life estate is to be determined by reference to the life interest valuation tables promulgated by the United States Treasury Department. * * * They disagree whether to use the table in effect in 1980, at the time of the testatrix's death * * * or the one in effect at the time of the sale in 1986. * * * The difference is considerable. The 1980 table, which differentiated by gender, was predicated on a six percent interest factor and would value the plaintiff's life estate (based on his life expectancy at the time of sale) at 49.585% of $580,000 (the sale price). The 1986 table, which is gender-blind, was predicated on a ten percent interest factor and would value the plaintiff's life estate at 69.352% of the sale price.

The basic contention underlying the defendant's advocacy of the 1980 table is that the testatrix naturally would have contemplated that the plaintiff's life estate would diminish in value as * * * the years passed, that the use of the table in effect at her death would be consistent with her presumed expectation, and that this approach is consonant with the usual rule that a will speaks as of the time of the testator's death and refers to the state of things then existing. * * *

The argument is not persuasive. The testatrix did not mention life estate valuation tables. When she spoke of the "then current value of [James's] life interest," she must be taken to have meant the actual market value of so much of the life estate as remained at the time of the sale. The actual market value of such an interest would necessarily be affected not only by the diminishing expected duration of the life estate but also by market forces reflected both in fluctuating real estate values and in fluctuating interest rates. The actual market value of the life estate at the time of sale will be approximated by the actuarial tables in use at the time of sale, reflecting current market conditions and actuarial assumptions, rather than those in effect at an earlier time when conditions were different. * * * It could be argued that the 1986 table marginally overvalued the plaintiff's share, either because the interest factor was higher than market conditions in 1986 actually warranted, or because of the gender-blinding; but the parties foreclosed consideration of such questions by stipulating to the use of one or the other of the two treasury tables as reflective of market conditions at the two pertinent dates.

The "judgment" appealed from, ostensibly a final disposition, was entered on cross-motions for partial summary judgment which were addressed only to the valuation issue. The parties had indicated that they thought they would be able to settle amicably the other issues raised in the pleadings. A judgment, however, should not be entered until the record reflects that those issues have been resolved by settlement or otherwise. * * *

Notes and Questions

1. The property interest in Thomas and his brother was created and had value at the time of Mrs. Summers's death—at the moment James's life interest was created and became possessory. The argument here was over (i) how much that "future interest" was worth, not over (ii) whether there was such an interest, nor (iii) whether it had value. The thing to notice about spreading ownership on the plane of time is that the ownership of future interests is a *present* ownership: Future interests have value now. They are not only a chance at something; they *are* something. And they are something even when they are only a chance at something. The law of "waste" is an example. James Summers is entitled to exclusive possession of this property under his wife's will; he can exclude his sons from entering on or using it, as much as he can exclude strangers to the family. But he is obliged to preserve the value of his sons' future interests. If the property had a house on it, the life tenant would be obliged to fix the roof, see that property taxes were paid, and to obtain fire insurance. The facts in *Summers* indicate that it was James who sold the property in 1986; a life tenant cannot normally sell the entire ("fee simple") ownership of property that has been spread on the plane of time. The source of Mr. Summers's extraordinary power was a power given to him in Mrs. Summers's will; if the will had not conferred this power on Mr. Summers, his sons could have consented to his selling the property (which would mean, strictly speaking, that they would all three do the selling).

2. The variables that affect the value of future interests are, the court here says, "current market conditions" and "actuarial assumptions":

    (a) Who would have benefitted here if the neighborhood had become a slum?

    (b) Who would have benefitted if oil had been discovered on the land?

    (c) Who would have benefitted if the actuarial tables the court had approved had not been "gender blind"?

3. The parties to this lawsuit stipulated that one of two valuation tables was to be used. Both tables are promulgated by the Commissioner of Internal Revenue, under federal legislative authority having to do with the administration of federal tax laws. The "current market conditions" variable in these tables is a rate-of-return variable that supposedly turns on current interest rates; that is, the "market" involved is the market for borrowed money. The "actuarial assumptions" variable is life expectancy, which is an empirical figure based on how long people live. The experience of a population in this regard is what is used to set life-insurance and annuity premium rates and many other things. What the Commissioner does, for federal tax purposes, is to recognize what the market for borrowed money is and to take account of life expectancies. The issues that may arise with regard to the generalizations in the Commissioner's tables—or any other tables—are whether his restatement of these factual matters is accurate and whether the omission of other relevant factual matters is justified. Here are some pieces of the current table, which uses a ten per cent rate of return, Revenue Regulations, Sec. 20.2031–7(f) (Table A):

Age	Life Estate	Remainder
24	.96841	.03159
	* * *	
56	.79006	.20994
	* * *	
80	.43659	.56341

Some states provide similar tables in their codified statutes.

4. Suppose, in the *Summers* case, that James Summers could be shown to have been terminally ill, so that, in fact, his life expectancy was shorter than the life expectancy indicated by actuarial tables. Who would have benefitted from that fact? Should such specific facts be taken into account in arriving at the present (market) values of specific interests?

5. White people live longer than black people. Non-smokers live longer than smokers. Protestants live longer than Catholics, Episcopalians longer than Baptists. Women live longer than men. None of these variables is used in the tables at issue in this case, although some of them are used in other tables. James Summers was (say) a white Protestant non-smoker, as well as a male. His lawyer, in agreeing to use federal tax tables, eliminated advantages James might have had if other tables had been used. Did James's lawyer serve him well in this? If James's lawyer argued for use of any of these distinctions that would help James, which ones should the court have applied?

BLACK v. BLACK

Supreme Court of Appeals of West Virginia, 1982.
171 W.Va. 307, 298 S.E.2d 843.

McHUGH, JUSTICE.

E.E. Black and Minnie Black, both of whom are now deceased, had a farm near Seneca Rocks, Pendleton County. That farm contained approximately 460 acres. Their children, Claude Black, I.D. Black and the appellant [Jessie Black], became joint owners of the farm.

By a document dated January 3, 1950, and referred to in the complaint as a "written joint survivorship and partnership agreement," Claude Black, I.D. Black and the appellant agreed as follows:

WHEREAS the parties hereto are the joint owners of the E.E. Black home farm * * * and they having mutually agreed among themselves that in the event of the death of any one or more of said parties the survivor or survivors shall receive their interest therein.

NOW, THEREFORE, THIS AGREEMENT WITNESSETH, that in the event of the death of any of the parties to this agreement the other parties hereto shall receive the interest of said deceased party, and

WHEREAS, we, the said parties hereto, being the joint owners of said farm and operate the same jointly and are the joint owners of the personal property used in connection of said farm, it is agreed between us that all personal property owned by either of us shall go to the survivor or survivors upon the death of each or any of us.

That agreement was recorded in the office of the Clerk of the County Commission of Pendleton County.

Subsequently, Claude Black, I.D. Black and the appellant executed a joint will. That will named Paul Black and James Paul Geary as executors and was dated August 11, 1969. That will provided, in part, as follows:

FIRST: It is the desire of each of us that all of our property, both real and personal, shall remain and continue in the family, and to carry into effect that intention, it is the will of each of us, to-wit: I.D. Black, Claude Black and Jessie Black, that upon the death of any one of us, all the property, both real and personal, belonging to him or her, shall go to the survivors of that one; and upon the death of either of said survivors, all of the property of that one shall go to the remaining survivor, this being the joint and several will of each and all of us.

SECOND: Providing, further, however, that upon the death of the last survivor of I.D. Black, Claude Black, and Jessie Black, all of the estate, both real and personal, then remaining, shall go to and become the property in fee of the following named nieces and nephews and in the share and interest so shown.

There were seven nieces and nephews named in the will and each was to receive a one-seventh interest in the estate "then remaining." Those nieces and nephews and the executors are appellees in this action.

Neither Claude Black nor I.D. Black ever married. They died without issue. Claude Black died on April 30, 1971, and I.D. Black died on March 14, 1976. The joint will was recorded in both instances in Pendleton County during probate proceedings. Appraisement and final settlement reports were recorded. * * *

In July, 1979, [Jessie Black] filed a complaint in circuit court in which she asserted that having survived the deaths of Claude Black and I.D. Black, both the 1950 agreement and the joint will vested her with fee simple title to the 460 acre farm and 36 acre tract and all the personal property located upon that real estate. Specifically, the appellant alleged that inasmuch as she owned all the property in question, she could sell or dispose of it in fee simple, and none of the appellees had any interest in the property. * * *

The appellees filed an answer in which they denied the essential allegations of the complaint. They also filed a counterclaim in which they asserted that * * * the two deeds dated February 17, 1979 [from Jessie Black to others], were null and void.

With respect to the issue of the appellant's interest in the property in question, the circuit court resolved the matter upon the record without a jury and without taking evidence. By order dated March 10, 1981, the circuit court held that pursuant to the joint will, the appellant had a life estate only in the 460 acre farm and the 36 acre tract, and a life interest only in the personal property, with the right to consume that personal property through normal use. The circuit court declared that the interests in the remainder of both the real and the personal property were held by the seven nieces and nephews or their heirs. Furthermore, the circuit court held the deeds dated February 17, 1979, to be null and void to the extent those deeds purported to convey more than the appellant's life interest in the property. * * *

The reasons for the ruling of the circuit court against the appellant were stated in the circuit court's memorandum of opinion dated January 7, 1981. The circuit court concluded as follows concerning the joint will:

> There is no intent by the three Testators to vest the survivor with the assets of the estate absolutely, but the intent is clearly expressed that the survivor shall have a lifetime interest only, then the assets shall vest in the third parties, nieces and nephews, named in the will.
>
> The * * * agreement dated January 3, 1950, entered into by the parties was completely modified and superseded by their subsequent agreement as set forth and contained in their joint will.

[Jessie Black] contends that, having survived Claude Black and I.D. Black, she acquired fee simple title to the real property and personal property in question, because (1) the language of the will so indicates, and (2) the will does not contain phrases such as "life estate" limiting her interest. * * *

The [nephews and nieces] contend, however, that the will clearly provides them with a remainder in fee to the property in question. In this regard, the appellees contend that the appellant is bound by the provisions of the will because Claude Black, I.D. Black and [Jessie Black] mutually agreed upon the will's provisions, one of which provisions allegedly provides the appellees with a remainder in fee to the property in question. * * *

W.Va.Code, 36–1–16 [1931] provides as follows:

> If any interest in or claim to real or personal property be given by sale or gift inter vivos or by will to one, with a limitation over either by way of remainder or of executory devise or any other limitation, and by the same conveyance or will there be conferred, expressly or by implication, a power upon the first taker in his lifetime or by will to use or dispose absolutely of such property, the limitation over shall not fail or be defeated except to the extent that the first taker shall have lawfully exercised such power of disposal. The proceeds of a disposal under such power shall be held subject to the same limitations and the same power of use or disposal as the original property, unless a contrary intent shall appear from the conveyance or will.

The effect of that statute is to preserve the initial validity of the limitation over, subject to the first taker's power of disposal. * * *

The common law rule * * * was as follows:

> Where there is a devise or bequest to one in *general terms* and there is a subsequent limitation over of what remains at the first taker's death, if there is also given to the first taker an unlimited and unrestricted power of absolute disposal, express or implied, the devise or bequest to the first taker is construed to pass a fee [simple], and the limitation over is invalid. * * *

The joint will in the action before this Court * * * does not expressly confer upon the appellant an estate "during the term of her natural life." Nevertheless, from a reading of the entire will, this Court concludes, as did the circuit court, that the appellant received under the will a life estate only in the property in question and that the named nieces and nephews received a remainder in fee simple.

That conclusion is clearly mandated by the provisions of the joint will, and, as the appellees assert, reference to extrinsic evidence is not appropriate. As indicated by the provisions of W.Va.Code, 36–1–16 [1931], the remainder or gift over to the named nieces and nephews does not fail but, rather, is subject to the appellant's power of disposal, if any, conferred by the will. No such power of disposal, either by express provision or by implication, was conferred upon the appellant by this particular will. Rather, the will, after stating the desire of the testators to keep the property in the family, directs that upon the death of the appellant, the property shall "become the property in fee" of the named nieces and nephews.

Although the joint will provides that the nieces and nephews shall receive the property "then remaining," we do not believe that the phrase "then remaining" is sufficient in this action to defeat the remainder or gift over to the named nieces and nephews. We agree with the circuit court that the phrase "then remaining" refers to the ordinary use and consumption of property by a life tenant during the course of a life estate. * * *

Notes and Questions

1. The court uses the phrase "remainder interest" to refer to the future-interest portion of ownership after it is divided on the plane of time. A bit of review might be useful. Remember that there are, in general, two possibilities when a life interest, or an interest for years, is created out of fee-simple ownership:

(a) The future interest may not be disposed of, in which case the grantor (that is, the person who owned the fee simple when the story began) has not disposed of the future interest. We saw in the "vocabulary lesson," *supra,* that the general term for such a grantor future interest is "reversion."

(b) The future interest may have been conveyed, when the story began, to someone other than the owner of the life interest or term of years; this was the interest the Black nephews and nieces were held to have had in this case; it was the interest the sons of Mr. Summers had in the *Summers* case. The general term for such a *grantee* future interest is "remainder." [8]

(c) Could a grantee own a reversion? Yes. See if you can guess how that might have come about in *Black v. Black.*

(d) Could a grantor own a remainder? Yes. See if you can imagine how that might have come about in *Black v. Black.*

(e) Could an owner own a life estate that was not measured by his own life? Yes. See if you can imagine how that might have come about in *Black v. Black.*

2. Many family situations—and the Black family is perhaps an example—are such that a division into life estates and remainders is too rigid to be workable. More exacting tools are needed. It is possible to put residential, or farm, or business property in one generation, with future interests in the next generation, but it may become necessary to sell some of the property during the life of the life tenant, or to use it in the present

---

8. The late Dean Oval Phipps of the University of South Dakota School of Law and Saint Louis University School of Law took a somewhat more mathematical approach to common-law estates than we do. Some students find mathematics useful, and in service to them we offer Dean Phipps's "Twelve Rules and Definitions." We are only going to offer five of them at this point, though, lest mathematics intrude too much on our image of the law office on Wednesday afternoon:

From Phipps, *Titles in a Nutshell* 216 (1968):

(A) Twelve Rules and Definitions

(1) Interest: An aggregate of rights, privileges, powers, and immunities appertaining to some person the exclusive enjoyment of which constitutes him owner or part owner of a particular property asset.

(2) Possessory Interest: A present interest which entitles the holder thereof to present possession of the asset.

(3) Future Interest: A present interest which does not [at present] entitle the holder thereof to present possession of the asset, but which will or may later entitle him to such possession.

(4) Reversion: A future interest, that part of his legal estate still retained by the grantor when he conveys away an estate smaller than he has.

(5) Remainder: A future interest in someone other than the grantor which according to its terms may become possessory upon the normal termination of some particular estate of freehold.

in a way that is not consistent with life ownership. The argued-for power of disposal in the *Black* case might be a way to make the life estate more flexible. What are the risks and benefits of using such a device? (You should assume, of course, that the lawyer using the device drafts the document so that it is clear that the device is being used.) It is also possible to give this life tenant power to convey interests in the property to grantees who otherwise would have no interest—power not only to dispose but also to *appoint*. How might a power of appointment have been useful in planning for the older generation of siblings in the Black family?

A NOTE ON THE LAW OF WASTE

It turned out here that Jessie Black had no interest other than a life estate. Once that problem was solved, as to nieces and nephews, the question was how to treat the attempted disposition of the property by deed in 1979. But even where that issue is clearly resolved—as, arguably, it should have been in the joint will—there are issues of power and use that have to be worked out as between the possessory ownership of the life tenant and the remainderman's (or reversioner's) present ownership of a future interest. That subject is taken up in the law of waste, which is extensive, complex, and legalistic. But there ought to be some discernible principles in it that would guide an inquiring student who doesn't have time just now to look at the precedents. Professors Cunningham, Stoebuck, and Whitman, in their valuable West Hornbook on the law of property (1984), §§ 4.1 through 4.3, pp. 163–177, point to the traditional distinction between *voluntary* waste and *permissive* waste.

Voluntary waste is "any affirmative act of a possessory tenant for life or for years which 'injured the inheritance'" of the owner of the future interest. The English cases our American lawyer forebears inherited and put to use said that "any substantial alteration of the land or the structures thereon would 'injure the reversion' because the reversion or remainderman in fee simple was legally entitled, at the termination of all preceding less-than-fee simple estates, to have possession of the property in substantially the condition it was in when the fee simple was divided into successive estates."

Using that as your test, see if you can answer two questions about the following situations. The first question is whether the law of voluntary waste would provide a remedy for the owner of the remainder, under the general "injury to the inheritance" standard the Hornbook quotes. The second question is whether modern American law should provide a different resolution when the owner of the future interest objects to what the owner of the possessory estate is doing.

(a) The life tenant cuts down an orchard of richly bearing, mature apple trees and turns the orchard site into a corn field.

(b) The life tenant cuts down an orchard of apple trees that are declining in yield, many of them half dead, and replaces them, not with young apple trees, but with a corn field.

(c) The life tenant discovers that there is coal under the tract, develops a coal mine, and extracts and sells the coal. Consider here whether it makes any difference that he gives a share of the proceeds to the owner of the remainder, using some evaluation device such as those stipulated in the *Summers* case. (Assume here that the mine will not significantly disturb use of the surface of the land.)

(d) Should it make any difference that the owner of the fee simple at the beginning of the story, the owner who spread subsequent ownership on the plane of time, had the coal mine in operation when the life estate was created?

(e) The neighborhood has become industrial since the life estate was created. It would increase the value of the property to tear down the house that is on it and use the land for a storage yard for the factory next door. The life tenant acts to increase the value of the property, even though the house being torn down is a solid house with artistic and historical value, and even though the owner of the remainder, the grand-niece of the person who created the life estate, places great sentimental value on the house.

The Cunningham, Stoebuck, and Whitman Hornbook defines *permissive* waste as "a limited duty to make repairs on the property and to pay all or part of certain carrying charges such as property taxes, mortgage interest, and special assessments for public improvements." The rule is "subject to the important limitation that the life tenant is under no duty to expend more than the income he receives from the land or, if he personally occupies the land, the rental value thereof, in order to discharge such duties."

(f) Vandals trespass on the property and break all the windows in the house. The life tenant wants the owner of the remainder to contribute to the cost of their replacement. (The loss could have been covered by a standard "homeowners" insurance policy, but the life tenant elected to buy only fire insurance, which is cheaper.)

PIGG v. HALEY

Supreme Court of Virginia, 1982.
224 Va. 113, 294 S.E.2d 851.

COMPTON, JUSTICE.

The focus of this appeal is upon the validity of an agreement, executed to settle uncertainties arising from the doubtful meaning of provisions in a will.

Edward F. Haley, a resident of Charlotte County, died testate on July 13, 1977, survived by his wife, appellee Eva F. Haley. The testator's one-page holograph, duly probated shortly after his death, provides in part:

"Third: Whatever land I may own, including buildings, furniture, farming equipment of all kinds, livestock of every description, automobiles, money in hand, or in banks, or owing to me, shall immediately upon my decease become the property of my wife, Eva F. Haley, to be used for her decent support during her natural life.

"Fourth: It is my will and desire that upon the death of my said wife whatever residue of my estate either real or personal which she has not consumed or disposed of shall become the property of Garland D. Pigg."

Appellant Pigg, a resident of Fairfax County, was a distant cousin of the testator.

At his death, Haley owned certain personal property and an undivided one-half interest in approximately 152 acres of land in Charlotte County; his wife owned the remaining one-half interest in the realty.

Because of doubt as to the meaning of the foregoing language in the will, the agreement in dispute was executed about two weeks after Haley's death by the widow and Pigg. Drafted by an attorney, the operative portions of the agreement provide:

"1. That all personal property, both tangible and intangible, in the Estate of Edward F. Haley, shall be the sole and exclusive property of Eva F. Haley, with complete right to dispose of the same in any manner that she might deem fit, and the party of the second part relinquishes any interest that he might acquire under the will of Edward F. Haley, in this regard.

"2. That the interest in any real estate that Edward F. Haley died seized and possessed of in Charlotte County, Virginia, shall be construed as to give his wife, Eva F. Haley, a life estate therein exclusively, with the remainder over to Garland D. Pigg, upon her death, in fee simple and absolutely."

Subsequently, the widow and appellees Donald F. Haley and Betty R. Haley, his wife, executed a real estate contract in May of 1979 for the sale by the widow to the Haleys of 30 acres from the 152–acre tract. Within a month, the present suit was filed by the widow and the Haleys against Pigg. By virtue of the contract, the Haleys claim "an equitable fee interest" in the 30 acres. * * *

Following an October 1979 ore tenus hearing, the trial judge ruled from the bench in favor of the plaintiffs, declaring the agreement [between Eva Haley and Garland Pigg] void. The court found the agreement lacked adequate consideration. In the January 1980 final decree, from which we awarded Pigg an appeal, the court decided that the effect of the will "was to vest in [the widow] the right to consume and dispose of, by sale, gift, or otherwise, the property of" the testator. Thus, the court implicitly held that Pigg received nothing under the will which he could relinquish in the agreement.

Upon appeal, as in the court below, the validity of the agreement depends upon the interpretation of the will. Our analysis, of necessity, will be in two steps. Initially, we must interpret the will. Because the words of the will are of doubtful meaning and the uncertainty is not resolved by reading the will as a whole, we will consider admissible extrinsic evidence to establish the relevant facts and circumstances that surrounded the testator at the time the will was executed. * * * Next, we must address the issue of consideration and, in so doing, we will consider all the relevant circumstances disclosed by the record. * * *

The decedent [Edward F. Haley] and his wife [Eva] married in 1937. He taught in an Alabama high school for a period of time and, because he was a native of Virginia, the couple moved to Charlotte County where both husband and wife worked. He farmed, taught, and sold life insurance; she was a registered nurse. During the 1940s, with their joint funds, the couple purchased the 152–acre "farm" in question, deeded to them "jointly" and without "a survivorship clause," and later built a residence on the property. They worked on the farm together, and actually participated in the construction of their home.

As a hobby, the decedent engaged in genealogical research. During the 1940s, when he was teaching at Hargrave Military Academy, the decedent "discovered" Pigg, a fourth cousin, while searching records in Chatham. Pigg, about seven or eight years old at the time, lived near Chatham with his parents. Thereafter, a close personal relationship developed between the decedent, who had no children, and Pigg, whose father died when he was a young person. Calling the decedent "Uncle Frank," young Pigg regularly visited the decedent and his wife on their farm, staying for periods of time during the summer months.

After Pigg completed high school, the decedent helped Pigg during the 1950s obtain entry to Ferrum College, the decedent's alma mater, and "arranged" for Pigg to have a scholarship there. Later, Pigg lived with the decedent and his wife while he attended one semester at Longwood College, where Mrs. Haley was employed as a nurse.

After finishing college, Pigg taught for a period of time at Staunton Military Academy. He married in 1962. Subsequently, Pigg, his wife, who was also a teacher, and their children spent a part of all the regular holidays—Thanksgiving, Christmas, Easter, and the summer— with the Haleys. The Piggs had possession of a key to the Haleys' home so they could enter if no one was there when they arrived for a visit. When asked to describe the relationship existing between her husband and Pigg in 1964, when the will in question was written, the widow testified they were "friends" and "[r]easonably close." Pigg stated he and Haley had a "close" relationship.

After 1964, the decedent advanced Pigg $10,000 to purchase a 130– acre tract adjacent to the property in question. The loan subsequently was repaid. According to the evidence, the regular visits and the personal relationship between the Piggs and the Haleys continued into the 1970s and past 1972 when Mrs. Haley retired from her employment at Longwood College.

During the decedent's final illness, while he was hospitalized in Farmville, the Piggs came from their home in Fairfax, having been called by Mrs. Haley. When Haley died, the Piggs assisted with the funeral arrangements.

Within a week of the death, an unwitnessed typewritten will dated in 1963 was found in Haley's desk at home. When the widow was advised the writing could not be admitted to probate, a further search among Haley's effects was made with the assistance of the Piggs. Finally, Mrs. Pigg discovered the will in question among Haley's voluminous genealogical notes.

On the day the will was probated, Lelia Hoy, a Charlotte County attorney who had reviewed the will, told the widow she had only a life interest in her husband's estate, observing: "You own nothing; you have the use of the property, the use of the farm; the proceeds of the farm until you die; and you have the interest from the money until you die."

The widow testified that this news was "overwhelming" because she had no knowledge of a will; in fact, Haley told his wife during his last illness "that he had no will." The widow testified she felt she had been "sabotaged" because in 1964, when the will was written, the couple "did not have any money;" they had recently finished making large, regular payments over a ten-year period on a joint annuity.

The widow, accompanied by the Piggs, then went to Farmville to consult R.A. Wilmouth, the proprietor of "a bookkeeping tax service." Wilmouth had prepared income tax returns for the testator for a number of years. In discussing the tax aspects of the estate, he said to the widow: " 'You will receive the interest from the money, and you will have the proceeds from the farm.' " Upon Wilmouth's recommendation, the widow, still accompanied by the Piggs, then consulted E. Preston Lancaster, Jr., a Farmville attorney.

Lancaster, noting the ambiguity in the will, mentioned that a court interpretation should be sought. But "the main thing on [the widow's] mind," according to Pigg, was that an agreement be prepared to fix the interests of the respective parties.

According to Pigg, the widow stated to him repeatedly, after realizing that the meaning of the will was uncertain: " 'Uncle Frank and I always wanted you to have the farm, and we didn't intend for you to have the money.' " The widow testified that she suggested the agreement in an effort to "salvage some property for myself." When asked whether the testator before his death mentioned "the possibility of leaving an interest in the farm" to Pigg, the widow said: "I did not recall that he said that." The widow previously had stated in a deposition in responding to a similar question: " 'Well, he might have mentioned it vaguely.' "

The record shows that the widow suggested the terms of the agreement to Lancaster who, on the date it was executed, dictated the language of the document to his secretary in the presence of the widow and the Piggs. According to Lancaster, the widow said to him that the agreement reflected "what her husband would have wanted." At the time the agreement was executed, Lancaster asked both parties whether they understood the document and whether "these were the terms that [they] wanted"; the widow responded "yes" and Pigg said: " 'If that's what she wants, that's okay with me.' "

Even though the agreement recites "in consideration of the sum of TEN DOLLARS ($10.00), and other good and valuable consideration, the receipt of which is hereby acknowledged, and the love and affection that exists between the parties," no money actually passed between the parties.

Before construing the will, Code § 55–11, the doctrine of *May v. Joynes*, 61 Va. (20 Gratt.) 692 (1857), and Code § 55–7 should be reviewed. Code § 55–11 provides:

> "When any real estate is conveyed, devised or granted to any person without any words of limitation such devise, conveyance or grant shall be construed to pass the fee simple or other whole estate or interest which the testator or grantor has power to dispose of in such real estate, unless a contrary intention shall appear by the will, conveyance or grant."

Under *May v. Joynes*, "where a life estate is given to the first taker coupled with the absolute power of disposition, the added power raises the life estate to a fee in real property and absolute ownership of personalty, and any limitations in the remainder over are void for repugnancy and uncertainty. * * * " But the foregoing rule has been modified by statute.

Code § 55–7 provides, in part:

> "A. If any interest in or claim to real estate or personal property be disposed of by deed or will for life, with a limitation in remainder over, and in the same instrument there be conferred expressly or by implication a power upon the life tenant in his lifetime or by will to dispose absolutely of such property, the limitation in remainder over shall not fail, or be defeated, except to the extent that the life tenant shall have lawfully exercised such power of disposal."

The effect of the statute is to validate the gift over "where the first taker is given an *express estate for life,* coupled with the absolute power of disposition" * * *.

It is against this background that the competing parties debate the meaning of the will. The widow says she acquired either an absolute fee simple interest, in which case § 55–7 would not apply, or she acquired "a life estate coupled with an absolute power of disposition during her life," in which case the savings provisions of § 55–7 would apply. But, the argument continues, under the latter alternative, the second taker must prove what property, if any, remains at the death of the first taker, and it is doubtful that Pigg will be able to prove at the widow's death that she did not dispose of all the testator's property. Thus, in either event, says the widow, Pigg received under the will nothing which he could surrender in the agreement.

Pigg contends that the will created an express life estate in the testator's property in Eva Haley, coupled with an absolute inter vivos power of disposition, and a remainder over to Pigg. He argues the widow took less than a fee simple interest in the realty and less than an absolute interest in the personalty. Consequently, Pigg urges, his interest acquired under the will was such as to constitute sufficient consideration for the agreement. We concur.

The extrinsic facts show the circumstances surrounding the testator in 1964 when he wrote the will. A strong bond existed between the Haleys who, at that time, had been married 27 years. They had labored together in operating their farm and in building their home, pooling their financial resources acquired from their respective occupations. There was also a close, avuncular relationship between the testator and Pigg, a tie based on mutual respect and affection that, at the time, had existed for over 20 years. Consequently, the parol evidence established that the objects of the testator's affection were, principally, his wife and, secondarily, Pigg. * * *

Against this background, we turn to the language of the clauses in issue. The testator provided in the Third clause that whatever land he owned, "including" items of personal property, should immediately upon his decease "become the property" of his wife, "to be used for her decent support during her natural life." Then, he wrote in clause Fourth: "It is my will and desire that upon the death of my said wife whatever residue of my estate either real or personal which she has not consumed or disposed of shall become the property of Garland D. Pigg."

We conclude, contrary to the widow's contention, that the words "shall immediately upon my decease become the property of my wife * * * to be used for her decent support during her natural life," created an express life estate in the testator's property. * * * Here * * * we believe the language points to the intention of the testator to provide for the support and comfort of his wife during her life, but, upon her death, such of the property which she had not consumed would pass to Pigg, his esteemed kinsman. Such a plan, under these facts and circumstances, would benefit both objects of the testator's affection.

The question then becomes whether Code § 55–7 is applicable to clauses Third and Fourth. We think it is. An express life estate was created, fulfilling the first requirement of the statute. The Fourth clause confers expressly a power upon the life tenant in her lifetime, as she agrees on brief, to dispose absolutely of the property, thus satisfying the second requirement. In addition, the language of the Fourth clause manifestly is a limitation in remainder over, thus fulfilling the third statutory requirement. Finally, there is a corpus; property remains undisposed of by the life tenant on which the "limitation in remainder over" can operate. * * *

And, as we have said, the interest Pigg acquired under the will affords the basis for adequate consideration in the agreement. * * * Pigg acquired a remainder interest under the will in the realty and personalty. In order to make certain that which the will rendered ambiguous and vague, the parties entered into this agreement, in which Pigg relinquished his interest in all of the decedent's personalty and acquired a "remainder * * * in fee simple" in the realty. While it is true, as the widow argues, that under our interpretation of the will eventually there may have been no property remaining undisposed of by the life tenant at the time of her death, nonetheless, Pigg in 1977 suffered a detriment by agreeing to surrender his interest in the personalty, at a time when the property had not been dissipated.

Finally, the widow argues the agreement is void because, as the trial judge found, there was a mutual mistake of fact. She contends that the parties entered into the agreement upon the mistaken assumption that she acquired under the will a life estate only, when "at a minimum" she was given "a life estate in her husband's property and, without any dispute, the unfettered right to dispose of it."

Generally, equity, while relieving mistakes of fact, will not give relief from a mistake of law, except in extraordinary cases. * * * But that rule has been confined to mistakes of the general rules of law, and does not apply to the mistakes made by individuals as to their own private legal rights and interests, such as to the ownership of property. Those private rights are treated as matters of fact, albeit the result of matters of law. * * * However, the latter rule has no application to cases of compromise, when doubts have arisen as to the rights of parties, and they have intentionally entered into an agreement to compromise and settle those doubts. * * * This is such a case.

Manifestly, the record shows that the parties to the agreement both were in doubt as to their respective interests under the will, that they intentionally made a sincere effort to settle their respective claims, and that they endeavored to avoid the litigation suggested by Lancaster. Consequently, and the transaction being devoid of overreaching or unfair dealing on either side, we will not annul the agreement on the ground of mutual mistake.

For the foregoing reasons, we conclude that the trial court erred in declaring the agreement of July 26, 1977 void and in removing the cloud on the title to the 30–acre tract. Accordingly, we will declare such agreement valid and enforceable, reverse the judgment appealed from, and enter final judgment dismissing the bill of complaint.

Notes and Questions

1. Wills statutes require that testators' signatures on wills be witnessed by two or three competent witnesses. ("Competent" means able to testify in court.) That requirement was not met as to the 1963 document that was found in Edward F. Haley's notes. The document that was given effect as Mr. Haley's will was holographic, which means it was written entirely in his own hand. In many states, including Virginia, such a will is valid even though there are no witnesses to its execution. Does *Pigg v. Haley* argue for or against permitting holographic wills?

2. Uniform Probate Code, § 3–912: "[S]uccessors may agree among themselves to alter the interests, shares, or amounts to which they are entitled under the will of the decedent * * * in any way that they provide in a written contract. * * * The [executor] shall abide by the terms of the agreement. * * * " The policy behind § 3–912, and the policy behind similar statutes or case-law doctrines in states that have not adopted the Uniform Probate Code, is the preservation of family concord, even when the agreement of the successors departs radically from the pattern the testator put in the will. The question in a case such as *Pigg v. Haley* is why the agreement (and the statute or case-law policy that encouraged the parties to make an agreement) failed of its purpose—so that the matter had to be resolved by judges:

(a) Both Mrs. Haley and the Piggs visited Mr. Lancaster's office in Farmville and were together, in fact, and perhaps in spirit, for the making of an agreement that would conform their ownership either to what Mr. Haley seemed to have had in mind, or to Mrs. Haley's needs, or to both. Is there something: (i) in the express agreement itself; or (ii) in the way the agreement was made, that gives a hint as to why the harmony did not last?

(b) Mr. Lancaster first suggested taking the will to court, so that a judge could tell the parties what Mr. Haley's will meant. But the policy of law such as U.P.C. § 3–912 is that Mrs. Haley and Mr. and Mrs. Pigg could decide for themselves what effect the will was to have on their property ownership, and on their relationship(s) with one another. They could have made their own law, and have been their own judges. And here, apparently, they were willing to do that, at least for a moment. What are the advantages and disadvantages of agreement versus litigation in such a situation?

(c) Drafting a will that is clear in terms of the property interests it purports to create is a matter of law-office skill. Could this rather tragic family quarrel have been avoided if Mr. Haley had had a lawyer draft his will? How would you have done the job?

(d) Drafting an agreement that settles a dispute, or makes clear what is otherwise unclear, also involves skill. Could this *agreement* have been drafted in such a way as to have avoided a lawsuit over its validity?

(e) Obtaining commitment from each party to a contract is another matter that involves skill. Here commitment was related to skill at resolving the dispute in an effective, lasting, mutually understood way. And that, in turn, involved skill at locating and describing the human conflict that a dispute involves—getting it out into the open, where it could have been dealt with. Is there indication here that better dispute-resolution skills in Mr. Lancaster's law office might have avoided the failure of this agreement? Are these skills appropriate for law offices?

(f) Many lawyers will say, in a case such as this, that the agreement failed because the parties were not separately represented: When Mrs. Haley went to consult Mr. Lancaster, Mr. and Mrs. Pigg should have hired their own lawyer. This assertion is sometimes given an "ethical" form, in which case reference may be made to the profession's formal rules on acting for parties whose interests are in conflict. The traditional rules would have required here, for example, that Mr. Lancaster: (i) explain to all three parties the risks and benefits of his working with both the Piggs and Mrs. Haley; (ii) obtain from all parties their consent to his doing so; and (iii) determine in his own mind that he could act with "independent professional judgment" for all three parties. If Mr. Lancaster took these steps, acting in the way he did is within the practice and tradition of property lawyers.

(g) A lawyer's acting, beyond that, as a resolver of disputes, would have involved a somewhat more elaborate routine. Rule 2.2 of the American Bar Association's proposed Rules of Professional Conduct, identifies this lawyer function as separate from those of advocate and counselor; it refers to this function as "lawyer as mediator," and sets down these requirements for the exercise of the function:

1. Explanation to all parties, and consent from each of them, as in the case of common representation of conflicting interests.

2. The lawyer's judgment that (A) the interests that the parties have in common and (B) the individual interests of each of the parties, will be served by the lawyer acting as mediator.

3. The lawyer's judgment that she or he is able to do the job as mediator.

4. Continuing consultation with each of the individual clients (probably separate consultation).

5. Withdrawal from mediation if any of these conditions comes not to be met or if any of the clients asks the lawyer to withdraw as mediator.

Some questions: (i) Are these requirements generous enough to permit a lawyer who is in the position Mr. Lancaster was in to do a good job of dispute resolution? (ii) Might two lawyers, negotiating as advocates for the two sides, do better? (iii) Might a judge do better? Notice that the parties could have selected their own private judge—an arbitrator. What advantages would arbitration have had?

The parties told Mr. Lancaster that they were willing to agree, and apparently did so over Mr. Lancaster's initial misgivings, on whether an agreement was best; this was not a case where agreement was imposed or coerced. It is, rather, a case in which the questions raised are: (i) whether resolution by agreement is a good idea; and, if it is, (ii) whether the process by which agreement was reached was as skillful as it should have been. Here are three paragraphs from the A.B.A. comment on Rule 2.2:

> A lawyer acts as intermediary in seeking to establish or adjust a relationship between clients on an amicable and mutually advantageous basis; for example, in helping to organize a business in which two or more clients are entrepreneurs, working out the financial reorganization of an enterprise in which two or more clients have an interest, arranging a property distribution in settlement of an estate or mediating a dispute between clients. The lawyer seeks to resolve potentially conflicting interests by developing the parties' mutual interests. The alternative can be that each party may have to obtain separate representation, with the possibility in some situations of incurring additional cost, complication or even litigation. Given these

and other relevant factors, all the clients may prefer that the lawyer act as intermediary.

In considering whether to act as intermediary between clients, a lawyer should be mindful that if the intermediation fails the result can be additional cost, embarrassment and recrimination. In some situations the risk of failure is so great that intermediation is plainly impossible. For example, a lawyer cannot undertake common representation of clients between whom contentious litigation is imminent or who contemplate contentious litigation. More generally, if the relationship between the parties has already assumed definite antagonism, the possibility that the clients' interests can be adjusted by intermediation ordinarily is not very good.

The appropriateness of intermediation can depend on its form. Forms of intermediation range from informal arbitration, where each client's case is presented by the respective client and the lawyer decides the outcome, to mediation, to common representation where the clients' interests are substantially though not entirely compatible. One form may be appropriate in circumstances where another would not. Other relevant facts are whether the lawyer subsequently will represent both parties on a continuing basis and whether the situation involves creating a relationship between the parties or terminating one.

B. OWNERSHIP IN THE FAMILY

We need here to take a somewhat more careful look at the rise and fall of the fee-tail estate.

It is possible to look at the long history of Anglo–American property law and say that the government and the family are natural enemies, that that is the lesson of history. It is possible to say even that government fears the power of families and associations that can seriously claim the metaphor of family in identifying themselves. In any event, our law has never provided a form of property ownership in which a family, as a legal person, is owner (although it provides for ownership by corporations as legal persons); there are forms of ownership for married couples, but these do not reach the principal goal family ownership would attempt to reach—a solution to the "problem of death," a means of immortality, a way for the property owner to defeat the grim reaper and to live on in his family and on his land. This is the issue that is usually put in terms of the property owner wanting to keep property in the family.

In most of the history of the subject, by the way, English law and custom dealt with family ownership by putting legal ownership in the oldest male in the family. "Heir" meant *one person,* the oldest son or a circumstantial substitute where the oldest son could not take ownership or where there were no sons. Ownership in any generation was, typically, in one person; and even after this form of inheritance—primogeniture—was no longer imposed by law (after 1540), law-office practice preserved it as the conventional form in England until into the twentieth century. Notice, for example, the substantial suffering that falls on families of women in the novels of Jane Austen, or the thousands of pages of plot that Anthony Trollope develops from the fact that one person among a dozen is in line to take all of a family's wealth—to take it, in the usual case, from a doddering old uncle or an unadmirable if conventional ancestor such as the Duke of Omnium of the parliamentary novels, or old Vavasour in *Can You Forgive Her?*

The old duke was a bachelor; his heir apparent was his nephew, but a legitimate son would come in ahead of the nephew if the Duke married and his wife had a son. The Duke caused prolonged anxiety in his nephew's family when he proposed marriage to Madame Max Goessler, who was possibly still within her child-bearing years. Old Vavasour's choice was between his granddaughter Alice, an able and virtuous young woman, and his grandson George, a weak and dishonest young man. The dramatic tension of the story turns on the conventional pressure to give the property to George instead of Alice. All of this may render references to "the family" a bit hollow, but we, in fidelity to our forebears in the offices of family solicitors, will say it as they would wish us to say it.

In the thirteenth century, in the sort of quarrel between barons and king that produced *Magna Carta* (and, for that matter, *Quia Emptores*), the law had been that property could (but need not) be held in such a way that descent in ownership was descent within the grantor's family. (Descent within the family, a rule having to do with inter-generational *transfers* in ownership, might serve as family ownership would, if we had it. It is not the same thing.) In order to invoke that form of descent, the grantor of the property to, say, Sam of Sussex, would say as he conveyed the property: "to Sam and the heirs of his body." The result was that Sam was not able to convey the property; the idea was that he would use and hold the property during his life, but the transfer of ownership at his death would be a transition within the family. The common way of referring to Sam's disability, and a reference that is still used today, is to say that the property is "entailed." This estate in land was known as the *fee simple conditional.*[9]

Sam, of course, came into circumstances in which he wanted to convey the property, to turn it into a more liquid asset. And he went to a lawyer. Lawyers (over generations, no doubt) had figured out ways for Sam to convey property that he held in fee simple conditional. The common law had come eventually to say that, if a child were born to Mrs. Sam, Sam could convey a fee simple (*i.e.,* full ownership): He still owned a fee simple conditional, but he could give someone else full ownership, a *fee simple.* (There are many instances in the law of property in which a person can give away more than he has. Even so, judges in property cases and professors who use cases to oppress students continue to explain their decisions by saying or writing *nemo*

---

9. These three little words are used only for this estate. It was abolished in 1285. Except in one or two American states that did not recognize *De Donis* as common law, the fee simple conditional is not a modern form of ownership.

dat quod non habet. Retaining the maxim in Latin is apparently a way to hide the fact that it is not dependable.)

This meant that property could rather easily be taken out of the substitute for family ownership that was possible with the fee simple conditional. The great English landowners, who were, no doubt, mostly grandfathers, were not happy with that result: If your daughter was about to marry Sam of Sussex, and you were about to give the happy couple a thousand acres of England, you wanted to see to it that the property descended to your grandchildren and not to Sam's race-course companions, or, even worse, to members of *his* family. The law had at one time assured that result with the fee simple conditional; the lawyers had ruined the fee simple conditional; the cure was legislation. The barons got their legislation in 1285, in the statute *De Donis Conditionalibus.*

Under this statute, after the common-law judges construed it, a new form of ownership was created: *the fee tail.* A grantor to Sam of Sussex created this form of ownership in Sam with the same words that had been used to create the fee simple conditional: "to Sam and the heirs of his body." The statute abolished the fee simple conditional. The new estate, the fee tail, was not "disentailable"; that is, the "tenant in tail" (Sam) could not convey any more than he had; Sam's heir took the estate Sam had, whether Sam conveyed to a third person or not. If the family ran out of "issue" (that is, lineal descendants of Sam), and whenever it did—even if that were 200 years away—the property reverted. Ownership in Sam's family ended, by the terms of the original deed. The power to possess the land returned to the original grantor. The original grantor had owned this reversion all along; it had value, in him, all along. It was an interest he had because he did not give it away when he gave Sam the fee-tail deed. The original grantor retained this interest. There were four possibilities when Sam's line of lineal descendants ran out (in five years, or ten, or five hundred) and possession shifted out of Sam's family: [10]

(i) The grantor might be living; possession would revert to him.

(ii) The grantor might not be living; possession would "revert" to the grantor's heir (or the heir's heir, or the heir of the heir's heir) who, for property-law purposes, *is* the grantor.

(iii) The grantor might, at the time of the deed to Sam, have given his reversion to someone else ("to Sam and the heirs of his body, then to Elmer and his heirs"),[11] in which case

10. That is, out of primogeniture ownership in one male. There might still be a family of women left, as in Jane Austen's *Pride and Prejudice* and Anthony Trollope's *The Small House at Allington.*

11. If we haven't made it clear yet, we had better make it clear now that the creation of these common-law estates required magic words in the conveyance. These words at first were spoken within the hearing of the community; in time

Elmer or his heir could claim possession. Elmer held a remainder while Sam or one of his descendants held the fee tail. Elmer's remainder in this case was in fee simple. It could have been a remainder in fee tail ("to Sam and the heirs of his body, then to Elmer and the heirs of his body"), in which case the grantor had a reversion.

(iv) The grantor might have conveyed to Sam in fee tail without creating a remainder at that time ("to Sam and the heirs of his body"), and then, at a later time, have given his reversion to Elmer ("all of my interest in the land to Elmer and his heirs"), in which case:

(a) Sam would at first have had a fee tail with reversion in the grantor; and then (b) Sam would have had a fee tail with reversion in Elmer in fee simple.

Just to make sure you understand this so far, what are the interests created in the following deeds, all after 1285?

(A) Henry conveys to Sam and the heirs of his body. Sam and his wife have a son Eric.

(B) Henry conveys to Sam and the heirs of his body, and then to Dorothy and her heirs.[12] Sam and his wife have no children (yet).

(C) Henry conveys to Sam and the heirs of his body and then to Dorothy and her heirs. Sam and his wife have no children (yet). Henry dies; Henry's heir is Elmer.

(D) Henry conveys to Sam and the heirs of his body. Sam and his wife have no children (yet). Henry dies; Henry's heir is Elmer.

The fee tail arrangement for keeping property in the family appears to have worked for about two centuries. No doubt lawyers for people like Sam kept chipping away at it, though. And no doubt, in the long run, government was going to side with people like Sam, rather than with the family of his wife, which is where the land came from, for three reasons: (i) Government wanted transactions in land, especially transitions of ownership between generations, as occasions for imposing transfer taxes. (ii) Government did not favor family ownership of large amounts of land. Land was power, and Government suspected and tended to eliminate aggregations of power other than its own. (iii) As the sustaining economy of England (and then Great Britain) became a

---

they came to be written in documents. The magic words for the fee simple conditional, until 1285, and the magic words for the fee tail thereafter, were: "to [grantee] and the heirs of her/his body." The magic words for the fee simple were "to [grantee] and her/his heirs." If the magic words were not spoken ("to [grantee]" without more), the estate conveyed was only a life estate.

12. "And her heirs" does not create an interest in heirs. The phrase has always been a matter of magic words; and the magic words designate that the grantee (Dorothy) has a fee simple. If Dorothy's heir ends up owning the land it will be because Dorothy gave it to him, or he took it at her death by operation of law, not because this conveyance created a future interest in him.

trading economy, concentrations of wealth in land were undesirable because wealth tied up in land did not circulate and drive the economy.

In any event, by the end of the fifteenth century, the common-law courts had recognized a form of *disentailment,* through which people in Sam's situation could do what they had been able to do before 1285; they could, as the county-seat lawyers in America came to say later, *dock the entail.* The fifteenth-century procedure for docking entails was devious, complex, and expensive. The eventual form (the form Atticus Finch used in his law office, in 1935, in rural Alabama) was a piece of paper that the tenant in tail signed and recorded in the land records. The historical lesson is that, after 1500, the fee tail was not a dependable way to keep property in the family.

The fee tail was used, from the sixteenth century on, as part of an extensive scheme invented by family solicitors, called the strict settlement. The key to the strict settlement was not the fee tail, though; the key was to bring the heir before his (male) elders, and the family solicitor, as soon as he was of age, and bribe him into surrendering his ability to disentail the family estates. In itself the fee tail began to fade from its medieval prominence and become a quaint old tool in the plane-of-time part of the property-lawyer's tool box.

For some reason, though, the disentailable fee tail was widely used in property practice in the United States in the nineteenth and early twentieth centuries. It is still used in some places. It was available, and was disentailable, and still is in some places, because most states accepted the statute *De Donis* and the fifteenth-century case law on disentailment, as part of American common law. The fact that the fee tail was, when used, vulnerable to disentailment would seem to indicate that its main value in county-seat practice was as a will substitute: If I take title to my farm in tail, the farm will, at my death, go to my children. If that is what I want to happen, I won't have to make a will saying so. (Primogeniture never caught hold in American law and has had only spotty acceptance in American convention, so that "heirs of his body" in a fee-tail deed meant, in American practice, all of the grantee's children.) In any case, the fee tail has now been abolished in most American states, and one or two never recognized it in the first place, holding that *De Donis* was not part of their common law. The legal question in most places, when a lawyer comes across a fee-tail deed, is what ownership it creates, since, by statute in most jurisdictions, it cannot create a common-law fee tail. There are four common statutory possibilities:

(i) The tenant in tail (Sam) may have, by statute, a life estate, with remainder in fee simple to his issue. If Sam has no issue, ownership will revert to the grantor. Sam never has more than a life estate.

(ii) The tenant in tail may have a fee simple.

(iii) The tenant in tail may have in effect what he would have had before *De Donis:* an estate for life that becomes a fee simple upon the birth of issue.[13]

    (iv)   In one or two states he will have a common-law fee tail and will have available (as in Atticus's law office) a simple form of disentailment.

II. OWNERSHIP DIVIDED INTO DIFFERENT PRESENT INTERESTS

JOHN P. FRANK, "THE LEGAL ETHICS OF LOUIS D. BRANDEIS,"

17 Stanford Law Review 683 (1965).

Louis D. Brandeis was no saint, but he * * * [did] guide his life by a standard more severe and exacting than most of us, and his appointment to the United States Supreme Court came close to being a rendezvous for a lynching.

The Brandeis appointment controversy was * * * [in] 1916. Woodrow Wilson had been elected as a minority President in the three-way election of 1912. [The other candidates were former President Theodore Roosevelt and incumbent President William Howard Taft.] * * *

Brandeis had richly earned both his appointment and his enemies. * * * The * * * appointment battle is almost fifty years old. * * * Taft made his peace with Brandeis when both were later on the Supreme Court. * * * Mr. Justice Brandeis died almost twenty-five years ago. But now, if ever, we should be able to assess the ethical charges made against him to determine their validity. We should also stop to consider what the practicing lawyer of today can gain for the guidance of his own life from the Brandeis experience.

I

The Brandeis appointment raised no question of competence. The long-time head of a great New England [law] firm was clearly able. After extended hearings, however, the Republican minority of the Judiciary Committee reported adversely to Brandeis. They adopted as their own the conclusion of six former presidents of the American Bar Association, including Taft, that Brandeis was "not a fit person to be a member of the Supreme Court of the United States." The minority listed, in summary, twelve specific counts of ethical unfitness on which they based this grave conclusion. * * *

THE WARREN MATTER

Charge: That he for a long time represented and collected fees from two clients whose interests were diametrically opposed to each other and when they, later, went to law over those same conflicting interests he took employment for one of them against the other.

---

13. "Issue" means lineal descendants. It is not limited to children but includes as many future generations as are in existence when the word is applied. It excludes collateral descendants (e.g., nephews and nieces).

Facts: The actual event has only a remote resemblance to the charge so succinctly stated. In 1888 and before, Brandeis and his partner, Sam Warren, were counsel for S.D. Warren and Company, a paper manufacturing concern dominated by Sam Warren's father. In 1888 the elder Warren died, leaving a wife, a daughter, and four sons—Sam, Fiske, Henry, and Edward, commonly referred to as Ned. The estate covered all the investment in the paper mills except the very substantial portion owned by a person named Mason.

The Brandeis firm represented the estate, as well as the entire family. It was apparent that only Sam and Mason could make the business prosper; Ned, for example, preferred to live in England where he was engaged in the antique business. An arrangement was finally made—with the full and complete concurrence of every member of the family—whereby the properties were placed in trust, the three trustees being the mother, Mason, and Sam Warren. The trustees leased the property to a newly formed company of which Sam and Mason were the principal members. As the mills prospered, the lessees were entitled to keep a portion of the revenue for their services. Another portion passed to the trustees as payment on the lease and was distributed by the trustees among the various beneficiaries, of whom Ned was one.

The arrangement continued throughout the last decade of the nineteenth century. Sam Warren resigned from the law firm to devote himself entirely to his business. * * * The Brandeis firm continued to handle the legal problems of the trustees and the lessees [as well, apparently, as legal matters for members of the Warren family].

After 1900, Ned Warren began to grow discontent with his brother's management of the family affairs. Finally, in 1909 he brought an action to void the lease and to secure an accounting. Ned was not a trustee, and all trustees—indeed all other members of the family—stood by Sam and supported the arrangement. In the resulting litigation the Brandeis firm represented the lessees. Any individual member of the family who became involved separately had individual counsel. In the course of the litigation, Sam Warren died. Ned's interest in the trust was bought out by the other members of the family, and the litigation was abandoned.

Ethical Problem: As this matter was presented to the Committee, there were essentially two charges. The first did not survive the investigation; and yet had it not been made, the second probably would never have been explored.

The first charge of the counsel who had represented Ned in the intra-family litigation was that the entire trust-lease arrangement had been a fraud upon their client and that the accounting methods used by Sam Warren were part of this fraud.

No one on the Committee, and no one likely to look into it at any subsequent time, could find any merit in this charge. The business prospered admirably under the direction of Sam Warren and Mason, and all interests seem to have been most fairly treated. Even the minority members of the Committee went out of their way to eliminate this issue.

The second charge, involving the true problem of legal ethics, was that the Brandeis firm could not properly represent the lessees in an action brought by a beneficiary of the trust. If there had been a dispute between the trustees and the lessees, the Brandeis firm could, of course, represent neither. There is an inherent possibility of conflict between the trustees and the lessees, it being the duty of the trustees to gain as much from the property as possible, and the natural inclination of the lessees to pay as little as possible. To this relationship, which involves a troublesome problem, we must return.

The Committee, however, did not raise this problem. To the criticism it did see fit to make there is little merit. The Committee report asserts that Brandeis represented two clients "whose interests were diametrically opposed to each other and when they, later, went to law over those same conflicting interests he took employment for one of them against the other." This is reckless talk. The only parties who ever "went to law" against each other were Ned and the lessees. Except as a member of the family group which had a common interest in the total situation, Ned was never represented by Brandeis. His interests as an heir in 1888 were represented in the sense that he was a member of a family which was making a common arrangement to deal with a common problem. Assuming that at that stage Ned's interest was technically in conflict with that of the lessees, Canon 6 [of the American Bar Association *Canons* of 1908] expressly provides that one is not "to represent conflicting interest, except by express consent of all concerned given after a full disclosure of the facts." Ned, whose dealings were essentially with his brother, Sam, completely consented to the whole arrangement and executed papers to that effect. As an individual he never paid a nickel to Brandeis. After 1890, except for drawing a will for Ned on one of his visits to Boston, Brandeis never—even in a technical sense—represented Ned or had any dealings with him.

We are here clearly concerned with three separate interests: those of the beneficiaries, the trust and the lessees. Simply because one of several beneficiaries becomes dissatisfied with the policies which a trust has been following and seeks to have them set aside does not require counsel to abandon the trustees who have employed him. As the majority of the Judiciary Committee said, "It would have been virtually a desertion if the counsel for the trustee and his firm had failed to act." Senator Walsh, noting that Ned had made no disclosures to the firm, confidential or otherwise, asked:

> Can it be that when the title of the trustee or his administration of the trust is attacked by one of the beneficiaries the attorney for the trustee can not represent him, because, forsooth, the former has been drawing pay out of funds which belong equitably in part to the suing *cestui?* Is an attorney for a corporation precluded from defending its directors when assailed in court for maladministration? Is the attor-

ney for an executor or an administrator? The suggestions must have been made unreflectingly.

The real problem is not whether Brandeis could properly represent either the trustees or the lessees against Ned, but whether he could ethically represent both the trustees and the lessees simultaneously. This was the principal matter that troubled Senator Works; his concern was not that Brandeis should have abandoned the representation in 1909, but that he erred in permitting the firm to represent both the trustee and the lessees in 1889. For a twenty-year period he was paid for services to both; and at the beginning of the relationship he represented the [legatees under S.D. Warren's will] as well.

Except where consent is given it is poor practice for an attorney to represent both a trust and someone leasing property from a trust. In Opinion No. 60 of the American Bar Association Committee on Legal Ethics, a trust company was trustee for an estate which it held for the life of A, with remainder over to various other persons. The remaindermen can be considered to be in a position roughly similar to that of the beneficiaries under the Warren trust. The trust company, having sold property to C, filed an action seeking a court order declaring this sale legal. The remaindermen objected to the sale. The same lawyer represented the trust company, the purchaser, and the life tenant. This was held to be a clear violation of Canon 6 on Conflicts of Interest. The Committee said:

> The attorney for the purchaser * * * could not properly also act for the trustee. * * * The litigation that followed was caused by the different estimates of value placed on the property by the purchasers and the beneficiaries of the trust funds. The real question then was one between the purchaser and the beneficiaries of the trust. It was the duty of the trustee, inherent in its fiduciary capacity, to protect the interest of these beneficiaries. That duty could not be performed for it by an attorney who represented an adverse interest.

Assuming Opinion No. 60 to be correct, it differs from the Warren case first, as has been noted, because of the element of consent. It differs even more fundamentally because of the family nature of the transaction. When the elder Warren died, the Warren family faced a problem together. There is no canon of legal ethics which requires each of the relatives of the deceased to take different counsel to the funeral: if a half-dozen heirs were required to pay a half-dozen counsel, they would indeed have additional grounds for grief. Sherman L. Whipple, trial counsel for Ned in the 1909 litigation, testified at the 1916 hearing that given a situation of "perfect understanding and accord among all the members of the family" at the time the trust and lease arrangement was established, there could be no criticism of Brandeis's role. "[I]f that was so, and all parties assented, there was no moral wrong."

Presumably the reason the Republican minority did not rest its argument on the original multiple representations was that Senator

Cummins rejected the suggestions that "it was improper for Mr. Brandeis to represent the heirs, trustees, and lessees in the original arrangement, because there were or might be conflicting interests. * * *" Senator Works, however, saw the problem differently. While his position is ambiguous, he seemed to think it was a "bad practice" to represent a group in this situation. Moorefield Storey—a distinguished Boston attorney, a regular adversary of Brandeis, and a former president of the American Bar Association—was one of Ned Warren's counsel. Storey on the one hand seemed to agree with Works that this was a "bad practice," and yet he testified, "[I]f I had been in Mr. Brandeis's shoes when that situation came up, I think I would have taken the same course."

Once the facts of family representation and general consent of all parties to the basic arrangement are recognized as the essentials of the situation, the Warren charge evaporates. Granting that, as a fresh matter under Opinion No. 60, a scrupulous attorney might not enter such a situation after conflicts have already arisen, once he is innocently in the situation, there is no direction to go but forward. The lawyer cannot lightly withdraw from a representation once undertaken; as Canon 44 provides, he "should not throw up the unfinished task to the detriment of his client except for reasons of honor or self-respect." From 1889 to 1903, Ned Warren, both by express writing and by complete absence of objection, accepted the trust and lease arrangements. In 1903 he obtained independent counsel and was well represented at all subsequent times. In 1909 he brought a lawsuit. For Brandeis to have failed to defend against that suit would have been, as the majority concluded, desertion of a plain duty.

Notes and Questions

1. Please review the discussion of the American legal profession's modern regulatory rules on conflicts of interest and "inter-mediation," in our notes after *Pigg v. Haley,* supra. Would those rules have made it easier for Mr. Frank to analyze Brandeis's behavior in the Warren matter?

2. Mr. Frank says that Ned Warren "was never represented by Brandeis." What other word would he prefer to use for the services Brandeis performed in Ned's behalf as legal counsel for: (a) Mr. and Mrs. S.D. Warren; (b) the Warren family (all living generations); (c) Mrs. S.D. Warren; (d) the estate of S.D. Warren; (e) the trust established by the family and the S.D. Warren estate; (f) the business; and (g) the three operators of the business?

3. The professional rules that have developed from Canon 60 of the A.B.A. *Canons* of 1908 have repeated the importance of informed consent when a lawyer acts for a group of clients. They have tended also to emphasize a second requirement that may or may not be implicit in Mr. Frank's discussion: the lawyer's personal judgment, about the situation and about the lawyer's own abilities and temperament, when it comes to undertaking the delicate mediative tasks involved in being a family lawyer in property matters. That requirement of honest self-assessment was

expressed in the 1969 A.B.A. *Code* in terms of "independent professional judgment." It includes, under Rule 2.2 of the proposed *Rules* of 1983, the lawyer's ability to seek the "best interests" of the "clients" (plural) who employ him, on the one hand, and, at the same time, the individual interests of *each* of the individuals who belong to the group for whom he is working. How does it affect such a complex judgment to notice, as Mr. Frank does, "the family nature of the transaction"?

4. Mr. Frank notes that Ned Warren made no confidential disclosures to the trustees or to Brandeis. Two questions about that:

(a) How likely is it that Ned, in need of money, in London, would have made no confidential disclosures to his mother and his older brother? What is Mr. Frank doing with this word "trustees"?

(b) What difference would it have made, in Mr. Frank's analysis of Brandeis's behavior, if Ned had made confidential disclosures to Brandeis or to one of the trustees? (Maybe a context is possible if we think of Ned, living in London as an antique dealer in the Edwardian era, and doing the expensive things Edwardian gentlemen did, some of which—as in the case of King Edward VII himself—were probably best kept confidential.)

Notice, in this regard, the comment to A.B.A. Model Rule 2.2, in a situation where one member of the family has a legitimate interest in keeping information secret and other members have a legitimate interest in having the same information: "In a common representation, the lawyer is still required both to keep each client adequately informed and to maintain confidentiality of information relating to the representation. * * * Complying with both requirements while acting as intermediary requires a delicate balance. If the balance cannot be maintained, the common representation is improper."

5. "Estate planning" for two-generation family businesses is one of the most ordinary and complex assignments a property lawyer has. Division of interests is an important compartment in the property-lawyer's tool box in this sort of work. For examples:

— conveyance of the property to a corporation, with issuance of corporate stock to members of the family: The property ownership is then in the corporation, a legal person in its own right; it will not die; ownership of the stock passes among generations and between people in one generation.

— division of ownership interests, as in the Warren family, into ownership-as-burden (management of the property) and ownership-as-benefit (what Ned Warren had), so that some members of the family can carry on (and therefore control) the business, and others can take the profits from it without responsibility for business decisions. This can be done through the corporate form; for example, a family-business corporation can issue different classes of stock, divided according to dividend rights or voting rights. It can also be done with partnership interests (including division of interests between limited-partnership interests and "general" partnership interests).

— Brandeis used corporate division of ownership interests. He also used the two other kinds of division of property interests that we have been discussing:

(i) He divided S.D. Warren's business property into legal and equitable interests, by putting the property in a trust, so that the trustees thereafter had the common-law property ownership and the beneficiaries of the trust had the equitable property ownership. This was what the lawyer for the Franciscan friars did with property that pious landowners in medieval England wanted to give to them. It was a matter of invoking both of the two systems of English property law.

(ii) He divided the legal ownership into a leasehold interest—a term of years—and a reversion. The business entity (a corporation or a partnership; maybe bits of both) was the tenant of the paper mill; the trustees were the fee-simple title holders, which meant they held the reversion. Brandeis spread the ownership of the paper mills on the plane of time.

6. For some reason these divisions of ownership were not established in S.D. Warren's will. They were fashioned by the family lawyer and agreed to by all members of the family, after Mr. Warren died. Mr. Frank does not describe what the will provided; it might have differed radically from what the family, with Brandeis's help, did with S.D. Warren's property. The legal policy that allows even radical readjustments of the plan of a deceased property owner is expressed in § 3–912 of the Uniform Probate Code: "[C]ompetent successors may agree among themselves to alter the interests, shares, or amounts to which they are entitled under the will of the decedent, or under the laws of intestacy, in any way that they provide in a written contract executed by all who are affected by its provisions. The personal representative [executor] shall abide by the terms of the agreement. * * * " If this is the law, why do property owners such as Mr. Warren bother to employ lawyers to "plan" their "estates" and draft wills for them? Among all of the answers that may occur to you to that question, please consider the relevance of the following passages from a study of decedents' estates, families, and property lawyers in Cuyahoga County (Cleveland), Ohio:

MARVIN B. SUSSMAN, JUDITH N. CATES, AND DAVID T. SMITH, THE FAMILY AND INHERITANCE, CH. 6, "CONCEPTIONS OF JUSTICE: THE HEIRS"

pp. 121–145 (1970).[14]

The decedent's conception of justice is embodied in his last will and testament, in which his worldly goods are distributed among specified persons or institutions. His conception may or may not correspond to that of his heir.[15] If it does not, the heirs may react with anger or guilt

---

14. Excerpts from a study of the distribution of property interests, after the deaths of owners, in Cuyahoga County (Cleveland), Ohio.

15. The term heirs is used [by Sussman, Cates, and Smith] in a lay person's sense, to indicate those who inherit either by testate or intestate succession. As lawyers

and proceed to rectify the situation. In some cases, these testate successors may make a redistribution of the property of the decedent.

Society's conception of justice may be considered to be shown by the [statutes prescribing intestate distribution]. The heirs in the intestate case may * * * react with anger or guilt if this distribution is not fair, and they may also attempt to change the distribution. In the absence of a will that would express the decedent's wishes, the heirs may redistribute the estate according to their own ideas of justice or in accordance with their interpretation of the decedent's wishes.[16]

* * *

The number of testate cases in which the [legatees under the will] redistributed the estate was small. From this, it may be inferred that the testator's disposition of the estate was satisfactory in most instances or that the [legatees] were unable to agree on a more satisfactory disposition.

There were only 50 cases of redistribution among the 360 testate cases for which interviews were obtained. In 21 of these cases, the redistribution involved a car; most often a spouse who was the sole beneficiary gave the car to a son or daughter. Some of these cars might almost be considered mementos. * * *

In 29 cases, the redistribution concerned something other than a car. In 17 of these cases, the survivors were a spouse and lineal descendants. Where the spouse was the sole beneficiary, the redistribution involved giving part or all of the estate to the children. The most interesting cases were those involving real estate.

    Case 361. The decedent willed the house, which was not held jointly, to his 80–year–old wife, who then transferred it to their only son. The son and his wife lived with the parents; and the father had wanted to put the house in the son's name several years before, but the son felt at that time it would "be rushing things."

    Case 391. The decedent left her estate, which consisted of half a house, to her 78–year–old husband. He has deeded the house to their daughter and also made his own bank account joint with her. The daughter, who is single, does not live with him but in another state. Another daughter is deceased. His first will left everything to his wife. He does not plan to make a new will since he has signed everything over to his daughter.

    Case 256. The decedent left her half of the house to her 79–year–old husband. He sold the house and divided the money among his two sons and a deceased son's widow. Each of them has put $1,000 of the $2,500 received into a bank account to take care of the father if he should need medical care. "So far this money hasn't been touched, but

---

use the word heir means a person entitled to an intestate's realty and, at most, the successor to either real or personal property via intestate succession.

16. Cf. the modern statutes on "family settlements" discussed in Note "2" of the Notes and Questions after *Pigg v. Haley, supra.*

he is getting old and senile and we may have to put him in a nursing home. He is getting too hard for us to handle."

Case 632. The decedent willed her half of two houses to her 69–year–old husband. The husband has deeded the houses to their son and daughter. The children make their homes in these properties, and the widower lives with his daughter. The son commented that he and his sister signed a statement guaranteeing that they will provide for their father if this becomes necessary. * * *

Where lineal heirs were the surviving kin, redistribution occurred in only nine cases. In three of these cases, the redistribution was of a minor nature. Three other cases involved disinheritance or a situation bordering on disinheritance.

Case 586. The decedent was a 75–year–old widow whose only property was a house worth $14,000. The will had been made thirteen years before her death, when her husband was still living. Five of the six children were contingent beneficiaries. One daughter had been disinherited because she had married a divorced man. After a period of years, there was a reconciliation, but the will was not changed. Instead, the widow called her five children together and told them to include their sister. This they did. The decedent's oldest daughter had lived with her and according to the will should have received $1,000 more than her siblings. The relationships between the siblings were so precarious, however, that this daughter felt it would be wiser to take only an equal share. "I didn't take it because I didn't want any bad feelings." Although some disapproval of her care of the mother was voiced by other members of the family, the sentiment expressed to us by several members was that she deserved the extra portion. "All the money in the world couldn't repay her care of Mother." It was also mentioned that one of the sons disapproved of sharing the estate with the disinherited daughter.

Case 611. A widowed male divided his $19,000 estate among four of his five children. To the fifth child, a son, he left $300 and notes from a $400 debt. The son had borrowed the money during the Depression to help pay college expenses. Otherwise, he had paid his own way and was the only one to go to college. He renounced his inheritance, and his legacy reverted to the residue. * * *

There were three cases of redistribution where collateral kin were the survivors and [legatees].

Case 509. A second cousin of the decedent put her $14,000 inheritance in a trust fund for her daughter. She felt the decedent wanted the daughter to have the inheritance.

Case 636. Ten nieces and nephews inherited. "Three of the rich relatives turned their shares over to the niece who had the least money of the living relatives."

Case 589. The decedent's two sisters were her only legatees. They gave $500 to their disinherited brother.

The last will and testament accurately depicts the disposition of the decedent's assets in the vast majority of testate cases; there was a redistribution in only 14 per cent of the cases. Where redistribution did occur, it generally reflected differential services or needs of the heirs....

[M]ajor redistributions occurred in over 50 per cent of [all] cases. [This means the rate of redistribution where the decedent had no will was much higher than the rate where there was a will.] Knowledge of such redistribution was obtained from interviews with the heirs. Thus, for the single purpose of knowing how the decedent's estate was actually distributed, the interviews with intestate heirs were more important than those conducted with the survivors of testate decedents.
* * *

There were 74 cases in which the spouse and lineal descendants or ascendants survived. * * * In 38 cases, the spouse received all or more than the intestate share, most often because others who had claims to the estate signed over their shares. * * *

Why do people give up their rights in property by signing over their share to the decedent's spouse? * * *

The remarks of the children who had given up a share in their deceased parent's estate indicated that they made no searching analysis in reference to this decision. It was a matter-of-fact action; in their family it was the right and proper thing to do. "Why take the home away from an older parent who is still living? It is my mother's home." "Mother is more entitled to it than anyone else. She worked hard for that home." "The wife should be entitled to everything unless it's a second marriage." "Mother needs everything, she has many years ahead of her; she shouldn't have to be dependent on her children."

The parents who were the recipients of their children's generosity similarly took the action for granted for the most part. "My children wouldn't do that—not see that I have enough to live on." "The intestate pattern isn't fair. The wife should get it all. She should be able to do what she needs to do. My daughter is further ahead in her twelve years of marriage than we were much later." "If I get sick, I need the money; it is my security." * * *

[I]n testate cases, the testator usually willed the entire estate to the spouse. In intestate cases, adult children usually signed over their shares of the estates to the surviving parents. * * *

An exception to the spouse-all pattern occurred in the case of remarriage. In both testate and intestate cases, these estates were more likely to be divided between spouse and children than were those in which the spouse was the parent of the surviving children. * * *

Equality of distribution among descendants is subscribed to by more descendants than decedent testators. Among the testators, 43 per cent deviated from equality of distribution among equally related lineal kin. Nearly 75 per cent of the intestate descendants were content with equality and did not redistribute the estate. Where one child assigned his share to a sibling, it was often in payment for the final care rendered the deceased parent.

KEVIN J. CROY, "EXECUTIVE RIGHT IN A MINERAL ESTATE IS A SEPARATE INTEREST IN REAL PROPERTY SUBJECT TO PROPERTY LAW PRINCIPLES: *DAY & CO. V. TEXLAND PETROLEUM, INC.,* 786 S.W.2D 667 (TEX. 1990)"

22 Texas Tech Law Review 281 (1991).

(Most footnotes omitted.)

Mildred Keaton and Francell Young conveyed eighty acres of land by warranty deed to Day & Company, Inc. ("Day, Inc.") By the deed, Keaton and Young reserved an undivided one-half mineral interest but expressly conveyed all executive rights. Thus, Keaton and Young owned a nonexecutive, one-half mineral interest in the eighty acres, and Day, Inc. owned the surface estate, one-half the mineral estate, and all of the executive rights. Thereafter, Day, Inc. conveyed ten acres of the eighty acre tract by warranty deed to John and Genelda Shoaf, excepting and reserving an undivided one-fourth mineral interest. Although the deed excepted the one-half mineral interest previously reserved to Keaton and Young, it did not mention the executive right granted to Day, Inc. by the conveyance from Keaton and Young.

The Shoafs and Day, Inc. executed mineral leases.[17] Texland Petroleum, Inc. ("Texland") subsequently acquired the leases covering all eighty acres. However, Day Inc., believing that Texland's predecessor in interest had failed to maintain his lease to Keaton and Young's nonexecutive mineral interest, attempted to exercise the executive right to the Keaton and Young interest by leasing the minerals to Bobby G. Day. After executing this lease, Day, Inc. and Bobby Day sued Texland and the Shoafs for a declaration that Day, Inc. owned three-fourths of the executive rights covering the Shoaf's ten acre tract. The trial court granted Texland's motion for summary judgment, and the court of appeals affirmed. On Appeal, the Texas Supreme Court initially reversed the lower courts. However, upon granting Texland's motion for rehearing, the court withdrew its opinion and substituted a new opinion affirming the court of appeals. In the new opinion, the supreme court held that the executive right in a mineral estate, even when severed from the other rights incident to the mineral estate, is an interest in real property subject to principles of property law. * * *

An overwhelming number of American jurisdictions recognize that land may be severed into two estates—the surface estate and the mineral estate. The mineral estate is the most complete ownership of oil and gas recognized in law, and, as a consequence, essential rights,

---

17. Specifically, the deed conveyed to Day, Inc. "the power to execute any and all future leases for the development of said lands or any portion thereof, for oil, gas or other minerals."

powers, privileges and attributes are attendant to the estate. Generally, there are five essential attributes of the severed mineral estate: 1) the right to develop; 2) the right to receive royalty payments; 3) the right to receive bonus payments; 4) the right to receive delay rentals; and 5) the right to lease. The right to lease, also known as the "leasing right" or the "executive right," is defined as the right to execute oil and gas leases to secure the exploration and development of the minerals. It is well established that the executive right may be severed from the mineral estate. Once severed, the executive right may be conveyed or reserved upon any terms that the mineral owner deems proper. * * *

Although courts clearly recognize the existence of the executive right, they have found themselves confronted with problems concerning alienability and duration of the right. In this regard, a question arises as to whether the right may be inherited or assigned when the original deed reserves or conveys the executive right to the grantor or grantee, but is silent as to "heirs and assigns." A survey of case law reveals that in California, Kentucky and Oklahoma, the executive right is inheritable or assignable where expressly provided for by words of duration. However, where the deed is silent as to words of duration, and the executive right holder fails to exercise the right while alive, Oklahoma classifies the executive right as a personal nonassignable, noninheritable right that terminates upon the holder's death.[18] Until recently, Texas was in accord with these jurisdictions in determining whether the executive right was assignable or inheritable. * * *

[T]he court's opinion eliminates the requirement that there be "something to indicate that the parties intended that the power should survive and be exercised by others." In other words, now that the executive right is recognized as an interest in land as opposed to a contractual right, there is no need for words of duration in the original deed conveying or reserving the right to indicate that the grantor and grantee intended the right to be assignable or inheritable. Furthermore, as an interest in real property, the executive right possesses the attributes commonly associated with a fee simple absolute. Accordingly, the executive right is now freely assignable, devisable, and inheritable. * * *

The *Day* court's rejection of the [old Texas] rationale appears logical and sound. No valid reason exists for treating a severed executive right any differently from an executive right that remains bundled with the other attributes of the mineral estate. The character, purpose and consequence of the executive right remains the same whether the mineral owner retains the right with all or a portion of the mineral estate, severs the right and reserves it in himself, or severs the right and conveys it to another. In the latter two situations, the power

18. In terms of ownership spread on the plane of time, the Oklahoma executive right in the mineral estate, when the deed is silent as to words of duration, looks very much like a medieval deed of real estate "from A to B." Compare Texas law on the point, as a result of this case, and modern treatment of the "from A to B" deed. (Eds.)

of the executive right is not diminished by its severance from the mineral estate. Indeed, the executive right holder in all three situations would have identical rights and privileges in exercising the power to lease. * * *

Notes and Questions

1. Why might an owner of the fee simple in a piece of promising Texas land want to reserve, or give to a separate grantee, the executive right in his mineral estate? Suppose the owner is a busy lawyer whose law practice takes more of his time than it should.

2. Why would anyone want to own the mineral estate but not own the executive right in a piece of promising Texas land? Suppose the potential owner is an investor in oil and gas properties (but not a developer of oil and gas wells). Suppose the mineral estate without the executive right is all the investor is interested in purchasing. Or, in the alternative, suppose the investor seeks to buy the surface estate, but not the mineral estate, and the executive right is in a developer.

III. OWNERSHIP SUBJECT TO CONDITION

It is possible to put conditions on common-law and equitable forms of property ownership. It is possible to put: (i) conditions that must be satisfied before any ownership will occur (conditions precedent); and (ii) divesting conditions that will end ownership after it begins (divesting conditions):

— *precedent:* to Mary and her heirs when she marries a Presbyterian;

— *divesting* : to Mary and her heirs, but if she marries a Presbyterian she loses the property.

In the first example, Mary has a future interest in fee simple; in the second she has a possessory fee simple subject to a divesting condition. It is possible to put conditions such as these on any of the interests that occur when a lawyer spreads ownership on the plane of time or divides up the bundle of present possessory property interests an owner has:

— *precedent* : to Henry for life then to Mary and her heirs if Mary has by then married a Presbyterian (contingent remainder in fee simple);

— *divesting* : subsurface water rights to Henry for life so long as he uses the water to make moonshine whiskey and at his death to Mary and her heirs but if Mary marries a Presbyterian she loses the water rights (life estate in water rights subject to a divesting condition, followed by a remainder in fee simple in the water rights, which remainder is subject to a different divesting condition).

And it is possible, as we will see in more detail in the next section, to put these conditions on forms of ownership that are created under equitable rules, as well as on forms of ownership that are created under common-law rules:

— *example* : to Uncle Theodore and his heirs, for the use of (or in trust for) Henry for life then to the children of Mary *then living* and their heirs (legal fee simple in Theodore; equitable life estate in Henry followed by a contingent remainder in fee simple in those of Mary's children who survive Henry).

Conditions take up an important compartment in the property-lawyer's tool box; they do not make it possible to see into the future, but they make it possible to plan for the future by providing for changes in ownership based on foreseeable events. The effective use of conditions benefits from clients' and their lawyers' creative imagination as they think about what might happen.

The effective use of conditions also requires careful use of language in drafting wills, deeds, and trust documents. One of the principal sources of litigation over conditions are muddles from lawyers' language that might have created a condition, but might also have created some other device that can be used to hedge against the future. A condition on ownership is a definitive limit on what the owner has. It is not (i) a statement of desire, which is not legally enforceable but may (as we saw, above, in the Cuyahoga County probate study) be a powerful influence on members of the family:

— *example* : "to my son John, and I hope he will use the land as a farm."

Nor is a condition (ii) a promise (or covenant), which may be legally enforceable through damages:

— *example* : Alfonso grants Blackacre to Bianca in fee simple; Bianca promises not to keep animals on the property. She nonetheless installs goats in the front yard. Alfonso has a cause of action for breach.[19]

With those distinctions in mind, it is possible for a lawyer to provide clients with forms of ownership that will become vested or come into possession when conditions are met, or will terminate on the happening of conditions, or will do both. The ability to prescribe conditions is important to clients, both when clients want to control what happens with their property, and when clients want to control people through defining interests in property:

— to Mary and her heirs, but if she marries John she will lose the land;

— to Henry until he is of age;

— to Alice for ten years, then to Sam and his heirs so long as he remains a Catholic;

— to the school board so long as it uses the property for a school;

— to the lodge but if the lodge does not use the property for its lodge building, the property reverts to the grantor.

---

19. He may also have a cause of action for equitable enforcement, as we will see   when we study the law of neighbors.

MAYOR AND CITY COUNCIL OF
OCEAN CITY v. TABER

Court of Appeals of Maryland, 1977.
279 Md. 115, 367 A.2d 1233.[20]

ORTH, JUDGE.

This appeal concerns the ownership of an improved lot of ground at the northwest corner of Atlantic Avenue and Caroline Street in Ocean City, Maryland, which was occupied and used by the United States of America as a Life Saving Station for almost a hundred years. At the hub of the controversy is whether the United States acquired title in fee simple absolute through adverse possession or lost all its right, title, interest and estate in the property by realization of a possibility of reverter.

I

The relevant record title to the property devolves through three conveyances: 1) a deed dated 28 July 1876 from Stephen Taber and wife to Hillary R. Pitts, Benjamin Jones Taylor and George W. Purnell,

20. This opinion is difficult to read; you may find yourself wishing that Judge Orth had not studied Latin in prep school. And we realize that you will be reading it to find something that fits our outline (i.e., ownership that is subject in some way to a condition). But you will be rewarded here, we think, by spending some extra time to locate broader property-law context in it.

For instance, the four or five deeds and the local judicial decree the court identifies in the county land records show how "record title" to land is established by a search in the public records in the county courthouse. In times past (and still in some communities), you could almost always find two or three lawyers in the county recorder's office, hauling down and looking through the massive tomes the court here identifies by number. In most cases the search was to back up a lawyer's opinion that her client, or someone her client proposed to deal with, owned the land in question. In a rare case, as here, the "chain of title" is part of the evidence in a lawsuit.

The recorder's office as a place to keep such documents makes the evidentiary agenda easier for trial lawyers and handy for the routine weekday searches of property lawyers. The fact that the documents are there, indexed so that a lawyer can find them, has an effect on ownership, as we will see when we look at the law of conveyancing: In all jurisdictions the presence of the documents in the office gives "constructive" notice to the world of the owner's claim, and in that way controls the assertion, by injured parties, of the claim that they were purchasers without notice of prior conflicting claims to the land. In many jurisdictions a document that is not recorded is by statute, and for most purposes, not even valid.

Another instance of broader context here is the presence of mistakes in documents and the use of devices such as the statute of limitations on property claims to overcome the effect of mistakes: The recorder does not inspect or validate documents; they go into the land records warts and all. And, of course, people go into possession of land thinking that the document with the mistakes in it establishes their titles. Lawyers seeking to protect their clients' title have to take steps to correct mistakes, which steps include quitclaim deeds and the assertion of the statute of limitations (adverse possession). Both devices appear in this story.

Finally, the facts of this case show how property fits into a community with civic purposes and leaders who are out to serve the common good. A town gets started and grows through control of large tracts of real estate. Planners of towns, one way or another, have to provide for essential public services, such as a public life-saving station by the ocean and space for streets and parks. The lawyers for the government of Ocean City failed in this case to gain control of land they thought belonged within these public purposes; but, as you can see by the court's last footnote, they had other cards to play. (Eds.)

Trustees (the Trustees), recorded among the Land Records of Worcester County in Liber I.T.M. No. 4, folios 536–537 (the 1876 deed); 2) a deed dated 11 September 1878 from the Trustees to the United States of America, recorded among the aforesaid Land Records in Liber I.T.M. No. 6, folios 400–402 (the 1878 deed); 3) a deed dated 23 June 1967 from the United States of America to the Mayor and City Council of Ocean City, recorded among the aforesaid Land Records in Liber F.W.H. No. 220, folios 449–451 (the 1967 deed). * * *

II

On 15 January 1869 Stephen Taber and Hepburn S. Benson obtained a patent from the State of Maryland. The patent, preserved in the Hall of Records in Liber W.L. & W.S. No. 2, folios 326–327, gave Taber and Benson "The Lady's Resort to the Ocean," a 280 acre tract of land along the Atlantic Ocean in Worcester County. Taber acquired Benson's interest by deed dated 9 October 1871 and recorded among the aforesaid Land Records in Liber I.T.M. No. 1, folios 591–592.

Stephen Taber created Ocean City, "desirous," as he explained in the 1876 deed, "of conforming to the views and general public sentiment of the people of Worcester and the adjacent counties in their desire to establish a place as a seaside Summer Resort and the promotion of the growth of the same." Fifty acres of "The Lady's Resort to the Sea," with his acquiescence and approval, were "laid off into a town, with lots, streets and avenues, as is called and known as Ocean City," and he granted the fifty acres to the Trustees by the deed of 1876, appending a plat of the proposed town.[21] The terms of the trust were set out in the habendum clause. The Trustees were to hold the property

> upon trust, that they or their successors shall convey the same, with as little delay as practicable, at the expense of the grantee or grantees named in the deeds in lots as they are described on said plat and according to their numbers; to such persons as draw the same at a distribution of said lots, made by the Stockholders of the Atlantic Hotel Company at the Atlantic Hotel at Ocean City on the thirty first day of August Eighteen Hundred and Seventy Five. And if there are any lots remaining which are not drawn at the aforesaid distribution, then and in that event, the said trustees or their successors are hereby authorized and empowered to sell and convey the same to such persons as they think proper or to make any other disposition of said lots they

21. The conveyance excepted and reserved from the fifty acres "so much thereof as has been by deed bearing even date herewith, conveyed to the Atlantic Hotel Company of Berlin, and also so much thereof as has been by deed bearing even date herewith granted to Wiscomico and Pocomoke Rail Road Company, together with the right of said Rail Road Company to occupy not to exceed sixteen feet in width for the construction, maintenance and operation of a rail road through and along Baltimore Avenue its entire length." The grant was also subject to streets and avenues (except Caroline Street) as laid down on the plat. There were 205 lots laid out between Atlantic Avenue on the east, Synepuxent Bay on the west, past Caroline Street on the north and to Division Street on the south.

think proper and appropriate the proceeds thereof in such manner as they shall deem most advantageous to the interest of said Ocean City.

Lot no. 3, as laid out on the plat, was at the northwest corner of Atlantic Avenue and Caroline Street. Its exact size is not shown, for the plat reflects neither lot dimensions nor a scale. It was, however, much larger than the size of the other lots except that of the Atlantic Hotel. It was bounded by the west side of Atlantic Avenue on the east, the north side of Caroline Street on the south and the east side of Baltimore Avenue on the west and was of irregular width.

The deed of 1878 conveyed a part of lot no. 3 to the United States of America. The part conveyed was described as "beginning at the northwest corner of Atlantic Avenue and Caroline Street thence running westerly by and with the north side of Caroline Street one hundred feet thence northerly by a line parallel with Atlantic Avenue fifty feet then easterly by a line parallel to Caroline Street one hundred feet to Atlantic Avenue, hence by and with the west side of Atlantic Avenue fifty feet to the place of beginning, all in Ocean City, County of Worcester and State of Maryland." The deed declared that lot no. 3 had not been drawn in the distribution and that a part thereof had been sold to the United States by the Trustees for the sum of one dollar. The deed recited that the Secretary of the Treasury of the United States had been authorized by Act of Congress of 3 March 1875 "whenever he shall deem it advisable, to acquire, by donation or purchase in behalf of the United States, the right to use and occupy sites for life saving, or life boat stations * * * " and that the Secretary of the Treasury deemed "it advisable to acquire on behalf of the United States the right to use and occupy, the hereinafter described lot of land, as a site for Life Saving Station, as is indicated by his signature hereto. * * * " The Part of lot no. 3 granted by the deed was "for the purpose of a Life Saving Station, and also the right to erect such structures, upon the said land, as the United States may see fit, and to remove any and all such structures and appliances at any time, the said premises to be used and occupied, for the purpose named in said act of March 3, 1875. * * * " The habendum clause read:

> to have and to hold the said lot of land and privileges, unto the United States from this date for the purpose aforesaid. And it is further stipulated, that when the United States shall fail to use the said Life Saving Station, the land hereby conveyed for the purpose aforesaid, shall, without any legal proceedings, suit or otherwise, revert to the said Trustees, their successors and assigns, absolutely, and they shall be entitled to re-enter upon and take possession thereof free from all encumbrances of every nature or kind.

The deed was signed and acknowledged by the Trustees and signed by the Secretary of the Treasury.

The 1967 deed was designated a "quitclaim Deed." The United States of America was "Grantor", and the Mayor and City Council of Ocean City, Maryland, was "Grantee." It witnessed that "the Grantor has remised, released and forever quitclaimed, and by these presents does remise, release and forever quitclaim any and all right, title and interest which [the United States] may have, on an 'as is, where is' basis" to two parcels of land and designated improvements thereon. The first parcel described was the lot conveyed by the 1878 deed.[22] The habendum clause read: "TO HAVE AND TO HOLD the premises herein granted unto the Grantee, its successors and assigns forever." The deed expressly declared that it was "executed and delivered to the Grantee without representations, warranties or covenants, either express or implied."

III

On 17 July 1973 an equity action for a declaratory judgment was instituted in the Circuit Court for Worcester County by Thomas T. Taber, Jr., et alii (appellees) against the Mayor and City Council of Ocean City (appellant), et alii. Motions for Summary Judgment filed by appellees and by appellant were determined without hearing or argument by agreement. The motions were denied on 4 December 1975 with the suggestion that the parties "submit the entire proceeding to the Court upon the pleadings and exhibits in the file." The suggestion was followed. On 17 December all parties, through their counsel, requested that the court "render an Opinion and Order based upon the pleadings and exhibits presently on file herein, after giving due consideration to the memoranda of the various parties filed herein, and render its decision hereon at its earliest convenience without a hearing or taking of testimony on this matter." The court honored the request, and its order came forth on 8 April 1976. Only the Mayor and City Council of Ocean City noted an appeal therefrom to the Court of Special Appeals. We granted a writ of certiorari before decision by that Court.

Appellant would have the 1878 deed be ineffective. Thus, it reasons, the United States, and appellant through privity of estate * * * would have acquired legal title to the property by adverse possession. * * *

The 1878 deed conveyed an estate in fee simple determinable. Such an estate has long been recognized in Maryland. * * * The estate is discussed in 1 H.T. Tiffany, The Law of Real Property § 220 (3rd ed. B. Jones 1939):

> An estate in fee simple determinable, sometimes referred to as a base or a qualified fee, is created by any limitation which, in an otherwise effective conveyance of land, creates an estate in fee simple

---

22. The description of the first parcel in the 1967 deed is the same as the description in the 1878 deed except that the beginning point in the 1967 deed is given as "the northeast corner of Atlantic Avenue and Caroline Street." This is an obvious error, probably arising in the deciphering of the handwriting in the 1878 deed.

The second parcel as described in the 1967 deed was a lot fifty feet wide and one hundred feet deep immediately adjoining the rear of the first parcel. The deed did not contain a "being" clause, and the source of the title to the second parcel was not disclosed therein and does not appear in the record before us. It follows that the resolution of the case *sub judice* does not affect this second parcel.

and provides that the estate shall automatically expire upon the occurrence of a stated event.

* * *

No set formula is necessary for the creation of the limitation, any words expressive of the grantor's intent that the estate shall terminate on the occurrence of the event being sufficient. * * * So, when land is granted for certain purposes, as for a schoolhouse, a church, a public building, or the like, and it is evidently the grantor's intention that it shall be used for such purpose only, and that, on the cessation of such use, the estate shall end, without any re-entry by the grantor, an estate of the kind now under consideration is created.

* * *

If one who has an estate in fee simple creates a determinable fee in favor of another, he has thereafter merely a possibility of re-acquiring the land by reason of the occurrence of the contingency named or indicated, this possibility being known as a possibility of reverter.

See Restatement of Property § 44 (1936). We described a possibility of reverter in *Ringgold v. Carvel* * * * (1950):

A possibility of reverter is any reversionary interest which is subject to a condition precedent. * * * When the owner of an estate in fee simple absolute transfers an estate in fee simple determinable, the transferor has a possibility of reverter. In other words, if one who has an estate in fee simple creates a determinable fee in another, he has thereafter merely a possibility of reobtaining the land by reason of the occurrence of the indicated contingency. Thus, where land is devised for a certain purpose, and it is the testator's intention that it shall be used for that purpose only, and that on the cessation of such use, the estate shall end without re-entry by the grantor, a possibility of reverter arises. * * * In case of a diversion of the land from the purpose for which it was devised, the heirs of the testator may be entitled to have the land again by reverter.[23]

What the United States acquired in the property was a determinable fee and nothing more. Of course, the United States had the power to convey what it owned. "The owner of a determinable fee has all the rights of an owner in fee simple * * *; conveyance of the property does not necessarily terminate the fee, but the grantee takes it subject to the same liability to termination as existed before the grant." 1 H.T. Tiffany, The Law of Real Property, § 220 (3rd ed. B. Jones 1939). Thus, having validly acquired a determinable fee, the United States could convey it. This it did by the 1967 deed, which remised, released and forever quitclaimed any and all right, title and interest which it had

---

23. A reversion, on the other hand, is "any reversionary interest which is not subject to a condition precedent. * * * It is the residue of an estate left in the testator to commence in possession after the determination of some particular estate devised by him. Hence, a reversion arises whenever the owner of real estate devises or conveys an interest in it less than his own. The logical conception of it in the common law is that it is a return by operation of law to the owner of a portion of that which he owned before and in reality had never lost."

and on an "as, where is" basis. The United States expressly made no warranties or covenants with reference to the property. The most that appellant acquired from the United States as to the first parcel described in the 1967 deed was a determinable fee, subject to the liability to termination set out in the 1878 deed. The trial judge "specifically" found that the 1967 deed established "the fact that the United States of America, as of that date, did 'fail to use the said Life Saving Station.' " This finding was not clearly erroneous. Maryland Rule 886. It is ironic that evidence of the occurrence of the event terminating the estate was supplied by delivery of the 1967 deed conveying the determinable fee. The estate in fee simple determinable having terminated, the property reverted, and appellant was left with no right, title, interest or estate whatsoever. * * *

We note that, as the 1878 deed was in full force and effect, the statutory period for adverse possession would not start to run until 23 June 1967, the date of the occurrence of the event terminating the estate of fee simple determinable as found by the trial judge. Code (1957, 1973 Repl.Vol.) Art. 21, § 6–103 (now Real Property Art. § 6–103) provides:

> Possession of land * * * after termination of an estate of fee simple determinable shall be deemed adverse and hostile * * * from the occurrence of the event terminating an estate of fee simple determinable.

The trial judge correctly found that appellant had not acquired title by virtue of adverse possession.

Appellant asks if the appellees are "estopped from asserting a claim to the premises under the theories of estoppel, waiver or laches?" In the circumstances, it is patent that they are not. The 1878 deed divided the fee simple absolute estate in the property into the fee simple determinable estate conveyed by the Trustees and a possibility of reverter which remained in the hands of the Trustees. As we have observed, when the United States stopped using the property for a Life Saving Station, there was a diversion of the land from the purpose for which it was conveyed, the estate held by the United States was determined, and automatically a fee simple absolute estate was reestablished in those entitled under the original grantors. * * * It was not necessary for appellees to assert a claim to the fee simple absolute estate or to take any other positive action. They acquired a fee simple absolute estate by the realization of the possibility of reverter. * * *

[O]ur holding here goes only to the first parcel and does not determine any rights with respect to the second parcel.[24]

---

24. In a trial memorandum submitted by appellees and included in the joint record extract, it is averred that by ordinance dated 3 December 1968 appellant enacted legislation to condemn "the land which is the subject matter hereof." Pursuant to the ordinance, appellant instituted a condemnation action in the Circuit Court for Worcester County. We do not know whether this action covered both parcels of land. The outcome of the action is not disclosed in the record before us.

Judgment Affirmed; Costs To Be Paid By Appellant.

HIGBEE CORPORATION v. KENNEDY, EXECUTOR

Superior Court of Pennsylvania, 1981.
286 Pa.Super. 101, 428 A.2d 592.

PRICE, JUDGE.

* * * [A]ppellant, James J. Kennedy * * * contends that the trial court erred in determining that his interest in the disputed tract of land was a fee simple determinable. For the following reasons we agree with appellant and, therefore, reverse the order and remand for further proceedings consistent with this opinion. * * *

The trial court relied upon the following provision contained in the original grant to Kennedy's property in reaching its determination.

To have and to hold the said piece of land above-described the hereditaments and premises hereby granted or mentioned and intended so to be with the appurtenances unto the said party of the second part his heirs and assigns to and for the only proper use and behoof of the said party of the second part his heirs and assigns forever provided the party of the second part his heirs and assigns wishes to make use of it for the purpose of a road. The party of the second part agrees to keep a good fence around the above-mentioned lot, failing to do so forfeits his claim, whenever the party of the second part wishes to give up his claim to said lot he is to have full privilege to remove all fencing materials whenever the party of the second part his heirs and assigns fails to fulfill this agreement the land is to revert to the party of the first part. * * *

The sole issue for our consideration is whether the estate created by the deed was a fee simple determinable or a fee simple subject to a condition subsequent. A fee simple determinable is an estate in fee that automatically reverts to the grantor upon the occurrence of a specified event. * * * The interest held by the grantor is termed a possibility of reverter. * * * Words of indubitable limitation, such as "so long as," "during," "while" and "until," are generally used to create the fee simple determinable. * * *

"If, on the other hand, the deed conveyed a fee simple subject to a condition subsequent, then upon the noncompliance with the stated condition the grantor or his successor in interest would have the power to terminate the preceding estate. Thus, the grantors would have a right of re-entry." *Stolarick v. Stolarick* [1976]. * * * At common law conditional language in conjunction with a clause granting the grantor or his successors the right to re-enter and terminate the estate upon breach of condition was required to create the fee simple subject to a condition subsequent. * * * "The principal distinction between the two estates is that a right of re-entry requires some action to perfect title by the grantor or his successor, while a reverter vests automatically." Restatement of Property § 57 (1936). * * * "

A grantor and his successor are capable of transmitting both a possibility of reverter and a right of re-entry by inheritance, conveyance, assignment or lease. * * * [25] The grantor is characterized as retaining these interests because when he creates a fee simple determinable or a fee simple subject to a condition subsequent he does not dispose of his entire interest in the land. Therefore, the interests are deemed vested at the time of their creation. * * *

We first examine the effect of the following clause: "forever *provided* the [grantee] his heirs and assigns wishes to make use of it for the purpose of a road." (Emphasis added.) We concur with the parties' consensus that the portions of the deed preceding this phrase create a fee simple. However, we cannot agree with appellee's contention that this conditional language limits the estate to a fee simple determinable. Words such as "provided," "if," or "upon the condition that" express condition and, therefore, indicate the existence of a fee simple subject to a condition subsequent. In *Stolarick v. Stolarick* * * * we held that when conditional language is followed by reverter clause, absent a showing of contrary intent, we will find a fee simple subject to a condition subsequent. * * * [26]

The term "wishes" refers to the state of mind of the grantee. Thus, it is evident that mere nonuse of the property as a road does not establish that the condition has been broken. The estate can be deemed forfeited only upon a showing that the grantee has no inclination to use the property as a road. Since the record does not contain any evidence maintaining that appellant had no desire to use the property as a road, we cannot agree that this provision has been breached.

> We find the following clause more perplexing: the [grantee] agrees to keep a good fence around the above-mentioned lot, failing to do so *forfeits* his claim, whenever the [grantee] wishes to give up his claim to said lot he is to have full privilege to remove all fencing materials whenever the [grantee] his heirs and assigns fail to fulfill this agreement the land is to revert to the [grantor]

---

25. At common law a possibility of reverter was generally viewed as "a mere possibility that a right, or an estate in land, might arise in the future upon the happening of a contingency." *London v. Kingsley* * * * (1951). It could be disposed only by release since it was not categorized as an actual estate in land. * * * However, Pennsylvania has long recognized that the power to alienate a possibility of reverter is in accordance with the public policy favoring the alienability of land, and thus permits the disposition of all reversionary interests, including the possibility of reverter, by devise, grant, assignment or release. * * *

26. In reaching our decision in * * * we cited with approval the following provision of the Restatement of Property [Sec. 45]:

When an otherwise effective conveyance contains a clause which provides that "if," or "upon the condition that," or "provided that" a stated event occurs, then the estate created "shall be null and void" or "shall revert back," a problem in construction is presented as to whether such conveyance creates an estate in fee simple subject to a condition subsequent or an estate in fee simple determinable. Such a conveyance more commonly manifests an intent to create an estate in fee simple subject to a condition subsequent. * * *

(emphasis added). The term "forfeits" is conditional language and, coupled with the absence of words of incontestable limitation, indicates the existence of a fee simple subject to a condition subsequent. The provision of reverter to the grantor, on the other hand, infers that the estate is a fee simple determinable. Since a fee simple determinable automatically divests a grantee of his interest in an estate, without regard to the current status of a grantor or his successors in interest, it is more cumbersome upon the alienability of land than a fee simple subject to a condition subsequent.[27] It is our opinion that the grantor, as draftsman of the deed, bears the heavy burden of using clear and unambiguous language to make explicit his intent to create this type of onerous limitation to an estate in land. * * * Therefore, only in the absence of ambiguity will we find in favor of a fee simple determinable. * * * Accordingly, in absence of contrary intent, we view the conflicting terminology herein as creating a fee simple subject to a condition subsequent.

The order of the court of common pleas is reversed and this action is remanded for further proceedings consistent with this opinion.

Notes and Questions

1. As the *Higbee* court's footnote says, at common law the grantor future interest after either of these defeasible estates was inalienable. That is, (a) no grantee future interest could be created at the time the defeasible interest was created: whatever the future interest was, possibility of reverter or right of entry, it was a grantor future interest; it could only be in the grantor; and (b) the grantor could not separately convey the future interest; he could not one day give a deed that said, "to the bishop so long as the property is used as a cemetery" and then, the next day, give a deed that said, "my possibility of reverter in the cemetery to John." (The reason for this had to do with the common law's horror of assigning causes of action.) But grantors—even altruistic grantors—do not live forever, and these grantor future interests have to survive the deaths of the grantors or the defeasible estate is not, after all, a useful tool for clients. Which is to say that, even though possibilities of reverter and rights of entry are inalienable, as they are in some jurisdictions, they are descendible; they pass to the grantor's heirs. In most American states they are now both alienable and descendible. In some states they cannot be alienated by deed but can be given in the grantor's will (devisable even though not otherwise alienable).

2. Neither *Ocean City* nor *Higbee* involved controversy over whether the event foreseen by the words of condition had occurred. Neither does the Henrico Courthouse case, just ahead, although it clearly could have. That can be a question of fact, a question of local politics, and a question of political policy as well. The Appellate Court of Illinois has dealt with several phrases in such a case, in a series of opinions that span the decade

---

27. Indeed, since a possibility of reverter is not subject to the rule against perpetuities, it can work to divest a party of property centuries after both the grantor and the reason for the condition have ceased to exist.

of the 1980s. It involves a gift made in 1941 by Mr. and Mrs. W.E. Hutton to the trustees of a school in Allison, Illinois, "for school purposes only." A school was built on the property and students studied there until 1973. Since that time, the school authorities have been using the school building for storage.

The Huttons' heirs, a family named Mahrenholz, have been arguing in court since 1974 that the use of the school building for storage caused the "automatic" reversion of possession of the land to them as holders of a possibility of reverter. In a series of opinions in the 1980s, the Appellate Court decided ambiguous language in the deed created a fee simple determinable, which decision vindicated the Mahrenholz's property theory, but, as they found out when they went back to court, did not establish that a reversion of possession had taken place in 1973.

In Mahrenholz v. County Board, 188 Ill.App.3d 260, 135 Ill. Dec. 771, 544 N.E.2d 128 (1989), the court had to consider what "school purposes" means. That appears to be a question of fact, but, as the court treated it, it is more fundamentally (or, if you prefer, more evasively) a question:

—(a) of judicial policy (deference to the local finder of fact, in this case the trial judge, who "conducted a personal inspection and examination of the school and its contents");

—(b) of politics, and politics of a familiar local and often virulent sort, between people who run the public schools and people who disapprove of the way the schools are being run;

—(c) of political theory, that is, of the appropriate deference higher government should, in sound philosophical theory, accord to lower government. It was possible to say that, since "school purposes" were words in a deed, the appellate judges should have asked what those words meant to Mr. and Mrs. Hutton. But the court can be taken to have treated the grant of land here as if it had come from a higher level of government.

See what you think: "The question * * * becomes whether storage of school property constitutes a legitimate 'school purpose.'" Why, we wonder, is *legitimacy* important; the deed says "school purposes only."

The court continued: "We believe that, in general, the answer is yes. School populations are not static. They change from year to year. * * * In order to accommodate such changes, storage facilities are necessary. * * * Clearly, having such equipment and supplies on hand furthers the ultimate goal of educating students. * * * [P]laintiffs contend defendants are using the building for nothing more than a 'dumping ground' * * * while allowing the building to deteriorate. * * * The evidence at trial, however * * * [shows the Board] spent substantial amounts of money to maintain the structure. * * * We * * * will not substitute our judgment for that of the trial court when faced with conflicts in the evidence and issues of the credibility of witnesses. * * *

"We agree with plaintiffs that defendants could have found more convenient storage facilities, which were less expensive to maintain. It is not for us, however, to determine whether defendants' use of the premises is in the best economic interest of the district and its taxpayers."

What, we ask, has sound economy in local government to do with the meaning of "school purposes" in a deed? [28]

PAUL FLETCHER, "COURTHOUSE HEIRS"

Virginia Lawyers Weekly.
July 25, 1988, p. 1.

James Cocke was a man who planned ahead. Some 237 years ahead.

Cocke deeded a half-acre of land to Henrico County in 1751, stipulating that the property be used for a courthouse. In the hand-written deed, Cocke inserted language providing that if the county ever moved the courthouse, "then the said lot shall revert and be the property of James Cocke and his heirs forever."

The following year, Henrico built a courthouse on the corner of what is now 22nd and Main Streets in Richmond. There it stayed until 1840, when it was moved slightly because part of the building was in Main Street. In 1896, the county built the current brick structure, replacing a building burned during the Civil War. At all times, the county courthouse remained on the Cocke property.

Then, in 1975, Henrico moved its courthouse to a new government center in the suburbs of Richmond. The Cocke clan, led by Richmond real estate lawyer Richard Cocke, filed a chancery suit in 1984 [and successfully reclaimed] the property.

[Now the owners have to be found. Who are the heirs, in 1988, of James Cocke?] A thick, two-volume family history entitled "Cockes and Cousins" may * * * prove helpful. Cocke originally filed one volume of the genealogy with his initial suit papers.

Locating all owners may be time-consuming. When asked how long the process might take, Cocke said, "I hope I'm not pipedreaming to say a couple years."

Cocke said he will request that the property be sold, saying it is "unrealistic and impractical" to keep the property in the hands of so many people. * * *

Richard Cocke, the great-great-great-great-grandson of James Cocke, said his "conservative estimate" is that potentially 1,000 heirs might have an interest. * * *

Cocke declined to specify exactly what steps will be taken to locate the heirs, because, he said, he had not met with the commissioner.

However, he thought they would set up some kind of guidelines to insure that reasonable notice is given to potential heirs. "We expect to use the services of a professional genealogist," he said.

28. We pursue this issue further in Ch. Seven.

Notes and Questions

1. *Burby's Real Property 213–214 (3d ed. 1965):* "Usually, the termination of an estate will be denied if there is impossibility of performance with respect to the event or condition involved and the owner of the possessory estate is without fault. * * *

"The termination of an estate cannot be based upon the happening of an event that is illegal or contrary to public policy. * * * A public policy issue may * * * arise in the following situations. The general rule is that a restriction placing a *total* restraint upon marriage is contrary to public policy and void. Some decisions support the rule that while a condition in restraint of marriage is void, a valid gift may be made until the donee remarries. It is considered that such a *limitation* is not designed to prohibit marriage. * * * The preferred view is that partial restraints upon marriage are valid if they are reasonable, such as in a case where the restraint is limited to the minority of the subject. So also, the restraint may prohibit marriage to a particular person, or to a person of a particular religious faith. There is also authority for the view that there may be a restraint against remarriage if a gift is made by one spouse to the other.

"If an otherwise valid restraint upon marriage is embodied in a will, some authorities hold that it is void unless there is a *gift over* upon breach of the condition. It is reasoned that in the absence of a gift over the testator did not intend to make a conditional gift. His purpose was merely to frighten the donee into compliance with the condition. * * * The prevailing rule is that valid restraints may be imposed respecting religious training and practices. Constitutional guarantees as to religious belief are limitations on the powers of government and do not prohibit restraints imposed by individuals."

2. *Review Notes.* What are the interests of Alice and of George after each of the following conveyances:

(a) Alice to George and his heirs.

(b) Alice to George and the heirs of his body.

(c) Alice to George and his heirs so long as the property is used for residential purposes.

(d) Alice to George and his heirs, but if the property is not used for residential purposes, Alice and her heirs shall have a right of entry.

(e) Alice to George for life.

(f) Alice to George for life, then to George's heirs and their heirs.

(g) Alice to George and the heirs of his body, then to the heirs of George and their heirs.

(h) Alice to George and his heirs, and Alice earnestly desires that George use the property only for residential purposes.

(i) Alice to George and his heirs, and George covenants, in consideration of the transfer, that the property will be used only for residential purposes.

3. *Limits on the Creation of Common–Law Future Interests.* There were two limits on the use of conditions under the medieval common-law rules:

First, there could not be a lapse of ownership (or, as the medieval lawyers called it, of seisin). If there was, the interest pegged to a condition precedent would fail. Property lawyers have usually learned this rule as a rule against *springing* interests:

(a) "to Giovanni when he marries Lucia" is a springing interest. It is not the same as "to Carlo for life, then to Giovanni if Giovanni marries Lucia." In the latter case there may not be any springing of ownership in Giovanni; we can wait until Carlo dies to find out. The law can wait until then to see if ownership will lapse. Under the common-law rules, the conveyance failed at the death of Carlo if by then Giovanni and Lucia had not married. If they married during Carlo's life, what was Giovanni's future interest?

(b) "to Carlo for life and then, one day later, to Giovanni and his heirs." The attempt to create a future interest in Giovanni was bad from the beginning because the conveyance had a built-in, one-day lapse in ownership.

The second rule was a rule against *shifts* in ownership after a fee simple. This rule did not forbid conditions subsequent—divesting conditions—on a fee simple. It forbad the creation of further *grantee* interests to take effect after the divestment occurred:

(a) So: "To Maria and her heirs so long as she uses the property as a farm" left a future interest in the grantor.

(b) But: "To Maria and her heirs so long as she uses the property as a farm, then to Juan and his heirs" was an invalid attempt to create a shifting interest in Juan.

The rules permitted the condition on Maria's ownership. When Maria stops farming, her ownership ends and the possession of the property is once again in the grantor. The rules did not permit the creation of a *grantee* future interest (after Maria's fee simple) in Juan. This was an invalid *shifting* interest.

Springing and shifting future interests could be created prior to 1536, but not under common-law rules. The lawyer who was employed to create a shifting or springing future interest had to use the Chancellor's rules, the rules of *equity.* We will look at how that was done, and at what happened in 1536, in the next section.

4. *More Review Notes.*

(a) Assume that O, A, B, and C are alive, unless otherwise indicated, and determine the estate of each of the parties indicated in parentheses:

(i) O → A for life, then to B and his heirs (O, A)

(ii) O → A for life (O, A)

(iii) O → A for life, then to A's children who survive her and their heirs (O; A; C, a child of A, who is living)

(iv) O → A and his heirs so long as he remains in Missouri (O; A; C, A's only son; A is living)

  (v) O → A and his heirs so long as the land is farmed; if the land is not farmed to B and his heirs (O, A, B)

  (vi) O → A and his heirs. The land is to be used for farm purposes only (O, A; C, devisee and sole taker under the will of O, who died last month)

  (vii) O → A and his heirs, but if A fails to graduate from law school, to B and his heirs (O, A, B)

  (viii) O → A for life, then to A's children and their heirs:

    (A) Assuming that A has no children, the interests are * * * (O, A)

    (B) Assuming that A has a child B, the interests are * * * (O, A, B)

    (C) Assuming that A has child B and dies, the interests are * * * (O, B)

  (ix) O → A for life, then to B for life, then to C and his heirs (O, A, B, C)

  (x) O → A for life, then to B and his heirs if B survives A, but if B does not survive A, then to C and his heirs (O, A, B, C)

  (b) O conveys to A and his heirs "so long as the land is farmed." Subsequent to this conveyance, O enters a life-care center to which he is required to transfer all assets, which he does. At his death, he is survived by one heir, B. Last week A quit farming the land. Who owns the land?

IV. CHOICE OF LAW ON OWNERSHIP

A. LEGAL INTERESTS IN MODERN AMERICAN LAW—OFFICE PRACTICE

Consider the situation of a client named Lois Stephens.[29] Mrs. Stephens is a middle-aged wife, mother, and farmer. She has a husband, Carl, and six children. The family farm is owned by her, an inheritance from her family; it has been in her family for more than a century. Their two oldest children are adults: Howard, a 30–year–old bachelor, lives with Carl and Lois and works on their farm; Marie, 27, is married, to Bill; Marie and Bill have two pre-school-age children. Mrs. Stephens has come to the law office to "see about my will," as she puts it. She wants to leave the farm in such a way that Carl and Howard are provided for after her death, if she dies before both of them die. Then, she says, she wants the farm to go to Marie. She says the choice of Marie as ultimate taker is not because of a preference for her daughter over her son, but is because Marie and Bill have children and Howard is, as Mrs. Stephens puts it, "only a bachelor." Mrs. Stephens says this in such a way as to invite the impression that she doesn't think Howard will ever marry. (He is, we know, a reclusive sort and has been heard to express more affection for the hogs he raises than for

---

29. Based loosely on "The Stephens Family of Iowa," one of the six segments in "Six American Families," a series produced on public television in the 1970s by the United Methodist Church.

people outside his own family.) Mrs. Stephens wants to keep the farm in the family.

We raised with Mrs. Stephens the possibility that Howard might marry and have children. We got her to thinking; she does not exclude that possibility and may even hope for it. She went home and pondered, and in a second visit, she tells us she thinks we were right and she has changed her mind: She now wants to leave the farm to Carl for his life, if he survives her, and then to Howard *if* Howard has children. Only if Howard does not have children does she want the farm to go to Marie. This is not a preference for son's children over daughter's children, Mrs. Stephens says, but is due to the fact that Marie and Bill already have a farm.

Suppose we, with our 14–inch yellow pads in hand, come up with this possibility:

> to Carl for life, then to Howard and his heirs, but if Howard dies childless to Marie and her heirs.

And suppose Mrs. Stephens says, "Yes. That's what I want. Just like that."

The problem with that draft is that it involves an attempt to create a grantee future interest after a fee simple, and the common-law rules will not allow that sort of future interest. It is a shifting interest, one of the two kinds of conditional future interests the common-law does not allow. The future interest this draft would create in Marie would come into possession as the result of shifting out of a prior estate. Or, to put it another way, the common law will not allow a remainder after a divesting condition subsequent on a fee-simple estate. (A third way to put it—and you may find any or all of these expressions in the books—is that there cannot be a fee upon a fee.)

We like to create the impression in our law office that there is no difficulty with which we cannot cope. There are three ways to cope with this one:

First: We could draft a different sort of future interest in Marie, one the common law rules will allow. The rule we're having trouble with is a rule about remainders after divesting conditions—that is, conditions subsequent to ownership. The common law will allow a condition *precedent* to ownership, a condition that must be satisfied before a fee simple estate vests. We could say, under common-law rules,

> to Carl for life, then to Howard for life, then, if Howard dies childless, to Marie and her heirs, and, if not, to Howard and his heirs.

That alternative was unattractive in the law offices of our forebears, though, and may be unattractive in ours, because it created contingent remainders (in both Howard and Marie), and contingent remainders could be destroyed. This is probably no longer the case, but it was a serious concern until fairly recently for property lawyers whose clients wanted to keep property in their families and out of the market.

Second: We could do this in two bites: In most (but not all) modern jurisdictions, the problem of the invalid future interest in Marie can be solved by allowing it to remain a grantor future interest instead of drafting so as to create a grantee future interest. This is done by first conveying the present interest (leaving the future interest in the grantor) and then conveying the future interest separately, so that it keeps its character as a grantor interest rather than a grantee interest, a reversionary interest (possibility of reverter or right of entry), rather than an attempted remainder:

> By deed: "I give the farm to Carl for life, then to Howard and his heirs, but if Howard dies childless, the farm shall revert to my estate."

> By will: "I give my right of entry to Marie and her heirs."

In the old English common law, and today in some jurisdictions in the U.S., we could not do it. A right of entry cannot be given by will or by deed in some jurisdictions. (It is, as we have seen, descendible, but it is neither alienable nor devisable.) In some other jurisdictions the conveyance of a grantor interest is valid, but it requires two documents, as above, not merely two paragraphs in the same document.

The third alternative is to use the property rules of equity rather than those of common law: Use the *Chancellor's rules*. Under those rules, we can, as the medieval lawyers put it, *raise a use*. If we do that, we can create in Marie an equitable future interest; the Chancellor did not (and does not) have a rule against shifting future interests. The Chancellor will enforce such an interest in Marie.

If we use the Chancellor's rules, Marie's future interest will not have a common-law name; this is, after all, a different legal system. (The difference is convenient for us in any case; it means we can reserve the word "remainder" to refer to grantee future interests under common-law rules.) The shifting interest under the Chancellor's rules is an *executory interest*. Some scholars, with varying jurisprudential arguments, use other words for it, but we will ignore them.

We create an executory interest by raising a use. A use is one of the ways a property lawyer invokes the Chancellor's rules. It is what the property lawyers of legend did for the Franciscan friars; see the Introduction to Common Law Estates, at the beginning of this chapter. We "raise a use" by conveying legal title to a "feoffee to uses" who will hold the property for "the use of" Carl, Howard, and Marie. The feoffee to uses is a real person, who holds real legal title, but his office is fictional. He doesn't *do* anything. The reason for his existence is to satisfy the common law's demand that property have a *legal* owner (that is, an owner under common-law rules). Carl, or Howard, or Marie, or Marie's family is in possession and for all practical purposes responsible as owners. Their equitable interests, spread on the plane of time, are treated under the Chancellor's rules; they would, but for the use, be treated under common-law rules.

Marie owns the future interest; the difference (which changes in 1536) between her owning it under common-law rules and her owning it under the Chancellor's rules, is the court to which she will repair if she has to sue somebody to get possession of the farm. (After 1536, as we will see, Marie would enforce her interest in the common-law courts.) The vested remainder in fee simple that Howard would have under our original idea, with a shifting interest in Marie, is, then, possible, using the Chancellor's rules: "To T and his heirs for the use of Carl for life, then to Howard and his heirs, but if Howard dies childless to Marie and her heirs." Marie's interest, which cannot be a remainder, is an *executory interest;* [30] and Howard's vested remainder is in fee simple subject to the executory interest (or, as the scholars more commonly put it, to "executory limitation").

This bit of terminology permits a pause in which we can fill out a chart of present possessory and corresponding future interests:

Present	**Future–Grantor**	**Future–Grantee**
Fee Simple	—	—
Fee Tail	Reversion	Remainder
Life Estate	Reversion	Remainder
Fee Simple Defeasible		
a) Fee Simple Determinable	Possibility of Reverter	—
b) Fee Simple Subject to Condition Subsequent	Right of Entry	—
c) Fee Simple Subject to Executory Interest (Chancellor's rules)	—	Executory Interest (Chancellor's rules)

* * *

By the end of the fifteenth century the use of uses by property lawyers had proliferated to the point where it had become a major concern to the common-law bar and to the King. The King was a Tudor in those days, and the Tudors were the architects of the modern English (now British) nation-state; they labored for more than a century—three generations of them—to increase central power in the monarchy. Aggregations of power elsewhere—in the church, in the barons, and even among a certain group of lawyers—was a threat to royal power.

The most memorable of the Tudor kings, Henry VIII (he of the multiple spouses, persecutor of Thomas More), formed a political alliance with the common-law bar, aimed at reducing the power of the

---

30. Dean Phipps (see footnote 8, supra): "Executory Interest: A future interest in someone other than the grantor which according to its terms if it becomes possessory must do so otherwise than as would a remainder." A springing-interest example would be "to T and his heirs for the use of Carl for life, then, one month after the death of Carl, to Marie and her heirs."

chancery (equity) bar, which meant reducing the use of uses. The King was interested in reducing uses because uses were devices for avoiding death taxes payable to the crown. The common-law bar was interested in reducing uses because the chancery bar threatened to dominate green-eyeshade law practice. In one way and another the King and the lawyers managed to get the votes they needed to get corrective legislation through Parliament.

The most enduring result of this property-law alliance was the Statute of Uses, 1536. The novel statutory device invented to cut down the influence of the Chancellor's property rules was to *execute uses*. This device, with characteristic English attachment to the way things are done, left the property tools intact but changed the courts in which the tools were employed: It moved equity's business to the common-law courts. It was as if from henceforth Chevrolets, which will continue in every way to be Chevrolets, will be sold and repaired by Ford dealers.[31]

The Statute of Uses eliminated the jurisdictional distinction between common-law and the Chancellor's rules by making executory interests common-law devices. Executory interests after the Statute were legal interests, not equitable interests. But the Statute did this in a characteristically English way: The English change things by adding to them, not by taking anything away. An old church in England may have a Norman tower built before the year 1200; an Elizabethan central structure, put there twenty years after the Statute of Uses, when all but the tower fell down; a vestry put on in the 18th century; and a sheet-metal lean-to in the back that was put there in 1962 to house the vicar's rather modern lawn tractor. British property law is like that old church. Or, rather, it was until 1925—but we won't get into what happened to British property law in 1925.

The Statute of Uses did not take away or even affect common-law remainders, or defeasible estates, or rights of entry, or possibilities of reverter. We still use them all the time. It did not take away or change any of the possessory estates. It did not take away the executory interest; what it did was to put the executory interest among a different set of lawyers and judges. These were new *common-law* interests, but they were not new property interests. Until modern times (and even in modern times, by force of professional habit) exec-

---

31. The Statute of Uses, as it existed in Missouri until 1983:

456.020 Operation of conveyances to use (Statute of Uses).—Where any person or persons stand or be seized, * * *, of and in any lands, * * *, to the use, confidence or trust of any other person or persons, * * * case all and every such person or persons that have, any such use, confidence or trust, in fee simple for term of life or of years, or otherwise, or any use, confidence or trust, in remainder or reversion, shall from thenceforth stand and be seized, * * * to all intents, constructions and purposes in law, of and in such like estates, as they had or shall have in use, confidence or trust of or in the same; and that the estate, right, title and possession that was or shall be in such person or persons, that were or hereafter shall be seized of any lands, tenements or hereditaments, to the use, confidence or trust of any such person or persons, * * *, be from henceforth clearly deemed and adjudged to be in him, her or them that have or hereafter shall have such use, confidence or trust * * *.

utory interests were (are) set up the same way the old equitable interests had been set up by the chancery lawyers, prior to Henry VIII. *You have to raise a use to create an executory interest:* [32]

(a) In 1600, by common-law conveyance, Oswald conveys Purpleacre to Aiken and his heirs so long as the land is farmed, then to Boswell and her heirs. Immediately after this conveyance, what do Aiken, Boswell, and Oswald own?

(b) What would they have owned if the conveyance had been "to Thompson and her heirs for the use of Aiken and his heirs so long as the land is farmed, then to Boswell and her heirs"?

(c) The common-law rules did not regard a term of years as a form of real-property ownership for purposes of creating future interests. This meant that a contingent interest after a term of years was a springing interest: "to Apple for ten years, then to Burpee and his heirs if Burpee is then living." The future interest in Burpee is void unless the drafter has raised a use. The common-law rules would permit a *vested* interest after a term of years, on the fiction that the vested interest took the ownership immediately, subject to the term of years. So: "to Apple for ten years, then to Burpee and his heirs" was all right under common-law rules; a use was not necessary. Burpee held a possessory fee simple subject to a term of years in Apple.

The Statute of Uses did not change the results in these examples: An attempt to create a shifting or springing interest without raising a use was still void. Executory interests were still valid. What the Statute did was make executory interests—which still had to be created in the same way—legal interests rather than equitable interests. What happened to the "feoffee to uses," the friendly, virtually fictional legal owner who held title under common-law rules? What the Statute of Uses did was to "execute" the use, so that legal and equitable ownership were the same. When legal and equitable ownership are in the same person, they merge into legal ownership only. But the fiction of executing the use still required separation, and a separate legal owner, for a metaphysical instant: The feoffee to uses was still necessary, and was still a fictional office, but he was necessary only for a moment, only

---

32. Does that mean you still raise a use? Maybe. You do not need these days to use "magic words" in creating shifting and springing executory interests. One way to explain that is to say that you still have to raise a use and that the law has dispensed with the magic words. The value of thinking of it that way is that it helps you to remember that it was necessary until fairly recently to use the magic words. In some places in 19th century America, for example, if the drafter wrote, "To A for life and one day later to B and her heirs," the attempt to create an interest (a common-law springing interest) in B would fail. You had to say "To T and his heirs for the use of A for life and one day later to B and her heirs," or in some other way define the interest in a way that, prior to 1536, would have made it equitable. It is not now necessary to convey to the "feoffee to uses" (or to use one of the other ways 16th century English lawyers used to raise a use), but you could argue, if you like metaphysics, that the use is still raised—raised by the necessity to use an executory interest rather than a remainder. One could also argue that such a position is sterile historicism. Take your pick—but remember: (1) If you are asked about the situation in, say, 1700, lawyers then were still using magic words to raise uses; and (2) there remains in modern law a distinction between the remainder and the executory interest, and the distinction makes a difference.

for as long as it took to execute the use and move legal ownership from the feoffee to uses to the beneficial owner of the property. "To Thompson and his heirs for the use of Boswell and her heirs" created a legal fee simple in Thompson, which the statute then executed (meaning it became a legal fee simple in Boswell). The transfer of legal title to the feoffee to uses (Thompson) still occurred, but then, in the twinkling of an eye, his legal title ended. The equitable owner (Boswell) was an equitable owner only for a moment, and then his equitable ownership ended and he was thereafter the legal owner.

Another way to look at this is to say that the statute eliminated the feoffee to uses but not the conveyance to him. You still raised a use by a transfer to the feoffee to uses, but the Statute then "executed" the use by making the beneficial owner's equitable interest a common-law legal interest instead. Whatever equitable ownership the real owner had held in use he now held in common law:

> To T and his heirs for the use of A and his heirs so long as the land is farmed, then to B and his heirs.

Before the Statute, A held an equitable fee simple determinable; after the Statute, A held a legal fee simple determinable. Before the Statute, B held an executory interest under the Chancellor's rules (no interest under common-law rules); after the Statute, B held a legal executory interest. B's interest was still not a remainder; it would not be today. Before the statute T held the legal fee simple; after the statute he still got a legal fee simple but it disappeared as soon as he got it.

To Eustace and her heirs when Eustace marries Tregrear

creates a springing interest in Eustace. To accomplish what the client wants, the lawyer has to raise a use. This was as true after 1536 as it was before. The grantor aims for a fee-simple interest in Eustace at a time in the future. That cannot be done by way of remainder. We will need to say:

> To Thompson and his heirs for the use of Eustace and her heirs when Eustace marries Tregrear.

Before 1536, that would result in an equitable executory interest in Eustace. It could not be a remainder because it sprang. It would not be a remainder today, for the same reason. Before 1536 it was an executory interest under the Chancellor's rules (no interest under common-law rules); after 1536, it was a legal executory interest.

By 1600, then, the use had become a fiction—a matter, merely, of magic words. It had not begun as a fiction, though. The medieval landowner who, in his charity, really wanted to help a band of St. Francis's little brothers of the poor, made his gift to his neighbor "for the use of the friars." He wanted his neighbor to own and use the land for the friars and not for himself. The *benefit* of ownership was divided from the *burden* of ownership. One question judges first construing the Statute of Uses had to answer was whether the statute eliminated the use, as a way to divide the benefit of ownership from the burden of ownership, from the property-owner's tool box. You will be happy to learn that the answer is: No. It will help, in reading the following material, to know that the modern word for the modern device that separates the burden of property ownership from the benefits of it is *trust*.

B. TRUSTS IN MODERN AMERICAN LAW OFFICE PRACTICE

The trust has been, for a century and a half, a principal device for gathering together borrowed capital for American business purposes. It is also a principal device for pooled investments; many "mutual funds" that are marketed to the public are trusts. And the trust is the basic tool used by property lawyers in arranging property ownership for members of families. Here are some examples:

1. *Family Businesses*

Where clients need to find ways to separate management of the business from enjoyment of business profits and to do this in reference to a range of people that may include an ailing 90–year–old founder of the firm, who still "comes in to the office every morning," to an unborn child who will one day win the Nobel Prize for her poetry and will never come into the office at all. The agenda suggests Louis D. Brandeis's work for the Warren family. It also suggests work we will have to do for the Stephens family, after we employ future-interest tools to settle the ownership of the farm: Carl and Lois Stephens have four school children to consider; none of the children is a farmer (yet).

2. *Disability*

The trust as a means of providing fiduciary management for disabled clients is not the only device available, but it is the most flexible. The trust may be the only device that will work well for the client who has business to do or investment to see to but who fears her own disability—especially mental disability—from age or poor health, and who needs a device that will be available to provide as much substitute management as the occasion requires, from no management of her property to a substitute for guardianship.

An example is the use of a "discretionary" trust to permit middle-class elderly people to obtain access to benefits for the poor and at the same time retain both the benefit of their savings and their ability to leave wealth to the next generations: Widowed Grandpa Villalobos, for instance, has savings of half a million dollars and may soon need to go into a nursing home. His lawyer (or a lawyer employed by his children) transfers his savings to his eldest daughter, as trustee, with directions to provide funds to Grandpa in whatever way she decides. Grandpa is equitable owner of the trust assets, but it is almost impossible to say what he owns in a welfare-office sense since he cannot get at any of it; he owns only what his daughter decides he can have. Under judge-made law analogous to the 19th century law we discuss, just below, involving restraints on alienation, Grandpa is held to have no income or assets for welfare-law purposes, and nothing the state can reach to reimburse itself for the costs of his care. (See T. Shaffer and C. Mooney, The Planning and Drafting of Wills and Trusts, ch. 11, 1991.)[33]

Professor Joel C. Dobris, in "Medicaid Asset Planning by the Elderly: A Policy View of Expectations, Entitlement and Inheritance," 24 Real Property, Probate and Trust Journal 1 (1989):

[T]his * * * is really about a rather remarkable use by the middle class, under particular circumstances, of a social welfare program initially intended only for the poor. * * * And they are doing it with the assistance of lawyers. Why lawyers? First, for the typical family there is a great deal of money at stake. * * * Second, this is a serious social problem and, when there is such a problem, lawyers often are called upon to help. Third, this is a classic situation in which people will pay a lawyer. * * *

A major piece of social engineering is at work—a popular conversion of a need-based program for the poor to a more universal entitlement program. * * * The glue that holds this project together is the feeling on the part of applicants, and their children, that they are entitled to these benefits. * * * When they choose to, they are taking [them] without a twinge of conscience. * * *

[Even though] elderly individuals may change their minds about the propriety of divestment planning, it seems fair to say that middle-aged children have much less concern about propriety than their elderly parents. The funds are there, at least for the moment, the planning is legal, and the stakes are high. The chances are the children do not care what people think. * * * [T]he social sanction is gone * * *.

Grandpa Villalobos may care what people think. He may be affected by the moral considerations Professor Dobris hints at. He may also believe (with considerable justification) that nursing-home care paid for from his savings will be better than nursing-home care paid for by the welfare department.

3. Tax Planning

Clients dislike the very idea of death taxes, particularly the thought that the federal government will impose huge tax bills on their families under the federal uniform transfer (estate and gift) tax. There are in that tax legislation two examples that give occasion for tax planning: (a) deductions for transfers to a surviving spouse; and (b) exclusions for (relatively) small annual transfers to individuals. The

---

33. Trusts are often combined with a modern statutory version of the power of attorney, a venerable property-law tool in which one person ("attorney in fact," not necessarily a lawyer) can convey another person's property. The modern version keeps the power intact—for property purposes and for making health-care decisions—when the owner is in a coma or otherwise cannot act for himself. This would be a way for Grandpa to convey his property to a welfare-proof trust even after he becomes incompetent to act for himself. It is also a way for members of the family to make "pull the plug" medical decisions for Grandpa.

pure case of qualification for either tax benefit is an outright transfer (a fee simple, in other words), but clients often do not want such transfers to be made outright. Of course, they want to obtain the marital deduction and per-donee exclusion for their families, though, and they employ lawyers to get them the best of both worlds (tax advantage and retained control). The array of trusts crafted to comply with Sections 2056 and 2503 of the Internal Revenue Code is one of the wonders of 20th century trust law. When you add this family-trust business to management of pension and profit-sharing trusts, you describe a hundred-billion-dollar enterprise.

4. *Children Who Might Become Orphans*

Parents in young families want (or, after they talk to their lawyers, come to want) "estate planning" devices to protect their minor children from some of the material effects of the unlikely but disastrous death of both parents before the children "come of age." Transfer and ownership are usually not the problem: The law will allow a child to own property (a fractional share of the family home, say, or the Stephens farm, or cash from life-insurance policies and retirement plans). And the law will provide a fiduciary to make contracts for the minor owner: a court-appointed guardian, usually, or, in some cases, a custodian under the Transfers to Minors Act. But these devices are inflexible: Betty's share cannot be used for her brother Enrico's benefit, even if Enrico is dangerously ill or is a prodigy on the piano. Some standard legal devices for the protection of children are also expensive; legal fees for a guardian's periodic and probably unnecessary accountings to a court are an example. Guardianship is also rejected by many clients because the protection it offers ends at the child's 18th birthday: Being "of age" in our middle-class American culture means after one has graduated from college; the provision of the age of 18 in our voting and competency statutes is viewed by many clients as dysfunctional sentimentality. A trust allows parents (or grandparents or aunts or uncles) to continue management to an age chosen by the settlor (grantor) of the trust; clients have been known to choose the age of 50; many choose ages between 25 and 30. A trust can avoid using any age and define "coming of age" in terms of an event (such as graduation from college or marriage), or it can leave the matter to a trustee's judgment.[34]

5. *Restraints on Alienation*

The common law came to hate restraints on alienation as it came to favor the availability of real property for commerce. It is generally not possible to convey property and fasten on the grantee a condition that he not sell the property; the rule was (and is) applied strictly on attempts to restrain alienation of a legal fee simple, although a judicious use of the fee simple determinable or the fee simple subject to

---

34. See T. Shaffer and C. Mooney, The   ch. 3, 10 (3d ed. 1991).
Planning and Drafting of Wills and Trusts,

condition subsequent is still possible, as we saw in the *Ocean City* and *Higbee* cases:

> "To Monique and her heirs so long as the property is used for agricultural purposes, and then to Henry and his heirs" (assuming the jurisdiction permits alienation of the shifting executory interest)

may amount in the circumstances to the same thing as saying "to Monique and her heirs so long as she does not sell the property."

The safer way to do this is in a trust. A series of 19th–century American cases held that a restraint on alienation—even a restraint on the alienation of a fee simple—is possible when the interest being restrained is an *equitable* interest:

> to Manon and her heirs, in trust for Monique and her heirs, and Monique shall not alienate her interest, voluntarily or involuntarily.

("Involuntary" alienation occurs when the property is vulnerable to Monique's creditors.) This rule—which was not developed in Britain but is now followed in all but a couple of the United States—was justified with the arguments: (i) that the property had not been removed from the market (since the trustee held an unrestrained legal fee simple); or, if it had, (ii) that such removal had been the will of the settlor of the trust, who held an unrestrained legal fee simple and should have been able to do what he wanted with his own property. You may enjoy commenting on these arguments; here is a context:

George Vavasour is a young man about town. He drives an expensive Italian sports car, lives in a gentrified high rise in the center of town, and has a condominium vacation place on the banks of trendy Lake Link, with his own dock and sailing boat. He neither labors nor toils, and those who are in the know say that is because he was provided for lavishly by his late mother Matilda. You are in law practice, with an understandable amount of envy for George, when you are consulted by Prego Motors, Inc., the auto dealer from which George obtained his sports car. George owes Prego $10,000 for accessories and repairs to the car, and he refuses to pay. Prego, through its in-house lawyer, filed suit against George and obtained a default judgment; George didn't bother to come to court. When Prego's in-house lawyer went to collect the judgment, she found that George doesn't own anything she can levy on: The apartment and condo are rented; so is the Alpha Romeo; and the sail boat belongs to George's cousin Alice. George has no earnings and no savings accounts.

George lives well because he gets weekly payments in excess of $2,000 each from a trust established by his late mother. The trust is funded with $2 million in securities. George is the only beneficiary; the trustee is directed to pay George all of the income from the trust property and, when George dies, to distribute the trust property to his cousin Alice or, if she is dead, among her descendants. The trust has a spendthrift clause such as Monique's trust had in the example just above: If that clause means what it says, George's income interest in the trust cannot be assigned by him or reached by his creditors.

Payments of income are given to George in cash every Tuesday at 7 p.m. at the back door of the trustee's cottage on the shores of Lake Link. George spends his money from a supply of cash held by a solid gold money clip that he carries in his pants pocket. When Prego decides to turn this matter over to you, you call George to see whether he plans to pay Prego or not. George says, "No. Not really. Why should I? But I'll tell you what I will do, just to show I am a sport: Come out to the lake and take a ride on my boat. I'll buy you a drink."

Many of these modern uses of the trust avoid (some would say evade) legal requirements. An additional, common example in many states is the trust to protect lenders of money used to purchase residences. In that case the trust is used to avoid the protections that have grown up to inhibit the foreclosure of mortgages. The modern trust is, in these respects, a worthy descendant of the medieval use: Professor Austin Scott's treatise on trusts quotes an eighteenth-century chancery barrister who said to the court of equity, "The parents of the use were fraud and fear, and the court of conscience was its nurse."

C. THE UNEXECUTED USE

The modern trust grew out of a little open space—a loophole, if you like—in the Statute of Uses. The statute by its terms executed all uses, which meant: (i) ownership in equity became ownership in law; and (ii) the feoffee to uses (the person we would today call a trustee) remained necessary, but only for a moment. That worked as it was supposed to work for the cases—most cases, no doubt—in which the use was a fiction and the feoffee to uses (trustee) had nothing to do. It did not work, though, for cases in which the grantor of the use (whom we would today call a settlor or a trustor) wanted the property to be managed for the equitable owner (whom we today call a beneficiary, or—for the quaint among us—a *cestui que trust*). This is the case of the "active" use (trust), as distinguished from the "passive" or "dry" use (trust). The judges, as you will by now have no doubt guessed, construed the Statute of Uses not to reach active trusts. The way you tell which is which is to ask if the feoffee to uses (trustee) has duties: If the trustee has duties, the trust survives the Statute of Uses. The trustee has legal title and fiduciary duties to the beneficiary ("the punctilio of an honor the most sensitive," Judge Cardozo said). The beneficiary has equitable title.

Not all states have pervasive rules forbidding dry trusts. It is possible in some states to separate legal and equitable ownership without imposing duties on the trustee. One dubious advantage this device offers, where it is available, is that land ownership can be concealed from the public and even from local government. An owner who does not want it known that he is an owner transfers title to (or, more likely, takes title in) a trust. The deed conveying title is recorded in the public land records, but it shows only the name of the trustee. If there is a written agreement between the trustee and the equitable owner, it is not recorded. Standard Statute-of-Uses (common) law would hold the trust executed—that is, no trust at all. A few states permit such dry trusts; some of these justify the device by construction of the Statute of Uses; in some states it is provided for by statute—for example, this provision in the Indiana Trust Code:

> If the trust property consists only of real property, and, under the terms of the trust,
>
> (a) the beneficiary has the power to manage the trust property, including the power to direct the trustee to sell the property; and
>
> (b) the trustee may sell the trust property only on direction by the beneficiary or other person or may sell it after a period of time stipulated in the terms of the trust in the absence of a direction: the [Statute of Uses] shall not apply to defeat the trustee's title.

This provision was part of a (relatively) new code, a relatively elaborate revision and modernization of trust law. Indiana had not theretofore provided for dry trusts, a circumstance that caused some annoyance among practitioners whose offices are near the Illinois border, because Illinois does allow them. If you had been a Hoosier legislator, would you have voted for this part of the Trust Code? Would the addition of the following provision (also from the Indiana Trust Code) have made a difference?

> (a) Any person may petition the court for disclosure of information concerning beneficiaries of the trust estate. The court may order the disclosure of all or any part of the information requested in the petition only after the petitioner has shown both a reasonable need for it and the trustee has either refused or neglected to provide the information on written request delivered to the trustee.
>
> (b) The court shall, upon petition, order the disclosure of the identity of the beneficiaries or their agents, if any, and any other information concerning the trust, in any case in which:
>
>> (1) in a trust of real estate, there is a violation of a state law or an ordinance or resolution of a political subdivision relating to the structure or condition of buildings, or the health and safety of occupants of or visitors to buildings; or
>>
>> (2) there has been or may be a deed, sale, lease, purchase, mortgage, assignment or similar transfer of any interest in trust property to or from any unit of state or local government or agency or official thereof; and the trustee has refused to disclose the identities of the beneficiaries within a reasonable time after written demand.

V.   THE DESTRUCTION OF FUTURE INTERESTS

Families, from the time of De Donis (1285) on, have asked their lawyers to arrange ownership so that property stays in the family. This was the history of the fee tail and its predecessor estate, the fee simple conditional, of disentailment, and of the remarkably complex devices used by British lawyers of the eighteenth and nineteenth centuries to control profligate tendencies in "the heir" (the eldest male in each generation, who had sometimes nominal ownership of the family estates). Descriptions of these devices, and of the family cultures that surrounded them, sound quaint to a modern ear; but concern for family ownership is as strong in our culture as it was in theirs. That seems clear from reflection on prominent families in 20th century America (Rockefeller, Ford, Kennedy); it is clear also in the modern Wednesday-afternoon, county-seat law practice, when clients, such as the farmer Lois Stephens, come in to get their wills done.

There are two powerful social forces resisting perpetual or even indefinite family ownership of property. The first is government, which fears aggregations of power other than its own (remember the political forces that supported the Statute of Uses) and which needs the tax revenue that transitions in ownership provide. The other is the mercantile economy, which came to dominate England after the Tudor monarchs (the last of whom, Elizabeth I, died in 1603). A trading economy needs circulating wealth, which means, as to land, property that can be sold by those who possess it:

Example (a): One of the principal ways to tax wealth, in the Middle Ages, and now, and at all times in between, is to tax it at the death of the current owner. One of the principal means of avoiding such a tax is to spread ownership on the plane of time, so that the death of a possessor is not a transition in ownership. Lawmakers who seek to protect sources of revenue for the government therefore need to invent ways to frustrate the use of life estates and future interests. This agenda explains the rule in Shelley's Case and the doctrine of worthier title, of which more below, and the modern, American generation-skipping transfer tax.

Example (b): Division of property between possessory estates and vested future interests complicates but is not an insurmountable obstacle to the sale of property. After the conveyance "to Alicia for life, then to Bartolomeo and his heirs," a buyer can obtain a possessory fee simple by getting deeds from both Alicia and Bartolomeo; if either or both of them is a minor or otherwise disabled, the conveyance can be in whole or in part from guardians. But the division of property ownership between possessory estates and *contingent* future interest tends to keep property out of the market: "to Alicia for life, then to the heirs of Bartolomeo and their heirs" creates a contingent remainder in persons who cannot be ascertained until after Bartolomeo's death; "to my children for life, then to my grandchildren who survive them" creates contingent remainders in a similar class of unascertained persons and, in addition, puts a condition of survival on their future interests that may not be insurmountable but is difficult. Mercantile forces will favor legal rules that make it possible to eliminate (destroy) conditional future interests and place the power to convey ownership in the possessory generation (e.g., the destructibility of contingent remainders, of which more below). Mercantile forces will also favor limits on the creation of conditional future interests. One such limit—one that has endured through centuries of tax schemes—is the rule against perpetuities.

These forces do not operate as cleanly as the examples suggest—government and the implacable forces of commerce in momentary alliance on the ridge; the family in its manor house, searching the horizon for signs of harm. Pressure to put property on the market will come from the generation that possesses the property and sometimes even from generations that will possess it later. The possibility of these pressures will be present in the minds of clients, such as Mrs. Stephens, who come in to see about their wills.

In addition, tax avoidance devices have negative as well as positive economic impact on the taxpayer; saving taxes usually costs something: You can get an income-tax deduction for the ten dollars you put in the collection plate at church, but to get the deduction you have to give up the ten dollars. There is, as a result, pressure from within the family to forego tax-avoidance devices and increase short-run prosperity. The point is this: It is not possible to separate the law office from the legislatures and courts in considering the policies that tend to inhibit us lawyers from using the tools we have to keep property in the family.

We propose in this section to look at three historic ways the common law resisted forms of ownership that keep property in the family:

(A) the destructibility of contingent remainders;

(B) the rule in Shelley's case and the doctrine of worthier title (considered together because they are a lot alike); and

(C) the rule against perpetuities.

A. THE DESTRUCTIBILITY OF CONTINGENT REMAINDERS

This set of doctrines is no longer important for law practice, but the dynamic that made destructibility possible still is. For that reason, and for historical interest, we need to pause briefly over this first category.

Consider a couple of examples:

(1) Grandma, by deed, gave the family property "to my son Saul for life, then, if she reaches the age of 21, to his daughter, my beloved grand-daughter, Leah and her heirs." Leah was then 12. Grandma's deed made a valid transfer under common-law rules: Saul had a possessory life estate; Leah had a contingent remainder in fee simple (contingent on her reaching her 21st birthday). If Leah had reached her 21st birthday during Saul's life, her remainder would have become a vested remainder in fee simple.

But suppose she did not; suppose that Leah was only 18 when Saul died. In that case, Leah's remainder failed. To give it effect in such circumstances would be to allow the ownership to lapse (i.e., revert to Grandma) between Saul's death and Leah's birthday, and then to spring up again when Leah had her birthday party. The old common-law lawyers spoke of this as a lapse in the seisin, meaning a lapse in "freehold" possession of the sort Grandma and Saul had. This would be to allow a springing interest and, under common-law rules, a remainder cannot spring; it must take effect at the expiration of the prior estate—or fail. In this case it failed. The contingent remainder was destroyed. At Saul's death the fee ownership reverted to Grandma. If Grandma were then dead, the fee ownership would have reverted to her heirs. Leah, as one of Grandma's heirs, would have had to share it with her sisters, and maybe even with her repulsive cousins.

(2) Same facts except suppose that Saul does not die when Leah is 18. He lives on to experience the frustration and pain of having a rebellious and disobedient 19–year–old daughter. She has taken up with a Lothario from across the tracks. If she gets her hands on Grandma's property, she will spend it on the Lothario. Saul goes to see his lawyer; the lawyer (let's assume) still has in his tool-box an antique destructibility tool—a tool modern reform has taken away from us. By using this old tool, the lawyer can destroy Leah's contingent remainder and keep Lothario at bay until Leah becomes responsible. It works this way:

  (i)   Grandma is still living.
  (ii) There is a reversion after Leah's contingent remainder. There is always a reversion after a contingent remainder; in this case there is a realistic, non-fictional reversion, because Leah may not be 21 when poor Saul dies, which, in view of the way Leah is treating him, could be any day now. Possession may revert to Grandma between Saul's death and Leah's 21st birthday.
  (iii) Saul holds the life estate and is in possession.
  (iv) Grandma agrees with Saul that something must be done about Leah.
  (v)   Grandma conveys her reversion to Saul.

The result of this last conveyance was to put both the possessory life estate and the reversion in the same person. The doctrine was that the two then merged to become a fee simple, and any intervening contingent remainders were destroyed:

  (i)   This would not be the case if Leah's remainder had been vested (e.g., she had already become 21). In that case the reversion would have disappeared when Leah became 21 and there would be no future interest to merge with Saul's life estate.
  (ii) But it would have been possible, even if, logically, there could be no return of possession to the grantor under the terms of the deed ("Saul for life, then, if she reaches her 21st birthday, to Leah and her heirs, and if not, to Rachel and her heirs"). There is always a reversion after contin-

gent remainders. The fiction is essential to the doctrine. The doctrine is that both remainders are destructible.

Lawyers of course found a way to make conditional future interests indestructible. By the year 1700 they had successfully argued to the common-law courts that executory interests should not be destructible, so that all Grandma had to do, if she wanted Leah's future interest to be indestructible, was to—what?

B. THE RULE IN SHELLEY'S CASE AND THE DOCTRINE OF WORTHIER TITLE

Lily Bart wants to keep her seaside summer place in Maine in the family by providing for Lawrence, her husband, for life, and then she wants the farm to go to their only child, a daughter named Agnes, and her family. She wants to make these arrangements by deed or by will; she does not want to depend on the law of inheritance. But the people she wants to benefit in the next generation are Agnes or those of Agnes's children who are living when Lawrence dies—the same people who would inherit if Lily made no deed and had no will.

You can imagine, perhaps, some modern reasons for her preferring a conveyance over dependence on inheritance law—families are more reluctant to rearrange a will plan than an intestate distribution; the legislature may change the inheritance statute; a will provides more control and less expense than intestate succession; and a deed is even less expensive. British lawyers in the 17th and 18th centuries had an even more potent reason: Death taxes were imposed on inheritance but not on transition of ownership under a deed or will.

Suppose Mrs. Bart conveys, in a deed from her, "to Lawrence for life and then to the heirs of Lawrence." The heirs of Lawrence will be Agnes or her children—all in the family.

SEYMOUR v. HEUBAUM
Appellate Court of Illinois, 1965.
65 Ill.App.2d 89, 211 N.E.2d 897.

DAVIS, JUSTICE.

This is a suit seeking construction of a will and a declaratory judgment that plaintiff is owner in fee simple absolute of certain real estate. The issue before the Court is the applicability of the rule in Shelley's case to a certain devise contained in the will of Effie Seymour, who died in 1939. If the rule is applicable * * * its abrogation by statute in 1953 * * * will not affect the determination here as the statute has no retroactive application. * * *

After making certain specific bequests, Effie Seymour provided. * * *

" * * * I give, devise and bequeath all the rest and residue of my estate real or personal, wherever situate, including all my right, title and interest in and to the real estate known as * * * to J. Harter Kirkpatrick * * * as trustee, to be held in trust for the benefit of my son William H. Seymour during his lifetime and upon his death to be paid to his lawful heirs. * * * "

[W]illiam died in 1960 leaving a will in which he devised all of his property to his wife, the plaintiff, who brought this suit seeking a construction of Effie Seymour's will and a judgment declaring that her husband took a fee interest under his mother's will, capable of being devised to her. This contention is premised upon the applicability of the rule in Shelley's case to the mother's will, converting the remainder to William's lawful heirs into a remainder in fee in William. The trial court held that the rule in Shelley's case was applicable and that William thus took the remainder as well as the life estate, which constituted the fee; and that, therefore, he had the power to dispose of the same by will. The defendants, the heirs of William other than his widow, prosecuted this appeal.

Stated simply, the rule in Shelley's case is that whenever, in the same instrument, an estate of freehold is limited to the ancestor, and a remainder to his heirs, either mediately or immediately, in fee, or in tail, the word "heirs" is one of limitation of the estate, and not of purchase, and the ancestor takes the fee. * * * Whenever the grants of the freehold and remainder are contained in the same instrument, there are three requisites for application of the rule: First, a freehold estate must be granted to the ancestor; second, a remainder must be limited to "his heirs," general or special, as such—that is, by the name of heirs and without explanation as meaning sons, children, etc.; and third, the two estates, freehold and the remainder, must both be of the same quality,—that is, both must be either legal or equitable. * * *

[I]t matters not that the creator of the instrument in question manifested an intent that the property pass in a manner different than that resulting from the application of the rule. That is, in fact, the necessary result of the rule. It operates on the remainder alone, taking it from the heirs and vesting it in the ancestor; and although the preceding estate of freehold is a circumstance necessary to its application, such estate is not directly affected by it. The ordinary rules of construction are applicable only in first determining if there is a "freehold"; [35] if there is a remainder in the "heirs," and if the two estates are of the same quality. These determinations are made wholly independently of the rule in Shelley's case itself. * * *

It is not disputed that the will of Effie Seymour granted an equitable life estate, and thus a freehold, to her son, William. The defendants contend, however, that the second and third requisites for the application of the rule are not present. They argue that the second requisite is absent because the word "heirs" was intended to designate

---

35. A freehold is a fee simple, a fee tail, or a life estate. For purposes of this rule a   freehold is a fee tail or a life estate. (Eds.)

certain persons other than those ordinarily encompassed within the meaning of the word, and it was thus used as a "word of purchase" not of "limitation"; and that the third requisite is missing in that the life estate was equitable and the remainder was legal. Hence, they urge that the two estates were not of the same quality. Lastly, they contend that the plaintiff is guilty of laches and is further estopped from asserting the application of the rule in Shelley's case.

Defendants contend that since Effie Seymour's will contained two specific bequests of $100.00 each to her two step-daughters, described as "my daughters," she thus evidenced an intent that the two named step-daughters were to take under her will as her own son's "heirs," although not technically such. If this intention were clearly manifested, we concede that the word "heirs" would not have been used in its technical and legal sense and the rule in Shelley's case could not be applied. However, it is not readily apparent to us how the two specific bequests of $100.00 each to her respective step-daughters, designated as "daughters," manifests an intent that they are to be included in the devise of the entire residue of her estate to the "lawful heirs" of her son upon his death. We think rather, that such bequests to each of her step-daughters would indicate an intent to exclude them from the residuary estate; and that the designation of her son's "lawful heirs" as the ones to ultimately take upon his death indicated that Effie Seymour had exhausted her specific wishes by prior bequests and when disposing of her residuary estate, she was content to let the law then take its course. * * *

That the word "heirs" is preceded by the word "lawful" does not affect its ordinary or technical meaning. * * * The word "heirs" as used by Effie Seymour in her will, was used as a word of limitation and not of purchase, and the second requisite for the application of the rule in Shelly's case is present.

Whether the remainder interest is legal or equitable must depend upon the character of the trust created by Effie Seymour's will. If the trustee was vested with the fee simple title under the trust created by the will, coupled with the power to sell, convey, rent, mortgage, etc., it follows that the life estate limited to William H. Seymour was equitable and the remainder interest given to his "lawful heirs," was likewise equitable—the same as the life estate. * * *

The quantity of the estate taken by the trustee is not determined from the particular form of the devise to the trustee, but, rather, from the intention manifested by the testator in defining the scope, extent and purpose of the trust and the duties of the trustee thereunder. The trustee will take whatever legal estate is necessary for him to carry out the purpose of the trust and his duties thereunder. If a fee is required, a fee will be taken; if a lesser estate will suffice, then only such an estate will vest. * * *

Our courts have long held that a devise to a trustee in which there is a power in the trust to sell, necessarily vests the fee in the trustee. * * *

While we do not deem it crucial to our determination, two other provisions of the will are consistent with the apparent intent to convey a fee to the trustee. The trustee was directed to pay for a proper burial for the life tenant. The fact that the trustee has duties to perform after the death of the life tenant suggests a legal fee in the trustee, rather than life estate coupled with powers. * * *

If the legal estate continued in the trustee after the death of the life tenant, no matter how short the period, there cannot during that same period be a legal vested remainder in the heirs of the life tenant. The remainder interest given to the heirs must then, of necessity, be equitable in nature. * * *

The will further provided that upon the death of William Seymour, the rest and residue of the estate that was devised and bequeathed in trust, was then "to be paid" to his lawful heirs. The defendants urge that the word "paid" cannot be interpreted to mean "convey" and suggest that it might be construed to mean "descend," in which case, they argue, the trust became passive immediately upon the death of the life tenant, and was executed by the Statute of Uses, and the remainder interest was then legal. * * * This argument, however, is more ingenious than persuasive. The wording of the fifth paragraph of the will does not suggest or require the liquidation of the trust estate. Nor do the words "to be paid" lend themselves to the interpretation of being synonymous with "descend". * * *

As to whether the Statute of Uses may ever operate to execute a trust in which the trustee has obtained full legal title or whether, in such cases, the trustee retains the active duty of conveying the legal title upon the termination of all other active duties, it appears that our courts have not always reached consistent conclusions. * * * Insofar as the application of the rule in Shelley's case is concerned, however, the determination of whether or not the Statute of Uses becomes operative, is irrelevant. For if we concede the operation of the Statute of Uses which would convert the remainder from an equitable into a legal interest, even then the statute may not execute the trust until all of the active duties of the trustee have been performed and nothing remains to be done. * * * The inquiry to be made regarding the applicability of the rule in Shelley's case is as to the effect of the instrument creating the freehold and remainder estates on the date such an instrument becomes effective. In the case of a will, it is as of the date of the testator's death. Thus, if a trust is created in a will, with the result that the freehold is equitable, the inquiry to be made in determining the quality or nature of the remainder must be as to the quantum or size of the trustee's estate at the inception of the trust. If it is a fee interest, then the freehold and remainder must be equitable in nature. * * * If both estates—the freehold and remainder—are of the same quality at the time the trustee takes title, it matters not that the quality or nature of one of the estates might, or might not, be altered at some later time. * * *

All of the requisites for the application of the rule in Shelley's case are here present, with the result that the life tenant, William Seymour, was given the fee to the real estate in question under the will of Effie Seymour. The application of the rule in Shelley's case to a particular case depends, not upon the quantity of the estate intended to be given to the ancestor, but upon the estate devised to his heirs. It conclusively expresses the intention of the testator, and governs and controls in determining the estate devised, notwithstanding the expression of an intention on the part of the testator that the ancestor shall take a less estate than the fee. It changes the remainder to the heirs of the devisee, into a remainder to the ancestor, so that he has a life estate with the remainder in fee to himself. * * *

Note

Smith v. Wright, 300 Ark. 416, 779 S.W.2d 177, 179–181 (1989): "Arkansas is one of the few states that continues to recognize the Rule in Shelley's case. * * * The Rule * * * is a rule of law, and we will apply it whenever the language of the conveyance fits under the rule without regard to the conveyor's intention. * * *

"[A] remainder is limited under the Rule in Shelley's case, when the language used to describe it is construed to refer to the persons who as heirs or heirs of the body would inherit the property of the designated person on his or her death intestate. * * * In our case, the chancellor found that the remaindermen were not limited to the heirs or heirs of the body of Buren Hardin for two reasons: (1) his widow was named as one of the remaindermen, and (2) Buren's heirs did not become fixed at the time of his death. We agree. * * *

"[T]he widow was a remainderman in fee simple interest. * * * [W]hen Buren died, his widow was not an heir under Arkansas law. * * * Thus, because the remainder interest was not limited to Buren's heirs, the Rule in Shelley's case cannot apply.

"In addition * * * Buren's heirs [as described in the will] were not fixed at the time of his death. In the fee simple conveyance, those in a class of beneficiaries consisting of Buren's widow and his legitimate descendants who are alive at the time of the expiration of the trust will share in the fee simple interest. The Rule in Shelley's case is not applicable if the heirs are to be determined as of some other time than the death of the ancestor. * * * In the present case, the beneficiaries of the fee simple interest clearly are to be determined at the end of the trust and not upon Buren's death."

THE DOCTRINE OF WORTHIER TITLE

Back to Mrs. Bart, and our interest in drafting a deed for her that will provide for the possession of the farm by her husband Lawrence, until he dies, with a remainder in fee in the Barts' daughter and her children. We could draw a deed for our client that said "to Lawrence for life and then to *my* heirs" (i.e., the heirs of Lily Bart, our client, the grantor). The children and their children are the people our client wants to benefit ultimately and (as she sees it) permanently. If we take care of this by deed now, we will save the costs of putting the summer place through the probate process, after our client's death, and we might even save some death taxes.

This second alternative attempts to create a remainder in the heirs of the *grantor*. Effie Seymour's will created a remainder in the heirs of the *grantee*. In this second situation (remainder in heirs of the grantor), the common-law tax rule was called the doctrine of worthier title, and it was construed so that the future interest was not a remainder in heirs, but a reversion in the grantor. (That way, the heirs of the grantor took by inheritance, not under the deed, and their title was "worthier"—which seems to have meant that it was taxable.) "A purported devise of an estate to heirs is inoperative if it is the identical estate that they are entitled to take in case of intestacy. * * * The doctrine is [also] * * * applicable if an *inter vivos* gift is followed by a gift to the [grantor's] 'heirs' or 'next of kin'. * * * " [36]

The rule in Shelley's case has been abolished in Illinois and virtually everywhere else. There may be as many as four states where it is still in force, but generalizations on the point are not to be trusted. In Indiana, for example, the issue has not been presented in the appellate courts for more than a century. The last time it was presented, the Supreme Court condemned the rule but refused to abolish it judicially. The Indiana Trust Code has abolished it as to trusts. Some writers say the rule may still obtain in Arkansas, Colorado, and Delaware.

The doctrine of worthier title has not been so clearly abolished, mostly because Judge Benjamin Nathan Cardozo, in Doctor v. Hughes, 225 N.Y. 305, 122 N.E. 221 (1919), turned it into a rule of construction—so judges don't have to abolish it; they can keep it around in case it might come in handy some time. A dozen states, including Cardozo's New York, have abolished it by legislation. It has been applied, relatively recently, in federal death-tax cases of this sort:

Deed: Lois to Carl for life, then to the heirs of Lois.

It appears that there is no asset in Lois's estate which can be taxed at her death. But if she has the remainder (reversion), there is an asset left after her death that is taxable (market value less the value of Carl's life estate).

C. THE RULE AGAINST PERPETUITIES

Neither of the three old rules we have discussed thus far in this section is likely to be an obstacle to modern drafting. Not so the old

36. Burby, Real Property 336–337 (3d ed. 1965), tracking Coke on Littleton.

common-law rule against perpetuities, which has been balkanized by modern judicial policy in virtually all states and by statute in several, but is, in some version of its old self, still the law everywhere.

Recall that a common-law lawyer could create an indestructible conditional future interest if he used the executory-interest tool rather than the contingent-remainder tool:

Not: "to Saul for life and then to Leah if Leah is then 21,"

But: "to Lawyer and his heirs for the use of Saul for life and then, one day after Saul's death, to Leah and her heirs, if Leah is then 21."

The second form raised a use, which the Statute of Uses then executed, with the result that equitable interests became legal interests and the feoffee to uses disappeared from the transaction. Saul's interest was a legal life estate under either form. If the second form had said " * * * for the use of Saul for life and then to Leah if Leah is then 21," Leah would have had a contingent remainder under the second form, which contingent remainder would have been destructible. But the (clever) drafter here put a one-day gap between the end of the life estate and the beginning of the remainder,[37] which made Leah's future interest under the second form a legal springing executory interest, not a remainder. And executory interests were not destructible.

But if contingent future interests could be made non-destructible, there was no law in place to prevent family property being made permanently inalienable—through, for example, a succession of conditional executory interests for life that would go on indefinitely:

to Lawyer and his heirs for the use of Saul for life and then, one day after Saul's death, to Leah for life; and then, one day after Leah's death, to Leah's oldest daughter living at the death of Leah, for life, and then, one day after the death of such daughter. * * *

There was a case in the House of Lords, early in the nineteenth century, in which counsel argued that a family that could retain property indefinitely would soon own all of England. The rule against perpetuities was invented, in the 17th century, to quell such concerns and keep England safe.

NORTH CAROLINA NATIONAL BANK v. NORRIS

Court of Appeals of North Carolina, 1974.
21 N.C.App. 178, 203 S.E.2d 657.

Action for a declaratory judgment to determine whether certain provisions of the last will of B.F. Montague violated the rule against perpetuities. * * *

---

37. The common-law rule is that where a future interest according to its terms might be either a remainder or an executory interest, it is construed to be a remainder.

B.F. Montague died a resident of Wake County on or about 1 April 1928, leaving a will dated 19 November 1927. At the time of his death, he left surviving a widow, three daughters who were then 38, 40 and 43 years of age, and one grandchild, Thomas A. Norris, Jr., who was then six years of age; there were no children or grandchildren born subsequent to the death of B.F. Montague. Montague's widow, daughters, and only grandchild have successively deceased. Thomas A. Norris, Jr., the grandchild, died 10 January 1973, leaving surviving four children, who are the defendants herein, and a last will naming plaintiff herein as the Executor.

The pertinent provisions of the will of B.F. Montague are the following:

"FOURTH: I give, devise and bequeath to my three daughters, May M. Allison and Annie M. Hunter and Marjorie M. Norris, all of my estate, below described, during their natural lives and at the death of either of my said daughters, I give, devise and bequeath all of said property to the survivor or survivors alike, and at the death of the last survivor, I give, devise and bequeath all of my estate below described to the child or children of my said daughters for and during the natural life or lives of such child or children (my grandchild or grandchildren) with remainder over to the lawful issue of such grandchild or grandchildren forever. In default of such issue from such grandchild or grandchildren, the remainder shall go to Peace Institute of Raleigh, N.C., absolutely and forever. First of all, however, I give, devise and bequeath to my wife, Bettie L. Montague, a life estate in and to all the property below described in this section (Section FOURTH), and at her death, the same shall descend to my said daughters in the manner and form above specified in this section (Section FOURTH)."

There then follows a description of certain tracts of real property in Raleigh, N.C.

If the rule against perpetuities was violated by the foregoing provisions of Montague's will, title to the real property in question would have been vested in his grandchild, Thomas A. Norris, Jr., immediately prior to Norris's death and would now be vested in plaintiff by virtue of Norris's will. If the rule was not violated, title to such property would now be vested in defendants, Montague's great-grandchildren.

The trial court, concluding as a matter of law that the attempted devise of the remainder interest to the testator's great-grandchildren violated the rule against perpetuities, entered judgment that title to the property in question is now vested in plaintiff as Executor under the will of Thomas A. Norris, Jr., subject to the provisions of Norris's will.
* * *

PARKER, JUDGE.

The common-law rule against perpetuities has been long recognized and enforced in this jurisdiction, and its application has the continuing sanction of our State Constitution. This rule, which is "not one of construction but a positive mandate of law to be obeyed irrespective of the question of intention" * * * has been stated by our Supreme Court as follows:

> "No devise or grant of a future interest in property is valid unless the title thereto must vest, if at all, not later than twenty-one years, plus the period of gestation, after some life or lives in being at the time of the creation of the interest. If there is a possibility such future interest may not vest within the time prescribed, the gift or grant is void". * * *

The devise which B.F. Montague attempted to make in Item Fourth of his will to his great-grandchildren of the remainder interest after the termination of the successive life estates granted to his widow, his daughters, and his grandchildren, clearly violated the rule. As of the date of the testator's death, which in case of wills is the time at which the validity of the limitation is to be ascertained, the possibility existed, at least insofar as the law views the matter, that one or more children might thereafter be born to one or more of the Montague's three surviving daughters. Had this occurred, the life estates which he provided for his grandchildren might well have extended and postponed vesting of the remainder in his great-grand-children to a date beyond the time prescribed by the rule. It is the possibility, not the actuality, of such an occurrence which renders the grant void. As stated by the author of [an American Law Reports annotation], "it should be noted that a remainder to great-grandchildren whose vesting is not limited upon termination of a secondary life estate in a named grandchild, but upon the death of all the creator's grandchildren as a class, is invalid, since other grandchildren might be born after the creation of the future interests and postpone the vesting of the remainder beyond the permitted period."

Appellant here acknowledges the possibility that a grandchild or grandchildren might have been born after Montague's death with the result that vesting of at least portions of the remainder might have been postponed beyond the period permitted by the rule, but seeks to invoke the so-called "Doctrine of Separability" to save the devise to the great-grandchildren in the present case. That doctrine has been stated by the author of the last-cited Annotation as follows:

> "While a class gift may not be split and is either good or bad in toto, it has been held that where a creator makes a gift of remainder to his great-grandchildren following life estates successively in his children and grandchildren in such a manner as to constitute separate and distinct devises or bequests to different classes, which take effect at different times, upon the respective death of the life tenants, and the number of classes or shares is definitely fixed within the period of the rule, although not until after the creator's death, the question of remoteness is to be considered with reference to each share separately. * * *"

As we read Item Fourth of Montague's will, however, we find the doctrine of separability simply not applicable in the present case.

Montague did not devise life estate[s] successively to his children and grandchildren "in such a manner as to constitute separate and distinct devises or bequests to different classes, *which take effect at different times, upon the respective death of the life tenants*." (Emphasis added.) Quite to the contrary, he devised all of the property described in Item Fourth of his will, first to his wife for life, then to his three daughters for life and at the death of any of them to the survivors or survivor for life, then, upon the death of the last to survive of his daughters, and still dealing with *all* of his estate, "to the child or children" of his daughters "for and during the natural life or lives of such child or children" (his grandchild or grandchildren), and finally, and still dealing with *one* property interest, "with remainder over to the lawful issue of such grandchild or grandchildren forever." In default of such issue, "the remainder" is devised to Peace Institute. All the way through the testator dealt with only *one* remainder to take effect at *one* time. Though he obviously contemplated the possibility that he might have more than one grandchild, he did not provide any "separate and distinct" devise of separate portions of the remainder interest to the issue of each grandchild to take effect at different times upon the respective death of each grandchild. Nothing in his will indicates any intention that each of his grandchildren should have a separate life estate in a separate share that each such separate share should vest separately at the death of such grandchild in such grandchild's issue.

* * *

Notes and Questions

1. It is not clear who cared enough about the issue in *Norris* to pay for litigating it. What is clear is that the remaindermen Mr. Montague intended to take—"lawful issue of grandchildren"—cannot take as remaindermen. They may take the same property as heirs. Suppose, though, that Mr. Montague's will provided that any property not passing under Article "Fourth" was to go to his synagogue. Or suppose he gave this "residue" to a daughter other than Thomas's mother.

2. The rule against perpetuities is not a reliable way to keep property alienable against the schemes of lawyers to keep property in the family. There are many tools, in our green-eyeshade tool box, that work well when it comes to tying property up, for, say, as much as three generations. It should be clear to you how a drafter could have avoided the problem in *Norris*.

Suppose our client Plantagent Palliser wants to leave his country estate to his descendants, in his will, and to do so in such a way as to take the maximum time the rule against perpetuities allows him:

(a) try your hand at a draft;

(b) then pass judgment on this:

> * * * income to my descendants until 21 years after the death of the last to die of those of the descendants of the late John D.

Rockefeller who are living at my death, then to my descendants and their heirs.

Such a client is unlikely to appear even one Wednesday afternoon in a property lawyer's life. The more common concern for the rule against perpetuities is to avoid it in more reasonable dispositions.

T. SHAFFER AND C. MOONEY, THE PLANNING AND DRAFTING OF WILLS AND TRUSTS
173–179 (3d ed. 1991).

An occasional client has dispositions in mind which could easily violate the rule. They are not absurdities, but are genuinely dynastic. They call for pushing to the limits of the rule. A case in the Court of Appeals of North Carolina, *North Carolina National Bank v. Norris* ... is an example. The disposition there ... was "to my Wife, W, for life, then to my children, A, B, and C, for life, then to my grandchildren for life, and then to my great grandchildren." At the time of the will, the testator, Mr. Montague, had only one grandchild, Thomas, and no more grandchildren were ever born. The draftsman avoided problems with unborn widows,[38] fertile octogenarians,[39] and precocious toddlers [40] by naming names, so that wife and all three children were lives in being. But the draftsman did not interview enough, or draft well enough, to repeat that precaution in the next generation, which meant that no one in the grandchild's generation could be used as a life in being—even though there was only one grandchild, Thomas, and he had been living at the time Montague's will became effective. The rule does not operate on facts as they occur *after* the testator's death, but on facts as they might occur, or, rather, *might have occurred* after that time: Mr. Montague's will said "grandchildren" and he left three living children. At the time of the litigation it was clear that the only grandchild was Thomas, but, looking at the family on the day Mr. Montague died, there might have been additional children. The final remainder in great-grandchildren therefore failed. It would not have failed if the instrument had said "then to my grandchild Thomas for life" or "then for life to those of my grandchildren who are living at my death." Careful

---

38. "To S for life, then to S's widow for life, then to the lineal descendants of S" violates the rule because the widow of S may not be a life in being at the effective date of the conveyance. (Eds.)

39. " 'To my nieces and nephews for life and then to my descendants.' The grantor's parents are living and aged 79 and 77. They have had two children * * * but, the common law said, they may have more children * * * so that not everyone who is a parent of anyone who meets the description 'nieces and nephews' would be a life in being. It is presumed that anyone can have children, and it is the rule that no member of a class may be used as a measuring life unless every other member is also a life in being." Shaffer and Mooney 173. (Eds.)

40. " 'Income to Q for life and thereafter principal to those of Q's grandchildren who are living at my death or born within five years thereafter, and who attain the age of 21.' Q is a 65-year-old widow, but, the law says, she may marry again and have another child and that child may have children of his own, and all of this may happen within five years." Shaffer and Mooney 173. (Eds.)

drafting could even have added 21 years to this dynastic disposition without risking invalidity.

Another way to draft for dynastic safety is to grant a power to a fiduciary to reform the instrument if it proves invalid under the rule against perpetuities; several states now provide statutes which give this power to judges. A grantor can give the same power to a private fiduciary, in a clause (adapted from the Vermont statute) something like this: "An interest which would violate the rule against perpetuities shall be reformed by my trustee, within the limits of that rule, to approximate most closely my intention." In the case of Mr. Montague's will, the trustee could have reformed the life interest in grandchildren to confine it to Thomas, which would have made no difference at all, and thus have saved the remainder interest in great-grandchildren.

A third form of drafting, one that is common and advisable in instruments which do not create dynastic dispositions but which could run into trouble under one of the historic absurdities in the rule, simply limits interests to those allowed under the rule. Here is an example: "All interests created in this will shall vest no later than twenty-one years after the death of the last to die of me, my wife Jane, and those of my lineal descendants who are living at my death. Upon the expiration of this period all income interests shall terminate and principal shall be distributed to the persons entitled to receive income."

JUDICIAL REFORM

Judges have [often] been * * * liberal about perpetuities—usually by way of construing interests before applying the rule to them. * * * [P]erpetuities is a less serious problem than failures to follow statutory formalities for will execution, or defects in trust conveyancing, and certainly less serious than mistakes made about tax law. Judges commonly avoid problems with perpetuities by construing interests away from the rule. Consider the example * * * "to the children of T, but if any of them becomes a Unitarian, his interest to the children of X." The courts early held the shifting executory interest in X's children invalid, but they also held that the grantor's object could have been achieved in two conveyances: (1) "to the children of T, so long as none of them becomes a Unitarian;" (2) "All of my remaining interest to the children of X." The reasoning was that the left-over after the first conveyance was a vested interest, a reversion in the grantor, and that its vested character was retained when it was conveyed separately. That sort of result is sophistry, of course, but it is not offensive to a judge unless he finds moral quality in the rule against perpetuities. It is a delightful bit of evasion for those who find the rule too restrictive. It is less interesting as stating a rule (the *two bites* rule, the late Professor Barton Leach called it), than as stating a relatively modern judicial attitude.

Another way for judges to avoid problems with the rule is to hold that courts have an inherent equitable power to reform interests so that they do not violate the rule. A couple of American courts have held that judges have this power. * * *

A third judicial alternative is to reject formal applications of the rule; for example, there is nothing to prevent a modern court from rejecting the presumption that any woman can bear a child; from applying common sense to gravel pits; [41] from presuming that a testator who says "my son's widow" means the person to whom his son is married either when the testator makes his will or when the testator dies; or, more commonly, from construing "to the children of S when they are 25" as an interest vested subject to divestment, rather than as a contingent interest.

The last example is probably the most common sort of judicial reform, and may justify a few additional words of explanation. If the grantor says "to A for life and then to the children of A when the youngest is 25," the rule, classically applied, invalidates the gift, since any given child of A could reach 25, or fail to reach 25, at a time which is beyond lives in being and 21 years. But that reasoning depends on regarding the interest of each child of A as a contingent interest. Some cases support that construction, but there are also cases which construe as vested a gift "to the children of A, to be distributed when the youngest of them is 25," which probably means the same thing, perpetuities aside. The task of a judge bent on avoiding the rule is to apply the rule in the second line of cases, and to hold that the interests of children of A are vested subject to the divesting condition that a child survive until the youngest of his siblings dies or reaches 25. This is a practical, everyday sort of example. Clients often want to postpone distribution of trust principal to children until they reach an age regarded by parents as mature, and until their youngest child has grown up and been educated. [42]

41. B. Leach, "Perpetuities in a Nutshell," 51 Harvard Law Review 638, at 644–645: "T was in the sand and gravel business. He owned gravel pits which, at the time of his death, would have been exhausted in four years if worked at the rate which was habitual with T. T died, leaving a will which devised to trustees the gravel pits in trust to work until the same were exhausted, then to sell the pits and divide the proceeds among T's issue then living. The pits were already exhausted in six years. But the gift to issue was held bad." This one Leach called the case of the Magic Gravel Pit; he also invented—from decided cases—the titles "unborn widow," "precocious toddler," and "fertile octogenarian." (Eds.)

42. This enlightened construction takes care of the basic gifts by regarding them as vested subject to divestment. It does not, though, take care of "gifts over" that occur after divestment, when there is divestment:

(i) "to A for life and then to the children of A when the youngest is 25" is saved by a construction that vests shares in the children of A at the effective date of the instrument. But the testator's lawyer asked him, "What should happen if the children don't survive?" And the testator said, "to the Rollison United Methodist Church." Is the gift to the church valid?

(ii) "to the children of A when the youngest is 25" is saved by the same construction. If A has two children, one of whom does not survive to age 25, the usual rule of construction would say that the other child takes both shares, but he takes one share by way of gift over, and, as to that share, the gift to him is not vested.

One non-perpetuities problem with this judicial behavior is that it cuts off any children born after the effective date of the instrument. In both of these examples, A

LEGISLATION

* * * There are four broad categories, ranging from drastic to trivial—(1) "wait and see" reform; (2) *cy pres*; (3) specific; and (4) miscellaneous.

The "wait and see" statutes mandate courts to regard "actual events" rather than the "might have been" factual perspective upon which the common-law rule depends. The actual-events statute would eliminate almost all * * * absurd cases, since octogenarians and five-year-olds will not in fact have children, gravel pits will quickly be exhausted, and youngest children will attain 25 within 21 years of the end of all lives in being. What judges will do under the statutes, apparently, is to dismiss actions which assert invalidity so long as defending litigants can show that the actual-events period has not elapsed. This possibility raises questions about what lives can be selected for measuring an actual-events period. Some commentators feel that "wait and see" reform destroys the rule against perpetuities because litigation based on the rule will virtually never succeed. The defender will always be able to find someone who was alive at the effective date of the instrument and who died fewer than 21 years before the lawsuit. The late Professor Lewis Simes, commenting on these statutes, entitled his essay "Is the Rule Against Perpetuities Doomed?". * * *

Cy pres [43] statutes give jurisdiction to the courts to reform dispositions which violate the rule. They do not modify the rule; they modify the sanction for violation. They are in three forms: (1) A broad form: "No interest * * * is * * * void * * * to the extent that it can be reformed or construed * * * to give effect to the general intent of the creator. * * * This section shall be liberally construed * * * to validate such interest. * * *" (2) A second form combines "wait and see" and *cy pres,* so that interests which offend the rule, even after a "wait and see" time period is applied, can be reformed. (3) A few states limit the *cy pres* remedy to specific situations, such as the reduction of age limitations (so that "to the children of A when the youngest is twenty five" is reformed to read "when the youngest is twenty one").

A few statutes are directed to *specific* situations, usually to * * * absurd constructions. * * * The California statute, for instance, overrules the unborn-widow construction by providing that a disposition measured by the life of a widow is deemed to be measured by a life in being, whether it is or not. An Illinois statute overrules the magic-

---

may have more children after the effective date of the instrument, and the testator would probably want those children included in the gift. But "early vesting" to avoid the rule against perpetuities will cut them off, and "vested subject to open" is *not* vested for perpetuities purposes. (Eds.)

43. "Cy pres" is law French meaning, here, "as close as possible." The notion is borrowed from the law of charitable trusts. (Eds.)

gravel-pit result. Statutes in New York and the New England states establish presumptions on human fertility.

Finally, there are, in the miscellaneous category, several statutes which set up novel experiments. Two of the most interesting are statutes in the United Kingdom and in California which establish gross periods longer than twenty-one years. At common law, a disposition was valid if limited for a gross period of twenty one years or less ("to the children of A twenty one years after my death"). Under the new statutes, the time can be much longer. The California statute, for instance, says: "No interest * * * which must vest, if at all, not later than 60 years after the creation of the interest" violates the rule. A proposed statute promulgated by the Commissioners on Uniform State Laws recommends a 90–year gross period.

More common miscellaneous examples are statutes exempting from the rule employment fringe-benefit trusts, trust for the maintenance of cemeteries, or dispositions over to charity. At common law, charitable trusts are exempt from the rule if the interest vests in some charity within the common-law period or shifts, beyond the period, from charity to charity. "To the Baptist Church in 25 years" is, therefore, void, but "to the Baptist Church so long as it uses the property for purposes of worship, and then to the Methodist Church" is all right.

Notes

Mr. Croy's note on *Day & Co. v. Texland Petroleum, Inc.,* supra, describes the recent decision of the Texas Supreme Court that recognizes an "executive right" in mineral interests as a right in property. Mr. Croy, at 22 Texas Tech Law Review 281, 300–303, considers the implications of the decision for Texas law on the rule against perpetuities:

"Now that the executive right is recognized as an interest in real property, the right is clearly subject to the rule against perpetuities. As a result, Texas courts may soon be called upon to contend with violations of the rule. For example, the question may arise as to whether a "bare" executive right, severed from the mineral interest, violates the rule when it is held in perpetuity. Since the executive right and an option contract to purchase real estate could be considered analogous in some ways, courts may decide to rely upon the area of law regarding option contracts to answer questions concerning perpetual ownership of a "bare" executive right.

"In Texas, an option of indefinite duration that extends to the optionee's "heirs and assigns" violates the rule because the option does not expire within the optionee's lifetime. Generally, where no fixed period of duration is stated in the option, Texas courts will imply a reasonable time so as to save the option from violating the rule. However, courts will not imply a reasonable time for performance if the option extends to the optionee's heirs and assigns. Thus, an option of indefinite duration that does not extend to the optionee's "heirs and assigns" may be saved from violating the rule if the court implies a reasonable time for performance.

"Applying Texas law regarding option contracts to the 'bare' executive right would arguably do little to rescue the right from violating the rule. For example, where the deed expressly conveys or reserves the right to 'A, his heirs and assigns,' with no period of duration stated, the executive right might violate the rule and courts would probably refuse to imply a reasonable time for performance. Moreover, since the executive right is now freely alienable, devisable and inheritable, the executive right extends to the optionee's heirs and assigns as a matter of law. As a result, an executive right of unstated duration may violate the rule even in the absence of the words 'heirs and assigns.' In this latter situation, it is likely that courts will not imply a reasonable time period in order to save the executive right. * * *

"Since the executive right is now recognized as an interest in real property, contingent remainders and executory interests, both of which are subject to the rule against perpetuities, may now be created in the executive right. For example, O could convey a one-half mineral interest and all of the executive rights to A for life, with a remainder in B's grandchildren who graduate from college. The contingent remainder in B's grandchildren would violate the rule because there is no guarantee that a grandchild will graduate from college within twenty-one years after the death of O, A, B or B's child. Moreover, O could convey a one-half mineral interest and all of the executive rights to A and his heirs as long as the land is farmed, and then to B and his heirs. The executory interest in B would be void because there is no guarantee that the land will cease being farmed within twenty-one years after O, A or B's death.

"Although Texas utilizes the doctrine of *cy pres* to reform a future interest in real property that violates the rule, a survey of Texas case law suggests that the doctrine has only been applied in the context of charitable testamentary transfers. Thus, if the contingent remainder and executory interest illustrated above were created by testamentary devise, a strong argument would exist for invoking the doctrine of *cy pres* to reform the devise and effectuate the intent of the testator. The doctrine should also be applicable if the same interests were crated by way of an inter vivos gift. However, if the contingent remainder or executory interest in question was created in a commercial oil and gas context, the doctrine of *cy pres* would probably not be invoked and the interests would be void and struck from the grant.

"Alternatively, any future rule against perpetuities violations resulting from application of the *Day* court's holding could be avoided altogether if Texas courts would follow the suggestion of some commentators and declare that the rule does not apply to commercial oil and gas transactions. A convincing argument in support of this proposition arises in light of the fact that the seventeenth century rule was originally intended to restrain the 'dead-hand control of perpetual family settlements.' Thus, modern-day commercial oil and gas transactions do not offend the policy behind the rule. This is especially true in Texas after the supreme court's holding in *Day*. For example, when the executive right is conveyed or reserved, the power of alienation is not suspended because all of the nonexecutive interests, as well as the executive right, are freely alienable by the present owners.[44]   In fact, transfer of the executive right actually promotes the purpose behind the rule.   When the executive right is separated from a nonexecutive interest, alienability is increased by eliminating the need for nonexecutive interest owners to join the lease.

"If the Texas Supreme Court is faced with an issue regarding future interests in the executive right and the rule against perpetuities, one can hope the court will exercise the same sound legal reasoning and foresight evidenced in *Day* and declare that the rule is inapplicable in commercial oil and gas transactions.   * * *"

VI. REVIEW PROBLEMS

A.   Describe the enforceable property interests of all parties in the following instruments.   In working through these problems assume that the jurisdiction accepts the rule in Shelley's case, the doctrine of worthier title, the destructibility of contingent remainders, the Statute of Uses, and the rule against perpetuities.

1. Oswald to Adams and her heirs so long as the land is farmed.
2. Oswald to Adams for life; if Adams dies having borne live children, then to Boswell and his heirs, but if Adams dies without having borne live children, then to Chambers and her heirs.
3. Oswald to Adams for life, then to Boswell and his heirs, unless Adams dies unmarried, then to Oswald and his heirs.
4. Oswald to Adams for life, then to Adams's heirs.
5. Oswald to Adams for life, then to Boswell and his heirs, but if Adams dies without children, to Chambers and her heirs.
6. Oswald to Adams and the heirs of her body, then to Boswell and his heirs.
7. Oswald to Adams for life, then to Adams's children for life, then to Adams's grandchildren and their heirs.
8. Oswald to Adams when she graduates from law school (Adams is a first year law student).
9. Oswald to Adams for life, then to Boswell for life, but if Boswell dies before there is peace in the world, to Chambers and her heirs.
10. Oswald to Adams and her heirs as long as she remains unmarried, then Boswell and his heirs.
11. Oswald to Boswell for life, then to Chambers's heirs for the life of the longest liver of them, then to Boswell's heirs and their heirs.
12. Oswald to Boswell for life, then to Chambers and her heirs if Boswell dies unmarried.
13. Oswald to Adams for life, then to Oswald's heirs and their heirs.

---

44.   See 2 H. William and C. Meyers, Oil and Gas Law § 325, at 76 (separating executive right from nonexecutive interest does not violate policy of Rule because there is no suspension of power of alienation, no restraint on practical alienation, and no interference with full development of land).

14. Oswald to Adams for life, then to Adams's grandchildren who reach 21 and their heirs.

15. Oswald to Adams and her heirs so long as liquor is not served, then to Boswell for life.

16. Oswald to Adams and her heirs so long as liquor is not served, then to Boswell and his heirs.

17. Oswald to Adams for 99 years, then to Boswell and his heirs, but if Boswell marries Chambers, to Duncan and her heirs.

B. Describe the enforceable property interests of all parties in the following instruments. Answer the question where a question is asked. And draft where drafting is requested. In working through these problems assume that the jurisdiction has abolished the rule in Shelley's case, the doctrine of worthier title, and the destructibility of contingent remainders. This was done in a single act of the legislature that reads: "The rule in Shelley's case, the doctrine of worthier title, and the destructibility of contingent remainders, are hereby abolished." The jurisdiction follows the common-law rule against perpetuities without statutory modification and is famous throughout the world for its enlightened judiciary. It is not necessary that a use be raised expressly in order to create executory interests.

18. Otero to Annunzio and his heirs, but if Annunzio fails to graduate from law school, to Boaz and her heirs.

19. Otero to Annunzio and her heirs upon Annunzio's reaching the age of 21; Annunzio is now two.

20. Otero, in his will, "to my widow for life, then to my children alive at the time of her death and their heirs."

21. Otero, in his will, "to my son Juan for life, then to St. Louis University as long as the land is used for student parking. * * * The residue of my estate to the Rollison United Methodist Church and its successors."

22. Otero, by deed, "to John Jones, then to John's children and their heirs." John takes possession of the land and later dies childless and testate; his will devises all of his property to his wife.

23. Otero, by deed in 1990: "My real property in St. Louis to the Denise Salsich Art Museum and its successors, so long as it remains open to the public free of charge." Before he died in 1992, Otero deeded all of his real estate, in fee simple absolute, to the Art Institute of Chicago and its successors.

24. Otero, in his will: "Twenty-five thousand dollars to my wife Alicia; my real property to the Denise Salsich Art Museum and its successors, so long as it remains open to the public free of charge; all of the rest of my property, real and personal, to my daughter Emily and her heirs."

25. Ochs, in her will, gave her entire estate "to my son Karl so long as he lives, then to his wife if she survives him, and then to his children and their heirs."

26. Ochs, by deed, "to Anna for life, then to the first daughter of Anna who reaches 21 and her heirs." At the time of the deed, Anna has two daughters, Bette, who is 20; and Clara, who is 18.

27. Ochs, in her will, "to Anna for life, then to Bette and her heirs, but if Bette does not survive Anna, then to Clara and her heirs."

   An extra task: After you have identified the interests created by this will, draft two conveyances with the identical condition but using different future interests.

28. Ochs, by deed, "to Mary for life, then to her children and their heirs." Mary wants to tear down the single-family residence that is on the deeded land and build a multi-unit condominium for well-to-do law students. She asks if the law will allow her to do so.

29. In No. 28, would your answer be different if the deed said, "to Mary for life, then to her heirs and their heirs"?

30. Ochs, by deed, "to Alpheus for life, then to the heirs of Ochs and their heirs." After the deed is delivered, Ochs dies testate; his will leaves all of his property to the Roman Catholic Archdiocese of St. Louis.

31. O'Brien to Avia for life then to the children of Avia who reach 30 and their heirs. Avia has one child at the effective date of this instrument. Then, two years later, she has a second child, who dies at the age of six. Then, four years after the death of the second child, she has a third child. The first and third children reach the age of 30.

32. O'Brien, in his will, "to my widow for life, then to my children and their heirs."

33. O'Brien, in his will, "to Atticus for life, then to the children of Atticus who have reached the age of 30 by the time of Atticus's death and their heirs."

34. O'Brien, by deed, "to Agatha for life, then to the grandchildren of Agatha who reach the age of 21 and their heirs."

TWO-BITES

Chapter Three

JOINT OWNERSHIP

INTRODUCTION: PROPERTY IN FAMILIES

Anglo–American property law has developed forms of collective property ownership for business. It is possible for partners in a business to put the title to their property in a form that will not be affected by the death or defection of a partner. The Uniform Partnership Act provides a form of tenancy in partnership that will accomplish that. The most common form of collective ownership in business planning is ownership of business property in a business corporation, a fictional legal person who neither dies nor defects. Similar forms of ownership have been developed for voluntary and charitable organizations, such as lodges and churches, and even for ownership by communities: The equitable "ownership" of property held in a charitable trust, for example, is in theory in the community; ownership interests are enforced by a governmental official.

But property law has not developed a form of collective property ownership for families. There is no moral or conceptual reason we can think of to explain why family ownership of property has not been accommodated in a similar way. (Of course, a family business can be put into partnership or into a family business corporation. Examples are in the legal work Louis D. Brandeis did in the Warren matter, which was discussed in Chapter Two. We are thinking of property as family property, not primarily as business property—the family home, the family estate in the country, the family farm as home as much as business.) Our guess is that family ownership has not been so accommodated because the transition of ownership at death has been a convenient time for government to assert control over family property or to impose taxes on it. Attempts by the current owner of family property, to assure continued ownership in the family, have in any case been a major occasion for governmental interference in family life.

It is easier to approximate family ownership in a current generation than it is to approximate family ownership that reaches across generations (as business ownership in a corporation reaches across generations). It is possible to create collective ownership of property, in *married* partners, in the current generation: Marital ownership is possible; that is the most common instance of joint ownership. Lawyers will, of course, try to use forms of marital ownership as a means to family ownership that reaches across generations; we will want to keep an eye on those attempts and on how they work.

What property lawyers for families have done is to take old forms of collective ownership and use them as forms of marital ownership. It has been possible for centuries for two or more people to own a single tract of land in undivided shares (*the tenancy in common*). Such common ownership can be spread on the plane of time, divided among interests, made subject to conditions, and held in equity as well as in law. It has also been possible to own undivided shares in such way that the surviving co-owners take the share of the co-owner who dies first (*the joint tenancy*). The common law even developed a form of this collective ownership that it limited to married partners, probably so that the husband could control the wife's interest (*the tenancy by the entirety*). Except for the third form of ownership, these devices were not exclusively for married people, but they have come in modern practice to be used by married people more than in any other personal relationship, and they have come to be the dominant form of ownership of residential and agricultural real estate in the United States. Whatever their history, the tenancy in common, the joint tenancy, and the tenancy by the entirety have become our culture's answer to the family's need to own as a family. These concurrent, marital forms of property ownership are the subject of the first section in this chapter.

The subject of the second section in this chapter is the porous nature of ownership by one member of the family: Not all family property is owned collectively. Much of it is still owned by one member of the family. Members of the family other than the owner are likely to mount moral and political pressure to have the family's interest in the property recognized despite the name that is put on the land records in the courthouse.

The family's interest is most likely to appear when the current or nominal owner of the property dies. Most likely, inheritance will be to members of the family. Most cultures force inheritance in this way. English and American property law has generally not forced inheritance. (The common law did not allow for wills of real estate until 1540, but it was possible after *Quia Emptores* to convey to people other than the heir, during life. Before 1540, medieval chancery barristers adapted the use to the equivalent of a will.)

But a disdain for forced inheritance (such as continental legal systems have) does not mean that English law had no way to recognize property claims from members of the family other than the property owner. A man's widow, for example, was not an heir of his real property, in Anglo–American law, until relatively recently. "The heir," from *De Donis* through nineteenth-century English novels, meant the oldest son, or some functional substitute for the oldest son who was in a younger generation. But the widow had a moral (and therefore, ultimately, in some way or other, legal) claim to her husband's property. Even if the culture did not regard her as a partner of her husband, it pretty much had to regard her as a dependent, and she had at least a claim to means of supporting herself during widowhood. The law's response to the claim was the widow's right to *dower*. In Professor Moynihan's definition, "the widow was entitled on the death of her husband to a life estate in one-third of the lands of which he had been seised at any time during the marriage of an estate in fee simple or in fee tail, provided that the estate was one capable of being inherited by issue of the marriage."

The surviving husband was a different case with a similar result. The widower was not his wife's heir, and her family's solicitor had probably arranged things so that her property would go to her children after she and her husband were dead. But the husband, until relatively recently, controlled his wife's property during their lives together. His moral (and therefore legal) claim to his wife's property, after she died, was probably based on the fact that he had grown accustomed to controlling her property while she was alive—that and the possibility that he might have children to look after. (Of course, he often needed his wife's property in order to support himself: The young Victorian gentleman, according to the novels, had either to marry a rich woman or ruin his whole life and go to work. But a patriarchical culture was not likely to phrase the widower's claim in terms of dependence, even if he was in fact dependent, as—according to the novels—he usually was.) The law's response to his claim was the widower's right to *curtesy*. In Professor Moynihan's definition, curtesy was "a life estate to which the husband was entitled in all lands of which his wife was seised in fee simple or in fee tail at any time during the marriage provided that there was issue born alive capable of inheriting the estate."

Finally, continental community-property theories found their way into American law through the French settlement of Louisiana and Spanish settlements in the Southwest and on the Pacific coast. Spanish law recognizes marriage as a community, and the community as the owner of property earned by the community. The husband controlled the community's property (as the husband in England controlled both the jointly-owned property and his wife's property), but the property was, in ownership theory, half his wife's. This form of collective marital ownership survives in the nine community-property states and is the basis of modern marital-property proposals in several of the common-law states.

I. CONCURRENT OWNERSHIP

Imagine a couple, Frank and Mary Tregrear, who have located and signed a broker's form contract to buy their first home in the suburbs. They have heeded the advice of the newspaper financial columnists—as not every couple does—and have consulted a lawyer for representation

in the formalities of purchase. The lawyer is talking to them, on
Wednesday afternoon, her green eyeshade tilted back for purposes of
conversation, and she says: "How do you want to take title?" They
looked puzzled, and the lawyer says, "Whose names do you want on the
deed?" And Mary says: "What do you advise?"

The evident choices are: (i) Mary; (ii) Frank; (iii) Mary and Frank
as tenants in common; (iv) Mary and Frank as joint tenants; and, in
some (but not all) states, (v) Mary and Frank as tenants by the entirety.
If one of the first two forms is chosen, the spouse not mentioned will
have claims on the property of the sort we will consider in Section II of
this chapter.

A. TENANCY IN COMMON

In modern law, the *basic* form of joint ownership is the tenancy in
common. It is not the most widely used, but it is the form the law
presumes where the words of the deed are not clear. In a tenancy in
common:

— The parties own in undivided shares which need not be equal.

— Each co-owner has a cause of action to have his share, as we
lawyers say it, "set off by metes and bounds." That can be done,
and almost always is, by agreement; but if the owners do not agree,
any one of them can ask a judge to *partition* the property. The
judge will appoint commissioners to go to the land and divide it up.
The judge has the power to adjust unequal shares by imposing
obligations of cash payment to make the shares work out. If the
property cannot be divided equally, the judge has the power to order
it sold so that the money equivalent of the land can be divided.

— Each cotenant's interest can be conveyed, given by will, inherited,
or burdened with secured debt. The unsecured creditors of each of
them can reach that cotenant's interest for the satisfaction of
claims that have been reduced to judgment. If a creditor succeeds
to ownership by foreclosure or execution, the creditor then owns as
a tenant in common.

— Tenants in common have been treated in the law as a group of
owners. Any one of them can get out if he wants to, but, until he
does, he consents to being treated as the member of a group. For
example, no cotenant has a legal claim on the others for time and
expense spent in making improvements. However, if one cotenant
makes a profit on the land, from outsiders, the other cotenants have
a claim to a share of the profits.

— The tenancy in common is the presumed form of joint ownership.
If there is doubt about what a joint estate is, it is a tenancy in
common. Most states have statutes to this effect. The common-law
presumption favored joint tenancy: If modern owners want to own
as joint tenants, or as tenants by the entirety, they probably have to
make their intention explicit. If property is conveyed to two or
more people, with no statement of how it is to be held, they will
hold as tenants in common. (However, in states that recognize the

tenancy by the entirety, identification of the joint owners as married to one another is probably enough to establish a tenancy by the entirety.)

CHOSAR CORPORATION v. OWENS

Supreme Court of Virginia, 1988.
235 Va. 660, 370 S.E.2d 305.

STEPHENSON, JUSTICE.

The principal questions in this appeal are (1) whether mining of coal owned by cotenants without the consent of all owners constitutes waste and the exclusion of the interests of the nonconsenting owners entitling them to injunctive relief, and (2) if such mining does constitute waste and the exclusion of the nonconsenting owners' interests, whether the consenting coal owners may permit a third party to transport coal from adjoining land through an underground passageway created by such mining, over the objection of the nonconsenting owners.

In this chancery cause, Beulah Owens and others (collectively, Owens) seek to enjoin Chosar corporation and William H. Drake (collectively, Chosar) from mining coal in which Owens owns an undivided fractional interest and from hauling coal from the land of a third party through an underground passageway created by such mining. The trial court ruled that "the mining of coal by Chosar and its lessees * * *, without the consent of all cotenants, is the commission of waste, the exclusion by [Chosar] of [Owens] from their interest in the property, and an appropriation thereof to [Chosar]." The court also ruled that fewer than all cotenants could not permit the haulage of coal, produced from other lands, through underground passages carved out of the jointly-owned coal. Consequently, the trial court permanently enjoined Chosar from such mining and haulage, ordered an accounting, and referred the cause to a special commissioner. * * *

The relevant facts are undisputed. The coal in controversy lies within a 61–acre tract of land in Dickenson County (the Willis tract). The coal is owned by the heirs and successors in title of Andrew and Crissie Willis (collectively, Willis). At present, approximately 90 persons own undivided interests in the coal.

Approximately 85 percent of the co-owners executed leases transferring to Chosar "all their right, title and interest" in all the merchantable seams of coal on the Willis tract. The leases provided for a royalty that is the greater of two dollars per 2,000 pounds of coal or eight percent of the price obtained from the coal. The leases also granted Chosar the right to transport coal from adjoining lands through underground passageways on the leased premises.

The most valuable coal on the Willis tract is the "Splashdam seam," which is several hundred feet beneath the surface of the land. Chosar subleased the right to mine the Splashdam seam to coal operators at a royalty rate of 14 percent of the selling price.

Because the Splashdam seam does not outcrop on the Willis tract, access for underground mining had to be achieved from other lands. Consequently, Chosar obtained a lease from Pittston Resources, Inc. (Pittston), to mine coal from land owned by Pittston that adjoins the Willis tract. Thus, a portal was established at the outcropping of the Splashdam seam on the Pittston tract, approximately 200 feet from the Willis tract's boundary.

The mining operation proceeded from the portal to the Willis tract, thence through the Willis tract to Pittston's land on the opposite side. Thereafter, coal mined from Pittston's property was transported underground through the passageways on the Willis tract and thence to the surface. The passageways on the Willis tract were created by the mining operation.

Although a cotenant may transfer to another his undivided interest in the common property without the consent of his cotenants * * * nonconsenting cotenants are not bound by an agreement purporting to lease the entire property or any specific portion thereof * * *. A lessee claiming under such a lease acquires rights no greater than those of his lessor. * * * Consequently, our inquiry here necessarily focuses upon the extent of the consenting cotenants' rights in the common coal lands.

We first consider whether Chosar's mining of the coal without the consent of all owners constituted waste. Generally, waste is defined as "[a] destruction or material alteration or deterioration of the freehold, or of the improvements forming a material part thereof, by any person rightfully in possession, but who has not the fee title or the full estate." Black's Law Dictionary 1425 (5th ed. 1979). At common law, a cotenant was not liable to his cotenants for waste. * * * The common law, however, has been changed by statute: "If a tenant in common, joint tenant or parcener commit waste, he shall be liable to his cotenants, jointly or severally, for damages." Code § 55–212. Injured parties also have a remedy at law for waste committed by "any tenant of land * * * while he remains in possession." Code § 55–211.

Notwithstanding these statutory remedies, a court of equity, in a proper case, may grant an injunction to prohibit waste. * * * What constitutes waste sufficient to entitle the injured party to injunctive relief depends upon the circumstances of each particular case. * * * For example, the cutting of timber in some instances may constitute waste, while in other cases it may be a benefit. * * *

In the case of tenants in common, no tenant can change or alter the common property to the injury of his cotenants without their consent. * * * Injunctive relief against a cotenant is proper where the injury is material, continuing, and not adequately remedied in damages. * * *

In the present case, the extraction of coal from the Willis tract is a material and continuing destruction of the very substance of the mineral estate. The consenting cotenants had no right to remove coal from the common property without the consent of Owens. Consequently, the consenting cotenants could not authorize Chosar to mine coal from the property without the consent of the other cotenants. We conclude, therefore, that the trial court correctly ruled that Chosar's mining within the Willis tract constituted the commission of waste. Because continued mining would cause irreparable harm to Owens, we further conclude that the trial court properly enjoined Chosar from committing further waste.

We next consider whether Chosar's mining of the Willis tract excluded the nonconsenting cotenants from their interest in the property. At common law, one cotenant who used the common land exclusively was not required to account to the other cotenants unless his use resulted in an ouster or exclusion of his cotenants. * * * Now, however, an accounting may be had against a cotenant "for receiving more than comes to his just share or proportion." Code § 8.01–31.

In his use of the common property, a cotenant cannot appropriate to himself the entire estate * * * or unilaterally partition the property by appropriating to himself any specific portion of the property. * * * If a cotenant desires partition, he may seek relief under Code § 8.01–81. That section also authorizes courts to compel partition of "mineral rights east and south of the Clinch River."

Significantly, however, courts had no authority to partition mineral rights until 1964.[1] In that year, the General Assembly amended the predecessor to Code § 8.01–81 to permit the partition of mineral rights "east of the Blue Ridge mountains." Acts 1964, c. 167. Subsequently, the General Assembly again amended that section, empowering courts to partition mineral rights "east and south of the Clinch River." Acts 1968, c. 412.

Thus, by negative implication, Code § 8.01–81 prohibits the partitioning of mineral rights west and north of the Clinch River, which is where the mineral rights in the Willis tract are located. If a court has no authority to partition mineral rights west and north of the Clinch River, a fortiori, such mineral rights cannot be partitioned without the consent of all cotenants.

In the present case, however, Chosar's conduct of mining operations was such an appropriation of a specific portion of the Splashdam seam, and in effect, a unilateral partitioning of the mineral estate. Thus, we conclude that the trial court correctly ruled that Chosar's mining excluded the nonconsenting cotenants from their interests in the property.

1. In a situation where there is no common-law partition remedy for tenants in common, and no statutes such as Justice Stephenson is about to describe, partition is nonetheless possible when all cotenants agree. Suppose a case in which they *do* agree; even there judicial partition is not available (and hardly seems necessary anyway). How does a Wednesday-afternoon lawyer go about the task, though? Note that, in a case such as this, it is going to be important to show clear title in the records in the courthouse: Third parties are not going to risk investment under conveyances that might be subject to challenge—particularly not in Virginia after this case. (Eds.)

Similarly, the transporting of coal from Pittston's adjoining land through the underground passageway created in the Willis tract by Chosar's mining constitutes an exclusion of the nonconsenting owners' interest in the property. Moreover, the underground passageway is a product of the waste of the estate. Allowing Chosar to use the tunnel to transport coal would permit Chosar to profit from its own wrongdoing. We conclude, therefore, that the trial court properly enjoined Chosar from further haulage. * * *

Affirmed and remanded.

THOMAS, JUSTICE, dissenting.

This is an extremely important property case which, in my opinion, has been wrongly decided by the majority in a decision that could have dire adverse consequences for the Commonwealth. The basic dispute is over the mining of coal. The owners of 85% of the coal in question want to mine. The owners of the remaining 15% of the coal do not want to mine. As the majority acknowledges, because of Code § 8.01–81, the dispute between the owners cannot be resolved by a partition suit. Thus, the owners are locked in battle with no way out. The result of the majority opinion is that the rights of the 15% who do not want to mine have been made paramount to the rights of the 85% who want to mine. Indeed, the principle of the majority opinion is such that if the mineral rights here in dispute were jointly owned by 1,000,000 people and 999,999 of these co-owners wanted to mine, one solitary co-owner could enjoin all mining. The majority's decision is neither required nor justified by existing Virginia law; moreover, it is not sound in principle or logic.

Two issues were presented to the trial court. The first was whether Chosar, the 85% owner of the mineral rights in the Willis tract, committed waste by mining coal from the property. The second was whether Chosar committed a trespass by hauling coal belonging to third parties through tunnels in the Willis tract which had been created by the mining that was claimed to be waste. The trial court ruled against Chosar on both points. * * *

* * *

Chosar has never claimed exclusive right to all the coal from the mine in question. Chosar has always acknowledged the ownership interest of its co-owners. Further, Chosar attempted to leave unmined sufficient coal to represent the interest of the 15% who did not want to mine and Chosar also set up a fund into which it made royalty payments for the benefit of those who had refused to mine. * * * Chosar never contended that it had a right to all the coal and all the proceeds from the sale of the coal. * * *

I would treat the present problem as a case of first impression in the commonwealth and establish a rule that protects the property rights of both the minority and the majority. * * *

* * *

With regard to the issue of trespass and waste, I would consider the totality of the circumstances, including the fact that coal can be enjoyed only through extraction and is valuable only as a result of extraction. * * * Moreover, I would consider the fact that an overwhelming majority of the interest holders want to mine yet are prohibited from partitioning the property. Then I would adopt a rule such as that which is said to be the majority rule regarding extraction of oil and gas: "Under the rule which is applied in the majority of states which have decisions on the point, a cotenant in the fee may enter to explore for and produce oil and gas without consent of his cotenants. *He must, however, account to his cotenants for their proportionate share of production*" (emphasis added). By such rule, in the special class of cases represented by the instant appeal, I would undertake to prevent a tyranny of the minority interest holders. Without such a rule, the majority's interest in otherwise valuable mineral rights could be absolutely destroyed on the whim of one recalcitrant co-owner.

The portion of the majority opinion which concerns the haulage issue does not even address the issue which was presented to this Court. That issue is whether Chosar trespassed upon its own property when it transported a third party's coal through passageways located in the Willis tract. The facts are that the haulage does nothing to damage the mineral estate.

I cannot understand, and the majority does not explain, how a co-owner of property can trespass on his own property simply by moving through that property. The haulage issue does not involve a question of entering the property to commit waste. Hauling coal through tunnels is not the same as removing coal from the property. The theory of trespass in the context of waste is that not even a co-owner of property will be permitted to enter the property to commit waste. In that limited situation, the law says that even the co-owner has no right to be on the property. But where no act of waste is being committed, the co-owner's original rights to enter his property will obtain.

The majority has, by brute force, simply declared that because it was waste to extract coal in the first instance, it is trespass to move through the tunnels created by the original extraction even if no more extraction is being done. I disagree with the first proposition. But even if it were true, the second proposition does not follow from the first. I would reverse the judgment of the trial court on both issues.

Notes and Questions

Justice Thomas's moral argument depends on the disproportionate power of "one recalcitrant co-owner." Perhaps his argument is that such an arrangement is anti-democratic; if so, it is an argument that might be raised in many property situations. In one sense all of property law is anti-democratic: Property is power and the more you own the more power you have. Perhaps Justice Thomas only wants to bring the law governing co-ownership of coal fields within that sort of regime.

It is more likely, though, that his argument is that mining coal is a progressive thing to do in southwestern Virginia—that development of this natural resource in that part of the Commonwealth is for the common good. We will evade that interesting issue, to the dismay of both capitalists and environmentalists among our readers, by turning from the appellate reports to the law office:

In law-office property law, the governing morality is not the morality of judges; it is almost always the morality of one's client. For example: Assume our client, Miss Elizabeth Lupton, spinster heiress, owns 500 acres in a more opulent part of Virginia—in the horse country not far from Washington, D.C. She is talking to us about her will; and it is clear that what she wants, more than anything, is to leave our office with the assurance that her horse farm will not be turned into a bedroom subdivision for bureaucrats from the nation's capital. The "objects of her bounty," as we lawyers put it, are five nephews and nieces. They are also her heirs. All of them except one are urban people who don't have much interest in horses or where horses live.

One niece, Lucy, is different and is of one mind with Miss Lupton on the preservation of horses in Northern Virginia. If Miss Lupton's will said "my horse farm to my nephews and nieces," they would hold, after her death, as tenants in common. Development of the land might end up being impeded by Lucy, that "one recalcitrant co-owner," but not for long, since in this case, unlike *Chosar,* partition would be available and four-fifths of the farm could be partitioned, then developed (and the remaining one-fifth would not be much of a horse farm). Tenancy in common will not get what our client wants. Make some alternative suggestions for her, please. In doing so, review in your mind some of the devices we discussed in Chapter Two.

B. JOINT TENANCY AND TENANCY BY THE ENTIRETY

The logic of concurrent ownership should be coming clear by now; we are going to suppose that it is and introduce this section with some questions.

Robert J. Bruss writes a Saturday column in the Washington Post, called "Real Estate Mailbag." On July 11, 1988, he reprinted and answered the following question:

"Dear Bob: My best friend and I want to buy a house together. I am putting up 75 percent of the down payment and he is putting up 25 percent. Since I earn more money than he does, we have agreed he will pay 25 percent of the expenses and I will pay 75 percent. I will own 75 percent of the house and he will own 25 percent. We want to hold title as joint tenants with right of survivorship, but our attorney says that doing so requires equal 50–50 ownership. If anything happens to either of us we want the other to own the house. Can we do this with joint tenancy?—John R."

"Dear John: Yes, but * * * joint tenancy ownership requires equal property ownership shares. To illustrate, each of two joint tenants would own 50 percent and each of three joint tenants would own one-third. The survivorship feature means the surviving joint tenant winds up owning the entire property.

"But joint tenancy ownership is inconsistent with your desire to own 75 percent of the house while your friend owns 25 percent. That can be accomplished by holding title as tenants in common because joint tenants cannot own unequal shares.

"However, tenant-in-common ownership does not automatically pass to the survivor and is subject to a deceased's will. Sorry, you can't have both unequal ownership and the survivorship benefit of joint tenancy. Your attorney is correct."

Question One: Is there a way to get Bob what he wants?

* * *

Since the *joint tenancy* was the basic common-law joint estate, we can expect to find residues of common law in modern law. There is, for example, a common-law requirement that joint tenancies must have four unities: They must be created; (1) at the same time; (2) by the same title; (3) with the same possession; and (4) with the same interests. Modern courts are not often fussy about the law of unities. The unities are invoked, when they are noticed at all, to explain a result the judges reach on other grounds. In any case, as Mr. Bruss said, shares in joint tenancy are equal:

— Joint tenancy prevails over descent by will and inheritance. That makes it attractive as a will substitute. It is, in American rural legal folklore, the poor man's will. Wife and husband own homes as joint tenants so that when he dies, it will be hers—period. Without her going to a probate judge, or a lawyer, or even to the courthouse. All she needs to establish her ownership are; (i) the deed, which is already recorded in the courthouse, or bank records creating a joint account, or transfer-agent records showing joint ownership of securities; and (ii) evidence of her husband's death, which will also be a matter of public record.

— The other side of that feature is that neither spouse's will disposes of the joint-tenancy house, account, or securities unless the spouse of the testator dies first (in which case the property is not held in joint tenancy when the testator dies).

— Each joint tenant can, though, convey his interest during life. If the spouse of the testator makes a deed to her brother John of her interest in the house—

  Will John have exactly what she had (undivided possession with Frank, while Frank and Mary are both alive, with a chance for full ownership if Mary survives Frank, or nothing if she doesn't)?

  Answer: No. Mary's deed will *sever* the joint tenancy—that is, convert it into a tenancy in common between John and Frank. Either can then seek partition and get his interest out by metes and bounds.

* * *

Finally, there is the *tenancy by the entirety,* which is in most ways a joint tenancy that is not severable except by divorce. We say in most ways because in some states the tenancy by the entirety retains the old patriarchy of the English common law: Husband and wife are one and that one is the husband. The unseverability feature has some advantages, in those states that recognize the common-law tenancy by the entirety (and most do not): Suppose, for example, that Frank and Mary may be able to take title in an old-fashioned tenancy by the entirety. Suppose Mary is a director of a public corporation. Lawsuits against directors are beginning to proliferate: lawsuits that might leave her with million-dollar personal liabilities that could be executed on their home. How would you suggest the Tregrears take title to their house?

Question Two: Would joint tenancy serve the clients as well as tenancy by the entirety?

Question Three: Can the Tregrears protect themselves from liabilities to other creditors in one of those ways—furniture companies, for example, or plumbers and garbage collectors?

The possibility of secret severance is one of the main disadvantages of joint tenancy. Harms v. Sprague, 105 Ill.2d 215, 85 Ill.Dec. 331, 473 N.E.2d 930 (1984) [reproduced in Chapter Five], tells a story about secret severance that illustrates the disadvantage. The case puts us in mind of Garrison Keillor, of "Prairie Home Companion," and the Norwegian bachelor farmers of Lake Woebegone, Minnesota. John and William held their farm as joint tenants. They fell out and John fell in with their neighbor Charlie Sprague. Charlie needed some money and the bank wouldn't lend it to him without a guarantor. John said he would be the guarantor for Charlie's loan. But the bank said it needed collateral from John as guarantor, and John put up the farm: He mortgaged his and William's farm to secure Charlie Sprague's note. Then he moved off the farm and moved in with Charlie. Then he died. Then William found out about the mortgage and went to a lawyer, who brought a quiet-title action joining as defendants both Charlie and the bank.

The circuit judge said that the mortgage severed the joint tenancy—which pleased the bank (we trust you understand why). The appellate court reversed and held that the mortgage did not sever the joint tenancy—which pleased William.

Question Four: "Why was William pleased?"

The Supreme Court of Illinois affirmed and took a firm line on what causes a severance. A mortgage does not. A mortgage is not like a grant of "title." But if John had secretly *deeded* his interest to Charlie Sprague, the joint tenancy would clearly have been severed and Charlie and William would hold the farm as tenants in common.

Another example: One of us was once asked to talk to a "Parents Without Partners" meeting, about wills. (A not infrequent request made of lawyers is to speak to meetings of clubs and church organizations about property-law matters—more often than not about making wills. Lawyers have always been generous about giving their time in the community in this way—no doubt, usually, for reasons attributable to civic virtue, although less altruistic reasons may occur to you.) After the talk, a member of the audience came up (a frequent occurrence on such occasions), possibly for some free legal advice, but, for all that appeared, in order to teach this lawyer something he had not learned in law school.

This man said he was a widower and had one child, an 18–year–old son who had recently graduated from high school. The man said he owned his house now; it had been held in a tenancy by entirety until his wife died two years before the club's meeting. And he had several thousand dollars in a bank account, which had been "held jointly" before his wife died. He had, he said, just a month before, made it unnecessary to see a lawyer about a will. How had he done that? He had "put the boy's name on everything." He had, as the conversation then showed, placed his savings in a joint bank account ("JTWROS," father and son) and filled out and signed a dime-store form deed that put the house in joint tenancy. The lawyer (one of us) nodded and asked how the son was doing. (There was no malice in this question; the lawyer was just trying to change the subject.) The father said, "Just fine. He joined the Marines. He is in basic training at Camp Pendleton [San Diego], California."

Question Five: Please evaluate what this parent without a partner did.

IN RE ESTATE OF THOMPSON

Supreme Court of Ohio, 1981.
66 Ohio St.2d 433, 423 N.E.2d 90.

In 1954, Richard L. Thompson, appellee herein, opened two joint and survivorship savings accounts, one with Banc–Ohio (then Ohio National Bank), and the second with Hub Federal Savings & Loan Association. Thompson's wife, Carma Lee, was the other party to the accounts.

By June of 1978, the Thompsons were having marital problems, although neither party had taken legal action prior to that month. On June 8, 1978, Richard Thompson closed both accounts and transferred the funds into two new accounts in his name only.

On June 9, 1978, Richard Thompson was served with a complaint that his wife had filed on June 2, 1978, seeking a divorce, separate maintenance and alimony. The complaint was coupled with a motion seeking a restraining order prohibiting, *inter alia,* withdrawal of any funds in the original two joint and survivorship savings accounts.

On July 19, 1978, Carma Lee Thompson became comatose and on September 26, 1978, she succumbed.

Carma Lee Thompson's daughter, Pamela Lee Botts, appellant herein, was appointed executrix of her estate by the Probate Division of the Court of Common Pleas of Franklin County on October 25, 1978.

She filed an inventory which included two unliquidated claims against Richard Thompson as constructive trustee for one-half of the amounts which had been in the joint and survivorship accounts.

Richard Thompson filed exceptions to the inventory, including among the items excepted to the above two unliquidated claims. A hearing was held before a referee.

At the hearing it was established that Thompson had transferred the money, which consisted largely of his contributions from the joint and survivorship accounts, after talking with an attorney regarding his marital problems. On cross-examination, Thompson testified that the accounts had been intended as "safekeeping," to be used by his wife in the event of his death or illness. According to Thompson, approximately ten years before his wife's death, when his wife had taken one or two hundred dollars out of one of the accounts, he had advised her that in the event she persisted in such conduct, he would remove her name from the account. Thompson admitted that in his opinion the accounts belonged to both of them, although he maintained possession and control over the passbooks throughout their existence.

The referee's report, approved by the Probate Judge, found that one-half of the balance in the accounts was properly included in the inventory, and that Richard Thompson had improperly withdrawn the funds from the joint and survivorship accounts, breaching a fiduciary relationship he had with his wife who was determined to be co-owner of the funds.

The Court of Appeals reversed, finding that the survivorship aspect of the accounts continued in effect after the transfer because the transfer was a good faith effort to preserve the funds for the mutual benefit of both Richard and Carma Lee Thompson. * * *

CELEBREZZE, CHIEF JUSTICE.

This court has traditionally utilized contract law concepts to enforce the survivorship rights of the parties to accounts on deposit in financial institutions which are designated as joint and survivorship accounts. * * *

* * *

In the case of *Cleveland Trust Co. v. Scobie, Admr.,* 114 Ohio St., 241, 151 N.E., 373, 48 A.L.R., 182, this court laid down the rule, since adhered to in principle, that where one opens a savings account in a bank to the joint credit of himself and another, payable to either or the survivor, and it is apparent that the depositor intended to transfer to the person, to whom he made the account jointly payable, a present joint interest therein equal to his own, the person to whom the account is made jointly payable is entitled to the balance of the money in the account upon the death of the depositor as against the claim thereto of the depositor's personal representative.

Because both a survivorship interest and a present joint interest are created by contract, we have held that the property can be transferred at one of the party's death even though the formal requisites of a will are not present.

Joint and survivorship accounts, however, are frequently utilized without their legal ramifications being fully understood by their creators. As a result, this court has held that the creation of such accounts raises a rebuttable presumption that the parties to the account share equally in the ownership of the funds on deposit, allowing the presumption to be rebutted by a showing of the "realities of ownership." * * *

The case at bar illustrates a common problem with this approach. The primary and foremost contributions made to the accounts were by Richard Thompson. When he created the accounts, he intended to maintain control over them during his lifetime; however, he also intended to create a survivorship interest in them. Under a strict contractual analysis, he could not do both.

R.C. 1107.08(A) states:

"When a deposit is made in the name of two or more persons, payable to either, or the survivor, such deposit or any part thereof, or any interest thereon, may be paid to either of said persons, or the guardian of his estate, whether the other is living or not, and the receipt or acquittance of the person paid is a sufficient release and discharge of the bank for any payments so made."

R.C. 1151.19(A) states in part:

"A building and loan association may receive money on deposit or stock deposits from any persons, firms, corporations, and courts, or their agents, officers, and appointees and may pay interest thereon. When such deposits are made to the joint account of two or more persons, whether adults or minors, with a joint order to the association that such deposits or any part thereof are to be payable on the order of any of such joint depositors, and to continue to be so payable notwithstanding the death or incapacity of one or more of the persons making them, such account shall be payable to any of such survivors or order notwithstanding such death or incapacity. No recovery shall be had against such association for amounts so paid and charged to such account."

In the past this court has held that these sections and their predecessors were enacted solely for the benefit and protection of financial institutions and did not affect the relationships of the parties to joint and survivorship accounts nor authorize use of such accounts to transfer property. * * *

These sections authorizing financial institutions to create and make payments on joint and survivorship accounts implicitly permit use of such accounts to transfer property at death even though such transfers are not pursuant to a testamentary disposition. Because these statutes authorize the use of such accounts, it is not necessary to utilize the rigid contractual analysis of our earlier cases. Instead, our goal should be to effectuate the intent of the party or parties creating such accounts.

In order to do so, we must first realize that such accounts are not necessarily the most desirable means of effectuating intent. Justice Locher recognized this in his concurrence in *Vetter v. Hampton* * * * when he stated, 54 Ohio St.2d at pages 233, 234, 375 N.E.2d 804:

"This writer is cognizant that R.C. 1107.08 and 1151.19 make provision for joint and survivorship accounts. My personal observation is that these accounts are frequently litigated. It is thus apparent that there exists an abysmal flaw in their creation. All too frequently, the parties entering into this type of contractual agreement with banks or savings and loan associations are not *really* apprised of all the ramifications that exist when such a contract is consummated. Often depositors are advised that these accounts are the best way to 'avoid probate.' Seldom, if ever, are the clerks in banks and savings and loan associations attorneys or well versed in the legal aspects of this contract. Thus, the end result, in numerous instances, is a defective estate plan that successfully avoids probate at the cost of litigation, great expense, disruption of the deceased's intention and hardship to his family. * * *

[T]he joint and survivorship account is, in essence, a substitute testamentary disposition stripped of all its normal safeguards. * * * "

Use of a rebuttable presumption offers a means by which the relationships of the parties to joint and survivorship accounts can be stabilized. To a certain extent, our earlier case law has done this, but because the presumption used failed to distinguish between the treatment of such accounts during the parties' lifetimes and the treatment of such accounts after the death of a party, the effort to effectuate intent was not entirely successful.

* * *

Section 6–103(a) of the Uniform Probate Code states:

"A joint account belongs during the lifetime of all parties, to the parties in proportion to the net contributions by each to the sums on deposit, unless there is clear and convincing evidence of a different intent."

Section 6–104(a) of that Code states:

"Sums remaining on deposit at the death of a party to a joint account belong to the surviving party or parties as against the estate of the decedent unless there is clear and convincing evidence of a different intention at the time the account is created. If there are two or more surviving parties, their respective ownerships during lifetime shall be in proportion to their previous ownership interests under Section 6–103 augmented by an equal share for each survivor of any interest the decedent may have owned in the account immediately before his death; and the right of survivorship continues between the surviving parties."

We hold that the presumptions created in these two sections accurately reflect the common experiences of mankind in regard to joint and survivorship accounts. As a result, we adopt these specific sections as the law of this state.

Use of these rules does not significantly alter our earlier case law; it merely amends our earlier analytic framework so that the intent of the parties to create joint and survivorship accounts can be better effectuated.

In our earlier cases we ordinarily dealt with the right of survivorship to such accounts, not the right to control the funds on deposit during the lifetimes of the parties to the accounts. The presumption in favor of holding that such an interest exists has been essentially in accord with creator intent and the Uniform Probate Code even though we have required an intent to transfer a present interest, as well as a survivorship interest.

For example, in In re Estate of Svab (1967), 11 Ohio St.2d 182, 228 N.E.2d 609, this court held that a survivorship interest was not created because it was shown that the creator of the account had placed the other party's name on the account solely to allow that other person to assist her in conducting her business affairs. Such evidence of the "realities of ownership" can be used to rebut the presumption of survivorship which we have adopted from Section 6–104(a) of the Uniform Probate Code and of course would buttress the presumption adopted from Section 6–103(a).[2] Similarly, in a case dealing with ownership during the lives of the parties * * * the court affirmed a determination that the sole depositor to the account had sole ownership of the funds on deposit after it was shown that the other party's name was placed on the account because an injury prevented the depositor from going to the bank. The presumption adopted from Section 6–103(a) leads to the same result.

In the case at bar, appellee, in forbidding his wife from making withdrawals, in maintaining possession of the passbooks for the accounts, and in stating that the money was being held for use in the event of his death or illness, exhibited an intent to maintain control of his contributions to the account. In this context, his statement that he considered the accounts to belong to him and his wife reflected his intention to create a survivorship interest and to authorize use at some future time should he become disabled. Certainly he did not exhibit an intent to make his wife a co-owner of the accounts.

As a consequence, on June 8, 1978, appellee was entitled to withdraw from the accounts that amount which was proportionally attributable to his contributions to those accounts. That proportion of the accounts clearly belonged to him. A constructive trust can be imposed over any amounts withdrawn which exceeded those amounts attributable to his contributions. His withdrawal of any such amounts would be

2. On the other hand, it appears that treatment of the accounts as available for the use and benefit of all parties could be used to show that co-ownership of the accounts was intended.

a breach of his fiduciary duty to his wife. Any survivorship rights appellee had in such sums was forfeited.

We modify the judgment of the Court of Appeals and remand the cause to the Probate Division so that it may determine what proportion of the net contributions to the savings accounts is attributable to appellee and so that it may order any amount remaining be included in the inventory.

PAUL W. BROWN, JUSTICE, dissenting.

The lower courts found, and the parties agreed, that the funds in the joint and survivorship accounts were owned equally by Mr. and Mrs. Thompson. Had the funds not been removed, Mr. Thompson would have been entitled to all the funds on Mrs. Thompson's death pursuant to the survivorship provision of the accounts.

When Mr. Thompson closed out the joint and survivorship accounts, he terminated the contract, including the contractual right to survivorship. He has practically admitted that half the funds were his wife's. If he was afraid that she would dissipate the accounts, he should have withdrawn his one-half of the funds and left hers alone. Mr. Thompson should not be permitted to withdraw all the funds from the joint and survivorship accounts and to transfer them to an account to which only he has access, and then argue that the right to survivorship survived so that he can legally keep everything he took. This is especially true because this is a marital situation in which assets acquired by joint effort are usually considered by the contracting parties to be the property of both, absent agreements or circumstances demonstrating a contrary purpose. Here the joint account is some further acknowledgment that the funds were the property of both. The husband's threat to take his wife's name off the account made at an earlier date is not a claim of exclusive ownership, it is merely the act of a spouse who considers himself the dominant financial party with a veto power over expenditures and has no real legal significance. I consider this a poor case in which to generalize about joint and survivorship accounts. I would reverse the Court of Appeals and reinstate the Probate Judge's order.

WILLIAMS v. STUDSTILL

Supreme Court of Georgia, 1983.
251 Ga. 466, 306 S.E.2d 633.

HILL, CHIEF JUSTICE.

From revolutionary times until 1976, the law was that joint tenancy as it existed at common law [3] was abolished in this state. * * * [4]

---

3. At common law an estate in joint tenancy, with right of survivorship, was created in any case where land was granted to two or more persons. The creation of the estate in two or more persons, without more, carried with it the right of survivor-

ship. * * * If a joint tenant conveyed his interest to another, the joint tenancy was severed and converted to a tenancy in com-

---

4. See note 4 on page 215.

This case involves an attempt to create a joint tenancy by will in 1970. The trial court held that a joint tenancy was created, but was destroyed by severance. This appeal followed.

Alice C. Studstill died in 1970, possessed of 750 acres of land in Dodge County, Georgia, which she devised as follows: "I give, bequeath and devise that track of land known as the Daniel Mill Pond Place * * * containing approximately 750 acres, to my children, James H. Studstill and Mary Ella S. Studstill [now Williams], *as joint tenants and not as tenants in common and to the survivor of them in fee simple.*" (Emphasis supplied.) * * *

In 1980, Mary Ella S. Studstill Williams conveyed her interest to her nephew, James Arthur Williams, reserving a life estate and timber rights to herself. In June, 1982, James H. Studstill died testate leaving his widow, Louise, as his executrix and sole heir. In her suit against Mary Ella and James A. Williams, Louise claims a one-half interest in the property.

Louise contends that under the case law, a joint tenancy could be expressly created before the 1976 statute, that Mary Ella's deed to James severed the four unities required of a joint tenancy and created a tenancy in common, and that thereafter upon her husband's death, she inherited his interest in the tenancy in common. Mary Ella and James contend that the case law prior to the 1976 statute clearly establishes that although joint tenancies, as such, were abolished, the creation of a right of survivorship is not prohibited, and that the right of survivorship is enforceable where expressly created and is not destroyed by severance. The trial court found that the joint tenancy was converted into a tenancy in common by virtue of severance and found in favor of Louise. * * *

[W]herever an instrument creates an estate which at common law would be held to be a joint tenancy, in this State the instrument would be held to take effect as to all its terms, except so far as it provided by implication for survivorship among the tenants, and such tenants would be held to occupy to each other, so far as this question is concerned, the relation of tenants in common. While the doctrine of survivorship as applied to joint tenancies has been distinctly abolished

mon and the right of survivorship was defeated by the severance. * * *

4. In 1976, the General Assembly provided that a true joint tenancy could exist in Georgia: "(a) Deeds and other instruments of title, including any instrument in which one person conveys to himself and one or more other persons, any instrument in which two or more persons convey to themselves or to themselves and another or others, and wills taking effect after January 1, 1977, may create a joint interest with survivorship in two or more persons. Any instrument of title in favor of two or more persons shall be construed to create interests in common without survivorship between or among the owners unless the instrument expressly refers to the takers as 'joint tenants,' 'joint tenants and not as tenants in common,' or 'joint tenants with survivorship' or as taking 'jointly with survivorship.' *Any instrument using one of the forms of expression referred to in the preceding sentence or language essentially the same as one of these forms of expression shall create a joint tenancy estate or interest that may be severed as to the interest of any owner by his lifetime transfer of all or a part of his interest.*" * * *

and does not exist in this State, there is no law of this State that we are aware of which prevents parties to a contract, or a testator in his will, from expressly providing that an interest in property shall be dependent upon survivorship. Of course all presumptions are against such an intention; but where the contract or will provides, either in express terms or by necessary implication, that the doctrine of survivorship shall be recognized, we know of no reason why a provision in the contract or will dependent upon such doctrine may not become operative under the laws of this State. * * * At common law an estate in joint tenancy, with the incident of survivorship, was created in any case where lands or tenements were granted to two or more persons, to be held in fee simple, fee tail, for life, for years, or at will. The mere creation of the estate in two or more persons, without more, drew to it the incident of survivorship. * * * In Georgia the mere creation of the estate in two or more persons never draws to its survivorship as an incident, and the presumption is in all cases that survivorship was not intended. But where by express terms or necessary implication a survivorship is provided for, the law of Georgia allows it to exist. * * *

In his article entitled "Joint Tenancy in Georgia," 3 Ga.St.Bar J. 29 (1966), William H. Agnor * * * said * * *: "All that was suggested * * * was that a right of survivorship could be created. This meant that property, real or personal, could be transferred to A and B so that they would hold as tenants in common until one of them died and at that time the survivor would take a fee simple. They held life estates and each of them had a contingent remainder interest in fee simple. Specifically, they held cross, alternative, contingent remainders. Neither A nor B acting alone could defeat the contingent remainder held by the other." * * *

Despite the presumption to the contrary, Alice C. Studstill clearly intended by the language in her will to create a right of survivorship in her son James and her daughter Mary Ella, and we so hold. * * *

Although a right of survivorship created by contract or by will was recognized, under the Georgia law at the time this will was executed, the joint tenancy with its unity of time, title, interest and possession had long been abolished in this state. * * * Thus, the doctrine of severance also had no place in our law at the time that the interests of these parties were created. * * * As Agnor observed (above) "Neither A [Mary Ella] nor B [James Studstill] acting alone could defeat the contingent remainder held by the other." We decline to engraft the doctrine of severance into pre–1976 deeds and wills as we find the result reached here to be consistent with the testator's intent. The trial court erred in holding otherwise.

Judgment reversed.

Notes and Questions

1. Michigan case law also makes the distinction between; (i) a joint tenancy; and (ii) "a joint life estate with indestructible survivorship." In

one of the 1988 Michigan bar examinations, the examiners put this problem to applicants:

Grant, owner of Goldacre, Irons, Michigan, in 1981, deeded Goldacre to his unmarried adult daughters, Amy and Betty, by a deed which described the grantees as "my daughters Amy and Betty, jointly, with the right of survivorship." Goldacre is an apartment building, which at all relevant times has been fully rented and well-run by an on-site manager. After Grant deeded to Amy and Betty, net rental income was simply divided evenly and paid in equal shares to Amy and to Betty. This continued until 1986 when Amy deeded "my interest in Goldacre" to her favorite nephew, Norman. Thereafter, net rent distributions, which had been paid to Amy, were paid to Norman.

In late 1987, Betty, a Michigan resident, died, willing her entire estate to Environmental Awareness, a recognized charitable organization. Amy survived. Who now owns what interest in Goldacre? Discuss and decide.

2. In one of the 1986 bar examinations, the Michigan examiners put this question:

In 1978 valuable vacant lakefront land in Michigan was deeded to "Joe and Ann, husband and wife, as tenants by the entireties." The grantor thought Joe and Ann were married, but they never were, and knew they weren't. Joe and Ann lived together until 1980, then parted, unable to agree as to what to do about the land, except that each would pay half the property taxes.

This arrangement continued until 1985, and the land grew increasingly valuable. A developer, Don, approached Joe about buying it for a high price. Joe said, "I'll sell you my half, but you'll have to deal with Ann about hers." Don agreed, and paid Joe well for a deed conveying to Don "my (Joe's) interest" in the land. A few weeks later, before Don had approached Ann, Joe was killed in an automobile accident. When Don soon after contacted Ann and offered to buy her half, he learned that Ann claims to own the entire interest in the land. Don, of course, insists that *he* owns an undivided half bought from Joe.

(a) What are the four possible types of tenancies which might be argued by the parties?

(b) Discuss the effects on the parties.

(c) What is the probable result under Michigan law?

SCHWAB v. KRAUSS

Supreme Court of New York, Appellate Division, 1991.
165 A.D.2d 214, 566 N.Y.S.2d 974.

LEVINE, JUSTICE.

In July 1984, defendant obtained a judgment in the amount of $36,893 against Allen Abrahams in Supreme Court, New York County. Some three months later, that judgment was docketed in Rockland County where Abrahams and his wife, Helen Abrahams, owned real property as tenants by the entirety. Subsequently, in May 1985, the

Abrahamses filed a joint petition in bankruptcy; however, Allen Abrahams' debt to defendant was not discharged during the bankruptcy proceeding.

While in bankruptcy, the Abrahamses, in December 1986, attempted to sell their Rockland County property to plaintiffs without the consent of the trustee in bankruptcy. Plaintiffs concede on this appeal that the deed they received was void. The following November Allen Abrahams died, and in March 1988 plaintiffs obtained a second deed to the Rockland County property from Helen Abrahams' trustee in bankruptcy in exchange for an additional $10,000.

In April 1988, defendant sought to execute his previously acquired judgment lien on the property purchased by plaintiffs. Plaintiffs then commenced the instant action seeking a judgment declaring that they are the lawful owners of the property free of defendant's lien. Defendant counterclaimed for dismissal of the complaint and enforcement of his judgment. Plaintiffs then moved for summary judgment. Supreme Court denied that motion and granted defendant summary judgment dismissing the complaint. Upon reargument, Supreme Court reversed its initial decision and granted summary judgment in favor of plaintiffs, concluding that the tenancy by the entirety survived the filing of the joint petition and that, upon Allen Abrahams' death, Helen Abrahams' interest in the property held by the trustee ripened into a fee absolute free from defendant's lien. This appeal by defendant followed.

Defendant's sole contention on this appeal is that the Abrahamses' filing of a joint bankruptcy petition and the resulting transfer into the bankruptcy estate of the real property held by them as tenants by the entirety effected a termination of the entireties estate. We disagree. When a husband and wife in this State take title to real property as tenants by the entirety, each spouse acquires an undivided one-half interest in the property with the right of survivorship, which right cannot be destroyed without the consent of both spouses. * * * Although either spouse may mortgage or convey his or her own interest in the tenancy, such act will not impair the nonconsenting spouse's survivorship interest. * * *

Here, upon the Abrahamses' filing of the joint bankruptcy petition pursuant to 11 USC § 302, the respective interest of each spouse was effectively transferred into his or her individual bankruptcy estate. * * * Despite defendant's assertion to the contrary, we cannot conclude that these transfers by way of the joint petition had the same effect as a joint consensual conveyance of the property, which clearly would have terminated the entireties estate. * * * The purpose of the joint bankruptcy petition is merely to ease administration and, in the absence of an order from the Bankruptcy Court consolidating the Abrahamses' estates * * * such estates existed separately in the hands of the trustee. * * * Thus, each estate contained what was essentially a survivorship interest. Following Allen Abrahams' death, the survivorship interest contained in Helen Abrahams' estate ripened into a fee interest by operation of law. * * * Consequently, defendant's lien, which was valid only as against Allen Abrahams' interest in the entireties estate, was extinguished along with his debtor's interest in the property and plaintiffs took title to the property from the trustee free and clear of that lien. Accordingly, Supreme Court was correct in granting summary judgment in favor of plaintiffs.

Order and judgment affirmed, with costs.

Notes

1. American states have varied the rigors of the common-law tenancy by the entirety. The most common reason for doing so is the effect on the estate of 19th-century statutes permitting married women to own property, make wills, enter into contracts, etc. All states adopted such legislation, commonly called married-women's property acts; but very few of these statutes addressed the effect of the reform on the tenancy by the entirety. The Supreme Court of Hawaii, in its opinion in Sawada v. Endo, 57 Hawaii 608, 561 P.2d 1291 (1977), concluded that 19 states at that time preserved the tenancy by the entirety. These included Hawaii, and in Hawaii, as is usually the case, the married-women's property act did not say what effect the statutory removal of common-law disabilities was to have on the tenancy by the entirety. In the *Sawada* case, as is typical, a creditor of one spouse was attempting to execute a judgment against that spouse on entireties property. The court divided the states into four groups on the question of whether a creditor can do that:

"In the Group I states * * * the estate is essentially the common law tenancy by the entireties, unaffected by the Married Women's Property Acts. As at common law, the possession and profits of the estate are subject to the husband's exclusive dominion and control. * * * [A]s at common law, the *husband* may convey the entire estate subject only to the possibility that the wife may become entitled to the whole estate upon surviving him. * * * As at common law, the obverse as to the wife does not hold true. * * * In [some of the Group I states] the use and income from the estate is not subject to levy during the marriage for the separate debts of either spouse.

"In the Group II states * * * the interests of the debtor spouse in the estate may be sold or levied upon for his or her separate debts, subject to the other spouse's contingent right of survivorship. * * * Alaska, which has been added to this group, has provided by statute that the interest of a debtor spouse in any type of estate, except a homestead [5] as defined and held in tenancy by the entirety, shall be subject to his or her separate debts. * * *

---

5. "Homestead rights" are statutory. They make certain property, or a certain amount of property value, immune from creditors. They often require that the property be part of a family home and that the family live in it; the property interest protected is usually an interest held for a family, but is not necessarily a marital interest; the statutes do not require that the owner be married. The statutory exemption in Alaska was unusual in the way it combined the homestead concept with the tenancy by the entirety. See the next note, on similar and more recent legislation in Massachusetts. (Eds.)

"In the Group III jurisdictions * * * an attempted conveyance by either spouse is wholly void, and the estate may not be subjected to the separate debts of one spouse only. * * *

"In Group IV * * * [courts] hold that the contingent right of survivorship appertaining to either spouse is separately alienable by him and attachable by his creditors during the marriage. * * * The use and profits, however, may neither be alienated nor attached during coverture."

The judges in Hawaii decided to join Group III: "[T]he interest of a husband or a wife in an estate by the entireties is not subject to the claims of his or her individual creditors during the joint lives of the spouses."

In those few Group I states in which, according to the *Sawada* court's opinion, the husband has exclusive control, the equal-protection clause of the fourteenth amendment probably requires a change in state law that makes the spouses equal—so that, for example, the spouses have equal control of the property while both are alive. That will not mean, though, that the creditors of one spouse can reach the entireties property; the *Sawada* court did not address the question of control under the equal-protection clause.

2. Alexander A. Bove, Jr., a Boston lawyer who writes about property-law matters in a weekly column in the Boston Globe, compared, in one of his columns (May 19, 1988), the relative protection afforded in his state by entireties ownership and a statutory homestead right (one that resembles homestead rights in other jurisdictions):

"The declaration of homestead is relatively simple and can be made on a principal residence by anyone with a spouse and/or children. It is a simple, one-page sworn statement by either of the spouses declaring a homestead in their principal residence and recorded at the registry of deeds. The declaration protects up to $100,000 of equity in the house from a creditor's attack.

"In addition to making a homestead declaration, a couple could hold their house under a 'new' tenancy by the entirety, one where the deed creating the tenancy is dated after Feb. 10, 1980. This prevents a creditor of either spouse from having the house sold. * * *

"In 1979 Massachusetts passed a law that exempts a couple's principal residence from seizure and sale by a creditor of either spouse. The non-debtor spouse must continue to occupy the property as the principal residence and the residency held under a tenancy by the entirety created after Feb. 10, 1980.

"The creditor protection, however, does not excuse a couple from paying on their mortgage, nor does it protect them or a dependent family member against debts for 'necessaries': food, clothing, medical costs.

"The protection does not extend to creditors of both spouses for the same debt, such as where they are jointly liable for income taxes.

"The typical debt that would be protected might be where the husband made a bad business decision and was sued by a customer for damages, or where he injured someone in an auto accident and was sued for personal injuries. In either case, if the husband's house were held under a qualified tenancy by the entirety, neither the customer nor the injured party could reach the house, even though each had a valid claim.

"If the husband has no other assets, therefore, the customer and the injured party may simply be out of luck, since the statute prohibits a creditor from forcing a sale of the house.

"All of this has been relatively clear. The unanswered question was: Even though a creditor could not force a sale of the house, could he place an attachment on it, thereby preventing the couple from disposing of the house or remortgaging it without paying off the creditor? If this were so, just how protective is the law that protects the house?

"Not that protective, says the Massachusetts Supreme Judicial Court. Although a couple's house may not be sold by a creditor, it may definitely be attached.

"In the deciding case, the wife, Maureen P., was involved in an automobile accident and was sued by the injured party. In the process, the injured party's lawyer sought to attach Maureen's house. Maureen's husband objected to the attachment, pointing to the Massachusetts law that prevented a seizure and execution (sale) of their residence, which was held under a 'new' tenancy by the entirety.

"In upholding the creditor's right to attach Maureen's house, however, the court said the law was designed only to protect the couple's right to continued possession of the house, and allowing a creditor to place an attachment on it did not upset this right. Therefore, Maureen and her husband could still live in the house, even though it had been legally attached. * * *

"Although a creditor can attach your house so you won't be able to sell it or refinance it, the decision does not mean your enjoyment and occupancy will be otherwise affected: a forced sale by a creditor is still prohibited while you live there.

"Unfortunately, this is not much consolation, since the attachment can remain on the house for 20 years or more after the judgment. Aside from winning the lawsuit or settling with the creditor, therefore, it appears your only hope in such a case is to survive the debtor spouse, but this is difficult to plan, in most cases.

"Previously Massachusetts law of tenancy by the entirety followed the antiquated common law rule that the husband was entitled to sole possession of the property, plus all the rents, if any, and the wife had nothing more than a survivorship right. A creditor of the husband, therefore, could conceivably acquire the right to occupy and rent the property to satisfy the husband's debt.

"For a time there was some confusion as to whether the special protection from creditors applied to all tenancies by the entirety or just to those created on or after Feb. 11, 1980, the effective date of the new law. After all, there were many thousands of Massachusetts couples who held their house under a tenancy by the entirety created long before the law was enacted, and if the protection did not extend to them, it might be possible for a creditor of the husband to have the couple evicted from their own house. This confusion and concern lasted a few years, until February 1984, when the Massachusetts Supreme Judicial Court decided the issue.

"In that case, a homeowner engaged a contractor, who, although already paid for the job, decided not to finish it. The homeowner sued the contractor and got a judgment against him for about $6,000, yet the contractor still stubbornly refused to pay.

"It so happened the contractor and his spouse owned their house under a tenancy by the entirety, and that title was taken before enactment of the 1979 law. Donald Orkin, the attorney for the homeowner, pursued the matter in Housing Court and subsequently got a sheriff to sell the contractor's house to satisfy the judgment against the contractor/husband.

"Despite this decision, however, there was apparently still some concern on the part of the Housing Court judge as to the confusion between the old and new tenancy by the entirety. Therefore, he asked the Supreme Judicial Court to consider it.

"The court held simply that tenancies by the entirety created before Feb. 11, 1980, were governed by the old law in such cases. * * * [T]he husband had sole right to possession and rents and, therefore, a judgment creditor of the husband could have the property sold. A principal residence held under a tenancy by the entirety created on or after Feb. 11, 1980, would be exempt from seizure and sale. * * *

"So what do you do if you already own your house under an old tenancy by the entirety (created before Feb. 11, 1980) and you want creditor protection as a new tenancy by the entirety? You must create a new tenancy. This is done by a transfer from you and your spouse to a straw (a third party who has no true interest in the property, but who merely acts as a go-between, since spouses cannot transfer to themselves), and the straw would immediately re-transfer the property back to the two of you as tenants by the entirety. * * * "

3. In United States v. One Single Family Residence, 894 F.2d 1511 (11th Cir.1990), federal prosecutors attempted to seize property held by the entireties, under the extraordinary power federal drug enforcers have to bring about the forfeiture of property used in drug trafficking (21 U.S.C. Sec. 881). The property was in Florida which, with 14 other states, holds that the entireties estate is not severable. The alleged offender's wife was not involved in the alleged drug dealing; she argued that she could not be deprived of her property under the government's statutory authority. Lawyers for the couple argued (and the court held) that the government's power does not extend to what the innocent cotenant has; the government gets what she doesn't have. Here the wife had an unseverable interest in the entire property, with the result that the government was not able to seize anything. In this case the couple took title to the house before the alleged offense by the husband; the court noted that its holding would not permit a drug offender to establish entireties ownership after the offense, under the apparently well-established principle that the government's seizure takes effect at the time of the offense.

JOHNSON v. HENDRICKSON

Supreme Court of South Dakota, 1946.
71 S.D. 392, 24 N.W.2d 914.

SICKEL, J.

This is an action for the partition of real property. Henry W. Bauman and Katie B. Bauman were husband and wife. Their children consisted of three, named Grace, Arthur, and Vernon. The husband died intestate in 1904, leaving an estate consisting of an improved quarter section of land in Clark County. The decree of the circuit court determined the right of inheritance to this land as follows: One-third to the widow, two-ninths to each of the three children. * * * The widow then married the defendant Karl Hendrickson. The children of this marriage consisted of twin boys named Kenneth and Karroll. Katie B. Hendrickson, widow of Henry W. Bauman, wife of Karl Hendrickson and mother of all the children, never moved from this land during her lifetime. Karl Hendrickson, her husband, lived there with her until she died, and still lives upon the land. All the children lived on this land during their minority and at various periods of time after attaining their majority. The mother died in May 1944 and left her property by will as follows: To her husband, Karl Hendrickson, one-half; to each of the children of the second marriage one-fourth; to the children of her first marriage, five dollars each. * * * Plaintiffs in this action are the three children of the first marriage of Katie B. Hendrickson. They allege in their complaint that the land is so situated that it cannot be partitioned among the various owners either individually or in groups, without prejudice to such owners, and ask that it be sold in one tract. Defendants deny that the partition in kind would be prejudicial to the owners. The circuit court determined the claims and liabilities of all the parties as to mortgages paid and improvements made, and adjudged that the land be sold. From this decree the defendants have appealed. * * *

The appellants * * * proposed that the partition in kind be made by allotting to them, as owners collectively of a one-third interest in the land, the southeast forty-acre tract with all the buildings and improvements situated thereon, and the hog house now on the southwest forty-acre tract, and by allotting to the three respondents, as owners of a two-thirds interest in the land, the other three forty-acre tracts with no buildings, but upon which is situated a forty-acre slough. The first question presented then is whether the court was justified in deciding that the land be sold. * * *

[A] sale may be ordered if it appear to the satisfaction of the court that the value of the share of each cotenant, in case of partition, would be materially less than his share of the money equivalent that could probably be obtained for the whole. * * * [A] sale is justified if it appears to the satisfaction of the court that the value of the land when divided into parcels is substantially less than its value when owned by one person. This land is now owned by six persons. The largest individual interest is two-ninths and the smallest is one-twelfth. Partition in kind would require the division of the land into not less than four parcels: Two-ninths to each of the three respondents, and one-third to appellants, collectively. It is a matter of common knowledge in this state that the division of this quarter section of land, located as it is, into four or more separate tracts would materially depreciate its value, both as to its salability and as to its use for agricultural purposes. * * *

Appellants * * * offer, as an alternative, to purchase the two-thirds interest of the three respondents in the land by paying to them the sum of $800 each. This latter proposition is an offer of settlement, not a proposed plan of partition. The law favors the compromise and settlement of disputed claims because it is the interest of the state that there should be an end to litigation, but such offer does not present a justiciable question. It is the function of the court to hear and decide questions of law and fact, not to use its influence to bring about the composition of disputes.

The widow inherited from her first husband an undivided one-third interest in the farm. After she married appellant Karl Hendrickson in 1909 she continued to occupy the farm * * * with her children, her second husband, and the children of the second marriage. During such occupancy they remodeled the house, built the barn, hog house, granary, wash house, milk house, chicken house, fences, and two wells, at a cost of over $9,000. Appellants Karl Hendrickson and the two sons of the second marriage claim in this action that as the devisees of Katie B. Hendrickson, and present owners of an undivided one-third interest in the farm, they are entitled to credit for such improvements.

The rule at common law is that a tenant in common cannot compel his cotenants to contribute to his expenditures for improvements placed by him on the common property without the consent or agreement of the cotenants. * * * It is also the general rule, with some exceptions not pertinent to this case, that a life tenant who makes permanent improvements upon real property with full knowledge of his title will be presumed to have made them for his own benefit, and that he cannot recover anything therefor from the remainderman. * * * The rule in regard to the rights of tenants in common as stated above has been modified by courts of equity in partition cases. * * *

[C]ourts generally make suitable allowance, on partition, for improvements made in good faith by a cotenant in possession, to the extent that the value of the property has been enhanced thereby. * * * This modification of the common law rule, however, does not alter the rule as to life tenants who have no interest in the remainder, or their successors in interest after the termination of the life estate.

In this case, Katie B. Hendrickson had a homestead interest in the land from the date of her first husband's death until she died in 1944. She also owned a one-third interest in it by right of inheritance from her first husband. She was, therefore a tenant in common with the children of the first marriage, and a life tenant by virtue of her homestead right. Under the rules to which we have referred she would be entitled in partition, as a tenant in common, to contribution for improvements made, but as a life tenant such contribution would be denied. Cases like this, where the person making the improvements has a life estate and is also a tenant in common, are generally decided by the court on equitable principles, that is, "according to its own notions of general justice and equity between the parties." * * *

This case does not deal with the right to offset the value of improvements against rents and profits accruing after the termination of the life estate. Such rents and profits have been accounted for in this action. Neither did the widow who made the improvements believe or understand that she was the sole owner of the remainder. Decisions of other courts dealing with such propositions are not pertinent to the facts in this case. Here the evidence shows that improvements consisting of a house, barn, granary, chicken house, and shed, all old, were situated upon this farm in 1909. In 1910 a granary was built, in 1911 a chicken house and in subsequent years the barn was torn down and a new one constructed in its place. The house was repaired and remodeled, a hog house, wash house, garage, milk house, fences, and wells were also constructed in the following years.

In the year 1909 the mortgage on the homestead was $2,500. It was increased to as much as $7,000 to pay for improvements, debts, and to buy another quarter section of land across the road. Arthur Bauman was born in 1893 and remained at home until he was twenty-seven years of age. Grace Bauman was born in 1895 and remained at home until her mother died in 1944. Vernon Bauman was born in 1898 and remained at home until he was thirty-six years of age. These three children of the first marriage worked but received no wages while at home, and none of them had separate incomes, except the daughter from some chickens and Vernon from some farming which he did on his own account. During all the time that these three children of the first marriage remained at home they and their mother occupied the homestead as such, and owned it as tenants in common. The second husband and the children of the second marriage were members of the same family. The mother was the head of this family. She owned all the personal property and managed all the family affairs. The improvements, incumbrances, and additional land were made and paid for out of the land by the combined efforts of all. The respondents made substantial contributions to the family income out of which these things were accomplished, during their minority, and also during their majority. The family had the use of the greater part of the improvements over a period of more than thirty years. These improvements and the payment of the mortgage have greatly enhanced the value of the estate. Karl Hendrickson and his two sons now own a one-third interest in the homestead, improved and free from debt, and the additional quarter section of land. The circuit court determined that under these circumstances an allowance to Karl Hendrickson and his sons for the improvements made and the indebtedness paid would be inequitable, and this conclusion is amply supported by the evidence. * * *

Finding no error in the record the judgment is affirmed.

Notes and Questions

1. In Wendell Berry's short story, "It Wasn't Me" (one of six stories in *The Wild Birds,* 1986), Wheeler Catlett, county-seat Kentucky property lawyer, drew a will for a farmer named Jack Beechum. Wheeler's client, a widower, had a daughter who was not interested in his farm. When Jack was forced by ill health to retire, he and Wheeler located tenant farmers, Elton and Mary Penn, to farm the place. Jack later wanted Elton and Mary to have the farm. The will Wheeler drew for him gave the farm to Jack's daughter, Clara Pettit, and the value of half the farm to Elton and Mary. (His estate would have only the farm in it, so that, in effect, and at the time he made the will, this amounted to giving Elton and Mary half the farm.) It occurred to him later that maybe Clara would not want to sell the farm to Elton and Mary, or that the value would appreciate. He left an undelivered, handwritten note to Wheeler, saying that he wanted Clara to sell the farm to Elton and Mary, at date-of-will value. The note was of no legal effect.

After Jack died, as Jack feared, Clara refused to sell to Elton and Mary and put the farm up for sale at auction. Wheeler devoted himself to seeing to it that Elton got the farm anyway. He got Elton to bid, successfully, much more than Elton thought he could afford. Wheeler then created a security fund to back Elton's debt. Why? Not only out of a sense of obligation to Jack, but also because, "Wheeler is a seer of visions—not the heavenly visions of saints and mystics, but the earthly ones of a mainly practical man who sees the good that has been possible in this world, and beyond that, the good that is desirable in it." Wheeler finally told Elton that he had to help him get the farm "because Mr. Beechum wanted it to happen, and because the farm * * * wanted it to, and because you wanted it to * * * [a]nd because what has happened has been desirable to a lot of people we never knew, who lived before us."

That solved the legal problem and probably solved the financial one, but it did not solve the human problem. The human problem was that Elton did not want to have to be grateful: "I want to make it on my own. I don't want a soul to thank." Wheeler, the lawyer for the situation, then undertakes to convert Elton to awareness of the fact that he is not alone in the world, and to the acceptance of having to thank the people he is in it with: "I don't think your old friend has left you in shape to live thankless," he says to Elton.

Wheeler Catlett's argument to his client is an argument about proper-ty. He says it is only possible to live without gratitude for property if it is "a kind of property you can put in your pocket. * * * But when you quit living in the price and start living in the place, you're in a different line of succession." There is no way Elton's debt can be paid back, Wheeler says: "We're dealing in goods and services that we didn't make, that can't exist at all except as gifts. Everything about a place that's different from its price is a gift. Everything about a man or woman that's different from their price is a gift. The life of a neighborhood is a gift. * * * Once the account is kept and the bill presented, the friendship ends, the neighborhood is finished, and you're back to where you started. The starting place doesn't have anybody in it but you." Elton is converted then. He laughs. "You're going to be my friend, it sounds pret' near like, because you can't get out of it."

2. Katie B. Hendrickson was the sort of prairie pioneer woman Willa Cather wrote about. Among modern novelists the one most likely to do justice to such a character is, no doubt, Anne Tyler (*Accidental Tourist, Breathing Exercises, Dinner at the Homesick Restaurant, The Clockwinder*). Tyler writes about bizarre families that are held together in bizarre ways— families that are put together by resilient heroines such as Katie Hendrickson, who put together two husbands and five children. Tyler's point, like Judge Sickel's, would be that, when Katie was alive, they were one family and were at home—even into the children's middle age. How does such a story end up in a set of oral arguments, by lawyers, in the highest court of the state, arguments over whether Katie Hendrickson's farm should be sold—should be sold not because efficiency or production require it, or because the bank is foreclosing its mortgage, but because Katie Hendrickson's family, now that she is gone, cannot live together on her farm? They have turned Katie's farm, the physical thing that held them together, into a battle field.

3. Title to the farm was originally taken in the name of Henry W. Bauman, Katie's first husband. All of the forms of marital ownership were available to the person who drew up that conveyance. Did that lawyer choose the one that was best for Henry and Katie and their children?

4. Henry Bauman did not make a will; the farm went to Katie and the children by intestate succession. (Note that by that time in the development of Anglo–American inheritance, the widow was an heir.) Was that pattern of distribution and control the best one for Katie and her children?

5. Katie, as Henry's widow, had both a homestead right and a share as Henry's heir. The homestead right gave her a life estate on the property that is analogous to common-law dower, which we will take up again in the next section. Might a lawyer working on Henry Bauman's will have pulled Katie's two interests together and used them as elements in a single planning scheme? (Katie could probably have waived her homestead interest.)

6. Katie did make a will. Suppose she had come to your law office for that purpose. What such a lawyer is asked to do is to contemplate the possibility that Katie will die leaving two sets of children, a husband, and this prosperous quarter section of South Dakota. The six people who live with her have, then, to have a substitute for her presence among them— and the thing available as building material for the substitute is this good farm. The will maker here is asked to fashion a substitute for Katie's presence in her family:

— It is evident why Katie left only five dollars each to her older children, but does it make sense? Was that the way to deal with the issue of equality among children? Come to that, how important is equality among children? Who do you suppose answered these questions in Katie's lawyer's office?

— Katie's lawyer has to deal with some givens, the most limiting of which was that she did not get the whole farm from her first husband. She has a life interest in her homestead and a one-third fee-simple interest. The older children, in middle age by the time of this lawsuit, own two-ninths of the farm. Katie apparently did not feel she could give them more. Is there anything else she could do to influence them to work for family harmony? Notice that the tragedy in a case like this—and there are thousands of such cases in the reports—is not that the land gets chopped up, but that the people do.

— Some facts that might be worth taking into account if we got into a time machine, one that could go to Clark County, South Dakota, and had a chance to work on Katie's will (or on Henry's, or on the original deed to Henry, or—best of all—on all three):

  — The possibility and advisability of equal distribution among all of the children. Notice that it may be possible to provide a mechanism here, rather than a recipe. Notice, too, that it is unlikely that five children in one farm family will all want to be farmers when they grow up, but very likely that at least one of them will want to be a farmer.

  — The possibility of providing a system for taking account of time and expense spent on improvements, and of taking into account who had a home on the farm and for how long (an alternative, that is, to the common-law rules on claims among cotenants).

  — The possibility of providing not only a mechanism but also a decision maker other than the circuit judge (who apparently got so angry at these squabbling relatives that he threw up his hands and ordered the property sold).

7. If a family could own land as a corporation does, as a single, separate, legal person, and if Henry and Katie had taken ownership of their quarter section of Clark County in the name of their family, would the result in this case have been less tragic? Would it have made it easier to do the sort of planning you were asked to think about in Question 6?

8. Many farm families today incorporate their farms—home, business, and all. If Henry and Katie had done that, presumably the quarter section would have been conveyed to Bauman Farm, Inc., and common stock would have been issued as Henry and Katie directed. Would that form of ownership have made any difference in this case? Would it have made it easier to do the sort of planning you were asked to think about in Question 6?

9. Is the law incapable of doing anything about this family tragedy? Is it inevitably the case, in an orderly commonwealth, that an offer of compromise presents nothing a judge can deal with? Is it even the case that the only reason for the law to favor settlement of disputes in a family is "because it is in the interest of state that there should be an end to litigation"?

C. CONDOMINIUMS

JAMES C. CLARK, "CONDOMINIUM: A RECONCILIATION OF COMPETING INTERESTS?"

18 Vanderbilt Law Review 1773 (1965).

As Americans have migrated to urban areas, the suburbs have grown at an astounding pace, principally by means of single home subdivisions. Of necessity, this march to the suburbs must cease at some point and people will begin to return to the central city and its close-lying peripheral areas if for no other reason than to lessen the heavy economic burden resulting from man-hours wasted in commuting great distances. Often the alternative to the suburban home is an apartment in the city. Apartment renting, however, runs counter to a deeply ingrained American tradition of individual home ownership, a tradition encouraged by favorable tax consequences. It seems only natural that in this period of increasing urbanization the condominium concept should be advanced as an attempt to reconcile these needs. Its arrival on the property scene has attracted the intense interest of potential apartment dwellers, developers, and legal writers.

Basically the condominium is a form of property ownership whereby the owner has fee simple title to a single unit within a multi-unit building with an undivided interest in the common elements—land, hallways, swimming pools, heating plants, *et cetera*. Condominium is a new form of ownership, not a new estate or different kind of property. It differs from the cooperative in that in the cooperative the building is owned by a corporate or business entity which holds title to all the premises and each cooperator is a shareholder with a proprietary lease for one apartment.

The present condominium activity was largely generated by section 234 of the National Housing Act which permits the Federal Housing Administration to issue mortgage insurance on individual condominium units. While the section does not expressly cover condominiums but rather speaks in terms of "a one-family unit in a multifamily structure and an undivided interest in the common areas and facilities which serve the structure," it clearly was intended to cover the condominium. At the time of the passage of this amendment, only Puerto Rico had a condominium statute. In a period of less than four years, forty-four states and the District of Columbia have passed condominium legislation giving statutory basis to this form of ownership. * * *

While the present interest in the condominium has been created principally by the rapid spread of condominium legislation, it should be recognized that a condominium may be created by contract if the following conditions are allowed under state common or statutory law:

(1) ownership of part of the building as an interest in land;

(2) restraint against the partition of the commonly-owned land and partitions of the building;

(3) restraint against the separation of the share in the commonly-owned property from the separately-owned unit;

(4) separate assessment of units for taxation;

(5) provision for the use, management, and maintenance of the commonly-owned property; or, more briefly stated, provisions for operation of the condominium.

Obviously, it is difficult to find all of these conditions co-existing in a particular jurisdiction. However, a number of condominiums were constructed upon a common law framework in Florida, California, and Utah; but the circumstances of their creation may be unique in that each of these states subsequently passed condominium legislation. Perhaps these common law condominiums were partly inspired by the belief that such enabling legislation was imminent.

The absence of a condominium statute necessitates convincing all parties involved that the division of the air space above the land surface is practical and legal. The difficulty of guaranteeing that the listed conditions exist places a heavy burden on the developer and creates doubt as to the feasibility of the condominium without specific legislation. As one condominium observer noted: "Condominium, it appears, can exist under the common law, but whether it will flourish without statutory provision is doubtful."

Assuming the necessity for permissive legislation in order to give the certainty required by the real estate community and institutional lenders, what form should it take? Broadly speaking, a condominium statute must: (1) provide for the establishment of the condominium; (2) accommodate existing legislation dealing with recording procedures, taxation of property, liens, land-use control, to the unique requirements of the condominium; (3) provide a means of preserving unity and harmony of condominium projects by prohibiting suit for partition of the common areas; and (4) provide for the dissolution of the condominium. * * *

The condominium statutes, or horizontal property acts as they are sometimes called, prescribe the exclusive means whereby property may be submitted to their terms. The FHA Model Act provides: "The Act shall be applicable only to property, the sole owner or all of the owners of which submit the same to the provisions hereof by duly executing and recording a Declaration as hereinafter provided." While some of the acts vary in wording, the uniform requirement of filing a declaration removes any doubt as to whether a particular building has been submitted to the terms of the condominium act.

The declaration provides for descriptions of the land on which the condominium is constructed, the building, the individual apartments, the common elements, and the limited common elements and the unit to which they are appurtenant. It sets forth the value of the property and of each apartment and the percentage of the undivided interest in the common elements. The name of a person to receive service of process and the purposes for which the building and each apartment are intended and restricted as to use are likewise included in the declaration. Finally, the declaration may contain any further details as to the condominium which may be deemed desirable, including the method by which the declaration may be amended, so long as they are consistent with the enabling legislation.

Once the declaration has been filed and the building constructed, the question may arise whether a purchaser of an apartment takes an interest in real property. The Model Act provides specifically that each apartment together with its common elements "shall for all purposes constitute real property." Such an express provision seems preferable to those statutes which remain silent on this point, for it eliminates possible litigation and quells any fears of mortgage lenders created by the statutory void. * * *

Once the condominium is established, attention must be turned to the preservation of the regime. By definition, the individual unit owners of the condominium hold the common elements in co-tenancy. One of the characteristics of a co-tenancy is the right of partition and, in the absence of a provision to restrain the exercise of this right, the condominium regime may be dissolved by a single disgruntled unit owner. Such partition could result in a physical division of the property with the individual unit owners receiving a several interest corresponding to his share of the individual interest or a sale and division of the proceeds.

The possibility of a single unit owner disappointing the expectations of the legal integrity of the regime would practically preclude condominium activity. To meet this threat, most of the statutes expressly provide that no action for partition may be maintained. * * * The Model Act recognizes the right of all of the unit owners to remove the property from the provisions of the condominium statute and that in the event of destruction with a decision not to rebuild, a partition suit may be maintained. * * *

A functional problem inherent in permitting the developer to retain apartment or commercial units for rental is reconciling the voting control exercised by the owners of the condominium. Since the owners of the individual units collectively own the entire condominium, they possess the right to manage its affairs. In the cooperative each member has one vote regardless of the value of his interest. But in the condominium, the weighing of the votes is generally determined by the proportion which the basic value of the unit bears to the total value of all units in the condominium. * * *

A functional problem arises when the developer retains units comprising a substantial percentage of the value of the condominium. If the voting power is proportioned strictly on the value of the interest, then the developer may have a dominant voice in the management. This would certainly be true where the retained units constituted more than fifty per cent of the value. It would seem that in many instances the interests of the developer as an investor in rental units would conflict with those of the individual unit owners, whose dominant interests are those of a homeowner. Of course, the declaration could exclude the developer from any voice in the management. * * *

It has been suggested that to base voting power on all matters effecting the condominium strictly in conformity with economic interests is undesirable. When the decisions are economic in character, then perhaps the economic test is proper. However, many decisions are basically social in nature, and in this area the economic test loses much of its appeal and unduly favors the owners of the more expensive units. It was suggested that the economic interests could be decided on the basis of the economic test, whereas the social questions by a majority of those owners affected. Such a distinction might be helpful in reconciling the conflicting interests of the developer and the homeowner. However, it is recognized that even with such a distinction a potential conflict exists, for the developer's interest in economic matters would seem to be to minimize expense in order to maximize profit. This could conflict with a desire on the part of the homeowner to make his place of abode as attractive and liveable as possible, with economic considerations playing a secondary role.

One method of reconciling these conflicting interests * * * would be to differentiate the common elements. Some statutes permit the reservation of particular common elements for the use of certain units to the exclusion of others. These limited common elements may be advantageously used in the mixed commercial and residential condominium. For example, the high rise condominium could have a swimming pool and sun deck on the roof as common elements appurtenant to the individually owned apartments, but not part of the common elements of the commercial units. In fact, even the rental apartment units could be excluded from participation in certain elements with a provision that, if subsequently sold, the purchaser might pay a sum to obtain an undivided interest in these common elements. Since only those persons having the dominant economic and social interest in these areas hold title to them, the conflict between the developer-investor and the apartment owner is lessened in a particularly sensitive area.

There still will remain elements common to both the rental units and the individually owned apartments, but the interests of the investor and the apartment owners begin to coincide in regard to these facilities and there is less likelihood of a conflict of interest. However, it might be preferable to place in the condominium declaration a provision calling for arbitration in the event of a conflict over maintenance or additions or improvements to the common elements when the developer and a majority of the owners of individual units take opposing views. * * *

COMMERCIAL WHARF EAST CONDOMINIUM ASSOCIATION v. WATERFRONT PARKING CORP.

Supreme Court of Massachusetts, 1990.
407 Mass. 123, 552 N.E.2d 66.

NOLAN, JUSTICE. * * *

The subject of this litigation is the land in Boston known as Commercial Wharf. In 1967, Commercial Wharf was purchased by the developer, which rehabilitated the granite block warehouse in the center of the wharf and, in 1978, decided to convert the building into condominium units. * * *

Immediately prior to recording the condominium master deed, which covers the granite building and a portion of the wharf known as the "parking and driveway area," the developer recorded a document entitled "Commercial Wharf East Condominium—Declaration of Covenants and Easements" (Declaration). The Declaration purports to retain certain rights for the benefit of the retained land over the parking area which was deeded to the condominium. The retained rights include the right "to control and collect fees for the parking of vehicles in such area." The Declaration also provides that the owner of the retained land must maintain and manage the parking area and rent parking spaces to condominium unit owners at reasonable and competitive rates. The condominium master deed, recorded shortly after the Declaration, recites that it is subject to the easement pronouncement in the Declaration. The master deed also provides that each unit owner has the right to rent one parking space, as stated in the Declaration.

From 1978 to 1984 the developer sold the condominium units in the granite building and managed the entire parking lot, including the parking and driveway area deeded to the Association. Then, in 1984, the developer began to sell its remaining interests on Commercial Wharf. First, in June, 1984, it conveyed lots 2 and 3 to the defendants Wharf Nominee Trust and Marina Nominee Trust (Nominee Trusts). The deeds to the Nominee Trusts include the right to irrevocable licenses to park ten cars in the parking and driveway area. In April, 1985, the developer conveyed lots 4, 5, and 6 and the right "to control and collect fees" in the parking and driveway area to the defendant Waterfront Park Limited Partnership (Waterfront). This deed grants the right to irrevocable licenses for sixteen parking spaces to Waterfront and retains the right to irrevocable licenses for fifty-two spaces in the developer, which then sold lot 1 and the right to twenty-six of its fifty-two irrevocable parking licenses to East Commercial Wharf Limited Partnership (East Commercial Wharf). Next, in February, 1986, the developer conveyed lot 8 to One Hundred Atlantic Avenue Limited Partnership (Atlantic). The deed to Atlantic includes the right to eleven parking licenses. The right to licenses for the remaining spaces of the fifty-two reserved by the developer is included in an option to purchase lot 7, granted to defendant Arthur B. Blackett.

Reference to the accompanying simplified map is helpful in visualizing the various interests on Commercial Wharf.

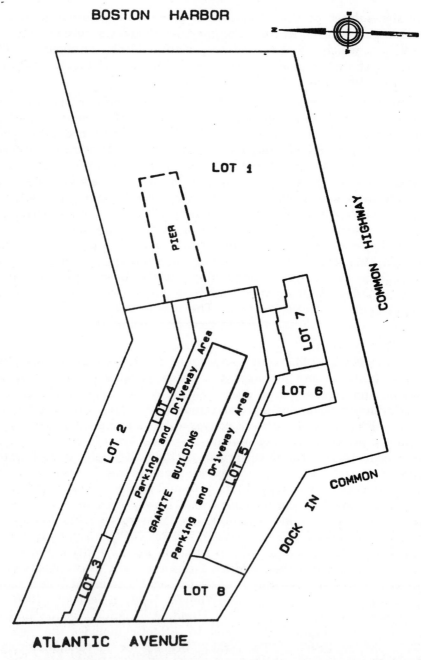

The granite building and the area surrounding it entitled "parking and driveway" area are condominium property. Lots 2 and 3 are owned by the Nominee Trusts. Lots 4, 5, and 6, together with the right "to control" parking in the parking and driveway area, are owned by Waterfront. Lot 1 and the surrounding marinas are owned by East Commercial Wharf. Lot 7 is under option to Arthur B. Blackett and lot

8 is owned by Atlantic. Further facts appear in our discussion of the various issues raised in the cross appeals. * * *

General Laws c. 183A, § 10(b)(1) (1988 ed.), provides that the condominium association "shall have" the right and power "[t]o lease, manage, and otherwise deal with such community and commercial facilities as may be provided for in the master deed as being common areas and facilities." Since the parking and driveway area is part of the common area, the Association contends that the developer's retention of control over that area cannot be reconciled with § 10(b)(1). * * *

We think it is clear that, by enacting G.L. c. 183A and providing that land can be placed into the condominium form of ownership, the Legislature did not intend to preclude the existence of nonownership interests in the condominium land. The law of real property has long recognized the coexistence of possessory interests in land with limited nonownership interests in the same land. Nothing in c. 183A expressly precludes such nonownership interests. We will not presume that the Legislature intended such a radical change in the common law without a clear expression of such intent. * * *

Similarly, the Association's argument under G.L. c. 183A, § 5(c) (1988 ed.), fails also. Section 5(c) provides that the common area shall remain undivided and that any provision to the contrary is void. The Association contends that the developer's retention of rights in the parking and driveway area is a division of the common area and is therefore void. * * * Section 5(c) provides: "The common areas and facilities shall remain undivided and no unit owner or any other person shall bring any action for partition or division of any part thereof. * * * Any covenant or provision to the contrary shall be null and void." The clear meaning of this provision is that the ownership of the common areas shall not be divided; in other words, the common areas must remain in common ownership with each unit owner entitled to an undivided interest in the common areas. Nothing in § 5(c) purports to prevent the existence of nonownership interests in the common areas. The fee interest remains undivided and in common ownership. That the master deed makes the fee interest subject to a prior interest is not violative of § 5(c).

A valid interest in a common area, to which the master deed is expressly subject, is not part of the common area. Section 1 of G.L. c. 183A makes it clear that certain land granted to a condominium, including the parking area, shall be considered part of the common area, but adds "except as otherwise provided or stipulated in the master deed." In this case the master deed makes it clear that the fee simple title to the parking and driveway area is in the Association. However, the master deed also makes that grant subject to the interests reserved in the Declaration. It follows that the interests retained by the developer in the Declaration are not "common areas." Since the interest retained by the developer never became part of the condominium common area, its retention does not constitute a division of the common area.   * * *

"Deeds should be 'construed as to give effect to the intent of the parties, unless consistent with some law or repugnant to the terms of the grant.'" *Harrison v. Marcus* * * * (1985). * * * The intent of the parties is gleaned from "the words used, interpreted in the light of the material circumstances and pertinent facts known to them at the time [the deed] was executed." * * * The Declaration provides that the retained land shall benefit from and the condominium land shall be subject to "the non-exclusive right and easement to use the Condominium Land for vehicular and pedestrian access to the Retained Land for all purposes over the * * * 'Parking and Driveway' [area] ... including the right * * * to control and collect fees for the parking of vehicles in such area.   * * *" While a strict grammatical reading of the latter phraseology might mean that the owner of the retained land only has the right to control the fees he collects, we think that the intent was to retain the right to control the parking of vehicles on the land. It is clear that the developer intended, when it executed and recorded the Declaration and the master deed, to convey the fee interest in the parking and driveway area to the Association. The Land Court judge found that the developer also intended to create a "common scheme" of sorts, whereby the parking rights of the wharf would be managed for the benefit of all the parcels on the wharf. To effectuate its plan, the developer intended to retain control over the parking activities in the parking and driveway area. Hence, it retained the right "to control and collect fees for the parking of vehicles."

The remainder of the Declaration is indicative of the developer's intent to retain the right to control all parking activities in the parking and driveway area. Paragraph 2 of the Declaration provides, in part, that "[t]he owners of the Retained Land at its [*sic*] own cost and expense shall maintain and manage the said Parking and Driveway area in the same condition as said land is in on the date hereof * * *." The remainder of paragraph 2 lists specific obligations, traditionally associated with management, which were imposed on the owner of the retained land. This implies that the power to control and manage the parking area was meant to be retained. Paragraph 3 obliges the owners of the retained land to rent parking spaces to condominium unit owners at reasonable rates, again indicating that the Declaration envisaged a retention of management rights by the owners of the retained land. In context we think that there is little doubt that the power "to control and collect fees" includes the power to manage the parking activities in the parking and driveway area.

To the extent that there remains any doubt, we think that the actions of the parties clarify the arrangement. "[W]here the language of an instrument is doubtful, evidence of the practical construction by the parties is admissible to explain and remove the doubt." *Oldfield v. Smith* * * * (1939). From 1978 until 1985, when it sold the management rights to Waterfront, the developer controlled all parking activities, set parking rates, and maintained the parking facilities. Neither the Association nor any of the unit owners objected to this control. This practical construction of the terms in the Declaration is in accord with our interpretation of that provision.   * * *

The Land Court judge held that the Declaration impliedly retained the right for the developer, as owner of the retained land, to park vehicles other than those of condominium unit owners on condominium land. We agree. As discussed above, the purpose of the Declaration was to retain control over parking for the benefit of all the parcels on the wharf. Absolutely essential to that purpose is the right to park noncondominium vehicles in the parking and driveway area. More-over, the unit owners and the Association acquiesced in such a con-struction of the Declaration from 1978 until 1985.

The Land Court judge determined that the Declaration and the master deed envisaged a "common scheme" of "unified control of parking on the Wharf for the benefit of all owners without differentia-tion of the parking areas on Condominium or Retained Land." What was earlier said about the nature of the expressly reserved right to control parking supports this conclusion, as does the impliedly reserved right to park vehicles other than those of condominium unit owners on condominium land. This is not a "common scheme" in the sense that similar restrictions were imposed upon all the lots in a subdivision. * * *

When it began to sell the remaining parcels on the wharf the developer included in the deeds the rights to obtain licenses to park in the parking lots on the wharf, including in the parking and driveway area. These rights are referred to as "deeded parking rights." In our view, this was a division of the easement rights retained by the developer. Such a division of rights is valid. * * * Indeed, since the retained rights were for the benefit of the land owners on the wharf, those rights were appurtenant to the land. There was nothing wrong with the manner in which the developer divided those rights, according to the needs of each parcel.

Thus, the "deeded parking rights" are valid.   * * *

The Land Court judge expressed the view that the retained rights are subject to some durational limit, but reserved the question of what that time limit is. The Land Court judge explicitly noted that she would rule on this question after any appeals from the judgment. * * *

In *Barclay v. DeVeau* * * * (1981), we suggested that a finding of overreaching or fraud might have invalidated the management agree-ment that we upheld in that case. The Association argues that the arrangement in this case, even if permissible, is invalid because it is the product of overreaching or a breach of fiduciary duty. We disagree.

The Association claims that both procedural and substantive as-pects of the parking arrangement are unconscionable. * * * The judge

found that the unit owners had notice of the terms of the Declaration.
* * * The judge also found that the design of the project was not
concealed from the unit owners, that many of the unit owners had
"considerable negotiating clout," and that there was no "bad faith" in
the submission of the property to c. 183A. The principal point relied
upon by the Association is that, despite the notice of the terms of the
Declaration, there was some uncertainty as to the extent of the right
"to control" parking on the wharf. In the circumstances, we think this
falls short of a showing that there was overreaching.

Substantively, we think the parking arrangement is fair and reasonable. The developer submitted the parking and driveway area to
condominium ownership in order to comply with zoning requirements.
It retained the right to control parking, however, because it had
concerns regarding the allocation of the limited parking rights among
the various parcels on the wharf. The Declaration and master deed
exhibit an attempt by the developer to allocate various burdens and
benefits among the parcels on the wharf. Thus, in addition to retaining
the right to control parking and to collect fees, the Declaration provides
that the owner of the retained land (the developer and its successors)
must maintain the parking area. Maintenance includes, "without
limitation, making necessary repairs and replacements thereto, clearing snow therefrom, providing for reasonable security at reasonable
hours and obtaining and maintaining public liability insurance on said
land with limits of not less than a single limit of $1,000,000 * * * said
insurance to name the owners of the Condominium Land as additional
insureds." The Declaration also provides that the owners of the retained land must assume the cost of maintaining the main horizontal
sewer line serving the properties. Unit owners are guaranteed the
right to rent parking spaces at "reasonable and competitive" rates.
Accordingly, there was both a legitimate reason for the arrangement
and a reasonable allocation of the burdens and benefits associated with
it. * * *

We need not address the Association's contention that a developer
of a condominium owes a fiduciary duty to the future residents. Even
if we so held, we would find no breach of that duty in the circumstances
presented here. For the reasons discussed above we think the developer acted in a fair and evenhanded manner.

Notes and Questions

1. Mitchell Rait, "Lollipop Condominiums: Air Rights, The Takings
Clause, and Disclosure Under New York's New Guidelines," 17 Real Estate
Law Journal 335, 337–340 (1989): "A lollipop condominium is a legally
separate residence built on top of an existing condominium. Since the New
York Condominium Act requires residential condominiums to be built on a
piece of property (leading to fee simple absolute ownership), the upper
condominium must be provided with an easement to touch the land. This
is usually accomplished through an elevator shaft or a column of the
building leading to the land directly beneath the shaft or column. This

piece of land is then assigned to the upper condominium. The result is a tall stem with a building balanced on top, hence the name 'lollipop.'

"A consequence of lollipop condominiums is the reduction in the share of common interests of the original owners. The new purchasers of the upper condominium cut into the portion of the shared facilities owned originally by the lower owners. This effect also occurs in 'phasing,' the lateral counterpart to lollipops. An obstacle is presented, however, by Section 339–i(1) of the New York Real Property Law. This section establishes a permanent character of the common interests, preventing any fluctuation of the interest shares. Similarly, New York State's attorney general requires specification of the undivided fractional interest attached to each unit for ownership.

"Virginia, on the other hand, unequivocally allows a developer to reserve the right to expand. The Virginia statute merely requires three criteria: (1) the explicit reservation of an option to expand the condominium; (2) a statement of any limitations on that option; and (3) a seven-year time limitation upon which the option to expand will expire. In 1965, the Association of the Bar of the City of New York disapproved a proposed amendment to Section 339–i(1) of the New York Real Property Law that would have provided developers with the leeway found in the Virginia statute: '[T]hat the declaration may specifically provide for an increase or decrease of the common interest upon the happening of one or more of the following events: (a) the addition of units to the condominium; (b) the removal of units from the condominium.' The Association * * * contended that the clause would place the unit purchaser in a position that was far too uncertain. The initial purchasers could never be certain what the extent of the finished development would be and, hence, what the unit owner's fractional interest, share of expenses, and proportionate voting strengths would be. * * *

"With the restriction of Section 339–i(1) of the New York Real Property Law and without the flexibility found in the proposed amendment, sponsors have nonetheless accomplished their goal. First, the sponsor would indeed comply with the rigid requirements of the Condominium Act by setting forth with particularity the common interests of the initial offering. Second, the sponsor would contractually arrange easements, covenants, and restrictions with the offerees. Such provisions, many of them blanket retentions, would satisfy the requirement of Section 339–i(2) of the New York Real Property Law, allowing alteration of the common interest applicable to each unit via the consent of all unit owners. Unanimity would be accomplished through the agreements. It is these contractual provisions that are the target of the attorney general's new guidelines. The Real Estate Financing Bureau prohibited vague boiler-plate reservations of expansion rights unless the sponsor disclosed future plans in great detail. The result was that developers who did not have firm construction plans within four or five years, according to the Real Estate Financing Bureau, were prevented from retaining developmental rights. * * *"

2. The guidelines of the Attorney General of New York, to which Mr. Rait refers, are one approach to the problem of unconscionability that was unsuccessfully offered for judicial resolution in *Commercial Wharf*. Anoth-

er and more common solution is in the moral conversation between the developer and the developer's lawyer. Business lawyers exercise moral influence on their clients constantly, and law professors occasionally ask them to be even more resolute than they are. Professor Harry W. Jones, an esteemed elder in the teaching part of the profession, for example: "J.M.L., fine lawyer and truly good man * * * behind his office desk as counselor and advisor. A major corporate client * * * is concerned about possible claims from its distributors and customers and wants something put into its standard form contracts to insulate the company from possible liability, even for losses caused by the company's own negligence, default or neglect. The corporation is a big fellow in its industry; the standard form contract will be offered on a take-it-or-leave-it basis, and the smaller distributors and consumers will have no alternative but to take it. J.M.L. would never for a moment think of putting such an oppressive clause into a contract of his own. Do the accepted ethical standards of the legal profession instruct or authorize him to do for his client what he would never do for himself? Should he be troubled in conscience if he drafts the requested insulation clause with technical precision, so as to make it legally enforceable, and, by including it in the client's standard contract, imposes it on every small businessman with whom the client deals? * * *

"There must be some point, short of running over one's grandmother, at which the lawyer's own personal and social morality will rebel against his traditional allegiance to his client. My revered mentor, J.M.L., unquestionably drew the line somewhere." ("Lawyers and the Uneasy Ethics of Partisanship," 23 Villanova Law Review 957 [1978].)

3. Mrs. Wylick: Mrs. Wylick is visiting your office to discuss the disposition of her estate. The visit is at the insistence of Mrs. Wylick's favorite granddaughter, Rose Jones. Both Mrs. Wylick and her granddaughter have come to the attorney's office.

Mrs. Wylick is 75 and has a slight hearing problem. Mrs. Wylick has been in the hospital for cancer twice in the last 15 years. In both cases, the cancer was surgically removed, and there has been no recurrence of the disease; however, Mrs. Wylick fears the return of the cancer. In addition, she has begun to suffer from periodic high blood pressure. Aside from the cancer, Mrs. Wylick is robust for her age and has no apparent health difficulties.

Mrs. Wylick becomes depressed frequently because she doesn't have anyone to talk with. She is also very distressed because she can't keep her house as clean as she used to because she can't see as well as she once did. Finally, she doesn't think she is eating right because she doesn't have the desire to cook only for herself.

Mrs. Wylick has three children and five grandchildren. She is not speaking to her eldest child, a son named John, and has not seen him for eight years. She has twins, Martha and George. The twins are 40 years old. Martha is married and has three children. Martha is Mrs. Wylick's favorite child, although they did not speak for a ten-year period about 20 years ago. The favorite granddaughter, Rose, is Martha's eldest child. George is single and lives with Mrs. Wylick.

Mrs. Wylick owns her own home in which both she and her son George live. She also owns a duplex from which she receives rental income, and a vacant lot on the city's south side.

Mrs. Wylick would like George to have a place to live even after she dies, but she doesn't want him to have "too much" because she considers him irresponsible. She doesn't want him to be able to sell the home, and she wants her home to go to her granddaughter after George dies.

She wants the duplex to go to Martha. In fact, because she has trouble getting around and fears that she may face a lengthy hospitalization, she would like to "add Martha's name" to the duplex now. Martha has always helped her maintain the duplex.

Mrs. Wylick's vacant lot is next to the Slovak church. Mrs. Wylick would like to give it to the Slovak church, but she is worried that the Archdiocese may take any income from the property's sale. She doesn't want to benefit the Archdiocese in any way. If that would happen, she would rather have the property go to her heirs.

Suggest will clauses to carry out our client's wishes.

II. PROPERTY CLAIMS IN MARRIAGE

The first part of this chapter considered common-law forms of joint (or concurrent) property ownership. Although these have not been, either conceptually or historically, forms of family or marital ownership, they have become, in our modern American culture, popular arrangements for ownership of property by people who are married to one another. The tenancy in common and the joint tenancy (including derivative personal-property arrangements such as joint bank accounts and joint tenancies in securities and safety deposit boxes) are forms of marital property ownership by planning. The tenancy by the entirety is a form of marital property ownership, but it is less useful than the joint tenancy because it is often not available for personal property.

In this section, we consider property claims in marriage, claims under policies maintained by the state to protect spouses. These are forms of ownership and claims on ownership that have to do with marriage. In most cases these forms and claims have to do with property in families, since marriages usually involve families in which property interests, like children, are his, hers, and ours. The most interesting question, often, is how ownership works out in families. Since families do not usually consult lawyers except in crisis, this question, in terms of Wednesday-afternoon law practice, is: How does ownership work out when the family is put through divorce or through the death of one of its property owners?

We carefully do not say when the family is "broken up" by one of these events. What is significant for present purposes is that such events bring families into law offices. Such events do not necessarily break up families, which are resilient old things—not easy to break. A follower of Anne Tyler, winner of the Pulitzer Prize and chronicler of the modern American family, is bound to say that families can survive death and divorce. We who follow Anne Tyler are going to notice, though, that property is involved in the question of whether a family breaks up over divorce or death—and that means that a property lawyer is involved: A property lawyer is present, in one way or another, making things better or making things worse.

A. CLAIMS AGAINST THE OWNER

Imagine a visit to the law office by two brothers who own a junkyard—a prosperous and growing junkyard. They have, with help from our law office, incorporated their business; in form, what the brothers own is stock in the junkyard corporation. Title to the land on which the business is conducted is in the corporation, Junkyard, Inc. Junkyard stock is all either of them owns, but it is a lot. Each brother is almost a millionaire.

One of the brothers, Morgan, is married; he and his wife, Charlotte, have two unmarried teen-aged children. Jake, Morgan's little brother, is not married and has no children—but he is engaged and planning to be married in a couple of months, to a dermatologist named Elizabeth.

These two brothers come to see their lawyer together, without appointment. They march into the office of the partner who does their legal work and say they want to disinherit their wives and children (or, in Jake's case, his fiancee). Each brother wants his stock in the business to go to the other brother—all of it.

A place to begin thinking about such a client agenda (certainly not the only place, and maybe not even the best) is in terms of what the law will let the brothers do: The doctrinal notion to begin with is that disinheritance is something a client can usually do in our property system. It could be accomplished even before wills were allowed in England: by the use of uses, for example. After the Statute of Wills (1540), it was possible to make a will of real property, and disinheritance was even easier. Your client, with your help, could see to it that the eldest son—the heir—got nothing. He could give his property to daughters or to his mistress or to his brother or to a hospital, or even, if he was a hopeless romantic, to his wife:

— There was not then and is not now any significant restraint on disinheriting children or other relatives; the most that even the most modern Anglo–American system provides is support for dependent children, and that is in many places limited to support during the judicially-supervised administration of the estate.

— There was not, for that matter, any significant restraint on *disinheriting* a spouse. The wife was not an heir anyway. After she became an heir, she could be disinherited as easily as anyone else could be. Spouses had claims to life interests in the dead person's property (dower and curtesy), but the idea there was not inheritance so much as to *provide for* the spouse during widowhood. These claims were not claims of forced inheritance; they were more like debts.

In terms, then, of what the law will allow our clients to do, things look about as promising as things ever look on Wednesday afternoon. (Of course, the situation would not be the same in a community-property state.) Morgan wants to disinherit Charlotte and their children. Jake wants to disinherit Elizabeth before he marries her. We can do both jobs. They may not be simple, but we can do them. Consider our nuts and bolts:

First, it will matter *when* the brothers got or get the *property* we are depriving these families of. Then it will matter *when* we are doing this *legal work* for them. Jake, for example, is a different case than Morgan, in both respects. And the value of their stock now is a different case from the additional value their stock will have at the time a spouse's claim is made on it. It matters whether we are talking about what will happen when one of these wives finds out about our legal work and files for divorce, or talking about what will happen when one of the brothers dies and his wife survives.

Take Jake first: Jake has property, but he is not married yet. If you are a lover of Victorian novels, you know that the visit to the family solicitor's office, before the wedding, was a big part of the mundane consequences of those chaste romances that Trollope and the Bronte sisters, Jane Austen, and Wilkie Collins wrote about. The implication of such a visit was that the solicitor (who was usually the family solicitor for the groom's family) had access to property rules that made it possible to disinherit the bride before she became a bride. If the wealth were on the bride's side of the marriage, it would fall under the husband's control after the wedding, and careful arrangements were necessary to arrange for its availability for her support if he died before she did, and then for its ownership by their children.

In most American states today, in our law office on Wednesday afternoon, as the professional descendants of the Victorian family solicitor, we would be considering Elizabeth and Charlotte as in the following situations:

— Neither would be, or would need to be, an heir in order to have a claim: In a narrow sense of the word, both Morgan and Jake can disinherit their wives by making wills that give their entire estates (*i.e.,* the property each will own when he dies) to one another.

— In Victorian society (and in a few American states still) each wife (assuming Elizabeth is by then a wife) has a common-law *dower* claim to a *life estate in one third of the real property that her husband owned during their marriage.* Only real property that was an *estate of inheritance,* and was held in a *legal* (as distinguished from equitable) form of ownership was vulnerable to this claim. So, for example, if the brothers had not yet incorporated their business, they could tend to that on the eve of Jake's marriage—put the land ownership in the corporation and ownership of stock in the brothers—and thereby defeat Elizabeth's dower claim. There is no dower in shares of stock; they are not real property. The dower claim thus became limited as wealth was put in stock markets rather than farms, but dower is persistent in other ways. It attaches at marriage or when property is acquired by the husband, and once it attaches it stays attached; it is "inchoate." Although the wife cannot do anything with her dower interest so long as the husband is alive, the husband cannot get rid of it so long as the wife is alive. Since the junkyard was real property, owned in part by Morgan, owned when he and Charlotte were married, the ante-nuptial devices of Victorian lawyers are not useful for disinheriting Charlotte. Charlotte had an inchoate dower interest that was not affected by incorporation. The husband, at common law, had a parallel inchoate interest in the wife's property (curtesy); it did not attach unless children were born to the couple, but then it was a life interest in *all* of the wife's property. Modern American constitutional law would probably require that the interests of spouses be equal. Most American states have abolished common-law dower and curtesy.

— Most states have adopted an "elective share" system in addition to or rather than dower and curtesy. The critical elective-share time, if we are working for Morgan and Jake, will be the time of the death of one of the brothers. At that point, a brother's wife can claim a significant share of the estate as a *statutory share*. A will giving everything to someone else—the decedent's brother, in this case—will not prevent this claim; it is a matter, in the popular phrase, of "taking against the will." But the critical moment is death; if the decedent has disposed of property prior to death (given it to his brother, say), the common elective share provided by American statutes won't reach that lifetime (or, as lawyers say, *inter-vivos*) transfer. The great disadvantage an elective-share system has over dower and curtesy (for Morgan and Jake) is that it reaches all kinds of property—real, personal, mixed, tangible and intangible—where dower and curtesy reach only real property. An elective-share statute will reach their corporate stock. The great advantage for our clients is that the elective share does not touch lifetime transfers. An elective-share claim by Elizabeth would reach Jake's junkyard stock, but not if Jake gave it to Morgan before Jake's death.

KNELL v. PRICE

Court of Special Appeals of Maryland, 1988.
77 Md.App. 331, 550 A.2d 413.

Wenner, Judge.

This appeal was spawned when appellant, Violet E. Knell, filed suit in the Circuit Court for Kent County against appellee, Jesse Annabelle Price, the personal representative of her husband's estate, to set aside certain deeds entered into by her husband during his lifetime. * * * She contends that: * * *

II.   The trial court erred when it found that the deeds executed by the decedent and trustee on December 19, 1978 were not for the purpose of fraudulently depriving appellant of her statutory share in the Mercer Avenue property.

We shall affirm the judgment of the circuit court.

Appellant and William A. Knell were married on January 11, 1938. They lived together until 1960 when, due to marital difficulties, they separated. Although they remained separated from 1960 until Mr. Knell's death in 1987, no separation agreement was ever executed nor were they ever divorced. During the separation, appellant continued to occupy the home on Haven Road in Rock Hall, Maryland, which she and her husband had purchased in 1955. Upon Mr. Knell's death, that property became hers as surviving tenant by the entirety.

In late 1960, after the separation, Mr. Knell began living with the appellee in Baltimore County. He continued to live with her until his death. During that time appellee served as Mr. Knell's nurse, homemaker, cook and companion.

In October 1978, Mr. Knell purchased a home on Mercer Avenue in Rock Hall, Maryland, which he shared with appellee and which is the subject of this litigation. The Mercer Avenue property was titled in his name. Two months after acquiring it, Mr. Knell conveyed the Mercer Avenue property to a trustee who immediately reconveyed the property to Mr. Knell. Although the granting clause of the deed from the trustee purported to convey the Mercer Avenue property to Mr. Knell in fee simple, the habendum clause provided that Knell held an estate in the property for his life only, "with the full power unto him to sell, mortgage, lease, convey and dispose (except by Last Will and Testment [sic]) of the whole and entire estate." Finally, the habendum clause provided that if any of the property remained, upon Knell's death it was to go to "Annabelle Price, her heirs and assigns, in fee simple." The deeds were dated and recorded on December 19, 1978. * * *

Appellant * * * asserts that the trial judge erred in not finding that, by arranging for the deeds complained of, Mr. Knell had fraudulently deprived her of her marital rights in the Mercer Avenue property. Specifically, she argues that since Mr. Knell exercised dominion and control over the Mercer Avenue property until he died, the trial judge should have found that the complained of deeds were merely devices contrived to deny her that portion of his estate which the law provides to her. We see it somewhat differently.

It is beyond cavil that a husband has the right to convey his property without the assent or knowledge of his wife. When the conveyance is an absolute, unconditional transfer, it is valid even if the husband made the transfer to deprive his wife of the property upon his death. * * * Thus, the threshold question is whether the decedent retained an interest in or control over the property he attempted to convey.

Where the decedent retains an interest in or control over the property, however, the trial judge must determine whether the transfer is a fraud upon the surviving spouse's marital rights. * * * The trial court is aided in making that determination by the factors explicated by the Court of Appeals in *Whittington v. Whittington* * * * (1954) * * *:

> In Maryland, the completeness of the transfer and the extent of control retained by the transferor, the motive of the transferor, participation by the transferee in the alleged fraud and the degree to which the surviving spouse is stripped of his or her interest in the estate of the decedent spouse have all been considered material, and no one test has been adopted to the exclusion of all other tests. * * * [T]here are several other factors which have been or may be considered as pertinent, such as the relative moral claims of the surviving spouse and of the transferees, other provisions for the surviving spouse, whether or not he or she has independent means and the interval of time between the transfer and the death of the transferor. * * *

In the case at hand, the lower court considered the *Whittington* factors and found that no fraud was committed. As we said earlier, appellee had lived with Mr. Knell for twenty seven years preceding his death, serving as his housekeeper, nurse, and companion. As we also said, the trial judge found that Mr. Knell intended to give the Mercer Avenue property to the appellee upon his death. Moreover, the trial judge found no evidence to support appellant's contention that Mr. Knell intended to defraud her. Indeed, the court said, "He seems to have regarded his action * * * as the moral and equitable thing to do under the circumstances."

The cases cited by appellant are distinguishable from the one before us. For example, in *Jaworski v. Wisniewski* * * * (1925), the decedent and her husband acquired property as tenants by the entirety. When marital difficulties arose, they separated, and as an incident of that separation, appellee bought her husband's interest in the property. Several years later, for the express purpose of preventing her husband from receiving the property upon her death, Mrs. Wisniewski arranged a transfer of the property whereby she retained the property for her life, with the remainder to her children. The Court of Appeals held that, since the clear and avowed purpose of Mrs. Wisniewski's conveyance was to deprive her husband of the property, in order for the conveyances to be valid, she would have had to give up all dominion and control over the property. It was upon that finding that the court held that the transfer was invalid.

In *Hayes v. Henry* * * * (1848) the decedent's widow brought an action claiming that her husband had conveyed certain property to his paramour solely for the purpose of preventing his wife from getting the property upon his death. The property in question was purchased by the decedent on April 2, 1844. The decedent immediately conveyed the property to his paramour. * * *

The court found that the decedent had not parted with possession but rather that he bought, lived on and died on the property. The court also found that the decedent's *sole* purpose for making that transfer was to deprive his widow of her share of his estate. It was upon that finding that the court held that the transfer was invalid.

In sum, in both *Jaworski* and *Hayes,* the court found that the decedents had transferred property for the sole purpose of depriving their spouses of their marital rights. On the other hand, in the case *sub judice,* the trial judge found from the evidence before him that Mr. Knell had no such intent. Rather, the trial judge concluded that Mr. Knell had intended to make a gift of the Mercer Avenue property to the person who had lived with him, cared for him, and been his companion for twenty seven years. We hold that in making that determination the trial judge was not clearly erroneous. * * *

Notes and Questions

1. The lawyer who seeks to set up either (i) conveyance of real property from Jake to the corporation, on the eve of his marriage; or (ii) conveyance of stock, by Jake, to Morgan, during Jake's life and after his marriage to Elizabeth, will have to proceed with some care to come to terms with the substantial body of case law having to do with eve-of-marriage transfers to frustrate dower claims or lifetime gratuitous transfers to frustrate statutory-share claims. (You can see how case law on one issue is authority on the other issue. Should it be?) Can you suggest how evidence might be assembled and preserved, at and before the time of transfer, to protect the transfers from attacks such as the one in *Knell?*

2. An alternative way to strengthen elective-share claims against gratuitous lifetime transfers is to seek legislation that will pull lifetime transfers back into the decedent's estate for the limited purpose of satisfying statutory-share claims. In some ways this extends the inchoate character of dower to an elective-share system and gives a surviving spouse the best of both worlds. The analogy might be (and has been) to death taxes. Those taxes, both state and federal, reach lifetime gratuitous transfers, including joint tenancies (where the decedent has placed her property in a joint tenancy with a donee), outright gifts, trust arrangements in which the decedent reserved a life interest, and even life insurance and survivor's retirement benefits. Such lifetime transfers are not invalid, but they are vulnerable to having to be partially undone in order to pay death taxes—or the elective share to the widow or widower: New York and Pennsylvania adopted "augmented estate" statutory-share systems a generation ago. The Uniform Probate Code provided such a system in 1969, and several states have adopted it. Statutes of this sort typically: (i) refer to and build on the existing elective-share statute (*e.g.,* a surviving spouse may claim his intestate share of the estate "against the will"); (ii) list a range of lifetime transfers that can be set aside to "augment" the estate against which the elective share can be taken (but are not otherwise set aside); (iii) provide that the same list of transfers be applied as to the surviving spouse, so that a tenancy by the entirety or an outright gift to the surviving spouse is also brought into the augmented estate; and (iv) direct a computation of the

elective-share fraction against the augmented estate, followed by reduction for amounts the surviving spouse already received.

Note: On Morals in the Law Office [6]

In my classes in wills and trusts we use Justice Holmes's bad-man theory of law when we discuss the rules * * * protecting spouses from disinheritance. * * *

[Even] in those few states which use "augmented estate" systems * * * the obstacles are surmountable. None of those systems of protection, for instance, covers life insurance. One way to disinherit a spouse is to reduce everything to cash and to buy life insurance with it—insurance which, in this case would be [on the life of Jake, with Morgan as beneficiary, or vice versa]. * * *

The students come to see that they are equal to a difficult bit of planning. They gather confidence in their own learning and ability. They discover that it is easier to defeat a family than it is to defeat the government.

And then I say to them: Now that you know you *can* do it, I want to know whether you *would* do it. I get three sorts of answers to this moral question: (1) Some students say that the moral question is not for a lawyer to answer; it is for the client. Our professional ideals point to doing for people what they want done, within the limits of the law. In fact, our system works best when each lawyer does his best for his client and the system itself irons out the differences. (2) Some students say they would not, under any conditions, do this work for this client. They argue that our professional ideals point toward clients' conduct which is moral as well as legal. Professional ideals do not suspend the lawyer's conscience; lawyers still have to answer for what they do. (3) A final answer is that the lawyers should talk to the client about this question. Lawyers have moral influence on their clients; a lawyer's work should include efforts to help clients make choices that are morally sound, and this is accomplished by sharing with the client the burden of hard choices.

[Maybe] those three schools of ethical thought sum up the morality of practicing law. The first is role-determined; it says, in effect, that lawyers are like plumbers, or clerks in hardware stores. They do what their customers want done. The second is a morality of conscientious objection; it says that a lawyer cannot base her behavior on what people expect of her as a lawyer, but that she has a conscience of her own. The third is a morality of care. * * * [I]t says that the moral life is a shared life: No person is an island, it says; "and therefore never send to know for whom the bell tolls, it tolls for thee." I care for my client and have a right to expect that my client will care for me.

Each of these three orientations has its promise and its limitations; the third, the morality of care, is, I think, the most difficult, but it is the morality I urge on my students.

6. Thomas L. Shaffer, "The Ethics of Estate Planning," Probate Notes, American College of Probate Counsel, Spring 1979, p. 19.

The morality of role depends on an idea about the function of the profession in society, and on an idea about the function of each lawyer within the profession. It offers security, as functional definitions of people always do, but it does not offer moral breadth or depth. Even so, the debate that goes on in our profession about the moral responsibility of lawyers takes place almost entirely within this limited morality of role. Those who defend the adversary system argue that lawyers should do what clients want done because the courts, or the free-enterprise economy, or Social Darwinism, will make things come out right. The more modern school of "public interest law," which argues that lawyers have a duty to see to the social usefulness of what their clients do, is morally similar in that it, like the adversary-ethic argument, bases its case on the principle that lawyers should serve the public interest.

The problem with either branch in the morality of role is that it is only as good as the system * * * the lawyer is said to serve. Professionalism does not contain within itself a basis for questioning the goodness of the system. Or, to put that thought another way, professionalism assumes that the system can provide goodness. It assumes that *power* can provide goodness. But power cannot provide goodness, and those who assume that power can provide goodness risk ending up in the service of evil. Albert Speer, or the S.S. colonel in "The Holocaust," did not set out to serve evil; they set out to serve power, on the assumption that power would provide a good society for themselves and their families. They fooled themselves, as many others did in the German establishment of their day, and the consequences were as bad as anything that has ever happened to the world.

The morality of conscientious objection depends on * * * moral isolation. It assumes that each lawyer and each client makes decisions alone, that these people in the law office do not depend upon and influence one another. That idea seems to me to be untrue. My observation, from more than 20 years [30 years now] of studying, teaching, and practicing law, is that clients are almost always influenced by lawyers, and that lawyers are influenced by clients. In fact, lawyers tend to become like their clients. Lawyers are, in a way, more influenced than influencing.

We Americans cherish a myth of rugged individualism, but our history, like the history of any people, is a history of dependence and influence. Dependence and influence are almost as pronounced in professional relationships as they are in the family. We tend to forget how dependent we are until we are stuck in an airline waiting room, wondering about a delayed flight across the country, or until we are out looking for a job. If we were capable of moral reflection at such moments, we would realize how much we depend on our clients, and they on us. In the moral life, dependence is a matter of fact and a matter of aspiration. As the great theologian Karl Barth put it:

> He who takes the risk of counseling must be prepared to be counseled in turn by his brother if there is need of it. Such mutual counseling in a concrete situation is an event. It is a part of the ethos which is realized ethics. The ethos * * * implies that he refrain from attempting too much and becoming thereby a lawgiver.

The prominent problem with the morality of conscientious objection is that it assumes a moral isolation that is not truthful. A more subtle problem is that it assumes a moral life without risk; if I set out to give moral assistance to my client, I must, as Barth says, be prepared to accept moral assistance, and that is scary. That is less secure than my students, who decide that they must do the right thing in their law offices, suppose it to be.

The morality of care is based on the dynamics of making up your mind. The most interesting examples of people making up their minds are in literature—in Trollope's novels *The Warden* and *The Duke's Children,* for two examples, or in C.P. Snow's novel about justice, *The Affair.* The process in which a strong, good person decides what to do, or decides to change her mind, is a wondrous and subtle process, but one thing that seems to be present in these literary cases is the influence of other people. I argue that the morality of care is not a matter of deciding to exert influence or to be influenced. It is a matter of admitting that we do influence and are influenced. It is a matter, in the first instance, of truthfulness. Once we tell ourselves the truth about influence, we can begin to take moral account of the influences we exert and the influences exerted on us.

If influence is admitted it is possible to work toward a morality of influences. Most lawyers would probably say that the most important principle in exerting moral influence on clients is respect for the freedom of the client. Modern philosophical ethics * * * sets down limits * * * which forbid coercion, dishonesty, and manipulation. Within the practice of respect for the moral freedom of clients, the influence lawyers choose to exert can range from acceptance of the moral choices of clients to advertent attempts at conversion. At one end of this spectrum of influence are lawyers who ask only that their clients consider moral choices seriously; at the other end are lawyers who ask their clients to pray with them. All along the spectrum is a realization that moral problems in professional relationships are shared. My concern for my client includes the concern that he become a better person. I have an investment in his goodness. It is not enough that he and I make moral choices that are right; our goal is moral choices that cause us to become better people. * * *

The morality of care also assumes skills. It requires the ability to listen and to elicit, the ability to focus on what worries the client, and not merely on the art of planning to do what the client says she wants done. In the example my students work with, the skills involved are skills for talking about the client's family and about the [client's brother and their business]. These are counseling skills, not advocacy or planning skills. * * * They are skills Carl Rogers pointed toward when he said to his client:

> To be of assistance to you I will put aside myself—the self of ordinary interaction—and enter into your world of perception as completely as I am able. I will become, in a sense, another self for you—an alter ego of your own attitudes and feelings—a safe opportunity for you to discern yourself more clearly * * * to choose more significantly.

There is no morally responsible way to limit the work of the law office to filling orders or to the naked assertion of moral choice. My client and I are in this thing together. * * *

B. MARITAL PROPERTY

The most coherent and consistent body of American marital-property law is the system of community property we inherited from our Spanish forebears. This system is in effect in Louisiana, Texas, New Mexico, Arizona, Nevada, California, Idaho, and Washington. The community-property system turns on the principle that earnings in a marriage belong to the marriage (the "community"). It is not determinative that record ownership of property traceable to the earnings of one spouse is in that spouse's name. Earnings and property traceable to earnings are community property and are *owned*, from the first, half and half.

The system has had its patriarchical past, as much as the common-law property system has. The old rule was that the husband controlled the community's property, so that, for all practical purposes, community ownership became an issue only at divorce or death. Legislation and judicial decisions parallel to *Knell* in community-property states limit the old principle, where it has not been abolished entirely, so that third persons dealing with a husband are much less able than they once were to assume that the husband's actions will bind the wife.

The system is also complicated by definitions of what is community property and what is not. Property a spouse owned at the time of marriage, inherited property, and gift property, are probably the clearest examples of "separate" (non-community) property. Paychecks, bank accounts into which earnings are deposited, and houses and automobiles bought from such accounts, are probably the clearest examples of community property. Employer-provided fringe benefits, such as life insurance and retirement pay, are a middle case. And damages recovered for torts committed on one of the spouses by a third party are a good example for discussion; such issues have not yet been dealt with everywhere by case law or statute.

The character of property is subject to the agreement of the spouses. Thus property can be "transmuted" from community to separate, or vice versa, or to a form that is functionally neither. A joint-and-survivor bank account, or joint securities ownership, are possible in community-property states, for example, as are joint tenancies in other property.

PROBATE, TRUST AND REAL PROPERTY SECTION, INDIANA STATE BAR ASSOCIATION, "UNIFORM MARITAL PROPERTY ACT"

Res Gestae, November 1984, p. 237.

In July of 1983, the Commissioners on Uniform State Laws approved for promulgation the Uniform Marital Property Act ("UMPA").

If adopted by Indiana, UMPA would change Indiana's present common law system of property ownership to a community property based system. This course has already been taken by Wisconsin, a former common law property state, which adopted a look-alike UMPA in the spring of 1984.

UMPA was designed to address property problems occurring as a result of increases in the incidences of divorce and the numbers of marriages in which both spouses are employed outside the home.

Moreover, it reflects increased pressures to recognize the services of the full time homemaker as a contributor to a couple's economic success. UMPA treats the property acquired during a marriage ("marital property") as "ours" rather than as "yours or mine." * * *

UMPA's *determination date* is the last to occur of (i) the parties' marriage, (ii) the date the parties move into the enacting state, or (iii) the effective date of UMPA's enactment in the state.

UMPA provides for three categories of property: "marital," "individual" and "mixed." Property owned by an individual prior to marriage is individual property, as is property acquired by gift made by, or inheritance received from, a third person to a spouse. Except as specifically provided in UMPA, the interest of a spouse in property owned immediately before UMPA's enactment is individual property.

Property acquired by a spouse through exchange for or with the proceeds of the spouse's individual property remains individual property as does appreciation of individual property. Other examples of individual property include recoveries from the other spouse for UMPA "breaches" and recoveries for personal injuries.

Except as noted above, and unless reclassified by * * * agreement * * *, all other property acquired by a couple after UMPA's determination date is "marital" property.

Earnings, income earned or accrued by a spouse on marital property, and income earned or accrued by a spouse on individual property *after* UMPA's determination date are "marital" property. Each spouse is the owner of an undivided one-half interest in all marital property.

Marital and individual property may be commingled, resulting in "mixed" property under UMPA. Mixed property (other than life insurance and deferred employment benefits) is deemed to be "marital" property unless the component of the mixed property which is not marital property can be traced. This rule is in line with UMPA's general presumption that all property owned by spouses is marital property. * * *

Mixed property can * * * result from "sweat equity"—defined as the application by one spouse of substantial labor, effort, inventiveness, physical or intellectual skill, creativity, or managerial activity with respect to the other spouse's individual property.

Marital property attributable to that application is created if reasonable compensation is not received by the spouse applying the sweat equity and if substantial appreciation results from the spouse's labor. * * *

The classification rules would introduce a new element in Indiana practice when marriages terminate either by death or dissolution. It would be necessary to determine the source of property, trace the income of individual and marital property, and trace the growth in asset value realized from appreciation of individual property. Additional problems would be presented by mixed property. * * *

[M]arried persons may, by way of a marital property agreement, agree to just about any matter relating to their property that is not illegal or immoral. Marital property agreements cannot be used to vary some provisions of UMPA, such as its good faith requirement, the provisions protecting third parties, and the provisions concerning the support of dependent children.

The fact that a marital property agreement can be revoked or amended only by a later marital property agreement provides considerable protection to spouses in probate matters. A will or trust can be altered unilaterally, while a marital property agreement alteration would require the signatures of both spouses. There are some similarities between these agreements and the antenuptial agreements effective under current Indiana law. * * *

Both spouses must act together to control marital property held in the names of both spouses. * * * Either spouse has sole management and control rights over a marital property asset which is titled in that spouse's name alone.

Thus the precise language of title may be determinative of control and will necessitate careful attention when titling real or personal property. UMPA specifically authorizes the titling of marital property.

UMPA contains rules restricting the ability of one spouse to make a gift to a third party of marital property controlled by that spouse. UMPA leaves the amount of the gift which can be made without joinder by the other spouse to the discretion of the adopting state, but sets forth $500.00 as a suggested limit. * * *

Creditors' rights are not diminished by UMPA and may, in fact, be somewhat enlarged. UMPA (1) establishes a presumption that any obligation (including one attributable to an act or omission) incurred by a spouse during marriage is incurred in the interest of the marriage or family; and (2) allows the obligation to be satisfied out of all the marital property and the incurring spouse's individual property.

Any other obligation (also including one attributable to an act or omission) incurred by a spouse is satisfied first out of that spouse's individual property and then out of his or her interest in marital property.

Thus creditors' rights are expanded through an ability to [garnish] a non-contracting spouse's wages to satisfy debts, unless it can be shown that those debts were not incurred in the interest of the marriage or family.

On the other hand, the non-contracting spouse's interest in marital property is protected against creditor's claims arising out of the purely personal obligations of the incurring spouse. * * *

In addition to creditors, UMPA provides protection to bona fide purchasers for value. This is the same bona fide purchaser that all lawyers get to know and love in law school—with one exception. A bona fide purchaser *with* notice is protected. Therefore, third party purchasers of marital property are under no duty of inquiry and may rely on record title. * * *

Survivorship Marital Property. UMPA creates a new designation of property known as "survivorship marital property." By using these words in a title, rather than the words "marital property," total ownership rights in the marital property will rest in the surviving spouse upon death. In this way, among others, probate may be avoided. * * *

Because UMPA creates vested interests in marital property while still permitting individual management and control of that property, some method is necessary to allow the noncontrolling spouse to review the activities of the controlling spouse and to remedy any injustice to the noncontrolling spouse's interests.

UMPA's method is to give the noncontrolling spouse a claim against the controlling spouse for a breach of the controlling spouse's good faith duty.

To remedy the breach, a court can order an accounting of all property and obligations of the spouses and can determine each spouse's rights of ownership in, beneficial enjoyment of, or access to, marital property. It can adjust their interests as may be necessary to remedy an injustice unless these interests fall within particular classes. * * *

[A]fter dissolution or death, each spouse would own an undivided one-half interest in the marital property. However, this result could be changed on dissolution by an agreement or court order.

The adoption of UMPA would require some rethinking of Indiana's intestate and elective share statutes. Since the surviving spouse would, under UMPA, own one-half of the marital property, this one-half share would not pass as part of a deceased spouse's probate estate (although it may be administered as part of it).

If UMPA were enacted and present Indiana law were not changed, the surviving spouse would be entitled to one-half of the couple's marital property and to an intestate or elective share of the deceased spouse's individual property and share of marital property.

Notes

1. The Indiana State Bar Association has consistently (and as of 1991 successfully) opposed enactment of UMPA in Indiana.

2. When the marital property act became effective in Wisconsin, James Bartelt, a reporter for the Green Bay Press–Gazette, interviewed legislators from his newspaper's region, and reported their comments (November 17, 1985):

> Senator Alan Lasee, noting that couples can, by agreement, keep their property in common-law forms of ownership: "There is this concept of man and wife sitting at the kitchen table working things out. But the result is going to be going to an attorney to find out what to do to protect their property. Even attorneys who have attended seminars say, 'My God, what did you do down there?'"

> Senator Jerome Van Sistine * * * voted for the new property system "with very mixed emotions." It could cause problems for small business, and some couples with one spouse having a long and terminal illness might even consider divorce to preserve property, he said.

> Senator Lloyd Kincaid * * * said a big plus for the new system is the transfer of property when there is no will. "If there is a will, there is safety. But for the thousands of people without a will, the widow is left in trouble," he said. Kincaid said he "formulated my position on equal opportunities for women. Women have always played a second-place role as far as pay is concerned". * * *

> Rep. Cletus Vanderperren * * * said he supported the * * * bill "very reluctantly. I suppose now that 50 percent of marriages end in divorce it can be a good idea to divide property. It's more of an attorneys' bill," he said.

> Rep. Sharon Metz * * * said she "voted for marital property right down the line. Under the English common law system, men own all the property and almost own the women. This provides for sharing. When a couple prospers, each shares equally."

3. In common-law states, when one spouse holds most or all of the couple's property, divorce-court judges often have the power to rearrange legal ownership. It is not fatal to fairness for a wife in divorce that the property is all held by the husband. (Judges will usually respect the spouses' agreement on division of property, by the way, and that also will normally involve re-arrangement of ownership.) The argument is therefore made that a marital-property act is more symbolic than anything else in changing the situation of women in divorce cases. Or, to put that point another way, opponents argue that, if the evil to be corrected is unfairness in divorce cases, the price of dual control of property during an intact marriage is too great a price to pay for reform. The counter-argument is that pooled ownership and dual control recognizes in the law the philosophical and moral understanding of what marriage is.

Chapter Four

THE LANDLORD–TENANT RELATIONSHIP

INTRODUCTION

As we have seen, it is possible in our property system for two or more persons to hold interests in the same piece of property at the same time. Examples previously studied include Indian title, finders, the common law system of estates in land, and concurrent ownership.

In this chapter, we will study the law governing the landlord-tenant relationship, an important form of property sharing, in which possession and ownership of land are held voluntarily by two different persons. We will examine the common law concept, a non-freehold estate in which possession, or tenure, of land formed the basis for the relationship. We will also study the revolutionary changes in the law that took place in a 20–year period beginning in the mid–1960s, particularly with respect to residential landlord-tenant relationships, as well as the rules for entering into and exiting from the relationship. In addition, we will introduce the idea of mediation as a non-adversarial method of resolving disputes that may be particularly useful in a landlord-tenant setting.

The following problem, which will be the focal point of our dispute resolution discussion, can also provide a useful setting for consideration of the other materials in this chapter. As you study the materials in this chapter, ask yourself what Kelly Green and Lance Lord did or did not do to provoke the controversy, what specific laws govern their relationship, and what they might have done differently to prevent the dispute from arising or to resolve it once it had arisen.

In considering this problem, you may wish to consult Wexler, Practicing Law for Poor People, 79 Yale L.J. 1049 (1970), discussed in T. Shaffer, American Legal Ethics: Text, Readings, and Discussion Topics 36–39 (1985), (arguing that the client, not the lawyer, should decide objectives and tactics). Review also the materials on lawyer-client relations in the adverse possession section of Chapter One and in the estates and family property sections of Chapters Two and Three.

THE INEXPERIENCED LANDLORD:
A MEDIATION EXERCISE FOR PROPERTY LAW *

Assume it is now February. Nearly two years ago, Kelly Green signed a one-year lease, renting an attractive older apartment for herself, her two-year old daughter, Susan, and her twelve-year old son, Michael. The rent was $600.00 a month, with heat furnished. There were nineteen other units in the building, which was fully rented at the time. The lease that Kelly signed contained a printed clause requiring the tenant to make all repairs. Kelly crossed out this clause and initialled the change. The lease also contained a typed clause stating that the landlord did not warrant the habitability of the premises.

At the time the lease was signed, Lance Lord, the landlord, and owner of the building promised Kelly that he would make certain repairs in the apartment and would provide screens for all the windows. Kelly asked for the screens because the apartment was on the second floor, and she was worried about her children's safety. When Kelly and the children moved in three weeks later, the screens had been placed in the windows, but other promised repairs had not been made. Moreover, the floor was wet with fresh varnish and as a result Kelly and her children had to spend the night in a motel.

During the first year that Kelly lived there, Lance's brother, Ray, lived in the building and provided some maintenance in return for a lower rent. He kept the common areas clean and made occasional minor repairs. Despite letters from Kelly, however, Lance never sent anyone to repair a malfunctioning oven and a broken kitchen cabinet door.

Believing that Lance would eventually fulfill his promises, Kelly renewed her lease the following July. The situation began to deteriorate soon thereafter. Ray moved out of the building, and Lance hired a series of incompetent maintenance men to replace him. The hall and stairways were rarely swept. The trash was not regularly carried out to the curb to be picked up, so the trash containers often overflowed. There were roaches in all the apartments. Often Kelly could hear them scurrying around in the dark.

Kelly's son, Michael, usually was home alone after school, and often brought friends over to play ball. They were noisy and broke windows from time to time. They also played in the back yard with the Airedale that belonged to Kelly's upstairs neighbor in the process trampling the grass and destroying some of the bushes.

The new maintenance men made haphazard attempts at building repairs that were beyond their capabilities. One of them tried to

* An earlier version appeared in L. Riskin & J. Westbrook, Instructor's Manual, Dispute Resolution and Lawyers 398, 402–404 (1987). Reprinted with permission from West Publishing Co.

Revisions were contributed by Professor Barbara Fick, Notre Dame Law School.

unclog a stopped-up drain in Kelly's kitchen by using a commercial drain cleaner. The drain had become clogged when a plastic top of a milk bottle fell into it as Michael was fixing an afternoon snack. After the drain cleaner was used, the sink continued to back-up. One day, water saturated with the powerful drain cleaner chemicals spilled onto the kitchen floor when Susan was playing while her mother was washing the dinner dishes. The overflow ruined the kitchen carpeting which Kelly had personally installed.

After Labor Day, Lance announced that he was going ahead with plans to install separate heating units in each apartment. The tenants had agreed to this contingency when they renewed their leases. (The renewed leases also provided for a twenty-dollar reduction in monthly rent as soon as the new furnaces were installed because of the expected energy efficiency of the new heating units.) Lance stated in a letter to the tenants that the work would be done in an orderly fashion and would be completed within a month.

As it turned out, the work was not completed until the middle of December because the workmen did not come every day. Each apartment was in a state of upheaval for a week or more while the new furnace was being installed. Plaster dust accumulated because the contractor did not clean up daily as he had agreed to do. The workmen were very careless—leaving dangerous tools around and leaving rings of keys to all the apartments where anyone could have taken them. They also left apartment doors standing open when they left for the day. During this time one of the apartments, rented by Gene Fitzsimmons, was burglarized and his stereo was taken.

The weather turned cold in early November before the new furnaces were working. Lance did not turn on the old boiler which was still functional, although he had promised to provide heat until the new furnaces were working. The building was without heat during all of November and the first two weeks of December, although the lease agreements expressly provided that the landlord was to furnish heat from October 1 through May 1 unless there were circumstances beyond his control.

Installation of the furnaces finally was completed by mid-December. As the weather turned colder, however, it became apparent that the new furnaces did not work very well. Most of the tenants found that their kitchens were now unheated. As a result, while Kelly was out of town during Christmas vacation, the pipes in her kitchen froze, then burst and flooded the kitchen. When Kelly returned from vacation, she walked into an apartment that smelled like a cave from the resulting dampness. Several of her kitchen appliances had suffered water damage. Lance had not repaired the pipes while she was gone. Eventually, the maintenance man made a half-hearted and unsuccessful attempt to repair the pipes. Now, whenever Kelly washes her dishes, water seeps into the apartment below which is rented by Jane

Hughett. Before Hughett noticed the leak, her sofa had sustained water damage.

In January, Kelly helped organize a tenants meeting. Tenants from twelve of the twenty units attended. (Four units were vacant and four elderly tenants did not come because they were afraid Lance might not renew their leases if they did.) At this meeting, all those present voted to withhold their rent until the building was properly maintained and repaired, and to discourage prospective tenants from leasing the vacant units. They have informed Lance Lord of their decision to withhold the rent and to hire a lawyer to pursue their legal rights. Lance responded by telling them that he would begin eviction proceedings against anyone who withheld the rent.

I. NONADVERSARIAL RESOLUTION OF LANDLORD–TENANT DISPUTES

Landlord-tenant disputes, particularly ones involving conditions within particular apartments or interpretations of specific lease provisions, may be better suited to nonadversarial forms of dispute resolution such as negotiation and mediation than to the traditional adversarial model of litigation. Landlords and tenants both generally want "good" counterparts and both generally want the landlord-tenant relationship to continue once established. When disputes flare up, communication between the parties, rather than communication to a judge, may allow the parties to preserve their relationship while resolving their dispute.

RISKIN, MEDIATION AND LAWYERS *
43 Ohio State L.J. 29–30, 34–36, 43–46 (1982).

A mediator helps disputants toward resolving their disagreement. Unlike a judge or arbitrator, however, the mediator lacks authority to impose a decision on the parties; he can only facilitate the process. Mediation has been and remains the dominant method of processing disputes in some quarters of the world. In parts of the Orient litigation is seen as a shameful last resort, the use of which signifies embarrassing failure to settle the matter amicably. Though it is unclear to what extent philosophy influences practice, the connection between the prominence of mediation and a Confucian heritage has been noted repeatedly by scholars. In the Confucian view,

> [a] lawsuit symbolized disruption of the natural harmony that was thought to exist in human affairs. Law was backed by coercion, and therefore tainted in the eyes of Confucianists. Their view was that the optimum resolution of most disputes was to be achieved not by the exercise of sovereign force but by moral persuasion. Moreover, litiga-

* Reprinted with permission of the Ohio
State Law Journal and Professor Riskin.

tion led to litigiousness and to shameless concern for one's own interest to the detriment of the interests of society.

This idea—that the natural and desirable condition is harmony—contrasts sharply with the predominant Western perspectives which focus on freedom as an absence of restraint and on autonomy and individual liberty as the highest goal. These Western notions, crystallized in the adversary system, pervade the American legal process and the lives of most of its citizens, including its lawyers. In recent years, though, mediation as a means of dispute processing has sent vines through the adversarial fence. They differ somewhat in purpose, orientation, and direction, but share a rapid growth rate. The development of mediation promises much that is good for American society and carries significant dangers as well.

* * *

I. Mediation in the United States

* * *

C. Mediation and the Law

Mediation offers some clear advantages over adversary processing: it is cheaper, faster, and potentially more hospitable to unique solutions that take more fully into account nonmaterial interests of the disputants. It can educate the parties about each other's needs and those of their community. Thus, it can help them learn to work together and to see that through cooperation both can make positive gains. One reason for these advantages is that mediation is less hemmed-in by rules of procedure or substantive law and certain assumptions that dominate the adversary process. There are, of course, assumptions that affect the procedure and results achieved in mediations—assumptions about mutuality, cooperation, and fairness, and general principles that ought to govern; in some systems, rules that approximate applicable law even serve as starting points. But in mediation—as distinguished from adjudication and, usually, arbitration—the ultimate authority resides with the disputants. The conflict is seen as unique and therefore less subject to solution by application of some general principle. The case is neither to be governed by a precedent nor to set one. Thus, all sorts of facts, needs, and interests that would be excluded from consideration in an adversary, rule-oriented proceeding could become relevant in a mediation. Indeed, whatever a party deems relevant is relevant. In a divorce mediation, for instance, a spouse's continuing need for emotional support could become important, as could the other party's willingness and ability to give it. In most mediations, the emphasis is not on determining rights or interests, or who is right and who is wrong, or who wins and who loses because of which rule; these would control the typical adjudicatory proceeding. The focus, instead, is upon establishing a degree of harmony through a resolution that will work for these disputants.

A danger inheres in this alegal character: individuals who are not aware of their legal position are not encouraged by the process to develop a rights-consciousness or to establish legal rights. Thus, the risk of dominance by the stronger or more knowledgeable party is great. Accordingly, for society to maximize the benefits of mediation while controlling its dangers, it must carefully adjust the role of lawyers in the mediation process.

Though mediation agreements typically neither set nor follow legal precedent, they often have important legal consequences. Frequently, the mere making of an agreement defers legal action by one of the disputants or the government. The agreement itself may establish or avoid legally enforceable rights. To reduce the danger that less powerful persons unwittingly will give up legal rights that would be important to them, they must be afforded a way of knowing about the nature of the adversary process and the result it would likely produce. But the very presentation of the rules that would probably govern a decision if the matter were litigated may impel parties toward adopting the predicted results, rather than regarding the law as simply one factor—to be blended with a variety of economic, personal, and social considerations—in reaching a decision. At the same time, if such information is not readily available to them, they are not necessarily free from influence by the law; they may be basing their decisions to mediate and their judgments during mediation upon inaccurate assumptions about what result would follow from adversary processing.

D. The Role of the Mediator

Nearly all mediators seek to help the disputants achieve an agreement. Most have educational objectives as well, especially where the parties will have a continuing relationship. There are, however, enormous differences in procedures and in roles that mediators adopt. Some will act merely as go-betweens, keeping open lines of communication. They may or may not give their own suggestions when the parties have deadlocked. Some mediators will separate the parties physically; others will insist on keeping them together. Some mediators will urge that the parties propose solutions; others will make their own proposals and try to persuade the parties to accept them and may even apply economic, social, or moral pressure to achieve a "voluntary" agreement.

One of the principal functions of the mediator is managing the communications process. He must intervene carefully at the correct moments. Accordingly, he must understand interpersonal relations and negotiations. He must be able to listen well and perceive the underlying emotional, psychological, and value orientations that may hold the keys to resolving more quantifiable issues. And he must arrange for these to be honored in the mediation process, the agreement, and the resulting relationship. A like sensitivity is essential for good lawyering as well, but it occupies a more prominent place on the list of skills required of a mediator.

* * *

II. HEADWINDS: PRESSURES AGAINST LAWYERS' PROPER
INVOLVEMENT IN MEDIATION

Most lawyers neither understand nor perform mediation nor have a strong interest in doing either. At least three interrelated reasons account for this: the way most lawyers, as lawyers, look at the world; the economics and structure of contemporary law practice; and the lack of training in mediation for lawyers.

A. The Lawyer's Standard Philosophical Map

E.F. Schumacher begins his *Guide for the Perplexed* with the following story:

> On a visit to Leningrad some years ago, I consulted a map * * * but I could not make it out. From where I stood, I could see several enormous churches, yet there was no trace of them on my map. When finally an interpreter came to help me, he said: "We don't show churches on our maps." Contradicting him, I pointed to one that was very clearly marked. "That is a museum," he said, "not what we call a 'living church.' It is only the 'living churches' we don't show."
>
> It then occurred to me that this was not the first time I had been given a map which failed to show many things I could see right in front of my eyes. All through school and university I had been given maps of life and knowledge on which there was hardly a trace of many of the things that I most cared about and that seemed to me to be of the greatest possible importance to the conduct of my life.

The philosophical map employed by most practicing lawyers and law teachers, and displayed to the law student—which I will call the lawyer's standard philosophical map—differs radically from that which a mediator must use. What appears on this map is determined largely by the power of two assumptions about matters that lawyers handle: (1) that disputants are adversaries—*i.e.,* if one wins, the others must lose— and (2) that disputes may be resolved through application, by a third party, of some general rule of law. These assumptions, plainly, are polar opposites of those which underlie mediation: (1) that all parties can benefit through a creative solution to which each agrees; and (2) that the situation is unique and therefore not to be governed by any general principle except to the extent that the parties accept it.

The two assumptions of the lawyer's philosophical map (adversariness of parties and rule-solubility of dispute), along with the real demands of the adversary system and the expectations of many clients, tend to exclude mediation from most lawyers' repertoires. They also blind lawyers to other kinds of information that are essential for a mediator to see, primarily by riveting the lawyers' attention upon things that they must see in order to carry out their functions. The mediator must, for instance, be aware of the many interconnections between and among disputants and others, and of the qualities of these connections; he must be sensitive to emotional needs of all parties and recognize the importance of yearnings for mutual respect, equality, security, and other such non-material interests as may be present.

On the lawyer's standard philosophical map, however, the client's situation is seen atomistically; many links are not printed. The duty to represent the client zealously within the bounds of the law discourages concern with both the opponents' situation and the overall social effect of a given result.

Moreover, on the lawyer's standard philosophical map, quantities are bright and large while qualities appear dimly or not at all. When one party wins, in this vision, usually the other party loses, and, most often, the victory is reduced to a money judgment. This "reduction" of nonmaterial values—such as honor, respect, dignity, security, and love—to amounts of money, can have one of two effects. In some cases, these values are excluded from the decision makers' considerations, and thus from the consciousness of the lawyers, as irrelevant. In others, they are present but transmuted into something else—a justification for money damages. Much like the church that was allowed to appear on the map of Leningrad only because it was a museum, these interests—which may in fact be the principal motivations for a lawsuit—are recognizable in the legal dispute primarily to the extent that they have monetary value or fit into a clause of a rule governing liability.

The rule orientation also determines what appears on the map. The lawyer's standard world view is based upon a cognitive and rational outlook. Lawyers are trained to put people and events into categories that are legally meaningful, to think in terms of rights and duties established by rules, to focus on acts more than persons. This view requires a strong development of cognitive capabilities, which is often attended by the under-cultivation of emotional faculties. This combination of capacities joins with the practice of either reducing most nonmaterial values to amounts of money or sweeping them under the carpet, to restrict many lawyers' abilities to recognize the value of mediation or to serve as mediators.

The lawyer's standard philosophical map is useful primarily where the assumptions upon which it is based—adversariness and amenability to solution by a general rule imposed by a third party—are valid. But when mediation is appropriate, these assumptions do not fit. The problem is that many lawyers, because of their philosophical maps, tend to suppose that these assumptions are germane in nearly any situation that they confront as lawyers. The map, and the litigation paradigm on which it is based, has a power all out of proportion to its utility. Many lawyers, therefore, tend not to recognize mediation as a viable means of reaching a solution; and worse, they see the kinds of unique solutions that mediation can produce as threatening to the best interests of their clients.

"One of the central difficulties of our legal system," says John Ayer, "is its capacity to be deaf to the counsel of ordinary good sense."

A law school classroom incident shows how quickly this deafness afflicts students—usually without anyone noticing. Professor Kenney Hegland writes:

> In my first year Contracts class, I wished to review various doctrines we had recently studied. I put the following:
>
> In a long term installment contract, Seller promises Buyer to deliver widgets at the rate of 1000 a month. The first two deliveries are perfect. However, in the third month Seller delivers only 999 widgets. Buyer becomes so incensed with this that he rejects the delivery, cancels the remaining deliveries and refuses to pay for the widgets already delivered. After stating the problem, I asked "If you were Seller, what would you say?" What I was looking for was a discussion of the various common law theories which would force the buyer to pay for the widgets delivered and those which would throw buyer into breach for cancelling the remaining deliveries. In short, I wanted the class to come up with the legal doctrines which would allow Seller to crush Buyer.
>
> After asking the question, I looked around the room for a volunteer. As is so often the case with the first year students, I found that they were all either writing in their notebooks or inspecting their shoes. There was, however, one eager face, that of an eight year old son of one of my students. It seems that he was suffering through Contracts due to his mother's sin of failing to find a sitter. Suddenly he raised his hand. Such behavior, even from an eight year old, must be rewarded.
>
> "OK," I said, "What would you say if you were the seller?"
>
> "I'd say 'I'm sorry'."

I do not mean to imply that all lawyers see only what is displayed on the lawyer's standard philosophical map. The chart I have drawn exaggerates certain tendencies in the way many lawyers think. Any good lawyer will be alert to a range of nonmaterial values, emotional considerations, and interconnections. Many lawyers have "empathic, conciliatory" personalities that may incline them to work often in a mediative way. And other lawyers, though they may be more competitive, would recognize the value of mediation to their clients. I do submit, however, that most lawyers, most of the time, use this chart to navigate.

L. RISKIN & J. WESTBROOK, DISPUTE RESOLUTION AND LAWYERS
231–233 (1987).

ALVAREZ v. GRANT *
A LANDLORD–TENANT DISPUTE IN A NEIGHBORHOOD JUSTICE CENTER [1]
by Leonard Riskin.

The first case I mediated at the Houston Neighborhood Justice Center involved a dispute between a landlord and tenant. The landlord, Mr. Alvarez, had served an eviction notice ordering the tenant, Mrs. Grant, to be out in three days. In her initial presentation, Mrs. Grant complained that Mr. Alvarez had not kept the apartment in repair. Mr. Alvarez retorted that she had not paid the rent and then admitted that he had not kept the apartment in repair because he could not afford to do so.

I asked Mrs. Grant what outcome she wanted, and she said, "I'm willing to leave. I'm glad to leave. But I need a month." Mr. Alvarez responded, "I can't give her a month but I can give her two weeks." "Fine," Mrs. Grant replied. The process had taken only two minutes, and we had an agreement. Then I asked another question: "Is there anything else that you want to say to each other?" Mrs. Grant told Mr. Alvarez that she respected him and thought he did the best he could, and that she appreciated his efforts. Mr. Alvarez told Mrs. Grant, in turn, that she had been a valuable tenant and was a good person; that he regretted he could not make the repairs; and that he was sorry she was leaving. Healing took place in the relationship between these people.

Notes and Questions

1. As suggested earlier, mediators have different ideas about their obligations. Many would have ended the session when the parties reached an agreement and would not have asked whether they wanted to say anything else to each other. Such mediators' goal would have been to help the parties reach an agreement with which the parties were satisfied. On the other hand, the mediator in this case wanted the participants to have the opportunity to broaden the dispute to make their emotional needs or their relationship relevant. Both these orientations are found among neighborhood justice center mediators. Sibley and Merry, Mediator Settlement Strategies, 8 Law & Policy 7 (1986).

What would you have done as a mediator? Why?

2. This mediation fostered some good outcomes. The parties worked out an arrangement that satisfied both their needs to the extent feasible. Because they spoke directly to one another and because they discussed their feelings about each other a kind of psychological healing took place, which put their relationship back in balance. These are among mediation's principal potential advantages over both adjudication and negotiation through lawyers.

---

* These names are fictitious.

1. This draws upon Riskin, The Special Place of Mediation in Alternative Dispute Processing, 37 U.Fla.L.Rev. 19, 26–27 (1985).

On the other hand, this mediation illustrates some significant dangers. Mrs. Grant gave up a possible legal right to remain in the apartment for a longer time. In addition, she and the mediator acquiesced in the landlord's continuing violation of the housing code. These outcomes illustrate two risks of mediations in which law or lawyers do not play significant roles. The first is the possibility of unfairness that springs from an imbalance in skill or power or information. The second problem is broader. Because this case was settled, the courts and government lost an opportunity to articulate and enforce the public policy behind the housing code, which might have required the landlord to improve his properties or close them. This problem would have remained even if the parties had agreed that Mr. Alvarez would bring Mrs. Grant's apartment into compliance with the housing code. Such an agreement, in contrast to a court ruling, would not necessarily serve as a precedent that would require the landlord to maintain other apartments at a similar level. Note also that Mr. Alvarez escaped any fine to which he might have been subject under the housing code.

How do you balance the advantages and disadvantages of mediation here? See Fiss, Against Settlement, 93 Yale L.J. 1073 (1984).

3. The role of law and lawyers in neighborhood justice center mediations is problematic. Most such centers discourage the presence of lawyers for the parties because they might make the process unduly formal and legalistic. Some disputants, of course, see lawyers before the mediation, and a few do bring their lawyers into the sessions. Others who want or need lawyers are given referrals by the centers.

At many neighborhood justice centers, some of the mediators are lawyers. If the mediator in Alvarez v. Grant had been a licensed lawyer familiar with the relevant law, would it have been appropriate for him to tell the parties about the law? Would you be more likely to say "yes" if the law were very clear? Plainly, knowledge of the law could affect the direction of the mediation. How important is it for disputants in neighborhood justice center mediations to have access to information about law? How should it be provided, given the (presumed) importance of speed and efficiency? * * *.

Many commentators have maintained that neighborhood justice centers can be used to oppress poor and otherwise disadvantaged persons. See, e.g., Hofrichter, Neighborhood Justice and Social Control Problems of American Capitalism: A Perspective, I The Politics of Informal Justice 207 (R. Abel, ed. 1982); Delgado, Dunn, Brown, Lee, and Hubbert, Fairness and Formality: Minimizing the Risks of Prejudice in Alternative Dispute Resolution, 1985 Wis.L.Rev. 1359.

II. THE LANDLORD–TENANT CONCEPT: SEPARATING POSSESSION FROM OWNERSHIP OF LAND

The terms, landlord and tenant, describe the relationship created when the right to exclusive possession of land is transferred but the owner ("landlord") retains a reversionary interest in the rest of the property bundle. The transferee ("tenant") gains a present possessory interest in the land in return for the payment of a bargained-for consideration called rent.

Modern landlord-tenant law is a blend of contract and property law spiked with dashes of public policy and seasoned with a heavy dose of history. Landlord-tenant relationships are created by contracts, and thus are governed by contract law. But these contracts rearrange property rights in land, and thus also are governed by property law. The lease, which is the written document evidencing the relationship, therefore is both a contract and a conveyance.

The history of landlord-tenant law is the story of a continuing struggle for domination of the landlord-tenant relationship by principles of contract law and principles of property law, set against a rich tapestry of Anglo–American social and political history. An excellent historical summary is found in C. Moynihan, Introduction to the Law of Real Property 56–76 (2d ed. 1988). More detailed discussions are found in A.W.B. Simpson, A History of the Land Law (2d ed. 1986), R. Schoshinski, American Law of Landlord and Tenant (1980 & Supp 1991), and Plucknett, Concise History of the Common Law (5th ed. 1956).

For a variety of reasons, holders of leasehold interests in land did not achieve the same status in medieval English communities as did holders of fee simple, fee tail, and life estates. To distinguish leasehold interests from the freehold estates, the common law used the term "nonfreehold" estates or "tenancies." Three types of nonfreehold estates were recognized by the common law, estates for years, periodic estates, and estates at will. In addition, a tenancy at sufferance commonly was recognized along with, in recent years, what has come to be called a statutory tenancy.

The characteristics of nonfreehold estates are discussed in the following excerpt.

MOYNIHAN, INTRODUCTION TO THE LAW OF REAL PROPERTY

58–60, 65–71 (2d ed. 1988).

A. THE ESTATE FOR YEARS

An estate for years is any estate having a duration for a fixed or computable period of time, usually expressed in terms of a unit of a year or of a multiple or fraction of a year. Thus, a lease for one thousand years creates an estate for years; so also does a lease "for two weeks commencing July 1 next year." The requirement of definiteness of duration is satisfied if the estate has a certain ending even though its commencement in possession is stated to depend on the happening of a specified event. The stipulated event may be the completion of a building by the lessor on the land subject to the lease. But if the termination date is indefinite the estate does not meet the traditional requirement for a term of years. This requirement of certainty of duration relates to the maximum period of duration. The estate for years may, like an estate in fee simple or a life estate, be defeasible by reason of being subject to a special limitation or a condition subsequent or an executory limitation. In fact, most leases create estates for years on condition subsequent by reason of the presence in the instrument of a clause giving the lessor a right of re-entry or power of termination on breach by the lessee of any of the specified conditions set out in the lease.

B. THE PERIODIC TENANCY

A periodic estate is a tenancy which will continue for a year or a fraction of a year and for successive similar periods unless terminated by either party by proper notice. There are various kinds of periodic tenancies but the most common are those from year to year and from month to month. By its nature, the periodic tenancy is continuous and of indefinite duration. Thus, if the tenancy is from month to month it is a single, continuous tenancy until terminated, not a tenancy for one month which comes to an end at the expiration of the month and is renewed for the following month.

Although historically the periodic estate was derived from the tenancy at will, its general characteristics are similar to those of the estate for years. The interest of the tenant is assignable, he is liable for permissive waste, and the death of either landlord or tenant leaves the estate unaffected. But unlike the estate for years which terminates without notice at the end of the specified term, the periodic estate continues until terminated by the giving of proper notice by either party. The common law required a six months' notice to terminate a tenancy from year to year, and for lesser periods a notice equal to the period. Thus, in a tenancy from month to month the notice of termination must be a month's notice. In all cases the notice must terminate the estate at the end of a period, not at some intermediate day.
* * *

A periodic tenancy may be created by express agreement of the parties, or by a letting for an indefinite time with rent payable at periodic intervals, or by holding over with the assent of the lessor after the expiration of an estate for years, or by entry into possession under an invalid lease. * * *

A more common method of creating such tenancies is by inference on a general letting when the rent is payable periodically. * * *

C. THE TENANCY AT WILL

An estate at will is an estate which is terminable at the will of either landlord or tenant and has no other specified period of duration. Such a tenancy is properly an estate since the tenant has an exclusive right to possession and may maintain an action of trespass or ejectment against persons interfering with his possessory interest. Its duration is dependent on the will of both parties and, unlike the periodic estate, no formal notice of a prescribed length of time is required for its termination at common law.

A tenancy at will may be created by an express agreement between the landlord and tenant that the tenant shall hold possession so long as both parties agree. Such explicit agreements are relatively infrequent and more often a tenancy at will is inferred in situations where the holding is indefinite and a periodic tenancy cannot be presumed. Thus, if the premises are let for an indefinite time and no rent is reserved the natural inference is that the parties intended a tenancy at will. * * *

At common law a tenancy at will could be terminated by either party, without formal notice, by expressing an intention to treat the tenancy as ended. In the event of termination by the landlord, the tenant was allowed a reasonable time to remove his personal property and was entitled to emblements. Since the relation assumes the assent of both parties to a continuance of the tenancy the death of either landlord or tenant terminates the estate. So also, a conveyance of the reversion by the landlord ends the tenancy at will. A lease for years made by the landlord to a third person has the same effect and it is immaterial that the lease was made for the purpose of putting an immediate end to the tenancy. An assignment by the tenant terminates his estate but, according to the modern view, a sublease by the tenant is effective between the parties thereto. Because the common law liability of the estate at will to abrupt termination gave security to neither landlord nor tenant, statutes in most states require that either party desiring to terminate shall give the other written notice of a specified length of time, usually thirty days or a period equal to the interval between rent days. These statutes have generally been construed as not prescribing an exclusive mode of termination and the estate, therefore, comes to an end on the death of either party and on conveyance or lease by the landlord. Hence, the estate at will even as modified by statute is not the precise equivalent of a periodic estate.

D.   THE TENANCY AT SUFFERANCE

A tenancy at sufferance is a possessory interest in land which exists when a person who had an estate in land wrongfully continues in possession after the termination of such estate. * * *

In view of the minimal interest of the tenant at sufferance, one may inquire why in modern law that interest is still included in the catalogue of estates. The main justification seems to be that it lends support to the doctrine that the landlord may at his election convert the tenancy at sufferance of the holdover tenant into a periodic tenancy, or, in some states, into a tenancy for a definite period. In a few jurisdictions the interest of the tenant at sufferance has been enlarged by statutes requiring that the landlord give written notice, usually thirty days, before commencing an action against the tenant to recover possession. And an occasional statute makes the tenant liable for "rent" in order to broaden the basis of common law liability for use and occupation which required at least an implied contract to pay.

E.   STATUTORY TENANCIES

In recent years there has developed a form of tenancy unknown to the common law: a tenancy that, apart from express agreement, is terminable at will by the tenant but is terminable by the landlord not at will but only under limited circumstances. For example, a tenant of public housing cannot be evicted except for cause and after the landlord follows a procedure prescribed in the public housing regulations. In effect the tenant has a determinable life estate. So also, the protected tenancy of a tenant occupying premises subject to rent control gives him a more extensive estate than under the common law rules. And an occasional statute gives the residential tenant the right to continue occupancy despite the termination of the duration of the term specified in the lease. These anomalous modern tenancies may be conveniently grouped under the heading of "Statutory Tenancies."

Notes and Questions

1.   Suppose the owner of a house signed a document transferring the right to possession "for the full term of while [the grantee] shall wish to live in the city, from and after the 1st day of August, 1991." Assuming an agreement to pay rent, has a landlord-tenant relationship been established? If so, what type of tenancy was created? See Thompson v. Baxter, 107 Minn. 122, 119 N.W. 797 (1909) (life estate, rather than nonfreehold interest, created). An interpretation often given is that language permitting one to stay as long as desired or wished creates only a tenancy at will on the theory that by implication the desire/wish provision is applicable to both parties. See R. Cunningham, W. Stoebuck & D. Whitman, Property 279 (1984).

2.   Requirements that landlords and tenants give notice of their intentions respecting renewal of tenancies are an important part of modern landlord-tenant law. The common law requirements were geared to an agricultural society and often required lengthy notice periods (e.g., six months) for decisions not to renew periodic tenancies from year to year and decisions to renew tenancies for a term of years. Modern statutes and leases typically impose a shorter notice requirement, usually based on rental payment periods, such as 30 days. Longer notice periods, such as 90 or 180 days, are commonly required for multi-year commercial leases. Examine the notice requirements in the sample leases that follow the next two cases. What do the leases provide if those notice requirements are not met? What if a tenant fails to provide the required notice of intent to renew a tenancy for a term of years, but the landlord continues to transact business with the tenant in person? See Perrotti v. Chiodo, 21 Conn.App. 288, 573 A.2d 342 (1990) (landlord's personal transaction of business with tenant constituted waiver of lease requirement for notice of intent to renew by registered mail).

3.   A major feature of nonfreehold estates is the requirement that the tenant pay rent. A popular textbook of the 19th Century describes rent as follows:

[W]e may consider rent simply as a periodical compensation, in money or otherwise, agreed to be given by the tenant to the landlord for the use of realty, the payment of which may be enforced like any other demand. I say agreed to be given, because where one occupies another's land without a lease containing a special agreement to pay a fixed rent, the compensation which may be recovered, is not in the shape of rent, but of damages in an action for *use and occupation,* or for *mesne profits.* * * * When the relation of landlord and tenant has been created, the estate of the landlord is denominated a *reversion,* to which rent is said to be incident. If therefore he conveys the reversion, the future rent passes with it, and when he dies it goes to his heirs; but it is otherwise if the rent be already due. If the tenant be evicted by a paramount title in a stranger, or actually expelled by the landlord, his obligation to pay rent ceases; but no destruction of the premises by fire, flood, or other inevitable accident, will discharge the obligation, unless the lease contains a provision to that effect. * * *

T. Walker, Introduction to American Law, Designed as a First Book for Students 305 (4th Ed.1860).

4. John and Mary Byers signed a contract to purchase a house in St. Louis from Robert Owens. Closing, at which title was to be transferred, was to take place within 90 days. Because the Byers were moving from Chicago and needed a place to stay before the closing, Robert Owens agreed to permit them to move into the house before the closing if they signed a form lease that he had prepared with a beginning date of September 1 and ending date the following August 31. The Byers signed the form lease on August 15. However, before they could move to St. Louis, they received word that the employment opportunity which was bringing them to St. Louis had been canceled. As a result they were unable to purchase the house and remained in Chicago. Do the Byers have any legal obligations under common law landlord-tenant principles? See Arthur Treacher's Fish & Chips of Fairfax v. Chillum Terrace, 272 Md. 720, 327 A.2d 282 (1974) (tenancy for a term was conveyed as a future interest, but obligation to pay rent did not arise until tenant actually entered and took possession. Until that point, damages for breach of contract, but not back rent, are recoverable).

Suppose that you are counsel to the Byers and you discover that the lease was not properly executed and the local statute of frauds requires a writing (see § III(a) infra). What advice can/should you give them? What concerns would you raise with them?

Problem

Lander and Toner signed the following written memorandum:

"I, Lander, lease to Toner the property known as 'Camp Happy Trails' for the sum of $500 per year, with the option to renew the lease as long as the camp is run as a business for profit."

Have the parties established a valid landlord-tenant relationship? If so, what type of tenancy was created? See Womack v. Hyche, 503 So.2d 832 (Ala.1987) (clause permitting renewal as long as camp is run for a profit held unenforceable as "tending to create a perpetuity" without the "plain and unambiguous" language expressing such intention that courts have required when applying the non-freehold exception to the rule against perpetuity).

If you were asked to correct the legal problem created by the original memorandum, how would you redraft it? In redrafting, pay attention to the advice of Professor David Mellinkoff: "Some day someone will read what you have written, trying to find something wrong with it. This is the special burden of legal writing, and the special incentive to be as precise as you can." D. Mellinkoff, Legal Writing: Sense and Nonsense 15 (St. Paul, Minn., 1982), as quoted in Burnham, Teaching Legal Ethics in Contracts, 41 J. of Legal Educ. 105, 116 (1991).

———

As the Walker excerpt indicates, the heart of the landlord-tenant transaction is an exchange of possession for a valuable consideration called rent. Under the common law, the obligation of the tenant to pay rent was considered absolute in return for which the tenant received the full possessory rights discussed in Chapter One. The following cases explore this concept.

PARADINE v. JANE
King's Bench, 1647.
82 Eng.Rep. 897.

In debt the plaintiff declares upon a lease for years rendering rent at the four usual feasts; and for rent behind for three years, ending at the Feast of the Annunciation, 21 Car. brings his action; the defendant pleads, that a certain German prince, by name Prince Rupert, an alien born, enemy to the King and kingdom, had invaded the realm with an hostile army of men; and with the same force did enter upon the defendant's possession, and him expelled, and held out of possession from the 19 of July 18 Car. till the Feast of the Annunciation, 21 Car. whereby he could not take the profits; whereupon the plaintiff demurred, and the plea was resolved insufficient.

* * *

It was resolved, that the matter of the plea was insufficient; for though the whole army had been alien enemies, yet he ought to pay his rent. And this difference was taken, that where the law creates a duty or charge, and the party is disabled to perform it without any default in him, and hath no remedy over, there the law will excuse him. As in the case of waste, if a house be destroyed by tempest, or by enemies, the lessee is excused. * * * Now the rent is a duty created by the parties upon the reservation, and had there been a covenant to pay it, there had been no question but the lessee must have made it good, notwithstanding the interruption by enemies, for the law would not protect him beyond his own agreement, no more then in the case of reparations; this reservation then being a covenant in law, and whereupon an action of covenant hath been maintained (as Roll said) it is all one as if there had been an actual covenant. Another reason was added, that as the lessee is to have the advantage of casual profits, so he must run the hazard of casual losses, and not lay the whole burthen of them upon his lessor; and Dyer 56.6. was cited for this purpose, that though the land be surrounded, or gained by the sea, or made barren by wildfire, yet the lessor shall have his whole rent: and judgment was given for the plaintiff.

MERZ v. PROFESSIONAL HEALTH CONTROL OF AUGUSTA, INC.

Court of Appeals of Georgia, 1985.
175 Ga.App. 110, 332 S.E.2d 333.

SOGNIER, JUDGE.

Oscar and Johanna Merz brought suit against Professional Health Control of Augusta, Inc. (PHC) under various tort theories to recover damages which allegedly resulted when PHC filmed four television commercials on property owned by the Merzes while under lease to Mark and Donna Plants (lessees). The trial court granted summary judgment in favor of PHC. The Merzes appeal.

1. Appellants contend the trial court erred by granting summary judgment to appellee because questions of fact remain as to their claims of breach of contract and quantum meruit. Appellee entered onto appellants' property and filmed four pool-side commercials promoting appellee's diet and weight loss business with the permission of the lessees, who had leased the residence during the year appellants were out of the country. Appellants contend appellee breached those parts of the lease which provided that the premises would be "occupied only as a residence" and "used only for residential purposes." However, appellants' claim of breach of contract fails in view of the uncontroverted evidence that appellee was not a party to the lease contract between appellants and the lessees and no third-party beneficiary issue is involved. [ ] As to appellants' claim of quantum meruit, there is no allegation or inference of an allegation in appellants' complaint or amended complaint from which it fairly could be determined that appellants were asserting any claim in quantum meruit against appellee. Therefore, the trial court did not err by granting summary judgment to appellee in regard to this issue. [ ]

2. We find no merit in appellants' argument that summary judgment was erroneously granted to appellee on appellants' claim of trespass. It is uncontroverted that appellee was on the property at the express invitation of the lessees, and although appellants allege there was physical damage to the freehold estate, appellants presented no evidence to rebut lessee Mark Plants' affidavit that appellee's activities on the property were not the cause of any alleged damage. [ ]

3. Appellants contend the trial court erred by granting summary judgment in favor of appellee on their claim of invasion of privacy. Appellants argue that appellee's filming of commercials on property leased by the Plants and with the permission of the lessees while appellants were in Borneo, Indonesia, constituted an "intrusion upon [appellants'] seclusion or solitude, or into [their] private affairs." *Cabaniss v. Hipsley,* 114 Ga.App. 367, 370, 151 S.E.2d 496 (1966). [ ] "It would seem to require no argument that there was no physical intrusion into [appellants'] seclusion, solitude or private affairs here. * * *" *Williams v. Church's Fried Chicken,* 158 Ga.App. 26, 32, 279 S.E.2d 465 (1981). Nor do we find appellants have a cause of action for the wrongful invasion of the leased premises since, even assuming arguendo that appellee's activities on the property constituted a "wrongful invasion," appellants, by executing the lease, contracted away any expectations of privacy as to the leased property. [ ] Any wrongs to be redressed for a wrongful invasion of the leased property would accrue to those directly injured by the wrong—the lessees who inhabited the residence—rather than appellants, whose sensibilities as landlords of the leased property could have been injured indirectly at best. [ ] Accordingly, the trial court did not err by granting summary judgment to appellee on this issue.

Judgment affirmed.

Notes and Questions

1. As you will learn in your Contracts course, the Common Law has long since recognized an exception to the rule of *Paradine v. Jane* for contracts that are impossible to perform through no fault of the obligor. See, e.g., Albert M. Greenfield & Co. v. Kolea, 475 Pa. 351, 380 A.2d 758 (1977) (accidental destruction of building by fire excused tenant from obligation to pay rent when building was an essential part of the bargain and parties had not otherwise allocated the risk of loss); Restatement, (Second), of Property § 5.4 (1976) (landlord breaches obligation if, after entry by tenant, building is destroyed suddenly by non man-made force, landlord fails to correct situation within a reasonable time after being requested to do so by tenant, and parties have not validly agreed otherwise). But does this mean that *Paradine* is dead? Should a person who leases land near a river be excused from paying rent because the river flooded and destroyed her crops? See Jensen v. Haynes, 633 S.W.2d 154 (Mo.App.1982) (flooding of farmland did not excuse rent obligation because flooding was a foreseeable risk).

2. Do you believe the result in *Merz* would have been different if the landlords had returned from Borneo in time to seek injunctive relief? Suppose PHC had been trying unsuccessfully for years to get the owners' consent to film a pool-side commercial on this property? Might the owners actually have had a stronger case if this were commercial property?

III. CREATION OF THE RELATIONSHIP: THE LEASE

As the preceding materials indicate, a landlord-tenant relationship can be created orally by the voluntary transfer of possession of land. Such relationships are governed generally by the common law rules discussed in the Moynihan excerpt.

Most people, however, prefer to reduce their understanding of the relationship to writing in a document called a lease. In fact, a writing is required to create enforceable longer term landlord-tenant obligations through the application of the Statute of Frauds, a statute you will study in your Contracts course.

The following leases are examples of residential landlord-tenant transactions. One might be said to be "landlord friendly," the other "tenant friendly." Can you see the difference?

APARTMENT LEASE

_____ hereinafter referred to as Lessor, for and in consideration of the agreements hereinafter made between it and _____, hereinafter referred to as Lessee, does hereby lease to Lessee for a private residence or dwelling only, the premises known and described as follows, to wit:

Apartment _____ in the building known as _____ in the City of _____, County of _____, State of _____

1. TERM. The term of this lease shall be twelve (12) months commencing on _____, 19__ and ending on the _____ day of _____, 19__ which term shall be automatically renewed for a like term unless notice in writing is sent by either party to this lease to the other at least thirty (30) days prior to the end of the current term.

2. RENT. As rent, Lessee hereby agrees to pay Lessor the sum of _____ Dollars ($_____) per month, for each month during the term of this lease, such rent to be paid in advance on the first day of each calendar month, without relief from valuation or appraisement laws. A late charge will be added to Lessee's account, in the amount of $10.00, if payment is not received by the 5th day of the month. A penalty of $10.00 will be added to Lessee's account for any check returned by the bank for non-payment.

3. SECURITY DEPOSIT. Lessee hereby deposits with Lessor the sum of _____ Dollars ($_____) as security for Lessee's performance of this lease. In the event Lessee complies fully with all covenants and conditions of the lease, security deposit agreement, and rules and regulations, said sum shall be returned to Lessee within thirty (30) days following the satisfactory termination of this lease. In the event of a breach or default by Lessee in respect to any of the terms or conditions

of this lease, Lessor may apply sum or any part thereof to any costs, damages, losses, or injuries caused by Lessee by such breach or default and without in any manner waiving or limiting Lessor's rights to further hold Lessee for costs, damages, losses, or injuries otherwise due. *This security deposit is not and shall not be considered the rent payment for the last or any other month of the term of this lease.*

4. RULES AND REGULATIONS. The rules and regulations are incorporated by reference and made a part of the written lease between Lessor and Lessee, and are to be strictly followed by all residents. Lessee shall comply with all the rules and regulations now or at any time hereafter during the existence of this lease adopted by Lessor, which are brought to the notice of Lessee, both in regard to the apartment community as a whole and as to the premises herein leased. Lessee further acknowledges receiving and reading a copy of said rules and regulations and agrees to abide by them.

5. OCCUPANCY. Lessee agrees not to assign or transfer this lease or any interest therein or sublet the premises or any part thereof without the prior written consent of Lessor. The premises shall be used and occupied in a safe, careful, and proper manner by Lessee without waste of water; that no trade, business or occupation shall be carried on therein; that premises shall not be used or permitted to be used for any unlawful purpose; nor shall premises, or any part thereof, be used for any purpose that, in the judgment of Lessor, will injure the reputation of the premises or building of which they are a part; or disturb or annoy the residents of the building or the neighborhood. No additional lock or fastening shall be placed upon any door without written permission of Lessor.

6. CONDITION OF PREMISES. Lessee agrees that no representation as to condition or repair of the premises, and no promise to decorate, alter, repair or improve the premises, has been made, except such as is contained in the lease. Lessee agrees that he shall examine the premises prior to his occupancy thereof and that his occupancy of the premises shall be conclusive evidence of his satisfaction and approval of the premises as being in good physical condition and in good order and repair.

7. PETS. Lessee shall not keep any pets of any kind or description in the leased unit or on the premises of which the unit forms a part without the prior written consent of Lessor. In the event consent is given to the keeping of a pet, Lessee shall pay to Lessor a one-time fee of $50.00, as set forth in the Pet Agreement.

8. UTILITIES AND MAINTENANCE. Lessor agrees to maintain and care for the lawns, parking areas and common grounds, to provide reasonable snow and trash removal, and to furnish janitor service at reasonable times for and to maintain the hallways and corridors of the community of which the unit is a part. Lessor shall provide heat, water and sewage facilities to the premises. Lessor shall also make available such other utility services as may be necessary to serve the

leased premises, including telephone and electricity, but Lessee shall individually pay for his/her use of such utility services.

9. ALTERATIONS. Lessee shall make no alterations or additions to the premises, nor shall Lessee install or have done any painting or decoration of the unit without written consent of Lessor. Lessee shall not attach any article of a permanent character or any sign containing writing or printing to any window, floor, ceiling, door or wall, without the written consent of Lessor. Lessee shall, on termination of this lease, surrender to Lessor the quiet and peaceable possession of the premises in as good order as it was at the commencement of the term, reasonable wear and tear excepted.

10. OWNER'S OR AGENT'S RIGHT TO ENTER. Lessor shall have the right to show the premises to prospective lessees for a period of thirty (30) days prior to the termination of this lease. Lessee shall permit Lessor to enter the said premises at all reasonable times to inspect the premises or for any purpose connected with the repair, improvement, care and management of the premises in which the same are situated.

11. FIRE OR CASUALTY. In the event the leased premises are destroyed by fire, wind, or other causes beyond the control of Lessor, or are torn down by properly constituted authorities of the federal, state, county or city governments, or any other governmental authority, then in any of these events the lease shall cease and terminate as of the date of such destruction. If the leased premises are injured by fire, wind, rain, or other causes, so as to render the same partially unrentable or partly unfit for use, but are repairable within a reasonable time, then this lease shall remain in full force and effect, but Lessee's rent shall be proportionally reduced until the premises are repaired.

12. RIGHTS OF LESSOR UPON DEFAULT. Upon failure to pay any installment or rent of any part thereof when due, or if Lessee shall violate any other term, condition or covenant of this lease, or if Lessee shall fail promptly to take possession of or shall abandon the premises, Lessor shall have the right to re-enter and repossess the premises. Lessor shall have the option to change the lock on the entry door to prevent Lessee's re-entry into the unit until such defaults are corrected, and to remove all persons therefrom and to remove all property therefrom and, in such event, this lease and all rights of Lessee as resident shall terminate, but Lessee shall remain liable for the rent herein specified during the remaining term of this lease plus Lessor's cost of repossessing the premises. Lessee hereby waives notice of any failure or default and any demand of Lessor for possession of the premises. In the event Lessor shall repossess the premises, Lessor shall not be required to exercise diligence in reletting the premises in order to mitigate Lessee's obligations hereunder, nor will it be required to accept any resident for the premises offered by Lessee. The failure on the part of Lessor to re-enter or repossess the premises, or to exercise any of its rights hereunder upon any default, shall not preclude Lessor

from the exercise of any such rights during the continuance of such default or upon any of Lessor's right to terminate the lease for nonpayment of rent when due, and no notice or demand shall be required for the enforcement thereof. If Lessee shall violate or breach any term or condition of this lease, Lessee shall pay all costs and expenses, including attorney's fees, incurred by Lessor in connection with its exercising any right or remedies it may have under this lease because of such violation or breach.

13. NOTICES AND RENTS. All notices and demands authorized or required to be given Lessee hereunder may be served upon Lessee in person or by regular mail and addressed to him/her at the leased premises. All notices required to be given hereunder to Lessor, and all rent payments, shall be given or sent Lessor at this office or such other place as Lessor may designate and shall not be effective until received.

14. RIVER, PONDS AND LAGOONS. The involved unit is one of several, all of which constitute a residential project which adjoins the * * * River. In addition there [are] situated on such project ponds or lagoons. Lessor owns to the eastern water's edge of such River and has no authority or jurisdiction thereover, and accordingly cannot police same. Lessee, the members of his/her family, invitees and guests enter into or onto such River at their sole risk and responsibility, and Lessor shall not be liable for any injury or damage to person or property by reason of any such ponds or lagoons.

15. EQUIPMENT AND PERSONALTY. Lessor is furnishing equipment and other items of personalty for use by Lessee in the involved unit. Lessee shall not make any substitutions therefor or remove same without prior written consent of Lessor. None of such items, including articles substituted with the consent of Lessor, shall be removed from the leased premises at any time. Furthermore, on the yielding of possession of the involved unit, either by reason of termination or expiration of this lease, or otherwise, all of such items of equipment and personalty so furnished by Lessor (including any articles substituted by either Lessee or Lessor) shall be delivered up to Lessor along with the involved unit in the same condition as when received, ordinary wear excepted. Lessee shall be charged and shall pay for all costs of cleaning, repair, replacement and redecorating not occasioned by normal wear.

16. LESSEE YIELDING POSSESSION. At the termination of this lease, Lessee shall yield up immediate possession of the premises to Lessor and return the keys to said apartment/townhouse to Lessor at the office of the Manager, and failing to do so shall pay liquidated damages for the whole time such possession is withheld, a sum equal to twice the amount of the rent herein reserved prorated for each day of withholding. Any such holding over shall not create a new term of this lease if notice to terminate the lease has prior thereto been given by Lessor or Lessee. It is understood, however, that the acceptance of any

such liquidated damages by Lessor shall not constitute waiver by Lessor of its right of re-entry as herein set forth.

RULES AND REGULATIONS

It is our intent that _____ be the finest residential neighborhood in our area. In order to attain that objective, we shall strive at all times to render prompt and efficient service to the property. Since residents must also cooperate if the community is to be highly regarded, the following rules will be in effect. * * *

RENTAL PAYMENTS: All rents are due and payable in advance on the first day of each lease month. Rents may be paid either by mail or in person. Rents will be considered delinquent if not paid in full within five days. There will be a ten dollar ($10.00) late fee on all delinquent rents.

MAINTENANCE: PLEASE MAKE REQUESTS FOR REPAIRS BY PHONING THE OFFICE DURING NORMAL OFFICE HOURS. THE NUMBER IS _____. FOR EMERGENCY SERVICE WHEN THE OFFICE IS CLOSED, CALL _____. Your cooperation will enable the management to provide you with quick and efficient service. Emergency calls, however, will be handled immediately. No charge is made for normal repairs. Any repairs or replacements necessitated by a resident's negligence will be charged to the resident and will be due and payable with the following [month's] rent.

SOLICITING: Soliciting is strictly forbidden. It is requested that residents notify the office if a solicitor appears, and appropriate action will be taken.

NOTICE OF INTENT TO VACATE: After the first year of occupancy, residents are required to sign a new lease in order to continue living in their unit. Management will notify the resident of his lease expiration approximately thirty (30) days in advance.

SUBLETTING: According to the terms of your lease, you do not have the right to sublet without prior consent. However, under certain conditions we may permit you to do so, providing you secure another resident whose application to lease is approved by the office prior to the date on which you wish to vacate the premises under lease.

VACATING APARTMENT: After a resident has vacated his/her apartment, we will make a formal inspection of that apartment, room by room, looking for any damages such as: floors, windows, baseboards, plumbing fixtures, chips on sinks or tubs, broken tile, cabinets, dirty appliances, etc. The inspection will also include the checking of each appliance to make certain they all operate properly. After writing the inspection report, a final letter is sent to the resident returning the deposit minus any charges.

CARPET: All residents are required to have their carpet cleaned at their own expense once a year. The work must be done by a professional cleaning service. Please retain receipts for management's approval upon vacating the apartment. If carpet has not been correctly cleaned annually, a pro-rated charge will be deducted from the security deposit. * * *

TRASH: Bottles, cans, newspapers, magazines, and all garbage or trash not disposable through the disposal must be taken to the trash containers outside the building. Please use plastic bags large enough to be closed at the top.

PATIO & LAWN AREAS: When using barbecue grills, braziers or other outside means of preparing food, residents shall assume any and all liability arising from this. Absolutely no plants are to be planted in the grounds by residents.

ADDITIONS: Any additions that will be attached to the walls, floors or ceilings must be approved by management. Such additions will be considered permanent and will become the property of _____, unless otherwise specified in writing by the management. No change in color of walls will be permitted without written permission.

KEYS: Keys are the responsibility of the resident. Each resident will be given two (2) keys for the apartment door and one (1) key for the mail box at the time of occupancy. There is a $2.00 charge for each replacement. If the resident needs to be let into his/her unit at any time other than during office hours, there will be a $5.00 charge.

STORAGE: Individual storage areas have been assigned to each unit. They should not be used for storage of newspapers or other materials creating a fire hazard. Individual padlocks should be provided by the resident. The use of these rooms is entirely gratuitous, and we accept no responsibility whatsoever for the care or custody of any articles deposited therein.

PARKING: One (1) parking space is provided for each unit. Other unassigned guest parking is also available. Dead storage parking of cars as well as the parking of boats, trailers, or commercial vehicles is not permitted, and these items will be removed by the management at the owner's expense. * * *

THE UNDERSIGNED, HAVING READ THE AFORESAID RULES AND REGULATIONS, HEREBY AGREE(S) TO ABIDE BY THEM AT ALL TIMES DURING RESIDENCY AT _____.

TENANT(S) _____

LANDLORD _____

RENTAL AGREEMENT *

This lease, made this _____ day of _____, 19__, by and between _____, the landlord, and _____, the tenant(s). The landlord and tenant(s) agree to the following mutually dependent provisions:

1. The landlord has this day leased to the tenant(s) the premises known and described as _____, Number _____ in the City of _____, County of _____ to be occupied only as a residence of said tenant(s) and no more than _____ other persons upon the terms and conditions set forth in this lease. The premises, which shall be placed in actual possession of the tenant(s), are partly/fully furnished. The term of this lease shall be from _____, 19__ to _____, 19__.

2. The tenant(s) shall pay to the landlord as rent, for the term stated, $ _____ per month payable on the _____ of each month. If the tenant(s) remain in the premises at the termination of the lease, they shall be considered hold over tenant(s) and the landlord shall be entitled to collect the daily rent for each day that the tenant(s) remain.

3. The tenant(s) shall:

    a. Pay all rents promptly when due.

    b. Pay for any damage to the leased premises or to the appliances and fixtures therein, caused by any act of negligence of the tenant(s) or any member of his or her family or a guest—damage due to ordinary and normal wear and tear, or loss or damage by fire excepted.

    c. Place garbage and refuse inside the containers provided by the landlord.

    d. Keep the apartment/house and grounds in a clean and sanitary condition.

    e. Abide by municipal code regulations regarding care and occupancy of the premises.

    f. Surrender possession of the premises to the landlord upon the end of the term above, and be allowed to remove any fixtures they attached, provided they repair or pay cost of repairing any damage done by such removal.

4. The landlord or his or her agent(s) shall have the right to enter the leased premises for the following purposes: inspecting the premises for damage or needed repairs or improvements only, without intruding into a tenant(s) personal effects; making necessary repairs or improvements; exhibiting the premises to prospective tenants, purchasers or mortgagees. Such entry may be made only between the hours of 10:00 a.m. and 7:00

---

* Off–Campus Housing Guide, University of Notre Dame (1988). Reprinted with permission.

p.m. after advance notice of at least 24 hours to the tenant(s) of the date, time, and purpose of the entry. Entry may be made without prior notice if the landlord or his or her agent reasonably believes that an emergency exists, such as a fire or broken water pipe, and requires immediate entry without notice.

5. In addition to the requirements herein understood as a binding covenant of habitability and quiet enjoyment, the landlord shall be specially responsible for the following maintenance duties.

    a. Repairs to the exterior of the premises.

    b. Repairs to sewers, heating, all appliances, wiring and plumbing facilities.

    c. Repairs to all common areas, doors, windows, and stairs.

    d. Maintaining an extermination service for the premises, providing for the elimination of all vermin and rodents prior to and throughout occupancy.

    e. Painting all interior areas of the premises with interior non-lead base paint of a grade capable of being washed without streaking.

    f. Installing and maintaining locks on all exterior windows and doors, and on the door to all common areas.

    g. Providing and installing screens, storm windows, and window shades in good condition for all windows in the premises.

    h. Maintaining the premises and common areas in accordance with city or county housing, building and zoning standards.

    i. The landlord shall be responsible not only for his own, but also any agent(s) negligent maintenance or non-maintenance of the premises and agrees to pay tenant(s) or any member of his or her household or guest for damages for personal injuries resulting from such negligence.

6. All notices to quit and evictions shall be issued in strict adherence to the laws of Indiana regarding forcible entry and detainer. Notice of any lease violations and opportunity to correct them must be given at least one week before beginning legal proceedings.

7. The tenant(s) have this day paid a security or damage deposit of $_____ to be returned within thirty (30) days of the expiration of this lease minus the cost of repairing any damage (except ordinary wear and tear) caused by the tenant(s) or anyone legally acting under tenant(s) control, the cost of putting the premises in as clean a condition as the tenant(s) found them, and any rent due. The security deposit shall be forfeited only to extent it reflects actual damages. The landlord will also be under a duty to mitigate damages.

8. If the landlord fails to perform necessary repairs within the one month following written notification, such repairs may be effected by the tenant. The cost of such repairs may then be deducted from the rent provided that a written notification of such intention precedes the repairs by a period of ten (10) days and an itemized statement, including cost of agent, of such repairs is provided by the tenant to the landlord after completion.

9. If the premises become uninhabitable through acts of third parties, an act of God, a condemnation order, the tenant(s) may at his option elect to terminate the lease, or to remain and pay a proportional amount of the rent.

10. The tenant(s) shall, in addition to the rent, provide for the following utilities:

water _____   oil _____

gas _____   telephone _____

electricity _____   refuse pick-up _____

11. The tenant(s) may sublet or assign the leased premises for any part of the term of this lease, upon written consent of the landlord, which consent shall not unreasonably be withheld.

12. Should any tenant(s) become unable to fulfill his obligation due to extraordinary circumstances defined exclusively as severely debilitating illness, death, suspension or expulsion from the University, all obligations of the parties to this lease shall cease on that date and the tenant shall be responsible for only the rent then owing.

13. Exhibits A and B attached hereto are made a part of this lease.

14. If at the time of initial occupancy all defects enumerated in Exhibit B have not been remedied, the lessee reserves the right of termination of this lease and all obligations contained herein within twenty (20) days. At such time, the tenant shall be entitled to recovery of all money paid.

15. The landlord hereby assures the tenant that the housing covered under this lease conforms to all appropriate local housing ordinances and codes. In the event that the tenants are advised by local administrative agencies that they must move as a result of non-conformance with housing ordinances or codes, the landlord shall allow the students to move from the premises immediately without any further obligation for lease payments and the refund of any security deposits shall also be made immediately in full subject only to deduction of any clean-up or damage problems as covered more specifically elsewhere in this lease.

16. This lease and written notations upon it constitute the entire lease agreement between landlord and tenant(s). It may be later modified only by a signed agreement between the landlord and tenant(s).

SIGNED

_____

LANDLORD

_____

TENANT(S)

_____

TENANT(S)

_____

TENANT(S)

CONDITION OF PREMISES AT THE TIME OF OCCUPANCY

1. STOVE
2. REFRIGERATOR
3. WASHER
4. DRYER
5. FURNITURE
   A. LIVING ROOM
   B. DINING ROOM
   C. BEDROOMS
   D. AUXILIARY ROOMS
6. BATHROOM FACILITIES
7. WINDOWS
8. WALLS & CEILING
   A. LIVING ROOM
   B. DINING ROOM
   C. KITCHEN
   D. BEDROOMS
   E. BASEMENT
   F. ATTIC
   G. AUXILIARY ROOMS
9. DRAPES

10. CARPETS AND/OR FLOORS
11. STEPS
    A. EXTERIOR
    B. INTERIOR
12. GARAGE
13. MIRRORS & DECORATIONS
14. PAINT
    A. EXTERIOR
    B. INTERIOR
15. GUTTERS & DOWNSPOUTS
16. GARBAGE CANS
17. YARD
18. ELECTRICAL FACILITIES
19. WALKWAYS & ACCESS AREAS
20. FURNACE & WATER HEATER
21. PLUMBING

SIGNED

_____

LANDLORD

_____

TENANT(S)

_____

TENANT(S)

_____

EXHIBIT A

THE FOLLOWING IS AN INVENTORY OF FURNITURE PROVIDED IN THE PREMISES:

ROOM _____

_____

_____

ROOM _____

_____

_____

ROOM _____

_____

_____

ROOM _____

_____

_____

_____

EXHIBIT B

THE FOLLOWING IS A LIST OF DAMAGES OR DEFECTS IN THE PREMISES EXISTING AS OF THE _____ day of _____ 19___.

ROOM _____

_____

_____

ROOM _____

_____

_____

ROOM _____

_____

_____

ROOM _____

_____

_____

INITIALED

LANDLORD _____

TENANT(S) _____

TENANT(S) _____

Notes and Questions

1. Examine the two lease forms carefully. Do they appear to be balanced, or do they give one or the other party a more favorable position? Do the leases attempt to do more than simply create a tenancy? What about allocation of risk of loss? Responsibility for maintenance and repairs? Use of facilities? Transferability?

2. If you or a friend of yours have ever been a landlord or a tenant, make a list of problems that you or your friend experienced in that situation. Do the leases address your experiences? Adequately? What modifications would you suggest to the lease forms based on your experiences?

3. In studying the lease forms, identify places in each lease where common law rules appear to be relied upon, and places where such rules appear to be varied. Does the common law, for example, require that landlord-tenant relationships be in writing? Are there reasons why a landlord or a tenant would favor an oral arrangement rather than a written one?

A. NECESSITY FOR A WRITING (STATUTE OF FRAUDS)

LONGMIER v. KAUFMAN

Missouri Court of Appeals, 1983.
663 S.W.2d 385.

GAERTNER, JUDGE.

Plaintiffs, the general partners of I.M. Simon and Company, (Simon) are engaged in the investment and stockbrokerage business. From January 27, 1970 to July 31, 1975 Simon occupied space in the Security Building in the City of St. Louis pursuant to a written lease. After the expiration of the lease Simon continued to occupy the space as a month to month tenant. The Security Building is owned by defendant St. Louis Real Estate Ventures, a partnership, which in turn leases the building to defendant Pierre Chouteau Properties, Inc., a corporation. Defendant Burt W. Kaufman is the executive director of St. Louis Real Estate Ventures and the President and sole shareholder of defendant Pierre Chouteau Inc. and is the manager of the Security Building.

In March 1977, Kaufman initiated negotiations with certain partners of Simon for a new lease. Factors included in these negotiations were the rent per square foot, extra space to be occupied by Simon, renovation, remodeling and alterations. It is Simon's position that the negotiations did not culminate in a final agreement on all terms of a new lease. Defendants, although admitting that no new written lease was ever executed, contend that the terms of a new lease were orally agreed upon on December 5, 1977 and that remodeling work was commenced shortly after that date. On March 10, 1978 Simon gave written notice to defendants of its intention to terminate its tenancy and vacate the premises as of May 31, 1978. On that latter date, Simon did move to new quarters but left behind certain cabinets, shelving and other items. On July 31, 1978 most of these items were removed by Simon and the following day, August 1, 1978, Simon delivered the keys to the premises to Kaufman.

This litigation was initiated by the filing of a petition for declaratory judgment by Simon. In three counts Simon prayed the court to declare: (1) that no lease agreement had been entered into, (2) that its month to month tenancy terminated as of May 31, 1978, and (3) that it had no obligation to defendants to pay any cost of improvements. Defendants filed a joint answer to this petition in which they sought a declaration that Simon was bound by a five year lease and owed unpaid rental of $158,620.00 thereon, in Count II, a declaration that no month to month tenancy existed in 1978, and in Count III, a declaration that Simon owed defendants $30,000 for the cost of remodeling and renovation.

Defendant Pierre Chouteau Properties, Inc. also filed a counterclaim alleging in Count I, the repudiation of Simon of a five year lease allegedly entered into as of January 1, 1978 and, seeking damages in the amount of $158,620.00 in Count II, alleging that in reliance upon Simon's representations that a five year lease would be executed, it undertook to remodel and renovate the premises at a cost of $30,000, but that Simon's representations were false and made with the intent to defraud. Count II prayed for actual damages of $30,000 and punitive damages of $100,000.

* * *

[The counterclaim for remodeling and renovation expenses was severed. Plaintiff moved for summary judgment on its petition as well as on the counterclaim alleging repudiation of a new five-year lease. Plaintiff was granted summary judgment on one count and prevailed at trial on the other counts, except for a ruling that it owed additional rent for time it remained in possession. Cross appeals followed.—Eds.]

* * *

Defendants' first point on appeal alleges error in the sustaining of the motions for summary judgment as to Count I of the petition and Count I of the counterclaim. These counts concerned the existence vel non of a new five year lease. Defendants do not dispute the fact that no new lease was executed by the parties. However, they contend that Simon is estopped from denying the creation of a five year lease commencing January 1, 1978.

* * *

The affidavits filed in support of the motion for summary judgment and those filed in opposition reflect a dispute over whether or not an agreement to all the terms of the proposed lease had been reached. However, in view of the undisputed fact that no written lease was signed, the disputed facts do not relate to a material or controlling issue. Accepting as true defendants' contention that the oral agreement to enter into the lease was made on December 5, 1977, until the lease was signed by the parties it could amount, by operation of law, to no more than a month to month tenancy. Section 441.060(2) RSMo 1978 provides as follows:

> "2. All contracts or agreements for the leasing, renting or occupation of stores, shops, houses, tenements or other buildings in cities, towns or villages, and of stores, shops, houses, tenements or other buildings except when such leasing, renting or occupation is as tenant of real estate used or rented for agricultural purposes, other than garden purposes, not made in writing, signed by the parties thereto, or their agents, shall be held and taken to be tenancies from month to month, and all such tenancies may be terminated by either party thereto, or his agent, giving to the other party, or his agent, one month's notice, in writing, of his intention to terminate such tenancy."

Attempting to avoid the destructive impact of § 441.060(2) upon their theory, defendants argue that Simon is estopped from asserting the statute. This argument is completely refuted by *Shaffer v. Hines*, 573 S.W.2d 420, 422 (Mo.App.1978). There, in rejecting the invocation of the doctrine of estoppel in an attempt to evade the strictures of the Statute of Frauds, this court stated: "[t]he doctrine is often referred to as a shield against fraud. It is not, however, available for use as a sword. It cannot be used to create a cause of action, if the action did not otherwise exist. Its purpose is not to bring about a gain but to protect from loss."

Defendants' reliance on *Hamburger v. Hirsch,* 212 S.W. 49 (Mo.App. 1919) is misplaced. There the predecessor of this court approved the admission of parol evidence of an agreement to extend the date for the giving of notice of a termination of a written lease. It was there held the plaintiff was estopped from asserting the Statute of Frauds. The decision has not been followed in any other case involving a lease or the sale of an interest in land. Further, it has been tacitly overruled by this court in *Shaffer.* More importantly, however, admission of parol evidence regarding a modification of a single provision of a written lease is far different than the creation of a long term lease which is prohibited by the statute. The above quoted language from *Shaffer* has much more applicability to this case where we are concerned with the lease statute, § 441.060, than in *Shaffer,* which concerned the Statute of Frauds, § 432.010. The latter is a rule of evidence, rendering inadmissible testimony regarding oral agreements pertaining to matters within its purview so as to cause such agreements to become legally unenforceable. The former, however, relates to a matter of substantive law, declaring the legal relationship of parties to an unwritten lease to be that of month to month tenancy. It deals neither with the admissibility of evidence nor with the enforceability of the agreement. Rather the statute enunciates the public policy of Missouri that unwritten lease agreements shall not be construed as creating any obligation beyond that of a month to month tenancy. Paraphrasing *Shaffer,* it is the legislature, not the plaintiffs, which has made the contract in this case.

* * *

Simon's cross-appeal from the judgment declaring the month to month tenancy was not terminated until September 30, 1978 and that Simon is liable to defendants for rental payments for the months of June, July, August and September, 1978, is equally without merit. The letter of March 10, 1978 notifying defendants of Simon's intention to terminate the tenancy on May 31, 1978 would have sufficed to comply with the requirements of § 441.060(2), as Simon contends. However, the retention of keys to the premises plus the failure to remove items of property until August 1, 1978 are indications of continued control and possession which adequately support the trial court's finding of a holding over until that date. [ ] The trial court, after hearing evidence and seeing photographs of items left on the premises, did not accept Simon's argument that this property was valueless and abandoned. We find this ruling amply supported by evidence and not clearly erroneous. Therefore, we are constrained to uphold the judgment of the trial court. [ ]

The judgment of the trial court is affirmed in all respects.

Notes and Questions

1. Note that there were two statutes involved in *Longmier,* the Statute of Frauds which requires that all leases "for a longer period than one year" must be in writing to be enforceable, Mo.Rev.Stat. § 432.010, and a statute providing that all oral leases, except ones for agricultural purposes, are to be construed as periodic tenancies from month-to-month, Mo.Rev.Stat., § 441.060. What did the court say was the significant difference between the two statutes?

2. Why did the court refuse to permit the defendants in *Longmier* to raise the estoppel defense? What did the court mean by its quotation from an earlier case that the Statute of Frauds may be a "shield" against fraud, but not a "sword" to create something that did not exist?

3. Note the significance of the retention of keys by the tenant and the failure to remove all personal property after the premises were vacated. Should those actions override the intent expressed in the March 10 letter? Suppose the tenant simply forgot to return an extra set of keys? Suppose the tenant kept the keys, but the landlord had a duplicate set?

B. Allocating Risks through Leases—Public Policy and Ethical Questions

VERMES v. AMERICAN DISTRICT TELEPHONE CO.

Supreme Court of Minnesota, 1977.
251 N.W.2d 101.

SCOTT, JUSTICE.

These are separate appeals by two of the defendants in an action brought by Harry Vermes, owner of a jewelry store in the Foshay Tower in Minneapolis, to recover losses sustained when his store was burglarized. Defendants were the American District Telegraph Company (ADT), which had supplied Vermes with a burglary detection system; the Apache Corporation (Apache), which had leased the space to Vermes; and The Towle Company (Towle), which managed the Foshay Tower at the time of the burglary.

Trial was by jury in the district court. In a special verdict, the jury allocated negligence percentages among the parties and set damages at $23,000. Plaintiff's post-trial motion to increase damages to $47,185.03 was granted. Defendants' motions for judgment notwithstanding the verdict and a new trial were denied. These appeals are by ADT and Apache from the judgment below and the order denying the various post-trial motions.

In 1968 Harry Vermes leased space in the Foshay Tower's first floor for his jewelry store. A few weeks later Vermes entered into a contract with ADT for burglar alarm service. In 1970 Towle replaced Apache as building manager.

On Monday morning, August 23, 1971, Vermes discovered that his store had been burglarized. The police investigation determined that entry had been made through the ceiling of the vault area. A mechanical-equipment access room was located over the plaintiff's store and the thin floor of this room formed the ceiling of plaintiff's store. The construction design allowed easy entry into the vault from above. The wholesale value of the property taken was $47,185.03.

* * *

The liability of a landlord to a tenant is necessarily based upon different considerations than that owed a tenant by a third party with whom the tenant merely contracts for certain specific services. The lease between Vermes and Apache contained the following clause:

> "Lessee also agrees to be responsible for and to relieve Lessor from all liability by reason of any damages or injuries to any person or thing which may arise from or be due to the use, misuse or abuse of all or any of the elevators, hatches, openings, stairways, hallways of any kind whatsoever which may exist or hereafter be erected or constructed on the said premises, or from any kind of injury which may arise from any other cause whatsoever on the said premises or the building of which the demised premises are a part, whether such damage, injury, use, misuse or abuse be caused by or result from the negligence of Lessor, its servants or agents or any other person or persons whatsoever."

On appeal Apache contends that this clause is valid and applies with full force to plaintiff. Vermes responds by arguing that (1) the negligence alleged (i.e., leasing Vermes space not suitable for a jewelry store) occurred prior to the lease, and (2) the exculpatory clause may be void as against public policy, citing the following language from *Rossman v. 740 River Drive*, Minn., 241 N.W.2d 91 (1976):

> " * * * The enforceability of a lease clause which exculpates a landlord from liability for negligence is a question of balance. The public policy favoring freedom of contract is weighed against the policy favoring the landlord's observance of the particular duty he is alleged to have breached. Thus, the balance depends on the nature of the particular duty breached. If the landlord's duty is basic and his observance of it is of extreme importance * * *, then the policy favoring his observance of that duty may well be stronger than the policy favoring freedom of contract. * * * [I]f the duty the landlord breaches is less basic and his observance of it is not of such grave importance * * *, then freedom of contract may well be the dominant policy."

The question then becomes whether the alleged duty of the landlord in this case is "basic."

The duty of Apache, if it can be defined as such, was to sufficiently inform Vermes concerning the store which was being considered for rental to the extent that Vermes had enough information from which he would be able to properly assess the store's suitability for his jewelry business. In the commercial context this would seem to be a "basic" duty. A commercial tenant will often have specific needs peculiar to his business which will require the premises to be leased to have certain attributes. Space suitable for a restaurant, for example, might be completely unsuitable for a bank. A part of a building where the air conditioning is ineffective might suit a tenant in need of storage space, but could be useless for a doctor or a business office. In cases where suitability factors might not be obvious upon casual inspection, as with ineffective air conditioning if the premises were inspected in winter, it would be a basic duty of the landlord to inform the prospective tenant of any qualities of the premises which might reasonably be undesirable from the tenant's point of view.

A jewelry store, in addition to the usual requirements for a retail store, requires physical security. The landlord's duty, prior to the signing of the lease, would be to point out any facts about the premises which would tend to make them insecure; for example, a side door accessible from the street or a thin partition separating them from a storage room. In this case it was, in the language of *Rossman v. 740 River Drive, supra,* the "particular duty" of Apache to point out to Vermes any facts about the proposed premises which might reasonably make them unsuitable for his use. As noted by Vermes in his brief, this duty was basic to the relationship between Apache and Vermes. It is fair to say that if Vermes had been informed of his insecure ceiling, he might have insisted that changes be made as conditions to the lease. He did so as to lighting.

Thus, under the *Rossman* decision, the broad exculpatory clause in the lease here should not operate to bar Vermes' negligence claim against Apache. It is not necessary to reach plaintiff's other arguments on precontractual negligence, contractual ambiguity, misrepresentation, and strict construction. * * *

Reversed in part, affirmed in part, and remanded with instructions.

Notes and Questions

1. Should prospective landlords or tenants be allowed to contract away rights or duties? Should the type of intended use of the property being rented—agricultural, commercial, residential—make a difference? As we progress through these materials, we will see that courts and legislatures have tended to create different rules for adjusting rights and responsibilities of landlords and tenants based on the type of intended use.

2. Suppose the rent for the space leased in the principal case was less than half of that for other, more secure buildings that were available at the time the jewelry store owner signed the lease containing the exculpatory clause. Should that have a bearing on cases of this type? Might the lower rent suggest that the parties were allocating the risk of physical security to the tenant?

3. What risk was being allocated by the exculpatory clause in *Vermes?* Did the court allocate the risk differently, or did the court enforce a different duty (disclosure of latent defects)? Did the language of the

exculpatory clause cover potential liability to tenants, or was it designed to insulate the landlord from potential claims of third parties?

4. Are there exculpatory clauses in the sample residential leases discussed supra? If so, would you expect the *Vermes* court to enforce them?

5. Statutes in some states prohibit lease clauses that are designed to protect landlords from the legal consequences of their conduct or the conduct of third parties. See, e.g., the Maryland Real Property Code Ann., § 8–105 (1988), which declares void as against public policy lease provisions that "indemnify the landlord, hold the landlord harmless, or preclude or exonerate the landlord from any liability * * * for any injury, loss, damage, or liability arising from any * * * negligence * * * of the landlord on or about the leased premises or any * * * appurtenances used in connection with them, and not within the exclusive control of the tenant." Prince Philip Partnership v. Cutlip, 321 Md. 296, 582 A.2d 992 (1990) (landlord's failure to install handicapped-accessible public toilet facilities in medical office building in violation of applicable building code not protected by exculpatory clause in lease to physician whose patient fell and broke her legs while attempting to use a non-handicapped accessible bathroom in the physician's office because the landlord's negligence involved "appurtenances [that were] not within the exclusive control" of the tenant).

6. Another frequent source of disputes is the allocation of repair responsibilities, particularly when it is not articulated clearly in the lease. Who, for example, should be responsible for repairing a pre-existing hole in the roof of a leased building under a lease that required the tenant to keep the building "in as good condition as when received, ordinary wear and tear excepted"? See Jacobi v. Timmers Chevrolet, Inc., 164 Ga.App. 198, 296 S.E.2d 777 (1982) (distinguishing capital "repairs" from ordinary "maintenance" and requiring the landlord to repair the roof as a capital improvement of greater benefit to the landlord than to the tenant).

If the parties do not allocate repair responsibilities in their lease, how should that allocation be made? What reasons can you articulate in favor of an allocation to the landlord? to the tenant? Are there reasons to restrict the ability of the parties to make the allocation decision themselves? Might the parties make the allocation decision without expressly saying so, for example, by adjusting the rent or other terms? Should the rules regarding allocation of repair responsibility be different for commercial and residential tenancies? What about multi-family residential as opposed to single-family residential? What about mixed-use buildings in which both commercial and residential spaces are leased?

7. How much should a landlord be required to disclose to a prospective commercial tenant, particularly if the prospective tenant does not make known specific needs? What about lack of storage space for a retail business such as a shoe store? A narrow driveway adjacent to loading docks? Space leased to a competitor in the next block? The traditional common law answer has been *caveat emptor*—let the actor beware. Later we will see that this principle became the focal point for the movement to reform the law affecting residential landlord-tenant relationships.

Is the real issue for lawyers what clients should disclose rather than what the law requires to be disclosed? Suppose one's client asks if a prospective tenant must be told about a situation such as the one in *Vermes*. Would the lawyer be providing better service to the client by responding in a spirit of friendship (collaboration in the good) with suggestions regarding what is morally admirable even though it may not be legally required, or should the lawyer simply stick to the rules of law? See ABA Model Rules of Professional Conduct, Comment to Rule 2.1 (Purely technical legal advice can sometimes be inadequate. It is proper for a lawyer to refer to relevant moral and ethical considerations in giving advice).

T. SHAFFER, AMERICAN LEGAL ETHICS
453–455 (1985).

Here is a landlord-tenant situation from Professors Louis M. Brown and Edward Dauer:

Lawyers * * * are enlisted not only in the defense of virtue; they also participate in a process which most often does not occur before or within an impartial tribunal. The lawyer is often engaged as a planner, and as a counsellor for clients not then involved in any dispute whatsoever. There are still decisions that are made, and these decisions may still have better or worse outcomes, but they involve neither adversaries nor the safeguard of a tribunal: In the preventive law area of practice the lawyering process is final and decisive. There is virtually no appeal from the lawyer's preventive law decision that his client sign the irrevocable trust, or the deed conveying property, or a contract, or engage in numerous other events having legal consequences.

Consider then the difficulties which are raised when the role predicate of the profession's responsibilities seems exclusively adversarial. More to the point, consider the following hypothetical problem: Five years ago the state legislature enacted a statute specifically authorizing residential tenants to offset against their liability for rent payments any sums which they expended in improving the premises so that they would conform to the existing housing code's minimum standards of habitability. The intended effect of the act was to prevent evictions for nonpayment of rent when the tenant made necessary repairs, and as a practical matter to encourage such repairs to be made. Almost immediately after the statute became effective the great majority of residential lease forms began including a clause (a lawyer's product, no doubt) whereby the tenant waived his right to offset under section so-and-so of the statutes. Having thus had its purposes thwarted, the legislature recurred to the offensive: three years ago a further statute was enacted, this one making such waivers void. No criminal or other penalties were listed with the second statute. Such a waiver would be a null act—the courts would not aid in its enforcement, and it would not serve to defeat the statutory defense to eviction. The legislative history is clear, and it is well-known that such waivers were considered by the legislature to be against public policy.

A landlord now becomes a client and requests that a lawyer draft a standard lease form for use in his leasing all of the dozen or so tenements which he owns. The client asks that a waiver of the offset right be included. He is advised that such a waiver is unenforceable, but persists: The waiver will have an *in terrorem* effect on those tenants who are not aware of the later statute (all of them, we can suppose *arguendo*) and who are unlikely ever to have their claims adjudicated by a knowing tribunal or with the aid of a knowing counsellor (ditto). The clause will, in addition, deter tenants from unilaterally making repairs at the landlord's expense.

In a somewhat related situation, the Association of the Bar of the City of New York said:

> In the opinion of our Committee it is not within the proper standards of ethics for a lawyer to insert such a waiver in a contract if the lawyer knows that such a waiver is against public policy and void as a matter of law.

> A lawyer must himself observe and advise his client to observe the statute law * * *. If a waiver in a contract has been held by a court of last resort to be void as against public policy as a matter of law, he should so advise his client. If the client should nevertheless insist on its incorporation in the contract, the lawyer should refuse to do so, for if he should comply with his client's request he would thereby become a party to possible deception of the other party to the contract.

It is the lawyer's duty, the Association said, "to uphold the honor of the profession. He should strive at all times to uphold the honor and to maintain the dignity of the profession and to improve not only the law but the administration of justice."

Professor Monroe Freedman, in his widely discussed book, *Lawyers' Ethics in an Adversary System* (1975), indicated that he and many lawyers might have disagreed with the Association. The cases might be said to turn on a lawyer's obligation to carry out the law—or at least to obey it—and therefore to be within the limitations adopted in Canon Seven. It does not go as far as the cases * * * where the client's means or goal are clearly legal but the lawyer nonetheless believes them to be immoral. That suggests a distinction that may not be defensible, of course, particularly if the relationship between law and morals is one of dependence (of law on morals) rather than of peaceful coexistence.

Problems

(a) First year law students Ann Bucki, Susie Lewis, and Colleen O'Hara signed a one-year lease for a small house about a mile or so from campus. Willing to accept a Spartan life style during law school and anxious to save money where possible, they negotiated a lease to rent the property "as is" for a 20 per cent reduction in rent. The lease contained the following provisions:

4. In consideration of the reduced rental provided for, the tenant covenants not to sue the landlord and the landlord will not be

liable to the tenant for any damage, loss or injury to property or person by reason of any existing or future defect in the premises, including acts, omissions, negligence or nuisance of other persons or tenants or of the landlord or his agent, and including that arising from falling plaster, leaking roofs, or faulty or inadequately lighted or repaired sidewalks, stairs, halls, alleys, yards or cellars.

5. It is understood that the landlord has no public liability insurance. If the tenant desires to eliminate clause four, written notice thereof should be given the landlord, in which event the rent will be increased $10 a month. Following termination of clause four by the tenant, the landlord's liability shall be that provided by the general laws of the State. The landlord *shall not* become an insurer by virtue of such termination.

A New Jersey court in deciding a case involving a clause similar to Clause Four, but without the provision for a reduction in rent, stated that a clause which attempts to immunize the landlord from all liability is contrary to public policy, particularly in situations where the relative bargaining positions of the landlord and tenant are substantially unequal. Kuzmiak v. Brookchester, Inc., 33 N.J.Super. 575, 111 A.2d 425 (1955). Does the addition of Clause Five cure any public policy questions arising from Clause Four? See Cardona v. Eden Realty Company, 118 N.J.Super. 381, 288 A.2d 34 (1972) (clauses in question invalidated as "legalistic effort[s] to circumvent the positive public policy of the State"); Jones v. Hanna, 814 S.W.2d 287, 289 (Ky.Ct.App. 1991), distinguishing exculpatory clauses for causing personal injury or for wilful and wanton conduct (invalid as against public policy) from clauses excusing simple negligence affecting property or business activities (public policy not affected). See generally Burnham, Teaching Legal Ethics in Contracts, 41 J.Leg.Ed. 105 (1991).

Can you redraft the lease to reflect the parties' agreement so that it will pass muster under the New Jersey rule?

(b) The *Vermes* case and the *Shaffer* excerpt raise the point about drawing a distinction between (i) moral behavior and legal advice consistent with it, and (ii) what the law will allow. One is as much the business of the law office as is the other. Note also that there is a distinction between the profession's regulatory rules and moral behavior. Would, for example, an attorney who drafts clauses such as those contained in Problem (a), violate her professional responsibility under Rule 1.2(d) of the American Bar Association's Model Rules of Professional Conduct:

A lawyer shall not counsel a client to engage, or assist a client, in conduct that the lawyer knows is criminal or fraudulent, but a lawyer may discuss the legal consequences of any proposed course of conduct with a client and may counsel or assist a client to make a good faith effort to determine the validity, scope, meaning, or application of the law.

Would the drafting of such clauses be a moral act? Cf. Burnham, Teaching Legal Ethics in Contracts, 41 J.Leg.Ed. 105, 118, n. 42 (1991), noting that the following clause was deleted prior to adoption of Rule 1.2(d): A lawyer shall not counsel or assist a client in conduct "or in the preparation of a written instrument containing terms" the lawyer knows or reasonably should know are legally prohibited.

IV. SELECTION OF TENANTS

Although the power to exclude incidental to property ownership discussed in Chapter One gives landlords the general right to choose whomever they please as tenants, the following constitutional and statutory prohibitions against various forms of discrimination impose important limitations on landlords' freedom of choice.

UNITED STATES CONSTITUTION

Amendment XIII

Section 1. Neither slavery nor involuntary servitude, except as a punishment for crime whereof the party shall have been duly convicted, shall exist within the United States, or any place subject to their jurisdiction.

Section 2. Congress shall have power to enforce this article by appropriate legislation.

Amendment XIV

Section 1. All persons born or naturalized in the United States, and subject to the jurisdiction thereof, are citizens of the United States and of the State wherein they reside. No State shall make or enforce any law which shall abridge the privileges or immunities of citizens of the United States; nor shall any State deprive any person of life, liberty, or property, without due process of law; nor deny to any person within its jurisdiction the equal protection of the laws. * * *

CIVIL RIGHTS ACTS—EXCERPTS

42 U.S.C. § 1982

All citizens of the United States shall have the same right, in every State and Territory, as is enjoyed by white citizens thereof to inherit, purchase, lease, sell, hold, and convey real and personal property.

Fair Housing Act of 1968, as amended—excerpts

42 U.S.C. § 3602 Definitions

(b) "Dwelling" means any building, structure, or portion thereof which is occupied as, or designed or intended for occupancy as, a residence by one or more families, and any vacant land which is offered for sale or lease for the construction or location thereon of any such building, structure, or portion thereof.

* * *

(h) "Handicap" means, with respect to a person—

(1) a physical or mental impairment which substantially limits one or more of such person's major life activities,

(2) a record of having such an impairment, or

(3) being regarded as having such an impairment, but such term does not include current, illegal use of or addiction to a controlled substance (as defined in section 102 of the Controlled Substances Act (21 U.S.C. 802)).

* * *

(k) "Familial status" means one or more individuals (who have not attained the age of 18 years) being domiciled with—

(1) a parent or another person having legal custody of such individual or individuals; or

(2) the designee of such parent or other person having such custody, with the written permission of such parent or other person.

The protections afforded against discrimination on the basis of familial status shall apply to any person who is pregnant or is in the process of securing legal custody of any individual who has not attained the age of 18 years.

42 U.S.C. § 3604   Discrimination in sale or rental of housing and other prohibited practices

As made applicable by section 803 of this title and except as exempted by sections 803(b) and 807 of this title, it shall be unlawful—

(a) To refuse to sell or rent after the making of a bona fide offer, or to refuse to negotiate for the sale or rental of, or otherwise make unavailable or deny, a dwelling to any person because of race, color, religion, sex, familial status, or national origin.

(b) To discriminate against any person in the terms, conditions, or privileges of sale or rental of a dwelling, or in the provision of services or facilities in connection therewith, because of race, color, religion, sex, familial status, or national origin.

(c) To make, print, or publish, or cause to be made, printed, or published any notice, statement, or advertisement, with respect to the sale or rental of a dwelling that indicates any preference, limitation, or discrimination based on race, color, religion, sex, handicap, familial status, or national origin, or an intention to make any such preference, limitation, or discrimination.

(d) To represent to any person because of race, color, religion, sex, handicap, familial status, or national origin that any dwelling is not available for inspection, sale, or rental when such dwelling is in fact so available.

(e) For profit, to induce or attempt to induce any person to sell or rent any dwelling by representations regarding the entry or prospective entry into the neighborhood of a person or persons of a particular race, color, religion, sex, handicap, familial status, or national origin.

(f)(1) To discriminate in the sale or rental, or to otherwise make unavailable or deny, a dwelling to any buyer or renter because of a handicap of—

(A) that buyer or renter,

(B) a person residing in or intending to reside in that dwelling after it is so sold, rented, or made available; or

(C) any person associated with that buyer or renter.

(2) To discriminate against any person in the terms, conditions, or privileges of sale or rental of a dwelling, or in the provision of services or facilities in connection with such dwelling, because of a handicap of—

(A) that person; or

(B) a person residing in or intending to reside in that dwelling after it is so sold, rented, or made available; or

(C) any person associated with that person.

(3) For purposes of this subsection, discrimination includes—

(A) a refusal to permit, at the expense of the handicapped person, reasonable modifications of existing premises occupied or to be occupied by such person if such modifications may be necessary to afford such person full enjoyment of the premises, except that, in the case of a rental, the landlord may where it is reasonable to do so condition permission for a modification on the renter agreeing to restore the interior of the premises to the condition that existed before the modification, reasonable wear and tear excepted.

(B) a refusal to make reasonable accommodations in rules, policies, practices, or services, when such accommodations may be necessary to afford such person equal opportunity to use and enjoy a dwelling; or

(C) in connection with the design and construction of covered multifamily dwellings for first occupancy after the date that is 30 months after the date of enactment of the Fair Housing Amendments Act of 1988, a failure to design and construct those dwelling in such a manner that—

(i) the public use and common use portions of such dwellings are readily accessible to and usable by handicapped persons;

(ii) all the doors designed to allow passage into and within all premises within such dwellings are sufficiently wide to allow passage by handicapped persons in wheelchairs; and

(iii) all premises within such dwellings contain the following features of adaptive design:

(I) an accessible route into and through the dwelling;

(II) light switches, electrical outlets, thermostats, and other environmental controls in accessible locations;

(III) reinforcements in bathroom walls to allow later installation of grab bars; and

(IV) usable kitchens and bathrooms such that an individual in a wheelchair can maneuver about the space.

* * *

(8) Nothing in this title shall be construed to invalidate or limit any law of a State or political subdivision of a State, or other jurisdiction in which this title shall be effective, that requires dwellings to be designed and constructed in a manner that affords handicapped persons greater access than is required by this title.

(9) Nothing in this subsection requires that a dwelling be made available to an individual whose tenancy would constitute a direct threat to the health or safety of other individuals or whose tenancy would result in substantial physical damage to the property of others.

MARABLE v. H. WALKER & ASSOCIATES

U.S. Court of Appeals for the Fifth Circuit, 1981.
644 F.2d 390.

FRANK M. JOHNSON, JR., CIRCUIT JUDGE:

Sylvester Marable brought this suit alleging that defendants Harold and Francis Walker refused to rent an available apartment to him because he is black, in violation of the Fair Housing Act, 42 U.S.C.A. § 3604 et seq., and 42 U.S.C.A. §§ 1981, 1982. After defendants answered that their policy was to rent only to married couples and that Marable was denied tenancy because he applied as a single male, Marable amended his complaint to add a claim of sex discrimination in violation of 42 U.S.C.A. § 3604. The district court rendered judgment for defendants after a non-jury trial, concluding that the defendants did not discriminate against Marable on the basis of either race or sex. The district court found that the apartment was denied to Marable because he had a credit report that showed him to be an unacceptable tenant, he was single and the apartment complex had a policy of renting to families and married persons only, and he "constantly harassed" defendants about his application after it was submitted.

Marable appeals, contending that the district court erred first in failing to conclude that defendants' policy of not renting to single males is a violation of 42 U.S.C.A. § 3604 because it is explicitly sexually discriminatory, and second in failing to conclude that the single male exclusionary policy was not applied equally between blacks and whites since defendants had made exceptions for white single males, but no blacks—single or married—had ever been accepted as tenants at the Traces Apartments. Marable also assigns error in the trial court's failure to consider whether the putative reasons for his rejection as a tenant were standards or criteria that were applied equally to white rental applicants and in its failure to consider the related question whether the asserted reasons were a mere pretext for racial discrimination.

Defendants Harold and Francis Walker own the Traces Apartments, a 56–unit apartment complex located in a predominantly white suburb of Birmingham, Alabama. Each of the apartments has either two or three bedrooms. When these apartments were first being rented, beginning in April 1974, defendants rented to at least eight single males and also to tenants with poor or no credit histories, with poor or unverified employment records, and with poor or no rental histories. Thereafter, defendants adopted a policy of renting to married couples and families, in part, Mrs. Walker stated, because they had some trouble with single male tenants. Francis Walker became the managing partner of the Traces Apartments on February 3, 1976. She testified at trial that since that time no single males had rented apartments and that only three single females and one widow had rented at the Traces. However, she stated that applications were taken from singles on a case by case basis. Mrs. Walker testified that from 1974 until 1978, the time of trial, out of 209 tenancy turnovers, defendants had rented to 22 non-married tenants, including ten single white males. She testified that the Traces Apartments had never had a black tenant.

Sylvester Marable submitted his application for tenancy in the Traces Apartments in November 1976. The resident manager, Mark Hammond, showed Marable a vacant apartment and told him that he would be contacted in a few days about his application. Marable was accompanied during his first visit to the Traces Apartments by his fiancee. He testified that he told Hammond of his anticipated marriage in December 1976 but Hammond contradicted this testimony, although Hammond stated that he assumed at that time that Marable and his companion were married. After Hammond showed him the apartment, Marable and his fiancee returned to the resident manager's office where he completed a credit application. No deposit was placed. Shortly after Marable left, Hammond telephoned the credit information to a credit reporting company named Equifax, which proceeded to prepare a credit report on Marable. Several days later, Marable was contacted by a Mrs. Sims, from Equifax, for the purpose of interviewing Marable concerning the facts stated on the credit application given to Hammond.

The Equifax credit report on Marable, which was defendants' only source of information regarding his credit standing, disclosed that Marable had worked for the Feather Corporation as a public affairs consultant at an estimated annual salary of $14,000 for the previous 8½ months. The report noted that Equifax had been unable to contact Feather or determine the type of business in which it was engaged; it described the nature of the business as an "independent corporation." However, the report also indicated that Marable worked full time steadily and that his prospects for continued employment were regarded as good.

The Equifax credit report also contained the results of an investigation of credit references supplied by Marable. The report listed his account with a music company as satisfactory and noted that an account that he had set up with a furniture company had never been used. A jewelry store at which Marable had an account was listed as having a policy of not disclosing credit information. A bank loan account (for an automobile) listed in the report showed that Marable had borrowed $10,689, that $6,104 was owed at the time of the report, and that the loan terms included 42 payments at $254.72 per month. The amount past due was listed as none and Marable's credit rating was listed as "I–2." The report also stated that Marable had never been subject to any foreclosures, garnishments, suits or judgments regarding debts, or bankruptcies. The report also indicated that Marable had not previously rented or owned a home and that before working for the Feather Corporation he had worked for the State of Alabama as a parole officer for 1½ years. Marable's net worth was estimated at $7,000. The report concluded that there were no factors that might affect doing business with Marable on a credit basis.

Later on the same day that Marable was interviewed by Mrs. Sims from Equifax, he phoned Mrs. Walker who told him that as soon as she received the Equifax report she would contact him. Mrs. Walker testified that Marable accused her of stalling and of not wanting to rent to him because he was black. She testified that until Marable informed her she was unaware that he was black. Mrs. Walker received the report on December 10, 1976, and on that day Marable phoned Mrs. Walker. Marable testified that Mrs. Walker asked him why he wanted to live on that side of town and then laughed at him and told him that she did not rent to unmarried applicants. Mrs. Walker testified that until she received the credit report she was unaware that Marable was single. Later that same day Marable again phoned Mrs. Walker requesting an explanation as to why he was rejected as a tenant.

Marable claimed at trial that Mrs. Walker refused to give him any further explanation, but Mrs. Walker testified that she told him that, in addition to his single marital status, he lacked sufficient credit and had no previous rental history, and that his employer and his income could not be verified. She also testified that Marable "got a little smart" with her during the phone call when she told him that he would not get the apartment.

The apartment for which Marable had applied remained vacant for three months, until it was rented to a white single female with no children.

After being refused as a tenant, Marable then went to the United States Department of Housing and Urban Development (HUD) on December 20, 1976, and filed a charge against defendants alleging that they discriminated against him on the basis of his race in refusing to rent to him. Defendants told the HUD investigator that Marable was rejected as a tenant because he had minimal credit references and had never previously rented an apartment. Mrs. Walker did not tell HUD that she had earlier stated that she refused to rent to Marable because of his single marital status. She admitted at trial that she gave other reasons for rejecting Marable because she was not certain that it was legal to refuse to rent to Marable on the ground of single marital status. HUD concluded from its investigation that defendants denied Marable an apartment because of his race.

This suit was filed on May 2, 1977, after efforts at conciliation failed. Defendants have asserted different reasons at different times for rejecting Marable as a tenant. As mentioned above, they told a HUD investigator that Marable's inadequate credit and rental history were the reasons he was rejected. In their answer to the complaint the only asserted reason was Marable's single marital status. In their answers to Marable's first interrogatories, Marable's alleged credit deficiencies were listed as the reason for defendants' refusal to rent to him. At trial, two more reasons were stated: Marable was "a little smart" with Mrs. Walker during one phone call, and he was employed with a "new" company.

The district court found that Marable was denied the apartment because of his single marital status, his credit report and his constant harassment of defendants. The court discounted the testimony of two of Marable's witnesses on the ground that they evidenced clear bias because one of the witnesses was under indictment for stealing from defendants and the other was involved in civil litigation with defendants. The court further stated that "[p]laintiff demonstrated a lack of credibility in his testimony both because of contradictions in his testimony and by his own manner and demeanor in court." The court found that Marable's credit report was unacceptable because he claimed an estimated $14,000 yearly income with a "nonexistent corporation" and he had "no significant employment history." The court concluded that defendants were justified in refusing to rent to Marable solely on the basis of his credit report.

A plaintiff bringing a claim under the Fair Housing Act of 1968, 42 U.S.C.A. § 3601 et seq., charging defendants with refusal to provide housing on the basis of racial discrimination is not required to establish that his denial of housing was motivated *solely* by racial discrimination. [ ]

It is sufficient that race was one significant factor considered by the defendants in dealing with the plaintiff. [ ]

Similarly, a plaintiff bringing suit under the Civil Rights Act of 1866, [ ] is not required to show that discrimination was the sole reason for defendants' refusal to provide housing. [ ] The race of an applicant for tenancy is not to be considered and the presence of other factors also motivating the refusal to rent cannot justify racial discrimination. * * *

Several of the district court's findings of subsidiary facts are not supported by the record and are clearly erroneous. The finding that Marable claimed an estimated annual salary of $14,000 "with what proved to be a nonexistent corporate employer" was refuted by defendants' own exhibit which consisted of a copy of the article of incorporation of the Feather Corporation. The finding that Marable had "no significant employment history" is belied by Marable's credit report itself, which informed the defendants that he had been working full time for 8½ months and had previously worked as a parole officer for the State of Alabama for 1½ years, and which described his prospects for continued employment as good.

The finding that Marable was denied the apartment because he was single and the Traces had a policy of renting only to families and marrieds is contradicted by Mrs. Walker's own testimony that applications were accepted from singles on a case by case basis and that 22 of the total 209 tenants at the Traces had been singles. It is manifest from the documentary evidence and the testimony of Mrs. Walker that apartments were in fact rented to singles, and the exceptions made by defendants constitute over 10% of all the tenants who had ever rented at the Traces.

The finding that one of defendants' reasons for refusing to rent to Marable was because he "constantly harassed" the defendants is without support in the record. Even the testimony of Mark Hammond, the resident manager of the Traces, and that of Mrs. Walker does not warrant a finding that three phone calls to Mrs. Walker and two to Hammond constituted constant harassment. Neither Mrs. Walker nor Hammond claimed that they were "harassed" by Marable. Mrs. Walker testified merely that Marable got "a little smart" during one phone call but her perception that Marable, a young black man, was uppity toward her does not support the court's finding.

The findings of fact mandated by Fed.R.Civ.P. 52(a) "must be sufficient in detail and exactness to indicate the factual basis for the ultimate conclusion reached by the court." *Corley v. Jackson Police Department,* 566 F.2d 994, 1003 (5th Cir.1978), *quoting Lettsome v. United States,* 434 F.2d 907, 909 (5th Cir.1970). The district court in this case failed to consider in its findings the evidence indicating that the defendants' credit and employment requirements and their single male exclusionary policy were unequally applied as between Marable and white applicants. The court also failed to consider whether defendants' rejection of Marable's application for tenancy was a pretext for racial discrimination.

Marable introduced documentary evidence consisting of applications for tenancy listing credit references and credit reports prepared by a credit agency, which demonstrated that defendants rented to numerous white persons with significant credit problems far greater than any deficiencies indicated by Marable's credit report. Similarly, the undisputed evidence indicated that defendants had rented to (1) numerous tenants with unverified incomes, (2) several who were unemployed or who worked for companies with which the defendants were unfamiliar when they were accepted as tenants, and (3) several others for whom defendants ordered no independent credit report to be prepared. Also, by defendants' own admission in the testimony of Mrs. Walker, at least 10 single white males had rented at the Traces. The defendants' disparate treatment of white applicants and Marable, as reflected by their patterns of accepting white applicants who were credit risks or who were single, is clearly reflected by the evidence.

The district court also erred in failing to make any finding concerning whether the defendants' asserted reasons for refusing to rent to Marable were a pretext for racial discrimination. The asserted reasons given by defendants have included virtually every possible reason except Marable's race. They have asserted, alternatively or cumulatively, at different times during this dispute, that the reasons for Marable's rejection were his poor credit, his unverified income and unverified employer, his "smartness," and his single marital status. The district court erred in failing to consider the comparative evidence of the unequal application of defendants' rental criteria as between Marable and white applicants, which demonstrated that defendants' reasons for rejecting Marable were a pretext. [ ] The district court never considered the qualifications of Marable in relation to the qualifications of white applicants; rather, it considered Marable's qualifications only against the defendants' alleged absolute standards. However, even Mrs. Walker testified that the defendants' rental standards were not absolute and that tenants' applications were considered on a case by case basis. The defendants' tenant selection process and criteria were shown by the testimony of Mrs. Walker and Mark Hammond to be subjective. Finally, the defendants admitted that no black applicants had ever been accepted as tenants at the Traces Apartments.

The district court discounted the testimony of Marable on the ground that it lacked credibility because of contradiction and Marable's demeanor at trial. The court also discounted the testimony of two of Marable's witnesses on the ground that they were biased. Even if it is accepted as true that Marable and two of his witnesses lacked credibility—a district court finding that is binding on this Court unless it is clearly erroneous—documentary evidence in the record clearly indicates that Marable's race was a significant factor in his rejection as a tenant. A district court may not "bootstrap" its findings and conclusions by stating that they are based upon credibility when the documentary evidence and undisputed testimony reflected in the record show the findings and conclusions to be clearly erroneous.

We conclude, after careful examination of the record, that the unequal application of defendants' rental criteria, including marital status and employment and credit histories, as between Marable and white applicants demonstrates disparate treatment on the basis of race violating the Fair Housing Act, 42 U.S.C.A. § 3604, and 42 U.S.C.A. §§ 1981 and 1982. * * *

Reversed.

Notes and Questions

1. Would the Fair Housing Act be violated by a refusal to rent to someone because of her occupation, e.g., a lawyer? See Kramarsky v. Stahl Management, 92 Misc.2d 1030, 401 N.Y.S.2d 943 (1977) (refusal to rent to black woman lawyer not violative of New York fair housing statute when decision was based on occupation). "[T]here is nothing illegal in a landlord discriminating against lawyers as a group, or trying to keep out of his building intelligent persons, aware of their rights, who may give him trouble in the future." Id. at 944.

2. Does the Fair Housing Act prohibit a landlord from refusing to rent to unmarried, cohabiting couples because such activity offends the landlord's religious beliefs? How should the interest of landlords and tenants be balanced when their life styles differ? See Hann v. Housing Authority of City of Easton, 709 F.Supp. 605 (E.D.Pa.1989) (Federal Housing Act violated by exclusion of unmarried couples from subsidized housing); Foreman v. Anchorage Equal Rights Com'n, 779 P.2d 1199 (Alaska 1989) (state and local fair housing acts barring discrimination based on "marital status" violated by private landlord's policy of refusing to rent to unmarried couples).

For a case resolving the conflict in values in favor of the landlord's religious beliefs, see State by Cooper v. French, 460 N.W.2d 2 (Minn.1990), holding that the prohibition against discrimination on the basis of marital status in the Minnesota Human Rights Act was not intended by the legislature to include unmarried, cohabiting couples, and that the religious liberty clause of the Minnesota Constitution protected the "rights of conscience" of a landlord who refused to rent to unmarried, cohabiting couples. The court held that unless the state can show a "compelling and overriding state interest," the landlord must be granted an "exemption" from the state human rights act. A similar result was reached in Illinois on the issue of statutory construction without considering the constitutional question. Mister v. A.R.K. Partnership, 197 Ill.App.3d 105, 113–14, 143 Ill.Dec. 166, 171, 553 N.E.2d 1152, 1157 (1990). See also Donahue v. Fair Employment and Housing Commission, 1 Cal.App.4th 387, 2 Cal.Rptr.2d 32 (1991) (granting exemption from state marital status discrimination ban on state constitutional grounds, finding no compelling state interest to override landlords' free exercise of religion claim).

One of the reasons the Minnesota Supreme Court gave for overturning a conviction under the Minnesota Human Rights Act was that there was a "less restrictive" alternative to "forc[ing] a person to break one statute [prohibiting fornication] to obey another [prohibiting discrimination based on marital status]." Is the "exemption" the court granted an appropriate way to resolve such disputes? If so, how should it be worded? Should it make a difference whether the landlord is "some faceless corporation" or an elderly couple who acquired the apartment "as wholly personal investments for their retirement years"? J. Kilpatrick, Living–in–Sin Suit Pits Rights Against Rights, St. Louis Post–Dispatch, August 29, 1989, at p. 313, suggesting that such a line be drawn. Suppose the landlord were in his mid–30s and rented units as a source of investment income? Layle French, the landlord in the Minnesota case, was 34 at the time of the supreme court decision. Associated Press, Landlord Ruling Reversed, The Cincinnati Enquirer, September 2, 1990, at p. A–12. Should the number of units involved make a difference? In the *French* case, a single two-bedroom house was involved. Is the following compromise, worked out by Congress in the debate over the Fair Housing Act of 1968, an acceptable one?

42 U.S.C. § 3603

* * *

(b) Nothing in section 804 of this title (other than subsection (c)) shall apply to—

(1) any single-family house sold or rented by an owner: **Provided,** That such private individual owner does not own more than three such single-family houses at any one time: **Provided further,** That in the case of the sale of any such single-family house by a private individual owner not residing in such house at the time of such house or who was not the most recent resident of such house prior to such sale, the exemption granted by this subsection shall apply only with respect to one such sale within any twenty-four month period: **Provided further,** That such bona fide private individual owner does not own any interest in, nor is there owned or reserved on his behalf, under any express or voluntary agreement, title to or any right to all or a portion of the proceeds from the sale or rental of, more than three such single family houses at any one time: **Provided further,** That after December 31, 1969, the sale or rental of any such single-family house shall be excepted from the application of this subchapter only if such house is sold or rented (A) without the use in any manner of the sales or rental facilities or the sales or rental services of any real estate broker, agent, or salesman, or of such facilities or services of any person in the business of selling or renting dwellings, or of any employee or agent of

any such broker, agent, salesman, or person and (B) without the publication, posting or mailing, after notice, of any advertisement or written notice in violation of section 804(c) of this title; but nothing in this proviso shall prohibit the use of attorneys, escrow agents, abstractors, title companies, and other such professional assistance as necessary to perfect or transfer the title, or

(2) rooms or units in dwellings containing living quarters occupied or intended to be occupied by no more than four families living independently of each other, if the owner actually remains and occupies one of such living quarters as his residence.

3. The Fair Housing Amendments Act of 1988 expanded the coverage of the Act to include persons with disabilities and families with children. For a discussion of the changes, see Kushner, The Fair Housing Amendments Act of 1988: The Second Generation of Fair Housing, 42 Vanderbilt L.Rev. 1049 (1989). Examine the statutory excerpts. May a landlord require an elderly person to be able to "live independently" as a condition of admission? See Cason v. Rochester Housing Authority, 748 F.Supp. 1002 (W.D.N.Y.1990) (ability to live independently requirement held violative of Fair Housing Act and Rehabilitation Act of 1973). What about a mentally ill person who suffers from auditory hallucinations? Cf. City Wide Associates v. Penfield, 409 Mass. 140, 564 N.E.2d 1003 (1991) (eviction violated Federal Rehabilitation Act where landlord received public subsidies including reimbursement for tenant-caused damage and adverse impact on other tenants was not shown). Suppose a landlord denies an application of a couple who told the landlord that they planned to adopt a foster child. See Gorski v. Troy, 929 F.2d 1183 (7th Cir.1991) (couple evicted after telling landlord of their plans to adopt foster child were "aggrieved persons" within meaning of Fair Housing Act). Could a landlord deny an application to a homosexual couple? See Braschi v. Stahl Associates Co., 74 N.Y.2d 201, 544 N.Y.S.2d 784, 543 N.E.2d 49 (1989), discussed in Comment, Braschi v. Stahl: Family Redefined, 8 J. Human Rts. 289 (1990) (homosexual couple held legal equivalent of family under state rent control statute).

Would a requirement that prospective tenants have gross monthly incomes of at least three times the rent to be charged be a violation of the Act? Suppose a prospective tenant alleges race or sex discrimination because of findings that minorities and women tend to have lower average incomes than Caucasian men. The Supreme Court of California construed the state civil rights statute to require a showing of intentional discrimination rather than discriminatory impact and upheld the minimum income policy as a reasonable economic test in Harris v. Capital Growth Investors XIV, 52 Cal.3d 1142, 278 Cal.Rptr. 614, 805 P.2d 873 (1991). The court reasoned as follows:

The minimum income policy is no different in its purpose or effect from stated price or payment terms. Like those terms, it seeks to obtain for a business establishment the benefit of its bargain with the consumer: full payment of the price. In pursuit of the objective of securing payment, a landlord has a legitimate and direct economic interest in the income level of prospective tenants, as opposed to their sex, race, religion, or other personal beliefs or characteristics. For nearly all tenants, current income is the source of the monthly rental payment. When a tenant ceases paying rent during the term of the tenancy, the landlord must resort to legal process to obtain possession of the premises and to collect any back rent that may be due. [ ]

Even with the use of summary unlawful detainer proceedings, an eviction may take several months, during which the tenant remains in possession, enjoying the benefits of the leasehold without paying rent. [ ] Thus, the landlord bears the economic burdens (what an economist might call the "transaction costs of default") resulting from: (1) loss of income from default to eviction; (2) administrative time and the legal and other expenses incurred in the eviction process; and (3) the delays and expense of collection of back rent from the tenant, as well as the risk of noncollection.

In order to minimize the transaction costs of default, the economically rational landlord might adopt one or more of several approaches. First, a landlord might simply charge higher rents to all tenants to absorb the additional expense. Such a policy, of course, contains its own element of arbitrariness because it penalizes the majority of tenants who pay their rent on a regular basis. Moreover, the charging of higher rents as a means of subsidizing defaults necessarily excludes even more low income persons from tenancy. Second, a landlord might require larger amounts from all tenants as advance rent or security deposits. This policy, too, imposes additional burdens on the paying tenants. In apparent recognition of this fact, it is also subject to statutory limitations on the amount of advance payment a landlord may demand. [ ] Third, a landlord might adopt one or more policies or practices designed to screen out prospective tenants who are likely to default.

The minimum income policy adopted by defendants is, of course, an example of the third approach. It assumes that, at some ratio of rent to income, the burden of paying rent, along with other living expenses, will impose a hardship on a tenant, resulting in default. Although there may be myriad of individual factors operating in cases of particular prospective tenants that might affect the predictive value of the ratio, it does not thereby become "arbitrary" in the same way that race and sex discrimination are arbitrary. On the contrary, it is based on the rational economic interest of the landlord to minimize defaults and maintain the solvency of his business establishment, while extending the opportunity for rental housing to all persons regardless of race, sex, religion, etc. * * * Id., 805 P.2d 885–886, 893.

UNITED STATES v. STARRETT CITY ASSOCIATES

Court of Appeals for the Second Circuit, 1988.
840 F.2d 1096.

MINER, CIRCUIT JUDGE:

The United States Attorney General, on behalf of the United States ("the government"), commenced this action under Title VIII of the Civil Rights Act of 1968 ("Fair Housing Act" or "the Act") against defendants-appellants Starrett City Associates, Starrett City, Inc. and Delmar Management Company (collectively, "Starrett") in the United States District Court for the Eastern District of New York (Neaher, J.). The government maintained that Starrett's practices of renting apartments in its Brooklyn housing complex solely on the basis of applicants' race or national origin, and of making apartments unavailable to black and hispanic applicants that are then made available to white applicants, violate section 804(a), (b), (c) and (d) of the Act, 42 U.S.C. § 3604(a)(d) (1982).

The parties made cross-motions for summary judgment based on extensive documentary submissions. The district court granted summary judgment in favor of the government and permanently enjoined appellants from discriminating on the basis of race in the rental of apartments. Starrett appeals from this judgment.

BACKGROUND

Appellants constructed, own and operate "Starrett City," the largest housing development in the nation, consisting of 46 highrise buildings containing 5,881 apartments in Brooklyn, New York. The complex's rental office opened in December 1973. Starrett has made capital contributions of $19,091,000 to the project, the New York State Housing Finance Agency has made $362,720,000 in mortgage loans, and the U.S. Department of Housing and Urban Development subsidizes Starrett's monthly mortgage interest payments. The United Housing Foundation abandoned a project to build a development of cooperative apartments at the Starrett City site in 1971. Starrett proposed to construct rental units on the site on the condition that the New York City Board of Estimate approve a transfer to Starrett of the city real estate tax abatement granted to the original project. The transfer created "substantial community opposition" because "the neighborhood surrounding the project and past experience with subsidized housing" created fear that "the conversion to rental apartments would result in Starrett City's becoming an overwhelmingly minority development." *United States v. Starrett City Assocs.*, 660 F.Supp. 668, 670 (E.D.N.Y.1987). The transfer was approved, however, "upon the assurance of Starrett City's developer that it was intended to create a racially integrated community." *Id.*

Starrett has sought to maintain a racial distribution by apartment of 64% white, 22% black and 8% hispanic at Starrett City. [ ] Starrett claims that these racial quotas are necessary to prevent the loss of white tenants, which would transform Starrett City into a predominantly minority complex. Starrett points to the difficulty it has had in attracting an integrated applicant pool from the time Starrett City opened, despite extensive advertising and promotional efforts. Because of these purported difficulties, Starrett adopted a tenanting procedure to promote and maintain the desired racial balance. This procedure has resulted in relatively stable percentages of whites and minorities living at Starrett City between 1975 and the present. [   ]

The tenanting procedure requires completion of a preliminary information card stating, *inter alia,* the applicant's race or national origin, family composition, income and employment. The rental office at Starrett City receives and reviews these applications. Those that are found preliminarily eligible, based on family composition, income, employment and size of apartment sought, are placed in "the active file," in which separate records by race are maintained for apartment sizes and income levels. Applicants are told in an acknowledgement letter that no apartments are presently available, but that their applications have been placed in the active file and that they will be notified when a unit becomes available for them. When an apartment becomes available, applicants are selected from the active file for final processing, creating a processed applicant pool. As vacancies arise, applicants of a race or national origin similar to that of the departing tenants are selected from the pool and offered apartments.

In December 1979, a group of black applicants brought an action against Starrett in the United States District Court for the Eastern District of New York. The district court certified the plaintiff class in June 1983. [   ] Plaintiffs alleged that Starrett's tenanting procedures violated federal and state law by discriminating against them on the basis of race. The parties stipulated to a settlement in May 1984, and a consent decree was entered subsequently. [   ] The decree provided that Starrett would, depending on apartment availability, make an additional 35 units available each year for a five-year period to black and minority applicants. [   ]

The government commenced the present action against Starrett in June 1984, "to place before the [c]ourt the issue joined but left expressly unresolved" in the * * * consent decree: the "legality of defendants' policy and practice of limiting the number of apartments available to minorities in order to maintain a prescribed degree of racial balance." *United States v. Starrett City Assocs.,* 605 F.Supp. 262, 263 (E.D.N.Y.1985). The complaint alleged that Starrett, through its tenanting policies, discriminated in violation of the Fair Housing Act. Specifically, the government maintained that Starrett violated the Act by making apartments unavailable to blacks solely because of race, 42 U.S.C. § 3604(a); by forcing black applicants to wait significantly longer for apartments than whites solely because of race, *id.* § 3604(b); by enforcing a policy that prefers white applicants while limiting the numbers of minority applicants accepted, *id.* § 3604(c); and by representing in an acknowledgement letter that no apartments are available for rental when in fact units are available, *id.* § 3604(d). Because the government had refused to intervene in the [first] suit, defendants moved to dismiss this suit as barred under the judicial estoppel doctrine. On April 2, 1985, that motion was denied. [   ]

Following a period for taking discovery, the government moved for summary judgment on January 30, 1986. Defendants made a cross-motion for summary judgment on May 5, 1986. Extensive documentary submissions were made, and arguments on the motion were heard on August 26, 1986.

Starrett maintained that the tenanting procedures "were adopted at the behest of the [s]tate solely to achieve and maintain integration and were not motivated by racial animus." 660 F.Supp. at 673. To support their position, appellants submitted the written testimony of three housing experts. They described the "white flight" and "tipping" phenomena, in which white residents migrate out of a community as the community becomes poor and the minority population increases, resulting in the transition to a predominantly minority community. [ ] Acknowledging that " 'the tipping point for a particular housing development, depending as it does on numerous factors and the uncertainties of human behavior, is difficult to predict with precision,' " one expert stated that the point at which tipping occurs has been estimated at from 1% to 60% minority population, but that the consensus ranged between 10% and 20%. [ ] Another expert, who had prepared a report in 1980 on integration at Starrett City for the New York State Division of Housing and Community Renewal, estimated the complex's tipping point at approximately 40% black on a population basis. [ ] A third expert, who had been involved in integrated housing ventures since the 1950's, found that a 2:1 white-minority ratio produced successful integration. [ ]

The court, however, accepted the government's contention that Starrett's practices of making apartments unavailable for blacks, while reserving them for whites, and conditioning rental to minorities based on a "tipping formula" derived only from race or national origin are clear violations of the Fair Housing Act. The district court found that apartment opportunities for blacks and hispanics were far fewer "than would be expected if race and national origin were not taken into account," while opportunities for whites were substantially greater than what their application rates projected. [ ] Minority applicants waited up to ten times longer than the average white applicant before they were offered an apartment. [ ] Starrett City's active file was 21.9% white in October 1985, but whites occupied 64.7% of the apartments in January 1984. Although the file was 53.7% black and 18% hispanic in October 1985, blacks and hispanics, respectively, occupied only 20.8% and 7.9% of the apartments as of January 1984. [ ] Appellants did not dispute this. Further, the court found that appellants' tipping argument was undercut by the "wide elasticity of that standard" and the lack of difficulty they had in increasing their black quota from 21% to 35% "when it became necessary to avoid litigating the private *Arthur* lawsuit which threatened their unlawful rental practices." [ ] The court also found that Starrett violated the Act by making untrue representations of apartment unavailability to qualified minority applicants in order to reserve units for whites. [ ] Finally, the court rejected Starrett's claim that the duty imposed upon government to achieve housing integration justified its actions, stating that "[d]efendants cannot arrogate to themselves the powers" of a public housing authority. [   ]

The court concluded that Starrett's obligation was "simply and solely to comply with the Fair Housing Act" by treating "black and other minority applicants * * * on the same basis as whites in seeking available housing at Starrett City." [   ] The court noted that Starrett did not dispute any of the operative facts alleged to show violations of the Fair Housing Act. [   ] Accordingly, Judge Neaher granted summary judgment for the government, enjoining Starrett from discriminating against applicants on the basis of race and "[r]equiring [them] to adopt written, objective, uniform, nondiscriminatory tenant selection standards and procedures" subject to the court's approval. [   ] The court retained jurisdiction over the parties for three years. [   ]

On appeal, Starrett presses arguments similar to those it made before the district court. We affirm the district court's judgment.

DISCUSSION

Title VIII of the Civil Rights Act of 1968 ("Fair Housing Act" or "the Act"), 42 U.S.C. §§ 3601–3631 (1982), was enacted pursuant to Congress' thirteenth amendment powers, [   ] "to provide, within constitutional limitations, for fair housing throughout the United States." 42 U.S.C. § 3601. Section 3604 of the statute prohibits discrimination because of race, color or national origin in the sale or rental of housing by, *inter alia:* (1) refusing to rent or make available any dwelling, *id.* § 3604(a); (2) offering discriminatory "terms, conditions or privileges" of rental, *id.* § 3604(b); (3) making, printing or publishing "any notice, statement, or advertisement * * * that indicates any preference, limitation, or discrimination based on race, color * * * or national origin," *id.* § 3604(c); and (4) representing to any person "that any dwelling is not available for * * * rental when such dwelling is in fact so available," *id.* § 3604(d).

Housing practices unlawful under Title VIII include not only those motivated by a racially discriminatory purpose, but also those that disproportionately affect minorities. [   ] Section 3604 "is designed to ensure that no one is denied the right to live where they choose for discriminatory reasons." *See Southend Neighborhood Improv. Ass'n v. County of St. Clair,* 743 F.2d 1207, 1210 (7th Cir.1984). Although "not every denial, especially a temporary denial, of low-income public housing has a discriminatory impact on racial minorities" in violation of Title VIII, *see Arthur v. City of Toledo,* 782 F.2d 565, 577 (6th Cir.1986), an action leading to discriminatory effects on the availability of housing violates the Act. [   ]

Starrett's allocation of public housing facilities on the basis of racial quotas, by denying an applicant access to a unit otherwise available solely because of race, produces a "discriminatory effect * * * [that] could hardly be clearer," *Burney v. Housing Auth.,* 551 F.Supp.

746, 770 (W.D.Pa.1982). Appellants do not contend that the plain language of section 3604 does not proscribe their practices. Rather, they claim to be "clothed with governmental authority" and thus obligated, under *Otero v. New York City Housing Auth.*, 484 F.2d 1122 (2d Cir.1973), to effectuate the purpose of the Fair Housing Act by affirmatively promoting integration and preventing "the reghettoization of a model integrated community." We need not decide whether Starrett is a state actor, however. Even if Starrett were a state actor with such a duty, the racial quotas and related practices employed at Starrett City to maintain integration violate the antidiscrimination provisions of the Act.

Both Starrett and the government cite to the legislative history of the Fair Housing Act in support of their positions. This history consists solely of statements from the floor of Congress. [ ] These statements reveal "that at the time that Title VIII was enacted, Congress believed that strict adherence to the anti-discrimination provisions of the [A]ct" would eliminate "racially discriminatory housing practices [and] ultimately would result in residential integration." [ ] Thus, Congress saw the antidiscrimination policy as the means to effect the antisegregation-integration policy. [ ] While quotas promote Title VIII's integration policy, they contravene its antidiscrimination policy, bringing the dual goals of the Act into conflict. The legislative history provides no further guidance for resolving this conflict.

We therefore look to analogous provisions of federal law enacted to prohibit segregation and discrimination as guides in determining to what extent racial criteria may be used to maintain integration. Both the thirteenth amendment, pursuant to which Title VIII was enacted, and the fourteenth amendment empower Congress to act in eradicating racial discrimination, [ ] and both the fourteenth amendment and Title VIII are informed by the congressional goal of eradicating racial discrimination through the principle of antidiscrimination. [ ] Further, the parallel between the antidiscrimination objectives of Title VIII and Title VII of the Civil Rights Act of 1964, 42 U.S.C. §§ 2000e–2000e–17 (1982), has been recognized. [ ] Thus, the Supreme Court's analysis of what constitutes permissible race-conscious affirmative action under provisions of federal law with goals similar to those of Title VIII provides a framework for examining the affirmative use of racial quotas under the Fair Housing Act.

Although any racial classification is presumptively discriminatory, [ ] a race-conscious affirmative action plan does not necessarily violate federal constitutional or statutory provisions. [ ] However, a race-conscious plan cannot be "ageless in [its] reach into the past, and timeless in [its] ability to affect the future." [ ] A plan employing racial distinctions must be temporary in nature with a defined goal as its termination point. [ ] Moreover, we observe that societal discrimination alone seems "insufficient and over expansive" as the basis for adopting so-called "benign" practices with discriminatory effects "that work against innocent people," [ ] in the drastic and burdensome way that rigid racial quotas do. Furthermore, the use of quotas generally should be based on some history of racial discrimination, [ ] or imbalance, [ ] within the entity seeking to employ them. Finally, measures designed to increase or ensure minority participation, such as "access" quotas, [ ] have generally been upheld. [ ] However, programs designed to maintain integration by limiting minority participation, such as ceiling quotas, [ ] are of doubtful validity because they " 'single [ ] out those least well represented in the political process to bear the brunt of a benign program.' " [ ]

Starrett's use of ceiling quotas to maintain integration at Starrett City lacks each of these characteristics. First, Starrett City's practices have only the goal of integration maintenance. The quotas already have been in effect for ten years. Appellants predict that their race-conscious tenanting practices must continue for at least fifteen more years, but fail to explain adequately how that approximation was reached. In any event, these practices are far from temporary. Since the goal of integration maintenance is purportedly threatened by the potential for "white flight" on a continuing basis, no definite termination date for Starrett's quotas is perceivable. Second, appellants do not assert, and there is no evidence to show, the existence of prior racial discrimination or discriminatory imbalance adversely affecting whites within Starrett City or appellants' other complexes. On the contrary, Starrett City was initiated as an integrated complex, and Starrett's avowed purpose for employing race-based tenanting practices is to maintain that initial integration. Finally, Starrett's quotas do not provide minorities with access to Starrett City, but rather act as a ceiling to their access. Thus, the impact of appellants' practices falls squarely on minorities, for whom Title VIII was intended to open up housing opportunities. Starrett claims that its use of quotas serves to keep the numbers of minorities entering Starrett City low enough to avoid setting off a wave of "white flight." Although the "white flight" phenomenon may be a factor "take[n] into account in the integration equation," *Parent Ass'n of Andrew Jackson High School v. Ambach*, 598 F.2d 705, 720 (2d Cir.1979), it cannot serve to justify attempts to maintain integration at Starrett City through inflexible racial quotas that are neither temporary in nature nor used to remedy past racial discrimination or imbalance within the complex.

Appellants' reliance on *Otero* is misplaced. In *Otero* the New York City Housing Authority ("NYCHA") relocated over 1800 families in the Lower East Side of Manhattan to make way for the construction of new apartment buildings. [ ] Pursuant to its regulations, NYCHA offered the former site occupants first priority of returning to any housing built within the urban renewal area. [ ] However, because the response by the largely minority former site residents seeking to return was nearly seven times greater than expected, NYCHA declined to follow its regulation in order to avoid creating a "pocket ghetto" that would "tip" an integrated community towards a predominantly minority community. [   ] It instead rented up half of these apartments to non-former site occupants, 88% of whom were white. [   ]

In a suit brought by former site occupants who were denied the promised priority, the district court held as a matter of law that "affirmative action to achieve racially balanced communities was not permitted where it would result in depriving minority groups" of public housing, and thus granted summary judgment in favor of plaintiffs. [   ] This court reversed the grant of summary judgment, stating that public housing authorities had a federal constitutional and statutory duty "to fulfill, as much as possible, the goal of open, integrated residential housing patterns and to prevent the increase of segregation, in ghettos," but we recognized that "the effect in some instances might be to prevent some members of a racial minority from residing in publicly assisted housing in a particular location." [   ]

Otero does not, however, control in this case. The challenge in *Otero* did not involve procedures for the long-term maintenance of specified levels of integration, but rather, the rental of 171 of 360 new apartments to non-former site occupants, predominantly white, although former site residents, largely minority, sought those apartments and were entitled to priority under NYCHA's own regulation. The *Otero* court did not delineate the statutory or constitutional limits on permissible means of integration, but held only that NYCHA's rent-up practice could not be declared invalid as a matter of law under those limits. In fact, the court in *Otero* observed that the use of race-conscious tenanting practices might allow landlords "to engage in social engineering, subject only to general undefined control through judicial supervision" and could "constitute a form of unlawful racial discrimination." [   ]

It is particularly important to note that the NYCHA action challenged in *Otero* only applied to a single event—the initial rent up of the new complexes—and determined tenancy in the first instance alone. NYCHA sought only to prevent the immediate creation of a "pocket ghetto" in the Lower East Side, which had experienced a steady loss of white population, that would tip the precarious racial balance there, resulting in increased white flight and inevitable "non-white ghettoization of the community." [   ] Further, the suspension of NYCHA's regulation did not operate as a strict racial quota, because the former site residents entitled to a rental priority were approximately 40% white. [   ] As a one-time measure in response to the special circumstances of the Lower East Side in the early 1970's, the action challenged in *Otero* had an impact on non-whites as a group far less burdensome or discriminatory than Starrett City's continuing practices.

CONCLUSION

We do not intend to imply that race is always an inappropriate consideration under Title VIII in efforts to promote integrated housing. We hold only that Title VIII does not allow appellants to use rigid racial quotas of indefinite duration to maintain a fixed level of integration at Starrett City by restricting minority access to scarce and desirable rental accommodations otherwise available to them. We therefore affirm the judgment of the district court.

JON O. NEWMAN, Circuit Judge, dissenting.

[omitted]

Notes and Questions

1. *Starrett City* considered the problem of "integration maintenance," the process of maintaining integration once it has been achieved. What would you tell a landlord client can be done to prevent loss of an integrated environment through "tipping" toward a predominant racial group? What about a special marketing plan, leaflets, advertisements in targeted newspapers, etc., to attract one racial group without deterring others? See South Suburban Housing Center v. Greater South Suburban Board of Realtors, 935 F.2d 868 (7th Cir.1991) (affirmative marketing plan to foster integration without denying equal housing opportunities to all persons upheld). Is the court's distinction in *Starrett City* between the permissible use of "race-conscious tenanting practices" in the "single event" of initially renting new units from the impermissible use of such techniques to maintain an integrated status persuasive? Should admission standards be "race blind"?

2. The selection of sites for governmentally-assisted housing developments has been a source of conflict in a number of communities. Federal public housing units, constructed under a program that began in the 1930s and expanded in the 20 years following World War II, along with federally-subsidized private apartment developments constructed in the 1960s and 1970s, often have been located in racially-segregated neighborhoods. Protracted litigation has ensued in an attempt to dismantle segregated public housing and to provide opportunities for persons in subsidized housing to live in an integrated neighborhood. Notable success has been achieved in establishing that site selection procedures which cater to segregated housing patterns violate constitutional protections against racial discrimination if intentional and violate the Fair Housing Act if such practices have the effect of racial discrimination. See, e.g., Hills v. Gautreaux, 425 U.S. 284, 96 S.Ct. 1538, 47 L.Ed.2d 792 (1976) (intentional discrimination in the selection of sites for public housing in Chicago); Huntington Branch, N.A.A.C.P. v. Town of Huntington, 844 F.2d 926, (2d Cir.1988), review declined in part, judgment affirmed 488 U.S. 15, 109 S.Ct. 276, 102 L.Ed.2d 180 (1988) (refusal to rezone to permit construction of a subsidized multi-family development in a white neighborhood violated Fair Housing Act); United States v. Yonkers, 837 F.2d 1181 (2d Cir.1987) (city and board of education held liable for intentionally maintaining segregated housing and public schools through "pattern and practice of confining subsidized housing" to southwest portion of city and "selective adherence to a neighborhood-school policy in light of the City's segregative housing practices"); Young v. Pierce, 628 F.Supp. 1037 (E.D.Tex.1985); 685 F.Supp. (E.D.Tex. 1988) (maintenance of racially segregated public and subsidized housing in 36 East Texas counties enjoined).

3. However, fashioning an appropriate remedy has proved to be extraordinarily difficult, primarily because of tension between the "flexible but not unlimited power" of federal courts to remedy constitutional violations, United States v. Yonkers, 837 F.2d at 1235, and the separation of powers principle which allocates to the legislative branch the power and responsibility for spending public funds and exercising public regulatory authority.   For discussion of the remedy question, see Spallone v. United States, 493 U.S. 265, 110 S.Ct. 625, 107 L.Ed.2d 644 (1990) (enforcement of order to build subsidized housing outside southwest area of Yonkers); Jenkins v. Missouri, 639 F.Supp 19 (W.D.Mo.1985), aff'd in pertinent part, 807 F.2d 657 (8th Cir.1986), cert. denied, 484 U.S. 816, 108 S.Ct. 70, 98 L.Ed.2d 34 (1987) (order enjoining property tax rollback and requiring submittal of tax levy increase to voters to implement school desegregation plan); Low–Income Black Children in White Suburban Schools (1986) and Economic and Social Impacts of Housing Integration (1990), Center for Urban Affairs and Policy Research, Northwestern Univ., Evanston, Ill. (evaluating the success of a consent decree following *Gautreaux* that has enabled over 4,000 households to obtain certificates entitling them to federal subsidies for private rental housing in non-racially impacted neighborhoods of Chicago and surrounding suburbs); Polikoff, Gautreaux and Institutional Litigation, 64 Chicago–Kent L.Rev. 451 (1988).   See also Roisman, Establishing a Right to Housing, 25 Clearinghouse Review 203, 225–226 (1991) ("People who work full-time should have access to decent, affordable housing.   The old, the blind, the disabled, needy dependent children—all should be assured a decent place to live.")

V. TENANTS' RIGHTS/LANDLORDS' RESPONSIBILITIES

A. RIGHT TO POSSESSION

ADRIAN v. RABINOWITZ

Supreme Court of New Jersey, 1936.
116 N.J.L. 586, 186 A. 29.

HEHER, JUSTICE.

On April 30, 1934, defendant, by an indenture, leased to plaintiff certain store premises in the main business district of the city of Paterson for the term of six months, commencing on June 15th next ensuing, at a stipulated monthly rent payable in advance; and the gravamen of this action is the breach of an obligation thereby imposed upon the lessor, as is said, to deliver to the lessee possession of the demised premises at the beginning of the term so prescribed. The state of demand is in two counts: The first seems to be grounded upon an asserted implied duty "to give and deliver possession" of the demised premises on the first day of the term; and the second, upon what plaintiff conceives to be an express covenant to put the lessee in possession on that day.

The lessee stipulated to devote the premises to the conduct of the shoe business; and he was given an option to renew the lease for an additional term of six months. Rent for the first month of the term was paid upon delivery of the lease, and the payment was acknowledged therein.

At the time of the execution of the contract, the premises were tenanted by another, who failed to respond to the landlord's notice to vacate on June 15. The landlord deemed himself obliged to institute dispossess proceedings, which terminated in a judgment of removal. This judgment was executed on July 7, 1934, and plaintiff took possession two days later.

The district court judge, sitting without a jury, found for the plaintiff on the basic issue, and measured the damages at $500, "the loss sustained by plaintiff in the resale of the seasonable merchandise." He also ruled that plaintiff was not liable for rent for the portion of the term he was deprived of possession, and, making allowance for this, he awarded $25 to defendant on her set-off for rent due for the month beginning July 15, 1934.

It is apparent that the tenant in possession when the lease was executed wrongfully held over after the termination of the tenancy; and the primary question, raised by motions to nonsuit and direct a verdict in defendant's favor, is whether, expressly or by implication, the contract imposed upon the lessor the duty of putting the lessee in actual and exclusive possession of the demised premises at the beginning of the term.

It seems to be the rule in this state that a covenant for quiet enjoyment, as one of the covenants of title, is not to be implied from the mere relation of landlord and tenant, even when that relation springs from a deed. [ ] But here the lessor expressly covenanted that the lessee, "on paying the said monthly rent, and performing the covenants aforesaid, shall and may peaceably and quietly have, hold and enjoy the said demised premises for the term aforesaid." And it has been held elsewhere that a covenant for quiet enjoyment, similarly phrased, imposed upon the lessor the obligation to deliver possession of the premises on the first day of the term. [ ] Yet a covenant for quiet enjoyment is generally interpreted to secure the lessee against the acts or hindrances of the lessor, and persons deriving their right or title through him, or from paramount title, and does not protect the lessee from interference by strangers with his possession. [ ] It remains to consider whether the lessor, in the absence of an express undertaking to that effect, is under a duty to put the lessee in actual as well as legal possession of the demised premises at the commencement of the term. We are of the view that he is. There seems to be no dissent from the doctrine that the lessor impliedly covenants that the lessee shall have the legal right of possession at the beginning of the term. But there is a contrariety of view as to whether this implied obligation extends as well to actual possession, especially where, as here, the prior tenant wrongfully holds over. [ ]

In some of our American jurisdictions, the rule obtains that, while the lessee is entitled to have the legal right of possession, there is no implied covenant to protect the lessee against wrongful acts of strangers. [ ] The English rule is that, where the term is to commence in futuro, there is an implied undertaking by the lessor that the premises shall be open to the lessee's entry, legally and actually, when the time for possession under the lease arrives. This rule has the support of respectable American authority. [ ] And in an early case in this state, where the premises, while tenanted, were let for a term to begin on a fixed day in the future, and the lessor, in an action of covenant brought by the lessee for failure to deliver possession on the first day of the term, or any time thereafter, pleaded inability to deliver possession because of the wrongful holding over by the tenant, this court construed the stipulation for possession at the commencement of the term "as an express covenant to let the premises, and give possession" on the first day of the term, and held that the lessor, having failed in the performance of the duty thus undertaken, was liable to the action. [ ]

The English rule, so-called, is on principle much the better one. It has the virtue, ordinarily, of effectuating the common intention of the parties—to give actual and exclusive possession of the premises to the lessee on the day fixed for the commencement of the term. This is what the lessee generally bargains for; and it is the thing the lessor undertakes to give. Such being the case, there is no warrant for placing upon the lessee, without express stipulation to that effect, the burden of ousting, at his own expense, the tenant wrongfully holding over, or the trespasser in possession of the premises without color of right at the commencement of the term; and thus to impose upon him who is not in possession of the evidence the burden of establishing the respective rights and duties of the lessor and the possessor of the lands inter se, as well as the consequences of the delay incident to the adjudication of the controversy, and the obligation to pay rent during that period. As was said by Baron Vaughan in Coe v. Clay, supra: "He who lets agrees to give possession, and not merely to give a chance of a law suit." This doctrine is grounded in reason and logic. The underlying theory is that the parties contemplated, as an essential term of their undertaking, without which the lease would not have been made, that the lessor should, at the beginning of the term, have the premises open to the entry and exclusive possession of the lessee. This is certainly the normal course of dealing, and, in the absence of stipulation to the contrary, is to be regarded as the parties' understanding of the lessor's covenant to deliver possession of the demised premises at the time prescribed for the commencement of the term.

There is an obvious distinction, which seems to have been overlooked in some of the cases rejecting the English doctrine [ ] between a wrongful possession at the time fixed for the commencement of the term and the acts of trespassers who intrude after the lessee has been given the possession provided by the contract. [ ]

It is worthy of note that here the lessor, apparently conscious of a contractual obligation in the premises, initiated and prosecuted to a conclusion the proceedings requisite for dispossession of the hold-over tenant. She interpreted the contract as imposing the duty.

Therefore, the motions for a nonsuit and a direction of a verdict in defendant's favor on the ground that there was no evidence of a breach of defendant's undertaking to deliver possession of the demised premises at the stipulated time were rightly denied. * * *

Notes and Questions

1. The Restatement has adopted the English rule of actual possession over the American rule of legal possession, in the absence of a valid lease provision to the contrary, Restatement (Second) of Property, § 6.2, Reporter's Note 2 (1976).

2. Does it surprise you that the American rule has been the majority rule in the United States? The leading case for the American rule is Hannan v. Dusch, 154 Va. 356, 153 S.E. 824 (1930). Clearly, delivery of the right to possession will give the new tenant a host of legal and equitable remedies that can be asserted against a person wrongfully in possession. Who might be said to have a greater incentive to use the available remedies, the landlord (English rule) or the successor tenant (American rule)?

3. Examine the sample leases, supra. Which rule do those leases adopt?

B. TRANSFER OF LEASEHOLD INTERESTS

DAVIS v. VIDAL

Supreme Court of Texas, 1912.
105 Tex. 444, 151 S.W. 290.

DIBRELL, J. This is a suit by Antoinette W. Davis brought in the district court of El Paso county against Lewis Vidal, to recover the sum of $1,200 alleged to be due her by Vidal for the use of certain premises situated in the city of El Paso, of which Vidal was in possession as the assignee of the Dallas Brewery. The sole question of law involved in the case is whether a certain instrument of writing executed by the Dallas Brewery to the defendant, Vidal, on October 1, 1907, was an assignment of its lease from the plaintiff, Antoinette W. Davis, of date April 26, 1907, or a subletting of the premises in question. If the instrument referred to was an assignment of the lease, then plaintiff was authorized to recover of the defendant the rent due on her contract of lease with the Dallas Brewery, by virtue of the privity of estate and contract that subsists between them; but if, on the other hand, the instrument was a subletting of the premises to Vidal by the original lessee, the plaintiff could not recover against defendant as a subtenant, since in such case there is neither privity of estate nor of contract between the original lessor and the undertenant. [ ]

The instrument in question was construed by the trial court and the Court of Civil Appeals to be a subletting of the premises by the Dallas Brewery to the defendant, Vidal, and in accordance with that holding judgment was rendered for the defendant. Upon appeal of the case to the Court of Civil Appeals the judgment of the lower court was affirmed.

That the question involved and decided may be fully understood we embody the instrument executed by the Dallas Brewery to Vidal: "Know all men by these presents, that, whereas, on the 26th day of April, 1907, Mrs. Antoinette W. Davis, acting by her agents, A.P. Coles & Brother, did lease to the Dallas Brewery the following parcel of land with the tenements thereon in the city of El Paso, county of El Paso, state of Texas, to wit, being the one-story and adobe composition roof building situated on lot 1 and south 24 feet of lot 2, block 135, Campbell's addition to the city of El Paso, Texas, known as Nos. 415–419 Utah street, same being leased from the 1st day of May, 1907, for three years, to be ended and completed on the 30th of April, 1910 and in consideration of same lease the said Dallas Brewery yielding and paying therefor during said term the sum of $100.00 per month, payable in advance on the first day of each and every month; and, whereas, said lease provides that said premises or any part thereof may be sublet by said Dallas Brewery without the consent of said Mrs. Davis; and, whereas, it is desired to transfer, assign and sublet all of said above premises so leased by the said Mrs. Davis to said Dallas Brewery to Lou Vidal: Now, therefore, in consideration of the premises and the sum of $300.00 to it in hand paid, the receipt whereof is hereby acknowledged, said the Dallas Brewery does hereby sublet, assign and transfer the said above premises and does assign and transfer the above said lease, to the said Lou Vidal, and in consideration therefor the said Vidal does well and truly agree and promise to pay the rents in said lease agreed to be paid, to wit, the sum of one hundred ($100.00) dollars per month, each and every month hereafter ensuing, beginning on the first day of November, 1907, in advance on the first day of each month so hereinafter ensuing. And the said Vidal does agree and bind himself and obligates himself to in all respects indemnify, save and hold harmless said Dallas Brewery by reason of any of the terms or conditions in said lease contained, including the payment of rent therein provided to be paid, and should the said Dallas Brewery elect to pay any rent therein provided, or be called upon to pay any rent therein provided, upon same being done the said Vidal agrees to pay the same with interest at the rate of ten per cent. per annum; or if the said Vidal neglects or fails to pay said rent promptly, as in said lease provided to be paid, then and in such event the Dallas Brewery can and may at its option declare this transfer null and void, and thereupon oust the said Vidal, and assume possession thereof, and this without notice of any character or kind to the said Vidal; and the failure to pay any rent as in said lease provided to be paid, at the election of the said Dallas

Brewery, can and may authorize it without notice to re-enter and repossess said premises."

In construing the effect of the foregoing instrument it is not conclusive as to its form, since it may be in form an assignment and yet be in effect a sublease. The question is one of law to be determined from the estate granted by the instrument. As a general proposition, if the instrument executed by the lessee conveys the entire term and thereby parts with all of the reversionary estate in the property, the instrument will be construed to be an assignment; but, if there remains a reversionary interest in the estate conveyed, the instrument is a sublease. The relation of landlord and tenant is created alone by the existence of a reversionary interest in the landlord. Out of this fact arises the distinction made between assignments and subtenancies. To state the test slightly different from that already stated, if the instrument is of such character by its terms and conditions that a reversionary interest by construction remains in the grantor of the property, he becomes the landlord and the grantee the tenant. The tenant who parts with the entire term embraced in his lease becomes an assignor of the lease, and the instrument is an assignment; but where the tenant by the terms, conditions, or limitations in the instrument does not part with the entire term granted him by his landlord, so that there remains in him a reversionary interest, the transaction is a subletting and not an assignment. [ ] It will be observed that, in stating the general rule as to what constitutes an assignment of a lease as distinguished from a sublease, the requirement is that the instrument must convey the whole *term*, leaving no interest or reversionary interest in the grantor.

By the word "term," as used in the statement of this principle of law, is meant something more than the mere *time* for which the lease is given, and the instrument must convey not only the entire time for which the lease runs, but the entire estate or interest conveyed by the lease. Mr. Blackstone in his Commentaries (book 2, p. 144), in commenting on the significance of the word "term," when used in leases, says: "Thus the word, *term*, does not merely signify the time specified in the lease, but the estate also and interest that passes by the lease; and therefore the *term* may expire, during the continuance of the *time*, as by surrender, forfeiture and the like." The meaning of the word "term," as defined by Blackstone above, was adopted by the Supreme Court of Massachusetts in the case of Dunlap v. Bullard, 131 Mass. 162, and by a number of text-writers on the subject of assignments and subleases.

Mr. Blackstone, in his Commentaries (book 2, p. 327), defines an assignment to be, and draws the distinction between an assignment and a lease of property, as follows: "An *assignment* is properly a transfer, or making over to another, of the right one has in *any* estate; but it is usually applied to an estate for life or years. And it differs from lease only in this: That by a lease one grants an interest less than his own, reserving to himself a reversion; in an assignment he parts with the whole property, and the assignee stands to all intents and purposes in the place of the assignor." If we may accept this definition from so eminent authority upon the common law, which definition and distinction so concisely stated and drawn seems to have met the approval of this court in other cases, and apply it to the facts of the case at bar, the conclusion must be reached that the instrument executed by the Dallas Brewery to Vidal was a sublease and not an assignment. The instrument speaks for itself. By its terms the whole estate granted to the Dallas Brewery by its lease from Mrs. Davis is not conveyed, for the reason there is reserved to the Dallas Brewery a contingent reversionary interest in the estate, to be resumed summarily upon the failure of Vidal to pay rent. More than this, and of equal significance, by the terms of the instrument the Dallas Brewery reserved the right to pay the rent to the original lessor, and thereby the right was reserved to forestall Mrs. Davis, upon the failure of Vidal to pay the rent, from exercising the right to re-enter and possess the premises. That right was reserved to the Dallas Brewery and gave it the power to control the estate in the premises upon failure by Vidal to pay it the rent.

If the instrument was an assignment of the lease, the Dallas Brewery must of necessity have parted with all its estate and interest in said premises, and could therefore exercise no right in or control over the premises. If the instrument was an assignment of the lease, the legal effect was to substitute Vidal in lieu of the Dallas Brewery. But this was not the case. By the terms of the instrument the Dallas Brewery retained the control of the possession of the leased premises, thereby denying the legal effect of an assignment, which would have given Mrs. Davis the right of re-entry and possession of the property upon Vidal's failure to pay the rent.

We are aware that there is great conflict of authority upon this subject, and that it would be futile to attempt to reconcile such conflict. Many of the authors of the textbooks on the subject of the assignment of leases and subletting under leases, and the decisions of a great many of the states in this Union, hold that the fact that the right of re-entry is reserved in the assignment to the assignor upon failure of the assignee to pay rent does not change the instrument of assignment from such to a sublease. The holding of such authors and decisions is based upon the theory that the right of re-entry is not an estate or interest in land, nor the reservation of a reversion. They hold that the reservation of the right of re-entry upon failure to pay rent is neither an estate nor interest in land, but a mere chose in action, and when exercised the grantor comes into possession of the premises through the breach of the condition and not by reverter.

Those authorities which hold the contrary doctrine base their ruling upon the idea that the reservation in the instrument of the right of re-entry is a contingent reversionary interest in the premises resulting from the conveyance of an estate upon a condition subsequent where there has been an infraction of such condition. * * *

We are not able to discern why there may not be a contingent reversionary estate or interest in land, as well as any other contingent estate or interest. It certainly cannot be contended upon sound principle that, because the right of re-entry and resumption of possession of land is contingent, it is thereby any the less an estate or interest in land. The very definition of a contingent estate as distinguished from a *vested* estate is that "*the right to its* enjoyment is to accrue on an event which is dubious and uncertain." 1 Washburn on Real Property, 38.

We think it deducible from respectable authority that where the tenant reserves in the instrument giving possession to his transferee the right of re-entry to the premises demised, upon failure to pay rent, he necessarily retains a part of or an interest in the demised estate which may come back to him upon the happening of a contingency.

The instrument under consideration does not convey the entire estate received by the Dallas Brewery by its lease from Mrs. Davis, but retains by the right of possible re-entry a contingent reversionary interest in the premises. That the interest retained is a contingent reversionary interest does not, it seems to us, change the rule by which an assignment may be distinguished from a sublease. If by any limitation or condition in the conveyance the entire term, which embraces the estate conveyed in the contract of lease as well as the length of time for which the tenancy is created, may by construction be said not to have passed from the original tenant, but that a contingent reversionary estate is retained in the premises the subject of the reversion, the instrument must be said to constitute a subletting and not an assignment.

The following test may be applied to determine whether the instrument in question is an assignment of the original lease, or a subletting of the premises: If it is an assignment, its legal effect must be a transfer of the right of possession of the property conveyed to Vidal and the creation of a privity of estate and contract between Mrs. Davis, the original lessor, and Vidal, to whom the possession was granted by the Dallas Brewery. This would be essential to constitute the instrument an assignment, and if it was an assignment Vidal obligated himself to pay the rent to Mrs. Davis, and the Dallas Brewery had no further connection with or interest in the transaction. But such a result can by no fair or reasonable construction of the language and provisions of the instrument be deduced therefrom. On the contrary, the Dallas Brewery reserved the privilege of paying the rent to its lessor, and upon nonpayment of rent by Vidal it reserved the right to declare the instrument forfeited and to repossess the premises without notice to or the consent of Vidal. There can be but one theory upon which the Dallas Brewery considered itself interested in seeing that the rent was promptly paid by Vidal, and that is that it desired to control the property in question, and therefore intended, and by the language and reservation in the instrument made, it a sublease.

We do not think the proposition tenable that by the express terms of the agreement between the Dallas Brewery and Vidal, or by implication, Vidal obligated himself to pay the rent to Mrs. Davis. The provision of the contract relied upon to establish the fact that Vidal obligated himself to pay the rent to the lessor in the original lease is the following, "and in consideration therefor the said Vidal does well and truly agree and promise to pay the rents in said lease agreed to be paid, to wit, the sum of one hundred dollars per month." Under the uniform rule of construction the latter part of the above sentence explains and qualifies the preceding part. The obligation of Vidal was to pay the rents in said lease agreed to be paid, that is, the sum of $100 per month, payable on the 1st day of each month in advance. There is nothing in the agreement from which it may be inferred that Vidal obligated himself to pay the rents directly to Mrs. Davis.

Having reached the conclusion that the instrument executed by the Dallas Brewery to Vidal conveying the premises in question was a sublease and not an assignment, * * * we conclude there exists no privity of estate or contract between the plaintiff, Mrs. Davis, and the defendant, Lewis Vidal, and that Mrs. Davis has no cause of action authorizing her to recover judgment against Vidal. * * *

The court is of opinion the judgments of the Court of Civil Appeals and of the trial court should be affirmed, and it is, accordingly, so ordered.

Notes and Questions

1. At common law, for a covenant respecting land, such as a promise to pay rent, to "run with the land" and thus be binding on successors in interest to that land, three requirements must generally be met: 1) the parties to the covenant must intend it to run; 2) the covenant must "touch and concern" the land; and 3) there must be privity of estate. Some formality in the making of the covenant may also be required, such as that the covenant be in writing.

In the landlord-tenant context, as *Davis v. Vidal* illustrates, there is privity of estate between landlord and assignee, but not between landlord and subtenant. The intention of the parties is supplied in most leases by a catch-all "successors and assigns" clause. The absence of a clause binding successors and assigns, however, will not necessarily mean that a covenant does not run with the land. Conversely, the presence of such a clause will not necessarily mean that a covenant does run with the land. This topic is discussed in greater detail in Chapter Six, The Law of Neighbors.

2. Why should it make a difference whether a transfer of a leasehold interest is an assignment or a sublease? While the original tenant can transfer her property interest, doesn't she remain liable to the landlord under her contract? Are landlords more likely to seek to have a transfer characterized as an assignment and successor tenants to have it deemed a sublease? What about the original tenant? Will she likely have a preference? Might the presence of income-producing property that is appreciating or depreciating in value affect the parties' viewpoints?

3. The intention of the parties, rather than the presence or absence of a reversionary interest, often is said to be the determining factor in deciding whether a transfer is an assignment or a sublease. See e.g., Ernst v. Conditt, 54 Tenn.App. 328, 390 S.W.2d 703 (1964). How does one determine the intention, if not by examining whether a reversionary interest is present?

4. Assume a five-year commercial lease with four consecutive options to renew for additional five-year periods. The lease contains covenants on the part of the tenant to pay rent, to return the property at the end of the lease term, and to repaint the interior of the leased premises annually.

(a) Tenant transfers her interest in the property "for the balance of my term." Who is responsible for the rent? Is the transferee responsible for repainting the interior? Can the transferee exercise an option to renew?

(b) Suppose instead that tenant transfers her interest for two years. Who is responsible for the rent? Is the transferee responsible for repainting the interior? Can the transferee exercise the option to renew? If the tenant defaults on the lease covenants, can the landlord evict the transferee?

(c) If you represented the landlord, the tenant, or the transferee, what interests would you expect your client to have and what clauses would you seek to add to the lease in anticipation of the situations described in (a) and (b) above. Consider the following observations by an experienced real estate lawyer.

> Preparing and defending a one-sided unfair lease form is a wasteful and foolish activity. It doesn't take long for a property owner or a tenant to fill in the blanks of a printed form or word processing document. On the other hand, the negotiators who have to read the document must spend many boring hours just to discover what everybody knows to begin with—the lease is one-sided, every provision is one-sided, and every sentence is one-sided. * * *

> The fact that a form is printed should be a signal that it is not fair. It is unrealistic to expect a real estate board or a corporation that leases many offices, stores or warehouses to go to the trouble of printing a lease form that is fair to landlords and tenants alike. Landlords and tenants who print their forms often do so to intimidate the other party with the notion that, if it's printed, it can't be changed. * * *

> * * * I've heard of more than one tenant who violently threw a lease proposed by his landlord in the garbage after checking out a few clauses. Most likely, a few chain store printed forms have found their way to landlords' garbage cans as well. The main advantage of drafting a fair lease is that you might get it signed.

Halper, Can You Find a Fair Lease? 14 Real Est.L.J. 99, 100–101, 121 (1985).

JULIAN v. CHRISTOPHER

Court of Appeals of Maryland, 1990.
320 Md. 1, 575 A.2d 735.

CHASANOW, JUDGE.

In 1961, this Court decided the case of *Jacobs v. Klawans*, 225 Md. 147, 169 A.2d 677 (1961) and held that when a lease contained a "silent consent" clause prohibiting a tenant from subletting or assigning without the consent of the landlord, landlords had a right to withhold their consent to a subletting or assignment even though the withholding of consent was arbitrary and unreasonable. * * *

In the instant case, the tenants, Douglas Julian and William J. Gilleland, III, purchased a tavern and restaurant business, as well as rented the business premises from landlord, Guy D. Christopher. The lease stated in clause ten that the premises, consisting of both the tavern and an upstairs apartment, could not be assigned or sublet "without the prior written consent of the landlord." Sometime after taking occupancy, the tenants requested the landlord's written permission to sublease the upstairs apartment. The landlord made no inquiry about the proposed sublessee, but wrote to the tenants that he would not agree to a sublease unless the tenants paid additional rent in the amount of $150.00 per month. When the tenants permitted the sublessee to move in, the landlord filed an action in the District Court of Maryland in Baltimore City requesting repossession of the building because the tenants had sublet the premises without his permission.

At the district court trial, the tenants testified that they specifically inquired about clause ten, and were told by the landlord that the clause was merely included to prevent them from subletting or assigning to "someone who would tear the apartment up." The district court judge refused to consider this testimony. He stated in his oral opinion that he would "remain within the four corners of the lease, and construe the document strictly," at least as it pertained to clause ten. Both the District Court and, on appeal, the Circuit Court for Baltimore City found in favor of the landlord. The circuit judge noted: "If you don't have the words that consent will not be unreasonably withheld, then the landlord can withhold his consent for a good reason, a bad reason, or no reason at all in the context of a commercial lease, which is what we're dealing with."

* * *

Traditional property rules favor the free and unrestricted right to alienate interests in property. Therefore, absent some specific restriction in the lease, a lessee has the right to freely alienate the leasehold interest by assignment or sublease without obtaining the permission of the lessor.[2] [   ]

Contractual restrictions on the alienability of leasehold interests are permitted. [   ] Consequently, landlords often insert clauses that restrict the lessee's common law right to freely assign or sublease.

Probably the most often used clause is a "silent consent" clause similar to the provision in the instant case, which provides that the

---

2. The common law right may have some limitations. For example, a lessee may not sublet or assign the premises to be used in a manner which is injurious to the property or inconsistent with the terms of the original lease.

premises may not be assigned or sublet without the written consent of the lessor.

In a "silent consent" clause requiring a landlord's consent to assign or sublease, there is no standard governing the landlord's decision. Courts must insert a standard. The choice is usually between 1) requiring the landlord to act reasonably when withholding consent, or 2) permitting the landlord to act arbitrarily and capriciously in withholding consent.

Public policy requires that when a lease gives the landlord the right to withhold consent to a sublease or assignment, the landlord should act reasonably, and the courts ought not to imply a right to act arbitrarily or capriciously. If a landlord is allowed to arbitrarily refuse consent to an assignment or sublease, for what in effect is no reason at all, that would virtually nullify any right to assign or sublease.

Because most people act reasonably most of the time, tenants might expect that a landlord's consent to a sublease or assignment would be governed by standards of reasonableness. Most tenants probably would not understand that a clause stating "this lease may not be assigned or sublet without the landlord's written consent" means the same as a clause stating "the tenant shall have no right to assign or sublease." Some landlords may have chosen the former wording rather than the latter because it vaguely implies, but does not grant to the tenant, the right to assign or sublet.

There are two public policy reasons why the law enunciated in *Klawans* should now be changed. The first is the public policy against restraints on alienation. The second is the public policy which implies a covenant of good faith and fair dealing in every contract.

Because there is a public policy against restraints on alienation, if a lease is silent on the subject, a tenant may freely sublease or assign. Restraints on alienation are permitted in leases, but are looked upon with disfavor and are strictly construed. [ ]

If a clause in a lease is susceptible of two interpretations, public policy favors the interpretation least restrictive of the right to alienate freely. Interpreting a "silent consent" clause so that it only prohibits subleases or assignments when a landlord's refusal to consent is reasonable, would be the interpretation imposing the least restraint on alienation and most in accord with public policy. * * * [T]his Court has recognized that in a lease, as well as in other contracts, "there exists an implied covenant that each of the parties thereto will act in good faith and deal fairly with the others." *Food Fair v. Blumberg,* 234 Md. 521, 534, 200 A.2d 166, 174 (1964). When the lease gives the landlord the right to exercise discretion, the discretion should be exercised in good faith, and in accordance with fair dealing; if the lease does not spell out any standard for withholding consent, then the implied covenant of good faith and fair dealing should imply a reasonableness standard.

We are cognizant of the value of the doctrine of *stare decisis,* and of the need for stability and certainty in the law. However, as we noted in *Harrison v. Mont. Co. Bd. of Educ.,* 295 Md. 442, 459, 456 A.2d 894, 903 (1983), a common law rule may be modified "where we find, in light of changed conditions or increased knowledge, that the rule has become unsound in the circumstances of modern life, a vestige of the past, no longer suitable to our people." The *Klawans* common law interpretation of the "silent consent" clause represents such a "vestige of the past," and should now be changed.

REASONABLENESS OF WITHHELD CONSENT

In the instant case, we need not expound at length on what constitutes a reasonable refusal to consent to an assignment or sublease. We should, however, point out that obvious examples of reasonable objections could include the financial irresponsibility or instability of the transferee, or the unsuitability or incompatibility of the intended use of the property by the transferee. We also need not expound at length on what would constitute an unreasonable refusal to consent to an assignment or sublease. If the reasons for withholding consent have nothing to do with the intended transferee or the transferee's use of the property, the motivation may be suspect. Where, as alleged in this case, the refusal to consent was solely for the purpose of securing a rent increase, such refusal would be unreasonable unless the new subtenant would necessitate additional expenditures by, or increased economic risk to, the landlord.

PROSPECTIVE EFFECT

The tenants ask us to retroactively overrule *Klawans,* and hold that in all leases with "silent consent" clauses, no matter when executed, consent to assign or sublease may not be unreasonably withheld by a landlord. We decline to do so. In the absence of evidence to the contrary, we should assume that parties executing leases when *Klawans* governed the interpretation of "silent consent" clauses were aware of *Klawans* and the implications drawn from the words they used. We should not, and do not, rewrite these contracts. * * *

For leases entered into after the mandate in this case, if the lease contains a "silent consent" clause providing that the tenant must obtain the landlord's consent in order to assign or sublease, such consent may not be unreasonably withheld. If the parties intend to preclude any transfer by assignment or sublease, they may do so by a freely negotiated provision in the lease. If the parties intend to limit the right to assign or sublease by giving the landlord the arbitrary right to refuse to consent, they may do so by a freely negotiated provision of the lease clearly spelling out this intent. For example, the clause might provide, "consent may be withheld in the sole and absolute subjective discretion of the lessor."

[Reversed and remanded—Eds.]

Notes and Questions

1. If a tenant sublets contrary to the transfer provision in her lease, yet continues to pay the monthly rent in a timely fashion, has the landlord

been harmed? What remedies are available to the landlord? If the landlord elects to terminate the lease under a provision authorizing that remedy, would the sublessee have any rights? Against whom?

2. Four graduate students leased a large house for one year, beginning August 1 and ending July 31 the next year. The lease, signed by all four students, contained no provisions limiting assignment or subletting. By December, two of the tenants had moved out because of a dispute among the tenants over parties in the house. During the semester break, one of the remaining tenants who lived in town assigned the lease to four law students, assuring the law students that the fourth tenant, who was in Florida for the holidays, was anxious to be relieved of the large rent payment. The third tenant moved out but left the fourth tenant's clothing and furniture. When school resumed for the second semester, the fourth tenant returned and was surprised to find the law students occupying the house. Who is entitled to possession of the house? Who is obligated to pay rent? See Dozier v. Wallace, 169 Ga.App. 126, 311 S.E.2d 839 (1983) (tenant in common has no power to lease the common property without the consent of the remaining co-tenants).

3. Consider the tenant's remedies if the landlord unreasonably withholds consent. If the landlord specifically covenants and agrees not to unreasonably withhold or delay consent, failure to act reasonably subjects the landlord to liability for the tenant's damages. However, if the landlord's agreement is merely a qualification or condition to tenant's covenant not to assign or sublet, then tenant's only remedy is declaratory judgment. ("T's right to sublet or assign shall be subject to its having first obtained the prior written consent of L, which may be withheld by L in the good faith exercise of its reasonable business judgement.") Suppose, after extensive negotiation, the landlord finally concedes the point of not unreasonably withholding consent, but asks in return for tenant's agreement not to sue for damages for breach. If tenant agrees, it has won the battle but may have lost the war. A declaratory judgment that the landlord unreasonably withheld consent may provide little solace to the tenant seeking to assign the leased premises because, during the litigation delay, the typical office or retail space assignee is likely to rent elsewhere.

4. Review the sample residential leases discussed, supra. What do they say about assignments and subleases?

5. Restatement (Second) of Property, § 15.2, Comment i (1976) adopts the "freely negotiated" standard for determining the validity of clauses giving landlords the absolute right to withhold consent. What is meant by a "freely negotiated" transfer provision? As tenant, what would you seek? As landlord? Should it make a difference whether the proposed use is commercial or residential? Consider the following excerpt.

BERGER, HARD LEASES MAKE BAD LAW

74 Colum.L.Rev. 791, 814–815 (1974).

While this may be so, a larger issue remains that the present system fails to moot. It is the issue of "contract integrity"—the integrity of the paper that seals the bargain. Here I use "integrity" in a dual sense. I refer both to the honesty or fairness of the contract and to its even-handed completeness.

In the context of the lease, let me illustrate what I mean. A and B make a lease. What they negotiate, however, is far less detailed than the instrument they sign. The negotiated oral transaction seldom goes beyond the monthly rental and the duration of the lease. These terms often are flexible, and the final bargain responds to the urgency with which each party needs to obtain or get rid of the space. Thus, even during an apartment shortage, some owners may readily make a rent concession if their buildings are renting poorly. Conversely, some tenants will pay dearly for apartments they badly want even during a market glut. Thus, as to the *negotiated* bargain, chronic disparity between landlord and tenant would be hard to prove.

If the negotiated bargain were the entire transaction, the written lease would be one paragraph long. But, of course, the landlord-tenant relation is far more complex, and the non-bargained part of the transaction occupies most of the written form. This is where the principle of contract integrity enters. It would require:

1. That the lease fairly describe all the unspoken expectations of the parties. For example, if the tenant expects to receive and the landlord expects to furnish heat, hot and cold running water, trash removal, a minimum level of security, or janitorial service, these rights and duties should be set forth.

2. That the lease fairly describe all basic statutory and common-law rights of the parties. For example, where statute requires landlord to hold the tenant's security deposit in an interest-bearing account, interest payable annually to the tenant, the lease should say so.

3. That the lease describe the tenant's remedies with the same completeness and detail that it describes the landlord's remedies. Thus, tenants would read in their leases of rent-withholding, repair-and-offset, or rescission, where these remedies were available.

4. That the lease distinguish *fairly* between major ("substantial") and minor ("insubstantial") duties, and indicate what penalties follow the breach of each.

5. That the lease not contain any surprises. A tenant who expected to get delivery of the apartment on April 1 should not discover, if the previous tenant unlawfully holds over, that the landlord may recover rent even though the apartment is not ready. If the landlord wants to bargain for such a surprising right, he must *ask* for it during the oral negotiations.

6. That the lease be written for a layman's understanding.

Contract integrity and contract unconscionability occupy the opposing ends of a spectrum. Between them lie many shades of tolerated agreement. Since unconscionability is a doctrine of last resort, virtually any contract that does not shock the conscience is presumptively valid. But I suggest that the legal system should espouse a higher norm, one that contract integrity can help fulfill. Each party who signs an agreement should sense its truth and essential fairness and should believe that the paper fully states his rights and remedies, that it captures both parties' understanding, that it conceals no hookers, and that it is understandable. Uninformed or misinformed parties to a contract are easily terrorized or disarmed into foregoing their rights and remedies, and contract integrity would help prevent that. I also believe, and have tried to show, that hard leases often make bad law, and while no reform can root out the defects of intellect or of fairness among our judges, contract integrity would allow courts to apply their powers of reason and their spirit of impartiality to a dispute far more readily than does today's standard form lease.

C. QUIET ENJOYMENT AND CONSTRUCTIVE EVICTION

DYETT v. PENDLETON

Court of Errors of New York, 1826.
8 Cow. 727.

[John B. Pendleton sued Joshua Dyett for nonpayment of rent under a lease with a term of "two, three, five or eight years, but not for a less term than two years" for several rooms in a house in New York City. Dyett defended by alleging that Pendleton had "introduced divers lewd women or prostitutes" into portions of the house remaining in Pendleton's control, causing "such noise and riotous proceedings" at night that Dyett was forced to leave the premises. The trial court refused to admit evidence concerning Dyett's allegations. From a verdict in favor of Pendleton, Dyett appealed—Eds.]

SPENCER, SENATOR. It seems to be conceded, that the only plea which could be interposed by the defendant below, to let in the defense which he offered, if any would answer that purpose, was, that the plaintiff had entered in and upon the demised premises, and ejected and put out the defendant. Such a plea was filed, and it is contended on the one side that it must be literally proved, and an actual entry and expulsion established; while on the other side it is insisted that a constructive entry and expulsion is sufficient, and that the facts which tended to prove it, should have been left to the jury. * * *

This distinction, which is as perfectly well settled as any to be found in our books, establishes the great principle that a tenant shall not be required to pay rent, even for the part of the premises which he retains, if he has been evicted from the other part by the landlord. As to the part retained, this is deemed such a disturbance, such an injury to its beneficial enjoyment, such a diminution of the consideration upon which the contract is founded, that the law refuses its aid to coerce the payment of any rent. Here, then, is a case, where actual entry and physical eviction are not necessary to exonerate the tenant from the payment of rent; and if the principle be correct as applied to a part of the premises, why should not the same principle equally apply to the whole property demised, where there has been an obstruction to its beneficial enjoyment, and a diminution of the consideration of the contract, by the acts of the landlord, although those acts do not amount to a physical eviction? If physical eviction be not necessary in the one case, to discharge the rent of the part retained, why should it be essential in the other, to discharge the rent of the whole? If I have not deceived myself, the distinction referred to settles and recognizes the principles for which the plaintiff in error contends, that there may be a constructive eviction produced by the acts of the landlord. * * *

[Reversed—Eds.]

Notes and Questions

1. The decision in Dyett v. Pendleton was based on the principle that the landlord impliedly covenants not to disturb the tenant's enjoyment of his possessory interest. While the tenant's promise to pay rent was said to be "independent" of any promises the landlord may have made about the condition of the premises being leased, the importance of the tenant's possessory interest was such that interference by the landlord with its "quiet enjoyment" constituted a "total breach of consideration," depriving the landlord of any remedy for the tenant's failure to pay rent. Thus, the duty to pay rent became "dependent" upon the landlord's observing the implied covenant of quiet enjoyment.

2. While early cases applying the principle of constructive eviction were not sympathetic to tenants who complained of vermin, see, e.g., Jacobs v. Morand, 59 Misc. 200, 110 N.Y.S. 208 (1908), it is now well settled that vermin infestation which is outside the control of tenants can constitute constructive eviction. See, e.g. Mayers v. Kugelman, 81 Misc.2d 998, 367 N.Y.S.2d 144 (1975); Ianacci v. Pendis, 64 Misc.2d 178, 315 N.Y.S.2d 399 (1970); Streep v. Simpson, 80 Misc. 666, 141 N.Y.S. 863 (1913).

BLACKETT v. OLANOFF
Supreme Judicial Court of Massachusetts, 1977.
371 Mass. 714, 358 N.E.2d 817.

WILKINS, JUSTICE.

The defendant in each of these consolidated actions for rent successfully raised constructive eviction as a defense against the landlords' claim. The judge found that the tenants were "very substantially deprived" of quiet enjoyment of their leased premises "*for a substantial time*" (emphasis original). He ruled that the tenants' implied warranty of quiet enjoyment was violated by late evening and early morning music and disturbances coming from nearby premises which the landlords leased to others for use as a bar or cocktail lounge (lounge). The judge further found that, although the landlords did not intend to create the conditions, the landlords "had it within their control to correct the conditions which * * * amounted to a constructive eviction of each [tenant]." He also found that the landlords promised each tenant to correct the situation, that the landlords made some attempt to remedy the problem, but they were unsuccessful, and that each tenant vacated his apartment within a reasonable time. Judgment was entered for each tenant; the landlords appealed; and we transferred the appeals here. We affirm the judgments.

The landlords argue that they did not violate the tenants' implied covenant of quiet enjoyment because they are not chargeable with the noise from the lounge. The landlords do not challenge the judge's conclusion that the noise emanating from the lounge was sufficient to constitute a constructive eviction, if that noise could be attributed to the landlords.[3] Nor do the landlords seriously argue that a constructive eviction could not be found as matter of law because the lounge was not on the same premises as the tenants' apartments. [ ] The landlords' principal contention, based on the denial of certain requests for rulings, is that they are not responsible for the conduct of the proprietors, employees, and patrons of the lounge.

Our opinions concerning a constructive eviction by an alleged breach of an implied covenant of quiet enjoyment sometimes have stated that the landlord must perform some act with the intent of depriving the tenant of the enjoyment and occupation of the whole or part of the leased premises. [ ] There are occasions, however, where a landlord has not intended to violate a tenant's rights, but there was nevertheless a breach of the landlord's covenant of quiet enjoyment which flowed as the natural and probable consequence of what the landlord did, what he failed to do, or what he permitted to be done. [ ] Although some of our opinions have spoken of particular action or inaction by a landlord as showing a presumed intention to evict, the landlord's conduct, and not his intentions, is controlling. [ ]

The judge was warranted in ruling that the landlords had it within their control to correct the condition which caused the tenants to vacate their apartments. The landlords introduced a commercial activity into an area where they leased premises for residential purposes. The lease for the lounge expressly provided that entertainment in the lounge had to be conducted so that it could not be heard outside the building and would not disturb the residents of the leased apartments. The potential threat to the occupants of the nearby apartments was apparent in the circumstances. The landlords complained to the tenants of the lounge after receiving numerous objections from residential tenants. From time to time, the pervading noise would abate in response to the landlord's complaints. We conclude that, as matter of law, the landlords had a right to control the objectionable noise coming

---

3. There was evidence that the lounge had amplified music (electric musical instruments and singing, at various times) which started at 9:30 P.M. and continued until 1:30 A.M. or 2 A.M., generally on Tuesdays through Sundays. The music could be heard through the granite walls of the residential tenants' building, and was described variously as unbelievably loud, incessant, raucous, and penetrating. The noise interfered with conversation and prevented sleep. There was also evidence of noise from patrons' yelling and fighting.

from the lounge and that the judge was warranted in finding as a fact that the landlords could control the objectionable conditions.

This situation is different from the usual annoyance of one residential tenant by another, where traditionally the landlord has not been chargeable with the annoyance. [   ][4] Here we have a case more like *Case v. Minot*, 158 Mass. 577, 33 N.E. 700 (1893), where the landlord entered into a lease with one tenant which the landlord knew permitted that tenant to engage in activity which would interfere with the rights of another tenant. There, to be sure, the clash of tenants' rights was inevitable, if each pressed those rights. Here, although the clash of tenants' interests was only a known potentiality initially, experience demonstrated that a decibel level for the entertainment at the lounge, acoustically acceptable to its patrons and hence commercially desirable to its proprietors, was intolerable for the residential tenants.

Because the disturbing condition was the natural and probable consequence of the landlords' permitting the lounge to operate where it did and because the landlords could control the actions at the lounge, they should not be entitled to collect rent for residential premises which were not reasonably habitable. Tenants such as these should not be left only with a claim against the proprietors of the noisome lounge. To the extent that our opinions suggest a distinction between nonfeasance by the landlord, which has been said to create no liability [ ] and malfeasance by the landlord, we decline to perpetuate that distinction where the landlord creates a situation and has the right to control the objectionable conditions.

Judgments affirmed.

Notes and Questions

1. What is the difference between malfeasance and nonfeasance noted by the court in the principal case? Should it make a difference whether the condition which forms the basis of a tenant's complaint is the result of landlord malfeasance or nonfeasance? See Fidelity Mutual Life Ins. Co. v. Robert P. Kaminsky, M.D., 768 S.W.2d 818 (Tex.App.1989) (constructive eviction resulted from failure to prevent demonstrators from blocking access to leased premises from common areas).

2. To what extent should a landlord be held responsible for behavior of tenants that is offensive to other tenants? Should it make a difference whether the behavior complained of is a violation of published rules and regulations, such as the ones incorporated into the lease reproduced earlier in this chapter? Would the following clause make a difference?

4. The general, but not universal, rule in this country is that a landlord is not chargeable because one tenant is causing annoyance to another [   ] even where the annoying conduct would be a breach of the landlord's covenant of quiet enjoyment if the landlord were the miscreant. * * *

A tenant with sufficient bargaining power may be able to obtain an agreement from the landlord to insert and to enforce regulatory restrictions in the leases of other, potentially offending, tenants. [   ]

Nothing contained in this lease shall be construed to impose upon landlord any duty or obligation to enforce the rules and regulations, or the terms, conditions or covenants in any other lease, as against any other tenant, and landlord shall not be liable to tenant for violation of the same by any other tenant, its employees, agents or invitees.

Would you suggest to a landlord-client, or possibly accept the suggestion from him that he be willing to surrender some of his power as owner to tenants who would meet and decide what they want from one another with regard to the control of offensive behavior? Is this what is done when home owners and condominium owners form community associations? See Chapter Six.

3. Restatement (Second) of Property, § 6.1 Comment d (1976), states: "The conduct of a third person outside of the leased property that is performed on property in which the landlord has an interest, which conduct could be controlled by him, is attributable to the landlord for the purpose of applying the rule of this section [describing remedies for impermissible interference with use and enjoyment]."

Illustrations 10–12 indicate that the section is intended to apply to the landlord's failure to control noisy tenants. The Reporter's Note points out, however, that the noisy tenant rule is a special exception to the "well settled" rule that the landlord is not responsible for third party inference after the tenant has taken possession. Restatement (Second) of Property, § 6.1 Reporter's Note 3, at 231–32 (1976).

4. One of the main elements, and perhaps the chief weakness, of the constructive eviction defense is the requirement that the tenant vacate the premises within a reasonable time after the condition causing the constructive eviction arises. The Supreme Court of New Jersey described the dilemma this can pose for a tenant as follows:

> Plaintiff's final claim is that assuming the tenant was exposed to a constructive eviction, she waived it by remaining on the premises for an unreasonable period of time thereafter. The general rule is, of course, that a tenant's right to claim a constructive eviction will be lost if he does not vacate the premises within a reasonable time after the right comes into existence. [ ] What constitutes a reasonable time depends upon the circumstances of each case. In considering the problem courts must be sympathetic toward the tenant's plight. Vacation of the premises is a drastic course and must be taken at his peril. If he vacates, and it is held at a later time in a suit for rent for the unexpired term that the landlord's course of action did not reach the dimensions of constructive eviction, a substantial liability may be imposed upon him. That risk and the practical inconvenience and difficulties attendant upon finding and moving to suitable quarters counsel caution.

> Here, plaintiff's cooperative building manager died about nine months before the removal. During that period the tenant complained, patiently waited, hoped for relief from the landlord, and tried to take care of the water problem that accompanied the recurring rainstorms. But when relief did not come and the "crowning blow" put five inches of water in the leased offices and meeting rooms on

December 20, 1961, the tolerance ended and the vacation came ten days later after notice to the landlord. The trial court found as a fact that under the circumstances such vacation was within a reasonable time, and the delay was not sufficient to establish a waiver of the constructive eviction. We find adequate evidence to support the conclusion and are of the view that the Appellate Division should not have reversed it.

Reste Realty Corporation v. Cooper, 53 N.J. 444, 251 A.2d 268, 277 (1969).

5. Statutes in some states have codified the covenant of quiet enjoyment and permit the recovery of damages, including reasonable attorney's fees, for breach. See, e.g., Mass.Ann.Laws ch. 186, § 14 (Michie/Law Co-op 1981); Manzaro v. McCann, 401 Mass. 880, 519 N.E.2d 1337 (1988) (upholding award of three months rent as damages along with reasonable attorney's fees for landlord's failure to silence smoke alarms that sounded for over 24 hours).

6. An interesting distinction has been drawn between actual eviction of part of the premises and constructive eviction. When actual eviction of part of the leased premises occurs, such as by blocking access to an elevator, a hallway or an entrance way, the tenant receives full abatement of rent but does not have to vacate the rest of the premises. See Bijan Designer v. St. Regis Sheraton, 142 Misc.2d 175, 536 N.Y.S.2d 951 (1989) (discussing concept but finding no actual partial eviction from renovation of hotel in which tenant leased space). Suppose one room in an apartment develops a serious leak in the ceiling. Does it make sense to require the tenants to vacate the apartment in order to use constructive eviction as a defense for non-payment of rent or should they be allowed to merely close off the room?

Problem

Robert Nugent, a newcomer to the city, leased an apartment in a "gentrified" neighborhood that had become popular with young professionals. When he signed the lease, he gave the landlord a check for $1000, representing rent for one month and an equal amount as a security deposit. When he arrived with his family and furniture to take possession, he found the apartment infested with vermin and rodents. Rather than move in, he chose an available apartment in a different building nearby. Can Robert recover his advance rent and security deposit? See Mayers v. Kugelman, 81 Misc.2d 998, 367 N.Y.S.2d 144 (Dist.Ct.1975); Ianacci v. Pendis, 64 Misc.2d 178, 315 N.Y.S.2d 399 (Civ.Ct.1970).

D. CONDITION OF THE PREMISES

JAVINS v. FIRST NATIONAL REALTY CORPORATION

Court of Appeals for the District of Columbia Circuit, 1970.
428 F.2d 1071, cert. den., 400 U.S. 925, 91 S.Ct. 186, 27 L.Ed.2d 185 (1970).

J. SKELLY WRIGHT, CIRCUIT JUDGE:

These cases present the question whether housing code violations which arise during the term of a lease have any effect upon the tenant's obligation to pay rent. The Landlord and Tenant Branch of the District of Columbia Court of General Sessions ruled proof of such violations inadmissible when proffered as a defense to an eviction action for nonpayment of rent. The District of Columbia Court of Appeals upheld this ruling. [ ]

Because of the importance of the question presented, we granted appellants' petitions for leave to appeal. We now reverse and hold that a warranty of habitability, measured by the standards set out in the Housing Regulations for the District of Columbia, is implied by operation of law into leases of urban dwelling units covered by those Regulations and that breach of this warranty gives rise to the usual remedies for breach of contract.

I

The facts revealed by the record are simple. By separate written leases, each of the appellants rented an apartment in a three-building apartment complex in Northwest Washington known as Clifton Terrace. The landlord, First National Realty Corporation, filed separate actions in the Landlord and Tenant Branch of the Court of General Sessions on April 8, 1966, seeking possession on the ground that each of the appellants had defaulted in the payment of rent due for the month of April. The tenants, appellants here, admitted that they had not paid the landlord any rent for April. However, they alleged numerous violations of the Housing Regulations as "an equitable defense or [a] claim by way of recoupment or set-off in an amount equal to the rent claim," as provided in the rules of the Court of General Sessions. They offered to prove

> "[t]hat there are approximately 1500 violations of the Housing Regulations of the District of Columbia in the building at Clifton Terrace, where Defendant resides some affecting the premises of this Defendant directly, others indirectly, and all tending to establish a course of conduct of violation of the Housing Regulations to the damage of Defendants * * *."

Settled Statement of Proceedings and Evidence, p. 2 (1966). Appellants conceded at trial, however, that this offer of proof reached only violations which had arisen since the term of the lease had commenced. The Court of General Sessions refused appellants' offer of proof and entered judgment for the landlord. The District of Columbia Court of Appeals affirmed, rejecting the argument made by appellants that the landlord was under a contractual duty to maintain the premises in compliance with the Housing Regulations. [ ]

II

Since, in traditional analysis, a lease was the conveyance of an interest in land, courts have usually utilized the special rules governing real property transactions to resolve controversies involving leases. However, as the Supreme Court has noted in another context, "the body of private property law * * *, more than almost any other branch of law, has been shaped by distinctions whose validity is largely historical." Courts have a duty to reappraise old doctrines in the light of the facts and values of contemporary life—particularly old common law doctrines which the courts themselves created and developed. As we have said before, "[T]he continued vitality of the common law * * * depends upon its ability to reflect contemporary community values and ethics."

The assumption of landlord-tenant law, derived from feudal property law, that a lease primarily conveyed to the tenant an interest in land may have been reasonable in a rural, agrarian society; it may continue to be reasonable in some leases involving farming or commercial land. In these cases, the value of the lease to the tenant is the land itself. But in the case of the modern apartment dweller, the value of the lease is that it gives him a place to live. The city dweller who seeks to lease an apartment on the third floor of a tenement has little interest in the land 30 or 40 feet below, or even in the bare right to possession within the four walls of his apartment. When American city dwellers, both rich and poor, seek "shelter" today, they seek a well known package of goods and services—a package which includes not merely walls and ceilings, but also adequate heat, light and ventilation, serviceable plumbing facilities, secure windows and doors, proper sanitation, and proper maintenance. * * *

Some courts have realized that certain of the old rules of property law governing leases are inappropriate for today's transactions. In order to reach results more in accord with the legitimate expectations of the parties and the standards of the community, courts have been gradually introducing more modern precepts of contract law in interpreting leases. Proceeding piecemeal has, however, led to confusion where "decisions are frequently conflicting, not because of a healthy disagreement on social policy, but because of the lingering impact of rules whose policies are long since dead."

In our judgment the trend toward treating leases as contracts is wise and well considered. Our holding in this case reflects a belief that leases of urban dwelling units should be interpreted and construed like any other contract.[5]

---

5. This approach does not deny the possible importance of the fact that land is involved in a transaction. The interpretation and construction of contracts between private parties has always required courts to be sensitive and responsive to myriad different factors. We believe contract doctrines allow courts to be properly sensitive to all relevant factors in interpreting lease obligations.

We also intend no alteration of statutory or case law definitions of the term "real property" for purposes of statutes or decisions on recordation, descent, conveyancing, creditors' rights, etc. We contemplate only that contract law is to determine the rights and obligations of the parties to the lease agreement, as between themselves. The civil law has always viewed the lease as a contract, and in our judgment that perspective has proved superior to that of the common law. *See* 2 M. Planiol, Treatise on the Civil Law § 1663 *et seq.* (1959); 11 La.Stat.Ann., Civil Code, Art. 2669 (1952).

III

Modern contract law has recognized that the buyer of goods and services in an industrialized society must rely upon the skill and honesty of the supplier to assure that goods and services purchased are of adequate quality. In interpreting most contracts, courts have sought to protect the legitimate expectations of the buyer and have steadily widened the seller's responsibility for the quality of goods and services through implied warranties of fitness and merchantability. Thus without any special agreement a merchant will be held to warrant that his goods are fit for the ordinary purposes for which such goods are used and that they are at least of reasonably average quality. Moreover, if the supplier has been notified that goods are required for a specific purpose, he will be held to warrant that any goods sold are fit for that purpose. These implied warranties have become widely accepted and well established features of the common law, supported by the overwhelming body of case law. Today most states as well as the District of Columbia have codified and enacted these warranties into statute, as to the sale of goods, in the Uniform Commercial Code.

Implied warranties of quality have not been limited to cases involving sales. The consumer renting a chattel, paying for services, or buying a combination of goods and services must rely upon the skill and honesty of the supplier to at least the same extent as a purchaser of goods. Courts have not hesitated to find implied warranties of fitness and merchantability in such situations. In most areas product liability law has moved far beyond "mere" implied warranties running between two parties in privity with each other.

The rigid doctrines of real property law have tended to inhibit the application of implied warranties to transactions involving real estate. Now, however, courts have begun to hold sellers and developers of real property responsible for the quality of their product. For example, builders of new homes have recently been held liable to purchasers for improper construction on the ground that the builders had breached an implied warranty of fitness. In other cases courts have held builders of new homes liable for breach of an implied warranty that all local building regulations had been complied with. And following the developments in other areas, very recent decisions and commentary suggest the possible extension of liability to parties other than the immediate seller for improper construction of residential real estate.

Despite this trend in the sale of real estate, many courts have been unwilling to imply warranties of quality, specifically a warranty of habitability, into leases of apartments. Recent decisions have offered no convincing explanation for their refusal; rather they have relied without discussion upon the old common law rule that the lessor is not obligated to repair unless he covenants to do so in the written lease contract. However, the Supreme Courts of at least two states, in recent and well reasoned opinions, have held landlords to implied warranties of quality in housing leases. [ ] In our judgment, the old no-repair rule cannot coexist with the obligations imposed on the landlord by a typical modern housing code, and must be abandoned[6] in favor of an implied warranty of habitability.[7] In the District of Columbia, the standards of this warranty are set out in the Housing Regulations.

IV

A. In our judgment the common law itself must recognize the landlord's obligation to keep his premises in a habitable condition. This conclusion is compelled by three separate considerations. First, we believe that the old rule was based on certain factual assumptions which are no longer true; on its own terms, it can no longer be justified. Second, we believe that the consumer protection cases discussed above require that the old rule be abandoned in order to bring residential landlord-tenant law into harmony with the principles on which those cases rest. Third, we think that the nature of today's urban housing market also dictates abandonment of the old rule.

The common law rule absolving the lessor of all obligation to repair originated in the early Middle Ages.[8] Such a rule was perhaps well suited to an agrarian economy; the land was more important[9] than whatever small living structure was included in the leasehold, and the tenant farmer was fully capable of making repairs himself.[10] These historical facts were the basis on which the common law constructed its rule; they also provided the necessary prerequisites for its application.[11]

6. As far as tort liability is concerned, we have previously held that the old common law rule has been changed by passage of the housing code and that the landlord has a duty to maintain reasonably safe premises. * * *

7. Although the present cases involve written leases, we think there is no particular significance in this fact. The landlord's warranty is implied in oral and written leases for all types of tenancies.

8. The rule was "settled" by 1485. 3 W. Holdsworth, A History of English Law 122–123 (6th ed. 1934). The common law rule discussed in text originated in the even older rule prohibiting the tenant from committing waste. The writ of waste expanded as the tenant's right to possession grew stronger. Eventually, in order to protect the landowner's reversionary interest, the tenant became obligated to make repairs and liable to eviction and damages if he failed to do so. *Ibid.*

9. The land was so central to the original common law conception of a leasehold that rent was viewed as "issuing" from the land: "[T]he governing idea is that the land is bound to pay the rent * * *. We may almost go to the length of saying that the land pays it through [the tenant's] hand." 2 F. Pollock & F. Maitland, The History of English Law 131 (2d ed. 1923).

10. Many later judicial opinions have added another justification of the old common law rule. They have invoked the time-worn cry of *caveat emptor* and argued that a lessee has the opportunity to inspect the premises. On the basis of his inspection, the tenant must then take the premises "as is," according to this reasoning. As an historical matter, the opportunity to inspect was not thought important when the rule was first devised.

* * *

11. Even the old common law courts responded with a different rule for a landlord-tenant relationship which did not conform to the model of the usual agrarian lease. Much more substantial obligations were placed upon the keepers of inns (the only multiple dwelling houses known to the common law). Their guests were interested solely in shelter and could not be expected to make their own repairs. "The modern apartment dweller more closely resembles the guest in an inn than he resembles an agrarian tenant, but the law has not generally recognized the similarity." J. Levi, P. Hablutzel, L. Rosenberg & J. White, Model Residential Landlord–Tenant Code 6–7 (Tent.Draft 1969).

Court decisions in the late 1800's began to recognize that the factual assumptions of the common law were no longer accurate in some cases. For example, the common law, since it assumed that the land was the most important part of the leasehold, required a tenant to pay rent even if any building on the land was destroyed. Faced with such a rule and the ludicrous results it produced, in 1863 the New York Court of Appeals declined to hold that an upper story tenant was obliged to continue paying rent after his apartment building burned down. The court simply pointed out that the urban tenant had no interest in the land, only in the attached building.

Another line of cases created an exception to the no-repair rule for short term leases of furnished dwellings. The Massachusetts Supreme Judicial Court, a court not known for its willingness to depart from the common law, supported this exception, pointing out:

" * * * [A] different rule should apply to one who hires a furnished room, or a furnished house, for a few days, or a few weeks or months. Its fitness for immediate use of a particular kind, as indicated by its appointments, is a far more important element entering into the contract than when there is a mere lease of real estate. One who lets for a short term a house provided with all furnishings and appointments for immediate residence may be supposed to contract in reference to a well-understood purpose of the hirer to use it as a habitation. * * * It would be unreasonable to hold, under such circumstances, that the landlord does not impliedly agree that what he is letting is a house suitable for occupation in its condition at the time. * * * " [12]

These as well as other similar cases demonstrate that some courts began some time ago to question the common law's assumptions that the land was the most important feature of a leasehold and that the tenant could feasibly make any necessary repairs himself. Where those assumptions no longer reflect contemporary housing patterns, the courts have created exceptions to the general rule that landlords have no duty to keep their premises in repair.

It is overdue for courts to admit that these assumptions are no longer true with regard to all urban housing. Today's urban tenants, the vast majority of whom live in multiple dwelling houses, are interested, not in the land, but solely in "a house suitable for occupation." Furthermore, today's city dweller usually has a single, specialized skill unrelated to maintenance work; he is unable to make repairs like the "jack-of-all-trades" farmer who was the common law's model of the lessee. Further, unlike his agrarian predecessor who often remained on one piece of land for his entire life, urban tenants today are more mobile than ever before. A tenant's tenure in a specific apartment will often not be sufficient to justify efforts at repairs. In addition, the increasing complexity of today's dwellings renders them much more difficult to repair than the structures of earlier times. In a multiple dwelling repair may require access to equipment and areas in the

---

12. Ingalls v. Hobbs, 156 Mass. 348, 31 N.E. 286 (1892).

control of the landlord. Low and middle income tenants, even if they were interested in making repairs, would be unable to obtain any financing for major repairs since they have no long-term interest in the property.

Our approach to the common law of landlord and tenant ought to be aided by principles derived from the consumer protection cases referred to above. In a lease contract, a tenant seeks to purchase from his landlord shelter for a specified period of time. The landlord sells housing as a commercial businessman and has much greater opportunity, incentive and capacity to inspect and maintain the condition of his building. Moreover, the tenant must rely upon the skill and *bona fides* of his landlord at least as much as a car buyer must rely upon the car manufacturer. In dealing with major problems, such as heating, plumbing, electrical or structural defects, the tenant's position corresponds precisely with "the ordinary consumer who cannot be expected to have the knowledge or capacity or even the opportunity to make adequate inspection of mechanical instrumentalities, like automobiles, and to decide for himself whether they are reasonably fit for the designed purpose." Henningsen v. Bloomfield Motors, Inc., 32 N.J. 358, 375, 161 A.2d 69, 78 (1960).

Since a lease contract specifies a particular period of time during which the tenant has a right to use his apartment for shelter, he may legitimately expect that the apartment will be fit for habitation for the time period for which it is rented. We point out that in the present cases there is no allegation that appellants' apartments were in poor condition or in violation of the housing code at the commencement of the leases. Since the lessees continue to pay the same rent, they were entitled to expect that the landlord would continue to keep the premises in their beginning condition during the lease term. It is precisely such expectations that the law now recognizes as deserving of formal, legal protection.

Even beyond the rationale of traditional products liability law, the relationship of landlord and tenant suggests further compelling reasons for the law's protection of the tenants' legitimate expectations of quality. The inequality in bargaining power between landlord and tenant has been well documented. Tenants have very little leverage to enforce demands for better housing. Various impediments to competition in the rental housing market, such as racial and class discrimination and standardized form leases, mean that landlords place tenants in a take it or leave it situation. The increasingly severe shortage of adequate housing further increases the landlord's bargaining power and escalates the need for maintaining and improving the existing stock. Finally, the findings by various studies of the social impact of bad housing has led to the realization that poor housing is detrimental to the whole society, not merely to the unlucky ones who must suffer the daily indignity of living in a slum.

Thus we are led by our inspection of the relevant legal principles and precedents to the conclusion that the old common law rule imposing an obligation upon the lessee to repair during the lease term was really never intended to apply to residential urban leaseholds. Contract principles established in other areas of the law provide a more rational framework for the apportionment of landlord-tenant responsibilities; they strongly suggest that a warranty of habitability be implied into all contracts for urban dwellings.

B. We believe, in any event, that the District's housing code requires that a warranty of habitability be implied in the leases of all housing that it covers. The housing code—formally designated the Housing Regulations of the District of Columbia—was established and authorized by the Commissioners of the District of Columbia on August 11, 1955. Since that time, the code has been updated by numerous orders of the Commissioners. The 75 pages of the Regulations provide a comprehensive regulatory scheme setting forth in some detail: (a) the standards which housing in the District of Columbia must meet; (b) which party, the lessor or the lessee, must meet each standard; and (c) a system of inspections, notifications and criminal penalties. The Regulations themselves are silent on the question of private remedies.

Two previous decisions of this court, however, have held that the Housing Regulations create legal rights and duties enforceable in tort by private parties.

* * *

This principle of implied warranty is well established. Courts often imply relevant law into contracts to provide a remedy for any damage caused by one party's illegal conduct. In a case closely analogous to the present ones, the Illinois Supreme Court held that a builder who constructed a house in violation of the Chicago building code had breached his contract with the buyer:

> " * * * [T]he law existing at the time and place of the making of the contract is deemed a part of the contract, as though expressly referred to or incorporated in it. * * *

> "The rationale for this rule is that the parties to the contract would have expressed that which the law implies 'had they not supposed that it was unnecessary to speak of it because the law provided for it.' * * * Consequently, the courts, in construing the existing law as part of the express contract, are not reading into the contract provisions different from those expressed and intended by the parties, as defendants contend, but are merely construing the contract in accordance with the intent of the parties." [13]

13. Schiro v. W.E. Gould & Co., 118 Ill.2d 538, 544, 165 N.E.2d 286, 290 (1960). As a general proposition, it is undoubtedly true that parties to a contract intend that applicable law will be complied with by both sides. We recognize, however, that reading statutory provisions into private contracts may have little factual support in the intentions of the particular parties now before us. But, for reasons of public policy, warranties are often implied into contracts by operation of law in order to

We follow the Illinois court in holding that the housing code must be read into housing contracts—a holding also required by the purposes and the structure of the code itself. The duties imposed by the Housing Regulations may not be waived or shifted by agreement if the Regulations specifically place the duty upon the lessor.[14] Criminal penalties are provided if these duties are ignored. This regulatory structure was established by the Commissioners because, in their judgment, the grave conditions in the housing market required serious action. Yet official enforcement of the housing code has been far from uniformly effective. Innumerable studies have documented the desperate condition of rental housing in the District of Columbia and in the nation. In view of these circumstances, we think the conclusion reached by the Supreme Court of Wisconsin as to the effect of a housing code on the old common law rule cannot be avoided:

> " * * * [T]he legislature has made a policy judgment—that it is socially (and politically) desirable to impose these duties on a property owner—which has rendered the old common law rule obsolete. To follow the old rule of no implied warranty of habitability in leases would, in our opinion, be inconsistent with the current legislative policy concerning housing standards. * * * "[15]

We therefore hold that the Housing Regulations imply a warranty of habitability, measured by the standards which they set out, into leases of all housing that they cover.

V

In the present cases, the landlord sued for possession for nonpayment of rent. Under contract principles,[16] however, the tenant's obligation to pay rent is dependent upon the landlord's performance of his obligations, including his warranty to maintain the premises in habitable condition. In order to determine whether any rent is owed to the landlord, the tenants must be given an opportunity to prove the housing code violations alleged as breach of the landlord's warranty.[17]

---

meet generally prevailing standards of honesty and fair dealing. When the public policy has been enacted into law like the housing code, that policy will usually have deep roots in the expectations and intentions of most people. *See* Costigan, Implied-in-Fact Contracts and Mutual Assent, 33 Harv.L.Rev. 376, 383–385 (1920).

14. Any private agreement to shift the duties would be illegal and unenforceable. The precedents dealing with industrial safety statutes are directly in point:

> " * * * [T]he only question remaining is whether the courts will enforce or recognize as against a servant an agreement express or implied on his part to waive the performance of a statutory duty of the master imposed for the protection of the servant, and in the interest of the public, and enforceable by crimi-

nal prosecution. We do not think they will. To do so would be to nullify the object of the statute. * * * "

Narramore v. Cleveland, C., C. & St. L. Ry. Co., 6 Cir., 96 F. 298, 302 (1899). *See* W. Prosser, Torts § 67 at 468–469 (3d ed. 1964) and cases cited therein.

15. Pines v. Perssion, 14 Wis.2d 590, 596, 111 N.W.2d 409, 412–413 (1961). *Accord*, Buckner v. Azulai, 251 Cal.App.2d Supp. 1013, 59 Cal.Rptr. 806 (1967).

16. In extending all contract remedies for breach to the parties to a lease, we include an action for specific performance of the landlord's implied warranty of habitability.

17. To be relevant, of course, the violations must affect the tenant's apartment or common areas which the tenant uses.

At trial, the finder of fact must make two findings: (1) whether the alleged violations [18] existed during the period for which past due rent is claimed, and (2) what portion, if any or all, of the tenant's obligation to pay rent was suspended by the landlord's breach. If no part of the tenant's rental obligation is found to have been suspended, then a judgment for possession may issue forthwith. On the other hand, if the jury determines that the entire rental obligation has been extinguished by the landlord's total breach, then the action for possession on the ground of nonpayment must fail.[19]

The jury may find that part of the tenant's rental obligation has been suspended but that part of the unpaid back rent is indeed owed to the landlord. In these circumstances, no judgment for possession should issue if the tenant agrees to pay the partial rent found to be due. If the tenant refuses to pay the partial amount, a judgment for possession may then be entered.

The judgment of the District of Columbia Court of Appeals is reversed and the cases are remanded for further proceedings consistent with this opinion.[20]

Notes and Questions

1. Judge J. Skelly Wright's eloquent opinion in *Javins* generally is credited with supplying the impetus for one of the most striking reforms in

Moreover, the contract principle that no one may benefit from his own wrong will allow the landlord to defend by proving the damage was caused by the tenant's wrongful action. However, violations resulting from inadequate repairs or materials which disintegrate under normal use would not be assignable to the tenant. Also we agree with the District of Columbia Court of Appeals that the tenant's private rights do not depend on official inspection or official finding of violation by the city government. Diamond Housing Corp. v. Robinson, 257 A.2d 492, 494 (1969).

18. The jury should be instructed that one or two minor violations standing alone which do not affect habitability are *de minimis* and would not entitle the tenant to a reduction in rent.

19. As soon as the landlord made the necessary repairs rent would again become due. Our holding, of course, affects only eviction for nonpayment of rent. The landlord is free to seek eviction at the termination of the lease or on any other legal ground.

20. Appellants in the present cases offered to pay rent into the registry of the court during the present action. We think this is an excellent protective procedure. If the tenant defends against an action for possession on the basis of breach of the landlord's warranty of habitability, the trial court may require the tenant to make future rent payments into the registry of the court as they become due; such a procedure would be appropriate only while the tenant remains in possession. The escrowed money will, however, represent rent for the period between the time the landlord files suit and the time the case comes to trial. In the normal course of litigation, the only factual question at trial would be the condition of the apartment during the time the landlord alleged rent was due and not paid.

As a general rule, the escrowed money should be apportioned between the landlord and the tenant after trial on the basis of the finding of rent actually due for the period at issue in the suit. To insure fair apportionment, however, we think either party should be permitted to amend its complaint or answer at any time before trial, to allege a change in the condition of the apartment. In this event, the finder of fact should make a separate finding as to the condition of the apartment at the time at which the amendment was filed. This new finding will have no effect upon the original action; it will only affect the distribution of the escrowed rent paid after the filing of the amendment.

the common law of property. In less than 20 years after his opinion, virtually all of the states adopted the implied warranty of habitability, either by judicial opinion or by statute, and in the process reversed the common law view of residential landlord-tenant relationships that had been in vogue for centuries. For a thorough history and analysis of the reform, see Rabin, The Revolution in Residential Landlord–Tenant Law: Causes and Consequences, 69 Cornell L.Rev. 517 (1984) and Glendon, The Transformation of American Landlord–Tenant Law, 23 B.C.L.Rev. 503 (1982). See also Cunningham, The New Implied and Statutory Warranties of Habitability in Residential Leases: From Contract to Status, 16 Urb. L.Ann. 3 (1979).

2. How should "habitability" be defined? Suppose an apartment building in an older section of town has hot and cold running water in the kitchens, but only cold water in the bathrooms. Does the fact that a tenant cannot take a hot shower and must fill a tub with hot water from the kitchen in order to take a bath constitute a breach of the warranty of habitability? See City of St. Louis v. Brune, 515 S.W.2d 471 (Mo.1974) (hot shower a "convenience" rather than a "necessity" for health or safety). Suppose a housing code requires window screens to keep out insects. If such screens are installed, but fail to prevent a young child from falling through an open window and suffering serious injury, is the apartment uninhabitable in violation of the warranty? See Mudusar by Baloch v. V.G. Murray & Co., 100 N.C.App. 395, 396 S.E.2d 325 (1990) (screens that keep out insects but do not keep in children not violative of statutory implied warranty of habitability).

3. Note the importance Judge Wright placed on the adoption of local housing codes. Can landlord interests avoid the warranty of habitability by persuading local legislators not to enact a housing code, or is the code simply evidence of how the community believes the term "habitability" should be defined?

4. Judge Wright in *Javins* stressed that all contract remedies, including actions for specific performance, are available for breach of the implied warranty of habitability (IWH). Examples of available remedies include:

(a) *rent withholding*—Green v. Superior Court, 10 Cal.3d 616, 111 Cal.Rptr. 704, 517 P.2d 1168 (1974) (defense of breach of IWH may be raised in action for possession because of non-payment of rent);

(b) *rent abatement*—Berzito v. Gambino, 63 N.J. 460, 308 A.2d 17 (1973) (retroactive rent abatement, as well as other affirmative contract remedies, recognized for breach of IWH);

(c) *self-help repairs and deduction of rent*—Marini v. Ireland, 56 N.J. 130, 265 A.2d 526 (1970) (tenant may deduct costs of necessary repairs when landlord fails to maintain premises in livable condition after timely notice);

(d) *damages*—Mease v. Fox, 200 N.W.2d 791 (Iowa 1972) (damages for breach of implied warranty of habitability are the difference between fair rental value as warranted and fair rental value as is; if tenant vacates, damages are based on loss of bargain difference between fair rental value as warranted and promised rent for balance of term).

5. Courts have had difficulty with the measure of damages for breach of the warranty of habitability. Most have applied the contract measure of damages for breach of warranty. If the buyer keeps the product, his general damages are the difference between the value of the product as promised (warranted) and the value of the product he received. He is obligated to pay the purchase price less his damages. If the buyer returns the product to the seller, his damages are the difference between the value of what he was promised and the amount he promised to pay, i.e., the value of his bargain. In that case, of course, he does not pay the purchase price.

The "value" of what was promised or received is the fair market value (in the lease context, the fair rental), i.e., the price a willing buyer would pay to a willing seller in an arms-length transaction in a free market. The problem with determining the fair rental value of property, especially for lower income or slum housing, is that there are not many willing sellers of slum housing which meet the warranty of habitability standards or willing buyers of unsafe and unsanitary housing. The absence of a free market in housing, resulting from housing shortages and the tenants' consequent lack of bargaining power, was one of the primary reasons for the development of the implied warranty of habitability.

The absence of data on fair rental value has led many courts to assume that the agreed rental represents the fair rental value as warranted, since that is what the tenant bargained for (or would have bargained for if he had enough bargaining power). See, e.g., Hilder v. St. Peter, 144 Vt. 150, 478 A.2d 202, 209 (1984); Berzito v. Gambino, 63 N.J. 460, 469, 308 A.2d 17, 22 (1973). Even if this assumption were valid at the time the lease was made, it is not necessarily so at the time of the breach, since rental values can rise or fall. Other courts have assumed that the agreed rent is equivalent to the fair rental value of the dwelling in its defective condition, i.e. unfit for human habitation. In addition to ignoring possible market fluctuations, does this approach also overlook the tenant's lack of free choice in the market by assuming that he got what he bargained for? See generally R. Schoshinski, American Law of Landlord and Tenant § 3:25 (1980 & 1991 Supp.) (discussing four different views regarding measure of damages that courts have adopted).

6. Suppose the apartment did not meet habitability standards at the time the tenant rented it. Would that affect her legal position?

In Brown v. Southall Realty Co., 237 A.2d 834 (D.C.App.1968), the court held that a lease of property containing violations of the housing code is void. A subsequent case, William J. Davis, Inc. v. Slade, 271 A.2d 412 (D.C.App.1970), also involved a lease that was void because substantial violations of the housing code existed at the time the lease was executed. The court held that the tenant, while in possession of the premises under the void lease, was a tenant at sufferance. Consequently the landlord was entitled to receive the reasonable rental value of the premises in the defective condition for the period of the tenant's occupation.

7. If T's utility bills are excessive because of the uninhabitable condition of the premises, can T recover the difference between what the bills actually were and what they should have been if the premises had been in a habitable condition? See Fair v. Negley, 257 Pa.Super. 50, 390 A.2d 240

(1978). (Yes. Court also held that boilerplate "as is" clause did not constitute an effective waiver of the implied warranty of habitability.)

8. Should a tenant be able to recover for mental distress caused by the landlord's breach of the warranty of habitability?

Restatement (Second) of Torts § 46 provides in part:

(1) One who by extreme and outrageous conduct intentionally causes severe emotional distress to another is subject to liability for such emotional distress, and if bodily harm to the other results from it, for such bodily harm.

Several courts have held that § 46 extends to a landlord who intentionally inflicts emotional distress on a tenant by breaching the implied warranty of habitability. Simon v. Solomon, 385 Mass. 91, 431 N.E.2d 556 (1982); Fair v. Negley, 257 Pa.Super. 50, 390 A.2d 240 (1978); Aweeka v. Bonds, 20 Cal.App.3d 278, 97 Cal.Rptr. 650 (1971).

The Supreme Court of Oregon has held that a tenant "cannot charge to the landlord the tenant's emotional or psychological distress over nonculpable shortcomings of rented quarters, but that the tenant can recover for actual psychological harm suffered from the landlord's deliberate, willful, retaliatory, or malicious acts as proscribed by [the Uniform Residential Landlord and Tenant Act (URLTA) §§ 4.107 or 5.101]." Brewer v. Erwin, 287 Or. 435, 453, 600 P.2d 398, 409 (1979). Psychological harm for which recovery will be allowed is limited to "tangible consequences such as physical illness, medical bills, inability to sleep, to eat or work in one's dwelling, separation of family members or similar disruptions in one's personal life [which] result from the events or conditions that breach the standards of secure occupancy and essential services guaranteed by the act, rather than from the strain of preoccupation and vexation with the dispute itself." Id. at 449, 600 P.2d at 407. In Detling v. Edelbrock, 671 S.W.2d 265 (Mo.1984), the Missouri Supreme Court held that a tenant cannot recover for emotional harm unless physical injury also was suffered or the emotional distress was "medically diagnosable and medically significant."

9. What obligation does a tenant have to notify her landlord of conditions affecting habitability? Should failure to notify the landlord affect her ability to pursue a cause of action for breach of the warranty? See Detling v. Edelbrock, 671 S.W.2d 265, 270 (Mo.1984) (tenant must give landlord notice of defects not known to landlord and a reasonable opportunity to cure).

10. Statutes in a number of states have codified landlord and tenant responsibilities for conditions of the premises, generally following the implied warranty of habitability. The best known statute, the Uniform Residential Landlord and Tenant Act (URLTA), contains the following provisions.

UNIFORM RESIDENTIAL LANDLORD AND TENANT ACT

§ 2.104 [Landlord to Maintain Premises]

(a) A landlord shall

(1) comply with the requirements of applicable building and housing codes materially affecting health and safety;

(2) make all repairs and do whatever is necessary to put and keep the premises in a fit and habitable condition;

(3) keep all common areas of the premises in a clean and safe condition;

(4) maintain in good and safe working order and condition all electrical, plumbing, sanitary, heating, ventilating, air-conditioning, and other facilities and appliances, including elevators, supplied or required to be supplied by him;

(5) provide and maintain appropriate receptacles and conveniences for the removal of ashes, garbage, rubbish, and other waste incidental to the occupancy of the dwelling unit and arrange for their removal; and

(6) supply running water and reasonable amounts of hot water at all times and reasonable heat [between [October 1] and [May 1]] except where the building that includes the dwelling unit is not required by law to be equipped for that purpose, or the dwelling unit is so constructed that heat or hot water is generated by an installation within the exclusive control of the tenant and supplied by a direct public utility connection.

(b) If the duty imposed by paragraph (1) of subsection (a) is greater than any duty imposed by any other paragraph of that subsection, the landlord's duty shall be determined by reference to paragraph (1) of subsection (a).

(c) The landlord and tenant of a single family residence may agree in writing that the tenant perform the landlord's duties specified in paragraphs (5) and (6) of subsection (a) and also specified repairs, maintenance tasks, alterations, and remodeling, but only if the transaction is entered into in good faith.

(d) The landlord and tenant of any dwelling unit other than a single family residence may agree that the tenant is to perform specified repairs, maintenance tasks, alterations, or remodeling only if

(1) the agreement of the parties is entered into in good faith and is set forth in a separate writing signed by the parties and supported by adequate consideration;

(2) the work is not necessary to cure noncompliance with subsection (a)(1) of this section; and

(3) the agreement does not diminish or affect the obligation of the landlord to other tenants in the premises.

(e) The landlord may not treat performance of the separate agreement described in subsection (d) as a condition to any obligation or performance of any rental agreement.

———

The Wisconsin statute is another example of codification of the implied warranty of habitability.

WISCONSIN STATUTES ANNOTATED

§ 704.07   Repairs; untenantability

(1) Application of section. This section applies to any nonresidential tenancy if there is no contrary provision in writing signed by both parties and to all residential tenancies. An agreement to waive the requirements of this section in a residential tenancy is void. Nothing in this section is intended to affect rights and duties arising under other provisions of the statutes.

(2) Duty of landlord. (a) Unless the repair was made necessary by the negligence or improper use of the premises by the tenant, the landlord is under duty to:

1. Keep in reasonable state of repair portions of the premises over which the landlord maintains control;

2. Keep in a reasonable state of repair all equipment under his control necessary to supply services which he has expressly or impliedly agreed to furnish to the tenant, such as heat, water, elevator or air-conditioning;

3. Make all necessary structural repairs;

4. Except for residential premises subject to a local housing code, repair or replace any plumbing, electrical wiring, machinery or equipment furnished with the premises and no longer in reasonable working condition, except as provided in sub. (3)(b).

5. For a residential tenancy, comply with a local housing code applicable to the premises.

(b) If the premises are part of a building, other parts of which are occupied by one or more other tenants, negligence or improper use by one tenant does not relieve the landlord from his duty as to the other tenants to make repairs as provided in par. (a).

(c) If the premises are damaged by fire, water or other casualty, not the result of the negligence or intentional act of the landlord, this subsection is inapplicable and either sub. (3) or (4) governs.

(3) Duty of tenant. (a) If the premises are damaged by the negligence or improper use of the premises by the tenant, the tenant must repair the damage and restore the appearance of the premises by redecorating. However, the landlord may elect to undertake the repairs or redecoration, and in such case the tenant must reimburse the landlord for the reasonable cost thereof; the cost to the landlord is presumed reasonable unless proved otherwise by the tenant.

(b) Except for residential premises subject to a local housing code, the tenant is also under a duty to keep plumbing, electrical wiring, machinery and equipment furnished with the premises in reasonable working order if repair can be made at cost which is minor in relation to the rent.

(c) A tenant in a residential tenancy shall comply with a local housing code applicable to the premises.

(4) Untenantability. If the premises become untenantable because of damage by fire, water or other casualty or because of any condition hazardous to health, or if there is a substantial violation of sub. (2) materially affecting the health or safety of the tenant, the tenant may remove from the premises unless the landlord proceeds promptly to repair or rebuild or eliminate the health hazard or the substantial violation of sub. (2) materially affecting the health or safety of the tenant; or the tenant may remove if the inconvenience to the tenant by reason of the nature and period of repair, rebuilding or elimination would impose undue hardship on him. If the tenant remains in possession, rent abates to the extent the tenant is deprived of the full normal use of the premises. This section does not authorize rent to be withheld in full, if the tenant remains in possession. If the tenant justifiably moves out under this subsection, the tenant is not liable for rent after the premises become untenantable and the landlord must repay any rent paid in advance apportioned to the period after the premises become untenantable. This subsection is inapplicable if the damage or condition is caused by negligence or improper use by the tenant.

––––––––

11. What if a tenant was aware of habitability standards but was willing to accept an apartment "as is" because of a lower rent? Is the warranty available under URLTA? The Wisconsin statute? Should it be? Suppose a landlord cannot meet habitability standards and still make a profit on investment in residential rental housing because required repairs are too costly or persons who would consider renting the apartments would not or could not pay the rent the landlord would have to charge to recover the costs of repairs. What is a landlord is this situation likely to do? Should the parties be able to bargain for a lower standard of quality?

12. Are the statutory standards broader or narrower than the standard adopted by Judge Wright in *Javins?* Who is better able to define an inherently vague term such as habitability, the judiciary or the legislature? Are the legislative definitions based on notions of a *contract* between a residential landlord and a residential tenant, as Judge Wright envisioned his definition, or is it based on what the legislature believes the *status* of residential landlord and residential tenant should mean? Cf. Cunningham, The New Implied and Statutory Warranties of Habitability in Residential Leases: From Contract to Status, 16 Urb.L.Ann. 3 (1979).

13. Does the implied warranty of habitability pose ethical dilemmas for low income tenants, landlords who rent to them, and lawyers who advise them? Suppose a tenant does not have enough money to pay the agreed rent, regardless of whether the apartment meets habitability standards. Would use of the implied warranty and related tenant-protective rules to delay eviction for months be an abuse of the landlord? Suppose the tenant can afford a lower rent, but the landlord cannot afford to charge

the lower rent unless repairs necessary to meet habitability standards are not made. What should be done?

DAVIDOW v. INWOOD NORTH PROFESSIONAL GROUP

Supreme Court of Texas, 1988.
747 S.W.2d 373.

SPEARS, JUSTICE.

This case presents the question of whether there is an implied warranty by a commercial landlord that the leased premises are suitable for their intended commercial purpose. Respondent Inwood North Professional Group—Phase I sued petitioner Dr. Joseph Davidow for unpaid rent on medical office space leased by Dr. Davidow. The jury found that Inwood materially breached the lease agreement and that the defects rendered the office space unsuitable for use as a medical office. The trial court rendered judgment that Inwood take nothing and that Dr. Davidow recover damages for lost time and relocation expenses. The court of appeals reversed the trial court judgment and rendered judgment that Inwood recover unpaid rents for the remainder of the lease period and that Dr. Davidow take nothing. 731 S.W.2d 600. We affirm in part and reverse and render in part.

Dr. Davidow entered into a five-year lease agreement with Inwood for medical office space. The lease required Dr. Davidow to pay Inwood $793.26 per month as rent. The lease also required Inwood to provide air conditioning, electricity, hot water, janitor and maintenance services, light fixtures, and security services. Shortly after moving into the office space, Dr. Davidow began experiencing problems with the building. The air conditioning did not work properly, often causing temperatures inside the office to rise above eighty-five degrees. The roof leaked whenever it rained, resulting in stained tiles and rotting, mildewed carpet. Patients were directed away from certain areas during rain so that they would not be dripped upon in the waiting room. Pests and rodents often infested the office. The hallways remained dark because hallway lights were unreplaced for months. Cleaning and maintenance were not provided. The parking lot was constantly filled with trash. Hot water was not provided, and on one occasion Dr. Davidow went without electricity for several days because Inwood failed to pay the electric bill. Several burglaries and various acts of vandalism occurred. Dr. Davidow finally moved out of the premises and discontinued rent payments approximately fourteen months before the lease expired.

Inwood sued Dr. Davidow for the unpaid rent and costs of restoration. Dr. Davidow answered by general denial and the affirmative defenses of material breach of the lease agreement, a void lease, and breach of an implied warranty that the premises were suitable for use as a medical office. The jury found that Inwood materially breached the lease, that Inwood warranted to Dr. Davidow that the lease space was suitable for a medical office, and that the lease space was not suitable for a medical office. One month after the jury returned its verdict, but before entry of judgment, the trial court allowed Dr. Davidow to amend his pleadings to include the defense of constructive eviction. The trial court then rendered judgment that Inwood take nothing and that Dr. Davidow recover $9,300 in damages.

With one justice dissenting, the court of appeals reversed the trial court judgment and rendered judgment in favor of Inwood for unpaid rent. The court of appeals held that because Inwood's covenant to maintain and repair the premises was independent of Dr. Davidow's covenant to pay rent, Inwood's breach of its covenant did not justify Dr. Davidow's refusal to pay rent. The court of appeals also held that the implied warranty of habitability does not extend to commercial leaseholds and that Dr. Davidow's pleadings did not support an award of affirmative relief.

Inwood contends that the defense of material breach of the covenant to repair is insufficient as a matter of law to defeat a landlord's claim for unpaid rent. In Texas, the courts have held that the landlord's covenant to repair the premises and the tenant's covenant to pay rent are independent covenants. [ ] Thus, a tenant is still under a duty to pay rent even though his landlord has breached his covenant to make repairs. [ ]

This theory of independent covenants in leases was established in early property law prior to the development of the concept of mutually dependent covenants in contract law. At common law, the lease was traditionally regarded as a conveyance of an interest in land, subject to the doctrine of *caveat emptor*. The landlord was required only to deliver the right of possession to the tenant; the tenant, in return, was required to pay rent to the landlord. Once the landlord delivered the right of possession, his part of the agreement was completed. The tenant's duty to pay rent continued as long as he retained possession, even if the buildings on the leasehold were destroyed or became uninhabitable. The landlord's breach of a lease covenant did not relieve the tenant of his duty to pay rent for the remainder of the term because the tenant still retained everything he was entitled to under the lease—the right of possession. All lease covenants were therefore considered independent. [ ]

In the past, this court has attempted to provide a more equitable and contemporary solution to landlord-tenant problems by easing the burden placed on tenants as a result of the independence of lease covenants and the doctrine of *caveat emptor*. [ ] In *Kamarath v. Bennett*, [568 S.W.2d 658 (Tex.1978)], we reexamined the realities of the landlord-tenant relationship in a modern context and concluded that the agrarian common-law concept is no longer indicative of the contemporary relationship between the tenant and landlord. The land is of minimal importance to the modern tenant; rather, the primary subject of most leases is the structure located on the land and the services which are to be provided to the tenant. The modern residential tenant seeks to lease a dwelling suitable for living purposes. The landlord usually has knowledge of any defects in the premises that may render it uninhabitable. In addition, the landlord, as permanent owner of the premises, should rightfully bear the cost of any necessary repairs. In most instances the landlord is in a much better bargaining position than the tenant. Accordingly, we held in *Kamarath* that the landlord impliedly warrants that the premises are habitable and fit for living. We further implicitly recognized that the residential tenant's obligation to pay rent is dependent upon the landlord's performance under his warranty of habitability. [   ]

When a commercial tenant such as Dr. Davidow leases office space, many of the same considerations are involved. A significant number of commentators have recognized the similarities between residential and commercial tenants and concluded that residential warranties should be expanded to cover commercial property. [   ]

It cannot be assumed that a commercial tenant is more knowledgeable about the quality of the structure than a residential tenant. A businessman cannot be expected to possess the expertise necessary to adequately inspect and repair the premises, and many commercial tenants lack the financial resources to hire inspectors and repairmen to assure the suitability of the premises. [   ] Additionally, because commercial tenants often enter into short-term leases, the tenants have limited economic incentive to make any extensive repairs to their premises. [   ] Consequently, commercial tenants generally rely on their landlords' greater abilities to inspect and repair the premises. [   ]

In light of the many similarities between residential and commercial tenants and the modern trend towards increased consumer protection, a number of courts have indicated a willingness to apply residential property warranties to commercial tenancy situations. [   ]

There is no valid reason to imply a warranty of habitability in residential leases and not in commercial leases. Although minor distinctions can be drawn between residential and commercial tenants, those differences do not justify limiting the warranty to residential leaseholds. Therefore, we hold there is an implied warranty of suitability by the landlord in a commercial lease that the premises are suitable for their intended commercial purpose. This warranty means that at the inception of the lease there are no latent defects in the facilities that are vital to the use of the premises for their intended commercial purpose and that these essential facilities will remain in a suitable condition. If, however, the parties to a lease expressly agree that the tenant will repair certain defects, then the provisions of the lease will control.

We recognized in *Kamarath* that the primary objective underlying a residential leasing arrangement is "to furnish [the tenant] with quarters suitable for living purposes." *Kamarath*, 568 S.W.2d at 661. The same objective is present in a commercial setting. A commercial tenant desires to lease premises suitable for their intended commercial use. A commercial landlord impliedly represents that the premises are in fact suitable for that use and will remain in a suitable condition. The tenant's obligation to pay rent and the landlord's implied warranty of suitability are therefore mutually dependent.

The existence of a breach of the implied warranty of suitability in commercial leases is usually a fact question to be determined from the particular circumstances of each case. Among the factors to be considered when determining whether there has been a breach of this warranty are: the nature of the defect; its effect on the tenant's use of the premises; the length of time the defect persisted; the age of the structure; the amount of the rent; the area in which the premises are located; whether the tenant waived the defects; and whether the defect resulted from any unusual or abnormal use by the tenant. [ ]

The jury found that Inwood leased the space to Dr. Davidow for use as a medical office and that Inwood knew of the intended use. The evidence and jury findings further indicate that Dr. Davidow was unable to use the space for the intended purpose because acts and omissions by Inwood rendered the space unsuitable for use as a medical office. The jury findings establish that Inwood breached the implied warranty of suitability. Dr. Davidow was therefore justified in abandoning the premises and discontinuing his rent payments.

* * *

Notes and Questions

1. Most courts have rejected an implied warranty of habitability or suitability in commercial leases without analyzing whether the distinctions between residential and commercial leases justify limiting the warranty to residential leases. A standard argument is that commercial lessees normally do not occupy inferior bargaining positions. See, e.g., Service Oil Co. v. White, 218 Kan. 87, 542 P.2d 652 (1975). Is that a persuasive reason for the distinction? What about commercial tenants on the first floor of an apartment building? Do they have a stronger bargaining position than the residential tenants?

2. The American Law Institute, in adopting the implied warranty of habitability as a warranty that premises will be "suitable for residential use," stated that it was taking "no position at this time" on whether the warranty should be implied in commercial leases. Restatement (Second) of Property §§ 5.1, Caveat; 5.5, Caveat to subsection (1) (1976).

3. *Davidow* suggests some differences in the application of the implied warranty of suitability for leased commercial space. For example, the warranty can be waived if "the parties to a lease expressly agree that the tenant will repair certain defects." 747 S.W.2d at 377; Kerrville HRH, Inc. v. City of Kerrville, 803 S.W.2d 377, 389 (Tex.App.1990). In a mixed-use building, with both residential and commercial tenants, should different standards be applied concerning waivability?

4. What is the proper scope of an implied warranty of commercial suitability? Should it be confined to latent physical or structural defects in the leased premises? Or should it extend to the failure of a landlord to provide adequate parking for customers of the commercial tenant? See Coleman v. Rotana, Inc., 778 S.W.2d 867 (Tex.App.1989) (implied warranty covers only physical defects of leased premises and not inadequacies in use of parking facilities).

5. Suppose a commercial tenant inspects the premises prior to entering into a lease and negligently fails to discover a structural defect. Is the warranty defeated by the tenant's negligence? See Kerrville HRH, Inc. v. City of Kerrville, 803 S.W.2d 377, 386 (Tex.App.1990) (contributory negligence no bar to cause of action for breach of implied warranty of suitability).

E. RETALIATORY EVICTION

EDWARDS v. HABIB

Court of Appeals for the District of Columbia Circuit, 1968.
397 F.2d 687, cert. den., 393 U.S. 1016, 89 S.Ct. 618, 21 L.Ed.2d 560 (1969).

J. SKELLY WRIGHT, CIRCUIT JUDGE:

In March 1965 the appellant, Mrs. Yvonne Edwards, rented housing property from the appellee, Nathan Habib, on a month-to-month basis. Shortly thereafter she complained to the Department of Licenses and Inspections of sanitary code violations which her landlord had failed to remedy. In the course of the ensuing inspection, more than 40 such violations were discovered which the Department ordered the landlord to correct. Habib then gave Mrs. Edwards a 30–day statutory notice to vacate and obtained a default judgment for possession of the premises. Mrs. Edwards promptly moved to reopen this judgment, alleging excusable neglect for the default and also alleging as a defense that the notice to quit was given in retaliation for her complaints to the housing authorities. Judge Greene, sitting on motions in the Court of General Sessions, set aside the default judgment and, in a very thoughtful opinion, concluded that a retaliatory motive, if proved, would constitute a defense to the action for possession. At the trial itself, however, a different judge apparently deemed evidence of retaliatory motive irrelevant and directed a verdict for the landlord.

Mrs. Edwards then appealed to this court for a stay pending her appeal to the District of Columbia Court of Appeals, and on December 3, 1965, we granted the stay, provided only that Mrs. Edwards continue to pay her rent. [ ] She then appealed to the DCCA, which affirmed the judgment of the trial court. [ ] In reaching its decision the DCCA relied on a series of its earlier decisions holding that a private landlord was not required, under the District of Columbia Code, to give a reason for evicting a month-to-month tenant and was free to do so for any reason or for no reason at all. The court acknowledged that the landlord's right to terminate a tenancy is not absolute, but felt that any limitation on his prerogative had to be based on specific statutes or very special circumstances. Here, the court concluded, the tenant's right to report violations of law and to petition for redress of grievances was not protected by specific legislation and that any change in the relative rights of tenants and landlords should be undertaken by the legislature, not the courts. We granted appellant leave to appeal that decision to this court. We hold that the promulgation of the housing code by the District of Columbia Commissioners at the direction of Congress impliedly effected just such a change in the relative rights of landlords and tenants and that proof of a retaliatory motive does constitute a defense to an action of eviction. Accordingly, we reverse the decision of the DCCA with directions that it remand to the Court of General Sessions for a new trial where Mrs. Edwards will be permitted to try to prove to a jury that her landlord who seeks to evict her harbors a retaliatory intent.

* * *

[Discussion of constitutional issues that were not decided is omitted.—Eds.]

III

* * *

45 D.C.Code § 910, in pertinent part, provides:

"Whenever * * * any tenancy shall be terminated by notice as aforesaid [   ], and the tenant shall fail or refuse to surrender possession of the leased premises, * * * the landlord may bring an action to recover possession before the District of Columbia Court of General Sessions, as provided in sections 11–701 to 11–749."

And 16 D.C.Code § 1501, in pertinent part, provides:

"When a person detains possession of real property * * * after his right to possession has ceased, the District of Columbia Court of General Sessions * * * may issue a summons to the party complained of to appear and show cause why judgment should not be given against him for restitution of possession."

These provisions are simply procedural. They neither say nor imply anything about whether evidence of retaliation or other improper motive should be unavailable as a defense to a possessory action brought under them. It is true that in making his affirmative case for possession the landlord need only show that his tenant has been given the 30–day statutory notice, and he need not assign any reason for evicting a tenant who does not occupy the premises under a lease. But while the landlord may evict for any legal reason or for no reason at all, he is not, we hold, free to evict in retaliation for his tenant's report of housing code violations to the authorities. As a matter of statutory construction and for reasons of public policy, such an eviction cannot be permitted.

The housing and sanitary codes, especially in light of Congress' explicit direction for their enactment, indicate a strong and pervasive congressional concern to secure for the city's slum dwellers decent, or at least safe and sanitary, places to live. Effective implementation and enforcement of the codes obviously depend in part on private initiative in the reporting of violations. Though there is no official procedure for the filing of such complaints, the bureaucratic structure of the Department of Licenses and Inspections establishes such a procedure, and for fiscal year 1966 nearly a third of the cases handled by the Department arose from private complaints. To permit retaliatory evictions, then, would clearly frustrate the effectiveness of the housing code as a means of upgrading the quality of housing in Washington.

As judges, "we cannot shut our eyes to matters of public notoriety and general cognizance. When we take our seats on the bench we are not struck with blindness, and forbidden to know as judges what we see as men." Ho Ah Kow v. Nunan, C.C.D.Cal., 12 Fed.Cas. 252, 255 (No. 6546) (1879). In trying to effect the will of Congress and as a court of equity we have the responsibility to consider the social context in which our decisions will have operational effect. In light of the appalling condition and shortage of housing in Washington, the expense of moving, the inequality of bargaining power between tenant and landlord, and the social and economic importance of assuring at least minimum standards in housing conditions, we do not hesitate to declare that retaliatory eviction cannot be tolerated. There can be no doubt that the slum dweller, even though his home be marred by housing code violations, will pause long before he complains of them if he fears eviction as a consequence. Hence an eviction under the circumstances of this case would not only punish appellant for making a complaint which she had a constitutional right to make, a result which we would not impute to the will of Congress simply on the basis of an essentially procedural enactment, but also would stand as a warning to others that they dare not be so bold, a result which, from the authorization of the housing code, we think Congress affirmatively sought to avoid.

The notion that the effectiveness of remedial legislation will be inhibited if those reporting violations of it can legally be intimidated is so fundamental that a presumption against the legality of such intimidation can be inferred as inherent in the legislation even if it is not expressed in the statute itself. Such an inference was recently drawn by the Supreme Court from the federal labor statutes to strike down under the supremacy clause a Florida statute denying unemployment insurance to workers discharged in retaliation for filing complaints of federally defined unfair labor practices. While we are not confronted with a possible conflict between federal policy and state law, we do have the task of reconciling and harmonizing two federal statutes so as to best effectuate the purposes of each. The proper balance can only be struck by interpreting 45 D.C.Code §§ 902 and 910 as inapplicable where the court's aid is invoked to effect an eviction in retaliation for reporting housing code violations.

This is not, of course, to say that even if the tenant can prove a retaliatory purpose she is entitled to remain in possession in perpetuity. If this illegal purpose is dissipated, the landlord can, in the absence of legislation or a binding contract, evict his tenants or raise their rents for economic or other legitimate reasons, or even for no reason at all. The question of permissible or impermissible purpose is one of fact for the court or jury, and while such a determination is not easy, it is not significantly different from problems with which the courts must deal in a host of other contexts, such as when they must decide whether the employer who discharges a worker has committed an unfair labor practice because he has done so on account of the employee's union activities. As Judge Greene said, "There is no reason why similar factual judgments cannot be made by courts and juries in the context of economic retaliation [against tenants by landlords] for providing information to the government."

Reversed and remanded.

McGOWAN, CIRCUIT JUDGE (concurring except as to Parts I and II)

[omitted]

DANAHER, CIRCUIT JUDGE (dissenting)

[omitted]

ROBINSON v. DIAMOND HOUSING CORPORATION

Court of Appeals for the District of Columbia Circuit, 1972.
463 F.2d 853.

J. SKELLY WRIGHT, CIRCUIT JUDGE:

In Edwards v. Habib, 130 U.S.App.D.C. 126, 397 F.2d 687 (1968), cert. denied, 393 U.S. 1016, 89 S.Ct. 618, 21 L.Ed.2d 560 (1969), this court held that a tenant may assert the retaliatory motivation of his landlord as a defense to an otherwise proper eviction. In Brown v. Southall Realty Co., D.C.App., 237 A.2d 834 (1968), the District of Columbia Court of Appeals held that a lease purporting to convey property burdened with substantial housing code violations was illegal and void and that hence the landlord was not entitled to gain possession for rent due under the invalid lease. [ ] The case before us involves the intersection of these two principles. Specifically, it raises the question whether a landlord who has been frustrated in his effort to evict a tenant for nonpayment of rent by successful assertion of a *Southall Realty* defense may automatically accomplish the same goal by serving a 30–day notice to quit.

Appellant argues that she should be permitted to show that her landlord, Diamond Housing, was motivated by a retaliatory intent when it served the notice to quit. Diamond Housing contends that a retaliatory eviction defense has no place in a situation where, as here, the landlord is unable or unwilling to make the repairs on the premises that would entitle it to rent under *Southall Realty* and alleges an intent to take the property off the housing market. When the District of Columbia Court of General Sessions granted summary judgment to appellee, appellant renewed her arguments in the District of Columbia Court of Appeals. That court affirmed, holding:

> " * * * [T]he retaliatory defense of Edwards v. Habib * * * is not available to a tenant in a case such as this where she was successful in a prior Landlord and Tenant action and is being evicted after the expiration of a thirty-day notice because the landlord wishes to withdraw the property from the rental market. The *Edwards* case involved a situation where the landlord attempted to evict the tenant because of her complaints to the housing authorities and it should be, we think, limited to its facts."

Robinson v. Diamond Housing Corp., D.C.App., 267 A.2d 833, 835 (1970).

We can find nothing about the *Edwards* principle which necessitates such a drastic limitation on its applicability. Indeed the prohibition against retaliatory evictions generally, without limitation to the facts of *Edwards,* and in terms applicable to *Southall Realty* rights, has become part of the housing code of the District of Columbia. We see no reason why the rights protected in *Southall Realty* and *Javins* should be rendered nugatory by a restrictive reading of *Edwards* or by a judicial failure to respect the legislative will. We are therefore of the view that appellant should have been given the opportunity to prove the facts necessary to make out an *Edwards* defense and that the trial judge erred in aborting this opportunity by prematurely granting summary judgment. It follows that the decision of the District of Columbia Court of Appeals must be reversed.

I

If lawsuits were won by perseverance alone, Diamond Housing could hardly lose this suit. Appellee has been attempting to evict Mrs. Robinson for over three and a half years. It has proceeded under no fewer than three legal theories and has remained undaunted through an adverse jury verdict, a dismissal of its action by the Court of General Sessions, an adverse decision by the District of Columbia Court of Appeals, and action by the District of Columbia City Council which seemingly cut the heart out of its case.

The saga begins on May 2, 1968, when Mrs. Robinson and her four children moved into a row house owned by Diamond Housing in Northwest Washington. Mrs. Robinson signed a lease making her a month-to-month tenant with the apparent understanding that the landlord would repair the deteriorating condition of the premises. [ ]

When the landlord failed to keep this promise, Mrs. Robinson began withholding rent, and Diamond Housing sued for possession. Mrs. Robinson defended on the ground that substantial housing violations existed at the time the lease was signed and that the lease was therefore unenforceable under the principles announced in Brown v. Southall Realty Co., *supra.* Specifically, Mrs. Robinson introduced evidence showing that large pieces of plaster were missing throughout the house, that there was no step from the front walk to the front porch, that the front porch was shaky and unsafe, that there was a wall in the back bedroom which was not attached to the ceiling and which moved back and forth when pressed, that nails protruded along the side of the stairway, that there was a pane of glass missing from the living room window, and that the window frame in the kitchen was so far out of position that one could see into the back yard through the space between it and the wall. [ ] At the completion of the trial, the jury returned a special verdict finding that housing code violations existed at the inception of the lease rendering the premises unsafe and unsanitary. [ ] The trial court then granted judgment to Mrs. Robinson, as required by *Southall Realty*. [ ]

Unwilling to admit defeat, Diamond Housing instituted a second suit for possession on the theory that, since the lease was void, Mrs. Robinson was a trespasser and hence no longer entitled to possession. When the trial court granted Mrs. Robinson's motion to dismiss, Diamond Housing appealed to the District of Columbia Court of Appeals. That court affirmed, holding that "an agreement entered into in violation of the law creates no rights upon the wrongdoer. The defense of illegality does not rescind the illegal agreement, but merely prevents a party from using the courts to enforce such an agreement." Diamond Housing Corp. v. Robinson, D.C.App., 257 A.2d 492, 495 (1969). (Footnote omitted.) It followed that Mrs. Robinson, "having entered possession under a void and unenforceable lease, was not a trespasser but became a tenant at sufferance." [ ] The court added, however, that Mrs. Robinson's tenancy, "like any other tenancy at sufferance, may be terminated on thirty days' notice. The Housing Regulations do not compel an owner of housing property to rent his property. Where, as here, it has been determined that the property when rented was not habitable, that is, not safe and sanitary, and should not have been rented, and if the landlord is unwilling or unable to put the property in a habitable condition, he may and should promptly terminate the tenancy and withdraw the property from the rental market, because the Regulations forbid both the rental and the occupancy of such premises." *Ibid.* (Footnote omitted.)

Seizing upon this dicta, Diamond Housing instituted a third action for possession, this time on the basis of a 30–day notice. In support of its action, Diamond filed an affidavit stating that it was unwilling to make the repairs necessary to put the housing in compliance with the housing code and that it presently intended to take the unit off the rental market. [ ] In defense, Mrs. Robinson asserted that she was being evicted in retaliation for successfully asserting her *Southall Realty* rights in the previous actions, and that the eviction was therefore illegal under the principles announced in Edwards v. Habib, *supra*. Mrs. Robinson also argued that the eviction was barred under general equitable principles since Diamond Housing, having allowed its housing to fall into disrepair, lacked the requisite "clean hands."

On this record, Diamond Housing moved for summary judgment. In an oral opinion, Judge Hyde recognized that "there wouldn't be but one way this issue [Diamond's retaliatory motive] could be decided by the jury, because as a matter of fact, I should think that if the landlord is honest at all, he would admit that he's upset, angry, wanted the tenant out of there." [21]

[ ] Nonetheless, the court found that "[i]t would seem to be the height of absurdity to permit retaliation, at this juncture, even to be entertained," *ibid.,* and granted Diamond's motion. [ ]

While this decision was on appeal to the District of Columbia Court of Appeals, Mrs. Robinson apparently vacated the premises. [ ] However, the precise circumstances surrounding her move are not clear on this record. Mrs. Robinson alleges that she was forced to leave involuntarily by the continued existence of the unremedied housing code violations. [ ] Diamond Housing asserts that Mrs. Robinson voluntarily made the premises uninhabitable by failing to pay her heating bills which led to a discontinuance of heat and the freezing of all pipes in the building. [ ]

Whatever the truth of these competing contentions, the District of Columbia Court of Appeals apparently found that they had no effect on the justiciability of the controversy, since that court proceeded to affirm the judgment of the Court of General Sessions on the merits. The court found that the procedures followed by Diamond were in accord with the statutory requirements for recovery of property from a tenant at sufferance and that the retaliatory defense of Edwards v. Habib, *supra,* was unavailable as a matter of law in this situation. [ ] We thereupon granted leave to appeal, and it is this judgment which is now before us for review.

II

A panel of this court recently had occasion to observe that there is an "apparently rising incidence of possessory actions based on notices to quit following closely on the heels of possessory actions based on nonpayment of rent." Cooks v. Fowler, 141 U.S.App.D.C. 236, 240, 437 F.2d 669, 673 (1971). This trend is disturbing because, if judicially encouraged, it would vitiate tenants' rights recognized in *Southall Realty* and *Javins* and now protected by statute in the District of Columbia. * * *

The *Javins* and *Southall Realty* decisions—as well as the District of Columbia regulations patterned after them—were based on the express premise that private remedies for housing code violations would increase the stock of livable low-cost housing in the District. If exercise of those remedies leads instead to eviction of tenants and abandonment of what little low-cost housing remains in the District, the great goal of "a decent home and a suitable living environment for every American

---

21. Even counsel for Diamond seems to have conceded that a jury would find the landlord to have been motivated by retaliatory purposes. At one point in oral argument he stated, "Any jury is going to have to practically say that there is retaliation. Certainly, it's understandable—only human nature, that a person who can't collect the rent is going to try and get them out. That's going to be the basic reason." Transcript of Record in DCCA No. 5194 at 39.

family," Section 1 of the Housing Act of 1937, 50 Stat. 888, as amended by the Housing Act of 1949, 63 Stat. 413, will be frustrated. [   ]

Of course, if the housing market is structured in such a way that it is impossible for landlords to absorb the cost of bringing their units into compliance with the housing code, there may be nothing a court can do to prevent vigorous code enforcement from driving low-cost housing off the market. But the most recent scholarship on the subject indicates this danger is largely imagined. In fact, it appears that vigorous code enforcement plays little or no role in the decrease in low-cost housing stock. When code enforcement is seriously pursued, market forces generally prevent landlords from passing on their increased costs through rent increases. *See generally* Ackerman, Regulating Slum Housing Markets On Behalf of the Poor: Of Housing Codes, Housing Subsidies and Income Redistribution Policy, 80 Yale L.J. 1093 (1971). The danger stems not from the possibility that landlords might take low-cost units off the market altogether, but rather from the possibility that they will do so selectively in order to "make an example" of a troublesome tenant who has the temerity to assert his legal rights in court. We can be fairly confident that most landlords will find owner-ship of property sufficiently profitable—even with vigorous code en-forcement—to remain in business. But it is undoubtedly true that the same landlords would be able to make a greater profit if the housing code were enforced laxly or not at all. There is thus a real danger that landlords may find it in their interest to sacrifice the profits derived from operation of a few units in order to intimidate the rest of their tenants.

Fortunately, this is a danger with which the law is better equipped to deal. While the judiciary may be powerless to control landlords who no longer wish to remain landlords, it can prevent landlords from conducting their business in a way that chills the legally protected rights of tenants. [   ] Indeed, this court's decision in Edwards v. Habib, *supra,* was premised on the belief that retaliatory evictions had a "chilling effect" on assertion of rights protected by the housing code, and that the courts could and should eliminate this inhibition. The *Edwards* court expressly recognized the vital role which private tenants play in the District's system of housing code enforcement, and held that it would violate congressional intent to permit eviction of tenants for the purpose of preventing exercise of private remedies.

It would thus appear, at first blush at least, that the *Edwards* principle should control disposition of this case. Applying this princi-ple Diamond Housing would prevail if it were able to prove to the satisfaction of a jury that it evicted Mrs. Robinson because it could not afford to repair the premises, or for some other valid reason, or for no reason at all. But questions of motivation are particularly inappropri-ate for resolution on a motion for summary judgment. [   ] There is also the possibility—indeed, the trial judge viewed it as a near certain-ty—that the jury would find Mrs. Robinson's eviction to be based on an illicit motive. Given the legal sufficiency of the *Edwards* defense, Mrs.

Robinson should have been permitted to make her case if she could, and the factual issue should have been left in the hands of a jury.

This argument assumes, however, that an *Edwards* defense is in fact legally sufficient in this situation. Although the broad principles which underlie *Edwards* would seem squarely applicable, it is possible that something special about this fact pattern would make it unwise or impermissible to utilize *Edwards* here. Diamond Housing takes the position that this case is, in fact, special and that the special circumstances surrounding it make an application of *Edwards* unjust. Diamond's argument begins with the premise—apparently shared by the District of Columbia Court of Appeals—that *Edwards* should be narrowly "limited to its facts." Since *Edwards* involved reporting of code violations to city officials while this case involves setting up those violations as a defense to an action for eviction, it is contended that *Edwards* does not compel reversal here. Moreover, Diamond argues that, even if *Edwards* is more broadly read, it still should not be applied to a case such as this where the landlord is prevented from collecting rent by *Southall Realty,* refuses to repair the premises, and wishes to take the housing off the market altogether. Closely allied to this contention is the further argument that Mrs. Robinson is precluded from remaining in possession by Section 2301 of the Housing Regulations which makes it illegal to occupy premises which are in violation of the Regulations. Finally, Diamond argues that in any event this case is now moot since Mrs. Robinson has voluntarily surrendered possession and Diamond has chosen to forego any claim it might have to back rent.

We have carefully examined each of these arguments and have concluded that none of them sufficiently distinguishes this case from *Edwards* or precludes application of the District of Columbia law against retaliatory evictions. If we resolve all reasonable doubts in favor of appellant—as we must when reviewing a summary judgment, [ ]—it becomes plain that a jury might find Diamond Housing to be using the eviction machinery to punish Mrs. Robinson for exercising her legal rights. *Edwards* squarely holds that the state's judicial processes may not be so used, and nothing which has transpired since *Edwards* was decided has caused us to change our view. Indeed, if anything, the creation by the District of Columbia City Council of new private remedies for code violations since *Edwards* reinforces our belief in the necessity for a broad retaliatory eviction defense. If the housing code were effectuated solely by a system of comprehensive public enforcement, the situation might perhaps be different. But by legislating a system of private remedies conforming to the *Javins* and *Southall Realty* decisions, the City Council has made plain that the code is to be enforced in large part through the actions of private tenants. Having put at least some of its eggs in the private enforcement basket, the legislature should not at the same time be taken as having authorized use of legal processes by those who seek to frustrate private enforcement. The right to a decent home is far too vital for us to assume that government has taken away with one hand what it purports to grant with the other. * * *

III

We do not pretend that allowing Mrs. Robinson to assert an *Edwards* defense will solve the housing crisis in the District of Columbia. That crisis is the product of a constellation of social and economic forces over which no court—and indeed perhaps no legislature—can exercise full control. But while the judicial process is not a *deus ex machina* which can magically solve problems where the legislature and the executive have failed, neither is it a mere game of wits to be played without regard for the well-being of the helpless spectators. We cannot expect judges to solve the housing dilemma, but at least they should avoid affirmative action which makes it worse. The District's legislative body has formulated a comprehensive plan, including criminal sanctions, public inspections, subsidies and rent withholding, to tackle our housing difficulties. In the end, that plan may not work. But if it fails, at least the failure should be caused by inherent weaknesses rather than by judicial subversion.

Thus all we hold today is that when the legislature creates a broad based scheme for dealing with a problem in the public interest, courts should not permit private, selfishly motivated litigants to undermine it. This result is required by the clear wording of the applicable statute, by the dictates of legislatively declared social policy, and, in the final analysis, by respect for the separation of powers and the rule of law.

Reversed and remanded with instructions.

ROBB, CIRCUIT JUDGE (dissenting)

[omitted]

Notes and Questions

1. Restatement (Second) of Property § 14.8, Caveat (1976) takes no position on whether the retaliatory eviction defense should be extended to residential leases not involving code violations, residential leases from landlords who are not in the rental business, or to commercial leases. Are there any policy reasons for limiting the retaliatory eviction defense in this manner? See Custom Parking, Inc. v. Superior Court, 138 Cal.App.3d 90, 187 Cal.Rptr. 674 (1982) (extending retaliatory eviction defense to commercial tenancies).

2. For purposes of retaliatory eviction, is there any reason to distinguish termination and refusal to renew? See Restatement (Second) Property § 14.8 (1976) (both covered) and URLTA § 5.101 (covers any action for possession).

3. A number of states have prohibited retaliatory eviction and related acts by statute. For a review of the statutes and commentary, see Restatement (Second) of Property §§ 14.8 & 14.9 (1976). Other acts prohibited include retaliatory rent increases and retaliatory reductions in services.

PROBLEM

Leaders of a tenants' union filed complaints with local code enforcement authorities because of alleged housing code violations. While the complaints were pending, the landlord offered to renew leases that were due to expire in 60 days, but with an average rent increase of 15%. The tenants sued to block the increase alleging retaliation for their complaints. During the pendency of this suit, the leases expired but the landlord was enjoined from evicting the tenants so long as timely rental payments required by the expired leases were made. The tenants subsequently failed to prove their allegations of retaliatory rent increases. Thereupon, the landlord filed suits to evict the tenants as holdovers. What result? See Bradley v. Gallagher, 14 Ill.App.3d 652, 303 N.E.2d 251 (1973) (concept of retaliatory eviction presupposes existence of a valid lease or tenancy); Schweiger v. Superior Court of Alameda County, 3 Cal.3d 507, 90 Cal.Rptr. 729, 476 P.2d 97 (1970) (retaliatory rent increase may be asserted as defense to unlawful detainer action for restitution of premises for nonpayment of rent).

A NOTE ON LANDLORD TORT LIABILITY

(a) *Traditional rules*

Historically, landlords have been immune from tort liability because a lease was viewed as a conveyance of land. The landlord gave up control of the premises once possession was transferred to the tenant. With the transfer of possession went the power to exclude the landlord and the responsibility for conditions of the premises. Without control, the landlord had no duty of care for the premises. Several exceptions to the general rule of landlord tort immunity have been recognized.

(1) *Where the premises are under the landlord's control or are leased for a public use.* Landlords are obligated to keep in repair the parts of a building over which they retain control, and buildings that are leased for public activities, such as movie theaters. For example, they must keep in a reasonable state of repair common areas of apartment buildings such as hallways and stairs, shared heating and plumbing systems, and any other area or system over which they retain control. The general standard here is negligence.

(2) *Latent defects.* Landlords may be liable for injuries if they fail to reveal dangerous conditions of the premises of which they are or should be aware that bear an unreasonable risk of harm to the tenant. Landlords normally are not liable for injuries caused by obvious defects, but may be held responsible if a tenant is aware of a defect, but does not realize the degree of risk. Landlords have been held liable for failure to warn of a disease-infested house, steep basement stairs with no handrail, and polluted wells.

(3) *Where the landlord and tenant contract for repair.* Traditionally, courts have refused to impose tort liability on the landlord in this situation, reasoning that the tenant's only remedy is for breach of contract. Now, however, a majority of jurisdictions and the Restatements of Torts and Property recognize a tort duty on the part of landlords, but only if: (i) they have notice of the need for repair; (ii) they fail to exercise reasonable care; and (iii) the resulting state of disrepair creates an unreasonable risk of harm.

(4) *Negligence in making repairs.* Landlords who begin to make repairs and do not exercise reasonable care may be liable in tort for a tenant's injuries. While there may be no duty to act for another's protection, a landlord who undertakes repairs must act reasonably. Some jurisdictions distinguish contracts for repairs, imposing an ordinary negligence standard, from gratuitous repairs for which liability is imposed only for gross negligence.

(5) *Violation of statutes.* Some statutes specifically provide a cause of action for damages for violation of statutes. For those statutes that do not provide for such, the court must decide whether to give the statute any effect in a tort action. Generally, courts recognize that such statutes create duties of care, but require a showing of harm of the type the statutes were designed to prevent and that the plaintiff is a member of the class of people the statute was intended to protect. After a duty is established, courts place varying degrees of importance on a statutory violation. Some courts view violation of a statute as negligence per se, others view it as some evidence of negligence, and still others view it as a presumption of negligence.

(b) *Impact of the Implied Warranty of Habitability*

Some courts have used the implied warranty of habitability to impose a duty of due care on landlords for conditions of the leased premises. The Supreme Court of New Hampshire, in Sargent v. Ross, 113 N.H. 388, 308 A.2d 528, 533–534 (1973), stated that " * * * now is the time for the landlord's tort immunity to be relegated to the history books where it more properly belongs." The court found that "landlords, as other persons, must exercise reasonable care not to subject others to an unreasonable risk of harm." The Supreme Court of Wisconsin, in Pagelsdorf v. Safeco Ins. Co. of America, 91 Wis.2d 734, 284 N.W.2d 55, 60 (1979), extended this duty of due care to people on the premises with the tenant's permission, concluding that "[i]t would be anomalous indeed to require a landlord to keep his premises in good repair as an implied condition of the lease, yet immunize him from liability for his failure to do so." In Kline v. 1500 Massachusetts Avenue Apartment, 439 F.2d 477, 483–485 (D.C.Cir.1970), the District of Columbia Circuit Court held that the landlord was bound to protect the tenant against foreseeable risks of crime and that this duty derived from the "logic of the situation itself," the implied warranty of habitability in the lease, which had been recognized three months earlier by the court in *Javins,* and common law precedents regarding innkeepers and guests also used in *Javins* to support the implied warranty rationale.

The Supreme Court of California in Becker v. IRM Corp., 38 Cal.3d 454, 213 Cal.Rptr. 213, 220, 698 P.2d 116, 123 (1985), held a landlord strictly liable in tort for a defect in the premises. In that case, a tenant suffered severe cuts when he slipped and fell against an untempered glass door. The court held that "a landlord engaged in the business of leasing dwellings is strictly liable in tort for injuries resulting from a * * * defect in the premises when the defect existed at the time the premises were let to the tenant." In reaching this conclusion, the court drew heavily on the implied warranty of habitability concept recognized in California 11 years earlier in Green v. Superior Court, 10 Cal.3d 616, 111 Cal.Rptr. 704, 517 P.2d 1168 (1974).

In Aaron v. Havens, 758 S.W.2d 446 (Mo.1988), the Missouri Supreme Court held that a landlord could be liable for the injuries sustained by a tenant as a result of a sexual assault by an intruder who gained entry to her apartment via a window adjoining a fire escape. The court stated that the owner of the building had a recognized duty of due care to make the premises safe against foreseeable risk, and that, in this situation, the landlord had ample reason to know of the danger of the fire escape leading to the tenant's window. Thus, the landlord could be liable for damage resulting from this dangerous condition. The court made no mention of the implied warranty of habitability which had been accepted by the court four years earlier in Detling v. Edelbrock, 671 S.W.2d 265 (Mo.1984).

In Bellikka v. Green and Columbia Christian College, 306 Or. 630, 762 P.2d 997 (1988), the issue was whether a landlord owed a duty to a third person not a tenant. There, plaintiff fell and was injured when she stepped into a partially concealed hole in the front yard of a landowner's rental property. Plaintiff proceeded on three theories: statutory warranty, implied warranty of habitability and common law negligence. Her statutory theory claims were held to have been properly dismissed at the trial court level. The Supreme Court of Oregon refused to recognize an implied warranty of habituality, stating that the state's statutory warranty of habitability was sufficient. But the court allowed the plaintiff to proceed on a common law negligence claim using the statute to develop the necessary standard of care.

Not all courts have accepted the argument that the implied warranty of habitability should be used to abrogate landlords' traditional common law immunity from tort liability. The Supreme Court of Vermont refused to apply the implied warranty of habitability to a case in which a tenant was injured by falling down a steep stairway on the leased premises. The court reasoned as follows:

> We believe, however, that in the adjudication of a lawsuit for relief from personal injury, the concepts of tort and negligence law provide the more straightforward way to describe the respective duties and

liabilities of the parties. Where a tenant leases substandard premises, she ought recover from the landlord her excess rental payments, her consequential damages for "annoyance and discomfort" and, in certain instances, punitive damages. The landlord broke a promise—at least one implied by the law—and the tenant has the right to recover her losses. But where the tenant seeks a damage award for her personal injuries, other questions arise: What caused the injuries? Were they the result of the landlord's breach? Did they flow from the tenant's own carelessness? The law of negligence is best suited to answer these questions and has developed rules for their accommodation. For example, under Vermont's comparative negligence statute, a plaintiff can recover only if her own negligence contributed to no more than half the cause of the accident, and even then only in proportion to the amount of negligence attributed to the defendant. 12 V.S.A. § 1036. If she was primarily to blame for her fall and injuries, she cannot recover. In essence, plaintiff is asking us to do away with these principles, for, in her view, all damages stemming from defendant's breach of the warranty would be recoverable. Fault would not enter the calculation. We believe it is unwise to abandon negligence principles in this context absent legislative direction.

Favreau v. Miller, 591 A.2d 68, 73 (Vt.1991).

A Texas court, noting that "no majority rule has emerged regarding whether property damages are recoverable in an action for breach of this warranty," concluded that permitting property damages to be recovered would be inconsistent with earlier decisions of the Supreme Court of Texas that damages for personal injury are not recoverable for breach of the warranty. Both personal injury and property damages could be recovered in a negligence action if the elements of negligence could be established. Bolin Development Corp. v. Indart, 803 S.W.2d 817, 819–820 (Tex.App.1991).

For discussion of the tort liability issue, see J. Page, The Law of Premises Liability 193–253 (2d Ed 1988); R. Schoshinski, American Law of Landlord and Tenant § 3.9 (1980 & 1991 Supp); Browder, The Taming of a Duty—The Tort Liability of Landlords, 81 Mich.L.Rev. 99 (1982); Annot., Dangerous Condition of Rented Premises, 64 A.L.R.3d 339 (1975); Restatement (Second) of Property §§ 17.1–17.7, 18.1–18.4, 19.1–19.3 (1976).

F. PUBLIC REGULATION OF THE LANDLORD–TENANT RELATIONSHIP

CHICAGO BOARD OF REALTORS v. CITY OF CHICAGO
Court of Appeals for the Seventh Circuit, 1987.
819 F.2d 732.

CUDAHY, CIRCUIT JUDGE.

On September 8, 1986, the Chicago City Council enacted the Chicago Residential Landlord and Tenant Ordinance (the "Ordinance"), Municipal Code of Chicago, ch. 193.1 (repealing § 193.11), recasting the relative rights and obligations of most residential landlords and tenants in Chicago. On October 14, 1986, the day before the Ordinance was to become effective, this lawsuit began. Plaintiffs-appellants are Chicago property owners or managers and organizations representing their interests. Defendants-appellees are the City of Chicago and its Mayor. Also before the court are three individual tenants and nine organizations representing Chicago tenants. Plaintiffs challenged the constitutionality of the Ordinance and sought a temporary restraining order and a preliminary injunction to prevent its enforcement. A TRO was issued on October 14. On November 3, 1986, the district court denied the preliminary injunction and dissolved the TRO, pending plaintiffs' immediate interlocutory appeal. We granted an expedited appeal schedule but denied plaintiffs' emergency motion for a stay and an injunction pending appeal. We now affirm the district court's denial of plaintiffs' motion for a preliminary injunction.

I. THE ORDINANCE

The Ordinance, by its own terms, was passed by the Chicago City Council:

> in order to protect and promote the public health, safety and welfare of its citizens, to establish the rights and obligations of the landlord and the tenant in the rental of dwelling units, and to encourage the landlord and the tenant to maintain and improve the quality of housing.

Ordinance, § 193.1–1. By its terms the Ordinance applies to all rental agreements for dwelling units located in Chicago, with exceptions for owner-occupied buildings of six or fewer units; dwelling units in hotels, motels, boarding houses and the like; accommodations in hospitals, not-for-profit shelters and school dormitories; and units in cooperatives occupied by holders of proprietary leases. [ ] The Ordinance governs leases either entered into or to be performed after October 15, 1986.

Landlords are required to maintain dwelling units in compliance with all applicable municipal code provisions and with certain other specified standards. [ ]

Landlords have the authority, after notice to the tenant, to terminate a lease if the tenant fails to pay rent or otherwise comply with lease requirements. If the landlord accepts the full rent due under a lease knowing that payments are in default, the landlord thereby waives the right to terminate the lease for that default.

[ ] Except in case of emergency, the landlord must provide notice two days before entering a unit for maintenance, repairs or inspections. [ ]

After notice to the landlord, tenants are granted authority to withhold rent in an amount reflecting the reasonable value of any material noncompliance with the lease by the landlord. Alternatively, tenants can, again after notice, opt to repair certain minor defects or deficiencies and deduct their reasonable cost from the rent.

[   ] Tenants are required to keep their units clean and safe, to use appliances and utilities in a reasonable manner and to avoid disturbing neighbors' "peaceful enjoyment of the premises."

The Ordinance prohibits a charge greater than ten dollars per month for late payment of rent. [   ] In addition, all security deposits received after January 1, 1987 must be maintained in a federally insured account in a financial institution located in Illinois. * * *

A. The Contract Clause

The Constitution prohibits a state from passing "any * * * law impairing the Obligation of Contract," U.S. Const. art. I, § 10, cl. 1. The plaintiffs contend that the Ordinance violates this provision by destroying pre-existing contractual rights and bargained-for expectations contained in leases entered into before October 15, 1986. Despite the mandatory language of the contract clause, however, the Supreme Court has repeatedly affirmed that the clause does not abrogate a state's inherent power to protect the interests of its citizens. * * *

The extent of this prior regulation [of the landlord-tenant relationship] suggests that the Ordinance in fact might not substantially impair any contract obligations. [   ]

At the least, prior regulation dictates a lowered level of scrutiny.

With a relaxed level of scrutiny, then, we ask whether legitimate and significant purposes support the Ordinance and the contractual impairments that it works. The plaintiffs suggest that the actual purpose behind the Ordinance is simply to "provide[ ] one group with an economic advantage over another group," [   ] rather than to protect the public health or welfare. Of course, regulatory legislation may frequently tip the economic scales but at the same time serve entirely legitimate purposes. The expressed purpose of the Ordinance is to promote public health and welfare by improving the quality of housing in the city. The city apparently concluded that this purpose could be furthered by enacting the Ordinance and redefining some rights and obligations for landlords and tenants. On the record before us, we cannot say that the Ordinance is without a legitimate and significant public purpose. * * *

In any event, and certainly without passing judgment on its advisability, we believe that the Ordinance may represent a rational allocation of rights and responsibilities between landlords and tenants. This is an allocation that the city rationally could have believed would lead to improved public health and welfare.

Accordingly, we agree with the district court that the plaintiffs did not show a reasonable probability of prevailing on their contract clause claim. We have found no case, and none has been cited to us, in which a similar landlord-tenant law has been found unconstitutional under the contract clause. The plaintiffs have failed to present persuasive reasons why the present Ordinance should not similarly pass muster.

B. Procedural Due Process

The plaintiffs assert that the Ordinance deprives them of protected property rights without procedural due process as guaranteed by the fourteenth amendment. The essence of this argument seems to be that the Ordinance is unconstitutional because it delegates to tenants— inherently biased decisionmakers—a broad discretion to withhold rent while retaining possession of a landlord's property. [ ]

The first step in this inquiry, of course, is to determine what, if any, state action exists. We are not convinced that actions taken by tenants, pursuant to the Ordinance, comprise state action. A law that defines rights, obligations or remedies among private parties does not thereby transform every private enforcement of that law into state action. [ ] The Supreme Court considered the issue of what action by a private citizen constitutes state action in *Flagg Brothers, Inc. v. Brooks,* 436 U.S. 149, 98 S.Ct. 1729, 56 L.Ed.2d 185 (1978), where the Court held that a warehouseman's forced sale of a debtor's goods, pursuant to New York law, was not state action, because by merely delegating a power to resolve disputes, New York had not delegated any "exclusive public function." *Id.* at 161, 98 S.Ct. at 1739. To the extent that the Ordinance shifts from the landlord to the tenant the power initially to determine whether the premises are in accordance with the lease terms (and with municipal standards embodied in the terms), the Ordinance has readjusted property rights. But this is not a delegation of an exclusive public function; it does not import state action into every action a tenant or landlord might take. We believe that neither a landlord's unlawful lock-out of a tenant nor a tenant's unlawful withholding of rent from a landlord would of itself involve state action.

[ ] This analysis does not end the matter, however, because the plaintiffs charge that the Ordinance itself, enacted by the City, works a deprivation of protected property rights.

The enactment of the Ordinance itself undoubtedly represents state action. The Ordinance, however, does not deprive the plaintiffs of rights in property without due process. The plaintiffs' strongest argument is that the Ordinance provides inadequate post-deprivation remedies by which a landlord can challenge rent withholdings and regain possession. But the Ordinance does not significantly alter the preexisting post-deprivation remedy, the Illinois Forcible Entry and Detainer Act, Ill.Rev.Stat. ch. 110, ¶ 9–101 *et seq.* Plaintiffs have not shown that the Forcible Entry and Detainer Act is an unconstitutionally slow or onerous procedure. [ ] If the Ordinance had established a new post-deprivation procedure by which, for instance, a landlord could not recover possession for five years after a rent default, the plaintiffs would have a much stronger case.

The Ordinance prohibits a late payment penalty exceeding $10 per month. This undoubtedly will cost some landlords some money. But a law that imposes heavier economic burdens on some group of citizens is not thereby rendered unconstitutional. The procedure the landlords were due in this respect was accorded them—in the legislature. [   ]

In addition, the Ordinance requires that landlords attach a copy of the Ordinance to each lease. It is inconceivable that this violates procedural due process.

We conclude that the Ordinance simply readjusts the balance in the long-standing landlord-tenant relationship. Nothing suggests that the Ordinance itself works a deprivation of property without procedural due process. Rather, the Ordinance appears merely to shift some bargaining power to the tenant. This in itself does not violate procedural due process. [   ] * * *

[The Court's discussion of void-for-vagueness, substantive due process, equal protection and preemption is omitted.—Eds.]

The judgment of the district court is Affirmed.

POSNER, CIRCUIT JUDGE, with whom EASTERBROOK, CIRCUIT JUDGE, joins.

We agree with Judge Cudahy's opinion as far as it goes, and we therefore join it. But in our view it does not go far enough. It makes the rejection of the appeal seem easier than it is, by refusing to acknowledge the strong case that can be made for the unreasonableness of the ordinance. It does not explain how the district judge's denial of a preliminary injunction against such an interference with contract rights and economic freedom can be affirmed without violating the contract clause and the due process clause of the Constitution. So we are led to write separately, and since this separate opinion commands the support of two members of this panel, it is also a majority opinion.

The new ordinance rewrites present and future leases of apartments in Chicago to give tenants more legal rights than they would have without the ordinance. It requires the payment of interest on security deposits; requires that those deposits be held in Illinois banks; allows (with some limitations) a tenant to withhold rent in an amount reflecting the cost to him of the landlord's violating a term in the lease; allows a tenant to make minor repairs and subtract the reasonable cost of the repair from his rent; forbids a landlord to charge a tenant more than $10 a month for late payment of rent (regardless of how much is owing); and creates a presumption (albeit rebuttable) that a landlord who seeks to evict a tenant after the tenant has exercised rights conferred by the ordinance is retaliating against the tenant for the exercise of those rights.

The stated purpose of the ordinance is to promote public health, safety, and welfare and the quality of housing in Chicago. It is unlikely that this is the real purpose, and it is not the likely effect. Forbidding landlords to charge interest at market rates on late payment of rent could hardly be thought calculated to improve the health, safety, and welfare of Chicagoans or to improve the quality of the housing stock. But it may have the opposite effect. The initial consequence of the rule will be to reduce the resources that landlords devote to improving the quality of housing, by making the provision of rental housing more costly. Landlords will try to offset the higher cost (in time value of money, less predictable cash flow, and, probably, higher rate of default) by raising rents. To the extent they succeed, tenants will be worse off, or at least no better off. Landlords will also screen applicants more carefully, because the cost of renting to a deadbeat will now be higher; so marginal tenants will find it harder to persuade landlords to rent to them. Those who do find apartments but then are slow to pay will be subsidized by responsible tenants (some of them marginal too), who will be paying higher rents, assuming the landlord cannot determine in advance who is likely to pay rent on time. Insofar as these efforts to offset the ordinance fail, the cost of rental housing will be higher to landlords and therefore less will be supplied—more of the existing stock than would otherwise be the case will be converted to condominia and cooperatives and less rental housing will be built.

The provisions of the ordinance requiring that interest on security deposits be paid and that those deposits be kept in Illinois banks are as remote as the provision on late payment from any concern with the health or safety of Chicagoans, the quality of housing in Chicago, or the welfare of Chicago as a whole. Their only apparent rationale is to transfer wealth from landlords and out-of-state banks to tenants and local banks—making this an unedifying example of class legislation and economic protectionism rolled into one. However, to the extent the ordinance seeks to transfer wealth from landlords to tenants it could readily be undone by a rent increase; the ordinance puts no cap on rents. Cf. Coase, *The Problem of Social Cost*, 3 J.Law & Econ. 1 (1960).

The provisions that authorize rent withholding, whether directly or by subtracting repair costs, may seem more closely related to the stated objectives of the ordinance; but the relation is tenuous. The right to withhold rent is not limited to cases of hazardous or unhealthy conditions. And any benefits in safer or healthier housing from exercise of the right are likely to be offset by the higher costs to landlords, resulting in higher rents and less rental housing.

The ordinance is not in the interest of poor people. As is frequently the case with legislation ostensibly designed to promote the welfare of the poor, the principal beneficiaries will be middle-class people. They will be people who buy rather than rent housing (the conversion of rental to owner housing will reduce the price of the latter by increasing its supply); people willing to pay a higher rental for better-quality housing; and (a largely overlapping group) more affluent tenants, who will become more attractive to landlords because such tenants are less likely to be late with the rent or to abuse the right of withholding rent—a right that is more attractive, the poorer the tenant. The losers from the ordinance will be some landlords, some out-of-state banks, the poorest class of tenants, and future tenants. The landlords are few in number (once owner-occupied rental housing is excluded—and the ordinance excludes it). Out-of-staters can't vote in Chicago elections. Poor people in our society don't vote as often as the affluent. See Filer, An Economic Theory of Voter Turnout 81 (Ph.D. thesis, Dept. of Econ., Univ. of Chi., Dec. 1977); Statistical Abstract of the U.S., 1982–83, at pp. 492–93 (tabs. 805, 806). And future tenants are a diffuse and largely unknown class. In contrast, the beneficiaries of the ordinance are the most influential group in the city's population. So the politics of the ordinance are plain enough, cf. DeCanio, *Rent Control Voting Patterns, Popular Views, and Group Interests,* in Resolving the Housing Crisis 301, 311–12 (Johnson ed. 1982), and they have nothing to do with either improving the allocation of resources to housing or bringing about a more equal distribution of income and wealth.

A growing body of empirical literature deals with the effects of governmental regulation of the market for rental housing. The regulations that have been studied, such as rent control in New York City and Los Angeles, are not identical to the new Chicago ordinance, though some—regulations which require that rental housing be "habitable"— are close. The significance of this literature is not in proving that the Chicago ordinance is unsound, but in showing that the market for rental housing behaves as economic theory predicts: if price is artificially depressed, or the costs of landlords artificially increased, supply falls and many tenants, usually the poorer and the newer tenants, are hurt. See, e.g., Olsen, *An Econometric Analysis of Rent Control,* 80 J.Pol.Econ. 1081 (1972); Rydell et al., The Impact of Rent Control on the Los Angeles Housing Market, ch. 6 (Rand Corp. N–1747–LA, Aug. 1981); Hirsch, *Habitability Laws and the Welfare of Indigent Tenants,* 61 Rev.Econ. & Stat. 263 (1981). The single proposition in economics from which there is the least dissent among American economists is that "a ceiling on rents reduces the quantity and quality of housing available." Frey et al., *Consensus and Dissension Among Economists: An Empirical Inquiry,* 74 Am.Econ.Rev. 986, 991 (1984) (tab. 2).

Article I, § 10, cl. 1 of the Constitution—the "contract clause"— forbids a state to pass "any * * * Law impairing the Obligation of Contracts." If the contract clause were taken seriously, the Chicago ordinance, to the extent it modifies existing leases as well as prescribing terms for future ones, would certainly violate the clause. And even though the clause isn't taken very seriously nowadays by those whose views matter the most (Justices of the Supreme Court), the plaintiffs may conceivably be able to prove a violation when the case is tried on the merits. No one argues that the ordinance is not a "law" for purposes of the contract clause or that a lease is not a contract, and no one could doubt that the ordinance impairs the contractual obligations of the tenants: abrogating an obligation impairs the obligation. One might suppose, by analogy to the just-compensation clause, that the hardest cases under the contract clause would be those where the state, without actually abrogating a contract in whole or part, did something that made a person's contractual rights much less valuable. [ ]

This is not such a case. The ordinance transfers contractual entitlements from the party on one side of the contract to the party on the other side.

The Supreme Court, however, has rewritten the contract clause, by inserting the word "unreasonably" before "impairing" and by adopting a radically undemanding definition of "reasonableness." * * *

At all events it is clear that the plaintiffs in this case have an extremely uphill battle against the ordinance on contract clause grounds, [ ] a battle they cannot possibly win on the basis of the evidence they presented in seeking a preliminary injunction. An even stronger conclusion is possible with regard to their challenge on the ground of "substantive due process." The due process clauses of the Fifth and Fourteenth Amendments forbid government to deprive a person of life, liberty, or property without due *process* of law; and if due process is accorded, it is very hard to see how the person can complain about the *substance* of the government's action. So the text is inhospitable to the concept of "substantive due process"; nor does the history of the Constitution support it.

* * *

The plaintiffs have brought their case in the wrong era. Chicago's new ordinance indeed strikes at the heart of freedom of contract, but the Supreme Court's current conception of substantive due process does not embrace freedom of contract; a provision once questionably interpreted to guarantee economic freedom is now questionably interpreted to guarantee sexual and reproductive freedom instead. The Court is not about to cut the welfare state down to size by invalidating unreasonable economic regulation such as the ordinance under attack in this case. [ ] Thus it is clear that the Chicago ordinance does not deny "substantive due process," though not because it is a reasonable ordinance, which it is not.

Clearly, if reasonableness means the same thing in applying the contract clause as in applying the due process clause, the plaintiffs' claim of impairment of contract is also doomed, no matter what evidence they put in at the trial on the merits. Maybe, though, * * * it is a somewhat more demanding requirement in the former than in the latter setting. * * *

Notes and Questions

1. Although concurring in the decision, Judge Posner criticized the Chicago ordinance based on the economic theory that artificial depression of prices (e.g., through public regulation of rents) or increases in costs (e.g., through public imposition of higher standards of quality) will cause the supply of affordable housing to fall. Most ordinances regulating rents also restrict the ability of landlords to refuse to renew tenancies so long as tenants are paying the controlled rent and abiding by reasonable rules and regulations. Landlords often argue that these provisions amount to an illegal taking of their power to exclude, discussed in Chapter One, without

payment of just compensation, discussed in Chapter Seven. The results have been mixed. See Pennell v. City of San Jose, 485 U.S. 1, 108 S.Ct. 849, 99 L.Ed.2d 1 (1988) (taking issue held premature); Pinewood Estates of Michigan v. Barnegat Township Leveling Board, 898 F.2d 347 (3d Cir.1990) (illegal taking of power to exclude by owners of mobile home park); Troy Ltd. v. Renna, 727 F.2d 287 (3d Cir.1984) (no taking resulted from law prohibiting conversion of apartments occupied by elderly and disabled into condominiums).

Should the landlord's power to exclude outweigh a tenant's "right to shelter (tenure)" in a situation where the landlord wishes to convert occupied apartments to condominiums for wealthier persons? Would your answer be different if the building in question was a dilapidated, unoccupied, single room occupancy hotel that the city believes can provide housing for homeless persons? See Seawall Associates v. City of New York, 74 N.Y.2d 92, 544 N.Y.S.2d 542, 542 N.E.2d 1059 (1989), cert. den., ___ U.S. ___, 110 S.Ct. 500, 107 L.Ed.2d 503 (1989) (requirement that owners of SROs restore units and offer them at controlled rents held a taking requiring compensation). Do the selections in Chapter One from different perspectives on the concept of property help in answering these questions?

2. A number of studies, some cited by Judge Posner, have found that low income tenants often are not represented by lawyers and thus do not raise available defenses to eviction actions. In addition, these studies have found that often little or no positive improvement in housing quality results when warranty of habitability issues are raised by low income tenants, primarily because of the inability of such tenants to pay the fair rental value of housing that has been brought up to warranty quality. If these findings are true, should tenant-protective changes continue to be supported without a corresponding willingness to publicly subsidize land owners who are willing to rent to low income families?

A NOTE ON MAINTAINING AFFORDABLE HOUSING THROUGH LONG TERM LEASES

While homeownership has been and remains the dream of most Americans, it is little more than a faint glimmer for millions of persons in the bottom economic quartile. For the most part, persons making less than $20,000 per year (which will include two-income families if both incomes do not exceed full-time minimum wage rates) must depend on rental housing for their shelter. Increasing pressures on rents resulting from a variety of factors, including inflation and higher standards of housing quality, have reduced the number of affordable units of decent quality in the private rental market.

Governments and non profit organizations have responded to this situation in a number of ways.

Public housing. Since 1937, the United States has offered financial assistance to local communities for the development and management of rental units that are owned by local public bodies called housing authorities. The public housing program is a complex exercise in federalism, with the federal government offering financial assistance, state governments regulating the governing public authorities through state enabling legislation, and local governments establishing public authorities that own the housing units. Financial assistance comes in several forms: 1) sale of government backed, tax-free bonds to finance construction, 2) long-term "annual contributions contracts" for the payment of interest and principal on the bonds, 3) annual operating subsidies, and 4) periodic grants for maintenance and repairs. Controversial from its inception, the public housing program remains the most significant form of government housing assistance for low income persons. A new program designed to encourage transfer of ownership of public housing units to tenant organizations and individuals was authorized by the Cranston–Gonzales National Affordable Housing Act of 1990.

Assisted Housing. Since the 1960s, the federal government has offered a variety of incentives to private owners of rental housing, including subsidies to lenders to reduce the cost of financing the development of housing, rental subsidies tied to particular units that were constructed or renovated in accordance with government standards, and vouchers issued to eligible low income persons that can be redeemed for rental subsidies by owners of existing units who agree to rent to the persons holding the vouchers. Concerns over the cumulative budgetary effect of multi-year interest and rental subsidies led to sharp reductions in appropriations for new expenditures after 1978.

While leases in both public and assisted housing typically offer one year terms, legislative and judicial restrictions on refusals to renew except for "good cause" effectively convert the leases into long-term tenancies.

Rent Control. As noted by Judge Posner, governmental restriction on the amount of rent that can be charged by private landlords is an approach often advocated and sometimes implemented in tight housing markets. Rent control usually is coupled with a restriction on refusing to renew leases for other than "good cause," similar to good cause restrictions on public housing and assisted housing landlords.

Long Term Leases. Public controversies over abandonment of apartment buildings by private owners, conversion of apartments to condominiums, and withdrawal of apartments from the assisted housing market have dramatized the importance of maintaining a predictable supply of affordable rental units. A number of techniques involving long term leases have been used.

(a) *Limited equity cooperatives.* In a limited equity cooperative, a non profit corporation owns the building and maintains it as affordable housing. Members of the cooperative purchase shares of stock in the corporation, which entitle them to a vote on corporate governance and a long-term lease of one of the units in the cooperative. Transfer of memberships is regulated by the cooperative and members agree to limit their profit potential should the units appreciate in value.

(b) *Mutual Housing Associations.* The housing cooperative principle is expanded in the mutual housing association through the addition of representatives of business, community groups and government to the governing board, although a majority of the board is made up of residents. Mutual housing associations emphasize long term affordability by offering a life-time right to occupy, along with a right to pass on the unit to a family or household member.

(c) *Community land trusts.* Community land trusts are non profit corporations that are organized to acquire and hold land for the benefit of a particular community. Community land trusts may emphasize goals of protecting agricultural land, preserving the environment and safeguarding cultural treasures, as well as providing permanent affordable housing. When affordable housing is the goal, long term leases of the land will be executed, enabling lessees to acquire existing units or build new units on the land. Private restrictions on land use, discussed in Chapter Six, combined with long term leases and repurchase options for improvement, are used to ensure that the land is permanently dedicated to affordable housing. See, generally, Institute for Community Relations, The Community Land Trust Handbook (1982).

Problem

Suppose you are a new associate assigned to represent an important client of your law firm who has inherited rental property in a low-income neighborhood.

Current tenants generally are long-standing residents, some with month-to-month tenancies and others with one-year term leases that have been renewed on a regular basis. Some tenants have lost their jobs because of a recent plant closing. Most of the rental units need repairs, and the client is weighing alternatives of retaining the rental units "as is," making repairs and raising rents, converting the units to condominiums for middle income persons, or demolishing the building in favor of commercial use. You have been asked to advise the client concerning property law aspects of the alternatives under study, including consideration of the harm that might be caused the tenants and steps that might be taken to alleviate that harm. Prepare a memorandum discussing your analysis and conclusions.

Suppose the client does not ask about potential hardships that might result. Should you raise that possibility? If so, how would you do it?

VI.   A SECOND LOOK AT DISPUTE RESOLUTION

SALSICH AND FITZGERALD, MEDIATION OF LANDLORD–TENANT DISPUTES: NEW HOPE FOR THE IMPLIED WARRANTY OF HABITABILITY?

19 Creighton L.R. 791–795, 809–815 (1986).

* * *

While the revolution in residential landlord-tenant law has resulted in one of the quickest and most dramatic changes in American history to a major aspect of law, it has not produced the improvement in housing standards for low- and moderate-income families that its leaders expected. Legal literature is replete with analysis and commentary about the implied warranty of habitability as a legal concept and about the expectations that were created by it. In many locations, the results have fallen far short of the expectations. Empirical studies in Boston, Chicago, Detroit, and San Francisco, as well as observations of activity in Kansas City and St. Louis, have noted a disappointing, harsh, but observable reality: landlord-tenant law reform, as administered by the courts, has not improved the housing conditions of low- and moderate-income tenants. One of the most distressing findings is the evidence that some courts, responsible for administering landlord-tenant law, have taken a hostile view to the doctrine of implied warranty of habitability or have ignored the doctrine and its attendant tenant remedies.

This Article does not attempt to reanalyze this problem but, instead, looks at a parallel development, alternative dispute resolution, as a possible approach to the administration of the new landlord-tenant law. This approach may enable some of the hopes regarding better housing to be realized. Some particular characteristics of the residential landlord-tenant relationship, particularly with respect to the low- and moderate-income tenants in urban environments, suggest that alternatives to litigation as a means of resolving disputes and administering this relationship have greater potential for success than a continued tinkering with the litigation process.

* * *

Because the landlord remains the owner of the property, a complexity is introduced into this relationship. Two people share the property "bundle" represented by the leased premises. The landlord has an obligation not to harm the tenant's possessory interest, while the tenant has both an obligation not to harm the landlord's ownership interest and an obligation to pay rent. The technical articulation of the tenant's responsibility is that the tenant may not commit waste. Most written leases incorporate the tenant's responsibility through language providing that the tenant agrees to return the property in the same condition as received, normal wear and tear excepted. When a dispute develops involving allegations that waste has been committed, the security deposit usually becomes the center of attention.

Another point of importance, particularly with respect to residential rental property occupied by families of low- and moderate-income, is that short-term tenancies often are created by oral agreements. Most states require written leases for tenancies that are one year or longer in duration. Many low- and moderate-income urban tenants occupy housing under oral arrangements that can be terminated by either party at the end of a rental period, which is usually one month in duration. Traditionally, landlord-tenant law focused on the administration of the termination process by concentrating on notice requirements, summary eviction proceedings, and regulation of the use of self-help.

* * *

III. NONADVERSARIAL DISPUTE RESOLUTION

A parallel development of potential significance to landlords and tenants has been the increased attention given to non-adversarial methods of resolving disputes. A wide range of techniques are being touted, with arbitration and mediation the most popular. The basic distinction between arbitration and mediation is the role assumed by the person to whom the dispute has been brought and the amount of pressure which that person can bring to bear on the parties to the dispute.

Under an arbitration system, the parties usually transfer control over the dispute to a neutral arbitrator who will impose a resolution which will bind the parties if they have agreed in advance to be bound. Arbitration resembles adjudication in this respect, but it is conducted in a far less formal manner. If the parties have agreed in advance to accept the arbitrator's decision, courts will enforce that decision unless the arbitrator clearly exceeded his authority.

Mediation, on the other hand, focuses primarily on the parties themselves coming to an agreement. In these situations, the mediator acts only as a facilitator without the authority to impose a decision on the parties. The mediator seeks to be accepted by the parties as a neutral conciliator rather than a partisan participant or adjudicator.

Proponents of both mediation and arbitration emphasize the speed, lack of expense, informality, de-emphasis of adversary relationships, voluntary nature, privacy, and potential expertise of the dispute resolution officials as factors favoring the use of alternatives to litigation. They, however, caution that mediation typically presumes the possibility of compromise between the parties. If one of the parties is considerably more powerful than the other, that party may not have sufficient incentives to compromise.

In addition to the benefits noted, proponents argue that more extensive use of mediation and arbitration would alleviate some of the problems arising from use of the traditional judicial system. The courts are often a hostile environment for landlord-tenant disputes. This hostility can flow from such things as overburdened caseloads, the built-in conflict between human and property rights, traditional court procedures, lack of familiarity with conditions of housing involved, and even the lack of standards for determining such things as damages from a breach of the implied warranty of habitability. Some courts, recognizing these difficulties, have begun encouraging parties to participate in a mediation process before the court enters its final judgment.

Landlord-tenant disputes—especially conflicts between individual tenants and their landlords over conditions within their particular apartments because of which rent payments or security deposits are held hostage, while emotions rage out of control—may be particularly suited to nonadjudicatory, dispute-resolution processes. In dealing with these issues, property law in general, and landlord-tenant law in particular, has traditionally recognized few legal theories that permit courts to compromise claims. Thus, litigation takes the form of an "either/or, winner/loser" process. Because of the continuing nature of the relationship and the often blurred facts as to who bears responsibility for the damages, litigation may be the least satisfactory approach toward resolving the typical landlord-tenant dispute.

In part, this ineffectiveness is due to the subject matter of the dispute. When parties are in litigation over possessory or ownership rights to real property, usually one side must be declared the winner, with the corresponding right to possess or exclude, and the other, the loser. Ownership and possessory interests and corresponding responsibilities for maintenance and protection of those interests generally must be clear and undiluted in order to enhance the property's productivity and transferability. The long-term nature of most property investments makes predictability an essential element of property law.

The "either/or" choices that prevail in property law litigation can destroy the continuity that is an essential attribute of landlord-tenant relationships. The modern residential landlord-tenant relationship resembles a family in one crucial aspect—mutual interdependence. Because the landlord normally does not live in the building that is being rented, and may, in fact, not even be present in the same jurisdiction, the landlord depends upon the tenants to be "good" tenants and to take care of the landlord's property. At the same time, the tenants depend upon the landlord to be a "good" landlord and to provide the essential services which enable the tenants to live in peace and dignity. The reality of these mutual but often unstated interests was recognized in the pathbreaking, implied-warranty-of-habitability cases. The nature of mediation, with its emphasis on direct communication between the parties to the relationship, assists in defining such interests.

These mutual interests often stem from the purely interpersonal disputes which arise among parties involved in an ongoing relationship. For example, a landlord might believe that a tenant's young children will be likely to damage the common areas of the premises and, therefore, will be less tolerant of any normal childlike activity. The tenant, on the other hand, might believe that the landlord has failed to provide an adequate area where the children may play without them worrying about damage to the premises. In this situation, mediation can be of immeasurable help because it can get the parties talking to one another. With this conversation, the parties may realize that there is no genuine conflict between them. Meshing the concept of "kids will be kids" with the landlord's legitimate concern for the preservation of his property is just one circumstance which is better suited for dispute resolution through communication rather than through a formal judicial process.

Satisfactory protection of the mutual interests of landlords and tenants requires a stable, predictable relationship in which each party can rely on the other to perform in accordance with the mutual understandings. It, however, does not require that landlords or tenants subordinate their self-interests. In fact, responding to the others' concerns actually maximizes the responders' self-interests. The landlord who wants the tenants to be "good" tenants and to take care of the property, as well as to pay the rent on time, is more likely to get these results if he delivers the services that his tenants justifiably expect to receive. Conversely, the tenant who seeks services of a particular quality, such as prompt responses to repair and maintenance requests, is more likely to obtain such responses if he pays the rent on time and takes reasonable care of the premises. In short, both parties desire that the other be "good."

Unfortunately, as is the case with all families, disputes often mar the day-to-day life of the landlord-tenant family. Comparable to other families, resorting to the courts for a resolution of a landlord-tenant dispute generally presages the destruction of the relationship. Whatever possibilities for conciliation and compromise which might exist and which could save the relationship are generally lost once litigation is commenced. This loss is due to the way an adversarial proceeding often transforms a dispute over competing interests into a conflict over hardened positions. Regardless of who wins a landlord-tenant lawsuit, whatever trust and respect that might have been present at one time and which is so essential to the achievement of a "good" landlord-tenant relationship, has probably been destroyed by the bitterness engendered in the litigation. Litigation can be quite costly to both the winner and the loser. If the tenant leaves as a result of the conflict, the landlord faces the additional expense and uncertainty of a vacant apartment until a new tenant can be found, plus the cost of redecorating or repairing the apartment to attract a new tenant. Likewise, the departing tenant faces the cost and uncertainty of seeking a new place to live. If the tenant stays after the litigation has been completed, the obstacles that must be overcome before a "good" relationship can be restored are enormous.

The seeds of urban tragedy can be found in this state of affairs. The great hope that the revolution in residential landlord-tenant law would result in improved housing conditions for low-income families has dissolved like a desert mirage. Wholesale abandonment of apartment buildings or their conversion into condominiums has occurred in many urban neighborhoods. Of course, placing all of the housing ills of the urban poor on the doorstep of the landlord-tenant courthouse is about as fair as blaming all of the ills of society on the failure of the public school system. However, the fact remains that reliance on litigation, even after the substantial shift in the law toward the tenant's point of view, has not resulted in a measurable improvement in the living conditions of the low- or moderate-income urban tenant. Continued reliance on litigation as the basic mechanism for resolution of landlord-tenant disputes is, thus, open to serious question.

The shift in landlord-tenant law has laid the foundation for the use of alternatives to litigation in dispute resolution. Two of the major concerns that have been raised about the use of arbitration and mediation in landlord-tenant disputes are: (1) the perceived imbalance of power between the landlord and the tenant; and (2) the corresponding lack of incentive for the landlord to participate in noncoercive dispute resolution proceedings. Under the common law, the landlord certainly held the upper hand, in that the tenant had an absolute obligation to pay rent and usually had all the responsibility for maintenance and repair, even if he did not have control or the wherewithal to discharge that responsibility. The typical response of the landlord to a tenant's protest of that state of affairs was that no one was forcing the tenant to stay. This has changed. Society, through the courts and the legislatures, has shifted much of the repair and maintenance responsibility back to the landlord. In the eyes of the law, a state of equilibrium has been approached. If anyone may cry in the future that the system is out of balance, it may be the landlords.

While these changes in the law are not yet reflected in the realities of the landlord-tenant courts, they can dispel the power-imbalance concern because the tenant today has a wide range of legal weapons at his disposal. Effective dissemination of information about the power-shifts in the landlord-tenant law may help tenants overcome the intimidation which results from their sense of powerlessness, while also giving landlords a greater incentive to accept and, perhaps, even to seek out nonadversarial means of settling disputes. If a seeking of nonadversarial means were to occur, the use of the techniques of conciliation and compromise, heart of the mediation process, could enable the disputing parties to preserve the essential unity of the landlord-tenant relationship, while resolving their differences in a reasonably efficient and less costly manner. One of the most positive results that could come about is an increase in direct communication regarding the disputed matter. Communication between the affected parties could occur at an earlier stage so as to prevent irreparable damage to the landlord-tenant relationship. * * *

Dispute Resolution Exercises

1. Write a memorandum of law analyzing the legal issues in Green v. Lord, the problem at the beginning of the chapter.

2. Prepare a draft agreement for consideration by the disputants, including a short memorandum of your reasons for your recommendations.

3. Write a memorandum discussing your reactions to your observation or participation in mock arbitration/litigation and mediation exercises involving Green v. Lord. Include a discussion of the utility of landlord-tenant rules such as implied warranty of habitability for resolving disputes of this type.

VII. LANDLORDS' RIGHTS/TENANTS' RESPONSIBILITIES

A. DUTY TO OCCUPY PREMISES

SLATER v. PEARLE VISION CENTER, INC.

Superior Court of Pennsylvania, 1988.
376 Pa.Super. 580, 546 A.2d 676.

BECK, JUDGE:

This is a commercial lease dispute between Maurice Slater and Peter Kanton, t/a Bloomsburg Shopping Center, Associates (the "Shopping Center") and Pearle Vision Center, Inc. ("Pearle"). Appellant Shopping Center is the lessor and appellee Pearle is the tenant under a lease of premises located in Shopping Center's strip shopping mall. Although Pearle has paid the rent under the lease, it has never occupied the leased premises. Apparently because of Shopping Center's concern that the presence of a vacant store would damage the business of the shopping mall as a whole, in August 1986 Shopping Center filed a complaint in equity seeking an injunction requiring Pearle to occupy and use the premises.

Pearle filed preliminary objections in the nature of a demurrer. Pearle basically alleged that Shopping Center had failed to state a claim for breach of either an express or implied obligation to occupy and use the premises and indeed could not since the lease contains none. Pearle also alleged that Shopping Center had an adequate remedy at law and had no standing to claim relief on behalf of other tenants in the mall.

The trial court sustained Pearle's preliminary objection on the ground that the lease does not expressly obligate Pearle to occupy and use the premises and that as a matter of law, no such obligation could be implied. * * *

We reverse and remand because we find that the complaint, which incorporates the lease in full, is sufficient, albeit minimally, to state a claim for relief based on an implied obligation of Pearle to occupy the premises.   * * *

Shopping Center argues that the lease contains both an express and an implied requirement that Pearle occupy the premises. The express requirement is alleged to be found in Section 10 of the lease, which states:

> A. Tenant covenants and agrees that it shall use the Premises solely as a "Pearle Vision Center" or such other name as is used by the other Tenant's businesses within the State of Pennsylvania for the retail sale and repair of eyeglasses, lenses and other optical merchandise and optical services, and eye examinations and lens grinding and preparation and for no other purpose * * *.

The quoted language on its face would appear to impose an obligation on Pearle to occupy the premises and to use it as a vision center. However, Pennsylvania case law requires us to interpret such language in commercial leases to mean only that no use other than the use specified in the lease is permitted. The language does not address the question of the lessee's duty to occupy the premises.

In the seminal case of *Dickey v. Philadelphia Minit–Man Corp.*, 377 Pa. 549, 105 A.2d 580 (1954), the lease provided that the leased premises were to be occupied by the lessee in the business of washing and cleaning automobiles and for no other purpose. [ ] The lease also provided for rent based on a percentage of gross sales, with a fixed minimum annual rental. The defendant tenant occupied and used the premises for a number of years in accordance with the lease, but then limited its business to waxing cars and largely eliminated the car washing aspect of its business.

The lessor sought to eject the defendant, contending that it was in breach of the lease. The Supreme Court affirmed the trial court's grant of a demurrer to the landlord's complaint. * * *

The lessor argued that in a lease where the rental is based upon gross sales, there is an implied obligation of the tenant to continue the business on the premises to the fullest extent possible. The Court rejected this argument, finding that the tenant's decision to change its business was made in good faith and in the exercise of legitimate business judgment and was not forbidden by any implied term of the lease.

* * *

Thus, the holding of *Dickey* would appear to be that a use covenant like that presented here cannot be read as an express requirement that the tenant use the premises for the precise permitted business purpose. Moreover, *Dickey* holds that there is no implied obligation that the tenant under a percentage lease refrain from conducting its business in good faith and in accordance with sound business judgment simply because doing so may decrease the rent payable.

More pertinent to the instant case is the fact that *Dickey* specifically does not address a situation where the tenant conducts no business on the leased premises. It also does not address a lease for premises which are part of a strip of stores where the economic health of each store may be dependent on the others.

Certain of these considerations were addressed, however, in *McKnight–Seibert Shopping Center, Inc. v. National Tea Co.*, 263 Pa.Super. 292, 397 A.2d 1214 (1979). In *McKnight,* the lessor of a shopping center brought an action for ejectment of the tenant, a food market operator, and its assignee and for damages for wrongful retention of the premises. The lease contained a use provision similar to that involved herein and a fixed rental provision. When the tenant experienced financial difficulties, it attempted to assign the lease, which was permitted by the lease, and notified the lessor that it would close the store temporarily to allow for transfer to the assignee. The temporary closing lasted longer than contemplated due to labor difficulties of the tenant, who paid the fixed monthly rental throughout. Eventually, possession of the premises was surrendered to the lessor, but the claim for damages for wrongful retention survived.

The *McKnight* court recognized the general rule expressed in *Dickey* regarding the limited meaning of a use clause. However, it also recognized that "[a] clause that a shopping center tenant 'shall use the demised premises * * * for the purpose of * * * displaying and selling [merchandise]' probably does not contemplate a permanently idle store front." *Id.* at 298, 397 A.2d at 1217. On the other hand, the court noted that the absence of provisions like a percentage rental clause, a continuous operations clause or a clause mandating that the store be open during certain hours would indicate that there was no obligation of continuous use.

Since the only issue before the *McKnight* court was whether the temporary cessation of the tenant's business to accommodate a legitimate assignment, lengthened due to circumstances beyond the tenant's control, was wrongful and in breach of the lease, the court did not specifically hold as to whether permanent vacancy of a store might constitute a breach of the lease. The court simply held that under the facts presented, a temporary vacancy did not constitute a breach of the lease. *Id.* at 298, 397 A.2d at 1218.

The trial court in the instant matter found *Dickey* and *McKnight* controlling and read them as mandating the dismissal of plaintiff's complaint. As the foregoing discussion of these cases indicates, we do not consider them completely dispositive in this case. Although we recognize that *Dickey* precludes our finding that the use provision requires that the tenant actually used the premises for the precise permitted use, and thus precludes our accepting Shopping Center's argument that this provision alone is an express imposition of a use requirement on Pearle, that does not conclude our inquiry. Shopping Center also argues that in consideration of all of the circumstances of this case, including consideration of all of the provisions of the lease, we should find that it has stated a claim for relief based on an implied obligation to occupy and use the premises. Neither *Dickey* nor *McKnight* precludes such a claim since neither of those cases address the specific situation presented here, i.e. a completely vacant store front in an interdependent shopping mall where the lease itself contains provisions other than the use clause from which an obligation to use and occupy might be implied.

Since there is no other directly controlling Pennsylvania precedent, we must necessarily rely on more general principles of lease construction in our analysis of this issue. As our Supreme Court has recently reiterated, "a lease is in the nature of a contract and is controlled by principles of contract law." *Cimina v. Bronich*, 517 Pa. 378, 383, 537 A.2d 1355, 1357 (1988). One such principle of contract law applicable to this case is sometimes called the doctrine of necessary implication, which has been described as follows:

> In the absence of an express provision, the law will imply an agreement by the parties to a contract to do and perform those things that according to reason and justice they should do in order to carry out the purpose for which the contract was made and to refrain from doing anything that would destroy or injure the other party's right to receive the fruits of the contract.

Frickert v. Deiter Bros. Fuel Co., Inc., 464 Pa. 596, 347 A.2d 701 (1975) (Pomeroy, J., concurring) (quoting *D.B. Van Campen Corp. v. Building and Const. Trades Council of Phila.*, 202 Pa.Super. 118, 122, 195 A.2d 134, 136 (1963)). Thus, where it is clear that an obligation is within the contemplation of the parties at the time of contracting or is necessary to carry out their intentions, the court will imply it. [ ] This is true even where the contract itself is not ambiguous. [ ] Since the doctrine of necessary implication serves not to instruct the court as to which of two possible interpretations of a contract should be adopted, but rather to allow the court to enforce the clear intentions of the parties and avoid injustice, the court does not need to find an ambiguity before it will employ the doctrine.

Applying this doctrine to the case at bar, we find ample evidence in this lease that these parties may well have contemplated and intended that Pearle was obligated to occupy and use the premises. For example, sub-paragraph 9(E) of the lease provides that the tenant agrees to "open the Premises for business to the public not later than ninety (90) days after Landlord's approval of Tenant's plans and specifications." Although we recognize that Shopping Center's complaint does not specifically allege when or if it ever approved Pearle's "plans and specifications", thus triggering this provision, the complaint does allege that Pearle "failed to open the premises and utilize it in accordance with" this provision. Although admittedly unclear, the lack of specificity in the complaint on this point should not herald its demise. This is precisely the genre of pleading deficiency that may often be cured by amendment and that should not, therefore, constitute grounds for dismissal.

Moreover, we find that there are other provisions in the lease that suggest that actual occupancy and use of the premises by Pearle was in the contemplation of the parties when they executed the lease. Section 10(B) states that the tenant agrees "that it will conduct its business in the entire Premises." Section 30 includes "abandonment" as an Event of Default and contains the following noteworthy exception:

> Notwithstanding anything to the contrary herein, Tenant may allow the demised premises to be vacant for a period not exceeding sixty (60) days, provided Landlord is given not less than ninety (90) days written notice that such vacancy will occur: said vacancy being necessary due to repairs or remodeling of the demised premises or transfer of possession to a franchisee or assignee pursuant to the terms of this lease.

This exception appears in type that differs from the body of the lease, which otherwise appears to be largely based on a standard form, thus creating at least the suggestion that this provision was a separately negotiated term. The necessary implication of this provision, which severely circumscribes Pearle's ability to leave the premises vacant, is that except under the circumstances specifically outlined, Pearle *cannot* allow the premises to be vacant.

Finally, the lease contains references to the obligations of Pearle vis-a-vis the viability of the shopping mall as a whole. The "affirmative obligations" of Pearle set forth in Section 20(A) refer to Pearle's obligation to keep the premises in a manner consistent with the general character of the shopping mall and to refrain from any action or practice that "may damage, mar or deface the Premises or any other part of the Shopping Center."

In the face of such provisions, we cannot agree with the trial court's conclusion, based only on the complaint and the *Dickey* and *McKnight* decisions, that no implied-in-fact obligation to occupy and use the premises can be found as a matter of law. We note that a similar conclusion has been reached in cases involving similar facts decided in other jurisdictions. * * *

These cases further buttress our conclusion that in construing the lease to ascertain what obligations respecting use and occupancy it imposes on Pearle, and thus in ascertaining the intentions of the parties to the lease, we must construe the lease as a whole in light of the circumstances surrounding its execution. Having done so, we are convinced that Shopping Center has pleaded a minimally sufficient claim for relief, perhaps capable of further support through an amended pleading, based on an implied obligation to occupy and use. In the instant case, the lease is not completely silent on the tenant's duty to occupy. If it were, we would conclude that the tenant had no duty to occupy because the landlord failed to include such a condition in the lease. Here, several provisions on the lease can arguably lead to the conclusion that the parties intended that Pearle would occupy the premises. * * *

Notes and Questions

1. Whether the tenant has a duty to occupy leased premises normally arises only in commercial settings where a portion of the rent, called percentage rent, is derived from the income generated by the tenant's business. In those situations, the landlord has a direct stake in the tenant's occupation of the leased premises.

Consider, however, whether the landlord might also have a direct interest in a tenant's occupation of residential space. Even if the tenant pays rent on time, might the landlord also desire and expect physical occupation to forestall vandalism and trespass by squatters?

2. Note the use by the court of the contract law doctrine of necessary implication to hold the tenant obligated to occupy the premises in *Slater*. What provisions of the lease, other than the "use" clause, led the court to the "necessary implication" that the parties contemplated regular occupancy? Are any of these provisions the type that might lead to a similar conclusion with respect to a residential lease? Are any of them present in the sample leases supra?

B. ACTIONS FOR WASTE

RUMICHE CORPORATION v. EISENREICH

Court of Appeals of New York, 1976.
40 N.Y.2d 174, 386 N.Y.S.2d 208, 352 N.E.2d 125.

FUCHSBERG, JUDGE.

The issue is whether certain repairs and alterations made by a tenant to his rent-controlled apartment constitute grounds for eviction under the provisions of subdivision a of section 52 of the New York City Rent, Eviction and Rehabilitation Regulations.

The Civil Court of the City of New York granted the landlord's petition for eviction; the Appellate Term and the Appellate Division, successively, each affirmed. The tenant appeals to this court by leave of the Appellate Division. For the reasons which follow, we believe there should be a reversal.

Subdivision a of section 52 of the Rent, Eviction and Rehabilitation Regulations, in pertinent part, reads:

[A]n action or proceeding to recover possession of any housing accommodation shall be maintainable * * * upon one or more of the following grounds:

"a. The tenant is violating *a substantial obligation of his tenancy* other than the obligation to surrender possession of such housing accommodation and has failed to cure such violation after written notice by the landlord that the violation cease within 10 days; *or within the 3 month period immediately prior to the commencement of the proceeding, the tenant has wilfully violated such an obligation inflicting serious and substantial injury upon the landlord"*. (Emphasis added.)

Turning to the facts, the record on this appeal discloses that the tenant has lived in his one-room studio apartment for approximately 10 years. In May of 1973, the building was purchased from its former owner by the landlord, who immediately requested the existing rent-controlled tenants to vacate the building so that he could renovate the premises, offering at least some of them a sum of money as inducement to do so. The tenant before us received such an offer but declined to move. He also called the landlord's attention to the fact that his ceiling was falling in and asked that it be repaired. The landlord did not do so.

The tenant thereupon replaced it with one constructed of three-eighths inch sheetrock and, in the course of doing so, had a licensed electrician install a working ceiling light fixture controlled from a wall switch in place of the pre-existing malfunctioning, old-fashioned, pull-chain one. He also attached a single wooden closet to a wall and erected a small decorative wooden frame around the room's only window. That is the sum total of the "repairs and alterations" involved here.

In essence, in its petition brought pursuant to subdivision a of section 52, the landlord alleged that the repairs to the ceiling did not conform to section 60 of New York City's Fire Code, which specifies five-eighths inch rather than three-eighths inch sheetrock be used, and that the lighting fixture, the closet and the window frame were so permanent or lasting in nature and so materially altered the premises that they violated the "substantial obligation" of the tenancy contemplated by the section. * * *

The question then is whether the repairs and alterations before us constituted waste.

Basically, at common law waste had three different definitions, each related to particular types of conduct on the part of tenants. Involuntary waste was defined as failure to prevent damage to the premises, in other words negligence. Equitable waste was defined as failure to do what a prudent owner would do and was available as a cause of action only in limited circumstances, neither of these concepts is relevant to the facts at hand. But the third, voluntary waste, is. It occurs when a tenant injures the premises by an affirmative act. [ ]

Voluntary waste as a concept stems from early English common law concern that the interests in land held by reversioners or remaindermen be protected from depredations by life tenants of scarce natural resources. [ ]

For instance, the cutting of trees or exhaustion of coal supplies were regarded as waste because their effects extended well beyond the term of the tenant's temporary interest in the land or premises. It is the impingement upon the ultimate estate of the landlord which is the keynote to the definition of waste.   * * *

Its application in a modern landlord-tenant setting is well described in *Pross v. Excelsior Cleaning & Dyeing Co.,* 110 Misc. 195, 201, 179 N.Y.S. 176, 179: "[S]uch a change as to affect a vital and substantial portion of the premises, as would change its characteristic appearance, the fundamental purpose of the erection, or the uses contemplated, or a change of such a nature, as would affect the very realty itself—extraordinary in scope and effect, or unusual in expenditure".

Other courts have also emphasized the definition of waste as permanent or lasting damage. [   ]

Thus, not every change or alteration made by a tenant constitutes waste. For instance, prior to modern leasing developments, except as provided in tenement house legislation [   ] it was, and is, the tenant's and not the landlord's obligation to make repairs. [   ]

Short of waste, a tenant may also make nonstructural alterations consistent with the use of the premises contemplated by his possession of them. [   ]

The ready removability of installations is a significant factor. * * *

In this perspective, it becomes apparent that in the case before us there was insufficient proof of any repair or alteration which could be characterized as one causing permanent or lasting injury to the premises. The apartment in issue remains a one-room studio. Its four walls are intact and remain in place. The closet and windowframe built by the tenant are merely nailed to and not built into the walls; there was no showing that either cannot be taken down and removed at minimal, if any, expense or damage. They are clearly consistent with the tenant's use of the apartment as a residence. The ceiling light fixture is a straight replacement of the old and unworkable one by a new and functioning equivalent; the addition of a modern wall switch could hardly have been more *de minimis*. The replacement for the defective ceiling itself, though, according to the parties' stipulation, not as thick as that required by the fire code, was of the required composition and, interestingly, no violation because of it had ever been issued by the city. More pointedly, the landlord made no showing whatsoever, whether by stipulation or otherwise, that the thickness of the falling ceiling which it replaced was any greater than the one of which it complained in this proceeding.

Significant too, especially on the question of the regulation's requirement that there be a showing of willfulness, is the fact that the tenant, though compelled to remedy the ceiling problem on his own and unaware that his choice of materials could be cause for complaint, upon learning that it was, offered to correct it. His offer, never withdrawn, was refused, the landlord insisting on nothing less than eviction.

We conclude, therefore, that, as a matter of law, the landlord did not establish that the tenant inflicted serious and substantial injury upon the landlord by willfully violating a substantial obligation of his tenancy. Accordingly, the order of the Appellate Division should be reversed and the petition dismissed.

COOKE, JUDGE (dissenting) [omitted.]

Notes and Questions

1. As noted in *Rumiche*, the concept of waste stems from the fact that landlord and tenant share contemporaneous property interests, as do the holders of life estates and remainders discussed in Chapter Two and the holders of concurrent interests discussed in Chapter Three. While the tenant enjoys the benefits of present possession, she must respect the fact that the landlord expects to experience similar possessory enjoyment in the future—when the tenancy ends. In a sense, the tenant is a steward of the landlord's property. The modern doctrine of waste attempts to balance that stewardship responsibility with the recognition that physical changes to the leased property may be necessary to enable the tenant to use the property as intended. See, e.g., Wingard v. Lee, 287 S.C. 57, 336 S.E.2d 498 (App.1985) (clear cutting of unimproved land covered with trees by tenant who had 25–year lease for development of mobile home park held reasonable use and not waste); Restatement (Second) of Property § 12.2(1) (1976) (tenant may change physical condition to extent necessary to permit reasonable use).

2. Many states regulate waste by statute, with remedies ranging from multiple damages (double or treble) to forfeiture of the lease. See Restatement (Second) of Property, Statutory Note to Section 12.2 (1976) for a review of the statutes.

3. Waste is a fact-specific doctrine. Courts use a multi-factor test to decide controversies involving allegations of waste, with the key factors being "the nature, purpose and duration of the tenancy; the character of the property; whether the acts complained of are related to the use and enjoyment of the property; whether the use is reasonable in the circumstances; and whether the acts complained of are reasonably necessary to effectuate such use." Wingard v. Lee, 287 S.C. 57, 336 S.E.2d 498, 500 (App.1985). For a well-known analysis of the waste multi-factor test in the life tenant-remainder setting, see Melms v. Pabst Brewing Co., 104 Wis. 7, 79 N.W. 738 (1899) (permitting family home to be demolished by life tenant because of "radical and permanent change in surrounding conditions" (industrial development)).

4. The Uniform Residential Landlord and Tenant Act allocates certain specific responsibilities to tenants, as noted in the following excerpts.

UNIFORM RESIDENTIAL LANDLORD AND TENANT ACT

§ 3.101. [Tenant to Maintain Dwelling Unit]

A tenant shall

(1) comply with all obligations primarily imposed upon tenants by applicable provisions of building and housing codes materially affecting health and safety;

(2) keep that part of the premises that he occupies and uses as clean and safe as the condition of the premises permit;

(3) dispose from his dwelling unit all ashes, garbage, rubbish, and other waste in a clean and safe manner;

(4) keep all plumbing fixtures in the dwelling unit or used by the tenant as clear as their condition permits;

(5) use in a reasonable manner all electrical, plumbing, sanitary, heating, ventilating, air-conditioning, and other facilities and appliances including elevators in the premises;

(6) not deliberately or negligently destroy, deface, damage, impair, or remove any part of the premises or knowingly permit any person to do so; and

(7) conduct himself and require other persons on the premises with his consent to conduct themselves in a manner that will not disturb his neighbors' peaceful enjoyment of the premises.

§ 3.102. [Rules and Regulations]

(a) A landlord, from time to time, may adopt a rule or regulation, however described, concerning the tenant's use and occupancy of the premises. It is enforceable against the tenant only if

(1) its purpose is to promote the convenience, safety, or welfare of the tenants in the premises, preserve the landlord's property from abusive use, or make a fair distribution of services and facilities held out for the tenants generally;

(2) it is reasonably related to the purpose of which it is adopted;

(3) it applies to all tenants in the premises in a fair manner;

(4) it is sufficiently explicit in its prohibition, direction, or limitation of the tenant's conduct to fairly inform him of what he must or must not do to comply;

(5) it is not for the purpose of evading the obligations of the landlord; and

(6) the tenant has notice of it at the time he enters into the rental agreement, or when it is adopted.

(b) If a rule or regulation is adopted after the tenant enters into the rental agreement that works a substantial modification of his bargain it is not valid unless the tenant consents to it in writing.

§ 3.103. [Access]

(a) A tenant shall not unreasonably withhold consent to the landlord to enter into the dwelling unit in order to inspect the premises, make necessary or agreed repairs, decorations, alterations, or improvements, supply necessary or agreed services, or exhibit the dwelling unit to prospective or actual purchasers, mortgagees, tenants, workmen, or contractors.

(b) A landlord may enter the dwelling unit without consent of the tenant in case of emergency.

(c) A landlord shall not abuse the right of access or use it to harass the tenant. Except in case of emergency or unless it is impracticable to do so, the landlord shall give the tenant at least [2] days' notice of his intent to enter and may enter only at reasonable times.

(d) A landlord has no other right of access except

(1) pursuant to court order;

(2) as permitted by Sections 4.202 and 4.203(b); or

(3) unless the tenant has abandoned or surrendered the premises.

§ 3.104.   [Tenant to Use and Occupy]

Unless otherwise agreed, a tenant shall occupy his dwelling unit only as a dwelling unit. The rental agreement may require that the tenant notify the landlord of any anticipated extended absence from the premises [in excess of [7] days] no later than the first day of the extended absence.

Concerns over waste are one of the main reasons that landlords usually require tenants to pay security deposits.

R. CUNNINGHAM, W. STOEBUCK & D. WHITMAN, THE LAW OF PROPERTY

357–359 (1988).

§ 6.57   Security and Damage Deposits

Presumably on the theory of "a bird in the hand," landlords frequently require their tenants to deposit a sum of money with them at the beginning of the term, to serve as security for the tenant's paying rent and performing other lease covenants. A specialized form of security deposit is the so-called "damage deposit," which the landlord holds to cover the cost of repairing physical damage or perhaps extraordinary cleaning costs caused by the tenant's acts. It is common for leases to require both deposits to secure rent and performance and to pay for damage. * * *

The first and most straightforward mechanism is for the tenant to deposit money or securities upon the understanding that the landlord may draw upon the fund to make up for the tenant's defaults or to pay for physical damage but that all sums not thus withdrawn will be returned to the tenant at the end of the term. Courts agree that the fund remains the tenant's property; for instance, with this kind of deposit, the landlord does not receive income for federal income tax purposes when the deposit is made but only if and when a breach occurs. There is disagreement, however, over the relationship between landlord and tenant with respect to the fund. Most courts consider the landlord to be the tenant's debtor. A few states, New Jersey notably, regard the parties as pledgor and pledgee. Under the creditor-debtor view or the pledgor-pledgee view, the landlord generally is not required to keep the deposit separate from his own funds or to pay interest on it unless, as in a number of jurisdictions, a statute imposes one or both duties. * * *

A second form of security clause is one that, on its face anyway, allows that landlord to retain the entire deposit if the tenant breaches in any way. This is in essence a liquidated damages mechanism. Questions about commingling, interest payment, federal income tax, and accounting should be resolved the same as for the deposit described in the preceding paragraph. A new issue is whether the provision for liquidated damages may be declared void on the ground that it calls for a penalty. Decided cases go both ways on this question. The correct approach, which seems to reconcile most of the decisions, is to begin with the principle that parties may agree for liquidated damages as long as the amount is "reasonable." * * *

The third form of security device, the prepayment of rent for the last period or periods of the term, is not truly a "deposit." When paid at the commencement of the term, the money is the landlord's absolute property. He is required to include it in that year's income for federal income tax purposes. Though it is probably not often done, because advance rent and a security deposit serve overlapping functions, there seems no reason the parties might not use both devices, which do not completely overlap. Apparently the main legal reason a landlord would want rent in advance for the latter part of the term is to avoid the common-law rule that if the landlord entered during the term because the lease authorized it for the tenant's breach, the landlord could not recover rent for the balance of the term. * * *

Statutes in most states affect, to a greater or lesser extent, what has been said thus far about security and damage deposits. Likewise, the Uniform Residential Landlord and Tenant Act and the Model Residential Landlord–Tenant Code regulate such deposits. * * *

C. HOLDOVERS

BOCKELMANN v. MARYNICK

Supreme Court of Texas, 1990.
788 S.W.2d 569.

PHILLIPS, CHIEF JUSTICE.

The issue in this appeal of a landlord-tenant dispute is whether a tenant who has vacated the leased premises before the end of the term is liable for rent and repairs accruing during a cotenant's holdover tenancy. The court of appeals held that the tenant is liable unless the tenant gives notice to the landlord that he or she ceases to hold the leased premises. [ ] We reverse the judgment of the court of appeals and render judgment for the vacating tenant, holding that one tenant is not jointly liable for the holding over of another.

Brenda Bockelmann and her then husband, Hermann Bockelmann, rented one side of a duplex from Samuel and Sharon Marynick for several years. Their last written lease was jointly executed in 1984, for a twelve-month term ending on February 28, 1985. The lease included the following holdover provision:

> Should Tenant remain in possession of the demised premises with the consent of Lessor after the natural expiration of this lease, a new tenancy from year to year shall be created between Lessor and Tenant which shall be subject to all the terms and conditions hereof but shall be terminable by 60 days notice.

Ten days before the lease expired, Brenda separated from her husband and vacated the premises.

After the lease expired, Hermann remained in possession of the duplex and continued to pay rent. During part of 1985, however, Hermann was unable to pay his rent. Hermann and Samuel agreed, in writing, to a "loan" that suspended Hermann's rent payments for seven months and required repayment with interest. Hermann resumed his rent payments in November 1985 and began making loan payments in January 1986.

At the conclusion of the first holdover year, Hermann again retained possession of the duplex. He continued to make both rent and loan payments through June 1986, when he defaulted on both obligations. At the insistence of the Marynicks, Hermann vacated the duplex on September 7, 1986.

The Marynicks brought suit against Hermann and Brenda to recover unpaid rent, the expense of repairs, and the balance due under the loan contract. The trial court rendered summary judgment for the Marynicks against Hermann but ordered that they take nothing against Brenda. The Marynicks appealed from the take-nothing judgment against Brenda. The court of appeals, with one justice dissenting, affirmed in part and reversed in part. The court agreed that Brenda was not liable under the loan contract, thus affirming part of the trial court's judgment. However, the court reversed the remainder of the trial court's judgment, holding that Brenda was liable for unpaid rent and repairs because her "joint obligations under the lease continued through the first and second holdover terms by virtue of Hermann's holding over." [ ]

Although this issue is one of first impression in this state, it has been addressed by at least four other jurisdictions. The earliest reported decision was by the South Carolina Supreme Court, which held that when a lease is executed by two tenants jointly and only one occupies after expiration of the term, the law will presume that both tenants are holdovers unless the tenant not in actual possession gives notice to the landlord that he or she ceases to hold. *Fronty v. Wood,* 20 S.C.L. (2 Hill) 367 (1834). The court below relied on this decision. The Supreme Court of Arizona and an appellate court in New York, however, have rejected the South Carolina presumption, holding instead that one tenant cannot be involuntarily bound to a new tenancy by the acts of another. *Mosher v. Sabra,* 34 Ariz. 536, 541, 273 P. 534, 535 (1929) (the contract arising from a holdover is between the tenant continuing to occupy the premises and the landlord; the cotenant not in possession is not liable simply because he or she jointly leased the premises); *Foster v. Stewart,* 196 A.D. 814, 816, 188 N.Y.S. 151, 152 (App.Div.1921) (a cotenant cannot, by the act of holding over, exercise an option to renew and thereby create a new contract which would bind a cotenant not in possession). More recently, a California intermediate court followed *Fronty v. Wood* and distinguished the Arizona and New York decisions by concluding that California treats a holdover tenancy as an extension of the original agreement rather than a new tenancy. *Schmitt v. Felix,* 157 Cal.App.2d 642, 645, 321 P.2d 473, 475 (1958) (a cotenant who vacates remains in constructive possession of the premises by virtue of the other cotenant's continuing occupancy and, in the absence of notice to the landlord of any change in the occupancy of the premises, may be bound as a holdover).

The court below held that notice was required in order to terminate Brenda's continuing obligations under the joint lease. We disagree. The lease created a tenancy for a definite term (a tenancy with a specified beginning and ending date). The general rule is that a tenancy for a definite term does not require a tenant to give notice in order to terminate the tenancy, because a tenancy for a definite term simply expires at the end of the contract period. [ ] The tenancy created under this lease thus terminated regardless of notice and regardless of whether either tenant vacated.

A tenant who remains in possession of the premises after termination of the lease occupies "wrongfully" and is said to have a tenancy at sufferance. [ ] Under the common law holdover rule, a landlord may elect to treat a tenant holding over as either a trespasser or as a tenant holding under the terms of the original lease. [ ] The lease incorporated this rule of holdover, providing that, if the landlord consents, a "new tenancy" would be created if the tenant remained in possession beyond expiration of the lease. The lease stated that this new tenancy would be subject to the same terms and conditions as the original tenancy, except that the holdover tenancy would be "from year to year * * * terminable by 60 days notice." Thus, under the express terms of the lease, this holdover tenancy was a new tenancy rather than an extension or renewal of the original lease. Therefore, Hermann's holdover tenancy was not, as the court below held, a continuation of the original tenancy he held jointly with Brenda, but was rather a new tenancy for which he alone was liable.

The court of appeals bound Brenda to this new tenancy by presuming that a holding over by Hermann was also a holding over by Brenda, absent notice to the contrary. However, a presumption that one cotenant's holding over binds another cotenant is contrary to the general principles of cotenancy under Texas law. The relationship of cotenancy exists only so long as the parties own rights in common property. [ ] At the moment the original lease expired, neither Hermann nor Brenda had any legal right to possession of the duplex, and their relationship as cotenants was extinguished. Because they were no longer cotenants, there was no basis from which to presume a joint holding over. Moreover, under Texas law, "each owner in a cotenancy acts for himself and no one is the agent of another or has any authority to bind him merely because of the relationship." *Lander v. Wedell,* 493 S.W.2d 271, 274 (Tex.Civ.App.—Dallas 1973, writ ref'd n.r.e.). Thus, where a lease contains an option to renew, one tenant may not unilaterally exercise that option and bind nonconsenting cotenants. [ ] Since Texas does not permit Hermann to renew the lease for another term on Brenda's behalf, it similarly should not presume that he was authorized to hold over on her behalf.

Accordingly, the judgment of the court of appeals is reversed, and we render judgment that the Marynicks take nothing.

Notes and Questions

1. What constitutes "holding over"? Suppose a tenant sends a letter to the landlord stating an intention not to renew a lease upon its expiration in compliance with the notice provisions of the lease. The tenant vacates on the appointed date, but retains the keys and leaves items of personal property in the vacated premises. Is the tenant holding over? See Longmier v. Kaufman, 663 S.W.2d 385 (Mo.App.1983), reproduced in Sec. III of this chapter (retention of keys and failure to remove property constitutes sufficient control to support finding of a holding over).

2. As noted in the principal case, the common law holdover rule gives the landlord a choice to treat the holdover as a trespasser or as a tenant under the terms of the original lease. Controversies often arise over the terms of the new lease when the parties do not anticipate the holdover possibility. For example, if a tenant holding over after the expiration of a five year term tenders rent equal to one month under the expired lease and the landlord accepts it, has a new five year term been created, or a periodic tenancy from year to year or month to month? See R. Cunningham, W. Stoebuck & D. Whitman, Property 276 (1984) (new tenancy is periodic, by same period if prior tenancy was periodic for less than a year, by year to year if old tenancy was for a term of a year or more).

D. SELF–HELP

SPINKS v. TAYLOR

Supreme Court of North Carolina, 1981.
303 N.C. 256, 278 S.E.2d 501.

[Tenants sued to recover damages allegedly incurred as a result of defendant's wrongful padlocking of leased premises. The landlord followed a practice of padlocking apartments and placing cards marked "Legal Notice" on apartment doors when rent was past due. At least ten days prior to the padlocking notice of default and demand for payment was given. From summary judgments in favor of the defendant, John R. Taylor Company, Inc., plaintiffs appealed—Eds.]

BRANCH, CHIEF JUSTICE.

Plaintiffs first contend that the trial court erred in granting summary judgment for defendant since North Carolina law does not recognize a landlord's right to use peaceful self-help to evict tenants who are subject to forfeiture for non-payment of rent. Defendant maintains on the other hand that at common law a landlord had the right to reenter peacefully and take possession of leased premises subject to forfeiture, and that nothing in the statutory or case law of this state abrogates that common law right.

At early common law, a lessor was permitted to reenter leased premises and use necessary force, not amounting to death or bodily harm, to take possession. [   ] In 1381, however, Parliament enacted the statute of Forcible Entry, 5 Richard II stat. 1, c. 8, making forcible entry without legal process a crime. That statute provided:

> That none from henceforth make any entry into any lands and tenements but in case where entry is given by the law; and in such case, not with strong hand nor with multitude of people, but only in peaceable and easy manner. And if any man from henceforth do to the contrary, and thereof be duly convict, he shall be punished by imprisonment of his body, and thereof ransomed at the King's will.

2 *Bishop on Criminal Law* § 492 (9th Ed.1923). In England it was held that, while the use of necessary force may be a crime under the forcible entry statute, a dispossessed tenant still had no civil remedy in the absence of excess force. [   ] In numerous jurisdictions in this country, including North Carolina, statutes similar to that of 5 Richard II were enacted, and the various constructions placed upon the statutes in the states have produced at least three distinct approaches to the question of self-help evictions.

First, a number of states adhere to the English rule that a landlord may use necessary and reasonable force to expel a tenant and may do so without resort to legal process. [   ] A second line of authority holds that a landlord must in any case resort to the remedy provided by law, usually summary ejectment proceedings, in order to evict an overstaying tenant. [   ] Finally, a third line of cases, and one which tends to overlap the second line, holds that a landlord entitled to immediate possession may "gain possession of the leased premises by peaceable means, and necessity for recourse to legal process exists only where peaceable means fail and force would otherwise be necessary." *Annot.,* 6 ALR 3d 177, § 6 (1966). Within this third category are cases which hold that, while peaceful means technically may be used, *any* retaking which is against the will of the tenant constitutes a forceful retaking and thus is not permitted. [   ]

Turning now to the law of North Carolina, we find that our forcible entry statute reads substantially as did the old English statute and that *Mosseller v. Deaver,* 106 N.C. 494, 11 S.E. 529 (1890), is the pivotal case dealing with the issue before us. In *Mosseller* the landlord entered the tenant's house while the tenant was present and did so "under such circumstances as to constitute a forcible entry under the [forcible entry] statute * * *." The trial judge instructed the jury that the landlord " 'had the right to go there and put him out by force, if no more force was used than was necessary for that purpose.' " *Id.* at 495, 11 S.E. at 530. This Court disapproved such an instruction, * * *, and noted that public policy required "the owner *to use peaceful means or resort to the courts* in order to regain his possession * * *." *Id.* [Emphasis added.] It seems clear to us, then, that this state recognizes the right of a lessor to enter peacefully and repossess leased premises which are subject to forfeiture due to nonpayment of rent.

Even so, plaintiffs urge that the existence of statutory summary ejectment procedures precludes the use of self-help measures in evicting a tenant in default of rental payments. We are not inadvertent to the fact that some jurisdictions view the statutory remedies as exclusive and as precluding self-help. [ ] However, nothing in our summary ejectment statutes indicates a legislative intent to make those remedies exclusive. [ ] Furthermore, despite the widespread existence of summary statutory remedies, the majority view still recognizes some degree of self-help. [ ]

Having determined that the law of this state permits a landlord to employ peaceable self-help measures in repossessing leased premises, we turn now to an inquiry into what acts constitute acts of force which would subject a landlord to civil liability for the reentry.

In *Reader v. Purdy,* 41 Ill. 279 (1866), relied upon by this Court in *Mosseller,* the court examined the prohibition against the use of force:

> It is urged that the owner of real estate has a right to enter upon and enjoy his own property. Undoubtedly, if he can do so without a forcible disturbance of the possession of another; but the peace and good order of society require that he shall not be permitted to enter against the will of the occupant * * *. He may be wrongfully kept out of possession, but he cannot be permitted to take the law into his own hands and redress his own wrongs. The remedy must be sought through those peaceful agencies which a civilized community provides for all its members. A contrary rule befits only that condition of society in which the principle is recognized that

> He may take who has the power,

> And he may keep who can.

> If the right to use force be once admitted, it must necessarily follow as a logical sequence, that so much may be used as shall be necessary to overcome resistance, even to the taking of human life.

Id. 41 Ill. at 285. The Illinois court concluded, "In this State, it has been constantly held that *any entry is forcible,* within the meaning of this law, *that is made against the will of the occupant."* *Id.* at 286. [Emphasis added.] [ ] We find the reasoning of *Reader* persuasive and perceive no reason for departing from its rule. We therefore hold that while a landlord is permitted to use peaceful means to reenter and take possession of leased premises subject to forfeiture, he may not do so against the will of the tenant; an objection by the tenant elevates the reentry to a forceful one, and the landlord's sole lawful recourse at that time is to the courts.

In the instant case, defendant submitted affidavits in support of his motion for summary judgment which averred, *inter alia,* that: Tenants were given several days' notice of the padlocking. On that day scheduled for the padlocking, the apartment manager would go and knock loudly, announcing the purpose of the visit. If the tenant pays the rent, the procedure ceases; likewise, if the tenant protests, the manager ceases padlocking and tells the tenant that court proceedings will be begun. If the tenant is not at home, the manager checks the apartment to make sure no children or pets are present, and then proceeds to padlock the door. Notice of the padlocking is posted and the manager attempts to notify the tenant personally. According to defendant's affidavit, if the tenant requests personal property from the apartment, he is permitted to enter and remove the property. At any time a tenant objects to the padlocking, the self-help procedures cease and resort is made to the courts.

* * *

[The court held that one tenant, Spinks, had effectively pleaded that her objections to the padlocking had been disregarded by the landlord, but that the other tenant had not. The court also held that the padlocking practices did not constitute unfair trade practices and that the posted notices were not illegal attempts to collect debts by deceit.—Eds.]

Likewise, we hold that summary judgment was improperly rendered for defendant on the issue of conversion of plaintiff Spinks' personal property. In this state, conversion is defined as

> an unauthorized assumption and exercise of the right of ownership over goods or personal chattels belonging to another, to the alteration of their condition *or the exclusion of an owner's rights.*

Peed v. Burleson, Inc., 244 N.C. 437, 439, 94 S.E.2d 351, 353 (1956) [Emphasis added.]. The landlord's actions in denying plaintiff access to her personal goods, if believed by a jury, would constitute a conversion of those goods, and plaintiff would be permitted to recover at least nominal damages.

* * *

[Affirmed in part; reversed in part; and remanded—Eds.]

Notes and Questions

1. Are there any reasons for treating commercial tenants differently from residential tenants with respect to permissible levels of self-help?

Also, should the activities of the tenants be taken into consideration in determining whether self-help is available to recover possession of leased premises? Suppose, for example, tenants are suspected of associating with criminal elements and the landlord feels threatened by their activities. Should the landlord be able to use self-help, say by changing locks while the tenants are out, to remove such "threatening" tenants? See Restatement (Second) of Property § 14.2 (1976) (landlord or incoming tenant may not use self-help if a speedy judicial remedy for recovery of possession is available unless self-help is permitted by controlling law).

2. Restrictions on landlord self-help often are justified as the "quid pro quo" for enactment of summary proceeding statutes enacted in all the states. While the statutes were designed to provide a quick and simple forum to determine who has the right to possession when disputes arise between landlords and tenants, landlords often complain that recalcitrant tenants can manipulate the statutory process to delay eviction by weeks and months. For a review of the use of summary proceeding statutes and recommendation that landlord self-help be prohibited, see DeGraffe, The Development of Unlawful Evictions and Tenant Remedies for Injurious Conduct in New York, 41 Syracuse L.Rev. 1179 (1990).

R. CUNNINGHAM, W. STOEBUCK & D. WHITMAN, THE LAW OF PROPERTY

395–397 (1984).

§ 6.77 Summary Eviction Statutes

Every state, as well as the District of Columbia, Guam, Puerto Rico, and the Virgin Islands, has some form of statute allowing the landlord to evict a tenant who breaches his lease covenants, by a special, summary proceeding. All but a few jurisdictions allow the landlord to use the action even though the lease does not contain a termination clause. In a broad sense, these statutes constitute an exception to the traditional common-law rule that one may not rescind a lease.

The types of breaches that will trigger the statutory remedy known as summary eviction or unlawful detainer may be limited. Some statutes allow the remedy only for nonpayment of rent; others may allow it for other kinds of breaches, some for any tenant's breach. The usual scheme is that the landlord must give the tenant a notice in a prescribed manner, requiring the tenant either to cure the breach, if it is curable, within a certain period of time or to vacate. Times of notice, generally short, vary from state to state and according to the nature of the breach; from three to 10 days' notice is typical for a rent default. If the tenant vacates, lease and leasehold terminate. If not, the tenant falls into a status usually called "unlawful detainer." At that point the landlord has the summary court action for possession and, in most states, for back rent with perhaps a penalty. In Lindsey v. Normet the United States Supreme Court upheld the constitutionality of the summary form of action with accelerated trial date.

Because the statutory actions are summary, courts have traditionally limited the issues to whether the tenant has committed the breach alleged. Most frequently this principle has been applied to prevent a tenant's presenting evidence of an offset or counterclaim against his unpaid rent. If rent is unpaid, he is liable to be placed in unlawful detainer, and his affirmative claim will have to await a separate action. Lindsey v. Normet held this limitation of issues valid. In recent years, however, the traditional rule has been changed in a number of jurisdictions, to allow tenants to prove offsets or counterclaims against unpaid rent. The decisions in which this has occurred have generally involved a residential tenant who claimed an offset for breach of the landlord's newly found implied warranty of habitability. In popular parlance, this allows a form of "rent withholding" by a tenant whose premises do not come up to the habitability standard. A number of states that have recently adopted residential landlord-tenant codes, exemplified by the Uniform Residential Landlord and Tenant Act and the Model Residential Landlord–Tenant Code, have accomplished the same result legislatively.

Under some summary eviction statutes, the landlord's sole remedy is possession. Most statutes also permit recovery of rent due, and some permit even a penalty in a multiple of the rent, such as double. When there is a statutory penalty, courts certainly may award it, but they have frequently refused to do so when tenants have had a reasonable excuse for holding over after the statutory notice to quit.

Problem

Margaret Thomas placed an advertisement in the local newspaper seeking a roommate. She had several responses, but decided to lease her extra bedroom to Laura Witt. Laura gave Margaret a security deposit and moved in. The next day, Margaret asked Laura to sign a lease. Laura refused. Therefore Margaret asked Laura to move out. She refused to do that as well.

About 20 days later, Margaret decided she'd had enough. She demanded that Laura leave immediately. Laura refused this request and locked herself in the bedroom. Margaret called the police, who arrested Laura for trespass.

What do you think of Laura's actions? Of Margaret's? Should Margaret have used a different approach? See People v. Evans, 163 Ill.App.3d 561, 114 Ill.Dec. 662, 516 N.E.2d 817 (1987) (summary proceedings statute provided sole means for resolving dispute concerning who had "better right of possession").

One of the complaints landlords have about the summary eviction process is that sometimes it is nearly impossible to get tenants out once they have taken possession. Consider this problem in light of both the traditional view of the lease as a conveyance of property and the view that a lease is simply a contractual arrangement. What about the situation, as with Margaret and Laura, where there is no written lease? Should self help be available?

A 1990 movie, "Pacific Heights", portrayed a situation similar, although more extreme, to that of Margaret and Laura. A tenant moved in before he signed a lease, did not sign the lease and proceeded to systematically destroy the apartment before the landlords were finally able to have him evicted.

E. MITIGATION OF DAMAGES

SOMMER v. KRIDEL

Supreme Court of New Jersey, 1977.
74 N.J. 446, 378 A.2d 767.

PASHMAN, J.

We granted certification in these cases to consider whether a landlord seeking damages from a defaulting tenant is under a duty to mitigate damages by making reasonable efforts to re-let an apartment wrongfully vacated by the tenant.

* * *

I

A.

Sommer v. Kridel

This case was tried on stipulated facts. On March 10, 1972 the defendant, James Kridel, entered into a lease with the plaintiff, Abraham Sommer, owner of the "Pierre Apartments" in Hackensack, to rent apartment 6–L in that building. The term of the lease was from May 1, 1972 until April 30, 1974, with a rent concession for the first six weeks, so that the first month's rent was not due until June 15, 1972.

One week after signing the agreement, Kridel paid Sommer $690. Half of that sum was used to satisfy the first month's rent. The remainder was paid under the lease provision requiring a security deposit of $345. Although defendant had expected to begin occupancy around May 1, his plans were changed. He wrote to Sommer on May 19, 1972, explaining

> I was to be married on June 3, 1972. Unhappily the engagement was broken and the wedding plans cancelled. Both parents were to assume responsibility for the rent after our marriage. I was discharged from the U.S. Army in October 1971 and am now a student. I have no funds of my own, and am supported by my stepfather.

> In view of the above, I cannot take possession of the apartment and am surrendering all rights to it. Never having received a key, I cannot return same to you.

> I beg your understanding and compassion in releasing me from the lease, and will of course, in consideration thereof, forfeit the 2 month's rent already paid.

Please notify me at your earliest convenience.

Plaintiff did not answer the letter.

Subsequently, a third party went to the apartment house and inquired about renting apartment 6–L. Although the parties agreed that she was ready, willing and able to rent the apartment, the person in charge told her that the apartment was not being shown since it was already rented to Kridel. In fact, the landlord did not re-enter the apartment or exhibit it to anyone until August 1, 1973. At that time it was rented to a new tenant for a term beginning on September 1, 1973. The new rental was for $345 per month with a six week concession similar to that granted Kridel.

Prior to re-letting the new premises, plaintiff sued Kridel in August 1972, demanding $7,590, the total amount due for the full two-year term of the lease. Following a mistrial, plaintiff filed an amended complaint asking for $5,865, the amount due between May 1, 1972 and September 1, 1973. The amended complaint included no reduction in the claim to reflect the six week concession provided for in the lease or the $690 payment made to plaintiff after signing the agreement. Defendant filed an amended answer to the complaint, alleging that plaintiff breached the contract, failed to mitigate damages and accepted defendant's surrender of the premises. He also counterclaimed to demand repayment of the $345 paid as a security deposit.

The trial judge ruled in favor of defendant. Despite his conclusion that the lease had been drawn to reflect "the 'settled law' of this state," he found that "justice and fair dealing" imposed upon the landlord the duty to attempt to re-let the premises and thereby mitigate damages. He also held that plaintiff's failure to make any response to defendant's unequivocal offer of surrender was tantamount to an acceptance, thereby terminating the tenancy and any obligation to pay rent. As a result, he dismissed both the complaint and the counterclaim. The Appellate Division reversed in a *per curiam* opinion, [　], and we granted certification. [　]

B.

Riverview Realty Co. v. Perosio

* * *

[Omitted.—Eds.]

II

As the lower courts in both appeals found, the weight of authority in this State supports the rule that a landlord is under no duty to mitigate damages caused by a defaulting tenant. [　] This rule has been followed in a majority of states, [　] and has been tentatively adopted in the American Law Institute's Restatement of Property. [　]

Nevertheless, while there is still a split of authority over this question, the trend among recent cases appears to be in favor of a mitigation requirement. [　]

The majority rule is based on principles of property law which equate a lease with a transfer of a property interest in the owner's estate. Under this rationale the lease conveys to a tenant an interest in the property which forecloses any control by the landlord; thus, it would be anomalous to require the landlord to concern himself with the tenant's abandonment of his own property.

* * *

Yet the distinction between a lease for ordinary residential purposes and an ordinary contract can no longer be considered viable. As Professor Powell observed, evolving "social factors have exerted increasing influence on the law of estates for years." 2 *Powell on Real Property* (1977 ed.), § 221[1] at 180–81. The result has been that

> [t]he complexities of city life, and the proliferated problems of modern society in general, have created new problems for lessors and lessees and these have been commonly handled by specific clauses in leases. This growth in the number and detail of specific lease covenants has reintroduced into the law of estates for years a predominantly contractual ingredient. [*Id.* at 181]

Thus in 6 *Williston on Contracts* (3 ed. 1962), § 890A at 592, it is stated:

> There is a clearly discernible tendency on the part of courts to cast aside technicalities in the interpretation of leases and to concentrate their attention, as in the case of other contracts, on the intention of the parties, * * *.

[   ]

This Court has taken the lead in requiring that landlords provide housing services to tenants in accordance with implied duties which are hardly consistent with the property notions * * *.

Application of the contract rule requiring mitigation of damages to a residential lease may be justified as a matter of basic fairness. Professor McCormick first commented upon the inequity under the majority rule when he predicted in 1925 that eventually

> the logic, inescapable according to the standards of a 'jurisprudence of conceptions' which permits the landlord to stand idly by the vacant, abandoned premises and treat them as the property of the tenant and recover full rent, while yield to the more realistic notions of social advantage which in other fields of the law have forbidden a recovery for damages which the plaintiff by reasonable efforts could have avoided. [McCormick, "The Rights of the Landlord Upon Abandonment of the Premises by the Tenant," 23 *Mich.L.Rev.* 211, 221–22 (1925)]

Various courts have adopted this position. [   ]

The pre-existing rule cannot be predicated upon the possibility that a landlord may lose the opportunity to rent another empty apartment because he must first rent the apartment vacated by the defaulting tenant. Even where the breach occurs in a multi-dwelling building, each apartment may have unique qualities which make it attractive to certain individuals. Significantly, in *Sommer v. Kridel*, there was a specific request to rent the apartment vacated by the defendant; there is no reason to believe that absent this vacancy the landlord could have succeeded in renting a different apartment to this individual.

We therefore hold that antiquated real property concepts which served as the basis for the pre-existing rule, shall no longer be controlling where there is a claim for damages under a residential lease. Such claims must be governed by more modern notions of fairness and equity. A landlord has a duty to mitigate damages where he seeks to recover rents due from a defaulting tenant.

If the landlord has other vacant apartments besides the one which the tenant has abandoned, the landlord's duty to mitigate consists of making reasonable efforts to re-let the apartment. In such cases he must treat the apartment in question as if it was one of his vacant stock.

As part of his cause of action, the landlord shall be required to carry the burden of proving that he used reasonable diligence in attempting to re-let the premises. We note that there has been a divergence of opinion concerning the allocation of the burden of proof on this issue. [ ] While generally in contract actions the breaching party has the burden of proving that damages are capable of mitigation, [ ] here the landlord will be in a better position to demonstrate whether he exercised reasonable diligence in attempting to re-let the premises. [ ]

III

The *Sommer v. Kridel* case presents a classic example of the unfairness which occurs when a landlord has no responsibility to minimize damages. Sommer waited 15 months and allowed $4658.50 in damages to accrue before attempting to re-let the apartment. Despite the availability of a tenant who was ready, willing and able to rent the apartment, the landlord needlessly increased the damages by turning her away. While a tenant will not necessarily be excused from his obligations under a lease simply by finding another person who is willing to rent the vacated premises, [ ] here there has been no showing that the new tenant would not have been suitable. We therefore find that plaintiff could have avoided the damages which eventually accrued, and that the defendant was relieved of his duty to continue paying rent. Ordinarily we would require the tenant to bear the cost of any reasonable expenses incurred by a landlord in attempting to re-let the premises, [ ] but no such expenses were incurred in this case.

In *Riverview Realty Co. v. Perosio*, no factual determination was made regarding the landlord's efforts to mitigate damages, and defendant contends that plaintiff never answered his interrogatories. Consequently, the judgment is reversed and the case remanded for a new trial. Upon remand and after discovery has been completed, [ ] the trial court shall determine whether plaintiff attempted to mitigate damages with reasonable diligence, [ ] if so, the extent of damages remaining and assessable to the tenant. As we have held above, the burden of proving that reasonable diligence was used to re-let the premises shall be upon the plaintiff. [ ]

In assessing whether the landlord has satisfactorily carried his burden, the trial court shall consider, among other factors, whether the landlord, either personally or through an agency, offered or showed the apartment to any prospective tenants, or advertised it in local newspapers. Additionally, the tenant may attempt to rebut such evidence by showing that he proffered suitable tenants who were rejected. However, there is no standard formula for measuring whether the landlord has utilized satisfactory efforts in attempting to mitigate damages, and each case must be judged upon its own facts. [ ]

IV

The judgment in *Sommer v. Kridel* is reversed. In *Riverview Realty Co. v. Perosio*, the judgment is reversed and the case is remanded to the trial court for proceedings in accordance with this opinion.

* * *

Notes and Questions

1. What is the basis for the traditional common law rule that the landlord has no responsibility to mitigate damages in cases of tenant abandonment? Are there reasons for continued adherence to the no-mitigation rule, or has the rule outlived its usefulness? See Restatement (Second) of Property, § 12.1 (3), Comment i (1976) (no-mitigation rule helps discourage tenant abandonment and subsequent threat of vandalism). See generally Weissenberg, The Landlord's Duty to Mitigate Damages on the Tenant's Abandonment: A Survey of Old Law and New Trends, 53 Temple L.Q. 1 (1980).

2. What constitutes abandonment? Suppose a tenant leaves on a trip for three weeks without telling the landlord. Is the landlord justified in treating the tenant as having abandoned the premises? Would it make a difference whether the rent was not yet due, or that it was overdue? Would a landlord be justified in including in a lease the requirement that tenants inform the landlord whenever they will be absent for more than seven days, and that failure to do so would enable the landlord to treat the tenant as having abandoned? See URLTA, § 3.104, reproduced earlier (authorizing notice requirement for extended absences).

3. Suppose a landlord re-lets an abandoned apartment for more than the original contract rent. Who is entitled to the difference? Suppose the apartment is re-let for half the remaining time of the original lease but for twice the contract rent. How would the landlord's damages be calculated?

4. Ordinarily, the landlord who refuses to accept surrender and elects to leave the property vacant must wait to collect rent until it falls due. If the abandoning tenant refuses to pay, and the landlord does not want to sue for each installment, he may wait until several installments have accrued or even until the term has expired to begin legal action. Some

jurisdictions, however, will allow the landlord to recover damages on a theory of breach by anticipatory repudiation. What would be the measure of the landlord's damages under that theory?

5. To enable the landlord to sue for the rent for the balance of the term immediately upon a tenant's abandonment, leases frequently include rent acceleration clauses, which render the balance of the rent due, at the landlord's option, if any rental installment is past due. Should the rent acceleration clause be enforceable in a no-mitigation jurisdiction? In a mitigation jurisdiction? See Ricker v. Rombough, 120 Cal.App.2d Supp. 912, 261 P.2d 328 (1953) (held unenforceable as either a penalty or an agreement for liquidated damages when actual damages are readily ascertainable); R. Cunningham, W. Stoebuck & D. Whitman, The Law of Property 365–366 (1984) (majority of courts accept acceleration clauses under freedom of contract principles, but apply strict construction rules).

VIII. A THIRD LOOK AT DISPUTE RESOLUTION

Problems

1. Review the Green v. Lord problem at the beginning of the chapter. As counsel for either Kelly Green or Lance Lord, prepare a proposal for a negotiated settlement. Identify the issues upon which agreement may be relatively easy to obtain, and the ones which will most likely require hard bargaining. To use a baseball analogy, prepare a list of goals, from "homerun" (best possible achievement) through "triple," "double," "single," and "strikeout," for review with your client.

2. Consider the use of a grievance procedure to resolve landlord-tenant disputes. For example, Federal law requires local public housing authorities to offer administrative grievance procedures for disputes which "adversely affect the tenant's rights, duties, welfare or status." 24 C.F.R. § 966.50 (1990). The grievance procedure includes an informal settlement conference, a hearing before an impartial hearing officer, and an administrative appeal. What advantages or disadvantages might such a procedure have over litigation? Over mediation?

Mediation From a Law Student Perspective *

Two Case Studies

During the Spring, 1984 Semester, five Saint Louis University law students participated in an experimental settlement program designed to resolve disputes among litigants in the small claims division of the St. Louis City Circuit Court. As court-appointed mediators, the students met with litigants on the date their cases were scheduled to be

* Reprinted with permission of Timothy Blanchard (J.D., M.H.A., 1986, Saint Louis University) and William K. Meehan (J.D., 1985, Saint Louis University). Names of parties are changed to protect privacy.

heard and attempted to settle the disputes without the need for adjudication. The judge explained to the parties that they were under no obligation to settle, but he expressed his desire that they attempt settlement before requesting a trial of their cause.

Students generally followed a three-step procedure. First, they explained their role as a neutral third party whose duty was simply to facilitate an agreement. Second, they met with each party to the dispute in a private conference for ten to fifteen minutes to obtain a basic understanding of the dispute and gauge the interests of the respective parties. Finally, they met with both parties in a joint conference in which they attempted to help the parties reach agreement. Each student was assigned four or five cases during a one-month period. Following are illustrative case evaluations from two students who participated in the program.

JOHN O. MARLEY v. HOUSE CIRCLE APARTMENTS

Marley v. House Circle Apartments, was an action for property damage arising out of a landlord-tenant relationship. One morning in December, 1983, John Marley, a tenant in defendant's building, noticed a leak emanating from his dishwasher before leaving for work. Marley reported the leak to the management and left for work. He returned later that evening and found his kitchen flooded by approximately a foot and a half of water. Marley again called the management, which responded the next day to remove the water and clean up the mess. As a result of the flooding, Marley claimed damage to his personal effects, groceries, and household items in the amount of $338.00.

The events in question occurred during a prolonged period of unreasonably cold temperatures in the St. Louis area. While the flooding could have logically been caused by the rupture of frozen water pipes, Marley ruled out this possibility since he had taken the precaution of letting his taps run in an effort to avoid this problem. Thus, he concluded that management had been negligent in responding to his report of a leaky dishwasher. Marley made several requests for compensation with regard to his damaged property, but received only a letter dated two days after the incident. The letter, authored by the unit manager, denied his claims for compensation and implied that he was negligent in failing to let his taps run during the cold snap. In the face of this response, Marley brought this action.

The apartment complex was represented by the community director, the unit manager, and the maintenance supervisor. At the time of the letter, the source of the flooding had yet to be determined. By the time of the hearing, management had ascertained the source of the flooding and they brought a detailed account of the problem with them to the hearing. Acting as spokesman for the group, the maintenance supervisor explained, with the aid of graphics, that the flooding of the apartment had been caused by a rupture in a water main leading to the outside of the building. The main was located in a locked access area behind the wall of the kitchen and was not an area regularly checked by the management's maintenance staff. When the break occurred, management was unaware of its existence and the water flowed into the apartment.

After speaking with both sides, I became convinced that this dispute had arisen due to poor communication between the parties. Marley had been informed of the true cause behind the flooding and still was under the impression that the apartment complex was unjustly attempting to hold him negligent. House Circle contributed to this misconception by failing to clear the matter up and ignoring his claims for compensation. I believed that once the misunderstanding was corrected, the parties would be able to reach some sort of settlement.

To their credit, both sides to this dispute were extremely objective. Although I sensed a bit of tension and annoyance on both sides, the parties were able to separate their emotions from the merits of the dispute. The maintenance supervisor was especially adept in his handling of the negotiations. Judging from his performance, it was obvious to me that he was well experienced in just this type of bargaining. Using his graphics and citing relevant portions of the lease agreement, he explained to Marley the cause behind the flooding, noted the unanticipated cold spell, and reminded Marley that management was not responsible for damage resulting from breaks in water or gas lines pursuant to the lease. The argument was flawless in that it employed an objective criterion and was tied to a rationale supported by evidence. Marley was equally objective in his response to the maintenance supervisor's explanation and argument. He didn't attack its premise, but, rather, accepted the explanation as plausible. Yet, he adhered to principle by arguing that he was not responsible for the flooding and felt victimized.

Once the misunderstanding had been resolved, I recognized each party desired to settle the dispute without going to trial. The maintenance supervisor acknowledged that Marley had been a good tenant and House Circle wanted him to continue residency there. Marley also indicated that he had been satisfied with the House Circle management and wished to continue his residence there. This gave me the opening I was looking for. Both sides had recognized their mutual interests at stake (their desire to preserve the satisfactory landlord-tenant relationship) and now needed an option which would allow both to gain at neither's expense. This meant that the issue of culpability would have to be resolved.

Marley had worded his complaint in terms alleging that House Circle had been negligent. House Circle would not settle if it meant they would be held negligent. Such a judgment would have reflected poorly on their maintenance man, and it was clear he was not at fault. At this point, I suggested that Marley waive his allegation of negligence in return for a cash settlement. Moreover, I reviewed Marley's list of damages and suggested he drop some of the more frivolous items. Both parties were receptive to such a proposed settlement, and after a short discussion over some of the damage items, they agreed on terms. In return for $170.00 as settlement of his claims, Marley agreed to waive his claim of negligence on the part of House Circle Apartments.

In summary, this was simply a case of failed communication between parties engendering a lawsuit. Acting out of ignorance of the true cause behind the disputed event, both sides retreated to positions and resisted any effort to move towards rational discussion. After the addition of a disinterested third party, the parties were able to recognize their interests, improve their communications, and work towards an option meeting both of their needs. The parties preserved their existing relationship and avoided the risk of realizing their perceived BATNAs (Best Alternative to Negotiated Agreement) which would have resulted in dismissal of Marley's claim or a judgment against House Circle for the entire amount asked. Mediation allowed both parties to walk away content, if not pleased.

ROSS v. GRAHAM

This case involved a dispute between a landlord and a former tenant. The Grahams rented the upper flat from Ross, who lived in the lower flat. There was no written lease, but the parties agree that rent of $225.00 was due monthly. It is disputed whether the term began on the eleventh or the seventh of the month, however, and with the exception of the first month, the rent had been tendered and accepted in installments as the Grahams were able to pay. In December the Grahams were unable to pay rent, but they paid the December rent, less $19.00, in early January. They then agreed to pay the January rent at $50.00 per week for two weeks then $125.00 two weeks later. The Grahams made the first $50.00 payment then moved out without notice, leaving a balance due of $194.00. Mrs. Ross's prayer for $234.00 included $194.00 in rent due, a penalty of $25.00 for failure to give 30 days notice prior to vacating, and $15.00 for an allegedly missing fluorescent lamp fixture.

During Mrs. Ross's rendition of the facts, neither of the Grahams gave any indication of disagreement with anything she said, so, rather than ask for their side of the story, I simply asked if what she said was correct. They admitted that they owed the $194.00 and that they were willing to pay. They were unable to pay the total due at one time, however, because of cash flow problems. They maintained, however, that no penalty was discussed at any time prior to their moving out, and that they did not take the lamp fixture. Mrs. Graham then began an attempt to legitimate the fact that they moved out by complaining that promised repairs had not been effected by Ross. For a moment I was afraid that the momentum generated by the Graham's quick admission of responsibility would be lost in counterproductive ancillary counter-claims. In order to avoid this without having to separate them, which would likewise destroy the momentum, I interrupted by asking,

"Excuse me, but was there a written lease?" The response was that there was not. Since I suspected that Ross's primary objective was to recover the rent due, I wanted to reduce her expectation of recovering the penalty. Toward this end I pointed out that in the absence of a written lease, the court would probably require the landlord to prove that such a clause had been agreed to from the outset. I also recognized that the Grahams already felt guilty about not having been able to pay the rent. Since this coupled with their admission gave Mrs. Ross a stronger power position, I sought to equalize the bargaining positions because when one side is in the dominant position or perceives itself to be, effective negotiation is less likely to occur. More powerful parties tend to exhibit behavior leading to inequitable agreements. Therefore, effective bargaining should be enhanced to the extent that a mediator can bring about a perception of balance of power.

I think I was able to do this by phrasing my comments in such a way as to make Ross feel a bit guilty or at least foolish for not having a written lease. Ross admitted that the provision for a penalty had never been discussed. I then asked, "Your real interest then is that $194.00," to which she responded, "Yes," and that she would settle for that, but that it had to be all in one payment. The Grahams both interjected that they couldn't do that. When I asked why it had to be a single payment she said that was how the rent was to have been paid all along, and that she couldn't wait for it anymore. She was in effect saying to the Grahams, We've been nice to you, but now that you're going we want our money now. The perceived balance of power was shifting once again, so to avoid the risk of losing the "bargaining relationship," I once again sought to equalize the relative power positions. I pointed out that the law may imply a waiver of even explicit terms in light of a course of dealing to the contrary, such as the payment schedule in this case. To this Ross responded that she just wanted to be sure that she got the money once and for all. Thus, her primary concern was certainty of collection. I then explained that even if the judge ruled in her favor, it would be up to her to collect on the judgment, that this would involve another court appearance in a collection or garnishment proceeding (making it sound as complicated and cumbersome as possible), and that given the Grahams' income, even this would not pay her "all at once."

Having adequately reduced her expectations, I restated the situation as I saw it in a light most favorable to both parties. I said that it looked to me as though the Grahams really just wanted a chance to pay what they owed, and that Ross was mainly interested in the certain recovery of her money as quickly as reasonably possible. My goal in making this statement was to make use of an impression I had drawn from observing Ross. It was my impression that she was not there for the purpose of punishing the Grahams but only to insure the recovery of the rent due. I further speculate that Mr. Ross actually decided to sue, but that Mrs. Ross had to appear since he was at work. At one point Mrs. Ross said that Mr. Ross had demanded a single payment of the late January rent but she had convinced him to allow them to make installments—to give them another chance, as it were. Thus, through this statement and my delivery, I was attempting to reinforce Ross's self-perception as a good, generous person and at the same time revive her prior perception of the Grahams as good people having some tough times, who deserved one more chance. One might have expected an entirely different attitude from Mrs. Ross, who might have felt double-crossed by the Grahams, who had, in effect, bitten the hand that fed them (with another chance). Accordingly were it not for the contrary impression I got from non-verbals, I would have expected "face-restoration" behavior since the Grahams' vacation of the flat with rent past due must have made Ross look foolish to her husband. Fortunately, this was not the case.

I waited for both parties to volunteer agreement to this characterization of the situation. Having put the rationale before the solution, I suggested, "Suppose I can work it out to where both of these interests are met—do you think we can settle this case?" When both parties had agreed, I explained that a payment schedule could be set forth in a consent judgment entered by the Judge, and that this would afford Ross the security of a judgment which she could execute if the Grahams failed to make the scheduled payments. We then worked out a payment schedule with three payments of $50.00 every other week and the balance due two weeks after the third payment. I then asked if this was entirely agreeable to everyone. Both sides answered affirmatively and I simply allowed the allegedly missing lamp fixture to be forgotten. The case was settled.

I made an error, however, that could have ruined the whole thing. I forgot to deal with court costs. When the issue arose before the judge the Grahams accepted it as a formality and the costs were added on to the final payment. This could have been a serious practical problem, given the Grahams' cash flow situation, even though they acknowledged their duty to pay the back rent and that they would have lost on that issue at trial. Even if the issue of victory at trial had been at issue, I could have suggested that the court costs be set up to cancel out the $15.00 lamp fixture. In spite of feeling a bit foolish if not negligent, about forgetting the issue of court costs, I left the courtroom tired but strangely satisfied, despite the rain.

Notes and Questions

1. Compare the approaches of the two students. In the first case, the student emphasized the use of mediation techniques, while in the second one, greater use was made of landlord-tenant law in an attempt to persuade the parties that they may achieve a more satisfactory result by themselves than one that might be imposed through litigation.

2. The author of the first paper was more successful in mediating the four disputes assigned to him than the author of the second paper. Does this suggest that:

    a.   mediation skills and their effective use by the mediator,

    b.   the cases/parties themselves and their suitability for mediation, or

    c.   some necessary combination of the above,

is the distinguishing feature of those cases which are successfully resolved without litigation?

    3.   Did the student mediators maintain neutrality? Were their statements of law accurate? Did the student mediators appear to have achieved success?

Chapter Five

REAL ESTATE TRANSACTIONS

With this chapter we finally arrive at the subject that most lay persons assume real property law is really about: conveyancing. We begin with an examination of the participants in the real estate transfer process and their roles in that process. Next we examine the primary legal documents involved in real estate transfers and legal problems that arise with respect to them. Finally we turn to the primary problems with which conveyancing law is concerned: protection against defects in the condition or title of the property and the financing of real estate purchases.

I. THE PARTICIPANTS AND THEIR ROLES

A. THE SERVICE GROUPS

JOHNSTONE, LAND TRANSFERS: PROCESS AND PROCESSORS

22 Valparasio University Law Review 493 (1988).

The buying and selling of land is a complex process that normally involves a series of procedures and the assistance of service specialists skilled in implementing these procedures. This article * * * considers the land transfer process by focusing on the principal service specialists who operate the process and who in large measure are responsible for how well it functions. The principal service specialists in the land transfer field are real estate brokers, lawyers, title companies, and lenders.[1]

* * *

1. Other generally less important specialists may also become involved in land transfer servicing, including such groups as appraisers, escrow agents, surveyors, contractors, land planners, and termite inspectors. Some of the principal service specialists may themselves act as these ancillary servicers. In the western United States, escrow agents have become particularly common participants in servicing real estate sale transactions. * * *

1. *Real Estate Brokers*

The major services provided by real estate brokers are bringing buyers and sellers together, assisting them to make informed decisions on whether or not to enter into sales contracts, and assisting them with the terms of any such agreements.[2] Most brokered real estate sales are of single family residences and one or both parties to these sales agreements usually know little about land transfer procedures and often know little about the housing market. Furthermore, the buyers usually have a limited capacity to evaluate the merits of the properties being purchased. Thus, in these residential transactions, brokers commonly assume important educational and advisory roles in relation to the parties. * * *

* * *

Real estate brokers for their sales work almost universally are paid on a commission basis, commonly six percent of the contract price, and estimates indicate that gross commissions nationally can total as much as $10 billion per year. * * *

Broker-principal contracts vary as to the exclusiveness of the broker's right to sell. What brokers prefer and often obtain from their principals is an exclusive right-to-sell listing, one in which only the broker may attempt to sell the property. If another broker or the seller arranges for the sale, the exclusive right-to-sell broker is entitled to the contracted for commission. Another listing format is the exclusive agency, under which the broker receives a commission if another broker sells, but not if the sale is effectuated by the seller. Still another format is the *open listing,* one entitling the broker to a commission only if he makes the sale, not if it is made by another broker or by the seller's efforts. Listing agreements often expressly set an *expiration date* for the listing, and if no such date appears in the agreement, a reasonable time is usually implied.

* * *

In most communities, marketing of single-family residences is greatly enhanced by a form of cooperative venture among brokers, the *multiple listing service* (MLS). The MLS device, well-established in the United States since at least the 1920s, is a pooled marketing arrangement, * * * in which listings of properties for sale made with any participating broker are circulated to all other brokers participating in the scheme. Prospective buyers who contact any participating broker then are informed of the types of available properties that are listed through the exchange. If a listed property is sold, the sales commission

2. On real estate brokers and their work, see D. Burke, Law of Real Estate Brokers ch. 1 (1982); P. Rohan, B. Goldstein & C. Bobis, Real Estate Brokerage Law and Practice (1985); U.S.Fed.Trade Comm'n, The Real Estate Brokerage Industry (1983); Currier, Finding the Broker's Place in the Typical Residential Real Estate Transaction, 33 U.FLA.L.REV. 655 (1981). Functions of industrial real estate brokers are discussed in Society of Industrial Real Estate Brokers, Industrial Real Estate chs. 6–7 (4th ed. 1984).

is split between the listing broker, the one with whom the property was originally listed, and the so-called selling broker, the one who finds a buyer. * * *

* * *

Compared to many occupations, real estate brokers are not extensively regulated by government. Real estate brokers are licensed, although license acquisition is relatively easy to obtain; and real estate brokers are, of course, subject to the limitations of antitrust law and to laws restricting performance of many law-related services to lawyers. There are few other significant regulatory restrictions on them of much significance.[3] * * * Salespersons, those persons working for a broker as employees or independent contractors, are separately licensed, although the examination and other prerequisites for these licenses ordinarily are less demanding than for broker licenses. A high percentage of licensed salespersons work only part-time at selling real estate. * * *

* * *

2. Lawyers

Historically, land transfer servicing was one of the principal types of work performed by American lawyers, and although of less overall significance to contemporary lawyers than to their predecessors, it is still of tremendous importance to many in practice today. * * * Small private law firms and solo practitioners in the general practice of law are particularly active in sales of single-family residences and family farms, with larger law firms concentrating on sales of more expensive properties, such as large apartment buildings, hotels, office buildings, and industrial properties. Legal work required in connection with the ordinary single-family home sale tends to be a routine procedure including preparation of the contract of sale; title search, title examination, and perhaps clearing of title defects; drafting or review of a mortgage; drafting of a deed; preparation of a closing statement showing expenses and receipts; and a final closing session in which the seller is paid and the deed delivered to the buyer. Supplemental steps often are involved, such as ordering a survey and reviewing the surveyor's report, and ordering and approving a title insurance policy. The period between the contract of sale and closing usually is eight or ten weeks, during which time the buyer ordinarily arranges for financing and the necessary title work is performed. Added problems, of course, may emerge in connection with the sale transaction which lawyers may be asked to resolve, such as controversies over the broker's commission or deed covenant compliance. In sales of properties for large sums of money, a much wider range of legal problems typically exists, including

3. Federal and state fair housing laws, although difficult to enforce, also impose major restrictions on residential real estate brokers in many communities by prohibiting discrimination on such grounds as race, sex, and national origin in the marketing of housing. On these laws see D. Burke, supra note 2, ch. 6; Note, Racial Steering: The Real Estate Broker and Title VIII, 85 Yale L.J. 808 (1976).

intricate financing arrangements, complicated income tax considerations, zoning and other land use control issues, and frequently construction problems, as these sales often are tied into major development projects.

* * *

In the sale of a single-family residence, the buyer and seller each may be represented by a different lawyer or to save expense, the same lawyer may represent both, only one may be represented by a lawyer, or neither may be represented. Also, in single family residence sales, there are considerable variations in lawyers' roles depending on the geographic area. In many places, lawyers do not become involved in such sale transactions until after the contract of sale has been signed because brokers commonly prepare the sales contracts. In some areas, lawyers in private practice do little or no title work unless title curing litigation is necessary; title insurers, relying on their private title plants and their own staff, perform the requisite search and examination tasks. In still other areas, lay abstracters do most of the title searching, and lawyers' title work is restricted largely to legal evaluation of titles based on summaries of public title records prepared by the abstracters. Similarly, lawyers do not have a monopoly on final closings in many regions. In many communities, title companies, lenders, brokers, or escrow companies have taken over much of the final closing or settlement work. Lawyers in larger firms often refuse to do single-family residence closings or will do them only as an accommodation for their better clients. * * *

Mortgage lenders are usually represented by lawyers who make certain that in individual transactions the lenders' interests are adequately protected. Some home buyers do not retain their own counsel because they are willing to gamble that transaction approval by the lenders' lawyers sufficiently protects the buyers' generally similar, but in some respects quite different, interests.

* * *

* * * Relative to land transfer servicing, there are several respects in which the [lawyer's professional ethical] standards are of particular importance: in particular, they severely restrict the conflict of interest situations in which an individual lawyer or law firm may become involved,[4] and they permit lawyer advertising but prohibit in-person solicitation of prospective clients.[5] The conflict of interest proscriptions do not prevent a lawyer from representing both the buyer and seller or borrower and lender in the same real estate sale transaction, provided that neither party is likely to be harmed thereby and both parties consent. However, some lawyers consider the possibilities of conflict so

---

4. Model Rules of Professional Conduct Rules 1.7–1.9 (1980) [hereinafter Model Rules]; Model Code of Professional Responsibility DR5–101 to –106 (1980) [hereinafter Model Code].

5. Model Rules, supra note 15, Rules 7.1–7.5; Model Code, supra note 15, DR2–101 to –106.

serious that they will never represent both parties to a real estate transaction; and there is case law which indicates that when such dual representation occurs the consents must be knowing and based on full and timely disclosure. * * *

* * *

* * * [A] federal enactment of importance regulating certain aspects of the land transfer servicing work of lawyers is the Real Estate Settlement Procedures Act (RESPA).[6] * * * RESPA applies to settlement services pertaining to mortgage loans and covers the vast majority of mortgage loans made in the United States. Settlement services include most types of work performed by lawyers in relation to loans covered by the Act. Some examples are title search and examination, document preparation, and final closing. Lawyers, of course, can be compensated for this work, but only for services actually performed. Referrals are not compensable services under the Act. Thus, RESPA outlaws fees, commissions, kickbacks, rebates, or fee splits to lawyers for referring settlement work to others, including the referring of work to title companies and real estate brokers.[7] The prohibition of referral fees has proven especially troublesome in relations between lawyers and title insurers. * * *

With respect to unauthorized practice in providing land transfer services, lawyers are in a fairly favorable position, although subject to some significant restrictions. * * * In some states, lawyers are permitted to perform one of the most important nonlegal land transfer services—brokerage, merely by being licensed to practice law. However, in other states, lawyers are exempt from real estate broker licensing requirements only when acting within the scope of their duties as lawyers. There are also deterrents to integration of legal and brokerage aspects of land transfer servicing. These include restrictions on lawyers using another business as a front for attracting legal work, and prohibitions against lawyers aiding in the unauthorized practice of law, against sharing legal fees with nonlawyers, and against carrying on a law practice with lay co-owners.

3. Title Insurers

The principal service provided by title insurers is making title insurance coverage available to land owners and lenders.[8] Incidental to this service, insurers provide interested parties, in advance of coverage, with important information about title quality, including outstanding title defects of which the insurer is aware. Insurers may also provide information about the insurability of title and the terms for insuring title. Most title insurance is applied for during the process of

6. 12 U.S.C. §§ 2601–2617 (1982).

7. The section of RESPA prohibiting referral fees and fee-splitting is 12 U.S.C. § 2607 (1982).

8. On title insurance generally, see A.B.A. Section of Real Property, Probate and Trust Law, Title Insurance: The Lawyer's Expanding Role (1985) [hereinafter The Lawyer's Expanding Role]; A. Axelrod, C. Berger & Q. Johnstone, Land Transfer and Finance, Cases and Materials 764–851 (3d ed. 1986); D. Burke, [Law of Title Insurance (1986)].

selling land, and title quality information can be crucial in determining whether or not loans will be made and sales will take place. Loan commitments and sales contracts are normally conditioned on title to the property involved being marketable, insurable with only specified exceptions, or meeting some other quality standard. Furthermore, owners and contract buyers may want precise title quality information for reasons other than insurance, reasons such as estimating how much it will cost to clear any title defects or determining if the title is adequate to merit major physical improvements on the premises. Thus, providing information, in addition to providing insurance, is a major title insurer service. Further services that many title insurers have long performed are supervising closings and acting as escrow agents in real estate transactions. A few title insurers also act as trust companies and administer a considerable number of trust accounts.

Determining with accuracy the outstanding legal interests in any particular parcel of land, especially in the United States, usually is an onerous, expensive, and time-consuming process. There is also the possibility that even with a careful search some interests will not be discovered, either because they are undiscoverable by the searcher or because they cannot be found without a prohibitively expensive search. This inability-to-discover risk ordinarily is remote, yet troublesome, particularly to buyers and lenders. Negligence in the search and examination process also is a serious risk which title policies can protect against. Title insurance thus has made a cumbersome and somewhat chancy system of title protection, more viable by compensating insureds when and if insured-against losses are incurred. Title insurance also has provided, through standardized policy coverage, a substantial degree of national uniformity in title protection, a feature highly desirable to the increasingly significant national market in mortgages. Each land parcel has unique characteristics, the terms in mortgages often differ, and title and mortgage laws vary considerably among the states, but title insurance superimposes an element of fungibility to mortgages that is highly attractive to lenders. This helps explain why a major reason for the spread of title insurance in the United States has been the demand for this type of protection by mortgage lenders, particularly national mortgage lenders.

* * *

Public land title records in many counties, particularly in counties with large populations and many land parcels, are ill-suited to efficient title searches. * * * To streamline searches, private so-called title plants have been set up in a minority of counties. These plants duplicate, centralize, and organize data from local public land title records in a manner far more conducive to rapid and accurate searches than when searches are made in the original public records. Title plants are kept up to date by the expensive procedure of making daily take-offs of all new additions to the public records and incorporating these additions into the private plants. * * * Some plants are extensively automated. Most large title plants are owned and operated by title insurers and are used for making searches on parcels for which title insurance orders have been received. Some plants are now shared by more than one title insurer, either as joint ventures or by the owner selling access to other insurers.

* * *

To the extent that title insurers or their agents do not make title searches and examinations, title insurance policies are issued in reliance on opinions of nonagent lawyers as to title quality of the parcels in question. The underlying title searches for these opinions are in some places customarily made in the public records by the lawyers who provide title opinions. In other places, the searches customarily are made by abstracters who prepare written reports of their searches, and lawyers' title opinions are then based on data in the abstracts. Each abstract summarizes every public record entry that has been located pertaining to the parcel being searched. The abstract usually includes entries dating back to origin of the title, and the summaries are sufficiently detailed so that the examining lawyer can give an adequate opinion on present ownership and outstanding encumbrances. In some parts of the country, buyers and lenders, in acquiring their interests, still commonly rely solely on lawyers' opinions and do not obtain the added protection of title insurance.[9] However, title insurance has become so widely accepted that the number of areas in which it is customary to rely only on lawyers' opinions are far fewer than thirty or forty years ago. * * *

Compared to most forms of insurance, title coverage premiums are low. Whether title insurance premiums are low in relation to the actual risks underwritten, however, is a separate question. An important reason for comparatively low title insurance premiums is the scope and character of coverage. A title policy covers the state of the title as of the time the policy is taken out and does not protect against subsequently-created defects. Also, title policies are issued only after a search is made for title defects, and known material defects are then excepted from coverage. In addition, some types of risks are usually excluded or excepted as standard provisions, including risks arising from building or zoning ordinances; government eminent domain or police power rights unless apparent in the public records; and mechanics liens which are not of public record. For an added premium, some standard exclusions or exceptions will be covered. In effect, the princi-

---

9. The practice of relying on lawyers' title opinions without title insurance is still fairly frequent in Midwestern and Southeastern small towns and in New England, but title insurance based on a lawyer's opinion has become much more common even in these areas. In many smaller Midwestern counties, lawyers' opinions are based on abstracts prepared by local abstract companies. Title insurers do most of the title search and examination work, relying usually on their own title plants, in the Far West and in many larger urban areas elsewhere in the United States. An appreciable percentage of land parcels are registered under the Torrens system of registration in a few small counties plus a few major urban areas: Boston, Chicago (Cook County), Honolulu, and Minneapolis–St. Paul. In Chicago, however, it is not uncommon for Torrens titles to be insured by commercial title insurers in addition to the insurance provided by the Torrens system.

pal risks insured against are negligence in search, examination, and private plant maintenance; and off-record risks or those that might be located only by an unduly onerous and costly search of the public records. As a result, in comparison to most types of insurance, title insurance losses are low.[10]

Apart from exclusions and exceptions, the existence of marketable title is usually covered in title insurance policies. Important differences, however, exist between lenders' policies and owners' policies, including the greater number of standard exceptions in most owners' policies and the right usually granted lenders to assign their policies to mortgage assignees. The effect of this latter difference between policies is that if owners sell their properties, the buyers must take out new policies if they want coverage; but if mortgagees sell their mortgages, as is common, the transferees normally are covered by the original policies. Under both types of policies, however, the insurer agrees to defend the insured in litigation that may arise involving allegations that the title as insured is defective.

* * *

One group of title insurers that nationally have only a small fraction of the title insurance market, and yet as competitors have been feared and bitterly opposed by other title insurers, is the bar-related title insurance companies which are also known as lawyers' title guaranty funds. * * * Each bar-related company provides similar title insurance coverage to that written by commercial insurers, but only to clients of practicing lawyers who are members of the bar-related insurer. * * * Most bar-related companies pay commissions to members insuring through them, and some companies pay dividends to their stockholders. * * *

* * *

Title insurers are subject to government regulation, largely at the state level, but this control generally is less restrictive than that pertaining to most other kinds of insurers. One set of insurer regulations is designed to protect policy holders by safeguarding company solvency and the ability to pay insured losses that may occur. * * * Another form of government control of title insurers is rate regulation, and about half the states impose some kind of control over premium rates charged by title insurers, although rate requests are rarely denied. * * *

4. Lenders

Most land purchases are financed in substantial part with borrowed money, the land serving as security for the loan. The lenders' service of making loan funds available is usually crucial to land sales

---

10. Only about five to ten percent of a title insurer's gross premium income is used to pay actual losses while over 90 percent is absorbed by operating expenses, mainly the cost of searching and examining title. In contrast, the average loss ratio for homeowner's multiple peril insurance is approximately 65 percent, and the ratio for other lines of casualty insurance is still higher.

taking place, and closings of sales contracts are often contingent on the arrangement of adequate secured funding. * * * Mortgage loans are regularly made to finance land purchases and can therefore become an essential step in the land transfer process. But it is common, as well, for owners to borrow on the security of their land for other purposes. Land is such a valuable asset that its owners can use it to borrow funds for an endless variety of purposes, on-site construction being one of the most frequent.

The overwhelming proportion of mortgage loans is held by institutional lenders that specialize in this form of finance. These lenders fall into a number of well-recognized sub-groups. * * * The major private institutional mortgage lenders, in order of the total amount of outstanding real estate mortgage loans they hold, are savings and loan associations, commercial banks, life insurance companies, and savings banks. The total amount of real estate mortgage loans held by these institutions in 1985 was about one and a half trillion dollars, up from less than half a trillion dollars in 1970.[11] * * * In addition to the four major types of private institutional mortgage lenders, large volumes of mortgage loans are held by federally-chartered credit agencies and mortgage pools.[12] Also, individuals, particularly sellers who are financing buyers by means of purchase-money mortgages, hold a sizable volume of mortgage loans. * * *

In terms of relevance to the land transfer process, originators of mortgage loans should be distinguished from those who later purchase this form of debt. Originators make the decisions as to whether or not to loan, negotiate loan terms, and advance loan funds on the security of land interests. In many instances, the originators continue to hold the mortgage loans they originate until the loans are paid off or otherwise terminated, but increasingly, originators are selling their loans in the secondary market. A vast secondary market in mortgages has developed in the United States with federally-chartered credit agencies contributing greatly to its successful operation. * * * The federally-chartered agencies most involved in secondary market operations have been the Federal National Mortgage Association (FNMA), the Federal Home Loan Mortgage Corporation (FHLMC), and the Government National Mortgage Association (GNMA). * * *

It is estimated that recently as high as sixty-five to seventy percent of all new mortgage loans annually have been sold in the secondary market. Persons who have acquired mortgages and wish to sell them are provided, by the secondary market, with a ready outlet in which

---

11. As of 1985, these institutions held a total of $1,337 billion in construction, long-term mortgage, and land loans, allocated as follows: savings and loan associations, $658 billion; commercial banks, $401 billion; life insurance companies, $168 billion; and savings banks, $110 billion. U.S. Bureau of the Census, Statistical Abstract of the United States 1987, at 488, table 820

(1986) [hereinafter Statistical Abstract]. Total real estate secured mortgage debt outstanding in the United States as of 1985 was $2,250 billion. Id. at 489, table 822.

12. As of 1985, these agencies held $189 billion in real estate mortgage debt, and mortgage pools held $392 billion. Id. at 488, table 820.

there are purchasers willing to buy. Many institutional lenders shift their mortgage holdings by buying or selling in the secondary market and operate in this market to further perceived investment opportunities, to avoid excessive holdings of long-term loans, to keep their asset allocations within legal limits, or because they need cash. Also, some mortgage lenders do not have the organization or staff to originate mortgages effectively or in markets that they want to tap outside areas where they maintain offices. Therefore, some lenders must rely on the secondary market for some or all of the mortgages they acquire. * * *

Many lenders also rely on mortgage banks, also known as mortgage companies, to originate mortgages for them. Mortgage banks are in the business of originating mortgages for others, ordinarily for regular customers who are expected to take the loans. The major customers of mortgage banks are life insurance companies, but all types of mortgage lenders acquire mortgages through these intermediaries to some extent. * * *

* * *

An important means of reducing risks to mortgage lenders is by shifting risks to third parties through mortgage insurance or guarantees. Such shifts long have been significant in expanding the housing market and increasing the number of persons who can qualify for financing to purchase their own homes. In many instances, lenders are more willing to make mortgage loans on more favorable terms if a financially responsible third party is underwriting some or all of the loan. Since the Depression of the 1930s, the federal government has been the principal underwriter of real estate mortgages, although coverage is also available through private companies. Federal government underwriting has been handled almost entirely by two agencies, the Federal Housing Administration (FHA), that insures—charges premiums to borrowers, and the Veterans Administration (VA), that guarantees—charges no premiums. The two federal agencies place restrictions on the coverage they provide by restricting the amounts and kinds of mortgage loans that they will underwrite. They have had a major impact on the residential mortgage market, including the secondary market. * * *

Government regulation of most mortgage lending institutions is substantial, despite recent deregulatory moves. To a considerable extent, each lender subgroup has been separately regulated with separate statutes, administrative codes, and regulatory agencies for each major type of mortgage lender such as savings and loans, savings banks, commercial banks, and insurance companies. Extensive legal controls over lenders have been imposed by both state and federal governments, and the principal regulatory objective generally has been to protect lender solvency. * * *

* * *

B. CONVEYANCING AND THE PRACTICE OF LAW

As the Johnstone excerpt notes, the importance of lawyers in real estate transactions has diminished in recent years as other professionals or institutions have taken on an increasingly dominant role. Under these circumstances, three questions must be addressed: Is there a continuing role for lawyers in real estate transactions? If so, is it necessary that all participants in a real estate transaction be represented by their own lawyer? Is it appropriate for non-lawyers to undertake tasks traditionally performed by lawyers as part of the conveyancing process?

As to the first question, lawyers clearly have a role in conveyancing, if only to review documents for lenders and for title insurers. Certainly, major commercial transactions cannot go forward without extensive involvement of lawyers. Lawyer involvement in residential transactions, however, varies at this point from locality to locality. In some jurisdictions, representation of the buyer or seller or both is common; in others it is rare. In favor of lawyer involvement, it can be argued that the purchase of a dwelling is the biggest investment most lower and middle-class persons make in their lifetime, and is, as should be clear by the end of this chapter, potentially fraught with legal perils. On the other hand, individual residential real estate transactions rarely result in serious legal problems, and real estate transactions are costly enough without adding lawyer's fees. Buyers often assume that their interests are adequately protected by their lender, title insurer, and loan guarantor (such as the Federal Housing Administration, FHA), who also have a stake in the transaction. Ask again when you finish these materials whether lawyers are necessary. As to how many lawyers are necessary, consider the following case:

IN THE MATTER OF EDWARD J. DOLAN

Supreme Court of New Jersey, 1978.
76 N.J. 1, 384 A.2d 1076.

Per Curiam.

A complaint was filed with the Middlesex County Ethics Committee charging respondent with conflicts of interest in connection with certain real estate transactions. After receipt of the Committee's report the Court directed the Central Ethics Unit to file a petition for an Order to Show Cause, which issued in due course. That petition asserts that respondent's conduct constituted violations of DR 5–105, DR 8–101, and DR 9–101, dealing respectively with conflicts, abuse of public position, and the appearance of impropriety.

I

The public position which respondent held during the times pertinent hereto was that of municipal attorney for the Borough of Carteret, to which he was appointed at the beginning of 1971. For some time prior to the events in question the Borough had implemented a policy of urban renewal pursuant to Federal Housing Authority (FHA) procedures. By ordinance it created the Carteret Redevelopment Agency (Agency) * * *. The Agency's function was to solicit proposals from developers for utilization of certain tracts for low and moderate income multi-family dwelling units. Gulya Brothers, Inc., a developer, submitted a proposal for a townhouse project on one of the tracts, which the Agency accepted. * * *

Upon acceptance of Gulya's proposal the Agency was required to obtain the necessary approvals from the municipal planning board, board of adjustment and governing body. Additionally, it was obliged to convey to the developer marketable title to the tracts involved. In due course the Agency, which was represented by its own counsel, successfully processed applications before the appropriate municipal bodies, and on November 15, 1971, the Borough gave final approval to the project.

Thereafter Gulya's attorney sought financing for the project on behalf of the developer but was unsuccessful. To aid in this endeavor the developer's attorney sought out the respondent, who had "handled matters for him in the past", was "familiar with mortgage financing", and had done "some extensive real estate work." In May or June of 1972 respondent, at the instance of Gulya's attorney, discussed the project with the principals of Gulya and at that point took over the representation of the developer, with the full consent of previous counsel. Prior to this respondent had not represented Gulya in any capacity whatsoever. Specifically, he had not appeared on the developer's behalf before the Agency; neither had he represented either the planning board or board of adjustment at the time of the Agency's applications to those bodies or at any other time. Respondent was, however, attorney for the Borough when the Council acted favorably on the board of adjustment's recommendation to grant the Agency's application for the necessary variances for this project.

Respondent's efforts on Gulya's behalf produced the required financing through a New Jersey mortgage company. The financing consisted of both the construction mortgage and permanent mortgages available to the buyers of the townhouses. Respondent's representation of the developer continued throughout the initial construction stage of the project, during which time he was, as has been indicated, attorney for the municipality in which the development was located, albeit that representation of the municipality was not in any wise in connection with any business of or application on behalf of the developer.

Respondent also represented the mortgage company in sales involving permanent mortgages used in the purchase of townhouses from Gulya. In those same transactions he came to act as well on behalf of purchasers-mortgagors of the housing units at their closings of mortgage loan and title, under the following circumstances. In order to market the townhouses the developer engaged a real estate agent, whose function it was to attract buyers and assist those buyers in obtaining FHA approvals. It was the agent who led the buyers through whatever preliminary steps were required leading to execution of the contracts, and it was the agent who secured execution of those contracts. Respondent did not enter the picture until after the contracts had been signed by the buyer. The contract forms utilized by the agent, pursuant to these procedures, contained the following clauses: [13]

> Purchaser shall be responsible for paying the closing attorneys for the mortgage (sic) their legal fee for examination of title and recording of deed and mortgage and shall also be responsible for and shall pay for survey, mortgage title insurance, hazard insurance premium, escrow funds for taxes and insurance, appraisal and inspection fees and a one percent processing fee except as may be otherwise provided herein.
> * * *

> If purchaser uses seller's attorney, the seller will pay the legal fee for title examination, recording of deed and mortgage, survey, mortgage title insurance, appraisal and inspection fees.

By virtue of the arrangement last referred to either respondent or an associate in his office attended closings not only for the seller in sixteen instances, but also for the purchasers-mortgagors in at least fourteen of those closings. At these closings purchasers were notified for the first time of the potential conflicts of interest arising out of respondent's multiple representations. They were presented with and executed two separate waiver and consent forms, one acknowledging and approving respondent's representation of purchaser and seller and the other acknowledging and approving his representation of mortgagor, mortgagee and seller.

As may be seen, then, there are two separate areas of potential conflict of interest called to our attention by the Committee report and the Central Ethics Unit's presentment.[14] The first centers about respondent's representation of the builder-developer while at the same time serving as attorney for the Borough of Carteret. The second focuses on his representation at the closing of the seller, the purchasers-mortgagors and the mortgagee under circumstances casting doubt on the informed nature of the consents given by the buyers to this multiple representation.

II

We address first the asserted conflict presented by respondent's representation of the developer while concurrently acting as borough attorney. Respondent points out that at no time did his representation of Gulya involve any dealings or transactions with the Borough. All

---

13. These clauses have not been directly attacked in these proceedings and we do not pass on their propriety.

14. A third area emerges, although it was not touched upon in the complaint, testimony, report or presentment. It is the arrangement under which respondent represented both Gulya and the mortgage company with respect to the construction mortgage again at a time when he was municipal attorney. Much of the thrust of this opinion can be directed with equal force to that relationship even though it has not been presented to us directly.

applications to municipal boards necessary to permit the Agency to convey clear title to the developer had been completed before respondent's representation of the developer commenced. Throughout the course of negotiations with the Agency involving Borough-related matters, Gulya was represented by its own attorney who eventually called on respondent for assistance when financing loomed as an obstacle.

With all of this, however, the fact remains that respondent's conduct was directly contrary to the mandate of this Court in In re A. and B., 44 N.J. 331, 209 A.2d 101 (1965). There it was noted that while in some situations it may be proper (within the proscription of DR 5–105) for an attorney to engage in dual representation, nevertheless

> the subject of land development is one in which the likelihood of transactions with a municipality and the room for public misunderstanding are so great that a member of the bar should not represent a developer operating in a municipality in which the member of the bar is the municipal attorney or the holder of any other municipal office of apparent influence. We all know from practical experience that the very nature of the work of the developer involves a probability of some municipal action, such as zoning applications, land subdivisions, building permits, compliance with the building code, etc.

> It is accordingly our view that *such dual representation is forbidden even though the attorney does not advise either the municipality or the private client with respect to matters concerning them. The fact of such dual representation itself is contrary to the public interest.* (44 N.J. at 334–35, 209 A.2d at 103 (emphasis added).)

* * *

In this case the affirmative action of those municipal boards, while made at the Agency's behest, inured to the benefit of Gulya. Those applications were, in a very real sense, in Gulya's interest, were made at a time when respondent represented the Borough, and were then followed by respondent's representation of Gulya in connection with the same development project. This representation ignored the clear admonition of In re A. and B., supra, and hence merits our disciplinary action.

III

We turn our attention to the conflict presented by respondent's multiple representation of seller, purchaser-mortgagor, and mortgagee. At the outset we recognize the emphasis that our disciplinary rules place on the desirability of completely independent counsel. Specifically, DR 5–105 prohibits multiple representation except under certain severely circumscribed circumstances. [ ] The sense of our rules is that an attorney owes complete and undivided loyalty to the client who has retained him. * * *

In a real estate transaction, the positions of vendor and purchaser are inherently susceptible to conflict. [ ] This is likewise the case with a borrower-lender relationship. [ ]

* * *

In the application of these principles to the matter before us we are mindful of the circumstances surrounding this type of transaction, namely, the purchase of low and moderate income dwellings with federally guaranteed financing, which serve to distinguish it from the conventional transfer of real estate. There is less flexibility in the terms. Federal auspices in this context brings with it a certain rigidity which leaves little room for negotiation of price and such other commonly negotiable features as limits and rates on borrowed money. The prescribed forms for bond and mortgage contain fixed terms from which variance is rarely, if ever, permitted. Nevertheless, the severely strictured nature of the relationship between mortgagor and mortgagee in no wise serves to diminish the essential obligation of full and timely disclosure. The opportunity for conflict to arise for instance, in terms of a condition of title acceptable to one party but not the other while perhaps remote is by no means non-existent. More apparent is the possibility that as between buyer and developer-seller there may ripen some disagreement respecting the physical condition of the premises. Without presuming to suggest an exhaustive list of potential areas of conflict, we draw attention to these as the kinds of matters of which consenting purchasers-mortgagors should be made aware before they consent to the attorney representing another party to the transaction.

Here the consent forms executed by purchasers at the eleventh hour amounted to little more than a perfunctory effort formally to comply with Kamp's admonition. After the respondent was retained, he had an "immediate" duty to explain to the client the nature of his relationship with the seller and inform the client of the significance of any consent that the client may have given to dual representation. [   ]

The problems that can arise from the failure to heed that instructive warning are graphically demonstrated in the matter before us. The record reveals that a purchaser objected to signing one of the consent forms after the conflict of interest situation had been explained to him (because he believed it might place him in the position of approving a conflict which was "illegal"), but ultimately he executed the form as the result of persuasion from his wife and a desire to avoid the serious disruption of his moving plans resulting from any adjourned or cancelled closing. Although we agree with the Committee's conclusion that the consent form was signed voluntarily in the literal sense that neither respondent nor the seller exerted any overt pressure on the client, nevertheless we are left with the impression, as was the Committee, that execution of the form was due more to the exigencies of the situation than to an unfettered will. And this need not and should not have been. * * * The record before us reveals that respondent's office dealt with the purchasers "for several weeks before * * * the closing." Somewhere in that interval the time should have been taken and the opportunity created to explain to the purchasers the potential conflicts—the "pitfalls"—so as to allow for execution of the consent forms after due deliberation.

While the practicalities of this type of purchase may generate joint representation of low or middle income purchasers-mortgagors and their sellers and mortgagees by a single attorney, those practicalities in no sense justify any relaxation of the requirement of full, complete and timely explanation of the pitfalls and implications of such representation and the potential for conflict. Indeed, given the increased likelihood that this class of clients may be without the resources to obtain separate representation, the need for meticulous observance of the requirement of full disclosure and informed consent is underscored.

IV

While tenable arguments have been made in favor of a complete bar to any dual representation of buyer and seller in a real estate transaction, see e.g., In re Lanza, supra, 65 N.J. at 353, 322 A.2d 445 (Pashman, J., concurring); In re Rockoff, 66 N.J. 394, 397, 331 A.2d 609 (1975) (Pashman, J., concurring), on balance we decline to adopt an inflexible per se rule. Confining ourselves to the type of situation before us (assuredly there are others, entirely unrelated to financial pressures), the stark economic realities are such that were an unyielding requirement of individual representation to be declared, many prospective purchasers in marginal financial circumstances would be left without representation. That being so, the legal profession must be frank to recognize any element of economic compulsion attendant upon a client's consent to dual representation in a real estate purchase and to be circumspect in avoiding any penalization or victimization of those who, by force of these economic facts of life, give such consent.

This opinion should serve as notice that henceforth where dual representation is sought to be justified on the basis of the parties' consents, this Court will not tolerate consents which are less than knowing, intelligent and voluntary. Consents must be obtained in such a way as to insure that the client has had adequate time manifestly not provided in the matter under consideration to reflect upon the choice, and must not be forced upon the client by the exigencies of the closing. This applies with equal force to the dual representation of mortgagor and mortgagee.

In view of respondent's impeccable record, including a history of significant public service and contributions to the legal profession, we conclude that appropriate discipline is exercised by the imposition of this public reprimand.

PASHMAN, J., concurring and dissenting.

While I applaud the Court's tightening of the rules governing multiple representation in real estate transactions by further narrowing its permissible circumstantial basis, I am afraid that its effort to provide an additional safeguard for consumers of legal services simply does not go far enough. The prophylactic rule announced herein will do little to enhance the likelihood that the quality of representation provided in such circumstances will duplicate that which would be provided by counsel with undivided loyalty. Similarly, the Court's admonition that attorneys must avoid "any penalization or victimization" of clients who, as a result of economic constraints, consent to dual representation will be far from effective to prevent the various abuses endemic in such situations.

* * * The result herein continues the Court's acceptance of dual representation in circumstances where, notwithstanding full disclosure and knowing consent by the derivative client,[15] the intrinsic degree of divided allegiance is so intolerable that the proscribed adverse effect on the exercise of the attorney's independent professional judgment on behalf of that client must ipso facto be conclusively presumed. See D.R. 5–105(B). In so doing, the Court relies on the fiction that a lay client can effectively consent to dual representation and perpetuates the cruel myth that adequate representation can be provided in such cases by an attorney who supposedly can simultaneously protect the inevitably adverse interests of his two masters. The reality, of course, is that it is well-nigh impossible for the derivative client to be so well attuned to the numerous legal nuances of the transaction that his consent can be said to have been truly informed.[16] The propriety of according dispositive effect to consent so obtained is further undermined when it is frankly acknowledged that the consent is induced by the derivative client's reliance on a promise by the attorney which cannot be fulfilled—the promise of adequate representation of each of his two clients.

Surely the Court is not so naive as to the economic realities of such transactions as its utopian stance would indicate. Any conflicting interests which are potentially disruptive of the ultimate goal the expeditious consummation of the sales transaction must inevitably be resolved in favor of the primary client and for that same reason will probably not even be brought to the attention of the derivative client. This problem is even more aggravated in circumstances such as those of

---

15. The derivative client is the client whose representation by the attorney derives from his participation in a transaction with the party who is the primary client of the attorney. The derivative client is the client to whom disclosure is made and from whom consent to the dual representation is sought.

16. The most frequent topics of controversy at closing are:

(A) Difficulties with the quality of title deliverable by the seller.

(B) Disputes over alleged structural defects.

(C) Warranties.

(D) Unfinished work.

(E) Leaks.

(F) Cellar problems.

(G) Construction of roads and sidewalks in the development on schedule.

(H) Drainage problems.

(I) Problems as to utilities.

(J) Defective masonry foundations.

(K) Mortgage and tax escrows amount and interest.

(L) Escrows of a part of seller's money to assure compliance with above problems, including schedule for release of funds.

(M) Appropriate remedies for compliance with any agreements concerning the above.

There are, of course, innumerable variations of such problems within the above general areas. These are in addition to the many subjects as to which intolerable conflicts of interest result if the attorney provides dual representation at the contract negotiation stage as well as at the closing of title.

the instant case where the primary client of the attorney is a developer with whom the attorney has a potentially long-term and profitable relationship. Consequently, the attorney has a substantial economic stake in maintaining the continued goodwill of this primary client. * * *

* * *

Even assuming that dual representation in an "ordinary isolated" real estate transaction should not be per se impermissible, the practice is wholly unsupportable where the attorney involved is the representative of a developer. The attorney's economic disincentive to be vigilant in safeguarding the buyer's interests in such a case is too strong, and a per se prohibition is absolutely imperative. * * *

* * *

Moreover, the Court's assumption that adoption of a per se prohibition of dual representation in a real estate transaction would somehow prevent persons of modest means from being represented at all is unwarranted. The more likely result of a per se rule will be to alert such persons to the gravity of the contemplated transaction and consequently impel them to secure their own counsel. In this regard it is not inappropriate for us to notice the greater access by consumers to information concerning the cost of legal services as a result of fee advertising in this post-Bates [17] era. Considering the more than adequate number of attorneys in this state, it is very likely that representation in such relatively uncomplicated matters as residential real estate settlements at moderate fees will be readily available. Furthermore, the cost of obtaining independent counsel is normally only an incremental addition to the cost of the entire transaction and is a cost that most purchasers would willingly bear if they were aware of its potentially significant benefit. * * *

Were these purchasers not induced to believe that the quality of the derivative representation they would receive from the seller's attorney is the equivalent of any representation they could receive from their own counsel, it is reasonable to assume that they would have obtained independent representation. In short, the Court allows dual representation to be a self-justifying practice by accepting the theory that its sine qua non role in the provision of housing to persons of limited means is proven by the fact that so many persons consent to it. I am unable to concur in that assessment. * * *

* * *

Notes and Questions

1. Whose assumptions as to the realities of a modern real estate transaction are more realistic, the majority's or the dissent's? Consider the following quote:

17. Bates v. Arizona State Bar Association, 433 U.S. 350, 97 S.Ct. 2691, 53 L.Ed.2d 810 (1977).

MORGAN, THE EVOLVING CONCEPT OF
PROFESSIONAL RESPONSIBILITY

90 Harv.L.Rev. 702 (1977).

A lawyer certainly cannot sit at both counsel tables in contested litigation. However by no means all legal problems involve going to court, and when they do not, having more than one lawyer to accomplish the parties' objectives may be an unnecessary and wasteful luxury. Individuals entering upon a contractual relationship, for example, might find it significantly less expensive and less disruptive to hire a single lawyer to draft a contract incorporating the business consensus of both sides than to have two lawyers, each trying to exact the marginal pound of flesh for his client. * * *

The response to this argument from many lawyers is that a situation which appears nonlitigious at the moment may develop into a contested situation in the future. This is not an unreasonable concern and may appear to go in part to the interest of the client. But having two lawyers from the outset in every case is expensive insurance against the unknown. Moreover, in many situations where things go badly, both sides can simply bring in separate counsel. The only person hurt by such a procedure would be the first lawyer who will now represent neither party. That the lawyer might not like this result is understandable. That his unhappiness should rise to the level of an ethical precept is less clear.

Do you agree or disagree? Is involvement of lawyers representing all parties necessarily an unnecessary extravagance? See Residential Real Estate Transactions: The Lawyer's Proper Role—Services—Compensation, 14 Real Prop., Prob., & Trust J. 581, 590–595 (1979) (Each party to the transaction needs separate representation.)

2. If a lawyer chooses to represent both the buyer and the seller (or any other two or more parties in a real estate transaction), how should the lawyer disclose the potential conflict? Is an oral disclosure sufficient? If a written disclosure is necessary, how should it be worded? Should it disclose some or all potential areas of conflict between the parties? What must the lawyer do if a conflict actually emerges? Is ABA Model Rule 1.7 helpful in resolving these issues?

3. A lawyer representing the purchaser in a real estate transaction drafts both a deed granting the property to the purchaser and a deed of trust—securing the interest of the vendor for later payment of the purchase price. The lawyer fails to advise the vendor of the necessity of recording the deed of trust to protect her security interest in the property. The vendor fails to record the deed of trust. Subsequently the property is sold to a purchaser who takes free of the unrecorded deed of trust under the recording act, and the original purchaser declares bankruptcy. Can the initial seller sue the lawyer for malpractice? See Stinson v. Brand, 738 S.W.2d 186 (Tenn.1987) (recognizing a cause of action on similar facts).

4. Can a lawyer adequately represent both a buyer and a title insurer? Are the title insurer's interests necessarily more compatible with those of the buyer than are the interests of the seller or broker? See, ABA

Formal Opinion 331. (No necessary conflict of interest between representing buyer and acting as agent for title insurance company if full disclosure and no breach of other rules.)

5. Ask many real estate broker whether lawyers should be involved in real estate transactions and they will tell you that lawyers kill deals. This is clearly a good reason for brokers to not want lawyers involved. Is it a good reason for buyers to not want lawyers involved?

6. If neither the buyer nor seller is represented by counsel, someone other than a lawyer must draft the documents necessary to consummate the conveyance. These are likely to be drafted by the real estate broker, the title company, or the lender. In drafting these documents, and in advising the buyer and seller as to what should be included in these documents, are these entities practicing law? If so, is their conduct illegal or unethical?

In State Bar of Arizona v. Arizona Land Title and Trust Co., 90 Ariz. 76, 366 P.2d 1 (1961), the integrated State Bar of Arizona and individual attorneys filed complaints for a declaratory judgment against several real estate brokers and title companies claiming that in connection with the conduct of their businesses and transactions the real estate brokers and title companies regularly prepared, drafted, and formulated documents affecting title to real property, and that their giving legal advice regarding the transactions and instruments constituted the unauthorized practice of law. The bar sought an injunction restraining and enjoining the real estate brokers and title companies from any further legal involvement in real estate transactions, except preparation of the customary preliminary purchase agreement executed on printed forms.

The Arizona Supreme Court held that, while it was impossible to give an exhaustive definition of "the practice of law," it was "sufficient to state that those acts, whether performed in court or in the law office, which lawyers customarily have carried on from day to day through the centuries must constitute 'the practice of law'." It was "obvious to anyone familiar with the work of attorneys that most of the activities engaged in by [the real estate brokers and title companies], traditionally have been and presently are conducted in the regular course of their practice by members of the bar." The court rejected the argument that the defendants were not practicing law since they did not charge separately for preparing legal documents, noting that "[r]eliance by the client on advice or services rendered, rather than the fact that compensation is received, is more pertinent in determining whether certain conduct is the purported or actual practice of law."

The court was particularly concerned that the title company employees who prepared the documents for customers of the title companies owed their first allegiance to "the company's rights and obligations rather than [to] the parties to the transaction." This the court contrasted with the position of lawyers representing the buyer or seller, who under professional ethics owed sole allegiance to the interest of their clients. The court further observed that "[t]itle company witnesses consistently testified that when dealing with customers, they carefully avoided conversation which would involve a discussion of the customers' objectives, or legal rights and obligations with respect to the property being conveyed. Nevertheless, the title company employee, in 'filling in a form,' obviously exercises his own discretion as to what form should be used, and what language is to be inserted in the blank spaces. * * * The title company employee, treading on doubtful ground, is hesitant to ask relevant questions and even more reluctant to make positive recommendations regarding the legal aspects of a prospective transaction, although he is nevertheless willing to draft legal instruments in order that a title policy may be issued. * * * "

The court rejected the argument that the complained-of acts were not the practice of law because of long-standing custom and because experience had proved that protection of the public interest did not require that the acts in question be performed by lawyers. The court argued: "This is tantamount to saying, 'We have been driving through red lights for so many years without a serious mishap that it is now lawful to do so.'" It went on to say that, "neither the public blissful acquiescence nor the bar's confessed lethargy can clothe the activities with validity. There is no prescriptive right to practice law." The court concluded by enjoining the title companies and realtors from assisting or advising in the preparation of documents affecting the title to real or personal property, including filling in the blanks in legal forms.

Subsequent to the Arizona decision, a popular initiative, sponsored by the real estate industry, amended the Arizona Constitution as follows:

Article XXVI

§ 1. Powers of real estate broker or salesman

Section 1. Any person holding a valid license as a real estate broker or a real estate salesman regularly issued by the Arizona State Real Estate Department when acting in such capacity as broker or salesman for the parties, or agent for one of the parties to a sale, exchange, or trade, or the renting and leasing of property, shall have the right to draft or fill out and complete, without charge, any and all instruments incident thereto including, but not limited to, preliminary purchase agreements and earnest money receipts, deeds, mortgages, leases, assignments, releases, contracts for sale of realty, and bills of sale.

What arguments can be made in favor of or in opposition to such an amendment? See Marks, The Lawyers and the Realtors: Arizona's Experience, 49 A.B.A.J. 139 (February 1963). In the course of the debate concerning the initiative, Marks relates, a Tuscon attorney offered a $100 prize to any real estate salesman (not a lawyer) who could pass a real property examination at the College of Law of the University of Arizona (supra at 141).

In subsequent cases, Arizona courts have held that real estate brokers completing legal documents can be held to full understanding of the implications and ramifications of legal doctrines, Olson v. Neale, 116 Ariz. 522, 570 P.2d 209 (App.1977), and to an obligation to inform their clients as to the legal consequences of documents they draft, Morley v. J. Pagel Realty and Ins., 27 Ariz.App. 62, 550 P.2d 1104 (1976).

Most jurisdictions faced with this problem have equivocated, permitting realtors, for example, to fill out standardized forms that advise clients that the form is legally binding, and that clients have the right to consult an attorney, See New Jersey State Bar Ass'n v. New Jersey Ass'n of Realtor Boards, 93 N.J. 470, 461 A.2d 1112 (1983), modified, 94 N.J. 449, 467 A.2d 577 (1983); Duncan & Hill Realty, Inc. v. Department of State, 62 A.D.2d 690, 405 N.Y.S.2d 339 (1978), appeal denied, 45 N.Y.2d 821, 409 N.Y.S.2d 210, 381 N.E.2d 608 (1978); Cultum v. Heritage House Realtors, Inc., 103 Wash.2d 623, 694 P.2d 630 (en banc 1985). Are participants in real estate transactions adequately protected by form contracts?

Professor Michael Braunstein, in a study of 132 recent home buyers in Columbus, Ohio, found that only 41 per cent hired their own lawyer to represent them in some aspect of the purchase. Twenty-one per cent of the buyers who did not use lawyers stated that they relied on the realtor to assist them with title matters, while 40 per cent of the purchasers stated that they relied mainly on the title insurance company. Seventy-eight per cent of the purchasers believed that if their lender was satisfied with the condition and title of the house, their investment was in all likelihood safe. Others stated that they relied on the seller's or builder's attorney to take care of the legalities. Braunstein found that the purchasers were remarkably uninformed as to basic matters like the type of deed they received or their coverage under the title insurance policy (only seven per cent realized that there were exceptions in the title insurance policy). He also found, however, that purchasers represented by lawyers were: (i) no better informed than those who were not; (ii) slightly less satisfied with the purchase transaction (78 per cent compared to 84 per cent satisfied); (iii) just as likely to find after signing the contract that it contained matters not explained to them; and (iv) no less likely to avoid disputes. See Braunstein, Odd Man Out: Preliminary Findings Concerning the Diminishing Role of Lawyers in the Home–Buying Process, 52 Ohio St.L.J. 469, 479–480 (1991).

II. THE BASIC DOCUMENTS IN THE REAL ESTATE TRANSACTION

Real estate lawyering is fundamentally green eyeshade work. It is primarily concerned with drafting documents (or filling in the blanks in printed documents) to achieve the client's goals. Thus we begin with the consideration of the documents that commonly govern real estate transactions, and the relationships they establish and memorialize.

A. THE BROKERAGE AGREEMENT

EXCLUSIVE RIGHT TO SELL LISTING CONTRACT

Adopted by the Multiple Listing Service of the Columbus Board of Realtors®, Inc.

In consideration of your efforts to find a purchaser for my property, your submitting this Listing Contract to the Multiple Listing Service (MLS) of the Columbus Board of Realtors, Inc. _____ broker, the exclusive

and the payment of all costs incurred by you in connection therewith, I hereby grant to you _____

right for _____ days, commencing (LIST Date) [Day(N)] [Month] [Year(N)] through (EXP) [Day(N)] [Month] [Year(N)] , to sell or exchange said property known generally

as _____ and more fully described above, for the sum of $ _____ payable

_____ or for such other price or on such other terms to which I may consent in writing.

I hereby agree to pay to you a fee of _____ of the selling price of said property if during the period of this listing contract 1) it is sold or exchanged or 2) if you produce a purchaser ready, willing and able to purchase said property

on the above terms. Owner authorizes broker to compensate other brokers through subagency. Owner further authorizes broker to compensate buyer-brokers from the fee paid (_____)Yes. (_____) No.

In addition, such fee shall be paid if said property is sold or exchanged within _____ DAYS _____ after the expiration of this listing contract (or any extension thereof) to anyone with whom broker has had negotiations prior to expiration,

provided I have received notice in writing, including the names of the prospective purchasers, before or upon expiration of this listing contract (or any extension thereof). However, I shall not be obligated to pay you such fee if I enter into

a valid listing contract during the term of said protection period with another licensed real estate broker.

You are hereby authorized to place a "For Sale" sign on said property and to remove all other "For Sale" signs; to actively market the property; and you and all brokers and salespersons authorized by you shall have access to the

property at all reasonable times for the purpose of showing it.

In the event of a sale or exchange. I hereby agree to furnish satisfactory evidence of marketable title to the property and to convey the property by transferrable and recordable warranty deed, with release of dower if any or fiduciary

deed, as appropriate.

The undersigned Owner(s) direct(s) the above named broker to immediately submit this listing to the Multiple Listing Service of the Columbus Board of Realtors, Inc. to be published and disseminated to participants therein. Further the

owner(s) have read this agreement and the information contained herein, and warrant that said information is correct and accurate to the best of their knowledge.

In compliance with existing Fair Housing Laws, the undersigned will not in any manner discriminate against any prospective purchaser or purchasers because of race, color, sex, national origin, ancestry, religion, physical

handicap, or familial status.

Remarks _____

Signature of Owner(s) _____

Signed this (LIST Date) _____ day of _____ 19 ____

Accepted _____ Address _____

By _____ Broker _____ City _____ State _____ Zip Code _____

Salesperson _____ Telephone _____

BROKER COPY

[G8348]

FEARICK v. SMUGGLERS COVE, INC.

District Court of Appeal of Florida, Second District, 1980.
379 So.2d 400.

HOBSON, JUDGE.

Appellant, a licensed real estate broker, appeals the dismissal with prejudice of his fourth amended complaint. In five counts, he sought to recover a brokerage commission for services allegedly performed in connection with the sale of certain property owned by Smugglers Cove, Inc.

The factual allegations in appellant's complaint state that he and Bauer, the president of Smugglers Cove, orally entered into an exclusive listing agreement in August of 1973 for the sale of property owned by the corporation. The sale price was set at $925,000, with the purchaser to assume a $200,000 mortgage, and appellant was to receive a 6% Commission if he procured a ready, willing and able purchaser. Thereafter, appellant undertook certain steps to advertise and sell the property, including placing signs on the property.

Although the purchase price had twice been reduced, the property remained unsold as of early February, 1976, resulting in a further reduction to $750,000. Thereafter, appellant contacted Hollopeter, president of Outer Island Development of Florida, Inc., which was in the process of developing a tract of land adjacent to the property. Hollopeter was informed that appellant was the exclusive broker and of the terms and conditions of the sale. After appellant had had several meetings with Hollopeter and had informed Bauer that a potential purchaser had been located, Bauer contacted another broker and offered him $4,000 if he would arrange an introduction with Hollopeter and if a sale resulted. Thereafter, Hollopeter told appellant that he was no longer interested in purchasing the property.

On July 1, 1976, the shareholders of Smugglers Cove consented to dissolution of the corporation, pursuant to Section 607.254, Florida Statutes (1975), and executed articles of dissolution pursuant to Section 607.267. After the filing of the articles of dissolution, a quit-claim deed was executed on July 7, 1976, transferring the subject property to the shareholders of the corporation. The property was then sold to Outer Island for $650,000. Appellant alleges that he demanded payment of his commission, but received only $2,500 for his services.

Appellant filed a complaint against appellee in February, 1977; the fourth amended complaint was filed in September, 1978, and dismissed with prejudice in January, 1979. Count I of the complaint is an action against Smugglers Cove for the real estate commission; Count II is against Bauer individually for entering into an unauthorized contract on behalf of the corporation; Count III is a claim against Bauer and Erb as trustees for payment of corporate debts in their capacity as directors; Count IV is an action against the shareholders of Smugglers Cove for the real estate commission; and Count V is an action against Hollopeter for tortious interference with the contract for the real estate brokerage commission.

We agree with the trial judge's dismissal of Counts II, and IV; however, we find that there was error in his dismissal of Counts I, III and V.

* * *

Count I of appellant's fourth amended complaint alleges facts which, if proven, will entitle him to his brokerage commission from Smugglers Cove, Inc. The parties had orally entered into an exclusive listing (agency to sell) agreement.[18] Under such an agreement, the owner retains the right to sell the property *independently* of the broker. However, if the sale is to a ready, willing and able purchaser *procured* by the broker, the owner is liable for the broker's commission. [ ]

Whether a broker is a procuring cause is a question of fact to be determined from the surrounding circumstances. [ ] Generally, to be the procuring cause of a sale, "a broker must show that he called the potential purchaser's attention to the property and that it was through his efforts that the sale * * * was consummated." B & B Super Markets, Inc. v. Metz, 260 So.2d 529, 531 (Fla.2d DCA 1972). If the broker locates a purchaser, inaugurates negotiations with him, and so informs the seller, he is the procuring cause and is entitled to his commission even though the seller interrupts the negotiations and sells to the purchaser at a price lower than the one which the broker was authorized to accept. [ ]

* * *

Count III also states a cause of action against Bauer and Erb, who were the directors at the time of dissolution of Smugglers Cove, in their capacity as trustees for property owned by the dissolved corporation. * * *

Finally, the facts alleged in Count V also state a cause of action against the purchaser for the tortious interference with the contract between the broker and seller.[19] The elements of this tort are three-fold: the existence of a business relationship under which the plaintiff has legal rights; an intentional and unjustified interference with that relationship by the defendant; and damage to the plaintiff as a result of the breach of the business relationship. [ ]

The business relationship need not be founded on an enforceable contract. [ ] A business relationship may be established if a commission was discussed by the broker and seller and the latter was aware that the broker was rendering services on his behalf. [ ] Such a relationship was alleged to have existed here.

The purchaser was informed by the broker that he had an exclusive listing with the seller. Nonetheless, the purchaser broke off negotiations with the broker and dealt directly with the seller after an introduction by another broker. This would supply the element of intent. [ ] There is no doubt that the broker suffered damage as a result of the purchaser's conduct.

---

18. Such agreements need not be in writing. [ ]

19. The fact that the broker has a cause of action against the seller does not deprive him of a cause of action against the purchaser if the latter helped induce the breach. [ ]

For the foregoing reasons, we find that the trial judge erred in dismissing Counts I, III and V of appellant's fourth amended complaint. Accordingly, we reverse and remand with directions that those counts be reinstated.

Notes and Questions

1. Though the Statute of Frauds in most states requires that most transactions affecting real property must be in writing (see below), the statutes of a majority of states exclude brokerage agreements, permitting oral agreements to be enforced. Even where the Statute of Frauds does not explicitly extend to brokerage agreements, some agreements may still need to be in writing under other provisions of the Statute, for example, agreements that cannot be performed within one year. Where a state statute of frauds requires brokerage commissions to be in writing, it is important that essential terms, such as the fact of employment, the authority of the agent, and the description of the property, be clearly spelled out.

2. The principal case involved an "exclusive listing" agency agreement. Several other types of listings are commonly used. Under an "open listing", the seller authorizes a broker to attempt to sell the property, while also retaining for himself the right to sell the property independently, or to procure the services of other brokers in marketing the property. Where several brokers hold an open listing on a property, the broker who actually was the procuring cause of a sale can claim the commission. An "exclusive agency" limits the seller to one broker during the duration of the agreement, but permits the seller to attempt to sell the property also on his own to buyers other than those procured by the broker. Finally, an "exclusive right to sell" authorizes only the broker to sell the property. If any buyer purchases the property during the duration of the agreement, a commission is owed.

A "multiple listing" arrangement permits brokers holding exclusive listings in a particular area to pool their listings through a common clearing house. Any broker belonging to the multiple listing arrangement may attempt to sell multiple listed properties. If a broker is successful, the commission will be split between the listing and the selling broker. The courts are split on the question of whether multiple listing arrangements that restrict access of realtors are restraints on trade, but the trend seems to be to permit multiple listing where restrictions on access are reasonable. See 7 R. Powell & P. Rohan, Real Property, ¶ 938.16[2].

3. The principal case recognizes the right of a broker to recover a commission for producing a "ready, willing, and able" purchaser. The majority of jurisdictions still permit a broker who procures a ready, willing and able buyer to recover a commission, whether or not the deal is ultimately consummated. Thus, if the seller ultimately refuses to convey, or is unable to convey the property, the broker still must be paid. Some jurisdictions go further, and hold that a broker has earned her commission once a valid, enforceable contract is signed by both the buyer and seller, even though the buyer later is found financially unable to perform, see Scully v. Williamson, 26 Okl. 19, 108 P. 395 (1910).

A minority of courts, however, hold that the broker has not earned his commission until the deal in fact closes or the seller's conduct precludes a closing. This rule, called the Ellsworth Dobbs rule after the leading case supporting it (Ellsworth Dobbs, Inc. v. Johnson, 50 N.J. 528, 236 A.2d 843 (1967)), represents the modern trend. The New Jersey court stated:

> There can be no doubt that ordinarily when an owner of property lists it with a broker for sale, his expectation is that the money for the payment of commission will come out of the proceeds of the sale. He expects that if the broker produces a buyer to whom the owner's terms of sale are satisfactory, and a contract embodying those terms is executed, the buyer will perform, i.e. he will pay the consideration and accept the deed at the time agreed upon. Considering the realities of the relationship created between the owner and broker, that expectation of the owner is a reasonable one, * * *.
>
> The present [ready, willing and able] New Jersey rule as exemplified by the cases cited above is deficient as an instrument of justice. * * * It seems to us that fairness requires that the arrangement between broker and owner be interpreted to mean that the owner hires the broker with the expectation of becoming liable for a commission only in the event a sale of the property is consummated, unless the title does not pass because of the owner's improper or frustrating conduct.
>
> * * * Since the broker's duty to the owner is to produce a prospective buyer who is financially able to pay the purchase price and take title, a right in the owner to assume such capacity when the broker presents his purchaser ought to be recognized. It follows that the obligation to inquire into the prospect's financial status and to establish his adequacy to fulfill the monetary conditions of the purchase must be regarded logically and sensibly as resting with the broker. * * * In reason and in justice it must be said that the duty to produce a purchaser able in the financial sense to complete the purchase at the time fixed is an incident of the broker's business; * * *. In a practical world, the true test of a willing buyer is not met when he signs an agreement to purchase; it is demonstrated at the time of closing of title, and if he unjustifiably refuses or is unable financially to perform then, the broker has not produced a willing buyer." 236 A.2d at 852–853.

What policies argue for the traditional position? Is the recognition in the principal case of a cause of action on the part of the broker against a purchaser who deals in bad faith relevant to the question of under what circumstances the broker ought to be able to recover from the seller?

Might the Ellsworth Dobbs rule encourage brokers who have identified purchasers of marginal financial ability to arrange risky financing arrangements to close the deal and secure a commission? If so, should the broker be liable upon the purchaser's default? Is such conduct less likely under the majority rule?

In a jurisdiction that has adopted the Ellsworth Dobbs rule, should the broker be permitted to contract for the traditional rule? Ellsworth Dobbs, 236 A.2d at 856, held such agreements unconsionable and against public policy, other courts merely subject them to close scrutiny, see Tristram's Landing, Inc. v. Wait, 367 Mass. 622, 327 N.E.2d 727 (1975).

4. The broker's primary fidiciary obligation is to the seller of real estate rather than to the buyer. When the property turns out be be defective, however, the buyer often attempts to hold the broker responsible. We examine the broker's obligations under these circumstances in Section IV below.

B. THE CONTRACT

The residential real estate purchase contract normally begins as an offer from the purchaser (responding to the vendor's listing of the property) which in turn results in a counter-offer or acceptance from the vendor. Negotiations can go on for some time, and in the case of commercial real estate, normally do. The contract, once signed, governs the relationship between the vendor and purchaser during the time, often lasting several weeks or months, between the contract and the closing—the date on which the deed is delivered. In some instances, as will be explored further below, some contractual obligations extend beyond the closing as well.

During the period between the signing of the contract and the closing, important tasks must be completed. In the course of completing those tasks, numerous problems can arise. It is during this period that the title record of the property is usually examined to discover any defects. (Why would the seller wait until a contract is signed to examine the title, rather than having a title examination completed before placing the property on the market?) Providing evidence of good title is usually the obligation of the seller, though in some eastern states the buyer undertakes the responsibility of examining the title. Once defects are uncovered (as they often are), the vendor must undertake to resolve them. The buyer must usually secure financing for part of the purchase price during this time. This will often require satisfying the lender as to the value of the property through an appraisal. Often the buyer or lender will also require a survey of the premises and the purchase of title insurance. The buyer may want to have buildings on the property examined for defects: leaky roofs, termite infestation, structural problems, defective appliances.

During the time that these tasks are underway, other problems may arise. The buildings on the property may be destroyed by fire, eminent domain proceedings against the property may be initiated, mechanics liens or tax liens may be filed encumbering the property.

Ideally, the contract will be sufficiently clear and detailed to resolve any disputes that may arise prior to the closing. As residential real estate contracts are often drafted, however, by brokers more eager to make a sale than to identify potential problems, this is not always the case. Examine the following contract, and compare it to one commonly used in your jurisdiction. Consider how they address common real estate transaction problems.

RESIDENTIAL
REAL ESTATE SALE CONTRACT

THIS CONTRACT IS APPROVED BY THE BAR ASSOCIATION OF METROPOLITAN ST. LOUIS
FOR USE BY BUYERS AND SELLERS OF RESIDENTIAL REAL ESTATE.

CAUTION TO BUYER: BUYER SHOULD CONSULT AN ATTORNEY IF BUYER EXPECTS TO CONDUCT AN ACTIVITY ON THE PROPERTY WHICH IS NOT PART OF THE CURRENT USE OR PLANS TO MAKE ADDITIONS OR IMPROVEMENTS TO THE OUTSIDE OF THE PROPERTY.

THIS CONTRACT ("Contract") is made by and between: (Print names and indicate marital status)

BUYER: _____

ADDRESS (For notices): _____

SELLER: _____

ADDRESS (For notices): _____

and is effective as of the date and time of acceptance by delivery as shown on the signature page of this Contract.

1. **OFFER**: Buyer hereby offers and agrees to buy and Seller hereby agrees to sell the following described Property, known and numbered as (Address) _____,

in the County/City of _____, State of Missouri. Legal description on Seller's title:

The term "Property" as used in this Contract means the land described above, all improvements and fixtures thereon and appurtenances thereto, and any of the following items, whether affixed or not (unless otherwise specified), as are now on the Property (**unless stricken**): heating, ventilating and air conditioning systems; electrical and plumbing systems; attached lighting and light bulbs; curtain rods, window coverings, awnings and window treatments; storm doors and storm windows; window and door screens; water heaters; water softeners; radiator covers; built-in appliances; ovens; stove or range; attached safes; wall-to-wall carpeting; garage door openers, controls and keys; all door keys; smoke detectors; fire detectors and security systems; television towers, antennas and satellite dishes; fencing, gates and landscaping; fireplace grates, screens, andirons and doors; attached mirrors; storage and outbuildings; and _____

_____

2. **PURCHASE PRICE**: The Purchase Price for the Property is: $ _____
   - (a) Earnest Money: Buyer herewith tenders to Seller earnest money which shall be deposited with Escrow Agent pursuant to Section 8, and which shall be applied against the purchase price at closing. $ _____

   - (b) Additional Earnest Money on or before_____. $ _____
   - (c) Payment on Closing: The balance due from Buyer at closing, subject to adjustment by closing costs charged or credited to Buyer, payable by cash, wire transfer or cashier's check drawn on a local bank. $ _____

3. **CLOSING COSTS**: Subject to closing costs responsibility directed by FHA, VA or other governmental agency financing, the parties agree to be responsible for the following costs, if any, to be paid at closing, or sooner as may be requested by Closing Agent named in Section 5:

   - (a) Buyer shall pay:
     1. Title insurance premium(s);
     2. Fire and extended coverage hazard insurance premium(s);
     3. Flood insurance premium(s), if required, and flood letter;
     4. Appraisal fees and charges of lender;
     5. Title company service charges, survey, Buyer's attorney's fees, Closing Agent and/or Escrow Agent fees charged to Buyer, recording fees, other customary closing costs, and accruals and prorations as otherwise provided in this Contract;
     6. Other Buyer's costs as provided in this Contract.
     7. Other_____

(b) Seller shall pay:
    1. Real estate sales commissions to:

_____ in the sum of_____% of Purchase Price;

_____ in the sum of_____% of Purchase Price;

    2. Recording fees for lien releases;
    3. Closing Agent and/or Escrow Agent fees charged to Seller, Seller's attorney's fees, other customary closing costs, and accruals and prorations as otherwise provided in this Contract;
    4. Other Seller's costs, including repairs pursuant to Section 10 and as otherwise provided in this Contract.
    5. Other_____

4. FINANCING CONTINGENCY: This Contract is contingent upon Buyer obtaining a loan secured by a first Deed of Trust on the Property upon the following or better terms:
    Loan Amount: $_____
    Interest rate not to exceed: _____% (Initially, if an Adjustable Rate Loan).
    Note term:_____years. Amortization term: _____ years.

    Point(s) to be paid by: Seller _____ Point(s); Buyer_____ Point(s).
    In addition, Buyer to pay for Mortgage Insurance, if required.

Type of Loan:	Fixed	Adjustable
Conv	_____	_____
VA	_____	_____
FHA	_____	_____

    Other provisions_____
_____

    Buyer shall apply for the loan within 7 Days of the acceptance of this contract with a lender who regularly makes real estate loans. Buyer shall furnish all necessary information and documents and pay all fees and charges required with such application. Failure to perform as provided herein shall be a default by Buyer.

    If a written commitment for a real estate loan ("Loan Commitment") is not obtained by 5:00 p.m. St. Louis time on _____, 19____, then this contract shall be null and void and the earnest money shall be returned to Buyer subject to the conditions of Section 8, unless Seller agrees in writing to provide the financing set forth above within 7 Days of being notified in writing by Buyer that a Loan Commitment was not obtained. A Loan Commitment containing contingencies or requirements shall satisfy this section unless they are unique to the Buyer or to the Property and are not usually found in Loan Commitments. Notwithstanding the above, Buyer may accept loan terms different from those set forth in this Section 4 provided Seller is advised in writing of the acceptance of the different terms by the date set forth in this Section 4.

    Buyer shall immediately provide Seller or Seller's Agent with written notice that the Loan Commitment was or was not obtained within the required time. Failure to comply with all requirements of the Loan Commitment in a timely manner shall be a default by Buyer.

5. CLOSING: The closing of the sale shall be on or before _____, 19 _____

at_____
("Closing Agent") during its normal business hours.

6. TITLE TRANSFER: Title shall transfer at closing.

7. POSSESSION: Seller shall deliver possession of the Property to Buyer upon completion of closing unless otherwise agreed to in writing. Except for rental property, Seller **WARRANTS** the property shall be vacant at the time specified for possession. Property shall be delivered in its present or repaired condition, ordinary wear and tear excepted.

8. EARNEST MONEY: All earnest money shall be deposited when received, and shall be held without interest, pending closing, by _____, "Escrow Agent". If the sale is not closed, Escrow Agent shall continue to hold the funds until the funds are released by Buyer and Seller. Escrow Agent shall retain funds sufficient to pay for expenses incurred on Buyer's behalf and upon invoice shall pay for such expenses, including but not limited to attorney fees, inspections, survey, and title search, which have been advanced in anticipation of closing but not already paid. If there is no release within 60 Days after the last date for closing provided for by this Contract or amendment, then, at the written request of either Buyer or Seller, the Escrow Agent shall file suit in interpleader. The successful claimant shall recover the costs of litigation, including a reasonable attorney's fee and interest at the rate of 10% per annum.

9. CONDITION OF THE PROPERTY: If not provided by Seller prior to acceptance of this Contract, then within 2 Days of acceptance of this Contract Seller shall provide Buyer with a written list of all material defects of which Seller has personal knowledge including, but not limited to: pest infestations, toxic or hazardous substances, wastes, materials, or gases, in, on, or under the Property or of any underground storage repository. Seller's failure to provide such a list or Seller's omission from such list of material defects required to be disclosed shall be deemed to be a **WARRANTY** by Seller that Seller has no personal knowledge of such material defects. Seller's disclosure relieves Seller from any warranty regarding the disclosed defects; however, the disclosure is subject to the repair provision of Section 10; unless such newly disclosed matter cannot be repaired and warranted or removed from the Property. Then Buyer may give written notice to Seller within 2 Days of such disclosure that Buyer is terminating this Contract.

10. INSPECTIONS AND OCCUPANCY PERMIT: Buyer, at Buyer's cost, may have the property inspected by one or more of the following: qualified building inspector, contractor, engineer, architect, termite and other pest inspectors, and inspectors or appraisers for lender. Seller, at Seller's cost, shall order a Laclede Gas Company inspection, and a municipal code compliance inspection (if required by the municipality).

The parties shall have 15 Days after acceptance to have the foregoing inspections completed, except for inspections or appraisals for lender, and 3 Days thereafter to deliver a copy of the inspection reports to the other party or his agent. However, if a Laclede Gas, municipal code compliance and/or hazardous or toxic gases or materials or hazardous substances or waste inspection is ordered within seven (7) Days of acceptance, then the 15 Day time limit shall not apply to those inspections, but the 3 Day time limit shall apply. If any party fails to cause the Property to be inspected or the reports not to be delivered within the above time periods, or if there is no time limit, then fails to deliver such report at least 7 Days prior to closing, Seller's failure shall be deemed a default; and Buyer's failure shall be deemed a waiver of any required repairs.

> **NOTE:** *The following paragraph governs the cost of repairs and/or removals. The blank to be filled in represents a limit on the amount the Seller will be required to pay for Buyer's requested repairs and/or removals. The amount could affect Seller's net proceeds. If the amount is $ zero or left blank, Seller is not obligated to make any repairs and/or removals and Buyer accepts the Property in "as is" condition.*

Seller agrees to make all repairs and/or removals required by Buyer but not to exceed $_____ ("Seller's Limitation") as a result of any inspection completed pursuant to this Contract or by FHA or VA or municipal code or in the Seller's disclosure provided pursuant to Section 9. All repairs shall be made in a workmanlike manner with comparable quality materials to that which is repaired. But if the Seller estimates the cost of such repairs and/or removals

[G8351]

to exceed Seller's Limitation or the repairs cannot be made, then (a) Seller shall give written notice of Seller's repair estimate to Buyer within 4 Days of the delivery to him of the last inspection report; and then (b) if Buyer does not agree in writing, within 4 Days of delivery of Seller's notice either (i) to bear any excess cost above Seller's Limitation, or (ii) accept a credit at closing for Seller's Limitation and also release Seller from any obligation for the repairs and/or removals, this Contract shall be null and void. Said credit shall not effect any real estate commission payable herein.

Upon timely receipt of a municipal code compliance inspection from Seller, Buyer shall obtain an occupancy permit, if required. In the event Buyer is unable to obtain an occupancy permit when required after a diligent attempt, this Contract shall be null and void. Except as provided in this Section 10, and subject to Seller's warranty in Section 9, Buyer accepts the Property in its current condition, and Seller shall deliver the Property in its present or repaired condition at closing, ordinary wear and tear excepted.

11. <u>**TOXIC OR HAZARDOUS SUBSTANCES, WASTES, MATERIALS OR GASES**</u>: Buyer, in addition to any other right to make inspections, may at its cost within seven (7) Days of acceptance of the Contract, order inspections and tests for toxic or hazardous substances, wastes or materials or gases including but not limited to urea-formaldehyde foam insulation, asbestos, PCBs, dioxin and radon gases. This Contract shall be contingent upon the inspection and/or test results showing no toxic or hazardous substances, wastes or materials or gases being in or on the Property at levels above those set by the United States Environmental Protection Agency and the Missouri Department of Natural Resources as acceptable, or if there is no such level for the particular substances, wastes or materials or gases then not above such level as would be expected to occur naturally on the Property or not be a health hazard ("Acceptable Levels"). If an inspection and/or test is not ordered within the seven (7) Day period, this contingency shall be deemed waived.

Seller shall not interfere with any testing materials which must temporarily be placed on the Property and shall cooperate with those persons performing the test or inspection.

If the inspection or test results show levels above the Acceptable Levels, Buyer shall deliver a copy of the inspection or test report to the Seller or Seller's agent within 3 Days of receipt of same. The parties shall then follow the procedures set forth in Section 10 regarding the making of repairs to have the toxic or hazardous substances, wastes or materials or gases removed or reduced to Acceptable Levels prior to closing; subject to the provisions regarding Seller's Limitation. If the repairs are made, Seller, at Seller's expense, will provide re-inspection or testing for same prior to closing; the result of which will show that the toxic or hazardous substances, wastes or materials or gases have been removed or reduced to Acceptable Levels.

12. <u>**ACCESS TO PROPERTY**</u>: Seller agrees to permit timely inspections of the Property by appraisers, inspectors and other parties who will need access to the Property pursuant to this Contract. Further, Buyer may inspect the Property within 24 hours of the time set for closing to determine if the Property complies with this Contract and amendments. Buyer shall indemnify, defend and hold Seller harmless from any damage caused by any inspector Buyer sends to the Property.

13. <u>**CLOSING ADJUSTMENTS AND CHARGES**</u>: General taxes (based upon the assessment and rate for the current year or, if both are not available, previous year), condominium or subdivision assessments and flat-rate utilities, shall be pro-rated on the basis of a 30-day month, day of closing to be charged to Seller. Special taxes and special condominium or subdivision assessments against the Property which are due and payable prior to closing shall be charged to Seller. Unless otherwise stated, Seller WARRANTS that Seller has no knowledge and has no notice of pending or proposed ordinances or resolutions authorizing special taxes or assessments.

14. <u>**TITLE AND DEED**</u>: Title shall be marketable in fact and Seller shall convey marketable title by general warranty deed (or fiduciary deed where applicable) subject to the following exceptions: (a) easements, liens or encumbrances created by or assumed by Buyer in writing; (b) deed, building and use restrictions, building lines, rights of way, mineral rights or conditions, all of record, if any; (c) recorded easements, provided that such easements do not adversely affect the use of the Property for residential purposes as presently built, or underlie any structures; and (d) easements apparent upon inspection of the Property. Seller WARRANTS that any personal property included in this Contract shall be conveyed free of any encumbrances. This Contract shall constitute a bill of sale for personal property sold herein upon closing. If Buyer orders title insurance, Buyer shall place the order within 10 Days after acceptance of this Contract, and shall direct the title company to furnish Seller with a copy of the title commitment. After receipt of the title commitment, if Buyer determines that any matter of record (a) which is not within the Seller's control to correct and (b) which would adversely affect the use of the Property for residential purposes as presently built or underlie any structures, Buyer may (a) declare the Contract null and void; provided Buyer shall notify Seller, in writing, of such declaration within 7 Days of receipt of the title commitment, or (b) Buyer may accept a title insurance policy insuring against any title defects beyond the Seller's control. If Seller fails to meet the requirements of the title commitment and eliminate any title defects within Seller's control by the final Contract closing date, Buyer may declare a default. Nothing in this section is to be construed to require Buyer to accept title which is not marketable in fact unless Buyer expressly waives such right or closes and thereby accepts title which is not marketable in fact.

15. <u>**ZONING AND OTHER ORDINANCES**</u>: Seller WARRANTS that the Property may be used as a single family residence or that the Buyer will be able to use the Property as it is presently being used, if not a single family residence. Seller WARRANTS that Seller has not received notice of any uncorrected violations of housing, building, condominium or subdivision safety, fire ordinance, or other regulations affecting the Property, except as may have been disclosed in writing to Buyer. See Caution to Buyer at the top of the first page.

16. **LOSS**: Risk of loss to the improvements on the Property shall be borne by Seller until title is transferred. If any improvements covered by this Contract shall be damaged or destroyed, Seller shall immediately notify Buyer in writing of the damage or the destruction, the amount of insurance proceeds payable, if any, and whether Seller will, prior to closing, restore the Property to its original condition. In the event the Property is not to be restored to its original condition by Seller before the last day fixed for closing, Buyer may (a) proceed with the transaction and be entitled to all insurance money, if any, payable to Seller under all policies insuring the improvements, or (b) rescind the Contract, and thereby release all parties from liability hereunder, by giving written notice of its election to Seller or Seller's Agent within ten (10) Days after Buyer has received written notice of such damage or destruction and the amount of insurance proceeds payable. Failure by Buyer to notify Seller or Seller's Agent within the ten (10) Days after receipt of the notice shall constitute an election for (b) above. In the event Seller's notice advises the Property will be restored to its original condition by Seller before the last day fixed for closing, and if Seller fails to complete such restoration as required herein, Buyer may declare Seller in default and Buyer shall have the remedies as provided in Section 17.

17. **REMEDIES UPON DEFAULT**: If any party defaults in the performance of any obligation provided by this Contract, the party claiming a default shall notify the other party in writing of the nature of the default, the time allotted for curing the default (if not otherwise specified in this Contract), and his election of remedy if the default is not cured by the specified time.

    If default is by the Buyer, the Seller may elect to release the Buyer from this Contract in return for the payment of a sum equal to the full amount of the Earnest Money without deduction, or alternatively may authorize return of Buyer's Earnest Money and pursue any remedy at law or in equity. The parties hereby stipulate that, without resale, the Seller's damages are difficult of ascertainment, and that if the Seller claims the Earnest Money in satisfaction of the Buyer's default, it shall be as liquidated damages and not a penalty. [G8352]

    If default is by the Seller, the Buyer may release the Seller from this Contract upon the Seller's release of the Earnest Money and reimbursement to the Buyer for all direct costs and expenses, as specified in the Buyer's notice of default, including but not limited to, appraisal, credit report, inspection, loan application fee, title examination, survey, and attorney's fee. The Buyer may elect, alternatively, to pursue any remedy at law or in equity.

    If default results in litigation, the prevailing party shall recover, in addition to damages or equitable relief, the cost of litigation, interest from the date of default at the rate of 10% per annum, and a reasonable attorney's fee.

18. **TIME IS OF THE ESSENCE**: Time is of the essence in this Contract.

19. **BINDING EFFECT**: This Contract shall be binding on and shall inure to the benefit of the parties hereto, and their respective heirs, personal representatives, executors, administrators or assigns.

20. **GOVERNING LAW**: This Contract shall be considered a Contract for the sale of real property and shall be construed in accordance with the laws of the State of Missouri, including the requirement to act in good faith.

21. **WARRANTIES SURVIVE**: All Seller's **WARRANTIES** shall survive closing of the sale of the Property. **WARRANTIES** do not cover events which first occur after closing.

22. **ENTIRE AGREEMENT**: This Contract constitutes the **ENTIRE AGREEMENT BETWEEN THE PARTIES HERETO AND THERE ARE NO OTHER UNDERSTANDINGS, WRITTEN OR ORAL, RELATING TO THE SUBJECT MATTER HEREOF**, and may not be changed, modified or amended, in whole or in part, except in writing signed by all parties.

23. **DEFINITIONS**: Defined terms begin with an upper case letter and shall have the meaning as defined in the appropriate paragraph where first used unless defined below.

    A. **DAY**: Day means any calendar day.
    B. **POINT**: Point means any charge equal to one percent (1%) of the principal of a real estate loan amount paid separately, in cash or by check before or at consummation of a transaction, or withheld from proceeds of the loan at any time, but excludes payments for mortgage insurance.

24. **CONSTRUCTION**: Words and phrases shall be construed as in the singular or plural gender, and as masculine, feminine or neuter gender, according to the context.

25. **RIDERS**: The following riders are attached hereto and incorporated herein as part of this Contract: Each rider must be signed by all parties to be effective.

[ ] TRANSFER OF POSSESSION BEFORE CLOSING	[ ] SELLER FINANCING
[ ] CONTINGENCY ON SALE OF BUYER'S PROPERTY	[ ] LOAN ASSUMPTION
[ ] CONDOMINIUM RIDER	[ ] RENTAL PROPERTY
[ ] SUBDIVISION RIDER	
[ ] OTHER _____	

26. **AGENT REPRESENTS SELLER**: Unless otherwise disclosed in writing, all Real Estate Agents (Brokers, Salespersons, Licensees, Broker's Employees) ("Agent") represent the Seller and not the Buyer, and Agent has a duty to disclose to Seller any relevant information from Buyer. Agent's commission will come either directly or indirectly from Seller. The Selling Agent named below acknowledges that this disclosure was given orally to Buyer at the time Agent obtained personal and financial information from Buyer, or provided other specific assistance. Buyer's signature below acknowledges that disclosure of the above was made. No Agent shall incur any expense on behalf of Buyer without Buyer's express written consent, and with such consent, the expense shall be charged to Buyer at closing.

SPECIMEN

_____   _____
Selling Agent signature   Selling Broker and MLS Code

THIS OFFER SHALL BE ACCEPTED BY DELIVERING A SIGNED COPY TO BUYER AT _____
_____ **PRIOR TO** _____ **M. ON** _____ **19** _____.

YOUR SIGNATURE BINDS YOU TO ALL OF THE TERMS OF THIS CONTRACT. CONSULT AN ATTORNEY FOR ADVICE, EXPLANATION, MODIFICATIONS OR ADDITIONS. FILL IN ALL BLANKS BEFORE SIGNING.

Buyer _____   Date_____   Time _____ M

Buyer _____   Date_____   Time _____ M

Seller hereby [ ] **accepts** [ ] **counter offers** the offer set forth above on the terms and conditions specified herein, effective on the date and year last written below.

Seller hereby [ ] **rejects** the foregoing offer.

SELLER'S COUNTER OFFER, IF APPLICABLE, SHALL BE ACCEPTED BY DELIVERING A SIGNED COPY TO SELLER AT _____ **PRIOR TO** _____ **M ON** _____ , **19** _____.

YOUR SIGNATURE BINDS YOU TO ALL OF THE TERMS OF THIS CONTRACT. CONSULT AN ATTORNEY FOR ADVICE, EXPLANATION, MODIFICATIONS OR ADDITIONS. FILL IN ALL BLANKS BEFORE SIGNING.

| Seller _____ | Delivery Date _____ | Time _____ M |
| Seller _____ | Delivery Date _____ | Time _____ M |

Buyer accepts the seller's counter offer as set forth above on the terms and conditions specified herein, effective on the date and year written below.

| Buyer _____ | Delivery Date _____ | Time _____ M |
| Buyer _____ | Delivery Date _____ | Time _____ M |

[G8350]

Notes and Questions

1. Examining both the contract above and a contract commonly used in your jurisdiction, determine the rights of the parties to a residential real estate transaction if after the contract is signed but prior to the closing:

(a) The residence is destroyed by fire. (We return shortly to the issue of allocation of risk of loss if the contract is silent on this issue.)

(b) Extensive termite damage and active termite infestation are discovered.

(c) The roof of the residence leaks during a heavy rain storm, causing serious damage to the plaster and carpets in several rooms.

(d) The main drain leading from the house to the city sewer line is found to be seriously damaged by a tree in the front yard.

(e) An inspection reveals that the level of radon gas in the house is ten times acceptable levels.

(f) The financial markets suffer a shock and the purchaser finds that she can only secure financing by paying interest rates three per cent higher than the rates on which she had planned.

(g) A title examination discovers an unreleased 1903 mortgage and a possible outstanding dower interest in the wife of a previous owner who sold the property in 1948.

(h) A survey reveals easements for telephone, electric, gas, water, sewer, and cable TV lines. It also establishes that the residence is only nine feet, nine inches from the west lot line, in violation of ten–foot set back requirements established by the municipal zoning ordinance and by private covenants.

(i) The purchaser is transferred to a different part of the country by his employer.

2. The Statute of Frauds of 1677 provided:

And be it further enacted by the authority aforesaid that * * * no action shall be brought * * * (4) or upon any contract for sale of lands, tenements or heriditaments, or any interest in or concerning them; * * * (6) unless the agreement upon which such action shall be brought, or some memorandum or note thereof, shall be in writing and signed by the party to be charged therewith, or some other person thereunto by him lawfully authorized." Stat. 29 Car. II, ch. 3 § 17 (1677).

Every American jurisdiction similarly provides that contracts for the sale of land must be in writing, though the statutes vary somewhat as to whether unwritten agreements are void or just unenforceable, and as to how long the term of a lease may be before it must be in writing. Though there is considerable variation among jurisdictions as to what contract terms must be in writing for a contract to be enforceable, most require identification of the parties, a description of the premises to be conveyed, language indicating intention to sell or purchase, and a signature of the party against whom the contract is to be enforced. Many jurisdictions also require the price term to be in writing, though some courts will imply a reasonable price if no price term is included.

Despite the absolute language of the statute, many jurisdictions will enforce oral land-sale contracts under the exception of part performance. The extent of performance necessary to take a contract out of the Statute of Frauds varies considerably. In most jurisdictions, partial payment alone is not sufficient, but a combination of partial payment with taking of possession or making improvements might suffice. A few jurisdictions require all three elements to establish part performance; a few refuse to recognize any exception for partial performance. Some courts treat part performance as the evidentiary equivalent of a writing, others liken part performance to estoppel, grounding the exception in justifiable reliance. The exception causes considerable uncertainty and contributes to a great deal of litigation. See, on the Statute of Frauds and its exceptions, R. Cunningham, W. Stoebuck and D. Whitman, The Law of Property, §§ 10.1, 10.2 (1984); 3 American Law of Property, §§ 11.2–11.12 (J. Casner, ed., 1952); Braunstein, Remedy, Reason and the Statute of Frauds: A Critical Economic Analysis, 1989 Utah L.Rev. 383.

3. One of the most common conditions in contemporary residential real estate contracts is the "subject to financing" clause. This condition makes the purchaser's obligation to purchase the property subject to the purchaser being able to secure a financing commitment from a lending institution to finance that part of the purchase which the purchaser cannot afford to pay from his own funds. Subject to financing clauses can be drafted with great specificity—"subject to the purchaser obtaining a commitment for a thirty-year conventional fixed mortgage at a rate not exceeding 12% per annum and two points"—or with great generality— "subject to the purchaser obtaining satisfactory financing."

Obviously, subject to financing clauses, particularly vague and indefinite clauses, provide a great opportunity for the purchaser who has second thoughts about a purchase commitment to back out of a real estate transaction. Indeed a sufficiently vague subject to financing clause may raise questions as to whether a contract obligates the buyer at all, and if not, whether it is unenforceable for not creating mutual obligations. See Imas Gruner & Associates, Limited v. Stringer, 48 Md.App. 364, 427 A.2d 1038 (1981); Nodolf v. Nelson, 103 Wis.2d 656, 309 N.W.2d 397 (App.1981).

Courts commonly interpret subject to financing clauses as creating an obligation on the buyer to exercise good faith in pursuing financing. See, Brack v. Brownlee, 246 Ga. 818, 273 S.E.2d 390 (1980); Smith v. Vernon, 6 Ill.App.3d 434, 286 N.E.2d 99 (1972). If the buyer is unable to secure financing, despite good faith efforts, his performance is excused. If, however, the buyer fails to make good faith efforts, he can be held in breach of contract. Other conditions, such as that of the purchaser selling another home to raise the down payment, have similarly been held to impose an obligation of good faith effort.

4. A contract may or may not specify the time by which conditions specified in the contract must be met and the closing occur. If it fails to do so, compliance must occur within a reasonable time. If a date for compliance with conditions or for closing is specified in the contract, it may not be determinative. Delay, if it does not become unreasonable, may subject the party in breach to damages, but not excuse performance by the other party. The party whose performance was delayed may still sue the other party at equity for specific performance.

If, however, the contract uses the magic formula, "time is of the essence," performance must be tendered on the date specified in the contract. See Doctorman v. Schroeder, 92 N.J.Eq. 676, 114 A. 810 (1921) (performance 30 minutes late not acceptable). Even if the contract fails to contain this formula, however, time may be made essential by either party giving the other reasonable notice that strict compliance must be forthcoming by a set date. As is often the case where form triumphs over fairness, courts often attempt to mitigate the strict application of these doctrines, usually by finding waiver by the party demanding performance. R. Cunningham, W. Stoebuck, and D. Whitman, The Law of Property, § 10.10 (1984).

C. THE DEED

KNOW ALL MEN BY THESE PRESENTS

THAT _____, Grantors, of the City of _____, County of and State of _____, in consideration of the sum of _____

paid by _____ Grantees, of the City of _____, County of and State of _____, the receipt of which is hereby acknowledged, do hereby GRANT, BARGAIN, SELL AND CONVEY to the said Grantee, _____ their heirs and assigns forever, the following REAL ESTATE situated in the County of in the State of _____, and in the City of _____ described as follows:

TO HAVE AND TO HOLD said premises, with all the privileges and appurtenances thereunto belonging, to the said Grantees, their heirs and assigns forever. The said Grantors do for themselves and their heirs hereby covenant that they are lawfully seized of the premises; that the said premises are free and clear from all encumbrances, and that they will forever warrant and

defend and guarantee the quiet enjoyment of the same, against the lawful claims of all persons whomsoever.

IN WITNESS WHEREOF, the said Grantors, who hereby release their respective rights of dower in the premises, have set their hands this ___ day of _____ in the year of our Lord one thousand nine hundred and

Signed and acknowledged in the presence of

Acknowledgment

The State of _____, County of

BE IT REMEMBERED that on this the ___ day of _____, A.D. ___, personally appeared before me the above named, _____ Grantors in the foregoing Deed and acknowledged the signing of the same to be their voluntary act and deed,

IN TESTIMONY WHEREOF, I have hereunto sub- scribed my name and affixed my official seal on the day and year aforesaid. DEED

Notes and Questions

1. Conveyancing by deed replaced the earlier process of foeffment by livery of seisin. Livery of seisin, as you recall, was accomplished by the parties going to the parcel of land to be conveyed and there, in the sight of witnesses, handing over a clod or twig to symbolize the transfer of owner- ship. The ingenuity of conveyancers and the rise of the use made possible a variety of alternatives to transfer by livery of seisin, which was too public and inconvenient for many grantors. These alternatives included the bargain and sale deed, the lease and release, and the covenant to stand seized. They were supplemented as devices for transferring property by the fine and common recovery, which were used to defeat the fee tail, and the grant for non-freehold interests. The Statute of Uses of 1536 and the Statute of Frauds of 1677 effectively ended transfer of property by livery of seisin, and gave birth to the modern deed. Many deeds remain archeologi- cal artifacts, however, containing all the atavistic formulae effective at one time or another for transferring one interest or another in real property: i.e. "The grantor * * * does give, grant, bargain, sell, release, and convey unto the grantee * * *." Many states now have statutes establishing simple formulae which are effective to serve as deeds, and increasingly, these appear in deed forms, see Cal.Civ.Code § 1092, Ill. Ann. Stat. ch. 30, ¶ 8.

2. Under the Statute of Frauds, a deed must be in writing. The essential elements which must be written include the names of the grantor and grantee, a description of the property, and a statement of intention to convey. The deed must also be signed by the grantor. Historically, a seal

was also required for some forms of conveyancing, and a deed may still require a seal in a few states. Many states require that a deed be acknowledged before it can be recorded. A few require attestation by witnesses as an alternative to, or in addition to, acknowledgment.

Occasionally deeds are executed by a grantor with the grantee's name left blank. Traditionally, such deeds were considered void and of no effect. If the grantee's name is inserted subsequently, however, some courts uphold the validity of the transfer for equitable reasons. See Mehus v. Thompson, 266 N.W.2d 920 (N.D.1978); Kindred v. Crosby, 251 Iowa 198, 100 N.W.2d 20 (1959).

As a deed is not a contract, neither consideration nor recitation of consideration is necessary to its validity. Recitation of consideration may be significant, however, for purposes of determining whether a grantee is a bona fide purchaser for value, protected by a recording act. Some states also require that deeds specify the amount of consideration for which the property was transferred as a "condition for recordation" to facilitate determination of the transfer tax and for property tax assessment.

To effectively transfer property, a deed must adequately describe the property transferred. In the United States, several methods of property description are in use. In the Atlantic seaboard states, Kentucky, Tennessee and West Virginia, property is commonly described through the use of metes and bounds descriptions. Such descriptions commonly begin at a geographic point of beginning, then specify, or call, the direction and distance of each boundary line around the lot back to the beginning. Where possible, reference is made to natural or artificial monuments. An example is found in the *Providence Property* case that follows.

The old Northwest territories and most of the land added to the United States since the colonial period has been surveyed according to the Government Survey System designed by Thomas Jefferson and adopted by the Continental Congress in 1785. Pursuant to this system the nation has been divided into six-mile-square blocks known as Townships, which each in turn are subdivided into mile square Sections, all numbered according to the same formula. Sections can be further divided into halves, quarters, or smaller units for describing properties located within them. Each township in the country can be located with reference to Range lines, running north and south parallel to Principal Meridian lines, or to township lines running east and west parallel to Base lines. There are 36 sets of such Principal Meridian and Base lines within the Government Survey System. So for example, a property could be described under the government system as the S ½ of the SW ¼ of Section 25 of Township 3 North, Range 3 West, First Principal Meridian.

Finally, residential property in the United States is commonly described by reference to a subdivision plat. A plat is a recorded survey map of a subdivided property. A deed may describe a property by lot and block number in a particular subdivision, and then refer to the recorded plat of that subdivision, and, perhaps to the location of the subdivision under the Government Survey System. For example, a property could be described as "Lot 7, West River Terrace, part of Sections 3 and 10, Township 8 South,

Range 17 West, Bertrand Township, Berrein County, Michigan, according to the Plat thereof, recorded July 23, 1957, in Book 15 of Plats, page 40."

Because surveying was not an exact science at the time much of the United States was surveyed, and because of transcription errors as descriptions in deeds have been transcribed or copied over time, inconsistencies and conflicts in the deeds of neighboring lots, or within the description of a single lot, occur not infrequently, as is illustrated by the following case.

PROVIDENCE PROPERTIES, INC. v. UNITED VIRGINIA BANK/SEABOARD NATIONAL

Supreme Court of Virginia, 1979.
219 Va. 735, 251 S.E.2d 474.

COCHRAN, JUSTICE.

United Virginia Bank/Seaboard National, Trustee under the Will of William S. Reid, deceased, and Olivia M. Reid (the Reids), instituted an action in ejectment in the court below against Providence Properties, Inc. (Providence). We granted Providence a writ of error to the order of the trial court, acting through Judge Owen, awarding the Reids final judgment (Record No. 770599). * * *

The land in controversy, containing approximately 4½ acres, is a portion of a tract of 92.58 acres conveyed to Thomas R. Norris and Ralph T. Norris by deed of M.F. Forbes and Nannie P. Forbes, his wife, dated February 23, 1912. The land was situated near Lynnhaven, then in Princess Anne County, but now within the city of Virginia Beach, between the right-of-way of the Norfolk and Southern Railroad and the road extending from Mapleton to Lynnhaven. A plat of the tract made by C.F. Petrie, C.E., showing metes and bounds and the names of adjoining landowners, was attached to the deed. The plat showed that the property of one of the adjoining landowners, Harper, fronted on the Mapleton to Lynnhaven road.

Prior to 1926, the Norrises made from the larger tract the following conveyances, listed in the order in which they were recorded:

1. Deed dated March 21, 1912 to M.F. Forbes

20 acres described by metes and bounds, and an easement over a 19–foot–wide roadway.

2. Deed dated March 21, 1912 to M.F. Forbes

an easement of right-of-way over a 32–foot–wide parcel leading from lands of Forbes to the Norfolk and Southern right-of-way, the easement to be located by the Norrises.

3. Deed dated November 20, 1913 to Thomas N. Kelly

10 acres, extending thirty rods (495 feet) along a line parallel to and 16 feet from the Norfolk and Southern right-of-way, extending back between parallel lines "a sufficient distance" to make the parcel, with a rear line parallel to the front line, contain 10 acres. The Norrises

reserved for road purposes the strip 16 feet wide lying between the parcel conveyed and the Norfolk and Southern right-of-way.

4. Deed dated March 9, 1915 to H.C. Hill

10 acres described by metes and bounds and by plat, showing the lot fronting 439 feet on 15–foot road adjacent to Norfolk and Southern right-of-way, with a western line extending along a 12–foot roadway.

5. Deed dated April 2, 1917, to J.L. Burgess

16.35 acres described by metes and bounds and by plat, showing the parcel extending 770.5 feet along the eastern line of a roadway.

6. Deed dated March 9, 1915 to D.B. Waterfield

10 acres described by metes and bounds and by plat showing this parcel separated from the parcel described in (4) by a 12–foot roadway.

7. Deed dated August 31, 1920 to Frederick C. Fockelman

4¼ acres, more or less, described by metes and bounds.

8. Deed dated February 24, 1913 to J.T. Harper

10 acres, beginning 20 feet east of J.T. Harper's property on the Mapleton to Lynnhaven road, extending back between parallel lines 692 feet 5 inches to a ditch, with front and rear lines parallel and of sufficient length to embrace 10 acres. The Norrises reserved title to the strip of land 20 feet wide extending northwardly from the Mapleton to Lynnhaven road between this parcel and the other land of Harper.

9. Deed dated March 11, 1921 to H.C. Hill

3½ acres described by metes and bounds, extending 360 feet along a private road, with a southern line of 385 feet extending to land of Those. N. Kelly.

10. Deed dated August 31, 1920 to Frederick C. Fockelman

corrects (7) and conveys the same 4¼ acres described in the earlier deed.

By the foregoing deeds the Norrises conveyed a total of approximately 84.10 acres from the parcel of 92.58 acres. In the same deeds, they reserved title to several roadways, including a roadway 15 feet wide in part and 16 feet wide in part extending a distance of approximately 1,080 feet along the Norfolk and Southern right-of-way; a roadway 32 feet wide extending approximately 715 feet along the western line of the tract; a roadway 12 feet wide extending a distance of approximately 746 feet between the two 10–acre parcels conveyed to Hill (4) and Waterfield (6), respectively; and a 20–foot-wide strip extending from the Mapleton to Lynnhaven Road approximately 692.4 feet along the western line of the 10–acre parcel conveyed to Harper (8).

Moreover, the deeds to J.L. Burgess (5) and H.C. Hill (9) indicate that the 12–foot private road originally extending between the Hill (4) and Waterfield (6) 10–acre parcels continued along the Hill and Burgess lines to connect with the private road leading to the Mapleton to Lynnhaven Road. Thus, after accounting for the lands aggregating approximately 84.10 acres conveyed to various grantees and for the property retained by the Norrises, presumably for highway purposes, containing one to one and one-half acres, the Norrises still retained a parcel of land from the original tract containing 6½ to 7 acres. Of course, these figures are based upon the assumption that the descriptions in the deeds were accurately followed. However, the plat dated November 29, 1977, made by Miller–Fox, Civil Engineers, and introduced into evidence by stipulation to locate the parcels conveyed by the Norrises from the 92.58–acre tract, shows that the deed descriptions were not always followed. For example, the parcel conveyed to Kelly, as shown on the 1977 plat, does not have a rear line parallel to the Norfolk and Southern, and contains approximately 12 acres rather than the 10 acres called for in the deed. On the other hand, the parcel conveyed to H.C. Hill in 1915 as 10 acres with a northern line of 439 feet parallel to the Norfolk and Southern, actually has a northern line, as shown on the 1977 plat, of only 384 feet. It is apparent, therefore, that there are many discrepancies between the deed descriptions and the parcels as platted in 1977. These discrepancies were not explained by engineers or surveyors. Since the deed descriptions were not accurately followed, it appears that the Norrises actually held title to a parcel of land approximately 9½ acres after the conveyances listed above had been consummated.

By deed dated December 21, 1926, the Norrises conveyed to D.B. Waterfield the following parcel:

"ALL THAT TRACT, PIECE OR PARCEL OF LAND situate in the Town of Lynnhaven, County of Princess Anne and State of Virginia, being 4 & ⅞ acres of land more or less adjoining land formerly deeded by the parties of the first part to the party of the second part, and bounded as follows: Beginning at the North East corner of said land running South 650 ft. along a 12 ft. right of way to lands owned by J.T. Harper thence West 270 ft. along the land of J.T. Harper to land formerly owned by M.F. Forbes, thence North 654 ft. along land formerly owned by M.F. Forbes, thence East along land owned by the party of the second part 388 ft. to the place of beginning. Containing 4 & seven eights acres of land more or less being part of the lands deeded to the parties of the first part by M.F. Forbes and wife, on the 23rd day of February, 1912."

Subsequently, the Waterfield parcels were acquired by William S. Reid and Olivia M. Reid, his wife. William S. Reid died testate, leaving his Will under which United Virginia Bank/Seaboard National qualified as Trustee.

A rough diagram is appended hereto for the purpose of showing the various parcels of land relevant to this controversy. It is to be noted that if the measurements of the lines in the metes and bounds description in the 1926 deed from the Norrises to Waterfield are used, only 4⅞ acres of the 9½ acres retained by the Norrises were conveyed, and title to a parcel of approximately 4½ acres remained in the Norrises. However, if the land conveyed is defined by the adjacent boundaries mentioned in the deed, the entire 9½–acre tract passed to Waterfield. Thus it is the area of 4½ acres lying between the land of J.T. Harper and the 4⅞ acres admittedly conveyed to Waterfield which is in dispute.

There were no conveyances by the Norrises, or their heirs, devisees, or successors in title, between 1926 and 1974. According to stipulation, Thomas R. Norris, widower, died intestate in 1929 in the State of New York, leaving as his sole heir at law, his son, Ralph T. Norris. Ralph T. Norris died in 1938 in Yates County, New York, leaving his Will under which he provided for a life estate in his realty for his wife, who died in 1951, with the remainder to his daughter, Sarah Norris Becker. According to probate records in New York State, Ralph T. Norris owned no property outside that state at the time of his death. In 1974, an attorney, Frank E. Butler, III, obtained special warranty deeds from Sarah Norris Becker and her husband, conveying to Butler the parcel in controversy containing approximately 4½ acres. By general warranty deed dated September 28, 1974, Butler and his wife conveyed the parcel to Providence, which conveyed this land and other tracts by deed of trust to John Thomas and William H. White, Jr., Trustees, to secure certain indebtedness payable to Virginia National Bank. Thereafter, the Reids filed their motion for judgment in ejectment against Providence.

* * *

Providence relied upon the metes and bounds and acreage descriptions set forth in the 1926 deed to Waterfield, and repeated in the deed from Waterfield's widow and heirs at law to William S. Reid and Olivia M. Reid, as tenants by the entireties, with right of survivorship, and in the deed from William S. Reid and Olivia M. Reid to themselves as tenants in common, and upon the testimony of Frances Pritchard and Frank E. Butler, III, heard *ore tenus* by the trial court.

* * *

Butler testified that he sought out Sarah Norris Becker and arranged to purchase the parcel in controversy from her and her husband. Testifying as an expert title examiner, Butler said that since the description in the 1926 deed to Waterfield did not call for a line extending to a point on the line of J.T. Harper's line, he concluded that the call "to lands owned by J.T. Harper" merely "gave an indication of the direction" of the line. Based upon the metes and bounds description, the specified acreage, his interpretation of the call to Harper's land, and the fact that the 1926 deed did not recite that the parcel comprised the remaining lands of the Norrises, he concluded that the deed did not convey the disputed property to Waterfield. Butler testified that prior to his purchase, the property in dispute was assessed in the name of "unknown owner". After his purchase, Butler had the land assessed for three years in the name of Sarah Norris Becker, and paid these taxes.

The trial court rejected Butler's rationalization of the call to Harper's lands, noting that the next call in the deed description was "thence west 270 ft. along the land of J.T. Harper". We agree with the trial court's reasoning in this respect. Moreover, in view of the reservations by the Norrises of acreage included in roadways, the 1926 deed could not have stated correctly that it was a conveyance of all remaining Norris lands embraced in the original tract of 92.58 acres. Except for these reservations, of course, the trial court correctly stated that just prior to the 1926 conveyance the Norrises had conveyed all of the 92.58–acre tract other than the parcel bounded by other lands of Waterfield, a 12–foot right-of-way, lands of J.T. Harper, and lands of M.F. Forbes.

The general principles applicable in actions for ejectment are well settled. The plaintiff has the burden of proving that he has good title and the right to possession, and he must recover upon the strength of his own title rather than upon the weakness of the defendant's title.
[   ]

The 1926 deed to Waterfield contains inconsistent descriptions. The distance between the 10–acre parcel of Waterfield and the lands of J.T. Harper is far greater than the side line measurements specified in the deed, and the acreage of the parcel lying between the Waterfield 10–acre parcel and the Harper lands is more than 9 acres rather than 4⅞ acres, more or less, as stated in the deed. Virginia National contends that it is inconceivable that the Norrises intended to convey a parcel almost double the area specified in the deed. We disagree.

In construing a deed, the intention of the grantor must be ascertained from the entire instrument. [   ] We have held that where a deed contains two descriptions of land equally explicit, but repugnant to each other, we will adopt that description which best expresses the intention of the parties. * * *

We consider quantity to be the least reliable method of describing land. [   ] Therefore, a description by acreage is inferior to all other deed descriptions.

We have also approved the principle of construction that where there is conflict, descriptions by distances give way to calls for known boundaries. [   ] In Fentress v. Pocahontas Club, 108 Va. 155, 159, 60 S.E. 633, 634 (1908), we affirmed the universal rule that a description by course and distance must yield to a description by natural or permanent objects called for as a boundary. And in Stacy v. Ritter Lumber Co., 114 Va. 133, 75 S.E. 1038 (1912), we held that a call to an adjoining property would prevail over a call for course and distance based upon a survey by a surveyor who did not go upon the land. Moreover, in Richmond Cedar Works v. West, 152 Va. 533, 540, 147 S.E. 196, 198 (1929), we stated that calls for adjoining tracts of land are monuments and where they are certain are monuments of the highest dignity. See also Clarkston v. Virginia Coal & Iron Co., 93 Va. 258, 24 S.E. 937 (1896).

From the foregoing cases has evolved the following order of preference rule applicable, in the absence of contrary intent, where deed descriptions are inconsistent:

(1) natural monuments or landmarks;

(2) artificial monuments and established lines, marked or surveyed;

(3) adjacent boundaries or lines of adjoining tracts;

(4) calls for courses and distances;

(5) designation of quantity.

We reaffirm our approval of this rule. See 2 Minor, Real Property, § 1076, at 1419, n. 3 (2d ed. Ribble 1928). The rule, however, is not inflexible and will not be applied if to do so would frustrate the intent of the parties to the deed. Indeed, the rule is designed to effectuate the presumed intent of the parties.

Providence attaches great significance to the correlation between the acreage of $4\frac{7}{8}$ acres specified in the deed and the distances set forth in the metes and bounds description. Providence argues that under its construction of the deed the southern boundary line of the parcel conveyed by the 1926 deed would be approximately 270 feet in length, the exact distance specified in the deed, whereas if the entire $9\frac{1}{2}$ acres passed to Waterfield the southern boundary line would be only 255 feet in length. This discrepancy, if it exists, and we cannot verify it from the record, loses its significance, however, in light of the fact that the northern boundary line of the same parcel is shown as 400 feet on the Miller–Fox plat, although the 1926 deed calls for this line to be 388 feet in length. We believe that this discrepancy probably occurred through error on the part of the Norrises in deducting the width of the 12–foot right-of-way from the 400–foot line.

We believe that any discrepancy in the length of the southern boundary line which would exist if the Reids' interpretation of the deed is accepted, most likely results from a similar error. This is particularly true in light of the fact that the 12–foot roadway, now known as Pritchard Lane, was widened to 30 feet sometime prior to 1974. In any event, there are further discrepancies between the northern and southern lines of the $4\frac{1}{2}$–acre parcel as shown on the 1974 plat attached to the deed to Butler and as shown on the 1977 Miller–Fox plat. Indeed, the numerous discrepancies in courses and distances in the various deeds and plats in the record reveal the unreliability of this method of describing property and compel us to conclude that the order of preference rule must be applied in this case.

The 1912 plat of the 92.58–acre tract conveyed to the Norrises showed that Harper owned an adjoining parcel. Harper still owned this parcel in 1926 when the Norrises conveyed to Waterfield. The adjoining Waterfield 10–acre parcel had been shown on a plat attached to the deed to that land, the adjoining M.F. Forbes parcel had been shown on a plat attached to the deed to that land, and the 12–foot right-of-way had been referred to in several deeds. It is a reasonable inference, therefore, that the Norrises knew the location of the boundary on the south as well as the lands adjoining the parcel on the north, east and west.

* * *

The intent of the parties to the 1926 deed is determinative. In the absence of evidence to the contrary, the order of preference rule establishes what is presumed to have been the intent. After a careful review of the record before us, we hold that the trial court was justified in applying the order of preference rule and in finding that the intent of the Norrises and of Waterfield in 1926 was to consummate the conveyance to Waterfield of the parcel bounded on the north by the 10–acre Waterfield parcel, on the east by the 12–foot right-of-way, on the south by land of J.T. Harper, and the west by land of M.F. Forbes, regardless of dimensions and area. Consequently, we find no reversible error in the order of the trial court awarding judgment in ejectment to the Reids.

* * *

Affirmed

APPENDIX

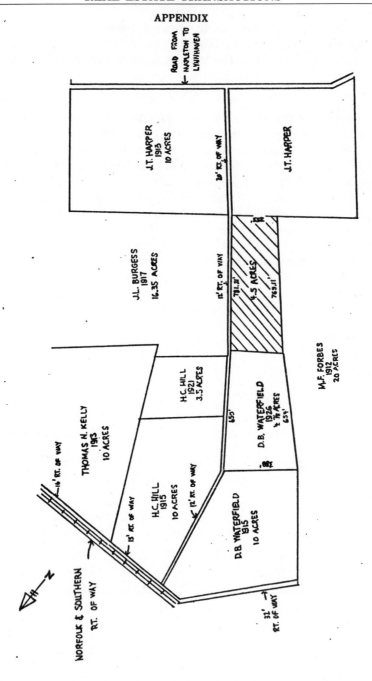

Notes and Questions

1. The principle on which the court relies for construction is supplemented by others, such as: "the construction prevails which is most favorable to the grantee"; "if the deed contains two descriptions, one ambiguous and the other unambiguous, the latter prevails in order to sustain the deed" or "when a tract of land is bound by a monument which has width, such as a highway or stream, the boundary line extends to the center * * *." See J. Cribbet & C. Johnson, Principles of the Law of Property, 210–212 (3rd ed. 1989) listing and commenting on these and other principles.

2. What was Butler up to in this case? Is this an appropriate activity for a lawyer?

3. According to the old chestnut, a deed is effective when "signed, sealed, and delivered." Though the seal has fallen into desuetude, execution and delivery are still key to the passage of property by deed, with delivery being the final act necessary before the deed becomes effective. Delivery is often straightforward; after signing the deed, the grantor hands it to the grantee. Increasingly, however, deeds are handled through commercial escrows supervised by financial institutions or title companies, where the deed may be delivered to the grantee sometime after the grantor executes it. In commercial escrows, an escrow agent is appointed with instructions from both the grantor (vendor) and grantee (purchaser). The escrow agent receives the deed from the vendor and the purchase money from the purchaser and lender. The agent determines the various charges and credits due each party, and ultimately records the deed and security interests and makes disbursements. Because escrow closings do not require the presence of the purchaser and vendor, the ceremony that attended traditional delivery of the deed is absent from them.

Delayed delivery of a deed is also used by grantors from time to time as an estate planning device. Whenever delivery is delayed problems can arise, as is evidenced in the following case.

PIPES v. SEVIER

Missouri Court of Appeals, 1985.
694 S.W.2d 918.

SHANGLER, JUDGE.

This action, an intra-family squabble over the title to certain parcels of land under successive—and incompatible—conveyances from the mother to several family members, commenced as a petition for declaratory judgment, and was adjudicated on a petition [the fourth amendment] to remove a cloud from the title. The dispute ranged the two children of Leone Pipes—Keith and Beverly—against the other, while the mother aligned first with the cause of Keith, and then after his death, with the cause of Beverly.

The action was tried to the court, and the court adjudged that the fee simple title to the subject parcel [the Home Place] was vested in Violet Pipes and children Jerry, Gary, Walter and Kathy—all as heirs at law of grantee Keith Pipes, then deceased, subject only to the life estate reserved in the grantor, Leone Pipes.

The appellants, Beverly Sevier and son Roddy and mother Leone Pipes, contend that the evidence does not support the judgment, and other errors.

The evidence was that Ralph and Leone Pipes, parents of Keith and Beverly, owned three tracts of land in Sullivan County: the Cott Farm, the Sheppy Farm and the Home Place. The parents purchased the Home Place in 1948. That acquisition [a tract of some 297 acres] was induced by the agreement of son Keith to remain with the father in the farm operation. The son Keith faithfully worked with the father from that time until year 1967, when the elder Pipes died, and thereafter continued to operate or work all three farms on a crop-share basis with mother Leone Pipes, until Keith died in 1982.

In about the year 1960, Ralph Pipes had a will prepared by attorney Leman Atherton whereby the Home Place was devised to son Keith and the Cott Farm and the Sheppy Farm to daughter Beverly, in the event wife Leone predeceased the children. The widow of son Keith, Violet Pipes, testified that it was understood within the family that the ultimate division of the farms intended by the parents was as provided in the Ralph Pipes will. Accordingly, in order to give effect to that shared intention, in November of 1972, Leone Pipes directed attorney Atherton to prepare two sets of deeds—a conveyance of the Home Place to son Keith and conveyances of the Cott Farm and the Sheppy Farm to daughter Beverly. She instructed attorney Atherton to keep them, and to deliver them only upon her death. The attorney advised her that upon delivery of the deeds to him for that purpose, "nobody could get them, not even herself." Leone Pipes understood and responded that was exactly what she wanted, "what she and [deceased husband] Ralph wanted." The attorney thereupon prepared the deeds as directed, Leone Pipes executed them, the attorney acknowledged them and affixed the notary seal, and then placed them in envelopes. There was a legend on the outside of each wrapper, respectively:

"This envelope is to be delivered to my daughter Beverly J. Sevier on my death.

/s/Leone Pipes"

and

"This envelope is to be delivered to my son Keith Pipes on my death.

/s/Leone Pipes"

These containers, sealed, were kept by attorney Atherton until they were produced as exhibits in the litigation we review.

The daughter, Beverly, accompanied the mother to the office of attorney Atherton on that occasion, but was excluded from their company at the direction of the attorney. She left at the request of Atherton. That was the version of the events given by the attorney. The narrative of daughter Beverly was different. She testified that she was present during the discussions between her mother and the attorney. The mother wanted the deeds "so that she could sell it at any time." Attorney Atherton advised, Beverly testified, that the deeds could be recalled at any time, whenever the mother decided that "[she] wanted to do anything different." That was the sense, also, of the testimony of the conveyancer, mother Leone Pipes—then, from her own choice, a party defendant to the suit. The mother freely acknowledged that she directed the deeds and signed them, but only on the assurance that "I could get them when I wanted them." The mother testified also that, although it was her signature that appeared upon the face of each envelope, there was no "printing on it" when she signed each one. That testimony, however, was contradicted by her written statement made to [then] attorney Kenneth Lewis [now circuit judge] who was counsel for Keith Pipes, and given at a time before mother Pipes aligned formally with any party to the suit. That statement recited that she directed attorney Atherton to make the three deeds, two to daughter Beverly and the Home Place to son Keith, that she signed the instruments, delivered the deeds to Atherton with the direction that they were to be recorded upon her death, and that she understood the counsel of attorney Atherton "that the delivery of the deeds to him was final and that I could not thereafter cancel the deeds or change my mind. I knew that the delivery of the deeds to Mr. Atherton was unconditional."

In March of 1981, almost ten years after mother Leone executed the deeds, Beverly accompanied her mother to the office of attorney Atherton to retrieve the deeds, but he refused to deliver them up. The mother then made two visits to another attorney, Merrill Montgomery—first in the company of son Keith and wife Violet, and then in the company of daughter Beverly. [The relations between the brother and sister were strained.] On that first visit, Leone informed attorney Montgomery concerning the deeds executed by her and given over to attorney Atherton, and of his refusal to give them back. Montgomery advised that those deeds were of no effect because unrecorded. The mother, Leone, on that first visit informed Montgomery that she wanted son Keith to have a lifetime share in the Home Place but that neither Violet nor her children were "to have any of it." The deeds to the other lands were to be "fixed" to Beverly and herself. Keith and Violet became displeased, and they left. Leone returned with Beverly the next day, and the deeds were fixed as the mother had directed. To begin with, Montgomery presented to the mother a deed which conveyed the Home Place to son Keith and mother Leone as joint tenants, but she refused it. The attorney then prepared two other deeds at the direction of Leone Pipes. One conveyed a life estate in the Home Place to Keith, and reserved a life estate to Leone, herself. The other conveyed one of the two other properties to daughter Beverly and to Leone, herself, as joint tenants. They were recorded. In April of 1981, Leone fell ill and was interned in the hospital. While there, she executed another deed which purported once again to convey the Home Place—this time to daughter Beverly in fee "subject to any interest that Keith Pipes has, if any." That deed was also duly recorded. Then, in August of 1981, Beverly conveyed the Home Place—now titled of record in her sole name—to Beverly J. Sevier and Roddy Sevier [her son] as joint tenants. That deed was also promptly recorded.

On September 1, 1981, Keith brought a petition against Beverly Sevier and Roddy Sevier for a declaratory judgment that all the conveyances of the lands, other than the deeds executed by Leone Pipes and delivered to attorney Atherton for recordation upon her death, are null and void. The mother, Leone Pipes, joined the suit as a party plaintiff, by amendment. The plaintiffs were represented by attorney Atherton. When it became evident that his witness would be necessary, attorney Atherton withdrew from the case, and [then] attorney Kenneth Lewis entered appearance and filed a second amended petition for declaratory judgment. In November of 1982, attorney Lewis assumed duty as circuit judge, and attorney Gordon Cox, a partner, assumed the representation. The plaintiff Keith Pipes died on November 9, 1982, and his widow, Violet Pipes and their four children, Jerry, Gary, Kathy and Walter, were substituted as plaintiffs in lieu. The mother, Leone Pipes, in turn, moved to be deleted as a party plaintiff and to be added as a party defendant, and for leave to file a counterclaim. The petition was amended into a petition to remove a cloud from the title and for the cancellation of deeds. The defendants [Beverly and Roddy] counterclaimed to quiet title and for trespass. The counterclaim of [now] defendant Leone Pipes to remove a cloud from the title was not thereafter repleaded.

The judgment adjudicated that the title to the Home Place was vested in fee simple absolute in Violet Pipes, widow of the deceased Keith Pipes, and in their children, Jerry, Gary, Walter and Kathy, subject to the life estate reserved by the grantor, Leone Pipes. The judgment rested on findings of fact that the deeds drafted by attorney Atherton were drawn upon the instructions of mother Leone Pipes, executed by her, then deposited in the envelopes with the written instructions for delivery to Keith and Beverly upon her death subscribed by the signature of the grantor mother, and then only after full explanation by attorney Atherton that the delivery of the enveloped deeds to him for that purpose—made without a reserved right of recall—was a final and irrevocable act. The court found as a fact, also, that the deed was accepted by the grantee, Keith Pipes, during his lifetime, and that he thereafter died intestate and was survived by the wife and four children. The judgment also adjudicated the counterclaims against the defendants. The demand for a jury trial was properly refused.

* * *

THE ATTORNEY-CLIENT PRIVILEGE

The defendants contend that at the times described in the testimony of attorney Atherton and [then] attorney Lewis, the attorney-client relationship subsisted between Leone Pipes and each of the named attorneys, hence the communications between them on subject matter encompassed by the professional relationship were privileged and could not be disclosed without the consent of the client. Atherton, as our discussion discloses, prepared the three deeds in November of 1972 to the three tracts then owned by Leone Pipes: the Home Place to son Keith, and the Cott Farm and the Sheppy Farm to daughter Beverly. Atherton testified in detail as to the circumstances of the preparation, execution and delivery of the instruments to his care with directions from the grantor mother Leone. * * * Atherton testified, most tellingly, that he informed Leone Pipes if he carried out her instructions as to the transactions "there was no way she or anyone else could get them [the deeds]." The defendants contend that these communications were incidents of the attorney-client relationship, and therefore were privileged and incompetent as evidence, over objection. The defendants did lodge objection at the trial, but that objection was ineffectual and properly refused for the simple reason that Leone Pipes had executed a formal waiver of her privilege—a waiver obtained from the witness by [then] attorney Lewis, counsel for Keith and Violet Pipes. That waiver [received as Exhibit 19] was executed by Leone Pipes on July 19, 1982, and recites:

> "I, Leone Pipes, hereby waive the attorney-client privilege regarding confidential communications with L.E. Atherton and hereby authorize him to testify in any legal action pertaining to any land which I now own or formerly owned.

> /s/Leone Pipes"—

The attorney-client privilege dates from the common law. Section 491.060, RSMo 1978 enacts that developed principle:

> "The following persons shall be incompetent to testify:

> * * *

> (3) An attorney, concerning any communication made to him by his client in that relation, or his advice thereon, without the consent of such client."

* * * There is no doubt that the communications between Leone Pipes and attorney Atherton were at the time the attorney-client relation subsisted between them, and that his advice on them was given in that capacity and on that account. That is to say, that the communications were privileged. Nor is there doubt that the privilege that they remain confidential, owned by the client, was waived by the client. Thus, the testimony of attorney Atherton was properly received.

The defendants assert that the testimony of [then] attorney Lewis was incompetent, and for the same reason. The original suit for declaratory judgment and for cancellation of the post-Atherton deeds was filed on September 11, 1981 by attorney Atherton on behalf of Keith Pipes as plaintiff and against Beverly Sevier and son Roddy as defendants. It became evident that the testimony of attorney Atherton was necessary to prove the cause of action, so he withdrew as counsel and referred the suit to [then] attorney Lewis. On June 15, 1982, Keith Pipes and wife Violet engaged the Lewis firm: Cleaveland, Macoubrie, Lewis and Cox as counsel to prosecute the petition. The contract of employment specified payment at a designated rate per hour, and required an advance of $2000. The Pipes husband and wife executed the contract at the home, and the mother Leone was then present. The retainer for $2000 was paid by a check signed by Leone Pipes. On that occasion, Lewis interrogated all three—Leone, Keith and Violet—in the presence of each other concerning the transactions involved, particularly the three Atherton deeds. On that June 15, 1982 occasion, attorney Lewis took from Leone Pipes a written statement subscribed by her signature concerning the Atherton deeds transactions—received at the trial as Exhibit 20. * * *

Attorney Lewis returned to the Pipes residence on July 19, 1982, to prepare Leone Pipes for her deposition on the next day. * * * Attorney Lewis testified at the trial that during the course of the deposition testimony, witness Leone Pipes was asked several times, and answered without variance, that Atherton advised her that "a delivery to him was final, absolute, unconditional and irrevocable and that she could not get the deed back." * * *

The defendants contend that the statements contained in Exhibit 20, as well as the testimony narrated by attorney Lewis at the trial concerning the communications from Leone Pipes were disclosures of confidential communications between attorney and client, and hence incompetent as evidence upon objection of the client.

The contention that the attorney-client relation subsisted between Lewis and Leone from June 15, 1982, rests altogether on the circumstance that the $2000 retainer was paid by a check signed by Leone and drawn upon her account. * * * The contract of employment in evidence, executed on June 15, 1982, was between attorney Lewis and Keith and Violet Pipes exclusively. The mother, Leone, was not a party. Attorney Lewis considered the retainer check, albeit drawn by Leone, as payment from the clients, Keith and Violet. The trial court expressly accepted that evidence as true. To be sure, Leone Pipes later [in October of 1982] joined son Keith as a party plaintiff on the petition against Beverly and son Roddy to cancel the latter deeds, but the attorney-client relationship did not arise until some time after July 20, 1982 [when the deposition of Leone was taken] and before October of 1982 [when Leone was formally joined as a plaintiff]. The trial court expressly found that the attorney-client relationship between attorney Lewis and Leone Pipes did not come into being until after July 20, 1982, so that the evidence given by Lewis at the trial concerning the

Leone Pipes communications to him as to the Atherton transactions was competent.

To exclude the testimony of an attorney on the ground of privilege, the relation of attorney and client must have actually subsisted between the principals at the time the communication was made or the advice given. [　] The communication, moreover, must have been made to the attorney on account of the relation of attorney and client. * * * Nor does the circumstance that the declarant herself later becomes a client cloak communications between them before the onset of that relation with confidentiality and privilege from disclosure. [　] The determination by the trial court that Leone was not a client of attorney Lewis until after the deposition event is valid, and we sustain it.

THE DELIVERY OF THE ATHERTON DEEDS

The defendants contend that the evidence does not sustain a valid delivery of the Home Place deed to Atherton. They argue the evidence given by Leone Pipes [by then, no longer a plaintiff, but a defendant aligned with daughter Beverly] that she gave the deed [and the two others] over to attorney Atherton for "safekeeping," and not as an irrevocable conveyance. The defendants argue that her attempt to retrieve them ten years later and the execution of the successor deeds when Atherton refused to yield them up prove that the placement into his escrow was without intention to pass title—that is, make delivery. They argue, moreover, that the legend on the envelope: "This envelope is to be delivered to my son, Keith Pipes, on my death" not only does not evince an intention for delivery, but expressly contradicts any such purpose.

The intention of the principals, particularly that of the grantor, determines whether a delivery of a deed has been accomplished. The essential inquiry, therefore, is whether the grantor intended a complete transfer: that is, whether the grantor parted with the instrument with the intention to relinquish all dominion and control over it so as to make the deed a presently effective and operative conveyance of title to the land. [　] It is not essential to delivery that the deed be manually given over to the grantee or to another person for the grantee; there may be delivery notwithstanding that the deed remains in the custody of the grantor. [　] A delivery to a third party, to be held by that party for delivery to the grantee upon the death of the grantor operates as a valid delivery when there is no reservation in the deed nor any right of control over the instrument retained by the grantor. In such case, the deed in the hands of the custodian has the same effect "as if it had been manually delivered by the grantor to the grantee." [　] A deed unconditional in terms and placed beyond control of the grantor upon its delivery to the third party escrow holder, moreover, although not a conferral of an immediate right to present possession, constitutes "such an investiture of title as to give the grantee a present fixed right of future enjoyment although the use of the premises [is] retained by the grantor during [her] life * * * The time of acceptance will not affect the validity of the transfer * * * Acceptance after the death of the grantor dates back to the time of the delivery of the deed to the * * * [escrow holder] and renders it a transfer as of that date." [ ] On this principle, upon final delivery by the depositary of the deed given in escrow, "the instrument will be treated as relating back to, and taking effect at the time of the original deposit *in escrow * * * [and this] appl[ies] even though one of the parties to the deed dies before the second delivery.* [ ] On this principle, the death of the grantee Keith Pipes which intervened before the second delivery from depositary Atherton is of no legal consequence—the validity of the delivery by Leone to Atherton in the first instance, assumed.

The defendants argue that Leone did not intend a delivery, but only to vouchsafe the keeping of the executed deeds. The evidence on the essential issue of delivery was in conflict—and in the case of Leone, herself, in utter contradiction. The court found her trial testimony not credible, and gave it no belief. * * * The court found as fact that Leone executed the deed to the Home Place in favor of son Keith and delivered the instrument in escrow with attorney Atherton with instruction to deliver to Keith upon her death only after full advice from him that such an act of delivery, when made without a reserved right of recall, was irrevocable and final. The court also found the testimony of attorney Atherton disinterested and credible, believed his testimony of the deed transactions with Leone Pipes, and rendered judgment accordingly. We concur in the thoughtful and meticulously-wrought judgment of the trial court: that the deed executed by Leone Pipes and delivered to attorney Atherton as escrow holder placed fee simple title to the Home Place in Keith Pipes, subject only to a reserved life estate in the grantor, Leone Pipes; that on the death of Keith Pipes, that interest passed to his wife and children as his sole heirs at law, and that the counterclaims of the defendants be disallowed with prejudice.

The judgment is affirmed.

Notes and Questions

1. What advantages and disadvantages of having an attorney serve as an escrow agent are illustrated by the *Pipes* case? Although the court held the testimony of Atherton and Lewis to be unprivileged, was it ethical for them to testify against a client? Would it have been ethical for them to have failed to testify? Do A.B.A. Rules 1.6 and 3.7 help? See also A.B.A. Model Code of Professional Responsibility, Disciplinary Rules 4–101, 5–102.

2. The *Pipes* case recites the traditional law with respect to "death escrows": that unconditional delivery to the escrow agent with instructions to deliver to the grantee on the death of the grantor effectively creates a vested remainder in the grantee, subject to a life estate in the grantor. Grantors occasionally attempt to achieve the same result through other forms of conditional delivery. The key issue in litigation resulting from these transfers is (or should be) the grantor's intent, as delivery is primarily a question of intent.

First, a grantor may deliver to a grantee a deed which conveys an interest to commence on the death of the grantor. The grantor's intent in such transactions is to transfer a future interest, and this intent is uniformly enforced. A grantor may also deliver to a grantee a deed absolute on its face, but accompanied by an oral condition that the deed will only take effect upon the occurrence of a certain contingency. If the contingency is the grantor's death, many cases hold the deed void as an improper testamentary transfer. If the contingency is other than death, some courts hold the deed valid and the condition void, others the deed void (because the grantor lacked intent presently to deliver the deed), and still others hold both the condition and the deed valid. A few cases have also upheld deeds expressly on their face conditional on the death of the grantor, and also reserving in the grantor the power to dispose of the property in fee and revoke the future interest, though such deeds seem clearly testamentary in nature. Whenever a deed is delivered conditionally and not recorded, of course, the opportunity exists for the grantor to subsequently transfer the property unconditionally to a bona fide purchaser for value, whose rights may be superior to those of the conditional grantee under the jurisdiction's recording acts. For a fuller discussion of conditional delivery, see R. Boyer, H. Hovenkamp, & S. Kurtz, Survey of the Law of Real Property, § 16.4 (4th ed. 1991); R. Cunningham, W. Stoebuck and D. Whitman, The Law of Property, § 11.3 (1984); 6A R. Powell & P. Rohan, Powell on Real Property, ¶ 898[2][a].

3. Under a commercial escrow, the vendor/grantor delivers a signed deed to the escrow agent (an escrow company, financial institution, title insurer, abstract company or lawyer) to be released to the purchaser/grantee upon the grantee's compliance with the terms of the sales contract, including, most importantly, payment for the property. If the grantor delivers the deed to the escrow agent pursuant to an enforceable contract of sale, retaining no right to recover the deed if the purchaser complies with the terms of the sales contract, the ultimate delivery from the escrow agent to purchaser is considered to relate back and to be effective as of the date the grantor delivered the deed to the escrow agent. Thus, if the grantor dies or becomes incapacitated in the interim period, an effective transfer can still be accomplished. If the escrow agent improperly releases the deed to the grantee prior to the fulfillment of the conditions of the contract, the deed is void and unenforceable against the grantor by the grantee, and, in most jurisdictions, also by subsequent purchasers from the grantee.

III. TITLE SECURITY

A person purchasing an interest in real property normally demands and expects to receive the most secure and unrestricted title to that interest that our legal system allows. Productive use of property requires that one who invests in purchasing or improving property be able to do so with assurance that he or she will be able to claim and enjoy the fruits of the investment and not lose it to one with a superior claim to the property. A purchaser of a fee estate in residential property should realistically expect some limitation on her rights to that property—reasonable public zoning regulations, servitudes limiting the property to uses appropriate to the neighborhood, and beneficial easements for sewer, water, gas, electric, telephone and cable TV lines. The purchaser should insist, however, that the vendor in fact has title to the property that would be recognized by a court of law and that all encumbrances affecting the property—unpaid taxes, liens, mortgages, easements, use restrictions—are fully disclosed and either removed or accepted before the purchase is completed. What is needed, therefore, is a system that encourages the vendor to identify and cure title defects prior to the completion of the sale. Finally, the purchaser wants insurance, either provided by the vendor or a third party, against undisclosed risks that may appear after the closing either as adverse claims or suits asserted against the purchaser as owner or as hindrances to a future resale.

Several approaches have evolved in the United States for protecting the title of purchasers of real property. First, most real estate contracts require the vendor to produce title of a certain quality (usually stipulated as marketable, merchantable, record, or insurable) before the purchaser is obligated to accept the property and to come forth with the purchase price. Second, the vendor through common law covenants of title warrants the title she conveys to the purchaser. Third, the recording acts protect the title of purchasers who search carefully before purchase and promptly record thereafter. Fourth, a few jurisdictions have adopted systems of title registration that offer further protection of titles. Finally, title insurance insures against title defects.

A. THE CONTRACTUAL OBLIGATION OF THE VENDOR TO PROVIDE MARKETABLE TITLE

The contract reproduced above requires the vendor to provide the purchaser with marketable title. As the following case illustrates, marketable title is not perfect title. It can, indeed, be very imperfect.

TACCONE v. DiRENZI

New York Supreme Court, Ontario County, 1978.
92 Misc.2d 786, 401 N.Y.S.2d 722.

DAVID O. BOEHM, JUSTICE.

This is a motion for summary judgment requiring the specific performance of a contract for the sale of real property brought by plaintiff, Paul N. Taccone, as administrator of the Estate of Sirie P. Taccone, deceased, against defendant, William DiRenzi.

On June 25, 1976 plaintiff and defendant entered into a contract for the sale of real property, consisting of lots numbered 640 to 659, inclusive, plus three mobile homes located on the property, all for $15,000. The property, known as the Crystal Beach Trailer Park, is located on East Lake Road in the Town of Gorham in Ontario County,

New York. It has been used as a trailer park for approximately ten years.

The agreement requires that the "Seller shall tender to Buyer a Warranty Deed with lien covenant conveying good, marketable title in fee simple to said premises." The contract also provides that if the buyer makes valid written objection to the marketability of title, the contract will nevertheless remain in full force and effect if the seller is able to cure the objection prior to the closing date or "if either party secures a commitment for title insurance * * * to insure the marketability of title against the objections raised * * * "

On October 20, 1976, the Monroe Abstract & Title Corporation agreed to issue title insurance for all lots except lots 640 through 645 and 655. As to these lots, Monroe Abstract stated that it "affirmatively insured that its insured hereunder will have full use, possession and quiet enjoyment of the premises to the exclusion of all not claiming under said insured." By letter dated February 1, 1977, plaintiff, by his counsel, sent a letter to defendant stating that time was of the essence and that he would be present in the Monroe County Clerk's office on Friday, February 11, 1977 at 2:00 P.M. "ready, willing and able to complete said transfer of said properties."

By letter dated February 4, 1977, counsel for defendant replied that his client was also ready, willing and able to perform his part of the bargain upon delivery of good and marketable title. He stated, however, that based upon his examination of the abstract of title and the Monroe Abstract title report, it was his opinion that plaintiff was unable to convey marketable title. On February 11, 1977, counsel for plaintiff was present in the Monroe County Clerk's office to close the deal and transfer title, but neither defendant nor his counsel appeared.

Plaintiff then commenced this action to declare title to the lots "good and marketable" and for specific performance. Defendant interposed an answer consisting of a general denial. Plaintiff has now brought this motion for summary judgment.

It is undisputed that decedent, Taccone, purchased the lots in question more than fifteen years prior to the execution of the contract and that no claim of other title has ever been asserted against the land. Included in plaintiff's papers is an affidavit of Carmella Taccone, widow of the decedent, dated December 1, 1976, prepared for purposes of the closing. In it, Mrs. Taccone states that "her deceased husband was the owner in possession and occupation of the premises described * * * for 20 years last past", that "the use of said premises by the deceased was open, notorious and adverse", and that "said ownership, possession, occupation and use of said premises by deceased was never challenged or questioned, nor has any claim of title or ownership thereof ever been filed or instituted against deceased by anyone or any lawsuit commenced whatsoever."

Although the answer contains only a general denial, the defendant in opposing this motion for summary judgment, raises a number of objections to the title. Most of the objections relate to minor defects which have been cured or are easily and ministerially curable. However, the defendant raises a serious objection as to the tax sales in the chain of title of twelve of the lots, asserting that they were jurisdictionally defective because notices of the tax sales were published in only one newspaper and because notice of sale was not given to the record owner, Finger Lakes Land Co., Inc. Further, he points out that there are also gaps in the chain of title of seven of these same twelve lots, rendering title to them wholly unmarketable.

Finally, the defendant makes a general observation that "constitutional questions are presented by the tax sales." For purposes of later discussion, it is significant to note here that defendant does not controvert decedent Taccone's continuous, open and notorious possession of the land from the date he first purchased and began occupying the property.

However, because Monroe Abstract agreed to insure the marketability of title of five lots which do not have gaps in their chain of title, the defendant is precluded from raising objections as to their marketability. The availability of title insurance is all that is required by the contract between plaintiff and defendant [   ]

As to the other seven lots, the Abstracts of Title reveal that they were owned in 1929 by the Finger Lakes Land Company and were sold at tax sales by Ontario County between 1940 and 1944. While the notices of tax sales set forth the names of the parties listed in the tax account for each lot, neither the grantor nor grantee indices has any record of deeds being conveyed by the Finger Lakes Land Company to any of the parties so listed.

Ontario County subsequently sold these seven lots to certain individuals by quit claim deeds and, between 1954 and 1959, the decedent acquired title to these lots from different grantors.

The issue here presented involves the effect of the tax sale transfers and the gaps in the chain of title on the marketability of the seven lots in question.

Marketable title has traditionally been defined as "good title, one that is free and clear from encumbrances or from material defects in the title * * * a title that is free from all reasonable doubt but not necessarily from all doubt" (3 Warren's Weed, New York Real Property, Marketability of Title, § 2.01 at p. 7 [   ]). While a tax title does not have the same presumption of validity as other transfers of title, such title may nevertheless be marketable (see, 3 Warren's Weed, New York Real Property, Marketable Title, supra, § 2.14; 62 N.Y.Jur., Vendor and Purchaser, supra, § 54). A subsequent conveyance by the County is presumptive evidence that the sale and all prior proceedings relating thereto "were regular and in accordance with all the provisions of law * * *" (Real Prop.Tax Law § 1020(3) [   ]).

Of course, marketability depends upon strict compliance with the tax foreclosure statutes [ ] including publication of the notice of sale in two newspapers "at least once in each week for six weeks in two newspapers." (Real Prop.Tax Law § 1002(1), formerly Tax Law § 150).

While the Abstracts of Title show that the various notices of sale for the seven lots were published once each week for six successive weeks, the Abstracts also disclose by the affidavits filed in the Ontario County Clerk's office that the respective notices of sale were published in only one newspaper.

* * *

Non-compliance with the notice of sale provisions has been held to be a jurisdictional defect, not a mere irregularity [ ] Failure to give proper notice of redemption is also considered a jurisdictional defect [ ].

However, as the plaintiff points out, the five year statute of limitations established in Real Property Tax Law § 1020(3) (formerly Tax Law § 132) renders any jurisdictional defects or claims immaterial. A reading of this section indicates that upon the expiration of the 5-year period of limitations, the legislature created a conclusive presumption of regularity of the tax sale and the prior proceedings relating thereto [ ].

* * *

The question which the defendant raises tangentially as to the constitutionality of tax sales need not detain us. He is not an aggrieved party and thus lacks standing to question the constitutionality of the notice provisions * * *.

The defendant raises the more forceful argument that although the expiration of the period of limitations may operate as a conclusive presumption of the regularity of the proceedings, this does not of itself render a title marketable. Indeed, it has been held that the statute of limitations only creates a bar to an action when the new record owner is in possession [ ].

Furthermore, the courts have distinguished between voidable and void tax deeds. As the Court of Appeals has pointed out: "There is a vast difference between a tax deed voidable for irregularities in the proceedings and a tax deed void because the proceedings were a nullity due to prior payment of the tax. A Statute of Limitations ordinarily does not start to run until the right sought to be barred has accrued * * * " [ ].

Thus, although title may be good, the five-year statute of limitations will not by itself render a title marketable without more, such as a curative judicial declaration of marketability, as in an action such as this one for specific performance (See, [ ]; Pedowitz, Tax Titles— Would You Insure One? 49 N.Y.S.B.J. 550, 592 (Nov., 1977)).

Although the above principles would apply to the five lots which the title company agreed to insure, they obviously would not correct the serious flaws resulting from the gaps in the title of the seven lots. The curative provisions of § 1020(3) of the Real Property Tax Law would not apply as to such defects and, consequently, title to these seven lots would not be marketable.

However, the passage of a sufficient period of time may operate to transform even a defective title into a good and marketable one. All that is required is for title to ripen by adverse possession. For this to occur the possession must be actual, open, notorious, exclusive, continuous and under a claim of right [   ] for a period of ten years * * *.

It is undisputed that decedent was in continuous possession of the property for over fifteen years. The possession was open and notorious and the land was held under claim of right. Conceding the validity of defendant's argument that plaintiff has the burden of proving the marketability of title [   ] the plaintiff's sworn and unrebutted statements in his pleadings and motion papers are sufficient to meet that burden [   ]. Accordingly, this court finds plaintiff's title to be good and marketable.

Policy and common sense also dictate this conclusion. Plaintiff's decedent has held recorded title to the land for a substantial period of time and no one has asserted any claims against it [   ]. All seven lots were transferred by tax deed by Ontario County more than thirty years ago, thereby rendering any possible claim stale [   ]. The decedent, no doubt, paid good and valuable consideration for his land, the boundaries of which are carefully described and defined [   ]. No individual, such as a prior owner contesting title, is being divested of or is forfeiting any right [   ]. Indeed, the holding here will have just the opposite effect and prevent a future forfeiture by quieting title [   ]. Whenever, possible, in situations such as this, title should be held good and marketable so that land transactions may be freely transferable in the open real estate market.

Accordingly, plaintiff's motion for summary judgment and for specific performance is granted.

Notes and Questions

1. Assume for a moment that the tax sale statute is unconstitutional. Who would have standing to raise the issue? What effect would a ruling of unconstitutionality on behalf of that person or persons have on the title to the land?

2. Few titles to property are record perfect. A thorough search of the title records of a particular property will often turn up old unreleased mortgages, potential dower interests, questionable legal descriptions, flawed acknowledgments, outstanding mineral interests, and a host of other problems. If a contract requires that the vendor produce marketable or merchantable title, the parties must determine whether such flaws render the title unmarketable. The question is usually one of judgment—in the

first instance the judgment of an attorney, abstractor, or insurer—then the judgment of the parties, and ultimately, possibly, the judgment of a court. As the principal case notes, the question is one of reasonableness: Is the title free from reasonable doubt? Or, conversely, does it subject the purchaser to sufficiently great risks of future litigation or unmarketability on resale that it would not be equitable to force him to go through with the purchase?

If the parties do not stipulate the quality of title that the purchaser expects, the law will imply an obligation to provide marketable title. The parties may alter this standard, however, for example, by agreeing instead to accept insurable title or insisting on record title. How would *Taccone* come out under either of these standards? The purchaser may also agree to accept certain disclosed defects in the vendor's title.

Defects that render a title unmarketable can either be defects in the vendor's ownership of the property (e.g. claims of adverse possessors or of holders of paramount title), or encumbrances that do not affect the vendor's fee title but limit the use of the land. *Taccone* illustrates the former type of problem. Why might the purchaser find the court's resolution of the issue of marketability in *Taccone* wholly unsatisfying? A host of encumbrances—liens, mortgages, easements, covenants, equitable servitudes, leases, dower interests, boundary disputes and encroachments, etc.—can raise the latter sort of problem. Visible servitudes that benefit the land, such as utility easements or public roads along the edge of the property, usually are held not to affect marketability. Similarly, public zoning laws are not usually considered encumbrances, though violation of zoning ordinances may be. However, any encumbrances on title that detract from the value of the property to any significant extent, render the property unmarketable.

3. Whether the vendor is obligated to provide evidence of marketable title or the purchaser is responsible for discovering title defects depends on the contract between the parties and the custom of the jurisdiction. Normally, however, the purchaser is responsible for giving the vendor notice of any objections he may have to the vendor's title. Failure to object may result in waiver of defects that the vendor could have cured had they been called to her attention.

4. At what point must the vendor be able to produce marketable title? One position the law could have taken would be that a vendor should not contract to sell more than she owns at the time the contract is signed. What problems would this approach cause? Another logical approach would be to require the vendor to be able to produce marketable title on "law day," the day set by the contract for closing. In fact, unless the contract specifies that "time is of the essence," courts usually allow the vendor a reasonable time to cure defects identified by the purchaser, even if the vendor is in fact not fully able to provide marketable title by the date set for closing.

5. The remedy sought by the vendor in the *Taccone* case was specific performance. Full consideration of contract remedies will be left for your contracts course, but note here that specific performance is granted much more commonly with respect to property transactions than elsewhere in

contract law because of the belief that land is unique and damages for the breach of land-sale contracts are difficult to determine. Should this rule apply when the vendor is suing for specific performance, rather than the purchaser, since the vendor is seeking money (the purchase price) which is certainly not a unique commodity? Should it apply when the sale of a condominium in a large development of similar condominia is at issue? See Centex Homes Corporation v. Boag, 128 N.J.Super. 385, 320 A.2d 194 (Ch.1974) (seller limited to damages where breach concerned one of 360 nearly identical condominium units).

6. Alternatively the injured party may sue for damages. The vendor often holds the earnest money deposit as liquidated damages specified by the contract, a permitted remedy where the damages are reasonable. The vendor may also sue for compensatory damages where the purchaser is in breach.

If the vendor is in breach, the purchaser may sue for restitution of any earnest money deposit and for compensatory damages. Where the vendor is unable to perform, however, because of a defect in the title, but is not in bad faith or willful breach, the common law limited the purchaser to recovery of the earnest money deposit, interest, and expenses. This rule, the "English" rule, was justified by the problems faced by a title examiner in determining clear title in eighteenth and nineteenth century England at the time the rule was formed. Many states have abandoned this rule, permitting purchasers loss-on-the-bargain damages where the seller is unable to provide good title. See Donovan v. Bachstadt, 91 N.J. 434, 453 A.2d 160 (1982) (abandoning English rule in favor of allowing compensatory damages to buyer where vendor unable to provide good title).

7. The suit for specific performance is a potent weapon in the hands of a disappointed purchaser. Whether or not the purchaser ultimately prevails in a suit for specific performance, once such a suit is filed, it renders the property unmarketable in the hands of the vendor. If court dockets portend lengthy litigation and the vendor must pay carrying charges until the litigation is resolved, the vendor has little choice but to settle with the purchaser for whatever terms can be obtained. See, e.g. Safeco Title Ins. Co. v. Moskopoulos, 116 Cal.App.3d 658, 172 Cal.Rptr. 248, 18 A.L.R. 4th 1301 (1981). Is it unethical for a purchaser to sue for specific performance where his rights under a real estate contract are doubtful if the main purpose of the suit is to extract a favorable settlement from the vendor? Does A.B.A. Model Rule 3.1 help resolve this dilemma?

B. DEED COVENANTS

If a grantor of real property fails to provide a grantee with marketable title as promised under the contract of sale at the time the deed is delivered, the merger doctrine may very well preclude the grantee from further recourse under the contract. Under the merger doctrine, acceptance of a deed that conveys a lesser title than that promised by a contract excuses the grantor from any obligation to provide any greater title. Questions as to the title would almost never be held collateral to the deed, thus it would rarely be the case that an agreement to provide marketable title would expressly survive the deed.

Subsequent to the closing, therefore, recourse by the grantee against the grantor must normally be based on covenants as to title found expressly in the deed or incorporated into the deed by statute. Subsequent grantees may also sue a grantor on the basis of deed covenants if it turns out that the title the grantor warranted was defective. The following case illustrates the limitations of reliance on deed covenants for title security.

ST. PAUL TITLE INSURANCE CORPORATION v. OWEN

Supreme Court of Alabama, 1984.
452 So.2d 482.

MADDOX, JUSTICE.

The question here is what liability do grantors have to remote grantees or their assigns under a warranty deed and a statutory warranty deed where certain covenants of title contained in the deeds are found to run with the land?

On February 18, 1976, Albert M. Owen, an unmarried man, executed a warranty deed purporting to convey certain real property in Baldwin County to his brother and sister-in-law, James R. Owen, Jr., and Cheryl C. Owen. The deed, which was recorded on March 8, 1976, in Baldwin County, contained the following covenants of title:

"The party of the first part [Albert Owen] for himself, his heirs, executors and administrators, hereby covenants and warrants to and with the said parties of the second part [James and Cheryl Owen], their heirs and assigns, that he is seized of an indefeasible estate in and to the said property; that he has a good right to convey the same as herein contained; that he will guarantee the peaceable possession thereof; that the said property is free from all liens and encumbrances, and that he will, and his heirs, executors and administrators will forever warrant and defend the same unto the said parties of the second part, their heirs and assigns, against the lawful claims of all persons."

The warranty deed form was obtained from the law office of James R. Owen, Sr., the father of Albert and James Owen.

Subsequently, James and Cheryl Owen conveyed the Baldwin County property, purportedly conveyed to them, by statutory warranty deed[20] to Dennis C. Carlisle Jr., the brother of Cheryl Owen. The property was conveyed June 6, 1976, and the deed recorded in Baldwin County on July 14, 1976.

On June 10, 1976, Dennis Carlisle mortgaged the property to United Companies Mortgage and Investment of Mobile 2, Inc., for

---

20. The deed provided that " * * * the Grantee, does hereby Grant, Bargain, Sell and convey unto said Grantee * * *."

$17,159.52. This mortgage was recorded on July 14, 1976, in both Mobile and Baldwin counties.

Dennis Carlisle mortgaged the property to GECC Financial Services (GECC) for $17,671.29, on November 8, 1977, apparently substituting mortgages and paying off the original mortgage. The mortgage to GECC was recorded in Baldwin County and a policy of title insurance naming GECC as the insured was issued shortly thereafter by Eastern Shore Title Insurance Corp., of Daphne, the agent for St. Paul Title Insurance Corp. (St. Paul Title). The title insurance was issued at the request of Dennis Carlisle.

When Dennis Carlisle subsequently defaulted on his mortgage payments, GECC attempted to foreclose on the property. The Circuit Court of Baldwin County found, however, that because Dennis Carlisle held no right, title, or interest in or to any of the property on the day the mortgage was executed, GECC was not entitled to foreclose on the property. GECC then brought suit against St. Paul Title, to collect its debt, and in addition the costs of litigation involved, all as provided for under the terms of the title insurance policy.

St. Paul Title, as subrogee of GECC, then filed a complaint against Albert Owen, James R. Owen, Jr., and Cheryl Owen, wherein St. Paul alleged that they had breached the covenants of title contained in the deeds executed and delivered by them. The trial court, after a non-jury trial, entered a judgment on behalf of the defendants. St. Paul appeals.

I. The liability of Albert Owen under the express covenants of title contained in his warranty deed.

The deed executed by Albert Owen, an unmarried man, purporting to convey property to James and Cheryl Owen, contained the following express covenants of title: a covenant of seizin; a covenant of right to convey; a covenant for quiet enjoyment; a covenant against encumbrances; and a covenant of warranty. [ ] Of these covenants, however, only the covenants of quiet enjoyment and warranty are said to operate in futuro for the benefit of the ultimate grantee. [ ] Until broken, these two covenants run with the land to the heirs of the grantee, or if the land is conveyed or assigned, to the assignee, so that when they are broken, the heir or assignee injured by the breach can maintain an action against the covenantor. [ ] Thus, it is generally recognized and held that when a covenant of title runs with the land, all grantors, back to and including the original grantor-covenantor, become liable upon a breach of the covenant to the assignee or grantee in possession or entitled to the possession at the time, and the latter may sue the original or remote grantor, regardless of whether he has taken from the immediate grantor with a warranty. [ ]

Because the covenants of quiet enjoyment and of warranty are virtually identical in operation, whatever constitutes a breach of one covenant is a breach of the other. [ ] Neither covenant is breached until there is an eviction under paramount title. [ ] The eviction may be either actual or constructive. [ ]

It has been said that an outstanding title that could be asserted in a judicial proceeding against the party in possession is equivalent to an eviction. [ ] Likewise, a final judgment or decree adverse to the covenantee's title or right to possession constitutes a sufficient constructive eviction to entitle the covenantee to sue for breach of the covenant of warranty. [ ]

Here, the breach occurred when the trial court ruled in the foreclosure proceedings that Dennis Carlisle possessed no interest in the property which had been mortgaged, thereby frustrating GECC's attempt to foreclose on the property purportedly conveyed to Carlisle in fee simple.

We hold that the covenant of quiet enjoyment and warranty provided by the terms of the warranty deed executed by Albert Owen ran with the land purportedly conveyed by that instrument. We further hold that because someone other than the original grantor-covenantor in fact possessed paramount title, appellant is entitled to assert a claim for the breach of the covenants of title, as its subrogor was the ultimate grantee or assignee who was in possession at the time the covenants were broken.

II. The liability of James and Cheryl Owen under the covenants of title contained in their statutory warranty deed.

The deed executed by James and Cheryl Owen contained no express covenants of title, but it did use the words, "grant, bargain, sell and convey." In all conveyances of estates in fee where the words "grant, bargain, and sell" appear, the deed is construed by statute as containing the following covenants of title: a covenant of seizin; a covenant against encumbrances; and a covenant of quiet enjoyment. Code 1975, § 35–4–271.

Appellant asserts that James and Cheryl Owen are liable for a breach of the implied covenant of quiet enjoyment contained in the statutory warranty deed, and that such a covenant runs with the land so as to benefit a remote grantee or assign. Unlike the express covenants of title found in a general warranty deed, however, the implied covenants of title contained in a statutory warranty deed are more limited in effect.

In the early case of Heflin v. Phillips, 96 Ala. 561, 11 So. 729 (1892), the Court noted: "In construing this statute [predecessor of § 35–4–271] this Court declared that the words 'grant, bargain, sell' do not import an absolute general covenant of seizin against incumbrances and for quiet enjoyment, but that they amount to a covenant only against acts done or suffered by the grantor and his heirs." [ ] More than twenty years after Heflin, the Court remarked: "All authorities hold that the covenants implied by statute are limited to the acts of the grantor and those claiming under him, and do not extend to defects of title anterior to the conveyance to him." Mackintosh v. Stewart, 181 Ala. 328, 333, 61 So. 956, 958 (1913).

* * *

James and Cheryl Owen conveyed their complete, albeit non-existent interest, in the subject property to Dennis Carlisle by statutory warranty deed. By so doing, they merely warranted that they had not conveyed title to anyone else; that they had not allowed the property to become encumbered while they held purported title; and that they had not caused or suffered anyone to do anything that would interfere with the property's quiet enjoyment by the grantee, the grantee's heirs or assigns. Because the record indicates that James and Cheryl did nothing to affect the purported title they conveyed, they did not breach any of the covenants of title contained in the statutory warranty deed delivered to Dennis Carlisle and are therefore not liable to the appellant, as subrogee of GECC.

III. Damages for breach of covenants of title.

Appellant asserts that it is entitled to recover, as damages, the amount of mortgage proceeds paid to Dennis Carlisle by its subrogor, plus litigation costs and interest. Appellant further contends its recovery should neither be barred nor be limited to merely nominal damages, even though appellees received no consideration for their conveyances.

In situations where there has been a complete failure of title and a grantee has sought recovery from his immediate grantor, the maximum recovery allowed has been the purchase price paid. [ ] With respect to an action against a remote grantor, however, there appears to be a difference of opinion as to whether damages are to be determined by the consideration paid by the grantee bringing the suit to his immediate grantor or by the consideration paid to the original grantor or covenantor, not exceeding in either case, however, the consideration paid for the conveyance by the defendant in the action. [ ] Here, however, the facts indicate that no consideration was ever paid to or received by any of the appellees, Albert Moore Owen, James R. Owen, Jr., or Cheryl C. Owen. Consequently, since there was no evidence that the remote grantors received any consideration for their conveyances purportedly conveying title to the subject property, appellant, as subrogee of GECC, is entitled to an award of nominal damages only, for the breach of the covenant of quiet enjoyment contained in Albert Owen's deed, and not the amount of the mortgage made by GECC. [ ]

* * *

The judgment of the trial court is hereby reversed and the cause remanded to that court for a determination of the amount of nominal damages appellant is entitled to recover as consistent with the holding of this opinion.

Notes and Questions

1. The "general warranty" deed from Albert Owen to James and Cheryl Owen contained five of the six common deed covenants. The

covenant of seisin guaranties that the grantor is seised of an estate in the land to be conveyed. In most jurisdictions this means that the grantor owns the land, but in a few it means that the grantor is in possession of the land. The covenant of right to convey promises that the grantor has the right to convey the property. Normally, a grantor with a right to convey a property is seised of it, and visa versa. Under what circumstances might one be true, but not the other?

The covenant against encumbrances promises that the land is free from a variety of potential rights and interests encumbering the land that could exist in third parties. First, it promises freedom from interests that affect the use and enjoyment of the land physically, i.e. servitudes. Second, it promises freedom from liens and charges. Third, it guarantees the absence of other interests that might limit the rights of the grantee, while not affecting seisin, such as leases, dower interests, etc. It is not breached by the existence of zoning ordinances that affect use of the property.

The covenants of warranty and of quiet enjoyment are identical. Under these covenants the grantor promises to defend the grantee's title and use of the property against any future adverse claims put forward by others. A sixth covenant, further assurances, is more common in England than in the United States, but appears in some warranty deeds. This promise to execute any documents or take further steps necessary to protect the grantee's title is specifically enforceable.

2. The first three covenants, seisin, right to convey, and against encumbrances, are present covenants. This means that they are breached only to the extent that the grantor's title is defective or encumbered at the time the deed is delivered. Several consequences follow from this. First, the statute of limitations for enforcing these covenants begins to run at the date of delivery of the deed. Even though outstanding claims and interests exist in third parties, if these claims are not asserted during the statutory period, the grantee may only claim nominal damages, and is barred from claiming damages under the present covenants thereafter. Further, these covenants, being present covenants, do not run with the land for the benefit of future grantees. They only benefit the immediate grantee of the land and covenant. A few jurisdictions permit a cause of action for breach of these covenants to be assigned with the resale of the property to remote grantees, Rockafellor v. Gray, 194 Iowa 1280, 191 N.W. 107 (1922), but in most jurisdictions the cause of action for breach of the present covenants may only be brought by the original grantee to whom the covenant was made.

3. The covenants of warranty, quiet enjoyment, and further assurances are future covenants. They are breached whenever a third party successfully asserts paramount title against the beneficiary of the covenant, and they run with the land. They thus benefit both immediate and future grantees. They are breached only in the event of actual or constructive eviction of the grantee. It is not sufficient that a claim is asserted, or even that it affects marketability of the title. Purchase of an outstanding interest to avoid eviction, however, may constitute a sufficient breach to ground an action.

4.   In most jurisdictions, the rule of damages established in the principal case is followed: Damages for failure of title are limited to the consideration received by the original covenantor. If title is lost to only a portion of the total area covered by the deed, recovery is limited to a proportionate share of the consideration. Where the defect that appears is an encumbrance, the damages recoverable are measured by the cost of removing the encumbrance, or, alternatively in some jurisdictions, the diminution in value of the property. Interest expenses for the time the grantee is deprived of the property and attorney's fees for defending against adverse claims may also be recoverable damages.

5.   Statutes in many jurisdictions imply the presence of certain covenants from the use of specific language or deed forms. For example, in Illinois the use of the word "warrants" in a deed implies the covenants of seisin, right to convey, freedom from encumbrances, warranty and quiet enjoyment. Ill.Stat.Ann. ch. 30 ¶ 9. The use of the term in Iowa only implies a covenant of general warranty, Iowa Code Ann. § 558.19. See 6A Powell on Real Property, ¶ 897[2].

6.   The deed of Albert Owen in the principal case is a "general warranty" deed. It covenants against any problems that subsequently may arise affecting the property, regardless of the covenantor's responsibility for causing those problems. The deed from James and Cheryl Owen to Dennis Carlisle is a "special warranty" deed. The grantor of a special warranty deed only warrants against problems which he may himself have caused or created while owning the property, not those attributable to predecessors in title. Finally, a grantor may "quitclaim" the property to the grantee, making no covenants at all as to the state of the title.

7.   Why did the plaintiff title insurance company in the principal case not sue on the present covenants against Albert Owen? Against James and Cheryl Owen? Assuming that a remote grantor has transferred property for consideration, why might a suit on the future covenants still yield an unsatisfactory result? Had James and Cheryl quitclaimed the property to Carlisle, what would be their liability? What would be the liability of Albert Owen, their grantor? See 6A R. Powell & P. Rohan, Powell on Real Property, ¶ 900[4]; R. Cunningham, W. Stoebuck, D. Whitman, The Law of Property § 11.13 (1984).

C. RECORDING ACTS

The most important device for protecting land titles in the United States, on which other forms of title assurance are ultimately based, is the recording system. The maintenance of pervasive records of land titles is an American innovation. Antecedents for it can be found in the English enrollment of bargain and sale deeds and in the local customs of some English counties, which required registration of land titles. See Cribbet, Conveyancing Reform, 35 N.Y.U.L.Rev. 1291, 1293–1296 (1960). Security of English land titles, however, was initially dependent on public enfeoffment ceremonies, and then, once written evidence of land transfers became more common, on the passing on at each transfer of relevant muniments of title. As early as 1640, however, the Massachusetts Bay colony adopted a recording act. Other colonies followed suit, and as the country spread westward, the practice of requiring recording of land-title transactions spread with it. See Marshall, A Historical Sketch of the American Recording Acts, 4 Cleve.–Mar.L.Rev 56 (1955). The laws of every state in the United States now provide for recording or registration of land-title transactions.

Nowhere is recording necessary to the validity of a transaction between the transferor and transferee: Regardless of whether a purchaser (or donee) of property records his title, it is good against the vendor (or donor). Recording does serve a number of other purposes, however. First, it provides a public record of land-title transactions. If a person wants to know who owns the trash-covered vacant lot down the street, or how much her neighbor's house just sold for, or whether a potential debtor really owns the property listed on a loan application, the public land records may provide an answer. In most states, properly authenticated copies of recorded documents are also admissible evidence in judicial proceedings in which questions relating to the land titles arise.

The most important purpose of the recording acts, however, is to assure the security of the title of land owners. They do this in two ways. First, a potential purchaser (or his title insurer), by examining a vendor's title to property, can discover any outstanding clouds on the title of the vendor. These can then be cleared up before the purchase is completed, or, if they cannot be, the purchaser can abandon the purchase as too risky. Second, once a purchase is completed, the recording acts protect the title of the purchaser (who, depending on the type of recording act, either takes without notice, records first, or both) from prior unrecorded interests in the property.

Recording systems are established by statute. Three different types of recording statutes are found in the United States.[21] The simplest, and most primitive are the race statutes. Under a pure race statute, the first to record of two holders of conflicting interests prevails. If O sells Blackacre first to A and second to B, and B records first, B's interest takes precedence over A's in a race jurisdiction. Pure race statutes operate very efficiently—the only question before a court in a title dispute is who recorded first, a matter usually quite simply

---

21. Some commentators recognize a fourth category of recording acts, grace-period acts, which allow a prior grantee of land to take precedence over a subsequent transfer if the earlier transaction is recorded within a "grace period" provided by statute. See 6A R. Powell & R. Rohan, Powell on Real Property, ¶ 905[1][c][iv]. Grace periods were common in early recording statutes, as the large areas covered by a single recorder's office and primitive means of transportation impeded immediate recordation of land transactions. It is obviously contrary to the policies underlying the recording acts, however, to hold a subsequent purchaser subject to an undiscoverable prior interest recorded after the subsequent purchase but within the grace period, thus grace-period statutes have been generally repealed. The only modern example of grace-period statutes are mechanic's lien statutes, which permit laborers or building suppliers to record a mechanics lien against a property if bills are not paid within a statutory period (usually 60–120 days). A purchaser of real property is well advised, therefore, to ascertain if any work has recently been done on the property, and, if so, to make certain that all bills are paid prior to closing.

determined. They are, however, inequitable in the situation where B was aware of A's prior unrecorded interest.

Faced with the potential for fraud and inequity raised by pure race recording acts, courts began to interpret them so as to refuse protection to subsequent purchasers with notice, even if the subsequent purchaser recorded first. Legislatures eventually amended the recording acts to incorporate notice requirements as well, resulting in notice acts. Notice statutes permit a purchaser to prevail in a dispute with a previous purchaser, even though the subsequent purchaser failed to record, thus defeating, to some extent, the goal of the recording acts to encourage universal recording of land transactions.

Under the final form of statute, the race-notice statute, a subsequent purchaser, to prevail in a dispute with a prior purchaser, must not only take without notice of the prior interests, but also must record before the holder of the prior interest records.

American states are today about evenly divided between notice and race-notice recording statutes, with a few pure race statutes remaining (see IV American Law of Property, § 17.5 for a complete list).

How would you classify each of the following statutes?

> All deeds, mortgages and other instruments of writing which are authorized to be recorded, shall take effect and be in force from and after the time of filing the same for record, and not before, as to all creditors and subsequent purchasers, without notice; and all such deeds and title papers shall be adjudged void as to all such creditors and subsequent purchasers, without notice, until the same shall be filed for record. Ill.Rev.Stat. ch. 30 ¶ 29.

> A conveyance of real property, within the state, on being duly acknowledged by the person executing the same, or proved as required by this chapter, * * *, may be recorded in the office of the clerk of the county where such real property is situated * * * Every such conveyance not so recorded is void as against any person who subsequently purchases or acquires by exchange or contracts to purchase or acquire by exchange, the same real property or any portion thereof, * * *, in good faith and for a valuable consideration, from the same vendor or assignor, his distributees or devisees, and whose conveyance, contract, or assignment is first duly recorded. * * * N.Y.Real Prop.L. § 291.

> No instrument affecting real estate is of any validity against subsequent purchasers for a valuable consideration, without notice, unless filed in the office of the recorder of the county in which the same lies, as hereinafter provided. Iowa Code Ann. § 558.41.

> No (i) conveyance of land, or (ii) contract to convey, or (iii) option to convey, or (iv) lease of land for more than three years shall be valid to pass any property interest as against lien creditors or purchasers for a valuable consideration from the donor, bargainor or lessor but from the time of registration thereof in the county where the land lies. * * * Gen.Stat.N.C. § 47–18.

Though the law of recording is fundamentally statutory, as with the law of adverse possession, the simple language of the statutes has been subjected to considerable judicial interpretation. See Mattis, Recording Acts: Anachronistic Reliance, 25 Real Prop., Prob. & Trust J. 17, 22–40 (1990).

The classic recording act dispute involved three parties: O, the original owner of the land; A, to whom O first transferred title to the land (or an interest in the land, such as a lien or an easement); and B, to whom O subsequently transferred a conflicting interest in the same land.[22] To determine who prevails in a dispute between A and B in a particular jurisdiction it is necessary to know:

(1) Does the jurisdiction have a race, notice, or race-notice statute?

(2) Is A's interest an interest that must be recorded under the recording act to be protected against subsequent purchasers?

(3) Is B a purchaser protected by the recording acts?

(4) Did A record before B's purchase?

(5) Did B record before A (relevant only in race and race-notice jurisdictions)?

(6) Did B purchase without notice (constructive, actual, or inquiry) of A's interest (relevant only in notice or race-notice jurisdictions)?

(7) Were the formalities of the recording act properly observed (instruments properly acknowledged, transcribed, indexed)?

(8) If A's interest was recorded prior to B's purchase, was A's interest recorded in B's chain of title?

All of these questions must be considered against the background of the common law which preceded the recording acts. Under the common law, the general rule was first in time, first in right. Between two conflicting interests if both were legal or both were equitable, the earlier created interest would prevail. Thus A would always win in the dispute we have posed above. This rule makes a great deal of sense: If O has transferred an interest in property to A, O no longer owns that interest and cannot transfer it subsequently to B, thus the transfer to B is a nullity, and in a dispute between A and B, A must prevail. The only exception to this rule at the common law was that if A's interest was equitable (for example a constructive or resulting trust) and B was a purchaser who took for value without notice of A's interest, B would prevail. Equity thus protected bona fide purchasers for value from

---

22. Note that, consistent with what was said earlier about the recording acts not affecting the validity of transfers between grantors and grantees, either A or B will prevail over O in a dispute regardless of considerations of recordation or notice.

Note also that, depending on the facts of the transaction, the losing party in the A versus B dispute may be able to recover from O under a fraud or constructive trust theory.

secret equities. See J. Pomeroy, Equity Jurisprudence, §§ 677–734 (5th ed. 1941)

We begin with the questions two and three above, which As must record to be protected by the recording act? Which Bs are protected by the act from unrecorded interests?

MUGAAS v. SMITH et ux.

Supreme Court of Washington, 1949.
33 Wash.2d 429, 206 P.2d 332.

HILL, JUSTICE.

This is an action by Dora B. Mugaas, a widow, to quiet title to a strip of land 135 feet in length and with a maximum width of 3½ feet which she claims by adverse possession, and to compel Delmar C. Smith and his wife to remove therefrom any and all buildings and encroachments. From a judgment quieting title to the strip in Mrs. Mugaas and directing the removal of any and all buildings and encroachments, the Smiths appeal.

The appellants contend that the respondent has failed to establish adverse possession of the tract in question. The character of the respondent's possession over the statutory period is one of fact, and the trial court's finding in that regard is to be given great weight and will not be overturned unless this court is convinced that the evidence preponderates against that finding. We are of the opinion that the evidence was sufficient to sustain the trial court's findings, and the conclusions based thereon, that the respondent had acquired title to the strip in question by adverse possession. The evidence would have warranted a finding that her adverse possession dated back to 1910.

The only serious questions raised by this appeal are attributable to the fact that the fence which between 1910 and 1928 clearly marked the boundary line for which respondent contends, disappeared by a process of disintegration in the years which followed, and, when appellants purchased the property in 1941 by a legal description and with a record title which included the disputed strip, there was no fence and nothing to mark the dividing line between the property of appellants and respondent, or to indicate to the appellants that the respondent was claiming title to the strip in question.

We have on several occasions approved a statement which appears in Towles v. Hamilton, 94 Neb. 588, 143 N.W. 935, 936, that:

> "* * * It is elementary that, where the title has become fully vested by disseisin so long continued as to bar an action, it cannot be divested by parol abandonment or relinquishment or by verbal declarations of the disseizor, nor by any other act short of what would be required in a case where his title was by deed." [ ].

The fact that the respondent had ceased to use the strip in question in such a way that her claim of adverse possession was apparent did not divest her of the title she had acquired.

Appellants' principal contention is that we have held, in a long line of cases, that a bona fide purchaser of real property may rely upon the record title. The cases cited by appellants construe our recording statute, Rem.Rev.Stat. §§ 10596–1, 10596–2, and involve contests between those relying upon the record title and those relying upon a prior unrecorded conveyance as conveyances are defined by Rem.Rev.Stat. § 10596–1. The holdings in the cases cited give effect to that provision of § 10596–2 which states that any unrecorded conveyance " * * * is void as against any subsequent purchaser or mortgagee in good faith and for a valuable consideration from the same vendor, his heirs or devisees, of the same real property or any portion thereof whose conveyance is first duly recorded. * * * "

Appellants cite no cases, and we have found none, supporting their contention that, under a recording statute such as Rem.Rev.Stat. §§ 10596–1, 10596–2, a conveyance of the record title to a bona fide purchaser will extinguish a title acquired by adverse possession. The trial judge, in his admirable memorandum decision, quoted the following from the opinion in Ridgeway v. Holiday, 59 Mo. 444, 454:

" * * * But it is contended by the defendant that he is a purchaser for value from Voteau who appeared from the record to be the owner, and was in possession, without any notice of the prior adverse possession which passed the title to Ridgeway, or of any claim on his part to the premises; and that as against him, the defendant, Ridgeway, cannot assert his title; that to permit him to do so, would be giving to an adverse possession greater force and efficacy than is given to an unrecorded conveyance. These objections, it must be admitted, are very forcible. The registry act, however, cannot, in the nature of things, apply to a transfer of the legal title by adverse possession, and such title does not stand on the footing of one acquired and held by an unrecorded deed, and of such title, the purchaser may not expect to find any evidence in the records."

He quoted, also, the following from Schall v. Williams Valley R. Co., 35 Pa. 191, 204:

* * *

"The first observation we have to make on his ruling is, that titles matured under the statute of limitations, are not within the recording acts. However expedient it might be to require some public record of such titles to be kept, and however inconvenient it may be to purchasers to ascertain what titles of that sort are outstanding, still we have not as yet any legislation on the subject, and it is not competent for judicial decision to force upon them consequences drawn from the recording acts. Those acts relate exclusively to written titles."

These cases seem to us to be directly in point, and to afford a complete answer to appellants' contention. * * *

* * *

The judgment is affirmed.

Notes and Questions

1. If A's interest is not subject to recordation and thus does not need to be recorded under the recording act, a dispute between A and a subsequent purchaser B will be settled under the common law rules, i.e. normally A will win (subject to the exception that prior equitable interests are subordinate to the interests of subsequent bona fide purchasers). A's interest may be exempt from recording for several reasons. First, as in the principal cases, A's interest may not be based on a document, and thus may not be recordable. Adverse possession claims, easements created by necessity, implication or prescription, (See Chapter 6), dower or courtesy rights, and beneficial interests in constructive or resulting trusts fall in this category. Second, there are interests that are noted on public records elsewhere, such as tax and assessment liens kept in the county treasurer or tax office, wills filed in the probate court, and bankruptcy records in the bankruptcy court, of which a purchaser will be treated as having constructive notice, whether or not the interests are recorded. See Leary and Blake, Twentieth Century Real Estate Business and Eighteenth Century Recording, 22 Am.U.L.Rev. 275, 283–84 (1973). Thus, these records must be checked as part of a thorough title search. Third, some instruments are specifically not recordable, and thus need not be recorded. In earlier times, many kinds of instruments were not subject to recordation, but today the most common example of this category is the short-term lease, see N.Y.Real Prop.Law § 290 (McKinney) (leases not over 3 years), Mass.Gen.L.Ann. ch. 183 § 4 (leases not over 7 years). Finally, federal land patents need not be recorded under state recording acts. Which As must record under each of the recording acts set out above?

2. The obvious effect of the fact that the recording acts do not protect Bs against the unrecorded interests of As who are not required by law to record their interests is that a simple search of the recording acts is not sufficient to protect prospective Bs from subsequent unpleasant surprises. This in turn means that a title search is not complete until the examiner has studied not only the records of the recorder's office, but also examined probate, bankruptcy and divorce court records and made a trip out to the property to discover the interests of those in possession. But what could the Smiths do to protect themselves against the claims of Dora Mugaas? If you cannot think of anything they could have done differently, what does that say about the protection afforded by the recording acts?

3. If B is protected by the recording act, B will prevail in a dispute with A who claims under a prior recordable but unrecorded interest. Most recording acts only protect Bs who are purchasers, defined as any person who acquires an interest in property for valuable consideration. The interest need not be a fee interest—mortgagors, purchasers of easements or mineral estates, and lessees are protected. Donees, heirs, devisees, persons who file a lis pendens, and, in many jurisdictions, general creditors, are not, however, protected by the recording acts. Neither are persons who pay a nominal consideration. Some acts explicitly identify those protected by the recording act ("purchasers for value"), others explicitly identify those not protected by the act ("the grantor, his heirs and devisees"). Which Bs are protected by each of the statutes set out above?

About half of the states protect general creditors. (See the North Carolina and Illinois statutes above). Even in these jurisdictions, however, only creditors who have filed a lien against the property by judgment or attachment are protected. Further, in most jurisdictions that protect creditors, only creditors who take without notice are protected. Purchasers at judgment sales are protected if they purchase without notice of prior unrecorded interests. If the recording act protects creditors, however, even a purchaser with notice is protected if the creditor who obtained a judgment against the property obtained her lien without notice. See, 4 American Law of Property, §§ 17.9, 17.10, 17.29, 17.30 (J. Casner, ed. 1952); Johnson, Purpose and Scope of Recording Statutes, 47 Iowa L.Rev. 231, 235–237 (1962).

4. Recording acts only protect Bs who are purchasers for "value." Problems arise if value is not extended at the same time the property interest is obtained: if, for example, the subsequent purchaser extends value first and acquires a property interest later; or acquires a property interest first and extends value later. Bs who acquire mortgages or transfers of title for an antecedent debt are not protected by the recording acts from prior unrecorded interests. Neither are Bs who receive an interest in property in exchange for a promise to pay, at least unless the promise to pay is in the form of a negotiable instrument which is negotiated to a holder in due course. Where the transfer and payment are part of the same transaction, the fact that one precedes the other will not be fatal unless in the interim between the transfer and the payment, the subsequent purchaser receives notice of the interest of an A in a notice or race-notice jurisdiction. Some courts have held that where B receives notice of the claim of an A after the B has given value but before the transfer has occurred, B will not be protected from A's interest by the recording act. On the other hand, a B who has obtained title but only paid part of the purchase price when she receives notice of the existence of an A, will only prevail to the extent of consideration already paid. See IV American Law of Property at § 17.10; Johnson, 47 Iowa L.Rev. at 234; Mattis, Recording Acts: Anachronistic Reliance, 25 Real Prop., Prob. & Trust J. 17, 55–94 (1990).

5. To be protected by the recording acts, a B must also, in a notice or race-notice jurisdiction, purchase without notice. Much more will be said about this below.

D. THE CHAIN OF TITLE

The recording acts seem literally to say that if A is first to place his interest of record in a race or race-notice jurisdiction, or if A places his interest of record before B purchases in a notice jurisdiction, then A will prevail over B in a dispute between them. In practice, however, A's obligation of prior recording has been largely replaced with an obligation to record within B's "chain of title." This change has been dictated by the nature of the American recording system.

In virtually any American recorder's office, far more instruments are of record than could ever be examined by a title searcher examining the title of a particular parcel of property. Title examiners must, therefore, depend on an index to identify documents relevant to a particular piece of property.[23]   Traditionally, and still in most jurisdictions, recorded documents are indexed under the names of the parties to the recorded transaction.   Separate indices are kept by the names of grantors and grantees.   When a document is brought in for recording, it is microfilmed or photocopied, and assigned an index number (traditionally a volume and page number) which will facilitate its retrieval. The recorder then notes the document in two indices, one listing grantors and the other listing grantees.

Traditionally, these indices were arranged alphabetically by the first two or three letters of the last name.   For example, a page might be headed Sho and include Shorrs, Shorts, Shooks, Shoops and Shopovskis, in chronological order of the filing of instruments rather than in strictly alphabetical order.   From time to time indices are consolidated, so that a search might require reviewing a current index, annual indices for the last several years, and decennial indices for earlier times.

To illustrate, assume that you represent a client who wants to purchase Greenacre, which Johnson claims to own.   You would search the grantee indices (probably searching the Jo pages) until you found the date where Johnson received the property from Salsich.   Noting the date and index number of that transaction, you would then search the grantee books further back looking for the name Salsich until you found a point where Salsich received the property from Shaffer.   Noting again the date and index number of the transaction, you would search back until you found the deed by which Shaffer had received the property.   You would continue your search backwards in time until you reached a deed from the sovereign, or until you reached the point where title searching standards in your jurisdiction or your marketable title act permit you to stop.   You would at that point have a list of successive owners of the property, and of the index numbers of the instruments by which they transferred title to the property.

At that point you would move over to the grantor books.   Starting from the earliest deed you discovered, you would search forward for the names of a grantor from the date of the deed to that grantor to the date at which a deed from that grantor to the next was recorded.   (Can you explain why your search would cover this time frame?)   You would note the dates and index numbers of all instruments recorded in the name of each grantor during the time he or she had title to the property.   If Shaffer, for example, had executed a mortgage to First Bank and Trust during the time he had title to the property, this would be noted.   So would the fact that Shaffer had granted an easement to Jost, a neighbor.   The grantor indices would then be searched forward under these names as well, to determine if the mortgage or easement

---

23. For a good description of title indices, see Leary and Blake, Twentieth Century Real Estate Business and Eighteenth Century Recording, 22 Am.U.L.Rev. 275, 283–286 (1973).

was ever released. When you finally had searched Johnson's name forward through the grantor index to the day of the search, your search of the indices would be completed. You would then retrieve the copies of the documents identified and examine them to determine which, if any, had any continuing effect on the title to Greenacre.

The series of successive interests in land identified by this search would constitute the chain of title for Greenacre. It is possible, however, that documents purporting to affect the title of Greenacre might be recorded out of this chain of title. Suppose, for example, that at some point in time Smith, who had no interest in Greenacre, deeded Greenacre to Jones and that Jones recorded the deed. This deed would in fact be prior of record to any deed your client could obtain or record, and thus literally, under the language of the recording act, would take precedence over that to your client. But should the claim of Jones prevail over that of your client? In fact, the courts have often placed a practical construction on the recording acts, holding a purchaser subject, not to all previously recorded deeds, but only to deeds recorded in that purchaser's "chain of title." The following cases explore the "chain of title" notion.

These cases also begin to explore the concept of "notice." Under notice or race-notice statutes, a B is only protected if he or she purchases without "notice" of prior unrecorded interests. Different types of notice are recognized by the cases. First, purchasers are considered to have "constructive" notice of all claims memorialized in recorded documents. Second, purchasers are held responsible for any claims to the property of which they have full "actual" notice. Finally, purchasers may be put on "inquiry" notice by various circumstances, most commonly by possession inconsistent with record title, or by information appearing in recorded documents suggesting unrecorded claims. A purchaser with inquiry notice has an obligation to make reasonable inquiries to discover the existence of prior adverse claims.

PALAMARG REALTY COMPANY v. REHAC

Supreme Court of New Jersey, 1979.
80 N.J. 446, 404 A.2d 21.

MOUNTAIN, J.

Plaintiffs brought suit to quiet title to two tracts of land in Burlington County. Title to one tract is claimed by defendants Joseph Rehac and Alexander Piatkowski; title to the other tract is claimed by defendants David W. Worth and Ezra B. Sharp. All defendants answered and filed counterclaims demanding relief similar to that sought by plaintiffs. Both plaintiffs and defendants moved for summary judgment. The trial court, in an unreported opinion, denied plaintiffs' motion and granted those of defendants. The Appellate Division reversed and entered judgment in favor of plaintiffs. * * *

Defendants Rehac and Piatkowski claim title to their tract by deed from Kupire Corporation dated November 21, 1973 and recorded November 26 of that year. The claim of title to the other tract, asserted by Worth and Sharp, rests upon a deed from the same grantor, Kupire Corporation, dated September 13, 1971 and recorded the following day. Although the two sets of defendants received deeds to their respective tracts from a common grantor on different dates, their back titles, to the extent here relevant, are otherwise identical.

Plaintiffs' chain of title as well as the common chain of all defendants derives from a common grantor, the Asbury Company. By quitclaim deed, on February 12, 1913, Asbury Company conveyed to a corporation named Appleby Estates a tract of land which included all the property here in question. The description in the deed is not by metes and bounds, but merely by reference to the earlier deeds that had conveyed the various parcels to the grantor. The instrument was recorded February 18, 1913. On February 15 of the same year, Asbury Company conveyed the particular land here in question (apparently all the land now claimed by both sets of defendants) [24] to one Robert E. Taylor by warranty deed,[25] the tract being described by metes and bounds. Taylor did not record this deed until April 25, 1913. Plaintiffs claim through the Asbury Company–Appleby Estates (Appleby Estates) chain; defendants, through the Asbury Company–Taylor (Taylor) chain.

The next instrument in plaintiffs' chain of title is a warranty deed from Appleby Estates back to Asbury Company dated and recorded in 1924. The description by earlier deed references only describes the lands that had been conveyed by Asbury Company to Appleby Estates in 1913, together with an additional tract. The description, however, includes the following proviso:

> Excepting therefrom the following named conveyances made by the said party of the first part; 429 acres to Robert E. Taylor,

(There follow like references to a number of other excepted tracts.) "The said party of the first part" was, of course, Appleby Estates, the grantor named as such in the deed, and Appleby Estates had made no conveyance to Robert E. Taylor. The conveyance of 429 acres to him had been made by its predecessor in title, Asbury Company. The exception quoted above made no reference to the date of the deed to Taylor, nor to the book and page where it had been recorded.

The next significant transaction in the plaintiffs' chain of title occurred about 40 years later. On August 15, 1966, Asbury Company, Appleby Estates and Appleby & Wood Company [26] conveyed to Anthony J. Del Tufo Agency, Inc., by quitclaim deed,

---

24. Some deed descriptions are so imprecise that we cannot make this statement with absolute certainty.

25. Inadvertently, the Appellate Division described this deed as being one of bargain and sale. 159 N.J.Super. at 290,

387 A.2d 1233. This point has importance, as will be seen below.

26. An earlier owner of some of the property.

* * * all of the real property owned by the grantors herein, wherever situate within the boundaries of the County of Burlington in the State of New Jersey.

This instrument was accompanied by a second quitclaim deed, dated August 12, 1966, running in favor of Anthony J. Del Tufo Agency, Inc., and executed by 34 persons purporting to be "all of the surviving heirs at law of J. Randolph Appleby and Maria DuBois Appleby, his wife, and their respective spouses," as well as by the five executors of the last will and testament of J. Randolph Appleby, deceased. The description of the property in this deed reads as follows:

> Being all of the real property owned by the grantors herein, wherever situate within the boundaries of the County of Burlington in the State of New Jersey, to which any of them may have derived title through the estates of J. Randolph Appleby or Maria DuBois Appleby, his wife, or from Appleby and Wood Company, Appleby Estates, or the Asbury Company, all being corporations of the State of New Jersey.

Plaintiffs are successors in title, by virtue of a number of mesne conveyances, to the Del Tufo Agency.

Two observations should be made with respect to Appleby Estates' chain of title. First, all instruments in the chain are quitclaim deeds with the exception of the deed of reconveyance in 1924 from Appleby Estates to Asbury Company. It is urged by defendants that plaintiffs' position is fatally weakened by this fact. The law is well settled, however, that a quitclaim deed passes the same estate to a grantee as does a deed of bargain and sale. [ ] The point is, therefore, without significance.

Secondly, J. Randolph Appleby was president and majority stockholder of both Asbury Company and Appleby Estates. In his capacity as president of the former he executed the first conveyance from Asbury Company to Appleby Estates and as president of the latter he executed the deed of reconveyance. This fact may be significant.

The Taylor chain, upon which all defendants rely, can be simply described. It will be recalled that Taylor ostensibly took title from Asbury Company by deed dated February 15, 1913 and recorded April 25, 1913. Taylor and his wife thereafter conveyed to Ruth McCrae on July 7, 1932, by deed of bargain and sale with covenant against grantors' acts. The deed was recorded May 23, 1933. There follow a series of warranty deeds culminating in the conveyances to defendants described above. The descriptions in all deeds in this chain of title are by metes and bounds.

The Appellate Division decided that plaintiffs should prevail. While we agree with much of the reasoning of the Appellate Division, we have concluded, for reasons set forth below, that the judgment of that court should be vacated and the case remanded to the trial court for further proceedings consistent with what is set forth herein.

Generally speaking, and absent any unusual equity, a court should decide a question of title such as this in the way that will best support and maintain the integrity of the recording system. The underlying purpose of the Recording Act is clear.

> An historical study of the (Recording) Act, as well as an analysis of the cases interpreting it, leads to the conclusion that it was designed to compel the recording of instruments affecting title, for the ultimate purpose of permitting purchasers to rely upon the record title and to purchase and hold title to lands within this state with confidence. The means by which the compulsion to record is accomplished is by favoring a recording purchaser, both by empowering him to divest a former non-recording title owner and by preventing a subsequent purchaser from divesting him of title. This ability to deprive a prior and bona fide purchaser for value of his property shows a genuine favoritism toward a recording purchaser. It is a clear mandate that the recording purchaser be given every consideration permitted by the law, including all favorable presumptions of law and fact. It is likewise a clear expression that a purchaser be able to rely upon the record title. (Jones, The New Jersey Recording Act—A Study of its Policy, 12 Rutgers L.Rev. 328, 329–30 (1957))

This policy is clearly established in the New Jersey Recording Act, pertinent parts of which provide as follows:

> Except as otherwise provided herein, whenever any deed * * * shall have been or shall be duly recorded * * * such record shall, from that time, be notice to all subsequent * * * purchasers * * * of the execution of the deed * * * so recorded and of the contents thereof. (N.J.S.A. 46:21–1)

> Every deed * * * shall, until duly recorded * * *, be void and of no effect against * * * all subsequent bona fide purchasers * * * for valuable consideration, not having notice thereof, whose deed shall have been first duly recorded * * *. (N.J.S.A. 46:22–1)

This legislation makes New Jersey a "notice/race" type jurisdiction. 4 American Law of Property § 17.5, at 541–45 & n. 63 (Casner ed. 1952). This means that if a common grantor sells the same land to two persons, the first to record even though he may have been the second to purchase will prevail, but only so long as he had no actual notice of the earlier sale. Id. at 544.

We examine first the deed from Asbury Company to Appleby Estates dated February 12, 1913 and recorded six days later. It was executed by J. Randolph Appleby as president of Asbury Company. It is not denied that Appleby was also at that time president of the grantee corporation, Appleby Estates. He, alone or with his wife, owned a substantial majority of the shares of both corporations. In fact it may also be reasonably inferred from the rather meager record though not certainly determined that the other shareholders of both corporations were all members of the Appleby family. It was also in his capacity as president of Asbury Company that he executed the deed dated February 15, 1913 from that corporation to Robert E. Taylor.

Were it not for these facts, we would agree with the Appellate Division's conclusion that, because the Asbury Company–Appleby Estates deed was the first recorded, "Appleby Estates title was, in 1913, superior to that of Taylor * * *." 159 N.J.Super. at 292, 387 A.2d at 1236.

Although Taylor, had he been made aware of the conflicting conveyance to Appleby Estates, might have brought a suit for damages against Asbury Company on the warranty in his deed, it is much more likely that he would have sought equitable relief against Asbury Company, Appleby Estates and J. Randolph Appleby by way of cancellation or removal of cloud on title. Had there been such a title contest in 1913, Taylor would most surely have won. We need cite no authority to support the obvious conclusion that J. Randolph Appleby's personal knowledge of the deed to Taylor would have been attributed to Appleby Estates. As far as the rights of third persons were concerned, one corporation was simply the *alter ego* of the other, and both stood in that position with respect to J. Randolph Appleby. This would have prevented Appleby Estates from successfully asserting its prior recording as a defense to Taylor's claim. It is, therefore, imprecise to say that Appleby Estates' title was superior to Taylor's in 1913. There was, however, no title contest at that time.

The prospects for a successful title suit by Taylor would not have been diminished by the deed of reconveyance to Asbury Company in 1924.[27] Notice of the Taylor deed still would have been attributed to both Appleby Estates and Asbury Company. In 1924 the latter, upon reacquiring title, did not become a purchaser for value without notice. Up to this point an action by Taylor, of the kind suggested above, presumably would have succeeded.

The superiority of the Taylor chain fades, however, with the 1966 conveyances to the plaintiffs' predecessor in interest, the Del Tufo Agency. It will be recalled that Asbury Company conveyed to Appleby Estates by deed dated February 12, 1913 and recorded February 18, 1913. The Taylor deed was dated February 15, 1913 and recorded April 25 of the same year. Therefore, when the Del Tufo Agency took title by virtue of the two deeds of which mention is made above, it did not have record notice of the Taylor deed. A leading treatise states that:

> If after the recording of a deed from an owner there is later recorded another deed from the same grantor to a different grantee, whether earlier or later in date, a purchaser from the first grantee is without notice of any rights of the second grantee unless it is by reason of some fact other than the record; the purchaser's obligation to examine the grantor's indices as to that grantor ceased at the date of recording of the first deed. This principle has general application in the case of two successive deeds from the same grantor, both deeds recorded in the

27. The question raised by the exception contained in the deed of reconveyance as well as the issue of estoppel by deed presented thereby, are both discussed below.

order of their execution; a party thereafter purchasing from the first grantee is not charged with notice by reason of the record then existing of the second deed. (4 American Law of Property § 17.21, at 596–97 (Casner ed. 1952))

Although the New Jersey Recording Act appears to say that a subsequent purchaser will *always* be deemed to have notice of, and be bound by, a prior recorded deed touching the same property, this is not in fact the case. The statutes have been consistently interpreted to mean that the subsequent purchaser will be bound only by those instruments which can be discovered by a "reasonable" search of the particular chain of title. That is, a prospective purchaser need only search the records to discover conveyances or other significant acts of an owner from the date the deed into that person was recorded until the date he relinquishes record title. A leading case in New Jersey is Glorieux v. Lighthipe, 88 N.J.L. 199, 96 A. 94 (E. & A.1915). There Justice Swayze, speaking for a unanimous court said,

A purchaser may well be held bound to examine or neglect at his peril, the record of the conveyances under which he claims, but it would impose an intolerable burden to compel him to examine all conveyances made by every one in his chain of title. (88 N.J.L. at 203, 96 A. at 96)

* * *

Although it is thus clear that Del Tufo Agency had no record notice, it still may have had *actual* notice. Because the case was decided on motion for summary judgment, this particular point was not adequately explored. Defendants will be given an opportunity to examine that question on remand.[28]

On remand, except in the respect noted below, the court need not concern itself with the 1924 deed of reconveyance from Appleby Estates to Asbury Company containing, as it does, the exception with respect to 429 acres described as having been previously conveyed by Appleby Estates to Robert E. Taylor.[29] As we have seen, there had been no such conveyance by Appleby Estates, although there had been such a convey-

---

28. It is appropriate in this connection to bear in mind that defendants would not be entitled to succeed merely by showing that Del Tufo Agency had actual notice. It must also be shown that subsequent purchasers had such actual notice.

Unless the contrary appears from the record, the question of whether prior owners in a chain of title were innocent purchasers is not material to an examiner, provided only his client is such at the time he completes his purchase. This is because, in all jurisdictions, a purchaser without notice from an owner who has notice is protected. This is not peculiar to the recording acts, but is merely the application of a long-established equity doctrine as to the effect of notice. It is further the case that a purchaser will be protected, even though he has notice of an unrecorded title or claim, provided his vendor was an innocent purchaser. (Patton on Titles, § 15 at 68–69 (1938))

3 Pomeroy, Equity Jurisprudence §§ 754, 754a, at 55–61 (5th ed. 1941).

29. We do not wish to be understood as foreclosing the possibility that expert testimony presented on remand may suggest that the exception in this deed should be deemed sufficient notice to spur further inquiry. In this latter event, the point should be considered anew in the light of such evidence and relevant law.

ance by its predecessor in title, Asbury Company. Defendant argues that this recital of an exception should be deemed to constitute notice of the Taylor deed to subsequent purchasers in plaintiffs' chain of title. Although we reserve final judgment, we tentatively feel that contention lacks merit. The recital gives notice only of a non-existent conveyance. Had the exception either referred to the proper grantor—Asbury Company—or to the book and page where the record of the instrument could be found, then indeed there would have been notice. Here, both were lacking. Nevertheless, final decision on this point should await the taking of expert proofs on remand.

Defendants' final and most vigorously pressed argument is that they are entitled to prevail upon a proper application of the doctrine of estoppel by deed. This issue was not addressed by the Appellate Division, perhaps because, as mentioned above, that court mistakenly thought the deed from Asbury Company to Taylor to have been one of bargain and sale rather than of warranty. Defendants contend that even if Taylor did not acquire title to the premises in question in 1913—the deed to Appleby Estates having been first recorded—nevertheless he did acquire title in 1924 when the property was reconveyed to Asbury Company.

Under the well-settled doctrine of estoppel by deed, a grantor who executes a general warranty deed purporting to convey land to which he has no title will not be heard to claim title against his grantee, if he (the grantor) subsequently acquires title. [ ] It will be seen that an application of this doctrine would, presumptively at least, either place title in Taylor upon the execution and delivery of the deed of reconveyance from Appleby Estates to Asbury Company in 1924 or give Taylor a right to equitable relief by way of specific performance. Plaintiffs answer by saying that estoppel by deed operates only to vest title in the original grantee and his successors in interest if the grantor, subsequent to his acquisition of good title, does not thereafter convey the property to a purchaser for value without notice. Such a conveyance apparently took place, plaintiffs point out, upon the transfer of title to the Del Tufo Agency in 1966.

Whether under circumstances such as this, title should be held to inure to the original grantee and his successors or pass to the subsequent grantee has been the subject of much controversy. See 3 American Law of Property § 15.22, at 849–50 (Casner ed. 1952). The case law in our state clearly favors the subsequent purchaser for value without notice. [ ]

Furthermore, this conclusion is in conformity with the requirements of our Recording Act and supports the integrity of the recording system. See especially, Philbrick, Limits of Record Search and Therefore of Notice, 93 U.Pa.L.Rev. 125, 181–86 (1944). It is likely that a correctly undertaken title search by the Del Tufo Agency in 1966 or by any of its successors in title would not have discovered the original deed from Asbury Company to Taylor. * * *

There is a further point that must be considered, but which has been neither briefed nor argued. As we set forth at the beginning of this opinion, defendants Rehac and Piatkowski ostensibly acquired title to the premises which they claim to own in November 1973. We may take judicial notice of the fact that it is the custom of title searchers and conveyancers in New Jersey to search a title only for sixty years and until a warranty deed is found in the chain of title. A sixty-year search undertaken in November, 1973 would extend back to November, 1913. A further search for a warranty deed would presumably end upon discovery of the Asbury Company to Taylor deed recorded in April of that year. Thus the deed from Asbury Company to Appleby Estates would not be discovered. Would such a title search meet the customary requirements as established by conveyancing practice in New Jersey? If so, how much force should be given to this fact? Should we adopt the custom of conveyancers and make the sixty-year search convention a rule of law? How could this be made to harmonize with the Recording Act and other relevant statutes? To what extent and over what period of time has reliance been placed on the sixty-year search? How did this custom develop and upon what law does it rest? What is the attitude of title companies to the problem that this case presents? We would prefer not to decide questions with such potentially far-reaching effects in a factual vacuum.

We are mindful that the art of title searching, upon which so much of our conveyancing practice rests, has been created in very large part without the aid of legislation and has received little attention in judicial decisions.

> No statute has ever mentioned search, much less indicated the time or records over which it must extend * * *. (Philbrick, supra, 93 U.Pa. L.Rev. at 137)

On remand to the trial court, expert testimony should be offered and received as to the customs and usages of the conveyancing bar and title companies with respect to what has been discussed above. * * *

* * *

Notes and Questions

1. The principal case illustrates two of the most commonly discussed chain of title problems. The archetype of the first problem is as follows: First O transfers to A. A does not record. Then O transfers to B. B takes with notice of A's claim, but records. Subsequently A records. Then B transfers to C, who takes without notice of A's claim. Analytically, at the point O transferred to B, B would, in a notice or race-notice jurisdiction, take subordinate to A's interest, since B had notice of it. Since B's claim is subordinate to A's, C can only prevail in a dispute between C and A if C can prevail in her own right. Assuming C takes without actual or inquiry notice of A's claim, C will prevail unless A's interest is considered to be of prior record to C's claim. In fact, A's claim is recorded before C's, but to discover A's claim, C would have to make a title search more extensive

than that described above. C could not stop searching for O's name in the indices once the first recorded O to B transfer was found, but would need to keep searching forward until the prior in time, but later in record, O to A transfer was found. Presumably, C would then need to further inquire as to whether B had knowledge of the O to A transfer to determine if C could claim shelter under the O to B transfer.

The *Palamarg* case raised the problem of when a title examiner can cease searching the indices as to a particular grantor, and with some twisting, its facts can be made to fit the aforementioned archetype. The Asbury Company is obviously O, Taylor is A, and the February 15, 1913 transfer from Asbury Company to Taylor is the O to A transfer. The transfer from Asbury Company to Appleby Estates on February 12, 1913 is the O to B transfer. (In fact this transfer was prior in time to the Asbury to Taylor transfer, but because of the identity of Asbury and Appleby, the court is willing to subordinate the transfer between them to the transfer between Asbury and Taylor, effectively treating Appleby Estates as a B rather than an A.) Asbury Company, of course, is on notice of its earlier transfer to Taylor, and therefore cannot claim the benefit of the fact that Appleby recorded before Taylor. Del Tufo may, however, be the C, who takes without notice, and who will not find the A (Taylor) record because it appears after the Asbury to Appleby deed is recorded.

Is the solution *Palamarg* reaches to this conundrum, limiting C to a "reasonable" search and permitting C to win over A unless C in fact had notice of A's claim, consistent with the language of the recording acts? Is it consistent with their policy? Should the answer to this question vary depending on whether the jurisdiction is a race or race-notice jurisdiction? See 4 American Law of Property, § 17.22 (J. Casner ed. 1952); Philbrick, Limits of Record Search and Therefore of Notice, 93 U.Pa.L.Rev. 125, 391–440 (1944); Cross, The Record "Chain of Title" Hypocrisy, 57 Colum.L.Rev. 787, 793–794 (1957); Mattis, Recording Acts: Anachronistic Reliance, 25 Real Prop., Prob. & Trust J. 17, 40–55 (1990). The jurisdictions are split on this issue, though a majority of the cases that have addressed the issue favor a literal reading of the recording acts, and give the victory to A.

2. Many areas of the country employ a tract index rather than a grantor-grantee index for locating recorded documents.[30] Normally under a tract index system, each parcel of property in the locality is given a parcel-identifier number. This can usually be discovered by locating the parcel on a map which gives the identifier numbers. Each parcel will then be assigned a page (or several pages) in the property indices. As documents are recorded, the recorder indexes them with respect to each tract which they affect. In a jurisdiction with a tract index, a title examiner need only study the pages of the indices affecting that particular piece of property to discover any interests affecting a particular parcel of property.

Would a tract index solve the problem identified in the preceding note? How?

---

30. A recent survey of recorder's offices found that of the 1330 respondent jurisdictions, 1059 used grantor-grantee indices, 271 used a tract index, U.S. Dept of Agriculture, Economic Research Serv. Natl. Resource Economics Div., Information Contained in Real Property Transfer Records, Rep. No. A–GE–S–840711 (August 1984).

3. The second problem encountered in the *Palamarg* case can be described as follows: A transfers an interest in property which A does not own to B by warranty deed. B records. Then O, the previous owner, transfers the property interest to A and A records. (Note at this point that by virtue of the doctrine of estoppel by deed, A's interest in the property becomes B's.) Finally, A transfers the property interest to C, who takes without notice of the earlier transfer to B and records. Subsequently C and B both claim the property interest. Note that, literally, B has recorded before C, and therefore ought to take priority under the recording acts. Again, however, this result would dramatically expand the scope of search required of C. He cannot begin his search with respect to each grantor in the chain, but must go back beyond that point for an undetermined previous period of time.

Under the facts of the *Palamarg* case, B is Taylor, who was transferred an interest in the property by warranty deed by Asbury (the A) at a time when Asbury had no interest in the property. Asbury subsequently receives the property from Appleby Estates (O) but then transfers it to Del Tufo (C).

The result reached by the *Palamarg* case to this problem, that C triumphs over B, is consistent with the weight of authority, though there are some cases to the contrary, See 4 American Law of Property, § 17.20; Philbrick, 93 U.Pa.L.Rev. at 303–306; Cross, 57 Colum.L.Rev. at 794–796; Mattis, 25 Real Prop., Prob. & Trust J. at 40–55.

Would a tract index solve this problem? How?

4. *Palamarg* dismisses offhandedly the notion that grantees under a quitclaim deed should be entitled to less protection under the recording acts than grantees under a warranty deed. A few jurisdictions hold, however, that a quitclaim grantee cannot claim recording act protection. The most common argument for this result is that the grantor's lack of confidence in his own title should put the grantee on notice of potential adverse claims. Other cases argue that a quitclaim transfers only the interest of the grantor, which, where there has been a prior conveyance, is no interest at all. Modern cases, following two Supreme Court decisions, Moelle v. Sherwood, 148 U.S. 21, 13 S.Ct. 426, 37 L.Ed. 350 (1893) and United States v. California and Oregon Land Co., 148 U.S. 31, 13 S.Ct. 458, 37 L.Ed. 354 (1893), generally take the *Palamarg* approach.

5. Do the concluding paragraphs of the opinion suggest that the court is proposing judicial adoption of a marketable title act? (See Section F infra.) It is perhaps sensible for the court not to get tied up in the literal language of the recording act, instead limiting searches to a reasonable time period. Is the court suggesting, however, that the defendants would win in 1973, the plaintiffs in 1974, despite the multiple intervening transfers of the land?

BALL v. VOGTNER

Supreme Court of Alabama, 1978.
362 So.2d 894.

TORBERT, CHIEF JUSTICE.

Appellant, Kitty Ball, filed suit against appellees, William and Rebecca Vogtner, to establish a judgment lien on certain real property in Mobile County. The Vogtners filed an answer and a third party claim against cross-appellant Mississippi Valley Title Insurance Company (hereinafter referred to as Mississippi Valley). The Vogtners denied the validity of the judgment lien and raised the defense that they were good faith purchasers for value without notice of appellant's judgment, and the judgment recorded in the probate court was outside their chain of title. The third party claim averred that the Vogtners had purchased a title insurance policy from Mississippi Valley and, if they were liable to appellant, then Mississippi Valley was liable to them. Mississippi Valley filed an answer denying liability based upon a policy exclusion, and the Vogtners filed an amended third party complaint alleging timely notice of the claim and asserting an additional claim for failure to defend.

The appellant then, with leave of court, amended the complaint to join as parties defendant in the original action Cooper Realty Company, Martin Ramon and Barbara Jolene Carrera, and Mississippi Valley alleging against such defendants, and the Vogtners, a count for fraud and conspiracy. The trial court dismissed with prejudice the count for fraud as to all parties, but allowed appellant to amend the original action against the Vogtners as a suit to impress a lien against the property.

The case was tried on the issues of the superiority of the judgment lien and the title company's duty to defend. The court entered its final decree holding that the Vogtners had neither actual nor constructive knowledge of the judgment against Mary Morgan; therefore, the judgment did not constitute a lien against the property. Furthermore, the trial court determined that Mississippi Valley had a duty to defend and awarded the Vogtners $1800 for attorney fees. After denial of her motion for new trial, appellant filed this appeal. Cross-appellant Mississippi Valley appeals that portion of the trial court's order awarding the Vogtners attorney fees which was based on the trial court's finding that Mississippi Valley had the duty to defend the action of appellant.

Appellant filed suit for damages for assault and battery on May 20, 1971 in the Circuit Court of Mobile County against Mary Morgan. Appellant recovered a judgment against Mary Morgan and recorded the judgment on May 17, 1972. During the interim between the filing of suit and judgment, Mary Morgan married B.B. Collins and subsequently acquired the property in question. Although appellant and her attorney knew of the marriage at the time of entry of judgment, the judgment was entered against Mary Morgan, not Mary Collins.

On December 15, 1971, the property in question consisting of a house and lot was conveyed to Mary C. Collins as grantee by Leon Gavin and Margaret Susan Young Helton, grantors. Mary Collins conveyed the property to Martin and Barbara Carrera on October 10,

1973 by a deed reciting a valuable consideration including the assumption of an existing mortgage. However, Mary Collins remained in possession of the house and lot and made the installment payments on the mortgage in lieu of rent to the Carreras. Both deeds were recorded.

Subsequently, the Vogtners became interested in the property and contacted Cooper Realty Company which had the listing. A representative of the company took them to the house where Mrs. Collins showed them around. Mrs. Collins had placed the house with Cooper Realty. Believing Mrs. Collins to be the owner, the Vogtners submitted a written offer through the realtor naming Mrs. Collins as owner. This offer was rejected. However, a subsequent offer was accepted but was signed by the Carreras as owners. Upon the Vogtners' inquiry concerning the signature of the Carreras, the agent of the realty company replied that there were some marital problems and they didn't want the house mixed up in the divorce.

Later, Mrs. Collins contacted the Vogtners in an effort to rescind the transaction, so the Vogtners retained counsel, Mr. Walter Lee, to represent them in the purchase of the home. Mr. Lee came to the conclusion that the Carreras were "straw people," and Mrs. Collins was the real owner of the property. Accordingly, he required a letter of attornment from Mrs. Collins and that the Vogtners' check at closing be endorsed by the Carreras over to Mrs. Collins.

Attorney Lee, before commencement of his representation of the Vogtners, learned through social contacts with appellant that she might have a judgment against Mary Collins whom he knew at that time only as "Mary." At the closing, he told the representative of Mississippi Valley, Mrs. Flinn, that there might be a judgment against Mary Collins, but he never communicated such to the Vogtners. Mrs. Flinn quickly checked the company's in-house records and found no judgment against Mrs. Collins, and the transaction was closed.

* * *

Appellant * * * contends that the property should be subject to the judgment lien since the Vogtners had actual or constructive notice of the lien.

For a judgment to create a lien on the property of the defendant, a certificate must be filed in the office of the judge of probate of the county in which the property is situated which shows: (1) the style of the court which entered the judgment, (2) the amount and date thereof, (3) the amount of costs, (4) the names of the parties thereto, (5) the name of the plaintiff's attorney, and (6) the address of each defendant or respondent, as shown in the court proceedings. Ala.Code §§ 6–9–210 to 211 (1975). To create a lien, the statutory requirements as to the contents of the certificate must be strictly observed. [ ]

Appellant properly filed a certificate; however, she listed the judgment debtor as Mary Morgan instead of Mary Collins. The certificate, as filed, does establish a valid lien between appellant and Mary

Collins, but not as to the Vogtners since the name shown in the certificate is insufficient to impart constructive notice to third parties.

As between the judgment creditor and judgment debtor a judgment may afford a valid lien despite inaccuracies or omissions in the docket or index in respect of the names or descriptions of the parties. In order to make the lien of a judgment effective as against third persons, however, it is ordinarily necessary that the docket and index should disclose the names of both parties, plaintiff as well as defendant, and designate them with such a degree of accuracy as to charge persons searching such records with notice of the judgments or to put them on inquiry. [ ]

Mary Collins both acquired and conveyed title to the property in her name as such. Nowhere in the Vogtners' chain of title does the name Mary Morgan appear. The Vogtners possessed no facts sufficient to put them on inquiry or to enable them to discover the existence of the judgment lien against Mary Morgan. An instrument executed by a married woman in her name prior to marriage without mention of her married name imparts no notice. [ ] 8 G. Thompson, Commentaries on the Modern Law of Real Property § 4300, at 275 (1963). In the absence of actual knowledge, the purchaser is charged with notice of that which appears on the face of all the instruments by which he takes title, but is not bound to inquire into collateral circumstances. [ ] A reasonable search of the records in the instant case would have revealed nothing of the judgment lien since the parties would be searching under the name Mary Collins, not Mary Morgan.

The Vogtners had no actual notice of the judgment lien. Their attorney did not inform them of the possibility of a judgment against Mrs. Collins. To impart constructive notice to the Vogtners, the certificate would have to be in their chain of title. [ ] Since it was not, the only way for the Vogtners to have any knowledge of the judgment is if the knowledge of their attorney, Mr. Lee, is imputed to them.

Our cases hold that for knowledge of the attorney to be imputed to the client, the knowledge must have come to the attorney while engaged in a service for his client after the attorney-client relationship began. [ ] "Information to an agent is not notice to the principal when given to the agent upon a casual conversation at a time when he is not engaged in business for his principal and no act or transaction of the agency is then pending." [ ] Mr. Lee acquired his knowledge of the possibility of a judgment during a "casual conversation" with social acquaintances approximately two years before his representation of the Vogtners; therefore, any knowledge he may have possessed is not imputed to the Vogtners. Since the Vogtners had neither actual nor constructive notice of the judgment lien, they acquired the property free of the lien.

Cross-appellant Mississippi Valley contends that it had no duty to defend the action against the Vogtners since a policy exclusion exempts the judgment lien from coverage. Therefore, awarding the Vogtners attorney fees was improper.

The policy provided that "(t)he company, at its own cost and without undue delay, shall provide for the defense of the insured in all litigations * * * founded upon defect, lien or encumbrance insured against by this policy." The policy expressly excluded from coverage: "(D)efects, liens, encumbrances, adverse claims against the title as insured or other matters * * * known to the Insured either at the date of this policy or at the date such Insured acquired an estate or interest insured by this policy and not shown by the public records, unless disclosure thereof in writing by the Insured shall have been made to the company prior to the date of the policy * * *." Public records are defined in the policy as "those records which impart constructive notice of matters relating to said land."

The certificate in this case did not impart constructive notice of the lien because it contained the judgment debtor's maiden name only, and accordingly, was outside the Vogtners' chain of title. The name Mary Morgan was insufficient to alert anyone interested in the property as to the existence of the lien. Therefore, the lien was not "shown by public records" and would be excluded from coverage if the Vogtners had knowledge of it and failed to notify the company in writing. However, since the Vogtners had no knowledge, either actual or constructive, of the judgment lien, the lien was not within those defects excluded by the policy and Mississippi Valley was obligated to defend.

For the above mentioned reasons, the order of the trial court is due to be affirmed.

AFFIRMED.

Notes and Questions

1. As the court views the facts in the principal case, it presents the classical wild deed problem: A (Mary Morgan) transfers Orangeacre to B (Kitty Ball), then O (Mary Collins), the record owner, transfers it to C (the Vogtners). (Here we have, of course, a variation on the classical problem in that O and A are, in fact, the same person. Normally A would be a complete stranger to the chain of title in which O was found.) A standard title search by C, as described above, will never find A's deed to B. How extensive a search would C have to carry out to find it? Courts uniformly rule for the subsequent purchaser without notice in this situation.

2. Who could most easily protect himself or herself in the principal case, Ms. Ball or the Vogtners? What would each have had to do to assure protection of his or her interest?

3. Would a tract index solve this problem? How?

4. Variances in names can arise not just from changes in marital status, but also from spelling variants and misspellings, or from variant usage of given names and initials. A reasonable title search should not require an examiner to check different letters of the alphabet for the same surname (Jost and Yost, Coons and Kuhns), but might require checking for

variant spellings beginning with the same letter (Frazier and Fraser, Johnson and Johnstone). See 4 American Law of Property § 17.18 (J. Casner ed. 1952).

5. Why are the Vogtners not treated as having "actual knowledge" of Ms. Ball's claim, since their attorney was aware of it? Is the decisive fact here that the information was obtained by their attorney through a "casual conversation" or that it was obtained before the attorney-client relationship began? The first question goes to what constitutes "actual notice" under the recording acts. Should it be sufficient to charge B with actual notice of A's claim that B is aware of the assertion of a claim, or must B have knowledge of the validity of the adverse claim? Surely the former information could be obtained through a casual conversation, the latter might require more. If a casual conversation cannot give actual knowledge of a claim, can it give inquiry notice? If so, was the extent of the inquiry in the principal case sufficient? See 6A R. Powell & P. Rohan, Powell on Real Property, ¶ 905[1][d]; Philbrick, Limits of Record Search and Therefore of Notice, 93 U.Pa.L.Rev. 125, at 259–273 (1944).

Turning to the second issue, under what circumstances should the knowledge of an attorney be attributed to a client? Clearly, if the information is gained during the attorney-client relationship as a result of work done for the client, it is attributable to the client. What if, however, the attorney became aware of the claim during a previous title search of the same property, for example for a previous owner? What if he learned of it representing Ms. Morgan Collins in previous litigation? What if he learned of it representing Ms. Ball? If, by the way, the attorney had represented Ms. Ball in the earlier litigation, would he have an ethical obligation to decline to represent the Vogtners in their efforts to purchase the property? See A.B.A. Model Rules 1.6, 1.9.

6. The Vogtners failed to discover the Ball claim because it was indexed under Ms. Collins' maiden name. Assume, however, that the lien was properly filed against Ms. Collins, but the recorder erroneously failed to index it, or indexed it under the wrong name or with respect to the wrong property (i.e., the legal description of the property in the index was in error). Should the courts treat such an improperly indexed document as a wild deed, and consider a subsequent purchaser to be without notice of it? Or should the court hold that once the instrument is recorded with the recorder, all subsequent purchasers have constructive notice of it? Who can most easily avoid this problem? What must Bs do to find such improperly indexed documents? What must As do to avoid mis-indexing?

In most states the first purchaser must make sure that in fact her instrument is placed of record. The effect of subsequent indexing errors, however, is less certain. The majority of states have held that a subsequent purchaser can be held to have constructive notice of a recorded claim even though it was not properly indexed. Brown v. United States, 496 F.Supp. 903 (D.N.J. 1980); Luthi v. Evans, 223 Kan. 622, 576 P.2d 1064 (1978); Cross, The Record "Chain of Title" Hypocrisy, 57 Colum.L.Rev. 787, 790–793 (1957). A significant minority, however, (probably representing the modern trend) hold that proper indexing is necessary to proper recording, Compiano v. Jones, 269 N.W.2d 459 (Iowa 1978); Badger v. Benfield, 78

N.C. App. 427, 337 S.E.2d 596 (1985). A party injured by recorder error may be able to sue the recorder, if permitted to do so by state law. Recovery will usually be limited to the amount of the recorder's bond, however, which is usually very low by modern standards. See Basye, A Uniform Land Parcel Identifier—Its Potential for All our Land Records, 22 Am.U.L.Rev. 251, n. 29 at 262 (1973).

7. A fourth situation in which the common law definition of "chain of title" may triumph over the literal words of the recording act commonly occurs in subdivision development. In the archetypical example of this problem, O conveys parcel 1 to A, conveying with it a servitude of some sort (easement, real covenant, equitable servitude) in his retained property. Subsequently he conveys parcel 2 to B, in which he previously granted a servitude when he transferred parcel 1 to A. If B searches only for transactions affecting parcel 2, she will not find the previously conveyed servitude unless the deed to parcel 1 was indexed as affecting parcel 2. There are, in effect, two chains of title branching from a common root.

Which party can more easily avoid the loss in this situation, the owner of parcel 1 or of parcel 2? Note that the deed to A here was from O, a grantor in B's chain of title, so the problem faced by B may not be as unmanageable as in other cases. Nevertheless, in large subdivisions with hundreds of lots the search can still be very burdensome. Would a tract index resolve this problem? Why or why not?

The courts seem fairly split on this issue. See 6A R. Powell & P. Rohan, Powell on Real Property, ¶ 906[2][b][iii]; Bishop v. Rueff, chapter six below.

8. The problem raised by the subdivision hypothetical is often resolved through a finding that B had inquiry notice of A's claim. If B purchases a property that clearly has a driveway leading across it to a neighboring property, the purchaser can realistically be required to inquire as to whether the neighbor owns an easement. The concept of inquiry notice is somewhat more problematic when applied to restrictions on the use of property imposed by real covenants and equitable servitudes. Should a purchaser in a subdivision be held responsible for inquiring as to the possible existence of restrictions limiting the property to residential use simply because all properties in the subdivision are occupied with dwelling units? See Sanborn v. McLean, 233 Mich 227, 206 N.W. 496, 60 A.L.R. 1212 (1925) (yes). Should the fact that all buildings in a subdivision are set back the same uniform distance from the street alert a purchaser to inquire regarding setback requirements?

9. The subdivision problem can easily be avoided. The subdivider can, for example, prior to subdividing the property, deed the entire subdivision to a straw and then back to himself with restrictions and easements attached. The servitudes are then easily discoverable in the chain of title of each purchaser in the subdivision. Alternatively, the subdivider can record a declaration of restrictions and reference it in every deed in the subdivision. Finally, in many jurisdictions he can record a plat for the subdivision, reciting restrictions and easements, which puts any purchaser of lots in the subdivision on notice of them. The paucity of cases in recent

years raising the subdivision problem indicates that subdividers are in fact pursuing these strategies.

E. NOTICE

HATCHER v. HALL

Court of Appeals of Missouri, 1956.
292 S.W.2d 619.

STONE, JUDGE.

In this action for a declaratory judgment [ ], plaintiff seeks a determination of rights and status under a written agreement between C.E. and Helen Whartenby, as "lessors," and Melvin Hall (one of the defendants herein), as "lessee," dated July 1, 1941, and recorded in the office of the Recorder of Deeds of McDonald County, Missouri, on September 20, 1941. (Except as otherwise specifically stated, statutory references herein are to RSMo 1949, V.A.M.S.) By this agreement, the "lessors," for a recited consideration of "One Dollar and other valuable consideration," purported to "lease, grant, bargain and sell unto the lessee the exclusive right to furnish all gasoline and oil products to be sold at a certain filling station" on a described tract (hereinafter called "the tract") at Lanagan, McDonald County, Missouri (then owned by the Whartenbys and presently owned by plaintiff), "for a period of ten years from the date of this instrument," with the further provision that "at any time said station is no longer used * * * to dispense motor fuel and lubricants, then this agreement shall suspend during such discontinuance and if re-opened then this agreement shall be reinstated and the time that such station was not being operated shall not run against this lease." By its terms, the agreement was "binding upon any and all persons or corporations which take possession of said premises" and granted to the "lessee * * * prior rights to renew this agreement for a like period of time." Since the case was tried below and has been presented here on that theory, we assume for the purposes of this opinion (without, however, so deciding) that the agreement was an instrument "whereby * * * real estate may be affected" [Section 442.-380], and that the obligation, which it purported to impose, might run with the land; and, adopting the terminology of the parties, we hereinafter refer to the agreement as "the lease."

Defendant Hall, a distributor of Phillips "66" products, supplied the filling station on the tract until the Whartenbys closed the station in September, 1946; but, the evidence is clear and undisputed that, when Gilbert F. Willard (joined as a defendant herein) purchased the tract on July 28, 1950, there were no pumps or "filling station equipment" on the tract, the abstract of title to the tract did not show the lease, and defendant Willard had no knowledge of it. As will become apparent from our subsequent discussion, we think it unnecessary to resolve the issue of credibility raised by the sharply-conflicting testimony as to whether Willard thereafter learned of the lease during the period of his ownership. "Right after" he purchased the tract, Willard leased a portion of it to one Norman Gast; and, under "a reseller's contract" with Gast, defendant Hall installed storage tanks, two pumps and some signs on the tract and supplied Phillips "66" products to Gast, who operated a filling station thereon from August 11, 1950, until he "went broke" about June 30, 1951.

When plaintiff purchased the tract from defendant Willard on May 15, 1952, a cafe and package liquor store were being operated on the tract, but the filling station was not in operation. The only description of the unused station equipment then on the tract came from plaintiff who said that there were "two abandoned pumps at the place," which "were broken down, doors off of them" and "weren't in condition to work," that there were "a couple of light globes, they were off," and that there was "a Phillips sign * * * at the other end of the property." At the time of his purchase, plaintiff was informed by Willard that Hall owned the filling station equipment on the tract. However, Willard also told plaintiff that he (Willard) had asked Hall "to come get those pumps"; and, in response to plaintiff's specific inquiry as to whether "Hall had any kind of lease whatsoever," Willard had replied, "No, he has not." The abstract of title still did not show the lease, and the conveyance by Willard to plaintiff made no reference thereto. Plaintiff first learned of the lease about two months after the date of his purchase of the tract, when defendant Hall notified plaintiff of his (Hall's) intention to enforce the lease. Upon the foregoing state of facts, the trial court found that plaintiff "had no actual knowledge or constructive notice of the lease" and that "the lease is not binding" upon the tract. Defendant Hall appeals.

The first issue is as to whether plaintiff, a subsequent purchaser of the tract, is charged with constructive notice of the lease by reason of its recordation on September 20, 1941. Plaintiff's position is that, for the reason (inter alia) that the acknowledgment was incomplete and insufficient, the lease was not entitled to record and that, therefore, recordation thereof did not impart constructive notice. The "acknowledgment" on the lease consists of the simple statement "Subscribed and sworn to before me this the 15th day of August, 1941," followed by the signature (without seal attached) of one "B.F. St. Clair," whose official status or position (if any) is not suggested and who remains utterly unidentified either in the lease or in the record before us.

We quickly recognize that the language of Section 442.210 (including the forms of acknowledgment which "may be used in * * * written instruments affecting real estate") is permissive and not mandatory, and we heartily endorse the salutary principle, which has found application in a variety of circumstances, that substantial compliance with statutory provisions pertaining to acknowledgments will suffice. But, although the law requires nothing more than such substantial compliance, it is satisfied with nothing less. And, since the power to take acknowledgments is derived from the statutory provisions pertaining thereto and acknowledgments may be taken only by a person designated by statute [ ], we do not impose "hypercritical requirements of technical nicety" [   ] in concluding, as we do, that "no rational liberality of construction can cure" [   ] the patent defects in the "acknowledgment" to the lease in the instant case, which does not even indicate whether the individual purporting to take such "acknowledgment" in 1941 was a person then authorized so to do. Section 3408, RSMo 1939. Lacking an acknowledgment substantially complying with statutory requirements, the lease was not entitled to record [see Sections 442.380 and 59.330(1)], and recordation thereof did not impart constructive notice under Section 442.390 to plaintiff, a subsequent purchaser for value.

* * *

Finally, defendant Hall asserts that plaintiff's knowledge, when he purchased the tract, that Hall owned the filling station equipment thereon should have provoked further investigation which would have disclosed existence of the lease, and that, therefore, plaintiff is chargeable with actual notice thereof. It is true that, as our courts have reiterated many times, notice is regarded in law as actual where the person sought to be charged therewith either knows of the existence of the particular fact in question or is conscious of having the means of knowing it, even though such means may not be employed by him; and that, since notice does not mean positive information brought directly home to the person sought to be affected thereby, whatever fairly is sufficient to put an ordinarily prudent person on inquiry constitutes notice to him of such facts as would be disclosed by reasonable pursuit and proper inquiry. For, justice is not so indulgent as to encourage one to shut his eyes to circumstances which would excite the zetetic impulse in an ordinarily prudent individual [   ] or to throw away the key to the door of exploration through which the facts reasonably might be ascertained [   ]; and, from early times, our courts "have always recognized that the still small voice of suggestion, emanating as it will from contiguous facts and surrounding circumstances, pregnant with inference and provocative of inquiry, is as potent to impart notice as a presidential proclamation, or an army with banners." [   ]

However, one is put on inquiry and charged with notice of the facts which would be disclosed thereby, only when "the inquiry becomes a duty, and the failure to make it a negligent omission" [   ] or, as otherwise stated, "(w)here there is a duty of finding out and knowing, negligent ignorance has the same effect in law as actual knowledge." Whether the circumstances are sufficient to give rise to a duty of further inquiry is ordinarily a question of fact [at least where the evidence is conflicting or is such that more than one inference of fact might be drawn therefrom (Merrill on Notice, Vol. 1, Section 64, p. 61)], frequently fraught with appreciable difficulty and always determinable in the light of the circumstances of the particular case under consideration; and whether, when one is put on inquiry, the exercise of common prudence and ordinary diligence [   ] in further investigation would have led to discovery of the information, knowledge of which is sought to be charged, likewise usually becomes a question of fact.

Being mindful that one of these questions of fact necessarily was found in favor of plaintiff [ ] and that, in this court-tried case, "(t)he judgment shall not be set aside unless clearly erroneous, and due regard shall be given to the opportunity of the trial court to judge of the credibility of the witnesses" [ ], we would not be inclined, upon the record before us, to disagree with the finding of the capable trial judge that plaintiff did not have actual notice of the lease. However, we need not and do not rest disposition of the case on this basis alone, for, on the undisputed testimony, defendant Willard, who was plaintiff's immediate predecessor in title, acquired the tract on July 28, 1950, as a bona fide purchaser for value without notice, either actual or constructive, of the lease. "(I)t is a commonplace of the law of real property that an innocent purchaser for value takes the title discharged of secret outstanding equities * * * not of record, and that, having a good title himself, he can transfer one to a grantee who even had notice" [subject only to the exception that the title may not be conveyed, free from such equities, to a former owner charged with notice [ ], the classic statement of the reason for the rule, in the words of Chancellor Kent, being "to prevent a stagnation of property, and because the first purchaser, being entitled to hold and enjoy, must be equally entitled to sell." Thus, the title to the tract being clear of "silent, unknown equities" when defendant Willard purchased in 1950 remained clear thereafter [ ] and so descended to plaintiff, a purchaser for value, irrespective of whether he had actual notice of the lease at the time of his acquisition.

The judgment of the trial court should be and is affirmed.

Notes and Questions

1. The "shelter rule," relied on by the court in *Hatcher v. Hall,* is a powerful tool for resolving recording act disputes. If O conveys to A, who fails to record, and then to B, who takes without notice (and in a race or race-notice jurisdiction records before A), it does not matter that C, a subsequent purchaser from B, has actual, constructive, or inquiry notice of A's claim. C is sheltered by B's good title.

2. Most states require that prior to recordation, an instrument affecting title to property must be witnessed or acknowledged. Some jurisdictions further require seals or transfer stamps. Where documents do not comply with these recording technicalities, they have no standing of record and do not give constructive notice to subsequent purchasers. See Messersmith v. Smith, 60 N.W.2d 276 (N.D.1953); 4 American Law of Property, §§ 17.27, 17.31 (J. Casner ed. 1952).

3. If Hatcher (or his attorney) had discovered the improperly acknowledged lease while searching the title to the property, would he have actual notice of it, and not be able to claim bona fide purchaser status? Alternatively, would his actual discovery of the defectively acknowledged lease put him on inquiry notice of Hall's claim, i.e. would he have a duty to inquire as to the validity of Hall's claim? How would Hatcher's status be affected if Willard had actually discovered the improperly acknowledged lease? Does the language of the recording acts set out above help with this

problem? See 6A R. Powell & P. Rohan, Powell on Real Property, ¶ 906[1]; Philbrick, Limits of Record Search and Therefore of Notice, 93 U.Pa.L.Rev. 125 at 281–296 (1944).

4. Recorded documents actually reviewed by a title examiner may also, in some instances, give notice of unrecorded claims. If a recorded document, for example, refers specifically to an unrecorded mortgage, or to a mortgage recorded outside of the purchaser's chain of title, most jurisdictions would hold the purchaser to a duty of inquiry to determine the status of the mortgage. Specific reference in a recorded interest to a deed on a specific date between two specific parties should probably excite the curiosity of a title examiner to determine whether such a document ever existed, and, if so, whether it supports an existing claim to the property. Many deeds, however, contain general exceptions such as "subject to existing encumbrances." Do such phrases give notice of anything? More specific statements such as "subject to existing mortgages" or "excepting so much of the described premises as have been heretofore conveyed" are more problematic. Though cases have imposed a duty of inquiry where such phrases appear in recorded documents, such decisions obviously have potential for undermining the protection the recording acts are supposed to afford subsequent purchasers. Thus some reform statutes take approaches similar to that of the Uniform Simplification of Land Transfers Act § 3–207(a):

> Unless a reference in a document is a reference to another document by its record location, a person by reason of the reference is not charged with knowledge of the document or an adverse claim founded thereon, and the document is not in the record chain of title by reason of the reference to it.

5. A purchaser of real property cannot rest secure even with a completely clear title examination unless the property itself has also been inspected. Signs of possession of the property inconsistent with the record should stimulate the "zetetic impulse" of potential purchasers as to adverse claims. Thus a purchaser is held, in most jurisdictions, to have inquiry notice of any claims that could have been discovered by an inspection of the premises.

Possession by a tenant in many jurisdictions gives notice, not only of the tenant's interest under her lease, but also of any other claims the tenant may have, such as the option in the principal case. Moreover, possession not only gives notice of the claim of the possessor, but also of those through whom the possessor claims. Thus, possession by a tenant gives notice of the landlord's title, possession by a vendee under an installment sales contract gives notice of the vendor's title. Possession consistent with the record, however, does not give notice of unrecorded claims of the party in possession. Thus, possession of property by a wife as a tenant in common with her husband under a recorded deed does not put a purchaser on notice of the fact that she also claims under an unrecorded quitclaim deed from the husband of his interest. Ildvedsen v. First State Bank, 24 N.D. 227, 139 N.W. 105 (1912). Possession is not limited to human occupancy. A form of possession adequate to ground a claim for adverse possession is likely also to be sufficient to put a purchaser on inquiry notice of a claim to the property.

F. TITLE RECORD REFORM

It should be clear by now that public title recording systems, as they have evolved in America, are far from perfect. An A may not be protected by the system, even if she promptly records her interest in a property, if: (i) a recording technicality is not properly complied with; (ii) the interest is not properly indexed (in some jurisdictions); or (iii) the record of the interest, for whatever reason, falls outside of the chain of title of a subsequent B. Bs are even more at risk of prior interests recorded outside of their chain of title or not subject to the recording acts.

Several approaches have been proposed, and to varying extents adopted, for improving the protections afforded property owners by public recording systems. First, a variety of statutes address specific defects such as defective acknowledgments, or problematic interests such as ancient mortgages or rights of entry and possibilities of reverter. More radical reform is offered by the marketable title acts, which attempt to set a statutory limit to the scope of a search necessary to identify interests affecting a piece of property, and eliminate interests recorded outside such a limited search. Finally, the most radical reform is title registration, which attempts to make the title records the sole and authoritative source of authentic title.

1. Specific Statutory Reform

Among the most basic of title reforms are curative acts. A curative act is "a form of retroactive legislation which reaches back into the past to operate upon past events, acts or transactions in order to correct errors and irregularities and to render valid and effective many attempted acts which would otherwise be ineffective for the purpose intended." Bayse, Clearing Land Titles § 201 (2d ed. 1970). Curative acts are generally aimed at specific types of commonly occurring mistakes and errors, and normally operate by validating acts taken before a certain date. Often they address trivial problems that are unlikely to result in litigation, but nevertheless clog commerce in real estate as overly scrupulous or anxious lawyers "fly-speck" a title.

One of the most common problems addressed by curative acts is that of formalities of recorded instruments, such as defective acknowledgments or missing seals. The Ohio statute is typical:

Ohio Rev.Code § 5301.07

> When any instrument conveying real estate, or any interest therein, is of record for more than twenty-one years * * * and the record shows that there is a defect in such instrument, such instrument and the record thereof shall be cured of such defect and be effective in all respects as if such instrument had been legally made, executed, and acknowledged, if such defect is due to any one or more of the following:

(A) Such instrument was not properly witnessed.

(B) Such instrument contained no certificate of acknowledgment.

(C) The certificate of acknowledgment was defective in any respect.

Curative acts also address defects regarding the capacity of the parties to an instrument or the interests of persons not explicitly parties to the instrument. Examples of such defects include improper exercise of powers of attorney, conveyances by corporate officers which are not properly authorized or not signed in representative capacity, conveyances by trustees, executors, or foreclosing mortgagees not fully complying with proper formalities, and conveyances without proper release of dower or homestead rights by the grantor's spouse. See Bayse, supra §§ 261–355. These defects are often not apparent from the face of the record, and are thus troublesome to a purchaser who desires a perfectly secure title. With respect to these problems, curative acts usually provide that if the defect is not raised to challenge the rights of a subsequent purchaser within a specified period of time, it cannot be raised thereafter.

Other statutes aim at specific troublesome interests. One common target of such statutes is ancient mortgages. Prior to this century, property was often purchased with borrowed money secured by short-term lump-sum mortgages. In time these mortgages were usually paid off, but often no formal discharge was recorded. Moreover, when mortgages were not paid off in a timely manner, payment was often extended through extension agreements or partial payment. Agreed-upon extensions were often not reflected on the record. Although suit on a mortgage is eventually barred by the statute of limitations, partial payment during the statutory period may extend the limitations period. As a result, within the title chains of many properties in the United States are found ancient mortgages of uncertain legal status. Ancient mortgage statutes address this problem, See Bayse, supra, ch. 5. The Oklahoma statute is a good example of such legislation:

Okl.St.Ann. tit. 46 § 301

A. No suit, action or proceeding to foreclose or otherwise enforce the remedies in any mortgage, contract for deed or deed of trust shall be had or maintained after the expiration of ten (10) years from the date the last maturing obligation secured by such mortgage, contract for deed or deed of trust becomes due as set out therein, and such mortgage, contract for deed or deed of trust shall cease to be a lien, unless the holder of such mortgage, contract for deed or deed of trust either:

* * *

2. After October 1, 1981, and within the above described ten-year period, files or causes to be filed of record a written notice of extension * * *

B. No suit, action or proceeding to foreclose or otherwise enforce the remedies in any mortgage, contract for deed or deed of trust filed of record in the office of the county clerk, in which the due date of the last maturing obligation secured by such mortgage, contract for deed or deed of trust cannot be ascertained from the written terms thereof, shall be had or maintained after the expiration of thirty (30) years from the date of recording of the mortgage, contract for deed or deed of trust, and said mortgage, contract for deed or deed of trust shall cease to be a lien, unless the holder of such mortgage, contract for deed or deed of trust either:

* * *

2. After October 1, 1981, and within the above described thirty-year period, files or causes to be filed of record a written notice of maturity date * * *

* * *

D. Any mortgage, contract for deed or deed of trust barred under this act shall not be a defect in determining marketable record title.

Similar statutes address the problem of ancient possibilities of reverter and rights of entry. As you remember, these interests are not subject to the rule against perpetuities and thus can persist almost indefinitely. Statutes limiting such interests take several different approaches. Some of the earlier statutes barred covenants, conditions and restrictions of "merely nominal, and of no actual and substantial benefit," Minn.Stat.Ann. § 500.20, effectively applying the equitable "changed conditions doctrine" to such interests. Other statutes bar such interests absolutely after a period of time, or bar such interests if not rerecorded within a statutory period. Unlike ancient repaid or abandoned mortgages, reversionary interests often serve an ongoing purpose in restricting land to a specific charitable or public purpose. Some state courts have therefore held statutes cutting them off to be unconstitutional as denying due process or impairing contract rights, Board of Educ. v. Miles, 15 N.Y.2d 364, 259 N.Y.S.2d 129, 207 N.E.2d 181 (1965); Biltmore Village v. Royal Baltimore Village, 71 So.2d 727 (Fla.1954). Other courts have held that the goal of protecting land from stale interests that unreasonably restrict the use of that land to be sufficiently important to justify such legislation, Trustees of Schools v. Batdorf, 6 Ill.2d 486, 130 N.E.2d 111 (1955); Presbytery of Southeast Iowa v. Harris, 226 N.W.2d 232 (Iowa 1975).

2. Marketable Title Acts

By the mid-twentieth century, advocates of conveyancing reform realized that piece-meal solutions were not adequate. The increasing frequency and variety of recorded interests affecting land made traditional title searches more cumbersome and less certain. What was needed was a new approach; one that would radically cut off dormant and outdated interests and limit the period of necessary search. See Aigler, Clearance of Land Titles—A Statutory Step, 44 Mich.L.Rev. 45 (1945); Basye, Trends and Progress—The Marketable Title Acts, 47

Iowa L.Rev. 261 (1962); Cribbet, Conveyancing Reform, 35 N.Y.U.L.Rev. 1291 (1960). In response to this need, a number of states enacted marketable title legislation. These formed the basis for the Model Marketable Title Act, drafted by Professor Lewis Simes and Charles Taylor in conjunction with the Michigan Research Project. L. Simes and C. Taylor, The Improvement of Conveyancing by Legislation (1960). The Ohio statute, to a considerable extent, tracks this Model.

OHIO REV.CODE §§ 5301.47 ET SEQ.

§ 5301.47 Definitions

As used in sections 5301.47 to 5301.56, inclusive, of the Revised Code:

(A) "Marketable record title" means a title of record, as indicated in section 5301.48 of the Revised Code, which operates to extinguish such interests and claims, existing prior to the effective date of the root of title, as are stated in section 5301.50 of the Revised Code.

(B) "Records" includes probate and other official public records, as well as records in the office of the recorder of the county in which all or part of the land is situate.

(C) "Recording," when applied to the official public records of the probate or other court, includes filing.

(D) "Person dealing with land" includes a purchaser of any estate or interest therein, a mortgagee, levying or attaching creditor, a land contract vendee, or any other person seeking to acquire an estate or interest therein, or impose a lien thereon.

(E) "Root of title" means that conveyance or other title transaction in the chain of title of a person, purporting to create the interest claimed by such person, upon which he relies as a basis for the marketability of his title, and which was the most recent to be recorded as of a date forty years prior to the time when marketability is being determined. The effective date of the "root of title" is the date on which it is recorded.

(F) "Title transaction" means any transaction affecting title to any interest in land, including title by will or descent, title by tax deed, or by trustee's, assignee's, guardian's, executor's, administrator's, or sheriff's deed, or decree of any court, as well as warranty deed, quit claim deed, or mortgage.

* * *

§ 5301.48 Unbroken chain of recorded title

Any person having the legal capacity to own land in this state, who has an unbroken chain of title of record to any interest in land for forty years or more, has a marketable record title to such interest as defined in section 5301.47 of the Revised Code, subject to the matters stated in section 5301.49 of the Revised Code.

A person has such an unbroken chain of title when the official public records disclose a conveyance or other title transaction, of record not less than forty years at the time the marketability is to be determined, which said conveyance or other title transaction purports to create such interest, either in:

(A) The person claiming such interest; or

(B) Some other person from whom, by one or more conveyances or other title transactions of record, such purported interest has become vested in the person claiming such interest; with nothing appearing of record, in either case, purporting to divest such claimant of such purported interest.

* * *

§ 5301.49 Record marketable title; exceptions

Such record marketable title shall be subject to:

(A) All interests and defects which are inherent in the muniments of which such chain of record title is formed; provided that a general reference in such muniments, or any of them, to easements, use restrictions, or other interests created prior to the root of title shall not be sufficient to preserve them, unless specific identification be made therein of a recorded title transaction which creates such easement, use restriction, or other interest; * * *;

(B) All interest preserved by the filing of proper notice or by possession by the same owner continuously for a period of forty years or more, in accordance with section 5301.51 of the Revised Code;

(C) the rights of any person arising from a period of adverse possession or user, which was in whole or in part subsequent to the effective date of the root of title;

(D) Any interest arising out of a title transaction which has been recorded subsequent to the effective date of the root of title from which the unbroken chain of title or record is started; provided that such recording shall not revive or give validity to any interest which has been extinguished prior to the time of the recording by the operation of section 5301.50 of the Revised Code;

(E) The exceptions stated in section 5301.53 of the Revised Code.

§ 5301.50 Prior interests

Subject to the matters stated in section 5301.49 of the Revised Code, such record marketable title shall be held by its owner and shall be taken by any person dealing with the land free and clear of all interests, claims, or charges whatsoever, the existence of which depends upon any act, transaction, event, or omission that occurred prior to the effective date of the root of title. All such interests, claims, or charges, however denominated, whether legal or equitable, present or future, whether such interests, claims, or charges are asserted by a person sui juris or under a disability, whether such person is within or without the state, whether such person is natural or corporate, or is private or governmental, are hereby declared to be null and void.

§ 5301.51 Preservation of interests

(A) Any person claiming an interest in land may preserve and keep effective the interest by filing for record during the forty-year period immediately following the effective date of the root of title of the person whose record title would otherwise be marketable, a notice in compliance with section 5301.52 of the Revised Code. No disability or lack of knowledge of any kind on the part of anyone suspends the running of the forty-year period. * * *

(B) If the same record owner of any possessory interest in land has been in possession of the land continuously for a period of forty years or more, during which period no title transaction with respect to such interest appears of record in his chain of title, and no notice has been filed by him on his behalf as provided in division (A) of this section, and such possession continues to the time when marketability is being determined, the period of possession is equivalent to the filing of the notice immediately preceding the termination of the forty-year period described in division (A) of this section.

§ 5301.52 Contents and filing of notice; false statements

* * *

(B) The notice shall be filed for record in the office of the recorder of the county or counties where the land described in it is situated. The recorder of each county shall accept all such notices presented to him which describe land situated in the county in which he serves, shall enter and record them in the deed records of that county, and shall index each notice in the grantee deed index under the names of the claimants appearing in that notice and in the grantor deed index under the names of the record owners appearing in that notice. Such notices also shall be indexed under the description of the real estate involved in a book set apart for that purpose to be known as the "Notice Index." Each recorder may charge the same fees for the recording of such notices as are charged for recording deeds.

* * *

§ 5301.53 provides that the Marketable Title Act shall not extinguish any lessor or reversioner following a lease, any railroad or public utility easement, and "easement or interest in the nature of an easement, the existence of which is clearly observable by physical evidence of its use"; easements, visible or invisible, for any "pipe, valve, road, wire, cable, conduit, duct, sewer, track, pole, tower, or other physical facility;" interests in coal; mortgages recorded by railroads, public utilities or government corporations; or interests of the United States, Ohio, or any of its political subdivisions.

Notes and Questions

1. The basic concept of marketable title acts is elegantly simple: The title examiner need only search the title indices back for 40 (or 30 or 50) years and then prior to that point to the "root of title," the most recently recorded instrument prior to that time purporting to transfer the interest in which the examiner is interested. The examiner thereafter need only concern herself with interests created subsequent to the root of title; all prior interests are nullified.

For example, assume O transferred Blackacre to X in 1948 and that X recorded this transfer. O then transferred the same interest again to Y in 1949, Y also recording. Under the common law, and under any form of recording act, X prevails over Y. Under the marketable title acts, however, as of 1990, Y would have marketable title as the most recently recorded interest prior to 1950 (1990—40 years), and X's interest would be nullified.

2. Like Hydra, however, title defects are not so easily slain. The interests of some property claimants are simply too powerful or sympathetic to be cut off summarily simply because they are more than 40 years old. First, note that § 5301.53 exempts a host of prior interests. One can certainly understand why the legislature would be hesitant to cut off these interests, but if a title examiner stops after a 40–year search, will she find them?

Second, any claimant of an interest more than 40 years old can preserve it by filing a notice of the interest within the 40 year period immediately following the root of title. This is certainly sensible. If an interest is of value, there ought to be a means to preserving it for more than 40 years. But, how will the title examiner discover such a claim in a jurisdiction that depends on grantor-grantee indices? (Do you see how this problem is solved by a tract index?) Section 5301.52 provides for indexing the claim under the name of the claimant in the grantee index and under the name of the record owner in the grantor index. If we return to our earlier example, however, if X records a properly drafted notice of his claim to the property in 1987, the interest will be indexed under X's name in the grantor indices, and will not be discoverable by an examiner searching only Y's chain back to the root of title in 1990. See Barnett, Marketable Title Acts: Panacea or Pandemonium? 53 Cornell L.Rev. 45, 81–83 (1967).

Third, what is meant by a defect "inherent in the muniments of which such chain of record title is formed."? If the root of title deed to Y is forged, or executed by one without capacity, does X remain the owner, even though a search terminating at the root of title will not discover X's interest? See Barnett, supra, 67–69.

Finally, what is the meaning of Ohio Rev.Code § 5301.49(D)?

HEIFNER v. BRADFORD

Supreme Court of Ohio, 1983.
4 Ohio St.3d 49, 446 N.E.2d 440.

In 1916, Elvira Sprague and her husband, owners in fee simple of a tract of real estate located in Monroe Township, Muskingum County, conveyed their interest by deed to Fred H. Waters. By this instrument, the grantors reserved the oil and gas rights in the land. This transaction was recorded in Muskingum County that same year.

Elvira Sprague died testate in Tuscarawas County in 1931. Her will was probated in Tuscarawas County and devised the reserved oil and gas rights in the land equally to her two daughters, Lottie E. Rogers and Sarah A. Bradford.

In 1936, Fred H. Waters and his wife, without mention of the reservation of the oil and gas rights, conveyed the property by warranty deed to Charles B. Waters, Emma M. Waters, Sarah K. Waters, and William H. Waters. This conveyance was recorded in 1936.

An authenticated copy of Elvira Sprague's will was filed in Muskingum County in 1957. In accordance with the terms of the will, an affidavit of transfer was filed and recorded in Muskingum County evidencing the transfer of the oil and gas rights by inheritance from Elvira Sprague to her daughters. However, both Lottie E. Rogers and Sarah A. Bradford had died intestate prior to this transfer. Thus, Lottie E. Rogers' one-half share in the oil and gas rights was divided equally among her four children and Sarah A. Bradford's share was equally divided among her three children. These conveyances were evidenced by affidavits of transfer which were duly recorded in Muskingum County in 1957.

In 1980, Charles B. Waters et al. conveyed their interest in the property to William H. Waters and his wife Shirley S. Waters.

Appellants, Charlotte Heifner, Jean Stewart and Doris Schaevitz, own three undivided fractional shares of the oil and gas rights in the property. Appellants instituted this action in the court of common pleas seeking to quiet title and partition the undivided fractional shares in the oil and gas rights. Defendants represent the remaining fractional oil and gas rights owners, as well as the record surface owner, William H. and Shirley S. Waters.

Relevant to this appeal, the record surface owners claim also to be owners of the oil and gas rights in the land contrary to the claim of appellants. Appellees, William H. and Shirley S. Waters, base their claim upon an operation of R.C. 5301.47 through 5301.56, Ohio's Marketable Title Act.

Upon appellants' motion for summary judgment, the trial court ruled that appellants were owners of the oil and gas rights and ordered a partition of the undivided fractional interests. The court of appeals reversed, holding that the Marketable Title Act operated to extinguish appellants' interest and vest complete ownership of the property in William S. and Shirley H. Waters.[31]

The cause is now before this court upon the allowance of a motion to certify the record.

* * *

FRANK D. CELEBREZZE, CHIEF JUSTICE.

This case involves a controversy between independent competing claims of ownership to the oil and gas rights in a particular tract of land. For purposes of this decision, appellants are the purported owners of the oil and gas rights while appellees are the undisputed owners of the surface land. The question involved is one of first impression in this state and deals exclusively with the operation of R.C. 5301.47 through 5301.56, otherwise known as the Ohio Marketable Title Act. The issue presented by this appeal is whether appellees, who have an unbroken chain of title of record of forty years or more, have a marketable record title even though appellants' competing interest arose from an independent chain of title recorded during the forty-year period subsequent to appellees' root of title.

At the outset, the Marketable Title Act sets forth several definitions germane to the instant cause. R.C. 5301.47(A) defines "marketable record title" as a "title of record, as indicated in section 5301.48 of the Revised Code, which operates to extinguish such interests and claims, existing prior to the effective date of the root of title * * *." A "root of title" is defined in subsection (E) as "that conveyance or other title transaction in the chain of title of a person, upon which he relies as a basis for the marketability of his title, and which was the most recent to be recorded as of a date forty years prior to the time when marketability is being determined. * * *" Subsection (F) defines "title transaction" as "any transaction affecting title to any interest in land, including title by will or descent * * *."

R.C. 5301.48 provides that one "who has an unbroken chain of title of record to any interest in land for forty years or more, has a marketable record title to such interest * * * subject to the matters stated in section 5301.49 of the Revised Code."

In relevant part, R.C. 5301.49 states:

"Such record marketable title shall be subject to:

" * * *

"(D) Any interest arising out of a title transaction which has been recorded subsequent to the effective date of the root of title from which

---

31. The trial court distributed the oil and gas interests as follows:

Charlotte Heifner an undivided 1/8
Jean Stewart an undivided 1/8
Doris Schaevitz an undivided 1/6
Lane S. Bradford an undivided 1/6
Jeanne Weaver Reed an undivided 1/12

Edith Morris Rogers an undivided 1/4
Charles Weaver an undivided 1/12

Further, the determination by the trial court with respect to the fractionalization of the oil and gas ownership is not before us.

the unbroken chain of title of record is started; provided that such recording shall not revive or give validity to any interest which has been extinguished prior to the time of the recording * * *."

Appellants' root of title is the 1916 deed from Elvira Sprague and her husband to Fred H. Waters which reserved to the grantors the oil and gas rights in the land. Appellees' root of title is the 1936 conveyance from Fred H. Waters and his wife to Charles B. Waters, Emma M. Waters, Sarah K. Waters, and William H. Waters which failed to mention the reservation of oil and gas rights. Consequently, unless subject to R.C. 5301.49, appellees hold a marketable record title to the oil and gas rights, as well as title to the surface land, by virtue of having an "unbroken chain" of record title for over forty years which extinguishes prior claims and interests, including that of appellants. R.C. 5301.47(A) and 5301.48.

The Act defines a "title transaction" to include the passage of "title by will or descent." Thus, the 1957 conveyance of the oil and gas rights which passed under the terms of Elvira Sprague's will must be considered a "title transaction" under R.C. 5301.49(D).

Appellees argue that we should construe R.C. 5301.49(D) to require that a title transaction under that section arise from the same chain of title as that under which there is claimed to be a marketable record title. For the reasons to follow, we feel the proper construction should be otherwise.

Ohio's Marketable Title Act is taken primarily from the Model Marketable Title Act.[32] In fact, R.C. 5301.49(D) is virtually identical to Section 2(d) of the Model Act.[33] This being the case, we are convinced that the General Assembly and the drafters of the Model Act intended that a title transaction under R.C. 5301.49(D) and Section 2(d), respectively, may be part of an entirely independent chain of title.

In Simes & Taylor, Model Title Standards (1960) 32, the drafters of the Model Act proposed comprehensive model title standards to accompany the Model Act. Standard 4.10 states:

> "The recording of an instrument of conveyance subsequent to the effective date of the root of title has the same effect in preserving any interest conveyed as the filing of the notice provided for in § 4 of the Act. (See § 2[d] of the Model Act.)"

Perhaps more significant is the comment to the above standard which provides that, "[t]his standard is operative both where there are claims under a single chain of title and where there are two or more independent chains of title." Id. (Emphasis added.)

---

32. The Model Marketable Title Act was first proposed in Simes & Taylor, The Improvement of Conveyancing by Legislation (1960).

33. Bayse, Clearing Land Titles (1970) 378, Section 174.

Moreover, the Ohio Standards of Title Examination drafted and adopted by the Ohio State Bar Association have embraced an identical approach. See 55 Ohio Bar No. 19 (May 10, 1982), at page 763.

Hence, we are satisfied that R.C. 5301.49(D) ought to be construed in the manner that Simes and Taylor, as drafters of Section 2(d) of the Model Act, intended.[34] Accordingly, a "marketable title," as defined in R.C. 5301.47(A) and 5301.48, is subject to an interest arising out of a "title transaction" under R.C. 5301.49(D) which may be part of an independent chain of title. Further, the effect of R.C. 5301.49(D) is identical to that obtained by the filing of a preservation notice. R.C. 5301.51 provides for the preservation of interests by the filing of a notice of claim during the forty-year period. As a result, the recording of a "title transaction" under R.C. 5301.47(F) and 5301.49(D) is equivalent to the filing of a notice of claim during the forty-year period as specified in R.C. 5301.51 and 5301.52.[35]

Thus, the 1957 conveyance under the terms of Elvira Sprague's will was a "title transaction" within the meaning of R.C. 5301.49(D), and appellants' interest was not extinguished by operation of the Market-

---

34. Appellees contend, however, that under the present grantor-grantee indexing system, in order to locate title transactions in an independent chain of title, the title examiner will have to search the title to its origin and then forward to discover such transactions. It is appellees' position that the purpose of the Act is to limit title searches to forty years.

The approach taken by the court of appeals and advanced by the appellees is not without support. See Barnett, Marketable Title Acts—Panacea or Pandemonium? 53 Cornell L.Rev. 45, 54–56 (1967). However, we are left unpersuaded by Professor Barnett's analysis. Initially, Barnett concedes his approach is contrary to that of the drafters of the Model Act [Barnett, supra, at page 89, fn. 122] and, further, Barnett views the purpose of marketable title acts solely to shorten title examinations. Barnett, at page 91.

We are not inclined to view the purpose of the Marketable Title Act so narrowly. The Supreme Court of Florida in Miami v. St. Joe Paper Co. (Fla.1978), 364 So.2d 439, 442, aptly stated that the purpose of marketable title acts is three-fold:

"The Marketable Record Title Act is a comprehensive plan for reform in conveyancing procedures. * * *

"The Marketable Record Title Act is also a statute of limitations in that it requires state demands to be asserted within a reasonable time after a cause of action has accrued. * * *

"The Marketable Record Title Act is also a recording act in that it provides for a simple and easy method by which the owner of an existing old interest may preserve it. If he fails to take the step of filing the notice as provided, he has only himself to blame if his interest is extinguished. The legislature did not intend to arbitrarily wipe out old claims and interests without affording a means of preserving them and giving a reasonable period of time within which to take the necessary steps to accomplish that purpose." [ ]

35. This precise conclusion was reached by the Supreme Court of Oklahoma in Allen v. Farmers Union Co–Operative Royalty Co. (Okl.1975), 538 P.2d 204, 209, in interpreting similar provisions of Oklahoma's Marketable Record Title Act.

We do recognize, as a practical matter, the difficulty faced by title examiners in locating these title transactions in a common title examination. We note that the General Assembly has mandated a "Notice Index" by which notices under R.C. 5301.51 are indexed under the description of the real estate. R.C. 5301.52. It would seem consistent to similarly require such an indexing procedure of at least the title transactions falling under R.C. 5301.49(D). See Webster, The Quest for Clear Land Titles—Making Land Title Searches Shorter and Surer in North Carolina via Marketable Title Legislation, 44 N.C.L.Rev. 89, 108–109 and 122 (1965). However, that is in the nature of a legislative determination beyond the scope of our consideration.

able Title Act. Accordingly, the judgment of the court of appeals is reversed.

Judgment reversed.

Notes and Questions

1. How extensive a search must a title examiner conduct to discover subsequently recorded interests under § 5301.49(D)? Is the search any less extensive than that necessary before the Marketable Title Act was adopted? If the Marketable Title Act does not, in fact, significantly limit the extent of the search necessary to assure perfect record title, is it therefore of no value? Is it more difficult to find or to clear up problematic interests?

2. Marketable Title Acts also have the potential for terminating property interests that can present sympathetic arguments for preservation. Returning to our original hypothetical, for example, X's interest in the property certainly seems worthy of some protection. What can X do to protect his claim?

First, X can possess the property continuously for 40 years or more, during which no title transactions appear in his chain of title and no notice is filed by another claimant. Apparently, however, if X transfers his interest to another during the 40–year period, the interest may be extinguished by Y's subsequently recorded interest, even if X and his grantee are continuously in possession. Alternatively, the marketable title acts of some states preserve interests carried on the real property tax roles for three years prior to the time marketability is to be determined. This serves to protect fee interests, but will not protect interests such as mortgages or servitudes ordinarily not subject to real estate taxes.

X can, of course, record a notice of his interest, but if he has no knowledge of Y's claim, what would cause him to do this? Assume, moreover, that the interest to be preserved is not a fee, but rather an equitable servitude imposing restrictions in favor of each lot owner in a 250 – lot planned subdivision against each other lot owner. Must each lot owner record a notice in the chain of each other lot owner in the subdivision to preserve the planned, restricted, nature of the community?

X can also establish title through adverse possession under § 5301.-49(c). When is such adverse possession established however? Does this exception help if interests are not possessory?

Finally, X's interest may be preserved under § 5301.49(A) if it is noted in the muniments of title of contrary chains. Note, however, that even though every deed in the chain of title states that it is subject to a specific interest (for example a possibility of reverter) held by a specific person but antedating the root of title, that interest will nevertheless be nullified if the documents do not also specify where that interest is recorded.

3. The constitutionality of the destruction of prior interests wrought by marketable title acts has been vigorously debated in the courts. The issue seems now, however, to have been settled in favor of such legislation by the United States Supreme Court in Texaco, Inc. v. Short, 454 U.S. 516, 102 S.Ct. 781, 70 L.Ed.2d 738 (1982).

PROBLEM: SUBURBAN SECRETS

One of the town's nicest residential areas, Orchard Hills, has been built on the site of an elegant old nineteenth-century farm house and orchard. Orchard Hills consists of 30 homes, several of which have changed hands in recent years. The transfers have taken place in amicable, green-eyeshade fashion. One of the older lawyers in town, however, knows that the deed from the family that owned the orchard to the developer 29 years ago contained a defective acknowledgment. This defect is beyond curing, as the deed to the developer was from a dozen heirs, some of whom are dead and some unavailable. The other lawyers in town, however, have not discovered the defect because title searching is done with abstracts and the abstracter did not note the defective acknowledgment.

Two years ago, Peter McPherson, a lawyer neither old nor young, discovered the fact of the defective acknowledgment from the older lawyer, who had had a bit too much to drink, at a bar-association golf outing. Peter dug up the deed in the recorder's office and found out that what the older lawyer said was so. Peter was at that time representing the seller of a lot in Orchard Hills; it was not to his client's advantage to call attention to the defect, and he did nothing.

Now Peter has as a prospective client the purchaser of another lot in Orchard Hills. Should Peter disclose the defective acknowledgment to his client? Is there here an obligation to keep confidences? See A.B.A. Rule 1.6. Can Peter represent the buyer at all? Is there a conflict of interest? What is the moral thing to do? Would your answer change if the jurisdiction had a marketable title act that would make the acknowledgment moot in two more years (30 years from the first transfer from the developer of the subject lot)?

G. TITLE REGISTRATION

The deficiencies of the recording acts both for securing the rights of owners of existing property interests, and for disclosing a definitive record of such interests for the benefit of potential purchasers, are manifest and manifold. Clearly a better system must be possible. In fact, such a system exists and is in use in central Europe, England, much of the former British empire (including Australia, New Zealand, and most of Canada) and in several American states. Title registration is often referred to as the "Torrens system," after Sir Richard Torrens, who introduced the system to South Australia in the mid–19th century.

Under a Torrens system property title is based on registration. A person claiming title to land and desiring to register that title must initiate judicial proceedings to determine ownership. The title history of the land is then searched and an abstract prepared. This abstract is in turn examined by an official examiner who reports to the court. Parties who are identified as possibly having an interest in the property are notified and a hearing is held to establish title. A final decree is then issued declaring title in the owner subject to any proven outstanding interests.

Title as established by the registration decree is considered absolute, subject to limited exceptions, such as claims based on federal law. Any challenges to the title must be brought by appeal of the original action. The decree is registered with the register of titles. Any subsequent transfers of the property or new interests created in the property must be registered and appear on the official certificate to be valid. Transfers may only be effected by surrender of the owner's duplicate certificate and issuance of a new duplicate certificate in the name of the new owner. Interests may not be gained by adverse possession or prescription. For a complete description of Torrens Systems, see B. Schick and I. Plotkin, Torrens in the United States (1978).

The theoretical advantages of title registration are obvious. The rights of a holder of a registered property interest are nearly indefeasible. In theory, at least, they are only subject to fraud or an error by the register, for which the owner may be able to recover against the compensation fund. A potential purchaser, on the other hand, need only review a certificate at most a few pages long to determine definitively all interests affecting a parcel of property. Virtually all of the uncertainties of the recording system could be eliminated.

Because of these obvious advantages, it would seem that title registration would have been widely adopted as an alternative to recording. In fact, title registration was quite popular in the United States in the early twentieth century, and at one point 21 states legally recognized the Torrens system. Since then nine states have repealed title registration however, and it has been extensively used only in parts of Hawaii, Illinois, Massachusetts, Minnesota, New York and Ohio. Though articles advocating giving title registration another chance appear from time to time,[36] its prospects in the United States at this point in time appear very dim.

Why has title registration failed to take hold in the United States? First, since Constitutional constraints required that registration be accomplished initially through a judicial rather than an administrative process, initial registration of title has proved quite costly and time consuming. Because title registration has always been voluntary rather than compulsory, landowners in jurisdictions with registration often opt to transfer unregistered land through the conventional system rather than through registration to avoid this initial expense. Second, registration statutes, like the marketable title acts, frequently except a variety of interests, weakening the conclusiveness of registered title. Subsequent judicial decisions upholding unregistered interests present-

36. See Bostick, Land Title Registration: An English Solution to an American Problem, 63 Ind.L.J. 35 (1987); Janczyk, Land Title Systems, Scale of Operations and Operating and Conversion Costs, 8 J.Leg. Studies 569 (1979).

ing appealing equities have further undermined the conclusiveness of registration. See Couey v. Talalah Estates Corp., 183 Ga. 442, 188 S.E. 822 (1936); Sheaff v. Spindler, 339 Ill. 540, 171 N.E. 632 (1930); Kirk v. Mullen, 100 Or. 563, 197 P. 300 (1921). Finally, it is widely believed that vigorous opposition from the conveyancing establishment, particularly from the title insurance companies, has contributed significantly to limiting and reversing the growth of title registration.

H. TITLE INSURANCE

In many parts of the United States, before a financial institution will agree to finance a real property purchase, it will insist that the seller or buyer procure a mortgagee policy of title insurance. If the financial institution intends to sell the mortgage on the secondary mortgage market, this will almost certainly be the case. Moreover, many purchasers of residential real property rely on their title insurance policy as the primary protection of their title. Indeed, in some jurisdictions general warranty deeds have been replaced by special warranty or quitclaim deeds and purchasers of residences rarely seek the assistance of attorneys because of the pervasiveness of reliance on title insurance as the primary means to securing title.

Title insurance is a peculiar form of insurance. Most forms of insurance cover the insured during a specified period of time against designated risks that may occur during that time period. In contrast, title insurance covers the insured only against risks already in existence at the time the policy is issued but for an unlimited time after issuance. Most forms of insurance insure against risks that are at least partially under the control of the insured. Title insurance insures against risks that are generally beyond the control of the insured, but often discoverable by, and thus, to some extent, subject to the control of the insurer.

Title insurance policies insure either the mortgagee or the owner. The mortgagee policy insures the title of the mortgagee against encumbrances and defects. It also insures the marketability and assignability of the mortgagee's title and access to and from the land subject to the mortgage. Mortgagee policies are generally assignable with the mortgage.

A copy of the current American Land Title Association owner's policy is reproduced below:

AMERICAN LAND TITLE ASSOCIATION
OWNER'S POLICY
(4-6-90)

CHICAGO TITLE INSURANCE COMPANY

SUBJECT TO THE EXCLUSIONS FROM COVERAGE, THE EXCEPTIONS FROM COVERAGE CONTAINED IN SCHEDULE B AND THE CONDITIONS AND STIPULATIONS, CHICAGO TITLE INSURANCE COMPANY, a Missouri corporation, herein called the Company, insures, as of Date of Policy shown in Schedule A, against loss or damage, not exceeding the Amount of Insurance stated in Schedule A, sustained or incurred by the insured by reason of:

1. Title to the estate or interest described in Schedule A being vested other than as stated therein;
2. Any defect in or lien or encumbrance on the title;
3. Unmarketability of the title;
4. Lack of a right of access to and from the land.

The Company will also pay the costs, attorneys' fees and expenses incurred in defense of the title, as insured, but only to the extent provided in the Conditions and Stipulations.

In Witness Whereof, CHICAGO TITLE INSURANCE COMPANY has caused this policy to be signed and sealed as of Date of Policy shown in Schedule A, the policy to become valid when countersigned by an authorized signatory.

CHICAGO TITLE INSURANCE COMPANY
By:

President

By:

Secretary

ALTA Owner's Policy (4-6-90)   [G8353]

EXCLUSIONS FROM COVERAGE

The following matters are expressly excluded from the coverage of this policy and the Company will not pay loss or damage, costs, attorneys' fees or expenses which arise by reason of:

1. (a) Any law, ordinance or governmental regulation (including but not limited to building and zoning laws, ordinances, or regulations) restricting, regulating, prohibiting or relating to (i) the occupancy, use, or enjoyment of the land; (ii) the character, dimensions or location of any improvement now or hereafter erected on the land; (iii) a separation in ownership or a change in the dimensions or area of the land or any parcel of which the land is or was a part; or (iv) environmental protection, or the effect of any violation of these laws, ordinances or governmental regulations, except to the extent that a notice of the enforcement thereof or a notice of a defect, lien or encumbrance resulting from a violation or alleged violation affecting the land has been recorded in the public records at Date of Policy.

    (b) Any governmental police power not excluded by (a) above, except to the extent that a notice of the exercise thereof or a notice of a defect, lien or encumbrance resulting from a violation or alleged violation affecting the land has been recorded in the public records at Date of Policy.

2. Rights of eminent domain unless notice of the exercise thereof has been recorded in the public records at Date of Policy, but not excluding from coverage any taking which has occurred prior to Date of Policy which would be binding on the rights of a purchaser for value without knowledge.

3. Defects, liens, encumbrances, adverse claims or other matters:

    (a) created, suffered, assumed or agreed to by the insured claimant;

    (b) not known to the Company, not recorded in the public records at Date of Policy, but known to the insured claimant and not disclosed in writing to the Company by the insured claimant prior to the date the insured claimant became an insured under this policy;

    (c) resulting in no loss or damage to the insured claimant;

    (d) attaching or created subsequent to Date of Policy; or

    (e) resulting in loss or damage which would not have been sustained if the insured claimant had paid value for the estate or interest insured by this policy.

4. Any claim, which arises out of the transaction vesting in the insured the estate or interest insured by this policy, by reason of the operation of federal bankruptcy, state insolvency, or similar creditors' rights laws.

[G8354]

CONDITIONS AND STIPULATIONS

1. DEFINITION OF TERMS

The following terms when used in this policy mean:

(a) "insured": the insured named in Schedule A, and, subject to any rights or defenses the Company would have had against the named insured, those who succeed to the interest of the named insured by operation of law as distinguished from purchase including, but not limited to, heirs, distributees, devisees, survivors, personal representatives, next of kin, or corporate or fiduciary successors.

(b) "insured claimant": an insured claiming loss or damage.

(c) "knowledge" or "known": actual knowledge, not constructive knowledge or notice which may be imputed to an insured by reason of the public records as defined in this policy or any other records which impart constructive notice of matters affecting the land.

(d) "land": the land described or referred to in Schedule A, and improvements affixed thereto which by law constitute real property. The term "land" does not include any property beyond the lines of the area described or referred to in Schedule A, nor any right, title, interest, estate or easement in abutting streets, roads, avenues, alleys, lanes, ways or waterways, but nothing herein shall modify or limit the extent to which a right of access to and from the land is insured by this policy.

(e) "mortgage": mortgage, deed of trust, trust deed, or other security instrument.

(f) "public records": records established under state statutes at Date of Policy for the purpose of imparting constructive notice of matters relating to real property to purchasers for value and without knowledge. With respect to Section 1(a)(iv) of the Exclusions From Coverage, "public records" shall also include environmental protection liens filed in the records of the clerk of the United States district court for the district in which the land is located.

(g) "unmarketability of the title": an alleged or apparent matter affecting the title to the land, not excluded or excepted from coverage, which would entitle a purchaser of the estate or interest described in Schedule A to be released from the obligation to purchase by virtue of a contractual condition requiring the delivery of marketable title.

2. CONTINUATION OF INSURANCE AFTER CONVEYANCE OF TITLE

The coverage of this policy shall continue in force as of Date of Policy in favor of an insured only so long as the insured retains an estate or interest in the land, or holds an indebtedness secured by a purchase money mortgage given by a purchaser from the insured, or only so long as the insured shall have liability by reason of covenants of warranty made by the insured in any transfer or conveyance of the estate or interest. This policy shall not continue in force in favor of any purchaser from the insured of either (i) an estate or interest in the land, or (ii) an indebtedness secured by a purchase money mortgage given to the insured.

3. NOTICE OF CLAIM TO BE GIVEN BY INSURED CLAIMANT

The insured shall notify the Company promptly in writing (i) in case of any litigation as set forth in Section 4(a) below, (ii) in case knowledge shall come to an insured hereunder of any claim of title or interest which is adverse to the title to the estate or interest, as insured, and which might cause loss or damage for which the Company may be liable by virtue of this policy, or (iii) if title to the estate or interest, as insured, is rejected as unmarketable. If prompt notice shall not be given to the Company, then as to the insured all liability of the Company shall terminate with regard to the matter or matters for which prompt notice is required; provided, however, that failure to notify the Company shall in no case prejudice the rights of any insured under this policy unless the Company shall be prejudiced by the failure and then only to the extent of the prejudice.

4. DEFENSE AND PROSECUTION OF ACTIONS; DUTY OF INSURED CLAIMANT TO COOPERATE

(a) Upon written request by the insured and subject to the options contained in Section 6 of these Conditions and Stipulations, the Company, at its own cost and without unreasonable delay, shall provide for the defense of an insured in litigation in which any third party asserts a claim adverse to the title or interest as insured, but only as to those stated causes of action alleging a defect, lien or encumbrance or other matter insured against by this policy. The Company shall have the right to select counsel of its choice (subject to the right of the insured to object for reasonable cause) to represent the insured as to those stated causes of action and shall not be liable for and will not pay the fees of any other counsel. The Company will not pay any fees, costs or expenses incurred by the insured in the defense of those causes of action which allege matters not insured against by this policy.

(b) The Company shall have the right, at its own cost, to institute and prosecute any action or proceeding or to do any other act which in its opinion may be necessary or desirable to establish the title to the estate or interest, as insured, or to prevent or reduce loss or damage to the insured. The Company may take any appropriate action under the terms of this policy, whether or not it shall be liable hereunder, and shall not thereby concede liability or waive any provision of this policy. If the Company shall exercise its rights under this paragraph, it shall do so diligently.

(c) Whenever the Company shall have brought an action or interposed a defense as required or permitted by the provisions of this policy, the Company may pursue any litigation to final determination by a court of competent jurisdiction and expressly reserves the right, in its sole discretion, to appeal from any adverse judgment or order.

(d) In all cases where this policy permits or requires the Company to prosecute or provide for the defense of any action or proceeding, the insured shall secure to the Company the right to so prosecute or provide defense in the action or proceeding, and all appeals therein, and permit the Company to use, at its option, the name of the insured for this purpose. Whenever requested by the Company, the insured, at the Company's expense, shall give the Company all reasonable aid (i) in any action or proceeding, securing evidence, obtaining witnesses, prosecuting or defending the action or proceeding, or effecting settlement, and (ii) in any other lawful act which in the opinion of the Company may be necessary or desirable to establish the title to the estate or interest as insured. If the Company is prejudiced by the failure of the insured to furnish the required cooperation, the Company's obligations to the insured under the policy shall terminate, including any liability or obligation to defend, prosecute, or continue any litigation, with regard to the matter or matters requiring such cooperation.

5. PROOF OF LOSS OR DAMAGE

In addition to and after the notices required under Section 3 of these Conditions and Stipulations have been provided the Company, a proof of loss or damage signed and sworn to by the insured claimant shall be furnished to the Company within 90 days after the insured claimant shall ascertain the facts giving rise to the loss or damage. The proof of loss or damage shall describe the defect in, or lien or encumbrance on the title, or other matter insured against by this policy which constitutes the basis of loss or damage and shall state, to the extent possible, the basis of calculating the amount of the loss or damage. If the Company is prejudiced by the failure of the insured claimant to provide the required proof of loss or damage, the Company's obligations to the insured under the policy shall terminate, including any liability or obligation to defend, prosecute, or continue any litigation, with regard to the matter or matters requiring such proof of loss or damage.

In addition, the insured claimant may reasonably be required to submit to examination under oath by any authorized representative of the Company and shall produce for examination, inspection and copying, at such reasonable times and places as may be designated by any authorized representative of the Company, all records, books, ledgers, checks, correspondence and memoranda, whether bearing a date before or after Date of Policy, which reasonably pertain to the loss or damage. Further, if requested by any authorized representative of the Company, the insured claimant shall grant its permission, in writing, for any authorized representative of the Company to examine, inspect and copy all records, books, ledgers, checks, correspondence and memoranda in the custody or control of a third party, which reasonably pertain to the loss or damage. All information designated as confidential by the insured claimant provided to the Company pursuant to this Section shall not be disclosed to others unless, in the reasonable judgment of the Company, it is necessary in the administration of the claim. Failure of the insured claimant to submit for examination under oath, produce other reasonably requested information or grant permission to secure reasonably necessary information from third parties as required in this paragraph shall terminate any liability of the Company under this policy as to that claim.

6. OPTIONS TO PAY OR OTHERWISE SETTLE CLAIMS; TERMINATION OF LIABILITY

In case of a claim under this policy, the Company shall have the following additional options:

(a) To Pay or Tender Payment of the Amount of Insurance.

To pay or tender payment of the amount of insurance under this policy together with any costs, attorneys' fees and expenses incurred by the insured claimant, which were authorized by the Company, up to the time of payment or tender of payment and which the Company is obligated to pay.

Upon the exercise by the Company of this option, all liability and obligations to the insured under this policy, other than to make the payment required, shall terminate, including any liability or obligation to defend, prosecute, or continue any litigation, and the policy shall be surrendered to the Company for cancellation.

(b) To Pay or Otherwise Settle With Parties Other than the Insured or With the Insured Claimant.

(i) to pay or otherwise settle with other parties for or in the name of an insured claimant any claim insured against under this policy, together with any costs, attorneys' fees and expenses incurred by the insured claimant which were authorized by the Company up to the time of payment and which the Company is obligated to pay; or

(ii) to pay or otherwise settle with the insured claimant the loss or damage provided for under this policy, together with any costs, attorneys' fees and expenses incurred by the insured claimant which were authorized by the Company up to the time of payment and which the Company is obligated to pay.

[G8355]

Upon the exercise by the Company of either of the options provided for in paragraphs (b)(i) or (ii), the Company's obligations to the insured under this policy for the claimed loss or damage, other than the payments required to be made, shall terminate, including any liability or obligation to defend, prosecute or continue any litigation.

7. DETERMINATION, EXTENT OF LIABILITY AND COINSURANCE

This policy is a contract of indemnity against actual monetary loss or damage sustained or incurred by the insured claimant who has suffered loss or damage by reason of matters insured against by this policy and only to the extent herein described.

(a) The liability of the Company under this policy shall not exceed the least of:

(i) the Amount of Insurance stated in Schedule A; or,

(ii) the difference between the value of the insured estate or interest as insured and the value of the insured estate or interest subject to the defect, lien or encumbrance insured against by this policy.

(b) In the event the Amount of Insurance stated in Schedule A at the Date of Policy is less than 80 percent of the value of the insured estate or interest or the full consideration paid for the land, whichever is less, or if subsequent to the Date of Policy an improvement is erected on the land which increases the value of the insured estate or interest by at least 20 percent over the Amount of Insurance stated in Schedule A, then this Policy is subject to the following:

(i) where no subsequent improvement has been made, as to any partial loss, the Company shall only pay the loss pro rata in the proportion that the amount of insurance at Date of Policy bears to the total value of the insured estate or interest at Date of Policy; or

(ii) where a subsequent improvement has been made, as to any partial loss, the Company shall only pay the loss pro rata in the proportion that 120 percent of the Amount of Insurance stated in Schedule A bears to the sum of the Amount of Insurance stated in Schedule A and the amount expended for the improvement.

The provisions of this paragraph shall not apply to costs, attorneys' fees and expenses for which the Company is liable under this policy, and shall only apply to that portion of any loss which exceeds, in the aggregate, 10 percent of the Amount of Insurance stated in Schedule A.

(c) The Company will pay only those costs, attorneys' fees and expenses incurred in accordance with Section 4 of these Conditions and Stipulations.

8. APPORTIONMENT

If the land described in Schedule A consists of two or more parcels which are not used as a single site, and a loss is established affecting one or more of the parcels but not all, the loss shall be computed and settled on a pro rata basis as if the amount of insurance under this policy was divided pro rata as to the value on Date of Policy of each separate parcel to the whole, exclusive of any improvements made subsequent to Date of Policy, unless a liability or value has otherwise been agreed upon as to each parcel by the Company and the insured at the time of the issuance of this policy and shown by an express statement or by an endorsement attached to this policy.

9. LIMITATION OF LIABILITY

(a) If the Company establishes the title, or removes the alleged defect, lien or encumbrance, or cures the lack of a right of access to or from the land, or cures the claim of unmarketability of title, all as insured, in a reasonably diligent manner by any method, including litigation and the completion of any appeals therefrom, it shall have fully performed its obligations with respect to that matter and shall not be liable for any loss or damage caused thereby.

(b) In the event of any litigation, including litigation by the Company or with the Company's consent, the Company shall have no liability for loss or damage until there has been a final determination by a court of competent jurisdiction, and disposition of all appeals therefrom, adverse to the title as insured.

(c) The Company shall not be liable for loss or damage to any insured for liability voluntarily assumed by the insured in settling any claim or suit without the prior written consent of the Company.

10. REDUCTION OF INSURANCE; REDUCTION OR TERMINATION OF LIABILITY

All payments under this policy, except payments made for costs, attorneys' fees and expenses, shall reduce the amount of the insurance pro tanto.

11. LIABILITY NONCUMULATIVE

It is expressly understood that the amount of insurance under this policy shall be reduced by any amount the Company may pay under any policy insuring a mortgage to which exception is taken in Schedule B or to which the insured has agreed, assumed, or taken subject, or which is hereafter executed by an insured and which is a charge or lien on the estate or interest described or referred to in Schedule A, and the amount so paid shall be deemed a payment under this policy to the insured owner.

12. PAYMENT OF LOSS

(a) No payment shall be made without producing this policy for endorsement of the payment unless the policy has been lost or destroyed, in which case proof of loss or destruction shall be furnished to the satisfaction of the Company.

(b) When liability and the extent of loss or damage has been definitely fixed in accordance with these Conditions and Stipulations, the loss or damage shall be payable within 30 days thereafter.

13. SUBROGATION UPON PAYMENT OR SETTLEMENT

(a) The Company's Right of Subrogation.

Whenever the Company shall have settled and paid a claim under this policy, all right of subrogation shall vest in the Company unaffected by any act of the insured claimant.

The Company shall be subrogated to and be entitled to all rights and remedies which the insured claimant would have had against any person or property in respect to the claim had this policy not been issued. If requested by the Company, the insured claimant shall transfer to the Company all rights and remedies against any person or property necessary in order to perfect this right of subrogation. The insured claimant shall permit the Company to sue, compromise or settle in the name of the insured claimant and to use the name of the insured claimant in any transaction or litigation involving these rights or remedies.

If a payment on account of a claim does not fully cover the loss of the insured claimant, the Company shall be subrogated to these rights and remedies in the proportion which the Company's payment bears to the whole amount of the loss.

If loss should result from any act of the insured claimant, as stated above, that act shall not void this policy, but the Company, in that event, shall be required to pay only that part of any losses insured against by this policy which shall exceed the amount, if any, lost to the Company by reason of the impairment by the insured claimant of the Company's right of subrogation.

(b) The Company's Rights Against Non-insured Obligors.

The Company's right of subrogation against non-insured obligors shall exist and shall include, without limitation, the rights of the insured to indemnities, guaranties, other policies of insurance or bonds, notwithstanding any terms or conditions contained in those instruments which provide for subrogation rights by reason of this policy.

14. ARBITRATION

Unless prohibited by applicable law, either the Company or the insured may demand arbitration pursuant to the Title Insurance Arbitration Rules of the American Arbitration Association. Arbitrable matters may include, but are not limited to, any controversy or claim between the Company and the insured arising out of or relating to this policy, any service of the Company in connection with its issuance or the breach of a policy provision or other obligation. All arbitrable matters when the Amount of Insurance is $1,000,000 or less shall be arbitrated at the option of either the Company or the insured. All arbitrable matters when the Amount of Insurance is in excess of $1,000,000 shall be arbitrated only when agreed to by both the Company and the insured. Arbitration pursuant to this policy and under the Rules in effect on the date the demand for arbitration is made or, at the option of the insured, the Rules in effect at Date of Policy shall be binding upon the parties. The award may include attorneys' fees only if the laws of the state in which the land is located permit a court to award attorneys' fees to a prevailing party. Judgment upon the award rendered by the Arbitrator(s) may be entered in any court having jurisdiction thereof.

The law of the situs of the land shall apply to an arbitration under the Title Insurance Arbitration Rules.

A copy of the Rules may be obtained from the Company upon request.

15. LIABILITY LIMITED TO THIS POLICY; POLICY ENTIRE CONTRACT

(a) This policy together with all endorsements, if any, attached hereto by the Company is the entire policy and contract between the insured and the Company. In interpreting any provision of this policy, this policy shall be construed as a whole.

(b) Any claim of loss or damage, whether or not based on negligence, and which arises out of the status of the title to the estate or interest covered hereby or by any action asserting such claim, shall be restricted to this policy.

(c) No amendment of or endorsement to this policy can be made except by a writing endorsed hereon or attached hereto signed by either the President, a Vice President, the Secretary, an Assistant Secretary, or validating officer or authorized signatory of the Company.

16. SEVERABILITY

In the event any provision of the policy is held invalid or unenforceable under applicable law, the policy shall be deemed not to include that provision and all other provisions shall remain in full force and effect.

17. NOTICES, WHERE SENT

All notices required to be given the Company and any statement in writing required to be furnished the Company shall include the number of this policy and shall be addressed to the Company at the issuing office or to:

Chicago Title Insurance Company
Claims Department
111 West Washington Street
Chicago, Illinois 60602

Form No. 8206
[G8356]

OWNERS

SCHEDULE A

OFFICE FILE NUMBER	POLICY NUMBER	DATE OF POLICY	AMOUNT OF INSURANCE
1	2	3	4 $

1. Name of Insured:

2. The estate or interest in the land which is covered by this Policy is:

   Fee Simple

3. Title to the estate or interest in the land is vested in the Insured.

4. The land herein described is encumbered by the following mortgage or trust deed, and assignments:

   and the mortgages or trust deeds, if any, shown in Schedule B hereof.

5. The land referred to in this Policy is described as follows:

SCHEDULE A
Owners Form
Reorder Form No. 3529 (Rev. 1/89)   **This Policy valid only if Schedule B is attached.**   [G8357]

SCHEDULE B

Policy Number: _____
                              Owners

EXCEPTIONS FROM COVERAGE

This policy does not insure against loss or damage (and the Company will not pay costs, attorneys' fees or expenses) which arise by reason of:

General Exceptions:

(1) Rights or claims of parties in possession not shown by the public records.

(2) Encroachments, overlaps, boundary line disputes, or other matters which would be disclosed by an accurate survey and inspection of the premises.

(3) Easements, or claims of easements, not shown by the public records.

(4) Any lien, or right to a lien, for services, labor, or material heretofore or hereafter furnished, imposed by law and not shown by the public records.

(5) Taxes or special assessments which are not shown as existing liens by the public records.

Special Exceptions: The mortgage, if any, referred to in Item 4 of Schedule A.

Countersigned

_____
Authorized Signatory

SCHEDULE B
Owner's Form
Reorder Form No 3528 (Rev 1/89)

Schedule B of this Policy consists of   pages.

[G8358]

Notes and Questions

1. The policy reproduced is the Form B policy. The form A policy differs only in that it does not insure marketability of the property. What difference does this make to the insured?

2. In addition to the general exceptions listed in the policy, the title policy will also generally except from coverage any non-trivial defects discovered during the title company's search. Indeed, it is possible to view the title insurer's job to be discovering all real risks to the title of a property and excluding these risks. Of course, the buyer or mortgagee dissatisfied with the exceptions specifically identified by the title insurer can refuse to issue a mortgage or to proceed with the property purchase.

3. Considering the exceptions and exclusions found in the policy, would a purchaser of property be insured against:

    (a) claims of an adverse possessor to part of the insured property?

    (b) a prescriptive easement across the property?

    (c) an encroachment across the boundary by a fence erected by a neighboring landowner?

    (d) a sewer line running across the property and used by a neighbor?

    (e) a mechanic's lien filed against the property after the closing for work performed before the closing, which under state law takes precedence over the title of the purchaser?

    (f) a violation of the zoning ordinance?

    (g) a preexisting unrecorded mortgage of which the purchaser has heard unconfirmed rumors?

    (h) a dower interest stemming from a sale of the property twenty years previously, which is discovered after the conveyance of the property to the purchaser, but never asserted against the property by its owner?

What exactly does a title insurance policy insure against?

4. When a defect is discovered that is covered by a title insurance policy, the extent of liability of a title insurer will usually be determined by interpreting the policy. One common measure where a claim is presented for a partial failure of title is the difference between the market value of the insured property with and the market value without the defect; another considers the cost of removing the defect. Where failure of title is complete, the measure of damages is usually the fair market value of the property to which title failed. Policies also vary as to the date on which damages are to be determined, some specifying the date of the policy; others specifying the date the defect was discovered. Damages can never exceed the total value of the policy (usually the purchase price of the property for owners' policies, the value of the loan for mortgagee policies) and the extent of the insured's loss. For a mortgagee, for example, the damages cannot exceed the amount unpaid on the loan at the time title fails. Most policies also provide for coverage of litigation costs for defend-

ing the title of the insured in addition to any damages recoverable by the insured. See D. Burke, The Law of Title Insurance (1986).

Though contract damages against title insurers are often quite limited, tort damages may be more substantial where tort liability is established. Tort litigation may also impose on title insurance companies responsibilities not clearly imposed by the insurance contract.

MOORE v. TITLE INSURANCE CO. OF MINNESOTA

Court of Appeals of Arizona, 1985.
148 Ariz 408, 714 P.2d 1303.

HOWARD, JUDGE.

Plaintiffs filed this action against the defendant title company alleging that the defendant was negligent in failing to discover certain liens against property plaintiffs were purchasing and further alleging that this misconduct resulted in a breach of contract. * * * [Plaintiffs appealed a judgment for the title company]

* * *

The facts considered in the light most favorable to defendant are as follows. On July 10, 1979, Michael C. Moore, acting on behalf of the partnership of Moore and Bale, attended a meeting at the offices of Title Insurance Company of Minnesota (Minnesota) in Tucson. The meeting concerned the purchase by the partnership of certain apartments located in Sierra Vista, Arizona, owned by Mr. Nieman. Present at the meeting were Nieman, his real estate broker, Moore, Bale and Roy Rogers, an escrow officer of Minnesota. The purpose of the meeting was to work out the details of a deposit receipt and agreement in connection with the partnership's proposed purchase of the apartments.

The partnership was concerned about purchasing the property because Sierra Solar Systems, Inc., a corporation owned by Nieman, was in bankruptcy and there were serious delinquencies on the first deed of trust on the apartments held by Security Savings and Loan. Unless immediate cash was provided to Security Savings it was going to foreclose. Moore informed everyone at the meeting that the partnership did not want to enter into the transaction at all if there was any danger that Nieman personally would file bankruptcy or if there was any problem concerning the property that would bring it into the bankruptcy court.

A deposit receipt and agreement was typed at the Minnesota office. It provided for a purchase price of approximately $100,000. It disclosed the existence of three liens on the property: first lien to Security Savings in the approximate sum of $30,000, a second lien to S & D Cattle Company in the approximate sum of $30,000 to $40,000 and a third lien to First National Bank in the approximate sum of $30,000. The agreement also contained the following terms and conditions:

"(1) If the subject property is subject to any liens other than the three liens described on page one, buyer shall have the option to terminate this agreement and all deposits shall be returned to buyer and buyer shall not be liable to seller for any amount nor may seller enforce this agreement."

* * *

Prior to signing the deposit receipt and agreement, Rogers told Moore that Minnesota had made a title search and there were no problems. Indeed, the record discloses that a preliminary title report was made searching the title up to July 10, 1979. It discloses no liens other than the realty mortgage owed to Security Savings, and the deeds of trust securing loans owed to S & D Cattle Company and First National Bank of Arizona.

The partners signed the agreement and took possession of the apartments. Although there were 14 apartments in existence at the time, only one of them was in shape to be rented and it was the duty of Bale to see to it that the remaining units were brought into a rentable condition. During their discussions with Nieman prior to signing the deposit receipt and agreement, Nieman represented to the partnership that the amount of money due and owing on the mortgage to S & D Cattle Company was closer to $30,000 with a discount and that the lienholder was cooperative. In fact, after taking possession, the partners discovered that the amount of the lien was claimed to be closer to $40,000 and that the S & D Cattle Company was not cooperative. It was also discovered that some of the fixtures and equipment in the apartments did not work and that there was cement in part of the sewer system. Bale commenced to repair the apartments and succeeded in getting six of them rented. Eventually the amount of rents came close to giving the partners a positive cash flow.

* * *

On December 13, 1979, the partners closed the deal in anticipation of persuading S & D Cattle Company to accept a lesser amount. At the time of the closing they did not have any financing.

Prior to the closing, Minnesota had prepared an amended preliminary title report which was given to the escrow officer. The only liens shown on this amended report were the liens that were previously known. Neither partner saw either of the preliminary title reports prior to closing the sale. The closing statement, which both partners saw, showed only the existence of the three liens previously mentioned and the closing statement showed that the partners were taking the property subject to these liens. Moore asked Rogers at the time about the three liens, and Rogers told him that he would let him know the balance due on each. Upon closing, the partnership released the $6,000 note which was given as security for the $45,000 earnest money and voided it. They also released Nieman's home in Sierra Vista, which was being held as security.

After the closing, Bale continued to work on improving the property. In April 1980, Bale moved to Kansas City. In November 1980, he made up a sales packet for the property showing a sale price of $155,000. He tried to sell the property to a prospect who, after checking into the deal, told Bale that the deal was not as represented since there were other outstanding liens on the property. About one month earlier, Moore was discussing financing with Lou Wallace of the First National Bank. Wallace told him that the bank would be happy to lend him money to pay off the first three liens, but asked Moore who was going to pay off the additional liens that his research showed existed on the property. This was the first time that Moore had any notice that there were additional liens.

Minnesota had failed to list the following liens of record on the property against Sierra Solar Systems, Inc.: Arizona Department of Economic Security, $329.36, recorded November 6, 1978; Arizona Department of Economic Security, $604.93, recorded November 29, 1978; United States Internal Revenue Service, $9,141.45, recorded January 15, 1979; Arizona Department of Economic Security, $214.82, recorded February 22, 1979, and United States Internal Revenue Service, $2,925.29, recorded March 13, 1979. Although a deed transferring the property from Sierra Solar Systems, Inc. to Nieman, individually, was executed and recorded on December 29, 1978, this deed was subsequently re-recorded by the title company on December 13, 1979 because of a defective acknowledgment.

Both personally and through his attorney, Moore communicated with Minnesota asking it to compensate the partnership for its failure to include all liens of record. The title company responded that it was responsible to protect and defend them with respect to the first two undisclosed liens on the subject property totalling about $1,000, but that it was not responsible for the other liens since they were filed after the debtor, Sierra Solar Systems, Inc., had transferred the property to Nieman in his individual capacity. This response did not satisfy the partnership. In the meantime, trustee's sales were noticed as to the deeds of trust held by S & D Cattle Company and First National Bank. Furthermore, the suit against S & D Cattle Company had not been resolved. Although the partnership had enough cash to pay off the liens that had not been disclosed by the title company, if they did so, they would not have the funds necessary to operate the apartments. First National Bank would not lend them the money unless they paid off the liens. The net result was that the partnership lost the property through the trustee's sales since it could not find permanent financing. This suit ensued.

At trial, both an expert witness on behalf of the plaintiffs and defendant's own employee, an escrow officer, testified that the title company had fallen below the standard of care of title companies under the circumstances by failing to discover and disclose all liens of record prior to closing.

It is plaintiffs' contention that the defendant was negligent in searching the title and that this negligence prevented them from exercising their option to terminate the contract. Plaintiffs contend that the title company should have the same liability as an abstractor of title. The title company contends that it is not an abstractor of title, that it is only an insurer and that it can only be liable for breach of contract. It argues that any duty on the part of an insurer to search the records has to be expressed and/or implied from the title policy issued to the plaintiff and that where, as here, the title company has no such duty under the title policy, any search that it may have actually undertaken was undertaken solely for its own protection against losses covered by its policy. See Anderson v. Title Insurance Company, 103 Idaho 875, 655 P.2d 82 (1982), and Horn v. Lawyers Title Insurance Corporation, 89 N.M. 709, 557 P.2d 206. See also Maggio v. Abstract Title & Mortgage Corporation, 277 App.Div. 940, 98 N.Y.S.2d 1011 (1950).

We start with the proposition that an abstractor of title is negligent as a matter of law when it fails to include in its abstract liens which are of record. Phoenix Title and Trust Company v. Continental Oil Company, 43 Ariz. 219, 29 P.2d 1065 (1934), overruled on other grounds, Donnelly Const. Co. v. Oberg/Hunt/Gilleland, 139 Ariz. 184, 677 P.2d 1292 (1984). Other jurisdictions have held that a title insurance company has the liability of an abstractor of title when it inspects records and prepares title reports. Garton v. Title Insurance and Trust Company, 106 Cal.App.3d 365, 165 Cal.Rptr. 449 (1980); Jarchow v. Transamerica Title Insurance Company, 48 Cal.App.3d 917, 122 Cal. Rptr. 470 (1975); Hawkins v. Oakland Title Insurance and Guaranty Company, 165 Cal.App.2d 116, 331 P.2d 742 (1958); Shada v. Title & Trust Company of Florida, 457 So.2d 553 (Fla.App.1984); Heyd v. Chicago Title Insurance Company, 218 Neb. 296, 354 N.W.2d 154 (1984);[37] and see the dicta in Laurence v. Kruckmeyer, 124 Ariz. 488, 605 P.2d 466 (App.1979).

The rationale for imposing liability is best expressed in Heyd v. Chicago Title Insurance Company, supra:

"We now hold that a title insurance company which renders a title report and also issues a policy of title insurance has assumed two distinct duties. In rendering the title report the title insurance company serves as an abstractor of title and must list all matters of public record adversely affecting title to the real estate which is the subject of the title report. When a title insurance company fails to perform its duty to abstract title accurately, the title insurance company may be liable in tort for all damages proximately caused by such breach of duty. A title company's responsibility for its tortious conduct is distinct from the insurance company's responsibility existing on account of its policy of insurance. Different duties and responsibilities

37. See also Shotwell v. Transamerica Title Insurance Company, 91 Wash.2d 161, 588 P.2d 208 (1978). The Washington court has discussed the issue but has not yet decided it.

imposed on the title insurance company, therefore, can be the basis for separate causes of action—one cause of action in tort and another in contract." 354 N.W.2d at 158–159.

Support for the foregoing can also be found in § 552(1) of the Restatement (Second) of Torts, which states:

"One who, in the course of his business, profession or employment, or in any other transaction in which he has a pecuniary interest, supplies false information for the guidance of others in their business transactions, is subject to liability for pecuniary loss caused to them by their justifiable reliance upon the information, if he fails to exercise reasonable care or competence in obtaining or communicating the information."

The preliminary title report was given to the escrow by the title insurance company. On the preliminary report, there is a section of "requirements." The requirements contained a list of documents that had to be drafted and executed by the escrow in order for the title insurance company to insure title. The title insurance company knew and intended that the escrow officer would use its preliminary title report both to comply with the requirements and to prepare a closing escrow statement for the parties. Clearly, the above section of the Restatement applies.

To hold otherwise would be to completely ignore reality. In addition, we note what one authority has said about this issue:

"Applicants for a title insurance policy are interested in obtaining the insurance coverage, but they are sometimes more interested in what the company examination of title discloses. This is perhaps partly at the base of the prevailing philosophy of title insurance companies—stressing the service of risk delineation rather than risk coverage." Johnstone, Title Insurance, 66 Yale L.J. 492, 494 (1957).

The insurance company holds itself out as a searcher of titles and provides the information for the applicants to act upon, and the applicants expect and rely on this information in closing their deals. We agree fully with the decision of the Nebraska court in Heyd v. Chicago Title Insurance Company, supra.

Having concluded that the title company can be held liable in tort for its negligence, we turn our attention to the issue upon which the trial court based its decision: reliance or, in other words, proximate cause. It is helpful to reiterate the plaintiffs' theory of liability. They claimed that the failure of the title company to disclose the liens of record prevented them from exercising their option to cancel the contract and that, had they known of the existence of the liens, they would have canceled.

Thus the case really hinged on their assertion that they would have canceled the contract. On the other hand, the trial court had the testimony of the plaintiffs saying they would have canceled, pointing out that they had included special provisions in the agreement regarding the existence of any other undisclosed liens. On the other hand, there was evidence that Nieman had lied to them about the S & D Cattle Company loan, that the sewage system was damaged, that there was defective fixtures and appliances and that the partners were unable to obtain satisfactory financing prior to closing. In spite of these deficiencies, the plaintiffs chose to close the sale. They did not have to do so because of another special provision which allowed them to cancel the contract if they did not have the necessary financing.

We believe that the evidence in this case was capable of two conclusions. The trial court could have believed that, in view of their decision to close the sale in the face of the adverse circumstances which were known to them, the partners would not have exercised the option of cancellation because of additional liens, but would have gone forward and closed the sale anyway in the hope of securing additional financing. Alternatively, it could have decided to believe the plaintiffs and found that the additional liens would have been the straw that broke the camel's back. It chose the former conclusion and not the latter.

An appellate court will not disturb the findings of fact of the trial court unless they are clearly erroneous. * * * Deciding what the plaintiffs would have done in this case, had they had knowledge of the liens, was peculiarly for the trial court to decide and there is substantial evidence to support its conclusion.

Affirmed.

Notes and Questions

1. Title insurance policies often attempt to limit the insurer's liability to the indemnity specified in the policy and to disclaim the insurer's responsibility to search the title. Nevertheless, the representations of title companies as to the services they provide frequently identify title searching as one of these services. Binders or title commitments provided prior to a closing also may create the bases of subsequent tort suits for negligent search. A recent review of the cases revealed that 18 states now impose a duty on title insurers to do a competent title search, seven reject such a duty. See Palomar, Title Insurance Companies' Liability for Failure to Search Title and Disclose Record Title, 20 Creighton L.Rev. 455 (1987). Note, however, that the insurer is only liable in these suits for a negligent search. It is not liable for a competent search that fails to reveal a title defect.

2. Who may claim the benefit of the title company's title search? May a mortgagor claim reliance on the search carried out before issuance of the mortgagee policy? See Fox v. Title Guaranty and Abstract Co. of Mobile Inc., 337 So.2d 1300 (Ala.1976) (yes). May a purchaser who relies on a title company's abstract prepared for the vendor? See Williams v. Polgar, 391 Mich. 6, 215 N.W.2d 149 (1974) (yes). When should the statute of limitations begin to run, on the date the search is completed, or on the date a defect is subsequently discovered?

3. A title insurance company may also be liable if it fails to afford the insured a good faith defense of a title defect. The leading case of Jarchow

v. Transamerica Title Insurance Co., 48 Cal.App.3d 917, 122 Cal.Rptr. 470 (1975), awarded the plaintiff $200,000 in tort damages for mental distress where the title insurer failed to report an easement and then for three years failed to compensate the insured for the easement or eliminate it.

4. Whenever a title insurance company hires a lawyer to represent an insured against an adverse claim, the potential exists for confusion as to whom the lawyer represents, the insured or the insurer. When the insured subsequently turns on the insurer, claiming inadequate defense or bad faith failure to settle within the policy limits, this conflict can raise major problems. In Lake Havasu Community Hospital, Inc. v. Arizona Title Insurance and Trust Co., 141 Ariz. 363, 687 P.2d 371 (App.1984), for example, the insurer hired an attorney, Miller, to represent the insured in litigation involving the insured property. During the course of the litigation, the attorney disclosed to the insurer his belief that the insured was trying to settle the litigation and then to make a claim against the company. The court stated: "There is no question that Miller's letter to Arizona Title includes confidential and privileged information obtained by Miller as attorney for Community Hospital." 687 P.2d at 384. The court then held, under earlier Arizona precedent, that " * * * when an attorney, who is an insurance company's agent, uses the confidential relationship between an attorney and a client to gather information so as to deny an insured coverage under the policy, such conduct constitutes a waiver of any policy defense, and is so contrary to public policy that the insurance company is estopped as a matter of law from disclaiming liability under an exclusionary clause in the policy." Id. Finally, the court held that the company was estopped from claiming that it would not have settled for the policy limits absent the disclosure of privileged information by Miller. It awarded the insured the full value of the policy limits, plus $50,000 in punitive damages against the insurer for the attorney's unfaithfulness (holding the insurance company vicariously liable for the attorney's acts), even though the court otherwise concluded that the insurer would have been liable only for a much smaller amount.

I. LENDER LIABILITY

Many purchasers of residential real property who purchase without legal representation apparently think that if the lender is willing to accept the title, the title must be acceptable for the purchaser as well. How valid is this reasoning? What does the lender stand to lose if the title to a property proves defective or encumbered? What does the purchaser stand to lose? How do the interests of each change over time? Can you think of encumbrances that might affect the use of the property by the purchaser but not the security of the lender's loan? Moreover, what recourse does the purchaser have against the lender or its attorney if title proves defective? Consider the following case.

PAGE v. FRAZIER

Supreme Judicial Court of Massachusetts, 1983.
383 Mass. 55, 445 N.E.2d 148 (1983).

LYNCH, JUSTICE.

The plaintiffs appeal from an adverse decision on the merits of their claims of negligent misrepresentation against defendants Attorney Charles E. Frazier, Jr., and the Cape Cod Five Cents Savings Bank (bank), which retained Frazier to perform a real property title examination on property being purchased by the plaintiffs. A judge of the Superior Court, who heard the case without a jury, dismissed the complaint after making comprehensive findings of fact and rulings of law, summarized below. We granted the plaintiffs' motion for direct appellate review. We affirm the judgments.

The plaintiffs, husband and wife, purchased a house in Wellfleet in 1964. Beginning in 1967, the plaintiff Robert G. Page (Page) sought to ascertain the ownership of an abutting, unimproved parcel of slightly over 1.1 acres; * * * In November, 1972, Page entered into an agreement to purchase the parcel for $14,500, from heirs of Lorenzo Dow Baker (sellers). * * * Page applied to the bank for an $8,700 mortgage loan on November 21, 1972. The bank's mortgage application form included the following language: "(1) The responsibility of the attorney for the mortgagee is to protect the interest of the mortgagee, notwithstanding the fact that (a) the mortgagor shall be obligated to pay the legal fees of said attorney, and (b) the mortgagor is billed for such legal services by the mortgagee. (2) The mortgagor may, at his own expense, engage an attorney of his own selection to represent his own interests in the transaction." [38]

Page's application was approved on November 22, 1972. Thereafter the bank retained Frazier, an experienced conveyancing attorney, and a vice-president and trustee of the bank as well, to certify the title to the property and to draft the necessary legal instruments. The judge found that it was the bank's practice at that time to require an attorney so retained to certify a good, clear, marketable title. The bank also requested from the sellers' attorney, and received on or about December 8, 1972, a general list of title references to deeds, probate decrees, and wills to assist Frazier in his examination of the title. In February, 1973, the sellers' attorney forwarded to the bank a proposed deed without title references. When executed ultimately in April, 1973, the quitclaim deed from the sellers to the plaintiffs was in the same form as the proposed deed. The title references in the December 8 communication from the sellers' attorney were photocopied and

38. The plaintiffs have noted the use of this language, which appeared on the application for a mortgage loan on unimproved land, and which the judge termed as "statutory." General Laws c. 184, § 17B, inserted by St.1969, c. 423, required the language to be printed in large type only on applications for loans "on real estate consisting of a dwelling house with accommodations for four or less separate households and occupied or to be occupied in whole or in part by the obligor on the mortgage debt." By St.1972, c. 547, § 2, approved June 29, 1972, and in effect at the time of Page's application, a portion of the language required to appear on application forms was deleted. As the judge noted, St.1972, c. 547, § 1, also amended G.L. c. 93, by inserting § 70, which provided for limited liability of a bank's attorney to a borrower paying the attorney's fee, subject to the same dwelling and occupancy conditions contained in c. 184, § 17B. The judge ruled that G.L. c. 93, § 70, had no application to the case at bar.

appended to the quitclaim deed and were recorded with it, on April 17, 1973, by Frazier, or at his direction. In his title examination Frazier had also relied on five separate survey plans of abutting owners and an unrecorded survey plan prepared in 1926 which, upon his research, yielded a reference to a deed to Lorenzo Dow Baker in 1900. Frazier searched that chain of title from 1926 onward. The 1900 deed, however, had no connection with the subject locus, and the property which it described had been conveyed out in 1909. A survey plan prepared for the sellers in January, 1973, and available to Frazier during his examination, referred to a 1932 deed which the parties stipulated during trial did not describe the subject locus.

The judge found that Page was not "particularly conversant with the intricate elements or ramifications of title examinations. However, Robert Page [was] a high-level executive possessing concomitant intelligence, ability and knowledge of business transactions. [He had] both purchased and sold real property for his personal use on a number of occasions prior to the transaction in issue." Page had engaged Frazier in 1967 to review his will and had from time to time inquired of Frazier as to possible real estate sites in Wellfleet. In purchasing property prior to 1972, Page had retained another attorney.

With respect to the instant transaction, in addition to the mortgage application form, the following documents involving Page or Frazier were in evidence: (1) a letter from Frazier to Page, dated March 3, 1973, requesting the plaintiffs' signatures on an enclosed proposed mortgage deed, mortgage note, and disclosure form showing a bank attorney's charge of $125 for recording and for title certification, payable by the plaintiffs;[39] (2) a letter from Page to Frazier, dated March 6, 1973, indicating that all forms forwarded on March 3 had been signed and were being returned; (3) a letter from Page to Frazier, dictated on March 28, 1973, enclosing a check for the balance of the purchase price, and adding: " * * * I would appreciate it very much if you would have the deed properly recorded for me. I will not be represented by an attorney in this transaction"; (4) a letter from Frazier to a vice-president of the bank, dated April 19, 1973, certifying that he had examined the record title to the parcel and had recorded the mortgage note on April 17, 1973, also stating that "[t]itle at the time of said recording was free and clear of any and all encumbrances of record," and requesting that a check for the mortgage loan proceeds be forwarded "payable to me as Attorney for the Pages." The bank assumed this letter indicated a good, clear, marketable title. A copy of the letter was sent to Page by the bank. In July, 1974, Page entered into an agreement of first refusal on the parcel with Stanford and Dorothy Ross. In December, 1975, the Pages and the Rosses executed a purchase and sale agreement. When the prospective buyers' attorney was unable to find good record and marketable title, Page contacted Frazier, who attempted without success to obtain a release of the

---

39. Page was neither billed for this charge nor did he pay it. This fact, how- ever, would not preclude a finding that an attorney-client relationship existed. * * *

Rosses' right of first refusal on the parcel. An attorney subsequently retained by the bank and a title researcher engaged by Page's attorney could not find title in the plaintiffs from the reference on their quitclaim deed. The title researcher determined that the deed reference upon which Frazier had relied did not convey the subject locus as a matter of record. The plaintiffs then commenced this action against Frazier and the bank.

The judge found that no record title had been established in the plaintiffs and that no good, clear, marketable title in them was ascertainable, based on Frazier's examination. She further found that, although the plaintiffs had shown by a fair preponderance of the evidence that Frazier was negligent in the performance of his title examination, they had failed to show the existence of an attorney-client relationship between them and Frazier.[40] As she found that Frazier was an independent contractor retained by the bank to represent its interests, the judge declined to impute his negligent performance to the bank, which she found had neither expressly nor impliedly warranted title to Page. On appeal, the plaintiffs argue that an attorney-client relationship did exist between Frazier and them; that even if such a relationship did not exist, their action for negligent misrepresentation against Frazier should not be barred; that Frazier's negligence must be imputed to the bank; and that the bank negligently misrepresented to them the sufficiency of title to the parcel.

We consider first the plaintiffs' contention that there is a statutory basis for their claim against Frazier. We recognize that the Legislature has modified the common law, to a certain extent, through the provisions of G.L. c. 93, § 70. As enacted by St.1972, c. 547, § 1, and in effect at the time of the present transaction, § 70 provided in material part: "Whenever, in connection with the granting of any loan or credit to be secured by a mortgage on real estate improved with a dwelling designed to be occupied by not more than four families and occupied or to be occupied in whole or in part by the mortgagor, the mortgagor is required or agrees to pay or to be responsible for any fee or expense charged or incurred by any attorney acting for or on behalf of the mortgagee, the mortgagor or his attorney shall be given a copy of any certification of title to the mortgaged property rendered by the mortgagee's attorney, and such certification shall be deemed to have been rendered for the benefit of the mortgagor to the same extent as it is for the mortgagee." * * * The plaintiffs urge us to extend the principle of G.L. c. 93, § 70, to the case before us. We can find, however, no suggestion or implication in the clear language of the statute that it is intended to be applicable to purchasers of unimproved land. * * *

---

40. The judge specifically found: "Despite the one statement to the [b]ank at the conclusion of the transaction wherein Frazier referred to himself as the 'Attorney for the Pages,' I find that the only express contract between the plaintiff and Frazier was relative to the recording of the deed. As Frazier was representing the bank, I find no privity of contract between Page and Frazier nor any attorney-client relationship."

* * *

We turn next to the plaintiffs' argument that an attorney-client relationship existed between them and Frazier. * * * Whether an attorney-client relationship existed between Frazier and the plaintiffs was a disputed issue to be resolved by the trier of fact. * * * The judge's finding that no attorney-client relationship was created between Frazier and the plaintiffs is amply supported by the evidence. [ ] Such a relationship may be, but need not be, express; the relationship can be implied from the conduct of the parties. [ ] Here, the judge weighed all the evidence, including Page's education and experience, his communications with Frazier, the mortgage application's language relative to the attorney's fee and representation, and Frazier's conduct in making no direct certification at all to Page and in certifying to the bank after the transaction had closed. She concluded, from conflicting evidence, that the plaintiffs had not carried their burden of proving an express or implied attorney-client relationship. * * *

The plaintiffs argue that the absence of an attorney-client relationship should not preclude them from recovering from Frazier for negligent misrepresentation of good, clear, marketable title to the property they wished to purchase. While they cite to us no case wherein a mortgagee's attorney has been held liable to a mortgagor for negligent performance of a real property title examination, the plaintiffs point to a general common law trend permitting recovery by injured nonclients for the negligent conduct of attorneys. Cf. Lucas v. Hamm, 56 Cal.2d 583, 15 Cal.Rptr. 821, 364 P.2d 685 (1961), cert. denied, 368 U.S. 987, 82 S.Ct. 603, 7 L.Ed.2d 525 (1962) (lack of privity was not a bar to an action by beneficiaries of a will alleging negligent drafting by the testator's attorney). We do not find the plaintiffs' authorities persuasive here, as we deal with the attorney's liability to another where the attorney is also under an independent and potentially conflicting duty to a client. [ ] See also Attorney Negligence in Real Estate Title Examination and Will Drafting: Elimination of the Privity Requirement as a Bar to Recovery by Foreseeable Third Parties, 17 New Eng.L.Rev. 955 (1982). As the judge noted in the instant case, "It is not only in the matter of items such as prepayment rights, disclosure law, late charge provisions and special mortgage provisions where a conflict of interest could arise if the attorney represented both bank and borrower, but many experienced conveyancers would acknowledge that there is a conflict of interest even with respect to title as there are some title defects which will not make the property unsatisfactory as a security but which would concern a buyer." Compare Lucas v. Hamm, supra, with Amey, Inc. v. Henderson, Franklin, Starnes & Holt, P.A., 367 So.2d 633 (Fla.Dist.Ct.App.1979) (allowance of defendants' motion for summary judgment on claims of attorney-client relationship and third-party beneficiary theory upheld where bank's attorneys were alleged by mortgagor to have negligently failed to discover a tax lien on the subject property).

* * *

* * * The present plaintiffs signed a mortgage application, conspicuous upon which was the bank's cautionary advice that its attorney would represent its interests, and that the plaintiffs might retain their own attorney to represent their interests. Because of what she termed this "strong exculpatory language," the judge concluded that the plaintiffs were not "entitled * * * to rely upon the defendant's performance." * * * In the case at bar, Frazier's contract with the bank was exclusively and expressly for the benefit and protection of the bank. Quite conceivably, the bank's interest could have differed materially from the plaintiffs' and the plaintiffs have not shown that they knew what type of certification the bank would require of Frazier at the time they claim reliance upon his performance. Nor do we think they have shown that Frazier could foresee their reliance from a letter dictated by Page five days before he expected the transaction to close, in which he informed Frazier that he was not represented by an attorney.

* * * The judge noted that Page's belief "that Frazier's role as the [b]ank's attorney in searching the title was representative of his interest as well * * * is not unusual * * * when a bank requires the borrower to pay the attorney's fee." Inherent in such a belief is the surmise that the client's interest is identical to the nonclient's. "However, this is a calculated risk, and if it proves to be unfounded, the buyer has no claim that the lawyer violates a duty owed to him." Amey, Inc. v. Henderson, Franklin, Starnes & Holt, P.A., 367 So.2d 633, 635 (Fla.Dist.Ct.App.1979). Where, as here, a nonclient takes the chance that the client's interests are in harmony with his own, and does so in the face of an express warning that the interests may differ, his claim of foreseeable reliance cannot be rescued simply because, in retrospect, the interests are shown not to have differed. * * *

The plaintiffs also seek recovery from the bank for its alleged negligent misrepresentation that Frazier's title examination had revealed no irregularities. * * * Page testified that he telephoned a vice-president of the bank to inquire whether his loan application had been approved, and that during the conversation he said that he "would be using the bank's attorney, * * * would not be using an attorney [because] it was a simple transaction * * * [and he] saw no sense in employing two attorneys to do the same job, or words to that effect." Beyond this testimony, the record does not show that the plaintiffs made any inquiry with respect to the condition of the title, nor does it show that either defendant made any representation whatsoever to the plaintiffs with respect to the status of the title examination or the sufficiency of the title prior to the closing. In the absence of some evidence of affirmative conduct on the part of the bank, there could be no reasonable understanding or reliance by the plaintiffs at the time the plaintiffs would have had to rely on such conduct, i.e., before they closed the sale. [ ] It follows that there could be no knowledge of reliance by the bank. [ ] The evidence supports the judge's finding of "no express or implied warranty on the part of the [b]ank to Page relative to the title of the locus." Since there was no evidence of any representations on behalf of the bank to Page, this finding also precludes recovery on the basis of negligent misrepresentation.

On our view that this case presents no demonstrated duty by Frazier or the bank to the plaintiffs with respect to performance of the title examination, the plaintiffs' arguments advancing liability on the theory that Frazier was an employee or agent of the bank are unavailing.

Judgment affirmed.

Notes and Questions

1. In addition to the theories argued in the principal case, a purchaser might also argue breach of contract, if contractual terms obligate the lender to establish clear title for the benefit of the purchaser, or breach of fiduciary duty. In the absence of a statute like the Massachusetts provision distinguished in the principal case, however, the courts are reluctant to find lenders liable to purchaser. See Note, Mortgage Lender Liability to the Purchasers of New or Existing Homes, 1988 U.Ill.L.Rev. 191.

2. Would it be unethical for an attorney to represent both a lender and a purchaser in conducting a title search?

3. What protection is in fact enjoyed by a purchaser of residential real property who does not retain an attorney for the transaction, but rather relies on the issuance of a title policy without significant specific exceptions and the fact that a lender will finance most of the purchase price? Would the purchaser be significantly better protected if she retained an attorney to handle the purchase? Would the purchaser be more or less likely to end up in disputes or litigation if he or she retained an attorney to handle the transaction? Does the added cost of an attorney exceed the added benefit? How would you go about answering these questions?

IV. THE CONDITION OF THE PREMISES

Under modern conditions the purchaser of real property is often at least as interested in the physical condition of the building that sits on the property as in the condition of the title to the property underlying the building. Legal disputes concerning the condition of the improvements on the premises commonly arise under two circumstances. First, if the condition of the improvements changes dramatically (because of fire, flood, or other disaster) while the property is under contract (i.e. between the time the contract is signed and the time that title changes hands), the parties argue over who bears the risk of loss. Second, if improvements prove to be defective, the purchaser turns to those who participated in the sale of the property for compensation for the damages attributable to the defects.

A. RISK OF LOSS WHILE THE PROPERTY IS UNDER CONTRACT

SKELLY OIL COMPANY v. ASHMORE

Supreme Court of Missouri, 1963.
365 S.W.2d 582.

HYDE, JUDGE.

* * *

This is a suit by the purchaser, Skelly Oil Company, a corporation, against the vendors, Tom A. Ashmore and Madelyn Ashmore, husband and wife, in two counts. Count One is for the specific performance of a contract to sell the north half of a certain described southwest corner lot (fronting 97½ feet on Main and 195 feet on 42nd Streets) in that part of Joplin lying in Newton County. Count Two seeks an abatement in the purchase price of $10,000, being the proceeds received by the vendors under an insurance policy on a building on the property, which building was destroyed by fire in the interim between the execution of the contract of sale and the time for closing of said sale by the exchange of the $20,000 consideration for the deed to the property. * * * The trial court found the issues in favor of the purchaser, decreed specific performance, and applied the $10,000 insurance proceeds on the $20,000 purchase price. The vendors have appealed.

The vendors acquired this property about 1953, and operated a grocery store in the concrete block building, with fixtures and furniture, and a one story frame "smoke house" thereon. * * *

Joe Busby, of the Kansas City office of the Skelly Oil Company real estate department, and Mr. Ashmore conducted the negotiations resulting in the contract of sale. * * * Busby secured the execution of a Skelly printed form of option by the vendors, dated July 31, 1957, for Skelly "to purchase" for the sum of $20,000, "payable in cash upon delivery of deed" said property, "together with the buildings, driveways, and all construction and equipment thereon, at any time before" August 31, 1957. * * * The option provided in typewriting (referring to the Jones lease): "Purchaser agrees to honor present lease on above property until expiration." * * *

* * *

[After attempts to terminate the lease proved unsuccessful] Busby informed Ashmore Skelly had decided to purchase under its option with Jones in possession under his lease. * * *

* * *

* * * By letter to the Ashmores under date of March 4, 1958, Skelly explicitly stated: "This letter is to inform you that Skelly Oil Company does hereby exercise its option to purchase the above described property for the sum of $20,000.00, subject to all the terms and conditions of the above referred to option, * * *"

The latter part of March Busby telephoned to Ashmore in Lawton and they agreed to meet in Joplin on April 16, 1958, to close the transaction.

The concrete block building, furniture and fixtures were destroyed by fire on April 7, 1958, without fault of either party.

Skelly's Kansas City headquarters advised Busby, who was in St. Joseph, on April 7 of the fire. The next day Busby telephoned Ashmore from Kansas City. In this conversation Ashmore said he had insurance on the building and fixtures, naming the company in Kansas City carrying it. * * * Busby called the insurance company and was informed there was $10,000 insurance on the building and $4,000 on the fixtures. He reported this to the purchaser's legal department. Then, after research, the legal department concluded that Skelly was entitled to have the insurance on the building applied on the purchase price. The closing papers were prepared accordingly.

The closing of the transaction was considered by the parties on April 15, 16 and 17. Busby [and Skelly's lawyer] * * * informed Ashmore * * * that Skelly thought it was entitled to the insurance proceeds on the building and would like an assignment of the insurance proceeds. When Ashmore disagreed, they informed him Skelly would close the deal and pay him the contract price but would not waive its rights to the insurance proceeds in so doing. Ashmore would not agree to this. * * *

By letter dated April 26, 1958, the Ashmores notified Skelly that the "option agreement" was rescinded "because it was given without consideration and is therefore not binding on us and for the further reason that you have refused to complete the purchase unless we reduce the agreed price, which constitutes a breach of the terms of the agreement."

A month or so later the Phoenix Insurance Company, under the standard mortgage clause, paid the Bank of Neosho the balance due on the vendors' notes, $7,242.46, and $2,757.54, the balance of the $10,000 insurance on the building, to the vendors, and also paid the vendors the $4,000 insurance carried on the furniture and fixtures.

This purchaser's claims are founded on the contract of sale in its letter of March 4, 1958, and the option therein referred to, which letter was "acknowledged and agreed to" by the vendors. * * *

* * *

The contract of sale here involved contained no provision as to who assumed the risk of loss occasioned by a destruction of the building, or for protecting the building by insurance or for allocating any insurance proceeds received therefor. When the parties met to close the sale on April 16, the purchaser's counsel informed vendors and their attorney he was relying on Standard Oil Co. v. Dye, 223 Mo.App. 926, 20 S.W.2d 946, for purchaser's claim to the $10,000 insurance proceeds on the building. Purchaser made no claim to the $4,000 paid vendors for the loss of the furniture and fixtures. It is stated in 3 American Law of Property, § 11.30, p. 90, that in the circumstances here presented at least five different views have been advanced for allocating the burden of fortuitous loss between vendor and purchaser of real estate. We summarize those mentioned: (1) The view first enunciated in Paine v. Meller (Ch. 1801, 6 Ves.Jr. 349, 31 Eng. Reprint 1088, 1089) is said to be the most widely accepted; holding that from the time of the contract of sale of real estate the burden of fortuitous loss was on the purchaser even though the vendor retained possession. (2) The loss is on the vendor until legal title is conveyed, although the purchaser is in possession, stated to be a strong minority. (3) The burden of loss should be on the vendor until the time agreed upon for conveying the legal title, and thereafter on the purchaser unless the vendor be in such default as to preclude specific performance, nor recognized in the decisions. (4) The burden of the loss should be on the party in possession, whether vendor or purchaser, so considered by some courts. (5) The burden of loss should be on the vendor unless there is something in the contract or in the relation of the parties from which the court can infer a different intention, stating "this rather vague test" has not received any avowed judicial acceptance, although it is not inconsistent with jurisdictions holding the loss is on the vendor until conveyance or jurisdictions adopting the possession test. As to the weight of the authority, see also 27 A.L.R.2d 448; Tiffany, Real Property, 3rd ed., § 309.

We do not agree that we should adopt the arbitrary rule of Paine v. Meller, supra, and Standard Oil Co. v. Dye, supra, that there is equitable conversion from the time of making a contract for sale and purchase of land and that the risk of loss from destruction of buildings or other substantial part of the property is from that moment on the purchaser. * * *

We take the view stated in an article on Equitable Conversion by Contract, 13 Columbia Law Review 369, 386, Dean Harlan F. Stone, later Chief Justice Stone, in which he points out that the only reason why a contract for the sale of land by the owner to another operates to effect conversion is that a court of equity will compel him specifically to perform his contract. He further states: "A preliminary to the determination of the question whether there is equitable ownership of land must therefore necessarily be the determination of the question whether there is a contract which can be and ought to be specifically performed *at the very time when the court is called upon to perform it.* This process of reasoning is, however, reversed in those jurisdictions where the "burden of loss" is cast upon the vendee. The question is whether there shall be a specific performance of the contract, thus casting the burden on the vendee, by compelling him to pay the full purchase price for the subject matter of the contract, a substantial part of which has been destroyed. The question is answered somewhat in this wise: equitable ownership of the vendee in the subject matter of the contract can exist only where the contract is one which equity will specifically perform. The vendee of land is equitably entitled to land, therefore the vendee may be compelled to perform, although the vendor is unable to give in return the performance stipulated for by his contract. The *non sequitur* involved in the proposition that performance may be had because of the equitable ownership of the land by the vendee, which in turn depends upon the right of performance, is evident. The doctrine of equitable conversion, so far as it is exemplified by the authorities hitherto considered, cannot lead to the result of casting the burden of loss on the vendee, since the *conversion depends upon the question whether the contract should in equity be performed.* In all other cases where the vendee is treated as the equitable owner of the land, it is only because the contract is one which equity first determines should be specifically performed.

"Whether a plaintiff, in breach of his contract by a default which goes to the essence, as in the case of the destruction of a substantial part of the subject matter of the contract, should be entitled to specific performance, is a question which is answered in the negative in every case except that of destruction of the subject matter of the contract. To give a plaintiff specific performance of the contract when he is unable to perform the contract on his own part, violates the fundamental rule of equity that * * * *equity will not compel a defendant to perform when it is unable to so frame its decree as to compel the plaintiff to give in return substantially what he has undertaken to give* or to do for the defendant.

"The rule of casting the 'burden of loss' on the vendee by specific performance if justifiable at all can only be explained and justified upon one of two theories: first, that since equity has for most purposes treated the vendee as the equitable owner, it should do so for all purposes, although *this ignores the fact that in all other cases the vendee is so treated only because the contract is either being performed or in equity ought to be performed;* or, second, which is substantially the same proposition in a different form, the specific performance which casts the burden on the vendee is an incident to and a consequence of an equitable conversion, whereas in all other equity relations growing out of the contract, the equitable conversion, if it exists, is an incident to and consequence of, a specific performance. Certainly nothing could be more illogical than this process of reasoning." (Emphasis ours.)

For these reasons, we do not agree with the rule that arbitrarily places the risk of loss on the vendee from the time the contract is made. Instead we believe the Massachusetts rule is the proper rule. It is thus stated in Libman v. Levenson, 236 Mass. 221, 128 N.E. 13, 22 A.L.R. 560: When "the conveyance is to be made of the whole estate, including both land and buildings, for an entire price, and the value of the buildings constitutes a large part of the total value of the estate, and the terms of the agreement show that they constituted an important part of the subject matter of the contract * * * the contract is to be construed as subject to the implied condition that it no longer shall be binding if, before the time for the conveyance to be made, the buildings are destroyed by fire. The loss by the fire falls upon the vendor, the owner; and if he has not protected himself by insurance, he can have no reimbursement of this loss; but the contract is no longer binding upon either party. If the purchaser has advanced any part of the price, he can recover it back. [ ] If the change in the value of the estate is not so great, or if it appears that the building did not constitute so material a part of the estate to be conveyed as to result in an annulling of the contract, specific performance may be decreed, with compensation for any breach of agreement, or relief may be given in damages." [ ] * * * The reason for the Massachusetts rule is that specific performance is based on what is equitable; and it is not equitable to make a vendee pay the vendor for something the vendor cannot give him.

However, the issue in this case is not whether the vendee can be compelled to take the property without the building but whether the vendee is entitled to enforce the contract of sale, with the insurance proceeds substituted for the destroyed building. We see no inequity to defendants in such enforcement since they will receive the full amount ($20,000.00) for which they contracted to sell the property. Their contract not only described the land but also specifically stated they sold it "together with the buildings, driveways and all construction thereon." While the words "Service Station Site" appeared in the caption of the option contract and that no doubt was the ultimate use plaintiff intended to make of the land, the final agreement made by the parties was that plaintiff would take it subject to a lease of the building which would have brought plaintiff about $6,150.00 in rent during the term of the lease. Moreover, defendants' own evidence showed the building was valued in the insurance adjustment at $16,716.00 from which $4,179.00 was deducted for depreciation, making the loss $12,-537.00. Therefore, defendants are not in a very good position to say the building was of no value to plaintiff. Furthermore, plaintiff having contracted for the land with the building on it, the decision concerning use or removal of the building, or even for resale of the entire property, was for the plaintiff to make. Statements were in evidence about the use of the building and its value to plaintiff made by its employee who negotiated the purchase but he was not one of plaintiff's chief executive officers nor possessed of authority to bind its board of directors. The short of the matter is that defendants will get all they bargained for; but without the building or its value plaintiff will not.

We therefore affirm the judgment and decree of the trial court.

STORCKMAN, JUDGE (dissenting).

I agree that the parties on March 7, 1958, entered into a valid contract for the transfer of the real estate, but in the circumstances I cannot assent to the holding that the plaintiff is entitled to specific performance on any terms other than those of the purchase contract without reduction in the contract price. * * *

The evidence is convincing that Skelly Oil Company was buying the lot as a site for a service station and that in so using it they not only wanted the Jones's lease terminated but intended to tear down and remove the building in question. * * * This conduct is consistent with its prior activities, but is inconsistent with plaintiff's present contention that the building and its rental under the lease represented a substantial part of the consideration for the purchase of the real estate.

* * *

The plaintiff introduced no evidence of the market value of the property before or after the fire in support of the allegations in Court 2. The amount paid by the insurance company is of little or no benefit as evidence of the actual value of the building * * *. Defendants' evidence tended to prove that the real estate was worth more as a site for a service station after the fire than before and that the value of the real estate after the fire was in excess of $20,000.

The claim of neither party is particularly compelling insofar as specific performance in this case is concerned. The destruction of the building by fire, its insurance, and the disposition of the insurance proceeds were matters not contemplated by the parties and not provided for in the purchase contract documents. Skelly's representative did not know that Mr. Ashmore carried insurance on the building until after the fire, and he then told Mr. Ashmore that despite the fire the deal would be closed on the agreed date. Skelly's present claims are an afterthought inconsistent with its conduct throughout the negotiations and prior to the closing date.

In short, as to both Skelly and the Ashmores, the destruction of the insured building was a fortuitous circumstance supplying the opportunity to rid the property of a vexatious lease, to dispose of the building, and at the same time resulting in a windfall of $10,000. And the problem, in fact the only seriously contested issue between the parties, is which of them is to have the advantage of this piece of good fortune. Skelly contracted to pay $20,000 for the property. If it is awarded the $10,000 windfall, it will receive a $20,000 lot for $10,000. If the Ashmores retain the $10,000, they will in fact have realized $30,000 for a piece of property they have agreed to sell for $20,000.

In claiming the proceeds of the Ashmores' fire insurance policy, Skelly did not contend that the value of the real estate as a service station site had decreased. * * * [Skelly relied on cases following Paine v. Meller, (1801) 6 Ves.Jr. 349, 31 Eng.Reprint 1088. The holding of that case] is "that a contract to sell real property vests the equitable ownership of the property in the purchaser, with the corollary that any loss by destruction of the property through casualty during the pendency of the contract must be borne by the purchaser." Annotation 27 A.L.R.2d 444, 446. The two-fold rationale of this doctrine is a maxim that "equity regards as done that which should have been done," from which it is said the "vendor becomes a mere trustee, holding the legal title for the benefit of the purchaser or as security for the price." 27 A.L.R.2d 444, 448, 449. All of the experts and scholars seem to agree that this doctrine and its rationale is misplaced if not unsound. To illustrate see only 4 Williston, Contracts, §§ 928–943B, pp. 2605–2639. As to the maxim, Williston said, "Only the hoary age and frequent repetition of the maxim prevents a general recognition of its absurdi- ty." 4 Williston, Contracts, § 929, p. 2607. As to the corollary, Williston points out that while the purchaser may have an interest in the property, it is equally clear that the vendor likewise has an interest, and as for the vendor's being a trustee for the purchaser observes, "However often the words may be repeated, it cannot be true that the vendor is trustee for the purchaser." 4 Williston, Contracts, § 936, p. 2622. See also Pound "The Progress of The Law—Equity", 33 Harv.L.R. 813, 830.

Nevertheless, adapting this doctrine and following a majority opin- ion in another English case, Rayner v. Preston, (1881) L.R. 18 Ch.Div. 1 (CA), the rule as stated in the Dye case has evolved: "Where the purchaser as equitable owner will bear the loss occasioned by a destruc- tion of the property pending completion of the sale, and the contract is silent as to insurance, the rule quite generally followed is that the proceeds of the vendor's insurance policies, even though the purchaser did not contribute to their maintenance, constitute a trust fund for the benefit of the purchaser to be credited on the purchase price of the destroyed property, the theory being that the vendor is a trustee of the property for the purchaser." Annotation 64 A.L.R.2d 1402, 1406. Many jurisdictions have modified or do not follow this doctrine, some take the view that the vendor's insurance policy is personal to him, and Parliament has enacted a statute which entirely changes the English rule. 4 Mo.L.R. 290, 296. The rule is not as general as the annotator indicated, and as with the rule upon which it is founded, all the experts agree that it is unsound, their only point of disagreement is as to what the rule should be. See 4 Williston, Contracts, ss 928–943; Vance, Insurance, § 131, p. 777, and 34 Yale L.J. 87; Vanneman, "Risk of Loss, Between Vendor and Purchaser", 8 Minn.L.R. 127; Pound, "The Progress of The Law", 33 Har.L.R. 813, and the excellent student note to Standard Oil Co. v. Dye in 4 Mo.L.R. 290. * * *

* * *

Automatic application of the doctrine that "equity regards that as done which ought to be done", in the circumstances of this case, begs the question of what ought to be done. Because the insurance proceeds may be a windfall to those legally entitled does not necessarily mean that justice will be accomplished by transferring them elsewhere. * * *

A valid legal excuse is a sufficient reason for refusal of specific performance. * * * Destruction of a particular thing upon which the contract depends is generally regarded as a legal excuse for nonper- formance. * * *

* * *

If plaintiff's contention is that there has been a substantial failure or impairment of the consideration of the contract by reason of the destruction of the building, then I do not think that the Ashmores should be entitled to specific performance, and because of the theory of mutuality it would seem that Skelly would not be entitled to specific performance unless it was willing to perform its legal obligations under the purchase contract as drawn. We would not be justified in making a new contract for the parties to cover the building insurance, and a court of equity will not decree specific performance of a contract that is incomplete, indefinite or uncertain. * * *

* * *

But Skelly did not after the fire or in this action elect to abandon the contract although the Ashmores gave it the opportunity to do so rather than to sell at the reduced price. It is quite evident that Skelly has received one windfall as the result of the fire in that the lease is terminated and the site can be cleared at less cost. It has not shown itself to be entitled to another, the one now legally vested in the Ashmores. Ideally the purchase contract should be set aside so that the parties could negotiate a new one based on the property in its present condition. But the plaintiff by its election to take title has foreclosed this possibility.

[The majority] * * * professes to repudiate the equitable conversion theory and to adopt unequivocally the Massachusetts rule, * * *.

Obviously the majority opinion did not find that the value of the building constituted "a large part of the total value of the estate" or "an important part of the subject matter of the contract", else it would have declared the sales contract no longer binding under the Massachusetts rule. What it had to find was that the value of the building was not so great or such a material part of the estate to be conveyed as to interfere with the decree of specific performance.

But at this point the majority opinion abandons any pretense of following the Massachusetts rule and switches back to the equitable conversion theory and awards the insurance proceeds as such to the vendee without a determination of compensation for breach or relief to be given in damages. The value of the building for insurance purposes or as a structure to house a retail store is not necessarily the proper measure of the compensation or damages to which the plaintiff is entitled. It might be considerably less than such a figure if Skelly intended to remove the building as soon as it had the legal right to do so. Obviously the Massachusetts rule is not tied in with insurance at all and that is as it should be. Logically the majority opinion should have remanded the case for a determination of the amount of actual damages suffered by Skelly or the compensation to which it is entitled if it still wants specific performance. This is undoubtedly what the Massachusetts rule contemplates. I would find no fault with such a procedure.

Such evidence would also have a bearing on whether specific performance should be decreed at all, which was the first matter to be determined. Actually without such evidence the court does not have any basis for its finding as to the value of the building to the vendee and whether it was "an important part of the subject matter of the contract". Such a determination is a necessary prerequisite to granting or denying specific performance under the Massachusetts rule before the assessment of damages is reached. As the opinion stands, the adoption of the Massachusetts rule is more imaginary than real. The equitable conversion theory is applied, not the Massachusetts rule.

* * *

Notes and Questions

1. How does the contract reproduced above at pages 446–450 handle the problem of risk of loss? Why does it not adopt the common-law equitable conversion approach?

2. The doctrine of equitable conversion represents the triumph of doctrinal elegance over common sense and the expectations of the parties to a transaction. The Skelley case explores fully the roots of the doctrine and its most important application: the situation where the property is destroyed during the contract period. The doctrine has been applied also, however, where a vendor or purchaser dies with real property passing to one person or groups of persons and the personal property passing to another by will or intestate succession. Under a rigorous application of the doctrine of equitable conversion, equitable title to the property would pass as realty to those who inherit the real property from the purchaser; the obligation to pay for, or exonerate, the land would be imposed on the personal representative, to be satisfied from the personal property. Conversely, legal title would pass to those who inherited real property from the vendor, but would be held subject to the equitable obligation to convey the property. The proceeds from the property equitably would belong to the personal representative of the vendor, to be turned over to the legatees or next-of-kin.

In most states, heirs and next-of-kin are the same persons, so the rule is only important if property passes under a will that distinguishes between those who inherit real and those who inherit personal property. Where a will is involved, courts should be more concerned with the intent of the testator than with doctrinal elegance, but the rule of equitable conversion is still applied in some cases, particularly where the testator's intent is unclear. To explore the vagaries of this application of the doctrine further, consult III The American Law of Property, §§ 11.26 and 11.27.

When creditors of the vendor attempt to attach a judgment lien against property under contract, some courts also apply the doctrine of equitable conversion, finding that the property is no longer equitably that of the vendor. The lien, which attaches to all real property of the judgment debtor, thus does not attach. Other cases reject the doctrine and allow the lien to attach. The rights of the purchaser, however, are not affected unless he has notice of the lien, and even then, he is merely obligated to pay the creditor rather than the vendor payments due under the contract.

Should the doctrine of equitable conversion apply if property under contract is seized under the eminent domain authority? Should it apply if changed zoning or environmental regulations deprive the land of much of its value between the contract and closing?

3. The Uniform Vendor and Purchaser Risk Act (UVPRA) is one of several model acts drafted to address the risk of loss problem. It was drafted by Professor Samuel Williston and has been adopted by twelve jurisdictions.

Any contract hereafter made in this State for the purchase and sale of realty shall be interpreted as including an agreement that the parties shall have the following rights and duties, unless the contract expressly provides otherwise:

(a) If, when neither the legal title nor the possession of the subject matter of the contract has been transferred, all or a material part thereof is destroyed without fault of the purchaser or is taken by eminent domain, the vendor cannot enforce the contract, and the purchaser is entitled to recover any portion of the price that he has paid;

(b) If, when either the legal title or the possession of the subject matter of the contract has been transferred, all of any part thereof is destroyed without fault of the vendor or is taken by eminent domain, the purchaser is not thereby relieved from a duty to pay the price, nor is he entitled to recover any portion thereof that he has paid.

See also § 2–406 of the Uniform Land Transactions Act.

Does the UVPRA solve the problem presented in the Skelley case? Was the loss material in *Skelley*? If not, what relief, if any, does the UVPRA afford *Skelley*?

B. REMEDIES FOR DEFECTS IN THE PREMISES AFTER THE PROPERTY IS TRANSFERRED

Not uncommonly the purchaser of real property is disappointed with the building he has bought. The land beneath it settles, the walls, ceilings, and basement floors crack, the roof leaks, termite infestation is discovered, the plumbing or wiring is defective, the well is poisoned. The purchaser then looks to those with whom he dealt in the conveyancing process for relief. If he bought the property from a builder or developer, he may make, along with other claims, a straightforward breach of warranty claim for defective merchandise. If the property was a used building, purchased from a previous owner, analogies to the commercial law setting are less obvious. The buyer also may look to those he trusted and depended on to protect his interests in the purchase process: the real estate broker, the lender, an appraiser, perhaps even a loan guarantor such as the VA or FHA. Traditionally, the doctrine of caveat emptor left the buyer unprotected, wherever he may have turned. But this is changing, as the following cases illustrate.

TUSCH ENTERPRISES v. COFFIN

Supreme Court of Idaho, 1987.
113 Idaho 37, 740 P.2d 1022.

DONALDSON, JUSTICE.

Tusch Enterprises appeals from an order of the district court granting summary judgment in favor of Robert and Elizabeth Vander Boegh, husband and wife, and Rex T. Coffin. Tusch Enterprises brought this action after discovering that residential duplexes it had recently purchased suffered from major structural infirmities. The complaint advanced the following theories of recovery: (1) negligence, (2) misrepresentation, (3) express warranty, and (4) implied warranty of habitability. We reverse the entry of summary judgment as to the misrepresentation and implied warranty of habitability counts.

I

FACTS

We present the facts in the light most favorable to Tusch Enterprises. Robert Vander Boegh, a man with considerable experience in the road construction business, and his wife owned land in Pocatello, Idaho, and decided to build three duplexes. The rolling foothill upon which the duplexes were to be built was levelled for construction by Bengal Construction. The Vander Boeghs then contracted with Rex Coffin, a building contractor, to erect the duplexes. Pursuant to their agreement, Coffin was to prepare plans for the duplexes, secure all the necessary building permits, and build the structures. The site preparation and the outside work, such as gutters, lawns, curbs, and grading, were left to Robert Vander Boegh to do, or to contract out.

Coffin began working on the site in the fall of 1975. In his deposition, he describes some difficulties he encountered in securing a permit:

* * *

Throughout his deposition, Coffin testifies that Robert Vander Boegh told him the site had been cut from the mountain, and that no fill dirt had been used. The presence of fill dirt is significant because it tends to compact more and is thus more likely to cause foundations to settle and crack. During construction, Coffin became concerned enough about the "softness" of the soil where the south duplex was to be built that he asked a building inspector to investigate. Coffin testifies that the softness was brought to Vander Boegh's attention:

* * *

In early 1976, after the duplexes were completed, the Vander Boeghs began renting out the duplex apartments. Later, they listed the properties for sale with a realtor. * * *

On June 7, 1978, Tusch Enterprises offered to purchase the duplexes for $125,000. The offer was rejected. During this time period, Marianne Tusch met with Robert Vander Boegh and his realtor. In her deposition, Marianne Tusch testifies that Vander Boegh informed her he worked for a construction company, had access to site preparation equipment, and had participated in the site preparation. She also testifies that Vander Boegh stated the buildings were of "good quality construction." By affidavit, she asserts that she relied upon these representations. On June 15, 1978, a second offer of about $140,000 was communicated to the Vander Boeghs. Vander Boegh told Marianne Tusch that he would either accept the second offer or take the property off the market. He chose the latter.

Sometime later, the duplexes were re-listed. Tusch Enterprises became aware of this, and on March 27, 1979, submitted an offer of $140,000. The Vander Boeghs accepted this third offer, though it was substantially the same as the one they had rejected only nine months earlier.

Prior to purchasing the units, Tusch Enterprises had inspected them and noticed no major defects. However, about one month after purchasing the duplexes, Tusch Enterprises discovered from a tenant that the south unit was having problems. The walls had begun cracking around the windows and many of the doors would not close properly. Further investigation revealed that the foundation was cracking. Geotechnical and construction experts have submitted affidavits and testified by deposition of their opinion that the foundation had been partially constructed on fill dirt, which had compacted causing the foundation to settle and crack. They are of the opinion that the foundation was improperly constructed given the fill dirt conditions.

Marianne Tusch testifies in her deposition that she was not told of the fill dirt conditions, or of the possible problems with the foundation. She further testifies that one of the cracks in the south unit appeared to have been filled in, or patched, with cement. After discovering the problems with the foundation, Tusch Enterprises learned from the Vander Boeghs that Coffin had actually constructed the duplexes and attempted, without success, to discuss the problems with Coffin. Tusch Enterprises expended a great deal of money remedying the problems. The structural defects have caused damage to the duplexes themselves and to the parking lot, and have caused losses in rental income, but Tusch Enterprises has suffered no personal injuries and has suffered no damage to property other than that which was the subject of the duplex sales transaction.

Suit was filed against the Vander Boeghs and Coffin to seek compensation for these structural defects. Tusch Enterprises alleged negligence, misrepresentation, express warranty, and implied warranty and prayed for damages for loss of rental value and costs of repair. The case was before a number of district judges at different stages, and eventually summary judgment was entered against Tusch Enterprises as to all four theories of recovery.

* * *

II

NEGLIGENCE

Tusch Enterprises alleges negligence on the part of the Vander Boeghs and Coffin in the design and construction of the duplexes. However, the only damages it alleges are lost rental income and property damage to the duplexes and the parking lot. These losses are economic. * * *

In Clark v. International Harvester Co., 99 Idaho 326, 581 P.2d 784 (1978), we had to decide whether the purchaser of a defective product who has suffered only economic losses may recover those losses in a negligence action against the manufacturer. We ruled that purely economic losses are not recoverable in negligence. Other courts have criticized limiting the negligence theory in this manner. See, e.g., Council of Co–Owners v. Whiting–Turner, 308 Md. 18, 517 A.2d 336, 344–45 (1986), and the cases cited therein. These courts argue that the distinction between economic and other loss is arbitrary. However, as we explained in Clark with the words of Justice Traynor, in our view:

> "[t]he distinction that the law has drawn between tort recovery for physical injuries and warranty recovery for economic loss is not arbitrary and does not rest on the 'luck' of one plaintiff in having an accident causing physical injury. The distinction rests, rather, on an understanding of the nature of the responsibility a manufacturer must undertake in distributing his products. He can appropriately be held liable for physical injuries caused by defects by requiring his goods to match a standard of safety defined in terms of conditions that create unreasonable risks of harm. He cannot be held for the level of performance of his products in the consumer's business unless he agrees [expressly or impliedly] that the product was designed to meet the consumer's demands." Clark, supra, 99 Idaho at 334, 581 P.2d at 792, quoting Seely v. White Motor Co., 63 Cal.2d 9, 45 Cal.Rptr. 17, 23, 403 P.2d 145, 151 (1965). (Addition ours.)

* * *

We adhere to the view expressed in Clark, and, accordingly, affirm the decision of the court below dismissing Tusch Enterprises' negligence claims.

III

MISREPRESENTATION

In its complaint, Tusch Enterprises alleges misrepresentation on the part of Robert Vander Boegh. Tusch Enterprises directs the court's attention to Faw v. Greenwood, 101 Idaho 387, 613 P.2d 1338 (1980), and argues that the elements of misrepresentation outlined therein have been satisfied. The elements are as follows:

"(1) a representation; (2) its falsity; (3) its materiality; (4) the speaker's knowledge of its falsity or ignorance of its truth; (5) his intent that it should be acted on by the person and in the manner reasonably contemplated; (6) the hearer's ignorance of its falsity; (7) his reliance on the truth; (8) his right to rely thereon; and (9) his consequent and proximate injury." Id., at 389, 613 P.2d at 1340, quoting Mitchell v. Siqueiros, 99 Idaho 396, 401, 582 P.2d 1074, 1079 (1978).

We do not believe Tusch Enterprises' misrepresentation claim should be analyzed only with reference to the elements recited in Faw, supra. It must also be considered whether the facts here fall within the category of cases finding a misrepresentation on the basis of nondisclosure.

We addressed the instances where nondisclosure may amount to misrepresentation in Bethlahmy v. Bechtel, 91 Idaho 55, 415 P.2d 698 (1966). In Bethlahmy, the defendant, Bechtel, was the builder and vendor of a residential home. Bechtel told the plaintiffs that the houses he built were the finest, and that the house at issue was of first quality construction. However, Bechtel did not disclose to the plaintiffs that a tiled water line ran underneath the garage and to within seven or nine feet of the north wall of the residence. * * *

Relying upon § 551 of a tentative draft of the Restatement (Second) of Torts,[41] the court found that the plaintiffs had presented facts entitling them to relief:

"Defendant did not testify that he called attention to, or advised plaintiffs of, the ditch running under the lot and garage; nor that the ditch was constructed of drainage tile without sealed joints; nor that the basement was not of waterproof construction. These facts were known to defendant and unknown to plaintiffs. They were not discoverable by inspection. Defendant had superior knowledge. Plaintiffs were ignorant of the facts. The parties did not deal at arms length. Defendant dealt from a position of superior knowledge. A confidential relationship arose between the parties. Stearns v. Williams, 72 Idaho 276, 288, 240 P.2d 833 (1952). Plaintiffs relied, and

41. The tentative draft provision relied upon in Bethlahmy was adopted after only minor cosmetic changes. Restatement (Second) of Torts § 551 (1977) provides in pertinent part: "§ 551. Liability for Nondisclosure (1) One who fails to disclose to another a fact that he knows may justifiably induce the other to act or refrain from acting in a business transaction is subject to the same liability to the other as though he had represented the nonexistence of the matter that he has failed to disclose, if, but only if, he is under a duty to the other to exercise reasonable care to disclose the matter in question. (2) One party to a business transaction is under a duty to exercise reasonable care to disclose to the other before the transaction is consummated, (a) matters known to him that the other is entitled to know because of a fiduciary or other similar relation of trust and confidence between them; and (b) matters known to him that he knows to be necessary to prevent his partial or ambiguous statement of the facts from being misleading; and * * * (e) facts basic to the transaction, if he knows that the other is about to enter into it under a mistake as to them, and that the other, because of the relationship between them, the customs of the trade or other objective circumstances, would reasonably expect a disclosure of those facts."

were entitled to rely, upon defendant's representation that the house would be a quality home. The facts essential to a finding of constructive fraud * * * are not in dispute." Id., at 62, 415 P.2d at 705.

The rationale for recognizing such a cause of action was explained in Bethlahmy with the following quotation from Kaze v. Compton, 283 S.W.2d 204, 207 (Ky.1955):

"It cannot be controverted that actionable fraud or misrepresentation by a vendor may be by concealment or failure to disclose a hidden condition or a material fact, where under the circumstances there was an obligation to disclose it during the transaction. If deception is accomplished, the form of the deceit is immaterial. And the legal question is not affected by the absence of an intent to deceive, for the element of intent, whether good or bad, is only important as it may affect the moral character of the representation." Bethlahmy, supra, 91 Idaho at 60, 415 P.2d at 703.

Kaze v. Compton explained that actual intent to deceive need not be shown where the seller knew of facts which would have apprised a person of ordinary prudence of the truth: if a reasonable person would have been so apprised, and the seller was under a duty to inform the buyer of the concealed facts, then intent to deceive is not necessary to make a prima facie showing. Kaze, supra, at 208.

After his conversation with Coffin, Vander Boegh knew, or should have known, that the south duplex was, at least partially, built upon fill dirt. A person of ordinary prudence with a background similar to Vander Boegh's (e.g., with extensive road construction experience and knowledge of compaction), who knew of the fill dirt would have been apprised of the truth (e.g., that problems with the foundation were likely). Yet, by Tusch Enterprises' account, Vander Boegh did not disclose the fill dirt problems, and, instead, assured Marianne Tusch that the duplexes were quality dwellings. * * *

We hold that it was error to dispose of Tusch Enterprises' misrepresentation claim against the Vander Boeghs at the summary judgment stage. Genuine issues of material fact exist whether the nondisclosure of the soil problems, coupled with the assurance that the duplexes were quality constructed, amounted to a misrepresentation. See Restatement (Second) of Torts § 551(2)(a), (b) and (e). * * *

IV

EXPRESS WARRANTY

Tusch Enterprises alleges that the Vander Boeghs and Coffin breached an express warranty to the effect that the duplexes were well-constructed. Regarding Coffin, Tusch Enterprises readily admits that it did not know of Coffin until after it had purchased the duplexes and problems had become evident. There being nothing in the record to show that Coffin made any warranties to the Vander Boeghs or had any discussions with Tusch Enterprises, we affirm the dismissal of the express warranty claim against Coffin. With regard to the Vander

Boeghs, the facts alleged in support of an express warranty are essentially those discussed in the preceding section under misrepresentation. Tusch Enterprises argues that these representations of quality construction became part of the bargain. However, we find that the parol evidence rule precludes Tusch Enterprises from making such an assertion and, accordingly, affirm the decision below dismissing the express warranty claim against the Vander Boeghs.

Before further addressing the applicability of the parol evidence rule, it is necessary to supplement the facts previously recited. When the third offer was accepted by the Vander Boeghs, they and Tusch Enterprises signed an earnest money agreement. This written document was prepared by Marianne Tusch, and included the following language with which she had become familiar through her employment with a real estate agency:

> "The undersigned Buyer hereby acknowledges further that he has not received or relied upon any statements or representation by the undersigned broker or his representatives or by the Seller which are not herein expressed. The Buyer has entered into this agreement relying solely upon information and knowledge obtained from his own investigation or personal inspection of the premises. This agreement constitutes the whole agreement between the parties and no warranties, agreements or representations have been made or shall be binding upon either party unless herein set forth."

A short time after executing the earnest money agreement, the parties entered into a written real estate contract, which was prepared by the Vander Boeghs. This contract provided that it incorporated the terms and conditions of the earnest money agreement, except as modified by the real estate contract. The portions of the real estate contract pertinent to the present inquiry are as follows:

> "12. EXCLUSIVE TERMS: This contract is the entire agreement between the parties and all other agreements heretofore entered into, either written or oral, are hereby either abrogated or contained in this agreement. All prior oral agreements and conditions are expressly waived unless stated in this agreement and the parties expressly understand they have no mutual understanding or agreement other than as herein set forth.

> "13. WARRANTIES: The Purchasers have fully inspected the above described premises and know just exactly what they are purchasing. Sellers warrant that they have a good and sufficient title, and that the premises have no code violations or governmental restrictions as of May 15, 1979, and that further as of May 15, 1979, Sellers warrant that they know of no defects in the sewers, plumbing, electrical items, and mechanical items in and about the property. Other than as set forth in this paragraph, Sellers make no further warranties with regard to the condition of the sewer lines, utility poles, fences, curbs, sidewalks, streets, patios or any other mechanical item of any description whatsoever within the described premises."

The features of the parol evidence rule are aptly stated in Chapman v. Haney Seed Co., Inc., 102 Idaho 26, 624 P.2d 408 (1981):

> "It is the general rule that when a contract has been reduced to writing, which the parties intend to be a complete statement of their agreement, any other written or oral agreements or understandings (referred to in many cases as extrinsic evidence) made prior to or contemporaneously with the written 'contract' and which relate to the same subject matter are not admissible to vary, contradict or enlarge the terms of the written contract." Id., at 28, 624 P.2d at 410.

* * *

From these facts, it is apparent that the parties intended the real estate contract, and the earnest money agreement by incorporation, to be a complete and exclusive statement of the terms of their agreement. The evidence proffered by Tusch Enterprises to the effect that the Vander Boeghs, prior to execution of these agreements, warranted that the duplexes were well-constructed is evidence that would vary, contradict or enlarge the terms of the written contract. Thus, under the parol evidence rule, this evidence was properly excluded, and the express warranty count against the Vander Boeghs was properly dismissed.[42]

V

IMPLIED WARRANTY

The final theory of recovery which we need address is implied warranty of habitability. Tusch Enterprises alleges a breach on the part of both Coffin and the Vander Boeghs. First, the Court will examine whether the integrated writings of the parties preclude the implied warranty of habitability. Next, we will address the issue whether the implied warranty of habitability extends to dwellings purchased for income-producing purposes which have never been occupied by the buyers. Then, we will determine if genuine issues of material fact exist as to whether the Vander Boeghs may have been builders or builder-developers and, thus, warrantors of habitability; and, if so, whether issues of material fact exist as to a breach of that warranty. Finally, we have to determine if genuine issues of material fact exist as to whether Coffin may have been a builder and, thus, a warrantor of habitability; and, if so, whether the implied warranty of habitability would extend to subsequent purchasers.

---

42. It may appear odd that we did not address the parties' merger clauses in our discussion above of misrepresentation, especially since Tusch Enterprises advances the same facts in support of both express warranty and misrepresentation, and since the merger clauses, when read together provide that the buyer has relied upon no representations other than those expressed in the two written agreements. The parol evidence rule, however, does not apply to averments of fraud, misrepresentation, mutual mistake or other matters which render a contract void or voidable. See 3 Corbin on Contracts § 580 (1960); and Restatement (Second) of Contracts § 214 (1981). * * *

A. Disclaimers

As noted in the preceding section, the integrated agreement of the parties purports to set forth all the warranties which attached to the duplexes. However, the warranty of habitability is not specifically mentioned or disclaimed in either the earnest money agreement or the real estate contract.

The majority of states permit a disclaimer of an implied warranty of habitability, but the disclaimer must be clear and unambiguous and such disclaimers are strictly construed against the builder-vendor. Belt v. Spencer, 41 Colo.App. 227, 585 P.2d 922, 925 (1978); Bridges v. Ferrell, 685 P.2d 409, 411 (Okla.Ct.App.1984); Crowder v. Vandendeale, 564 S.W.2d 879 (Mo.1978) (en banc). We agree with these courts * * *.

* * *

The disclaimers in the instant case fall woefully short of fulfilling these requirements. Because the implied warranty of habitability is a creature of public policy, public policy dictates that it be waived only with difficulty. The party asserting that it has been waived bears the burden of proving that it has been knowingly waived. Clearly, when no mention is made of the implied warranty of habitability in a contract, and the contract contains only general language stating there are no warranties other than those contained within its four corners, any purported waiver of the implied warranty of habitability is ineffective.

Because we find that the implied warranty of habitability has not been disclaimed, we proceed to the next topic.

B. Buyers

Next, we consider whether the implied warranty of habitability extends only to buyers who reside in dwellings after they are purchased. The uncontroverted facts show that Tusch Enterprises purchased the duplexes at issue for income-producing purposes and, rather than residing in them, has leased them to others. * * *

* * *

We refuse to restrict the implied warranty of habitability to buyers who personally reside in dwellings after they are purchased. It is of no matter who ultimately inhabits the home after purchase, be it the buyer, a relative or lessee. The implied warranty is that the structure will be fit for habitation, and resolution of the question whether the buyer has received that which he bargained for does not depend upon the status of the buyer or ultimate user; it depends upon the quality of the dwelling delivered and the expectations of the parties. In transactions in goods, our Uniform Commercial Code implies warranties of merchantability and fitness for a particular purpose when certain circumstances are present. See I.C. §§ 28–2–314 and 28–2–315 (1980). Yet, the UCC does not distinguish, as Hopkins does with sales of homes, between buyers who seek income through the use of purchased goods and buyers who merely acquire them for personal use. The focus must be upon the product, be it a typewriter or a home, and not upon the buyer. * * *

* * *

Therefore, we hold that the implied warranty of habitability extends to residential dwellings purchased for income-producing purposes which have never been occupied by the buyers.

C. Vander Boeghs

The court below granted summary judgment in favor of the Vander Boeghs on Tusch Enterprises' implied warranty of habitability count.

In Bethlahmy, supra, we recognized that when builder-vendors sell newly constructed buildings there is an implied warranty that the buildings will be habitable. Our rejection of the doctrine of caveat emptor as applied to the sale of new houses is consistent with the vast weight of authority. [ ] The trend away from the doctrine of caveat emptor in transactions of this nature is rooted in considerations of public policy:

> "The mores of the day have changed and the ordinary home buyer is not in a position to discover hidden defects in a structure. A home buyer should be able to place reliance on the builder or developer who sells him a new home, the purchase of which in so many instances, is the largest single purchase a family makes in a lifetime. Courts will judicially protect the victims of shoddy workmanship. Consumer protection demands that those who buy homes are entitled to rely on the skill of the builder and that the house is constructed so as to be reasonably fit for its intended use. The average purchaser is without adequate knowledge or opportunity to make a meaningful inspection of the component parts of a residential structure." Moxley v. Laramie Builders, Inc., 600 P.2d 733, 735 (Wyo.1979) (footnote omitted).

Economic policy considerations come into play as well:

> "[B]y virtue of superior knowledge, skill, and experience in the construction of houses, a builder-vendor is generally better positioned than the purchaser to know whether a house is suitable for habitation. He also is better positioned to evaluate and guard against the financial risk posed by a [latent defect], and to absorb and spread across the market of home purchasers the loss therefrom. In terms of risk distribution analysis, he is the preferred or 'least cost' risk bearer. Finally, he is in a superior position to develop or utilize technology to prevent such defects: and as one commentator has noted, 'the major pockets of strict liability in the law' derived from 'cases where the potential victims * * * are not in a good position to make adjustments that might in the long run reduce or eliminate the risk.' R. Posner, Economic Analysis of Law 140–41 (2d ed. 1977)." Gaito v. Auman, 70 N.C.App. 21, 318 S.E.2d 555, 559 (1984), aff'd, 313 N.C. 243, 327 S.E.2d 870 (1985).

Further, the implied warranty of habitability is not limited to builder-developers:

"We can see no difference between a builder or contractor who undertakes construction of a home and a builder-developer. To the buyer of a home the same considerations are present, no matter whether a builder constructs a residence on the land of the owner or whether the builder constructs a habitation on land he is developing and selling the residential structures as part of a package including the land. It is the structure and all its intricate components and related facilities that are the subject matter of the implied warranty. Those who hold themselves out as builders must be just as accountable for the workmanship that goes into a home * * * as are builder-developers." Moxley, supra, at 735.

However, the implied warranty of habitability only applies to those who are in the business of building dwellings. Hibbler v. Fisher, 109 Idaho 1007, 712 P.2d 708 (Ct.App.1985); Klos v. Gockel, 87 Wash.2d 567, 554 P.2d 1349, 1352 (1976) (en banc); Moxley, supra.

By adopting the implied warranty of habitability, we did not intend to make builders or developers the insurers against any and all defects in a home:

"The implied warranty of fitness [for habitability] does not impose upon the builder an obligation to deliver a perfect house. No house is built without defects, and defects susceptible of remedy ordinarily would not warrant rescission. But major defects which render the house unfit for habitation, and which are not readily remediable, entitle the buyer to [relief]. The builder-vendor's legitimate interests are protected by the rule which casts the burden upon the purchaser to establish the facts which give rise to the implied warranty of fitness [for habitability], and its breach." Bethlahmy, supra, 91 Idaho at 68, 415 P.2d at 711.

* * *

Construing the facts in favor of Tusch Enterprises, we note that Robert Vander Boegh had many years of experience in the road construction business. Regarding the duplexes, he contracted with Coffin to have the structures built. He contracted with others to level the land and make other site preparations. He periodically visited the site during the construction phase and consulted with Coffin about the possibility of fill dirt existing under the south duplex. Coffin stated that he relied upon Vander Boegh's expertise in these matters. From these facts it cannot be concluded that there is no genuine issue as to whether Vander Boegh was a developer-builder or merely an ordinary person with little expertise who contracted with others to have a house built for him. * * *

Having found that genuine issues of material fact exist, we hold that it was error for the court below to dismiss Tusch Enterprises' implied warranty of habitability claim against Vander Boeghs.

D. Coffin

Construing the facts again in favor of Tusch Enterprises, we conclude that they are sufficient to raise an issue as to whether Coffin was a builder in the sense that an implied warranty of habitability would flow from him. The Court, however, must consider a remaining issue: whether a subsequent purchaser of residential dwellings may assert a claim for breach of the implied warranty of habitability against the builder of the dwellings when there is no privity of contract between them.

The growing trend among other jurisdictions is to extend the implied warranty of habitability to subsequent purchasers. The following courts have so extended the doctrine: Barnes v. Mac Brown & Co., Inc., 264 Ind. 227, 342 N.E.2d 619 (1976) (cracks in basement walls); Moxley, supra, (Wyo.1979) (defective electrical wiring); Terlinde v. Neely, 275 S.C. 395, 271 S.E.2d 768 (1980) (foundation settled causing walls to crack, floors to sink, doors to not close properly, etc.); Hermes v. Staiano, 181 N.J. Super. 424, 437 A.2d 925 (N.J. Super. Ct. Law Div.1981) (defects in foundations wall and underground sewage disposal system); Blagg v. Fred Hunt Co., Inc., 272 Ark. 185, 612 S.W.2d 321 (1981) (strong odor and fumes from formaldehyde); Elden v. Simmons, 631 P.2d 739 (Okla.1981) (defective bricks); Redarowicz, supra, (1982) (defects in chimney and wall); Keyes v. Guy Bailey Homes, Inc., 439 So.2d 670 (Miss.1983) (foundation cracked); Gupta v. Ritter Homes, Inc., 646 S.W.2d 168 (Tex.1983) (foundation settled excessively causing walls to crack, roof to leak, and patio to pull away from house); and Richards v. Powercraft Homes, Inc., 139 Ariz. 242, 678 P.2d 427 (1984) (en banc) (faulty pipes, separation of floors from walls, cracking of walls, doors that would not close, etc.).

In choosing to follow this trend, the Arizona Supreme Court explained that limiting the implied warranty to first buyers would not only be arbitrary, but might encourage sham first sales calculated to insulate builders from liability. They explained further:

"The same policy considerations that lead to [our adoption of the implied warranty of habitability for sales of new homes]—that house-building is frequently undertaken on a large scale, that builders hold themselves out as skilled in the profession, that modern construction is complex and regulated by many governmental codes, and that home-buyers are generally not skilled or knowledgeable in construction, plumbing, or electrical requirements and practices—are equally applicable to subsequent homebuyers. Also, we note that the character of our society is such that people and families are increasingly mobile. Home builders should anticipate that the houses they construct will eventually, and perhaps frequently, change ownership. The effect of latent defects will be just as catastrophic on a subsequent owner as on an original buyer and the builder will be just as unable to justify improper or substandard work. Because the builder-vendor is in a better position than a subsequent owner to prevent occurrence of major problems, the cost of poor workmanship should be his to bear." Richards, supra, 678 at 430.

We adopt the reasoning of these courts, but with the following proviso:

"This extension of liability is limited to latent defects, not discoverable by a subsequent purchaser's reasonable inspection, manifesting themselves after the purchase. The standard to be applied in determining whether or not there has been a breach of warranty is one of reasonableness in light of surrounding circumstances. The age of the home, its maintenance, the use to which it has been put, are but a few factors entering into this factual determination at trial." Barnes, supra, 342 N.E.2d at 621.

This extension to subsequent purchasers is also limited to latent defects which manifest themselves within a reasonable time. Redarowicz, supra, 65 Ill.Dec. at 411, 441 N.E.2d at 331; Moxley, supra. Further:

"The burden is on the subsequent owner to show that the defect had its origin and cause in the builder-vendor. * * * Defenses are, of course, available. The builder-vendor can demonstrate [that the suit was not brought within the appropriate statute of limitations,] that the defects are not attributable to him, that they are the result of age or ordinary wear and tear, or that previous owners have made substantial changes." Richards, supra, 678 P.2d at 430.

* * *

We hold only that subsequent purchasers of residential dwellings, who suffer purely economic losses from latent defects manifesting themselves within a reasonable time, may maintain an action against the builder (or builder-developer, as the case may be,) of the dwelling based upon the implied warranty of habitability despite the fact that no privity of contract exists between the two. Any other holding would lead to an absurd result. For example, suppose an unscrupulous builder constructed a home of inferior quality and sold it to another. Suppose further, that for whatever reason, the buyer after three months sold the home to a second purchaser. And one month later the foundation of the house split apart rendering the home valueless. Should the common law deny the subsequent purchaser a remedy against the builder merely because there is no privity of contract and because the damages happen to be purely economic, when it was the conduct of the builder which created the latent defect in the first place?

We conclude that it was error for the court below to enter summary judgment in favor of Coffin on Tusch Enterprises' implied warranty of habitability count.

The decision of the court below is affirmed as to the negligence and express warranty counts. The decision granting summary judgment against Tusch Enterprises on the misrepresentation and implied warranty counts is reversed, and remanded for further proceedings not inconsistent with this opinion.

Notes and Questions

1. As the principal case illustrates, claims involving damages from latent defects in new or relatively new buildings may involve a variety of

combinations of plaintiffs and defendants. Such claims may be brought against either the builder, who constructed the building, or the developer, who is responsible for putting it on the market. The developer and builder may be the same or different entities. Claims may also be presented by initial or subsequent purchasers. Such claims may be asserted on a variety of theories based either in tort (negligence, strict liability, or misrepresentation), or contract (express or implied warranty).

The easiest case is probably an original purchaser's claim based on express warranty against an entity which is both the builder and developer. Many courts have also recognized implied warranty claims brought by initial purchasers against builders or developers. Several states have imposed warranties on new residential construction by statute. See Md. Real Prop.Code Ann. § 10–203; N.J.Stat.Ann § 46:3B; Va.Code Ann. § 55–70.1. Courts are generally receptive to tort claims where purchasers are injured because of defects in the premises, but where the only injuries are economic (i.e., loss of the expectancy interest), a number of courts have rejected tort claims for defects as noncompensable. Few courts have accepted strict liability claims.

Where claims are brought by subsequent purchasers against a builder or developer, or by an initial purchaser against a builder who was not the developer, the court must consider whether the lack of privity between the plaintiff and defendant defeats the claim. Lack of privity is probably a bar to recovery on an express warranty claim. The courts are split on the question of whether an implied warranty of habitability extends to subsequent purchasers of dwelling units, with a majority requiring privity. Jurisdictions permitting recovery to subsequent purchasers in tort are less likely to find lack of privity to be fatal, though the economic loss rule often effectively bars recovery by subsequent purchasers for the cost of the defects themselves.

The same requirements have barred suits against builders where the initial purchaser bought the property from a developer rather than from the builder itself; though if, as is sometimes the case, the developer is merely a shell corporation created by the builder, it can be argued that the court should consider the realities of the situation rather than its form. Jurisdictions permitting subsequent purchasers to recover do so for only a reasonable period of time, recognizing that as a home ages, defects are expected and are less often directly attributable to initial construction.

The principal case also addresses the efficacy of disclaimers of tort and contract liability. Disclaimers of tort liability for personal injury are generally held to be against public policy. Courts are more receptive to disclaimers against warranty liability, but are reluctant to accept vague or ambiguous attempts to disclaim liability. If a court permits a subsequent purchaser to recover, should disclaimers found in the contract between the initial purchaser and builder or developer be a bar?

Recovery is generally limited, in any event, to damages attributable to latent defects. Where defects are immediately evident, recovery is limited to rights that exist under contract.

Why might the right to recover against a builder or developer often prove an empty right? If you were representing a home purchaser, what protection would you prefer for your client? Is this a problem better handled through insurance rather than through tort or contract liability?

See, discussing these issues further, Annotation, Liability of Builder of Residence for Latent Defects Therein as Running to Subsequent Purchasers From Original Vendee, 10 A.L.R.4th 385 (1981); Annotation, Liability of Builder–Vendor or Other Vendor of New Dwelling for Loss, Injury or Damage Occasioned by Defective Condition Thereof, 25 A.L.R.3d 383 (1969); Barrett, Recovery of Economic Loss in Tort for Construction Defects: A Critical Analysis, 40 S.C.L.Rev. 891 (1989); Cherry, Builder Liability for Used Home Defects, 18 Real Est.L.J. 115 (1989); Grand, Implied and Statutory Warranties in the Sale of Real Estate: The Demise of Caveat Emptor, 15 Real Est.L.J. 44 (1986); Note, Latent Defects: Subsequent Home Purchasers Beware, 40 S.C.L.Rev. 1017 (1989).

ZIMMERMAN v. NORTHFIELD REAL ESTATE, INC.

Appellate Court of Illinois, First District, 1986.
156 Ill.App.3d 154, 109 Ill.Dec. 541, 510 N.E.2d 409.

Presiding Justice McNamara delivered the opinion of the court as modified upon denial of petition for rehearing:

Plaintiffs Irving R. and Geraldine C. Zimmerman purchased a single family residence and later discovered that the lot size was smaller than they had thought, and that the home had numerous defects. Plaintiffs filed this action, alleging fraud, negligent misrepresentation, and certain statutory violations, against defendants Northfield Real Estate, Inc. and its agent Ellen A. Reed (brokers), and sellers William Dunn and Mary Lou Dunn, who is now known as Mary Lou Steinbach.

Count I of the complaint alleges common law fraud against all defendants, and the trial court dismissed the common law fraud action against the brokers. The court denied the motion to strike and dismiss the common law fraud count against the sellers. Count II alleges negligent misrepresentation by all defendants, and that count was dismissed as to all defendants. Count II alleges violations by all defendants of the Consumer Fraud and Deceptive Business Practices Act (Ill.Rev.Stat.1983, ch. 121½, par. 262), and that count was dismissed as to all defendants. Count IV sets forth a private cause of action under the Real Estate Brokers and Salesmen License Act. (Ill.Rev.Stat. 1981, ch. 111, par. 5701 et seq.) against the brokers, and that count was also dismissed. Plaintiffs appeal from the dismissal of these counts. Defendant Steinbach cross-appeals from the order denying her motion to dismiss count I, * * *

The complaint alleges that during the period of April to October 1983, plaintiffs visited the sellers' home in Northfield, Illinois several times. In October 1983, plaintiffs signed a contract with the sellers agreeing to pay $325,000 for the home. The contract included an exculpatory clause:

"10(j). Purchaser acknowledges for the benefit of Seller and for the benefit of third parties that neither the Seller, broker nor any of their agents have made any representations with respect to any material fact relating to the real estate, its improvements and included personal property unless such representations are in writing and further that Purchaser has made such investigations as Purchaser deems necessary or appropriate to satisfy Purchaser that there has been no deception, fraud, false pretenses, misrepresentations, concealments, suppressions or omission of any material fact by the Seller, the Broker, or any of their agents relating to the real estate, its improvements and included personal property."

* * *

Plaintiffs contend that the trial court erred in dismissing the common law fraud count against the brokers. Defendant Steinbach cross appeals from the trial court order denying her motion to dismiss the common law fraud count against the sellers. The requisite elements of a common law fraud cause of action are that a false statement of material fact was intentionally made; that the party to whom the statement was made had a right to rely on it and did so; that the statement was made for the purpose of inducing the other party to act; and that reliance by the person to whom the statement was made led to his injury. [ ] Intentional concealment of a material fact is the equivalent of a false statement of material fact. [ ] Where a person has a duty to speak, his failure to disclose material information constitutes fraudulent concealment. [ ]

The complaint sufficiently alleges that defendants intentionally concealed, or made statements in regard to, material facts. The complaint alleges that defendant knew the lot size was less than one acre; knew the bathtubs and plumbing drain tile system did not work properly; knew the basement had four or five leaks; knew the south and east walls were badly deteriorated by moisture; knew the living room wall contained a substantial hole; and knew the basement had suffered massive flooding of up to four feet of water.

The trial court based its dismissal of the fraud count against the brokers partly on its belief that the complaint did not allege that the brokers "actively engaged in a course of conduct designed to deceive." The complaint alleges, however, that the brokers intentionally, with intent to deceive, issued a multiple listing sheet falsely advertising the lot size as one to three acres, or 43,650 square feet (equal to one acre).

The trial court also based its dismissal of the fraud count on its belief that the "only parties that could be concealing would seem to me to be the sellers." The court cited examples of wallpapering over cracks and leaks, and stated it did not believe "that the real estate broker could conceivably be guilty of that." Other well-pleaded facts, however, sufficiently allege the brokers' knowledge and fraudulent conduct. The complaint alleged that defendant Reed lived next door to the Dunn home for at least five years and was previously employed by the developer of the subdivision which had divided and sold much of the land surrounding the Dunn home. From these allegations it is reasonable to infer that Reed knew of the flooding and of the lot size.

The complaint also sufficiently alleged that the brokers had a duty to speak regarding material information of which they had knowledge. Realtors have a duty to disclose material facts under the Real Estate Brokers and Salesmen License Act. (Ill.Rev.Stat.1981, ch. 111, par. 5701 et seq.) Real estate brokers and salespersons occupy a position of trust with respect to purchasers with whom they are negotiating and owe a duty to exercise good faith in their dealing with such purchasers even absent the existence of an agency relationship. [   ] Thus, the brokers' silence may constitute fraudulent concealment of material facts. [   ] The broker defendants had a duty to disclose the massive flooding problems and the actual lot size. Concealment or misrepresentation of these material facts was fraudulent. Whether the brokers had knowledge of other claimed patent defects may be adduced at trial.

Plaintiffs sufficiently allege that the omissions and false statements were of material facts. * * * Here, in deciding whether to buy the home, plaintiffs could be expected to rely upon representations and omissions regarding matters relating to lot size, flooding, leaks and other defects in the home, and thus the matters are material. Defendants refer to the massive flooding which neighbors call "Dunn's Lake" as a mere "puddling." Defendants also refer to the 40% lot size difference as "somewhat smaller" and as being "not incorrect by much." We find defendants' characterizations unpersuasive.

The complaint further alleges that plaintiffs relied on the statements or silence and thereby acted to their detriment. Plaintiffs discovered the defects after signing a contract of sale, making a down payment, and taking possession. Plaintiffs also sufficiently allege that the statements were made for the purpose of inducing them to buy the house. * * * As a proximate result of these affirmative misrepresentations, concealments and omissions, plaintiffs allege they were required to spend large sums to cure the physical defects and that they now own a lot worth considerably less than the sale price because of the lot size which measured 40% less than the one acre advertised. Thus, we find the complaint states a cause of action for fraud against both the broker defendants and seller defendants. [   ]

We agree with defendants that the multiple listing description of the house as "magnificent" and "comfortable" is a subjective description and cannot qualify as a fraudulent misrepresentation of fact. [   ]

Plaintiffs next contend that the trial court erred in dismissing count II which set forth negligent misrepresentation causes of action against both the brokers and the sellers. The elements of a negligent misrepresentation cause of action include a duty owed by defendant to plaintiff, a breach of such duty, and injury proximately resulting from such breach. [   ] Count II of the complaint alleges that defendants had a duty to act with a reasonable degree of care to ascertain, disclose and not conceal the material facts regarding the lot size, flooding and other defects; that defendant acted negligently breaching this duty; and as a proximate result plaintiffs were required to spend sums to cure the physical defects, and plaintiffs owned less valuable property.

The test of negligent misrepresentation involves the breach of a duty to use due care in obtaining and communicating information upon which others may reasonably be expected to rely in the conduct of their economic affairs. The misrepresentations may result from failing to provide adequate information when there is a duty to do so, as well as providing information which is false. The person making a representation may believe it to be true, but because of negligent expression it is in fact false. [ ] We have already found that the broker defendants had such a duty and breached it. [ ] A realtor has no duty to prospective buyers to independently substantiate the representations of a seller unless the realtor is aware of facts which tend to indicate that such a representation is false. [ ] We have found that the complaint sufficiently alleges the broker defendants' knowledge of the flooding and lot size. Thus, plaintiffs have stated a cause of action for negligence against the broker defendants.

Plaintiffs here have not shown a loss beyond a consumer's commercial expectation and therefore have suffered only an economic loss, which is generally not recoverable in negligence actions. [ ] However, a plaintiff may recover solely economic losses in tort against those in the business of supplying information for the guidance of others in their business transactions. [ ] Realtors are in the business of supplying such information. [ ] Consequently, plaintiffs may recover economic losses from the broker defendants.

The sellers do not fall within the Moorman exception and thus plaintiffs cannot recover the economic losses they seek from the sellers under this negligence count. [ ] Damages for economic loss may be recovered, however, in a tort action where intentional misrepresentation is sufficiently alleged. [ ] Plaintiffs' cause of action against the sellers for intentional fraud, therefore, supports plaintiffs' request for damages incurred as a result of economic losses.

* * *

In regard to both the fraud count and the negligence count, defendants raise arguments concerning the exculpatory clause and the reasonableness of plaintiffs' reliance. Defendants argue that the contract's exculpatory clause quoted above protects them from liability for fraud. An exculpatory clause cannot protect persons from the results of their wilful and wanton misconduct. * * * We have found that count I sufficiently states a cause of action for fraud which is an intentional tort. Thus, the exculpatory clause in the present case would not shield defendants from liability for fraud.

Defendants also rely heavily on the exculpatory clause as a defense to the negligence count. * * *

Exculpatory clauses are not favored and are strictly construed and must have clear, explicit and unequivocal language showing that it was the intent of the parties. [ ] An exculpatory clause for simple negligence is valid unless it violates public policy, or involves certain semi-public relationships. [ ] One cannot exempt himself from negligence by a contractual exculpatory clause in cases where a positive duty has been imposed by law. [ ] The public policy of the State may be found in its statutes and judicial decisions. [ ]

Section 1 of the Real Estate Brokers and Salesmen Licensing Act (Ill.Rev.Stat.1981, ch. 111, par 5701 et seq., [ ] states that the legislature's intent in enacting the statute is to protect the public. (Ill.Rev. Stat.1981, ch. 111, par. 5701.) In Sawyer Realty Group, Inc. v. Jarvis Corp., our supreme court found that the plain purpose of the Act is to protect the public from incapable or dishonest persons who might aid in the perpetration of fraud. The legislature intended to compel brokers to practice their profession honestly and with integrity. The court also found that the broker owes an obligation to the prospective buyer because the broker occupies a position of trust, and thus must exercise good faith. Moreover, the Department of Registration and Education regulations require a broker to disclose all material knowledge to any and all purchasers. (Illinois Department of Registration and Education Regulation V(A), authorized by Ill.Rev.Stat.1981, ch. 111, par. 5715(a).) * * * We find that based on the specific duty which the law imposes on brokers, the overriding public policy expressed by the legislature in the Act, and the court's holding in Sawyer Realty, this court's enforcement of the exculpatory clause in favor of the broker defendants would violate public policy.

Defendants maintain, in regard to the fraud count, that plaintiffs' reliance was unreasonable. Steinbach contends that her statement to plaintiffs that the basement had one leak "effectively disclosed the existence of the flooding problem." * * * The statement that only one leak existed, however, may have left the buyers with a false sense of security. Where a plaintiff's inquiries are inhibited by a defendant's statements which create a false sense of security, the plaintiff's failure to investigate further is not fatal. * * * Steinbach argues that plaintiffs did not "seek to look behind the [basement wall] panelling which covered the disclosed defects." We find these arguments to be without merit. We cannot say as a matter of law that plaintiffs closed their eyes to available information by not ripping down the panelling in an effort to discover the true extent of the leakage and flooding damage after defendant told them there was only one leak. * * *

Defendants argue further that plaintiffs were not justified in relying on the statements and omissions at issue in regard to the negligence count. Whether an injured party justifiably relied upon defendants' words or silence depends on the surrounding circumstances. [ ] A party is not justified in relying on representations made when he had an ample opportunity to ascertain the truth of the representations. [ ] The question of whether defendants had a right to rely on the broker defendants' representations and omissions regarding the size of the lot and the defects in the home must be answered in light of all of the facts which plaintiffs had actual knowledge of as well as those which they might have discovered by the exercise of ordinary prudence. [ ] This raises substantial questions of fact. * * *

Moreover, the contract states that plaintiffs made any "necessary" or "appropriate" investigations. At this state of the pleadings, we cannot hold as a matter of law that plaintiffs should have known that a professional survey to measure the acreage was necessary. Persons may reasonably rely on a judgment where the broker or seller has some expert knowledge due to his previous work with the developer of the property. (See generally Anno., 90 A.L.R.3d 568.) Here, it is reasonable to infer from the complaint's allegations that Reed had special knowledge of "Dunn's Lake" and the flooding problems because she had lived next door for at least five years, and had knowledge of the lot size because she had previously worked for the developer of the property.

* * *

Plaintiffs next contend that the trial court erred in dismissing count III of the complaint which alleged that all defendants violated section 262 of the Consumer Fraud Act. (Ill.Rev.Stat.1983, ch. 121½, par. 262.) The trial court dismissed this count based on its belief that the Act only applies to merchants who are involved in the trade.

This court has held that section 262 of the Act applies to intentional misrepresentations made by real estate brokers to prospective purchasers. [ ] The broker must know of the false, misleading or deceptive character of the information he communicates. (Ill.Rev.Stat.1983, ch. 121½, par. 270b(4).) Section 262 expands a consumer's rights beyond those of the common law and provides broader protection than does the common law action of fraud. [ ] Thus, plaintiffs need not establish all of the elements of fraud. A plaintiff need not show actual reliance or diligence in ascertaining the accuracy of misstatements. [ ] We have already held that the complaint sufficiently alleged the elements of fraud. Our finding that plaintiffs have stated a cause of action for fraud is sufficient to warrant the conclusion that the same acts violate the Consumer Fraud Act because the Act prohibits any misrepresentation at all. The trial court erred in dismissing count III as to the brokers.

As to the sellers, the complaint alleges that the sellers "were conducting the trade or commerce of selling real estate." We find no support in Illinois law for the proposition that an individual selling his own home is liable to a purchaser under the Consumer Fraud Act. * * * The trial court properly dismissed count III as to the sellers.

Plaintiffs finally contend that the trial court erred in dismissing count IV of the complaint, which alleges that defendant brokers violated the Illinois Real Estate Brokers and Salesmen Licensing Act. (Ill. Rev.Stat.1981, ch. 111, par. 5701 et seq.) A private right of action exists under the Act. (Sawyer Realty Group, Inc. v. Jarvis Corp.) As we have stated, the relevant rule requires realtors to disclose any and all material knowledge. (Rule V(A).) Here, the alleged omissions and misrepresentations are the same as those upon which count I for fraud and count II for negligent misrepresentations are based, and the complaint sufficiently alleges facts to support these counts. Thus, plaintiffs have stated a cause of action against the brokers under the Licensing Act. The trial court erred in dismissing count IV.

* * *

Notes and Questions

1. The real estate broker, you will remember, is normally the agent of the seller. Therefore, imposing obligations on the broker to protect the purchaser confronts the broker with an inevitable and often difficult conflict of interest. In residential purchases, however, buyers often believe that the broker is on their side, and rely on the broker for assurances that the house they are buying is in good condition. Brokers often do little to disabuse buyers of either belief. Buyers can, of course, engage their own broker to represent their interests, but most do not.

Courts, and occasionally legislatures, have recognized the reality of buyer reliance on brokers, and have steadily expanded the responsibilities of brokers to buyers. Intentional misrepresentation of facts concerning the condition of the property relied on by the buyer will probably lead to broker liability, although mere "puffing" or statements of opinion may, as in the principal case, be excused. Most jurisdictions will also impose liability for intentional concealment of material facts that are known to the broker but which the broker knows are not known to the buyer.

Many, though not all, courts further hold the broker liable for negligent misrepresentation. If the broker merely passes on incorrect information supplied by the seller where the broker, by exercising reasonable care, could have discovered the falsity of the seller's statement, the broker may be liable. This theory does not require the broker to independently assess the conditions of the premises for the buyer; it merely requires the broker to avoid making statements about such conditions that the broker would have verified were the broker acting reasonably.

Some jurisdictions go further, holding the broker liable for innocent misrepresentation—i.e., for innocently passing on false information to the buyer, whether or not it was reasonable to expect the broker to verify the information. This effectively imposes a strict liability standard on the broker, though the broker may still avoid liability by disclaiming knowledge as to certain problems rather than making assertions regarding the premises.

Finally, a few courts have gone even further, imposing a duty on the broker to make a reasonable inspection of the premises and to disclose to the buyer any defects discovered in such an inspection. The California case of Easton v. Strassburger, 152 Cal. App. 3d 90, 199 Cal. Rptr. 383 (1984), which established the doctrine, held that a broker who failed to note soil defects that were suggested by various "red flags" and could have been discovered with reasonable diligence, was liable for not disclosing such defects. This position has also been endorsed by the California legislature, Cal.Civ.Code §§ 2079–2079.5.

Finally, various courts interpreting their states' consumer protection acts or real estate licensure acts have also imposed duties of disclosure on real estate brokers, as in the principal case.

As between the broker and the buyer, who is better able to discover defects in the premises? What difficulties does imposing a duty to disclose create for the broker? What alternatives does the buyer have to relying on the broker? Would a disclaimer, or disclosure of the broker's obligations to the seller, protect the buyer adequately? Might brokers object to such a requirement? Would greater involvement of attorneys representing buyers in real estate transactions alleviate this problem in any respect?

See, among the many sources addressing this topic, Annotation, Real–Estate Broker's Liability to Purchaser for Misrepresentation or Nondisclosure of Physical Defects in Property Sold, 46 ALR 4th 546 (1986); Hagglund & Weimer, Caveat Broker: The Brokers Liability for Negligent and Innocent Misrepresentation, 20 Real Est.L.J. 149 (1991); Murray, The Real Estate Broker and the Buyer: Negligence and the Duty to Investigate, 32 Vill.L.Rev. 989 (1987); Comment, Broker Liability After Easton v. Strassburger: Let the Buyer be Aware, 25 Santa Clara L.Rev. 651 (1985); Note, Imposing Tort Liability on Real Estate Brokers Selling Defective Housing, 99 Harv.L.Rev. 1861 (1986).

2. Purchasers of existing housing who find the premises to be defective may also sue their seller, the previous owner. The traditional rule here is, of course, caveat emptor—look it over well before you decide to buy it. Although, this rule still generally obtains, if a seller intentionally misrepresents or conceals defects in the premises and the buyer justifiably relies on these misrepresentations, the seller may be liable for fraud. A court that finds a seller liable for fraud may rescind the transaction and award damages to the purchaser. A seller will also be liable, of course, if it offers and breaches an express warranty as to the condition of the premises.

3. Several states have adopted statutes requiring sellers to disclose certain information about property that they sell. See e.g., Ind.Code Ann. § 13–7–22.5–10 (requiring disclosure of enviornmental defects.) Real estate brokers have often lobbied for such laws. Can you explain why? Note how this issue is handled in Clause 9 of the Contract at page 447 above.

BUTTS et al. v. ATLANTA FEDERAL SAVINGS & LOAN ASSOCIATION

Court of Appeals of Georgia, 1979.
152 Ga.App. 40, 262 S.E.2d 230.

DEEN, CHIEF JUDGE.

This is a suit for damages. The plaintiffs, husband and wife, purchased a lot and on January 28, 1972, contracted with a builder for the construction of a house. Under the terms of the contract the house was to be completed within ninety days. Plaintiffs obtained a construction loan in the amount of $27,500 from Atlanta Federal Savings & Loan Association on February 16, 1972. In September of 1972, plaintiffs filed suit against the contractor because they were dissatisfied with his work. The contractor then filed a petition in bankruptcy. Plaintiffs brought this suit against Atlanta Federal alleging that the association held the loan proceeds in trust and under the terms of the loan contract was required to disburse them to the contractor only upon order of the plaintiffs with the approval of the association, and that Atlanta Federal paid out funds to the contractor without their approval or the Association's inspection for work that had not been completed or had been poorly performed. Atlanta Federal answered claiming that the funds were disbursed only upon authorization of one or both of the plaintiffs and that the contract entered into between the parties did not impose the obligations alleged. The plaintiffs bring this appeal following the trial court's grant of Atlanta Federal's motion for summary judgment. Held:

The record shows that under the construction loan agreement the plaintiffs agreed to have the house completed in accordance with the plans and specifications submitted to the lender, that no change would be made in the building without written approval and that the lender was " * * * authorized to disburse the proceeds of said loan during the course of construction as work progresses and as approved by your inspector." The record also contains twelve disbursement requests signed by the contractor and one or both of the plaintiffs. The majority of them are notarized and state that the " * * * undersigned owner has personally inspected and accepts the above item." Atlanta Federal made eighteen inspections before disbursements to the contractor were stopped at the plaintiffs' request.

The Butts' claim that at the time they applied for the loan, they spoke with Atlanta Federal's vice-president and he told them that all work would be checked and approved for good workmanship before any funds were disbursed, and that they were advised by a bank official that they could sign some of the loan disbursements in blank in order to avoid a trip to the bank each time a request was made. In her deposition, Mrs. Butts, however, admits that only the first three of the twelve requests were signed in blank and that either she or her husband signed the remainder as they were presented by the contractor.

Any oral promises made by Atlanta Federal's vice-president prior to the signing of the loan agreement constitutes parol evidence and is " * * * inadmissible to add to, take from, or vary a written contract." Code Ann. § 20–704(1). * * * Therefore, the sole issue in this case is whether the Association's inspection, as provided in the contract, was for the benefit of Atlanta Federal. As this is a question of first impression in Georgia, we will examine cases from other jurisdictions.

It appears that the liability of a financing authority to the home purchaser for construction defects has only been rarely imposed. Annot. 39 A.L.R.3d 247. In Connor v. Great Western Savings & Loan Assoc., 69 Cal.2d 850, 73 Cal.Rptr. 369, 447 P.2d 609 (1968), the Association was held to be under a duty of reasonable care to protect the buyers from damages caused by major structural defects because of the closely connected business relationship between the lender and the developer which Great Western had voluntarily assumed. In the absence of such a close relationship, the lender has no legal duty to protect purchasers from construction defects when the association's financing activity does not extend beyond that of a conventional construction lender. Bradler v. Craig, 274 Cal.App.2d 466, 79 Cal.Rptr. 401 (1969). Even if an inspection fee is deducted from the loan proceeds, an action for damages based upon the theory of implied contract does not lie because the inspection is not made for the benefit of the buyers. " 'A lender of construction money has an interest in the progress and quality of the construction of its security proportional to the amount of money invested and would reasonably be expected to inspect the construction and be entitled to additional compensation for its additional costs in making such inspection.' " Rice v. First Federal Savings & Loan Assoc., 207 So.2d 22 (Fla.App.1968).

" * * * [C]onstruction inspection procedures are designed primarily as 'work-in-place' inspections in order to see to it that loan funds are being used by the builder on the particular site being financed and that they are not being diverted for other purposes. This is not to say that the construction lender has no interest in having the homes constructed so as to be free from defects. It *Does* have such an interest and if it does discover construction defects during the course of periodic inspections it can and *Should* use its financial power of withholding construction loan payments in order to make sure that the defects are remedied. The point is, however, that quality control is *Not* the primary purpose of the construction lender's inspection * * * In view of the fact that savings and loan associations do not have the specialized, technical competence to act as builders, and since they do not function as such or represent to potential home purchasers that they do, it seems unreasonable to hold them to a duty, the fulfillment of which not only would require them to acquire such competence but also would force them to share this function with the builders whom they finance. Imposing such a duty not only would require savings associations to hire high priced specialists in order to assure that they would be able to perform it, but since associations would be duplicating the primary function of the builder-vendor, the cost of tract financing would be increased substantially and unnecessarily and such cost, or course, ultimately would be passed on to the home purchaser." Pfeiler, Construction Lending and Products Liability, The Business Lawyer 1309, 1321–1323 (1970). It would appear that these reasons would also apply to a situation in which the lender makes a construction loan to the home buyer and does not have any dealings with the contractor. In the present case, there is no evidence that there was any business relationship between the contractor and the association and the plaintiffs have not alleged that the lender knew of the defects in the house. Indeed, the record shows that when the plaintiffs discovered serious defects and requested Atlanta Federal to stop future disbursements to the contractor, it complied with the request.

As the contract forbids changes in the plans for the construction of the house without the association's approval and requires the plaintiffs to approve the contractor's work before authorizing disbursement from their escrow account, we fail to see how the bank's final approval before disbursing funds could be construed to imply that the lender's inspection was for their benefit. 12 U.S.C.A. § 1464(c) permits savings and loan associations to lend construction funds only upon the taking of a security interest. The primary duty of a federal savings and loan association is to protect the assets of its members and depositors; it does not insure the assets of its borrowers. Shaw v. Cook County Federal Savings and Loan Assn., 139 Ga.App. 419, 228 S.E.2d 326 (1976).

Judgment affirmed.

Notes and Questions

1. Many home purchasers no doubt believe that if there were something seriously wrong with the property, the lender, who has had the home independently inspected and appraised, would not be willing to finance 80 per cent, 90 per cent, or more of the home's value. When defects subsequently appear, however, the buyer who turns to the lender or its appraiser to claim damages for reliance is usually disappointed. Courts are particularly reluctant to recognize obligations where the lender and purchaser have no direct contractual relationship. In *Connor,* discussed in the principal case, the California Supreme Court did hold a lender liable to subsequent purchasers for construction defects where the lender was extensively and intimately involved in the construction process. Subsequent cases have rejected *Connor* or limited it to its facts. A few courts have been willing to hold lenders liable to their own borrowers who have relied on appraisals done by the lender in purchasing a property. See Larsen v. United Federal Savings and Loan Association, 300 N.W.2d 281 (Iowa 1981). By and large, however, a purchaser's reliance on the lender will not render the lender liable for damages. See, on this topic, Note, Mortgage Lender Liability to the Purchasers of New or Existing Homes, 1988 U.Ill.L.Rev. 191 (1988).

2. Recent heightened sensitivity to environmental hazards has added a dimension to condition of the premises litigation. In particular, the discovery of high levels of radon in a house, or of pesticides in a water supply, or the presences of hazardous wastes previously disposed of on a property, create serious problems for a purchaser of property, which might well cause the purchaser to look elsewhere for relief. Moreover, federal superfund legislation holds purchasers (as well as prior owners) liable for the cost of cleaning up toxic wastes, unless a purchaser can prove that, despite diligent efforts to determine its presence, he was unaware of toxic contamination. 42 U.S.C. §§ 9601(35)(A). A purchaser tagged with such

liability may well look towards the prior owner who created the condition, a builder who built on contaminated property, or a real estate broker who failed to mention it, for indemnification. See Powell, Builder–Vendor Liability for Environmental Contamination in the Sale of New Residential Property, 58 Tenn.L.Rev. 231 (1991); Comment, A Toxic Nightmare on Elm Street: Negligence and the Real Estate Broker's Duty in Selling Previously Contaminated Residential Property, 15 B.C.Envtl.Aff.L.Rev. 547 (1988). See also pages 611–618 below, discussing further the implications of the superfund legislation for real estate transactions.

V. FINANCING THE ACQUISITION AND DEVELOPMENT OF LAND

Land is an expensive commodity, often costing several thousand dollars per acre. As expensive as land may be, it is only about 10–15 per cent of the total cost of a residential or commercial real estate transaction. With average costs of housing exceeding $100,000 in many parts of the country, the purchase of a home represents the largest single investment for the majority of Americans. Commercial developments, because of their size and complexity, can and often do require multi-million-dollar investments.

With rare exceptions involving very wealthy persons, land acquisition and development is accomplished with borrowed money. As discussed earlier in this chapter, a wide variety of financial institutions regularly lend money to finance real estate transactions. Real estate lenders generally have two basic interests: 1) recovery of borrowed money (the "principal"); and 2) realization of a profit on the transaction (the return on investment). In order to cover the costs of lending money and to make a profit on the transactions, lenders commonly charge "interest" on the "principal" amount of the loan. In this context, "interest" is an annual charge, expressed as a percentage of the amount of the loan, for the use of someone else's money.

Interest rates traditionally have been regulated by state laws prohibiting the charging of exorbitant rates, known as usury. However, in 1980 and 1982, Congress preempted state usury laws for most residential real estate loans. 12 U.S.C.A. § 3701 et seq.; 12 U.S.C.A. § 3801 et seq. See generally G. Nelson & D. Whitman, Real Estate Finance Law, 2d Ed, § 811–824 (1985). Actual rates charged for particular real estate loans represent a combination of limits established by the marketplace as well as by government regulators. In recent years, lenders have experienced sharp increases and substantial volatility in the cost of doing business. As a result, loan rates fluctuated widely while increasing steadily in the 1980s, then dropped dramatically during a recession in 1991. A banker in St. Louis once described the plight of the lending industry in the late 1970s and early 1980s to a group of law students by characterizing himself as a salesman whose product, money, was becoming increasingly costly to produce. When no one in the audience volunteered to predict what the cost of other products (e.g., automobiles, fuel or shoes) would be in five years, he asked rhetorically if his listeners could understand why he was no longer willing to make long-term loans (20–30 years) at fixed interest rates.

Although real estate loans come in all sorts of packages, each one contains combinations of four basic variables, termed the "credit quartet" by Professors Allan Axelrod, Curtis Berger and Quintin Johnstone, Land Transfer and Finance 131 (3d Ed.1986): 1) amount borrowed ("principal"); 2) length of time for repayment ("term"), 3) interest rate; and 4) method of repayment (amortization). The amount borrowed also is described in a loan-to-value ratio (amount of the loan expressed as a percentage of the value of the property offered as security for the loan, or of the value of the total real estate investment, e.g., an $80,000 loan secured by a house valued at $100,000, or being used to complete a $100,000 real estate investment, has a loan-to-value ratio of 80 percent and is known as an 80 percent loan).

The four variables can be manipulated to accomplish a variety of objectives. For example, young families with median-range incomes ($30–40,000), reasonable expectations for economic advancement, but little accumulated savings may be able to afford the monthly payments for a 20–year, $80,000 loan at ten per cent ($772.04/per month), but may not be able to purchase a $100,000 house because of the $20,000 down payment required to complete the transaction. However, if the loan-to-value ratio were increased to 95 per cent, their down-payment problem may be resolved, but they may find the monthly payments on a $95,000 loan at ten per cent ($916.80 per month) prohibitive. The monthly payment problem can be resolved either by lengthening the term of the loan, e.g., from 20 to 30 years (reducing the monthly payment to $702.07), or by reducing the interest rate, e.g., from ten per cent to eight per cent (lowering the monthly payment to $669.19) (20 years) or $587.03 (30 years). When a 95 percent loan-to-value ratio is combined with a 30 year term and an eight per cent interest rate, the resulting smaller down-payment ($5000) and lower monthly payments for principal and interest ($697.10), may make a $100,000 house affordable to a median-income family.

The Federal Housing Administration (FHA), established by Congress in the 1930s, pioneered the use of high loan-to-value, long term, lower interest, fixed-rate loans with self-amortizing features to reduce the cost of housing for moderate and middle-income families by offering mortgage insurance to lenders who would make such loans. FHA-insured loans also reduced a risk of default at the end of the loan term by providing for amortization of principal over the term of the loan through application of a gradually-increasing portion of each monthly payment to reduce the outstanding principal balance, rather than requiring a lump-sum ("balloon") payment at the end of the loan term.

The following table illustrates the effect of variations in loan-to-value ratio, down payment, length of term, and interest rate on the monthly principal and interest costs of a $100,000 house.

Interest Rate		Amount Borrowed	
8%	$80,000	$90,000	$95,000
Loan Term		**Monthly Payment**	
20 yrs.	$669.19/mo.	$752.84/mo.	$794.67/mo.
25 yrs.	617.48	694.67	733.26
30 yrs.	587.03	660.41	697.10
10%			
20 yrs.	$772.04/mo.	$868.54/mo.	$916.80/mo.
25 yrs.	726.97	817.85	863.28
30 yrs.	702.07	789.82	833.770
12%			
20 yrs.	$880.08/mo.	$990.09/mo.	$1045.95/mo.
25 yrs.	842.40	947.70	1000.35
30 yrs.	823.20	926.10	977.55

Effect of below-market interest rate subsidy

4%	**$80,000**	**$90,000**	**$95,000**
20 yrs.	$484.80/mo.	$545.40/mo.	$575.70/mo.
25 yrs.	442.40	475.20	501.60
30 yrs.	381.60	429.30	453.15

The concept of leverage plays an important role in real estate finance. Leverage in real estate finance is a reflection of the success a purchaser has in using other people's money to finance a real estate transaction. A highly-leveraged transaction is one with a high loan-to-value ratio and correspondingly low down payment (investment) by the purchaser. Leverage offers the potential for dramatically increasing the rate of return on a purchaser's investment. If, for example, property purchased for $100,000 in cash is sold in one year for $110,000, the seller obtains a 10 per cent return on her investment. If, however, that same property was purchased with a 90 per cent loan ($10,000 down payment), a sale for $110,000 nets the seller $20,000 or double her initial investment.

From a lender's standpoint, highly-leveraged loans are risky because highly-leveraged borrowers have less to lose from default, and thus may be less inclined to take steps to avoid default. In addition, a decline in real estate values may cause a lender to lose money on a loan default if the foreclosure sale price of highly-leveraged property is not sufficient to cover the unpaid balance of the loan.

The long-term nature of most real estate loans, coupled with the large amounts usually borrowed, make real estate loans inherently risky for both lender and borrower. Because of the high risks, it is common for real estate loans to be "secured" by property of the borrower. A "security interest" or "lien" on the property is conveyed by the borrower to the lender. The interest conveyed, called a mortgage, or in some states a deed of trust, is a non-possessory right to sell the property and use the proceeds of the sale to retire the loan should the borrower fail to make timely payments. It is called a security interest because the lender is supposed to feel more secure about the prospects of ultimate recovery of its investment should a default occur, and the borrower is supposed to be more motivated to honor her promise to repay because of the prospect of losing the property if the loan is not repaid.

Lenders commonly cluster their perceptions of the risks of real estate loans into two groups: 1) credit risks; and 2) interest rate risks.

Credit risks are of two types, the risk that the borrower will not have enough money to make the promised monthly payments, and the risk that, if a default occurs, the value of the property will not be high enough to generate sale proceeds sufficient to recoup the lender's investment. These risks are evaluated through a process called loan underwriting, using income and credit histories of the borrower, and appraisals of the value of the property which will secure the loan. Loan underwriting can be time consuming, and is one of the reasons why a substantial delay (30–90 days) usually occurs between the time a real estate sale contract is signed and a deed is transferred.

Interest rate risks arise out of increased unpredictability concerning the cost of money. Lenders typically obtain money for real estate loans by "buying" the use of other peoples' money through various types of deposit accounts, insurance premiums, pension accumulations, etc. They "pay" for such use by crediting interest to the accounts of the depositors. The interest rate risk that concerns lenders is the possibility that they may find themselves paying more to acquire money for lending purposes than they are receiving in repayment of previous loans. For example, lenders who routinely made 25 year-to-30–year loans at fixed interest rates in the six per cent range in the 1950s and early 1960s were not happy people when they had to offer 10–12 per cent rates in order to attract depositors in the 1970s and 1980s. Fears about interest rate risk returned in 1992 in the wake of a "tidal wave" of homeowners seeking to refinance home loans to take advantage of sharply lower interest rates. Labaton, Lower Interest Rates Revive Fears of Banks and S. & L.'s, New York Times, January 13, 1992, at p. A1, col. 3. The growth in popularity of various forms of adjustable rate mortgage loans (ARMs) is a result of lenders' concerns about interest rate risks.

A. ELEMENTS OF THE LOAN

The basic real estate loan consists of two parts: 1) a written promise to pay back the money borrowed upon the agreed terms (the note), and 2) a conveyance of a property interest to the lender to secure the borrower's performance of her promise (the mortgage or deed of trust).

1. *The Note*

The note is the contract between the borrower and the lender. It describes the particular cluster of variables described above that have been agreed upon by the parties, and expresses the borrower's promise to repay, along with agreements concerning the right to pay the loan off early ("prepayment"), late charges, rights of the lender upon default, notice requirements for exercising those rights, and an acknowledgment that the note is secured by a mortgage, deed of trust, or other property interest.

BOATMEN'S®

NOTE

_____ , 19____   _____ , _____
                                              [City]   [State]

_____
                               [Property Address]

1. BORROWER'S PROMISE TO PAY

In return for a loan that I have received, I promise to pay U.S. $ _____ (this amount is called "principal"), plus interest, to the order of the Lender. The Lender is _____ . I understand that the Lender may transfer this Note. The Lender or anyone who takes this Note by transfer and who is entitled to receive payments under this Note is called the "Note Holder."

2. INTEREST

Interest will be charged on unpaid principal until the full amount of principal has been paid. I will pay interest at a yearly rate of _____ %.

The Interest rate required by this Section 2 is the rate I will pay both before and after any default described in Section 6(B) of this Note.

3. PAYMENTS

(A) Time and place of payments

I will pay principal and interest by making payments every month.

I will make my monthly payments on the _____ day of each month beginning on _____ , 19 ____ . I will make these payments every month until I have paid all of the principal and interest and any other charges described below that I may owe under this Note. My monthly payments will be applied to interest before principal. If, on _____ , ____ , I still owe amounts under this Note, I will pay those amounts in full on that date, which is called the "maturity date."

I will make my monthly payments at _____ _____ or at a different place if required by the Note Holder.

(B) Amount of Monthly Payments

My monthly payment will be in the amount of U.S. $ _____

4. BORROWER'S RIGHT TO PREPAY

I have the right to make payments of principal at any time before they are due. A payment of principal only is known as a "prepayment." When I make a prepayment, I will tell the Note Holder in writing that I am doing so.

I may make a full prepayment or partial prepayments without paying any prepayment charge. The Note Holder will use all of my prepayments to reduce the amount of principal that I owe under this Note. If I make a partial prepayment, there will be no changes in the due date or in the amount of my monthly payment unless the Note Holder agrees in writing to those changes.

5. LOAN CHARGES

If a law, which applies to this loan and which sets maximum loan charges, is finally interpreted so that the interest or other loan charges collected or to be collected in connection with this loan exceed the permitted limits, then: (i) any such loan charge shall be reduced by the amount necessary to reduce the charge to the permitted limit; and (ii) any sums already collected from me which exceeded permitted limits will be refunded to me. The Note Holder may choose to make this refund by reducing the principal I owe under this Note or by making a direct payment to me. If a refund reduces principal, the reduction will be treated as a partial prepayment.

6. BORROWER'S FAILURE TO PAY AS REQUIRED

(A) Late Charge for Overdue Payments

If the Note Holder has not received the full amount of any monthly payment by the end of _____ calendar days after the date it is due, I will pay a late charge to the Note Holder. The amount of the charge will be ____ % of my overdue payment of principal and interest. I will pay this late charge promptly but only once on each late payment.

(B) Default

If I do not pay the full amount of each monthly payment on the date it is due, I will be in default.

(C) Notice of Default

If I am in default, the Note Holder may send me a written notice telling me that if I do not pay the overdue amount by a certain date, the Note Holder may require me to pay immediately in full as described above, the Note Holder will still have the right to do so if I am in default at a later time.

(D) No Waiver By Note Holder

Even if, at a time when I am in default, the Note Holder does not require me to pay immediately in full as described above, the Note Holder may require me to pay immediately the full amount of principal which has not been paid and all the interest that I owe on that amount. That date must be at least 30 days after the date on which the notice is delivered or mailed to me.

(E) Payment of Note Holder's Costs and Expenses

If the Note Holder has required me to pay immediately in full as described above, the Note Holder will have the right to be paid back by me for all of its costs and expenses in enforcing this Note to the extent not prohibited by applicable law. Those expenses include, for example, reasonable attorneys' fees.

7. GIVING OF NOTICES

Unless applicable law requires a different method, any notice that must be given to me under this Note will be given by delivering it or by mailing it by first class mail to me at the Property Address above or at a different address if I give the Note Holder a notice of my different address.

Any notice that must be given to the Note Holder under this Note will be given by mailing it by first class mail to the Note Holder at the address stated in Section 3(A) above or at a different address if I am given a notice of that different address.

8. OBLIGATIONS OF PERSONS UNDER THIS NOTE

If more than one person signs this Note, each person is fully and personally obligated to keep all of the promises made in this Note, including the promise to pay the full amount owed. Any person who is a guarantor, surety or endorser of this Note is also obligated to do these things. Any person who takes over these obligations, including the obligations of a guarantor, surety or endorser of this Note, is also obligated to keep all of the promises made in this Note. The Note holder may enforce its rights under this Note against each person individually or against all of us together. This means that any one of us may be required to pay all of the amounts owed under this Note.

9. WAIVERS

I and any other person who has obligations under this Note waive the rights of presentments and notice of dishonor. "Presentment" means the right to require the Note Holder to demand payment of amounts due. "Notice of dishonor" means the right to require the Note Holder to give notice to other persons that amounts due have not been paid.

10. UNIFORM SECURED NOTE

This Note is a uniform instrument with limited variations in some jurisdictions. In addition to the protections given to the Note Holder under this Note, a Mortgage, Deed of Trust or Security Deed (the "Security Instrument"), dated the same date as this Note, protects the Note Holder from possible losses which might result if I do not keep the promises which I make in this Note. That Security Instrument describes how and under what conditions I may be required to make immediate payment in full of all amounts I owe under this Note. Some of those conditions are described as follows:

Transfer of the Property or a Beneficial Interest in Borrower. If all or any part of the Property or any interest in it is sold or transferred (or if a beneficial interest in Borrower is sold or transferred and Borrower is not a natural person) without Lender's prior written consent, Lender may, at its option, require immediate payment in full of all sums secured by this Security Instrument. However, this option shall not be exercised by Lender if exercise is prohibited by federal law as of the date of this Security Instrument.

If Lender exercises this option, Lender shall give Borrower notice of acceleration. The notice shall provide a period of not less than 30 days from the date the notice is delivered or mailed within which Borrower must pay all sums secured by this Security Instrument. If Borrower fails to pay these sums prior to the expiration of this period, Lender may invoke any remedies permitted by this Security Instrument without further notice or demand on Borrower.

WITNESS THE HAND(S) and SEAL(S) OF THE UNDERSIGNED.

_____ (Seal)
-Borrower

_____ (Seal)
-Borrower

_____ (Seal)
-Borrower
(Sign Original Only)

Form RE 203 p2 of 2 (Rev. 6/89)

FNMA Form 3200 12/83
[G8360]

Notes and Questions

1. Examine the note carefully. Does the borrower have a grace period for making payments? What constitutes default? What procedure is to be followed when default occurs? Is the note transferable? By the lender? By the borrower? If the borrower wins the lottery, does she have the right to eliminate her debt by prepaying the note? If the borrower makes a double payment (two months), can she skip the next month's payment if she should become ill or be laid off from work? What happens to the balance of the double payment that remains after the regular monthly payment is credited? Does the note contain any restrictions on transfer of the property by the borrower?

2. The following excerpt describes a variety of mortgage loans designed to offer more flexibility to borrowers and lenders. As you study the excerpt, consider what changes you would make to the sample note in order to create a particular kind of mortgage note.

NELSON & WHITMAN, REAL ESTATE

Finance Law 776–780 (2nd Ed.1985).

§ 11.4 Alternative Mortgage Instruments

The great majority of mortgage loans which have been made in modern times are of the level-payment self-amortizing type * * *. Interest is fixed for the life of the loan and payments are the same each month or other period, and fully amortize the debt with no "balloon" payment upon maturity. While this format has resolved the problem of mandatory refinancing which existed in pre-depression mortgage loans, in which only interest was paid monthly, it also has certain disadvantages. The disadvantages fall into two basic categories, as do various proposals for reform.

The first troublesome aspect of the standard loan format is its failure to take into account changes in the ability of the mortgagors to make payments over their life spans. For example, young families purchasing a first house are likely to experience significant increases in income as they grow older. Yet the standard loan provides for level payments in terms of nominal dollars; in an inflationary economy, the real value of the monthly payments will decline over time, even though the mortgagors' ability to pay will probably be increasing. Hence their maximum initial loan amount will be fixed by an income which rapidly becomes irrelevant with the passage of time; after a few years they will easily be able to afford payments on a larger home, but can make such a change only through the rather costly method of selling the existing house and buying another.

At the other end of the mortgagors' life span an opposite mismatch occurs. The mortgagors frequently retire and experience a sharp drop in income, but their monthly mortgage payment obligation remains constant despite the fact that principal amortization and inflating house values have combined to produce a very low loan-to-value ratio. The mortgagors might prefer to reduce their payments, or even to stop them entirely, but the standard loan format makes no provision for doing so.

The second major problem with the standard loan relates not to the preferences and incomes of mortgagors, but to the ability of lenders, particularly thrift institutions, to retain deposits and hence to continue lending during periods of sharply increasing interest rates. The United States economy has experienced a series of large fluctuations in interest rates during the post-war period, especially since 1966. These credit cycles are largely produced by the interaction of a complex set of factors, including consumer behavior, federal and state borrowing demands, international trade and economic conditions, and the periodic efforts of the Federal Reserve Board to tighten the supply of money in the economy in order to slow inflation. Interest rate peaks can be clearly discerned in 1966, 1969–70, 1974, 1978, 1981, and 1984. In each case rates have subsequently fallen, but usually not as low as pre-peak levels.

The effect of these credit cycles on thrift institutions such as savings and loan associations and mutual savings banks is highly damaging. When short-term rates on alternative investments, such as Treasury bills and commercial paper, rise above the rates being paid on savings deposits by thrift institutions, many sophisticated depositors withdraw their funds from savings accounts and place them in these alternative investments. The institutions may literally run out of money to lend, and the housing market suffers. This phenomenon is known as disintermediation, since it involves the removal of funds from the thrift institutions, which are financial intermediaries. To forestall disintermediation, thrift institutions may attempt to raise the interest rates on their own deposits, thereby inducing investors to keep their funds on deposit. * * *

* * *

* * * [M]ortgage lenders which have historically been heavy investors in standard mortgages will still have difficulty raising their deposit rates to competitive levels during periods of generally rising rates. The reason is that their mortgage portfolios consist of mortgages made in prior years as well as those made in the current year. Even if the institution raises the interest rates on mortgage loans currently being made to very high levels, that action has relatively little impact on the overall yield of the portfolio, since it consists largely of fixed-interest loans made in earlier periods when rates were lower. This "portfolio lag" phenomenon virtually precludes the institutions from raising deposit interest rates quickly, no matter how much they would like to do so. The thrift institutions are caught in a fundamental structural dilemma; by their nature they violate the well-known axiom of finance: "Never borrow short and lend long." In an economy characterized by volatile interest rates, their problem is an acute one.

Two approaches to this problem can be taken, and the thrift institutions and their regulators have moved toward both. The first is to change the maturity structure of the institutions' liabilities—that is, their deposits—in order to make them less volatile. A number of regulatory changes have been made to allow thrifts to offer a broader range of longer-term instruments to savers.

The other approach is to shorten the effective maturity of the institutions' assets, their mortgage loans. Although most home mortgages today have nominal maturities of twenty-five to thirty years, they are typically prepaid in ten to twelve years or less. These early payments are due in part to rapidly inflating housing prices, which tend to make property sales with assumptions and subject-to transfers impractical within a few years after a mortgage loan has been placed on a home. The widespread use of due-on-sale clauses is also an important factor in causing early payoffs. But most portfolio lenders wish to reduce the effective term of the average home mortgage loan a great deal more than the reduction which results from ordinary prepayments associated with home transfers. Hence, since the beginning of the 1980's they have engaged in a major shift away from the standard fixed-rate loan and toward instruments with adjustable rates, with the adjustment indexed to some short-term or medium-term market rate such as that on United State government securities. Such mortgages are viewed as the economic equivalent of short-term loans, even though their monthly payment schedules might continue to be based on twenty-five or thirty year amortization of principal.

There are, then, two reasons for experimentation in recent years with alternative mortgage instruments: the desire to conform payment schedules to borrowers' abilities to pay, and the desire to make mortgage loans which are not locked into fixed interest yields for long time periods, but on which yields will tend to match those available in the current market from time to time. Certain types of new mortgage formats are associated with each of these two objectives.

* * *

———

3. As discussed earlier the secondary mortgage market plays a vital role in real estate finance. The rise of the secondary mortgage market gives added weight to the importance of the mortgage note, because secondary market investors must look to the note, as well as the mortgage, for their rights should disputes arise concerning payment or procedures to follow in case of default. Investors in the secondary market typically seek protection of the "holder in due course" concept of negotiable instruments in order to insulate themselves from defenses that may be raised by the original borrower against the original lender in case of default. For a case illustrating the importance of careful drafting of the mortgage note, see Taylor v. Roeder, 234 Va. 99, 360 S.E.2d 191 (1987) (adjustable mortgage note failed to qualify as negotiable instrument under Uniform Commercial Code).

2. *The Mortgage (and Mortgage Substitutes)*

The property part of a real estate loan transaction is the conveyance of a non-possessory property interest by the borrower to the lender. This takes place simultaneously with the execution of the note, and provides the "security" for repayment of the debt represented by the note. The document evidencing the conveyance is called a mortgage, although in some states a similar document called a deed of trust is used. Except where indicated, we can use the terms interchangeably. In reviewing the sample deed of trust below, pay particular attention to the language of conveyance. What legal relationships are created? What obligations are undertaken by the grantor (usually called the mortgagor)? By the grantee (the mortgagee)? By the trustee?

_____ [Space Above This Line For Recording Data] _____

DEED OF TRUST

THIS DEED OF TRUST ("Security Instrument") is made on _____ ,
19 _____ . The grantor is _____
_____ ("Borrower"). The trustee is _____
_____
_____ ("Trustee"). The beneficiary is
_____ , which is organized and existing
under the laws of _____ , and whose address is _____
_____ ("Lender").
Borrower owes Lender the principal sum of _____
_____ Dollars (U.S. $ _____). This debt is evidenced by
Borrower's note dated the same date as this Security Instrument ("Note"), which provides for monthly payments, with the
full debt, if not paid earlier, due and payable on _____
This Security Instrument secures to Lender: (a) the repayment of the debt evidenced by the Note, with interest, and all renewals,
extensions and modifications; (b) the payment of all other sums, with interest, advanced under paragraph 7 to protect the
security of this Security Instrument; and (c) the performance of Borrower's covenants and agreements under this Security
Instrument and the Note. For this purpose, Borrower irrevocably grants and conveys to Trustee, in trust, with power of sale,
the following described property located in _____ County, Missouri:

which has the address of _____ . _____ , _____ ,
　　　　　　　　　　　　　　　　　　　　[Street]　　　　　　　　　　　　　　　　　　　　　　　　　　[City]
Missouri _____ ("Property Address");
　　　　　　　　[Zip Code]

TOGETHER WITH all the improvements now or hereafter erected on the property, and all easements, rights,
appurtenances, rents, royalties, mineral, oil and gas rights and profits, water rights and stock and all fixtures now or hereafter
a part of the property. All replacements and additions shall also be covered by this Security Instrument. All of the foregoing
is referred to in this Security Instrument as the "Property."

BORROWER COVENANTS that Borrower is lawfully seized of the estate hereby conveyed and has the right to grant
and convey the Property and that the Property is unencumbered, except for encumbrances of record. Borrower warrants and
will defend generally the title to the Property against all claims and demands, subject to any encumbrances of record.

THIS SECURITY INSTRUMENT combines uniform covenants for national use and non-uniform covenants with limited
variations by jurisdiction to constitute a uniform security covering real property.

MISSOURI—Single Family—**FNMA/FHLMC UNIFORM INSTRUMENT**　　　　　　　　　　Form 3026 12/83
　　　[G8361]

Form RE 165 MO FNMA p1 of 4 (5/89)

UNIFORM COVENANTS. Borrower and Lender covenant and agree as follows:

1. Payment of Principal and Interest; Prepayment and Late Charges. Borrower shall promptly pay when due the principal of and interest on the debt evidenced by the Note and any prepayment and late charges due under the Note.

2. Funds for Taxes and Insurance. Subject to applicable law or to a written waiver by Lender, Borrower shall pay to Lender on the day monthly payments are due under the Note, until the Note is paid in full, a sum ("Funds") equal to one-twelfth of: (a) yearly taxes and assements which may attain priority over this Security Instrument; (b) yearly leasehold payments or ground rents on the Property, if any; (c) yearly hazard insurance premiums; and (d) yearly mortgage insurance premiums, if any. These items are called "escrow items". Lender may estimate the Funds due on the basis of current data and reasonable estimates of future escrow items.

The Funds shall be held in an institution the deposits or accounts of which are insured or guaranteed by a federal or state agency (including Lender if Lender is such an institution). Lender shall apply the Funds to pay the escrow items. Lender may not charge for holding and applying the Funds, analyzing the account or verifying the escrow items, unless Lender pays Borrower interest on the Funds and applicable law permits Lender to make such a charge. Borrower and Lender may agree in writing that interest shall be paid on the Funds. Unless an agreement is made or applicable law requires interest to be paid, Lender shall not be required to pay Borrower any interest or earnings on the Funds. Lender shall give to Borrower, without charge, an annual accounting of the Funds showing credits and debits to the Funds and the purpose for which each debit to the Funds was made. The Funds are pledged as additional security for the sums secured by this Security Instrument.

If the amount of the Funds held by Lender, together with the future monthly payments of Funds payable prior to the due dates of the escrow items, shall exceed the amount required to pay the escrow items when due, the excess shall be, at Borrower's option, either promptly repaid to Borrower or credited to Borrower on monthly payments of Funds. If the amount of the Funds held by Lender is not sufficient to pay the escrow items when due, Borrower shall pay to Lender any amount necessary to make up the deficiency in one or more payments as required by Lender.

Upon payment in full of all sums secured by this Security Instrument, Lender shall promptly refund to Borrower any Funds held by Lender. If under paragraph 19 the Property is sold or acquired by Lender, Lender shall apply, no later than immediately prior to the sale of the Property or its acquisition by Lender, any Funds held by Lender at the time of application as a credit against the sums secured by this Security Instrument.

3. Application of Payments. Unless applicable law provides otherwise, all payments received by Lender under the paragraphs 1 and 2 shall be applied: first, to late charges due under the Note; second, to prepayment charges due under the Note; third, to amounts payable under paragraph 2; fourth, to interest due; and last, to principal due.

4. Charges; Liens. Borrower shall pay all taxes, assessments, charges, fines and impositions attributable to the Property which may attain priority over this Security Instrument, and leasehold payments or ground rents, if any. Borrower shall pay these obligations in the manner provided in paragraph 2, or if not paid in that manner, Borrower shall pay them on time directly to the person owed payment. Borrower shall promptly furnish to Lender all notices of amounts to be paid under this paragraph. If Borrower makes these payments directly, Borrower shall promptly furnish to Lender receipts evidencing the payments.

Borrower shall promptly discharge any lien which has priority over this Security Instrument unless Borrower: (a) agrees in writing to the payment of the obligation secured by the lien in a manner acceptable to Lender; (b) contests in good faith the lien by, or defends against enforcement of the lien in, legal proceedings which in the Lender's opinion operate to prevent the enforcement of the lien or forfeiture of any part of the Property; or (c) secures from the holder of the lien an agreement satisfactory to Lender subordinating the lien to this Security Instrument. If Lender determines that any part of the Property is subject to a lien which may attain priority over this Security Instrument, Lender may give Borrower a notice identifying the lien. Borrower shall satisfy the lien or take one or more of the actions set forth above within 10 days of the giving of notice.

5. Hazard Insurance. Borrower shall keep the improvements now existing or hereafter erected on the Property insured against loss by fire, hazards included within the term "extended coverage", and any other hazards for which Lender requires insurance. This insurance shall be maintained in the amounts and for the periods that Lender requires. The insurance carrier providing the insurance shall be chosen by Borrower subject to Lender's approval which shall not be unreasonably withheld.

All insurance policies and renewals shall be acceptable to Lender and shall include a standard mortgage clause. Lender shall have the right to hold the policies and renewals. If Lender requires, Borrower shall promptly give to Lender all receipts of paid premiums and renewal notices. In the event of loss, Borrower shall give prompt notice to the insurance carrier and Lender. Lender may make proof of loss if not made promptly by Borrower.

Unless Lender and Borrower otherwise agree in writing, insurance proceeds shall be applied to restoration or repair of the Property damaged, if the restoration or repair is economically feasible and Lender's security is not lessened. If the restoration or repair is not economically feasible or Lender's security would be lessened, the insurance proceeds shall be applied to the sums secured by this Security Instrument, whether or not then due, with any excess paid to Borrower. If Borrower abandons the Property, or does not answer within 30 days a notice from Lender that the insurance carrier has offered to settle a claim, then Lender may collect the insurance proceeds. Lender may use the proceeds to repair or restore the Property or to pay sums secured by the Security Instrument, whether or not then due. The 30-day period will begin when the notice is given.

Unless Lender and Borrower otherwise agree in writing, any application of proceeds to principal shall not extend or postpone the due date of the monthly payments referred to in paragraphs 1 and 2 or change the amount of the payments. If under paragraph 19 the Property is acquired by Lender, Borrower's right to any insurance policies and proceeds resulting from damage to the Property prior to the acquisition shall pass to Lender to the extent of the sums secured by this Security Instrument immediately prior to the acquisition.

6. Preservation and Maintenance of Property; Leaseholds. Borrower shall not destroy, damage or substantially change the Property, allow the Property to deteriorate or commit waste. If this Security Instrument is on a leasehold, Borrower shall comply with the provisions of the lease, and if Borrower acquires fee title to the Property, the leasehold and fee title shall not merge unless Lender agrees to the merger in writing.

7. Protection of Lender's Rights in the Property; Mortgage Insurance. If Borrower fails to perform the covenants and agreements contained in this Security Instrument, or there is a legal proceeding that may significantly affect Lender's rights in the Property (such as a proceeding in bankruptcy, probate, for condemnation or to enforce laws or regulations), then Lender may do and pay for whatever is necessary to protect the value of the Property and Lender's rights in the Property. Lender's actions may include paying any sums secured by a lien which has priority over this Security Instrument, appearing in court, paying reasonable attorneys' fees and entering on the Property to make repairs. Although Lender may take action under this paragraph 7, Lender does not have to do so.

Any amounts disbursed by Lender under this paragraph 7 shall become additional debt of Borrower secured by this Security Instrument. Unless Borrower and Lender agree to other terms of payment, these amounts shall bear interest from the date of disbursement at the Note rate and shall be payable, with interest, upon notice from Lender to Borrower requesting payment.

Form RE 165 MO FNMA p2 of 4 (5/89)   [G8362]

If Lender required mortgage insurance as a condition of making the loan secured by this Security Instrument, Borrower shall pay the premiums required to maintain the insurance in effect until such time as the requirement for the insurance terminates in accordance with Borrower's and Lender's written agreement or applicable law.

8. Inspection. Lender or its agent may make reasonable entries upon and inspections of the Property. Lender shall give Borrower notice at the time of or prior to an inspection specifying reasonable cause for the inspection.

9. Condemnation. The proceeds of any award or claim for damages, direct or consequential, in connection with any condemnation or other taking of any part of the Property, or for conveyance in lieu of condemnation, are hereby assigned and shall be paid to Lender.

In the event of a total taking of the Property, the proceeds shall be applied to the sums secured by this Security Instrument, whether or not then due, with any excess paid to Borrower. In the event of a partial taking of the Property, unless Borrower and Lender otherwise agree in writing, the sums secured by this Security Instrument shall be reduced by the amount of the proceeds multiplied by the following fraction: (a) the total amount of the sums secured immediately before the taking, divided by (b) the fair market value of the Property immediately before the taking. Any balance shall be paid to Borrower.

If the Property is abandoned by Borrower, or if, after notice by Lender to Borrower that the condemnor offers to make an award or settle a claim for damages, Borrower fails to respond to Lender within 30 days after the date the notice is given, Lender is authorized to collect and apply the proceeds, at its option, either to restoration or repair of the Property or to the sums secured by this Security Instrument, whether or not then due.

Unless Lender and Borrower otherwise agree in writing, any application of proceeds to principal shall not extend or postpone the due date of the monthly payments referred to in paragraphs 1 and 2 or change the amount of such payments.

10. Borrower Not Released; Forbearance By Lender Not a Waiver. Extension of the time for payment or modification of amortization of the sums secured by this Security Instrument granted by Lender to any successor in interest of Borrower shall not operate to release the liability of the original Borrower or Borrower's successors in interest. Lender shall not be required to commence proceedings against any successor in interest or refuse to extend time for payment or otherwise modify amortization of the sums secured by this Security Instrument by reason of any demand made by the original Borrower or Borrower's successors in interest. Any forbearance by Lender in exercising any right or remedy shall not be a waiver of or preclude the exercise of any right or remedy.

11. Successors and Assigns Bound; Joint and Several Liability; Co-signers. The covenants and agreements of this Security Instrument shall bind and benefit the succesors and assigns of Lender and Borrower, subject to the provisions of paragraph 17. Borrower's covenants and agreements shall be joint and several. Any Borrower who co-signs this Security Instrument but does not execute the Note: (a) is co-signing this Security Instrument only to mortgage, grant and convey that Borrower's interest in the Property under the terms of this Security Instrument; (b) is not personally obligated to pay the sums secured by this Security Instrument; and (c) agrees that Lender and any other Borrower may agree to extend, modify, forbear or make any accommodations with regard to the terms of this Security Instrument or the Note without that Borrower's consent.

12. Loan Charges. If the loan secured by this Security Instrument is subject to a law which sets maximum loan charges, and that law is finally interpreted so that the interest or other loan charges collected or to be collected in connection with the loan exceed the permitted limits, then: (a) any such loan charge shall be reduced by the amount necessary to reduce the charge to the permitted limit; and (b) any sums already collected from Borrower which exceeded permitted limits will be refunded to Borrower. Lender may choose to make this refund by reducing the principal owed under the Note or by making a direct payment to Borrower. If a refund reduces principal, the reduction will be treated as a partial prepayment without any prepayment charge under the Note.

13. Legislation Affecting Lender's Rights. If enactment or expiration of applicable laws has the effect of rendering any provision of the Note or this Security Instrument unenforceable according to its terms, Lender, at its option, may require immediate payment in full of all sums secured by this Security Instrument and may invoke any remedies permitted by paragraph 19. If Lender exercises this option, Lender shall take the steps specified in the second paragraph of paragraph 17.

14. Notice. Any notice to Borrower provided for in this Security Instrument shall be given by delivering it or by mailing it by first class mail unless applicable law requires use of another method. The notice shall be directed to the Property Address or any other address Borrower designates by notice to Lender. Any notice to Lender shall be given by first class mail to Lender's address stated herein or any other address Lender designates by notice to Borrower. Any notice provided for in this Security Instrument shall be deemed to have been given to Borrower or Lender when given as provided in this paragraph.

15. Governing Law; Severability. This Security Instrument shall be governed by federal law and the law of the jurisdiction in which the Property is located. In the event that any provision or clause of this Security Instrument or the Note conflicts with applicable law, such conflict shall not affect other provisions of this Security Instrument or the Note which can be given effect without the conflicting provision. To this end the provisions of this Security Instrument and the Note are declared to be severable.

16. Borrower's Copy. Borrower shall be given one conformed copy of the Note and of this Security Instrument.

17. Transfer of the Property or a Beneficial Interest in Borrower. If all or any part of the Property or any interest in it is sold or transferred (or if a beneficial interest in Borrower is sold or transferred and Borrower is not a natural person) without Lender's prior written consent, Lender may, at its option, require immediate payment in full of all sums secured by this Security Instrument. However, this option shall not be exercised by Lender if exercise is prohibited by federal law as of the date of this Security Instrument.

If Lender exercises this option, Lender shall give Borrower notice of acceleration. The notice shall provide a period of not less than 30 days from the date the notice is delivered or mailed within which Borrower must pay all sums secured by this Security Instrument. If Borrower fails to pay these sums prior to the expiration of this period, Lender may invoke any remedies permitted by this Security Instrument without further notice or demand on Borrower.

18. Borrower's Right to Reinstate. If Borrower meets certain conditions, Borrower shalll have the right to have enforcement of this Security Instrument discontinued at any time prior to the earlier of: (a) 5 days (or such other period as applicable law may specify for reinstatement) before sale of the Property pursuant to any power of sale contained in this Security Instrument; or (b) entry of a judgement enforcing this Security Instrument. Those conditions are that Borrower: (a) pays Lender all sums which then would be due under this Security Instrument and the Note had no acceleration occured; (b) cures any default of any other covenants or agreements, (c) pays all expenses incurred in enforcing this Security Instrument, including, but not limited to, reasonable attorneys' fees; and (d) takes such action as Lender may reasonably require to assure that the lien of this Security Instrument, Lender's rights in the Property and Borrower's obligation to pay the sums secured by this Security Instrument shall continue unchanged. Upon reinstatement by Borrower, this Security Instrument and the obligations secured hereby shall remain fully effective as if no acceleration had occured. However, this right to reinstate shall not apply in the case of acceleration under paragraphs 13 or 17.

Form RE 165 MO FNMA p3 of 4 (5/89)   [G8363]

NON-UNIFORM COVENANTS. Borrower and Lender further covenant and agree as follows:

19. Acceleration; Remedies. Lender shall give notice to Borrower prior to acceleration following Borrower's breach of any covenant or agreement in this Security Instrument (but not prior to acceleration under paragraphs 13 and 17 unless applicable law provides otherwise). The notice shall specify: (a) the default; (b) the action required to cure the default; (c) a date, not less than 30 days from the date the notice is given to Borrower by which the default must be cured; and (d) that failure to cure the default on or before the date specified in the notice may result in acceleration of the sums secured by this Security Instrument and sale of the Property. The notice shall further inform Borrower of the right to reinstate after acceleration and the right to bring a court action to assert the non-existence of a default or any other defense of Borrower to acceleration and sale. If the default is not cured on or before the date specified in the notice, Lender at its option may require immediate payment in full of all sums secured by this Security Instrument without further demand and may invoke the power of sale and any other remedies permitted by applicable law. Lender shall be entitled to collect all expenses incurred in pursuing the remedies provided in this paragraph 19, including, but not limited to, reasonable attorneys' fees and costs of title evidence.

If lender invokes the power of sale, Lender or Trustee shall mail copies of a notice of sale in the manner prescribed by applicable law to Borrower and to the other persons prescribed by applicable law. Trustee shall give notice of sale by public advertisement for the time and in the manner prescribed by applicable law. Trustee, without demand on Borrorwer, shall sell the Property at public auction to the highest bidder for cash at the time and place and under the terms designated in the notice of sale in one or more parcels and in any order Trustee determines. Trustee may postpone sale of all or any parcel of the Property to any later time on the same date by public announcement at the time and place of any previously scheduled sale. Lender or its designee may purchase the Property at any sale.

Trustee shall deliver to the purchaser Trustee's deed conveying the Property without any covenant or warranty, expressed or implied. The recitals in the Trustee's deed shall be prima facie evidence of the truth of the statements made therein. Trustee shall apply the proceeds of the sale in the following order: (a) to all expenses of the sale, including, but not limited to, reasonable Trustee's and attorneys' fees; (b) to all sums secured by this Security Instrument; and (c) any excess to the person or persons legally entitled to it.

20. Lender in Possesion. Upon acceleration under paragraph 19 or abandonment of the Property, Lender (in person, by agent or by judicially appointed receiver) shall be entitled to enter upon, take possession of and manage the Property and to collect the rents of the Property including those past due. Any rents collected by Lender or the receiver shall be applied first to payment of the costs of management of the Property and collection of rents, including, but not limited to, receiver's fees, premiums on receiver's bonds and reasonable attorneys' fees, and then to the sums secured by this Security Instrument.

21. Release. Upon payment of all sums secured by this Security Instrument, Lender shall release this Security Instrument without charge to Borrower. Borrower shall pay any recordation costs.

22. Substitute Trustee. Lender, at its option, may from time to time remove Trustee and appoint a successor trustee to any Trustee appointed hereunder by an instrument recorded in the county in which this Security Instrument is recorded. Without conveyance of the Property, the successor trustee shall succeed to all the title, power and duties conferred upon Trustee herein and by applicable law.

23. Riders to this Security Instrument. If one or more riders are executed by Borrower and recorded together with this Security Instrument, the covenants and agreements of each such rider shall be incorporated into and shall amend and supplement the covenants and agreements of this Security Instrument as if the rider(s) were a part of this Security Instrument. [Check applicable box(es)]

☐ Adjustable Rate Rider   ☐ Condominium Rider   ☐ 2-4 Family Rider

☐ Graduated Payment Rider   ☐ Planned Unit Development Rider

☐ Other(s) [specify]

BY SIGNING BELOW, Borrower accepts and agrees to the terms and covenants contained in this Security Instrument and in any rider(s) executed by Borrower and recorded with it.

_____(Seal)
—Borrower

_____(Seal)
—Borrower

STATE OF MISSOURI)
) SS.
          OF   )

On this _____ day of _____, 19_____, before me personally appeared_____, to me known to be the person(s) described in and who executed the foregoing instrument, and acknowledged that_____ executed the same as_____free act and deed.

IN TESTIMONY WHEREOF, I have hereunto set my hand and affixed my official seal in the_____and State aforesaid, the day and year first above written.

_____
Notary Public

My term expires:

Form RE 165 MO FNMA p4 of 4 (5/89)   [G8364]

Notes and Questions

1. How would you describe the state of the title to property secured by the sample deed of trust? Who holds legal title? Equitable title? Are there encumbrances? If so, in favor of whom?

2. Suppose more than one person owns an interest in the property, such as a lessor and lessee, or concurrent owners? Can both persons pledge their property interest as security for a loan that one is obtaining without also becoming liable on the loan? See paragraph 11.

3. Can a borrower safely transfer her interest in secured property without obtaining permission from the lender, for example, by selling the property to someone who will assume the loan? See paragraphs 17 and 19. How do these paragraphs compare with regulations of assignment and subleasing by tenants?

4. What happens to the proceeds of insurance in the event of fire or other insured casualty? To the proceeds of condemnation? Why are these treated differently?

(a) The Mortgage Concept

PREBLE & CARTWRIGHT, CONVERTIBLE AND SHARED APPRECIATION LOANS: UNCLOGGING THE EQUITY OF REDEMPTION

20 Real Prop., Prob & T.J. 821, 823–824 (1985).

I. INTRODUCTION

For nearly six centuries, lenders have used mortgages on real property to secure loans made to individual and commercial borrowers. The mortgage of the fourteenth century, however, is but a distant cousin of the various security devices used by commercial lenders today. For most of the period since the fourteenth century, the evolutionary process has been a gradual one. The past ten years, however, have witnessed dramatic changes in real estate secured lending. Inflation, high real and nominal interest rates, the deregulation of financial institutions, the growth of pension funds, the changing role of life insurance companies, the impact of new tax laws and the development of computer programs for sophisticated financial forecasting have all combined to radically change the capital markets and the structure of real estate financing.

* * *

II. THE ENGLISH AUTHORITIES

A. *Evolution of the Mortgage*

The original mortgage form was the nominal equivalent of a fee simple subject to a condition subsequent. The borrower conveyed seisin and a deed to the lender, subject to a condition subsequent which would revest seisin in the borrower upon repayment of the debt. Payment had to be made on what came to be known as "law day." The right of repayment, which effectively defeated the lender's title, appeared as the "defeasance" clause in the deed.

In accordance with the common law courts' strict view of property law, a default by the borrower on law day destroyed the contingency and vested full title in fee simple absolute in the lender. The old English common law courts never mixed concepts of property law and contract law. Thus, no matter how much of the debt had been repaid, if the borrower failed to extinguish the obligation in full on law day, he lost the entire property.

* * * Under the Chancellor's parallel court system, "equity" responded to the harsh results perpetrated by common law decisions. As a result, in the seventeenth century, the chancery courts began a sustained attack upon the forfeiture imposed by the common law courts. Two significant legal rights were born: (i) the borrower was permitted to petition the King to set aside the deed; and (ii) if the debt was repaid, albeit not in strict compliance with the terms of the mortgage, the chancery courts would order reconveyance of the deed. It was the right of appeal to equity which spawned the equity of redemption.

Although the original purpose of the Chancellor's intervention was to protect the borrower against forfeiture and fraud, the remedy created by the equity courts, the borrower's equity of redemption, clouded every lender's title with the possibility that a defaulting borrower might eventually seek equitable relief. How long would the borrower have to redeem? When would the lender's title be immune from attack? A response and counterattack by the lender was inevitable. Thus, the lender was given the right to petition the chancery court to foreclose the equity of redemption. The court usually responded by setting a date at which the borrower's equity would be cut off if the default continued. Nevertheless, judicial relief was an uncertain, time-consuming and expensive process. In order to avoid the cumbersome appeals to equity and the uncertainty of property rights in the interim, lenders began a long process of changing the form and purpose of the mortgage deed. Not all of the steps in this evolutionary process met the standards of equity as viewed by the Chancellor.

Indeed, the initial step—a waiver of the equity of redemption executed by the borrower—was ultimately rejected by courts of equity. To protect the substantive equitable redemption right of the borrower, the equity courts countered the waiver and other unconscionable attempts to circumvent equitable jurisdiction with the doctrine against "clogging" the equity of redemption. In essence, the clogging doctrine restricted the lender to only one method of cutting off the borrower's equity of redemption—foreclosure. * * *

As the following case indicates, the concept of a mortgage has changed considerably since the days when it had the characteristics of a fee simple defeasible.

HARMS v. SPRAGUE

Supreme Court of Illinois, 1984.
105 Ill.2d 215, 85 Ill.Dec. 331, 473 N.E.2d 930.

THOMAS J. MORAN, JUSTICE.

Plaintiff, William H. Harms, filed a complaint to quiet title and for declaratory judgment in the circuit court of Greene County. Plaintiff had taken title to certain real estate with his brother John R. Harms, as a joint tenant, with full right of survivorship. The plaintiff named, as a defendant, Charles D. Sprague, the executor of the estate of John Harms and the devisee of all the real and personal property of John Harms. Also named as defendants were Carl T. and Mary E. Simmons, alleged mortgagees of the property in question. Defendant Sprague filed a counterclaim against plaintiff, challenging plaintiff's claim of ownership of the entire tract of property and asking the court to recognize his (Sprague's) interest as a tenant in common, subject to a mortgage lien. At issue was the effect the granting of a mortgage by John Harms had on the joint tenancy. Also at issue was whether the mortgage survived the death of John Harms as a lien against the property.

The trial court held that the mortgage given by John Harms to defendants Carl and Mary Simmons severed the joint tenancy. Further, the court found that the mortgage survived the death of John Harms as a lien against the undivided one-half interest in the property which passed to Sprague by and through the will of the deceased. The appellate court reversed, finding that the mortgage given by one joint tenant of his interest in the property does not sever the joint tenancy. Accordingly, the appellate court held that plaintiff, as the surviving joint tenant, owned the property in its entirety, unencumbered by the mortgage lien. * * *

Two issues are raised on appeal: (1) Is a joint tenancy severed when less than all of the joint tenants mortgage their interest in the property? and (2) Does such a mortgage survive the death of the mortgagor as a lien on the property?

A review of the stipulation of facts reveals the following. Plaintiff, William Harms, and his brother John Harms, took title to real estate located in Roodhouse, on June 26, 1973, as joint tenants. The warranty deed memorializing this transaction was recorded on June 29, 1973, in the office of the Greene County recorder of deeds.

Carl and Mary Simmons owned a lot and home in Roodhouse. Charles Sprague entered into an agreement with the Simmons whereby Sprague was to purchase their property for $25,000. Sprague tendered $18,000 in cash and signed a promissory note for the balance of $7,000. Because Sprague had no security for the $7,000, he asked his friend, John Harms, to co-sign the note and give a mortgage on his interest in the joint tenancy property. Harms agreed, and on June 12, 1981, John Harms and Charles Sprague, jointly and severally, executed a promissory note for $7,000 payable to Carl and Mary Simmons. The note states that the principal sum of $7,000 was to be paid from the proceeds of the sale of John Harms' interest in the joint tenancy property, but in any event no later than six months from the date the note was signed. The note reflects that five monthly interest payments had been made, with the last payment recorded November 6, 1981. In addition, John Harms executed a mortgage, in favor of the Simmonses, on his undivided one-half interest in the joint tenancy property, to secure payment of the note. William Harms was unaware of the mortgage given by his brother.

John Harms moved from his joint tenancy property to the Simmons property which had been purchased by Charles Sprague. On December 10, 1981, John Harms died. By the terms of John Harms' will, Charles Sprague was the devisee of his entire estate. The mortgage given by John Harms to the Simmonses was recorded on December 29, 1981.

Prior to the appellate court decision in the instant case [ ] no court of this State had directly addressed the principal question we are confronted with herein—the effect of a mortgage, executed by less than all of the joint tenants, on the joint tenancy. * * *

Clearly, this court adheres to the rule that a lien on a joint tenant's interest in property will not effectuate a severance of the joint tenancy, absent the conveyance by a deed following the expiration of a redemption period. [ ] It follows, therefore, that if Illinois perceives a mortgage as merely a lien on the mortgagor's interest in property rather than a conveyance of title from mortgagor to mortgagee, the execution of a mortgage by a joint tenant, on his interest in the property, would not destroy the unity of title and sever the joint tenancy.

Early cases in Illinois, however, followed the title theory of mortgages. In 1900, this court recognized the common law precept that a mortgage was a conveyance of a legal estate vesting title to the property in the mortgagee. [ ] Consistent with this title theory of mortgages, therefore, there are many cases which state, in *dicta*, that a joint tenancy is severed by one of the joint tenants mortgaging his interest to a stranger. [ ] Yet even the early case of *Lightcap v. Bradley*, cited above, recognized that the title held by the mortgagee was for the limited purpose of protecting his interests. The court went on to say that "the mortgagor is the owner for every other purpose and against every other person. The title of the mortgagee is anomalous, and exists only between him and the mortgagor * * *." *Lightcap v. Bradley* (1900), 186 Ill. 510, 522–23, 58 N.E. 221.

Because our cases had early recognized the unique and narrow character of the title that passed to a mortgagee under the common law title theory, it was not a drastic departure when this court expressly characterized the execution of a mortgage as a mere lien in *Kling v. Ghilarducci* (1954), 3 Ill.2d 455, 121 N.E.2d 752. In *Kling*, the court was confronted with the question of when a separation of title, necessary to create an easement by implication, had occurred. The court found that title to the property was not separated with the execution of a trust deed but rather only upon execution and delivery of a master's deed. The court stated:

> "In some jurisdictions the execution of a mortgage is a severance, in others, the execution of a mortgage is not a severance. In Illinois the giving of a mortgage is not a separation of title, for the holder of the mortgage takes only a lien thereunder. After foreclosure of a mortgage and until delivery of the master's deed under the foreclosure sale, purchaser acquires no title to the land either legal or equitable. Title to land sold under mortgage foreclosure remains in the mortgagor or his grantee until the expiration of the redemption period and conveyance by the master's deed." 3 Ill.2d 455, 460, 121 N.E.2d 752.
> * * *

[The Court also held that a joint tenancy is not severed by the execution of a mortgage by one joint tenant and that such a mortgage executed by one joint tenant does not survive the death of that joint tenant because the property right to which the mortgage lien originally attaches is extinguished automatically by the death of the mortgaging tenant—Eds.]

Judgment affirmed.

Notes and Questions

1. As a result of *Harms*, what should a lender do to protect itself if the borrower is a joint tenant of the property securing the loan? Does paragraph 11 of the sample deed of trust resolve the problem? Under *Harms*, is the surviving joint tenant a "successor" or "assign"? Should the lender insist that both joint tenants sign the security instrument?

2. As the court in *Harms* noted, the early view was that mortgagees held defeasible title to the mortgaged property, giving rise to the "title" theory of mortgages. Today, the majority of states follow the "lien" theory espoused in *Harms*. A third group of states follows an "intermediate" theory under which the mortgagee has a title, but no possessory right until after default and may only exercise the rights of a lienholder through foreclosure and sale of the property. See generally, G. Nelson and D. Whitman, Real Estate Finance Law 10–11 (2d Ed.1985).

(b) The Purchase Money Mortgage

Mortgages are used to secure a variety of loans, but one of the most common is the loan to enable someone to purchase land. A mortgage given to secure a loan to buy the property that is pledged as security for repayment of the loan is called a purchase money mortgage. It may be given either to a seller who is willing to accept a note and mortgage in lieu of cash or it may be given to a third party who advances the money for the purchase. In either event, the purchase money mortgage is given a special priority.

The theoretical basis for the special priority extended to purchase money mortgages was the common law belief that seisin did not leave the hands of the seller who accepted a purchase money note and mortgage in lieu of cash, but passed through the hands of the purchaser and came back immediately to the seller, albeit in altered form as a defeasible fee rather than an absolute fee. Since title had never left the seller, there was no time for a lien arising out of other actions of the purchase to attach to the land *ahead* of the seller's lien. See generally G. Nelson & D. Whitman, Real Estate Finance Law 675–684 (2d Ed.1985).

Is the special priority policy justified today, especially in lien or intermediate theory states? A creditor that has reduced a claim to judgment and obtained a lien against a purchaser's property prior to a purchase money mortgage land transaction clearly has priority in time against the seller's purchase money mortgage lien. Is the commonly accepted policy that creditor's rights follow debtor's rights sufficient basis for favoring the seller over the innocent and prior judgment creditor? Suppose the purchaser-mortgagor agreed with the prior creditor that the creditor's lien would attach to after-acquired property. Would that change the equation in favor of the prior creditor? Of the two innocent parties, the prior judgment creditor and the purchase money mortgage seller, who is better able to guard against the risk of loss from default? Should that be the basis for a decision regarding priority of lien claims? See G. Nelson & D. Whitman, Real Estate Finance Law 679–680 (2d Ed.1985).

(c) Mortgage Alternatives

DUVALL v. LAWS, SWAIN & MURDOCH, P.A.

Court of Appeals of Arkansas, 1990.
32 Ark.App. 99, 797 S.W.2d 474.

JENNINGS, JUDGE.

In 1982, appellant Fred Duvall was charged with theft in connection with the buying and selling of oil and gas leases. He asked Ike Allen Laws, Jr., the appellee, a Russellville lawyer, to represent him. The two had known each other since grade school.

Laws quoted Duvall a fee of $5,000.00. Duvall paid $2,498.00 but then he was unable to raise the balance. He and Laws entered into an agreement, which later became the subject matter of this lawsuit.

Duvall and his wife executed a deed which purported to convey outright the mineral rights to 160 acres of land in Pope County. The deed was dated September 27, 1982 and recited a consideration of $5,000.00. Revenue stamps were purchased reflecting that amount. Also on September 27 Laws sent Duvall the following letter:

> This will acknowledge that you have on this date transferred to our firm certain minerals by mineral deed, representing our attorney's fee of Five Thousand Dollars ($5,000.00) to defend Fred E. Duvall in the State of Arkansas v. Fred E. Duvall.
>
> This letter will serve as evidence of our agreement that you may repurchase these minerals at any time within one (1) year from the date of this letter upon payment in full of my said fee.

It is undisputed that the letter was received by Duvall. On October 5, 1982, the law firm sent Duvall an invoice showing a balance of $2,502.00. This was the last bill sent to Duvall.

During the summer of 1983, Duvall located a prospective purchaser for the mineral rights who was apparently willing to pay more than $30,000.00 for them. The transaction did not go through due to title problems. At trial, the testimony was conflicting as to whether Laws cooperated in the attempt to sell the mineral rights to the third party.

In 1987 Laws leased the mineral rights for $12,740.00. On June 28, 1988, Duvall sued Laws, alleging that their 1982 transaction ought to be construed as an equitable mortgage. The chancellor held that the transaction was a deed with an option to purchase and not an equitable mortgage. He nevertheless awarded Duvall judgment for $2,498.00. Duvall appeals the first holding; Laws cross appeals the second. We affirm on direct appeal and reverse on cross appeal.

On direct appeal, Duvall argues that the chancellor applied the wrong burden of proof and that his refusal to hold that the transaction was an equitable mortgage was clearly erroneous. The case is governed by two distinct sets of rules. In equity, a grantor may show that a deed, absolute on its face, was intended only to be security for the payment of a debt and thus was in actuality a mortgage. [ ] The burden of proving that the transaction was truly a mortgage rests upon the grantor because there is a presumption that the instrument is what it purports to be. [ ] The burden may be met only by clear and convincing evidence. [ ] When a vendor, at the time of a sale, is indebted to a purchaser, and continues to be indebted after the sale, with the right to call for a reconveyance upon payment of the debt, a deed absolute on its face will be considered in a court of equity as a mortgage. [ ] On the other hand the parties may enter into a contract for the purchase and sale of land, with a reservation to the vendor of a right to repurchase the property at a fixed price and at a specific time. If such a transaction is security for a debt, then it is a mortgage—otherwise it is a sale. [ ] The line of demarcation between the two has been said to be "shadowy." [ ] The question whether a deed to realty, absolute on its face, when construed together with a separate agreement or option to repurchase by the grantor amounts to a mortgage or is a conditional sale, depends on the intention of the parties in the light of all attendant circumstances. * * *

While it is true that during his testimony, Laws said that Duvall never made any attempt to "pay the balance of the fee," there was also evidence from which the chancellor could have found that Duvall's failure to pay "the balance" for more than six years indicates his awareness that the transaction was an absolute conveyance. * * * [O]ne test which may be helpful in determining whether a transaction is a mortgage or a conditional sale is to decide whether the grantee has the right to compel the grantor to pay the consideration named in the stipulation for reconveyance. In the case at bar it seems clear that Laws would not have been successful in a suit to compel the payment of "the balance" of his fee. In any event we cannot say that the chancellor's determination that the transaction was not intended as a mortgage is clearly erroneous.

In contending that the chancellor applied the "wrong burden of proof," Duvall relies upon the principle that an attorney who enters into a business transaction with a client has the burden of proving the fairness and equity of that transaction and the adequacy of the consideration therefor. [ ] We agree that the principle is applicable to the case at bar. Once the chancellor found that the grantor had not met his burden of proving by clear and convincing evidence that the transaction was intended as a mortgage, the burden was then upon Laws to establish that he dealt fairly and justly with Fred Duvall. [ ] In contending that the trial court applied the wrong burden, appellant relies on two remarks made by the chancellor.

> One of the problems in deciding this case that bothers me is the fact that the defendant is an attorney; [I] want to be very careful that he's not treated improperly one way or the other just because he's a lawyer.
>
> * * *
>
> If I ruled otherwise it would be simply because Mr. Laws is an attorney whom I have never met or seen before as far as I know ever in my life or had any correspondence with him. And I don't think that's right either.

When the two statements are viewed in the context of the court's other remarks, we are not persuaded that they indicate the chancellor was unaware of the burden imposed on Laws * * *. It is not an incorrect statement of the law to say that a decision should not be made *solely* on the basis that one of the parties is a lawyer. * * * In the case at bar there was evidence from which the trial court could find that mineral rights conveyed from Duvall to Laws were essentially without market value at the time of the conveyance. It was therefore not improper for the chancellor to find, as he clearly did, that the transaction was fair to appellant, viewed from the time of its making.

Finally, if the chancellor was correct in holding that the transaction was an absolute conveyance, we can find no justification for upholding his award of damages to the appellant and that award must be reversed.

Affirmed on direct appeal and reversed on cross appeal.

WRIGHT, ACTING CHIEF JUDGE, dissenting.

In September 1982, appellant and his wife, residents of Pope County, found themselves in a vulnerable position. Appellant was under criminal indictment in Conway County and needed an attorney to defend him. At trial he was acquitted. Appellant's wife had been seriously ill and the couple owed various debts, including a civil judgment in Conway County, hospital bills approximating $90,000.00 and other debts. Appellant was unemployed as he had been caring for his sick wife. Their assets were exhausted except for some mineral interests. Appellant's wife died after the commencement of this suit.

Appellant made an agreement with attorney Ike Laws, Jr. to defend him in the criminal case for a fee of $5,000.00. Appellant could raise only half of the fee at the time of employment. Appellant told Laws he had some mineral interests he wanted to sell and would pay the balance of the fee upon sale of the mineral interests. However, very shortly after half of the fee was paid, Laws called appellant on the phone and suggested appellant deed the mineral interests to him to assure payment of the balance of the agreed fee, and suggested further that appellant's judgment creditors could attach and execute upon the mineral interests and deprive appellant of all benefits in the mineral interests.

In keeping with Laws' recommendation, appellant and his wife on September 27, 1982, executed a deed prepared by Laws conveying to the appellee law firm the mineral rights in 160 acres of land in Pope County. On that date or shortly thereafter Laws sent appellant the letter set out in the majority opinion.

When the letter was written, Laws had already received $2,498.00 on the fee and was owed a balance of $2,502.00. However, the letter refers to the deed as "representing our attorney's fee of Five Thousand Dollars ($5,000.00)."

On October 5, 1982, some eight days after delivery of the deed to Laws, his office sent a statement to appellant reflecting a total fee of $5,000.00 in the criminal case, credits of $2,498.00 and a balance of $2,502.00 unpaid.

Laws gave testimony at the trial "so far as I'm concerned" the deed for the mineral interests was in settlement of the balance of the fee but that he gave appellant the right to have the minerals reconveyed upon payment of the balance within one year from date. However, during Laws' testimony with reference to a conversation he had with a Mr. Womack who was attempting in July 1983 to purchase for $30,000 the subject mineral interests, together with some 50 acres of additional mineral interests in which appellant and wife had an interest, he stated he told Mr. Womack his office had a deal with appellant and they wanted their name on the draft. In reference to his deposition, Laws admitted to the following at trial:

Q. "You stood to get your fee out of this?" And your answer was?

A. I stood to get what he still owed me on my fee.

The statement by appellee Laws was in direct conflict with his testimony at trial that the deed for the mineral interests was in settlement of the balance of the fee. The sale to Womack was never closed.

Appellant sought to employ attorney Ernie Witt to recover the mineral interests at least as early as July 1985. The evidence shows that attorney Cliff Hoofman had sent Laws a letter about appellant's claim for recovery of his mineral interests from Laws and Laws wrote Hoofman a letter in February 1988 in which he stated:

Dear Cliff: I thought you might be interested in a computer check I ran on judgments against Fred DuVall. With these judgments against him, it is my opinion that he would not be able to keep the minerals he claims, even if he could get them. I thought this may be of some interest to you in determining the manner that you took employment.

The letter was written after Laws had in December 1987 entered into two oil and gas leases for the mineral interests for an up front consideration of $12,700.00. Laws also wrote attorney Hoofman in February 1988 and in referring to appellant, stated: "he had not made any attempt to pay a single penny on our fee since his trial." The statement is in conflict with appellees' contention the mineral deed settled the fee.

Appellant gave the following unrebutted testimony:

A. I went to Ike's office and asked him if I borrowed the money, could I pay him in full and he issued a challenge to me if I could find an attorney to represent me.

Q. Was this following the * * * was this still within the one year period?

A. Yes, that was within the one year period.

Q. What did he say?

A. He said, "You just do whatever you think you're big enough to do."

Appellant testified that he had leased the mineral interests in years past for figures from $40.00 to $50.00 per acre and this was not rebutted.

Appellant testified he went to Laws' office promptly after he got the letter concerning his right to have the minerals reconveyed to him and complained that the letter did not show he would only be required to pay $2,500.00, the unpaid part of the fee, to have the minerals reconveyed, and also complained that the letter did not show the agreement was that the $2,500.00 would be paid when he sold the mineral interests. He said Laws' response was:

He said it was necessary for him to word the letter like that. That that represented the full fee in case the judgment people came out * * * came after me and said that I overpaid him 110 acres of minerals for just $2,500.00.

The chancellor found that the deed from appellant and wife to the appellees for the mineral interests was not a security for the debt, but was an absolute conveyance.

In an effort to show the $2,502.00 balance of the fee was fair consideration for the mineral interests appellees' witness Dale Braden, a fellow attorney and member of the Russellville Bar, who worked with Arkansas Oil and Gas Co., testified he offered "nothing" for the subject mineral interests in 1982. Of course, this had no significance for establishing the value of the mineral interests. There was no evidence any offer from him was solicited in 1982, and whether he offered "nothing" has no evidentiary value as to the market value. This witness admitted he paid Laws $129.00 per acre for a five-year lease on 80 acres of the mineral interests in 1987.

There are two reasons for reversing. First, when an attorney contracts with his client and litigation arises over the transaction, the attorney has the burden of proving that no advantage has been taken of the client. Appellant alleged that appellees' actions constituted a gross ethical breach of the duties a lawyer owes his client in an ongoing lawyer-client relationship. The reason for the rule is that the relation of attorney and client is one of trust and confidence requiring high degree of fidelity and good faith. The burden is upon the attorney to prove the fairness and equity of the transaction and the adequacy of the consideration. [ ] It is apparent from the findings and rulings of the chancellor from the bench that he did not follow this rule. * * * When the evidence as a whole is carefully weighed, it is apparent appellees failed to meet the burden of proving the transaction with appellant was fair and equitable. Appellees completely failed to present evidence of the market value of the mineral interests as of September 1982, the date of the deed. There is substantial evidence the value of the mineral interests greatly exceeded the amount of the balance of the fee. The court failed to make a finding as to the fairness of the transaction * * *. There is a total absence of evidence of negotiation between the parties as to the relative value of the minerals with relation to the balance of fee owed, and the testimony of Laws at trial was at variance with his own documentary evidence. His testimony sought to impeach his own documents and prior admissions. * * *

Secondly, it is clear from the evidence appellee Laws continued to consider appellant still owed the unpaid balance on the agreed fee after the receipt of the mineral deed as evidenced by the bill sent to appellant, Laws' letter to attorney Hoofman, and some of Laws' testimony that appellant had not paid the balance of the fee owed. When the evidence is considered in its entirety it is clear the chancellor's finding the mineral deed to Laws was in effect a sale with no equitable security interest attached was clearly against the preponderance of the evidence.   * * * The evidence is abundantly clear, not only from the testimony of appellant, but from evidence flowing from Laws that appellant continued to owe the balance of the fee after delivery of the mineral deed. The letter from Laws to appellant, coupled with the rest of the evidence, nails down the fact that the deed was security for the balance of the fee. It was after litigation was in the offing that Laws' posture about the nature of the transaction changed and in his testimony he sought to change the meaning of the bill for the balance of the fee sent after receipt of the deed and to impeach his prior statements about appellant still owing the balance of the fee. It is undisputed that appellant had the right to reconveyance on payment of the fee balance. The fact the letter purported to limit that right to one year is of no consequence here as the transaction constituted an equitable mortgage that required foreclosure.   * * *

* * *

This case should be reversed and judgment entered in favor of appellant against appellees for $12,700.00 less $2,502.00 and interest thereon from September 27, 1983. The mineral deed to appellee should be canceled, but appellant's mineral interests should be decreed subject to the rights of the two innocent purchasers of mineral leases who leased from appellees.

MAYFIELD, J., joins in dissent.

Notes and Questions

1. Since the essence of a mortgage is the conveyance of an interest in land to secure performance of a promise to repay borrowed money, it should come as no surprise that a variety of other property techniques can be used to accomplish the same result.

    (a) We have already mentioned the deed of trust, in which the property is conveyed to a third party as trustee for the benefit of the lender but also the borrower.

    (b) Another device is the installment land contract, or "contract for deed," in which the seller allows the purchaser to obtain possession while making periodic payments, and agrees to transfer title to the purchaser when the final installment of the purchase price is paid. In effect, the seller is financing the buyer's purchase of the land. Since title is not transferred at the time that possession is transferred, the relationship of purchaser and seller during the period before transfer of title resembles that of landlord and tenant. Thus, when a default occurs, the creditor-seller seeks to regain possession of the land by obtaining a judicial decree that the debtor-purchaser has forfeited her right to possession by defaulting on her obligations under the contract.

    (c) Still another technique is the long term ground lease, with or without an option to purchase at the end of the term. The ground lessee obtains long term control, which in many cases is the practical equivalent of a fee interest, and finances the acquisition of control through the periodic payments mechanism of the long term lease.

(d) The equitable mortgage, or deed absolute, illustrated by the principle case, is yet another device to accomplish the purpose of a mortgage. Courts will look through the form of a purported sale and construe the conveyance of a deed as the conveyance of a mortgage when they are persuaded that the parties really intended the transaction to serve as security for a deed.

For discussion of mortgage alternatives, see G. Nelson & D. Whitman, Real Estate Finance Law 29–142 (2d Ed.1985).

2. As noted by the *Duvall* court, whether a deed coupled with an agreement that the seller may repurchase the property should be construed as a sale with an option to repurchase or as a mortgage to secure repayment of a debt is a question of intent. What did the plaintiff in *Duvall* fail to prove? The presence of a debt? The desire to obtain repayment of that debt? The intent to use the mineral rights as security for the debt? Was the fact that the plaintiff apparently made no payments for six years persuasive? What about the fact that no bills were sent? What is the significance of construing the transaction in *Duvall* as a mortgage? Who would be entitled to the $12,000 proceeds from the mineral lease?

3. The dissent in *Duvall* was highly critical of the lawyer defendant's conduct in first entering into a property transaction with a client in a "vulnerable" position, and then being imprecise in the description of the transaction. Should attorneys be barred from business transactions of this sort with clients? If so, what should an attorney do in cases such as *Duvall* where a client cannot pay the full fee—waive the unpaid amount, accept an unsecured promise to pay, or refuse the case? Would a straight mortgage be acceptable? Cf. ABA Model Rules of Professional Conduct, Rule 1.8:

(a) A lawyer shall not enter into a business transaction with a client or knowingly acquire an ownership, possessory, security or other pecuniary interest adverse to a client unless:

(1) the transaction and terms on which the lawyer acquires the interest are fair and reasonable to the client and are fully disclosed and transmitted in writing to the client in a manner which can be reasonably understood by the client;

(2) the client is given a reasonable opportunity to seek the advice of independent counsel in the transaction; and

(3) the client consents in writing thereto.

* * *

(j) A lawyer shall not acquire a proprietary interest in the cause of action or subject matter of litigation the lawyer is conducting for a client, except that the lawyer may:

(1) acquire a lien granted by law to secure the lawyer's fee or expenses; * * *

(2) contract with a client for a reasonable contingent fee in a civil case.

(d) Possessory Rights of Mortgagees

As the Preble & Cartwright excerpt notes, the common law lender had an absolute right to take possession of the property if the borrower failed to repay the loan in full on "law day." What happens to the right to possession under *Harms?* See Martinez v. Continental Enterprises, 730 P.2d 308 (Colo.1986) (mortgage may not recover possession in the absence of foreclosure and sale).

Under Paragraph 20 of the sample deed of trust, a lender may take possession upon acceleration of the note, as provided for in Paragraph 19. Examine these provisions in light of *Harms*. Would a court that considers a mortgage to be a lien permit a lender to take possession of secured property by declaring the entire balance of a loan immediately due and payable (acceleration), or would the additional steps of foreclosure have to be taken? At what point in the process could the lender take possession? Suppose the borrower had vacated the premises, but under circumstances that a finding of the elements of abandonment, as discussed in Chapter Four (landlord-tenant), was unlikely? What steps could the lender take under the sample deed of trust to protect its security interest from devaluation because of waste or vandalism that would be acceptable to a lien theory court?

A lender who does take possession of secured property faces a new set of risks, as illustrated by the following case.

UNITED STATES v. MARYLAND BANK AND TRUST COMPANY

United States District Court, D. Maryland, 1986.
632 F.Supp. 573.

NORTHROP, SENIOR DISTRICT JUDGE.

This case presents the novel question of whether a bank, which formerly held a mortgage on a parcel of land, later purchased the land at a foreclosure sale and continues to own it, must reimburse the United States for the cost of cleaning up hazardous wastes on the land, when those wastes were dumped prior to the bank's purchase of the property.

The United States instituted this action pursuant to section 107 of the Comprehensive Environmental Response, Compensation, and Liability Act of 1980 ("CERCLA"), 42 U.S.C. § 9607 (1983), to recover the expenses incurred by the United States Environmental Protection Agency ("EPA") for removal of hazardous wastes from the toxic dump site known as the McLeod property or the California Maryland Drum site, located near the town of California in St. Mary's County, Maryland. Named as defendant in this suit is the Maryland Bank & Trust Company ("MB & T"), the owner of the property since May, 1982, and before that, the mortgagee of the tract beginning in December, 1980.

Pending before the Court are defendant Maryland Bank & Trust Co.'s motion for summary judgment and plaintiff United States' motion for partial summary judgment on the issue of liability.

FACTS

From July 7, 1944 to December 16, 1980, Herschel McLeod, Sr. and Nellie McLeod owned the piece of property now the subject of this litigation, a 117 acre farm located near the town of California, Maryland in St. Mary's County. The parties have dubbed this property the California Maryland Drum site or "CMD site".

During the period of the McLeod's ownership, the McLeods engaged in a business relationship with Maryland Bank & Trust Co., the contours of which are disputed by the parties. It is undisputed, however, that during the 1970's, MB & T loaned money to Herschel McLeod, Sr. for two of his businesses—Greater St. Mary's Disposal, Inc. and Waldorf Sanitation of St. Mary's, Inc. The bank knew that McLeod operated a trash and garbage business on the site, but the record does not state at what point the bank became aware of this.

During 1972 or 1973, McLeod permitted the dumping of hazardous wastes on the CMD site. The wastes included organics such as toluene, ethylbenzene and total xylenes and heavy metals such as lead, chromium, mercury, and zinc.

In 1980, Mark Wayne McLeod applied for a $335,000 loan from MB & T to purchase the CMD site from his parents. On or about September 2nd of that year, MB & T sent Farmers Home Administration a request for loan guarantees relating to the McLeod loan * * *. FmHA issued Loan Note Guarantees for 90% of the loan on January 2, 1981.

Mark Wayne McLeod purchased the CMD site on December 16, 1980 through the MB & T loan, but soon failed to make payments on the loan. Consequently, MB & T instituted a foreclosure action against the CMD site in 1981 and purchased the property at the foreclosure sale on May 15, 1982 with a bid of $381,500. MB & T then took title to the property. From that date to the present, MB & T has been the record owner of the CMD site. FmHA continues to be a 90% guarantor of that loan.

On June 20, 1983, Mark Wayne McLeod informed Walter E. Raum, Director of Environmental Hygiene for St. Mary's County Department of Health, of the existence of the dumped wastes on the CMD site. After inspecting the site the following day, the State of Maryland contacted the EPA. Tests were conducted to identify the substances. On the basis of the test results, the EPA requested and received funding to conduct a removal action under CERCLA. The agency notified MB & T president John T. Daugherty that MB & T would be given until October 24, 1983 to initiate corrective action at the site or EPA would use its funds to clean-up the wastes. The bank declined the EPA's offer, so the agency proceeded to clean the site itself, removing two hundred thirty-seven drums of chemical material and 1180 tons of contaminated soil at a cost of approximately $551,713.50. After completing the clean-up, the EPA sent a letter to MB & T President Daugherty summarizing the costs incurred in the response action and demanding payment. To date, MB & T has not tendered payment. This action ensued.

CERCLA

Congress enacted CERCLA in 1980 in response to the environmental and public health hazards posed by improper disposal of hazardous wastes. [ ] CERCLA empowers the federal government to clean-up and otherwise respond to hazardous dump sites. The EPA has been delegated primary responsibility for this task. [ ]

"Response" actions undertaken by the EPA are financed primarily from the Hazardous Substance Response Trust Fund, commonly known as the "Super Fund" * * *. The Act also authorizes the government to recover costs from certain "responsible parties". [ ] This section extends liability to four categories of persons: 1) current owners and operators of the hazardous substance facility; 2) past owners or operators of the hazardous substance facility at the time of disposal; 3) persons who arranged for treatment or disposal of hazardous substances at the facility; and 4) persons who transported hazardous substances for treatment or disposal at the facility selected by them.

To establish liability under section 107(a) of the Act, the government must establish the following:

1) The site is a "facility";

2) A "release" or "threatened release" of any "hazardous substance" from the site has occurred;

3) The release or threatened release has caused the United States to incur "response costs"; and

4) The defendant is one of the persons designated as a party liable for costs.

Section 107 imposes strict liability. * * *

DISCUSSION

Defendant Maryland Bank & Trust does not dispute the fact that the first three elements of the prima facie case under section 107(a) have been met by the United States. [ ] The question central to both the defendant's and the plaintiff's motions for summary judgment concerns the final element, specifically, whether Maryland Bank & Trust is an "owner and operator" within the meaning of sections 107(a)(1) and 101(20)(A).

Additionally, Maryland Bank & Trust has raised in its answer an affirmative defense based upon section 107(b)(3), the so-called "third party defense". The United States argues in its motion for partial summary judgment that the bank cannot meet its burden of proof on that defense, an assertion disputed by the defendant in its opposition memorandum.

* * *

A. The Court initially turns to the question of whether MB & T falls within section 107(a)(1). That section holds liable "the owner and operator" of the facility. It is undisputed that MB & T has been the owner of the facility since May, 1982. The parties dispute whether the bank has been the operator of the facility since that time. The dispute over the term "operator" is not determinative, however, for the Court holds that current ownership of a facility alone brings a party within the ambit of subsection (1). Notwithstanding the language "the owner and operator", a party need not be both an owner and operator to incur liability under this subsection.

The structure of section 107(a), like so much of this hastily patched together compromise Act, is not a model of statutory clarity. It is unclear from its face whether subsection (1) holds liable both owners and operators or only parties who are both owners and operators. This ambiguity stems in large part from the placement of the definite article "the" before the term "owner" and its omission prior to the term "operator". Proper usage dictates that the phrase "the owner and operator" include only those persons who are both owners and operators. But by no means does Congress always follow the rules of grammar when enacting the laws of this nation. In fact, to slavishly follow the laws of grammar while interpreting acts of Congress would violate sound canons of statutory interpretation. [ ] Misuse of the definite article is hardly surprising in a hastily conceived compromise statute such as CERCLA, since members of Congress might well have had no time to dot all the i's or cross all the t's. [ ]

An examination of the legislative history, sparse as it is, and the lone relevant case convinces the Court to interpret the language of subsection (1) broadly to include both owners and operators. The House Report accompanying H.R. 85, one of the four bills to coalesce into CERCLA, explains the definition of "operator" as follows: "In the case of a facility, an 'operator' is defined to be a person who is carrying out operational functions for the owner of the facility pursuant to an appropriate agreement." [ ] By its very definition, an operator cannot be the same person as an owner. Therefore, a class defined as consisting of persons who are both owners and operators would contain no members. Such a definition would render section 107(a)(1) a totally useless provision.

The Court of Appeals for the Second Circuit recently held a current owner of a facility responsible for response costs under section 107(a)(1) even though that party had not owned the site at the time of the dumping and had apparently not "operated" the facility. [ ] The court stated that "section 9607(a)(1) [107(a)(1)] unequivocally imposes strict liability on the current owner of a facility from which there is a release or a threat of release, without regard to causation." [ ] This Court agrees.

B. The definition of "owner or operator" contained in section 101(20)(A), 42 U.S.C. § 9601(20)(A), excludes from liability "a person, who, without participating in the management of a vessel or facility, holds indicia of ownership primarily to protect his security interest in the * * * facility." MB & T disclaims liability on the basis of this exemption.

Relying upon a statutory exemption to a Congressionally imposed rule of general liability, MB & T has the burden of proving that it is entitled to that exemption. [ ]

It is undisputed that MB & T held a mortgage on the site beginning on December 16, 1980, instituted foreclosure proceedings in 1981, and purchased the property at the foreclosure sale on May 15, 1982. MB & T contends that it is entitled to the benefit of this exclusion because it acquired ownership of the CMD site through foreclosure on its security interest in the property and purchase of the land at the foreclosure sale. The government asserts that the bank is not entitled to the exemption as a matter of law. The Court finds the government's position more persuasive and holds that MB & T is not exempted from liability by the exculpatory clause of section 101(20)(A).

The exemption of subsection (20)(A) covers only those persons who, at the time of the clean-up, hold indicia of ownership to protect a then-held security interest in the land. The verb tense of the exclusionary language is critical. The security interest must exist at the time of the clean-up. The mortgage held by MB & T (the security interest) terminated at the foreclosure sale of May 15, 1982, at which time it ripened into full title. [ ]

MB & T purchased the property at the foreclosure sale not to protect its security interest, but to protect its investment. Only during the life of the mortgage did MB & T hold indicia of ownership primarily to protect its security interest in the land. Under the law of Maryland (and twelve other states), the mortgagee-financial institution actually holds title to the property while the mortgage is in force. [ ] Congress intended by this exception to exclude these common law title mortgagees from the definition of "owner" since title was in their hands only by operation of the common law. The exclusion does not apply to former mortgagees currently holding title after purchasing the property at a foreclosure sale, at least when, as here, the former mortgagee has held title for nearly four years, and a full year before the EPA clean-up.

A review of the legislative history and policies underlying the Act support this narrow construction. * * * This [review] indicates that Congress intended to protect banks that hold mortgages in jurisdictions governed by the common law of mortgages, and not all mortgagees who later acquire title.

The interpretation of section 101(20)(A) urged upon the Court by MB & T runs counter to the policies underlying CERCLA. Under the scenario put forward by the bank, the federal government alone would shoulder the cost of cleaning up the site, while the former mortgagee-turned-owner, would benefit from the clean-up by the increased value of the now unpolluted land. At the foreclosure sale, the mortgagee could acquire the property cheaply. All other prospective purchasers would be faced with potential CERCLA liability, and would shy away from the sale. Yet once the property has been cleared at the taxpayers' expense and becomes marketable, the mortgagee-turned-owner would be in a position to sell the site at a profit.

In essence, the defendant's position would convert CERCLA into an insurance scheme for financial institutions, protecting them against possible losses due to the security of loans with polluted properties. Mortgagees, however, already have the means to protect themselves, by making prudent loans. Financial institutions are in a position to investigate and discover potential problems in their secured properties. For many lending institutions, such research is routine. CERCLA will not absolve them from responsibility for their mistakes of judgment.

* * *

Notes and Questions

1. Enactment of comprehensive environmental laws and decisions such as *Maryland Bank* spawned a whole new industry—environmental audits—involving engineers, lawyers and other professionals. Real estate departments of large law firms found themselves scrambling to hire lawyers with environmental law backgrounds, or sending members back to school to add environmental law to their repertoires.

A surprisingly large number of important issues were left ambiguous or simply unaddressed in the statute. CERCLA was passed during the final hectic days of the 96th Congress, a lame-duck Congress, just prior to the first inauguration of Ronald Reagan, under a suspension of the rules that precluded amendments. No House—Senate conference was held on the measure, so no conference report exists.

The cost to clean up the almost 400,000 hazardous waste sites identified through 1990 has been estimated to exceed $100 billion. To bridge the gap between the cost and available government resources, EPA has urged expansive theories of CERCLA liability. Does *Maryland Bank* represent acceptance of such theories, or is it consistent with a careful but not strained reading of the statute?

2. Note the Court's use of the distinction between "title" and "lien" theories of mortgages to support its decision to give a narrow construction to the secured creditor exemption from liability under the statute. Is the court's rationale persuasive or is it an example of form over substance?

3. What is a lender to do after *Maryland Bank*? Would the lender be better off not foreclosing and then asserting the "security interest" exception of CERCLA, which exempts from liability any "person, who, without participating in the management of a * * * facility, holds indicia of ownership primarily to protect his security interest in the * * * facility" (42 U.S.C. § 9601(20)(A))? If so, what happens to its possessory rights under the foreclosure process? How can it protect its security interest from additional devaluation? Note that the costs of cleanup that Maryland

Bank was assessed (more than $550,000) exceeded its investment in the property ($381,500).

4. In *Maryland Bank,* the lender became involved with CERCLA because it purchased the contaminated property at a foreclosure sale. Suppose that environmental cleanup costs are incurred before a secured lender takes title through the foreclosure sale process. If the landowner goes bankrupt, can the government recover from the secured lender? In United States v. Fleet Factors Corp., 901 F.2d 1550, 1556–1558 (11th Cir.1990), the court construed the "secured creditor" exemption as follows:

> The construction of the secured creditor exemption is an issue of first impression in the federal appellate courts. The government urges us to adopt a narrow and strictly literal interpretation of the exemption that excludes from its protection any secured creditor that participates in any manner in the management of a facility. We decline the government's suggestion because it would largely eviscerate the exemption Congress intended to afford to secured creditors. Secured lenders frequently have some involvement in the financial affairs of their debtors in order to insure that their interests are being adequately protected. To adopt the government's interpretation of the secured creditor exemption could expose all such lenders to CERCLA liability for engaging in their normal course of business.

> Fleet in turn, suggests that we adopt the distinction delineated by some district courts between permissible participation in the financial management of the facility and impermissible participation in the day-to-day or operational management of a facility * * *

> The court below * * * interpreted the statutory language to permit secured creditors to

>> provide financial assistance and general, and even isolated instances of specific, management advice to its debtors without risking CERCLA liability if the secured creditor does not participate in the day-to-day management of the business or facility either before or after the business ceases operation.

> *Fleet Factors Corp.,* 724 F.Supp. at 960 (S.D.Ga.1988); * * *

> [W]e find its construction of the statutory exemption too permissive towards secured creditors who are involved with toxic waste facilities. In order to achieve the "overwhelmingly remedial" goal of the CERCLA statutory scheme, ambiguous statutory terms should be construed to favor liability for the costs incurred by the government in responding to the hazards at such facilities.

> The district court's broad interpretation of the exemption would essentially require a secured creditor to be involved in the operations of a facility in order to incur liability. This construction ignores the plain language of the exemption and essentially renders it meaningless. * * *

> Under the standard we adopt today, a secured creditor may incur section 9607(a)(2) liability, without being an operator, by participating in the financial management of a facility to a degree indicating a capacity to influence the corporation's treatment of hazardous wastes. It is not necessary for the secured creditor actually to involve itself in the day-to-day operations of the facility in order to be liable—although

such conduct will certainly lead to the loss of the protection of the statutory exemption. Nor is it necessary for the secured creditor to participate in management decisions relating to hazardous waste. Rather, a secured creditor will be liable if its involvement with the management of the facility is sufficiently broad to support the inference that it could affect hazardous waste disposal decision if it so chose.
* * *

The Court of Appeals for the Ninth Circuit suggested, without deciding, that it believed the *Fleet Factors* rule was too broad, stating that "whatever the precise parameters of 'participation,' it is clear that there must be some actual management of the facility before a secured creditor will fall outside the exception." In re Bergsoe Metal Corporation (Hill v. The East Asiatic Company Ltd.), 910 F.2d 668 (9th Cir.1990). For an exhaustive analysis of the lender liability issue, see Howard and Gerard, Lender Liability Under CERCLA: Sorting Out the Mixed Signals, 64 S.Cal.L.Rev. 1187 (1991).

4. Note that under CERCLA, the United States can impose a lien on property to recover cleanup costs. This environmental lien, as a government lien, takes priority over all non-governmental liens. Review the material on title insurance earlier in this chapter. How should title insurance companies respond to environmental liens? Many state environmental laws provide for similar cleanup liens. See, e.g., N.J.Stat., § 58:10–23.11 f.f.

B. THE FORECLOSURE PROCESS—BALANCING DEBTOR AND CREDITOR INTERESTS

The vast majority of real estate loans are paid off on time and in accordance with the loan covenants. When the loan is retired, the mortgagee's lien is released, usually by the return of the note and mortgage to the borrower with a release notation added. In addition, the mortgagee should file with the recorder a deed of release, or request the recorder to enter a marginal note of release on the recorded mortgage or deed of trust.

However, when a mortgagor incurs a default by failure to pay as required, the mortgagee may take steps to protect its security interest. The following excerpt discusses the two most popular procedures, judicial foreclosure and power-of-sale foreclosure. Other procedures available to mortgagees are the common-law strict foreclosure, in which title is transferred directly to the mortgagee following a judicial decree of foreclosure, and acceptance by the mortgagee of a deed from the defaulting mortgagor in satisfaction of the debt, called a deed in lieu of foreclosure, or simply a deed in lieu.

NELSON & WHITMAN, REAL ESTATE FINANCE LAW
505–506, 534–538 (2nd Ed.1985).

D. Judicial Foreclosure

§ 7.11 Judicial Foreclosure—General Characteristics

Judicial foreclosure by sale in a court action in equity is the predominant method of foreclosure in the United States. It is the exclusive or generally used method of foreclosure in at least half of the states. Moreover, it is available in every jurisdiction, either by virtue of express statutory enactment or as an incident to the inherent jurisdiction of courts of equity. Even in jurisdictions where power of sale foreclosure is dominant, judicial foreclosure is required in certain special situations. For example, it will be necessary where the mortgage fails to create a power of sale. This situation will arise where the mortgage form omits any reference to a power of sale. It can also occur where one is seeking to foreclose an absolute deed as a mortgage because, by its very nature, the absolute deed will not contain a power of sale. Finally judicial foreclosure will be required where there is a serious lien priority dispute. In such a situation a judicial determination of lien priority will enable potential foreclosure sale purchasers to know the state of the title they will be bidding on and thus judicial foreclosure will be encouraged. On the other hand, if power of sale foreclosure were used, the uncertainty as to lien priority would discourage bidding and create title problems for the ultimate sale purchaser.

In spite of being the most pervasive method of foreclosure in America today, it has serious disadvantages. It is complicated, costly, and time-consuming. A typical action in equity to foreclose and sell involves a long series of steps: a preliminary title search to determine all parties in interest; filing of the foreclosure bill of complaint and lis pendens notice; service of process; a hearing, usually by a master in chancery who then reports to the court; the decree or judgment; notice of sale; actual sale and issuance of certificate of sale; report of the sale; proceedings for determination of the right to any surplus; possible redemptions from foreclosure sale; and the entry of a decree for a deficiency.

* * *

E. POWER OF SALE FORECLOSURE

§ 7.19 General Considerations

The other main foreclosure method, permitted in about twenty-five states, is power of sale foreclosure. After varying types and degrees of notice, the property is sold at a public sale, either by a public official, such as a sheriff, by some other third party, or by the mortgagee.

In some states utilizing the power of sale method, the deed of trust is the most commonly used mortgage instrument. The mortgagor-trustor conveys the real estate to a trustee who holds the property in trust for the mortgagee-beneficiary until full payment of the mortgage debt. In the event of foreclosure, the power of sale is exercised by the trustee, who holds a public sale of the mortgaged property; the sale is usually not judicially supervised.

As previously indicated, the notice requirements under power of sale foreclosure vary, but are usually less rigorous than those associated with judicial foreclosure. Notice, as used here, may be simply notice of foreclosure or notice of default or a combination of the two. While some states require that notice by mail or personal service be provided for any person having a record interest in the real estate junior to the mortgage being foreclosed, many do not. A few states require only notice of publication. This publication sometimes takes the form of newspaper advertisement and sometimes consists only of public posting. Other states, in addition to published notice, require notice either by mail or personal service to the mortgagor and the owner of the mortgaged real estate, but not to junior lienors and others holding an interest subordinate to the mortgage being foreclosed. A few states attempt to protect those interested parties who are neither mortgagors nor owners by requiring that the notice of foreclosure be mailed to any person who has previously recorded a request for such notice. In any event, whatever the notice requirements of the foregoing statutes, federal legislation makes power of sale foreclosure ineffective against a junior federal tax lien unless written notice is provided to the United States at least 25 days prior to the sale by registered or certified mail or by personal service. Finally, almost no power of sale foreclosure statutes provide for an opportunity for a hearing prior to the foreclosure sale.

* * *

The underlying theory of power of sale foreclosure is simple. It is that by complying with the above type statutory requirements, the mortgagee accomplishes the same purposes achieved by judicial foreclosure without the substantial additional burdens that the latter type of foreclosure entails. Those purposes are to terminate all interests junior to the mortgage being foreclosed and to provide the sale purchaser with a title identical to that of the mortgagor as of the time the mortgage being foreclosed was executed. Moreover, where it is in common use, power of sale foreclosure has provided an effective foreclosure remedy with a cost in time and money substantially lower than that of its judicial foreclosure counterpart.

Notwithstanding the fact that power of sale foreclosure generally works and that it is more efficient and less costly than judicial foreclosure, the titles it produces have been somewhat less stable than those resulting from judicial foreclosure. As we noted earlier, there are at least three reasons for this. First, the court supervision involved in judicial foreclosure will prevent many defects from arising. Second, because judicial foreclosure is an adversary proceeding, the presence of other parties who will bring possible defects to the court's attention constitutes added protection against a faulty end product. Finally, the concept of judicial finality provides substantial insulation against subsequent collateral attack even on technically defective judicial foreclosure proceedings. None of these protections are inherent in power of sale foreclosure. Moreover, as we will examine in detail later in this chapter, power of sale foreclosure has been subjected recently to the further uncertainty of constitutional attack because of its alleged notice and hearing deficiencies.

§ 7.20 Defective Power of Sale Foreclosure—The "Void–Voidable" Distinction

* * * Generally, defects in the exercise of a power of sale can be categorized in at least three ways. Some defects are so substantial as to render the sale void. In this situation no title, legal or equitable, passes to the sale purchaser or subsequent grantees, except perhaps by adverse possession. Such a result typically occurs where, notwithstanding mortgagee compliance with the prescribed foreclosure procedure, there was no right to exercise the power of sale. A forged mortgage, for example, would fall into this category. The most common example, however, of a defect that would render a sale void is where the power of sale is exercised when there has been no default in the mortgage obligation. So too will a sale be characterized as void where the person foreclosing did not own the note or where a trustee under a deed of trust forecloses without being authorized by the noteholder to do so. Moreover, the failure to follow certain fundamental procedural requirements may render a sale void. For example, the omission of part of the mortgaged real estate from the notice of sale has been held to render the sale of omitted land void.

Most defects * * * render the foreclosure *voidable* and not void. This means that bare legal title passes to the sale purchaser, subject to the rights of redemption of those injured by the defective foreclosure. Typically such a defect is "an irregularity in the execution of a foreclosure sale" and must be "substantial or result in a probable unfairness." A common example of a voidable sale in many jurisdictions is the purchase by a trustee under a deed of trust at his own sale. Further examples include the publication of the notice of sale for slightly fewer than the statutorily prescribed number of times or the sale at the east door instead of the west front door of the county courthouse. However, where the defect only renders the sale voidable, the rights of redemption can be cut off if the land falls into the hands of a bona fide purchaser for value. Where this occurs, an action for damages against the foreclosing mortgagee or trustee may be the only remaining remedy.

Finally, some defects are treated as so inconsequential as to render the sale neither void nor voidable. Such defects commonly involve minor discrepancies in the notice of sale. For example, where the first of four published notices of sale omitted the place of sale, the court held that since there was "substantial compliance" with the requirements specified by the deed of trust and since the parties were not affected in a "material way", the sale was valid. Similarly, a sale was deemed valid where the notice of sale was sent by regular rather than by the statutorily required certified or registered mail and the mortgagor had actual notice of the sale for more than the statutory period prior to the sale.

* * *

FIRST STATE BANK OF FORSYTH v. CHUNKAPURA

Supreme Court of Montana, 1987.
226 Mont. 54, 734 P.2d 1203.

SHEEHY, JUSTICE.

We hold in this case that a lender, electing to foreclose on its security under a trust deed by judicial procedure, is not entitled to remedies inconsistent with the Small Tract Financing Act of Montana, [ ] Specifically, the lender (mortgagee) may not recover a deficiency judgment against the borrower (mortgagor), and the borrower has no right of redemption as is accorded borrowers in judicial foreclosures of conventional mortgages.

First State Bank of Forsyth and William F. Meisburger appealed from an order of the District Court, Sixteenth Judicial District, Rosebud County, the Honorable C.B. Sande, District Judge, presiding, that § 71–1–317, MCA, prohibits the Bank from recovering a deficiency judgment on judicial foreclosure. No final judgment has been entered in the cause pending this appeal, and the cause has been properly certified to us for appeal * * *.

On October 20, 1980, the Chunkapuras executed a promissory note to the First State Bank of Forsyth in the amount of $17,000 with interest on the unpaid principal thereon accruing at the rate of 14% per annum to be paid by the Chunkapuras in monthly payments. The note was secured by a deed of trust executed the same day from the Chunkapuras to First Montana Title Insurance Company as trustee, naming the Bank as beneficiary, covering Lots 17 and 18 in Block 54 of the original town, now city, of Forsyth, Montana.

Under the terms of the note the Chunkapuras would have paid to the Bank $226.40 per month until October 20, 1995 to pay off the note, and under the terms of the deed of trust, were to provide such additional sums monthly as would be sufficient to pay taxes, assessments, insurance premiums, and other charges.

William S. Meisburger succeeded First Montana Title Insurance Company as trustee under the deed of trust. He appears in this action as a plaintiff trustee, and as attorney for the Bank and himself as plaintiffs. * * *

The Chunkapuras made payments under the note and deed of trust to the Bank until April 20, 1985, at which time they went into default, the principal of the indebtedness having been reduced to $14,957.02. On September 11, 1985, the plaintiffs filed an action in the District Court to foreclose judicially the security interest of the Bank. Their complaint was amended on October 4, 1985. Under the amended complaint plaintiffs prayed for judgment against the defendants for the unpaid principal, accrued interest and other costs, for a sale of the real estate premises by the sheriff of Rosebud County, and for a deficiency judgment against the defendants after applying all the proceeds of the sale of the premises.

By stipulation, the parties agreed that the District Court could enter judgment, issue an order for a sheriff's sale, and proceed with the sheriff's sale, reserving until a later time the question of whether a deficiency judgment could be recovered. At the sheriff's sale, the Bank, being the only bidder, bid on the property in the sum of $10,000.00 which after deducting sheriff's fees and attorneys fees, left a net sum of $8,965.50. Thereupon the plaintiffs sought a deficiency judgment in the amount of $8,556.93.

* * *

I.

The issues in this case involve interpretation of the Small Tract Financing Act of Montana, enacted in 1963. The history of the legislative adoption of that Act, not unknown to some members of this Court, needs telling at this point for perspective.

Prior to 1963, Montana was a "one action" state with respect to foreclosures of mortgages. Our statute provided that there was but one action for the recovery of debt, or the enforcement of any rights incurred by mortgage upon real estate, which action had to be in accordance with the foreclosure provisions of our statutes. [ ] Whereas in other states with differing statutes the lender had the option of suing on the promissory note, or suing to foreclose the mortgage securing the note, our "one action" statute was construed by us to mean that a creditor could not waive the mortgage and sue on the debt but was limited to foreclosure of the mortgage indebtedness. [ ] A mortgage instrument could and still may contain a power of sale provision to which the mortgagee could resort for foreclosure without judicial proceedings. [ ] No provision however is made in our statutes for a deficiency judgment where foreclosure under power of sale occurs. In a judicial foreclosure, after the court entered judgment that the mortgager had defaulted on his obligations and that the mortgagee was entitled to the benefit of his security, the court could and still can order sale of the secured premises by the sheriff of the county involved. If the proceeds from the sheriff's sale are insufficient and a balance still remains due, a deficiency judgment can then be docketed against the defendant or defendants personally liable for the debt which becomes a lien upon the real estate of the judgment debtors. [ ]

Two legal consequences attended, and still attend a judicial foreclosure of mortgaged real property. The judgment debtor has the right to redeem the property from the purchaser at the sheriff's sale any time within one year after the sale. [ ] The purchaser was not and is not now entitled to the possession of the real property as against the judgment debtor during the period of redemption while the debtor personally occupied the land as a home for himself and his family. [ ]

The banking and lending industry came to the legislature in 1963, contending that the "one action" rule and the attendant right of redemption and right of possession rules hampered the financing of improvements on small tracts in Montana because banks and investors were unwilling to invest in mortgages when on default their funds would be tied up during the period of redemption. A *quid pro quo* was proposed to the legislature: the lenders would give up their deficiency judgment rights on default, if the borrowers would give up their rights of possession and redemption. The result was the adoption by the legislature of the Small Tract Financing Act of Montana, originally limited to tracts of three acres, but now may involve tracts as large as fifteen acres.

Under the Small Tract Financing Act, instead of mortgages, trust indentures (sometimes called "deeds of trust" or "trust deeds") are authorized. Such instruments have the effect of transferring the title of the borrower to a private trustee to be held by the trustee to secure the performance of the obligation by the borrower. A power of sale is by the law granted to the trustee to be exercised after a breach of the obligation for which the trust transfer is security. [ ] The trust indenture is considered to be a mortgage on real property, [ ] and provisions are made in the law for the method whereby a trustee may foreclose a trust indenture by advertisement and sale. [ ] It is certain that when a trustee conducts a foreclosure sale, a deficiency judgment is not allowed [ ], and the purchaser at the trustee sale is entitled to possession of the property on the tenth day following the sale. [ ]

It may be safely said, although it does not appear in this record, that in the time since the enactment of the Small Tract Financing Act, the use of trust deeds for security purposes has become nearly exclusive in this state.

II.

The issues in this cause arise out of certain provisions of the Small Tract Financing Act which are subject to judicial interpretation. Section 71–1–304(3), MCA, provides that a trust indenture may be foreclosed by an advertisement and sale through the trustee, or at the option of the beneficiary (lender) by judicial procedure as provided by law for the foreclosure of mortgages on real property. The foreclosure of a trust indenture by advertisement and sale or by judicial procedure is limited to the times provided by law for the foreclosure of a mortgage on real property. Section 71–1–311, MCA. The provision prohibiting deficiency judgment states:

> *Deficiency judgment not allowed.* When a trust indenture executed in conformity with this part is foreclosed by advertisement and sale, no other or further action, suit, or proceedings shall be taken or judgment entered for any deficiency against the grantor or his surety, guarantor, or successor in interest, if any, on the note, bond, or other obligation secured by the trust indenture or against any other person obligated on such note, bond, or other obligation.

Section 71–1–317, MCA.

With respect to possession, the Act provides:

Possession. The purchaser at the trustee's sale shall be entitled to possession of the property on the 10th day following the sale, and any persons remaining in possession after that date under any interest, except one prior to the trust indenture, shall be deemed to be tenants at will.

Section 71–1–319, MCA.

The First State Bank of Forsyth contends that under the Act, it has the option of either foreclosing on the security by means of a trustee sale, or by resorting to judicial foreclosure. It further contends that when it elects to proceed by judicial foreclosure, it then becomes entitled to the legal consequences that follow the judicial foreclosure of a conventional mortgage, that is, the right to a deficiency judgment. It admits that if it is entitled to a deficiency judgment, the borrower also then becomes entitled to the right of redemption granted in the foreclosure of conventional mortgages.

The Chunkapuras on the other hand, contend that because the lender chose to finance this obligation under the Small Tract Financing Act, it thereupon elected the benefits conferred upon lending institutions by the Act, the immediate transfer of title in exchange for no deficiency judgment, and that these results apply whether the lender elects to proceed by trustee sale on default, or by judicial foreclosure. The Chunkapuras rely especially on § 71–1–305, MCA, which provides:

Trust indenture considered to be a mortgage on real property. A trust indenture is deemed to be a mortgage on real property and is subject to all laws relating to mortgages on real property except to the extent that such laws are inconsistent with the provisions of this part, in which event the provisions of this part shall control. For the purpose of applying the mortgage laws, the grantor in a trust indenture is deemed the mortgagor and the beneficiary is deemed the mortgagee.

They point also to the provisions of § 71–1–317, MCA, which we have quoted above, contending that whether a trustee sale occurs or a judicial foreclosure is utilized, the trust indenture is foreclosed "by advertisement and sale" in either case, and under § 71–1–317, a deficiency judgment is not allowed. To grant a deficiency judgment, the Chunkapuras contend, would be in effect giving life to a provision of the judicial foreclosure statutes which is inconsistent with the provisions of the Small Tract Financing Act under § 71–1–305.

III.

This Court is confronted in this case with a statutory situation wherein it is clear that in cases of trustee sales under trust deeds, there is no right of redemption given to the borrower, and the borrower must surrender possession within ten days; and the lender under a trustee sale has no right to a deficiency judgment. The provisions of the Small Tract Financing Act, permitting an election to the lender to resort to judicial foreclosure, [   ], and setting out time limitations [   ], do not clearly provide that under judicial foreclosures, the legal consequences of redemption and deficiency judgment follow. It becomes a matter of judicial interpretation whether the sense and intent of the legislature, in adopting the Small Tract Financing Act, and permitting judicial foreclosure, was also to permit deficiency judgments to the lenders and the rights of redemption to the borrowers.

* * *

We are directed to the case law of other states.

* * *

It may be stated therefore, as a broad general policy in the western states, with Alaska the sole exception, the lender has the option of proceeding by trustee sale under trust instruments, or by judicial foreclosure under the mortgage statutes; but if the latter procedure is elected, the deficiency judgment provisions of those statutes limit the deficiency judgment to the difference between the amount of the indebtedness sought and the fair market value of the property at the time of the sale, or the amount realized at the sale, whichever figure results in the lesser deficiency. Montana statutes on judicial foreclosure do not have a "fair market value" provision. A consideration of those provisions brings us to the crux of the problem in this case.

IV.

Generally, since 1963, with the exception of the last few years, real estate values in Montana have been subjected to the same inflationary pressures that existed elsewhere in the nation. At or about the time that the Chunkapuras borrowed on their property in this case, inflation had reached its highest stage. But Montana, since 1981, has been enduring a depressed economy of sorts, which has resulted in a marked depreciation in the values of real property. In the past five to six years foreclosures because of defaulted debts on farms, businesses, and homes have increased notably in this state. In this case, the Bank was the only bidder for the Chunkapuras property. Its bid of $10,000 may represent the fair market value of the property at the time of the sheriff's sale, or it may be an opportunistic bid which takes advantage of the circumstances so that later the Bank may sell the property for a sum in excess of $10,000. In the meantime the deficiency judgment of $8,556.93, plus accrued interest and costs, if allowed would become a lien on any other real estate the Chunkapuras now own or may own during the period that the judgment lien is in effect. The right of possession of their home which the Chunkapuras would have for one year might have some value, but the right of redemption is valueless, because if the Chunkapuras redeemed, the deficiency judgment lien would immediately adhere to the redeemed property. This result is not the *quid pro quo* which the legislature intended when it acceded to the lending industries' urging and adopted the Small Tract Financing Act in 1963.

We therefore determine and hold that District Judge Sande was correct when he determined that under § 71–1–317, MCA, a deficiency judgment may not be allowed when trust indentures are executed in conformity with the Act, and are foreclosed by advertisement and sale, whether through the trustee or by judicial proceedings; and that to allow a deficiency judgment would be inconsistent with the provisions of the Small Tract Financing Act of Montana and accordingly forbidden * * *.

The decision in the District Court therefore that no deficiency judgment may be obtained against the Chunkapuras is affirmed. It should go without saying that in like manner, the Chunkapuras are not entitled either to a right of possession after ten days from the sale, or to a right of redemption for a period of one year.

* * *

WEBER, JUSTICE, dissents. * * * [The dissent argued that the majority disregarded the interests of lenders and failed to follow the plain meaning of the statutes. If modification were necessary, that should be done by the legislature, the dissent concluded—Eds.]

ORDER ON REHEARING

[The Court limited its order to trust deeds related to occupied, single family residential property, holding that the restrictions on deficiency judgments did not apply to commercial lending or investment settings—Eds.]

Notes and Questions

1. Note the trade-offs in the Montana legislation: Lenders gave up the right to obtain deficiency judgments in return for borrowers giving up the right to retain possession after foreclosure while they attempted to raise money to pay off the debt and redeem the property. Does this strike you as a fair approach? Does this legislation increase or decrease the lenders' credit risk? The borrowers'?

2. A recurring theme of mortgage law development is the attempt to balance the risks of debtors and creditors. Creditors tend to have the upper hand because mortgage finance is a contractual activity in which persons with money generally can dictate the terms under which persons seeking money can obtain it. A major concern of lenders is the protection of their credit risk. To reduce this risk, lenders generally prefer to be able to transfer possession quickly to foreclosure sale purchasers, and to be able to recoup any deficiencies after foreclosure sale from the defaulting borrowers. Periodically courts of equity and legislatures have intervened, particularly in times of severe economic distress, such as the great depression, to cushion the impact of such risk-reduction techniques on defaulting borrowers in the hopes of alleviating some of the social problems resulting from residential default. As noted in *Chunkapura*, three basic techniques that originated in the depression are in use in a number of states: (a) "fair value" legislation that limits any deficiency that may be realized after foreclosure sale to the difference between an established "fair value" and the outstanding debt; (b) "anti-deficiency" legislation that prohibits deficiency judgments when power-of-sale foreclosure is used, or in cases where the foreclosed mortgage is a purchase money mortgage rather than a

construction mortgage; and (c) "one action" rules that require mortgagees to choose either a contractual action on the promissory note or a foreclosure action under the mortgage, or limit mortgagees to the foreclosure sale proceeds. For a succinct analysis of such legislative intervention, see G. Nelson & D. Whitman, Real Estate Finance Law 594–615 (2d ed. 1985).

3. During the inflationary-recessionary period of the late 1970s and early 1980s, high rates of default on farm and home mortgages led a number of states to enact additional consumer protection measures including temporary mortgage-payment forbearance periods of up to six months, court ordered restructuring of mortgage debt, and mortgage assistance payments to homeowners by state agencies. See e.g., Conn. Gen. Stat. §§ 49–31d through 49–31j; Minn. Stat. Ann. § 583.02; 35 Pa.Stat. § 1680, 13 401c et seq. For a review of the Connecticut, Minnesota and Pennsylvania programs, see Sclar, From the Legislatures: Mortgage Foreclosure Relief, 12 Real Est.L.J. 366 (1984).

4. The foreclosure relief statutes discussed above become effective after the foreclosure process has begun. An alternative approach, using mediation, is designed to intervene before debt problems reach the desperate stage of foreclosure. Farmer-lender mediation programs have been established in a number of midwestern states, some voluntary and some mandatory.

As we discussed in the landlord-tenant chapter, mediation is typically a voluntary procedure that depends in large measure for its success on the willing participation of the protagonists. Whether the mediation program is a required step in a loan default process, or merely a recommended step in the process, the parties must believe in mediation or at least be willing to approach mediation with an open mind if it is to have a chance to contribute to the resolution of a dispute. In Graham v. Baker, 447 N.W.2d 397 (Iowa 1989), the Supreme Court of Iowa held that an attorney for a lender who attended a mediation session but refused to cooperate with the mediator satisfied the Iowa statute requiring "participation" in mediation before foreclosing on farm loans. Did the court give the correct interpretation to the Iowa legislation, or should it have implied a standard of "good faith" before a mediation release could be obtained? Does such legislation make any sense the way the Iowa court construed it?

Would an attorney retained by a lender to pursue remedies upon default by a borrower be acting in an ethical/professional manner in refusing to cooperate with a mediation process? Would it make a difference whether the process was mandatory or voluntary? Would such an attorney merely be loyal to his client, or would he go beyond the bounds of loyalty and fail to live up to his obligation to serve the public as an officer of the court, particularly if the legislature had determined that efforts to resolve mortgage loan defaults short of forfeiture were required as a matter of public policy?

Proponents of mediation between farmers and creditors have identified "four outcomes that can be considered successful:

* clarification of the impasses including the recognition that the issues cannot be resolved;

* management of the communication system so that the parties can interact effectively;

* resolution of the goals and issues and management of the communications; and

* reconciliation of the relationship so that both parties' interests, issues and goals are met."

Thompson, Crisis in Rural America: The Genesis of Farmer–Lender Mediation, Nat. Inst. for Dispute Res. Forum, p. 4 (Fall 1990).

Chapter Six

THE LAW OF NEIGHBORS: SERVITUDES AND NUISANCES

This chapter is about the law of neighbors. Real property does not exist in a vacuum. Except perhaps for isolated islands, any particular parcel owned by one or more persons is bounded by other parcels owned by other persons. Correspondingly, the use of real property affects and is affected by the use of neighboring properties. The owner of a remote mountain ranch, for example, may need an access easement across a neighbor's land to get to a public road, or may damage neighboring properties through poor logging practices. Neighbors in a suburban residential development are far more interdependent. Their houses are hooked into pipes and wires that crisscross the neighborhood. They may be annoyed by each other's children, dogs, parties, fences, or satellite dishes. Developers attempt to define the character of neighborhoods through restrictions that limit permissible uses, or the placement of buildings, or the architectural style of the neighborhood. Neighbors litigate concerning these restrictions when nonconforming persons or uses attempt to settle in the neighborhood. Restrictions may also create property owners' associations—miniature private governments that may collect taxes (assessments), maintain common improvements, decide what sort of architecture will be permitted within the development, and amend their fundamental laws as the development progresses. Finally, residents in a cooperative or condominium are even more interdependent, and thus even more dependent on complex and detailed deed restrictions for accommodating each other as they live their common life.

Neighboring uses are accommodated through a variety of legal doctrines. The law of adverse possession, which you have already studied, is commonly used to decide boundary disputes between neighboring owners. The public law of zoning and planning, which comes later in this course, plays an increasingly important role in reconciling neighboring uses. Most of the law relevant to legal accommodations and disputes among neighbors, however, is found in this chapter.

The chapter begins with consideration of servitudes, then examines the law of nuisance, and concludes with a brief discussion of a variety of doctrines that play a lesser role in the law of neighbors: lateral and subjacent support and the law of surface waters.

I. SERVITUDES

Servitudes serve three primary functions. First, they permit persons affirmatively to use land that they do not own or possess. For example, A can own servitudes that allow her to get to her own land by driving down her neighbor, B's, lane; or to run telephone or electric wire, or gas, water, or sewer pipes across B's land to permit the development of her own land. Second, servitudes allow land owners to restrict their neighbors' use of their own land. A can own servitudes that forbid her neighbor, B, from using his property for uses other than residential development, from building within 30 feet of the street, from constructing a building not approved by an architectural review committee, or from posting political signs in his front yard. Finally, servitudes allow landowners to impose affirmative obligations on their neighbors. B, for example, may be obligated to pay $50 a year to a property owners' association, or to maintain a fence, or to provide his neighbor, A, with water from a stream.

Servitudes are most commonly based on agreements between or among landowners. They are often based on language in deeds or independent grants: A, for example, deeds the back half of her 320–acre farm to B and in doing so grants to B a servitude of way across A's retained 160 acres to get to B's purchased land. Increasingly servitudes are created by subdivision plats or declarations of restrictions. A developer establishes a 120–lot exclusive residential development, and before selling any lots, records a declaration binding the entire subdivision with certain restrictions.

Insofar as servitudes are based on agreements, they resemble contracts. They differ from contracts, however, in an important respect: they run with the land. A contract only binds parties who agree to be bound by it. When the appropriate requirements are met, however, a servitude binds and benefits not only the initial owners of the burdened and benefited properties, but also their successors. Moreover, unlike contracts, which bind their signatories until the obligations imposed by the contract are fulfilled or released, servitudes normally bind landowners only for so long as they own burdened land.

Though most servitudes are appurtenant to particular parcels of burdened and benefited properties, servitudes may also be created in gross. They may, that is, be created for the benefit of a particular individual or entity independent of property ownership. The telephone company may, for example, own an easement across a property to run its wires, or an environmental organization may own a conservation easement limiting the development of farmland.

Some kinds of servitudes may be created not only by express agreement, but also by implication. If A had not granted a servitude of way to B in the hypothetical above, for example, and if the conveyance cut B's land off from access to a public road, the law would in all likelihood imply a servitude of way across A's land in B's favor. If the deed failed to mention a servitude of way, but B continued to use A's lane to get to his land for 10 years, the law might recognize a servitude based on prescription. If the developer in the example above had not recorded a declaration of restrictions, but rather had advertised a restricted development and sold off successive lots each with identical restrictions in their deeds, the law might very well at some point imply the restrictions against a lot sold off subsequently without the restrictions. Because of a general public policy favoring preservation of land free from encumbrances, however, courts imply restrictions reluctantly and only under limited circumstances when they believe public policy requires it.

The law of servitudes could be relatively straightforward, but, unfortunately, it is not. Here, as elsewhere in property law, doctrine is a creature of history. Where the law of estates and future interests represents the continuous organic development of nearly a millennium of English and American law, servitude law in its modern form is largely a creation of the nineteenth and twentieth century. It thus represents the simultaneous uncoordinated attempts of the English law and chancery courts and of a number of American jurisdictions to arrive at a law suited to a period of rapid development.

The results are singularly confusing. Five primary tools—easements, licenses, profits, real covenants, and equitable servitudes—were created to serve the three functions set out above. To complicate matters further, several of these servitudes can serve more than one function. Real covenants and equitable servitudes can in many jurisdictions be used both to restrict land and to impose affirmative obligations on land owners. Easements permit one to use affirmatively another's property, but negative easements restrict the use of property, and, under very limited circumstances, easements can impose affirmative obligations.

The law of servitudes is also burdened by confusing doctrine which often either serves no contemporary purpose, or which strives by indirection to achieve goals more properly addressed directly. The requirement of horizontal privity for the creation of real covenants, for example, was probably created to deal with the lack of a recording system in Britain, but serves no purpose in modern America. The "touch and concern" requirement limits the subject matter of servitudes that impose negative restrictions or affirmative obligations on land, but often results in obfuscation and tautological reasoning instead of clear discussion of policy questions.

Much of this confusing doctrine was unfortunately enshrined in the 1944 Restatement of Property, which on the whole assumed a hostile attitude towards restrictions on real property, and adopted a variety of archaic doctrines of questionable authority to limit their use. A new Restatement, which adopts the more modern attitude recognizing the value of servitudes for many purposes, is now underway. It will greatly simplify servitude law once its reasoning is adopted by the courts. This goal may be achieved in your lifetime, but for the present, you must, regrettably, come to terms with the doctrine that still appears in court decisions.

Because existing traditional servitudes cannot be fit neatly into functional categories, this text adopts a functional as well as doctrinal approach. Affirmative rights to use the property of another—easements, licenses, and profits—are treated together first. Negative and affirmative obligations—real covenants, equitable servitudes, and negative easements—are considered next. Within each of these categories we consider creation; validity, succession, and scope; and modification and termination.

A. AFFIRMATIVE RIGHTS TO USE PROPERTY: EASEMENTS, LICENSES, AND PROFITS

1. *Definitions*

Three legal devices are used to permit affirmative use of property owned by another: easements, profits, and licenses. A license is a privilege to use property possessed by another. See Restatement, Property (1944) § 512. Examples of a license include tickets to a theatre or sporting event, or the privilege of being seated in a restaurant or of being allowed in a shopping mall. A license is revocable at the will of the licensor except where it has become irrevocable under one of several doctrines discussed below. An irrevocable license looks a great deal like an easement.

A profit (or profit à prendre) is the right to sever and take the "profits"—i.e. produce or substance—of the land of another. Examples of traditional English profits include turbary (the right to dig turf), estovers (the right to remove timber as needed for good husbandry), and pannage (the right to feed swine on acorns and mast). Of more contemporary importance, the right to remove oil and gas can be considered a profit, see Gerhard v. Stephens, 68 Cal.2d 864, 69 Cal.Rptr. 612, 442 P.2d 692, (1968).

The 1944 Restatement (§ 450, Special Note) took the sensible position that under contemporary American law there was no distinction between easements and profits, and that, therefore, the use of both terms was unnecessary. Other authorities have followed this approach (see 3 R. Powell & P. Rohan, Powell on Real Property, ¶ 404[1] (1991)) and use of the term profit in the courts has become increasingly rare but still occurs.

The most common device for creating affirmative rights in the property of another is the easement. The 1944 Restatement, § 450, defines an easement as:

"An interest in land in the possession of another which

(a) entitles the owner of such interest to a limited use or enjoyment of the land in which the interest exists;

(b) entitles him to protection as against third persons from interference in such use or enjoyment;

(c) is not subject to the will of the possessor of the land;

(d) is not a normal incident of the possession of any land possessed by the owner of the interest; and

(e) is capable of creation by conveyance."

Problem: Do the following situations involve easements, licenses, profits, or something else? How do you know?

(a) A permits B to place a billboard on the side of A's building.

(b) A University sells B student a parking permit which permits B to park in any available student parking place on campus.

(c) B purchases from A the right to dig gravel from a gravel pit on A's property.

(d) B parks her car in A's parking garage. B turns the car and its keys over to A upon entering the garage. A parks the car and keeps the keys until B returns.

(e) B permits A to hunt on B's property every year during hunting season.

(f) A uses B's lane to get from his farm across B's property to the county road.

(g) The eaves of A's house overhang B's property by one foot.

2. *Creation*

(a) By Express Conveyance

Most easements are created through express conveyances. Easements can be created in deeds conveying the fee to which they are appurtenant; through separate written grants; by reference to plats, maps, or declarations; and even by wills. Easements can also be created by contract to the extent that a contract to make an easement will be specifically enforced at equity. At common law, easements were incorporeal hereditaments, not subject to creation by livery of seisin. Instead, they had to be created through deeds, which had to be sealed instruments. The requirement of a seal has been abolished in most jurisdictions by statute or court decision, but appears to remain in force in a handful of jurisdictions.

Although there was some early confusion as to whether the Statute of Frauds applied to easements, since on its face it only applied to estates that could be created by livery of seisin or parole, it now clearly applies to easements. The Statute thus requires (subject to exceptions considered below) that grants of easements be in writing and signed. Though the writing must identify the burdened estate, it is not necessary to specify the location of the servitude upon the burdened estates, and grants are often indefinite in this particular. It is also not necessary that the grant identify the benefited estate if its identity is clear from the context. Finally, easements are often created by deeds that independently convey a fee, and which are signed only by the grantor. Even though the deed is a deed poll, not signed by the grantee (as is commonly the case), the grantor may retain an easement across the granted property, with the grantee's acceptance serving in place of a signature. Traditionally, the word "grant" was appropriate for creating an easement. While under contemporary practice other words can be used if their purpose is clear, lawyers never forget, and easements are still commonly granted. Easements are subject to the recording act and must normally be recorded to bind future parties.

Formalities retain their greatest vitality with respect to grants to third parties.

WILLARD v. FIRST CHURCH OF CHRIST, SCIENTIST, PACIFICA

Supreme Court of California, 1972.
7 Cal.3d 473, 102 Cal.Rptr. 739, 498 P.2d 987.

PETERS, ASSOCIATE JUSTICE.

In this case we are called upon to decide whether a grantor may, in deeding real property to one person, effectively reserve an interest in the property to another. We hold that in this case such a reservation vests the interest in the third party.

Plaintiffs Donald E. and Jennie C. Willard filed an action to quiet title to a lot in Pacifica against the First Church of Christ, Scientist (the church). After a trial judgment was entered quieting the Willards' title. The church has appealed.

Genevieve McGuigan owned two abutting lots in Pacifica known as lots 19 and 20. There was a building on lot 19, and lot 20 was vacant. McGuigan was a member of the church, which was located across the street from her lots, and she permitted it to use lot 20 for parking during services. She sold lot 19 to one Petersen, who used the building as an office. He wanted to resell the lot, so he listed it with Willard, who is a realtor. Willard expressed an interest in purchasing both lots 19 and 20, and he and Petersen signed a deposit receipt for the sale of the two lots. Soon thereafter they entered into an escrow, into which Petersen delivered a deed for both lots in fee simple.

At the time he agreed to sell lot 20 to Willard, Petersen did not own it, so he approached McGuigan with an offer to purchase it. She was willing to sell the lot provided the church could continue to use it for parking. She therefore referred the matter to the church's attorney, who drew up a provision for the deed that stated the conveyance was "subject to an easement for automobile parking during church hours for the benefit of the church on the property at the southwest corner of the intersection of Hilton Way and Francisco Boulevard * * * such easement to run with the land only so long as the property for whose benefit the easement is given is used for church purposes." Once this clause was inserted in the deed, McGuigan sold the property to Petersen, and he recorded the deed.

Willard paid the agreed purchase price into the escrow and received Petersen's deed 10 days later. He then recorded this deed, which did not mention an easement for parking by the church. While Petersen did mention to Willard that the church would want to use lot 20 for parking, it does not appear that he told him of the easement clause contained in the deed he received from McGuigan.

Willard became aware of the easement clause several months after purchasing the property. He then commenced this action to quiet title against the church. At the trial, which was without a jury, McGuigan testified that she had bought lot 20 to provide parking for the church, and would not have sold it unless she was assured the church could thereafter continue to use it for parking. The court found that McGuigan and Petersen intended to convey an easement to the church, but that the clause they employed was ineffective for that purpose because it was invalidated by the common law rule that one cannot "reserve" an interest in property to a stranger to the title.

The rule derives from the common law notions of reservations from a grant and was based on feudal considerations. A reservation allows a grantor's whole interest in the property to pass to the grantee, but revests a newly created interest in the grantor.[1] [ ] While a reservation could theoretically vest an interest in a third party, the early common law courts vigorously rejected this possibility, apparently because they mistrusted and wished to limit conveyance by deed as a substitute for livery by seisin. (See Harris Reservations in Favor of Strangers of the Title (1953) 6 Okla.L.Rev. 127, 132–133.) Insofar as this mistrust was the foundation of the rule, it is clearly an inapposite feudal shackle today. Consequently, several commentators have attacked the rule as groundless and have called for its abolition. [ ]

California early adhered to this common law rule. [ ] In considering our continued adherence to it, we must realize that our courts no longer feel constricted by feudal forms of conveyancing. Rather, our primary objective in construing a conveyance is to try to give effect to the intent of the grantor. [ ] In general, therefore, grants are to be interpreted in the same way as other contracts and not according to rigid feudal standards. [ ] The common law rule conflicts with the modern approach to construing deeds because it can frustrate the grantor's intent. Moreover, it produces an inequitable result because the original grantee has presumably paid a reduced price for title to the encumbered property. In this case, for example, McGuigan testified

---

1. The effect of a reservation should be distinguished from an exception, which prevents some part of the grantor's interest from passing to the grantee. The exception cannot vest an interest in the third party, and the excepted interest remains in the grantor. (6 Powell, The Law of Real Property (Rohan ed. 1971) § 892.)

that she had discounted the price she charged Petersen by about one-third because of the easement. Finally, in some situations the rule conflicts with section 1085 of the Civil Code.[2]

In view of the obvious defects of the rule, this court has found methods to avoid it where applying it would frustrate the clear intention of the grantor. In Butler v. Gosling, 130 Cal. 422, 62 P. 596 (1900), the court prevented the reserved title to a portion of the property from vesting in the grantee by treating the reservation as an exception to the grant. In Boyer v. Murphy, *supra*, 202 Cal. 23, 259 P. 38, the court, noting that its primary objective was to give effect to the grantor's intention (Id., at pp. 28–29, 259 P. 38), held that the rule was inapplicable where the third party was the grantor's spouse. [ ] Similarly, the lower courts in California[3] and the courts of other states[4] [ ] have found ways of circumventing the rule.

The highest courts of two states have already eliminated the rule altogether, rather than repealing it piecemeal by evasion. In Townsend v. Cable, 378 S.W.2d 806 (Ky.1964), the Court of Appeals of Kentucky abandoned the rule. It said: "We have no hesitancy in abandoning this archaic and technical rule. It is entirely inconsistent with the basic principle followed in the construction of deeds, which is to determine the intention of grantor as gathered from the four corners of the instrument." (Id., at p. 808.) [ ] Relying on Townsend, the

2. Section 1085 provides that "(a) present interest, and the benefit of a condition or covenant respecting property, may be taken by any natural person under a grant, although not named a party thereto." We have been unable to find a California case that cites the section. Similar provisions in the codes of other states have also lain unused on the books. (See Mont. Rev. Codes Ann. (1962) § 67–1524; N.D.Cent.Code (1962) § 47–09–17; R.I.Gen. Laws Ann. (1956) § 34–11–10.) The language of the section clearly does not apply in this case because the church is a corporation and not a natural person.

3. In Sutter Butte Canal Co. v. Richvale Land Co., 40 Cal.App. 451, 181 P. 98 (1919), a developer provided, in its subdivision proposal, that certain easements for streets were reserved to its assigns and successors. Faced with a challenge to the easement based on the rule against reservation to a stranger, the court noted that it was "not justified in resorting to technical refinement as to the meaning of 'reversions' to defeat the manifest intent of the parties * * *." (Id., at pp. 456–457, 181 P. at p. 100.) It held that the complaining landowner was estopped to object to the easement because of his express consent to it. Similarly, in Smith v. Kraintz, 201 Cal. App.2d 696, 20 Cal.Rptr. 471 (1962), the

court upheld a reservation to the general public because the intent to dedicate can be shown by even an ineffective instrument.

4. (See generally Harris, Reservations in Favor of Strangers to the Title, *supra*, 6 Okla.L.Rev. 127, 139–150.) Some courts, like the court in Butler, supra, mitigate the harshness of the rule by treating the reservation as an exception that retained the interest in the grantor. [ ]. While this approach did prevent the reserved interest from passing to the grantee, it did not achieve the grantor's intention of vesting that interest in the third party. Other courts gave effect to the grantor's intention by estopping those who claimed under a chain of title including the deed containing the reservation from challenging it on the basis of the common law rule. [ ] This approach has the effect of emasculating the common law rule without expressly abandoning it. One court found that a reservation created a trust in favor of the stranger [ ], but this approach seems unduly elaborate to achieve the grantor's intent. Finally, several courts, like the court in Boyer, supra, will disregard the rule entirely when the stranger is the grantor's spouse. [ ]. Thus, as in California, the rule has been riddled with exceptions in other states.

Supreme Court of Oregon, in Garza v. Grayson, 255 Or. 413, 467 P.2d 960 (1970), rejected the rule because it was "derived from a narrow and highly technical interpretation of the meaning of the terms 'reservation' and 'exception' when employed in a deed" (Id., at p. 961), and did not sufficiently justify frustrating the grantor's intention. Since the rule may frustrate the grantor's intention in some cases even though it is riddled with exceptions, we follow the lead of Kentucky and Oregon and abandon it entirely.

Willard contends that the old rule should nevertheless be applied in this case to invalidate the church's easement because grantees and title insurers have relied upon it. He has not, however, presented any evidence to support this contention,[5] and it is clear that the facts of this case do not demonstrate reliance on the old rule. There is no evidence that a policy of title insurance was issued, and therefore no showing of reliance by a title insurance company. Willard himself could not have relied upon the common law rule to assure him of an absolute fee because he did not even read the deed containing the reservation. This is not a case of an ancient deed where the reservation has not been asserted for many years. The church used lot 20 for parking throughout the period when Willard was purchasing the property and after he acquired title to it, and he may not claim that he was prejudiced by lack of use for an extended period of time.

The determination whether the old common law rule should be applied to grants made prior to our decision involves a balancing of equitable and policy considerations. We must balance the injustice which would result from refusing to give effect to the grantor's intent against the injustice, if any, which might result by failing to give effect to reliance on the old rule [6] and the policy against disturbing settled titles. The record before us does not disclose any reliance upon the old common law rule, and there is no problem of an ancient title. Although in other cases the balancing of the competing interests may warrant application of the common law rule to presently existing deeds, in the instant case the balance falls in favor of the grantor's intent, and the old common law rule may not be applied to defeat her intent.

Willard also contends that the church has received no interest in this case because the clause stated only that the grant was "subject to" the church's easement, and not that the easement was either excepted or reserved. In construing this provision, however, we must look to the clause as a whole which states that the easement "is given." Even if we assume that there is some ambiguity or conflict in the clause, the trial court found on substantial evidence that the parties to the deed intended to convey the easement to the church. [   ]

5. Although there was testimony at the trial as to the chain of title by an employee of a title insurance company, there was no evidence that a policy of title insurance was actually issued, or what its terms were.

6. In weighing claims of reliance, the court must, of course, give consideration to the several exceptions to the common law rule developed by the courts and partial abrogation of the rule by section 1085 of the Civil Code.

The judgment is reversed.

Notes and Questions

1. The first footnote in the case suggests that a different result might have obtained had the deed from McGuigan to Petersen "excepted" rather than "reserved" the easement in favor of the Church. What is the difference between an exception and a reservation? How does the court know that the deed creates a reservation rather than an exception? Should anything turn on such distinctions? See Mott v. Stanlake, 63 Mich.App. 440, 234 N.W.2d 667 (1975) (interpreting attempted grant to be an exception to benefit a third party rather than a reservation, since exceptions in favor of third party permissible). How can a drafter who understands the rules avoid them altogether?

2. If the reservation in favor of the third party is held invalid, is the land transferred free of the easement, or is the easement retained by the initial grantor? See Davis v. Gowen, 83 Idaho 204, 360 P.2d 403 (1961) (grantor retains reserved easement); Estate of Thompson v. Wade, 69 N.Y.2d 570, 516 N.Y.S.2d 614, 509 N.E.2d 309 (1987) (servient estate transferred free of easement). Are there any other alternatives? See Williams v. Stirling, 40 Colo.App. 463, 583 P.2d 290 (1978) (easement retained by grantor in trust for third party).

3. Since a landowner cannot own an easement in his own land, the early common law had difficulty conceiving of how an easement could be severed from the fee at the time of a conveyance to be reserved in the grantor. The early English law coped with this problem by treating the reservation as a "regrant": A would deed the fee to B, B would regrant an easement to A. This created further complexities, however. For example, if the deed was a deed poll and thus not signed by B, did the regrant fail under the Statute of Frauds? If the deed failed to regrant the easement to A "and his heirs," did it only grant a life estate in the easement? For a time, courts dealt with this problem by conceiving the regrant as conveying a preexisting "quasi-easement." Modern courts have wisely chosen to ignore the problem altogether.

4. Tentative Draft Number One of the Restatement of Property (Third) Servitudes § 2.6 (1989) permits the creation of easements in third party beneficiaries, rejecting the majority rule to the contrary:

Third party beneficiaries—easements, Comment e.

Substantial authority supports the proposition that a single instrument of conveyance can be used to create and convey the benefit of an easement to one party and to convey the servient estate to another. See 2 American Law of Property § 8.29 (Casner ed. 1952); 3 Powell, Real Property ¶ 407, p. 34–39 (Rohan Rev.Ed.1986). R. Cunningham, W. Stoebuck & D. Whitman, Property § 8.3 at 444 (1984) characterizes the jurisdictions allowing easements and profits to be created in favor of third persons by language of reservation as a minority, "probably representing a trend." The rationale varies. The most modern approach recognizes that the instrument creates rights directly in the intended beneficiary of the easement. Earlier approaches treated the reservation in favor of the third party as an exception retained by the grantor, or an exception of pre-existing rights held by the third party.

5. The principle of reliance invoked in Willard is an important one in property law, as we have seen before. Sometimes it may be more important to preserve a settled rule of property law than to establish a more correct one. This position was taken by the N.Y. Court of Appeals in Estate of Thompson v. Wade, supra:

> Although application of the stranger-to-the-deed rule may, at times, frustrate a grantor's intent, any such frustration can readily be avoided by the direct conveyance of an easement of record from the grantor to the third party. The overriding considerations of the "public policy favoring certainty in title to real property, both to protect bona fide purchasers and to avoid conflicts of ownership, which may engender needless litigation" [ ], persuade us to decline to depart from our settled rule. We have previously noted that in this area of law, "where it can reasonably be assumed that settled rules are necessary and necessarily relied upon, stability and adherence to precedent are generally more important than a better or even a 'correct' rule of law" [ ] Consequently, we hold here that any right-of-way reserved to plaintiff's predecessor-in-interest in the defendant's deed was ineffective to create an express easement in plaintiff's favor.

What are the economic implications of the positions taken respectively by the California and New York courts? Do any ethical problems arise if an attorney, relying on settled law, advises a client that it is permissible for the client to transfer a property free of an easement because an earlier reservation of an easement to a third party at the time the client purchased the land was of no effect as the law does not recognize such reservations?

(b) By Implication From Pre–Existing Use or Necessity

The Statute of Frauds has not precluded the creation of easements by implication where specified requirements are met:

CORDWELL v. SMITH

Court of Appeals of Idaho, 1983.
105 Idaho 71, 665 P.2d 1081.

ON DENIAL OF PETITION FOR REHEARING

SWANSTROM, JUDGE.

The Cordwells brought this quiet title action to extinguish the claims of defendants who were asserting a right to use certain roadways crossing the Cordwells' property. The defendants contended that the roads provided the only reasonable access to their nearby properties. The trial court found that only one defendant had acquired a right to cross the Cordwells' property, and entered a judgment quieting title in the Cordwells against the claims of the other defendants. Not all of the defendants chose to appeal from the judgment. Only those who did are listed in the caption of this opinion.

The issues raised by appellants are: (1) Was the trial judge correct in concluding that there was no public roadway across the Cordwells' property as the result of prior use and expenditure of public funds for maintenance? (2) Did the court err in concluding appellants had not acquired easements by implication either from (a) apparent continuous use or (b) as a way of necessity? * * * Because we find no reversible error in the trial court, the judgment quieting title in favor of the Cordwells is affirmed.

The record shows the following background facts. The Cordwells own about three hundred twenty acres at the bottom of Little Baldy Creek Canyon in Kootenai County, Idaho. The property is located a few miles south of Interstate Highway 90 near the towns of Cataldo and Kingston. There is a public road leading from the Interstate at Cataldo southwesterly to Latour Creek where it crosses a northern corner of the Cordwell property. The Cordwells use this Latour Creek public road to reach their lands.

There is another, more circuitous way to Little Baldy Creek Canyon, over a system of roads beginning at Kingston. * * * An old logging road—called the Nordstrom road—leaves the public road in the vicinity of Frost Peak and descends northward through the steep forested canyon, onto the Cordwell lands, where it joins the Latour Creek road on the northern corner of the property. We will call this way the French Gulch route.

The Nordstrom road and two other old logging roads come together on the Cordwell property near the Latour Creek county road. One, the Mack road, runs easterly from the fork. The other two, the Ladd road and the Nordstrom road generally parallel Little Baldy Creek. These three roadways are the focus of this lawsuit. They were built and extended at several times, starting about 1930, as haul roads for the timber that was logged from the canyon.

Appellants own various small parcels of land to the south and east of the Cordwell property. They assert a right to use the Ladd, Mack and Nordstrom roads across the Cordwell property in order to gain access to their properties from the Latour Creek county road. On the other hand, the Cordwells claim ownership of the roads, contending that the roads are private, and that appellants have no right to use them.

All three of the roads were, and still are, narrow, one-lane, primitive mountain roads. They were built by loggers and were named after the persons who helped in their construction. There was testimony that the Mack road was built in 1930 by Mack so he could log timber along the road. There was other testimony that the Ladd and Nordstrom roads were started in 1934 by Ladd and finished later by Nordstrom in the 1940's.

The part of the Cordwell property through which the three roads run was once owned by Ole Ladd and his wife. Ladd, a logger, at one time lived on Little Baldy Creek. Ladd constructed some of the roads; and he permitted other loggers to use them and to build additions to them. Nordstrom was one such logger. Over the years as the logging progressed, he pushed the Nordstrom road higher up the canyon until it eventually met the public road near Frost Peak.

In 1946 Ladd charged Nordstrom ten cents per thousand board feet for the privilege of logging over the Nordstrom road. As a result of this logging activity there are many old spur logging roads branching off the Nordstrom road above the Cordwell property.

By 1950 Ladd had acquired other lands in Little Baldy Creek Canyon to the south and east of what is now the Cordwell property. In 1951 Ladd sold the 320 acres on the east to Russell & Pugh Lumber Company. In March, 1954, Ladd sold 280 acres on the south to the same purchaser. Finally in July, 1954, he sold all of his remaining property to buyers named Turcottes. This latter piece, some 240 acres, went through a series of subsequent transfers, until it was purchased by the Cordwells in November, 1968. No mention was made of access roads in any of the original conveyances by Ladd.

The first two parcels sold by Ladd in 1951 and 1954 to Russell-Pugh went through several later transfers. The subsequent owners divided these tracts and some adjacent property into pieces and advertized them for sale in a national sporting magazine. Some pieces were as small as ten and twenty acres. The appellants were among those persons who responded to this advertising and who purchased small tracts to the south and east of the Cordwell property in 1969 or the early 1970's. The trial judge found that all of the appellants, except one, acquired their properties "sight unseen." Most of the appellants testified to a belief that the Nordstrom road was a public road, but none of them had inquired about the validity of the access to their property over the roadways in question.

The Cordwells, on the other hand, who bought their property in two separate purchases in 1968 and 1969, have always insisted that the so-called Mack, Ladd, and Nordstrom roads on their property were private. The Cordwells did not live on the property. They attempted to control the use of the roads by others by installing a locked gate on their property near the Latour Creek road but these efforts were ineffective. They had a caretaker for a time in an attempt to curtail trespassing and vandalism.

When the appellants and others continued to assert a right to use the roads, the Cordwells brought this action to quiet title. The defendants filed counterclaims setting forth several theories to support their claims of right to use one or more of the three roads. As noted above, when the trial court ruled against all defendants but one, this appeal followed.

I

[The court held that the roads had not become public roads through the expenditure of public funds.]

II

We next consider the assertion that the trial court erred in ruling appellants had not acquired right-of-way easements by implication. There are two types of such "common law" easements. They may arise where the owner of property severs it and—without making provision by deed for access—conveys a part in such a manner that either the part conveyed or the part retained is cut off from a public road.

One such implied easement may be termed an easement from apparent continuous use. It relates to an existing private roadway which was in "apparent continuous use" by the common owner before the severance. The second type of implied easement is a "way of necessity." This easement, as the term suggests, arises strictly from necessity and does not depend upon the prior existence of a roadway in apparent continuous use.

The creation of either type of implied easement rests upon exceptions to the rule that written instruments speak for themselves. Because implied easements are in derogation of this rule, they are not favored by the courts. Those who assert the existence of an implied easement have the burden of proving facts which establish it. Davis v. Gowen, 83 Idaho 204, 360 P.2d 403 (1961). [ ]

A

We will first discuss the appellants' claim of an implied easement arising from apparent continuous use. In Davis v. Gowen, supra, our Supreme Court stated the essentials to be as follows:

> To establish an easement by implication in favor of the dominant estate, three essential elements must be made to appear;
>
> (1) Unity of title and subsequent separation by grant of dominant estate;
>
> (2) Apparent continuous user;
>
> (3) The easement must be reasonably necessary to the proper enjoyment of the dominant estate.

83 Idaho at 210, 360 P.2d at 406–07.

* * *

Appellants assert that in 1950–51, when Ole Ladd owned 840 acres in Little Baldy Creek drainage, the three roads in question provided access to the various parts of Ladd's property. Appellants contend that when Ladd—the former common owner—conveyed two parcels to Russell & Pugh Lumber Company in 1951 and in 1954, easements by implication over the existing roadways were created in favor of each parcel conveyed. The district judge accepted appellants' proof that there once had been a "unity of ownership" followed by a "separation" of dominant and servient estates.

However, our view of the record discloses that some appellants are claiming easements to lands that were never part of Ole Ladd's holdings. An easement by implication can only arise as to the lands owned and severed by the former common owner. [ ] The parcels owned by appellants Fairbanks, Dotson, Sherick, and Long are all located in the east half of Section 17, Township 48 North, Range 1 East. Appellant Livich owns one parcel in the east half of Section 17 and another parcel, some distance away, in the west half of the section. Ole Ladd owned no property in the east half of Section 17. It is clear that no easement by implication arose as to any of the parcels located in the east half of Section 17. To this extent we agree with the Cordwells' contention, that no unity of ownership was proven. The district judge erred, but it was an error that benefited rather than harmed these appellants. The district judge's finding was correct with respect to the parcels located in the west half of Section 17, which are owned by Mathis, Livich, Solido, Smith, Schafer, and Smock. It was also correct as to the parcels owned by appellant Coyne in the northwest quarter of the southwest quarter of Section 8, Township 48 North, Range 1 East.

We next examine whether those appellants who did meet the unity of title test also met the second requirement—a showing of "apparent continuous user." We gather, from the discussion of this requirement in Close v. Rensink, [95 Idaho 72, 501 P.2d 1382 (1972)], that "apparent continuous user" refers to use before separation of the lands. That is, the common owner must have used the premises and the system of roadways long enough to show that the roadways were intended to provide permanent access to those lands which are later severed.

The district judge's findings, accurately summarizing the evidence, are not disputed. They show that all of the roads in question were originally constructed to haul logs from the Ladd property. The judge found "no evidence or presumption that they were to remain as permanent access roads." Most of the logging was done between 1930 and 1952. Mack, Ladd, and Nordstrom probably completed all logging use of the roads prior to 1953.

There is no evidence of the use of these roads by any of the appellants' predecessors in interest between 1951, when Ladd sold the first of two large tracts to Russell–Pugh, and 1969, when some of the appellants began acquiring smaller parcels of the same property. More importantly, it has not been shown that once Ladd completed his logging in the area, he used the roads for any purpose except to reach his home. His home was located on the tract of land he sold last, the one ultimately acquired by the Cordwells. Thus, at the times Ladd severed his ownership of the whole 840 acres, there was no continuous use being made of the roads leading from the parcel he retained and occupied to the parcels he conveyed to Russell–Pugh.

There also was no evidence to show what use, if any, Russell–Pugh made of the property during the ten years that it retained ownership before selling to subsequent owners who started subdividing the property. The trial court found that the only intervening use of the roads since 1953, shown by the evidence, was by hunters, woodcutters, berry pickers, and snowmobilers—all either trespassers or strangers to appellants' chain of title. We hold that the trial judge was correct in concluding that none of the appellants acquired easements by implication from "apparent continuous use" of the roads across the Cordwells' property. They failed to prove that the use made of the roads, before separation took place, was of a type and duration sufficient to satisfy the "apparent continuous user" test. Having reached that conclusion concerning this requirement, there is no need to discuss here whether the third part of the test for this type of implied easement was met by appellants.

We turn next to appellants' assertion that they have an implied easement by "way of necessity." Such necessity can arise when the owner of land conveys part thereof to another, and the part conveyed is without ingress or egress except over the lands retained. [ ] Martino v. Fleenor, 148 Colo. 136, 365 P.2d 247 (Colo.1961). The Idaho Supreme Court, quoting from Martino, and from 17A Am.Jur. 668–69, Easements, § 58, said in Burley Brick & Sand Company v. Cofer, 102 Idaho 333, 335, 629 P.2d 1166, 1168 (1981):

> Although a way of necessity is sometimes confused with an easement arising, on severance of title, from a pre-existing use, there is a definite distinction between them, mainly because a way of necessity does not rest on a pre-existing use but on the need for a way across the granted or reserved premises. A way of necessity is an easement arising from an implied grant or implied reservation; it is a common-law origin and is supported by the rule of sound public policy that lands should not be rendered unfit for occupancy or successful cultivation. Such a way is the result of the application of the presumption that whenever a party conveys property, he conveys whatever is necessary for the beneficial use of that property and retains whatever is necessary for the beneficial use of land he still possesses. Thus, the legal basis of a way of necessity is the presumption of a grant arising from the circumstances of the case. This presumption of a grant, however, is one of fact, and whether a grant should be implied depends upon the terms of the deed and the facts in each particular case.

> A way of necessity arises where there is a conveyance of a part of a tract of land of such nature and extent that either the part conveyed or the part retained is entirely surrounded by the land from which it is severed or by this land and the land of strangers. It is a universally established principle that where a tract of land is conveyed which is separated from the highway by other lands of the grantor or surrounded by his lands or by his and those of third persons, there arises, by implication, in favor of the grantee, a way of necessity across the premises of the grantor to the highway.

Thus, appellants here had the burden of proving they met three requirements: first, that their properties were once part of the larger tract held under one ownership prior to a division of the tract; second, that a necessity for the roadway existed at the time of the severance; and third, that the present necessity for the particular right-of-way is great. [   ]

As noted earlier, the trial court erred in finding that all appellants had met the first requirement of "unity of title" by a predecessor in interest. Some had not. As to the remaining appellants, the question is whether they proved that "necessity" existed at the time of severance and at the time of the lawsuit, and that the necessity was "great."

Concerning these two requirements, it should be reemphasized that the existence of a way of necessity does not depend upon what use the common owner was making of the roads existing at the time of severance. Such easement could arise even if at the time of severance there was no road across the grantor's property to the part conveyed. Thus, a remote grantee of land not being used at the time of severance—as in the present case—may nevertheless, when the use becomes necessary to the enjoyment of his property, claim the easement under this remote deed. [   ]

A way of necessity arises from public policy considerations. It is, literally, a creature of necessity. The necessity must exist at the time of the severance by the common owner, and the person claiming such an easement must also show there is a present necessity for it. Once established, a way of necessity exists only so long as the necessity lasts, for it is the policy of the law not to burden a servient estate more or longer than is necessary.

The trial court made no finding of necessity at the time of severance. Rather, the court noted, "There is no evidence or presumption that * * * [the Mack, Ladd, and Nordstrom roads] were to remain as permanent access roads." In any event, it cannot be presumed that the present owners have the same necessity for access roads which might have existed at the time of severance. When lands have been severed, the grantee—or his successors in interest—cannot, by subdividing, create a new and different "necessity" for rights-of-way, where no such necessity existed before the severance. [   ] A remote grantee cannot create the necessity upon which he relies. If the way of necessity was not implied at the time of the grants by Ladd in 1951 and 1954, it cannot be established by a subsequent necessity arising out of subdividing or other changed circumstances. [   ]

Moreover, the "present" necessity must be great.

* * *

Where a person claiming a way of necessity to a piece of property has other adjoining lands that abut on a public way, he may not be entitled to a way of necessity across lands of his grantor or across lands of strangers except in cases of "strict" necessity. [   ]

However, the degree of necessity is not so great where the lands of the person claiming a way of necessity are entirely cut off from access to a public way by the grantor's lands and by lands of strangers. In such a case the general rule is that the claimant need only establish a reasonable necessity for the claimed route. [ ] This standard for the degree of necessity required is comparable to the standard used in the Idaho private condemnation actions. * * *

In summation, we hold that the legal burden which each appellant had to carry on the issue of necessity was to establish by competent evidence that the route across the Cordwells' property was at the time of severance—and still is—the only reasonable means of access to the property of each appellant. Necessarily, this means proving that the French Gulch route was not reasonably adequate. Mere inconvenience would not suffice. Substantial inconvenience may be an important factor, but it must be weighed against the inconvenience and possible damage that could result to the Cordwells as a result of imposing an easement across their property. * * *

* * *

The trial court, "after weighing the pros and cons of each access," reached the conclusion that the French Gulch route provided appellants with reasonable access to their properties. He held they were not entitled to a way of necessity across the Cordwells' property. We are satisfied that the trial judge understood and applied the correct legal standard. We now examine whether his finding, that the French Gulch route provided appellants with reasonable access to their properties, was supported by substantial and competent evidence.

* * *

We focus our attention on the Nordstrom road, which is the subject of the other appellants' claims of easements by necessity. The trial judge determined, in essence, that these appellants had proven no present, great necessity to use the lower, northern end of the Nordstrom road, where it crosses the Cordwells' property, because the upper, southern end of the road provides access to each of the appellants' properties through the French Gulch route. In reaching this determination the trial judge made findings which we summarize as follows.

* * *

The area where appellants' tracts are located is steep, mountainous, forested country. The evidence shows that, until appellants purchased these scattered tracts there was no asserted need for year-round access to the area. None of the old logging roads beyond Ole Ladd's dwelling were kept open in the winter. With the exception of the Roush tract—not at issue in this appeal—none of the tracts has been occupied nor improved.

When weighing the relative convenience and practicality of the Cordwell road and the French Gulch route, the trial judge was faced with the undisputed fact that neither route would afford convenient, dependable access during several months of winter each year to many of the tracts involved in this suit. It would be necessary, with either route, to expend considerable money and effort in order to have year-round access by wheeled vehicles. Although many appellants apparently bought their property "site" unseen, they must have been aware they were purchasing property at a location, and in a climate, where there would be limited utility and access during the winter months.

In conclusion, the uncontroverted record shows that access through the Cordwell property would be easier, but both routes are presently available in fair weather and both are unavailable or treacherous during the winter. In view of this evidence, we hold that it was not clearly erroneous for the trial judge to find appellants had proven no present, great necessity to cross the Cordwell property. Therefore, we sustain the judge's determination that there was no easement by necessity.

* * *

We affirm the judgment. * * *

Notes and Questions

1. About 30 states have statutes permitting the acquisition of servitudes by necessity. These statutes usually provide that private landowners whose property is landlocked may petition a public authority to condemn a way for them across neighboring properties, with the cost of compensation to be borne by the landowner seeking the easement. See Iowa Code Ann. § 471.4(2); Kan.Stat.Ann. § 68–117. Where such laws exist, is there any need to imply easements (Idaho has such a law)? Do such laws violate the Fifth Amendment to the United States Constitution (applied to the states through the Fourteenth Amendment) which only permits taking of private property for public use?

2. Is the law of implied easements based on an attempt to discern and effectuate the intent of the parties whose conveyance originally severed the dominant and servient estate, or is it rather based on resolving the inefficiencies caused by cutting off property from access to public roads, sewers, etc? If the parties to the original conveyance clearly did not intend the creation of an easement, but did clearly intend that access be cut off, should the courts enforce this intent in spite of the public policy to the contrary? See Luthy v. Keehner, 90 Ill.App.3d 127, 45 Ill.Dec. 509, 412 N.E.2d 1091 (1980) (whether or not easement of necessity is created is question of intent at time of conveyance). White v. Landerdahl, 191 Mont. 554, 625 P.2d 1145 (1981) (easement will not be implied if intent to the contrary); Jones v. Weiss, 570 P.2d 948 (Okla.1977) (intent to create easement of way presumed unless evidence of intent clearly to contrary).

3. How necessary must the particular access route be to support the grant of an easement by necessity? Should it be sufficient that an alternative access route is sometimes impassible? See Broyhill v. Coppage, 79 N.C.App. 221, 339 S.E.2d 32 (1986) (yes); Justus v. Dotson, 168 W.Va. 320, 285 S.E.2d 129 (1981) (flooding 3 to 4 times a year of alternative access road that could be eliminated by drainage not enough to justify implication

of easement by necessity over road that remained dry). Should it be sufficient that no other route to a public road presently exists if it would in fact be possible to gain access by building a new road without traversing a neighboring property? See Schwob v. Green, 215 N.W.2d 240 (Iowa 1974) (no). Should the cost of gaining access by alternative routes be considered relative to the value of using the landlocked parcel productively? See Miller v. Schmitz, 80 Ill.App.3d 911, 36 Ill.Dec. 68, 400 N.E.2d 488 (1980) (yes, where pre-existing quasi-easement forms basis of implication). If access is possible by boat, can the court impose an easement by necessity over land? Compare Peasley v. State, 102 Misc.2d 982, 424 N.Y.S.2d 995 (Ct.Cl.1980) (no, if access over navigable water), with Attaway v. Davis, 288 Ark. 478, 707 S.W.2d 302 (1986); Hancock v. Henderson, 236 Md. 98, 202 A.2d 599 (1964) (yes, if access over water not suitable to reasonable use). A lower level of "reasonable" necessity is required to imply an easement from pre-existing use, Moody v. Sun, 127 A.D.2d 570, 511 N.Y.S.2d 646 (1987). See J. Bruce and J. Ely, The Law of Easements and Licenses in Land, ¶¶ 4.02, 4.03 (1988).

4. Should the court's decision whether or not to imply an easement turn on whether the easement is claimed by the grantor or grantee of the dominant parcel—i.e. whether the easement is claimed by implied grant or implied reservation? Would a claim of easement by implied reservation conflict with the covenants against encumbrances, of warranty, and of further assurances given in the initial deed? (See discussion in chapter five.) Though some cases reject the possibility of implying a servitude to the benefit of a grantor who failed expressly to retain such a servitude, the First Restatement states that "whether the claimant is the conveyor or conveyee" is merely a factor to consider in deciding whether to imply a servitude, § 476(a), and the proposed Third Restatement permits implication of servitudes by necessity in either the grantor or grantee of the dominant estate, § 2.15.

5. To imply an easement from the pre-existence of a quasi-easement, the courts normally insist that the prior use was "apparent", such that the grantor and grantee of the servient parcel were aware of its existence, and probable continued use. This requirement has been stretched a good deal in cases involving underground utilities, which often are not visible, but which usually are of great value to the dominant parcel and impose a minimal burden on the servient parcel. See Otero v. Pacheco, 94 N.M. 524, 612 P.2d 1335 (App.1980); Eichengrun, The Problem of Hidden Easements and the Subsequent Purchaser Without Notice, 40 Okla.L.Rev. 3 (1987).

6. The 1944 First Restatement of Property (Servitudes) attempted to consolidate the law of implied easements. Section 474 of the Restatement stated that when land under common ownership was divided, an implied easement could arise. Section 476 enumerated factors to consider in determining whether to imply an easement in this circumstance, including: "(a) whether the claimant is the conveyor or the conveyee, (b) the terms of the conveyance, (c) the consideration given for it, (d) whether the claim is made against a simultaneous conveyee, (e) the extent of necessity of the easement to the claimant, (f) whether reciprocal benefits result to the conveyor and the conveyee, (g) the manner in which the land was used prior to the conveyance, and (h) the extent to which the manner of prior

use was or might have been known to the parties." The 1989 Tentative Draft of the Third Restatement of Property, reflecting the continued practice of the courts, backs off from this consolidation and treats easements implied from pre-existing use, and easements implied from necessity, under two separate sections (§§ 2.12 and 2.15, respectively).

(c) By Prescription

PLETTNER v. SULLIVAN

Supreme Court of Nebraska, 1983.
214 Neb. 636, 335 N.W.2d 534.

SHANAHAN, JUSTICE.

Defendants, Earl W., Sr. and Ruth E. Sullivan, appeal the decree of the District Court for Douglas County that the plaintiffs, John J. and Doris E. Plettner, and Joel A. and Bernice Plettner, through adverse possession, have acquired title to certain real estate otherwise described in the defendants' deed and, further, have acquired a prescriptive easement in part of the road located in the disputed area. Sullivans claim that Plettners have not satisfied the elements of adverse possession and a prescriptive right. We affirm in part as modified and reverse in part.

Plettners' land, acquired by deed, adjoins Sullivans' land located to the east. Both Plettners and Sullivans have a common grantor, Lehar Valley Farms, which is also known as Fremont Hatchery (Hatchery).

In 1962 Plettners bought their parcel from the Hatchery. From 1962 until 1978 the Plettners and the Hatchery jointly used a road which provided access to the Plettner tract located west of the road. On the east side of this road and on the land owned by the Hatchery, there were buildings designated as "chickenhouse # 3" and "chickenhouse # 4." Chickenhouse # 4 was located near the southwest corner of the Hatchery tract and was some 300 feet in length, running north and south. Attached at the northeast corner of chickenhouse # 4 was a fence which, likewise, was attached to the southwest corner of chickenhouse # 3 located north of chickenhouse # 4. From chickenhouse # 3 a fence then ran north to the northern boundary of the property. The road which provided common access for Plettners and the Hatchery ran parallel with and the length of chickenhouse # 4.

In 1963 Plettners planted a row of trees 20 feet west of chickenhouse # 4 and parallel to the road. In 1972 Plettners improved the road by making it "rock-topped." From 1971 to 1973 the Plettners built three cabins west of the road, for which the only access was the road mentioned. Plettners believed the boundary was located 10 feet west of chickenhouses # 3 and # 4, respectively. The Hatchery did not conduct any of its activities on any land lying west of the road. This situation persisted until 1978, when the Hatchery ceased its operations on the tract east of the road.

On July 28, 1979, Sullivans bought their tract from the Hatchery and then obtained a survey for their property. The Sullivan survey disclosed that the true boundary between the Plettner parcel and the tract acquired by the Sullivans was actually 30 feet west of the chickenhouses. Based on the survey, Sullivans erected a fence on August 8, 1979. This fence was located in the road west of the chickenhouses and prevented access to the Plettner parcel from the road. On August 10, 1979, Plettners filed a quiet title action.

The trial court held that Plettners had acquired by adverse possession all land lying west of a line located 10 feet from the chickenhouses. Also, the trial court held that each party acquired a prescriptive easement 10 feet wide on each side of the boundary determined with respect to chickenhouse # 4, so that each of the parties acquired a "reciprocal easement" as a result of their adverse possession. Such "reciprocal easement" was restricted to access for land on either side of the road, with the additional restriction on the Sullivan prescriptive easement that it existed for "building maintenance purposes only." As a consequence of such determination by the District Court, Sullivans lost approximately one-half of the road to Plettners through adverse possession but gained a prescriptive easement in that part of the road gained by the Plettners.

On appeal the crucial question relates to exclusive possession on the part of Plettners.

* * *

To establish title by adverse possession the claimant must show by a preponderance of evidence that such claimant has been in actual, open, exclusive, continuous, and adverse possession under a claim of ownership for 10 years. [ ] To acquire a prescriptive easement a claimant must prove virtually the same elements required for adverse possession, namely, the claimant must show that the use and enjoyment of the land is exclusive, adverse, continuous, open, and under claim of right for 10 years. [ ]

Acquisition of a prescriptive easement differs in certain features from the acquisition of title by adverse possession. See, Annot., 27 A.L.R.2d 332, n. 5 at 334–35 (1953); [ ] Adverse possession provides the claimant with title to the land, while a prescriptive easement provides the claimant with only a limited use or enjoyment of another's land. [ ] Also, the conduct required for adverse possession differs from that required for a prescriptive easement. For adverse possession there must be possession and occupation of the land, which involves acts of dominion by a claimant which will place the owner on notice that the claimant is asserting ownership of the land. [ ] Such adverse possession must exclude all others, including the true owner. [ ] In contrast, to acquire a prescriptive easement there needs to be only an adverse use for the prescriptive period. [ ]

In the present case Plettners occupied the land lying west of the road. The Plettners planted trees at the west edge of that road in 1963. The evidence is clear that Plettners claimed as their own that land west of the road. Plettners demonstrated their dominion over the land west of the road, and their occupancy of the land was to the exclusion of all others. Plettners, by a preponderance of the evidence, have proved the elements of adverse possession regarding the land west of the road. The District Court judge was correct in determining the boundaries, but should have excluded the road from the area acquired by adverse possession. Regarding the road itself, Plettners have failed to prove that they occupied the road, to the exclusion of the Hatchery. The absence of the required exclusivity prevents Plettners' acquisition of title by adverse possession with respect to the road.

The question remains whether Plettners have acquired a prescriptive easement in the jointly used road. One acquires a prescriptive easement through use which is exclusive, adverse, under a claim of right, continuous and uninterrupted, and open and notorious for the full prescriptive period. [ ] Where the claimant-user shows that the use has been open, visible, continuous, and unmolested for the prescriptive period, the use is presumed to be under a claim of right. [ ]

The evidence establishes that Plettners used the road after their purchase of the land in 1962 until their use was prevented by the fence erected by Sullivans in 1979. The Hatchery acknowledged that Plettners had a right to use the road for access to Plettners' land, and certainly such use of the road was viewed by Plettners as vital to the continued enjoyment of their land west of the road. The common or joint use of the road by the Hatchery and Plettners existed for a period in excess of 16 years, until the Hatchery conveyed the land east of the road to Sullivans in 1979.

Finally, while Plettners lacked exclusive possession to acquire title to the road, they did have exclusive use to gain a prescriptive easement. Whereas the exclusivity required for adverse possession relates to "all others" or to "all the world," the exclusive use for acquisition of a prescriptive right or prescriptive easement is not so comprehensive. The word exclusive in reference to a prescriptive easement does not mean that there must be use only by one person but, rather, means that the use cannot be dependent upon a similar right in others, i.e., the user must exclude the public at large. [ ] Exclusion of the owner is not required for acquisition of a prescriptive easement. [ ] Here, the Plettners' use excluded the public at large.

Consequently, Plettners did acquire a prescriptive easement in the road. Sullivans, as successors to the Hatchery, still own the land on which the road in question is located, but Sullivans' land is subject to the prescriptive easement in the road.

For the reasons given above, the judgment and decree of the District Court is affirmed with respect to the adverse possession of Plettners, except there is no adverse possession of that land on which the road is located. The judgment and decree of the District Court is reversed concerning the reciprocal easements, and the District Court is directed to enter judgment that Plettners have a prescriptive easement regarding the road in question.

Affirmed in Part as Modified, and in Part Reversed.

Notes and Questions

1. English prescription law was based on use of the easement since "time immemorial" and, later, on a fiction that a prescriptive easement was created by a lost grant. See Stoebuck, The Fiction of Presumed Grant, 15 U.Kan.L.Rev. 17 (1966). The fiction of the lost grant (i.e., that the use of the easement was based originally on a grant from the owner of the servient estate which was subsequently lost) was picked up in early American cases, and persists in a few jurisdictions. It has largely been abandoned, however, in favor of approaches to prescription that rely on analogies to adverse possession. In theory, the lost grant and adverse possession approaches are diametrically opposed, the lost grant theory being based on an originally permissive use, the adverse possession approach, on adverse use. Results under the two doctrines may also diverge in some particulars. What, for example, would be the relevance of the disability of the owner of the property during the prescriptive period under a lost grant theory? See II American Law of Property, § 8.61 (J. Casner ed. 1952).

2. Though the law of prescription by and large has come to be based on the law of adverse possession, prescription and adverse possession diverge at several points. One difference, noted in the principal case is the role of exclusivity. Since the doctrine of prescription is based on use rather than possession, it makes little sense to require that the claimant of the easement establish exclusive dominion over the easement. Nonetheless, some courts have refused to recognize easements by prescription where the landowner and claimant both used the easement in common, holding that the use was permissive. See Howard v. Wright, 38 Nev. 25, 143 P. 1184 (1941). Where the public in general uses a road, it is more difficult for a private claimant to establish an exclusive adverse use unless his or her use was substantially different from the common use. Courts often treat public uses as permissive, and place a heavy burden on any one claimant to prove his use adverse to the owner.

3. It may also be more difficult for a claimant of a prescriptive use to establish that use of the easement was continuous, since use of an easement, unlike possession of property, is by its nature intermittent. For the same reason, it may be difficult to establish that use of an easement was open and notorious. Courts apply a reasonable construction to these requirements. Where state adverse possession statutes require color of title or payment of taxes to establish adverse possession, courts are split as to whether these requirements must also be fulfilled to establish prescription.

4. You are advising a client, A, who complains that his neighbor, B, repeatedly uses a lane that runs across A's field to get to B's own field. What must your client do to interrupt use of an easement and thus stop the running of the prescriptive period? Is it enough to post a no-trespassing sign? To build a fence across the easement? Would use be interrupted by construction of a fence containing a gate at the point where the claimed easement meets the fence? Would use be interrupted by a lawsuit that resulted in a judgment in favor of the landowner, but in fact did not end

use of the easement? See City of Derby v. Diyanno, 142 Conn. 708, 118 A.2d 308 (1955) (no trespassing sign not sufficient if it did not end use of easement); Margoline v. Holefelder, 420 Pa. 544, 218 A.2d 227 (1966) (to terminate prescription barrier must be erected that is intended to stop adverse use and that is effective in accomplishing this goal). See G. Korngold, Private Land Use Arrangements, § 3.33 (1990); 3 R. Powell, & P. Rohan, Powell on Real Property, ¶ 413 (1991).

5. You are instead advising B who used the lane. She has been driving across A's field for eight years to get her equipment in and out of her own adjacent field. The prescriptive period in your jurisdiction is ten years. A has recently placed a no trespassing sign at the entrance of the lane. You do a quick title search of both properties and find that they have never been under common ownership since they were owned by the federal government in the nineteenth century. How do you advise B to proceed?

6. Perhaps the most effective way for A to keep B from establishing prescriptive rights would be for A to grant B permission to use the lane, thus making B's use non-adverse. Determining when use of an easement is permissive is not always an easy task. Permission can of course be granted in writing or orally. It can also be inferred from a neighborly, cooperative relationship. See Hassigner v. Kline, 91 A.D.2d 988, 457 N.Y.S.2d 847 (1983). Cases have also held that the erection of fences with gates demonstrates an intention to assert ownership with an implied grant of permission to cross. See Pierce v. Jones, 207 Ark. 139, 142, 179 S.W.2d 454, 456 (1944). Should B be able to refuse A's permission, instead asserting an adverse claim? See generally on permission, G. Korngold, Private Land Use Arrangements, § 3.29 (1990).

(d) Irrevocable License

CAMP v. MILAM

Supreme Court of Alabama, 1973.
291 Ala. 12, 277 So.2d 95.

Jones, Justice.

* * *

In 1957 the Camps purchased a tract of land in Jefferson County, Alabama, for $9,000.00. Later the Camps wished to have an artificial lake constructed on the property. Mr. Camp discussed the plan to build a lake with Milam, who was an engineer and in the construction business. Milam offered to construct the dam for the Camps in return for part of the land and the right to use the lake. On October 26, 1959, Camp and Milam signed a written agreement which provided that Milam would construct an earthen dam on the Camp's property in exchange for 40 acres of the land, the description of which to be mutually agreed upon at a later date. The said agreement also contained the provision that "free access to the entire lake will be available to both parties, herein".

The dam was completed sometime in 1960 or 1961, and the Milams began to use the lake from time to time for recreational purposes. In

1965 the Milams decided to build a home at the lake and asked the Camps to convey the land as provided in the written agreement of October 26, 1959. The Camps did convey, at the Milams' request, a tract of about 25 acres in June, 1965, to A.C. Barrett & Associates, Inc. (Associates), a corporation owned and controlled by the Milam family. The deed executed by the Camps stated therein that the conveyance was subject to the restrictions and limitations contained in a certain written agreement between the Camps and "Associates" dated June 15, 1965. This agreement provided, inter alia, that the Camps would convey the described realty; that the Camps could at any time raise the level of the lake from 871.00 to 881.00; that there would be no construction on the property lying between the lake and the "Associates'" property (the Camps had retained a 10–foot strip of land all around the lake for use as a walkway or roadway); mutual easements would be granted to insure free access to their respective property.

The Milams completed their home on the 25–acre tract in July, 1965, and on August 1, 1965, that property was conveyed to the Milams by "Associates". Since 1965, the Milams have constructed a boathouse and stable on land owned by the Camps with their knowledge and consent. The lake has been used by the Milams for recreational purposes continually from the time of its completion until 1970, when the Camps sent the sheriff in to remove the Milams from "their" lake.

The bill of complaint in this case was originally filed by the Camps against the Milams and subsequently amended to add "Associates" as a party respondent. The bill charged that the Milams had been making use of a lake lying wholly on property owned by the Camps in such a manner as to interfere with the use and enjoyment of the lake by the Camps; specifically, by constructing a boathouse on the shore of the lake on property which was in exclusive possession of the Camps, and operating a motor boat in such a manner as to deprive the Camps of free use of the lake, and in building a stable on the Camps' property.

The prayer of the bill asked the court to declare that the Camps had sole and exclusive rights to the use of the lake and that the respondents had no interest therein. The bill also prayed that the court issue a permanent injunction barring the respondents from the use of the lake and ordering them to remove the stable and boathouse constructed upon the Camps' property.

The Milams filed an answer and crossbill in which they asserted that the Camps, on October 26, 1959, had agreed that the Milams, their heirs and assigns, would have free access to the lake and full water rights in the lake appurtenant to the ownership and title to certain real property described in a warranty deed dated June 15, 1965, executed by the Camps to "Associates". The cross-bill further averred that in reliance upon said agreement of October 26, 1959, the Milams constructed a dam to make the lake and that from the date of the completion of the dam until the present the Milams and "Associates" had exercised full possessory rights in and to all water rights of the lake including, but not limited to, fishing and swimming therein and operating power motor boats and skiing thereon.

The cross-bill further averred that in reliance on the agreement of October 26, 1959, the Milams constructed for themselves and for the benefit of "Associates" a brick home at a cost of approximately $55,-000.00 and a basement at a cost of approximately $4,000.00. The cross-bill further alleged that the water rights in the lake were necessary and incident to the real property conveyed in said deed from the Camps to "Associates" as to greatly and materially enhance the value of the property and that the water rights were necessary and incident to the reasonable and convenient use and enjoyment of the real property so conveyed. The cross-bill also averred that the water rights constituted an easement and covenant running with the land.

The prayer of the cross-bill asked the court to decree that "Associates", its successors and assigns (Milams), own and have complete and full water rights in the lake and that the said water rights were an easement appurtenant to and running with the land conveyed in said deed.

* * *

The trial court rendered its final decree in which the relief sought by the Camps was denied in its entirety. The court further decreed that "Associates", its successors and assigns (Milams), own and have title to all water rights in and to the lake and that such water rights are an easement appurtenant to and running with the real property conveyed by warranty deed dated June 15, 1965, from the Camps to "Associates". The decree also states that the Camps own and have title to all water rights in the lake, such water rights also being an easement appurtenant to and running with the real property owned by the Camps. The Camps' application for rehearing having been denied, they bring this appeal.

The Camps claim error and contend that they have exclusive ownership of the entire property on which the lake in question is situated and that no easement or other interest in and to said lake has been granted to the Milams, nor have the Milams otherwise acquired such interest. The Camps further contend that the use made of said lake by the Milams was at best a mere license revocable at the pleasure of the Camps.

The Milams, on the other hand, assert that they own full and complete water rights common with that of the Camps, and that the chancellor correctly construed the deed of June 15, 1965, giving effect to the intent of the parties as set forth in the final decree.

The court is of the opinion that the facts of this case, in keeping with the law applicable thereto, do not support the contentions of either party, we find no basis in the law for the legal conclusion of the court below that the Camps conveyed, or attempted or intended to convey, an easement to the water rights of said lake to "Associates" or its assigns (Milams).

The rules of construction of a written contract, including a deed, are well established by our cases. Where a court of equity is called upon to construe a deed (or other written contract), in ascertaining the intention of the parties, the plain and clear meaning of its terms must be given effect to, and the parties must be legally presumed to have intended what is plainly and clearly set out.

In the absence of fraud or mistake, it is only where the instrument is doubtful of meaning, or its language ambiguous, that the court may look beyond the "four corners" of the instrument to give clarity and specificity of meaning. [   ]

Our cases consistently hold that an easement can be created in only three ways: by deed; by prescription; or by adverse use for the statutory period. [   ] Since the latter two do not apply (use by permission in this case is neither adverse nor exclusive), we must look to the deed and referenced agreement made between the parties on June 15, 1965.

Our difficulty here lies in the fact that there is nothing unclear or ambiguous in either the deed or the referenced agreement, neither of which contain any language purporting to convey an easement in the lake. The trial court, then, was powerless to declare a new and different contract into which the parties did not enter. [   ]

Therefore, the trial court's interpretation of the deed, as set forth in its final decree, constitutes a reformation of the contract between the parties which is unauthorized by either the pleadings or the proof. [   ]

Having thus concluded, however, we are likewise constrained to the further conclusion that the relief sought by the complainants is also unauthorized. We hold that a legal interest did pass from the Camps to the Milams—not the granting of an easement as contended by the Milams and as found by the trial court, and not a revocable license as contended by the Camps—but an irrevocable license for the reasonable use of the lake commensurate with its size and nature and as originally contemplated and intended by the parties.

Generally speaking, the term "license" has been used in the common law to denote the doing of an act, i.e., the giving of one's consent. The revocability of a license is grounded on this concept. Since the granting of a license is the giving of one's permission to another to do a certain thing (or, in the case of a negative license, the consent for the benefit of another not to do a certain thing), this license is revocable at the will of the licensor, simply by the withdrawing of his permission. [   ] At the root of this concept is the familiar and often quoted language from Thomas v. Sorrell, 124 Eng.Rep. 1098, 1109:

> "A * * * licence properly passeth no interest, nor alters or transfers property in anything, but only makes an action lawful, which without it had been unlawful. As a licence to go beyond the seas, to hunt in a

man's park, to come into his house, are only actions, which without licence, had been unlawful."

To prevent possible injustice the law began to recognize that the giving of one's permission to another for the doing of certain acts with respect to the property of the former did not necessarily carry with it the unlimited right to withdraw the consent. The concept was broadened to look upon the license not merely as the giving of consent, but, in certain instances, the conferring of a legal right—a license coupled with an interest. From this broadened concept of a license came the ingrafting of the recognized exception to the general rule which may be stated thusly:

"A license has been generally defined as a mere personal privilege * * * revocable at the will of the * * * (licensor) unless * * * in the meantime expenditures contemplated by the licensor when the license was given have been made * * * " [7]

Thus, when expenditures contemplated by the licensor have been made by the licensee, the license, having been acted upon so as to greatly benefit the licensor, is said to have been executed. An executed license, for reasons founded upon the equitable principle of estoppel, becomes irrevocable and confers upon the licensee a substantive equitable right in the property.

This interpretation and rule was adopted by this court in our decision in Rhodes v. Otis, 33 Ala. 578, wherein this court stated that:

"It would be against all conscience to permit the defendant to revoke his license, after the plaintiff had acted upon it so far that great damage must necessarily result from the revocation. Every reason upon which the doctrine of estoppel In pais rests, applies. It is a plain case, where one party has, by his conduct, induced another to act in such a manner, that he cannot be allowed to retract without serious injury to that other person. We think a denial of the right of revocation, under such circumstances, is consistent with justice and right, supported by the analogies of the law, and many respectable decisions.[   ]"

* * *

Applying these legal principles to the facts of this case, we hold that the Milams became licensees and that this license extended to, and included, the reasonable use of the lake for purposes of swimming, fishing, boating, and other such reasonable uses as originally contemplated by the parties consistent with the Camps' right to common use thereof. We further hold that this license, when acted upon by the Milams through their expenditures in building the dam to the benefit of the Camps (constituting a consideration), became irrevocable; but this irrevocable status does not operate to expand or increase the nature and extent of its use.

7. City of Owensboro v. Cumberland Telephone & Telegraph Co., 230 U.S. 58, 64, 33 S.Ct. 988, 990, 57 L.Ed. 1389, 1393 (1913).

It is clear from the evidence that so long as the Milams so limited their use of the lake, and so long as both parties enjoyed its common use, the Camps registered no objection and made no attempt to withdraw their permission. It was only when the Milams exceeded the permission granted by monopolizing the use of the lake so as to impede the Camps' right of common use, that the Camps objected and attempted to withdraw all consent for the use of the lake by the Milams.

While it is our holding that the Camps have no legal standing to enjoin the Milams' use of the lake, this holding is not to be construed to mean that the Camps do not have legal authority to restrict the Milams to its reasonable use as contemplated by the parties.

We further hold that this license of the Milams, although irrevocable, is by its very nature personal; and, being a personal right, it is not an interest which attaches to or runs with the land, nor can it be assigned, conveyed or inherited. Neither can the use of the lake under this license ever ripen into an easement by prescription, however long continued. [ ]

In view of the above stated conclusions, we find that the trial court was correct in denying the complainants' prayer for the specific relief sought (i.e., to enjoin the Milams from all use of the lake). However, the trial court erred in granting the relief sought by the respondents in their cross-bills.

Consequently, this cause must be reversed and remanded for further proceedings not inconsistent herewith.

Affirmed in part and reversed in part and remanded.

Notes and Questions

1. Licenses were discussed briefly in the introduction to this section as revocable privileges. Under certain circumstances, however, illustrated by the principal case, licenses may become irrevocable by estoppel. See Restatement of Property (Third) Servitudes, Tentative Draft I (1989), § 2.10(1). Most commonly this occurs when the owner of a dominant estate makes substantial expenditures relying on a servitude created orally, and thus not in compliance with the Statute of Frauds. Licenses coupled with interests, i.e. licenses to come onto land to remove chattels, are also not subject to revocation until the chattel is removed. See II American Law of Property, § 8.114 (J. Casner ed. 1952); J. Bruce and J. Ely, The Law of Easements and Licenses in Land, ¶ 10.06 (1988).

2. How does the interest created in *Camp v. Milam* differ from an easement?

3. The court grants the Milams an interest, but holds that it is merely personal and not transferable. How does this effect the value of the interest? The 1944 First Restatement provides that duration of an irrevocable license is measured not by the tenure of the original owner, but rather by the length of time necessary to derive the fruits of the expenditures made by the original owner, § 519, comment g.

4.   Is litigation the most appropriate approach to resolving disputes as to the existence of a servitude found in cases such as *Camp v. Milam*, *Plettner v. Sullivan*, and *Cordwell v. Smith*? Design an alternative approach to resolving such disputes that might be more appropriate. Explain its advantages and disadvantages.

3. Scope, Succession, and Protection

AZTEC LIMITED, INC. v. CREEKSIDE INVESTMENT COMPANY

Supreme Court of Idaho, 1979.
100 Idaho 566, 602 P.2d 64 (1979).

BAKES, JUSTICE.

In 1976 appellant Aztec, Ltd., acting through its president, Roger Seaton, purchased a piece of real property in Pocatello, Idaho. At the time of the purchase, Seaton knew the approximate amount of land which had been purchased. He thought that the land lay to the north of Pocatello Creek Road, a public highway. After ordering a survey and title report, Seaton discovered instead that a small strip of Aztec's property lay to the south of the paved and traveled portion of Pocatello Creek Road.

Immediately to the west of Aztec's property, Pocatello Creek Road had been platted and offered for dedication to the public at a width of 70 feet. The portion of the road through Aztec's property has not been platted or dedicated to public use, although it has been used by the public for many years. At the time of purchase, there were no easements of record across Aztec's property. However, Aztec concedes that numerous years of public use have created a public prescriptive right of way on Pocatello Creek Road. The width of the prescriptive right of way or easement was in dispute at the trial. However, the trial court made no specific finding with respect to the width of the Pocatello Creek Road easement. Instead, it found other issues to be dispositive.

The heart of this controversy involves a roadway known as Freeman Lane, a dead end road that runs to the south off of Pocatello Creek Road. Freeman Lane came into existence when certain homeowners south of appellant's property (including respondent Creekside Investment Company's predecessors in interest) joined in the execution of reciprocal deeds which created a roadway easement, 50 feet wide, for access to their homes across their respective lands. This recorded easement extends from the homeowners' property north to the southern boundary of Aztec's property but falls a few feet short of the paved and traveled portion of Pocatello Creek Road. This gap between the end of the recorded Freeman Lane road easement and the traveled portion of Pocatello Creek road, which gap is part of Aztec's property, is the subject of this controversy.

Freeman Lane physically extends across the gap and intersects with the pavement of Pocatello Creek Road. Therefore, in order to get to Pocatello Creek Road from the Freeman Lane easement, one must pass over a portion of Aztec's property. The intervening strip of Aztec's land between Pocatello Creek Road and the deeded Freeman Lane easement is roughly six feet by fifty feet. This intervening strip is the alleged trespass area. The creators of the deeded Freeman Lane easement, as well as their successors, have for a considerable period of time been crossing the alleged trespass area in order to gain access to their homes. Thus, these individuals do, as Aztec freely acknowledges, enjoy a limited prescriptive easement across Aztec's land. The period of adverse use began at least eleven years ago and probably as early as 1959, but was limited to providing access to three or four homes.

The City of Pocatello paved Freeman Lane in 1973. Since such time, the city has also maintained Freeman Lane. The city has not acquired any interest of record in Freeman Lane. It has not been platted or dedicated to public use.

In 1976, respondent Creekside, which acquired its property from the owners who created the Freeman Lane easement, began construction of a 200–unit apartment development on its property to the south of appellant's property. When Seaton discovered that Creekside was utilizing Freeman Lane as the sole means of access for the project, he informed them of what he felt were Aztec's property rights in the area in question. Seaton further informed Creekside that he felt their activities constituted a trespass and demanded that they cease. Creekside continued construction on its project.

In May of 1977, appellant Aztec commenced an action against respondent Creekside for trespass to its land.

* * *

I

Appellant contends that the trial court erred in concluding that the Freeman Lane prescriptive easement was a public one; that the increase in traffic over the alleged trespass area did not amount to a trespass; and that the respondent's enlargement of the width of Freeman Lane in the alleged trespass area did not amount to a trespass. We agree.

The trial court found that Freeman Lane was a public easement. This finding is unsupported by any evidence and therefore is clearly erroneous. [ ] The only evidence which would support this finding is the fact that Freeman Lane has been paved and maintained by the city since 1973. This action was commenced in May of 1977. A similar action was commenced by Aztec against the City of Pocatello in December of 1977. The prescriptive period for a public road in Idaho is five years. [ ] While the evidence supports, and appellant admits, that the three or four homeowners, their visitors and invitees have a private easement, there is no competent evidence in the record which would tend to support a finding of adverse use and maintenance by the public for the full prescriptive period.

We next address the issue of whether Creekside's increased use of Freeman Lane amounts to an impermissible expansion of the original easement or merely an increase in degree of use. Generally, an easement acquired by prescription is confined to the right as exercised during the prescriptive period. It is limited by the purpose for which it is acquired and the use to which it is put. Gibbens v. Weisshaupt, 98 Idaho 633, 570 P.2d 870 (1977); [ ]. This general rule, however, admits of a single and narrow exception. In Gibbens, we stated:

"We do not mean to imply from our decision today that any increase in use of a prescriptive easement is an expansion. * * * We are aware that some changes in the character of the dominant estate are foreseeable and will necessitate changes in the use of a prescriptive easement. We emphasize, however, that any changes in the use of a prescriptive easement cannot result in an unreasonable increased burden on the servient estate and that the increase in use must be reasonably foreseeable at the time the easement is established." Gibbens v. Weisshaupt, 98 Idaho at 639, 570 P.2d at 876.

The record shows that during the prescriptive period Freeman Lane was an unpaved roadway approximately twenty feet in width which was used solely to provide access to three or four homes. In Gibbens, the easement in question was previously used only by a single family in order to gain access to their residence and farming operations conducted on the dominant estate. The increased use consisted of a commercial greenhouse and four additional residences. We reversed the trial court's finding that the increased use was not an expansion of the original easement, concluding "as a matter of law" that the use of the easement by both a commercial business and four additional homeowners constituted an impermissible expansion of the easement.

Here, Creekside seeks to increase the burden on the alleged trespass area by providing access to two hundred dwelling units in addition to the four homes which have in the past been serviced by Freeman Lane. We note that this is not a case where several families are building private homes bordering on Freeman Lane. Creekside's development is a commercial endeavor. Creekside seeks to provide residential accommodations for two hundred tenants and to use Freeman Lane as its access. This represents an increase by a factor of approximately fifty. This by far exceeds the increase in use present in the Gibbens case which we found resulted in an unreasonable increase in burden on the servient estate. Based on our decision in Gibbens, a similar conclusion is compelled here.

II

The increase in traffic which accompanies the construction of a two hundred unit apartment complex is not the only trespass about which appellant complains. The record reflects, and during oral argument counsel for Creekside conceded, that during the course of this controversy Creekside also improved and enlarged the physical dimensions of Freeman Lane in the alleged trespass area. To what extent the original width of twenty feet was expanded is not clear from the record. Generally, however, any increase in width of a prescriptive easement would constitute an impermissible expansion even if a contemporaneous increase in traffic over the easement would not. An increase in width does more than merely increase the burden upon the servient estate; it has the effect of enveloping additional land.

The trial court below and the respondent on appeal rely heavily on Illustration 1 to Comment b of the Restatement of Property § 479 (1944).[8] We find such reliance to be misplaced. First, in the Restatement illustration there was no attendant increase in the physical dimensions of the easement. The Restatement dealt only with an increase in traffic over the surface of the easement. Next, there is a significant difference between an increase in traffic by a factor of ten, as was the case in the Restatement illustration, and an increase in traffic by a factor of fifty, as is the case here. Finally, although we noted in Gibbens that our holding was consistent with Restatement §§ 478[9] and 479, we did not state that we would be inexorably bound by the Restatement and its illustrations. Gibbens v. Weisshaupt, 98 Idaho at 639, 570 P.2d 876. To the contrary, we held that since rights acquired by prescription should be closely scrutinized and strictly limited, the sections of the Restatement pertaining to the evolution and expansion of easements should be read "narrowly." Id. at 639, 570 P.2d at 876.

We conclude that the increased burden caused by Creekside's use constituted an impermissible expansion in the use of the Freeman Lane prescriptive easement and that any widening of Freeman Lane would constitute an impermissible expansion of Creekside's easement. Our conclusion does not, however, completely dispose of the case. The trial court below dismissed appellant's claim for damages before it determined whether or not there did exist a trespass. The court did so on the grounds that no actual damages were proven. However, in cases of trespass to land, the plaintiff need not prove actual harm in order to

---

8. § 479. Extent of Easements Appurtenant as Affected by Evolution of the Dominant Tenement. "In ascertaining whether a particular use is permissible under an easement appurtenant created by prescription there must be considered, in addition to the factors enumerated in § 478, the needs which result from a normal evolution in the use of the dominant tenement and the extent to which the satisfaction of those needs increases the burden on the servient tenement.

"Comment:

b. Normal evolution of condition of dominant tenement. * * *

"Illustrations:

1. By prescription, A acquires, as appurtenant to Blackacre, a right of

way to go by foot across Whiteacre. Though Blackacre was in the path of a growing city, only one family lived on it during the prescriptive period. Two tenement houses, in each of which five families dwell, have since been built on Blackacre. All of these families may use the way."

9. § 478. Factors in Ascertaining Extent of Easements Created by Prescription.

"In ascertaining whether a particular use is permissible under an easement created by prescription a comparison must be made between such use and the use by which the easement was created with respect to (a) their physical character, (b) their purpose, (c) the relative burden caused by them upon the servient tenement."

recover nominal damages. Nominal damages are presumed to flow naturally from a wrongful entry upon land. [ ] Moreover, there was some indication in the record that the respondent was given notice that its activities constituted a trespass and nonetheless continued construction on the project and widening of Freeman Lane in conscious disregard of the property rights of the appellant. The appellant therefore may be entitled to punitive damages. [ ] This Court has in the past held that a plaintiff may recover punitive damages without proving that he is entitled to more than nominal damages. [ ] The appellant also requested injunctive relief, which request was foreclosed by the trial court's finding that there was no trespass committed by Creekside. On remand the trial court must resolve these issues.

* * *

Notes and Questions

1. Discernment of the scope and duration of easements created by necessity, implication, or prescription presents somewhat different problems than those presented in the interpretation of express easements, where a writing is available to be interpreted. 3 R. Powell & P. Rohan, Powell on Real Property (1991) states that factors to consider in deciding whether specific uses are within the scope of a prescriptive easement include: "1) their similarity or dissimilarity of purpose, 2) their respective physical attributes, 3) the relative burden caused by them on the servient parcel." ¶ 416. Should a new use ever be permitted which increases the physical dimensions of a prescriptive easement? What factors should a court consider in deciding whether a novel use is within the scope of an easement of necessity? An easement implied from pre-existing use?

2. The principal case also addresses the problems raised by apportionment of appurtenant easements. An appurtenant easement is appurtenant to every part of the dominant estate, and if the dominant estate is subdivided, it remains appurtenant to each part of the subdivided estate. Where subdivision substantially increases the burden on the servient property, however, courts may consider, as in the principal case, whether the use is within the scope of the original easement.

3. Is Aztec responsible for maintaining the portion of Creekside's easement which crosses its property? Does Creekside have the privilege to maintain the easement? See Restatement of Property (Servitudes), §§ 480, 485 (1944); J. Bruce & J. Ely, The Law of Easements and License in Land, ¶ 7.09 (1988).

4. Assignment problems also arise as to easements in gross, i.e., easements not appurtenant to any tract of land. Easements in gross are not alienable under English law unless they include the power to sever and to remove a portion of the servient estate, i.e., unless they are attached to profits. Most American jurisdictions permit assignment of some, but not all, easements in gross. In general, utility-like easements are recognized as assignable: "Easements in gross for railroads, for telephones and telegraph and electric power lines, for pipelines, for stream facilities, for water ditches and for business structures have been held transferable by Ameri-

can courts almost without exception." 3 R. Powell & P. Rohan, Powell on Real Property, ¶ 419 (1991). The 1944 Restatement of Property further asserts that all easements in gross created for commercial purposes are alienable, § 489. Noncommercial easements—for example, a personal privilege to swim or fish in a stream—are often personal in nature, and not intended to be assignable. The 1944 Restatement, § 492, identifies as relevant considerations in determining the assignability of noncommercial easements in gross: "(a) the personal relations existing at the time of creation between the owner of the easement and the owner of the servient tenement; (b) the extent of the probable increase in the burden on the servient tenement resulting from the alienability of the easement either by increasing the physical use of the land or by decreasing its value; (c) the consideration paid for the easement."

5. Easements in gross can also, in some circumstances, be assigned to more than one person, and thus be apportioned or divided. The general rule is that exclusive easements are apportionable, non-exclusive easements are not. Why should exclusivity affect apportionability? If an easement is apportionable, there is authority for the proposition that all holders of the easement must use it as tenants in common and not as individuals, Mountjoy's Case, 1 And. 307, 123 Eng.Rep. 488 (1583); Miller v. Lutheran Conference & Camp Ass'n, 331 Pa 241, 200 A. 646, 130 A.L.R. 1245 (1938). What might be the economic motivation for this rule?

6. If a third party blocked Creekside's easement, could Creekside sue for damages? For injunctive relief? Could it remove the barrier itself? Should it have to prove actual pecuniary damages to recover a judgment? See 3 R. Powell & P. Rohan, Powell on Real Property, ¶ 420 (1991); J. Bruce & J. Ely, The Law of Easements and Licenses in Land, ¶ 7.07 (1988).

7. The principal case recognizes a prescriptive easement in the City of Pocatello over Pocatello Creek Road. Establishment of public ways over private land is more commonly handled through the doctrine of dedication. Dedications are most commonly express, as when a developer deeds to a municipality streets within a development. Implied dedication is also possible at the common law, based on a theory that a landowner who admits the public to use of his land over a long period of time is estopped from denying such use. Traditionally, courts would require proof of the owner's intent to dedicate an easement to the public, but courts are increasingly willing to imply intent, thus effectively creating a prescriptive public easement as in the principal case. For a dedication to be complete, it must also be accepted by the municipality. See Cunningham, Stoebuck, and Whitman, The Law of Property, § 11.6 (1984). Why would a developer give away the streets in a subdivision to a municipality? Why might a municipality be reluctant to accept such a gift?

8. Cases often arise involving interpretation of express easements. Courts interpreting express easements, like courts interpreting any other agreement, look for the intent of the parties. Factors normally considered include: "(1) whether the easement was created by grant or by reservation; (2) whether the conveyance was, or was not, gratuitous; (3) the use of the servient tenement prior to the conveyance; (4) the parties' practical construction of the easement's scope; and (5) the purpose for which the

easement was acquired." 3 R. Powell & P. Rohan, Powell on Real Property, ¶ 415[2]. Disputes frequently involve attempts to modernize or expand easements to accommodate developing uses. See, for example, Henley v. Continental Cablevision of St. Louis County, Inc., 692 S.W.2d 825 (Mo.App. 1985) interpreting a grant of easement to a telephone company to include the power to allow cable television lines. In these disputes, courts normally attempt to construe easements reasonably and flexibly to permit development of the dominant estate without unduly burdening the servient estate. See G. Korngold, Private Land Use Arrangements, § 4.08 (1990).

Problem: Drafting an Easement

James and Edward Russell, two brothers, recently inherited a two acre lot from their deceased parents. They have decided to subdivide the lot and both build houses on it. James will take the front half, Edward the back. Edward will need access to a lane which runs across James' property to gain access to the county road. Also electric and telephone lines will need to be run across James' land to reach Edward's house. Edward will need access to an existing well on James' property. County building regulations permit only one septic system on a two acre lot. The brothers have decided to locate this on Edwards' lot. Draft any easements that will be necessary to carry out the arrangements the brothers desire. What ethical problems might you encounter in carrying out the brothers' request?

4. Termination of Easements

While easements are useful property interests, they also interfere with the full enjoyment of the fee by its possessor. For that reason the law has provided a host of ways of terminating easements. 3 R. Powell & P. Rohan, Powell on Real Property, ¶ 421 (1991) helpfully classifies these approaches to termination in terms of whether they are based on the acts of the owner of the dominant estate (release, abandonment, or surcharge), of the servient estate (prescription or conveyance to a bona fide purchaser without notice), of both parties (merger and estoppel), or of others (eminent domain, mortgage foreclosure, or tax sale). Easements may also expire by their own terms. The principal case, like most cases in this area, addresses several of these arguments.

Tract Development Service, Inc. v. Kepler

California Court of Appeals, 4th District, 1988.
199 Cal.App.3d 1374, 246 Cal.Rptr. 469.

OPINION

McDANIEL, JUSTICE.

INTRODUCTION

Defendants John and Leona Kepler have appealed from a judgment in favor of plaintiff Tract Development which declared that Tract Development was entitled to an easement over the Keplers' property and which also awarded Tract Development $12,550 in damages for interference with Tract Development's easement.

FACTS

In 1980, the Keplers purchased some real property near Corona, in what is known as the Temescal Gardens Subdivision. The Keplers' property consists of 12 lots plus a portion of two other lots, an alley referred to as Lot T, and the property in question, which is a twenty-foot-wide strip of land running along the eastern edge of the Keplers' lots:

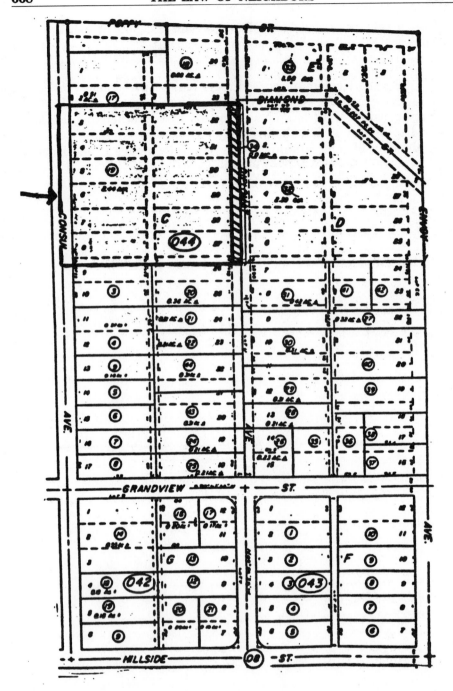

This strip of land corresponds to the western half of a forty foot right-of-way known as Diplomat Avenue. Diplomat Avenue was one of the streets shown on the Temescal Gardens subdivision map recorded in 1924. The portion of Diplomat Avenue in question was never developed or used as a right-of-way. The lots purchased by the Keplers were located in the northeast corner of Temescal Gardens, and represented a small portion of the entire subdivision:

* * *

In 1984, Tract Development purchased a number of lots to the east of the Keplers' property:

* * *

The property included the eastern half of Diplomat Avenue. Tract Development was aware of the existence of the streets outlined by the subdivision map, and began grading Diplomat Avenue as part of its plan to build homes on the lots it had just purchased.

Thereafter, Daryl Stark, Tract Development's Chief Executive Officer, noticed Mr. Kepler erecting a fence down the middle of Diplomat Avenue. He asked Mr. Kepler to honor the easement as shown on the subdivision map and to relocate his fence, but Mr. Kepler did not do so, and Tract Development thereupon instituted this action.

Judgment was entered in favor of Tract Development, and the Keplers now appeal, contending that the easement purportedly confirmed by the judgment no longer exists, either because (1) Tract Development did not acquire the easement when it purchased its property * * * (2) it was extinguished by common ownership of the dominant and servient tenements resulting in a merger of the two, or (3) it was abandoned, or (4) it was terminated by prescription.

In support of these contentions, the Keplers have set out a careful recitation of the chain of title to establish the common ownership of the dominant and servient tenements, and have also set out the evidence purportedly showing abandonment or termination by prescription. * * *

DISCUSSION

* * *

[The court held that Tract development had acquired an easement by its purchase.]

The Keplers' next argument is that the easement over the relevant portion of Diplomat Avenue *was* expressly excepted when, in 1956, Elvin and Ruth Downs, the then owners of Blocks C (the equivalent of the property now owned by the Keplers) and D and E (the equivalent of the property now owned by Tract Development) transferred Blocks D and E to Ernest and Bonnie Bill by a deed which referred to Diplomat Avenue "as now abandoned." In connection with this statement in the Downs-to-Bills deed, we note that in 1936, the Downs' predecessor in interest, A.J. Davis, had petitioned the board of supervisors to abandon portions of several streets in the subdivision, including the portion of

Diplomat Avenue involved here, and that the board of supervisors had passed a resolution to this effect.

Unfortunately for the Keplers, the reference to Diplomat Avenue in the Downs-to-Bills deed "as now abandoned" is not the equivalent of an express exception of the easement here. As stated in *Danielson v. Sykes, supra,* the initial reference to the subdivision map created a *private* easement entirely independent of the fact of dedication to public use. The abandonment by the board of supervisors could not have the effect of extinguishing this private easement nor did the reference to Diplomat Avenue "as now abandoned" evidence an unambiguous intent on the part of the Downs to except the private easement from the grant to the Bills.

The Keplers also urge that the easement was extinguished by the common ownership of the dominant and servient tenements which resulted in a merger. (Civil Code, §§ 805, 811(1).) This common ownership purportedly occurred when both Davis and the Downs owned fee title to all of blocks C, D and E.

As is apparent from the diagrams which precede this part of our opinion, Blocks C, D and E made up but a small portion of the Temescal Garden subdivision. The issue therefore is whether, in a case involving a network of streets laid out in connection with a subdivision, anything less than the entire subdivision can be said to be either the dominant or servient tenement for purposes of merger.

Here, each owner in the subdivision has the right to use every other owner's property to travel both within and through the subdivision. The easement enjoyed by each owner, which consists of the entire network of streets set out in the subdivision map, is not only appurtenant to that owner's particular lot, but is appurtenant to every lot in the subdivision, * * *, and conversely every lot in the subdivision is burdened by every other lot owner's right to use it. * * * In other words, each owner enjoys an easement which is not simply an easement over an abutting owner's land, but which is an easement over the land of non-abutting owners; the whole of the subdivision is in essence the servient tenement to each lot, and each lot is servient to every other lot. This being so, there can be no merger unless there is common ownership of the entire subdivision; such common ownership never occurred.

The Keplers next urge that the easement was abandoned. However, the evidence submitted by the Keplers to show that the prior owners (Davis, the Downs and the Bills) intended to abandon the private easement—that trees were planted on the avenue, or that the Downs and the Bills obtained a grant of easement to use another portion of Diplomat—was not exclusively susceptible to that interpretation; an easement created by grant is not lost by mere nonuse, no matter how long, and may be lost by abandonment only when the intention to abandon clearly appears. [   ]

* * * Abandonment hinges upon the intent of the owner to forego all future conforming uses of the property, and there must be conduct demonstrating that intent which is so decisive and conclusive as to indicate a clear intent to abandon. [   ]

Trees planted on a way may indicate nothing more than the property owners' intent not to use the way as a way until some time in the distant future, e.g., not until the lots fronting on the way are developed. Furthermore, the Downs' and Bills' act of obtaining an easement over another part of Diplomat Avenue is as susceptible to an inference that the Downs and Bills were under a misapprehension of the nature of their rights to a private easement over Diplomat Avenue * * * as it is to an inference that they intended to abandon their right to a private easement. If it is the case that the Downs and Keplers were in fact unaware of their right to a private easement, they could hardly be held to have ever *intended* to abandon such a right.

* * *

The Keplers also argue that the private easement was lost via adverse possession, because the Downs maintained a fence across Diplomat Avenue along the northerly line of Grandview from 1943 to 1960, thereby blocking not only the public's access, but other subdivision property owners' access, to the section of Diplomat Avenue here at issue.

An easement obtained by grant, such as the one here, may indeed be lost by prescription, e.g., when the owner of the servient tenement makes a use of his or her own land in a manner which is adverse to the rights represented by the easement. * * *

However, not every act which appears, at first blush, to be adverse to the rights represented by the easement will suffice to extinguish it by prescription. * * *

Here, the evidence showed that the Downs erected a fence around their property which bisected Diplomat Avenue at the northerly line of Grandview, and that this fence remained in place from 1943 to 1960. According to the Keplers, this is sufficient evidence to support a conclusion that the easement was terminated by prescription.

However, the evidence also indicated that there was a gate in the fence where it crossed Diplomat Avenue, from which it could be inferred that some person or persons used, or could use, if they desired, the right of way. Although the Downs' son testified as to the existence of this fence and the gate, and that the public did not have permission to pass through the gate, he did not testify that the gate was locked, or that other subdivision owners were actually effectively prevented from using the way if they so desired. * * *

Furthermore, the Downs' son did not testify that his parents had asserted that they held title to the property free of the easement or that they had a right to use the way in a manner adverse to other owners in the subdivision. * * * [T]he evidence as a whole supports a determination that the Downs' actions were not sufficiently hostile, open, notorious or under claim of right to constitute a prescriptive extinguishment, nor even so incompatible with the easement's nature or use as to constitute a prescriptive extinguishment. * * *

DISPOSITION

The judgment appealed from is affirmed.

CAMPBELL, P.J., and HEWS, J., concur.

Notes and Questions

1. Could a fee simple be lost by abandonment? Why should a different policy apply as to easement? Does allowing easements to be terminated by abandonment conflict with the Statute of Frauds? What evidence might establish intention to abandon if cessation of use alone is not sufficient? Can the court be serious in its assertion that mere non-use would never be enough to establish abandonment? Should abandonment be more easily established with respect to prescriptive or implied easements than with respect to easements created by grant? Easements may also be extinguished by a release from the owner of the dominant estate, in effect by express abandonment.

2. The owner of the servient estate in the principal case relies on his own acts as well as the acts of the owner of the dominant estate, arguing termination through prescription. How does termination by estoppel differ from termination by prescription, denominated in the principal case as adverse possession? Should construction of a building on an easement of way which has not been used for twenty years be sufficient to terminate the easement by estoppel, even though mere non-use in itself would not be sufficient?

3. If both the dominant and servient estate come under common ownership, an easement is terminated by merger for the simple reason that one cannot own an easement in his own land. Should the easement be terminated if the owner of the dominant estate acquires a term of years or life estate in the servient estate? What if the owner of the dominant estate acquires a security interest in the servient estate, or holds it in trust? See Restatement of Property (Servitudes), § 497, comments d, e, g (1944). An easement in gross is also extinguished if its owner acquires the servient estate, Restatement of Property (Servitudes), § 499 (1944).

4. Finally, easements, like any other property interest, may be terminated by actions of the sovereign through its eminent domain power or through seizure for nonpayment of taxes. The Fifth Amendment and provisions of state constitutions forbid the taking of property without payment of just compensation. An easement is clearly a property interest, thus a government entity must compensate the owner of an easement if the easement is blocked by government action. But what is just compensation? Is the value of the easement measured by the reduction in value of the dominant parcel if the easement is taken, or by the increase in the value of the servient parcel if the easement is terminated? See Restatement of Property (Servitudes), § 508, Comment c (1944); United States v. Welch, 217 U.S. 333, 30 S.Ct. 527, 54 L.Ed. 787 (1910) (value determined in

reference to dominant estate). Note that if the former measure is chosen, the combined value of the servient estate and of the easement may exceed the total value of a fee simple absolute in the servient estate. Yet if the latter measure is chosen, the owner of the dominant estate may not be fully compensated. Should sale of a servient property for non-payment of property taxes extinguish an easement across the property? Should the answer turn on whether the value of the easement was included in the assessment of the servient or dominant estate? Should it turn on whether the easement was appurtenant or in gross? See Restatement of Property (Servitudes) § 509 (1944), 3 R. Powell & P. Rohan, Powell on Real Property ¶ 426 (1991).

B. NEGATIVE RIGHTS AND AFFIRMATIVE OBLIGATIONS: COVENANTS, EQUITABLE SERVITUDES, NEGATIVE EASEMENTS

1. *Historical Development and Traditional Requirements*

To this point we have been focusing on one function of servitudes, that of permitting one person to use affirmatively the land of another. Now we turn to the two other functions of servitudes, the imposition of negative restrictions and affirmative obligations with respect to the use of land. Largely for historic reasons, several different legal labels have been applied to servitudes that serve these functions: easements, covenants, and equitable servitudes. A review of the historic background is useful to understand the confusion of current American law.

The law of easements as a means to gaining the right to affirmatively use the land of another was well established in England by the late eighteenth and early nineteenth century, and could have been expanded to fill the field of servitude law. The English courts opposed this expansion, however, and limited easements for purposes of negative restrictions and affirmative obligations to five categories: the right to receive light for a building, the right to receive air by a defined channel, the right to support of a building, the right to receive water from an artificial stream, and the right to maintenance of a fence.

The development of covenant law was also blocked by the English courts. Covenants, which find their historic roots in covenants of title, were used traditionally in England to specify the obligations of landlords and tenants in leaseholds. They could have been used to specify the affirmative and negative duties of freeholders as well, but this possibility was rejected by the English courts, which required "privity of estate", i.e., a tenurial relationship (such as between a landlord and tenant), for the enforcement of covenants. See Keppell v. Bailey, 39 Eng.Rep. 1042 (1834).

As we have seen before elsewhere in the development of English property law, equity stepped forward to remove the obstacles law imposed. In Tulk v. Moxhay, 41 Eng.Rep. 1143 (1848), the leading English case on equitable servitudes, the Chancery court enjoined the violation of a negative restriction by a landowner who purchased property with notice of the restriction. By the end of the nineteenth century, even this course of development had been blocked, however, as equity courts refused to enforce affirmative obligations, Haywood v. Brunswick Permanent Benefit Bldg. Soc'y, 8 Q.B.D. 403 (1881), or negative obligations in gross, London & South W. Ry. Co. v. Gomm, 20 Ch.D. 562 (1882).

American development was more hospitable to servitudes, but also much more confused. In early cases such as Hills v. Miller, 3 Paige Ch. 254 (N.Y.Ch. 1832), New York courts permitted the use of negative easements in situations where they would not have been permitted under English law. In Morse v. Aldrich, 36 Mass. (19 Pick.) 449 (1837), the Massachusetts court permitted the enforcement of an affirmative covenant for the benefit of an easement despite the absence of a tenurial relationship between the owners of the dominant and servient estate. The New York courts went even further in liberalizing real covenant law, recognizing that real covenants could run with the land even if the only "privity" between the dominant and servient estates was that they had been severed from the same estate at the time the covenant was created. Equitable servitudes were also quickly assimilated into American law.

By the turn of the century, therefore, American courts had recognized negative easements, real covenants, and equitable servitudes (sometimes called equitable easements), as tools available for restricting the use of land. Although some courts and commentators attempted to distinguish among these forms, noting the contractual nature of covenants (see H. Sims, Covenants Which Run With the Land (1901)), courts often used the terms indiscriminately, and sometimes in combination, to describe negative and affirmative obligations.

The 1944 Restatement combined negative and affirmative promises respecting the use of land into one category, but then distinguished between promises enforceable at law and at equity, § 539, effectively continuing the distinctions between real covenants and equitable servitudes. It also continued to recognize negative easements, § 452. The Restatement took a generally conservative approach to the running of obligations, relying on cases that had limited rather than encouraged the use of servitudes.

Thus at this point in the late twentieth century, American law is still bound up in doctrinal confusion. This state of affairs has been well analyzed, French, Toward a Modern Law of Servitudes: Reweaving the Ancient Strands, 55 S.Cal.L.Rev. 1261 (1982); Reichman, Toward a Unified Concept of Servitudes, 55 S.Calif.L.Rev. 1179 (1982). The proposed Restatement of Property, Third (Servitudes) would abandon the current complexities and adopt a single category of servitudes, including real covenants, equitable servitudes and negative easements (and also affirmative easements), but it is at this point merely a proposal. For the time being, therefore, the student of property law must, unfortunately, master the various categories to which American courts assign servitudes and the subtle, real, or imaginary, distinctions among those categories.

A brief orientation to that law at this point, however, may help you chart your path through that material.

According to the traditional law as set out in the 1944 Restatement, promises respecting the use of land only become property interests (i.e. obligations enforceable not only against the original promisor for the benefit of the original promisee, but also against successors in interest of the original promisor or by successors in interest of the original promisee) if several requirements are met. First, the parties to the original promise must intend it to "run with the land"—to bind and benefit successors. Second, the promise must "touch and concern" the land. Third, if the promise is to be enforced at law (in a suit for damages) as a real covenant, the following privity requirements must be met: (i) For the burden of the covenant to bind successors, there must be "horizontal privity" between the original promisor and promisee, i.e., the original promisor and promisee must have a relationship between themselves that meets certain requirements. (ii) There must be "vertical privity" between the original parties to the promise and their successors against or for whom enforcement is sought, i.e., the successor must succeed to a specified interest of the original promisor. For the promise to be enforced at equity (i.e., by injunction or specific performance), privity between the initial promisor and promisee, or between the original promisor and its successor, is not necessary. All that is necessary is that the successor to the promisor purchase with notice of the promise (and, perhaps, vertical privity between the promissee and a successor to the promissee).

The meaning and continuing validity of these requirements, as well as emerging additional limitations on negative and affirmative servitudes, will now be explored.

2. Creation

(a) Express Provision

Servitudes imposing negative and affirmative obligations, like easements, are most commonly created by express grants. Such restrictions are within the coverage of the Statute of Frauds and, unless they fall within an exception to the statute, must be in writing. A developer creating a restricted subdivision may record a declaration of restrictions establishing building lines, restricting construction to residential buildings, establishing the minimum square footage for buildings, and restricting, depending on the nature of the subdivision, such things as clotheslines, pets, satellite dishes, or signs. The declaration may also impose affirmative obligations, such as an obligation to pay an annual assessment for the support of a property owners' association or for the maintenance of common facilities. The declaration is then recorded and incorporated by reference into deeds from the developer to purchasers in the subdivision. Alternatively, the subdivider can deed the entire subdivision to a straw, incorporating the restrictions into this deed. This deed is then recorded, after which the straw deeds the subdivision back to the developer, with all property within it bound by the restrictions. Finally, a subdivider can attempt to incorporate the restrictions into each deed individually. This strategy is the most risky, because the subdivider may inadvertently (or intentionally) leave the restrictions out of some deeds. In this situation the courts must decide whether to imply restrictions, essentially rejecting the applicability of the Statute of Frauds.

(b) By Implication

WARREN v. DETLEFSEN

Supreme Court of Arkansas, 1984.
281 Ark. 196, 663 S.W.2d 710 (1984).

HICKMAN, JUSTICE.

Mike Detlefsen and others filed suit to enjoin the construction of two duplexes in the Warren Subdivision 3 in El Dorado, Arkansas. This subdivision is one of three adjoining residential neighborhoods which were part of a development by the Warrens through their partnership, the Warren Construction Company. The chancellor held that the Warrens should be enjoined from building the duplexes based on the restrictive covenants contained in the deeds of the appellees and the representations made by the Warrens concerning the development of the three subdivisions. In finding that these were enforceable restrictive covenants for single family use, the chancellor relied on the language in the deeds that the property was to be used for residential purposes, and that "carport" was used singularly in the deeds. Those factors coupled with the oral representations of the Warrens led the chancellor to conclude the restrictive covenants were enforceable. We find no error under these facts.

The chancellor received into evidence deeds to the lots which the Warrens had sold in each of the three units. In Unit One, there are nine lots, with five of the deeds containing covenants restricting use to "residential purposes only" and requiring a minimum of fourteen hundred square feet. One deed recites similar language except it requires a minimum of twelve hundred square feet. One deed states that the lot can be "used only for residential purposes" and requires a minimum cost of $30,000. Two deeds contain no covenants.

Unit Two consists of 21 lots with three of the deeds restricting use to "residential purposes only," "the dwelling," and require a minimum of fourteen hundred square feet. Four deeds are restricted to "residential purposes only," "the residence dwelling," and a minimum of fourteen hundred square feet. Four deeds contain this same language except the area is reduced to a minimum of twelve hundred square feet. Eight deeds in Unit Two contain no covenants.

In Unit Three, 20 lots had been sold at the time of trial. Of those, 11 deeds contain the restriction "for residential purposes only," "the residence dwelling," and require a minimum of twelve hundred square feet. One deed is restricted to "residential purposes only," "the residence," and requires a minimum of fourteen hundred square feet.

In promoting the development, the Warrens did not make a distinction between the three units, selling the area as a single neighborhood. There are no visible boundaries or divisions between the units. The Warrens, through Warren Construction Company, are the grantors, the developers, and the builders of the subdivisions. The Warrens displayed a master plat of the entire development on the wall of their office for prospective purchasers to view. This master plat was not recorded.

The Warrens argue that the chancellor erred in allowing witnesses to testify concerning oral representations allegedly made by them at the time the appellees were considering purchasing lots and homes within the units. This concerned the type of homes being built and the general scheme or plan of development which the Warrens intended to pursue. Testimony reflected that the Warrens had discussed these intentions with the prospective buyers, assuring them that only single family homes would be constructed, that no apartments would be constructed and that no mobile homes would be placed in any of the three units. Further, the appellees testified that they relied on these statements, at least in part, in deciding to purchase from the Warrens. At least one witness said he was told no duplexes would be built. Generally, duplexes were not mentioned.

While parol evidence is generally inadmissible to vary or contradict the language of a restrictive covenant, [ ] such evidence is admissible to establish a general building plan or scheme of development and improvement. Such plan or scheme can be proven by express covenant, by implication from a field map, or by parol representation made in sales brochures, maps, advertising, or oral statements upon which the purchaser relied in making his decision to purchase. [ ] This general scheme is shown by the deeds and by the oral statements of the Warrens. Seven of the nine deeds in Unit One are restricted to residential use. Thirteen of 21 deeds in Unit Two are restricted to residential use. In Unit Three, 12 of the 20 deeds contain similar restrictions. Mrs. Warren testified that she and Mr. Warren intended to insert the restrictions in all deeds in the three units. She also testified that they were aware that the prospective purchasers were relying on their oral representations in deciding whether or not to buy. The subdivisions, themselves, consisted of single-family dwellings only at the time the appellees purchased their lots and homes. Both Warrens testified that the economy dictated they change their plans and build the duplexes rather than single family residences.

The Warrens argue that the chancellor erred in finding that the restrictions contained in the deeds of the appellees were the proper basis for enjoining the construction of the duplexes. They contend that the wording of the restrictions does not limit their development to single family dwellings, but rather, that multi-family use was permissible, citing Shermer v. Haynes, 248 Ark. 255, 451 S.W.2d 445 (1970). There, we held that covenants which restrict use to "residence" or "dwelling" purpose alone, generally do not have the effect of forbidding the erection or maintenance of multiple family dwellings. However, the chancellor in this case had testimony and facts of a total building and selling scheme which indicate single residence purposes only. Further, the testimony reflects that the oral representations, combined with the express covenants, were the basis of the purchasers' decisions to buy lots in the neighborhood. The homes in the units display a uniformity of development, further indication of the general plan and scheme.

These restrictions are enforceable against the lots retained by the Warrens in the three units as a reciprocal negative easement. When the grantor places an express restriction in deeds to his grantees within the particular development, the restriction attaches to the lots retained to prevent their use in a manner detrimental to the enjoyment and value of neighboring lots sold with the restriction. 20 Am.Jr.2d Covenants § 173. The Warrens had the restrictions placed in their grantees' deeds, and the chancellor's findings support a conclusion that the Warrens intended to bind all the lots sold within the three units.

Finally, the Warrens challenge the standing of homeowners in Units One and Two to seek enforcement of the restrictions against the lots retained by the Warrens in Unit Three. They argue that these first two subdivisions are legally separate subdivisions and, as such, the owners within them can not have the restrictions enforced in the third, separate subdivision. However, in the negotiations leading to the purchase, the Warrens represented that the development would consist of some 350 homes, all being single family dwellings. The buyers were shown a master plat which depicted the three subdivisions as a single development, with only a line distinguishing the boundaries of each unit. Otherwise, there are no visible boundaries or divisions between the units. The buyers relied upon these factors in making their decision to purchase. Also, at least two of the appellees were homeowners in Unit Three.

While the chancellor based his decision on narrow reasoning, we must affirm unless the decision is clearly erroneous. [ ] The distinctive facts in this case support the chancellor's conclusion and since we cannot say he was clearly erroneous, we affirm his decision.

Affirmed.

Notes and Questions

1. The implied reciprocal servitudes doctrine is of use for addressing three problems. First, there is the situation found in the principal case. A developer purports to create a restricted subdivision, selling off lots with restrictions in the deeds. Subsequently the market changes and the developer decides to sell off or to develop lots in the subdivision in violation of the restrictions. Courts will then imply restrictions binding the retained

lots, essentially estopping the developer from developing the land for purposes other than those represented to earlier purchasers.

A second situation arises where a developer sells off some lots with deed restrictions, then subsequently, and perhaps inadvertently, sells others without. A purchaser of an unrestricted lot (or her successors) attempts to develop the lot for a purpose prohibited by the restrictions on the other lots. If a court finds that the earlier restrictions were imposed as part of a common scheme of which subsequent purchasers had notice, they will again imply a restriction, attaching with the earlier sale of restricted lots.

Finally, the implied reciprocal servitude doctrine addresses the conceptual problem raised when early purchasers in a subdivision attempt to enforce express servitudes against subsequent purchasers. There is no conceptual problem, of course, with subsequent purchasers in a subdivision enforcing written restrictions in the deeds of prior purchasers. Such restrictions are made for the benefit of the developer's retained land, and run to the benefit of subsequent purchasers of that land. Prior purchasers, however, are strangers to the transactions between the developer and subsequent purchasers and cannot claim to succeed to the benefit of that promise. Note there is no problem with the Statute of Frauds in these cases—the restrictions are in writing—rather the problem is how to connect them up with prior purchasers. Several theories have evolved for permitting enforcement. The prior purchasers could be treated as third-party beneficiaries to the subsequent agreement, the approach taken by the 1944 Restatement, § 541, comments c and f, and a few cases, Snow v. Van Dam, 291 Mass. 477, 197 N.E. 224 (1935). As courts do not commonly allow enforcement of negative servitudes by third-party beneficiaries, however, this theory is problematic, see 2 American Law of Property § 9.30 (J. Casner ed. 1952). More commonly, courts hold that at the time of the prior purchases, reciprocal servitudes were implied against the retained land of the developer of the common scheme for the benefit of the prior purchasers, and that these restrictions continue to bind the land in the hands of subsequent purchasers, see Sanborn v. McLean, 233 Mich. 227, 206 N.W. 496 (1925), Lehmann v. Wallace, 510 S.W.2d 675 (Tex.Civ.App.1974). This is the position taken by the 1989 Tentative Draft Restatement of Property (Third) Servitudes § 2.14.

2. Some jurisdictions continue to reject the implied reciprocal servitudes doctrine for any purpose because of its conflict with the Statute of Frauds, see Riley v. Bear Creek Planning Committee, 17 Cal.3d 500, 131 Cal.Rptr. 381, 551 P.2d 1213 (1976) (also relying on the parol evidence rule); Houghton v. Rizzo, 361 Mass. 635, 281 N.E.2d 577 (1972). What facts must a court find in such a jurisdiction before it would permit a prior (or a subsequent) purchaser in a subdivision to enforce a restriction against another lot owner in the subdivision? See Trahms v. Starrett, 34 Cal. App.3d 766, 110 Cal.Rptr. 239 (1973):

> * * * To create an equitable servitude, both the grantor and a grantee must intend that a parcel of land conveyed from the grantor to the grantee be restricted pursuant to a general plan. [ ] That intent must appear in the instruments exchanged between them. [ ] The

agreement between the two parties must show 'that the parcel conveyed (is) subject to restrictions in accordance with the plan for the benefit of all the other parcels and also that all other parcels (are) subject to such restrictions for its benefit.' [ ] The dominant and servient tenements must be shown. [ ] If these conditions have been met the grantee of the first deed from the developer of a tract will be entitled to enforce the covenants as to all the remaining area placed under equitable servitude; operation of the recording statutes will prevent the developer from exempting other grantees by omitting reference to restrictions in drawing later deeds. [ ]

* * * But a grantee possessed of a dominant interest could not enforce the restrictions as to lots that were deeded without restriction by Marinero prior to the execution of the grantee's deed. This conclusion follows from the fact that a grantor cannot place restrictions on land he does not own, or contract for third parties without their consent. * * *

Therefore the grantees whose deeds incorporated the restrictions, and were issued prior to the issuance of appellants' deeds, could enforce the restrictions on appellants. But neither appellants' deeds nor respondents' deed expressly or by reference adopted the restrictions. The facts that respondents may have known of the recorded tract restrictions by virtue of references in the report of the Real Estate Commissioner and in documents received from the title insurance company did not act as an agreement on their part to abide by the tract restrictions. [ ] The deed was the 'final and exclusive memorial of the intention and rights of the parties.' [ ]

Since neither appellants nor respondents agreed in their deeds to abide by the restrictions, appellants cannot enforce the restrictions on respondents. The fact that a few lot owners, who were granted deeds incorporating the restrictions prior to the grant to respondents, can enforce the restriction on respondents' lot does not determine the question whether appellants can enforce the restrictions. The servitudes created by those prior deeds run from respondents' lot to each of the lots conveyed by prior deeds which adopted the restrictions, not between appellants' lots and respondents' lot.

3. The principal case also raises the problem of what land will be included in the general plan for purposes of implying servitudes where a subdivision is not yet fully developed when a lot is sold off, or when the subdivision is developed in phases. Particular problems arise where an effort is made by a prior purchaser to enforce restrictions against land that was subsequently acquired by the subdivider but developed as part of the same scheme. The problem is usually handled as a question of fact, looking to the intentions and representations of the developer, see Draft Restatement of the Law of Property (Third) Servitudes § 2.14, comment g (1989).

4. Implied servitudes are generally negative restrictions enforced at equity and are denominated as negative easements or equitable servitudes. Traditional doctrine forbids implication of real covenants—servitudes enforceable at law. Cases implying affirmative obligations are rare, see R &

R Realty Co. v. Weinstein, 4 Ariz.App. 517, 422 P.2d 148 (1966) (implied reciprocal servitude to contribute to maintenance of park). Why should courts be more willing to imply negative than affirmative restrictions?

(c) By Prescription

PROBLEM: ANCIENT LIGHTS

Fifteen years ago, Samuel Kent bought a lot on a gentle hill on the north shore of Sandy's cove. Immediately after the purchase, he built a house with a sweeping view of the ocean. Eight years ago he built a swimming pool below the house, heated by a solar collector placed next to the swimming pool, ten feet from the southern boundary of Samuel's property. Last year Bill Littleton acquired the lot immediately south of Samuel's lot. Bill is building a two story A-frame home on his lot, which will substantially obstruct the view of the Ocean from Samuel's deck and cut off sunlight from the solar collector (as well as from the pool) much of the day during most of the year. There are no express restrictive servitudes affecting either lot, and Bill's proposed home complies with local zoning and development restrictions. The prescriptive period for establishing servitudes is five years. Samuel learns of the English "ancient lights" doctrine which permits acquisition of a negative easement for access to light by use for the prescriptive period. He brings a suit seeking an injunction against the construction of Bill's house, claiming that the courts of his jurisdiction should recognize the ancient lights doctrine. What result should obtain, and why? Would an argument of implication from necessity or pre-existing use fare any better? See Prah v. Maretti, 108 Wis.2d 223, 321 N.W.2d 182 (1982); Fontainebleau Hotel Corp. v. Forty–Five Twenty–Five, Inc., 114 So.2d 357 (Fla.App.1959); Maioriello v. Arlotta, 364 Pa. 557, 73 A.2d 374 (1950).

3. *Validity, Interpretation, and Scope*

When courts refuse to enforce restrictive and affirmative servitudes they usually offer one of two categories of reasons in explanation. First, they may refuse to enforce servitudes that violate explicit public policies, that, e.g., discriminate against protected groups, unduly restrain alienation, or restrain trade. Second, they may refuse to enforce restrictions created in violation of traditional servitude doctrine, e.g., where there was no "horizontal privity" between the initial covenantor and covenantee, or where the restriction does not "touch and concern" the land. The former doctrines normally render the servitude wholly unenforceable. The latter doctrines render the restrictions unenforceable against, and, sometimes, by, subsequent owners of burdened or benefited land, but do not affect their enforceability as contracts. This section begins with a consideration of restrictions imposed on servitudes by traditional law. It then moves on to consider public policy constraints on the enforcement of servitudes.

(a) Traditional Servitude Law

A traditional requirement for the enforcement of promises respecting the use of land against or by successors of the original promisor or promisee is that the original parties intend that the promise bind or benefit successors. Since servitudes originate in consensual relationships, it makes sense that the intent of the initial creators of the servitude should be considered in determining whether it runs with the land.

While this requirement has clear continuing validity, its operation has changed somewhat over time. At one time there was authority for the proposition that, at least for some servitudes, it was necessary to state that the servitude was binding on "assigns" to designate that the benefit or burden of the servitude was intended to run with the land. Modern courts try to discern the intent of the parties, unbound by particular verbal formulae. See American Law of Property, § 9.10 (J. Casner, ed. 1952).

Under the traditional law of servitudes, however, the mere intention of the parties that the promise "run with the land" was not enough to insure that it would. In addition, the law required that the promise "touch and concern" the land. Also, for a real covenant to be enforceable (i.e., for a negative or affirmative servitude to be enforceable at law), the initial covenantor and covenantee had to be in a special relationship known as "horizontal privity". What purposes do these doctrines serve? Do they, and should they, have continuing vitality? Consider these questions as you study the following materials.

(i) Horizontal Privity

MOSELEY v. BISHOP

Court of Appeals of Indiana, Fourth District, 1984.
470 N.E.2d 773.

YOUNG, JUDGE.

Edith Moseley brought suit against Merrill and Joanna Gates and sixteen others (hereinafter defendants) seeking damages for the defendants' failure to maintain a tile drain that served Moseley's farm and ran across the Gateses' land. This suit was based upon a contract made in 1896 by Henry Moseley, who then owned what is now the plaintiff's farm, and William Bohn, the defendants' predecessor in interest. The trial court ruled that this contract, which required Bohn to "permanently maintain" the drain at issue, did not run with the land and thus was not binding upon the defendants, Bohn's successors. The trial court also ruled that Moseley had not proved the defendants' failure to repair the drain caused the losses of which she complained. Moseley appeals, claiming the trial court's judgment was contrary to law.

We reverse.

In 1896, Henry Moseley and William Bohn owned adjoining farms in Miami County, Indiana. Moseley's land was drained by an open ditch across Bohn's land. In August, 1896, they entered into a contract (hereinafter termed the Moseley–Bohn agreement), which read in part as follows:

> That Whereas; There exists an open public ditch known as the 'Moseley Ditch' in the West half of the East half of Section 23 in Township 26 North, of Range 4 East, which real estate is owned by said Bohn, and Whereas; said Moseley is the owner of real estate lying immediately South of and adjoining said real estate and which has the ditch above referred to for the out-let for its drainage, and Whereas said Moseley and divers other persons have heretofore been assessed for the construction and repair of said Moseley Ditch, and said Bohn is desirous of straightening and placing drain tile the entire length of said ditch; Now Therefore, in consideration that said Moseley will consent to such straightening and tiling of said ditch, and in the further consideration of the sum of Forty Dollars to be paid by said Moseley when the tiling through that portion of said ditch which has been assigned to him for repairs shall have been completed, said William C. Bohn hereby agrees that he will place through the entire length of said ditch and permanently maintain drain tile of sufficient capacity to furnish adequate out-let for drainage from a twelve inch tile at the North line of said Moseley's land, being the south line of said Section 23. Backwater at said point to be conclusive evidence of lack of said capacity. In consideration of the foregoing premises, said Moseley hereby consents to the straightening and tiling of said ditch and agrees to pay to said Bohn the sum of $40.00 on the terms above stated.

This contract was duly recorded in the Miami County Recorder's Office.

In the course of time, Henry Moseley's farm came into the hands of Edith Moseley, the plaintiff. Bohn's farm has had several subsequent owners, most recently the Gateses—who farm the land—and the other defendants, most of whom own small residential tracts. Beginning in 1976, Moseley's son Harold noticed that her farm seemed to lack good drainage. This condition worsened each year to the point that, in 1981, there was standing water on Moseley's farm. In 1981 and again in 1982 Harold walked along the course of the drain at issue, which ran exclusively across the Gateses' land. On both occasions he observed eroded holes in the ground, some filled with water, indicating that the drain tile was broken or blocked. Harold requested Mr. Gates to fulfill his obligation under the Moseley–Bohn agreement and repair the drain tile. Gates refused to do so without Moseley's help, and he petitioned the Miami County Drainage Board to repair the drain and assess the cost equally against all the affected landowners. Moseley then brought this suit against the defendants, based on the Moseley–Bohn agreement, seeking damages for losses caused by flooding on her farm and asking that the defendants be made to pay any repair charges assessed against Moseley by the drainage board. After a bench trial the court entered judgment against Moseley, and this appeal ensued.

Moseley contends the trial court's ruling that the defendants had no contractual duty to repair the ditch was contrary to law. The central issue here is whether the Moseley–Bohn agreement runs with the land, so as to bind the defendants to "permanently maintain" the drain tile on their land. Generally, a covenant imposing an affirmative burden will run with the land if (1) the covenantors intend it to run, (2) the covenant touches and concerns the land, and (3) there is privity of estate between subsequent grantees of the original covenantor and covenantee. [ ] J. Cribbet, Principles of the Law of Property 353 (2d ed. 1975). Because Moseley had the burden of establishing these elements, we may reverse the trial court's ruling against her only if the evidence is undisputed and shows that she is entitled to judgment as a matter of law. [ ]

The first element, the parties' intent that their covenant should run with the land, must be determined from the specific language used and from the situation of the parties when the covenant was made. [ ] CRIBBET, supra, at 354. Although a statement in the covenant that it is binding on the covenantor's heirs and assigns is strong evidence of intent that the covenant should run with the land, the omission of such language here, as the defendants concede, does not conclusively prove the covenant was not intended to run. [ ]

In the contract at issue, Bohn agreed to "permanently maintain" a tile drain across his property. This language indicates an intention to bind not only Bohn but later grantees of the burdened property as well. Also relevant are the facts surrounding the covenant. Even before the agreement, Moseley's land was drained by an open ditch across Bohn's property. Thus, the installation of buried drain tile benefitted only Bohn, whose property gained additional usable surface area. Moseley, on the other hand, incurred an increased risk that his property might not be adequately drained, since it is more difficult to remove obstructions from a buried drain than from an open ditch. Under these circumstances, the importance of Bohn's promise to "permanently maintain" the drain is clear. Given the importance of this drain to Moseley's land, it is improbable that the parties intended their agreement to be purely personal and not binding on subsequent grantees of the land. Faced with similar agreements relating to ditches and drains, courts in other jurisdictions have generally found an intent that the covenant run with the land. See 20 Am.Jur.2d Covenants, Conditions, and Restrictions § 42 (1965). We find as a matter of law that the facts surrounding the written agreement and the language used in it show an intent to create a covenant running with the land.

Having proved this intent, Moseley was also required to show the covenant touched and concerned the land with which it was to run. This requirement ensures that one purchasing land will be bound by his grantor's contract only where the contract has some logical connection to his use and enjoyment of the land. Thus, a successor to the covenantor's interest in property may be bound by the covenant if it is logically connected to that property interest. Conversely, a successor to the covenantee's property interest may enforce the covenant if it is logically connected to his property. See C. Clark, Real Covenants and Other Interests Which "Run With Land" 97 (1947). The covenant to maintain the tile drain at issue here is logically connected both to the Gateses' property—in which the drain is buried—and to the plaintiff's land, which is served by the drain. Because the drain runs exclusively across the Gateses' land, however, the agreement to maintain it has no logical connection to the land held by the other defendants, who own residential tracts in the old Bohn farm. Thus, the "touch and concern" requirement is met as to Moseley, the plaintiff, and the Gateses, but not as to the other defendants.

Finally, to establish a covenant running with the land, Moseley was required to prove she was in privity of estate with the defendants. Where, as here, neither of the original covenantors is a party to the suit, both "vertical privity" and "horizontal privity" must be proved. "Vertical privity" is established where the party seeking to enforce the covenant and the party against whom it is to be enforced are successors in title to the property of the covenantee and covenantor respectively. See Cribbet, supra, at 354. Vertical privity clearly exists in this case.

The concept of "horizontal privity," however, is more difficult. "Horizontal privity" is generally established by evidence that the original parties to the covenant had some mutual or successive interest either in the land burdened by the covenant or the land benefitted by it. The requirement of horizontal privity may be met by proof that the covenantee has a leasehold and the covenantor has the reversion in the affected land. [ ] Similarly, the parties are in privity where one has an easement in land owned by the other, so long as the covenant concerns the easement. [ ] Finally, privity of estate may be found between the original covenantors even where they did not hold simultaneous interests in the land if the covenant concerns land transferred by one party to the other. [ ] Additionally, to establish privity, the plaintiff generally must prove the covenant was made in the context of a transfer of an interest in the affected land, whether by lease or by deed conveying the property or an easement therein. Wheeler v. Schad, 7 Nev. 204 (1871); Cribbet, supra, at 354.[10]

10. For several reasons, we make the foregoing statements of the law regarding horizontal privity with some trepidation. First, most of the legal scholars who have discussed real covenants argue that no privity of estate between the original covenantors should be required for their covenant to run with the land. Clark, supra, 111–37; O.W. Holmes, The Common Law 403, 404; Newman & Losey, Covenants Running with the Land, and Equitable Servitudes; Two Concepts, or One? 21 Hastings L.J. 1319 (1970); Stoebuck, Running Covenants: An Analytical Primer, 52 Wash.L.Rev. 861 (1977). These writers point out that the requirement of horizontal privity, while frequently stated in dictum, is seldom used to bar the running of an otherwise valid real covenant. Clark, supra, at 116. They also argue that this requirement is purely arbitrary, not vindicating any interest of the landowners involved or of society at large. Id. at 116–17. Second, the courts have made significant exceptions to the privity requirement. Thus, it has been held that a covenant need not be made as part of a transfer of an interest in land if "the promise is made in the adjustment of the mutual relationships arising out of the existence of an easement held by one of the parties to the promise in the land of the other." Restate-

We believe Moseley established the required privity of estate in this case. Where one landowner agrees to construct a drain across his property for the benefit of a neighbor's land, the agreement will generally create an easement appurtenant to the adjacent land. [ ] Thus, we find that Bohn's agreement to construct a tile drain across his land for Moseley's benefit created an easement appurtenant to Moseley's land. Since Bohn's agreement to maintain the drain was contained in the same document, the covenant was clearly made in the context of a transfer to Moseley of an easement in Bohn's land. This satisfies the requirement of privity of estate between the original covenantors. [ ] We accordingly hold that the Moseley–Bohn agreement runs with the land now held by Moseley and the Gateses. Because the agreement does not affect the other defendants' property, however, the trial court correctly found it did not run with their land.

* * *

Notes and Questions

1. The "horizontal" relationship in servitude law is the relationship between the initial promisor and promisee. Whether these two parties are in "privity" depends on the nature of that relationship, and the horizontal privity requirement applied in the jurisdiction. As the principal case points out, the requirement has been interpreted variously in different jurisdictions, with England requiring a landlord-tenant relationship, Massachusetts and other jurisdictions requiring that the servitude be attached to a "mutual" relationship, usually an easement, and other jurisdictions merely requiring that the servitude be created through a conveyance. Would the following landowners be in horizontal privity, and, if so, under what definition?

    a. Two neighbors who each promise to contribute half to the maintenance of a common sewer line that both use.

    b. A purchaser of a lot in a subdivision who accepts a deed which includes a promise to use the land only for residential purposes.

ment of Property § 534(b) (1944); see Morse v. Aldrich, 36 Mass. 449 (1837). Further, it is unnecessary to prove privity of estate where the benefit of the covenant, rather than the burden, is to run with the land. City of Reno v. Matley, 79 Nev. 49, 378 P.2d 256 (1963); Restatement of Property § 548 (1944); 21 C.J.S. Covenants § 58 (1940 & Supp.1984). Finally, the horizontal privity requirement has been undermined by the courts' frequent resort to the doctrine of equitable servitudes. Under this doctrine, a landowner who has actual or constructive notice of a covenant concerning the land made by his predecessor in interest may be bound by the covenant even though the original covenantors were not in privity of estate. Tulk v. Moxhay, 2 Phillips 774, 41 Eng.Rep. 1143 (1848); Cribbet, supra, at 356; see Howard D. Johnson Co. v. Parkside Development Corp., 169 Ind.App. 379, 348 N.E.2d 656 (1976). Because virtually all promises giving rise to a real covenant also create an equitable servitude, this equitable doctrine has become a popular means of circumventing the technical requirements that govern real covenants—most notably the requirement of horizontal privity. See, e.g., Neponsit Property Owners' Ass'n v. Emigrant Industrial Savings Bank, 278 N.Y. 248, 15 N.E.2d 793 (1938); Merrionette Manor Homes Improvement Ass'n v. Heda, 11 Ill. App.2d 186, 136 N.E.2d 556 (1956); see generally Stoebuck, supra, 52 Wash.L.Rev. at 919–21. For all these reasons, although we find the technical requirement of horizontal privity has been satisfied in this case, we doubt whether this requirement has much continuing vitality in Indiana.

c. Two neighbors who each agree to use their land only for residential purposes.

d. A person who buys a lot from his neighbor and promises not to build within 20 feet of the property line of the neighbor who sells him the lot.

2. The horizontal privity requirement is largely based on older cases; modern cases honor it principally in dicta. The 1989 Tentative Draft Restatement of the Law of Property (Third) Servitudes, states:

§ 2.4 No Horizontal Privity Required

No privity relationship between parties is necessary to create a servitude.

Its rationale for this position is:

b. *Rationale.* In American law, the horizontal privity requirement serves no function beyond insuring that most covenants intended to run with the land will be created in conveyances. Formal creation of covenants is desirable because it tends to assure that they will be recorded. However, the horizontal privity requirement is no longer needed for this purpose. In modern law, the Statute of Frauds and recording acts perform that function.

Application of the horizontal privity requirement prevents enforcement at law of covenants entered into between neighbors and between other parties who do not transfer or share some other interest in the land. The rule can easily be circumvented by conveyance to a strawperson who imposes the covenant in the reconveyance. Since the rule serves no necessary purpose and simply acts as a trap for the poorly represented, it has been abandoned. As a matter of common law, horizontal privity between the convenanting parties is no longer required to create a servitude obligation.

(ii) The Touch and Concern Requirement

The touch and concern requirement may prove more durable. The position is commonly taken that the benefit of a servitude must touch and concern some estate in the dominant parcel to run with the land. Similarly, the burden must touch and concern some estate in the burdened parcel to run with that land. See Cunningham, Stoebuck and Whitman, The Law of Property, § 8.15 (1984); G. Korngold, Private Land Use Arrangements, § 9.10 (1990). The content of the requirement, however, is subject to debate. Must the benefit or burden physically affect the land in some way, or would, for example, an obligation to pay money to a property owners association touch and concern the land? See Neponsit Property Owner's Ass'n v. Emigrant Industrial Savings Bank, 278 N.Y. 248, 15 N.E.2d 793 (1938) (the obligation to pay money touches and concerns the land where the money is used to maintain common easements). The most famous explication of the rule was created by Dean Harry Bigelow and elaborated by Judge Charles E. Clark:

If the promisor's legal relations in respect to the land in question are lessened—his legal interest as owner rendered less valuable by the promise—the burden of the covenant touches or concerns that land; if the promisee's legal relations in respect to that land are increased—his legal interest as owner rendered more valuable by the promise—the benefit of the covenant touches or concerns that land.

C. Clark, Covenants and Interests Running with the Land, 97 (2d ed. 1947).

Try to apply this test in the *Kotseas* case which follows.

Professor French, the author of the 1989 Restatement, proposes abolition of the requirement in favor of more policy oriented analysis:

FRENCH, SERVITUDES REFORM AND THE NEW RESTATEMENT OF PROPERTY: CREATION DOCTRINES AND STRUCTURAL SIMPLIFICATION

73 Cornell L.Rev. 928, 939–940 (1988).

* * *

The touch and concern doctrine has traditionally been stated in the form of an ex ante limit on the creation of servitudes. If the benefit or burden of the covenant does not touch or concern the land, then it does not run with the land. As it applies to benefits, I continue to regard the requirement as such as an ex ante control, and I have treated it as a prohibition on benefits in gross. As it applies to burdens, however, I think the touch and concern requirement is more in the nature of an ex post control, operating after the fact to give the court a discretionary power to terminate a servitude. The concept is so difficult to pin down that it can rarely be used as a basis for predicting the enforceability of a particular covenant. Each covenant must be litigated to determine whether it touches and concerns or not.

To the extent that the burden side of the touch and concern requirement does operate as a limit on covenant creation, I propose that it be eliminated along with the other old ex ante controls. Its only significant operation is in the realm of affirmative covenants, where it serves to prevent the creation of particular types of covenants. Why it prevents them, however, remains a mystery. Some have suggested that it only prevents creation of covenant obligations that people would expect not to be bound by if they bought the land. But why would they expect not to be bound? If there is notice of the covenant, and the intent that it run is clear, the only basis for such an expectation is precedent.

When a court invalidates a covenant obligation on the ground that it does not touch and concern the land, it makes a substantive judgment that the obligation should not be permitted to run with land. Such judgments have been passed with respect to mortgage covenants, a variety of lease covenants, and a few other covenants. The real reasons for the invalidation are seldom, if ever, given. Sometimes it appears that the covenant restrains trade or competition; sometimes it appears that the covenant takes unfair advantage of a consumer; sometimes it simply appears that the conditions have changed and the agreement no longer produces the benefits that the original covenantor expected.

In my view, servitudes law should separate initial-validity questions from modification and termination questions, and should tackle both directly. The vice of the touch and concern doctrine is that it permits commingling of the two types of questions and treats both behind such a screen of hocus-pocus that we have to guess at the reasons for a decision. It is often difficult to know whether the arrangement was invalidated because it violated some important public policy, or whether it was terminated because it was unfair in the beginning or had become obsolete or unduly burdensome later on.

We will make a major advance in improving the quality of servitudes law if we abandon the rhetoric of touch and concern. Servitudes law should address separately and directly the questions whether an arrangement would violate a constitutional, statutory, or public policy norm if permitted to operate as a servitude, and whether the arrangement, while valid as a servitude, should be terminated because it has become obsolete, unduly burdensome, or something else.

Professor Uriel Reichman, on the other hand, argues that the doctrine serves a useful purpose:

REICHMAN, TOWARD A UNIFIED CONCEPT OF SERVITUDES
55 S.Cal.L.Rev. 1177, 1232–1233 (1982).

In situations where a promise has no bearing on land use regulation, the courts treat the arrangement as a contract between the original parties and exempt the promisor's transferees from liability. In such cases, it is irrelevant whether or not the transacting parties clearly expressed their written intention that the promise would "run with the land," or that the promisor's transferee had actual or constructive notice of the obligation. As a matter of positive law, where land use efficiency gains could not conceivably be accomplished, servitudes are not recognized. By applying the "touch and concern" test, the courts are actually exercising their power to fix the boundaries of servitudes.

This somewhat unusual interventionist theory is justified because the permanent attachment to land of merely personal obligations is likely to frustrate the objectives of a private land holding system.

In the first place, obligations not related to actual property use are highly individualized. They tend, therefore to become inefficient in the short run following a transfer. Consensual termination of such rights might not occur because of prohibitive transaction costs. The best way to insure efficient termination of such arrangements is to shift the burden of negotiation; instead of making the transferee negotiate for a release, the aspiring beneficiary will have to reach agreement with each new owner. Personal contracts remain the subject of personal bargains.

There is another reason for the "touch and concern" rule. Private property is sanctioned by society not only to promote efficiency, but also to safeguard individual freedom. Servitudes are a kind of private legislation affecting a line of future owners. Limiting such "legislative powers" to an objective purpose of land planning eliminates the possibility of creating modern variations of feudal serfdom. There might be nothing objectionable in personal agreements concerning personal labor, adherence to ideologically prescribed modes of behavior, or promises to buy from a certain supplier. When such obligations however, become permanently enforced against an ever-changing group of owners, the matter acquires different dimensions. One point needs emphasis: The courts are not involved in measuring efficiency gains; this is clearly the prerogative of the parties. The courts only deny the permanency of agreements clearly unrelated to land use.

Consider how the touch and concern requirement was dealt with in a recent case, addressing one of the most persistent problems for which the touch and concern requirement has been invoked, the problem of covenants not to compete. Does the court's shift in analysis deal with the problem more rationally? Does it make the problem easier to deal with?

WHITINSVILLE PLAZA, INC. v. KOTSEAS

Supreme Judicial Court of Massachusetts, 1979.
378 Mass. 85, 390 N.E.2d 243.

QUIRICO, JUSTICE.

These are civil actions commenced by Whitinsville Plaza, Inc. (Plaza), against Charles H. Kotseas and Paul Kotseas (Kotseas) and against Whitinsville CVS, Inc. (CVS). In its further amended complaint against Kotseas, Plaza alleged imminent violations of certain anticompetitive deed restrictions and requested declaratory, injunctive, and monetary relief under theories of breach of contract and unfair acts or practices within the meaning of M.G.L.A. c. 93A, § 2. Plaza's amended complaint against CVS likewise alleged imminent violations of the deed restrictions, and it requested declaratory, injunctive, and monetary relief on theories of breach of contract, unfair trade practices, and interference with contractual relations. A judge of the Superior Court granted the defendants' motions to dismiss for failure to state a claim. [ ]

* * * We hold that dismissal for failure to state a claim was erroneous as to some counts of each complaint.

* * * [The allegations] are as follows. In 1968, Kotseas conveyed certain land identified as "Parcel A" to four individuals as trustees of the "122 Trust" (Trust), a wholly owned subsidiary of Plaza. The deed set forth numerous, detailed, reciprocal restrictions and covenants designed to assure the harmonious development of a shopping center on Parcel A and on abutting land retained by Kotseas. In particular, Kotseas promised (a) not to use the retained land in competition with

the discount store contemplated by the grantee and (b) to use the retained land only for enumerated business purposes. Among the permitted business uses of the land retained by Kotseas was a "drug store," defined in an appendix to the deed as a store selling prescribed types of merchandise. In addition, the deed recited that "(t)he foregoing restrictions shall be considered as covenants running with the land to which they are applicable and shall bind and inure to the benefit of the heirs and assigns of the respective parties to whom any part of the lands made subject to the above restrictions covenants and conditions shall at any time become or belong during the period hereinbefore set forth."

In 1975, the Trust conveyed Parcel A to Plaza and, thereafter, ceased operations. The deed to Plaza expressly made Plaza subject to, and gave it the benefit of, the restrictions and covenants in the 1968 deed from Kotseas to the Trust. At some later time, Kotseas leased a portion of its abutting land to CVS for use as a "discount department store and pharmacy." Plaza's complaints state that the lease to CVS, dated May 10, 1977, was expressly subject to the 1968 deed restrictions and that operation of the contemplated CVS store would violate those restrictions. Although the defendants controvert these allegations, we must, as we have said, accept them as true in ruling on the motion to dismiss.

As against Kotseas, Plaza sought (a) an injunction prohibiting the use of the retained land in violation of the restrictions and (b) damages suffered because of the alleged violations. In the alternative, Plaza prayed for a declaration that its own land was no longer subject to the anticompetitive restrictions. Plaza also requested the court to find that Kotseas had knowingly and wilfully violated M.G.L.A. c. 93A, § 2, and to award double or treble damages and counsel fees. As against CVS, Plaza requested similar relief and also requested damages on the theory that CVS had tortiously interfered with Plaza's contract by inducing Kotseas to violate its restrictions. The defendants filed motions to dismiss, stating as grounds that Plaza lacked standing to sue on the covenants and that the covenants were, in any event, unreasonable and in restraint of trade. * * *

I. Theories of Recovery

A. Real covenant analysis. Plaza has primarily sought to maintain its actions on the theory that the covenants contained in the 1968 deed run with the land. In our view, Plaza has alleged sufficient facts to be entitled to a hearing on its claims for legal and equitable relief on this theory. See generally 5 R. Powell, Real Property pars. 672–675, at 149–185 (Rohan rev. ed. 1979) (summarizing requirements for covenants to run with land). The covenants in question are evidenced by a writing signed by Kotseas, the covenantor. [ ] M.G.L.A. c. 259, § 1, Fourth (Statute of Frauds for interests in land). The language of the 1968 deed aptly expresses the intention of the original parties that the covenants run with the land. [ ] The deed also grants mutual easements sufficient to satisfy the requirement that Plaza and CVS be in privity of estate. See, e.g., Morse v. Aldrich, 19 Pick. 449, 454 (1837) (action at law). Plaza's complaint alleges that CVS had actual knowledge of the restrictions and shows, in any event, that the restrictions were recorded with the deed. [   ]

One additional prerequisite for either legal or equitable relief is, however, arguably lacking in this case on the present state of our case law. It is essential that both the benefit and the burden of a real covenant "touch and concern" the affected parcels of land before it will be considered to run. [   ] This court has long held that a covenant not to compete contained in a deed, such as is involved in this case, does not "touch and concern" the land to be benefited and that, in consequence, such a covenant does not run with the land. Shade v. M. O'Keefe, Inc., 260 Mass. 180, 183, 156 N.E. 867 (1927); Norcross v. James, 140 Mass. 188, 192, 2 N.E. 946 (1885). In Shell Oil Co. v. Henry Ouellette & Sons, 352 Mass. 725, 227 N.E.2d 509 (1967), we intimated that we might overrule Norcross and Shade in an appropriate case. Id. at 730–731 & n. 8, 227 N.E.2d 509. We believe this is such a case.

It is essential to our task that we identify precisely the holding and rationale of the cases we propose to overrule. Norcross was an action seeking specific performance of a covenant not to quarry stone from a parcel of land. The covenant in question was contained in a deed by which one Kibbe conveyed a stone quarry to one Flynt, and it concerned adjoining land retained by Kibbe. The defendant James, a successor to Kibbe's interest, began operating a quarry on the restricted land. The plaintiff Norcross, a successor to Flynt's interest, sought an injunction to halt that operation. 140 Mass. at 188, 2 N.E. 946. In an opinion by Justice Holmes, this court denied relief. Id. at 192, 2 N.E. 946.

Justice Holmes analyzed the case before him in two steps. He first noted a distinction drawn in early English decisions between promises resembling warranties of title and those resembling grants of easements. Warranty-like covenants ran "with the estate" to grantees from the convenantee, but were enforceable only against the covenantor. Easement-like covenants, on the other hand, ran "with the land" in favor of and against subsequent owners. Id. at 188–190, 2 N.E. 946. See also O.W. Holmes, The Common Law 371–409 (1881) (developing historical analysis summarized later in Norcross opinion).

Having traced the development of the law of real covenants, Justice Holmes proceeded to determine whether the covenant could be encompassed within the easement-like class.[11] He stated that a real covenant must "touch or concern" the land by conferring "direct physical advantage in the occupation of the dominant estate." 140 Mass. at 192, 2 N.E. at 949. The covenant against operating a quarry

---

11. Because Kibbe, the original covenantor, was not a party to the Norcross case, it was obvious that classifying the covenant with warranties of title would not assist the plaintiff.

did not do so because "(i)t does not make the use or occupation of (the dominant estate) more convenient. It does not in any way affect the use or occupation; it simply tends indirectly to increase its value, by excluding a competitor from the market for its products." Id. In addition, the covenant transgressed a supposed rule against attaching "new and unusual incidents" to land, for it attempted to create "an easement of monopoly, an easement not be competed with" not theretofore recognized. Id.

Two observations about Norcross are appropriate before we consider later developments. First of all, the benefit of the covenant surely touched and concerned the dominant estate within the ordinary sense and meaning of the phrase "touch and concern." Justice Holmes's analysis has been described as "overlook(ing) the purpose of all building restrictions, which is to enhance the market value of the promisee's land, whether for residential or for business purposes." 2 American Law of Property § 9.28, at 414 (Casner ed. 1952). It has been suggested that Justice Holmes's "real objection to (the covenant was) the policy against monopolies, and not any policy with reference to real covenants as such." C. Clark, Real Covenants and Other Interests Which "Run with Land" 84 n. 26 (1929). Cf. 140 Mass. at 193, 2 N.E. 946 (unnecessary to decide whether covenant would be invalid restraint of trade if enforcement attempted against Kibbe). If free-competition policies were indeed the basis for the Norcross decision, it would now seem preferable for us to deal with them explicitly rather than to condemn all anticompetitive covenants regardless of reasonableness.

Second, Norcross seems to turn on an assumption that there could be no other class of covenants, differing both from easements and from warranties, but which might nevertheless run with the land. Justice Holmes reasoned that neither the benefit nor the burden of the covenant could run because the benefit was personal to the original covenantee and was therefore inconsistent with the existence of any easement-like right appurtenant to the dominant land. Underlying such reasoning is the peculiar Massachusetts requirement of privity of estate, created by the existence of an easement between the parties to an action on a real covenant. Clark, *supra* at 88. Cf. Morse v. Aldrich, supra at 452–454 (statement of Massachusetts privity rule); 140 Mass. at 191, 2 N.E. 946 (citing Massachusetts privity cases). Yet, privity of estate in this sense had never been thought essential to an action in equity for specific performance of a covenant. [   ]

* * *

Massachusetts has been practically alone in its position that covenants not to compete do not run with the land to which they relate. It has long been the opinion of text writers that our rule is anachronistic and in need of change. See 2 American Law of Property § 9.28, at 414 (J. Casner ed. 1952); 5 Powell, *supra* par. 678, at 197. The American Law Institute has suggested that an otherwise enforceable covenant not to compete should be held enforceable in the same manner as an equitable servitude. Restatement of Property § 539, Comment k (1944). Reasonable anticompetitive covenants are enforceable in the great majority of States where the issue has arisen. See Comment, Covenants Not to Compete: Do They Pass?, 4 Cal.W.L.Rev. 131, 133–134 (1968). Modern judicial analysis of cases like the one at bar appears to concentrate on the effects of particular covenants on competition and to avoid the esoteric convolutions of the law of real covenants. See, e.g., Hall v. American Oil Co., 504 S.W.2d 313, 316 n. 3 (Mo.App.1973); Quadro Stations, Inc. v. Gilley, 7 N.C.App. 227, 231–235, 172 S.E.2d 237 (1970).

In addition to the doctrinal questions about the Norcross rule and the preference of most authorities for a more flexible approach, we may note the unfairness that would result from applying that rule to the facts of this case. In what appears to have been an arm's-length transaction, Kotseas agreed in 1968 not to use retained land in competition with the Trust. We may assume (a) that Kotseas received compensation for thus giving up part of his ownership rights by limiting the uses he could make of the retained land, and (b) that freedom from destructive, next-door competition was part of the inducement for the Trust's purchase and of the price paid by the Trust. Plaza, a closely associated business entity, succeeded to the Trust's interest in 1975. One of these entities established a business, presumably at great cost to itself and in reliance on the contractually obtained limitation of competition in its own narrow market area. Notwithstanding the promise not to do so, Kotseas proceeded to lease land to CVS for the purpose of carrying on the business that it knew would, at least in part, compete with Plaza and divert customers from Plaza's premises. Acting with full knowledge of the 1968 arrangement, CVS participated in this inequitable conduct by Kotseas. If we assume for the moment that the 1968 covenants are reasonable in their application to the present facts, we cannot condone the conduct of Kotseas and CVS. Yet, if Norcross remains the law, we are powerless to prevent Kotseas and CVS from indirectly destroying or diminishing the value of Plaza's investment in its business.

We think the time has come to acknowledge the infirmities and inequities of Norcross. Prior decisions by this court establish what we believe is the proper direction. With respect to covenants in commercial leases, we have long held that reasonable anticompetitive covenants are enforceable by and against successors to the original parties. [ ] We have applied a similar rule with respect to covenants between fee owners when we could identify intelligible land-use planning goals. * * * In short, our decisions support what we hereby state to be the law: reasonable covenants against competition *may* be considered to run with the land when they serve a purpose of facilitating orderly and harmonious development for commercial use. To the extent they are inconsistent with this statement, Norcross, Shade, and Ouellette are hereby expressly overruled.

We recognized in our decision in Ouellette that "(t)he fact of bar reliance in the past, however, must be given weight where a rule affecting real estate is involved." 352 Mass. at 730, 227 N.E.2d at 512. The fact of such reliance is a persuasive reason for excluding all covenants executed before June 13, 1967, the date of the Ouellette decision, from the operation and effect of the new rule which we have declared in the preceding paragraph of the present opinion. [ ] We believe that parties who, after the date of the Ouellette decision, executed restrictive covenants of the kind involved in this case could reasonably have relied on the expectation that on the next appropriate occasion thereafter this court would overrule the Shade and Norcross decisions, as we have done by our present decision. We believe further that parties who executed such covenants after Ouellette could not reasonably expect that the covenants would continue to be unenforceable under the rule of the Shade and Norcross decisions. We therefore hold that our overruling of the rule of the Shade and Norcross decisions shall apply to all such covenants executed after the Ouellette decision. [ ]

What we have said should not be construed as an invitation to legal draftsmen to insert unlimited, "boilerplate"-type covenants against competition in real estate documents. As we have said, an enforceable covenant will be one which is consistent with a reasonable overall purpose to develop real estate for commercial use. In addition, the ordinary requirements for creation and enforcement of real covenants must be met. We have summarized many of these requirements earlier in this opinion. Others are found in G.L. c. 184, §§ 27, 30, which regulate enforcement of land-use restrictions generally. Within these limits, however, commercial developers may control the course of development by reasonable restrictive covenants free from resort to devious subterfuges in their attempts to avoid the doubts created by the Norcross rule and our efforts to apply or reconcile it in later cases.

* * *

[The court proceeded to hold that claims of unreasonable restraint of trade raised factual questions that would have to be resolved on remand.]

III. Conclusion

To the extent that they dismiss Plaza's claims under c. 93A, the judgments are affirmed without prejudice to Plaza's right to amend its complaints within a reasonable time hereafter. To the extent they dismiss Plaza's claims for violation of real covenants or for interference with contractual relations, the judgments are erroneous and must be vacated. The cases are remanded to the Superior Court for further proceedings consistent with this opinion.

So ordered.

Notes and Questions

1. Was Kotseas' conduct inequitable and Plaza's reliance justified, given the previous state of Massachusetts law?

2. One implication of the position of the 1944 Restatement of Property (Servitudes) that the burden of a servitude was only enforceable as a real convenant if the benefit touched and concerned land was that covenants could not be created in gross. Restatement of the Law of Property (Servitudes) § 537(a) (1944). The Restatement did, however, permit equitable servitudes in gross, § 539, Comment k. Servitudes in gross serve a variety of useful purposes. Conservation groups, for example, can acquire development easements, permitting an owner to continue using his land for agricultural uses, but prohibiting development. Restrictions promoting historical preservation could also be owned by groups dedicated to that goal. Finally, property owners' associations often hold rights to enforce servitudes, including the right to enforce affirmative obligations like the payment of dues, even though they themselves own no property. Covenants against competition, like that found in the principal case, may be held in gross, as may covenants created for the benefit of governmental entities. The 1989 Tentative Draft Restatement of Property (Third) Servitudes takes the position that:

> (b) The benefit of a servitude may be held personally, in gross, or as an appurtenance to an estate or other interest in land., § 2.6

While decisions are divided on whether this statement accurately represents the law (see Roberts, Promises Respecting Land Use—Can Benefits be Held in Gross, 51 Mo.L.Rev. 933 (1986)) there is much to commend it.

3. The English courts prohibited running of servitudes that imposed affirmative obligations. A similar result has been reached by some American courts, which have held that affirmative covenants, such as covenants to pay money, do not touch and concern the land. See Eagle Enterprises, Inc. v. Gross, 39 N.Y.2d 505, 384 N.Y.S.2d 717, 349 N.E.2d 816 (1976) (obligation to purchase water from developer does not touch and concern the land). Most American courts, however, permit the running of affirmative servitudes.

(b) Interpretation or Invalidation to Promote Public Policy

Kotseas reaches beyond traditional servitude law to a more public policy-based approach to servitude law. Could an approach to questions of validity and interpretation be devised that was based solely on public policy, without consideration of traditional notions such as horizontal privity or touch and concern?

Some problems of servitude law are well-suited to such an approach. One of the most common uses of restrictive covenants in the early part of the twentieth century was to create racially restricted subdivisions. In some parts of the country virtually all deeds in new subdivisions had covenants or conditions prohibiting the sale of the property to African–Americans or limiting purchase to caucasians. Asians and Jews were also frequently singled out by such restrictions. In Shelley v. Kraemer, 334 U.S. 1, 68 S.Ct. 836, 92 L.Ed. 1161 (1948), the

United States Supreme Court held that, while such covenants were not void, enforcement of them by the courts through the grant of injunctive relief would violate the Fourteenth Amendment. Subsequently, the Court in Barrows v. Jackson, 346 U.S. 249, 73 S.Ct. 1031, 97 L.Ed. 1586 (1953), held that such covenants could not be enforced through the grant of money damages. They would also currently violate Title VIII of the Civil Rights Act of 1968, 42 U.S.C. §§ 3601–3631. Such covenants continue to exist pervasively, however, in the chains of title of American real estate. Can anything be done to remove such restrictions? Is there any reason for attempting to do so?

Since servitudes are based on private agreements, their existence does not require state action. Enforcement of servitudes requires judicial action, however, and it is here that the Court in Shelley found state action. How broad is this principle? Should a servitude that prohibits religious uses be found to violate the Free Exercise Clause? Compare West Hill Baptist Church v. Abbate, 24 Ohio Misc 66, 261 N.E.2d 196 (CP 1969) (yes), with Ireland v. Bible Baptist Church, 480 S.W.2d 467 (Tex.Civ.App.1972), cert. den., 411 U.S. 906, 93 S.Ct. 1529, 36 L.Ed.2d 195 (1973); Ginsberg v. Yeshiva of Far Rockaway, 45 A.D.2d 334, 358 N.Y.S.2d 477 (1974), aff'd, 36 N.Y.2d 706, 366 N.Y.S.2d 418, 325 N.E.2d 876 (1975) (no). Does a court's holding that a servitude is invalid constitute the taking of a property interest without compensation, also prohibited by the Constitution?

Servitudes can also under some circumstances be challenged as restraints on alienation.

Tentative Draft Number Two of the Restatement of Property (Third) Servitudes (1991) states at § 3.4:

> A servitude that imposes a direct restraint on alienation of the burdened estate is invalid if the restraint is unreasonable. Reasonableness is determined by weighing the utility of the restraint against the injurious consequences of enforcing the restraint.

Section 3.5 states:

> A servitude is not invalid because it indirectly restrains alienation by limiting the use that can be made of property, by reducing the amount realizable by the owner on sale or other transfer of the property, or by otherwise reducing the value of the property, unless there is no rational justification for the servitude.

For an example of this approach, see Taormina Theosophical Community, Inc. v. Silver, 190 Cal.Rptr. 38, 140 Cal.App.3d 964 (1983). In that case a covenant prohibited sales of land within a restricted community except to Theosophists over 50 years of age. The court held the covenant to be an invalid restraint on alienation, as there were only 6000 Theosophists in the United States, and even fewer over 50. Should a servitude that requires construction of a residence of at least 3000 square feet in area, or of at least $500,000 in value, also be held to be a restraint on alienation? Do not such restrictions substantially limit the number of prospective purchasers of a particular property?

Should cooperatives or condominiums be given greater latitude in restricting sales of units than developments involving separately owned single-family dwellings?

Another approach to dealing with discriminatory restrictions is to limit their restrictive nature through a broad interpretation rather than to eliminate them through invalidation. Such an approach leaves the restrictions intact, but may substantially diverge from the intent of the initial drafter of the servitude.

BLEVINS v. BARRY–LAWRENCE COUNTY ASSOCIATION FOR RETARDED CITIZENS

Supreme Court of Missouri, 1986.
707 S.W.2d 407 (Mo.1986).

WELLIVER, JUDGE.

This is an appeal from a circuit court judgment enjoining appellant, Barry–Lawrence County Association for Retarded Citizens, from using its property as a group home for retarded individuals. Respondents, Jess and Nedra Blevins, brought this equitable action alleging that said use violates a restrictive covenant on the lot. * * * We reverse.

Appellant owns Lot 23 and the residence thereon in the Wildwood Estates Subdivision of Cassville, Missouri, and it plans on establishing a group home for eight unrelated mentally retarded persons. Respondents own Lot 24, which is across the street from appellant's property. The subdivision is protected by restrictive covenants, which provide in relevant part:

1. The aforesaid real property shall be used for residential purposes only. No buildings shall be erected, altered, placed or permitted to remain on said real property other than single or double family dwellings not to exceed two and one-half stories in height and private garages for not more than two cars. No detached structures shall be permitted.

Respondents argue that appellant's intended use of its property will contravene this covenant. Appellant responds by alleging (1) that its intended use does not violate the covenant; (2) that awarding an equitable injunction would violate public policy, as illustrated by the recently enacted § 89.020, RSMo Supp.1985 which forbids either zoning ordinances or restrictive covenants from excluding group homes for mentally retarded individuals; and (3) that § 89.020 must be given retroactive effect and, therefore, the provision of the restrictive covenant is void.

* * *

It is a well-established rule that restrictive covenants are not favorites of the law, and when interpreting such covenants, courts should give effect to the intent of the parties as expressed in the plain language of the covenant; but, when there is any ambiguity or substantial doubt as to the meaning, restrictive covenants will be read narrowly in favor of the free use of property. [ ] It might be noted that respondent attempted to establish the intent of the parties to the covenant by offering the testimony of one of the original developers. Such evidence, however, is neither binding as a matter of law nor usually admissible. [ ]

The initial question is whether the group home for eight unrelated persons and two house parents violates the restriction against any use other than for "residential purposes only." In Shepherd v. State, 427 S.W.2d 382 (Mo.1968), this Court interpreted the phrase "residential purposes" in a restrictive covenant. This Court quoted with approval the following definition of "residential purposes":

> Giving the words their plain and ordinary meaning, we would say that * * * it is, one in which people reside or dwell, or which they make their homes, as distinguished from one which is used for commercial or business purposes.

Shepherd v. State, supra, at 388. [ ] Apartment buildings, therefore, were permitted under the covenant.

It is beyond doubt that the operation of the group home in question has all the characteristics of a residential as opposed to a commercial use. The home is owned and run by a non-profit organization, and the underlying theory behind establishing such a home is that it serves as a surrogate family arrangement. There is no commercial enterprise, and the home is neither a boarding house nor an institutional facility. The trial court found the following facts relative to the operation of the home:

> [Appellant] operates a number of "group homes" in which mentally retarded adults live in a residential setting with "house parents", often a husband and wife, who provide supervision and care for the retarded adults.

> * * *

> The group home as contemplated to be operated in Wildwood Estates by defendant is designed to allow the residents to develop their social, emotional and intellectual skills by living in a stable family-type environment. The house parents and residents function in an integrated family-style unit instead of as independent individuals who share only a place to sleep and eat. Residents are involved in performing simpl[e] household duties and participate in discussing, and if possible, resolving problems existing in the home and in making decisions as to the nature of group activities. Although ultimate decisions are left to house parents and/or the defendants board. The entire group often attends church, goes shopping and travels about the community in a body.

> * * * [F]ormal training for the retarded residents does not take place in the group home, but rather is conducted at an activity center or sheltered workshop during the workweek. Within the group home, the

house parents encourage the development of social skills and simple homemaking skills by the individuals living there. The primary purpose of a residential group home is to provide a living situation as normal as possible for developmentally disabled residents of the community and is ordinarily not a temporary living arrangement but, depending upon the individual, a resident may remain in the group home months, years or for their entire lifetime.

The trial court also found that prospective occupants of group homes are carefully screened and are admitted, at first, only on a trial basis. We believe that these findings of fact clearly indicate that appellant's intended use of Lot 23 as a group home is a residential purpose under the restrictive covenant.

Faced with a similar factual situation, a substantial number of courts have held that the operation of a group home is a residential purpose within the meaning of a covenant with such a restriction. [ ] See generally Annot., Restrictive Covenant Limiting Land Use to "Private Residence" or "Private Residential Purposes": Interpretations and Application, 43 A.L.R.4th 71 (1986); Annot., Use of Property for Multiple Dwellings as Violating Restrictive Covenant Permitting Property to be used for Residential Purposes Only, 99 A.L.R.3d 985 (1980).

* * *

The remaining question is whether appellant's intended use of the property violates the second sentence of the restrictive covenant, which prohibits erecting, altering, placing or permitting any building "other than single or double family dwellings not to exceed two and one-half stories in height and private garages for not more than two cars." Respondents argue that this restriction is a restriction on the use of the property; and, if a restriction on use, appellant's group home is neither a single nor a double family dwelling.

By its plain terms, however, this restriction applies only to structures and not to the use of the property.

* * *

A number of other jurisdictions have reached a similar conclusion.[12] [ ]

The record indicates that appellant does not intend to alter the structure of the residence on its lot. We hold, therefore, that appellant's intended use of its property does not violate the terms of the restrictive covenant. The trial court judgment granting the injunction is reversed.

---

12. We need not reach the issue of whether the group home would satisfy a single or double family use restriction. However, it might be noted that a number of jurisdictions, whether interpreting a restrictive covenant or a zoning ordinance, hold that certain group homes may be a "family" unless an explicit definition contained in the covenant or ordinance dictates otherwise. [ ] Recently the United States Supreme Court held that the application of a particular ordinance to prohibit a group home for mentally disabled persons was unconstitutional. City of Cleburne, Tex. v. Cleburne Living Center, 473 U.S. 432, 105 S.Ct. 3249, 87 L.Ed.2d 313 (1985). [ ]

Notes and Questions

Interpretation of negative or affirmative servitudes is necessary where a property owner wants to use the property for uses not clearly permitted by the restrictions. A host of cases, for example, address the question of whether restrictions limiting property to "residential purposes" or to a "dwelling house" excludes use for apartments, duplexes, or boarding homes, or for home occupations. Limitations governing types of commercial uses permitted or locations of buildings on lots also have resulted in litigation. Courts commonly construe restrictions strictly so as to promote the use of land, as in the principal case. See 5 R. Powell, & P. Rohan, Powell on Real Property, ¶ 674 (1991).

Interpretation may also be necessary where a land-owner proposes to use property for uses not contemplated at the time the restriction was drafted. In Breeling v. Churchill, 228 Neb. 596, 423 N.W.2d 469 (1988), a landowner was enjoined from erecting a satellite dish on her lot in violation of a 1972 restriction prohibiting any "outside radio, television, Ham broadcasting, or other electronic antenna or aerial." The court sensibly read the restriction to preclude satellite dishes, even though the technology was not in use at the time the restriction was granted.

4. Succession to Servitudes

If a servitude is determined to be valid and enforceable, and to run with the land generally to bind or benefit persons who subsequently hold interests in the burdened or benefited properties, the question still remains which particular individual subsequent purchasers will be bound or benefited.

(a) The Running of Burdens

(i) The Vertical Privity Requirement

The running of the burden of servitudes is limited both by the law of servitudes and by the recording acts. The most important of the limits imposed by the law of servitudes is the requirement of vertical privity, mentioned in the *Moseley* case above. While horizontal privity refers to the relationship between the initial promisor and promisee, vertical privity refers to the relationships between the initial promisor and promisee and their successors. The labels relate to a diagram used by generations of property teachers:

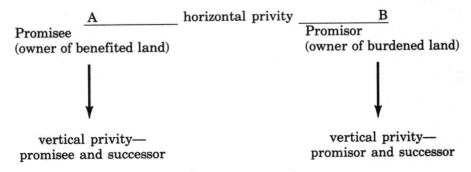

The 1944 Restatement of the Law of Property (Servitudes), § 535 describes the sorts of relationships that can meet the vertical privity requirements for succession to the benefit or burden of promises respecting the use of land enforceable at law.

§ 535. PRIVITY AS BETWEEN PROMISOR AND SUCCESSOR

The successors in title to land respecting the use of which the owner has made a promise are not bound as promisors upon the promise unless by their succession they hold

> (a) the estate or interest held by the promisor at the time the promise was made, or

> (b) an estate or interest corresponding in duration to the estate or interest held by the promisor at that time.

Note that the same relationship that can serve to establish horizontal privity can also serve to establish vertical privity. A purchaser purchasing a lot in a subdivision is in a successive relationship with the developer (i.e. the purchaser succeeds to the interest of the developer in the purchased lot). This successive relationship meets the requirements of either horizontal privity or vertical privity. Whether it is considered under one category or the other depends on the relationship of the purchaser to the promise which is being enforced. If the purchaser/developer relationship is the initial relationship pursuant to which the promise was made that is now being enforced, the relevant category is horizontal privity. If the purchaser succeeds to a previously burdened or benefited parcel (i.e., the developer has earlier made a promise binding or received a promise to benefit the retained land now being purchased), the relevant category is vertical privity.

What sorts of relationships meet the requirements of Restatement § 535? A sells Blackacre, bound by a servitude which requires the payment of an annual fee to a neighbor for maintenance of a common fence, to B. Is B bound by the servitude under Restatement § 535? A leases the property to B for one year. Must B make the payment? B takes the property from A by adverse possession. Must B continue to pay the fee? If you reach a different result for the different questions, is the result defensible in principle? Should the requirements be different if the servitude were negative in nature, e.g., a servitude prohibiting commercial uses in a residential neighborhood? Should tenants be treated differently from adverse possessors? Compare Reichman, Toward a Unified Concept of Servitudes, 55 S.Cal.L.Rev. 1179, 1249–1252 (vertical privity requirement makes no sense with respect to negative servitudes, affirmative obligations should be governed by rule that looked to nature of relationships and burdens) with French, Toward a Modern Law of Servitudes: Reweaving the Ancient Strands, 55 S.Cal.L.Rev. 1261, 1294–96 (vertical privity requirement as applied to limit the running of affirmative burdens is efficient and fair).

The 1944 Restatement required a looser privity—succession to title or possession of a property—for enforcement of the benefit of a servitude at equity. Does it make sense to have different standards for enforcement at law and at equity? Might your answer turn on whether affirmative obligations, as well as negative, were enforceable at equity?

(ii) Notice

Equitable servitudes are only enforceable against persons who take with notice. By virtue of the recording acts, the same is true with all servitudes. Questions of notice are often, therefore, very important when enforcement of servitudes is sought. The notice requirement seldom causes problems where a servitude is expressly placed in a recorded deed of a particular property against which the servitude is later enforced. A standard title search would find the servitude, and imposition of constructive notice is certainly defensible where such a title search is not done. Where servitudes are created by implication, however, or where the servitude is imposed by a deed from a common grantor to the owner of a benefited property but does not appear in the subsequent deed to the purchaser of the burdened parcel, locating the servitude through a title search becomes much more difficult. The question then arises whether the owner of the burdened parcel had sufficient notice of the servitude to be bound by it.

BISHOP v. RUEFF

Court of Appeals of Kentucky, 1981.
619 S.W.2d 718.

REYNOLDS, JUDGE.

Mrs. Nancy Bishop, appellant (plaintiff below), was awarded $1,801 damages in an action instituted against adjoining property owners, William and Patricia Rueff. This is an appeal and cross-appeal from the judgment.

The Rueffs had constructed a backyard patio and enclosed it with a 7–foot high "wooden slab" fence. One section of the fence was erected upon the parties' common boundary which was in near proximity to the side of the Bishop home. As a result of this improvement, appellant alleged damages resulting in changes from the water-flow across her property, as well as from the interference with her use and enjoyment of the property, and, additionally, she had sought injunctive relief to bring the fence into compliance with cited restrictive covenant.

Mr. George Imorde initially owned a sizeable tract of property, and from a portion of the tract he established four lots, one of which he sold to Mrs. Bishop in June of 1957, and her deed contained the following restriction:

> As a further consideration for this conveyance, it is hereby agreed that the property herein conveyed shall be subject to the following restrictions:

> No. 4 No solid board fence shall be erected on the property. Fencing, if any, shall be of rail, picket or shrub. Fences, other than shrub, shall not exceed four feet in height.

> It is further agreed that the restrictions hereinabove set out shall apply to and affect all the remaining property of the parties of the first part as was conveyed to George H. Imorde by deed of record in Deed Book 2672, Page 566, in the aforesaid Clerk's office.

Subsequent to this transaction, and before June 17, 1959, three additional lots were sold by Mr. Imorde, and with only one of those deeds (Lot 251 sold on July 3, 1957) containing notice of these restrictions. On March 29, 1962, Mr. Imorde disposed of a larger tract constituting the remainder of this property to developers David H. Wilson and Bobby J. Welsh. A subdivision containing eleven lots, being known as Trough Springs, was then developed with separate restrictions, none of which mentioned, nor did the deeds refer to, or notice, the restrictions contained in Mrs. Bishop's deed. On June 1, 1973, appellees became owners of a Trough Springs Subdivision lot which abutted the Bishop property.

Appellees were unaware of the restrictions until their backyard construction was substantially complete. This area had been graded, as well as elevated, which allowed water to flow/stand upon appellant's property.

In its instructions to the jury, the court ruled that the restrictions serving as the basis for appellant's claim for injunctive relief were inapplicable. The court reasoned that in the absence of notice in the direct chain of title, appellees were not charged with duty of notice. * * * [The jury awarded damages for diverted surface water and nuisance (not for violation of the servitude).]

Appellant argues that the deed restrictions ran with the land and were therefore binding on any subsequent purchasers of remaining portions of the original tract, and that the court's instructions were contrary to law and erroneous. On cross-appeal it is asserted that the court erred in not directing a verdict in their favor at the close of all evidence regarding the claims for water damage and nuisance.

Generally, the grantee is charged with notice of an encumbrance upon property created by an instrument which is of record, notwithstanding the fact that it may exist only collaterally in the chain of title. Harp v. Parker, 278 Ky. 78, 128 S.W.2d 211 (1939). The trial court determined that the restrictive covenant from the Bishop deed had no application to the lot subsequently acquired by appellees. The criteria for determining whether a covenant runs with the land or is merely personal between the grantor and the grantee include the intent of the parties, whether the covenant must affect or concern the land with which it runs, and whether privity of estate exists between the party claiming the benefit and the party who rests under the burden. 21 C.J.S. Covenants § 54. While the Bishops' deed was not in appellees' chain of title, we are aware of no rule that a restrictive covenant of this nature must meet such requirement. We believe that appellees were on constructive notice as to the restriction limiting fences, and there is some evidence of actual notice. The "chain of title" argument seems to have been disposed of by Harp v. Parker, supra.

We believe the governing principle involved is stated in McLean v. Thurman, Ky., 273 S.W.2d 825, 829 (1954). Where the owners of two or more lots situated near one another convey one of the lots with express restrictions applying thereto in favor of the land retained by the grantor, the servitude becomes mutual, and during the period of restraint the owner of the lots retained may do nothing that is forbidden to the owner of the lot sold. The restriction is enforceable against the grantor, or subsequent purchaser, with notice, actual or constructive.
[ ]

The deed of conveyance between Imorde and appellant contains words indicating that the parties intended for the restrictive covenants to run with Imorde's remaining lands and thus be binding on subsequent purchasers. After the Bishop sale, Imorde sold three additional residential lots. One of the deeds contained the restriction. We hold that the trial court erred by denying injunctive relief.

* * *

The judgment of the trial court is reversed in part, and appellant is entitled to the enforcement of the restrictive covenant which provides:

> No solid board fence shall be erected on the property. Fencing, if any, shall be of rail, picket or shrub. Fences, other than shrub, shall not exceed four feet in height.

The judgment of the trial court, in all other respects, is affirmed.

HOWERTON, JUDGE, concurring.

I would like to affirm Judge Eckert in all respects, but I must concur in the result reached by this Court. Perhaps our Supreme Court will see fit to bring the law regarding reciprocal negative easements and/or covenants running with the land into the late Twentieth Century. This case disturbs me, because we are giving effect to land restrictions which are not within a chain of title, nor are they contained in an instrument which should necessarily be checked to insure a clear title.

Three Kentucky cases which have dealt with the problem and which have helped establish the law are Anderson v. Henslee, 226 Ky. 465, 11 S.W.2d 154 (1928); Harp v. Parker, 278 Ky. 78, 128 S.W.2d 211 (1939); and McLean v. Thurman, Ky., 273 S.W.2d 825 (1954). Each of the cases, if limited to its facts, could be distinguished from the case at bar, but the language of the opinions expresses the law in such a way that such restrictions are enforceable, if reasonable. Constructive notice was considered to be given, because the restrictions were recorded in a deed from a common grantor, although the deed was outside the chain of title of the party to be bound by the restrictions.

* * *

Generally, the law is that reciprocal negative easements, which are enforceable against a grantor, are also enforceable against a subsequent purchaser of the common grantor's restricted remaining property, if the purchaser has notice, actual or constructive. I find no fault with that general principle, but the problem comes in what constitutes constructive notice of such off-shoot restrictions.

In attempting to "settle" the chain of title argument in Harp, the court adopted a passage from 2 Tiffany on Real Property, (2d Ed.) p. 2188. The passage concludes:

> And if, in conveying lot A the grantor enters into a restrictive agreement as to the improvement of lot B, retained by him, a subsequent purchaser of lot B would ordinarily be charged with notice of the agreement, by reason of its record as a part of the conveyance of lot A. Harp v. Parker, 278 Ky. 78, at 82, 128 S.W.2d 211.

Lot A is a conveyance from a common grantor with lot B, but the deed to lot A is outside the chain of title for lot B. The restrictive agreement is not in any conveyance to the common grantor.

It appears to me that the question of what is reasonable should not only apply to the nature of the restriction, but also to the manner of recording and what should constitute constructive notice. None of the three cited cases reach unreasonable results on the basis of their facts. However, to blindly apply Tiffany's principle in today's world is absurd. We are no longer dealing with a few conveyances or the examples of "blackacre" and "whiteacre."

Today, we may find a subdivision of 1,000 acres divided into 2,000 lots. If the owner of the subdivision agreed with the buyer of the twenty-fifth lot to have a reciprocal negative easement against fences on the remainder of his land, is every lot sold thereafter to be bound solely from the restriction written in the twenty-fifth deed? If so, it means that the buyer of lot number 2,000 would have to examine all 1,999 preceding deeds.

Buyers and lenders already have legitimate complaints regarding costs of title examinations, but we have heard nothing compared to what we will hear, if such useless and unreasonable burdens are mandated. It would be far more reasonable to require the buyer of lot A or 25 to require the grantor to record a separate instrument putting the restrictions squarely on the common grantor and in all chains of title from him. If the buyer of lot A or 25 desires to have the restrictions run with the land, he could require that the necessary instrument be prepared and recorded.

There will be times when a proper title examination will reveal restrictions which are nevertheless outside the chain of title. Examples of these situations would be similar to Anderson, Harp, and McLean, supra. Actual knowledge may come from any source, but constructive notice should not be applied to any situation where reciprocal negative restrictions are recorded only outside the chain of title.

Notes and Questions

1. In a jurisdiction that implies servitudes from the existence of a common scheme, what would a title examiner have to do before pronouncing whether or not a lot in a subdivision was bound by express servitudes? When searching the title of a subdivision lot in a jurisdiction which permits implication of restrictions, is it possible to do an adequate title search if the search is restricted solely to documents found in a recorder's office or title plant? See Sanborn v. McLean, 233 Mich. 227, 206 N.W. 496, 60 A.L.R. 1212 (1925) (inquiry notice from "strictly uniform" character of development of lots).

2. 4 The American Law of Property, § 17.24 (J. Casner ed. (1952)) states that the courts are equally divided between the positions of the majority and concurring opinion in principal case.

(b) Running of Benefits

The 1944 Restatement takes the position that the only privity necessary for the benefit of a servitude (either enforceable at law as a real covenant or at equity as an equitable servitude) is that the successor "succeeds to some interest of the beneficiary." § 547. This language was intended to exclude adverse possessors, but why should they be excluded if a servitude is in fact a property rather than a contract interest? Professor French, the author of the 1989 Draft Restatement, argues that there is no case authority to support the position of the 1944 Restatement, and no reason other than dislike of adverse possessors for barring them from enforcement of servitudes. French, Toward a Modern Law of Servitudes: Reweaving the Ancient Strands, 55 S.Cal.L.Rev. 1261, 1294–96 (1982).

C. TERMINATION

EL DI, INC. v. TOWN OF BETHANY BEACH

Supreme Court of Delaware, 1984.
477 A.2d 1066.

HERRMANN, CHIEF JUSTICE for the majority:

This is an appeal from a permanent injunction granted by the Court of Chancery upon the petition of the plaintiffs, The Town of Bethany Beach, et al., prohibiting the defendant, El Di, Inc. ("El Di") from selling alcoholic beverages at Holiday House, a restaurant in Bethany Beach owned and operated by El Di.

I.

The pertinent facts are as follows:

El Di purchased the Holiday House in 1969. In December 1981, El Di filed an application with the State Alcoholic Beverage Control Commission (the "Commission") for a license to sell alcoholic beverages at the Holiday House. On April 15, 1982, finding "public need and convenience," the Commission granted the Holiday House an on-premises license. The sale of alcoholic beverages at Holiday House began within 10 days of the Commission's approval. Plaintiffs subsequently filed suit to permanently enjoin the sale of alcoholic beverages under the license.

On appeal it is undisputed that the chain of title for the Holiday House lot included restrictive covenants prohibiting both the sale of alcoholic beverages on the property and nonresidential construction.[13] The same restriction was placed on property in Bethany Beach as early as 1900 and 1901 when the area was first under development.

As originally conceived, Bethany Beach was to be a quiet beach community. The site was selected at the end of the nineteenth-century by the Christian Missionary Society of Washington, D.C. In 1900, the Bethany Beach Improvement Company ("BBIC") was formed. The BBIC purchased lands, laid out a development and began selling lots. To insure the quiet character of the community, the BBIC placed restrictive covenants on many plots, prohibiting the sale of alcohol and restricting construction to residential cottages. Of the original 180 acre development, however, approximately ⅓ was unrestricted.

The Town of Bethany Beach was officially incorporated in 1909. The municipal limits consisted of 750 acres including the original BBIC land (hereafter the original or "old-Town"), but expanded far beyond the 180 acre BBIC development. The expanded acreage of the newly incorporated Town, combined with the unrestricted plots in the original Town, left only 15 percent of the new Town subject to the restrictive covenants.

Despite the restriction prohibiting commercial building ("no other than a dwelling or cottage shall be erected * * * "), commercial development began in the 1920's on property subject to the covenants. This

---

13. The restrictive covenant stated: "This covenant is made expressly subject to and upon the following conditions: viz; That no intoxicating liquors shall ever be sold on the said lot, that no other than dwelling or cottage shall be erected thereon and but one to each lot, which must be of full size according to the said plan, excepting, however, suitable and necessary out or back building, which may be erected on the rear of said lot, and no building or buildings shall be erected thereon within ten feet of the front building line of said lot and, if said lot be a corner lot within ten feet of the building line of the side street on which it abuts, and that all buildings erected or to be erected on said lot shall be kept neatly painted; a breach of which said conditions, or any of them, shall cause said lot to revert to and become again the property of the grantor, his heirs and assigns; and upon such breach of said conditions or restrictions, the same may be restrained or enjoined in equity by the grantor, his heirs or assigns, or by any co-lot owner in said plan or other party injured by such breach."

development included numerous inns, restaurants, drug stores, a bank, motels, a town hall, shops selling various items including food, clothing, gifts and novelties and other commercial businesses. Of the 34 commercial buildings presently within the Town limits, 29 are located in the old-Town originally developed by BBIC. Today, Bethany Beach has a permanent population of some 330 residents. In the summer months the population increases to approximately 10,000 people within the corporate limits and to some 48,000 people within a 4 mile radius. In 1952, the Town enacted a zoning ordinance which established a central commercial district designated C–1 located in the old-Town section. Holiday House is located in this district.

Since El Di purchased Holiday House in 1969, patrons have been permitted to carry their own alcoholic beverages with them into the restaurant to consume with their meals. This "brown-bagging" practice occurred at Holiday House prior to El Di's ownership and at other restaurants in the Town. El Di applied for a license to sell liquor at Holiday House in response to the increased number of customers who were engaging in "brown-bagging" and in the belief that the license would permit restaurant management to control excessive use of alcohol and use by minors. Prior to the time El Di sought a license, alcoholic beverages had been and continue to be readily available for sale at nearby licensed establishments including: one restaurant ½ mile outside the Town limits, 3 restaurants within a 4 mile radius of the Town, and a package store some 200–300 yards from the Holiday House.

The Trial Court granted a stay pending the outcome of this appeal.

II.

In granting plaintiffs' motion for a permanent injunction, the Court of Chancery rejected defendant's argument that changed conditions in Bethany Beach rendered the restrictive covenants unreasonable and therefore unenforceable. Citing Restatement of Property, § 564 [ ]. The Chancery Court found that although the evidence showed a considerable growth since 1900 in both population and the number of buildings in Bethany Beach, "the basic nature of Bethany Beach as a quiet, family oriented resort has not changed." The Court also found that there had been development of commercial activity since 1900, but that this "activity is limited to a small area of Bethany Beach and consists mainly of activities for the convenience and patronage of the residents of Bethany Beach."

The Trial Court also rejected defendant's contention that plaintiffs' acquiescence and abandonment rendered the covenants unenforceable. In this connection, the Court concluded that the practice of "brown-bagging" was not a sale of alcoholic beverages and that, therefore, any failure to enforce the restriction as against the practice did not constitute abandonment or waiver of the restriction.

III.

We find that the Trial Court erred in holding that the change of conditions was insufficient to negate the restrictive covenant.

A court will not enforce a restrictive covenant where a fundamental change has occurred in the intended character of the neighborhood that renders the benefits underlying imposition of the restrictions incapable of enjoyment. [   ] Review of all the facts and circumstances convinces us that the change, since 1901, in the character of that area of the old-Town section now zoned C–1 is so substantial as to justify modification of the deed restriction. We need not determine a change in character of the entire restricted area in order to assess the continued applicability of the covenant to a portion thereof. [   ]

It is uncontradicted that one of the purposes underlying the covenant prohibiting the sale of intoxicating liquors was to maintain a quiet, residential atmosphere in the restricted area. Each of the additional covenants reinforces this objective, including the covenant restricting construction to residential dwellings. The covenants read as a whole evince an intention on the part of the grantor to maintain the residential, seaside character of the community.

But time has not left Bethany Beach the same community its grantors envisioned in 1901. The Town has changed from a church-affiliated residential community to a summer resort visited annually by thousands of tourists. Nowhere is the resultant change in character more evident than in the C–1 section of the old-Town. Plaintiffs argue that this is a relative change only and that there is sufficient evidence to support the Trial Court's findings that the residential character of the community has been maintained and that the covenants continue to benefit the other lot owners. We cannot agree.

In 1909, the 180 acre restricted old-Town section became part of a 750 acre incorporated municipality. Even prior to the Town's incorporation, the BBIC deeded out lots free of the restrictive covenants. After incorporation and partly due to the unrestricted lots deeded out by the BBIC, 85 percent of the land area within the Town was not subject to the restrictions. Significantly, nonresidential uses quickly appeared in the restricted area and today the old-Town section contains almost all of the commercial businesses within the entire Town. [   ] Moreover, these commercial uses have gone unchallenged for 82 years. [   ]

The change in conditions is also reflected in the Town's decision in 1952 to zone restricted property, including the lot on which the Holiday House is located, specifically for commercial use. Although a change in zoning is not dispositive as against a private covenant, it is additional evidence of changed community conditions. [   ]

Time has relaxed not only the strictly residential character of the area, but the pattern of alcohol use and consumption as well. The practice of "brown-bagging" has continued unchallenged for at least twenty years at commercial establishments located on restricted property in the Town. On appeal, plaintiffs rely on the Trial Court finding that the "brown-bagging," practice is irrelevant as evidence of waiver inasmuch as the practice does not involve the sale of intoxicating liquors prohibited by the covenant. We find the "brown-bagging" practice evidence of a significant change in conditions in the community since its inception at the turn of the century. Such consumption of alcohol in public places is now generally tolerated by owners of similarly restricted lots. The license issued to the Holiday House establishment permits the El Di management to better control the availability and consumption of intoxicating liquors on its premises. In view of both the ready availability of alcoholic beverages in the area surrounding the Holiday House and the long-tolerated and increasing use of "brown-bagging," enforcement of the restrictive covenant at this time would only serve to subvert the public interest in the control of the availability and consumption of alcoholic liquors.

Plaintiffs contend that the covenant prohibiting the sale of intoxicating liquors is separate from the other covenants. In the plaintiffs' view, the alcohol sale restriction serves a purpose distinct from the prohibition of nonresidential uses. Plaintiffs argue, therefore, that despite evidence of commercial uses, the alcohol sale restriction provides a substantial benefit to the other lot owners. We find the cases on which plaintiff relies distinguishable:

In Jameson v. Brown, 109 F.2d 830 (D.C.Cir.1939), all of the lots were similarly restricted and there was no evidence of waiver or abandonment of the covenant prohibiting the sale of spiritous liquors. The court found evidence of one isolated violation—in contrast to the long-tolerated practice of "brown-bagging" in Bethany Beach. * * * In Benner v. Tacony Athletic Ass'n, Pa.Supr., 328 Pa. 577, 196 A. 390 (1938), it was found that commercial encroachments were few and that residential properties still closely surrounded the commercial lots. In Bethany Beach commercial uses have not simply crept in, but have been given official sanction through the 1952 Zoning Ordinance.

It is further argued that the commercial uses are restricted to a small area within the old–Town section. But significantly, the section in which Holiday House is located is entirely commercial. The business uses, the availability of alcohol in close proximity to this section, and the repeated use of "brown-bagging" in the C–1 district render the originally intended benefits of the covenants unattainable in what has become an area detached in character from the strictly residential surroundings to the west.

In view of the change in conditions in the C–1 district of Bethany Beach, we find it unreasonable and inequitable now to enforce the restrictive covenant. To permit unlimited "brown-bagging" but to prohibit licensed sales of alcoholic liquor, under the circumstances of this case, is inconsistent with any reasonable application of the restriction and contrary to public policy.

We emphasize that our judgment is confined to the area of the old–Town section zoned C–1. The restrictions in the neighboring residential area are unaffected by the conclusion we reach herein.

Reversed.

CHRISTIE, JUSTICE, with whom MOORE, JUSTICE, joins, dissenting:

I respectfully disagree with the majority.

I think the evidence supports the conclusion of the Chancellor, as finder of fact, that the basic nature of the community of Bethany Beach has not changed in such a way as to invalidate those restrictions which have continued to protect this community through the years as it has grown. Although some of the restrictions have been ignored and a portion of the community is now used for limited commercial purposes, the evidence shows that Bethany Beach remains a quiet, family-oriented resort where no liquor is sold. I think the conditions of the community are still consistent with the enforcement of a restrictive covenant forbidding the sale of intoxicating beverages.

In my opinion, the toleration of the practice of "brown bagging" does not constitute the abandonment of a longstanding restriction against the sale of alcoholic beverages. The restriction against sales has, in fact, remained intact for more than eighty years and any violations thereof have been short-lived. The fact that alcoholic beverages may be purchased right outside the town is not inconsistent with my view that the quiet-town atmosphere in this small area has not broken down, and that it can and should be preserved. Those who choose to buy land subject to the restrictions should be required to continue to abide by the restrictions.

I think the only real beneficiaries of the failure of the courts to enforce the restrictions would be those who plan to benefit commercially.

I also question the propriety of the issuance of a liquor license for the sale of liquor on property which is subject to a specific restrictive covenant against such sales.

I think that restrictive covenants play a vital part in the preservation of neighborhood schemes all over the State, and that a much more complete breakdown of the neighborhood scheme should be required before a court declares that a restriction has become unenforceable.

I would affirm the Chancellor.

Notes and Questions

1. The typical changed conditions case occurs because a residential neighborhood is gradually surrounded by commercial development, making the bordering lots of little value for residential use, but of great value for commercial development. The courts must then decide whether to lift the restriction, freeing the border lots up for their most valued use, or to retain it, thus protecting the interior lots from encroaching commercial develop-

ment. In applying the changed conditions doctrine, courts are effectively nullifying a property right (or a contract right, depending on how one views servitudes) of the owner of the dominant estate, in order to enhance the value of the servient estate. Whether or not courts should do this has proved quite controversial. The doctrine thus serves as a useful point of departure for considering a wider debate as to the proper role of the courts in enforcing servitudes, and, indeed, of the respective roles generally of private consent and public policy in property law.

Professor Richard Epstein takes a strong stance against judicial interference with contractual arrangements governing the use of land. He further argues that the protection of strangers to such contracts, including future purchasers of restricted property, is normally guaranteed adequately by recordation of restrictions. He then goes on to address the question of whether changed conditions justify modification or termination of private restrictions:

EPSTEIN, NOTICE AND FREEDOM OF CONTRACT IN THE LAW OF SERVITUDES
55 S.Cal.L.Rev. 1353 (1982).

This argument in favor of expanding the scope of the changed conditions doctrine contains three familiar elements. First, it is said that the original parties cannot anticipate changed circumstances and, therefore, cannot guard against them. Second, it is asserted that servitudes that persist over time give their holders the power to "blackmail" others long after their servitudes have become obsolete. Third, it is argued that such servitudes generate excessive transaction costs. Eliminating obsolete servitudes or allowing their modification is said to be beneficial on all three counts. A changed condition doctrine indeed is superior to a doctrine that strikes down many servitudes *ab initio* because its proponents are fearful of the future. But, even a limited doctrine of the sort advocated here is inferior to a complete denial of public intervention based on changed conditions.

The argument that parties who wish to create a servitude are incapable of providing for future contingencies presumes that such parties rarely, if ever, consider changed conditions in the course of their negotiations. The argument continues with the additional presumption that, even if the parties had considered the possibility of changed conditions, they would have agreed to apply the doctrine and allow for the modification or termination of the servitude in question. * * * [M]ost servitudes are not casual affairs. If they are recorded, there is a strong likelihood that the property in question is of sufficient value that both sides have been represented by lawyers. As a matter of construction, therefore, there is much to be gained by demanding that the parties to a transaction deal with the contingency of future uncertainty, just as they must deal with all other contingencies * * *

The parties involved in a transaction can be expected to shape their joint future in a way that promotes their mutual benefit. They may choose to create discretionary powers in anticipation of changed conditions. For example, in the case of planned unit communities, discretionary interests granted to the developer or the homeowners' association commonly function as a device for continuous corporate governance. The fact that discretion is often a good thing, however, is no justification for imposing it from without by terminating servitudes that are deemed obsolete. With discretion comes uncertainty, and this parties may rightly (and expressly) fear. * * * The point is that, given the pervasive ignorance over the trade-off between the virtues of flexibility and certainty, and between the vices of indefiniteness and rigidity, there is simply no persuasive reason to embrace one extreme to the exclusion of the other.

Professor Reichman suggest that courts should be permitted to modify as well as terminate servitudes that are considered obsolete because of changed conditions. Long temporal horizons make *any* present determination of utility imperfect by definition. The relevant question, therefore, is whether judicial determinations are superior to private ones. The original parties can provide for changed conditions if they so desire at the time when servitudes are created. And when disputes arise there is no apparent reason to consider judicial coercion superior to consensual renegotiation.

The second argument, that permanent easements encourage the holders of servitudes to extort large sums from those who wish to buy them out, is misplaced in principle. Here it is worth taking note of what ownership means in the context of the fee simple absolute in possession, i.e., the right to hold out. Suppose that *A* owns land which he does not wish to develop and that *B* wants this land as part of a larger parcel assembled for the most modern and productive use. *B* cannot simply take the land and escape all payment by showing the social superiority of his plans and intentions. Nor can *B* take the land from *A* even if he is prepared to pay him some reserve price, reflective of its value in current use. Ownership is meant to be a bulwark against the collective preferences of others; it allows one, rich or poor, to stand alone against the world no matter how insistent or intense its collective preferences.

In contrast Professor Sterk argues that servitudes create inefficiencies that under some circumstances justify public intervention:

STERK, FREEDOM FROM FREEDOM OF CONTRACT: THE ENDURING VALUE OF SERVITUDE RESTRICTIONS
70 Iowa L.Rev. 615 (1985).

This Article argues that to leave landowners unrestricted in their right to impose by contract obligations that run to successors-in-interest of land would be to ignore, or to subordinate as unworthy of decisive consideration, at least two problems. First, a number of servitudes create externalities. They affect not only the owners of burdened and benefited land, but third parties whose interests are not represented in the negotiation process. Second, many servitudes, particularly those that bind or benefit multiple parties, are difficult to remove because of high transaction costs. Even when parties to the original agreement consider the costs of removing the restrictions and take steps to reduce those costs, their actions do not eliminate the need for subsequent consideration. Current landowners have limited foresight; permitting their restrictions to govern land use for long periods or periods of unlimited duration might frustrate even their own preferences for the future. More important, even if current landowners possessed perfect foresight, to permit their preferences to govern for long periods or forever would be to resolve against future generations difficult questions of intergenerational fairness.

Of course, many servitudes impose no substantial external diseconomies. Nevertheless, high transaction costs—such as the cost associated with negotiating removal—may prevent removal of a servitude. Particularly if the servitude was imposed as part of a neighborhood scheme, with many parties holding the right to enforce the servitude, private negotiations for removal may be fraught with holdout and free rider problems. * * *

Sterk further argues that our legal system does not always protect the rights of hold-outs. The promisee of a contract, for example, cannot invariably insist on specific performance. He argues that leaving landowners to private negotiations when servitudes become inefficient may lead to strategic bargaining by hold-outs that ultimately prevents reaching agreements terminating the inefficient servitudes. He then states:

The chance that an exchange will not be completed is particularly high when multiple parties are involved. * * * When an exchange cannot be accomplished without the agreement of multiple parties, * * * both the difficulty of bringing all parties together and the uncertainty each party will face in assessing and reacting to the strategies of other parties make the exchange less likely. * * *

* * *

When landowners express their land use preferences in a privately negotiated servitude, the terms of the servitude establish the efficiency of the arrangement only as of the time of the agreement. But preferences and circumstances can change, and if modification of the original servitude cannot be achieved by private negotiation, the continued existence of the servitude would not establish its continued efficiency. It is true that the parties, in negotiating a servitude in the first instance, have the opportunity to consider the possibility that their preferences will change. An agreement that leaves the parties without flexibility to account for altered preferences is a strong indication that the parties expect their preferences to be stable over time. But no one is blessed with perfect foresight. There will be cases in which preferences have changed but the parties have left themselves no mechanism to accommodate the changes. In those cases the argument for governmental interventions is as strong as the argument for governmental intervention in any instance in which high transaction costs prevent private parties from reaching agreements that would promote their mutual interests.

Sterk concludes by arguing that the changed conditions doctrine is necessary to promote intergenerational equity:

Protecting future generations from dead-hand control has been a pervasive theme in property law. The rule against perpetuities, prohibitions against novel estates, and more modern regulations of the environment and of historic landmarks are all designed at least in part to prevent one generation from controlling the destiny of its successors. In the specific area of servitudes, the changed conditions doctrine, statutory limits on the duration of servitudes, and perhaps even the touch and concern requirement reflect in part a persistent if not easily quantifiable concern for intergenerational fairness. * * *

The [changed conditions] doctrine operates to protect present and future landowners from dead-hand control of land perpetuated through the use of servitudes that, because of high transaction costs, cannot be removed practically by private negotiations. The doctrine provides this protection by permitting judicial intervention to remove obsolete servitudes when private negotiations likely would be fruitless. This understanding of the changed conditions doctrine is supported by study of the doctrine's application. First, the doctrine is rarely, if ever, invoked to remove a servitude imposed on a single land-owner for the benefit of another. Instead, the doctrine relieves land-owners of burdens imposed on an entire neighborhood, where the transaction costs of removing restrictions are likely to be higher. * * * The doctrine itself is often framed to require a burdened landowner to establish changed conditions in the neighborhood—a difficult task if the only affected parcel is the benefited land and the benefited landowner refuses to consent to removal of the restriction.

In addition, in many jurisdictions changed conditions excuse the restricted landowner from specific enforcement of a servitude; the doctrine does not deprive benefited landowners of money damages for breach. * * * And because the litigation costs accompanying judicial removal are themselves substantial, affected landowners retain an incentive to remove obsolete restrictions by private agreement if at all possible. Only when the transaction costs accompanying private negotiations are higher than the litigation costs accompanying judicial removal will there be cause for invocation of the changed conditions doctrine.

For further elaboration of the consent-versus-intervention debate, see Alexander, Dilemmas of Group Autonomy: Residential Associations and Community, 75 Cornell L.Rev. 1 (1989); Ellickson, Cities and Homeowners Associations, 130 U.Pa.L.Rev. 1519 (1982); Korngold, Resolving the Flaws of Residential Servitudes and Owners Associations: For Reformation not Termination, 1990 Wis.L.Rev. 513; Natelson, Consent, Coercion, and "Reasonableness" in Private Law: The Special Case of the Property Owners Association, 51 Ohio St.L.J. 41 (1990); Winokur, The Mixed Blessing of Promissory Servitudes: Toward Optimizing Economic Utility, Individual Liberty and Personal Identity, 1989 Wis.L.Rev. 1; Winoker, Reforming Servitude Regimes: Toward Associational Federalism and Community, 1990 Wis.L.Rev. 537; Note, the Rule of Law in Residential Associations, 99 Harv.L.Rev. 472 (1985).

2. Do Epstein and Sterk adequately address the situation raised by the *El Di* case? What transactions would have had to take place for *El Di* to have freed itself from the servitude? Could the interests of the dominant estate (whatever that may be) be protected by damages? Is the problem in *El Di* an initial lack of foresight as to future efficient uses?

3. Note that the servitude in the principal case includes a defeasible fee. Are defeasible fees subject to the changed conditions doctrine, or can the initial grantor claim a reversion if the property is used in violation of the condition? See Jost, The Defeasible Fee and the Birth of the Modern Residential Subdivision, 49 Mo.L.Rev. 695, 731–732 (1984). Should the changed conditions doctrine apply to affirmative use servitudes (easements) if the law of servitudes is unified?

4. Absent changed conditions, should the owner of a servient estate be able to argue that the burden caused by the servitude far exceeds its value to the owner of the dominant estate? More specifically, if enforcement is sought through an injunction, should the equitable doctrine of balancing of the hardships apply, or should the injunction be granted regardless of the burdens this imposes on the defendant? Compare Beeler Development Co. v. Dickens, 254 Iowa 1029, 120 N.W.2d 414 (1963) (balancing of hardships inappropriate where injunction sought to enforce restriction to maintain the status quo of development) with Gilpin v. Jacob Ellis Realties, Inc., 47 N.J.Super. 26, 135 A.2d 204 (App.Div.1957) (damage award instead of injunction where injury to defendant if injunction issued grossly disproportionate to injury to plaintiff if injunction denied).

5. In addition to the changed conditions doctrine, several other means exist for terminating negative or affirmative obligation servitudes. The duration of a servitude is occasionally specified in the deed or declaration that creates it. In these instances, the servitude expires naturally at the end of the period specified in the document. Statutes in some states achieve the same result, see, e.g., Ga.Code Ann. § 44–5–60, limiting the running of a covenant to 20 years in a municipality that has adopted zoning. Why might the presence or absence of zoning be relevant to the duration of servitudes?

6. Negative and affirmative obligation servitudes may also be terminated by the same devices that would terminate affirmative-use servitudes (easements). They will be terminated by merger of the dominant and servient estate. See Aull v. Kraft, 286 S.W.2d 460 (Tex.Civ.App.1956). They may also be terminated by release by the owner of the dominant estate, see Chimney Hill Owners' Ass'n v. Antignani, 136 Vt. 446, 392 A.2d 423 (1978), or by an agreement to rescind or modify the servitude by all affected parties. Where a servitude binds all of the lots in a subdivision, however, merger and release issues can become complicated. Thus, if a developer reacquires lots it has earlier sold under a general plan of development, these lots are not thereby freed from servitudes which still benefit other lots the developer has sold. Similarly, the developer cannot unilaterally release a particular lot from restrictions that also benefit other lot owners in the subdivision.

7. When an attempt is made to enforce a servitude at equity, equitable defenses may also apply. These include abandonment, waiver,

estoppel, acquiescence, laches, and unclean hands. Estoppel is argued when the restriction has been violated following assurances that it would not be enforced; laches when enforcement attempts are tardy and the delay has prejudiced the defendant. Acquiescence is raised when violations of the servitude have been tolerated elsewhere in the neighborhood, unclean hands when the plaintiff himself has violated the servitude previously. Abandonment and waiver are vaguer and more general terms, which may include any of the other concepts. All of these defenses raise factual questions, and where servitudes vary from lot to lot, or where the servitudes that have been violated by the plaintiff or by others in the neighborhood are different from those violated by the defendant, these questions can become quite complex.

8. Finally, servitudes may be terminated by eminent domain, where the servient estate is used for a public use contrary to the restriction. This situation raises the questions of whether the servitude is a property interest, the loss of which must be compensated under the United States or state constitutions, and how it should be valued. Although it is clear that easements are property interests which must be paid for if taken, there is still controversy as to whether affirmative obligations or restrictive covenants are compensable interests. Compare Southern California Edison Co. v. Bourgerie, 9 Cal.3d 169, 107 Cal.Rptr. 76, 507 P.2d 964 (1973) (restriction is compensable property interest) and Restatement of Property (Servitudes) § 566 (1944), with Burma Hills Development Co. v. Marr, 285 Ala. 141, 229 So.2d 776 (1969) (restriction not property interest that must be compensated). Courts arguing the latter position hold that they are contract rather than property rights, that they were not intended to bind the government or to be enforced against government policy, or that compensation would be too expensive or procedurally cumbersome. The cost of compensating all property owners benefited by a terminated servitude is a real concern where the restriction runs to the benefit of a large subdivision.

Is it fair to permit a property benefited by a servitude to collect damages caused by a power station or prison built next door in violation of a restrictive covenant, but to refuse damages to an adjacent property not benefited by a restriction? Could the whole problem perhaps be better handled through nuisance rather than servitude law? See Note, Nuisance Damages as an Alternative to Compensation of Land Use Restrictions in Eminent Domain, 47 S.Cal.L.Rev. 998 (1974).

If a zoning ordinance inconsistent with a servitude is adopted (e.g., an ordinance permitting only commercial use in a neighborhood restricted to residential use), should the zoning ordinance or the servitude control future development? If the zoning ordinance controls, should the owners of the servitude be compensated for its termination?

II. NEIGHBORHOOD GOVERNANCE

A. GENERALLY

Servitudes make neighborhood governance possible. To the extent that the law also permits neighborhoods to choose those primarily responsible for enforcing servitudes, to amend the servitudes by which they govern themselves, to exercise discretion in the interpretation and enforcement of servitudes, to tax themselves through assessments, and to own and manage common facilities, neighborhoods begin to resemble municipalities, clothed in the powers traditionally exercised by governments. These functions are commonly exercised through property owners' associations.

Property owners associations can exist in residential subdivisions, condominia or cooperatives. Even without the existence of formal associations, some of the functions exercised by property owners associations can be carried on within neighborhoods. Neighbors can, for example, vote from time to time to modify the servitudes by which they govern themselves.

Servitudes found in deeds and in covenant declarations effectively serve as the constitutions of property owners associations. Problems addressed in the previous sections regarding the creation, interpretation, modification, and termination of servitudes take on new dimensions when the servitudes create and are enforced by residential private governments. These problems are explored in the materials that follow.

B. DEVELOPER–PROPERTY OWNER RELATIONS

BROWN v. McDAVID

Colorado Court of Appeals, 1983.
676 P.2d 714.

SMITH, JUDGE.

This case arises from the attempt, by the owners of a ranch in Grand County, to develop and subdivide their property.

Although several tracts were sold pursuant to a subdivision development plan, the original owners and their successors ultimately determined to abandon the entire plan. Plaintiffs Mackintosh and Sylvia Brown whose predecessors in title had purchased one of the tracts during the development stage, brought this action seeking to compel the developers and the owners of the ranch to provide them with certain easements, and to enforce certain covenants which were to be part of the development plan and upon which the tract purchasers alleged they relied at the time of the purchase of their respective tracts.

Ultimately, the owners of the other four tracts were made parties to this action, and at trial were aligned as plaintiffs. The case was tried to the court without a jury, and at the conclusion thereof, the trial court entered findings of fact and conclusions of law, and issued its decree determining, in essence, that the covenants, easements, and undertakings to provide easements, which had come into being during the developmental stage, ran with the land, were perpetual, and were not terminable. Having so decreed, the court entered certain orders designed to assure that the affirmative duties, which it found had arisen under the covenants, would be complied with. Upon appeal, we reverse and remand with directions.

Lewis, George, and J. Donald Yager were the joint owners of land in Grand County, commonly known as Devil's Thumb Ranch. In September of 1973, the Yagers entered into a contract with Charles Badsley, C.B. Jensen, and Jack Randall, who, as joint venturers, acting under the name "B.J.R. Associates" (BJR), agreed to develop and sell Devil's Thumb Ranch.

Under this contract, BJR was permitted to take possession of the ranch, have it surveyed, and to divide it into 26 separate parcels for resale as a ranch subdivision. Ultimately, a plan for development evolved which contemplated that certain protective and restrictive covenants were to be drafted and recorded as sales inducements in connection with the offering of Devil's Thumb Ranch. Pursuant to this plan, five lots were sold to various parties in November 1974. The purchasers were Bennett (Brown's predecessor in title), Mountain Valley Investment Corporation, the Greenwoods, Colskilo Inc., and the Hilbs.

Since the entire ranch was still under contract between the Yagers and B.J.R., it was necessary that the Yagers convey the five parcels to B.J.R., who in turn delivered deeds to the five respective purchasers. The promotional material used by B.J.R. included copies of the proposed restrictive covenants covering "Devil's Thumb Ranch Estates," and which we will refer to as the "Covenant Document."

The purchase contracts between B.J.R. and the above five parties had copies of the Covenant Document attached. At the time of closing of the five sales transactions, the Covenant Document had not been recorded nor was it attached, nor made a part of the deeds transferring title to the respective purchasers. By stipulation, however, the parties agreed that all of the purchasers (including McDavid) had relied on the Covenant Document at the time they purchased their respective lots.

The Hilbs, however, requested that their lot be exempted from the benefits and burdens of the Covenant Document in exchange for an express 60 foot easement, which was, in fact, granted to them across the southern end of the ranch.

B.J.R. recorded the Covenant Document in September 1975, with the county clerk and recorder. Subsequent to that recording, Bennett, Mountain Valley, the Greenwoods and Colskilo each executed a letter ratifying, adopting and confirming the recorded Covenant Document.

Eight months later, in May 1976, the Browns purchased their tract from Bennett. Later in 1976, the Browns and Mountain Valley made a request of B.J.R. and the Yagers for an express, legally described, written grant of easement. These demands were not met, and the Browns subsequently commenced this action and recorded a lis pendens in Grand County.

Following the commencement of this action and the filing of a lis pendens by the Browns, the Yagers, together with B.J.R. sold the balance of the tracts to McDavid. As a result of this transaction, McDavid became the title owner of 21 of the 26 tracts or lots which comprised "Devil's Thumb Ranch Estates."

On May 9, 1977, McDavid recorded with the county clerk and recorder a document entitled "Declaration and Consent to Elimination of Protective Covenants," which document we will refer to as the "Termination Document," and which was recorded for the purpose of terminating the Covenant Document. After McDavid had acquired title and recorded the termination document, he was made a party to this action. He thereafter conveyed his interest in "Devil's Thumb Ranch Estates" to a corporation, Devil's Thumb Ranch and Cross–Country Center, Inc.

I. The Covenant Document

The dispute here revolves around the language of the covenant document, and whether it could be, and was, properly terminated. This document, after describing generally its purposes, as being in furtherance of a plan for development, improvement, and sale of tracts within Devil's Thumb Ranch Estates, declares, inter alia:

> "These Covenants shall run with said property, and shall be binding upon and inure to the benefit of the Developer, each subsequent owner of said real property, or any part thereof, and each successor in interest of each such subsequent owner."

The document then discusses certain easements to be reserved to all of the owners for horseback riding, hiking, cross-country skiing, fishing, and other similar uses, and further purports to require each owner to grant a 60 foot wide easement for access and utility purposes to the owners of all other parcels. These easements were undescribed and unlocated at the time of the execution and recording of the Covenant Document.

The last two paragraphs of the document then read as follows:

> "ALL OF THE FOREGOING covenants, conditions, reservations and restrictions shall continue and remain in full force and effect at all times as against the owner of any parcel in Devil's Thumb Ranch Estates, regardless of how he acquired title, until the commencement of the calendar year 2000 A.D., on which date these covenants, conditions, reservations and restrictions shall terminate and end, and thereinafter be of no further legal or equitable effect on such premises, or any owner thereof.

> NOTWITHSTANDING THE FOREGOING, the Covenants agreements, conditions, reservations, restrictions and charges created and established herein for the benefit of the foregoing owners, and each parcel therein, may be waived, terminated or modified as to the whole of Devil's Thumb Ranch Estates only, with the written consent of the owners of sixty-six per cent (66%) of the parcels in Devil's Thumb Ranch Estates. No such waiver, termination or modification shall be effective until the proper instrument in writing shall be executed and

recorded in the office of the Clerk and Recorder in the County of Grand and State of Colorado."

The trial court, in construing this document, concluded, inter alia, as follows:

"[T]he recorded Covenants purport to provide for a grant of perpetual easements binding on the grantors, their successors and assigns, and then to provide that the easements are not perpetual and that they do not run with the land but have a fixed expiration date and are terminable at any time. These conflicting terms are irreconcilable and must therefore be construed against the drafters, particularly where, as here, the covenants affect substantial property interests of all the parties. The Court therefore concludes that those provisions of the covenants reserving or providing for a grant of easements should be preserved and specifically enforced in accord with the parties' clear intent."

Inasmuch as the trial court's determination proceeds solely from its interpretation of the written document, we are not bound thereby. [ ] We do not agree with the trial court's interpretation.

Despite the preliminary language in the covenant document providing that the covenants "run with the land," we conclude that there is no material ambiguity within the document. Reading it as a whole, it is apparent that the developers and owners of tracts who subsequently agreed to the document, intended that the covenants, easements, and other agreements, should terminate by the document's own terms, on the commencement of the calendar year 2000 A.D., unless they should be sooner terminated by the execution and recording of an appropriate document so reciting, consented to by the owners of 66% of the parcels in Devil's Thumb Ranch Estates. We construe the reference to covenants running with the land to express the intention that these covenants and agreements should be binding upon all owners of the land, their successors, and assigns, until the same be terminated, either by the terms of the agreement or by the filing and recording of a proper termination agreement.

Thus, reading the termination document as a whole, we conclude that it is not ambiguous, nor do we find in its terms any irreconcilable conflicts. We conclude that the trial court's interpretation is erroneous.

II. TERMINATION

Implicit in the trial court's lengthy ruling, however, is its conclusion that it would be inequitable to allow McDavid to terminate the covenants and thereby abandon the development plan upon which the other purchasers had relied in buying their lots. The parties argue here, in support of the trial court's ruling, that particularly the easements for utilities and access are essential to their use of the land. They assert that they should be, as the trial court determined, perpetual and not subject to termination. We disagree.

We do not disagree with the assertion that such easements may be a necessity, but rather with the argument that such necessity precludes exercise of the termination clause. No Colorado cases have been cited to us, nor have we found any dealing with the effect of similar termination clauses. However, the general law is well established that a covenant running with the land in a subdivision may be modified or terminated, when the covenant permits termination, upon the consent of a specified percentage of lot owners.

Such a case, closely analogous to the instant one, is Matthews v. Kernewood, Inc., 184 Md. 297, 40 A.2d 522 (1945). In Matthews, a development corporation subdivided parcels of land into thirty-four separate lots and imposed stringent protective covenants. Seventeen years later, only half of the lots had been sold. The developer then exercised his right which had been reserved in the covenants, to annul or change or modify the restrictions, and resubdivided the unsold lots into smaller parcels with reduced restrictions. Seven owners of the original lots filed suit, charging that they had purchased their lots in reliance on the development plan and original restrictions. The Maryland court observed that the rights of the parties who purchased the original lots must be determined by the agreement they voluntarily made, and that they could not be judicially relieved of a bad bargain into which they themselves had entered. Where covenants terminate on the consent of a specified percentage of lot owners, consent of the proper percentage will terminate the covenants. [ ]

Since developers and potential lot purchasers are free to contract for the price, terms, and conditions of any sale, when such parties elect to provide for covenants which, by their nature, may be terminated upon certain conditions, then a court must presume that such a contingency is reflected in the consideration paid, and will not rewrite the covenants years later for one of the parties. [ ] Where, as here, the covenant document containing the termination clauses in question, was admittedly relied upon and accepted by all parties, all parties knew the covenants could be terminated and this knowledge became part of the basis of their bargain. [ ]

We have examined the "Termination Document" and conclude that it is sufficient to comply with the provisions of the "Covenant Document" relative to termination. Thus, we hold that all of the covenants, easements, and servitudes created by the Covenant Document were terminated on the date that the Termination Document was recorded. Accordingly, we conclude that each tract owner has no rights or benefits in the land at Devil's Thumb Ranch Estates except those expressly granted by their deeds and as otherwise found in the law. It necessarily follows that the same rule applies as to burdens upon each of the parcels.

III. Issues Remaining

Our determination that the Covenant Document and all of the rights and obligations which it created has been properly terminated does not, however, resolve all of the issues existing between the parties.

There remain to be determined factual questions relative to location and extent of the access for ingress and egress and for utilities to certain of the parcels which appear to be landlocked. Easements may arise in any number of ways. They may arise by express grant or reservation, covenant, prescription, or implication. Colorado expressly recognizes implied easements which may arise by reason of grant and reservation, [ ] or even by preexisting use. [ ]

Here, Mountain Valley Investment Corporation appears to have an express easement created by grant apart from the terminated covenants. In its deed there appears the following language:

> "Purchasers are hereby granted an easement for access to this tract of land across the presently existing ranch road, a diagram of said road is attached hereto * * *."

Defendants Thomas and Susan Hilb likewise appear to have an express easement created by grant. As these grants are wholly separate from the easements granted in the covenant document, they are therefore unaffected by the termination document filed by McDavid. Plaintiffs, Mackintosh and Sylvia Brown, however, do not have a specific grant of easement. They may well, however, have an implied easement under one of the theories previously mentioned.

Because the evidence contained in the record before us discloses facts which may well entitle the Browns to an implied easement we remand this case to the trial court for location and determination of the extent of such easements as may have arisen outside of the covenants, specifically as to Mountain Valley and the Browns, as well as to consider if such easements should be decreed as to the other parcels.

The intent of the parties, as disclosed by the evidence, at the time the respective parcels were severed from the original tract, may provide guidance for the trial court in determining the location as well as the reasonable extent and dimensions of such easements. [ ]

We conclude that appellants' other contentions are without merit.

* * *

Notes and Questions

1. Modern residential developments are often quite large and represent a considerable capital investment for which a developer is responsible. In the early stages of the development, the developer faces a quandary. It may want to aim the development at a certain market—residential rather than commercial, upscale rather than moderate-income residential—and may want to include servitudes in the deeds or declaration of restrictions that will be attractive to this market. At the same time, the developer may not want to lock itself in. If it turns out that the developer's market research was faulty, it may want to change the nature of the subdivision to include some lower-priced housing or even rental units or commercial uses. In some jurisdictions, the developer may preserve this flexibility simply by not binding its retained land when it sells off restricted properties, but in many it cannot. Can you explain why?

In most jurisdictions, developers have attempted to retain flexibility by reserving to themselves the right to amend restrictions. This is often done through establishing the right to amend restrictions in the property owners association, and then retaining control of the property owners association until the development is substantially complete. This can be done, as in the principal case, by giving the developer one vote for each lot it retains, allowing it to retain control until it has sold off a considerable number of its lots. Model forms developed by the Urban Land Institute go further, allowing the developer three votes for every unit, effectively giving the developer control until 75% of the units in the development are sold. The developer may also want to retain control over architectural review committees and over the expenditure of funds collected through assessments.

Developer retention of control, however, poses problems for residents in a development. The developer can, as in the principal case, abandon the restrictions the lot owners thought they would be protected by, creating a much different sort of community. It could even use assessments from the community for its own purposes, such as marketing the development. Should these problems be addressed by the courts? By legislation? How? See Reichman, Residential Private Governments: An Introductory Survey, 43 U.Chi.L.Rev. 253, at 285–291 (1976).

2. As the development progresses and lots are sold, the developer will usually lose interest in the development. If the developer has maintained tight control over the property owners association until this point, however, there may not be any residents with the knowledge and ability to take over managing the association. Should a developer have an obligation to assist property owners in establishing a viable association once it loses interest? See Reichman, 43 U.Chi.L.Rev. at 290–291.

3. Other concerns that must be faced as a developer withdraws from management of a development and a property owners association takes over include transfer of common property, accounting for and transfer of funds collected to maintain common property, and transfer of books and records.

4. How should votes be allocated in an association once the developer has completed the development? Should they be distributed on a "one person, one vote" principle, or on a unit-by-unit basis, or with each owner having a number of votes proportionate to the value of his or her investment? What justifies the application of different principles than those followed with respect to public corporations, where one man, one vote is the rule? See Ellickson, Cities and Homeowners Associations, 130 U.Pa.L.Rev. 1519 (1982).

5. See generally on litigation by property owners associations against developers, R. Natelson, Law of Property Owners Associations, chapter 9 (1989).

C. INTERPRETATION AND ENFORCEMENT OF SERVITUDES BY PROPERTY OWNERS ASSOCIATIONS

SMITH v. BUTLER MOUNTAIN ESTATES PROPERTY OWNERS' ASSOCIATION, INC.

Court of Appeals of North Carolina, 1988.
90 N.C.App. 40, 367 S.E.2d 401.

JOHNSON, JUDGE.

Plaintiffs are the owners of a lot in Butler Mountain Estates. Butler Mountain Estates is a residential development containing 48 lots, and at the time of this action, consisted of twelve lots upon which houses have been constructed and three lots upon which houses are under construction. The lots in Butler Mountain Estates are subject to restrictive covenants set forth in a restrictive agreement. The restrictive covenants provide that the lots are to be used for single family residential houses and specify that any dwelling erected thereon is to have a habitable floor space on the main level of at least 1100 square feet. Furthermore, the restrictive covenants provide that:

> * * * all building plans * * * shall require the approval of the developer and/or Property owners Association * * *. No structure of any kind, the plan, elevations, and specifications which have not received the written approval of the developer and/or Property owners Association and which does not comply fully with such approved plans and specifications, shall be erected, constructed, placed or maintained upon any lot * * *

In the beginning, prior to the formation of an architectural review board, proposed plans were submitted to each existing homeowner and approved or disapproved, by the individual homeowners based on square footage and on the design.

On 29 February 1984, Elbert S. Brown and Dorothy S. Brown, the developers of Butler Mountain Estates, signed a Grant of Architectural Review, by the terms of which they granted to Butler Mountain Estates Property Owners Association Corporation, all rights of review and approval reserved by the developer under the above quoted restrictive covenant regarding building plans. In January of 1985, an architectural review board was formed to review all proposed building plans for each dwelling unit to be constructed. The architectural review board consists of the Board of Directors and the existing homeowners in Butler Mountain Estates.

In October, 1985, plaintiffs submitted a set of plans for a proposed dwelling unit to the architectural review committee for approval. Plaintiffs' plans, which were not for a geodesic dome house, were rejected solely because they failed to meet the restrictive covenant's square footage requirement.

In December 1985, plaintiffs submitted a second set of plans for a proposed dwelling unit, a geodesic dome house, to the architectural review committee for approval. The architectural review committee rejected these plans because of the roofline and the geodesic design of the house. It was also determined that the plans did not meet the minimum square footage requirement, but the architectural review committee did not express that failure as a prime consideration for rejecting plaintiffs' plans. On 23 January 1986, the president of the Property owners Association mailed plaintiffs a letter indicating that the "proposed structure reflects a marked departure from home-building styles prevailing throughout the area" and that plaintiffs "might consider a design closer to the home-building styles that exist on Butler Mountain Estates."

The primary manner in which this plan was such a radical departure from the existing homes was in its roofline. Plaintiffs' home would have an irregular domed roofline, which is built out of a series of triangles and pentagons, whereas the existing houses have conventional horizontal rooflines.

The architectural review committee did not have written standards as to design acceptability of plans but did establish among themselves a format to review plans submitted by owners. The committee believed that the homes should "conform and blend together." (See Illustrations.)

On 11 April 1986, plaintiffs filed their complaint seeking a declaratory judgment and alternatively for injunctive relief, against defendant. Defendant filed its answer on 13 June 1986. On 18 September 1986, plaintiffs filed a motion for summary judgment which was denied by order of the court on 5 November 1986. On 17 December 1986, a trial without jury was conducted before Judge Robert M. Burroughs, Sr. On 18 December 1986, after making findings of fact and conclusions of law, an order was filed granting defendant's motion for involuntary dismissal pursuant to Rule 41(b) of the North Carolina Rules of Civil Procedure. Plaintiffs appeal.

Plaintiffs bring forth sixteen assignments of error grouped into three arguments for this Court's review. For the following reasons, we find no error and affirm the order of the trial court.

Illustration of existing houses in
Butler Mountain Estates

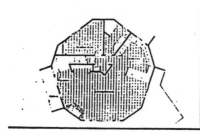
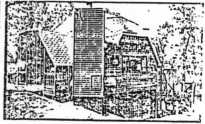
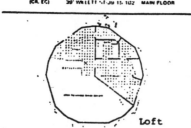

Illustration of
Plaintiffs' geodesic house plans

First, plaintiffs contend that the trial court erred in finding as fact and concluding as a matter of law that plaintiffs' second set of plans did not meet the restrictive covenant square footage requirement and that the plans were rejected on this basis. We disagree.

* * *

In the case *sub judice,* there was sufficient competent evidence to support the court's findings of fact and conclusions of law. The restriction in question states in part that:

> No structure or building shall be erected, altered, placed, or permitted to remain on any property or tract of land conveyed in Butler Mountain Estates other than one detached single family dwelling, permanent in nature, *the habitable floor space of which, exclusive of basements, porches, garages, is less than 1,100 square feet on the main level of said residence.* (Emphasis added).

Evidence was also admitted in response to questions tendered by plaintiffs, that the habitable living space on the main level of the house proposed by plaintiffs was 30 to 50 feet short of the required square footage. Thus, there was competent evidence to support the court's findings of fact and conclusions of law that plaintiffs failed to meet the 1100 minimum square footage requirement and that the architectural review committee "rejected [the plans] invariably" on that basis.

Next, plaintiffs contend the trial court erred in finding as fact that (a) defendants had developed an architectural style as construction took place; (b) that the existing housing was of a common, similar or like design; and (c) that the plaintiffs' second set of plans was a marked departure from existing homes in the development and did not meet the roofline designs of homes in the area. Again, we disagree.

We have thoroughly examined the record and find that there is sufficient evidence in the record to support the trial court's findings of fact. The photographs of the 12 houses that exist in the development establishes that they are of common, similar or like design, though they are not all exactly alike. The plans submitted by the plaintiffs revealed that the roofline of plaintiffs' house was not of the same or similar design of the other houses. The remaining houses had flat roofs, or pitched roofs with flat planes, and plaintiffs' geodesic home roofline was dome shaped. Furthermore, each house as it was built, maintained the same or similar design as each house previously built, thereby establishing the architectural style of the community. Therefore, plaintiffs' assignments of error on these findings of fact are overruled.

Finally, plaintiffs contend that the trial court erred in entering its judgment against them for the reason that the evidence showed that the restrictive covenants are void and unenforceable as applied because (1) they contain no standards by which proposed plans are to be judged; (2) they are not connected to any general plan or scheme of development; (3) they are ambiguous and (4) they were applied in an arbitrary and unreasonable manner and in bad faith. Again, we disagree.

"In North Carolina restrictive covenants are strictly construed against limitations upon the beneficial use of property, but such construction must be reasonable and not applied in such a way as to defeat the plain and obvious purposes of a restriction." Boiling Spring Lakes v. Coastal Services Corp., 27 N.C.App. 191, 195, 218 S.E.2d 476, 478 (1975). In Boiling Springs, a restrictive covenant required building plans to be submitted to and approved by the grantor prior to construction. This Court laid out the following rules governing approval of building plans by a grantor.

> The exercise of the authority to approve the house plans cannot be arbitrary. There must be some standards. Where these standards are not within the restrictive covenant itself, they must be in other covenants stated or designated, or they must be otherwise clearly established in connection with some general plan or scheme of development. (Citations omitted) * * * [A] restrictive covenant requiring approval of house plans is enforceable only if the exercise of the power in a particular case is reasonable and in good faith. (Citations omitted)

Id. at 195–96, 218 S.E.2d at 478–79.

In support of this rule, this Court relied upon decisions in other jurisdictions. See Syrian Antiochian Orthodox Archdiocese v. Palisades Associates, 110 N.J.Super. 34, 264 A.2d 257 (1970); Rhue v. Cheyenne Homes, Inc., 168 Colo. 6, 449 P.2d 361 (1969).

In Syrian, the court held that a covenant which prohibited the creation of structures or improvements unless plans and specifications in a grading plan of a plot to be built upon were approved by the grantor, and that the grantor could refuse to approve any such plans, which were not suitable in his opinion, was valid and enforceable, though no objective standards were set forth within the covenant to guide the grantor. The court stated,

> [t]he purpose of such a provision is to afford mutual protection to the property owners living in the development against injury, whether taking the form of diminished property values or otherwise, that would result from the construction of a residence or other improvement that was unsightly, in singularly bad taste, *discordantly at variance with neighboring homes in architectural appearance,* or otherwise offensive to the proposed or developed standards of the neighborhood.

Syrian, 110 N.J.Super at 40, 264 A.2d at 261. (Emphasis added).

Similarly, in Rhue, that court was called upon to consider a covenant which required plans for construction of houses to be submitted to an architectural committee for approval. In Rhue, an owner of property in whose chain of title the covenant appeared, wished to move to the site a 30–year old Spanish style home with a stucco exterior and a red tile roof. The development in which the house was to be located was 80% improved with modern ranch style and split level homes. The grantor refused approval upon the ground that the proposed improvement, if allowed would diminish the value of other properties in the neighborhood and would be an unsightly variation from the architectural pattern that had been established. In sustaining the disapproval the court observed:

> [i]t is no secret that housing today is developed by subdividers who, through the use of restrictive covenants, guarantee to the purchaser that his house will be protected against adjacent construction which will impair its value, and that a general plan of construction will be followed. Modern legal authority recognizes this reality and recognizes also that the approval of plans by an architectural control committee is one method by which guarantees of value and general plan of construction can be accomplished and maintained.

Rhue, 168 Colo. at 8, 449 P.2d at 362.

In the case *sub judice*, the restrictive covenant at issue requires building plans to be submitted to and approved by the Property owners Association which in turn formed an architectural review committee to serve the same function. The record establishes that this architectural review committee rejected plaintiffs' second set of plans because (1) the design of the house reflected a marked departure from the home building styles in the area and (2) the plans did not meet the general roofline design of the houses in the area. In addition, plaintiffs' plans did not meet the square footage requirement but the architectural review committee did not rely solely on this failure as the primary basis for rejection of the plans.

As shown earlier in the opinion, the plans of the main level of a proposed home had to contain 1100 square feet of habitable floor space. Thus, the architectural review committee could have justifiably rejected plaintiffs' second set of plans on this basis alone. Nevertheless, assuming arguendo, that plaintiffs had met the minimum square footage requirement, the record reveals that the 12 houses constructed were conventional type homes of the same or similar design, and had similar flat roof designs. Plaintiffs' second set of plans for their geodesic home was not of the same or similar design, and their dome shaped roofline, which is built out of a series of triangles and pentagons, was a radical departure from the other houses' rooflines.

Despite the architectural review committee's failure to put in writing the specific architectural style of the houses to be erected, all legitimate considerations which an architectural review committee may assess when determining the aesthetic value in approving house plans which fit into a general plan or development scheme of the neighborhood was attempted in the case sub judice. Without such consideration, there would have been no reasonable or good faith determination for approval or nonapproval of house plans.

The majority view, which this Court has adopted, with respect to covenants requiring submission of plans and prior consent to construction, is that such clauses, even if vesting the approving authority with broad discretionary power, are valid and enforceable so long as the authority to consent is exercised reasonably and in good faith. Therefore, applying the test of reasonableness and good faith to the case sub judice, we find that the rejection of plaintiffs' house plans was not arbitrary or capricious because the record clearly shows that plaintiffs' proposed house plans did not fit into the present and existing general plan or development scheme of the homes in the area.

Accordingly, for all the aforementioned reasons, the judgment is affirmed.

Notes and Questions

1. A recent study notes that reported state court appellate decisions involving property owners associations and servitudes increased seven-fold from 1977 to 1982, and doubled again between 1982 and 1987. Winokur, The Mixed Blessing of Promissory Servitudes: Toward Optimizing Economic Utility, Individual Liberty, and Personal Identity, 1989 Wis.L.Rev. 1, 63–64.

One classification of disputes within property owners associations breaks them down into six categories. First, are property disputes involving rights to the homeowner's unit or to common elements. Second, are financial disputes, involving assessments or money owed the association by third parties (such as the developer). Disputes involving services and maintenance of the common elements are third. Governance issues involving elections and board governance come next. Fifth are lifestyle disputes, involving noisy children, dogs, stereos, etc. Finally, are disputes involving personal injury or injury to reputation. Walker and Masotti, The Dynamics of Dispute Processing in Condominium Associations, CAI News, January 1983. Disputes involve both substantive issues—is the servitude itself valid—and procedural issues—did the association follow its own procedures and are these procedures reasonable?

Should courts follow a public or private-law model in addressing these questions? Is the property owners association a close enough cognate to the municipality to bring it under the requirements of the United States Constitution or state constitutions? The limits of the *Shelley v. Kramer* doctrine with respect to servitudes generally have been explored earlier. Should *Shelley v. Kramer* be applied more expansively where servitudes are enforced by a property owners association? In states where property owners associations exist by virtue of state enabling acts and are regulated by the state, does a sufficiently close nexus exist between the actions of the association and the state to find state action? Should state action be found under the public-function doctrine of Marsh v. Alabama, 326 U.S. 501, 66 S.Ct. 276, 90 L.Ed. 265 (1946). See Rosenberry, The Application of the

Federal and State Constitutions to Condominiums, Cooperatives and Planned Developments, 19 Real Prop., Prob. & Trust J. 1 (1985).

2. Alternatively, should property owners associations be viewed as private entities not subject to public-law controls? As such, should they be permitted to take actions the state is constitutionally barred from taking, such as barring religious uses or discriminating against certain societal groups? What limits may courts place on the procedures followed by associations?

3. The principal case considers the reasonableness and good faith of the substantive decision reached by the association. An alternative approach available in some cases is to focus on the procedures the association followed in making its decision or on the authority of the decisionmaker. In Ironwood Owners Association IX v. Solomon, 178 Cal.App.3d 766, 224 Cal.Rptr. 18 (1986), a property owners association sought a mandatory injunction requiring the removal of eight date palm trees planted by the Solomons. On appeal from the trial court grant of the injunction, the appellate court reversed, noting:

> When a homeowners' association seeks to enforce the provisions of its CCRs to compel an act by one of its member owners, it is incumbent upon it to show that it has followed its own standards and procedures prior to pursuing such a remedy, that those procedures were fair and reasonable and that its substantive decision was made in good faith, and is reasonable, not arbitrary or capricious. [ ]

The Court went on to hold that the record did not show either that the Architectural Control Committee had made findings on the compliance of the trees with the covenants, or that the board had made a decision with respect to the trees. Discussions at members' meetings or polls of the members were not, the court held, an adequate substitute for appropriate decisions by the governing body or proper committee. See, R. Natelson, Law of Property Owners Associations, chapters 4 & 5 (1989).

4. Litigation arises not only when associations sue their members for breach of servitudes, but also when members sue the association for failing to fulfill its responsibilities. This may happen, for example, when the association misuses assessments, acts beyond its authority, fails to maintain common property, or takes action which results in the injury of a member. A variety of arguments are raised in these actions, including corporate, fiduciary, and tort theories of liability. See R. Natelson, Law of Property Owners Associations, chapter 10 (1989); Rosenberry, Actions of Community Association Boards: When are They Valid and When do they Create Liability, 13 Real Est.L.J. (1985). Should the directors of property owners' associations be held to the same standard of care or to a higher or lower standard than the directors of commercial corporations? See Natelson, Keeping Faith: Fiduciary Obligations in Property Owners Associations, 11 Vt.L.Rev. 421 (1986).

5. Litigation is often a wholly unsatisfactory means of resolving disputes in property owners' associations. However irritated they may be with each other, neighbors must usually continue to coexist, and thus means of dispute resolution that emphasize cooperation and reconciliation rather than division and conflict are to be favored. How might documents

establishing property owners' associations be drafted so as to facilitate more helpful approaches to dispute resolution? What effect might the following Montgomery County, Maryland ordinance have?

MONTGOMERY COUNTY CODE, Chapter 24B.

Article 2. Dispute Resolution.

10B–2. Definitions.

In this Chapter, the following words have the following meanings:

(a) Commission means the Commission on Common Ownership Communities.

(b) Common ownership community includes:

(1) a development subject to a declaration enforced by a homeowners' association, as those terms are used in state law;

(2) a condominium, as that term is used in state law; and

(3) a cooperative housing project, as that term is used in state law.

(c) Office means the Office of Common Ownership Communities.

* * *

10B–8. Defined terms.

In this Article and Article 3, the following terms

* * *

(3) Dispute means any disagreement between 2 or more parties that involves:

(A) the authority of a governing body, under any law or association document, to:

(i) require any person to take any action, or not to take any action, involving a unit;

(ii) require any person to pay a fee, fine, or assessment;

(iii) spend association funds; or

(iv) alter or add to a common area or element; or

(B) the failure of a governing body, when required by law or an association document, to:

    (i) properly conduct an election;

    (ii) give adequate notice of a meeting or other action;

    (iii) properly conduct a meeting;

    (iv) properly adopt a budget or rule;

    (v) maintain or audit books and records; or

    (vi) allow inspection of books and records.

(4) Dispute does not include any disagreement that only involves:

    (A) title to any unit or any common area or element;

    (B) the percentage interest or vote allocable to a unit;

    (C) the interpretation or enforcement of any warranty;

    (D) the collection of an assessment validly levied against a party; or

    (E) the judgment or discretion of a governing body in taking or deciding not to take any legally authorized action.

* * *

(7) Party includes:

    (A) an owner;

    (B) a governing body; and

    (C) an occupant of a dwelling unit in a common ownership community.

10B–9. Filing of disputes; exhaustion of association remedies.

(a) The Commission may hear any dispute between or among parties.

(b) A party must not file a dispute with the Commission until the party makes a good faith attempt to exhaust all procedures or remedies provided in the association documents.

(c) However, a party may file a dispute with the Commission 60 days after any procedure or remedy provided in the association documents has been initiated before the association.

(d) After a community association finds that a dispute exists, the association must notify the other parties of their rights to file the dispute with the Commission. The association must not take any action to enforce or implement its decision for 14 days after it notifies the other parties of their rights.

(e) When a dispute is filed with the Commission, a community association must not take any action to enforce or implement the association's decision, except filing a civil action under subsection (f), until the process under this Article is completed.

(f) Any party may file a civil action arising out of an association document or a law regulating the association's powers and procedures at any time. However, the court may stay all proceedings for at least 90 days after the court is notified that a dispute has been properly filed under this Article so that a hearing under Section 10B–13 may be completed.

* * *

10B–11. Mediation.

(a) The Office may investigate facts and assemble documents relevant to a dispute filed with the Commission, and may summarize the issues in the dispute. The Office may notify a party if, in its opinion, a dispute was not properly filed with the Commission, and may inform each party of the possible sanctions under Section 10B–13(d).

(b) Any party may request mediation.

(c) If a party requests mediation, the Commission must notify all parties of the filing and of the mediation session.

(d) The Commission must provide a qualified mediator to meet with the parties within 30 days after a party requests mediation to attempt to settle the dispute.

(e) If any party refuses to attend a mediation session, or if mediation does not successfully resolve the dispute within 10 days after the first mediation session is held, the Commission must promptly schedule a hearing under Section 10B–13 unless a hearing has already been held under Section 10B–13.

10B–12. Hearing Panel.

(a) If a hearing is scheduled, the chair of the Commission must convene a 3–member panel to hear the dispute.

(b) The chair must choose 2 members of the panel from the voting members of the Commission. They must represent 2 different membership groups. At least one member must be a resident of a common ownership community. The 2 Commission members must designate the third member from a list of volunteer arbitrators trained or experienced in common ownership community issues maintained by the Commission. The third member must chair the panel.

(c) Each panelist must not have any interest in the dispute to be heard.

10B–13. Administrative hearing.

(a) A hearing panel appointed under Section 10B–12 must hold a hearing on each dispute that is not resolved by mediation under Section 10B–11 unless the Commission finds that:

(1) the dispute is essentially identical to another dispute between the same parties on which a hearing has already been held under this Section; or

(2) the dispute is clearly not within the jurisdiction of the Commission.

* * *

(d) The hearing panel may award costs, including a reasonable attorney's fee, to any party if another party;

(1) filed or maintained a frivolous dispute, or filed or maintained a dispute in other than good faith;

(2) unreasonably refused to accept mediation of a dispute, or unreasonably withdrew from ongoing mediation; or

(3) substantially delayed or hindered the dispute resolution process without good cause.

The hearing panel may also award costs or attorney's fees if an association document so requires and the award is reasonable under the circumstances.

* * *

(g) The court hearing an appeal must sustain the decision of the hearing panel unless the decision is:

(1) inconsistent with applicable law;

(2) not supported by substantial evidence on the record; or

(3) arbitrary and capricious, considering all facts before the hearing panel.

* * *

10B–14. Settlement of disputes; assistance to parties.

(a) Settlement of a dispute by mediation agreed to by the parties is binding, has the force and effect of a contract, and may be enforced accordingly.

* * *

6. A study of 599 condominium owners in Chicago, including 43 individuals who had been personally involved in condominium disputes, determined that nearly half of the disputants first attempted to resolve their disputes through negotiations, and one quarter through mediation. Only 2.3% began with litigation. Lifestyle and property disputes are most likely to be settled informally; disputes over finances, services, governance and personal well-being are less amenable to informal resolution. See Walker and Masotti, supra.

7. If the members of a property owners association are evenly divided on an issue—for example, whether to raise assessments, enforce a servitude, or undertake expensive remodeling of community facilities—who is the client of the association's lawyer? See A.B.A. Model Rule 1.13.

D. EXTENSION, MODIFICATION, AND TERMINATION OF RESTRICTIONS BY PROPERTY OWNERS ASSOCIATIONS

RIDGE PARK HOME OWNERS v. PENA

Supreme Court of New Mexico, 1975.
88 N.M. 563, 544 P.2d 278.

SOSA, JUSTICE.

This is a case involving building and use restrictions in a subdivision and concerns the effect of amending restrictive covenants of that subdivision. Plaintiffs-appellants filed an action in the district court of Bernalillo County to enjoin the construction of a drug store and physician's office on two lots in the Ridge Park Addition subdivision in Albuquerque. The lots in question were subject to residential restrictions of record that forbade such construction.

After granting a preliminary injunction, in a subsequent hearing the district court ruled that the restrictions had been amended by a vote of the majority of the owners in the Ridge Park Addition, and that such amendment allowed the construction of the drug store and physician's office on the two lots, and found that the objection was moot. From the dismissal of the complaint and their request for a permanent injunction, the plaintiffs appeal.

Since the amendment relieved only a small portion of the residential lots from the residential restrictions, changing them to multiple dwelling or commercial, it altered the existing restrictions to less than all of the property in the subdivision. The plaintiffs urge for reversal that the district court erred as a matter of law in upholding such amendment. We agree. This issue being dispositive of the appeal, we do not need to reach the other points raised by the appellants.

Building and use restrictions for the Ridge Park Addition were filed with the county clerk of Bernalillo County on January 18, 1951. The Ridge Park Addition to the city of Albuquerque provided for both a commercial and a residential area. The restrictions provided that all lots in all blocks would be used for residential, single dwelling purposes, except for blocks 4 and 9 which could be commercial or residential. Subsequent to the filing of the building and use restrictions, the city of Albuquerque zoned the two lots in question, lots 9 and 10 of block 8 (among others) as commercial, although these two lots were covered with the residential restrictive covenants. The general rule is that zoning ordinances if less stringent do not diminish the legal effect of more restrictive private building restrictions, and the rezoning of property for purposes other than residential does not supersede the original plat restrictions so as to prevent the enforcement of such restrictions. Kosel v. Stone, 146 Mont. 218, 404 P.2d 894 (1965); 20 Am.Jur.2d Covenants, Conditions, and Restrictions § 277 at 837–41 (1965).

Since the zoning did not abrogate the restrictive covenants, defendants assert that the consent of a majority of the owners of all of the lots in the Ridge Park Addition to the changing of lots 9 and 10 in block 8 from residential to commercial abrogated those covenants with respect to the two lots. The method for amending the restrictive covenants was contained in Provision VI of the restrictions which provided as follows:

> 1. All protective covenants herein shall apply to and be binding upon all parties to this agreement, and their successors in interest, from the date of recording of this agreement with the County Clerk of Bernalillo County, State of New Mexico, for a period of twenty years and shall run with the land. At the

expiration of twenty years said covenants shall be extended automatically for successive ten year periods unless a majority of the then owners of the lots vote to alter or eliminate said covenants.

The twenty year period had expired at the time the vote was taken. Passing by approximately an 85% majority, the amendment allowed all lots zoned C—1 by the city to be taken out of the residential restrictions and put under the business restrictions section of the subdivision agreement. The dissenting minority consisted mostly of the individuals living near and around the lots subject to the amendment.

The issue is whether the majority (or whatever percentage is required by an agreement) can amend or delete restrictive covenants on fewer than all lots subject thereto. Absent a specific provision in the agreement stating otherwise, we hold that the requisite vote cannot change the applicability of restrictive covenants to a few of the lots; the change must apply to all lots. Montoya v. Barreras, 81 N.M. 749, 473 P.2d 363 (1970). Defendants seek to distinguish Montoya supra by pointing out that the subdivision in that case was solely residential whereas Ridge Park is residential and commercial. This argument has little merit. "Restrictions as to the use of land are mutual, reciprocal, equitable easements in the nature of servitudes in favor of owners of other lots within the restricted area, and constitute property rights which run with the land." Montoya, 81 N.M. at 751, 473 P.2d at 365. In the instant case the residential restrictions burdened all residential lots; the commercial restrictions burden all commercial lots. The mutuality of restrictive covenants would be destroyed if we were to allow the majority of owners, who might not be adversely affected because of their insulated location in the subdivision, to authorize offensive consequences for the minority by removing or imposing restrictions only on certain lots within the minority's area. Thus, we find that the fact that the Ridge Park Addition was not merely residential, but was residential and commercial, makes no difference. No changes may be made with respect to any one lot without affecting all the others subject to the restrictions.

* * *

Notes and Questions

1. If the servitudes that establish and delineate the powers of a property owners' association are conceived of as its constitution, particular problems arise when an attempt is made to amend that constitution, especially when the modification will disadvantage some members of the community more than others. Is majority rule acceptable in these circumstances? Are supramajority voting requirements more acceptable, or should absolute unanimity be required? What problems does a unanimity requirement create? If a municipality could take the action at issue in the principal case, essentially a rezoning, why do we not permit it of a property owners association? Would such changes be more palatable if property owners associations were required to compensate losers in wealth-transfer modifications, along the lines of public eminent domain requirements? See

Ellickson, Cities and Homeowners Associations, 130 U.Pa.L.Rev. 1519, 1532–1539 (1982).

2. An impressive literature has arisen in the past decade debating whether property owners associations are on the one hand voluntary, consensual communities, that ought to be left largely free to chart their own course, or, on the other, tyrannical and oppressive arrangements that must be subjected to public control. See, e.g., Alexander, Dilemmas of Group Autonomy: Residential Associations and Community, 75 Cornell L.Rev. 1 (1989); Ellickson, Cities and Homeowners Associations, 130 U.Pa. L.Rev. 1519 (1982); Korngold, Resolving the Flaws of Residential Servitudes and Owners Associations: For Reformation not Termination, 1990 Wis.L.Rev. 513; Natelson, Consent, Coercion, and "Reasonableness" in Private Law: The Special Case of the Property Owners Association, 51 Ohio St.L.J. 41 (1990); Winokur, The Mixed Blessing of Promissory Servitudes: Toward Optimizing Economic Utility, Individual Liberty and Personal Identity, 1989 Wis.L.Rev. 1; Winokur, Reforming Servitude Regimes: Toward Associational Federalism and Community, 1990 Wis.L.Rev. 537; Note, The Rule of Law in Residential Associations, 99 Harv.L.Rev. 472 (1985). Do purchasers of property in a restricted subdivision in fact at the time of purchase consider and embrace the servitudes that bind that subdivision? Do most residents in restricted subdivisions experience the servitudes that govern their subdivision as limiting their individual creative expression or as facilitating the creation of a communal identity? Are restrictions the mindless creations of form-book writers or bureaucratic drones, or are they the market's response to the desires of consumers? What legal consequences should follow from how you answer these questions?

3. The issues raised in these materials are increasingly being addressed by state statutes and uniform laws. See, Codifying the Law of Homeowner Associations: The Uniform Planned Community Act, 15 Real Prop., Prob., and Trust J., 854 (1980); Geis, Beyond the Condominium: The Uniform Common–Interest Ownership Act, 17 Real Prop., Prob. & Trust J. 757 (1982).

SPRING LAKE ESTATES

Adapted from Riskin and Westbrook, Dispute Resolution
and Lawyers, Teachers' Manual (West 1988).

Spring Lake Estates is a planned residential development in an "exurban" part of the metropolitan area. Located approximately 25 miles from the central business district, it features a 200–acre lake and 300 acres of gently rolling meadows interspersed with strands of oak and pine. The developer, Spring Lake Properties, Inc., plans a first phase of 60 one-acre lots and a second phase of 40 additional lots. The first phase of 60 has been platted. The dam has been completed and the lake is filling. Roads have been laid out according to the plat, but have not yet been constructed. At present they are nothing more than dirt trails.

A brochure describing the development contains the following information. Spring Lake Estates will be "an outstanding residential community featuring amenities certain to appeal to executive home-owners." All lot owners will be expected to complete construction of a residence suitable for year-round occupancy or vacationing within two years of purchase. Lot owners and their guests will have full use of the lake, beaches, boat docks, club house, jogging trails, swimming pool, hot tub and tennis courts. Lot owners may have pets, but only if they do not constitute a nuisance. All roads will be paved within the next 12 months. The club house and sporting facilities will be completed within 24 months. All common facilities will be maintained by the developer until a property owners association is established.

Water supply must be purchased from a private utility company that will be organized by the developer. Water lines will be extended to the individual lots. A completion bond has been purchased by the developer. A well has been sunk by the developer that appears adequate for all anticipated water uses. A $10 per month flat rate has been established for each lot serviced by hookup.

Electricity and telephone services are available from local utilities regulated by the State Public Service Commission. Facilities will be extended to the individual lots upon request by a lot purchaser who constructs a residence. Costs of the facilities and service will be the responsibility of the lot owner. There is no gas service to the subdivision.

The sewage system is owned by the developer, which is responsible for the installation and operation of the system. Lines will be extended to individual lots. A connection (hookup) cost of $75 will be borne by the lot owner. No alternative method of sewage disposal will be permitted in the boundaries of the subdivision.

A home owners' association, Spring Lake Estates Home Owners' Association, will be organized when the development is complete. Title to the common areas, such as the lake, dam, roads, pools, clubhouse, and tennis courts will be conveyed to the home owners' association. Each lot owner will pay a maintenance fee of $250 per month. This fee may be modified annually if common area expenses so warrant. In addition, special assessments may be levied to respond to unanticipated repair and maintenance problems. Fees and assessments will be paid to the developer until such time as the home owners association is organized.

Fire and police protection, garbage and trash collection, schools, medical and dental facilities are available from local entities and are not the responsibility of the developer. A small shopping center will be developed at the periphery of the development, which will include a convenience store, drug store, laundromat, movie theater, gasoline station, and restaurant.

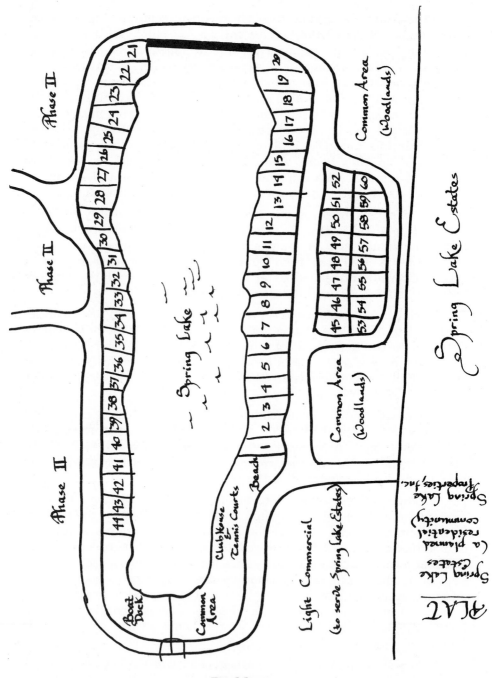

Problems

1. As attorney for the developer, describe the provisions that must be drafted to accomplish the developer's goals as outlined in the narrative. Identify the property interests those provisions create. Pay

particular attention to establishing a process to manage change as the development evolves through different stages.

2. Draft one clause creating an affirmative right to use the property of others, one negative obligation servitude, and one affirmative obligation servitude that will accomplish the developer's goals identified above.

3. Design a system for resolving disputes arising out of the relationships created by the common interest community and draft the appropriate clauses necessary to establish that system.

Dispute Resolution Exercise

Assume that it is now ten years later. Assume further that the following clauses were included, among others, in the declaration of restrictions:

"(1) No animals, livestock or poultry of any kind shall be raised, bred, or kept on any lot, except that dogs, cats and other household pets may be kept, provided that they are not kept, bred, or maintained for any commercial purpose.

"(2) The grantor reserves to itself the right to alter or amend these restrictions at any time, and such alterations and amendments shall apply to all lots in the subdivision whether owned by the grantor or its successors or assigns, provided that such amendment shall not diminish the protection provided by these restrictions.

"(3) The board of directors of the home owners' association may issue temporary permits to free owners of lots in the subdivision from any obligations express or implied by this declaration, provided the board of directors acts in accordance with adopted guidelines and procedures and shows good cause.

"(4) No noxious or offensive activity shall be carried on upon any lot, nor shall anything be done thereon which may be or may become an annoyance or nuisance to the neighborhood.

"(5) Lots within Spring Lake Estates shall only be used for single-family residential use."

As Spring Lake has developed over the past ten years, several problems have arisen.

(a) Lots 13, 14, and 15 have never been sold. Rather than drive to the common beach, the families owning lots 51 and 52 have simply cut across these lots to get to the lake. They have been doing this for as long as they have lived there. No one ever said anything to them about this, although a couple of "no trespassing" signs have been posted on the trees. Now Spring Lake Properties, Inc. (SLP) has strung a chain between the trees to block access to lots 13, 14 and 15. The owners of lots 51 and 52 seek your advice.

(b) SLP has had some financial difficulties. It recently sold ten acres in the area described as Phase II on the plat to Golden Age

Properties (GAP), which plans to construct a 100–unit retirement condominium development. SLP has also transferred "perpetual rights" to use the common area of the development, including the lake, beach, pools and tennis courts, to GAP. Homeowners from several of the lots in the original Spring Lakes development have sought your advice.

(c) The homeowners in the original development have recently discovered that the sewer lines for lots 44 through 33 pass under the land sold to GAP, and that SLP did not reserve an easement in the deed to GAP. GAP has recently discovered the sewer line and wishes to remove it as it interferes with construction in GAP. GAP has come to you for advice.

(d) The original purchaser of lot 5 sold her house and lot to a family that has placed a two bedroom, factory-built, modular house for their grandparents on the lot behind the existing house without seeking approval for the extra unit.

(e) Mrs. Smith's 100 pound golden retriever, Ginger, whom Mrs. Smith claims is "a very gentle animal," barked ferociously and terrorized the six year old daughter of the Brown's who live across the street, when she ran into Mrs. Smith's yard to retrieve a ball. Mrs. Smith has accused the eleven year old son of her next door neighbor, Ed Harris, of provoking the dog by constant teasing and harassment. The Browns are threatening legal action against Mrs. Smith unless she removes the dog from the development.

(f) Spring Lake Estates originally was situated about a quarter Mile from Highway 103, a two-lane state highway. The area between lots 53 and 60 and the highway was left heavily wooded as a barrier between the highway and Spring Lake Estates. Two years ago, the state made 103 a four-lane divided highway. In doing so, it condemned the wooded land. This area has been replaced with chain-link fence and non-descript highway foliage. The fronts of the homes on lot 53–60 face directly to the highway, separated only by the street and the chain-link fence. The homes were originally built at a cost of approximately $250,000 each.

The owner of lot 53 has a contract to sell his house to Le Petit Enfant Day Care Center. The center would serve about 40 children each day. The center is willing to purchase the house for $180,000. The center expects to do well because Spring Lake Estates is entirely residential, and there is an "office park" on the other side of the highway. The house has been for sale for nine months. The best offer received prior to that from the center was $150,000. The contract of sale is conditional on the absence of restrictions that would prohibit the day care center. What advice do you give the owner of lot 53?

III. NUISANCE

A. PRIVATE NUISANCE

Many disputes that arise between neighbors can be conceptualized alternatively as servitude or as nuisance problems. Servitude law invokes the authority of restrictions or affirmative obligations to which the parties have, at least constructively, consented. Nuisance law, on the other hand, invokes the authority of the more general obligations imposed by the law of tort.

The most general duty imposed by the law of nuisance is articulated by the latin phrase "Sic utere tuo ut alienum non laedas"—use your property so as not to injure others. The difficulty of applying this maxim in the context of relations between neighbors becomes readily apparent if one considers the contexts in which nuisance disputes are likely to arise. One neighbor's beloved pets create noise or odors that offend another. One neighbor's prized tree rains leaves and twigs into another's gutter. The diligent practice of one neighbor's son, an aspiring rock musician, arouses the fury of the entire block on a somnolent Sunday afternoon. Residential uses also come in conflict with agricultural, commercial or industrial uses, which uses in turn conflict among themselves. Feedlots breed odors and vermin, which afflict neighboring residences. Industries belch smoke, which their neighbors must breathe. Bright lights from shopping centers dim the screens of neighboring drive-in theatres. If an offending neighbor's conduct is sufficiently offensive or a receiving neighbor is sufficiently sensitive, offense becomes injury, and a nuisance dispute ends up in court. Courts must then struggle with whose rights must prevail, the rights of one landowner to use her land as she chooses, or the right of another landowner to be free from interference in the use of his land.

A private nuisance (more on public nuisances later) is defined by the Restatement (Second) of Torts (1979) as "a nontrespassery invasion of another's interest in the private use and enjoyment of land." § 821D. Nuisance is, therefore, an invasion of property which is not a trespass. Conceptually, trespass is a direct invasion of plaintiff's land, nuisance an indirect interference with use and enjoyment. If your neighbor walks across your land or dumps dirt onto it, he is guilty of trespass. If his noisy air conditioner keeps you awake at night, or flies from his manure pile keep you from enjoying barbecues on your deck, he may be guilty of a nuisance. The conceptual distinction between trespass and nuisance is important because a trespasser is liable irrespective of whether the trespass causes harm, Restatement (Second) of Torts, § 158 (1979), while one who commits nuisance is liable only if significant harm results, Restatement (Second) of Torts, Second, § 821F.

Why does this distinction exist between trespass and nuisance? Does it make economic sense? See Merrill, Trespass, Nuisance, and the Costs of Determining Property Rights, 14 J. Legal Stud. 13 (1985).

Practically, the distinction is often difficult to make. See, e.g., Martin v. Reynolds Metals Co., 221 Or. 86, 342 P.2d 790 (1959), cert. den., 362 U.S. 918, 80 S.Ct. 672, 4 L.Ed.2d 739 (1960) (invasion by gas held to be direct physical invasion).

BLANKS v. RAWSON

Court of Appeals of South Carolina, 1988.
296 S.C. 110, 370 S.E.2d 890.

CURETON, JUDGE:

This is a dispute between next door neighbors. Benjamin and Mary Ann Blanks claim their neighbor, Gary W. Rawson, has violated certain neighborhood restrictions by the construction of a dog pen, basketball goal, and ten-foot privacy fence. The trial judge ordered Mr. Rawson to remove or relocate the dog pen and basketball goal. He also ordered Rawson to remove or reduce the height of the fence. Rawson appeals. We affirm in part and reverse in part.

The Blanks and Rawson reside in the Indian Fork subdivision on Lake Murray in Lexington County. Both parties bought vacant lots and constructed homes. The subdivision was developed by Indian Fork Development Company. The company filed a "Declaration of Restrictions" which covered the lots in question. Rawson purchased his lot first. He constructed a home substantially identical to his prior home. In purchasing the property Mr. Rawson had discussions with a representative of Indian Fork Development Company. This representative was aware Rawson desired to build a house identical to his current home. The developer approved Rawson's house plans. The developer specifically gave permission to Rawson to vary the minimum set back requirements in the Declaration of Restrictions to accommodate his home on the lot and to locate the dog pen and basketball goal. The basketball goal is near the edge of the driveway close to the property line. The dog pen is on the property line behind the driveway.

Mr. and Mrs. Blanks purchased the lot to the right of Mr. Rawson. The developer advised the Blanks of Mr. Rawson's name because they desired to know who their neighbor would be. The Blanks rode by Rawson's old home to view it. At that time, the dog pen was behind the driveway on the property line. The dog pen in controversy is in the same location behind the driveway. The difference is Rawson has reoriented the new house so the driveway is on the right side of the house as opposed to the left. This is the side next to the Blanks.

As the homes were being constructed, Mr. Blanks expressed objections personally and through counsel to Rawson about the dog pen and basketball goal because he felt they violated the minimum setback limits. Rawson had already obtained the approval of the developer to vary the setback limits when these objections were raised. Paragraph Seven of the Declaration of Restrictions provides "no building shall be closer to any side boundary than fifteen (15) feet * * * provided further that the Declarant [Indian Fork Development Co. Inc.] reserves the right to vary all such setback lines at will."

Shortly after the complaint was served, Rawson constructed a ten foot privacy fence. The fence shields the basketball goal and dog pen from the Blanks. As with the dog pen and goal, Rawson obtained the permission of Indian River Development Company to build the fence. This permission was received in December of 1985 although construction of the fence did not occur until May 1986.

The Blanks complain the dog pen and basketball goal violate the minimum setback limits and are a nuisance. They claim the dog barks and the dog pen is not properly maintained thereby creating a foul odor. They complain Rawson's son plays loud music and his basketball comes into their yard. As to the fence, they complain it is too high and blocks the view of the lake they previously enjoyed across Rawson's property. The trial court found the nearness of the basketball goal to the property line created a nuisance whenever the basketball was thrown toward the goal. The court found that if the ball hits the goal it creates a noise and if it misses the goal, it can go into the Blanks' yard. The court found the nearness of the dog pen to the property line created a nuisance because it was not properly maintained and the sight and smell of dog feces was revolting. As to the fence, the court called it a "hate fence" not in keeping with the intentions of a high level residential neighborhood and not in keeping with what is right as opposed to what is wrong. The court held it was wrong for the fence to obstruct the Blanks' view of the lake across the Rawsons' backyard.

The complaint alleges violation of restrictions and seeks an injunction. As previously noted, Paragraph Seven of the Declaration of Restrictions deals with setback requirements. Paragraph Eight provides "no noxious or offensive activity * * * shall be had or done upon any lot in the subdivision and nothing shall be had or done thereon which constitutes or becomes an annoyance or nuisance to the neighborhood or constitutes an unsanitary condition." Paragraph Twelve indicates the restrictions shall run with the land. Paragraph Thirteen gives an owner a right to sue any other owner of real property in the subdivision in order to restrain a violation of the restrictions.

* * *

Mr. Rawson did not violate Paragraph Seven of the subdivision restrictions concerning the setback limits. The evidence is undisputed he received express permission from Indian Fork Development Company to locate the dog pen, basketball goal, and fence. The restrictions in Paragraph Seven concerning setbacks specifically provide the company has the right to vary all setback lines at will.

The trial court rested its conclusions on a concept of nuisance. Paragraph Eight prohibits the creation of an annoyance or nuisance to the neighborhood. Neither a basketball goal nor a dog pen is a nuisance per se. They may be a nuisance per accidens if they become a nuisance by reason of circumstances, location, or surroundings. A nuisance has been defined as "anything which works hurt, inconvenience, or damages; anything which essentially interferes with the enjoyment of life or property [   ]." Strong v. Winn–Dixie Stores, Inc., 240 S.C. 244, 253, 125 S.E.2d 628, 632 (1962).

The South Carolina Supreme Court has recognized that the resolution of the issue of a private nuisance involves the conflicting interests of landowners. "The right of one to make such lawful use of his property as he may desire must be applied with due regard to the correlative right of the other to be protected in the reasonable enjoyment of his property." Winget v. Winn–Dixie Stores Inc., 242 S.C. 152, 159, 130 S.E.2d 363, 367 (1963). Each case must be decided upon its own facts, and the observation of the Supreme Court regarding neighbors is particularly relevant:

> "[E]very annoyance or disturbance of a landowner from the use made of property by a neighbor does not constitute a nuisance. The question is not whether the plaintiffs have been annoyed or disturbed * * * but whether there has been an injury to their legal rights. People who live in organized communities must of necessity suffer some inconvenience and annoyance from their neighbors and must submit to annoyances consequent upon the reasonable use of property by others."

Winget, 242 S.C. at 159, 130 S.E.2d at 367.

From our review of the record, we do not find evidence to support the conclusion the basketball goal is a nuisance. Mr. Blanks testified to only one instance when Mr. Rawson's son was playing basketball and he asked the boy to turn down the radio. He also complained the ball could bounce over into his yard and damage his air conditioner unit or shrubs. There is no evidence this damage has occurred. The pictures in the record do not show any shrubs in the yard although Blanks stated they planned to plant some. At most, the Blanks complain about an anticipatory nuisance in this respect.

The debate over the dog pen concerns how often and how well it is cleaned. The trial court heard the testimony and reviewed photographs. The dog is a large breed. The Rawsons testified they cleaned the pen daily. Mr. Blanks stated it was not cleaned on a regular basis. Blanks testified the odor was still present with the fence in place. The trial court found the dog pen was maintained in a filthy condition and an odor was created by its condition. In this equity action, the Court of Appeals has the authority to make findings of fact in accordance with its own view of the preponderance of the evidence, however, it is not required to disregard the findings of the trial judge who saw and heard the witnesses and was in a better position to judge their credibility. [   ] Given the conflicting evidence on this issue, we affirm the trial judge.

The final issue is the fence. The Blanks object to its height primarily because it restricts their view of the lake. Before the fence was constructed, they could sit on their back porch and look at the lake across the Rawson property. Rawson received permission from the developer to construct the fence.

The Declaration of Restrictions does not contain language creating a covenant of view for any lot owner. South Carolina does not recognize a prescriptive easement of view. [ ]

Perhaps recognizing the inherent problem in arguing there could be no fence, Mr. Blanks testified he would be satisfied if the fence were reduced to eight feet near the basketball goal and six feet down to the water. The trial court apparently felt the fence was ill motivated, but did not find it was a nuisance. The court stated the fence was not in keeping with the intentions of a high-level residential development.

Motive in constructing the fence is not relevant to this case. The question is whether the fence violates a restriction. Based upon our view of the evidence, it does not. It is unfortunate relations among neighbors have degenerated to this point, but it appears the fence may be the best resolution of this controversy. While the Blanks no longer have a panoramic view of the lake, both parties have their privacy.

The decision of the trial court is affirmed in part and reversed in part.

Notes and Questions

1. What sorts of "annoyances and disturbances" rise to the level of a nuisance? The principal case rejects the plaintiff's position that interference with a view can constitute a nuisance. Should nuisance law ever be available to protect aesthetic sensibilities? Compare Cahill v. Heckel, 87 N.J.Super. 201, 208 A.2d 651 (1965); Robie v. Lillis, 112 N.H. 492, 299 A.2d 155 (1972) (unsightly commercial uses in residential neighborhood not nuisance), with Woodbury, Aesthetic Nuisances: The Time has come to Recognize It, 27 Nat.Res.J. 877 (1987). Should courts find "spite fences" to be nuisances? See 5 R. Powell, Powell on Real Property, § 696 (1991). Conduct that physically harms another's property (e.g., injury to crops or trees caused by polluting the soil or water) is grounds for nuisance litigation, as is conduct that diminishes the value of property. Should conduct that causes mental annoyance or physical discomfort also be grounds for a nuisance action independently of its affect on the value of the injured party's land? See Prosser & Keeton on Torts, § 88 (5th ed 1984). Could a use that causes psychological discomfort, such as a funeral home or cemetery, constitute a nuisance? See Frederick v. Brown Funeral Homes, Inc., 222 La. 57, 62 So.2d 100 (1952) (the majority rule permits enjoining a funeral home in a strictly residential neighborhood). Should a landowner be liable in nuisance if the natural condition of his land (e.g., as overgrown with weeds) injures an adjoining land owner? See Restatement (Second) of Torts, §§ 839, 840 (1977). As nuisance is a property tort, should it make any difference whether the person harmed is the owner of the property or merely another who lives there, such as a family member or employee? See Prosser & Keeton on Torts, § 87 (5th ed. 1984).

2. Nuisance law is permeated with Latin. The principal case raises the distinction between nuisance per se and nuisance per accidens. A

nuisance per se (or absolute nuisance) is a use that is unreasonable in itself, wherever located and however conducted. What uses fit that description? As a practical matter, a court will rarely hold a use to be a nuisance per se unless it is specifically outlawed by statute or ordinance. See Vianello v. State of Texas, 627 S.W.2d 530 (Tex.App.1982) (dog kennel illegal under local ordinance). Most nuisances fall into the per accidens category. They are offensive because of where or how they are conducted.

3. A related distinction applies when a suit is brought to enjoin a prospective nuisance. The plaintiff in such a suit must establish that it is highly probable that a nuisance will result, however the use is operated. It is not sufficient to merely show that a nuisance may result if the use is operated improperly. Usually this means showing that the use in itself is inappropriate for the locality for which it is proposed.

CARPENTER v. DOUBLE R CATTLE COMPANY, INC.

Court of Appeals of Idaho, 1983.
105 Idaho 320, 669 P.2d 643.

BURNETT, JUDGE.

* * *

This lawsuit was filed by a group of homeowners who alleged that expansion of a nearby cattle feedlot had created a nuisance. The homeowners claimed that operation of the expanded feedlot had caused noxious odors, air and water pollution, noise and pests in the area. The homeowners sought damages and injunctive relief. * * * The jury returned a verdict simply finding that no nuisance existed. The court entered judgment for the feedlot proprietors, denying the homeowners any damages or injunctive relief. This appeal followed. For reasons appearing below, we vacate the judgment and remand the case for a new trial.

The homeowners contend that the jury received improper instructions on criteria for determining the existence of a nuisance. The jury was told to weigh the alleged injury to the homeowners against the "social value" of the feedlot, and to consider "the interests of the community as a whole," in determining whether a nuisance existed. In Part I of this opinion we consider the adequacy of the record upon which to review the jury instructions. In Part II we establish an historical framework for reviewing the instructions, by examining the development of American nuisance law. In Part III we turn to pertinent sections from the nuisance chapter of the Restatement (Second) of Torts (1977). We explain how these sections limit the utilization of such concepts as "social value" and "the interests of the community as a whole" in determining whether a nuisance exists. We discuss the implications of these sections; and we adopt them. Finally, in Part IV, we return to the jury instructions in this case, holding them to be erroneous and offering guidance to the trial court upon remand.

I

* * *

Although the record on appeal is limited, the detailed minute records of the court and the exhibits indicate the general nature of evidence adduced. There was evidence tending to show a cattle operation involving several thousand head at the feedlot; swarms of insects on various properties near the feedlot; flocks of birds near the feedlot; manure piles at the feedlot; and drainage of waste water from the feedlot. The evidence identified the nature of the homeowners' properties and fixed their location relative to the feedlot. There was expert testimony regarding the economic values of the properties. * * * A comprehensive plan and a zoning ordinance of Washington County were presented. At the close of the homeowners' evidence, and at the conclusion of trial, the proprietors moved for dismissal of the homeowners' complaint. Both motions were denied.

* * *

II

The concept of nuisance originated in the law of property. At common law, a distinction was maintained between two encroachments upon property rights—interference with possession of land, and interference with the use and enjoyment of land. The first type of encroachment was subject to an "assize of novel disseisen," a remedy for trespass. The latter form of encroachment was subject to an "assize of nuisance," a remedy for a variety of invasions which diminished the owner's enjoyment of his property without dispossessing him of it. Thus, nuisance and trespass have common roots in property law, and occasionally it is difficult to distinguish between them. But where an invasion of property is merely incidental to the use of adjoining property, and does not physically interfere with possession of the property invaded, it generally has been classified as a nuisance rather than as a trespass. See cases collected in 58 Am.Jur.2d Nuisances, § 2, 556–57 (1971).

The early concepts of nuisance and trespass shared the common law's reverence for property rights. Invasions of property were deemed wrongful per se, and the parties responsible for such invasions were subject to a form of strict liability. * * *

The property-oriented, English concept of a nuisance had its analogue in early American law. In one illustrative case of the nineteenth century, an American court held that title to land gave the owner the right to impregnate the air with odors, dust and smoke, pollute his own water and make noises, provided that he did not substantially interfere with the comfort of others or injure the use or enjoyment of their property. Pennoyer v. Allen, 56 Wis. 502, 14 N.W. 609 (1883).

This broad description of nuisance was incorporated into Idaho law. Idaho Code § 52–101, which has antecedents dating to 1881, defines a nuisance as "[a]nything which is injurious to health or morals, or is indecent, or offensive to the senses, or an obstruction to the free use of property, so as to interfere with the comfortable enjoyment of life or property * * *."

However, as the English concept of nuisance was assimilated into American law, it underwent a transformation. It ceased to be solely a creature of property law. As exemplified by the Idaho statutes, nuisance law came to protect life and health, as well as property. * * *

American tort law in the nineteenth and early twentieth centuries was founded upon the rock of "fault." As the notion of fault burrowed into the concept of nuisance, the strict liability which had attended nuisance in property law began to deteriorate. American courts stressed that liability for nuisance would arise only from "unreasonable" uses of property. * * *

* * * Our courts also underscored the distinction between conditions which are inherently nuisances (nuisances per se) and those conditions which may or may not constitute nuisances, depending upon the surrounding circumstances (nuisances per accidens). Of cases in the latter category, it became customary for the courts to say that whether an invasion of another's enjoyment of property was unreasonable would depend upon all circumstances in the case. These circumstances typically would include the location of the claimed nuisance, the character of the neighborhood, the nature of the offending activity, the frequency of the intrusion, and the effect upon the enjoyment of life, health and property. [ ]

Moreover, the American transformation resulted in diminished application of the principle—derived from property law—that where property rights were substantially impaired by a nuisance, the complaining party was entitled to an injunction. This principle, which had complemented the property-based concept of strict liability, entitled a property owner to block an offensive activity on neighboring property, regardless of disparate economic consequences. American courts apparently found this approach ill-suited to the demands of a developing nation.

There evolved two lines of American response to the problem of injunctions. One response was to narrow the scope of cases in which injunctions would be granted, while continuing to recognize an entitlement to damages for injury to property rights. Thus, in Clifton Iron Co. v. Dye, 87 Ala. 468, 6 So. 192 (1889), the Alabama Supreme Court held that a mining company would not be enjoined from washing its ores simply because the operation polluted a stream below. The court held that the aggrieved parties' recourse was in damages. * * *

Ultimately, the approach exemplified by these cases developed into the "comparative injury" doctrine. Under this doctrine, the comparative benefits and hardships of discontinuing one activity for the protection of another would be weighed in determining whether injunctive relief or damages represented the more appropriate remedy for a nuisance. The Idaho Supreme Court adopted the comparative injury doctrine in Koseris v. J.R. Simplot Co., 82 Idaho 263, 352 P.2d 235 (1960). As explained later in this opinion, our Supreme Court in Koseris acknowledged the right to recover damages for the invasion of one's property, even where the comparative injury doctrine might bar injunctive relief.

The second line of American response to the injunction problem was to narrow the scope of cases in which nuisances were found to exist. This was achieved by incorporating the social value—the "utility"—of the offending activity into the litany of circumstances to be weighed in determining whether a particular use of property was "unreasonable." Thus, the utility of an offending activity militated not merely against the issuance of an injunction, but also against a determination that the offending activity was a nuisance at all. This second line of response found expression in the general ("black letter") principles set forth by the Restatement of Torts (1932) (herein cited as the First Restatement). Section 826 of the First Restatement declared that an invasion of another's enjoyment of property would be deemed unreasonable, and therefore a nuisance, unless the utility of the actor's conduct outweighed the gravity of the harm.

The Idaho Supreme Court never explicitly adopted the First Restatement. However, in McNichols v. J.R. Simplot Co., [74 Idaho 321, 262 P.2d 1012 (1953)], the Court may have intimated a similar approach. * * *

Thus, when confronted with a choice between the two American lines of response to the problem of injunctions in nuisance cases, Idaho appeared to choose both. Koseris adopted the "comparative injury" doctrine, restricting the cases qualifying for injunctions without narrowing the scope of nuisance cases in which an aggrieved party was entitled to be compensated in damages. However, McNichols and IDJI 491 allowed the offending activity's value to the community to be considered in determining whether any nuisance existed at all.

* * *

Dissatisfaction with the First Restatement also was expressed by the courts. In Boomer v. Atlantic Cement Co., 26 N.Y.2d 219, 309 N.Y.S.2d 312, 257 N.E.2d 870 (1970), the New York Court of Appeals held that parties adversely affected by dust from a cement plant would be entitled to recover damages for the harm, although the value of the cement plant to the community was so great that its operation would not be enjoined.

* * *

Thus, it was clear by 1970 that the First Restatement's black letter test for existence of a nuisance had ceased to be—if, indeed, it ever was—an adequate expression of case law. The days were drawing to a close when an economic activity could escape all liability under nuisance law for harm caused to its neighbors, simply because a large measure of social utility was ascribed to it.

III

The seeds of reform had been sown. They took root in fertile soil when the American Law Institute (ALI), which had begun to write a new restatement of the law of torts, turned its attention to the subject of nuisances in 1970.

* * *

B. *The Second Restatement*

Ultimately, the provisions of Tentative Draft No. 18 were approved and incorporated into the private nuisance sections of chapter 40, Restatement (Second) of Torts (1977) (herein cited as the Second Restatement). The Second Restatement, like its predecessor, divides such nuisances into two groups: (a) "intentional and unreasonable" invasions of another's interest in the use and enjoyment of property, and (b) invasions which are "unintentional" but otherwise actionable under general tort principles. Second Restatement at § 822.

The first category is broader than the term "intentional" at first glance might suggest. Section 825 of the Second Restatement explains that an invasion is "intentional" if the actor knows that the invasion is resulting, or is substantially certain to result, from his activity. Thus, the purpose of an activity, such as a feedlot, may not be to invade its neighbors' interests in the use and enjoyment of their property; but the invasion is "intentional" within the meaning of the Second Restatement if the proprietors of the activity know that such an invasion is resulting—or is substantially certain to result—from the intended operation of their business. We focus upon "intentional" invasion, in this sense, because it is the type of nuisance alleged to exist in the present case.

The Second Restatement treats such an "intentional" invasion as a nuisance if it is "unreasonable." Section 826 of the Second Restatement now provides two sets of criteria for determining whether this type of nuisance exists:

An intentional invasion of another's interest in the use and enjoyment of land is unreasonable if

(a) the gravity of the harm outweighs the utility of the actor's conduct, or

(b) the harm caused by the conduct is serious and the financial burden of compensating for this and similar harm to others would not make the continuation of the conduct not feasible.

The present version of § 826, unlike its counterpart in the First Restatement, recognizes that liability for damages caused by a nuisance may exist regardless of whether the utility of the offending activity exceeds the gravity of the harm it has created. This fundamental proposition now permeates the entire Second Restatement. * * *

* * *

C. Evaluation of The Second Restatement

The Second Restatement clearly has rejected the notion that if an activity's utility exceeds the harm it creates, the activity is not a nuisance and therefore is free from all liability in damages or for injunctive relief. * * * It discards those earlier authorities which had responded to the problem of disparate economic consequences of injunctions by narrowing the concept of nuisance. Thus, the Second Restatement today is inconsistent with the Idaho Supreme Court's decision in McNichols, supra, insofar as that decision is said to support IDJI 491. * * *

* * *

Both the Second Restatement and Koseris recognize that utility of the activity alleged to be a nuisance is a proper factor to consider in the context of injunctive relief; but that damages may be awarded regardless of utility. Evidence of utility does not constitute a defense against recovery of damages where the harm is serious and compensation is feasible. Were the law otherwise, a large enterprise, important to the local economy, would have a lesser duty to compensate its neighbors for invasion of their rights than would a smaller business deemed less essential to the community. In our view, this is not, and should not be, the law in Idaho.

Koseris and the Second Restatement also share a recognition of the fundamental difference between making an activity compensate those whom it harms, and forcing the activity to discontinue or to modify its operations. The damage question goes to a person's basic right in tort law to recover for harm inflicted by another. The injunction question is broader; it brings into play the interest of other persons who may benefit from the activity. * * *

We believe that Koseris and the Second Restatement furnish better guidance than IDJI 491 for the future path of nuisance law in Idaho. The law of nuisance profoundly affects the quality of life enjoyed by all Idahoans. It should be broad in coverage, as our statutes provide, and fair in its application. It should not contain blind spots for large or important enterprises.

However, our view is not based simply upon general notions of fairness; it is also grounded in economics. The Second Restatement deals effectively with the problem of "externalities" identified in the ALI proceedings. Where an enterprise externalizes some burdens upon its neighbors, without compensation, our market system does not reflect the true cost of products or services provided by that enterprise. Externalities distort the price signals essential to the proper functioning of the market.

This problem affects two fundamental objectives of the economic system. The first objective, commonly called "efficiency" in economic theory, is to promote the greatest aggregate surplus of benefits over the costs of economic activity. The second objective, usually termed "equity" or "distributive justice," is to allocate these benefits and costs in accordance with prevailing societal values. The market system best serves the goal of efficiency when prices reflect true costs; and the goal of distributive justice is best achieved when benefits are explicitly identified to the correlative costs.

Although the problem of externalities affects both goals of efficiency and distributive justice, these objectives are conceptually different and may imply different solutions to a given problem. In theory, if there were no societal goal other than efficiency, and if there were no impediments to exchanges of property or property rights, individuals pursuing their economic self-interests might reach the most efficient allocation of costs and benefits by means of exchange, without direction by the courts. See Coase, The Problem of Social Cost, 3 J.L. & Econ. 1 (1960). However, the real world is not free from impediments to exchanges, and our economic system operates within the constraints of a society which is also concerned with distributive justice. Thus, the courts often are the battlegrounds upon which campaigns for efficiency and distributive justice are waged.

* * *

In order to address the problem of externalities, the remedies of damages and injunctive relief must be carefully chosen to accommodate the often competing goals of efficiency and distributive justice. See generally Polinsky, Resolving Nuisance Disputes: The Simple Economics of Injunctive and Damage Remedies, 32 Stan.L.Rev. 1075 (1980); Ellickson, Alternatives to Zoning: Covenants, Nuisance Rules, and Fines as Land Use Controls, 40 U.Chi.L.Rev. 681 (1973). Koseris and the Second Restatement recognize the complementary functions of injunctions and damages. Section 826(a) of the Second Restatement allows both injunctions and damages to be employed where the harm created by an economic activity exceeds its utility. Section 826(b) allows the more limited remedy of damages alone to be employed where it would not be appropriate to enjoin the activity but the activity is imposing harm upon its neighbors so substantial that they cannot reasonably be expected to bear it without compensation.

We follow Koseris and adopt § 826 of the Second Restatement. To the extent that IDJI 491 is inconsistent with our decision today, we urge that it be modified. In any event, IDJI 491 is merely recommendatory in nature; it is not mandatory. I.R.C.P. 51(a)(2).

D. Implications of the Second Restatement

Each of the parties in the present case has viewed the Second Restatement with some apprehension. We now turn to those concerns.

The homeowners, echoing an argument made during the ALI proceedings, have contended that the test of nuisance set forth in § 826 grants large enterprises a form of private eminent domain. They evidently fear that if the utility of a large enterprise exceeds the gravity of the harm it creates—insulating it from an injunction and subjecting it to liability only in damages—the enterprise might interfere at will with the enjoyment and use of neighboring property, upon penalty only of paying compensation from time to time. Such a result might be consistent with the economic goal of efficiency, but it may conflict with the goal of distributive justice insofar as it violates a basic societal value which opposes forced exchanges of property rights. See Calabresi, Some Thoughts on Risk Distribution and the Law of Torts, 70 Yale L.J. 499, 536 (1961).

Even those legal scholars who advocate the most limited role for injunctions as a remedy against nuisances acknowledge that damages may be inadequate, and injunctions may be necessary, where the harm in question relates to personal health and safety, or to one's fundamental freedom of action within the boundaries of his own property. Ellickson, supra, 40 U.Chi.L.Rev. at 740–41. Ordinarily, plaintiffs in such cases would prevail on the test which balances utility against gravity of the harm. Moreover, in the exceptional cases, the offending activity might be modified or eliminated through legislative or administrative controls such as environmental protection laws or zoning. Therefore, we expect that few cases would remain in need of a judicial remedy. However, we do not today close the door on the possibility that an injunction might lie, to protect personal health and safety or fundamental freedoms, in cases missed by the balancing test and by non-judicial controls. To this extent, our adoption of the Second Restatement's test of nuisance stops short of being absolute.

The Second Restatement also has encountered a host of objections from the feedlot proprietors and from the amicus curiae. These objections reflect genuine, legitimate concerns of Idaho business, particularly the agricultural community. The concerns have been eloquently presented by able counsel. We recognize that business is an anchor of our state. We believe that Idaho business will find that it can operate responsibly and profitably within the contours of nuisance liability defined by the Second Restatement. Every business person is someone else's neighbor. Busienss people are as much benefited by protecting our quality of life as are other Idaho residents. We further note that business enterprises which do not depend for their viability upon an asserted right to impose serious harm upon their neighbors will not be threatened by the nuisance tests articulated in the Second Restatement.

Beyond these general observations, we address several particular objections to the Second Restatement. First, our attention has been invited to the Idaho "Right to Farm Act," I.C. §§ 22–4501 et seq. This Act recites the Legislature's concern that agricultural activities conducted on farmland in urbanizing areas often are subjected to nuisance lawsuits. The Act imposes restrictions upon such lawsuits. However, we find that these restrictions are inapposite to the present case. The Act does not apply to lawsuits commenced before March 31, 1981. See I.C. § 22–4504. The homeowners' complaint in the instant case was filed on March 28, 1978.

More fundamentally, even assuming, without deciding, that a feedlot constitutes an "agricultural operation" within the meaning of the Act, the Act precludes a finding of nuisance only with respect to an activity which would not have been a nuisance but for a change in surrounding non-agricultural uses more than one year after the activity began. See I.C. § 22–4503. In contrast, the pleadings in the present case disclose that the feedlot is alleged to be a nuisance, not because of changes in surrounding non-agricultural uses, but because of an expansion of the feedlot itself.

The proprietors and amicus curiae recognize that the Act does not strictly apply in this case, but they suggest that it is a legislative statement of policy which should inhibit our adoption of the Second Restatement. However, the Act in essence represents a statutory adaptation of the common law doctrine of "coming to the nuisance." This doctrine does not conflict with the Second Restatement.

At early common law, the doctrine of "coming to the nuisance" was thus expressed:

> If my neighbor makes a tan-yard so as to annoy and render less salubrious the air of my house or gardens, the law will furnish me with a remedy; but if he is first in possession of the air, and I fix my habitation near him, the nuisance is of my own seeking, and may continue.

2 W. Blackstone, Commentaries on the Laws of England, 402 (17th ed. 1830). This rigid doctrine later was changed to provide that coming to the nuisance was not an absolute bar to the finding of a nuisance, but was merely one factor to be considered. [ ] This change stemmed from recognition that an absolute bar to a finding of nuisance would, in effect, give the offending activity a perpetual servitude upon the land of its neighbors without the payment of any compensation.

In keeping with this case law development, the Second Restatement recites, at § 840D, that coming to the nuisance is not a total bar to relief, but is a factor to be considered * * *. We conclude that the Act affords no basis to view the Second Restatement as contrary to legislative policy.

The feedlot proprietors and amicus curiae also contend that the Second Restatement should be rejected because it assertedly contains a rule of absolute liability, making an enterprise liable in damages to anyone adversely affected by its operations. However, this argument overlooks the requirement in § 826(b) that the harm be "serious." A plaintiff who fails to demonstrate harm exceeding the utility of a defendant's conduct will fail to establish a nuisance under § 826(a). The plaintiff also will fail under § 826(b) unless the trier of fact is persuaded that the harm shown is "serious." * * *

In determining seriousness, the factors for evaluating gravity of harm, as set forth in § 827, may be utilized. They include the extent and character of the harm, the suitability of the particular use or enjoyment invaded to the character of the locality, the burden on the injured person to avoid such harm, and the value which the law attaches to the type of use or enjoyment invaded. The last factor—the value attached to the type of use or enjoyment invaded—obviously relates to its intrinsic value when applied under § 826(b); its relative value, in comparison with the utility of the offending activity, should be considered only when applying § 826(a).

* * *

The feedlot proprietors and amicus curiae also assert that the Second Restatement will prove uneven in its application, because damages may be awarded only in those cases where the payment of such compensation is "feasible." They contend that the element of feasibility subjects a profitable enterprise to greater potential liability than that which would attend a similar activity conducted by a marginal business. However, we believe this contention misperceives the thrust of the feasibility requirement.

As used in § 826(b), the term "feasible" does not refer to the financial condition of the business conducting the activity, but refers to the activity itself. Section 826(b) merely recognizes that if the burden of paying compensation in damages would make it unfeasible to continue the activity, the effect of a damage award would be to discontinue operation of the activity. In those circumstances, the result would be the same as an injunction. In order to qualify for injunctive relief under § 826(a), a plaintiff would be required to show that the gravity of the harm exceeded the utility of the defendant's conduct. Thus, as noted in comment f to § 826, "[i]f imposition of this financial burden would make continuation of the activity not feasible, the weighing process for determining unreasonableness is similar to that in a suit for injunction." * * *

The element of feasibility illustrates the interrelationship between § 826(a) and § 826(b). If a plaintiff suffers serious harm from an intentional invasion of the use and enjoyment of his property, he is entitled to injunctive relief or damages—or a mix of these remedies—if the trier of fact determines that the gravity of the harm exceeds the utility of the defendant's conduct. If the harm does not outweigh the utility, but remains serious, the plaintiff's remedy is limited to damages—subject, however, to the further limitation that if the nature of the activity (not the particular enterprise conducting it) is such that payment of compensation in damages would cause the activity to be discontinued, then the damage award will be viewed as having the same impact as an injunction. In those circumstances, full compensation will not be awarded unless the gravity of the harm has been found to exceed the utility of the defendant's conduct.

IV

We now resume our focus upon the instant case. * * *

* * * [T]he district judge gave the jury a set of instructions which did not conform precisely to, but were consistent with, the First

Restatement and IDJI 491 * * *. We conclude that the jury was improperly instructed, in light of our adoption today of the Second Restatement's criteria for determining existence of a nuisance.

The feedlot proprietors argue that even if the instructions failed adequately to state the entire standard contained in the Second Restatement, nevertheless, the instructions sufficiently stated the test of balancing harm against utility under § 826(a). Accordingly, the proprietors urge us not to disturb that part of the district court's judgment which denied injunctive relief. They contend that any remand in this case should be limited to a determination of damage liability—that is, whether the harm claimed by the plaintiff was "serious" and the payment of compensation was "feasible" under § 826(b). This argument is attractive because it comports with a surface reading of the tests set forth in the two subsections of § 826. However, we believe the argument overlooks the deeper interrelationships between these subsections, and between the remedies of damages and injunctive relief.

* * *

[W]e believe that a rigid separation of § 826(a) from § 826(b) would be inconsistent with the nexus between the remedies of damages and injunctive relief in nuisance cases. A nuisance may be alleviated by no fewer than four possible remedies: (1) an injunction; (2) damages; (3) a conditional injunction, which may be dissolved or modified upon payment of damages; or (4) in unusual circumstances, the "purchased injunction" which is imposed upon condition that a plaintiff may make some offsetting payment to the defendant. Calabresi & Malamed, Property Rules, Liability Rules, and Inalienability: One View of the Cathedral, 85 Harv.L.Rev. 1089 (1972). Moreover, where a nuisance can be abated, and the harm is not permanent but would stop when the nuisance is abated, a plaintiff would not necessarily be entitled to permanent damages. Rather, he could receive temporary or conditionally continuing damages, until the abatement occurs. [   ]

* * *

We conclude that the entire judgment of the district court, entered upon the verdict of a jury which had been improperly instructed, must be vacated. The case must be remanded for a new trial to determine whether a nuisance exists under the full criteria set forth in § 826 of the Second Restatement.

* * *

The judgment of the district court is vacated. The case is remanded for further proceedings consistent with this opinion.

Notes and Questions

1. The Court of Appeals decision in *Carpenter* was reversed by the Idaho Supreme Court at 108 Idaho 602, 701 P.2d 222 (1985). The Idaho Supreme Court rejected the Second Restatement approach, holding to the earlier McNichols precedent. In dissent Judge Bistline observed, "We have

before us today a most remarkable event: two appellate courts, each obviously unaware of its true appellate function. The Court of Appeals, in reviewing the instant case, acted as a court of law, while the Idaho Supreme Court functioned as a court of error correction. In my mind, the roles have been reversed—I always understood that the Court of Appeals was a court of error correction, and it was our function to act as a court of law."

2. The nineteenth-century transformation of nuisance law in the American courts from absolute protection of property rights to a balancing of relative interests is described in Bone, Normative Theory and Legal Doctrine in American Nuisance Law: 1850–1920, 59 S.Cal.L.Rev. 1101 (1986). This article is a masterful piece of legal scholarship, describing the evolution of nuisance law in the context of developing legal theory at the time, and illustrating how the law developed along different lines in different jurisdictions at the same time.

3. Nuisance disputes, as the principal case notes, are normally resolved by striking a balance between the utility of the defendant's conduct and the gravity of the harm experienced by the plaintiff. Relevant factors are outlined in the Restatement (Second) of Torts (1977): "(a) the extent of the harm involved; (b) the character of the harm involved; (c) the social value that the law attaches to the type of use or enjoyment invaded; (d) the suitability of the particular use or enjoyment invaded to the character of the locality; and (e) the burden on the person harmed of avoiding the harm." Restatement (Second) of Torts, § 827 (1977). Relevant factors for assessing the utility of the defendant's conduct include: "(a) The social value which the law attaches to the primary purpose of the defendant's conduct; (b) the suitability of defendant's activity to the character of the locality; and (c) the practicability of preventing or avoiding the invasion." Restatement (Second) of Torts § 828(a) (1977).

If the court finds the nuisance to be a nuisance per se, the balancing process may be short-circuited in the plaintiff's favor. The balance will also tilt more readily against the defendant where the defendant's conduct is motivated solely by malice, as it is clearly without utility. See Dunbar v. O'Brien, 117 Neb. 245, 220 N.W. 278 (1928).

A variety of defenses may also cut short the balancing process. First, the hypersensitive plaintiff, abnormally susceptible to conduct that would not bother most persons, is unlikely to recover. See Beckman v. Marshall, 85 So.2d 552 (Fla.1956) (day care center complained of by elderly neighbors not nuisance). Where the plaintiff has permitted the defendant's conduct, or led the defendant to believe that the plaintiff would not object to it, and the defendant has detrimentally relied on this, estoppel or acquiescence may be argued against a nuisance claim. Laches may also be asserted where the plaintiff fails to pursue a claim diligently, and the delay prejudices the defendant. Finally, the statute of limitations may bar a nuisance claim where the plaintiff has suffered substantial injury for the statutory period without taking action.

A more controversial defense is the "coming to the nuisance" defense. Should a person be permitted to construct a residence in the midst of an industrial area and then demand that all surrounding industries shut down? English courts have rejected the "coming to the nuisance" defense. Bliss v. Hall, 4 Bing (NC) 183, 132 Eng.Rep. 758 (1838). American courts have divided on the question, but the prevailing view is that "coming to the nuisance" is not, in itself, a total bar to a nuisance action. Curry v. Farmers Livestock Market, 343 S.W.2d 134 (Ky.1961) (only equitable consideration); Kellogg v. Village of Viola, 67 Wis.2d 345, 227 N.W.2d 55 (1975) (consideration in weighing equities). Should it be? Should notions of "first in time, first in right", which play such an important role elsewhere in property law, hold sway here? Further, if the plaintiff in a "coming to the nuisance" action acquired the property adjoining the existing offensive use for a price that reflected its limited value for development, is it fair to give the plaintiff a windfall by enjoining neighboring uses that caused the diminution in property value? On the other hand, allowing an offensive use in effect to block all conflicting uses for surrounding property for all time raises the specter of an unparalleled extension of private eminent domain. See, Wittman, First Come, First Served: An Economic Analysis of "Coming to the Nuisance," 9 J. Legal Stud. 557 (1980).

Legislative authorization of offensive conduct may also be raised as a defense to a nuisance action. This defense is particularly likely to be raised when the government is the source of the nuisance. Osborn v. City of Akron, 171 Ohio St. 361, 171 N.E.2d 492 (1960) (municipal garbage dump). "Right to farm laws" such as that discussed in *Carpenter,* are an example of this exception as applied to private uses. See, Comment: The Ethics and Economics of Right-to-Farm Statutes, 9 Harv.J.L. & Pub.Pol'y 525 (1986). Offensive uses must be specifically authorized, however. It is not sufficient that they be permitted under a general zoning ordinance.

The Second Restatement mandates consideration of the social value of both the plaintiff's and defendant's uses of their property. Historically, as *Carpenter* notes, courts have been more sensitive to this consideration in evaluating the defendant's conduct than in assessing the plaintiff's loss, particularly where the plaintiff is seeking injunctive relief. Thus, in Boomer v. Atlantic Cement Co., 26 N.Y.2d 219, 309 N.Y.S.2d 312, 257 N.E.2d 870 (1970), in denying injunctive relief, the court noted in passing that 300 jobs were at stake. On the other hand, more recent cases have also recognized the public interest in the plaintiff's uses as well. For example, in Prah v. Maretti, 108 Wis.2d 223, 321 N.W.2d 182 (1982), the court recognized the public interest in expanding alternative energy sources as one reason for recognizing the applicability of nuisance law for protecting the plaintiff's solar collector.

4. As *Carpenter* recognizes, a key problem in nuisance law is determining the appropriate role of the balancing process. One approach is to balance harm and utility up front to determine whether there is a nuisance at all, the approach ultimately taken by the Idaho Supreme Court. A second approach is to hold any substantial harm to be a nuisance, and then to apply a balancing test to determine whether the nuisance should be enjoined. Under this approach, even if the balance favors the defendant, damages may be appropriate. The Restatement (Second) of Torts (1977) seems to advocate the latter position, recognizing in § 821F that a nuisance should be found whenever there is significant harm, and then in § 826(b)

recognizing that it might be appropriate to find a nuisance and award damages in circumstances where conduct is serious, even if the gravity of harm did not outweigh the utility of the defendant's conduct.

5. Nuisance is generally regarded as an intentional tort (Prosser on Torts, § 87), though the Restatement (Second) of Torts takes the position that negligent or reckless conduct, or injuries caused by abnormally dangerous conditions or activities can also result in nuisance liability. What does it mean to say that nuisance results from intentional conduct, as the Restatement does? Must the actor intend the harm, or merely intend the action that causes harm? Is it sufficient that the actor knows (or should know) that his conduct is likely to result in harm? See Restatement (Second) Torts, § 825 (1977); Morgan v. High Penn Oil Co., 238 N.C. 185, 77 S.E.2d 682 (1953) (intention includes actions that the actor knows is substantially certain to result in injury); Keeton, Trespass, Nuisance and Strict Liability, 59 Columb.L.Rev. 457 (1959). If liability for intentional nuisance is only imposed after the court has balanced the utility of the defendant's conduct with the gravity of the harm, how does the test of liability differ from negligence, in which liability is found only when the harm of an action outweighs the cost of avoiding the harm?

6. Much of the scholarship regarding nuisance law over the last three decades has elaborated on themes developed in two seminal articles, Coase, The Problem of Social Cost, 3 J.L. & Econ. 1 (1960), and Calabresi and Melamed, Property Rules, Liability Rules, and Inalienability: One View of the Cathedral, 85 Harv.L.Rev. 1089 (1972). Nobel prize winner Coase noted that it is useful to view nuisance disputes as arising because neighboring lands are used for inconsistent purposes rather than because of wrongdoing. "The question [of nuisance] is commonly thought of as one in which A inflicts harm on B and what has to be decided is: how should we restrain A? But this is wrong. We are dealing with a problem of a reciprocal nature. To avoid the harm to B would inflict harm on A. The real question that has to be decided is: should A be allowed to harm B or should B be allowed to harm A? The problem is to avoid the more serious harm." Id. at 2.

If both polluting and receiving uses were under common ownership, Coase noted, conflicts would not arise, because the owner would choose whatever mix of polluting and receiving uses was optimal, thus achieving an efficient use of the land as a whole. In the absence of transactions costs independent neighboring landowners could reach the same result. Bargaining with each other, the polluting landowner could pay the receiving landowner enough to purchase his acquiesence in the polluting use, if the polluting use were more productive. Alternatively, the receiving landowner could pay the polluter enough to end the pollution if the receiving use was more valuable. The efficient result would be reached regardless of whether legal rules initially favored polluters or receivers, though the final allocation of wealth would differ depending on the legal rule.

The insight of the Calabresi and Melamed article is that there are four possible resolutions to nuisance disputes. Three of these are contemplated as possible results in *Carpenter.* First, the defendant might be found liable, and an injunction can issue restraining its conduct. Second, the defendant might be found liable, and damages may be ordered to compensate the plaintiff. Third, the defendant might be found innocent, and an injunction may be refused. The fourth possibility, necessary for the sake of symmetry, is to find the defendant innocent, but allow the plaintiff to terminate (or limit) the defendant's offensive conduct by paying damages as determined by the court to the defendant. As an illustration of this fourth alternative, in Spur Industries, Inc. v. Del E. Webb. Development Co., 108 Ariz. 178, 494 P.2d 700 (1972), a developer who had built a large housing development next to a feed lot was permitted an injunction against the feed lot, but was required to compensate the feed lot for the cost of moving or shutting down.

The synergy of these two articles has produced a torrent of commentary of ever increasing elaboration, elegance, and abstraction from reality. Coase's theorem argues that, absent transaction costs, regardless of which of the four remedies is chosen to resolve a nuisance dispute, the parties can bargain to an efficient result. Absent transaction costs, therefore, entitlements could be awarded solely on the basis of considerations of fairness or equity, with no need to worry about efficiency. Such fairness rules might be based on considerations such as normal neighborly behavior, or, first in time, first in right.

Transaction costs are always a factor in nuisance disputes, however, and in some cases play a larger role than they do in others. Where many parties are involved, for example, the costs of bargaining for the reallocation of an entitlement awarded by the court to the less productive use might be very high. Conversely, where only two parties are involved, strategic bargaining by the parties might prevent an efficient bargained resolution of the dispute.[14] Efficiency considerations, therefore, should be a factor in awarding entitlements, at least in some cases. Early solutions proposed, therefore, awarding the right to pollute or to be free from pollution initially to the most productive use, thus obviating the need for costly bargaining to reach an efficient result.

Further examination of the problem, however, suggested that both the efficient and fair result could be achieved by proper use of the four remedial options identified by Calabresi and Melamed. Assume, for example, that the fair thing to do is to protect the receiver, who was there first, but that it would be inefficient to close down the polluter, whose use is more productive. Assume also that transaction costs of bargaining to a solution are high. The efficient and fair result could be reached, it was argued, by awarding the entitlement to the receiver, but protecting it with damages rather than an injunction. Thus, the fair result would be reached

---

14. Strategic bargaining results when parties fail to bargain to an efficient result because each bluffs or misreads the other. For example, if continuation of the defendant's feedlot at a given level of production produces $120,000 in profits to the defendant, but will damage the plaintiff's property to the extent of $80,000, and an injunction shutting down the feedlot is awarded to the plaintiff, the defendant could pay the plaintiff any amount between $80,000 and $120,000 and both parties come out ahead. If, however, the plaintiff judges the defendant's use to be worth more, and refuses to accept a sum less than $121,000, or the defendant misjudges the plaintiff's injury, and refuses to offer more than $79,000, a bargain may not be struck, the feedlot will close, and both parties and society will be worse off than they would have been had the parties bargained successfully.

(the receiver is protected) but the efficient result would also obtain (the polluter continues to operate). Alternatively, if distributional concerns favored the polluter, but the receiving use was more efficient, solution four, the compensated injunction, might be appropriate.

For a time, damage and compensated injunction remedies enjoyed favor among the commentators. See Ellickson, Alternatives to Zoning: Covenants, Nuisance Rules, and Fines as Land Use Controls, 40 U.Chi. L.Rev. 681 (1973); Rabin, Nuisance Law: Rethinking Fundamental Assumptions, 63 Va.L.Rev. 1299 (1977). These commentators criticized reliance on injunctions to remedy nuisance injuries. If an injunction failed to achieve an efficient solution, it was argued, strategic bargaining on the part of the parties was likely to stand in the way of negotiations leading to an efficient solution. It was also argued that the party holding an injunction might use it to "extort" money from the enjoined party, if the enjoined party happened to be the one who could use the resource most efficiently. Finally, in a situation involving many parties, it was argued, it would be difficult to bargain to a more efficient solution once an injunction was issued or denied. In each of these situations, it was asserted, damage or compensated injunction solutions, were more likely to achieve the efficient result. This position was largely adopted by the appellate court in *Carpenter* with respect to the situation it faced.

The most recent scholarship in the area, however, returns to the injunction as the remedy of choice, or at least argues a more limited role for the damage or compensated injunction remedy. See Polinsky, Resolving Nuisance Disputes: The Simple Economics of Injunctive and Damage Remedies, 32 Stan.L.Rev. 1075 (1980); Compensated Injunctions and the Evolution of Nuisance Law, 71 Iowa L.Rev. 775 (1986) (arguing for more limited use of compensated injunctions); Travalio, Pay Up or Shut Down: Some Cautionary Remarks on the Use of Conditional Entitlements in Private Nuisance Cases, 38 U.Fla.L.Rev. 209 (1986). Assessing damages is a costly and uncertain business. Damage remedies also award all of the "profit" to be made in a transaction to the party against whom damages are awarded, a result that is not obviously fair.[15] Damage awards may further fail to consider the interests of the public or of persons not party to the litigation, which interests should be considered in equitable balancing. Damage awards may not take adequate account of the uncertainty present in modern pollution problems. Damages often, in effect, become a form of private eminent domain: the defendant can violate the plaintiff's property interest as long as it pays a court-determined sum. This raises serious constitutional problems. Finally, injunctions need not be all or nothing remedies. An injunction can be fine-tuned to permit a certain level of pollution, but not more, thus achieving an efficient result as effectively as might a damage remedy. See, reviewing the extensive literature on this

---

15. In the example given in the previous note, for example, the prevailing plaintiff would be, under a damage solution, awarded $80,000, and thus be compensated for his damages. The defendant would therefore clear $40,000 ($120,000 − 80,000) from the use of a resource, the air, in which both he and the plaintiff had rights. Why should not the plaintiff share in this wealth? Had the defendant desired to purchase land which the plaintiff owned to pursue a profitable activity, he would have to pay a price which shared the potential profit with the plaintiff. Why should not the same be true if he seeks to use the plaintiff's air?

subject, Lewin, Boomer and the American Law of Nuisance: Past, Present and Future, 54 Albany L.Rev. 189 (1990).

After three decades of debate, it is not clear that this literature yet gives courts much practical guidance for resolving nuisance disputes. Use of the damage remedy is probably more common now than formerly. With the exception of the Spur case, however, compensated injunctions have not been embraced by the courts. Few courts, moreover, have expressly relied on economic reasoning in resolving nuisance disputes.

B. PUBLIC NUISANCE

ARMORY PARK NEIGHBORHOOD ASSOCIATION v. EPISCOPAL COMMUNITY SERVICES IN ARIZONA

Supreme Court of Arizona, 1985.
148 Ariz. 1, 712 P.2d 914.

FELDMAN, JUSTICE.

On December 11, 1982, defendant Episcopal Community Services in Arizona (ECS) opened the St. Martin's Center (Center) in Tucson. The Center's only purpose is to provide one free meal a day to indigent persons. Plaintiff Armory Park Neighborhood Association (APNA) is a non-profit corporation organized for the purpose of "improving, maintaining and insuring the quality of the neighborhood known as Armory Park Historical Residential District." The Center is located on Arizona Avenue, the western boundary of the Armory Park district. On January 10, 1984, APNA filed a complaint in Pima County Superior Court, seeking to enjoin ECS from operating its free food distribution program. The complaint alleged that the Center's activities constituted a public nuisance and that the Armory Park residents had sustained injuries from transient persons attracted to their neighborhood by the Center.

The superior court held a hearing on APNA's application for preliminary injunction on March 6 and 7, 1984. At the commencement of the hearing, the parties stipulated that

> * * * there is no issue concerning any State, County, or Municipal zoning ordinance, or health provision, before the Court. And, the Court may find that defendants are in compliance with the same.

The residents then testified about the changes the Center had brought to their neighborhood. Before the Center opened, the area had been primarily residential with a few small businesses. When the Center began operating in December 1982, many transients crossed the area daily on their way to and from the Center. Although the Center was only open from 5:00 to 6:00 p.m., patrons lined up well before this hour and often lingered in the neighborhood long after finishing their meal. The Center rented an adjacent fenced lot for a waiting area and organized neighborhood cleaning projects, but the trial judge apparently felt these efforts were inadequate to control the activity stemming from the Center. Transients frequently trespassed onto residents' yards, sometimes urinating, defecating, drinking and littering on the residents' property. A few broke into storage areas and unoccupied homes, and some asked residents for handouts. The number of arrests in the area increased dramatically. Many residents were frightened or annoyed by the transients and altered their lifestyles to avoid them.

Following the hearing, ECS filed a motion to dismiss the complaint based on three grounds: 1) that compliance with all applicable zoning and health laws constituted a complete defense to a claim of public nuisance; 2) that there had been no allegation or evidence of a violation of a criminal statute or ordinance, which it argues is a prerequisite to a finding of public nuisance; and 3) that APNA lacked standing to bring an action to abate a public nuisance because it had neither pled nor proved any special injury differing in kind and degree from that suffered by the public generally.

Based on the hearing testimony, the trial court granted the preliminary injunction and denied ECS' motion to dismiss. In its order, the court noted that ECS could be enjoined because its activities constituted both a public and a private nuisance. After its motion for reconsideration was denied, ECS filed a special action in the court of appeals, and shortly thereafter filed a notice of appeal from the order granting the injunction. The court of appeals consolidated the proceedings and stayed enforcement of the trial court's order pending a final decision.

A divided court of appeals reversed the trial court's order. In the view of the majority, a criminal violation was a prerequisite to a finding of public nuisance; because plaintiff had alleged no criminal violation, the injunction was improperly granted. The majority also concluded that the trial court abused its discretion by finding both a public and a private nuisance when the plaintiff had not alleged a private nuisance. Finally, the court held that compliance with zoning provisions was a complete defense. The court vacated the order for preliminary injunction and remanded the matter to the trial court with directions to grant ECS' motion to dismiss. * * * We granted review in this case because of the importance of the following questions:

1) When does a voluntary association have standing to bring an action for public nuisance on behalf of its members?

2) May a lawful business be enjoined for acts committed off its premises by clients who are not under its control or direction?

3) Is it necessary to plead and prove a zoning or criminal violation by the defendant, or may a lawful activity be enjoined because the manner in which it is conducted is unreasonable and therefore constitutes a public nuisance?

THE CONCEPT OF "NUISANCE"

Now considered a tort, a public nuisance action originated in criminal law. Early scholars defined public nuisance as "an act or omission 'which obstructs or causes inconvenience or damage to the public in the exercise of rights common to all her Majesty's subjects.' "

Prosser, W. and W.P. Keeton, Handbook on the Law of Torts, § 90, at 643 (5th ed. 1984), quoting Stephen, General View of the Criminal Law in England 105 (1890). The sole remedy was criminal prosecution. Prosser, supra, § 86, at 618.

Historically, the remedy for a private nuisance was an action "upon the case," as it was an injury consequential to the act done and found its roots in civil law. Pearce, E. and D. Meston, Handbook on the Law Relating to Nuisances 2 (1926). A private nuisance is strictly limited to an interference with a person's interest in the enjoyment of real property. The Restatement defines a private nuisance as "a nontrespassory invasion of another's interest in the private use and enjoyment of land." Restatement (Second) of Torts § 821D. A public nuisance, to the contrary, is not limited to an interference with the use and enjoyment of the plaintiff's land. It encompasses any unreasonable interference with a right common to the general public. Restatement, supra, § 821B. Accord, Prosser, supra, § 86, at 618.

We have previously distinguished public and private nuisances. In City of Phoenix v. Johnson, 51 Ariz. 115, 75 P.2d 30 (1938), we noted that a nuisance is public when it affects rights of "citizens as a part of the public, while a private nuisance is one which affects a single individual or a definite number of persons in the enjoyment of some private right which is not common to the public." Id. at 123, 75 P.2d 34. A public nuisance must also affect a considerable number of people. Id. * * * The legislature has adopted a similar requirement for its criminal code, defining a public nuisance as an interference "with the comfortable enjoyment of life or property by an entire community or neighborhood, or by a considerable number of persons * * *." A.R.S. § 13–2917.

The defendant contends that the trial court erred in finding both public and private nuisances when the plaintiff had not asserted a private nuisance claim. The defendant has read the trial court's minute entry too strictly. While we acknowledge that public and private nuisances implicate different interests, we recognize also that the same facts may support claims of both public and private nuisance. As Dean Prosser explained:

> When a public nuisance substantially interferes with the use or enjoyment of the plaintiff's rights in land, it never has been disputed that there is a particular kind of damage, for which the private action will lie. Not only is every plot of land traditionally unique in the eyes of the law, but in the ordinary case the class of landowners in the vicinity of the alleged nuisance will necessarily be a limited one, with an interest obviously different from that of the general public. The interference itself is of course a private nuisance; but is none the less particular damage from a public one, and the action can be maintained upon either basis, or upon both. (Citations omitted.)

Prosser, Private Action for Public Nuisance, 52 Va.L.Rev. 997, 1018 (1966).

Thus, a nuisance may be simultaneously public and private when a considerable number of people suffer an interference with their use and enjoyment of land. [   ] The torts are not mutually exclusive. Some of plaintiff's members in this case have suffered an injury to the use and enjoyment of their land. Any reference to both a public and a private nuisance by the trial court was, we believe, merely a recognition of this well-accepted rule and not error. However, both because plaintiff did not seek relief under the theory of private nuisance and because that theory might raise standing issues not addressed by the parties, we believe plaintiff's claim must stand or fall on the public nuisance theory alone.

STANDING TO BRING THE ACTION

1. Do the residents have standing?

Defendant argues that the Association has no standing to sue and that, therefore, the action should be dismissed. The trial court disagreed and defendant claims it erred in so doing. Two standing questions are before us. The first pertains to the right of a private person, as distinguished from a public official, to bring a suit to enjoin the maintenance of a public nuisance. The original rule at common law was that a citizen had no standing to sue for abatement or suppression of a public nuisance since

> such inconvenient or troublesome offenses [sic], as annoy the whole community in general, and not merely some particular persons; and therefore are indictable only, and not actionable; as it would be unreasonable to multiply suits, by giving every man a separate right of action, by what damnifies him in common only with the rest of his fellow subjects.

IV Blackstone Commentaries 167 (1966). It was later held that a private individual might have a tort action to recover personal damages arising from the invasion of the public right. Y.B. 27 Hen. VIII, Mich, pl. 10, cited in Restatement, supra, § 821C comment a. However, the individual bringing the action was required to show that his damage was different in kind or quality from that suffered by the public in common. Prosser, supra, § 90, at 646; Harper & James, the Law of Torts § 1.23, at 64–5 (1956).

The rationale behind this limitation was two-fold. First, it was meant to relieve defendants and the courts of the multiple actions that might follow if every member of the public were allowed to sue for a common wrong. Second, it was believed that a harm which affected all members of the public equally should be handled by public officials. Restatement, supra, § 821C comment a. See also Engle v. Clark, 53 Ariz. 472, 90 P.2d 994 (1939). Considerable disagreement remains over the type of injury which the plaintiff must suffer in order to have standing to bring an action to enjoin a public nuisance. However, we have intimated in the past that an injury to plaintiff's interest in land is sufficient to distinguish plaintiff's injuries from those experienced by the general public and to give the plaintiff-landowner standing to bring the action. * * *

We hold, therefore, that because the acts allegedly committed by the patrons of the neighborhood center affected the residents' use and enjoyment of their real property, a damage special in nature and different in kind from that experienced by the residents of the city in general, the residents of the neighborhood could bring an action to recover damages for or enjoin the maintenance of a public nuisance.

2. May the Association bring the action on behalf of its members?

* * *

[The court found that under Arizona law the Association had standing to bring an action to redress injuries done to its members]

DEFENDANT'S DERIVATIVE RESPONSIBILITY

Defendant claims that its business should not be held responsible for acts committed by its patrons off the premises of the Center. It argues that since it has no control over the patrons when they are not on the Center's premises, it cannot be enjoined because of their acts. We do not believe this position is supported either by precedent or theory.

* * *

Under general tort law, liability for nuisance may be imposed upon one who sets in motion the forces which eventually cause the tortious act; liability will arise for a public nuisance when "one person's acts set in motion a force or chain of events resulting in the invasion." Restatement, supra, § 824 comment b. We hold, therefore, that defendant's activity may be enjoined upon the showing of a causal connection between that activity and harm to another.

The testimony at the hearing establishes that it was the Center's act of offering free meals which "set in motion" the forces resulting in the injuries to the Armory Park residents. * * * We find the testimony sufficient to support the trial judge's finding of a causal link between the acts of ECS and the injuries suffered by the Armory Park residents. * * *

REASONABLENESS OF THE INTERFERENCES

Since the rules of a civilized society require us to tolerate our neighbors, the law requires our neighbors to keep their activities within the limits of what is tolerable by a reasonable person. However, what is reasonably tolerable must be tolerated; not all interferences with public rights are public nuisances. As Dean Prosser explains, "[t]he law does not concern itself with trifles, or seek to remedy all of the petty annoyances and disturbances of everyday life in a civilized community even from conduct committed with knowledge that annoyance and inconvenience will result." Prosser, supra, § 88, at 626. Thus, to constitute a nuisance, the complained-of interference must be substantial, intentional and unreasonable under the circumstances. Restatement, supra, § 826 comment c and 821F. Our courts have generally used a balancing test in deciding the reasonableness of an interference. [ ] The trial court should look at the utility and reasonableness of the conduct and balance these factors against the extent of harm inflicted and the nature of the affected neighborhood. We noted in the early case of MacDonald v. Perry:

> What might amount to a serious nuisance in one locality by reason of the density of the population, or character of the neighborhood affected, may in another place and under different surroundings be deemed proper and unobjectionable. What amount of annoyance or inconvenience caused by others in the lawful use of their property will constitute a nuisance depends upon varying circumstances and cannot be precisely defined.

32 Ariz. 39, 50, 255 P. 494 (1927). [ ]

The trial judge did not ignore the balancing test and was well aware of the social utility of defendant's operation. His words are illuminating:

> It is distressing to this Court that an activity such as defendants [sic] should be restrained. Providing for the poor and the homeless is certainly a worthwhile, praisworthy [sic] activity. It is particularly distressing to this Court because it [defendant] has no control over those who are attracted to the kitchen while they are either coming or leaving the premises. However, the right to the comfortable enjoyment of one's property is something that another's activities should not affect, the harm being suffered by the Armory Park Neighborhood and the residents therein is irreparable and substantial, for which they have no adequate legal remedy.

Minute Entry, 6/8/84, at 8. We believe that a determination made by weighing and balancing conflicting interests or principles is truly one which lies within the discretion of the trial judge. [ ] We defer to that discretion here. The evidence of the multiple trespasses upon and defacement of the residents' property supports the trial court's conclusion that the interference caused by defendant's operation was unreasonable despite its charitable cause.

The common law has long recognized that the usefulness of a particular activity may outweigh the inconveniences, discomforts and changes it causes some persons to suffer. We, too, acknowledge the social value of the Center. Its charitable purpose, that of feeding the hungry, is entitled to greater deference than pursuits of lesser intrinsic value. It appears from the record that ECS purposes in operating the Center were entirely admirable. However, even admirable ventures may cause unreasonable interferences. [ ] We do not believe that the law allows the costs of a charitable enterprise to be visited in their entirety upon the residents of a single neighborhood. The problems of dealing with the unemployed, the homeless and the mentally ill are also matters of community or governmental responsibility.

ZONING

ECS argues that its compliance with City of Tucson zoning regulations is a conclusive determination of reasonableness. We agree that compliance with zoning provisions has some bearing in nuisance cases. We would hesitate to find a public nuisance, if, for example, the legislature enacted comprehensive and specific laws concerning the manner in which a particular activity was to be carried out. Accord Restatement, supra, § 821B comment f. We decline, however, to find that ECS' compliance with the applicable zoning provisions precludes a court from enjoining its activities. The equitable power of the judiciary exists independent of statute. Although zoning and criminal provisions are binding with respect to the type of activity, they do not limit the power of a court acting in equity to enjoin an unreasonable, albeit permitted, activity as a public nuisance. [   ]

The determination of the type of business to be permitted in a particular neighborhood, therefore, may be left to administrative agencies or legislative bodies. However, the judgment concerning the manner in which that business is carried out is within the province of the judiciary. Restatement, supra, § 821B comment f. See also J. Joyce, Treatise on the Law Governing Nuisances § 73, at 115 (1906). Zoning provisions may permit one's neighbor to operate a business. This does not give him license to use one's yard, nor permit his customers to do so.

* * *

CRIMINAL VIOLATION

Occasionally we have indicated that conduct which violates a specific criminal statute is an element of public nuisance for civil tort claims. [   ] These cases did not face the issue whether a tort claim for public nuisance exists independent of statute. * * *

In MacDonald v. Perry, supra, we indicated that the inquiry in a nuisance claim is not whether the activity allegedly constituting the nuisance is lawful but whether it is reasonable under the circumstances. The Restatement states that a criminal violation is only one factor among others to be used in determining reasonableness. That section reads:

(1) A public nuisance is an unreasonable interference with a right common to the general public.

(2) Circumstances that may sustain a holding that an interference with a public right is unreasonable include the following:

(a) Whether the conduct involves a significant interference with the public health, the public safety, the public peace, the public comfort or the public convenience, *or*

(b) whether the conduct is proscribed by a statute, ordinance or administrative regulation, *or*

(c) whether the conduct is of a continuing nature or has produced a permanent or long-lasting effect, and, as the actor knows or has reason to know, has a significant effect upon the public right. (Emphasis supplied.)

Restatement, supra, § 821B. Comment d to that section explains:

It has been stated with some frequency that a public nuisance is always a criminal offense. This statement is susceptible of two interpretations. The first is that in order to be treated as a public nuisance, conduct must have been already proscribed by the state as criminal. This is too restrictive * * *. [T]here is clear recognition that a defendant need not be subject to criminal responsibility.

Restatement, supra, § 821B comment d, at 89.

Our earlier decisions indicate that a business which is lawful may nevertheless be a public nuisance. * * *

We hold, therefore, that conduct which unreasonably and significantly interferes with the public health, safety, peace, comfort or convenience is a public nuisance within the concept of tort law, even if that conduct is not specifically prohibited by the criminal law.

* * *

Conclusion

The trial court's order granting the preliminary injunction is affirmed. By affirming the trial court's preliminary orders, we do not require that he close the center permanently. It is of course, within the equitable discretion of the trial court to fashion a less severe remedy, if possible. The opinion of the court of appeals is vacated. The case is remanded for further proceedings.

Notes and Questions

1. Public nuisance grows out of a class of crimes known as purprestures, involving encroachments on the king's right. Though the classic public nuisance was obstruction of a public road, the concept has encompassed publicly offensive conduct as various as keeping of diseased animals, Fevold v. Board of Supervisors of Webster County, 202 Iowa 1019, 210 N.W. 139 (1926); practice of medicine without a license, State ex rel. Collet v. Scopel, 316 S.W.2d 515 (Mo.1958); holding a rock concert, Planning & Zoning Commission v. Zemel Brothers, Inc., 29 Conn.Sup. 45, 270 A.2d 562 (1970); or nude sunbathing, State v. Rocker, 52 Hawaii 336, 475 P.2d 684 (1970). Creating a public nuisance is often proscribed by state statute or local ordinance. Because the concept is such an amorphous one, however, there is considerable potential for its abuse. Particular problems arise when public nuisance litigation is used to control conduct agreeably protected by the First Amendment, such as adult entertainment. Compare Vance v. Universal Amusement Co., 445 U.S. 308, 100 S.Ct. 1156, 63 L.Ed.2d 413 (1980) (enjoining future showings of allegedly obscene films under public nuisance statute was an unconstitutional prior restraint) with Arcara v. Cloud Books, Inc., 478 U.S. 697, 106 S.Ct. 3172, 92 L.Ed.2d 568

(1986) (use of nuisance statute to close adult book store used as place of prostitution does not violate First Amendment). See Gorman, The Demise of Civil Nuisance Actions in Obscenity Control, 14 Loy.U.Chi.L.J. 31 (1982); Note, Enjoining Obscenity as Public Nuisance and the Prior Restraint Doctrine, 84 Colum.L.Rev. 1616 (1984); Note, Pornography, Padlocks and Prior Restraints: The Constitutional Limits of the Nuisance Power, 58 N.Y.U.L.Rev. 1478 (1983).

2. As *Armory Park* illustrates, conduct that can be classified as a public nuisance may also harm neighbors in the use and enjoyment of their land. The injured neighbor may then either sue for private nuisance or attempt to establish the standing to sue for public nuisance. Armory Park presents a typical discussion of how a plaintiff may attempt to meet the special injury requirement for establishing a private right to sue for public nuisance. Unique or special injury may also be shown by establishing harm to health, physical harm to land or chattels, or pecuniary loss. Some state statutes, moreover, permit private suits to enjoin a public nuisance without showing special injury, See Wyo.Stat.Ann. § 6–6–202. Should private individuals be permitted to enjoin any conduct offensive to the public? Should they be permitted to sue for damages? Or should private litigation be limited to conduct that independently causes a private nuisance?

3. The *Armory Park* case illustrates the "not in my backyard" problem, a hardy perennial of property law. Society may need shelters for the homeless, group homes for ex-offenders, nuclear power plants, or hazardous waste dumps, but who wants to live next door to one? In reality, such uses often end up being imposed on neighborhoods or localities that are most politically vulnerable. Is this fair? How might the problem of siting such uses be addressed? Might solutions that depend on mediation or education be more effective than approaches based on litigation or on local politics? Might it be more appropriate to deal with these problems on a state, regional, or national level, because of the strength of opposition that appears when they are addressed locally? Might opposition to some of these uses suggest that they are never appropriate for any locality, and therefore should not be permitted anywhere? Do lawyers have any responsibility to society to seek equitable solutions to such problems, or is it enough that lawyers zealously represent their own clients opposing or supporting such uses?

C. NUISANCE LAW AND THE ENVIRONMENT

Nuisance law has obvious applications for protecting the environment. Persons whose property is damaged by air or water pollution from point sources, for example, can bring nuisance actions to enjoin the continuation of pollution. Alternatively, they can sue for damages against the polluter, thus forcing the internalization of the otherwise externalized costs of pollution. Public nuisance actions brought by municipal governments, for example, may be even more promising as an approach to dealing with widespread pollution. Increasingly, however, pollution has been addressed by federal and state statutory and regulatory law enforced by public administrative agencies.

This development results in obvious problems when the mandates of federal or state statutes and of court judgments enforcing nuisance law come in conflict. If the Environmental Protection Agency, for example, authorizes a certain level of discharge of a pollutant, or imposes a certain timetable for correcting a pollution problem, can a federal or state court impose stricter standards under a nuisance action? This question was addressed by a series of cases involving the attempts of the State of Illinois to stop the City of Milwaukee, Wisconsin, from discharging raw sewerage into Lake Michigan. In 1972, Illinois sued Milwaukee in the United States Supreme Court, seeking to enjoin this discharge. The Supreme Court's opinion, Illinois v. City of Milwaukee, 406 U.S. 91, 92 S.Ct. 1385, 31 L.Ed.2d 712 (1972), remanded the case to the district court for trial, but recognized a federal common law of nuisance giving the district court jurisdiction over the problem. By the time the case was resolved in the district court on remand, however, Congress had adopted the Federal Water Pollution Control Act Amendments of 1972, 33 U.S.C. § 1251 et seq., comprehensively amending the federal water pollution laws. The case reached the Supreme Court again in 1981 with the City of Milwaukee on the one hand subject to a state court judgment based on federal permit standards imposing on it one level of effluent discharge and a timetable for correction, and, on the other hand, a federal court nuisance judgment imposing stricter effluent limitations and a shorter time for correction. The Supreme Court held this time, in City of Milwaukee v. Illinois, 451 U.S. 304, 101 S.Ct. 1784, 68 L.Ed.2d 114 (1981), that the federal statute preempted the federal common law of nuisance for cases of interstate water pollution. In Middlesex County Sewerage Authority v. National Sea Clammers Association, 453 U.S. 1, 101 S.Ct. 2615, 69 L.Ed.2d 435 (1981), the Court held, two months later, that the federal water pollution statute had "entirely" preempted federal nuisance law with respect to water pollution, a decision followed by some lower courts as to federal air pollution laws. See New England Legal Foundation v. Costle, 666 F.2d 30 (2d Cir.1981); United States v. Kin–Buc, Inc., 532 F.Supp. 699 (D.N.J.1982); Connecticut v. Long Island Lighting Co., 535 F.Supp. 546 (E.D.N.Y.1982).

What institutional considerations might make legislative or regulatory strategies superior to nuisance litigation for addressing pollution problems? Why might a statewide, regional, or national program for regulating point sources of pollution be superior to a case-by-case approach under private nuisance law? Are there any respects in which nuisance litigation is a superior strategy to regulation for addressing pollution? Should courts in enforcing federal environmental protection law employ the discretion they traditionally exercise in nuisance litigation, or should they demand rigid compliance with the law? See, Farber, Equitable Discretion, Legal Duties, and Environmental Injunctions, 45 U.Pitt.L.Rev. 513 (1984). Why should federal water or air pollution control legislation be held to preempt nuisance litigation, when local zoning ordinances apparently do not? Might there be alternatives to nuisance litigation and regulatory strategies, superior to both?

IV. SURFACE WATER AND SUPPORT

WESTLAND SKATING CENTER, INC.
v. GUS MACHADO BUICK, INC.

Supreme Court of Florida, 1989.
542 So.2d 959.

GRIMES, JUSTICE.

* * *

This case involves a dispute among occupiers of adjacent parcels of land that used to be part of the Everglades and later became pasture-land, but which now comprise commercially developed property in Dade County. Petitioner, Westland Skating Center, Inc., operated a skating rink on property leased from petitioner, Hialeah Skating Center, Ltd. An auto dealership, now operated by respondent, Gus Machado Buick, Inc., occupied abutting property. There has been some alteration of all the land involved, but the parties agree that the natural drainage flow was generally and gradually toward the southwest, that is, from the skating rink property onto and toward the rear of the auto dealership property. When the auto dealership was built in 1970, a miniature-golf course occupied the skating rink property, and apparently neither landowner had unusual problems in dealing with rainwater.

Trouble began in April 1980, however, after the construction of the skating rink. The building's roof was 200 by 120 feet. A 200–by–60 foot section sloped toward the auto dealership; it ended about 10 feet from the property line. Water drained off the roof through five downspouts. During a rainstorm the auto dealership, then Seipp Buick, experienced flooding extensive enough to damage several cars. This sort of flooding had occurred only once before, and then during much heavier rain. Seipp blamed the new skating rink, with its sloping roof and downspouts, for increasing the flow of water onto his property.

Talks between Seipp and Revitz to alleviate the problem were unavailing, and in 1980 Seipp decided to take action. He built a wall, 8 feet high and 2 feet deep between the two tracts along the 900–foot length of his property. This project took several months to complete; the skating center did not object to the presence of the wall during that time.

August of 1981 brought a heavy rain and profoundly different results than the 1980 downpour. This time, water ran off the roof and down toward Seipp's wall, which acted as a dam. The water then backed up under the skating rink's floor, inflicting heavy damage. The floor was replaced, but another heavy rain a month or so later resulted in more flooding, which the skating rink's employees alleviated by sledgehammering holes in Seipp's wall. More repairs to the rink ensued, but eventually it closed.

Westland and Hialeah sued Seipp for damages and sought a mandatory injunction to remove the wall. Seipp counterclaimed for damages and to enjoin Westland from damaging the wall. During the litigation, Machado bought the Seipp land and the dealership and was substituted as a party.[16]

Before trial, Westland and Hialeah obtained a partial summary judgment to the effect that as long as the skating rink was constructed in accordance with the South Florida Building Code, Machado's lower-elevation lot remained the servient tenement for all surface water flowing from the skating center. The case proceeded to trial where the jury, after receiving an instruction that tracked the language of the partial summary judgment, found in favor of Westland and Hialeah in excess of one million dollars in damages.

The Third District Court of Appeal reversed the judgment against Machado in a six-to-three split decision. The court held that the trial judge had applied an incorrect rule of law in granting the summary judgment and that the jury instruction based on the summary judgment also was error.

Originally, disputes involving the interference of surface waters were resolved by one of two doctrines: the common enemy rule or the civil law rule. See generally F. Maloney, S. Plager, R. Ausness, B. Canter, Florida Water Law 589 (1980), [hereinafter Maloney & Plager]; Kunyon & McClure, Interference With Surface Water, 24 Minn.L.Rev. 891 (1940); Annotation, Modern Status of Rules Governing Interference With Drainage of Surface Waters, 93 A.L.R.3d 1216 (1979). The common enemy rule held that landowners had an unlimited privilege to deal with the surface water on their land as they pleased without regard to the harm which may be caused to others. The civil law rule recognized that higher elevation tracts had an easement or servitude over lower tracts for all surface water that naturally flowed downhill. However, anyone who increased or interfered with the natural flow of surface waters so as to cause invasion of another's interests was subject to liability to the other.

Neither of these doctrines, in its pure form, was perfect, especially as the population increased. While the common enemy rule permitted the free improvement of property, it also carried with it the potential of self-help engineering contests in which the winner was the person who most effectively turned the excess water upon his neighbor's land. On the other hand, the civil law rule acted as an impediment to the improvement of land since almost any development by an upper landowner was likely to increase the flow of surface water upon the land below and most efforts by the lower owner to dam the natural flow had

16. The counterclaim was dismissed in return for Westland and Hialeah agreeing not to seek punitive damages. The record is silent as to the fate of the injunction, but apparently improvements to both lots eliminated the flooding and mooted the issue.

the effect of throwing the water back onto the land of the upper owner. As a consequence, some jurisdictions adopted a third rule, known as the reasonable use rule. Under this rule, a possessor of land is not unqualifiedly entitled to deal with surface waters as he pleases nor is he absolutely prohibited from increasing or interfering with the natural flow of surface waters to the detriment of others. Each possessor is legally privileged to make reasonable use of his land even though the flow of surface waters is altered thereby and causes some harm to others. He incurs liability only when his harmful interference with the flow of surface waters is unreasonable.

Because of the inequities which would result from a strict application of either the common enemy or the civil law rule, most of the states which had adopted either of these rules began to apply modifications in given cases. Often, these hybrid rules produced the same result as would have occurred through the application of the reasonable use rule. The reasonable use rule has been adopted by Restatement (Second) of Torts § 833 (1979), which recommends that claims of interference with the flow of surface waters should be decided under principles of nuisance. See Pendergrast v. Aiken, 293 N.C. 201, 236 S.E.2d 787 (1977) (if the interference is intentional, the conduct of the offending party is measured in terms of reasonableness; if unintentional, the test is negligence).

The Florida position with respect to the interference with surface waters is not entirely clear. After explaining the common enemy and the civil law rules in Brumley v. Dorner, 78 Fla. 495, 83 So. 912 (1919), this Court noted that both of these rules had been modified considerably by the courts to the extent that each case must stand upon its own facts. The Court then stated:

The almost universal rule, as gathered from the decisions, is that no person has the right to gather surface waters that would naturally flow in one direction by drainage, ditches, dams, or otherwise, and divert them from their natural course and cast them upon the lands of the lower owner to his injury.

Id. at 501, 83 So. at 914. * * *

* * *

Upon analysis, we have elected to adopt the reasonable use rule in cases involving the interference with surface waters. In so doing, we join approximately twenty-one other states, Case Comment, Waters and Water Courses—Torts—Owners of Property Damaged by Unlawful Ditching or Unreasonable Discharge of Waters May Obtain Relief by Statute or by the Tort Concept of Reasonable Use, 60 N.D.L.Rev. 741, 745 (1984), many of which have taken this position in recent years. E.g., Page Motor Co. v. Baker, 182 Conn. 484, 438 A.2d 739 (1980); Cootey v. Sun Inv., Inc., 690 P.2d 1324 (Haw.App.), cert. granted, 67 Haw. 685, 744 P.2d 781 (1984), rev'd in part, 718 P.2d 1086 (Haw.1986); Hall v. Wood, 443 So.2d 834 (Miss.1983); McGlashan v. Spade Rockledge Terrace Condo. Dev. Corp., 62 Ohio St.2d 55, 402 N.E.2d 1196 (1980); Butler v. Bruno, 115 R.I. 264, 341 A.2d 735 (1975).

The rule we announce appears much like the modified civil law rule; however, we believe it desirable to state our position through the adoption of the separate rule of reasonable use. As noted by Maloney and Plager, supra, at 596:

> Although the courts have treated the doctrine of reasonable use as a separate rule on equal footing with the civil law and common enemy rules, it is in reality merely the general tort principle which would decide such cases in the absence of the application of either of the two "property" rules. The relationship between adjoining landowners, in the absence of specific property rights, has always been governed by the maxim "Sic utere two [sic] ut alienum non laedas" ("Use your property in such a manner as not to injure that of another"). Much confusion and strained reasoning could be avoided if the courts would limit the application of the traditional rules to the narrowest possible situation or discard them altogether.

The principle that an upper landowner enjoys an easement across the lower tract for all naturally occurring surface water continues to apply to land in its natural state. However, when any party improves his land, thereby causing surface waters to damage his neighbor's property, the reasonable use rule shall be applied in order to settle the controversy. The rule applies not only in cases involving the conduct of the upper owner but also to improvements by the lower owner, such as the construction of dams designed to protect against the natural flow of surface waters across the lower land. See Mulder v. Tague, 85 S.D. 544, 186 N.W.2d 884 (1971). Regardless of whether a counterclaim has been filed when both parties have made improvements, the reasonableness of the conduct of each will be in issue and may be compared in order to arrive at a fair determination.

We recognize that the application of the reasonable use rule may make the outcome of certain controversies less predictable. Yet, if the rigidity of the traditional doctrines made cases predictable, it also led to such arbitrary results that the courts began to modify those rules. Predictability should not be achieved at the expense of justice. We believe that the rule of reasonable use employs the proper balance and will best enable surface water controversies to be fairly decided. As stated in McGlashan v. Spade Rockledge Terrace Condominium Development Corp.:

> The basic issue in these controversies is normally whether liability for the damage resulting from an interference with surface water flow should be borne by the person causing it. In this regard, an analysis centering on the reasonableness of a defendant's conduct, in view of all the circumstances, is more likely to produce an equitable result than one based on arbitrary property concepts. It is true that the law should not inhibit reasonable land development, but neither should it allow a landowner to expel surface water without regard to the consequences. As eloquently stated by Justice Brennan in Armstrong

v. Francis Corp. (1956), 20 N.J. 320, 330, 120 A.2d 4, 10, "no reason suggests itself why, in justice, the economic costs incident to the expulsion of surface waters in the transformation of the rural or semi-rural areas of our State into urban or suburban communities should be borne in every case by adjoining landowners rather than by those who engage in such projects for profit. Social progress and the common well-being are in actuality better served by a just and right balancing of the competing interests according to the general principles of fairness and common sense which attend the application of the rule of reason."

62 Ohio St.2d at 59, 402 N.E.2d at 1199–1200.

While it is evident that we do not accept the application of the strict civil law rule by the district court of appeal, we do not disagree with its analysis of the disputed jury instruction. * * *

* * *

This instruction had the practical effect of requiring the jury to determine the reasonableness of Westland's conduct based upon whether or not it complied with the South Florida Building Code. As noted by the court below, while one's compliance with a statute or an ordinance may amount to evidence of reasonableness, such compliance is not tantamount to reasonableness as a matter of law. Thus, evidence of Westland's compliance with the code could be properly considered as evidence of the reasonableness of its conduct, but not to the exclusion of other relevant evidence on that issue. Moreover, this case involved an evaluation and comparison of the reasonableness of the conduct of both parties. Therefore, the entry of the partial summary judgment and the resultant giving of the disputed jury instruction constituted reversible error.

Accordingly, while we have expressed differing views with respect to the law applicable to the interference with surface waters, we approve the decision of the district court of appeal reversing the judgment and directing a new trial.

It is so ordered.

Notes and Questions

1. Does the law of nuisance adequately address problems caused by diversion of surface water, or is the development of separate doctrine necessary?

2. Stormwater runoff from intensely developed urban or suburban land (and from intensely farmed agricultural land) is a major source of water silting and pollution. The Washington, D.C. metropolitan area, for example, constituting 2% of the Potomac River Basin, contributes 25% of the Potomac's sediment load. Runoff from a typical American city during the first hour of a storm may carry many more pollutants than the cities untreated sewerage would carry. Surface water also causes far more significant erosion of soil in developing and developed areas than in areas covered by natural vegetation.

Does the common law of surface waters adequately address these problems? The law discussed in the principal case is supplemented by common-law doctrines regarding the quality of surface waters. In this area, the traditional application of the natural flow doctrine—a landowner cannot alter and diminish the natural quality of water flowing through her land—has increasingly given way to a reasonable-use doctrine, much like general nuisance law. Can such doctrines deal with the problem of surface water pollution?

Increasingly, governments at all levels have addressed the problem of surface water pollution through regulatory solutions. The 1987 Clean Water Act requires states to put in place management programs identifying "best management practices and measures" to control nonpoint pollution sources, and requires permits to regulate municipal and industrial stormwater discharges. 33 U.S.C. §§ 1329, 1342(p). A model stormwater runoff control ordinance similarly relies on approved water management plan, see Maloney, Hamann, & Canter, Stormwater Runoff Control: A Model Ordinance for Meeting Local Water Quality Management Needs, 20 Nat. Resources J. 713 (1980). For an example of stormwater management planning for a major development adjoining Austin, Texas, see Marsh & Hill–Rowley, Water Quality, Stormwater Management, and Development Planning on the Urban Fringe, 35 Wash.Univ.J.Urb. & Contemp.L. 3 (1989).

Will regulatory solutions help resolve disputes among neighbors, such as that involved in the principal case?

3. The principal case addresses the rights of persons over whose property water passes to get rid of that water. An even more important issue for landowners, particularly for those who own land in the drier parts of the western United States, is the rights of landowners to withdraw water from streams, rivers, or lakes that pass through or adjoin the landowner's land for domestic, industrial, or agricultural uses.

Different states approach this problem through three different doctrines, two of which are rough cognates of doctrines discussed in the principal case. First, the traditional common-law doctrine of natural flow allows only uses that do not reduce the natural flow of the water course. The owner could only consume water for domestic uses (personal human use and watering domestic animals) and for reasonable commercial uses that did not materially diminish the flow. This doctrine has in many states yielded to a "reasonable-use" doctrine that attempts to weigh economic and social considerations in accomodating uses of flowing water among riparian owners.

Finally, the prior-appropriation doctrine, applied exclusively, or in combination with reasonable-use doctrines, in the western United States, allows the first person to use water for beneficial purposes to establish property rights in the water. It is, like the common-enemy theory of surface water, a doctrine that favors individualism and development over communitarianism and balanced use, but unlike the common-enemy doctrine, establishes property rights in the first claimant that cannot be overcome by later developers. The prior-appropriation doctrine is now generally administered through administrative permit programs that allow the possibility of shifting water rights to later claimants with greater needs for the water, albeit often with compensation. What other doctrines that we have studied earlier does the prior-appropriation doctrine resemble? What incentives does it create? Why might it have been adopted in arid regions?

See generally, on water law, A.D. Tarlock, Law of Water Rights and Resources (1988).

4. Also related to nuisance law is the law of lateral support. At common law, a landowner had a right to have land left in its natural condition supported by the land of her neighbors. If a neighbor's excavation removed support from neighboring land in its natural state causing such land to subside, the excavating neighbor was strictly liable for damages caused thereby. Where supported land was altered or burdened by structures, however, a neighbor who gave notice and then proceeded to excavate without negligence, was not liable for damages to the neighboring land. Support rights of artificial structures can be obtained by contract or by implication. Should they also be obtained by prescription? American courts have generally said no. What supports this position? While American courts have neither permitted prescription nor adopted a general reasonableness standard, they have meliorated the harsh effects of the common law on burdened land by permitting consequential damages for damaged structures where the burdened land would have subsided even if left in its natural state, and by interpreting the concept of negligence rather broadly. The problem is also often addressed by statute or ordinance. Should it be wholly subsumed within the law of nuisance? Are there particular characteristics of the problem of excavation that make separate treatment necessary? See generally on support, 5 R. Powell & P. Rohan, Powell on Real Property ¶¶ 698–702 (1991).

Chapter Seven

PUBLIC REGULATION OF LAND USE

I. THE "TAKINGS" QUESTION

The Fifth Amendment to the Constitution of the United States, applicable to the States by operation of the Fourteenth Amendment, provides that **"private property [shall not] be taken for public use, without just compensation."** This short declaration has been the subject of thousands and thousands of pages of analysis in court opinions and in scholarly articles. Despite this attention, it can fairly be said that the meaning of this "Takings Clause" in application to particular situations is not entirely clear.

This is not surprising if one realizes that resolution of the takings question requires resolution of the irreducible tensions in private property ownership, especially ownership understood in its more complete sense of both a relationship of a person to a thing (in these cases most often land) *and* a relationship among persons with respect to a thing. The employment of government coercion in all of these cases only intensifies the issue. The cases clearly evidence changing perspectives on the relative balance of government power and private property rights through several generations.

The genesis of all conflicts involving a takings issue is a government action that, at least according to the claimant, interferes with constitutionally protected property rights. A broad range of federal, state or local government actions raises takings claims. In some, the government exercises its power of eminent domain by directly acquiring, through a judicial process, privately held land; for example, the government agency acquires privately owned land for a highway, for a park, for streets, or for a shopping mall or some other economic development. Eminent domain differs from other property transfers in that the owner's consent to the transfer is not required. If the owner rejects the government's offer, a court will settle the matter and may order the transfer and set the price. In other cases raising takings issues, the government simply restricts the ability of the property owner to use his or her property. Common examples of such regulation include historic preservation laws, environmental protection statutes and health and safety regulations.

In applying the constitutional standards of the Fifth Amendment to any of these situations, three separate questions must be answered. First, does the government action further a "public use"? Second, has property been "taken"? And third, has the property owner been justly compensated for his or her loss?

In reviewing the following cases, you will be making a return visit to some of the basic concepts presented early in this course. You will see, for example, some notion of the "column of dirt/column of air" description of property ownership and reliance on the bundle of rights/bundle of sticks description of property ownership. Should these metaphors have constitutional significance?

A. PUBLIC PURPOSE

HAWAII HOUSING AUTHORITY et al. v. MIDKIFF et al.

Supreme Court of the United States, 1984.
467 U.S. 229, 104 S.Ct. 2321, 81 L.Ed.2d 186.

JUSTICE O'CONNOR delivered the opinion of the Court.

* * * These cases present the question whether the Public Use Clause of [the Fifth] Amendment, made applicable to the States through the Fourteenth Amendment, prohibits the State of Hawaii from taking, with just compensation, title in real property from lessors and transferring it to lessees in order to reduce the concentration of ownership of fees simple in the State. We conclude that it does not.

I

A

The Hawaiian Islands were originally settled by Polynesian immigrants from the western Pacific. These settlers developed an economy around a feudal land tenure system in which one island high chief, the ali'i nui, controlled the land and assigned it for development to certain subchiefs. The subchiefs would then reassign the land to other lower ranking chiefs, who would administer the land and govern the farmers and other tenants working it. All land was held at the will of the ali'i nui and eventually had to be returned to his trust. There was no private ownership of land. [ ]

Beginning in the early 1800's, Hawaiian leaders and American settlers repeatedly attempted to divide the lands of the kingdom among the crown, the chiefs, and the common people. These efforts proved largely unsuccessful, however, and the land remained in the hands of a few. In the mid–1960's, after extensive hearings, the Hawaii Legislature discovered that, while the State and Federal Governments owned almost 49% of the State's land, another 47% was in the hands of only 72 private landowners.

* * * The legislature further found that 18 landholders, with tracts of 21,000 acres or more, owned more than 40% of this land and that on Oahu, the most urbanized of the islands, 22 landowners owned 72.5% of the fee simple titles. [ ] The legislature concluded that concentrated land ownership was responsible for skewing the State's residential fee simple market, inflating land prices, and injuring the public tranquility and welfare.

To redress these problems, the legislature decided to compel the large landowners to break up their estates. The legislature considered requiring large landowners to sell lands which they were leasing to homeowners. However, the landowners strongly resisted this scheme, pointing out the significant federal tax liabilities they would incur. Indeed, the landowners claimed that the federal tax laws were the primary reason they previously had chosen to lease, and not sell, their lands. Therefore, to accommodate the needs of both lessors and lessees, the Hawaii Legislature enacted the Land Reform Act of 1967 (Act), Haw.Rev.Stat., ch. 516, which created a mechanism for condemning residential tracts and for transferring ownership of the condemned fees simple to existing lessees. By condemning the land in question, the Hawaii Legislature intended to make the land sales involuntary, thereby making the federal tax consequences less severe while still facilitating the redistribution of fees simple. [ ]

Under the Act's condemnation scheme, tenants living on single-family residential lots within developmental tracts at least five acres in size are entitled to ask the Hawaii Housing Authority (HHA) to condemn the property on which they live. [ ] When 25 eligible tenants, or tenants on half the lots in the tract, whichever is less, file appropriate applications, the Act authorizes HHA to hold a public hearing to determine whether acquisition by the State of all or part of the tract will "effectuate the public purposes" of the Act. [ ] If HHA finds that these public purposes will be served, it is authorized to designate some or all of the lots in the tract for acquisition. It then acquires, at prices set either by condemnation trial or by negotiation between lessors and lessees, the former fee owners' full "right, title, and interest" in the land.

After compensation has been set, HHA may sell the land titles to tenants who have applied for fee simple ownership. HHA is authorized to lend these tenants up to 90% of the purchase price, and it may condition final transfer on a right of first refusal for the first 10 years following sale. [ ] If HHA does not sell the lot to the tenant residing there, it may lease the lot or sell it to someone else, provided that public notice has been given. [ ] However, HHA may not sell to any one purchaser, or lease to any one tenant, more than one lot, and it may not operate for profit. [ ] In practice, funds to satisfy the condemnation awards have been supplied entirely by lessees. [ ] While the Act authorizes HHA to issue bonds and appropriate funds for acquisition, no bonds have issued and HHA has not supplied any funds for condemned lots. [ ]

B

In April 1977, HHA held a public hearing concerning the proposed acquisition of some of appellees' lands. HHA made the statutorily required finding that acquisition of appellees' lands would effectuate the public purposes of the Act. Then, in October 1978, it directed appellees to negotiate with certain lessees concerning the sale of the designated properties. Those negotiations failed, and HHA subsequently ordered appellees to submit to compulsory arbitration.

Rather than comply with the compulsory arbitration order, appellees filed suit, in February 1979, in United States District Court, asking that the Act be declared unconstitutional and that its enforcement be enjoined. The District Court temporarily restrained the State from proceeding against appellees' estates. * * * Finally, in December 1979, it granted partial summary judgment to appellants, holding the remaining portion of the Act constitutional under the Public Use Clause. See 483 F.Supp. 62 (Haw.1979). The District Court found that the Act's goals were within the bounds of the State's police powers and that the means the legislature had chosen to serve those goals were not arbitrary, capricious, or selected in bad faith.

The Court of Appeals for the Ninth Circuit reversed. 702 F.2d 788 (1983). * * * It found that the transfers contemplated by the Act were unlike those of takings previously held to constitute "public uses" by this Court. The court further determined that the public purposes offered by the Hawaii Legislature were not deserving of judicial deference. The court concluded that the Act was simply "a naked attempt on the part of the state of Hawaii to take the private property of A and transfer it to B solely for B's private use and benefit." * * * We now reverse.

* * *

III

* * *

A

The starting point for our analysis of the Act's constitutionality is the Court's decision in *Berman v. Parker,* 348 U.S. 26 (1954). In *Berman,* the Court held constitutional the District of Columbia Redevelopment Act of 1945. That Act provided both for the comprehensive use of the eminent domain power to redevelop slum areas and for the possible sale or lease of the condemned lands to private interests. In discussing whether the takings authorized by that Act were for a "public use," *id.,* at 31, the Court stated:

We deal, in other words, with what traditionally has been known as the police power. An attempt to define its reach or trace its outer limits is fruitless, for each case must turn on its own facts. The definition is essentially the product of legislative determinations addressed to the purposes of government, purposes neither abstractly nor historically capable of complete definition. Subject to specific constitutional limitations, when the legislature has spoken, the public interest has been declared in terms well-nigh conclusive. In such cases the legislature, not the judiciary, is the main guardian of the public needs to be served by social legislation * * *.

* * *

There is, of course, a role for courts to play in reviewing a legislature's judgment of what constitutes a public use. But the Court in *Berman* made clear that it is "an extremely narrow" one. * * * In short, the Court has made clear that it will not substitute its judgment for a legislature's judgment as to what constitutes a public use "unless the use be palpably without reasonable foundation." [ ]

To be sure, the Court's cases have repeatedly stated that "one person's property may not be taken for the benefit of another private person without a justifying public purpose, even though compensation be paid." [ ] * * *

But where the exercise of the eminent domain power is rationally related to a conceivable public purpose, the Court has never held a compensated taking to be proscribed by the Public Use Clause. [ ]

On this basis, we have no trouble concluding that the Hawaii Act is constitutional. The people of Hawaii have attempted, much as the settlers of the original 13 Colonies did, to reduce the perceived social and economic evils of a land oligopoly traceable to their monarchs. The land oligopoly has, according to the Hawaii Legislature, created artificial deterrents to the normal functioning of the State's residential land market and forced thousands of individual homeowners to lease, rather than buy, the land underneath their homes. Regulating oligopoly and the evils associated with it is a classic exercise of a State's police powers. [ ]

* * * When the legislature's purpose is legitimate and its means are not irrational, our cases make clear that empirical debates over the wisdom of takings—no less than debates over the wisdom of other kinds of socioeconomic legislation—are not to be carried out in the federal courts. Redistribution of fees simple to correct deficiencies in the market determined by the state legislature to be attributable to land oligopoly is a rational exercise of the eminent domain power. Therefore, the Hawaii statute must pass the scrutiny of the Public Use Clause.

B

* * *

The mere fact that property taken outright by eminent domain is transferred in the first instance to private beneficiaries does not condemn that taking as having only a private purpose. * * * [G]overnment does not itself have to use property to legitimate the taking; it is only the taking's purpose, and not its mechanics, that must pass scrutiny under the Public Use Clause. * * * Accordingly, we reverse the judgment of the Court of Appeals, and remand these cases for further proceedings in conformity with this opinion.

Notes and Questions

1.   You notice that while the language of the Fifth Amendment refers to "public use," the Court in *Midkiff* instead requires only "public purpose." This is a change that was effected in *Berman v. Parker,* which is quoted in *Midkiff.* Is this a significant change? Does it anticipate or allow any broader government functions than might be allowed under a requirement that property may be taken only for a public use? Is this a case about whether the courts or elected bodies are in a "better" position to determine the common good?

2.   Does the Court in *Midkiff* set a substantive standard for "public purpose" or a process standard? Does its requirement that the public purpose be "conceivable" and the method chosen to achieve the purpose be "rational" limit the authority of the government? Or, is the standard in *Midkiff* a process standard; i.e., the government entity must simply "*determine* [that] there are substantial reasons for an exercise of the taking power"? (Emphasis added.)

3.   What purposes does the public purpose limitation serve? If the property owner is justly compensated, what more is needed?

4.   Under *Midkiff,* could a city council exercise its power of eminent domain, within the bounds set by the state, to acquire land for a privately owned shopping mall? What is the public purpose served by such an acquisition? Is a mall the modern equivalent of a public park? Could the council simply grant the power of eminent domain directly to the mall developers, skipping the middleman?

5.   One of the takings cases that has attracted the most passionate reaction is Poletown Neighborhood City Council v. City of Detroit, 410 Mich. 616, 304 N.W.2d 455 (Mich.1981), which is excerpted below. The second dissent describes in great detail the process through which the city of Detroit decided to acquire Poletown for a General Motors factory. Note that the Michigan Supreme Court decides the question as a matter of state constitutional law. Would the outcome have been different under federal constitutional law as applied in *Midkiff?*

What plaintiffs-appellants challenge is the constitutionality of using the power of eminent domain to condemn one person's property to convey it to another private person in order to bolster the economy. They argue that whatever incidental benefit may accrue to the public, assembling land to General Motors' specifications for conveyance to General Motors for its uncontrolled use in profit making is really a taking for private use and not a public use because General Motors is the primary beneficiary of the condemnation.

The defendants-appellees contend, on the other hand, that the controlling public purpose in taking this land is to create an industrial site which will be used to alleviate and prevent conditions of unemployment and fiscal distress. The fact that it will be conveyed to and ultimately used by a private manufacturer does not defeat this predominant public purpose.

There is no dispute about the law. All agree that condemnation for a public use or purpose is permitted. All agree that condemnation for a private use or purpose is forbidden. Similarly, condemnation for a private use cannot be authorized whatever its incidental public benefit and condemnation for a public purpose cannot be forbidden whatever the incidental private gain. The heart of this dispute is whether the proposed condemnation is for the primary benefit of the public or the private user.

The Legislature has determined that governmental action of the type contemplated here meets a public need and serves an essential public purpose. The Court's role after such a determination is made is limited.

* * *

As Justice Cooley stated over a hundred years ago "the most important consideration in the case of eminent domain is the necessity of accomplishing some public good which is otherwise impracticable, and * * * the law does not so much regard the means as the need." *People ex rel. Detroit & Howell R. Co. v. Salem Twp. Board*, 20 Mich. 452, 480–481 (1870).

When there is such public need, "[t]he abstract right [of an individual] to make use of his own property in his own way is compelled to yield to the general comfort and protection of community, and to a proper regard to relative rights in others." Id. Eminent domain is an inherent power of the sovereign of the same nature as, albeit more severe than, the power to regulate the use of land through zoning or the prohibition of public nuisances.

* * *

* * * The power of eminent domain is restricted to furthering public uses and purposes and is not to be exercised without substantial proof that the public is primarily to be benefited. Where, as here, the condemnation power is exercised in a way that benefits specific and identifiable private interests, a court inspects with heightened scrutiny the claim that the public interest is the predominant interest being advanced. Such public benefit cannot be speculative or marginal but must be clear and significant if it is to be within the legitimate purpose as stated by the Legislature. We hold this project is warranted on the basis that its significance for the people of Detroit and the state has been demonstrated.

RYAN, JUSTICE (dissenting).

This is an extraordinary case.

The reverberating clang of its economic, sociological, political, and jurisprudential impact is likely to be heard and felt for generations. By its decision, the Court has altered the law of eminent domain in this state in a most significant way and, in my view, seriously jeopardized the security of all private property ownership.

* * * The controversy arises in the context of economic crisis. While unemployment is high throughout the nation, it is of calamitous proportions throughout the state of Michigan, and particularly in the City of Detroit, whose economic lifeblood is the now foundering automobile industry. It is difficult to overstate the magnitude of the crisis. Unemployment in the state of Michigan is at 14.2%. In the City of Detroit it is at 18%, and among black citizens it is almost 30%. The high cost of doing business in Michigan generally has driven many manufacturers out of this state and to the so-called sunbelt states on a continuing basis during the past several years. Nowhere is the exodus more steady or more damaging than from the Metropolitan Detroit area.

* * *

It was in this economic context, fueled with talk of removal of its long-established Cadillac and Fisher Body manufacturing operations from the Detroit area and the construction of a new 3–million–square–foot plant in a sunbelt state, that in 1980 General Motors made its first overture to the City of Detroit about finding a suitable plant site in the city. * * *

It was, of course, evident to all interested observers that the removal by General Motors of its Cadillac manufacturing operations to a more favorable economic climate would mean the loss to Detroit of at least 6,000 jobs as well as the concomitant loss of literally thousands of allied and supporting automotive design, manufacture and sales functions. There would necessarily follow, as a result, the loss of millions of dollars in real estate and income tax revenues. The darkening picture was made even bleaker by the operation of other forces best explained by the social sciences, including the city's continuing loss of its industrial base and the decline of its population.

Thus it was to a city with its economic back to the wall that General Motors presented its highly detailed "proposal" for construction of a new plant in a "green field" location in the City of Detroit. In addition to the fact that Detroit had virtually no "green fields", the requirements of the "proposal" were such that it was clear that no existing location would be suitable unless the city acquired the requisite land one way or another and did so within the General Motors declared time schedule. The corporation told the city that it must find or assemble a parcel 450 to 500 acres in size with access to long-haul railroad lines and a freeway system with railroad marshalling yards within the plant site. As both General Motors and the city knew at the outset, no such "green field" existed. Unquestionably cognizant of its immense political and economic power, General Motors also insisted that it must receive title to the assembled parcel by May 1, 1981.

* * * In light of that demand, the uncommon speed and efficiency with which the city moved to * * * initiate proceedings to condemn the affected property is more understandable.

It is the less publicized site criteria prescribed by General Motors, however, and incorporated in the approved project plan by the City of Detroit, which suggest the withering economic clout of the country's largest auto firm.   * * * In all, the projected *public* cost of preparing a site agreeable to the board of directors of General Motors is over $200 million.   Remarkably, the site will be sold to General Motors for little more than $8 million.

* * *

From the beginning, construction of the new assembly plant in Detroit was characterized by the city administration as a do or die proposition.   Accordingly, the city, aided by the Michigan [eminent domain statute], marshalled and applied its resources and power to insure that [the "green field"] was a *fait accompli* before meaningful objection could be registered or informed opposition organized. Faced with the unacceptable prospect of losing two automotive plants and the jobs that go with them, the city chose to march in fast lock-step with General Motors to carve a "green field" out of an urban setting which ultimately required sweeping away a tightly-knit residential enclave of first- and second-generation Americans, for many of whom their home was their single most valuable and cherished asset and their stable ethnic neighborhood the unchanging symbol of the security and quality of their lives.

* * * As the new plant site plans were developed and announced, the property condemnation proceedings under the "quick-take" statute begun and the demolitionist's iron ball razed neighboring commercial properties such as the already abandoned Chrysler Dodge main plant, a crescendo of supportive applause sustained the city and General Motors and their purpose.

* * * It was in such an atmosphere that the plaintiffs sued to enjoin the condemnation of their homes.

The judiciary, cognizant of General Motors' May 1 deadline for the city's taking title to all of the property, moved at flank speed. The circuit court conducted a trial on defendants' motion to dismiss plaintiffs' complaint from November 17 to December 2, 1980, and the decision to dismiss the complaint was made on December 9, 1980. Application for leave to appeal prior to decision by the Court of Appeals was received in this Court on December 15, 1980. However, the trial transcript was not received by us until January 5, 1981. We promptly convened, conferred, and granted leave to appeal on January 29, 1981. The case was argued on March 3, 1981.

In less than two weeks, the lead opinions were filed by this Court and released. It is in such circumstances that we were asked to decide, and did decide, an important constitutional issue having towering implications both for the individual plaintiff property owners and for the City of Detroit and the state alike, to say nothing of the impact upon our jurisprudence.

* * *

Assume that you are one of the officials faced with a similar decision for your city. How would you go about deciding what to do? Would a consulting firm that could perform a cost-benefit analysis of the alternatives assist you? Does *Poletown* raise some of the same questions you considered in studying *Johnson v. McIntosh* in the first section of these materials?

The Poletown dispute has been described in a film entitled "Poletown Lives!" and in a book entitled "Poletown: Community Betrayed" by Jeanie Wylie. The case is also discussed in "In Our Defense: The Bill of Rights in Action" by Ellen Alderman and Caroline Kennedy. Alderman and Kennedy report that only 300 of Poletown's 3500 residents protested the acquisition of their property. The properties razed as the project progressed were those sold to the city for a negotiated price.

B. HAS PROPERTY BEEN TAKEN?

In *Midkiff* and *Poletown*, the government entities involved did not deny that they had "taken" property. They had, after all, acquired title to the land, extinguishing all property rights of the landowners, through eminent domain. Other situations are not so clear on this issue, however; and they produce the most difficult questions in takings litigation. Bright lines are hard to come by, but consider the following case:

LORETTO v. TELEPROMPTER MANHATTAN CATV CORP. et al.

Supreme Court of the United States, 1982.
458 U.S. 419, 102 S.Ct. 3164, 73 L.Ed.2d 868.

JUSTICE MARSHALL delivered the opinion of the Court.

This case presents the question whether a minor but permanent physical occupation of an owner's property authorized by government constitutes a "taking" of property for which just compensation is due under the Fifth and Fourteenth Amendments of the Constitution. New York law provides that a landlord must permit a cable television company to install its cable facilities upon his property. In this case, the cable installation occupied portions of appellant's roof and the side of her building. The New York Court of Appeals ruled that this appropriation does not amount to a taking. 53 N.Y.2d 124, 423 N.E.2d 320 (1981). Because we conclude that such a physical occupation of property is a taking, we reverse.

* * * The New York Court of Appeals described the installation as follows:

> "On June 1, 1970 TelePrompter installed a cable slightly less than one-half inch in diameter and of approximately 30 feet in length along the length of the building about 18 inches above the roof top, and directional taps, approximately 4 inches by 4 inches by 4 inches, on the front and rear of the roof. By June 8, 1970 the cable had been extended another 4 to 6 feet and cable had been run from the directional taps to the adjoining building at 305 West 105th Street."

TelePrompter also installed two large silver boxes along the roof cables. The cables are attached by screws or nails penetrating the masonry at approximately two-foot intervals, and other equipment is installed by bolts.

Initially, TelePrompter's roof cables did not service appellant's building. They were part of what could be described as a cable "highway" circumnavigating the city block, with service cables periodically dropped over the front or back of a building in which a tenant desired service. Crucial to such a network is the use of so-called "crossovers"—cable lines extending from one building to another in order to reach a new group of tenants. Two years after appellant purchased the building, TelePrompter connected a "noncrossover" line—*i.e.,* one that provided CATV service to appellant's own tenants—by dropping a line to the first floor down the front of appellant's building.

Prior to 1973, TelePrompter routinely obtained authorization for its installations from property owners along the cable's route, compensating the owners at the standard rate of 5% of the gross revenues that TelePrompter realized from the particular property. To facilitate tenant access to CATV, the State of New York enacted § 828 of the Executive Law, effective January 1, 1973. Section 828 provides that a landlord may not "interfere with the installation of cable television facilities upon his property or premises," and may not demand payment from any tenant for permitting CATV, or demand payment from any CATV company "in excess of any amount which the [State Commission on Cable Television] shall, by regulation, determine to be reasonable." The landlord may, however, require the CATV company or the tenant to bear the cost of installation and to indemnify for any damage caused by the installation. Pursuant to § 828(1)(b), the State Commission has ruled that a one-time $1 payment is the normal fee to which a landlord is entitled. The Commission ruled that this nominal fee, which the Commission concluded was equivalent to what the landlord would receive if the property were condemned pursuant to New York's Transportation Corporations Law, satisfied constitutional requirements "in the absence of a special showing of greater damages attributable to the taking."

* * *

* * * We conclude that a permanent physical occupation authorized by government is a taking without regard to the public interests that it may serve. * * *

The Court [has] noted that no "set formula" exists to determine, in all cases, whether compensation is constitutionally due for a government restriction of property. Ordinarily, the Court must engage in "essentially ad hoc, factual inquiries." [ ] But the inquiry is not standardless. * * *

When faced with a constitutional challenge to a permanent physical occupation of real property, this Court has invariably found a taking. * * *

* * *

The historical rule that a permanent physical occupation of another's property is a taking has more than tradition to commend it. Such an appropriation is perhaps the most serious form of invasion of an owner's property interests. To borrow a metaphor, [ ], the government does not simply take a single "strand" from the "bundle" of property rights: it chops through the bundle, taking a slice of every strand.

Property rights in a physical thing have been described as the rights "to possess, use and dispose of it." [ ] To the extent that the government permanently occupies physical property, it effectively destroys *each* of these rights. First, the owner has no right to possess the occupied space himself, and also has no power to exclude the occupier from possession and use of the space. The power to exclude has traditionally been considered one of the most treasured strands in an owner's bundle of property rights. [ ]

* * *

Second, the permanent physical occupation of property forever denies the owner any power to control the use of the property; he not only cannot exclude others, but can make no nonpossessory use of the property. Although deprivation of the right to use and obtain a profit from property is not, in every case, independently sufficient to establish a taking, [ ], it is clearly relevant. Finally, even though the owner may retain the bare legal right to dispose of the occupied space by transfer or sale, the permanent occupation of that space by a stranger will ordinarily empty the right of any value, since the purchaser will also be unable to make any use of the property.

Moreover, an owner suffers a special kind of injury when a *stranger* directly invades and occupies the owner's property. [P]roperty law has long protected an owner's expectation that he will be relatively undisturbed at least in the possession of his property. To require, as well, that the owner permit another to exercise complete dominion literally adds insult to injury. [ ] Furthermore, such an occupation is qualitatively more severe than a regulation of the *use* of property, even a regulation that imposes affirmative duties on the owner, since the owner may have no control over the timing, extent, or nature of the invasion.

The traditional rule also avoids otherwise difficult line-drawing problems. Few would disagree that if the State required landlords to permit third parties to install swimming pools on the landlords' rooftops for the convenience of the tenants, the requirement would be a taking. If the cable installation here occupied as much space, again, few would disagree that the occupation would be a taking. But constitutional protection for the rights of private property cannot be made to depend on the size of the area permanently occupied.

* * *

Finally, whether a permanent physical occupation has occurred presents relatively few problems of proof. The placement of a fixed structure on land or real property is an obvious fact that will rarely be subject to dispute. Once the fact of occupation is shown, of course, a court should consider the *extent* of the occupation as one relevant factor in determining the compensation due. For that reason, moreover, there is less need to consider the extent of the occupation in determining whether there is a taking in the first instance.

TelePrompter's cable installation on appellant's building constitutes a taking under the traditional test. The installation involved a direct physical attachment of plates, boxes, wires, bolts, and screws to the building, completely occupying space immediately above and upon the roof and along the building's exterior wall.

In light of our analysis, we find no constitutional difference between a crossover and a noncrossover installation. The portions of the installation necessary for both crossovers and noncrossovers permanently appropriate appellant's property. Accordingly, each type of installation is a taking.

* * * [O]ur holding today in no way alters the analysis governing the State's power to require landlords to comply with building codes and provide utility connections, mailboxes, smoke detectors, fire extinguishers, and the like in the common area of a building. So long as these regulations do not require the landlord to suffer the physical occupation of a portion of his building by a third party, they will be analyzed under the multifactor inquiry generally applicable to nonpossessory governmental activity.[1] [   ]

The judgment of the New York Court of Appeals is reversed, and the case is remanded for further proceedings not inconsistent with this opinion.

JUSTICE BLACKMUN, with whom JUSTICE BRENNAN and JUSTICE WHITE join, dissenting.

* * *

In a curiously anachronistic decision, the Court today acknowledges its historical disavowal of set formulae in almost the same breath as it constructs a rigid *per se* takings rule: "a permanent physical occupation authorized by government is a taking without regard to the public interests that it may serve." * * *

* * *

[W]hat does the Court mean by "permanent"? Since all "temporary limitations on the right to exclude" remain "subject to a more complex balancing process to determine whether they are a taking,"

---

1. If § 828 required landlords to provide cable installation if a tenant so desires, the statute might present a different question from the question before us, since the landlord would own the installation. Ownership would give the landlord rights to the placement, manner, use, and possibly the disposition of the installation. * * *

the Court presumably describes a government intrusion that lasts forever. But as the Court itself concedes, § 828 does not require appellant to permit the cable installation forever, but only "[s]o long as the property remains residential and a CATV company wishes to retain the installation." This is far from "permanent."

The Court reaffirms that "States have broad power to regulate housing conditions in general and the landlord-tenant relationship in particular without paying compensation for all economic injuries that such regulation entails." Thus, § 828 merely defines one of the many statutory responsibilities that a New Yorker accepts when she enters the rental business. If appellant occupies her own building, or converts it into a commercial property, she becomes perfectly free to exclude TelePrompter from her one-eighth cubic foot of roof space. But once appellant chooses to use her property for rental purposes, she must comply with all reasonable government statutes regulating the land-lord-tenant relationship. If § 828 authorizes a "permanent" occupation, and thus works a taking "without regard to the public interests that it may serve," then all other New York statutes that require a landlord to make physical attachments to his rental property also must constitute takings, even if they serve indisputably valid public interests in tenant protection and safety.

The Court denies that its theory invalidates these statutes, because they "do not require the landlord to suffer the physical occupation of a portion of his building by a third party." But surely this factor cannot be determinative, since the Court simultaneously recognizes that temporary invasions by third parties are not subject to a *per se* rule. Nor can the qualitative difference arise from the incidental fact that, under § 828, TelePrompter, rather than appellant or her tenants, owns the cable installation. * * *

In any event, under the Court's test, the "third party" problem would remain even if appellant herself owned the cable. So long as TelePrompter continuously passed its electronic signal through the cable, a litigant could argue that the second element of the Court's formula—a "physical touching" by a stranger—was satisfied and that § 828 therefore worked a taking. Literally read, the Court's test opens the door to endless metaphysical struggles over whether or not an individual's property has been "physically" touched. * * *

In sum, history teaches that takings claims are properly evaluated under a multifactor balancing test. By directing that all "permanent physical occupations" automatically are compensable, "without regard to whether the action achieves an important public benefit or has only minimal economic impact on the owner," the Court does not further equity so much as it encourages litigants to manipulate their factual allegations to gain the benefit of its *per se* rule. I do not relish the prospect of distinguishing the inevitable flow of certiorari petitions attempting to shoehorn insubstantial takings claims into today's "set formula."

Notes and Questions

1. The dissent spends considerable effort in arguing that the majority's distinction between permanent physical occupation and temporary physical occupation is not persuasive in the situation in *Loretto*. Aside from the question of whether the cable TV installations in *Loretto* are permanent or temporary, should the distinction generally make such a difference? Why or why not? Why did the majority want to draw such an impenetrable fortress around permanent physical occupations?

2. The majority holds that the Constitution requires that a landowner must be compensated for the value of the property lost due to the CATV installation, even though the financial loss is negligible. (The $1 compensation was found adequate by the New York Court of Appeal at *Loretto*, 58 N.Y.2d 143, 459 N.Y.S.2d 743, 446 N.E.2d 428 (1983).) But, it also states that regulations requiring landlords to install fire extinguishers or other devices, presumably at an expense far exceeding $1, would not be a *per se* taking requiring compensation, but would, instead, require a "multifactor" analysis. Why does the Court value, in terms of constitutional protection, what might be called the symbolic significance of property ownership in *Loretto* over the substantial financial losses of these other government-imposed burdens?

3. Loretto did not contest the public purpose of the cable TV statute. Could she have succeeded? In fact, did she "succeed" in her takings claim? Why might she have pursued this to the United States Supreme Court?

4. So far, we have seen two situations in which a taking is *always* found to have occurred and compensation is *always* required: 1) acquisition by the government of fee title, and 2) permanent physical occupation of property by the government or by a government-authorized third party. Beyond this lies the gray area of "regulation," sometimes a taking and sometimes not. Consider the following case in which the Court seventy years ago identified several of the factors that still define whether a taking has occurred in these gray areas.

PENNSYLVANIA COAL COMPANY v. MAHON

Supreme Court of the United States, 1922.
260 U.S. 393, 43 S.Ct. 158, 67 L.Ed. 322.

Mr. Justice Holmes delivered the opinion of the Court:

This is a bill in equity, brought by the defendants in error to prevent the Pennsylvania Coal Company from mining under their property in such way as to remove the supports and cause a subsidence of the surface and of their house. The bill sets out a deed executed by the Coal Company in 1878, under which the plaintiffs claim. The deed conveys the surface, but in express terms reserves the right to remove all the coal under the same, and the grantee takes the premises with the risk, and waives all claim for damages that may arise from mining out the coal. But the plaintiffs say that whatever may have been the Coal Company's rights, they were taken away by an Act of Pennsylvania, approved May 27, 1921, commonly known there as the Kohler Act.

The court of common pleas found that, if not restrained, the defendant would cause the damage to prevent which the bill was brought, but denied an injunction, holding that the statute, if applied to this case, would be unconstitutional. On appeal, the supreme court of the state agreed that the defendant had contract and property rights protected by the Constitution of the United States, but held that the statute was a legitimate exercise of the police power, and directed a decree for the plaintiffs. A writ of error was granted, bringing the case to this court.

The statute forbids the mining of anthracite coal in such way as to cause the subsidence of, among other things, any structure used as a human habitation, with certain exceptions, including among them land where the surface is owned by the owner of the underlying coal, and is distant more than 150 feet from any improved property belonging to any other person. As applied to this case, the statute is admitted to destroy previously existing rights of property and contract. The question is whether the police power can be stretched so far.

Government hardly could go on if, to some extent, values incident to property could not be diminished without paying for every such change in the general law. As long recognized, some values are enjoyed under an implied limitation, and must yield to the police power. But obviously the implied limitation must have its limits or the contract and due process clauses are gone. One fact for consideration in determining such limits is the extent of the diminution. When it reaches a certain magnitude, in most if not in all cases there must be an exercise of eminent domain and compensation to sustain the act. So the question depends upon the particular facts. The greatest weight is given to the judgment of the legislature, but it always is open to interested parties to contend that the legislature has gone beyond its constitutional power.

This is the case of a single private house. No doubt there is a public interest even in this, as there is in every purchase and sale and in all that happens within the commonwealth. Some existing rights may be modified even in such a case. [ ] But usually, in ordinary private affairs the public interest does not warrant much of this kind of interference. A source of damage to such a house is not a public nuisance even if similar damage is inflicted on others in different places. The damage is not common or public. [ ] The extent of the public interest is shown by the statute to be limited, since the statute ordinarily does not apply to land when the surface is owned by the owner of the coal. Furthermore, it is not justified as a protection of personal safety. That could be provided for by notice. Indeed, the very foundation of this bill is that the defendant gave timely notice of its intent to mine under the house. On the other hand, the extent of the taking is great. It purports to abolish what is recognized in Pennsylvania as an estate in land,—a very valuable estate,—and what is declared by the court below to be a contract hitherto binding the plaintiffs. If we were called upon to deal with the plaintiffs' position alone we should think it clear that the statute does not disclose a public interest sufficient to warrant so extensive a destruction of the defendant's constitutionally protected rights.

* * *

It is our opinion that the act cannot be sustained as an exercise of the police power, so far as it affects the mining of coal under streets or cities in places where the right to mine such coal has been reserved. What makes the right to mine coal valuable is that it can be exercised with profit. To make it commercially impracticable to mine certain coal has very nearly the same effect for constitutional purposes as appropriating or destroying it. This we think that we are warranted in assuming that the statute does.

It is true that in Plymouth Coal Co. v. Pennsylvania, 232 U.S. 531, 58 L.Ed. 713, 34 Sup.Ct.Rep. 359, it was held competent for the legislature to require a pillar of coal to be left along the line of adjoining property, that, with the pillar on the other side of the line, would be a barrier sufficient for the safety of the employees of either mine in case the other should be abandoned and allowed to fill with water. But that was a requirement for the safety of employees invited into the mine, and secured an average reciprocity of advantage that has been recognized as a justification of various laws.

The rights of the public in a street purchased or laid out by eminent domain are those that it has paid for. If in any case its representatives have been so shortsighted as to acquire only surface rights, without the right of support, we see no more authority for supplying the latter without compensation than there was for taking the right of way in the first place, and refusing to pay for it because the public wanted it very much.

* * *

The general rule, at least, is that while property may be regulated to a certain extent, if regulation goes too far it will be recognized as a taking. We are in danger of forgetting that a strong public desire to improve the public condition is not enough to warrant achieving the desire by a shorter cut than the constitutional way of paying for the change. As we already have said, this is a question of degree—and therefore cannot be disposed of by general propositions. * * *

But the question at bottom is upon whom the loss of the changes desired should fall. So far as private persons or communities have seen fit to take the risk of acquiring only surface rights, we cannot see that the fact that their risk has become a danger warrants the giving to them greater rights than they bought.

Decree reversed.

Mr. Justice Brandeis, dissenting:

The Kohler Act prohibits, under certain conditions, the mining of anthracite coal within the limits of a city in such a manner or to such an extent "as to cause the subsidence of any dwelling or other structure used as a human habitation, or any factory, store, or other industrial or mercantile establishment in which human labor is employed." Coal in place is land; and the right of the owner to use his land is not absolute. He may not so use it as to create a public nuisance; and uses, once harmless, may, owing to changed conditions, seriously threaten the public welfare. Whenever they do, the legislature has power to prohibit such uses without paying compensation; and the power to prohibit extends alike to the manner, the character, and the purpose of the use.

Every restriction upon the use of property, imposed in the exercise of the police power, deprives the owner of some right theretofore enjoyed, and is, in that sense, an abridgment by the state of rights in property without making compensation. But restriction imposed to protect the public health, safety, or morals from dangers threatened is not a taking. The restriction here in question is merely the prohibition of a noxious use. The property so restricted remains in the possession of its owner. The state does not appropriate it or make any use of it. The state merely prevents the owner from making a use which interferes with paramount rights of the public. Whenever the use prohibited ceases to be noxious—as it may because of further change in local or social conditions,—the restriction will have to be removed, and the owner will again be free to enjoy his property as heretofore.

The restriction upon the use of this property cannot, of course, be lawfully imposed, unless its purpose is to protect the public. But the purpose of a restriction does not cease to be public because incidentally some private persons may thereby receive gratuitously valuable special benefits. * * *

It is said that one fact for consideration in determining whether the limits of the police power have been exceeded is the extent of the resulting diminution in value; and that here the restriction destroys existing rights of property and contract. But values are relative. If we are to consider the value of the coal kept in place by the restriction, we should compare it with the value of all other parts of the land. That is, with the value not of the coal alone, but with the value of the whole property. The rights of an owner, as against the public, are not increased by dividing the interests in his property into surface and subsoil. The sum of the rights in the parts cannot be greater than the rights in the whole. The estate of an owner in land is grandiloquently described as extending ab orco usque ad coelum. But I suppose no one would contend that by selling his interest above 100 feet from the surface he could prevent the state from limiting, by the police power, the height of structures in a city. And why should a sale of underground rights bar the state's power? For aught that appears the value of the coal kept in place by the restriction may be negligible as compared with the value of the whole property, or even as compared with that part of it which is represented by the coal remaining in place, and which may be extracted despite the statute. Ordinarily a police regulation, general in operation, will not be held void as to a particular property, although proof is offered that, owing to conditions peculiar to it, the restriction could not reasonably be applied.

* * *

[W]here the police power is exercised, not to confer benefits upon property owners, but to protect the public from detriment and danger, there is, in my opinion, no room for considering reciprocity of advantage. * * *

Notes and Questions

1. Justice Brandeis argues that the Kohler Act merely prohibits a nuisance by regulating anthracite mining methods. Review the material on nuisance that you covered earlier. Clearly, there is no property right to use land in a manner that injures another; so, a regulation prohibiting a nuisance does not take property. Do the facts in *Mahon* better support Holmes' or Brandeis' conclusion as to nuisance?

In Hadacheck v. Sebastian, 239 U.S. 394, 36 S.Ct. 143, 60 L.Ed. 348 (1915), the Court upheld as a legitimate use of the police power a city ordinance that made the operation of a brickyard or brick kiln within city limits illegal. The Court was not persuaded by the property owner's claim that his operation had been a legal and appropriate use of his land. The Court stated that protection of a vested interest by first occupation and use "would preclude development and fix a city forever in its primitive conditions. There must be progress and if in its march private interests are in the way they must yield to the good of the community." The Court commented that the clay on the land could still be used by removing it to another location for processing. How elastic should the concept of nuisance be in a takings case? See, for example, Just v. Marinette County, 56 Wis.2d 7, 201 N.W.2d 761 (1972), in which a state wetlands protection act was held not to constitute a taking: "We have here a restriction on the use of a citizen's property, not to secure a benefit for the public, but to prevent a harm from the change in the natural character of the citizen's property."

See also, Sax, Takings and the Police Power, 74 Yale L.J. 36 (1964) and Sax, Takings, Private Property and Public Rights, 81 Yale L.J. 149 (1971).

2. Justice Holmes in *Mahon* established three of the factors that have been used ever since to determine whether a regulation effects a taking of property. The opinion in *Mahon* is a model of brevity, especially by more modern Supreme Court standards; and Holmes' "tests" are stated in no more than a few words. Perhaps his most cryptic rule is that only regulation that goes "too far" is a taking. The other Holmes' tests are:

(a) The Balancing Test: The public interest in *Mahon*, according to Holmes, was inconsequential while the loss was "great." Recall that all takings of property by the government, even those for which the owner is compensated, require a public purpose. Here, though, the intensity or strength or breadth of the purpose apparently is balanced against the loss to detect whether a taking has occurred and compensation for the loss caused by the regulation is constitutionally required.

(b) Reciprocity of Advantage: Property ownership exists in a society. Although some regulations restricting property rights result in some loss, they also create gains. Things tend to average out over the long run, at least if the loss is not too heavily visited on a few. This analysis is most often used to justify zoning.

(c) Diminution in Value: If the loss reaches a "certain magnitude," a taking occurs. Holmes' single sentence leaves some questions unanswered, and the Court has spent seventy years trying to answer them.

3. In 1987, the court decided a "triology" of cases in the takings area. In one of those cases, the Court revisited the coal mines. In Keystone Bituminous Coal Ass'n v. DeBenedictis, 480 U.S. 470, 107 S.Ct. 1232, 94 L.Ed.2d 472 (1987), the Court held that Pennsylvania's Bituminous Mine Subsidence and Land Conservation Act, which required that about 50 percent of the coal lying under certain structures be left unmined in order to avoid surface subsidence, did not take private property in violation of the Constitution. The 5–4 majority of the Court worked hard to distinguish *Keystone* from *Pennsylvania Coal.* According to the Court, "Unlike the Kohler Act, the character of the governmental action involved [in *Keystone*] leans heavily against finding a taking; the Commonwealth of Pennsylvania has acted to arrest what it perceives to be a significant threat to the common welfare." The Court in *Keystone* also commented that "there is no record in this case to support the finding, [unlike in *Pennsylvania Coal*], that the Subsidence Act makes it impossible for petitioners to profitably engage in their business, or that there has been undue interference with their investment-backed expectations." Observing that *Pennsylvania Coal* "has for 65 years been the foundation of our regulatory takings jurisprudence," the dissent by Justice Rehnquist argues that the public safety purpose of the Kohler Act was quite clear and, in fact, was quite similar in purpose to the Subsidence Act. The dissent also took issue with the majority's implication that this Act fell within the nuisance exception, discussed in the first note above: "We should hesitate to allow a regulation based on essentially economic concerns to be insulated from the dictates of the Fifth Amendment * * *". Finally the dissent criticizes the majority's conclusion that the Act did not take property because the mines could still be profitable: "There is no question that this coal is an identifiable and separable property interest. * * * [T]he 'bundle' of rights in this coal is sparse. * * * [T]his interest has been destroyed every bit as much as if the government had proceeded to mine the coal for its own use. The regulation, then, does not merely inhibit one strand in the bundle, but instead destroys completely any interest in a segment of property." Which analysis—the majority or the dissent—is more consistent with Holmes' opinion in *Pennsylvania Coal?* Does the result in *Keystone* simply reflect an increased acceptability of economic regulation?

PENN CENTRAL TRANSPORTATION COMPANY
v. CITY OF NEW YORK

Supreme Court of the United States, 1978.
438 U.S. 104, 98 S.Ct. 2646, 57 L.Ed.2d 631, reh. den.,
439 U.S. 883, 99 S.Ct. 226, 58 L.Ed.2d 198 (1978).

MR. JUSTICE BRENNAN delivered the opinion of the Court.

The question presented is whether a city may, as part of a comprehensive program to preserve historic landmarks and historic districts, place restrictions on the development of individual historic landmarks—in addition to those imposed by applicable zoning ordinances—without effecting a "taking" requiring the payment of "just compensation." Specifically, we must decide whether the application of New York City's Landmarks Preservation Law to the parcel of land occupied by Grand Central Terminal has "taken" its owners' property in violation of the Fifth and Fourteenth Amendments.

I

A

Over the past 50 years, all 50 States and over 500 municipalities have enacted laws to encourage or require the preservation of buildings and areas with historic or aesthetic importance. These nationwide legislative efforts have been precipitated by two concerns. The first is recognition that, in recent years, large numbers of historic structures, landmarks, and areas have been destroyed without adequate consideration of either the values represented therein or the possibility of preserving the destroyed properties for use in economically productive ways. The second is a widely shared belief that structures with special historic, cultural, or architectural significance enhance the quality of life for all. Not only do these buildings and their workmanship represent the lessons of the past and embody precious features of our heritage, they serve as examples of quality for today. * * *

New York City, responding to similar concerns and acting pursuant to a New York State enabling Act, adopted its Landmarks Preservation Law in 1965. See N.Y.C.Admin.Code, ch. 8–A, § 205–1.0 *et seq.* (1976). The city acted from the conviction that "the standing of [New York City] as a world-wide tourist center and world capital of business, culture and government" would be threatened if legislation were not enacted to protect historic landmarks and neighborhoods from precipitate decisions to destroy or fundamentally alter their character. § 205–1.0(a). The city believed that comprehensive measures to safeguard desirable features of the existing urban fabric would benefit its citizens in a variety of ways: *e.g.,* fostering "civic pride in the beauty and noble accomplishments of the past"; protecting and enhancing "the city's attractions to tourists and visitors"; "support[ing] and stimul[ating] business and industry"; "strengthen[ing] the economy of the city"; and promoting "the use of historic districts, landmarks, interior landmarks and scenic landmarks for the education, pleasure and welfare of the people of the city." § 205–1.0(b).

The New York City law is typical of many urban landmark laws in that its primary method of achieving its goals is not by acquisitions of historic properties,[2] but rather by involving public entities in land-use

---

2. The consensus is that widespread public ownership of historic properties in urban settings is neither feasible nor wise. Public ownership reduces the tax base,

decisions affecting these properties and providing services, standards, controls, and incentives that will encourage preservation by private owners and users. While the law does place special restrictions on landmark properties as a necessary feature to the attainment of its larger objectives, the major theme of the law is to ensure the owners of any such properties both a "reasonable return" on their investments and maximum latitude to use their parcels for purposes not inconsistent with the preservation goals.

The operation of the law can be briefly summarized. The primary responsibility for administering the law is vested in the Landmarks Preservation Commission (Commission), a broad based, 11–member agency [3] assisted by a technical staff. The Commission first performs the function, critical to any landmark preservation effort, of identifying properties and areas that have "a special character or special historical or aesthetic interest or value as part of the development, heritage or cultural characteristics of the city, state or nation." § 207–1.0(n); see § 207–1.0(h). If the Commission determines, after giving all interested parties an opportunity to be heard, that a building or area satisfies the ordinance's criteria, it will designate a building to be a "landmark," § 207–1.0(n), situated on a particular "landmark site," § 207–1.0(o), or will designate an area to be a "historic district," § 207–1.0(h). After the Commission makes a designation, New York City's Board of Estimate, after considering the relationship of the designated property "to the master plan, the zoning resolution, projected public improvements and any plans for the renewal of the area involved," § 207–2.0(g)(1), may modify or disapprove the designation, and the owner may seek judicial review of the final designation decision. Thus far, 31 historic districts and over 400 individual landmarks have been finally designated, and the process is a continuing one.

Final designation as a landmark results in restrictions upon the property owner's options concerning use of the landmark site. First, the law imposes a duty upon the owner to keep the exterior features of the building "in good repair" to assure that the law's objectives not be defeated by the landmark's falling into a state of irremediable disrepair. See § 207–10.0(a). Second, the Commission must approve in advance any proposal to alter the exterior architectural features of the

burdens the public budget with costs of acquisitions and maintenance, and results in the preservation of public buildings as museums and similar facilities, rather than as economically productive features of the urban scene. See Wilson & Winkler, The Response of State Legislation to Historic Preservation, 36 Law & Contemp.Prob. 329, 330–331, 339–340 (1971).

3. The ordinance creating the Commission requires that it include at least three architects, one historian qualified in the field, one city planner or landscape architect, one realtor, and at least one resident of each of the city's five boroughs. N.Y.C. Charter § 534 (1976). In addition to the ordinance's requirements concerning the composition of the Commission, there is, according to a former chairman, a "prudent tradition" that the Commission include one or two lawyers, preferably with experience in municipal government, and several laymen with no specialized qualifications other than concern for the good of the city. Goldstone, Aesthetics in Historic Districts, 36 Law & Contemp.Prob. 379, 384–385 (1971).

landmark or to construct any exterior improvement on the landmark site, thus ensuring that decisions concerning construction on the landmark site are made with due consideration of both the public interest in the maintenance of the structure and the landowner's interest in use of the property. See §§ 207–4.0 to 207–9.0.

In the event an owner wishes to alter a landmark site, three separate procedures are available through which administrative approval may be obtained. First, the owner may apply to the Commission for a "certificate of no effect on protected architectural features": that is, for an order approving the improvement or alteration on the ground that it will not change or affect any architectural feature of the landmark and will be in harmony therewith. See § 207–5.0. Denial of the certificate is subject to judicial review.

Second, the owner may apply to the Commission for a certificate of "appropriateness." See § 207–6.0. Such certificates will be granted if the Commission concludes—focusing upon aesthetic, historical, and architectural values—that the proposed construction on the landmark site would not unduly hinder the protection, enhancement, perpetuation, and use of the landmark. Again, denial of the certificate is subject to judicial review. Moreover, the owner who is denied either a certificate of no exterior effect or a certificate of appropriateness may submit an alternative or modified plan for approval. The final procedure—seeking a certificate of appropriateness on the ground of "insufficient return," see § 207–8.0—provides special mechanisms, which vary depending on whether or not the landmark enjoys a tax exemption, to ensure that designation does not cause economic hardship.

Although the designation of a landmark and landmark site restricts the owner's control over the parcel, designation also enhances the economic position of the landmark owner in one significant respect. Under New York City's zoning laws, owners of real property who have not developed their property to the full extent permitted by the applicable zoning laws are allowed to transfer development rights to contiguous parcels on the same city block. See New York City, Zoning Resolution Art. I, ch. 2, § 12–10 (1978) (definition of "zoning lot"). A 1968 ordinance gave the owners of landmark sites additional opportunities to transfer development rights to other parcels. Subject to a restriction that the floor area of the transferee lot may not be increased by more than 20% above its authorized level, the ordinance permitted transfers from a landmark parcel to property across the street or across a street intersection. In 1969, the law governing the conditions under which transfers from landmark parcels could occur was liberalized, see New York City Zoning Resolutions 74–79 to 74–793, apparently to ensure that the Landmarks Law would not unduly restrict the development options of the owners of Grand Central Terminal. See Marcus, Air Rights Transfers in New York City, 36 Law & Contemp.Prob. 372, 375 (1971). The class of recipient lots was expanded to include lots "across a street and opposite to another lot or lots which except for the intervention of streets or street intersections f[or]m a series extending to the lot occupied by the landmark building[, provided that] all lots [are] in the same ownership." New York City Zoning Resolution 74–79 (emphasis deleted).[4] In addition, the 1969 amendment permits, in highly commercialized areas like midtown Manhattan, the transfer of all unused development rights to a single parcel. *Ibid.*

B

This case involves the application of New York City's Landmarks Preservation Law to Grand Central Terminal (Terminal). The Terminal, which is owned by the Penn Central Transportation Co. and its affiliates (Penn Central), is one of New York City's most famous buildings. Opened in 1913, it is regarded not only as providing an ingenious engineering solution to the problems presented by urban railroad stations, but also as a magnificent example of the French beaux-arts style.

* * * The Terminal itself is an eight-story structure which Penn Central uses as a railroad station and in which it rents space not needed for railroad purposes to a variety of commercial interests. The Terminal is one of a number of properties owned by appellant Penn Central in this area of midtown Manhattan. * * * At least eight of these are eligible to be recipients of development rights afforded the Terminal by virtue of landmark designation.

On August 2, 1967, following a public hearing, the Commission designated the Terminal a "landmark" and designated the "city tax block" it occupies a "landmark site." The Board of Estimate confirmed this action on September 21, 1967. Although appellant Penn Central had opposed the designation before the Commission, it did not seek judicial review of the final designation decision.

On January 22, 1968, appellant Penn Central, to increase its income, entered into a renewable 50–year lease and sublease agreement with appellant UGP Properties, Inc. (UGP), a wholly owned subsidiary of Union General Properties, Ltd., a United Kingdom corporation. Under the terms of the agreement, UGP was to construct a multistory office building above the Terminal. UGP promised to pay Penn Central $1 million annually during construction and at least $3 million annually thereafter. The rentals would be offset in part by a loss of some $700,000 to $1 million in net rentals presently received from concessionaires displaced by the new building.

Appellants UGP and Penn Central then applied to the Commission for permission to construct an office building atop the Terminal. Two

4. To obtain approval for a proposed transfer, the landmark owner must follow the following procedure. First, he must obtain the permission of the Commission which will examine the plans for the development of the transferee lot to determine whether the planned construction would be compatible with the landmark. Second, he must obtain the approbation of New York City's Planning Commission which will focus on the effects of the transfer on occupants of the buildings in the vicinity of the transferee lot and whether the landmark owner will preserve the landmark. Finally, the matter goes to the Board of Estimate, which has final authority to grant or deny the application. [ ]

separate plans, both designed by architect Marcel Breuer and both apparently satisfying the terms of the applicable zoning ordinance, were submitted to the Commission for approval. The first, Breuer I, provided for the construction of a 55–story office building, to be cantilevered above the existing facade and to rest on the roof of the Terminal. The second, Breuer II Revised, called for tearing down a portion of the Terminal that included the 42d Street facade, stripping off some of the remaining features of the Terminal's facade, and constructing a 53–story office building. The Commission denied a certificate of no exterior effect on September 20, 1968. Appellants then applied for a certificate of "appropriateness" as to both proposals. After four days of hearings at which over 80 witnesses testified, the Commission denied this application as to both proposals.

* * *

Appellants did not seek judicial review of the denial of either certificate. Because the Terminal site enjoyed a tax exemption, remained suitable for its present and future uses, and was not the subject of a contract of sale, there were no further administrative remedies available to appellants. Further, appellants did not avail themselves of the opportunity to develop and submit other plans for the Commission's consideration and approval. Instead, appellants filed suit in New York Supreme Court, Trial Term, claiming, *inter alia,* that the application of the Landmarks Preservation Law had "taken" their property without just compensation in violation of the Fifth and Fourteenth Amendments and arbitrarily deprived them of their property without due process of law in violation of the Fourteenth Amendment. Appellants sought a declaratory judgment, injunctive relief barring the city from using the Landmarks Law to impede the construction of any structure that might otherwise lawfully be constructed on the Terminal site, and damages for the "temporary taking" that occurred between August 2, 1967, the designation date, and the date when the restrictions arising from the Landmarks Law would be lifted. The trial court granted the injunctive and declaratory relief, but severed the question of damages for a "temporary taking." [5]

Appellees appealed, and the New York Supreme Court, Appellate Division, reversed. 50 A.D.2d 265, 377 N.Y.S.2d 20 (1975). The Appellate Division held that the restrictions on the development of the Terminal site were necessary to promote the legitimate public purpose of protecting landmarks and therefore that appellants could sustain their constitutional claims only by proof that the regulation deprived them of all reasonable beneficial use of the property. * * *

5. Although that court suggested that any regulation of private property to protect landmark values was unconstitutional if "just compensation" were not afforded, it also appeared to rely upon its findings: first, that the cost to Penn Central of operating the Terminal building itself, exclusive of purely railroad operations, exceeded the revenues received from concessionaires and tenants in the Terminal; and second, that the special transferable development rights afforded Penn Central as an owner of a landmark site did not "provide compensation to plaintiffs or minimize the harm suffered by plaintiffs due to the designation of the Terminal as a landmark."

The New York Court of Appeals affirmed. 42 N.Y.2d 324, 397 N.Y.S.2d 914, 366 N.E.2d 1271 (1977). That court summarily rejected any claim that the Landmarks Law had "taken" property without "just compensation," *id.*, at 329, 397 N.Y.S.2d, at 917, 366 N.E.2d, at 1274, indicating that there could be no "taking" since the law had not transferred control of the property to the city, but only restricted appellants' exploitation of it. In that circumstance, the Court of Appeals held that appellants' attack on the law could prevail only if the law deprived appellants of their property in violation of the Due Process Clause of the Fourteenth Amendment. Whether or not there was a denial of substantive due process turned on whether the restrictions deprived Penn Central of a "reasonable return" on the "privately created and privately managed ingredient" of the Terminal. *Id.*, at 328, 397 N.Y.S.2d, at 916, 366 N.E.2d, at 1273.[6] The Court of Appeals concluded that the Landmarks Law had not effected a denial of due process because: (1) the landmark regulation permitted the same use as had been made of the Terminal for more than half a century; (2) the appellants had failed to show that they could not earn a reasonable return on their investment in the Terminal itself; (3) even if the Terminal proper could never operate at a reasonable profit some of the income from Penn Central's extensive real estate holdings in the area, which include hotels and office buildings, must realistically be imputed to the Terminal; and (4) the development rights above the Terminal, which had been made transferable to numerous sites in the vicinity of the Terminal, one or two of which were suitable for the construction of office buildings, were valuable to appellants and provided "significant, perhaps 'fair,' compensation for the loss of rights above the terminal itself." *Id.*, at 333–336, 397 N.Y.S.2d, at 922, 366 N.E.2d, at 1276–1278.

Observing that its affirmance was "[o]n the present record," and that its analysis had not been fully developed by counsel at any level of the New York judicial system, the Court of Appeals directed that counsel "should be entitled to present . . . any additional submissions which, in the light of [the court's] opinion, may usefully develop further the factors discussed." *Id.*, at 337, 397 N.Y.S.2d, at 922, 366 N.E.2d, at 1279. Appellants chose not to avail themselves of this opportunity and filed a notice of appeal in this Court. We noted probable jurisdiction. 434 U.S. 983 (1977). We affirm.

6. The Court of Appeals suggested that in calculating the value of the property upon which appellants were entitled to earn a reasonable return, the "publicly created" components of the value of the property—*i.e.*, those elements of its value attributable to the "efforts of organized society" or to the "social complex" in which the Terminal is located—had to be excluded. However, since the record upon which the Court of Appeals decided the case did not, as that court recognized, contain a basis for segregating the privately created from the publicly created elements of the value of the Terminal site and since the judgment of the Court of Appeals in any event rests upon bases that support our affirmance see *infra*, this page, we have no occasion to address the question whether it is permissible or feasible to separate out the "social increments" of the value of property. See Costonis, The Disparity Issue: A Context for the *Grand Central Terminal* Decision, 91 Harv.L.Rev. 402, 416–417 (1977).

II

* * *

* * * The question of what constitutes a "taking" for purposes of the Fifth Amendment has proved to be a problem of considerable difficulty. While this Court has recognized that the "Fifth Amendment's guarantee * * * [is] designed to bar Government from forcing some people alone to bear public burdens which, in all fairness and justice, should be borne by the public as a whole," *Armstrong v. United States,* 364 U.S. 40, 49, 80 S.Ct. 1563, 1569, 4 L.Ed.2d 1554 (1960), this Court, quite simply, has been unable to develop any "set formula" for determining when "justice and fairness" require that economic injuries caused by public action be compensated by the government, rather than remain disproportionately concentrated on a few persons. * * *

* * *

More importantly for the present case, in instances in which a state tribunal reasonably concluded that "the health, safety, morals, or general welfare" would be promoted by prohibiting particular contemplated uses of land, this Court has upheld land-use regulations that destroyed or adversely affected recognized real property interests. See *Nectow v. Cambridge,* 277 U.S. 183, 188, 48 S.Ct. 447, 448, 72 L.Ed. 842 (1928). Zoning laws are, of course, the classic example, see *Euclid v. Ambler Realty Co.,* 272 U.S. 365, 47 S.Ct. 114, 71 L.Ed. 303 (1926) (prohibition of industrial use); *Gorieb v. Fox,* 274 U.S. 603, 608, 47 S.Ct. 675, 677, 71 L.Ed. 1228 (1927) (requirement that portions of parcels be left unbuilt); *Welch v. Swasey,* 214 U.S. 91, 29 S.Ct. 567, 53 L.Ed. 923 (1909) (height restriction), which have been viewed as permissible governmental action even when prohibiting the most beneficial use of the property. See *Goldblatt v. Hempstead, supra,* 369 U.S., at 592–593, 82 S.Ct., at 988–989, and cases cited; see also *Eastlake v. Forest City Enterprises, Inc.,* 426 U.S. 668, 674, n. 8, 96 S.Ct. 2358, 2362 n. 8, 49 L.Ed.2d 132 (1976).

* * *

Pennsylvania Coal Co. v. Mahon, 260 U.S. 393, 43 S.Ct. 158, 67 L.Ed. 322 (1922), is the leading case for the proposition that a state statute that substantially furthers important public policies may so frustrate distinct investment-backed expectations as to amount to a "taking." There the claimant had sold the surface rights to particular parcels of property, but expressly reserved the right to remove the coal thereunder. A Pennsylvania statute, enacted after the transactions, forbade any mining of coal that caused the subsidence of any house, unless the house was the property of the owner of the underlying coal and was more than 150 feet from the improved property of another. Because the statute made it commercially impracticable to mine the coal, and thus had nearly the same effect as the complete destruction of rights claimant had reserved from the owners of the surface land, the Court held that the statute was invalid as effecting a "taking" without just compensation. [   ]

* * *

In contending that the New York City law has "taken" their property in violation of the Fifth and Fourteenth Amendments, appellants make a series of arguments, which, while tailored to the facts of this case, essentially urge that any substantial restriction imposed pursuant to a landmark law must be accompanied by just compensation if it is to be constitutional. Before considering these, we emphasize what is not in dispute. Because this Court has recognized, in a number of settings, that States and cities may enact land-use restrictions or controls to enhance the quality of life by preserving the character and desirable aesthetic features of a city, appellants do not contest that New York City's objective of preserving structures and areas with special historic, architectural, or cultural significance is an entirely permissible governmental goal. They also do not dispute that the restrictions imposed on its parcel are appropriate means of securing the purposes of the New York City law. Finally, appellants do not challenge any of the specific factual premises of the decision below. They accept for present purposes both that the parcel of land occupied by Grand Central Terminal must, in its present state, be regarded as capable of earning a reasonable return, and that the transferable development rights afforded appellants by virtue of the Terminal's designation as a landmark are valuable, even if not as valuable as the rights to construct above the Terminal. In appellants' view none of these factors derogate from their claim that New York City's law has effected a "taking."

They first observe that the airspace above the Terminal is a valuable property interest. They urge that the Landmarks Law has deprived them of any gainful use of their "air rights" above the Terminal and that, irrespective of the value of the remainder of their parcel, the city has "taken" their right to this superadjacent airspace, thus entitling them to "just compensation" measured by the fair market value of these air rights.

* * * "Taking" jurisprudence does not divide a single parcel into discrete segments and attempt to determine whether rights in a particular segment have been entirely abrogated. In deciding whether a particular governmental action has effected a taking, this Court focuses rather both on the character of the action and on the nature and extent of the interference with rights in the parcel as a whole—here, the city tax block designated as the "landmark site."

Secondly, appellants, focusing on the character and impact of the New York City law, argue that it effects a "taking" because its operation has significantly diminished the value of the Terminal site. Appellants concede that the decisions sustaining other land-use regulations, which, like the New York City law, are reasonably related to the promotion of the general welfare, uniformly reject the proposition that diminution in property value, standing alone, can establish a "taking," see *Euclid v. Ambler Realty Co.*, 272 U.S. 365, 47 S.Ct. 114, 71 L.Ed. 303

(1926) (75% diminution in value caused by zoning law); *Hadacheck v. Sebastian,* 239 U.S. 394, 36 S.Ct. 143, 60 L.Ed. 348 (1915) (87½% diminution in value); and that the "taking" issue in these contexts is resolved by focusing on the uses the regulations permit. * * *

Stated baldly, appellants' position appears to be that the only means of ensuring that selected owners are not singled out to endure financial hardship for no reason is to hold that any restriction imposed on individual landmarks pursuant to the New York City scheme is a "taking" requiring the payment of "just compensation." Agreement with this argument would, of course, invalidate not just New York City's law, but all comparable landmark legislation in the Nation. We find no merit in it.

* * *

* * * It is, of course, true that the Landmarks Law has a more severe impact on some landowners than on others, but that in itself does not mean that the law effects a "taking." Legislation designed to promote the general welfare commonly burdens some more than others. The owners of the brickyard in *Hadacheck,* of the cedar trees in *Miller v. Schoene,* and of the gravel and sand mine in *Goldblatt v. Hempstead,* were uniquely burdened by the legislation sustained in those cases.[7]
* * *

In any event, appellants' repeated suggestions that they are solely burdened and unbenefited is factually inaccurate. This contention overlooks the fact that the New York City law applies to vast numbers of structures in the city in addition to the Terminal—all the structures contained in the 31 historic districts and over 400 individual landmarks, many of which are close to the Terminal. Unless we are to reject the judgment of the New York City Council that the preservation of landmarks benefits all New York citizens and all structures, both economically and by improving the quality of life in the city as a whole—which we are unwilling to do—we cannot conclude that the owners of the Terminal have in no sense been benefited by the Landmarks Law. Doubtless appellants believe they are more burdened than

---

7. Appellants attempt to distinguish these cases on the ground that, in each, government was prohibiting a "noxious" use of land and that in the present case, in contrast, appellants' proposed construction above the Terminal would be beneficial. We observe that the uses in issue in *Hadacheck, Miller,* and *Goldblatt* were perfectly lawful in themselves. They involved no "blameworthiness, . . . moral wrongdoing or conscious act of dangerous risk-taking which induce[d society] to shift the cost to a pa[rt]icular individual." Sax, Takings and the Police Power, 74 Yale L.J. 36, 50 (1964). These cases are better understood as resting not on any supposed "noxious" quality of the prohibited uses but rather on

the ground that the restrictions were reasonably related to the implementation of a policy—not unlike historic preservation—expected to produce a widespread public benefit and applicable to all similarly situated property.

Nor, correlatively, can it be asserted that the destruction or fundamental alteration of a historic landmark is not harmful. The suggestion that the beneficial quality of appellants' proposed construction is established by the fact that the construction would have been consistent with applicable zoning laws ignores the development in sensibilities and ideals reflected in landmark legislation like New York City's.

benefited by the law, but that must have been true, too, of the property owners in *Miller, Hadacheck, Euclid,* and *Goldblatt.*

Appellants' final broad-based attack would have us treat the law as an instance, like that in *United States v. Causby,* in which government, acting in an enterprise capacity, has appropriated part of their property for some strictly governmental purpose. Apart from the fact that *Causby* was a case of invasion of airspace that destroyed the use of the farm beneath and this New York City law has in nowise impaired the present use of the Terminal, the Landmarks Law neither exploits appellants' parcel for city purposes nor facilitates nor arises from any entrepreneurial operations of the city. The situation is not remotely like that in *Causby* where the airspace above the property was in the flight pattern for military aircraft. The Landmarks Law's effect is simply to prohibit appellants or anyone else from occupying portions of the airspace above the Terminal, while permitting appellants to use the remainder of the parcel in a gainful fashion.   * * *

Rejection of appellants' broad arguments is not, however, the end of our inquiry, for all we thus far have established is that the New York City law is not rendered invalid by its failure to provide "just compensation" whenever a landmark owner is restricted in the exploitation of property interests, such as air rights, to a greater extent than provided for under applicable zoning laws. We now must consider whether the interference with appellants' property is of such a magnitude that "there must be an exercise of eminent domain and compensation to sustain [it]." *Pennsylvania Coal Co. v. Mahon,* 260 U.S., at 413, 43 S.Ct., at 159. That inquiry may be narrowed to the question of the severity of the impact of the law on appellants' parcel, and its resolution in turn requires a careful assessment of the impact of the regulation on the Terminal site.

Unlike the governmental acts in *Goldblatt, Miller, Causby, Griggs,* and *Hadacheck,* the New York City law does not interfere in any way with the present uses of the Terminal. Its designation as a landmark not only permits but contemplates that appellants may continue to use the property precisely as it has been used for the past 65 years: as a railroad terminal containing office space and concessions. So the law does not interfere with what must be regarded as Penn Central's primary expectation concerning the use of the parcel. More importantly, on this record, we must regard the New York City law as permitting Penn Central not only to profit from the Terminal but also to obtain a "reasonable return" on its investment.

* * *

On this record, we conclude that the application of New York City's Landmarks Law has not effected a "taking" of appellants' property. The restrictions imposed are substantially related to the promotion of the general welfare and not only permit reasonable beneficial use of the landmark site but also afford appellants opportunities further to enhance not only the Terminal site proper but also other properties.

Affirmed.

MR. JUSTICE REHNQUIST, with whom THE CHIEF JUSTICE and MR. JUSTICE STEVENS join, dissenting.

                              * * *

Only in the most superficial sense of the word can this case be said to involve "zoning." Typical zoning restrictions may, it is true, so limit the prospective uses of a piece of property as to diminish the value of that property in the abstract because it may not be used for the forbidden purposes. But any such abstract decrease in value will more than likely be at least partially offset by an increase in value which flows from similar restrictions as to use on neighboring properties. All property owners in a designated area are placed under the same restrictions, not only for the benefit of the municipality as a whole but also for the common benefit of one another. In the words of Mr. Justice Holmes, speaking for the Court in *Pennsylvania Coal Co. v. Mahon,* 260 U.S. 393, 415, 43 S.Ct. 158, 160, 67 L.Ed. 322 (1922), there is "an average reciprocity of advantage."

Where a relatively few individual buildings, all separated from one another, are singled out and treated differently from surrounding buildings, no such reciprocity exists. The cost to the property owner which results from the imposition of restrictions applicable only to his property and not that of his neighbors may be substantial—in this case, several million dollars—with no comparable reciprocal benefits. * * *

    * * * In a very literal sense, the actions of appellees violated this constitutional prohibition. Before the city of New York declared Grand Central Terminal to be a landmark, Penn Central could have used its "air rights" over the Terminal to build a multistory office building, at an apparent value of several million dollars per year. Today, the Terminal cannot be modified in *any* form, including the erection of additional stories, without the permission of the Landmark Preservation Commission, a permission which appellants, despite good-faith attempts, have so far been unable to obtain. Because the Taking Clause of the Fifth Amendment has not always been read literally, however, the constitutionality of appellees' actions requires a closer scrutiny of this Court's interpretation of the three key words in the Taking Clause—"property," "taken," and "just compensation."

                               A

Appellees do not dispute that valuable property rights have been destroyed. * * *

While neighboring landowners are free to use their land and "air rights" in any way consistent with the broad boundaries of New York zoning, Penn Central, absent the permission of appellees, must forever maintain its property in its present state. The property has been thus subjected to a nonconsensual servitude not borne by any neighboring or similar properties.[8]

B

Appellees have thus destroyed—in a literal sense, "taken"—substantial property rights of Penn Central. While the term "taken" might have been narrowly interpreted to include only physical seizures of property rights, "the construction of the phrase has not been so narrow." * * * [A]n examination of the two exceptions where the destruction of property does *not* constitute a taking demonstrates that a compensable taking has occurred here.

1

As early as 1887, the Court recognized that the government can prevent a property owner from using his property to injure others without having to compensate the owner for the value of the forbidden use. * * *

Thus, there is no "taking" where a city prohibits the operation of a brickyard within a residential area, see *Hadacheck v. Sebastian,* 239 U.S. 394, 36 S.Ct. 143, 60 L.Ed. 348 (1915), or forbids excavation for sand and gravel below the water line, see *Goldblatt v. Hempstead,* 369 U.S. 590, 82 S.Ct. 987, 8 L.Ed.2d 130 (1962). Nor is it relevant, where the government is merely prohibiting a noxious use of property, that the government would seem to be singling out a particular property owner. *Hadacheck, supra,* at 413, 36 S.Ct., at 146.[9]

The nuisance exception to the taking guarantee is not coterminous with the police power itself. The question is whether the forbidden use is dangerous to the safety, health, or welfare of others. * * *

Appellees are not prohibiting a nuisance. The record is clear that the proposed addition to the Grand Central Terminal would be in full compliance with zoning, height limitations, and other health and safety requirements. Instead, appellees are seeking to preserve what they believe to be an outstanding example of beaux-arts architecture. Penn Central is prevented from further developing its property basically because *too good* a job was done in designing and building it. The city of New York, because of its unadorned admiration for the design, has decided that the owners of the building must preserve it unchanged for the benefit of sightseeing New Yorkers and tourists.

Unlike land-use regulations, appellees' actions do not merely *prohibit* Penn Central from using its property in a narrow set of noxious

---

8. It is, of course, irrelevant that appellees interfered with or destroyed property rights that Penn Central had not yet physically used. The Fifth Amendment must be applied with "reference to the uses for which the property is suitable, having regard to the existing business or wants of the community, *or such as may be reasonably expected in the immediate future.*" *Boom Co. v. Patterson,* 98 U.S. 403, 408, 25 L.Ed. 206 (1879) (emphasis added).

9. Each of the cases cited by the Court for the proposition that legislation which severely affects some landowners but not others does not effect a "taking" involved noxious uses of property. See *Hadacheck; Miller v. Schoene,* 276 U.S. 272, 48 S.Ct. 246, 72 L.Ed. 568 (1928); *Goldblatt.* See *ante,* at 2660–2661, 2664.

ways. Instead, appellees have placed an *affirmative* duty on Penn
Central to maintain the Terminal in its present state and in "good
repair." Appellants are not free to use their property as they see fit
within broad outer boundaries but must strictly adhere to their past
use except where appellees conclude that alternative uses would not
detract from the landmark. * * *

2

Even where the government prohibits a noninjurious use, the Court
has ruled that a taking does not take place if the prohibition applies
over a broad cross section of land and thereby "secure[s] an average
reciprocity of advantage." *Pennsylvania Coal Co. v. Mahon,* 260 U.S.,
at 415, 43 S.Ct., at 160. It is for this reason that zoning does not
constitute a "taking." While zoning at times reduces *individual* property values, the burden is shared relatively evenly and it is reasonable
to conclude that on the whole an individual who is harmed by one
aspect of the zoning will be benefited by another.

Here, however, a multimillion dollar loss has been imposed on
appellants; it is uniquely felt and is not offset by any benefits flowing
from the preservation of some 400 other "landmarks" in New York
City. Appellees have imposed a substantial cost on less than one one-
tenth of one percent of the buildings in New York City for the general
benefit of all its people. It is exactly this imposition of general costs on
a few individuals at which the "taking" protection is directed. The
Fifth Amendment

> "prevents the public from loading upon one individual more than his
> just share of the burdens of government, and says that when he
> surrenders to the public something more and different from that which
> is exacted from other members of the public, a full and just equivalent
> shall be returned to him." *Monongahela Navigation Co. v. United
> States,* 148 U.S. 312, 325, 13 S.Ct. 622, 626, 37 L.Ed. 463 (1893).

* * *

As Mr. Justice Holmes pointed out in *Pennsylvania Coal Co. v.
Mahon,* "the question at bottom" in an eminent domain case "is upon
whom the loss of the changes desired should fall." 260 U.S., at 416, 43
S.Ct., at 160. The benefits that appellees believe will flow from
preservation of the Grand Central Terminal will accrue to all the
citizens of New York City. There is no reason to believe that appellants will enjoy a substantially greater share of these benefits. If the
cost of preserving Grand Central Terminal were spread evenly across
the entire population of the city of New York, the burden per person
would be in cents per year—a minor cost appellees would surely
concede for the benefit accrued. Instead, however, appellees would
impose the entire cost of several million dollars per year on Penn
Central. But it is precisely this sort of discrimination that the Fifth
Amendment prohibits.

Appellees in response would argue that a taking only occurs where
a property owner is denied *all* reasonable value of his property. The

Court has frequently held that, even where a destruction of property rights would not *otherwise* constitute a taking, the inability of the owner to make a reasonable return on his property requires compensation under the Fifth Amendment. See, *e.g., United States v. Lynah,* 188 U.S., at 470, 23 S.Ct., at 357. But the converse is not true. A taking does not become a noncompensable exercise of police power simply because the government in its grace allows the owner to make some "reasonable" use of his property. "[I]t is the character of the invasion, not the amount of damage resulting from it, so long as the damage is substantial, that determines the question whether it is a taking."

* * *

Over 50 years ago, Mr. Justice Holmes, speaking for the Court, warned that the courts were "in danger of forgetting that a strong public desire to improve the public condition is not enough to warrant achieving the desire by a shorter cut than the constitutional way of paying for the change." *Pennsylvania Coal Co. v. Mahon,* 260 U.S., at 416, 43 S.Ct., at 160. The Court's opinion in this case demonstrates that the danger thus foreseen has not abated. The city of New York is in a precarious financial state, and some may believe that the costs of landmark preservation will be more easily borne by corporations such as Penn Central than the overburdened individual taxpayers of New York. But these concerns do not allow us to ignore past precedents construing the Eminent Domain Clause to the end that the desire to improve the public condition is, indeed, achieved by a shorter cut than the constitutional way of paying for the change.

Notes and Questions

1. Who better understood Holmes' tests—the majority or the dissenters in *Penn Central?* Would Penn Central have been victorious if Holmes had been on the bench for this case? Does it matter? Should takings analysis change over time as the public view of the appropriate role of government and the nature of private property rights changes? Or should takings analysis be the firewall between the vagaries of public opinion and the security of private property?

2. *Penn Central* added another test—the "reasonable investment backed expectation." What does this add? Does it simply expand protection for wealth? Is this the same as protecting property?

NOLLAN v. CALIFORNIA COASTAL COMMISSION

Supreme Court of the United States, 1987.
483 U.S. 825, 107 S.Ct. 3141, 97 L.Ed.2d 677.

JUSTICE SCALIA delivered the opinion of the Court.

The Nollans own a beachfront lot in Ventura County, California. A quarter-mile north of their property is Faria County Park, an oceanside public park with a public beach and recreation area. Another public beach area, known locally as "the Cove," lies 1,800 feet south of their lot. A concrete seawall approximately eight feet high separates the beach portion of the Nollans' property from the rest of the lot. The historic mean high tide line determines the lot's oceanside boundary.

The Nollans originally leased their property with an option to buy. The building on the lot was a small bungalow, totaling 504 square feet, which for a time they rented to summer vacationers. After years of rental use, however, the building had fallen into disrepair, and could no longer be rented out.

The Nollans' option to purchase was conditioned on their promise to demolish the bungalow and replace it. In order to do so, under California Public Resources Code §§ 30106, 30212, and 30600 (West 1986), they were required to obtain a coastal development permit from the California Coastal Commission. On February 25, 1982, they submitted a permit application to the Commission in which they proposed to demolish the existing structure and replace it with a three-bedroom house in keeping with the rest of the neighborhood.

The Nollans were informed that their application had been placed on the administrative calendar, and that the Commission staff had recommended that the permit be granted subject to the condition that they allow the public an easement to pass across a portion of their property bounded by the mean high tide line on one side, and their seawall on the other side. This would make it easier for the public to get to Faria County Park and the Cove. The Nollans protested imposition of the condition, but the Commission overruled their objections and granted the permit subject to their recordation of a deed restriction granting the easement.

On June 3, 1982, the Nollans filed a petition for writ of administrative mandamus asking the Ventura County Superior Court to invalidate the access condition. They argued that the condition could not be imposed absent evidence that their proposed development would have a direct adverse impact on public access to the beach. The court agreed, and remanded the case to the Commission for a full evidentiary hearing on that issue.

On remand, the Commission held a public hearing, after which it made further factual findings and reaffirmed its imposition of the condition. It found that the new house would increase blockage of the view of the ocean, thus contributing to the development of "a 'wall' of residential structures" that would prevent the public "psychologically ... from realizing a stretch of coastline exists nearby that they have every right to visit." The new house would also increase private use of the shorefront. These effects of construction of the house, along with other area development, would cumulatively "burden the public's ability to traverse to and along the shorefront." Therefore the Commission could properly require the Nollans to offset that burden by providing additional lateral access to the public beaches in the form of an easement across their property. The Commission also noted that it had similarly conditioned 43 out of 60 coastal development permits along the same tract of land, and that of the 17 not so conditioned, 14 had been approved when the Commission did not have administrative regulations in place allowing imposition of the condition, and the remaining 3 had not involved shorefront property.

* * *

Had California simply required the Nollans to make an easement across their beachfront available to the public on a permanent basis in order to increase public access to the beach, rather than conditioning their permit to rebuild their house on their agreeing to do so, we have no doubt there would have been a taking. To say that the appropriation of a public easement across a landowner's premises does not constitute the taking of a property interest but rather, "a mere restriction on its use," is to use words in a manner that deprives them of all their ordinary meaning.

* * * We have repeatedly held that, as to property reserved by its owner for private use, "the right to exclude [others is] 'one of the most essential sticks in the bundle of rights that are commonly characterized as property.' "

* * * We think a "permanent physical occupation" has occurred, for purposes of that rule, where individuals are given a permanent and continuous right to pass to and fro, so that the real property may continuously be traversed, even though no particular individual is permitted to station himself permanently upon the premises.

* * *

Given, then, that requiring uncompensated conveyance of the easement outright would violate the Fourteenth Amendment, the question becomes whether requiring it to be conveyed as a condition for issuing a land use permit alters the outcome. We have long recognized that land use regulation does not effect a taking if it "substantially advance[s] legitimate state interests" and does not "den[y] an owner economically viable use of his land." [ ] Our cases have not elaborated on the standards for determining what constitutes a "legitimate state interest" or what type of connection between the regulation and the state interest satisfies the requirement that the former "substantially advance" the latter. They have made clear, however, that a broad range of governmental purposes and regulations satisfies these requirements. The Commission argues that among these permissible purposes are protecting the public's ability to see the beach, assisting the public in overcoming the "psychological barrier" to using the beach created by a developed shorefront, and preventing congestion on the public beaches. We assume, without deciding, that this is so—in which case the Commission unquestionably would be able to deny the Nollans their permit outright if their new house (alone, or by reason of the cumulative impact produced in conjunction with other construction) would substantially impede these purposes, unless the denial would interfere so drastically with the Nollans' use of their property as to constitute a taking.

The Commission argues that a permit condition that serves the same legitimate police-power purpose as a refusal to issue the permit should not be found to be a taking if the refusal to issue the permit would not constitute a taking. We agree. Thus, if the Commission attached to the permit some condition that would have protected the public's ability to see the beach notwithstanding construction of the new house—for example, a height limitation, a width restriction, or a ban on fences—so long as the Commission could have exercised its police power (as we have assumed it could) to forbid construction of the house altogether, imposition of the condition would also be constitutional. Moreover (and here we come closer to the facts of the present case), the condition would be constitutional even if it consisted of the requirement that the Nollans provide a viewing spot on their property for passersby with whose sighting of the ocean their new house would interfere. Although such a requirement, constituting a permanent grant of continuous access to the property, would have to be considered a taking if it were not attached to a development permit, the Commission's assumed power to forbid construction of the house in order to protect the public's view of the beach must surely include the power to condition construction upon some concession by the owner, even a concession of property rights, that serves the same end. If a prohibition designed to accomplish that purpose would be a legitimate exercise of the police power rather than a taking, it would be strange to conclude that providing the owner an alternative to that prohibition which accomplishes the same purpose is not.

The evident constitutional propriety disappears, however, if the condition substituted for the prohibition utterly fails to further the end advanced as the justification for the prohibition. When that essential nexus is eliminated, the situation becomes the same as if California law forbade shouting fire in a crowded theater, but granted dispensations to those willing to contribute $100 to the state treasury. While a ban on shouting fire can be a core exercise of the State's police power to protect the public safety, and can thus meet even our stringent standards for regulation of speech, adding the unrelated condition alters the purpose to one which, while it may be legitimate, is inadequate to sustain the ban. Therefore, even though, in a sense, requiring a $100 tax contribution in order to shout fire is a lesser restriction on speech than an outright ban, it would not pass constitutional muster. Similarly here, the lack of nexus between the condition and the original purpose of the building restriction converts that purpose to something other than what it was. The purpose then becomes, quite simply, the obtaining of an easement to serve some valid governmental purpose, but without payment of compensation. Whatever may be the outer limits of "legitimate state interests" in the takings and land use context, this is not one of them. In short, unless the permit condition serves the same governmental purpose as the development ban, the building restriction is not a valid regulation of land use but "an out-and-out plan of extortion." [   ]

* * *

* * * The Commission may well be right that [access to the beach] is a good idea, but that does not establish that the Nollans (and other coastal residents) alone can be compelled to contribute to its realization. Rather, California is free to advance its "comprehensive program," if it wishes, by using its power of eminent domain for this "public purpose;" but if it wants an easement across the Nollans' property, it must pay for it.

Reversed.

Justice BRENNAN, with whom Justice MARSHALL joins, dissenting.

There can be no dispute that the police power of the States encompasses the authority to impose conditions on private development. It is also by now commonplace that this Court's review of the rationality of a State's exercise of its police power demands only that the State "could rationally have decided" that the measure adopted might achieve the State's objective. In this case, California has employed its police power in order to condition development upon preservation of public access to the ocean and tidelands. The Coastal Commission, if it had so chosen, could have denied the Nollans' request for a development permit, since the property would have remained economically viable without the requested new development. Instead, the State sought to accommodate the Nollans' desire for new development, on the condition that the development not diminish the overall amount of public access to the coastline.

* * *

The Court's demand for this precise fit is based on the assumption that private landowners in this case possess a reasonable expectation regarding the use of their land that the public has attempted to disrupt. In fact, the situation is precisely the reverse: it is private landowners who are the interlopers. The public's expectation of access considerably antedates any private development on the coast. Article X, Section 4 of the California Constitution, adopted in 1879, declares:

> "No individual, partnership, or corporation, claiming or possessing the frontage or tidal lands of a harbor, bay, inlet, estuary, or other navigable water in this State, shall be permitted to exclude the right of way to any such water whenever it is required for any public purpose, nor to destroy or obstruct the free navigation of such water; and the Legislature shall enact such laws as will give the most liberal construction to this provision, so that access to the navigable waters of this State shall always be attainable for the people thereof."

It is therefore private landowners who threaten the disruption of settled public expectations. Where a private landowner has had a reasonable expectation that his or her property will be used for exclusively private purposes, the disruption of this expectation dictates that the government pay if it wishes the property to be used for a public purpose. In this case, however, the State has sought to protect *public* expectations of access from disruption by private land use. The State's exercise of its police power for this purpose deserves no less deference than any other measure designed to further the welfare of state citizens.

Even if we accept the Court's unusual demand for a precise match between the condition imposed and the specific type of burden on access created by the appellants, the State's action easily satisfies this requirement. First, the lateral access condition serves to dissipate the impression that the beach that lies behind the wall of homes along the shore is for private use only. It requires no exceptional imaginative powers to find plausible the Commission's point that the average person passing along the road in front of a phalanx of imposing permanent residences, including the appellants' new home, is likely to conclude that this particular portion of the shore is not open to the public. If, however, that person can see that numerous people are passing and repassing along the dry sand, this conveys the message that the beach is in fact open for use by the public. Furthermore, those persons who go down to the public beach a quarter-mile away will be able to look down the coastline and see that persons have continuous access to the tidelands, and will observe signs that proclaim the public's right of access over the dry sand. The burden produced by the diminution in visual access—the impression that the beach is not open to the public—is thus directly alleviated by the provision for public access over the dry sand. The Court therefore has an unrealistically limited conception of what measures could reasonably be chosen to mitigate the burden produced by a diminution of visual access.

The second flaw in the Court's analysis of the fit between burden and exaction is more fundamental. The Court assumes that the only burden with which the Coastal Commission was concerned was blockage of visual access to the beach. This is incorrect. The Commission specifically stated in its report in support of the permit condition that "[t]he Commission finds that the applicants' proposed development would present an increase in view blockage, *an increase in private use of the shorefront,* and that this impact would burden the public's ability to traverse to and along the shorefront." It declared that the possibility that "the public may get the impression that the beachfront is no longer available for public use" would be "due to *the encroaching nature of private use immediately adjacent to the public use, as well as* the visual 'block' of increased residential build-out impacting the visual quality of the beachfront."

* * *

The fact that the Commission's action is a legitimate exercise of the police power does not, of course, insulate it from a takings challenge, for when "regulation goes too far it will be recognized as a taking." *Pennsylvania Coal Co. v. Mahon,* 260 U.S. 393, 415, 43 S.Ct. 158, 160, 67

L.Ed. 322 (1922). Conventional takings analysis underscores the implausibility of the Court's holding, for it demonstrates that this exercise of California's police power implicates none of the concerns that underlie our takings jurisprudence.

In reviewing a Takings Clause claim, we have regarded as particularly significant the nature of the governmental action and the economic impact of regulation, especially the extent to which regulation interferes with investment-backed expectations. *Penn Central,* 438 U.S., at 124, 98 S.Ct., at 2659. The character of the government action in this case is the imposition of a condition on permit approval, which allows the public to continue to have access to the coast. The physical intrusion permitted by the deed restriction is minimal. The public is permitted the right to pass and re-pass along the coast in an area from the seawall to the mean high tide mark. This area is at its *widest* 10 feet, which means that *even without the permit condition,* the public's right of access permits it to pass on average within a few feet of the seawall.

* * *

Examination of the economic impact of the Commission's action reinforces the conclusion that no taking has occurred. Allowing appellants to intensify development along the coast in exchange for ensuring public access to the ocean is a classic instance of government action that produces a "reciprocity of advantage." *Pennsylvania Coal, supra,* 260 U.S., at 415, 43 S.Ct., at 160. Appellants have been allowed to replace a one-story 521–square–foot beach home with a two-story 1,674–square–foot residence and an attached two-car garage, resulting in development covering 2,464 square feet of the lot. Such development obviously significantly increases the value of appellants' property; appellants make no contention that this increase is offset by any diminution in value resulting from the deed restriction, much less that the restriction made the property less valuable than it would have been without the new construction. Furthermore, appellants gain an additional benefit from the Commission's permit condition program. They are able to walk along the beach beyond the confines of their own property only because the Commission has required deed restrictions as a condition of approving other new beach developments. Thus, appellants benefit both as private landowners and as members of the public from the fact that new development permit requests are conditioned on preservation of public access.

Ultimately, appellants' claim of economic injury is flawed because it rests on the assumption of entitlement to the full value of their new development. Appellants submitted a proposal for more intensive development of the coast, which the Commission was under no obligation to approve, and now argue that a regulation designed to ameliorate the impact of that development deprives them of the full value of their improvements. Even if this novel claim were somehow cognizable, it is not significant. "[T]he interest in anticipated gains has traditionally been viewed as less compelling than other property-related interests." *Andrus v. Allard,* 444 U.S. 51, 66, 100 S.Ct. 318, 327, 62 L.Ed.2d 210 (1979).

With respect to appellants' investment-backed expectations, appellants can make no reasonable claim to any expectation of being able to exclude members of the public from crossing the edge of their property to gain access to the ocean. It is axiomatic, of course, that state law is the source of those strands that constitute a property owner's bundle of property rights. "[A]s a general proposition[,] the law of real property is, under our Constitution, left to the individual States to develop and administer."

* * *

The foregoing analysis makes clear that the State has taken no property from appellants. Imposition of the permit condition in this case represents the State's reasonable exercise of its police power. The Coastal Commission has drawn on its expertise to preserve the balance between private development and public access, by requiring that any project that intensifies development on the increasingly crowded California coast must be offset by gains in public access. Under the normal standard for review of the police power, this provision is eminently reasonable. Even accepting the Court's novel insistence on a precise *quid pro quo* of burdens and benefits, there is a reasonable relationship between the public benefit and the burden created by appellants' development. The movement of development closer to the ocean creates the prospect of encroachment on public tidelands, because of fluctuation in the mean high tide line. The deed restriction ensures that disputes about the boundary between private and public property will not deter the public from exercising its right to have access to the sea.

Furthermore, consideration of the Commission's action under traditional takings analysis underscores the absence of any viable takings claim. The deed restriction permits the public only to pass and repass along a narrow strip of beach, a few feet closer to a seawall at the periphery of appellants' property. Appellants almost surely have enjoyed an increase in the value of their property even with the restriction, because they have been allowed to build a significantly larger new home with garage on their lot. Finally, appellants can claim the disruption of no expectation interest, both because they have no right to exclude the public under state law, and because, even if they did, they had full advance notice that new development along the coast is conditioned on provisions for continued public access to the ocean.

* * *

JUSTICE STEVENS, with whom JUSTICE BLACKMUN joins, dissenting.

The debate between the Court and JUSTICE BRENNAN illustrates an extremely important point concerning government regulation of the use of privately owned real estate. Intelligent, well-informed public officials may in good faith disagree about the validity of specific types of land use regulation. Even the wisest lawyers would have to acknowledge great uncertainty about the scope of this Court's takings jurisprudence.

* * *

Notes and Questions

1. Does the requirement of a public easement in *Nollan* represent a permanent physical invasion? Was the Nollans' proposed residence a nuisance? Does Justice Scalia hold that the public purpose requirement described in *Midkiff* is not met, or does he apply a form of Holmes' balancing test? Does he hold that California takes a segment of property, known as an easement? Or, do you conclude, along with dissenting Justice Stevens, that "even the wisest lawyers would have to acknowledge great uncertainty about the scope of this Court's taking jurisprudence"?

2. *Nollan* was one of the 1987 "trilogy" of Supreme Court takings cases. *Keystone,* described earlier, was another of this trio. The third, First English Evangelical Lutheran Church v. Los Angeles, 482 U.S. 304, 107 S.Ct. 2378, 96 L.Ed.2d 250 (1987), increased the risk to government of a wrong guess concerning the constitutionality of a land use statute or ordinance. In *First English,* the Court held that a property owner who is ultimately successful in arguing that the government action acted as a taking of property is entitled to compensation for recognized losses suffered for the "temporary taking" occurring during the period in which the law was in effect. Prior to *First English,* a court ruling that a taking existed allowed the government the choice of paying compensation or rescinding the offending act. *First English* would seem to require a more cautious approach on the part of government to land use control. One proposal suggests that "[I]t would be unfortunate if the only persons who benefit from [*First English*] are the lawyers and experts retained to argue the fine points of regulatory takings and compensation. The costs and uncertainties of the *First English* approach are so great that reason suggests that both land users and regulators seek an alternative * * *". Salsich, Keystone Bituminous Coal, First English and Nollan: A Framework for Accommodation?, 34 J. of Urb. and Contemp.L. 173 (1988). Salsich suggests that local government develop an "early-warning administrative review process" to alert regulators to problems and to encourage the affected parties to identify common interests and effect compromise through mediation or accommodation.

Salsich also argues that the 1987 trilogy effectively establishes a hierarchy of property interests that relates to the argument that property and personhood are closely intertwined, as has been argued by Radin in Property and Personhood, 34 Stan.L.Rev. 957 (1982). Salsich concludes:

> Those property interests in land that may be said to vindicate important personal rights, such as the right to privacy and the right to choose how to dispose of one's property, have received greater protection from the Court than have the interests associated with the accumulation of wealth through land development. Substantial impairment of a property interest that protects personal liberties, such as

the power to exclude others, may constitute a taking, even though the impairment occurs to only part of the property parcel. Substantial diminution in value that affects the profit potential of the property however, is not likely to be classified as a taking unless the regulation also impairs the use that can be made of the parcel as a whole.

Increased public concern with environmental and natural resource issues is likely to sharpen the distinction between property interests that protect personal liberties and property interests that permit the accumulation of wealth. The next question may be whether the pursuit of profit through land development should be recognized as a personal liberty entitled to the constitutional protection of property. Salsich, Life After the Takings Trilogy—A Hierarchy of Property Interests? 19 Stetson L.Rev. 795, 811 (1990).

Is a wetlands protection statute that prohibits a property owner from changing the character of an identified wetlands area a question of property serving personal liberties or property serving the accumulation of wealth?

For further views on the "temporary taking" issue, see Williams, Smith, Siemon, Mandelker & Babcock, The White Junction Manifesto, 9 Vt.L.Rev. 193 (1984).

3. Of the thousands of pages of commentary on the question of takings, there is one article that always emerges from the pack. Frank Michelman's article "Property, Utility, and Fairness: Comments on the Ethical Foundations of 'Just Compensation' Law," 80 Harv.L.Rev. 1165 (1967) is one of the most frequently cited law review articles in history and is clearly the most frequently cited by the courts in takings cases. In this article, Michelman argues that the constitutional requirements of just compensation are the "visible, formal expression of society's commitment to fairness as a constraint on its pursuit of efficiency." He examines the most common "takings rules" in terms of their service to fairness. Although Michelman recognizes that the "psychological shock" produced by "the stark spectacle of an alien, uninvited presence in one's territory" supports compensation for physical invasion, he criticizes the rule: "A physical invasion test * * * can never be more than a convenience for identifying *clearly compensable* occasions. It cannot justify dismissal of any occasion as *clearly non-compensable*." Even as a rule limited to identifying compensable events, the rule of compensation for physical invasion is arbitrary and unfair, Michelman argues, because "the relevant comparison is between large losses and small losses—not between those which are and are not accompanied by total evictions." What, then, would be Michelman's opinion of *Loretto?* Of *Nollan?* Michelman goes on to identify the limitations of each of the theories used by the courts to identify takings requiring compensation.

Michelman concludes that courts are simply inherently limited in their ability to meet a fairness standard in such cases and that reliance on the court as the source of fairness causes other, perhaps more productive, methods of deciding compensation to be ignored. Michelman specifically argues that settlement or negotiation of claims can reduce the "demoralization costs" experienced by property holders losing their property to the government and can compensate persons for real losses (such as tenants for relocation costs) not otherwise recognized as losing "property." Michelman places the responsibility on the legislature to identify, "cost out," and compensate for real losses, even if not required to do so by the Constitution. Should the California legislature have provided compensation to the Nollans? You might consider Michelman's argument on this point when you study the cases on just compensation in the next section.

4. If you are not persuaded by attempts to reconcile the Supreme Court cases on whether property has been taken, you are not alone. Commenting on these cases, Laura Underkuffler writes: "The * * * incoherence [in these cases] is profound. An easement, conceptually severed from the underlying land, is property and compensable if taken; twenty-seven million tons of coal are not. The right to occupy land, or to pass land to one's heirs, is property compensable if taken; the right to modify a building that one owns, or to prevent physical invasion, is not."

Underkuffler offers instead a "comprehensive approach to property," which "incorporates the historical tension between the individual and the collective," in contrast to the "absolute approach," which "advances a clear case for the supremacy of individual interests." According to Underkuffler, the reclamation of a collective approach would change takings jurisprudence:

> The Supreme Court's ostensible use of an absolute approach to property results in a kind of patent dishonesty; property is portrayed as a matter of technical understanding or definition, while the conception is artifically manipulated to reach a result that is compatible with social goals. * * * Explicit acknowledgement of the mediating function of property, and the involvement of the collective in determining the nature and scope of individual rights, makes explicit the real policy issues.

How would "explicit acknowledgement of the mediating function of property" change the result or analysis in *Loretto, Pennsylvania Coal,* and *Nollan?* (Underkuffler cites *Penn Central* as an exception to the rule, one in which the court did explicitly engage in balancing individual and collective interests.) Underkuffler, On Property, 100 Yale L.J. 127 (1990). For a different view of property, see Epstein, Takings: Private Property and Eminent Domain (1985).

4. How much of the confusion or lack of predictability in takings jurisprudence is due to changes in generally held views on the role of property and the role of government? For example, is a heightened environmental awareness relevant to cases challenging the constitutionality of environmental protection regulations? Should it be relevant? See Michelman, Takings 1987, 88 Colum.L.Rev. 1600 (1988).

C. JUST COMPENSATION

Whenever property is taken by the government, the Constitution requires that "just compensation" be paid for the property. In most cases the amount of compensation to be paid is resolved and settled between the government agency acquiring the property and the owner.

In cases where these parties fail to settle on a price, the amount is set by the court. State and federal statutes may establish compensation goals or requirements that exceed constitutional standards. Absent such statutes, however, the Constitution establishes the minimum standards for payment.

ALMOTA FARMERS ELEVATOR & WAREHOUSE CO. v. UNITED STATES

Supreme Court of the United States, 1973.
409 U.S. 470, 93 S.Ct. 791, 35 L.Ed.2d 1.

MR. JUSTICE STEWART delivered the opinion of the Court.

Since 1919 the petitioner, Almota Farmers Elevator & Warehouse Co., has conducted grain elevator operations on land adjacent to the tracks of the Oregon–Washington Railroad & Navigation Co. in the State of Washington. It has occupied the land under a series of successive leases from the railroad. In 1967, the Government instituted this eminent domain proceeding to acquire the petitioner's property interest by condemnation. At that time there were extensive buildings and other improvements that had been erected on the land by the petitioner, and the then-current lease had 7½ years to run.

In the District Court the Government contended that just compensation for the leasehold interest, including the structures, should be "the fair market value of the legal rights possessed by the defendant by virtue of the lease as of the date of taking," and that no consideration should be given to any additional value based on the expectation that the lease might be renewed. The petitioner urged that, rather than this technical "legal rights theory," just compensation should be measured by what a willing buyer would pay in an open market for the petitioner's leasehold.

As a practical matter, the controversy centered upon the valuation to be placed upon the structures and their appurtenances. The parties stipulated that the Government had no need for these improvements and that the petitioner had a right to remove them. But that stipulation afforded the petitioner only what scant salvage value the buildings might bring. The Government offered compensation for the loss of the use and occupancy of the buildings only over the remaining term of the lease. The petitioner contended that this limitation upon compensation for the use of the structures would fail to award what a willing buyer would have paid for the lease with the improvements, since such a buyer would expect to have the lease renewed and to continue to use the improvements in place. The value of the buildings, machinery, and equipment in place would be substantially greater than their salvage value at the end of the lease term, and a purchaser in an open market would pay for the anticipated use of the buildings and for the savings he would realize from not having to construct new improvements himself. In sum, the dispute concerned whether Almota would have to be satisfied with its right to remove the structures with their consequent salvage value or whether it was entitled to an award reflecting the value of the improvements in place beyond the lease term.

In a pretrial ruling, the District Court accepted the petitioner's theory and held that Almota was to be compensated for the full market value of its leasehold "and building improvements thereon as of the date of taking * * *, the total value of said leasehold and improvements * * * to be what the interests of said company therein could have been then sold for upon the open market considering all elements and possibilities whatsoever found to then affect the market value of those interests including, but not exclusive of, the possibilities of renewal of the lease and of the landlord requiring the removal of the improvements in the event of there being no lease renewal." The court accordingly ruled that the petitioner was entitled to the full fair market value of the use of the land and of the buildings in place as they stood at the time of the taking, without limitation of such use to the remainder of the term of the existing lease.

On appeal, the Court of Appeals for the Ninth Circuit reversed, 450 F.2d 125; it accepted the Government's theory that a tenant's expectancy in a lease renewal was not a compensable legal interest and could not be included in the valuation of structures that the tenant had built on the property. It rejected any award for the use of improvements beyond the lease term as "compensation for expectations disappointed by the exercise of the sovereign power of eminent domain, expectations not based upon any legally protected right, but based only * * * upon 'a speculation on a chance.'" [   ]

In view of [a] conflict in the circuits, we granted certiorari, to decide an important question of eminent domain law: "Whether, upon condemnation of a leasehold, a lessee with no right of renewal is entitled to receive as compensation the market value of its improvements without regard to the remaining term of its lease, because of the expectancy that the lease would have been renewed." We * * * reverse the judgment before us and reinstate the judgment of the District Court.

The Fifth Amendment provides that private property shall not be taken for public use without "just compensation." "And 'just compensation' means the full monetary equivalent of the property taken. The owner is to be put in the same position monetarily as he would have occupied if his property had not been taken." [   ] To determine such monetary equivalence, the Court early established the concept of "market value": the owner is entitled to the fair market value of his property at the time of the taking. [   ] And this value is normally to be ascertained from "what a willing buyer would pay in cash to a willing seller." [   ]

By failing to value the improvements in place over their useful life—taking into account the possibility that the lease might be renewed as well as the possibility that it might not—the Court of Appeals in this case failed to recognize what a willing buyer would have paid for the improvements. If there had been no condemnation, Almota would have continued to use the improvements during a renewed lease term, or if it sold the improvements to the fee owner or to a new lessee at the end of the lease term, it would have been compensated for the buyer's ability to use the improvements in place over their useful life. As Judge Friendly wrote for the Court of Appeals for the Second Circuit:

> "Lessors do desire, after all, to keep their properties leased, and an existing tenant usually has the inside track to a renewal for all kinds of reasons—avoidance of costly alterations, saving of brokerage commissions, perhaps even ordinary decency on the part of landlords. Thus, even when the lease has expired, the condemnation will often force the tenant to remove or abandon the fixtures long before he would otherwise have had to, as well as deprive him of the opportunity to deal with the landlord or a new tenant—the only two people for whom the fixtures would have a value unaffected by the heavy costs of disassembly and reassembly. The condemnor is not entitled to the benefit of assumptions, contrary to common experience, that the fixtures would be removed at the expiration of the stated term." *United States v. Certain Property, Borough of Manhattan*, 388 F.2d, at 601–602 (footnote omitted).

It seems particularly likely in this case that Almota could have sold the leasehold at a price that would have reflected the continued ability of the buyer to use the improvements over their useful life. Almota had an unbroken succession of leases since 1919, and it was in the interest of the railroad, as fee owner, to continue leasing the property, with its grain elevator facilities, in order to promote grain shipments over its lines. In a free market, Almota would hardly have sold the leasehold to a purchaser who paid only for the use of the facilities over the remainder of the lease term, with Almota retaining the right thereafter to remove the facilities—in effect, the right of salvage. "Because these fixtures diminish in value upon removal, a measure of damages less than their fair market value for use in place would constitute a substantial taking without just compensation. '[I]t is intolerable that the state, after condemning a factory or warehouse, should surrender to the owner a stock of secondhand machinery and in so doing discharge the full measure of its duty.'" *United States v. 1,132.50 Acres of Land*, 441 F.2d 356, 358 (1971).[10]

---

10. The compensation to which Almota is entitled is hardly "totally set free from [its] property interest," as the dissent suggests. The improvements are assuredly "private property" that the Government has "taken" and for which it acknowledges it must pay compensation. The only dispute in this case is over how those improvements are to be valued, not over whether Almota is to receive additional compensation for business losses. Almota may well be unable to operate a grain elevator business elsewhere; it may well lose the profits and other values of a going business, but it seeks compensation for none of that. *Mitchell v. United States*, 267 U.S. 341, 45 S.Ct. 293, 69 L.Ed. 644 (1925), did hold that the Government was not obliged to pay for business losses caused by condemnation. But it assuredly did not hold that the Government could fail to provide fair compensation for business improvements that are taken—dismiss them as worth no more than scrap value—simply because it did not intend to use them. Indeed, in *Mitchell* the Government paid compensation both for the land, including its "adaptability for use in a par-

United States v. Petty Motor Co., 327 U.S. 372, 66 S.Ct. 596, 90 L.Ed. 729 (1946), upon which the Government primarily relies, does not lead to a contrary result. The Court did indicate that the measure of damages for the condemnation of a leasehold is to be measured in terms of the value of its use and occupancy for the remainder of the lease term, and the Court refused to elevate an expectation of renewal into a compensable legal interest. But the Court was not dealing there with the fair market value of improvements. Unlike *Petty Motor,* there is no question here of creating a legally cognizable value where none existed, or of compensating a mere incorporeal expectation.[11] The petitioner here has constructed the improvements and seeks only their fair market value. *Petty Motor* should not be read to allow the Government to escape paying what a willing buyer would pay for the same property.

The Government argues that it would be unreasonable to compensate Almota for the value of the improvements measured over their useful life, since the Government could purchase the fee and wait until the expiration of the lease term to take possession of the land. Once it has purchased the fee, the argument goes, there is no further expectancy that the improvements will be used during their useful life since the Government will assuredly require their removal at the end of the term. But the taking for the dam was one act requiring proceedings against owners of two interests.[12] At the time of that "taking" Almota had an expectancy of continued occupancy of its grain elevator facilities. The Government must pay just compensation for those interests "probably within the scope of the project from the time the Government was committed to it." [ ] It may not take advantage of any depreciation in the property taken that is attributable to the project itself. [ ] At the time of the taking in this case, there was an expectancy that the improvements would be used beyond the lease term. But the Government has sought to pay compensation on the theory that at that time there was no possibility that the lease would be renewed and the improvements used beyond the lease term. It has asked that the improvements be valued as though there were no

ticular business," and for the improvements thereon.

11. Hence, this is not a case where the petitioner is seeking compensation for lost opportunities, see *United States ex rel. TVA v. Powelson,* 319 U.S. 266, 281–282, 63 S.Ct. 1047, ——, ——, 87 L.Ed. 1390 (1943); *Omnia Commercial Co. v. United States,* 261 U.S. 502, 43 S.Ct. 437, 67 L.Ed. 773 (1923). The petitioner seeks only the fair value of the property taken by the Government. * * *

12. "It frequently happens in the case of a lease for a long term of years that the tenant erects buildings or puts fixtures into the buildings for his own use. Even if the buildings or fixtures are attached to the real estate and would pass with a conveyance of the land, as between landlord and tenant they remain personal property. In the absence of a special agreement to the contrary, such buildings or fixtures may be removed by the tenant at any time during the continuation of the lease, provided such removal may be made without injury to the freehold. This rule, however, exists entirely for the protection of the tenant, and cannot be invoked by the condemnor. If the buildings or fixtures are attached to the real estate, they must be treated as real estate in determining the total award. But in apportioning the award, they are treated as personal property and credited to the tenant." 4 P. Nichols, Eminent Domain § 13.121[2] (3d rev. ed. 1971) (footnotes omitted).

possibility of continued use. That is not how the market would have valued such improvements; it is not what a private buyer would have paid Almota.

"The constitutional requirement of just compensation derives as much content from the basic equitable principles of fairness, [ ] as it does from technical concepts of property law." [ ] It is, of course, true that Almota should be in no better position than if it had sold its leasehold to a private buyer. But its position should surely be no worse.

The judgment before us is reversed and the judgment of the District Court reinstated.

MR. JUSTICE REHNQUIST, with whom THE CHIEF JUSTICE, MR. JUSTICE WHITE, and MR. JUSTICE BLACKMUN join, dissenting.

Petitioner is entitled to compensation for so much of its private "property" as was taken for public use. The parties concede that petitioner's property interest here taken was the unexpired portion of a 20-year lease on land owned by the Oregon–Washington Railroad & Navigation Co. near Colfax, Washington. The Court recognizes the limited nature of petitioner's interest in the real property taken, but concludes that it was entitled to have its leasehold and improvements valued in such a way as to include the probability that petitioner's 20-year lease would have been renewed by the railroad at its expiration.

There is a plausibility about the Court's resounding endorsement of the concept of "fair market value" as the touchstone for valuation, but the result reached by the Court seems to me to be quite at odds with our prior cases. Even in its sharply limited reading of *United States v. Petty Motor Co.,* 327 U.S. 372, 66 S.Ct. 596, 90 L.Ed. 729 (1946), the Court concedes that the petitioner's expectation of having its lease renewed upon expiration is not itself an interest in property for which it may be compensated. But the Court permits the same practical result to be reached by saying that, at least in the case of improvements, the fair market value may be computed in terms of a willing buyer's expectation that the lease would be renewed.

In *United States v. Petty Motor Co., supra,* the Government acquired by condemnation the use of a structure occupied by tenants in possession under leases for various unexpired terms. The Court held that the measure of damages for condemnation of a leasehold is the value of the tenant's use of the leasehold for the remainder of the agreed term, less the agreed rent. The Court considered the argument, essentially the same raised by petitioner here, that a history of past renewal of the leases to existing tenants creates a compensable expectancy, but held that the right to compensation should be measured solely on the basis of the remainder of the tenant's term under the lease itself. * * *

The holding in *Petty* was consistent with a long line of cases to the effect that the Fifth Amendment does not require, on a taking of a property interest, compensation for mere expectancies of profit, or for the frustration of licenses or contractual rights that pertain to the land, but that are not specifically taken and that are not vested property interests. [   ]

While the inquiry as to what property interest is taken by the condemnor and the inquiry as to how that property interest shall be valued are not identical ones, they cannot be divorced without seriously undermining a number of rules dealing with the law of eminent domain that this Court has evolved in a series of decisions through the years. The landowner, after all, is interested, not in the legal terminology used to describe the property taken from him by the condemnor, but in the amount of money he is to be paid for that property. It will cause him little remorse to learn that his hope for a renewal of a lease for a term of years is not a property interest for which the Government must pay, if in the same breath he is told that the lesser legal interest that he owns may be valued to include the hoped-for renewal.

The notion of "fair market value" is not a universal formula for determining just compensation under the Fifth Amendment.   * * *

It is quite apparent that the property on which the owner operates a prosperous retail establishment would command more in an open market sale than the fair value of so much of the enterprise as was "private property" within the meaning of the Fifth Amendment. Yet *Mitchell v. United States,* 267 U.S. 341, 45 S.Ct. 293, 69 L.Ed. 644 (1925), stands squarely for the proposition that the value added to the property taken by the existence of a going business is no part of the just compensation for which the Government must pay for taking the property:

> "No recovery therefor can be had now as for a taking of the business. There is no finding as a fact that the Government took the business, or that what it did was intended as a taking. If the business was destroyed, the destruction was an unintended incident of the taking of land." *Id.,* at 345.

* * *

In either *Mitchell* or *Powelson,* [319 U.S. 266, 63 S.Ct. 1047, 87 L.Ed. 1390 (1943)] the result would in all probability have been different had the Court applied the reasoning that it applies in this case. Here, too, the improvements on the property are not desired by the Government for the project in question, but the taking of petitioner's leasehold interest prevents its continuing to have their use for the indefinite future as it had anticipated. The Court says that although its "property" interest would have expired in 7½ years, the market value of that interest may be computed on the basis of expectancies that do not rise to the level of a property interest under the Fifth Amendment.

If permissible methods of valuation are to be thus totally set free from the property interest that they purport to value, it is difficult to see why the same standards should not be applied to a going business.

Although the Government does not take the going business, and although the business is not itself a "property" interest within the Fifth Amendment, since purchasers on the open market would have paid an added increment of value for the property because a business was located on it, it may well be that such increment of value is properly included in a condemnation award under the Court's holding today. And it will assuredly make no difference to the property owner to learn that destruction of a going business is not compensable, if he be assured that the property concededly taken upon which the business was located may be valued in such a way as to include the amount a purchaser would have paid for the business.

* * *

UNITED STATES v. 50 ACRES OF LAND et al.

Supreme Court of the United States, 1984.
469 U.S. 24, 105 S.Ct. 451, 83 L.Ed.2d 376.

Justice Stevens delivered the [unanimous] opinion of the Court.

The Fifth Amendment requires that the United States pay "just compensation"—normally measured by fair market value—whenever it takes private property for public use. This case involves the condemnation of property owned by a municipality. The question is whether a public condemnee is entitled to compensation measured by the cost of acquiring a substitute facility if it has a duty to replace the condemned facility. We hold that this measure of compensation is not required when the market value of the condemned property is ascertainable.

I

In 1978, as part of a flood control project, the United States condemned approximately 50 acres of land owned by the city of Duncanville, Texas.[13] The site had been used since 1969 as a sanitary landfill. In order to replace the condemned landfill, the city acquired a 113.7–acre site and developed it into a larger and better facility. In the condemnation proceedings, the city claimed that it was entitled to recover all of the costs incurred in acquiring the substitute site and developing it as a landfill, an amount in excess of $1,276,000. The United States, however, contended that just compensation should be determined by the fair market value of the condemned facility and deposited $199,950 in the registry of the court as its estimation of the amount due.

---

13. The United States initiated the condemnation proceedings by filing a declaration of taking under 40 U.S.C. § 258a. Under that procedure the Government deposits the estimated value of the land in the registry of the court. "Title and right to possession thereupon vest immediately in the United States. In subsequent judicial proceedings, the exact value of the land (on the date the declaration of taking was filed) is determined, and the owner is awarded the difference (if any) between the adjudicated value of the land and the amount already received by the owner, plus interest on that difference." *Kirby Forest Industries, Inc. v. United States,* 467 U.S. 1, 5, 104 S.Ct. 2187, ___, 81 L.Ed.2d 1 (1984).

Responding to special interrogatories, the jury found that the fair market value of the condemned property was $225,000, and that the reasonable cost of a substitute facility was $723,624.01. The District Court entered judgment for the lower amount plus interest on the difference between that amount and the sum already paid. 529 F.Supp. 220 (N.D.Tex.1981). The District Court explained that the city had not met its "burden of establishing what would be a reasonable cost of a substitute facility." In addition, the court was of the view that "substitute facilities compensation should not be awarded in every case where a public condemnee can establish a duty to replace the condemned property, at least where a fair market value can be established." The court found no basis for departing from the market value standard in this case, and reasoned that the application of the substitute-facilities measure of compensation would necessarily provide the city with a "windfall."

The Court of Appeals reversed and remanded for further proceedings. 706 F.2d 1356 (5th Cir.1983). It reasoned that the city's loss attributable to the condemnation was "the amount of money reasonably spent * * * to create a functionally equivalent facility." If the city was required, either as a matter of law or as a matter of practical necessity, to replace the old landfill facility, the Court of Appeals believed that it would receive no windfall. The court, however, held that the amount of compensation should be adjusted to account for any qualitative differences in the substitute site. Finding that the trial judge's instructions had not adequately informed the jury of its duty to discount the costs of the substitute facility in order to account for its increased capacity and superior quality, the Court of Appeals remanded for a new trial. We granted the Government's petition for certiorari, and we now reverse with instructions to direct the District Court to enter judgment based on the jury's finding of fair market value.

II

The Court has repeatedly held that just compensation normally is to be measured by "the market value of the property at the time of the taking contemporaneously paid in money." *Olson v. United States*, 292 U.S. 246, 255, 54 S.Ct. 704, ___, 78 L.Ed. 1236 (1934). "Considerations that may not reasonably be held to affect market value are excluded." *Id.*, at 256. Deviation from this measure of just compensation has been required only "when market value has been too difficult to find, or when its application would result in manifest injustice to owner or public." *United States v. Commodities Trading Corp.*, 339 U.S. 121, 123, 70 S.Ct. 547, ___, 94 L.Ed. 707 (1950); *Kirby Forest Industries, Inc. v. United States*, 467 U.S. 1, 10 n. 14, 104 S.Ct. 2187, ___ n. 14, 81 L.Ed.2d 1 (1984).

This case is not one in which an exception to the normal measure of just compensation is required because fair market value is not ascertainable. Such cases, for the most part, involve properties that are seldom, if ever, sold in the open market. Under those circumstances, "we cannot predict whether the prices previously paid, assuming there have been prior sales, would be repeated in a sale of the condemned property." *Lutheran Synod,* 441 U.S. at 513, ___ S.Ct. at ___. In this case, however, the testimony at trial established a fairly robust market for sanitary landfill properties, and the jury's determination of the fair market value of the condemned landfill facility is adequately supported by expert testimony concerning the sale prices of comparable property.

The city contends that in this case an award of compensation measured by market value is fundamentally inconsistent with the basic principles of indemnity embodied in the Just Compensation Clause. If the city were a private party rather than a public entity, however, the possibility that the cost of a substitute facility exceeds the market value of the condemned parcel would not justify a departure from the market value measure. *Lutheran Synod,* 441 U.S. at 514–517, ___ S.Ct. at ___–___. The question—which we expressly reserved in the *Lutheran Synod* case—is whether a substitute-facilities measure of compensation is mandated by the Constitution [14] when the condemnee is a local governmental entity that has a duty to replace the condemned facility.

III

The text of the Fifth Amendment certainly does not mandate a more favorable rule of compensation for public condemnees than for private parties. To the contrary, the language of the Amendment only refers to compensation for "private property," and one might argue that the Framers intended to provide greater protection for the interests of private parties than for public condemnees. That argument would be supported by the observation that many public condemnees have the power of eminent domain, and thus, unlike private parties, need not rely on the availability of property on the market in acquiring substitute facilities.

When the United States condemns a local public facility, the loss to the public entity, to the persons served by it, and to the local taxpayers may be no less acute than the loss in a taking of private property. Therefore, it is most reasonable to construe the reference to "private property" in the Takings Clause of the Fifth Amendment as encompassing the property of state and local governments when it is condemned by the United States. Under this construction, the same principles of just compensation presumptively apply to both private and public condemnees.

* * *

14. Congress, of course, has the power to authorize compensation greater than the constitutional minimum. See *United States v. General Motors Corp.,* 323 U.S. 373, 382, 65 S.Ct. 357, ___, 89 L.Ed. 311 (1945); see, *e.g.,* Uniform Relocation Assistance and Real Property Acquisition Policies Act of 1970, 84 Stat. 1894, 42 U.S.C. § 4601 *et seq.* (requiring the payment of relocation assistance to specified persons and businesses displaced as a result of federal and federally assisted programs).

V

In this case, as in most, the market measure of compensation achieves a fair "balance between the public's need and the claimant's loss." *United States v. Toronto, Hamilton & Buffalo Navigation Co.,* 338 U.S. 396, 402, 70 S.Ct. 217, ___, 94 L.Ed. 195 (1949). This view is consistent with our holding in *Lutheran Synod* that fair market value constitutes "just compensation" for those private citizens who must replace their condemned property with more expensive substitutes and with our prior holdings that the Fifth Amendment does not require any award for consequential damages arising from a condemnation.

The city argues that its responsibility for municipal garbage disposal justifies a departure from the market value measure in this case. This responsibility compelled the city to arrange for a suitable replacement facility or substitute garbage disposal services. This obligation to replace a condemned facility, however, is no more compelling than the obligations assumed by private citizens. Even though most private condemnees are not legally obligated to replace property taken by the Government, economic circumstances often force them to do so. When a home is condemned, for example, its owner must find another place to live. The city's legal obligation to maintain public services that are interrupted by a federal condemnation does not justify a distinction between public and private condemnees for the purpose of measuring "just compensation."

Of course, the decision in *Lutheran Synod* was based, in part, on a fear that a private condemnee might receive a "windfall" if its compensation were measured by the cost of a substitute facility and "substitute facilities were never acquired, or if acquired, were later sold or converted to another use." 441 U.S. at 516, ___ S.Ct. at ___. The Court of Appeals suggested that the city's obligation to replace the facility avoids this risk, 706 F.2d at 1360, but we do not agree. If the replacement facility is more costly than the condemned facility, it presumably is more valuable,[15] and any increase in the quality of the facility may be as readily characterized as a "windfall" as the award of cash proceeds for a substitute facility that is never built.

The Court of Appeals, however, believed that the risk of any windfall could be reduced by discounting the cost of the substitute facility to account for its superior quality. This approach would add uncertainty and complexity to the valuation proceeding without any necessary improvement in the process. In order to implement the Court of Appeals' approach, the factfinder would have to make at least two determinations: (i) the reasonable (rather than the actual) replacement cost, which would require an inquiry into the fair market value of the second facility; and (ii) the extent to which the new facility is superior to the old, which would require an analysis of the qualitative

---

15. "Obviously, replacing the old with a new facility will cost more than the value of the old, but the new facility itself will be more valuable and last longer." *Lutheran Synod,* 441 U.S., at 518 (White, J., concurring).

differences between the new and the old. It would also be necessary to determine the fair market value of the old property in order to provide a basis for comparison. There is a practical risk that the entire added value will not be calculated correctly; moreover, if it is correctly estimated, the entire process may amount to nothing more than a roundabout method of arriving at the market value of the condemned facility.

Finally, the substitute-facilities doctrine, as applied in this case, diverges from the principle that just compensation must be measured by an objective standard that disregards subjective values which are only of significance to an individual owner. As the Court wrote in *Kimball Laundry Co. v. United States,* 338 U.S. 1, 5, 69 S.Ct. 1434, __, 93 L.Ed. 1765 (1949):

> "The value of property springs from subjective needs and attitudes; its value to the owner may therefore differ widely from its value to the taker. Most things, however, have a general demand which gives them a value transferable from one owner to another. As opposed to such personal and variant standards as value to the particular owner whose property has been taken, this transferable value has an external validity which makes it a fair measure of public obligation to compensate the loss incurred by an owner as a result of the taking of his property for public use. In view, however, of the liability of all property to condemnation for the common good, loss to the owner of nontransferable values deriving from his unique need for property or idiosyncratic attachment to it, like loss due to an exercise of the police power, is properly treated as part of the burden of common citizenship."

The subjective elements in the formula for determining the cost of reasonable substitute facilities would enhance the risk of error and prejudice. Since the condemnation contest is between the local community and a National Government that may be thought to have unlimited resources, the open-ended character of the substitute-facilities standard increases the likelihood that the city would actually derive the windfall that concerned both the District Court and the Court of Appeals. "Particularly is this true where these issues are to be left for jury determination, for juries should not be given sophistical and abstruse formulas as the basis for their findings nor be left to apply even sensible formulas to factors that are too elusive." *Id.,* 338 U.S. at 20, 69 S.Ct. at __.

The judgment of the Court of Appeals is reversed.

It is so ordered.

Notes and Questions

1. What costs or damages does this interpretation of "just compensation" in *Almota Farmers* and *50 Acres of Land* leave uncompensated? Does it require payment for pain and suffering? Sentimental value? Assume that the condemned land is the site of a house that has been occupied by

the same family for a half-century. Does the family receive compensation for this history? What if the family was the Reagan family, most recently of California? Are these values "property"?

2. Federal and state statutes can require broader compensation. An example of such statutes is the federal Uniform Relocation Assistance and Real Property Acquisition Policies Act cited by the court in *50 Acres of Land*. Under what circumstances should a legislature mandate or undertake a broader compensation duty than that required by the Constitution?

3. The Court in *50 Acres of Land* addressed a question left open by a previous case, United States v. 564.54 Acres of Land, More or Less, 441 U.S. 506, 99 S.Ct. 1854, 60 L.Ed.2d 435 (1979). In this earlier case, the U.S. government condemned a summer camp owned by the Lutheran Church. The government offered $485,400 and the church claimed $5.8 million, the cost claimed for replacing the camp. The church claimed that the large difference was due to the fact that the condemned property enjoyed the benefit of exemption, by grandfathering from "financially burdensome" regulations applicable to any other property the church would acquire. The Court refused to depart from the fair market value measure of compensation, acknowledging that "just compensation" does not require that the property owner receive all value attached to the property.

II. ZONING—THE MOST POPULAR FORM OF PUBLIC LAND USE REGULATION

Public regulation of the use and development of land comes in a variety of forms which generally focus on four aspects of land use: 1) the type of use, such as whether it will be used for agricultural, commercial, industrial, or residential purposes; 2) the density of use, manifested in concerns over the height, width, bulk, or environmental impact of the physical structures on the land; 3) the aesthetic impact of the use, which may include the design and placement of structures on the land; and 4) the effect of the particular use of the land on the cultural and social values of the community, illustrated by community conflicts over adult entertainment, housing for service-dependent groups such as low-income families and developmentally disabled persons, and whether the term "family" should be defined in land use regulations to include persons who are not related by blood or marriage.

The basic forms of modern land use regulation were established in the 1920's when the Supreme Court approved the comprehensive zoning concept, in which land in cities and counties is divided into zones or districts, and uniform regulations for land use, building height and area, as well as building setbacks, are imposed within those districts. Earlier, the Court had approved land use regulations prohibiting specific uses from particular areas when those uses were deemed to be harmful to people and land in the immediate vicinity.

A. THE CONCEPT OF ZONING

AMBLER REALTY CO. v. VILLAGE OF EUCLID, OHIO

District Court, N.D. Ohio, E.D., 1924.
297 Fed. 307.

[On November 13, 1922, the village council of Euclid adopted an ordinance establishing a comprehensive zoning plan that regulated and restricted the location of trades, industries, apartment houses, two-family houses, single family houses, the lot area to be built upon, and the size and heights of buildings in Euclid. The comprehensive ordinance divided the area of the village into six classes of use districts, U-1 to U-6 inclusive; three classes of height districts, H-1 to H-3 inclusive; and four classes of area districts, A-1 to A-4 inclusive. Use restrictions were cumulative, meaning that permitted uses in the U-2 district included those permitted in the U-1 district and so on. U-1, the most restricted district, was limited to single family homes, farms, parks and related uses. U-6, the least restricted district, included industrial and manufacturing activities as well as uses permitted in U-1, U-2, U-3, U-4 and U-5 districts. A seventh category included uses prohibited altogether. A similar plan for cumulative restriction on the height of buildings and size of lots was imposed by the height and area district regulations. Ambler Realty Company owned 68 acres of vacant land in the western end of the village. It sought to sell and develop the land for industrial purposes. Portions of the land were zoned U-2 and limited to single-family and two-family dwellings, while other portions were zoned U-3, multi-family housing, and U-6, industrial—Eds.]

WESTENHAVER, DISTRICT JUDGE. This suit is brought to have declared null and void and enforcement enjoined of Ordinance No. 2812, enacted by the municipal council of the village of Euclid, November 13, 1922, and amended by Ordinances Nos. 3367 and 3368, enacted June 11, 1923. This ordinance is what is popularly called a "zoning ordinance," i.e., one imposing a variety of restrictions upon the use of land within the village limits. After issue joined, the evidence was taken and submitted in deposition form.

This case is obviously destined to go higher. On appeal in equity cases, a reviewing court weighs the evidence, and when taken in deposition form it can do so as well as the trial court; hence it is unnecessary to make special findings of fact. Much of the evidence is immaterial; still more of it is without weight. Upon the facts the case really comes down to the provisions of the ordinance, certain physical facts characterizing the situation as it affects plaintiff's land, and the nature and extent of the impairment of its value by the ordinance restrictions. None of the important or controlling facts are in dispute, with the single exception of the extent of that damage; but even here there is no substantial denial that this damage is not only in excess of the jurisdictional amount but is substantial. As an instance of immaterial testimony may be noted the large volume relating to the inadequacy of the present water supply of the village of Euclid. Manifestly, the police power of the village to legislate in the interests of the public health or public safety cannot be enlarged by its failure or refusal to perform its fundamental duty of providing an adequate water supply. Upon the whole case, it is sufficient to say that the material and substantial allegations of plaintiff's bill are sufficiently proved.

* * *

The argument supporting this ordinance proceeds, it seems to me, both on a mistaken view of what is property and of what is police power. Property, generally speaking, defendant's counsel concede, is protected against a taking without compensation, by the guaranties of the Ohio and United States Constitutions. But their view seems to be that so long as the owner remains clothed with the legal title thereto and is not ousted from the physical possession thereof, his property is not taken, no matter to what extent his right to use it is invaded or destroyed or its present or prospective value is depreciated. This is an erroneous view. The right to property, as used in the Constitution, has no such limited meaning. * * *

A similar misconception or confusion of thought appears to exist touching the nature and extent of the police power. In one brief it is said:

"As is well known, the police power is the whole reserved power of the community to legislate concerning persons and things in the interests of the promotion of the public health, the public morals, the public safety, the public convenience, the public order, the public prosperity, and the general welfare."

It is from this broad generalization that counsel deduce the conclusion that since the ordinance in question does not take away plaintiff's title or oust it from physical possession, the power of eminent domain has not been exercised, but that the police power has been. This conception recognizes no distinction between police power and sovereign power. The power asserted is not merely sovereign, but is power unshackled by any constitutional limitation protecting life, liberty, and property from its despotic exercise. In defendants' view, the only difference between the police power and eminent domain is that the taking under the former may be done without compensation and under the latter a taking must be paid for. It seems to be the further view that whether one power or the other is exercised depends wholly on what the legislative department may see fit to recite on that subject. Such, however, is not the law. If police power meant what is claimed, all private property is now held subject to temporary and passing phases of public opinion, dominant for a day, in legislative or municipal assemblies.

* * *

Obviously, police power is not susceptible of exact definition. It would be difficult, even if it were not unwise, to attempt a more exact definition than has been given. And yet there is a wide difference between the power of eminent domain and the police power; and it is not true that the public welfare is a justification for the taking of private property for the general good. The broad language found in the books must be considered always in view of the facts, and when this is done, the difficulty disappears. A law or ordinance passed under the guise of the police power which invades private property as above defined can be sustained only when it has a real and substantial relation to the maintenance and preservation of the public peace, public order, public morals, or public safety. The courts never hesitate to look through the false pretense to the substance. * * *

Nor can the ordinances here be sustained by invoking the average reciprocity of advantage rule. * * * It is a futile suggestion that plaintiff's present and obvious loss from being deprived of the normal and legitimate use of its property would be compensated indirectly by benefits accruing to that land from the restrictions imposed by the ordinance on other land. It is equally futile to suppose that other property in the village will reap the benefit of the damage to plaintiff's property and that of others similarly situated. The only reasonable probability is that the property values taken from plaintiff and other owners similarly situated will simply disappear, or at best be transferred to other unrestricted sections of the Cleveland industrial area, or at the worst, to some other and far distant industrial area. So far as plaintiff is concerned, it is a pure loss. In the average reciprocity of advantage there is a measureless difference between adjoining property owners as regards a party wall or a boundary pillar, and the owners of property restricted as in this case. In the former there may be some reciprocity of advantage, even though unequal in individual cases. In the present case, the property values are either dissipated or transferred to unknown and more or less distant owners.

The plain truth is that the true object of the ordinance in question is to place all the property in an undeveloped area of 16 square miles in a strait-jacket. The purpose to be accomplished is really to regulate the mode of living of persons who may hereafter inhabit it. In the last analysis, the result to be accomplished is to classify the population and segregate them according to their income or situation in life. The true reason why some persons live in a mansion and others in a shack, why some live in a single-family dwelling and others in a double-family dwelling, why some live in a two-family dwelling and others in an apartment, or why some live in a well-kept apartment and others in a tenement, is primarily economic. It is a matter of income and wealth, plus the labor and difficulty of procuring adequate domestic service. Aside from contributing to these results and furthering such class tendencies, the ordinance has also an esthetic purpose; that is to say, to make this village develop into a city along lines now conceived by the village council to be attractive and beautiful. The assertion that this ordinance may tend to prevent congestion, and thereby contribute to the health and safety, would be more substantial if provision had been or could be made for adequate east and west and north and south street highways. Whether these purposes and objects would justify the taking of plaintiff's property as and for a public use need not be considered. It is sufficient to say that, in our opinion, and as applied to plaintiff's property, it may not be done without compensation under the guise of exercising the police power.

* * *

My conclusion is that the ordinance involved, as applied to plaintiff's property, is unconstitutional and void; that it takes plaintiff's property, if not for private, at least for public, use, without just compensation; that it is in no just sense a reasonable or legitimate exercise of police power. * * *

VILLAGE OF EUCLID v. AMBLER REALTY CO.

Supreme Court of the United States, 1926.
272 U.S. 365, 47 S.Ct. 114, 71 L.Ed. 303.

Mr. Justice Sutherland delivered the opinion of the Court.

* * *

The ordinance is assailed on the grounds that it is in derogation of § 1 of the Fourteenth Amendment to the Federal Constitution in that it deprives appellee of liberty and property without due process of law and denies it the equal protection of the law, and that it offends against certain provisions of the Constitution of the State of Ohio. The prayer of the bill is for an injunction restraining the enforcement of the ordinance and all attempts to impose or maintain as to appellee's property any of the restrictions, limitations or conditions. * * *

Before proceeding to a consideration of the case, it is necessary to determine the scope of the inquiry. The bill alleges that the tract of land in question is vacant and has been held for years for the purpose of selling and developing it for industrial uses, for which it is especially adapted, being immediately in the path of progressive industrial development; that for such uses it has a market value of about $10,000 per acre, but if the use be limited to residential purposes the market value is not in excess of $2,500 per acre; that the first 200 feet of the parcel back from Euclid Avenue, if unrestricted in respect of use, has a value of $150 per front foot, but if limited to residential uses, and ordinary mercantile business be excluded therefrom, its value is not in excess of $50 per front foot.

It is specifically averred that the ordinance attempts to restrict and control the lawful uses of appellee's land so as to confiscate and destroy a great part of its value; that it is being enforced in accordance with its terms; that prospective buyers of land for industrial, commercial and residential uses in the metropolitan district of Cleveland are deterred from buying any part of this land because of the existence of the ordinance and the necessity thereby entailed of conducting burdensome and expensive litigation in order to vindicate the right to use the land for lawful and legitimate purposes; that the ordinance constitutes a cloud upon the land, reduces and destroys its value, and has the effect of diverting the normal industrial, commercial and residential development thereof to other and less favorable locations.

The record goes no farther than to show, as the lower court found, that the normal, and reasonably to be expected, use and development of that part of appellee's land adjoining Euclid Avenue is for general trade and commercial purposes, particularly retail stores and like establishments, and that the normal, and reasonably to be expected, use and development of the residue of the land is for industrial and trade purposes. Whatever injury is inflicted by the mere existence and threatened enforcement of the ordinance is due to restrictions in respect of these and similar uses; to which perhaps should be added—if not included in the foregoing—restrictions in respect of apartment houses. Specifically, there is nothing in the record to suggest that any damage results from the presence in the ordinance of those restrictions relating to churches, schools, libraries and other public and semi-public buildings. It is neither alleged nor proved that there is, or may be, a demand for any part of appellee's land for any of the last named uses; and we cannot assume the existence of facts which would justify an injunction upon this record in respect of this class of restrictions. For present purposes the provisions of the ordinance in respect of these uses may, therefore, be put aside as unnecessary to be considered. It is also unnecessary to consider the effect of the restrictions in respect of U–1 districts, since none of appellee's land falls within that class.

We proceed, then, to a consideration of those provisions of the ordinance to which the case as it is made relates, first disposing of a preliminary matter.

A motion was made in the court below to dismiss the bill on the ground that, because complainant [appellee] had made no effort to obtain a building permit or apply to the zoning board of appeals for relief as it might have done under the terms of the ordinance, the suit was premature. The motion was properly overruled. The effect of the allegations of the bill is that the ordinance of its own force operates greatly to reduce the value of appellee's lands and destroy their marketability for industrial, commercial and residential uses; and the attack is directed, not against any specific provision or provisions, but against the ordinance as an entirety. Assuming the premises, the existence and maintenance of the ordinance, in effect, constitutes a present invasion of appellee's property rights and a threat to continue it. Under these circumstances, the equitable jurisdiction is clear. [ ]

It is not necessary to set forth the provisions of the Ohio Constitution which are thought to be infringed. The question is the same under both Constitutions, namely, as stated by appellee: Is the ordinance invalid in that it violates the constitutional protection "to the right of property in the appellee by attempted regulations under the guise of the police power, which are unreasonable and confiscatory?"

Building zone laws are of modern origin. They began in this country about twenty-five years ago. Until recent years, urban life was comparatively simple; but with the great increase and concentration of population, problems have developed, and constantly are developing, which require, and will continue to require, additional restrictions in respect of the use and occupation of private lands in urban communities. Regulations, the wisdom, necessity and validity of which, as applied to existing conditions, are so apparent that they are now uniformly sustained, a century ago, or even half a century ago, probably would have been rejected as arbitrary and oppressive. Such regulations are sustained, under the complex conditions of our day, for reasons analogous to those which justify traffic regulations, which, before the advent of automobiles and rapid transit street railways, would have been condemned as fatally arbitrary and unreasonable. And in this there is no inconsistency, for while the meaning of constitutional guaranties never varies, the scope of their application must expand or contract to meet the new and different conditions which are constantly coming within the field of their operation. In a changing world, it is impossible that it should be otherwise. But although a degree of elasticity is thus imparted, not to the *meaning*, but to the *application* of constitutional principles, statutes and ordinances, which, after giving due weight to the new conditions, are found clearly not to conform to the Constitution, of course, must fall.

The ordinance now under review, and all similar laws and regulations, must find their justification in some aspect of the police power, asserted for the public welfare. The line which in this field separates the legitimate from the illegitimate assumption of power is not capable of precise delimitation. It varies with circumstances and conditions. A regulatory zoning ordinance, which would be clearly valid as applied to the great cities, might be clearly invalid as applied to rural communities. In solving doubts, the maxim *sic utere tuo ut alienum non laedas*, which lies at the foundation of so much of the common law of nuisances, ordinarily will furnish a fairly helpful clew. And the law of nuisances, likewise, may be consulted, not for the purpose of controlling, but for the helpful aid of its analogies in the process of ascertaining the scope of, the power. Thus the question whether the power exists to forbid the erection of a building of a particular kind or for a particular use, like the question whether a particular thing is a nuisance, is to be determined, not by an abstract consideration of the building or of the thing considered apart, but by considering it in connection with the circumstances and the locality. [ ] A nuisance may be merely a right thing in the wrong place,—like a pig in the parlor instead of the barnyard. If the validity of the legislative classification for zoning purposes be fairly debatable, the legislative judgment must be allowed to control. [ ]

There is no serious difference of opinion in respect of the validity of laws and regulations fixing the height of buildings within reasonable limits, the character of materials and methods of construction, and the adjoining area which must be left open, in order to minimize the danger of fire or collapse, the evils of over-crowding, and the like, and excluding from residential sections offensive trades, industries and structures likely to create nuisances. [   ]

Here, however, the exclusion is in general terms of all industrial establishments, and it may thereby happen that not only offensive or dangerous industries will be excluded, but those which are neither offensive nor dangerous will share the same fate. But this is no more than happens in respect of many practice-forbidding laws which this Court has upheld although drawn in general terms so as to include individual cases that may turn out to be innocuous in themselves. [   ] The inclusion of a reasonable margin to insure effective enforcement, will not put upon a law, otherwise valid, the stamp of invalidity. Such laws may also find their justification in the fact that, in some fields, the bad fades into the good by such insensible degrees that the two are not capable of being readily distinguished and separated in terms of legislation. In the light of these considerations, we are not prepared to say that the end in view was not sufficient to justify the general rule of the ordinance, although some industries of an innocent character might fall within the proscribed class. * * *

It is said that the Village of Euclid is a mere suburb of the City of Cleveland; that the industrial development of that city has now reached and in some degree extended into the village and, in the obvious course of things, will soon absorb the entire area for industrial enterprises; that the effect of the ordinance is to divert this natural development elsewhere with the consequent loss of increased values to the owners of the lands within the village borders. But the village, though physically a suburb of Cleveland, is politically a separate municipality, with powers of its own and authority to govern itself as it sees fit within the limits of the organic law of its creation and the State and Federal Constitutions. Its governing authorities, presumably representing a majority of its inhabitants and voicing their will, have determined, not that industrial development shall cease at its boundaries, but that the course of such development shall proceed within definitely fixed lines. If it be a proper exercise of the police power to relegate industrial establishments to localities separated from residential sections, it is not easy to find a sufficient reason for denying the power because the effect of its exercise is to divert an industrial flow from the course which it would follow, to the injury of the residential public if left alone, to another course where such injury will be obviated. It is not meant by this, however, to exclude the possibility of cases where the general public interest would so far outweigh the interest of the municipality that the municipality would not be allowed to stand in the way.

We find no difficulty in sustaining restrictions of the kind thus far reviewed. The serious question in the case arises over the provisions of the ordinance excluding from residential districts, apartment houses, business houses, retail stores and shops, and other like establishments. This question involves the validity of what is really the crux of the more recent zoning legislation, namely, the creation and maintenance of residential districts, from which business and trade of every sort, including hotels and apartment houses, are excluded. Upon that question this Court has not thus far spoken. The decisions of the state courts are numerous and conflicting; but those which broadly sustain the power greatly outnumber those which deny altogether or narrowly limit it; and it is very apparent that there is a constantly increasing tendency in the direction of the broader view.

* * *

The decisions enumerated * * * agree that the exclusion of buildings devoted to business, trade, etc., from residential districts, bears a rational relation to the health and safety of the community. Some of the grounds for this conclusion are—promotion of the health and security from injury of children and others by separating dwelling houses from territory devoted to trade and industry; suppression and prevention of disorder; facilitating the extinguishment of fires, and the enforcement of street traffic regulations and other general welfare ordinances; aiding the health and safety of the community by excluding from residential areas the confusion and danger of fire, contagion and disorder which in greater or less degree attach to the location of stores, shops and factories. Another ground is that the construction and repair of streets may be rendered easier and less expensive by confining the greater part of the heavy traffic to the streets where business is carried on.

* * *

The matter of zoning has received much attention at the hands of commissions and experts, and the results of their investigations have been set forth in comprehensive reports. These reports, which bear every evidence of painstaking consideration, concur in the view that the segregation of residential, business, and industrial buildings will make it easier to provide fire apparatus suitable for the character and intensity of the development in each section; that it will increase the safety and security of home life; greatly tend to prevent street accidents, especially to children, by reducing the traffic and resulting confusion in residential sections; decrease noise and other conditions which produce or intensify nervous disorders; preserve a more favorable environment in which to rear children, etc. With particular reference to apartment houses, it is pointed out that the development of detached house sections is greatly retarded by the coming of apartment houses, which has sometimes resulted in destroying the entire section for private house purposes; that in such sections very often the apartment house is a mere parasite, constructed in order to take advantage of the open spaces and attractive surroundings created by the residential character of the district. Moreover, the coming of one apartment house is followed by others, interfering by their height and bulk with the free circulation of air and monopolizing the rays of the sun which otherwise would fall upon the smaller homes, and bringing, as their necessary accompaniments, the disturbing noises incident to increased traffic and business, and the occupation, by means of moving and parked automobiles, of larger portions of the streets, thus detracting from their safety and depriving children of the privilege of quiet and open spaces for play, enjoyed by those in more favored localities,— until, finally, the residential character of the neighborhood and its desirability as a place of detached residences are utterly destroyed. Under these circumstances, apartment houses, which in a different environment would be not only entirely unobjectionable but highly desirable, come very near to being nuisances.

If these reasons, thus summarized, do not demonstrate the wisdom or sound policy in all respects of those restrictions which we have indicated as pertinent to the inquiry, at least, the reasons are sufficiently cogent to preclude us from saying, as it must be said before the ordinance can be declared unconstitutional, that such provisions are clearly arbitrary and unreasonable, having no substantial relation to the public health, safety, morals, or general welfare. [ ]

It is true that when, if ever, the provisions set forth in the ordinance in tedious and minute detail, come to be concretely applied to particular premises, including those of the appellee, or to particular conditions, or to be considered in connection with specific complaints, some of them, or even many of them, may be found to be clearly arbitrary and unreasonable. But where the equitable remedy of injunction is sought, as it is here, not upon the ground of a present infringement or denial of a specific right, or of a particular injury in process of actual execution, but upon the broad ground that the mere existence and threatened enforcement of the ordinance, by materially and adversely affecting values and curtailing the opportunities of the market, constitute a present and irreparable injury, the court will not scrutinize its provisions, sentence by sentence, to ascertain by a process of piecemeal dissection whether there may be, here and there, provisions of a minor character, or relating to matters of administration, or not shown to contribute to the injury complained of, which, if attacked separately, might not withstand the test of constitutionality. In respect of such provisions, of which specific complaint is not made, it cannot be said that the land owner has suffered or is threatened with an injury which entitles him to challenge their constitutionality. * * *

* * *

Decree reversed.

MR. JUSTICE VAN DEVANTER, MR. JUSTICE MCREYNOLDS and MR. JUSTICE BUTLER, dissent.

Notes and Questions

1. The *Euclid* case, which gave the stamp of approval to the technique which was to become the bedrock of the American law of public land use control, was decided by the narrowest of margins. Justice Sutherland, the authority of the majority opinion, was reported by a former law clerk of Chief Justice Stone to have been leaning in the other direction until "talks

with his dissenting brethren * * * shook his convictions and led him to request a reargument" of the case, after which he changed his mind and voted with the majority to uphold the ordinance. McCormack, Law Clerk's Recollection, 46 Colum.L.Rev. 710, 712 (1946). The person generally given credit for turning the case around was Alfred Bettman, a well-known land use attorney in Cincinnati who filed an amicus curiae brief on behalf of a number of national and state organizations who were promoting comprehensive planning and zoning as necessary tools to enable municipalities to guide and control their growth. For histories of the case, see Brooks, The Office File Box—Emanations from the Battlefield, in Zoning and the American Dream at 3, (C. Haar & J. Kayden eds. 1989); Tarlock, Euclid Revisited, 34 Land Use L. & Zoning Dig. 4 (1982); A. Bettman, City and Regional Planning Papers (1946). See also D. Mandelker, Land Use Law 107–116 (2d ed. 1988); D. Hagman & J. Juergensmeyer, Urban Planning and Land Development Control Law 39–51 (2d ed 1986); D. Kmiec, Zoning and Planning Deskbook 2–10 to 2–15 (1986); 1 R. Anderson, American Law of Zoning 96–115 (3d ed. 1986); R. Cunningham, W. Stoebuck & D. Whitman, The Law of Property 527–531 (1984); 1 N. Williams, American Land Planning Law 355–370 (1974).

2. The first comprehensive zoning ordinance in America was enacted by New York City in 1916. Supporters were greatly influenced by the use of zoning in German cities in the late nineteenth century. As Justice Sutherland noted in *Euclid*, building regulations in the United States began around the turn of the century to combat the deleterious effects of the Industrial Revolution: squalor, filth, disease, and fire, particularly in the inner cities populated by immigrants. A second force, which District Judge Westenhaver protested, sought to protect personal sensibilities and property values from encroachment by activities and individuals deemed to be undesirable. The two movements came together in the New York City zoning ordinance of 1916. From that ordinance, and a similar one in St. Louis a few years later, came a series of "standard" state planning and zoning enabling acts and corresponding local ordinances promulgated by the United States Department of Commerce under the leadership of then—Secretary of Commerce Herbert Hoover. Following the Supreme Court's decision in *Euclid*, comprehensive zoning swept the country. For a readable and thorough history of the enactment of the New York City ordinance and its influence on the development of zoning as a political process, see S. Toll, Zoned American (1969).

3. Zoning as a concept was tied to the notion of comprehensive planning. In theory, communities were supposed to prepare a comprehensive plan that was to be the basis for land use regulation. Zoning was then to become the device for implementing the plan that had previously been adopted by the community. In practice, many communities dispensed with the formal planning process, at least in written form, and went straight to a zoning ordinance. The courts acceded to this approach by concluding that adoption of a formal plan was not a condition precedent to a valid zoning scheme so long as the zoning ordinance itself contained evidence that the community had engaged in a rational process of deliberation about the future of the community. See, e.g., Town of Bedford v. Village of Mt. Kisco, 33 N.Y.2d 178, 351 N.Y.S.2d 129, 306 N.E.2d 155 (1973); Mott's

Realty Corp. v. Town Plan & Zoning Commission, 152 Conn. 535, 209 A.2d 179 (1965); Ward v. Montgomery Township, 28 N.J. 529, 147 A.2d 248 (1959). See generally, Haar, In Accordance With a Comprehensive Plan, 68 Harv L Rev 1154 (1955).

4. The comprehensive zoning approach tended to impose a grid pattern of development, partly because of the uniformity of treatment within districts requirement, which was based on the premise that homogeneity of use was desirable and that different types of land use should be segregated from one another. Comprehensive zoning was prospective in nature and thus was best suited for the regulation of new uses of previously undeveloped land. When it was imposed on the built-up areas of major cities, an extensive "non-conforming use" component had to be added to recognize the reality of the heterogeneous use, market-focused type of development that already was in place in the cities. See, e.g., State ex rel. Manhein v. Harrison, 164 La. 564, 114 So. 159 (1927) (upholding Shreveport ordinance which contained non-conforming use regulations); City of Aurora v. Burns, 319 Ill. 84, 149 N.E. 784 (1925) (upholding Illinois zoning enabling act containing non-conforming use regulations); Building Inspector of Lowell v. Stoklosa, 250 Mass. 52, 145 N.E. 262 (1924) and In re Opinion of the Justices, 234 Mass. 597, 127 N.E. 525 (1920) (upholding Massachusetts zoning enabling act and Middlesex ordinance containing non-conforming use regulations).

5. Note that the ordinance approved in *Euclid* was cumulative in nature, U–1 uses were permitted in the U–2 district and so on. This produced a "hierarchy" of uses, based on exclusivity, which placed single-family residences and the persons who occupied them, at the top of a status pyramid. Note that the highest status use did not necessarily comport with the highest economic use. Ambler Realty Company claimed that industrial use of its property would make it four times as valuable as residential use. Was Ambler deprived of a property interest because of its loss of an expected increase in value of its property? Is expectation of profit a stick in the property bundle? Recall *Penn Central Transportation Co. v. City of New York,* supra.

6. On what basis is the segregation inherent in zoning justified by the *Euclid* Court? Is it that incompatible uses, if not segregated, would become harmful to the public? Or is it that the quality of life for the people favored by the segregation will be improved? Is it sufficient to say, as the Supreme Court did in Mugler v. Kansas, 123 U.S. 623, 665, 8 S.Ct. 273, 299, 31 L.Ed. 205 (1887), that property owners hold their property subject to "the implied obligation that the owner's use of it shall not be injurious to the community"? Did Justice Douglas provide the answer in Berman v. Parker, 348 U.S. 26, 33, 75 S.Ct. 98, 102, 99 L.Ed. 27 (1954), when he declared: "The concept of the public welfare is broad and inclusive. The values it represents are spiritual as well as physical, aesthetic as well as monetary. It is within the power of the legislature to determine that the community should be beautiful as well as healthy, spacious as well as clean, well-balanced as well as carefully patrolled." Is the true test of zoning the impact that it has on property rights or its impact on personal relationships? Recall *State v. Shack,* supra, Chapter One.

7. Considering the history of the development of American cities and suburbs since the 1920s, who was more perceptive, District Judge Westenhaver or Justice Sutherland? Dr. Robert B. Reich, a political economist, has lamented the "secession" of the "top fifth of working Americans" from the rest of the populace, driven in part by a "near obsessive concern with maintaining or upgrading property values." Reich, Secession of the Successful, New York Times Magazine, January 20, 1991, at p. 17.

8. Two years after the *Euclid* decision, the Supreme Court sustained a due process challenge to the application of a zoning ordinance to a particular piece of property, in Nectow v. City of Cambridge, 277 U.S. 183, 48 S.Ct. 447, 72 L.Ed. 842 (1928). The zoning ordinance changed a 100–foot–wide strip of land from commercial to residential use, although the strip was surrounded by commercial and industrial development. The landowner argued that no practical use of the land could be made as it was rezoned. The Supreme Court upheld an injunction against implementation of the zoning amendment, based on the finding that the " * * * districting of the plaintiff's land in a residence district would not promote the health, safety, convenience and general welfare of the inhabitants of that part of the Defendant city, taking into account the natural development thereof and the character of the district and the resulting benefit * * * " Id. at 187.

Despite the Supreme Court's apparent signal in *Nectow* that it was prepared to supervise the application of zoning laws, it did not make another important zoning decision until upholding a restrictive definition of "family" in Belle Terre v. Boraas, 416 U.S. 1, 94 S.Ct. 1536, 39 L.Ed.2d 797 (1974), almost 50 years later.

9. One legacy of the *Nectow* decision and the Court's subsequent half-century abdication from the zoning field was an uncertainty about the appropriate relief to be awarded in zoning cases. For example, the Supreme Court of Michigan in Schwartz v. City of Flint, 426 Mich. 295, 395 N.W.2d 678, 686 (1986), quoted Professor Ellickson that *Nectow*:

> "has been construed to mean that a landowner's standard remedy against overly restrictive zoning should be some form of injunctive relief and not damages. [Also,] by failing to specify what type of injunctive relief the landowner was to receive, *Nectow* reinforced the judicial tendency toward sloppiness in the specification of remedies in zoning cases." Ellickson, Suburban Growth Controls: An Economic and Legal Analysis, 86 Yale L.J. 385, 490 (1977).

The Court in *Schwartz* declined to award damages, described as an "intriguing" concept, and settled for a declaration of invalidity when a zoning ordinance is applied unconstitutionally, along with a permissible judicial finding that the plaintiff's proposed use is reasonable when the plaintiff has met that burden, and an injunction against interference with that use. 395 N.W.2d at 692–693. The Court was particularly concerned about not invading the legislative prerogative of local governments. Do you think it succeeded?

Relief in the form of a "builder's remedy"—a judicial order that a building permit be issued so long as the developer complies with other valid local regulations—has been granted by some courts. See, e.g., Britton v. Town of Chester, 595 A.2d 492 (N.H.1991); Southern Burlington County

N.A.A.C.P. v. Township of Mount Laurel, 92 N.J. 158, 456 A.2d 390 (1983) (Mount Laurel II) discussed infra.

As we learn in contracts, torts and civil procedure courses, the traditional common-law remedy for injury is an award of monetary damages. Injunctive relief is an extraordinary remedy available only when damages would be inadequate. However, for a variety of reasons, including remnants of the tort doctrine of sovereign immunity, concern about potential budget-busting damages awards, and the delegation of taxing and spending decisions to the legislative branch of government by the separation of powers doctrine, the normal order of remedies is reversed in zoning cases: injunctive relief is ordinary and a damages award is extraordinary. See, e.g., Agins v. Tiburon, 24 Cal.3d 266, 157 Cal.Rptr. 372, 598 P.2d 25 (1979), aff'd on other grounds, 447 U.S. 255, 100 S.Ct. 2138, 65 L.Ed.2d 106 (1980).

Did the Supreme Court in *First English*, infra, reverse the normal remedy sequence in zoning cases? After *First English*, can a municipality avoid paying damages for invalid application of the zoning power by rescinding the offending regulation? See Bello v. Walker, 840 F.2d 1124 (3d Cir.1988) (unlawful denial of building permit not a taking when other permissible uses were possible); City of Virginia Beach v. Virginia Land Investment Ass'n No. 1, 239 Va. 412, 389 S.E.2d 312 (1990) (invalid piecemeal downzoning did not deprive owner of all economically viable uses of property).

B. MANAGING CHANGE THROUGH ZONING ADMINISTRATION

Zoning was initially thought to be a technique for preserving the status quo, as that status was articulated by the planning and legislative process leading to enactment of a comprehensive zoning ordinance. However, communities constantly change, either by growth or decline, and it soon became apparent that a major function of zoning would be the management of change. The following case explores the use of traditional zoning techniques to manage change.

BELL v. CITY OF ELKHORN

Supreme Court of Wisconsin, 1985.
122 Wis.2d 558, 364 N.W.2d 144.

CALLOW, JUSTICE.

This is an appeal from a judgment of the circuit court for Walworth county denying plaintiffs' request for a declaratory judgment and upholding a city of Elkhorn (City) amendatory zoning ordinance. The appeal was certified by the court of appeals and accepted by this court. * * * We affirm the circuit court.

The issues presented on appeal are whether the existence of a formal comprehensive plan is a condition precedent to the adoption of a valid zoning ordinance; whether Elkhorn's rezoning of certain property constituted illegal spot zoning; and whether the commercial-shopping district portion of Elkhorn's zoning ordinance is unconstitutional for failure to limit the City's legislative discretion.

This action arises out of the city of Elkhorn's approval of an application to rezone two parcels of land from multiple family use to commercial-shopping use. The subject property is located at the southeast corner of the intersection of East Geneva and South Lincoln Streets in Elkhorn. In 1972, Elkhorn enacted zoning ordinance No. 426, which divided the city into districts and provided certain regulations with regard to the use of property in those districts. Prior to the rezoning amendment which is the subject of this action, three corners of the intersection of East Geneva and South Lincoln Streets were zoned B-3, commercial-shopping district. The southeast corner, where the subject property is located, was zoned R-4, multi-family residential district. At the time this action was commenced, a gas station, muffler shop, and pizza parlor were located on the corners which were zoned B-3. Two residences were located on the subject property.

In October, 1982, the defendant, Hardees C & S Foods, Inc., applied to the Elkhorn common council to have the property at the southeast corner of the East Geneva and South Lincoln Street intersection rezoned from R-4 to B-3. Hardees intended to build a restaurant on the site. The city clerk-treasurer gave notice of a public hearing to be held before a joint meeting of the common council and the city plan commission on the proposed amendment to Elkhorn's zoning law, pursuant to sec. 62.23(7)(d)2, Stats. The plaintiffs, who are owners of more than twenty percent of the property located within 100 feet of the subject premises, filed a protest petition in opposition to the proposed rezone. The effect of the protest petition was that a three-fourths vote of the city council was required to pass the amendatory zoning ordinance.

A public hearing was held on November 1, 1982, and the city plan commission recommended to the common council that the petition to rezone be approved. On November 15, 1982, the council passed the amendment to the zoning ordinance, which changed the zoning of the subject property from R-4 to B-3, by a five to one vote. The amendatory zoning ordinance was published and became effective on December 23, 1982. A building permit was issued to Hardees on December 27, 1982, and the restaurant opened on April 19, 1983.

On December 13, 1982, the plaintiffs filed a declaratory judgment action challenging the City's passage of the amendatory zoning ordinance. An amended summons and complaint were filed on April 26, 1983. The plaintiffs' attack on the City's action was threefold. First, plaintiffs contended that Elkhorn's zoning ordinances were invalid because Elkhorn has not adopted a comprehensive plan. Second, plaintiffs charged that the rezone amendment amounted to spot zoning. Finally, plaintiffs contended that the portion of Elkhorn's original zoning ordinance establishing B-3 commercial-shopping districts was unconstitutional because it lacked proper standards.

The matter was tried to the court in July, 1983. On December 20, 1983, the court issued its memorandum decision denying plaintiffs' request for a declaratory judgment. The court found that a formal comprehensive plan is not a condition precedent to the enactment of a valid zoning ordinance. The court also found that the rezone of the property did not constitute spot zoning. Finally, the court upheld the constitutionality of Elkhorn's original zoning ordinance and rejected plaintiffs' argument that the portion of the ordinance establishing B–3 districts lacked proper standards. * * *

The first issue we decide is whether the existence of a formal comprehensive plan is a condition precedent to the adoption of a valid zoning ordinance. To resolve this issue, we must turn to sec. 62.23, Stats., which sets forth Wisconsin's statutory scheme for city planning. Section 62.23(1) provides that a city may create a city plan commission. Section 62.23(2), Stats. states:

"It shall be the function and duty of the commission to make and adopt a master plan for the physical development of the municipality * * *. The master plan, with the accompanying maps, plats, charts and descriptive and explanatory matter, shall show the commission's recommendations for such physical development, *and may include* * * * *a comprehensive zoning plan."* (Emphasis added.)

Section 62.23(7)(a) gives the city council the power to enact zoning ordinances "[f]or the purpose of promoting health, safety, morals or the general welfare of the community." Section 62.23(7)(c) requires that "[s]uch (zoning) regulations shall be made in accordance with a comprehensive plan. * * *" The statutes do not define the term "comprehensive plan," and the parties hold conflicting views as to its meaning. The defendants argue that the requirement of a "comprehensive plan" can be met by the enactment of a comprehensive zoning ordinance itself and that the statute does not require a comprehensive plan to be a separate document. The plaintiffs contend that a zoning ordinance does not qualify as a comprehensive plan and that a separate document must be prepared and adopted before a city may enact a zoning ordinance.

The question of whether a zoning ordinance may constitute a comprehensive plan is a matter of first impression in Wisconsin. * * *

Commentators have defined a comprehensive plan as a guide to community development. * * * The objectives sought to be achieved through the development of a comprehensive plan include: (1) improving the physical environment of the community; (2) promoting the public interest; (3) facilitating the implementation of community policies on physical development; (4) effecting political and technical coordination in community development; (5) injecting long-range considerations into the determination of short-range actions; and (6) bringing professional and technical knowledge to bear on the making of political decisions concerning the physical development of the community. [   ]

* * *

The majority view held by courts and commentators that have considered the issue is that a zoning ordinance itself may satisfy the requirement that zoning be in accordance with a comprehensive plan. In *Lanphear v. Antwerp Township,* 50 Mich.App. 641, 646, 214 N.W.2d 66 (Mich.Ct.App.1973), the court rejected the view that the plan must be embodied in a separate document.

> " * * * [T]here is no requirement in (the statute) that the 'plan' be written or be anything beyond 'a generalized conception by the members of the board as to how the districts in the township shall be * * * used'. This 'generalized conception' is exhibited in the zoning ordinance itself, since the document zones districts, prescribes variances, land uses, etc., for the entire township, and thus plans the township's future development."

* * *

Several courts have held that planning legislation requires the preparation and adoption of a separate comprehensive plan document and that the adoption of a formal comprehensive plan is a condition precedent to the enactment of a zoning ordinance. [ ]. However, none of those cases involved the interpretation of a statute containing the language that ordinances must be "in accordance with a comprehensive plan."

We find the majority view to be persuasive on this issue. * * * The purpose of a comprehensive plan is to provide an orderly method of land use regulation for the community. That purpose can be accomplished by the zoning ordinance itself without the need of a separate document labeled "Comprehensive Plan." The clear intent of the legislature in enacting sec. 62.23, Stats., was to have cities design a general plan to control the use of property in the community. This can be accomplished with or without the advice of a plan commission because the creation of a plan commission is at the discretion of the governing body of the community. [ ] The power to zone is exclusively vested in the city council. [ ]

Elkhorn's zoning ordinance divided the city into eleven districts and provided certain restrictions for the use of property in each district. It set forth regulations regarding nonconforming and conditional uses. It provided a procedure for changes and amendments to the ordinance. It established a board of appeals and specified its powers. Elkhorn's zoning ordinance serves as a general plan to control and direct the use and development of property in the city and serves as a guide to future community development. As such, we hold that the ordinance itself is a comprehensive plan * * *. No separate comprehensive plan document need be adopted by a city as a condition precedent to enacting a zoning ordinance.

The next issue we decide is whether Elkhorn's adoption of the amendatory zoning ordinance constituted spot zoning. Spot zoning has been defined as "the practice whereby a single lot or area is granted privileges which are not granted or extended to other land in the vicinity in the same use district." *Howard v. Village of Elm Grove*, 80 Wis.2d 33, 41, 257 N.W.2d 850 (1977); *Cushman v. Racine*, 39 Wis.2d 303, 306–07, 159 N.W.2d 67 (1968). This court has previously held that such zoning is not illegal per se because it is not necessarily inconsistent with the purposes for which zoning ordinances can be passed * * *. However, rezoning should be consistent with long-range planning and be based upon considerations which affect the whole community. [ ] Spot zoning "should only be indulged in where it is in the public interest and not solely for the benefit of the property owner who requests rezoning." [*Cushman v. Racine*, 39 Wis.2d 303,] 309, 159 N.W.2d 67 (1968), citing *Buhler v. Racine*, 33 Wis.2d 137, 150–51, 146 N.W.2d 403 (1966).

We do not believe the facts of this case support a finding that the amendatory zoning ordinance constituted spot zoning. Three corners of the intersection where the subject property was located were zoned commercial at the time Hardees applied for rezoning. Those lots which were already zoned commercial contained a gas station, pizza parlor, and muffler shop. This was not a case of a single commercial use encroaching on a strictly residential area. Testimony was presented at trial that single family residential use in the area was deteriorating. The amendatory zoning ordinance did not grant special privileges to a single parcel inconsistent with the use of property in the general area. Thus, we hold that the rezoning of Hardees' property was not spot zoning.

* * *

The judgment of the circuit court is affirmed.

Notes and Questions

1. In Schubach v. Silver, 461 Pa. 366, 336 A.2d 328 (1975), landowners sought to have a zoning amendment declared invalid as spot zoning. The change allowed construction of a nursing home on land located between residential and commercial areas. The Supreme Court of Pennsylvania characterized the spot zoning question as "whether the rezoned land is being treated unjustifiably different from similar surrounding land." Id. at 336. The court quoted 8 McQuillin on Municipal Corporations: "It is well-settled that an ordinance cannot create an 'island' of more or less restricted use within a district zoned for a different use or uses, where there are no differentiating factors between the 'island' and the district * * * thus, singling out one lot or a small area for different treatment from that accorded to similar surrounding land indistinguishable from it in character * * * " Id. at 336. The court upheld the rezoning, noting that the rezoned use was different from that of the surrounding area, but that by its location the land could actually only be used effectively as a "natural extension" of the already existing commercial use. Furthermore, the court took into consideration the fact that the area had been a problem spot because of its location between residential and commercial zoning areas. Construction of a nursing home would create a transition zone that would buffer the two

zones, and thus could be seen as the best possible use of this land, the court concluded.

2. Cases such as *Bell* and *Schubach* illustrate the traditional way that courts have approached rezoning decisions challenged by neighbors as illegal "spot" zoning—such decisions are clothed with a presumption of validity as legislative decisions, challengers have the difficult burden of overcoming the presumption, and "fairly debatable" decisions will not be second-guessed.

An alternative way of looking at rezoning decisions was advocated by the Supreme Court of Oregon in Fasano v. Board of County Commissioners of Washington County, 264 Or. 574, 507 P.2d 23 (1973). In *Fasano* the petitioners were a group of homeowners in Washington County who opposed a zoning change. The change anchored a previously-approved planned residential district (known as a floating zone because it does not receive a location designation on the zoning map when first approved) on 32 acres of land zoned residential to permit construction of a mobile home park. The court disallowed the change because "Once a [zoning scheme] is adopted, changes in it should be made only when such changes are consistent with the overall objectives of the plan and in keeping with changes in the character of the area or neighborhood to be covered thereby." Id. at 28.

The Court broke from the rigid pattern of characterizing all zoning decisions as legislative in character.

> At this juncture we feel we would be ingnoring reality to rigidly view all zoning decisions by local governing bodies as legislative acts to be accorded a full presumption of validity and shielded from less than constitutional scrutiny by the theory of separation of powers. Local and small decision groups are simply not the equivalent in all respects of state and national legislatures. * * *

> Ordinances laying down general policies without regard to a specific piece of property are usually an exercise of legislative authority, are subject to limited review, and may only be attacked upon constitutional grounds for an arbitrary abuse of authority. On the other hand, a determination whether the permissible use of a specific piece of property should be changed is usually an exercise of judicial authority and its propriety is subject to an altogether different test. An illustration of an exercise of legislative authority is the passage of the ordinance by the Washington County Commission in 1962 which provided for the formation of a planned residential classification to be located in or adjacent to any residential zone. An exercise of judicial authority is the county commissioners' determination in this particular matter to change the classification of A.G.S. Development Company's specific piece of property. Id. at 26.

As a quasi-judicial decision, the rezoning was not entitled to a presumption of legislative validity, the burden of proof was on the party seeking the change (the landowner), and the decision to change the zoning had to be justified by evidence of consistency with the adopted general plan or overriding public need, a test not met by a "conclusory and superficial" planning staff report, the Court held. 507 P.2d at 30.

Is the *Fasano* distinction between legislative policy-making zoning decisions and administrative, quasi-judicial, policy-implementing zoning decisions persuasive? Or does it permit courts to intrude too greatly into an inherently political process? See, e.g., Arnel Development Co. v. City of Costa Mesa, 28 Cal.3d 511, 169 Cal.Rptr. 904, 911–912, 620 P.2d 565, 572–73 (1980) (rejecting case-by-case adjudication of what is legislative or quasi-judicial, and approving use of generic classifications, e.g., zoning ordinances as legislative, and variances, special use permits, and subdivision map approvals as quasi-judicial). For a history of developments in Oregon after the *Fasano* decision, see Sullivan, Land Use in the Oregon Supreme Court: A Recent Retrospective, 25 Will.L.Rev. 259 (1989) (author was counsel for Washington County in *Fasano*).

3. In addition to zoning amendments, municipalities traditionally have used special use permits and variances in the administration of comprehensive zoning programs. Uses that require special permits are legislatively-authorized uses identified in the zoning ordinance that are regulated by a administrative agency "because of special problems the use * * * presents from a zoning standpoint. * * *" Tullo v. Millburn Tp., 54 N.J.Super. 483, 149 A.2d 620, 625 (App.Div.1959). Typical examples include day care centers, fast food stores and gas stations.

Decisions regarding special use permits generally are considered to be administrative rather than legislative in character, Arnel Development Co. v. City of Costa Mesa, 28 Cal.3d 511, 169 Cal.Rptr. 904, 911, 620 P.2d 565, 572 (1980), although some courts hold otherwise. See, e.g., Board of Supervisors of Fairfax County v. Southland Corp., 224 Va. 514, 297 S.E.2d 718 (1982) (special use permit is legislative act). Disputes over special use permits usually center on whether proper standards have been articulated for the delegation of authority, whether the standards have been met, and whether special permit requirements create unconstitutional classifications. See, e.g., City of Cleburne v. Cleburne Living Center, 473 U.S. 432, 105 S.Ct. 3249, 87 L.Ed.2d 313 (1985) (disapproving special permit requirement for group home in multi-family district). See generally P. Salsich, Land Use Regulation 190–194 (1991); D. Mandelker, Land Use Law 252–257 (2d ed. 1988); D. Hagman & J. Juergensmeyer, Urban Planning and Land Development Control Law 183–188 (2d ed. 1986); D. Kmiec, Zoning and Planning Deskbook 6–25 to 6–30 (1986); R. Cunningham, W. Stoebuck & D. Whitman, The Law of Property 549–553 (1984).

4. Variances are departures from the zoning regulations granted by an administrative body such as a board of zoning appeals in order to avoid overly harsh results from application of a zoning regulation. They originally were authorized by zoning enabling acts to avoid constitutional challenges to zoning ordinances that created "unnecessary hardship or practical difficulties." Strict application of the hardship standard ordinarily would limit variances to height and area restrictions, such as encroachment of a building into a required front, side or rear yard. In recent years, however, courts have been willing to approve the granting of variances to change permitted uses. The principal vice of the variance is that zoning map designations do not change when variances are granted, thus permitting municipalities to hide the "real" rules of the game by excessive use of variances to administer a zoning program. Like special use permits,

variances are administrative rather than legislative acts. See generally P. Salsich, Land Use Regulation 194–198 (1991); D. Mandelker, Land Use Law 239–251 (2d ed. 1988); D. Hagman & J. Juergensmeyer, Urban Planning and Land Development Control Law 172–182 (2d ed. 1986); D. Kmiec, Zoning and Planning Deskbook 6–12 to 6–25 (1986); R. Cunningham, W. Stoebuck & D. Whitman, The Law of Property 545–549 (1984).

PROBLEM

We have three clients in the office—representatives of three farming families who have come in together to talk to us: Mrs. Schmidt, Mr. Sanchez, and Mr. and Mrs. Ippolito. Among the three families they own 2,000 acres of good farm land, all within a ten-mile radius of the city limits, the closest part of which is four miles from town.

What brings them in is alarmed agreement. This is the first time in years they have ever agreed on anything. Their history of dealing with one another is a history of squabbles over boundaries, water rights, fences and drifting pesticides.

But today they are in agreement. They are alarmed at the way the town is growing out toward their farms, and they want a lawyer to tell them how to stop it.

— Last year a furniture dealer bought ten acres one mile from Mr. Sanchez's gate and built a warehouse on the tract.

— There are already three fast food places between their farms and the city limits.

— They love being farmers. Their many children want to be farmers after they are dead. They even have grandchildren who already want to be farmers.

— And, although they have never agreed on political candidates, they agree that farming is a good way of life, something that benefits everybody—that even city people benefit from having wide open spaces at the edge of town.

Assume that the lowest category of zoning under the county zoning ordinance provides for an industrial-agricultural category, that includes all of the higher categories, which means that, at present, any land use is permitted on this farm land.

1. What zoning strategies are available to you? In planning your approach, would you expect to function in an adjudicative or a negotiating mode? Is there a role for a mediator here?

2. Can you represent all three families, or will that present insurmountable ethical issues?

C. ADDING FLEXIBILITY TO THE PROCESS

Rezonings often are extremely controversial and municipalities may seek compromises between landowners and objecting neighbors.

One way to do this is to place conditions on the use of the land being rezoned. For example, neighbors may drop their opposition to a rezoning if they are assured that only small markets and restaurants may be built, but not taverns, gas stations, or fast food stores. Other conditions may address environmental issues, such as requiring landscaping or appropriate drainage. While the process may take on the appearance of a negotiated agreement among the landowner, neighbors, and the municipality, serious legal questions are raised by such efforts, as the following case illustrates.

COLLARD v. INCORPORATED VILLAGE OF FLOWER HILL

Court of Appeals of New York, 1981.
52 N.Y.2d 594, 439 N.Y.S.2d 326, 421 N.E.2d 818.

JONES, JUDGE.

Where a local municipality conditions an amendment of its zoning ordinance on the execution of a declaration of covenants providing, in part, that no construction may occur on the property so rezoned without the consent of the municipality, absent a provision that such consent may not be unreasonably withheld the municipality may not be compelled to issue such consent or give an acceptable reason for failing to do so.

Appellants now own improved property in the Village of Flower Hill. In 1976, the then owners of the subject premises and appellants' predecessors in title, applied to the village board of trustees to rezone the property from a General Municipal and Public Purposes District to a Business District. On October 4 of that year the village board granted the rezoning application by the following resolution:

"RESOLVED that the application of Ray R. Beck Company for a change of Zone * * * is granted upon the following conditions:

"(a) The Subject Premises and any buildings, structures and improvements situated or to be situated thereon, will be erected, altered, renovated, remodelled, used, occupied and maintained for the following purposes and no other;

"(i) Offices for the practice of the professions of medicine, dentistry, law, engineering, architecture or accountancy;

"(ii) Executive offices to be used solely for the management of business concerns and associations and excluding therefrom, but without limitation, retail or wholesale sales offices or agencies, brokerage offices of all types and kinds, collection or employment agencies or offices, computer programming centres or offices, counseling centres or offices and training offices or business or trade schools.

* * *

"(d) No building or structure situated on the Subject Premises on the date of this Declaration of Covenants will be altered, extended, rebuilt, renovated or enlarged without the prior consent of the Board of Trustees of the Village.

* * *

Subsequently, appellants' predecessors in title entered into the contemplated declaration of covenants which was recorded in the office of the Clerk of Nassau County on November 29, 1976. Consistent with paragraph (d) of the board's resolution, that declaration provided that "[n]o building or structure situated on the Subject Premises on the date of this Declaration of Covenants will be altered, extended, rebuilt, renovated or enlarged without the prior consent of the Board of Trustees of the Village."

Appellants, after acquiring title, made application in late 1978 to the village board for approval to enlarge and extend the existing structure on the premises. Without any reason being given that application was denied. Appellants then commenced this action to have the board's determination declared arbitrary, capricious, unreasonbale, and unconstitutional and sought by way of ultimate relief an order directing the board to issue the necessary building permits.

Asserting that the board's denial of the application was beyond review as to reasonableness, respondent moved to dismiss the complaint for failure to state a cause of action. Special Term denied the motion, equating appellants' allegation that the board's action was arbitrary and capricious with an allegation that such action was lacking in good faith and fair dealing—an allegation which it found raised triable issues of fact. The Appellate Division, 75 A.D.2d 631, 427 N.Y.S.2d 301, reversed and dismissed the complaint, holding that the allegation of arbitrary and capricious action by the board was not the equivalent of an allegation that the board breached an implied covenant of fair dealing and good faith. We now affirm.

At the outset this case involves the question of the permissibility of municipal rezoning conditioned on the execution of a private declaration of convenants restricting the use to which the parcel sought to be rezoned may be put. Prior to our decision in *Church v. Town of Islip,* 8 N.Y.2d 254, 203 N.Y.S.2d 866, 168 N.E.2d 680 in which we upheld rezoning of property subject to reasonable conditions, conditional rezoning had been almost uniformly condemned by courts of all jurisdictions—a position to which a majority of States appear to continue to adhere. Since *Church,* however, the practice of conditional zoning has become increasingly widespread in this State, as well as having gained popularity in other jurisdictions. [ ]

Because much criticism has been mounted against the practice, both by commentators and the courts of some of our sister States, further exposition is in order.

Probably the principal objection to conditional rezoning is that it constitutes illegal spot zoning, thus violating the legislative mandate requiring that there be a comprehensive plan for, and that all conditions be uniform within, a given zoning district. When courts have considered the issue [ ], the assumptions have been made that conditional zoning benefits particular landowners rather than the community as a whole and that it undermines the foundation upon which comprehensive zoning depends by destroying uniformity within use districts. Such unexamined assumptions are questionable. First, it is a downward change to a less restrictive zoning classification that benefits the property rezoned and not the opposite imposition of greater restrictions on land use. Indeed, imposing limiting conditions, while benefiting surrounding properties, normally adversely affects the premises on which the conditions are imposed. Second, zoning is not invalid per se merely because only a single parcel is involved or benefited [ ]; the real test for spot zoning is whether the change is other than part of a well-considered and comprehensive plan calculated to serve the general welfare of the community [ ]. Such a determination, in turn, depends on the reasonableness of the rezoning in relation to neighboring uses—an inquiry required regardless of whether the change in zone is conditional in form. Third, if it is initially proper to change a zoning classification without the imposition of restrictive conditions notwithstanding that such change may depart from uniformity, then no reason exists why accomplishing that change subject to condition should automatically be classified as impermissible spot zoning.

Both conditional and unconditional rezoning involve essentially the same legislative act—an amendment of the zoning ordinance. The standards for judging the validity of conditional rezoning are no different from the standards used to judge whether unconditional rezoning is illegal. If modification to a less restrictive zoning classification is warranted, then a fortiori conditions imposed by a local legislature to minimize conflicts among districts should not in and of themselves violate any prohibition against spot zoning.

Another fault commonly voiced in disapproval of conditional zoning is that it constitutes an illegal bargaining away of a local government's police power [ ]. Because no municipal government has the power to make contracts that control or limit it in the exercise of its legislative powers and duties, restrictive agreements made by a municipality in conjunction with a rezoning are sometimes said to violate public policy. While permitting citizens to be governed by the best bargain they can strike with a local legislature would not be consonant with notions of good government, absent proof of a contract purporting to bind the local legislature in advance to exercise its zoning authority in a bargained-for manner, a rule which would have the effect of forbidding a municipality from trying to protect landowners in the vicinity of a zoning change by imposing protective conditions based on the assertion that that body is bargaining away its discretion, would not be in the best interests of the public. The imposition of conditions on property sought to be rezoned may not be classified as a prospective commitment on the part of the municipality to zone as requested if the conditions are met; nor would the municipality necessarily be precluded on this account from later reversing or altering its decision [ ].

Yet another criticism leveled at conditional zoning is that the State enabling legislation does not confer on local authorities authorization to enact conditional zoning amendments [ ]. On this view any such ordinance would be *ultra vires*. While it is accurate to say there exists no explicit authorization that a legislative body may attach conditions to zoning amendments (see, e.g., Village Law, § 7–700 *et seq.*), neither is there any language which expressly forbids a local legislature to do so. Statutory silence is not necessarily a denial of the authority to engage in such a practice. Where in the face of nonaddress in the enabling legislation there exists independent justification for the practice as an appropriate exercise of municipal power, that power will be implied. Conditional rezoning is a means of achieving some degree of flexibility in land-use control by minimizing the potentially deleterious effect of a zoning change on neighboring properties; reasonably conceived conditions harmonize the landowner's need for rezoning with the public interest and certainly fall within the spirit of the enabling legislation [ ].

One final concern of those reluctant to uphold the practice is that resort to conditional rezoning carries with it no inherent restrictions apart from the restrictive agreement itself. This fear, however, is justifiable only if conditional rezoning is considered a contractual relationship between municipality and private party, outside the scope of the zoning power—a view to which we do not subscribe. When conditions are incorporated in an amending ordinance, the result is as much a "zoning regulation" as an ordinance, adopted without conditions. Just as the scope of all zoning regulation is limited by the police power, and thus local legislative bodies must act reasonably and in the best interests of public safety, welfare and convenience [ ], the scope of permissible conditions must of necessity be similarly limited. If, upon proper proof, the conditions imposed are found unreasonable, the rezoning amendment as well as the required conditions would have to be nullified, with the affected property reverting to the preamendment zoning classification.

Against this backdrop we proceed to consideration of the contentions advanced by appellants in the appeal now before us.   *   *   *

The focus of appellants' assault is the provision of the declaration of covenants that no structure may be extended or enlarged "without the prior consent of the Board of Trustees of the Village". Appellants would have us import the added substantive prescription—"which consent may not be unreasonably withheld". Their argument proceeds along two paths: first, that as a matter of construction the added prescription should be read into the provision; second, that because of limitations associated with the exercise of municipal zoning power the village board would have been required to include such a prescription.

Appellants' construction argument must fail. The terminology employed in the declaration is explicit. The concept that appellants would invoke is not obscure and language to give it effect was readily available had it been the intention of the parties to include this added stipulation. Appellants point to no canon of construction in the law of real property or of contracts which would call for judicial insertion of the missing clause. * * *

The second path either leads nowhere or else goes too far. If it is appellants' assertion that the village board was legally required to insist on inclusion of the desired prescription, there is no authority in the court to reform the zoning enactment of 1976 retroactively to impose the omitted clause. Whether the village board at that time would have enacted a different resolution in the form now desired by appellants is open only to speculation; the certainty is that they did not then take such legislative action. On the other hand, acceptance of appellants' proposition would produce as the other possible consequence the conclusion that the 1976 enactment was illegal, throwing appellants unhappily back to the pre–1976 zoning of their premises, a destination which they assuredly wish to sidestep.

Finally, we agree with the Appellate Division that the allegation of the complaint that the village board in denying appellants' application acted in an arbitrary and capricious manner is not an allegation that the board acted in bad faith or its equivalent.

For the reasons stated the Board of Trustees of the Incorporated Village of Flower Hill may not now be compelled to issue its consent to the proposed enlargement and extension of the existing structure on the premises or in the alternative give an acceptable reason for failing to do so. Accordingly, the order of the Appellate Division should be affirmed, with costs.

Notes and Questions

1. Is the court being realistic when it concludes that there is no bargaining process in conditional zoning? Why would a restrictive covenant, such as the one in dispute in *Collard*, be placed on the property except in expectation of, or in return for, a favorable zoning decision?

2. Why should "bargaining away of the police power" be a concern? Is it a means for reaching acceptable compromises in neighborhood land use disputes, or an invitation to corruption of the parties involved?

3. Developers seeking approval for large, complex projects often have to obtain permits and submit to a series of reviews under flexible "wait and see" techniques described infra. Because of the uncertainties created by the permit review process, developers often seek "Developers Agreements," authorized in a number of states, to set the "rules of the game" for the continued review of their project. For a superb analysis of the use of negotiated agreements as a basis for land use regulation, see Wegner, Moving Toward the Bargaining Table: Contract Zoning, Development

Agreements, and the Theoretical Foundations of Government Land Use Deals, 65 N.C.L.Rev. 957 (1987).

SALSICH, KEYSTONE BITUMINOUS COAL, FIRST ENGLISH AND NOLLAN: A FRAMEWORK FOR ACCOMMODATION?

34 J. Urb & Contemp L. 173, 187–190 (1988).

Although land use litigation is often framed as a contest between a developer and a land use regulator, scholars and practitioners have recognized a third party in most land use conflicts. An owner's proposed use of a particular tract often has an impact on two different groups of people. Adjacent landowners and residents experience the physical and aesthetic impacts of the size, shape, and density of the specific land use. A larger group of people, including residents and nonresidents of the governmental entity in which the land is located, may also experience a direct or indirect financial impact in the form of increased or decreased taxes. The degree of the impact on taxes depends on whether the particular land development increases the need for public services without a corresponding increase in the tax base, or whether the project increases the tax base without a corresponding increase in the demand for public services. It is also possible for this larger group to experience variations in choice of housing or employment, depending upon the nature of the particular development. These groups will also experience the environmental effects of the development.

These groups and the owner/developer may expect the governmental entity responsible for regulating land use to represent their best interests when making land use regulatory decisions. When subgroups emerge both to support and to oppose a land development project, the land use regulator may find itself caught in the middle of a struggle over competing values. The resulting relationship resembles a triangle with the owner/developer on one side, the neighbors on another, and the community at-large on the third. All three groups are locked into this relationship because of the external effects of a land development project, which varies with the nature and size of the development.

As with other relationships in which competing and common interests exist, owner/developers, neighbors, and the community at-large need to support one another for land use relationships to succeed. Although land does not depreciate in the sense that a building does, it is a finite resource that can be wasted by unnecessary or harmful development. When poorly executed development plans waste land, it may be lost for the current generation because of the enormous cost and difficulty of reclaiming such land. Although landowners and developers make the decisions that produce land waste, they are also members of the community at-large. As such, they too will benefit from land use regulations which effectively prevent land waste, and thus the community should urge developers to support such regulations.

Likewise, land use regulators need property users and developers. With the exception of land set aside in public parks and wilderness areas, legislators generally aim their regulations at balancing desirable and undesirable uses of privately owned land to benefit society. If regulations are so onerous that they discourage even desirable development, they do not benefit the community. Thus, the reaction of developers to land regulation provides important feedback to legislators concerning the utility of their regulations.

The availability of compensation as a remedy in taking cases is a significant addition to land use law. The compensation remedy supports those traditional arguments that accepted no difference in principle between "takings by dispossession" and "takings by excessive regulation." In addition, compensation can serve as a necessary check on government and as a means of retaining (or perhaps restoring) the consent of the people in their governments. Finally, compensation can be viewed as the price for public willingness to accept the "innovative," "flexible," and "comprehensive" land use regulations that today's legislators believe necessary.

The American system of property law, with its emphasis on private ownership of land, has two basic goals: to maximize and protect individual freedoms and to effectively utilize land. To achieve these goals, the chief actors in the American property law system—landowners, developers, users, neighbors, and regulators—must respect one another's interests. Additionally, state and local governments must provide the community with appropriate vehicles for asserting these competing interests. Ideally, these interests should exist in equilibrium. If one is perceived to have an unfair advantage, the cooperation necessary for the system's functioning breaks down. * * *

A Note on Planned Unit Developments and Other Techniques for Increasing Flexibility

Planned Unit Developments (Cluster Zoning)

The planned unit development (PUD) technique, popularized in the 1950s as part of a second generation of zoning, provides an opportunity for more flexible design and location of buildings and more creative use of open space than does the original Euclidean version of zoning. PUD zoning, also known as cluster zoning, permits developers to deviate from rigid lot size and building set-back requirements and, in some cases, to mix uses within a development.

The conceptual advance of the PUD concept was a shift in focus from individual lots in a development to the entire tract that comprises the development. For example, instead of requiring all houses in a

100–unit subdivision to be placed in the same spots on one-acre lots, with the same-sized front, rear and side yards, which often was the case under traditional zoning, a cluster zone provision permitting PUDs enables a developer to rearrange the houses in more attractive clusters around open spaces such as small ponds and parks, golf courses, village squares and woodlands.

PUDs have been praised for allowing more variety in appearance and for enabling developers to work with topographical features and terrain rather than against them. PUDs have been criticized for requiring more costly infrastructure such as roads and sewers and for contributing to a sense of isolation that residents of suburbia have sometimes experienced.

Cluster zoning usually is limited to relatively large tracts of land of at least 10 to 20 acres. Specific PUD proposals must be harmonious with the immediate environs and consistent with the municipality's land use plans.

Courts have been generally receptive to the cluster zone/PUD concept, including the extra scrutiny local officials may give a PUD proposal because of the contemplated relaxation of local land use regulations, but have required municipalities to deal fairly with developers by refraining from arbitrary denials or excessive requirements. See, e.g., Kenart & Associates v. Skagit County, 37 Wash.App. 295, 680 P.2d 439 (1984), rev. den., 101 Wash.2d 1021, ___ P.2d ___ (1984) (denial of PUD application reversed because planning commission findings failed to "provide guidance to the developer [or] permit meaningful appellate review").

Floating Zones

A close companion of the cluster zone/PUD concept is the floating zone, designed to add flexibility to the way that PUDs and other similar techniques are administered. Under the original Euclidean system of comprehensive zoning, all land in the municipality is divided into districts containing fixed boundaries that are identified on a zoning district map. If a zoning amendment is approved, a corresponding change is made on the zoning map.

Floating zones differ from traditional Euclidean zones in that they "have no such defined boundaries [but] 'float' over the entire area * * * where [they] may eventually be established." Bigenho v. Montgomery County Council, 248 Md. 386, 237 A.2d 53, 56 (1968). Creating a floating zone is a two-step process. First the municipality enacts an ordinance authorizing a particular range of activities such as planned unit development, commercial office parks, multi-family residential projects and mixed use developments, without specifying specific areas in the municipality where these activities can take place. A second ordinance is enacted that "anchors" the floating zone to a particular tract of land in response to specific development proposals.

After early doubts about the validity of the floating zone technique under traditional zoning enabling statutes, most courts have accepted the floating zone "as a recognition that municipal legislative bodies need a certain flexibility" in administering their zoning programs. Treme v. St. Louis County, 609 S.W.2d 706, 712 (Mo.App.1980), reviewing cases.

Overlay Zones

For a variety of reasons, municipalities may desire to impose different regulations on certain permitted uses in part of an existing zoning district. To accomplish this goal, the new regulations are "laid over" the existing zoning map. Existing regulations that do not conflict with the overlay district provisions remain in effect, but conflicting ones are pre-empted. See, e.g., Franchise Developers, Inc. v. City of Cincinnati, 30 Ohio St.3d 28, 505 N.E.2d 966, 968 (1987) (upholding as reasonable an environmental quality district that prevented development of a fast food restaurant on a particular site in Cincinnati even though the proposed use was permitted by the commercial zoning district in which the site was located).

Performance Standards

An alternative to the territorial division of zoning is the application of regulatory standards to control harmful effects of development, such as noise, pollution, and traffic, while permitting more heterogenous mixes of uses. The focus of regulation under a performance standard approach shifts from the type of use permitted to the impact of the use. Performance standard regulation requires municipalities to articulate meaningful and understandable standards and apply them in an even-handed manner. Most environmental regulation legislation has adopted the performance standard approach. For an excellent discussion of performance standards and other flexible techniques, see D. Porter, P. Phillips & T. Lassar, Flexible Zoning: How It Works (ULI, 1988). See generally, P. Salsich, Land Use Regulation 156–163 (1991).

D. FORBIDDEN SEGREGATION—RACE, SEX, RELIGION, FAMILY STATUS, AGE, DISABILITY

As we discussed in the chapter on landlord-tenant relations, federal, state, and local statutes now prohibit the denial of housing opportunities on the basis of race, sex, religion, age, family status, or disability. These statutes have been held to apply to local land-use regulations. Village of Arlington Heights v. Metropolitan Housing Development Corp., 558 F.2d 1283, 1288 (7th Cir.1977), cert. denied, 434 U.S. 1025, 98 S.Ct. 752, 54 L.Ed.2d 772 (1978) (discriminatory effect can in some instances establish Fair Housing Act violation); Huntington Branch, NAACP v. Town of Huntington, 844 F.2d 926 (2d Cir.1988), cert den. and appeal dism'd, 488 U.S. 15, 109 S.Ct. 276, 102 L.Ed.2d 180 (1988) (refusal to rezone to enable multi-family housing to be constructed outside of largely minority "urban renewal area" held violative of Fair Housing Act).

As is often the case with regulatory schemes, legitimate policy objectives may clash in the implementation phase. These clashes usually are first detectable in the law office, at least when a lawyer is contacted to help plan a proposed course of action.

Consider, for example, a family that wishes to build an addition on their house to create an accessory apartment for an elderly parent.

The apartment would have a separate entrance, as well as separate kitchen and bath facilities. The zoning code prohibits two-family units (duplexes) in the single-family district where the family lives. Assuming the addition will comply with all applicable building and fire codes, can the city deny a building permit to the family? Suppose the family wishes to rent it to any elderly or disabled person, whether related to them or not? See, e.g., 42 U.S.C. § 3607(b)(1) (Fair Housing Act does not limit the applicability of reasonable local regulations regarding maximum number of occupants permitted to occupy a dwelling).

Suppose a non-profit agency plans to acquire a house and convert it into a group home for six developmentally disabled students. The applicable zoning regulation requires special use permits for group homes, and prohibits group homes from being closer than 1000 feet from another group home. If another group home is operating on the same block, less than 1000 feet away, can the special use permit be denied? See Familystyle of St. Paul, Inc. v. City of St. Paul, 923 F.2d 91 (8th Cir.1991) (zoning ordinance requiring group homes for mentally impaired to be located at least a quarter of a mile apart upheld as reasonable accommodation of Federal goal of non-discrimination, and state goal of deinstitutionalization).

E. ZONING FOR AESTHETICS—PERMISSIBLE SEGREGATION OF UNDESIRABLE USES

STATE EX REL. STOYANOFF v. BERKELEY

Supreme Court of Missouri, 1970.
458 S.W.2d 305.

PRITCHARD, COMMISSIONER.

Upon summary judgment the trial court issued a peremptory writ of mandamus to compel appellant to issue a residential building permit to respondents. The trial court's judgment is that the below-mentioned ordinances are violative of Section 10, Article I of the Constitution of Missouri, 1945, V.A.M.S., in that restrictions placed by the ordinances on the use of property deprive the owners of their property without due process of law. Relators' petition pleads that they applied to appellant Building Commissioner for a building permit to allow them to construct a single family residence in the City of Ladue, and that plans and specifications were submitted for the proposed residence, which was unusual in design, "but complied with all existing building and zoning regulations and ordinances of the City of Ladue, Missouri."

It is further pleaded that relators were refused a building permit for the construction of their proposed residence upon the ground that the permit was not approved by the Architectural Board of the City of Ladue. Ordinance 131, as amended by Ordinance 281 of that city, purports to set up an Architectural Board to approve plans and specifications for buildings and structures erected within the city and in a preamble to "conform to certain minimum architectural standards of appearance and conformity with surrounding structures, and that unsightly, grotesque and unsuitable structures, detrimental to the stability of value and the welfare of surrounding property, structures and residents, and to the general welfare and happiness of the community, be avoided, and that appropriate standards of beauty and conformity be fostered and encouraged." It is asserted in the petition that the ordinances are invalid, illegal and void, "are unconstitutional in that they are vague and provide no standard nor uniform rule by which to guide the architectural board," that the city acted in excess of statutory powers (§ 89.020, RSMo 1959, V.A.M.S.) in enacting the ordinances, which "attempt to allow respondent to impose aesthetic standards for buildings in the City of Ladue, and are in excess of the powers granted the City of Ladue by said statute."

Relators filed a motion for summary judgment and affidavits were filed in opposition thereto. Richard D. Shelton, Mayor of the City of Ladue, deponed that the facts in appellant's answer were true and correct, as here pertinent: that the City of Ladue constitutes one of the finer suburban residential areas of Metropolitan St. Louis, the homes therein are considerably more expensive than in cities of comparable size, being homes on lots from three fourths of an acre to three or more acres each; that a zoning ordinance was enacted by the city regulating the height, number of stories, size of buildings, percentage of lot occupancy, yard sizes, and the location and use of buildings and land for trade, industry, residence and other purposes; that the zoning regulations were made in accordance with a comprehensive plan "designed to promote the health and general welfare of the residents of the City of Ladue," which in furtherance of said objectives duly enacted said Ordinances numbered 131 and 281. Appellant also asserted in his answer that these ordinances were a reasonable exercise of the city's governmental, legislative and police powers, as determined by its legislative body, and as stated in the above-quoted preamble to the ordinances. It is then pleaded that relators' description of their proposed residence as "'unusual in design' is the understatement of the year. It is in fact a monstrosity of grotesque design, which would seriously impair the value of property in the neighborhood."

The affidavit of Harold C. Simon, a developer of residential subdivisions in St. Louis County, is that he is familiar with relators' lot upon which they seek to build a house, and with the surrounding houses in the neighborhood; that the houses therein existent are virtually all two-story houses of conventional architectural design, such as Colonial, French Provincial or English; and that the house which relators propose to construct is of ultra-modern design which would clash with and not be in conformity with any other house in the entire neighborhood. It is Mr. Simon's opinion that the design and appearance of relators' proposed residence would have a substantial adverse effect upon the market values of other residential property in the neighborhood, such average market value ranging from $60,000 to $85,000 each.

As a part of the affidavit of Russell H. Riley, consultant for the city planning and engineering firm of Harland Bartholomew & Associates, photographic exhibits of homes surrounding relators' lot were attached. * * * According to Mr. Riley the standards of Ordinance 131, as amended by Ordinance 281, are usually and customarily applied in city planning work and are: "(1) whether the proposed house meets the customary architectural requirements in appearance and design for a house of the particular type which is proposed (whether it be Colonial, Tudor English, French Provincial, or Modern), (2) whether the proposed house is in general conformity with the style and design of surrounding structures, and (3) whether the proposed house lends itself to the proper architectural development of the City; and that in applying said standards the Architectural Board and its Chairman are to determine whether the proposed house will have an adverse effect on the stability of values in the surrounding area."

Photographic exhibits of relators' proposed residence were also attached to Mr. Riley's affidavit. They show the residence to be of a pyramid shape, with a flat top, and with triangular shaped windows or doors at one or more corners.

Although appellant has briefed the point that it is a constitutional exercise of the police power for the Legislature to authorize cities to enact zoning ordinances, it is apparent that relators do not contest that issue. Rather, relators' position is that "the creation by the City of Ladue of an architectural board for the purpose of promoting and maintaining 'general conformity with the style and design of surrounding structures' is totally unauthorized by our Enabling Statute." (§§ 89.020, 89.040, RSMo 1959, V.A.M.S.) It is further contended by relators that Ordinances 131 and 281 are invalid and unconstitutional as being an unreasonable and arbitrary exercise of the police power (as based entirely on aesthetic values); and that the same are invalid as an unlawful delegation of legislative powers (to the Architectural Board).

Section 89.020 provides: "For the purpose of promoting health, safety, morals or the general welfare of the community, the legislative body of all cities, towns, and villages is hereby empowered to regulate and restrict the height, number of stories, and size of buildings and other structures, the percentage of lot that may be occupied, the size of yards, courts, and other open spaces, the density of population, the preservation of features of historical significance, and the location and use of buildings, structures and land for trade, industry, residence or other purposes." Section 89.040 provides: "Such regulations shall be made in accordance with a comprehensive plan and designed to lessen congestion in the streets; to secure safety from fire, panic and other dangers; to promote health *and the general welfare;* to provide adequate light and air; to prevent the overcrowding of land; to avoid undue concentration of population; to preserve features of historical significance; to facilitate the adequate provision of transportation, water, sewerage, schools, parks, and other public requirements. *Such regulations shall be made with reasonable consideration, among other things, to the character of the district and its peculiar suitability for particular uses, and with a view to conserving the values of buildings and encouraging the most appropriate use of land throughout such municipality."* (Italics added.)

Relators say that "Neither Sections 89.020 or 89.040 nor any other provision of Chapter 89 mentions or gives a city the authority to regulate architectural design and appearance. There exists no provision providing for an architectural board and no entity even remotely resembling such a board is mentioned under the enabling legislation." Relators conclude that the City of Ladue lacked any power to adopt Ordinance 131 as amended by Ordinance 281 "and its intrusion into this area is wholly unwarranted and without sanction in the law." * * *

As is clear from the affidavits and attached exhibits, the City of Ladue is an area composed principally of residences of the general types of Colonial, French Provincial and English Tudor. The city has a comprehensive plan of zoning to maintain the general character of buildings therein. * * * [T]he character of the district, its suitability for particular uses, and the conservation of the values of buildings therein. * * * are directly related to the general welfare of the community. That proposition has support in a number of cases cited by appellant. [ ] The preamble to Ordinance 131, quoted above in part, demonstrates that its purpose is to conform to the dictates of § 89.040, with reference to preserving values of property by zoning procedure and restrictions on the use of property. This is an illustration of what was referred to in Deimeke v. State Highway Commission, Mo., 444 S.W.2d 480, 484, as a growing number of cases recognizing a change in the scope of the term "general welfare." In the Deimeke case on the same page it is said, "Property use which offends sensibilities and debases property values affects not only the adjoining property owners in that vicinity but the general public as well because when such property values are destroyed or seriously impaired, the tax base of the community is affected and the public suffers economically as a result."

Relators say further that Ordinances 131 and 281 are invalid and unconstitutional as being an unreasonable and arbitrary exercise of the police power. It is argued that a mere reading of these ordinances shows that they are based entirely on aesthetic factors in that the stated purpose of the Architectural Board is to maintain "conformity with surrounding structures" and to assure that structures "conform to certain minimum architectural standards of appearance." The argument ignores the further provisos in the ordinance: " * * * and that unsightly, grotesque and unsuitable structures, *detrimental to the stability of value and the welfare of surrounding property, structures, and residents,* and *to the general welfare and happiness of the community,* be avoided, and that appropriate standards of beauty and conformity be fostered and encouraged." (Italics added.) Relators' proposed residence does not descend to the " 'patently offensive character of vehicle graveyards in close proximity to such highways' " referred to in the Deimeke case, supra (444 S.W.2d 484). Nevertheless, the aesthetic factor to be taken into account by the Architectural Board is not to be considered alone. Along with that inherent factor is the effect that the proposed residence would have upon the property values in the area. In this time of burgeoning urban areas, congested with people and structures, it is certainly in keeping with the ultimate ideal of general welfare that the Architectural Board, in its function, preserve and protect existing areas in which structures of a general conformity of architecture have been erected. The area under consideration is clearly, from the record, a fashionable one. In State ex rel. Civello v. City of New Orleans, 154 La. 271, 97 So. 440, 444, the court said, "If by the term 'aesthetic considerations' is meant a regard merely for outward appearances, for good taste in the matter of the beauty of the neighborhood itself, we do not observe any substantial reason for saying that such a consideration is not a matter of general welfare. The beauty of a fashionable residence neighborhood in a city is for the comfort and happiness of the residents, and it sustains in a general way the value of property in the neighborhood." * * *

In the matter of enacting zoning ordinances and the procedures for determining whether any certain proposed structure or use is in compliance with or offends the basic ordinance, it is well settled that courts will not substitute their judgments for the city's legislative body, if the result is not oppressive, arbitrary or unreasonable and does not infringe upon a valid preexisting nonconforming use. [ ] The denial by appellant of a building permit for relators' highly modernistic residence in this area where traditional Colonial, French Provincial and English Tudor styles of architecture are erected does not appear to be arbitrary and unreasonable when the basic purpose to be served is that of the general welfare of persons in the entire community.

* * *

Relators claim that the * * * provisions of the ordinance amount to an unconstitutional delegation of power by the city to the Architectural Board. It is argued that the Board cannot be given the power to determine what is unsightly and grotesque and that the standards, "whether the proposed structure will conform to proper architectural standards in appearance and design, and will be in general conformity with the style and design of surrounding structures and conducive to the proper architectural development of the City * * * " and "the Board shall disapprove the application if it determines that the proposed structure will constitute an unsightly, grotesque or unsuitable structure in appearance, detrimental to the welfare of surrounding property or residents * * *," are inadequate. * * * Here, * * * the procedures are for public hearings with notice to the applicant, not only by the Architectural Board but also by the City Council on appeal on the factual issues to be determined under the ordinance. An applicant's rights are safeguarded in this respect * * *. Ordinances 131 and 281 are sufficient in their general standards calling for a factual determination of the suitability of any proposed structure with reference to the character of the surrounding neighborhood and to the determination of any adverse effect on the general welfare and preservation of property values of the community. * * *

The judgment is reversed.

Notes and Questions

1. *Stoyanoff* is an example of what has been called aesthetic zoning, the practice of discriminating against activities that depart from the norm, such as radical designs of buildings, unusual types of building materials (e.g., a plastic house), and the use of signs to convey messages. On what basis did the *Stoyanoff* court sustain the challenged zoning regulations? Was the offensive design threatening harm to the community? If so, what type of harm? Was the community's attack directed at the design of the building, or at the type of people who would live in such a house? Why were they perceived as threatening?

2. What defenses can a landowner raise to attacks against a proposed building design? Is there an unconstitutional "taking" of property? An arbitrary exercise of the police power? Must the offensive design or type of building materials constitute a nuisance in order for a ban to be sustained?

3. Signs raise particularly difficult First Amendment free speech issues, as well as property regulation issues. The Supreme Court has upheld the regulation, and in some cases the prohibition, of signs as a reasonable means of attacking "visual blight," but it has drawn the line against sign regulations that infringe on "political" speech or unreasonably restrict "commercial" speech. Members of City Council v. Vincent, 466 U.S. 789, 104 S.Ct. 2118, 80 L.Ed.2d 772 (1984).

Regulation of political speech is off limits except for compelling governmental reasons, usually not found in a land use context. Metromedia, Inc. v. City of San Diego, 453 U.S. 490, 101 S.Ct. 2882, 69 L.Ed.2d 800 (1981). Commercial speech, such as billboard advertisements of commercial products, can be subjected to reasonable "time, place and manner" regulations so long as the regulations do not affect the "content" of the speech. Central Hudson Gas & Elec. Corp. v. Public Service Com'n, 447 U.S. 557, 100 S.Ct. 2343, 65 L.Ed.2d 341 (1980).

How would you advise a city wishing to preserve the ambience of its well-to-do residential areas and considering a ban on all yard signs in those areas? Would it have to allow "For Sale" signs? Could it restrict the size or number of such signs on a lot? In a block? See Linmark Associates, Inc. v. Township of Willingboro, 431 U.S. 85, 97 S.Ct. 1614, 52 L.Ed.2d 155 (1977) (prohibition of For Sale and Sold signs invalidated).

What about signs advertising private garage or estate sales? Signs supporting political candidates? Could your client community ban a sign advocating peaceful negotiations rather than war as a means of resolving an international dispute? Would it be relevant that a neighbor attorney stated that he did not wish to be confronted with that message when he arrived home after a hard day at the office? See Gilleo v. City of Ladue, 774 F.Supp. 1564 (E.D.Mo.1991) (ban on sign advocating no war in Persian Gulf invalidated).

4. The segregative aspect of zoning has occasionally led to challenges under federal antitrust statutes from persons who are disappointed by decisions to deny zoning permission for commercial or industrial development proposals. The Supreme Court laid to rest most questions about potential antitrust liability for zoning decisions in City of Columbia v. Omni Outdoor Advertising, Inc., 111 S.Ct. 1344, 113 L.Ed.2d 382 (1991), a case in which major revisions to a municipal sign ordinance were challenged as illegally favoring one company that had erected billboards before the sign ordinance was enacted and hindering the ability of a competitor by restricting the number of additional billboards that could be installed.

In concluding that zoning ordinances come within a long-standing "state action" exemption to federal antitrust states, the Court stated

> The very purpose of zoning regulation is to displace unfettered business freedom in a manner that regularly has the effect of preventing normal acts of competition, particularly on the part of new entrants. A municipal ordinance restricting the size, location, and spacing of billboards (surely a common form of zoning) necessarily protects existing billboards against some competition from newcomers.

111 S.Ct. at 1350.

F. EXCLUSIONARY ZONING—IMPERMISSIBLE SEGREGATION OF UNDESIRABLE PEOPLE

SOUTHERN BURLINGTON COUNTY N.A.A.C.P. v. TOWNSHIP OF MOUNT LAUREL

Supreme Court of New Jersey, 1975.
67 N.J. 151, 336 A.2d 713, appeal dismissed, 423 U.S. 808, 96 S.Ct. 18, 46 L.Ed.2d 28.

HALL, J.

This case attacks the system of land use regulation by defendant Township of Mount Laurel on the ground that low and moderate income families are thereby unlawfully excluded from the municipality. The trial court so found, [ ] and declared the township zoning ordinance totally invalid. Its judgment went on, in line with the requests for affirmative relief, to order the municipality to make studies of the housing needs of low and moderate income persons presently or formerly residing in the community in substandard housing, as well as those in such income classifications presently employed in the township and living elsewhere or reasonably expected to be employed therein in the future, and to present a plan of affirmative public action designed "to enable and encourage the satisfaction of the indicated needs." Jurisdiction was retained for judicial consideration and approval of such a plan and for the entry of a final order requiring its implementation.

* * *

The implications of the issue presented are indeed broad and far-reaching, extending much beyond these particular plaintiffs and the boundaries of this particular municipality.

There is not the slightest doubt that New Jersey has been, and continues to be, faced with a desperate need for housing, especially of decent living accommodations economically suitable for low and moderate income families. The situation was characterized as a "crisis" and fully explored and documented by Governor Cahill in two special messages to the Legislature—*A Blueprint for Housing in New Jersey* (1970) and *New Horizons in Housing* (1972).

Plaintiffs represent the minority group poor (black and Hispanic) seeking such quarters. But they are not the only category of persons barred from so many municipalities by reason of restrictive land use regulations. We have reference to young and elderly couples, single persons and large, growing families not in the poverty class, but who still cannot afford the only kinds of housing realistically permitted in most places—relatively high-priced, single-family detached dwellings on sizeable lots and, in some municipalities, expensive apartments. We will, therefore, consider the case from the wider viewpoint that the effect of Mount Laurel's land use regulation has been to prevent various categories of persons from living in the township because of the limited extent of their income and resources. In this connection, we accept the representation of the municipality's counsel at oral argument that the regulatory scheme was not adopted with any desire or intent to exclude prospective residents on the obviously illegal bases of race, origin or believed social incompatibility.

* * *

I

The Facts

Mount Laurel is a flat, sprawling township, 22 square miles, or about 14,000 acres, in area, on the west central edge of Burlington County. It is roughly triangular in shape, with its base, approximately eight miles long, extending in a northeasterly-southwesterly direction roughly parallel with and a few miles east of the Delaware River. Part of its southerly side abuts Cherry Hill in Camden County. That section of the township is about seven miles from the boundary line of the city of Camden and not more than 10 miles from the Benjamin Franklin Bridge crossing the river to Philadelphia.

In 1950, the township had a population of 2817, only about 600 more people than it had in 1940. It was then, as it had been for decades, primarily a rural agricultural area with no sizeable settlements or commercial or industrial enterprises. The populace generally lived in individual houses scattered along country roads. There were several pockets of poverty, with deteriorating or dilapidated housing (apparently 300 or so units of which remain today in equally poor condition). After 1950, as in so many other municipalities similarly situated, residential development and some commerce and industry began to come in. By 1960 the population had almost doubled to 5249 and by 1970 had more than doubled again to 11,221. These new residents were, of course, "outsiders" from the nearby central cities and older suburbs or from more distant places drawn here by reason of employment in the region. The township is now definitely a part of the outer ring of the South Jersey metropolitan area, which area we define as those portions of Camden, Burlington and Gloucester Counties within a semicircle having a radius of 20 miles or so from the heart of Camden city. And 65% of the township is still vacant land or in agricultural use.

* * *

The location and nature of development has been, as usual, controlled by the local zoning enactments. The general ordinance presently in force, which was declared invalid by the trial court, was adopted in 1964. We understand that earlier enactments provided, however, basically the same scheme but were less restrictive as to residential development. The growth pattern dictated by the ordinance is typical.

Under the present ordinance, 29.2% of all the land in the township, or 4,121 acres, is zoned for industry. This amounts to 2,800 more acres than were so zoned by the 1954 ordinance. The industrial districts comprise most of the land on both sides of the turnpike and routes I–295, 73 and 38. Only industry meeting specified performance standards is permitted. The effect is to limit the use substantially to light manufacturing, research, distribution of goods, offices and the like. Some non-industrial uses, such as agriculture, farm dwellings, motels, a harness racetrack, and certain retail sales and service establishments, are permitted in this zone. At the time of trial no more than 100 acres, mostly in the southwesterly corner along route 73 adjacent to the turnpike and I–295 interchanges, were actually occupied by industrial uses. They had been constructed in recent years, mostly in several industrial parks, and involved tax ratables of about 16 million dollars. The rest of the land so zoned has remained undeveloped. If it were fully utilized, the testimony was that about 43,500 industrial jobs would be created, but it appeared clear that, as happens in the case of so many municipalities, much more land has been so zoned than the reasonable potential for industrial movement or expansion warrants. At the same time, however, the land cannot be used for residential development under the general ordinance.

The amount of land zoned for retail business use under the general ordinance is relatively small—169 acres, or 1.2% of the total. Some of it is near the turnpike interchange; most of the rest is allocated to a handful of neighborhood commercial districts. While the greater part of the land so zoned appears to be in use, there is no major shopping center or concentrated retail commercial area—"downtown"—in the township.

The balance of the land area, almost 10,000 acres, has been developed until recently in the conventional form of major subdivisions. The general ordinance provides for four residential zones, designated R–1, R–1D, R–2 and R–3. All permit only single-family, detached dwellings, one house per lot—the usual form of grid development. Attached townhouses, apartments (except on farms for agricultural workers) and mobile homes are not allowed anywhere in the township under the general ordinance. This dwelling development, resulting in the previously mentioned quadrupling of the population, has been largely confined to the R–1 and R–2 districts in two sections—the northeasterly and southwesterly corners adjacent to the turnpike and other major highways. The result has been quite intensive development of these sections, but at a low density. The dwellings are substantial; the average value in 1971 was $32,500 and is undoubtedly much higher today.

The general ordinance requirements, while not as restrictive as those in many similar municipalities, nonetheless realistically allow only homes within the financial reach of persons of at least middle income. The R–1 zone requires a minimum lot area of 9,375 square feet, a minimum lot width of 75 feet at the building line, and a minimum dwelling floor area of 1,100 square feet if a one-story building and 1,300 square feet if one and one-half stories or higher. Originally this zone comprised about 2,500 acres. Most of the subdivisions have been constructed within it so that only a few hundred acres remain (the testimony was at variance as to the exact amount). The R–2 zone, comprising a single district of 141 acres in the northeasterly corner, has been completely developed. While it only required a minimum floor area of 900 square feet for a one-story dwelling, the minimum lot size was 11,000 square feet; otherwise the requisites were the same as in the R–1 zone.

The general ordinance places the remainder of the township, outside of the industrial and commercial zones and the R–1D district * * *, in the R–3 zone. This zone comprises over 7,000 acres—slightly more than half of the total municipal area—practically all of which is located in the central part of the township extending southeasterly to the apex of the triangle. The testimony was that about 4,600 acres of it then remained available for housing development. Ordinance requirements are substantially higher, however, in that the minimum lot size is increased to about one-half acre (20,000 square feet). (We understand that sewer and water utilities have not generally been installed, but, of course, they can be.) Lot width at the building line must be 100 feet. Minimum dwelling floor area is as in the R–1 zone. Presently this section is primarily in agricultural use; it contains as well most of the municipality's substandard housing.

* * *

The record thoroughly substantiates the findings of the trial court that over the years Mount Laurel "has acted affirmatively to control development and to attract a selective type of growth" (119 N.J.Super. at 168, 290 A.2d at 467) and that "through its zoning ordinances has exhibited economic discrimination in that the poor have been deprived of adequate housing and the opportunity to secure the construction of subsidized housing, and has used federal, state, county and local finances and resources solely for the betterment of middle and upper-income persons." (119 N.J.Super. at 178, 290 A.2d at 473).

There cannot be the slightest doubt that the reason for this course of conduct has been to keep down local taxes on *property* (Mount Laurel is not a high tax municipality) and that the policy was carried out without regard for non-fiscal considerations with respect to *people*, either within or without its boundaries. This conclusion is demonstrated not only by what was done and what happened, as we have related, but also by innumerable direct statements of municipal officials at public meetings over the years which are found in the exhibits. The trial court referred to a number of them. [ ] No official testified to the contrary.

This policy of land use regulation for a fiscal end derives from New Jersey's tax structure, which has imposed on local real estate most of the cost of municipal and county government and of the primary and secondary education of the municipality's children. The latter expense is much the largest, so, basically, the fewer the school children, the lower the tax rate. Sizeable industrial and commercial ratables are eagerly sought and homes and the lots on which they are situate are required to be large enough, through minimum lot sizes and minimum floor areas, to have substantial value in order to produce greater tax revenues to meet school costs. Large families who cannot afford to buy large houses and must live in cheaper rental accommodations are definitely not wanted, so we find drastic bedroom restrictions for, or complete prohibition of, multi-family or other feasible housing for those of lesser income.

This pattern of land use regulation has been adopted for the same purpose in developing municipality after developing municipality. Almost every one acts solely in its own selfish and parochial interest and in effect builds a wall around itself to keep out those people or entities not adding favorably to the tax base, despite the location of the municipality or the demand for varied kinds of housing. There has been no effective intermunicipal or area planning or land use regulation. All of this is amply demonstrated by the evidence in this case as to Camden, Burlington and Gloucester counties. As to the similar situation generally in the state, see New Jersey Department of Community Affairs, Division of State and Regional Planning, *Land Use Regulation, The Residential Land Supply* (April 1972) (a study assembling and examining the nature and extent of municipal zoning practices in 16 counties as affecting residential land available for low and moderate income housing) and Williams and Norman, Exclusionary Land Use Controls: The Case of North–Eastern New Jersey, 22 Syracuse L.Rev. 475, 486–487 (1971). One incongruous result is the picture of developing municipalities rendering it impossible for lower paid employees of industries they have eagerly sought and welcomed with open arms (and, in Mount Laurel's case, even some of its own lower paid municipal employees) to live in the community where they work.

The other end of the spectrum should also be mentioned because it shows the source of some of the demand for cheaper housing than the developing municipalities have permitted. Core cities were originally the location of most commerce and industry. Many of those facilities furnished employment for the unskilled and semi-skilled. These employees lived relatively near their work, so sections of cities always have housed the majority of people of low and moderate income, generally in old and deteriorating housing. Despite the municipally confined tax structure, commercial and industrial ratables generally used to supply enough revenue to provide and maintain municipal services equal or superior to those furnished in most suburban and rural areas.

The situation has become exactly the opposite since the end of World War II. Much industry and retail business, and even the professions, have left the cities. Camden is a typical example. The testimonial and documentary evidence in this case as to what has happened to that city is depressing indeed. For various reasons, it lost thousands of jobs between 1950 and 1970, including more than half of its manufacturing jobs (a reduction from 43,267 to 20,671, while all jobs in the entire area labor market increased from 94,507 to 197,037). A large segment of retail business faded away with the erection of large suburban shopping centers. The economically better situated city residents helped fill up the miles of sprawling new housing developments, not fully served by public transit. In a society which came to depend more and more on expensive individual motor vehicle transportation for all purposes, low income employees very frequently could not afford to reach outlying places of suitable employment and they certainly could not afford the permissible housing near such locations. These people have great difficulty in obtaining work and have been forced to remain in housing which is overcrowded, and has become more and more substandard and less and less tax productive. There has been a consequent critical erosion of the city tax base and inability to provide the amount and quality of those governmental services— education, health, police, fire, housing and the like—so necessary to the very existence of safe and decent city life. This category of city dwellers desperately needs much better housing and living conditions than is available to them now, both in a rehabilitated city and in outlying municipalities. They make up, along with the other classes of persons earlier mentioned who also cannot afford the only generally permitted housing in the developing municipalities, the acknowledged great demand for low and moderate income housing.

II

THE LEGAL ISSUE

The legal question before us, as earlier indicated, is whether a developing municipality like Mount Laurel may validly, by a system of land use regulation, make it physically and economically impossible to provide low and moderate income housing in the municipality for the various categories of persons who need and want it and thereby, as Mount Laurel has, exclude such people from living within its confines because of the limited extent of their income and resources. Necessarily implicated are the broader questions of the right of such municipalities to limit the kinds of available housing and of any obligation to make possible a variety and choice of types of living accommodations.

We conclude that every such municipality must, by its land use regulations, presumptively make realistically possible an appropriate variety and choice of housing. More specifically, presumptively it cannot foreclose the opportunity of the classes of people mentioned for low and moderate income housing and in its regulations must affirmatively afford that opportunity, at least to the extent of the municipality's fair share of the present and prospective regional need therefor. These obligations must be met unless the particular municipality can sustain the heavy burden of demonstrating peculiar circumstances which dictate that it should not be required so to do.

We reach this conclusion under state law and so do not find it necessary to consider federal constitutional grounds urged by plaintiffs. We begin with some fundamental principles as applied to the scene before us.

Land use regulation is encompassed within the state's police power. Our constitutions have expressly so provided since an amendment in 1927. That amendment, now Art. IV, sec. VI, par. 2 of the 1947 Constitution, authorized legislative delegation of the power to municipalities (other than counties), but reserved the legislative right to repeal or alter the delegation (which we take it means repeal or alteration in whole or in part). The legislative delegation of the zoning power followed in 1928, by adoption of the standard zoning enabling act. * * *

It is elementary theory that all police power enactments, no matter at what level of government, must conform to the basic state constitutional requirements of substantive due process and equal protection of the laws. These are inherent in Art. I, par. 1 of our Constitution,[16] the requirements of which may be more demanding than those of the

---

16. The paragraph reads:
All persons are by nature free and independent, and have certain natural and unalienable rights, among which are those of enjoying and defending life and liberty, of acquiring, possessing, and protecting property, and of pursuing and obtaining safety and happiness.

federal Constitution. [ ] It is required that, affirmatively, a zoning regulation, like any police power enactment, must promote public health, safety, morals or the general welfare. (The last term seems broad enough to encompass the others.) Conversely, a zoning enactment which is contrary to the general welfare is invalid. [ ] Indeed these considerations are specifically set forth in the zoning enabling act as among the various purposes of zoning for which regulations must be designed. [ ] Their inclusion therein really adds little; the same requirement would exist even if they were omitted. If a zoning regulation violates the enabling act in this respect, it is also theoretically invalid under the state constitution. We say "theoretically" because, as a matter of policy, we do not treat the validity of most land use ordinance provisions as involving matters of constitutional dimension; that classification is confined to major questions of fundamental import. [ ] We consider the basic importance of housing and local regulations restricting its availability to substantial segments of the population to fall within the latter category.

* * *

This brings us to the relation of housing to the concept of general welfare * * * and the result in terms of land use regulation which that relationship mandates. There cannot be the slightest doubt that shelter, along with food, are the most basic-human needs. * * *

It is plain beyond dispute that proper provision for adequate housing of all categories of people is certainly an absolute essential in promotion of the general welfare required in all local land use regulation. Further the universal and constant need for such housing is so important and of such broad public interest that the general welfare which developing municipalities like Mount Laurel must consider extends beyond their boundaries and cannot be parochially confined to the claimed good of the particular municipality. It has to follow that, broadly speaking, the presumptive obligation arises for each such municipality affirmatively to plan and provide, by its land use regulations, the reasonable opportunity for an appropriate variety and choice of housing, including, of course, low and moderate cost housing, to meet the needs, desires and resources of all categories of people who may desire to live within its boundaries. Negatively, it may not adopt regulations or policies which thwart or preclude that opportunity.

It is also entirely clear, as we pointed out earlier, that most developing municipalities, including Mount Laurel, have not met their affirmative or negative obligations, primarily for local fiscal reasons. * * *

In sum, we are satisfied beyond any doubt that, by reason of the basic importance of appropriate housing and the long-standing pressing need for it, especially in the low and moderate cost category, and of the exclusionary zoning practices of so many municipalities, * * * judicial attitudes must be altered from that espoused in that and other cases cited earlier, to require, as we have just said, a broader view of the general welfare and the presumptive obligation on the part of developing municipalities at least to afford the opportunity by land use regulations for appropriate housing for all.

We have spoken of this obligation of such municipalities as "presumptive." The term has two aspects, procedural and substantive. Procedurally, we think the basic importance of appropriate housing for all dictates that, when it is shown that a developing municipality in its land use regulations has not made realistically possible a variety and choice of housing, including adequate provision to afford the opportunity for low and moderate income housing or has expressly prescribed requirements or restrictions which preclude or substantially hinder it, a facial showing of violation of substantive due process or equal protection under the state constitution has been made out and the burden, and it is a heavy one, shifts to the municipality to establish a valid basis for its action or non-action. [ ] The substantive aspect of "presumptive" relates to the specifics, on the one hand, of what municipal land use regulation provisions, or the absence thereof, will evidence invalidity and shift the burden of proof and, on the other hand, of what bases and considerations will carry the municipality's burden and sustain what it has done or failed to do. Both kinds of specifics may well vary between municipalities according to peculiar circumstances.

* * *

III

THE REMEDY

As outlined at the outset of this opinion, the trial court invalidated the zoning ordinance in toto and ordered the township to make certain studies and investigations and to present to the court a plan of affirmative public action designed "to enable and encourage the satisfaction of the indicated needs" for township related low and moderate income housing. Jurisdiction was retained for judicial consideration and approval of such a plan and for the entry of a final order requiring its implementation.

We are of the view that the trial court's judgment should be modified in certain respects. We see no reason why the entire zoning ordinance should be nullified. Therefore we declare it to be invalid only to the extent and in the particulars set forth in this opinion. The township is granted 90 days from the date hereof, or such additional time as the trial court may find it reasonable and necessary to allow, to adopt amendments to correct the deficiencies herein specified. It is the local function and responsibility, in the first instance at least, rather than the court's, to decide on the details of the same within the guidelines we have laid down. If plaintiffs desire to attack such amendments, they may do so by supplemental complaint filed in this cause within 30 days of the final adoption of the amendments.

We are not at all sure what the trial judge had in mind as ultimate action with reference to the approval of a plan for affirmative public action concerning the satisfaction of indicated housing needs and the entry of a final order requiring implementation thereof. Courts do not build housing nor do municipalities. That function is performed by private builders, various kinds of associations, or, for public housing, by special agencies created for that purpose at various levels of government. The municipal function is initially to provide the opportunity through appropriate land use regulations and we have spelled out what Mount Laurel must do in that regard. It is not appropriate at this time, particularly in view of the advanced view of zoning law as applied to housing laid down by this opinion, to deal with the matter of the further extent of judicial power in the field or to exercise any such power. * * *

The judgment of the Law Division is modified as set forth herein. No costs.

SOUTHERN BURLINGTON COUNTY N.A.A.C.P.
v. TOWNSHIP OF MOUNT LAUREL

Supreme Court of New Jersey, 1983.
92 N.J. 158, 456 A.2d 390.

WILENTZ, C.J.

This is the return, eight years later, of *Southern Burlington County N.A.A.C.P. v. Township of Mount Laurel*, 67 *N.J.* 151, 336 A.2d 713 (1975) (*Mount Laurel I*). We set forth in that case, for the first time, the doctrine requiring that municipalities' land use regulations provide a realistic opportunity for low and moderate income housing. The doctrine has become famous. The *Mount Laurel* case itself threatens to become infamous. After all this time, ten years after the trial court's initial order invalidating its zoning ordinance, Mount Laurel remains afflicted with a blatantly exclusionary ordinance. Papered over with studies, rationalized by hired experts, the ordinance at its core is true to nothing but Mount Laurel's determination to exclude the poor. Mount Laurel is not alone; we believe that there is widespread non-compliance with the constitutional mandate of our original opinion in this case.

To the best of our ability, we shall not allow it to continue. This Court is more firmly committed to the original *Mount Laurel* doctrine than ever, and we are determined, within appropriate judicial bounds, to make it work. The obligation is to provide a realistic opportunity for housing, not litigation. We have learned from experience, however, that unless a strong judicial hand is used, *Mount Laurel* will not result in housing, but in paper, process, witnesses, trials and appeals. We intend by this decision to strengthen it, clarify it, and make it easier for public officials, including judges, to apply it.

This case is accompanied by five others, heard together and decided in this opinion. All involve questions arising from the *Mount Laurel* doctrine. They demonstrate the need to put some steel into that doctrine. The deficiencies in its application range from uncertainty and inconsistency at the trial level to inflexible review criteria at the appellate level. The waste of judicial energy involved at every level is substantial and is matched only by the often needless expenditure of talent on the part of lawyers and experts. The length and complexity of trials is often outrageous, and the expense of litigation is so high that a real question develops whether the municipality can afford to defend or the plaintiffs can afford to sue.

There is another side to the story. We believe, both through the representations of counsel and from our own research and experience, that the doctrine has done some good, indeed, perhaps substantial good. We have tried to make the doctrine clearer for we believe that most municipal officials will in good faith strive to fulfill their constitutional duty. There are a number of municipalities around the State that have responded to our decisions by amending their zoning ordinances to provide realistic opportunities for the construction of low and moderate income housing. Further, many other municipalities have at least recognized their obligation to provide such opportunities in their ordinances and master plans. Finally, state and county government agencies have responded by preparing regional housing plans that help both the courts and municipalities themselves carry out the *Mount Laurel* mandate. Still, we are far from where we had hoped to be and nowhere near where we should be with regard to the administration of the doctrine in our courts.

These six cases not only afford the opportunity for, but demonstrate the necessity of reexamining the *Mount Laurel* doctrine. We do so here. The doctrine is right but its administration has been ineffective.

A brief statement of the cases may be helpful at this point. *Mount Laurel II* results from the remand by this Court of the original *Mount Laurel* case. The municipality rezoned, purportedly pursuant to our instructions, a plenary trial was held, and the trial court found that the rezoning constituted a bona fide attempt by Mount Laurel to provide a realistic opportunity for the construction of its fair share of the regional lower income housing need. Reading our cases at that time (1978) as requiring no more, the trial court dismissed the complaint of the N.A.A.C.P. and other plaintiffs but granted relief in the form of a builder's remedy, to a developer-intervenor who had attacked the total prohibition against mobile homes. Plaintiffs' appeal of the trial court's ruling sustaining the ordinance in all other respects was directly certified by this Court, as ultimately was defendant's appeal from the grant of a builder's remedy allowing construction of mobile homes. We reverse and remand to determine Mount Laurel's fair share of the regional need and for further proceedings to revise its ordinance; we affirm the grant of the builder's remedy.

* * *

I.

BACKGROUND

A. History of the Mount Laurel Doctrine

In *Mount Laurel I,* this Court held that a zoning ordinance that contravened the general welfare was unconstitutional. We pointed out that a developing municipality violated that constitutional mandate by excluding housing for lower income people; that it would satisfy that constitutional obligation by affirmatively affording a realistic opportunity for the construction of its fair share of the present and prospective regional need for low and moderate income housing. [ ] This is the core of the *Mount Laurel* doctrine. Although the Court set forth important guidelines for implementing the doctrine, their application to particular cases was complex, and the resolution of many questions left uncertain. Was it a "developing" municipality? What was the "region," and how was it to be determined? How was the "fair share" to be calculated within that region? Precisely what must that municipality do to "affirmatively afford" an opportunity for the construction of lower income housing? Other questions were similarly troublesome. When should a court order the granting of a building permit (*i.e.,* a builder's remedy) to a plaintiff-developer who has successfully challenged a zoning ordinance on *Mount Laurel* grounds? How should courts deal with the complicated procedural aspects of *Mount Laurel* litigation, such as the appointment of experts and masters, the joinder of defendant municipalities, and the problem of interlocutory appeals? These have been the principal questions that New Jersey courts have faced in attempting to implement the *Mount Laurel* mandate, and the principal questions dealt with in this opinion. * * *

B. Constitutional Basis for Mount Laurel and the Judicial Role

The constitutional basis for the *Mount Laurel* doctrine remains the same. The constitutional power to zone, delegated to the municipalities subject to legislation, is but one portion of the police power and, as such, must be exercised for the general welfare. When the exercise of that power by a municipality affects something as fundamental as housing, the general welfare includes more than the welfare of that municipality and its citizens: it also includes the general welfare—in this case the housing needs—of those residing outside of the municipality but within the region that contributes to the housing demand within the municipality. Municipal land use regulations that conflict with the general welfare thus defined abuse the police power and are unconstitutional. In particular, those regulations that do not provide the requisite opportunity for a fair share of the region's need for low and moderate income housing conflict with the general welfare and violate the state constitutional requirements of substantive due process and equal protection.

* * *

It would be useful to remind ourselves that the doctrine does not arise from some theoretical analysis of our Constitution, but rather from underlying concepts of fundamental fairness in the exercise of governmental power. The basis for the constitutional obligation is simple: the State controls the use of land, *all* of the land. In exercising that control it cannot favor rich over poor. It cannot legislatively set aside dilapidated housing in urban ghettos for the poor and decent housing elsewhere for everyone else. The government that controls this land represents everyone. While the State may not have the ability to eliminate poverty, it cannot use that condition as the basis for imposing further disadvantages. And the same applies to the municipality, to which this control over land has been constitutionally delegated.

* * *

Subject to the clear obligation to preserve open space and prime agricultural land, a builder in New Jersey who finds it economically feasible to provide decent housing for lower income groups will no longer find it governmentally impossible. Builders may not be able to build just where they want—our parks, farms, and conservation areas are not a land bank for housing speculators. But if sound planning of an area allows the rich and middle class to live there, it must also realistically and practically allow the poor. And if the area will accommodate factories, it must also find space for workers. The specific location of such housing will of course continue to depend on sound municipal land use planning.

While *Mount Laurel I* discussed the need for "an appropriate variety and choice of housing," [ ], the specific constitutional obligation addressed there, as well as in our opinion here, is that relating to low and moderate income housing. [ ] All that we say here concerns that category alone; the doctrine as we interpret it has no present applicability to other kinds of housing. [ ] It is obvious that eight years after *Mount Laurel I* the need for satisfaction of this doctrine is greater than ever. Upper and middle income groups may search with increasing difficulty for housing within their means; for low and moderate income people, there is nothing to search for.

No one has challenged the *Mount Laurel* doctrine on these appeals. Nevertheless, a brief reminder of the judicial role in this sensitive area is appropriate, since powerful reasons suggest, and we agree, that the matter is better left to the Legislature. We act first and foremost because the Constitution of our State requires protection of the interests involved and because the Legislature has not protected them. We recognize the social and economic controversy (and its political consequences) that has resulted in relatively little legislative action in this field. We understand the enormous difficulty of achieving a political consensus that might lead to significant legislation enforcing the constitutional mandate better than we can, legislation that might completely remove this Court from those controversies. But enforcement of constitutional rights cannot await a supporting political consensus. So while we have always preferred legislative to judicial action in this field, we shall continue—until the Legislature acts—to do our best to uphold the constitutional obligation that underlies the *Mount Laurel* doctrine. That is our duty. We may not build houses, but we do enforce the Constitution.

* * *

C. Summary of Rulings

Our rulings today have several purposes. First, we intend to encourage voluntary compliance with the constitutional obligation by defining it more clearly. We believe that the use of the State Development Guide Plan and the confinement of all *Mount Laurel* litigation to a small group of judges, selected by the Chief Justice with the approval of the Court, will tend to serve that purpose. Second, we hope to simplify litigation in this area. While we are not overly optimistic, we think that the remedial use of the SDGP may achieve that purpose, given the significance accorded it in this opinion. Third, the decisions are intended to increase substantially the effectiveness of the judicial remedy. In most cases, upon determination that the municipality has not fulfilled its constitutional obligation, the trial court will retain jurisdiction, order an immediate revision of the ordinance (including, if necessary, supervision of the revision through a court appointed master), and require the use of effective affirmative planning and zoning devices. The long delays of interminable appellate review will be discouraged, if not completely ended, and the opportunity for low and moderate income housing found in the new ordinance will be as realistic as judicial remedies can make it. We hope to achieve all of these purposes while preserving the fundamental legitimate control of municipalities over their own zoning and, indeed, their destiny.

* * *

[The Court summarized its rulings: every municipality has an obligation to provide housing opportunities for at least some of its residents as well as nonresidents desiring to move in; the fair share obligation extends to all municipalities in state-designated "growth areas," not just "developing" municipalities; results, not merely good faith attempts, are required; affirmative action may be necessary; providing least cost housing is acceptable only if all other alternatives have been unsuccessful; builder's remedies will be afforded on a case-by-case basis, and future Mount Laurel litigation will be assigned only to a panel of judges selected by the Court.—Eds.]

II.

RESOLUTION OF THE ISSUES

A. Defining the Mount Laurel Obligation

* * *

The Constitution of the State of New Jersey does not require bad planning. * * * There is nothing in our Constitution that says that we cannot satisfy our constitutional obligation to provide lower income housing and, at the same time, plan the future of the state intelligently.

Sound planning requires that municipalities containing "growth areas" have a *Mount Laurel* obligation and that, together, all of those municipalities affirmatively provide a realistic opportunity for the construction of sufficient lower income housing to meet the needs of New Jersey's lower income population. * * *

* * *

As noted before, *all* municipalities' land use regulations will be required to provide a realistic opportunity for the construction of their fair share of the region's present lower income housing need generated by present dilapidated or overcrowded lower income units, including their own. Municipalities located in "growth areas" may, of course, have an obligation to meet the present need of the region that goes far beyond that generated in the municipality itself; there may be some municipalities, however, in growth areas where the portion of the region's present need generated by that municipality far exceeds the municipality's fair share. The portion of the region's present need that must be addressed by municipalities in growth areas will depend, then, on conventional fair share analysis, some municipality's fair share being more than the present need generated within the municipality and in some cases less. In non-growth areas, however (limited growth, conservation, and agricultural), no municipality will have to provide for more than the present need generated within the municipality, for to require more than that would be to induce growth in that municipality in conflict with the SDGP.

* * *

C. Calculating Fair Share

The most troublesome issue in *Mount Laurel* litigation is the determination of fair share. It takes the most time, produces the greatest variety of opinions, and engenders doubt as to the meaning and wisdom of *Mount Laurel*. Determination of fair share has required resolution of three separate issues: identifying the relevant region, determining its present and prospective housing needs, and allocating those needs to the municipality or municipalities involved. Each of these issues produces a morass of facts, statistics, projections, theories and opinions sufficient to discourage even the staunchest supporters of *Mount Laurel*. The problem is capable of monopolizing counsel's time for years, overwhelming trial courts and inundating reviewing courts with a record on review of superhuman dimensions.

We have had enough experience with *Mount Laurel* litigation to warrant procedural modifications designed, over a period of time, to simplify these determinations. The procedural modification provided in this opinion (confining all *Mount Laurel* litigation to a limited number of judges) is well within conventional judicial techniques.

* * *

As for fair share, however, we offer some suggestions. Formulas that accord substantial weight to employment opportunities in the municipality, especially new employment accompanied by substantial ratables, shall be favored; formulas that have the effect of tying prospective lower income housing needs to the present proportion of lower income residents to the total population of a municipality shall be disfavored; formulas that have the effect of unreasonably diminishing the share because of a municipality's successful exclusion of lower income housing in the past shall be disfavored.

In determining fair share, the court should decide the proportion between low and moderate income housing unless there are substantial reasons not to do so. The provisions and devices needed to produce moderate income housing may fall short of those needed for lower. Since there are two fairly distinct lower income housing needs, an effort must be made to meet both.

* * *

D. Meeting the Mount Laurel Obligation

1. Removing Excessive Restrictions and Exactions

In order to meet their Mount Laurel obligations, municipalities, at the very least, must remove all municipally created barriers to the construction of their fair share of lower income housing. Thus, to the extent necessary to meet their prospective fair share and provide for their indigenous poor (and, in some cases, a portion of the region's poor), municipalities must remove zoning and subdivision restrictions and exactions that are not necessary to protect health and safety.

* * *

2. Using Affirmative Measures

Despite the emphasis in *Mount Laurel I* on the *affirmative* nature of the fair share obligation, [ ] the obligation has been sometimes construed * * * as requiring in effect no more than a theoretical, rather than realistic, opportunity. As noted later, the alleged realistic opportunity for lower income housing in *Mount Laurel II* is provided through three zones owned entirely by three individuals. There is absolutely no assurance that there is anything realistic in this "opportunity": the individuals may, for many different reasons, simply not desire to build lower income housing. They may not want to build any housing at all, they may want to use the land for industry, for business, or just leave it vacant. It was never intended in *Mount Laurel I* that this awesome constitutional obligation, designed to give the poor a fair chance for housing, be satisfied by meaningless amendments to zoning or other ordinances. "Affirmative," in the *Mount Laurel* rule, suggests that the *municipality* is going to do something, and "realistic opportunity" suggests that what it is going to do will make it *realistically* possible for lower income housing to be built. Satisfaction of the *Mount Laurel* doctrine cannot depend on the inclination of developers to help the poor. It has to depend on affirmative inducements to make the opportunity real.

* * *

There are two basic types of affirmative measures that a municipality can use to make the opportunity for lower income housing realistic: (1) encouraging or requiring the use of available state or federal housing subsidies, and (2) providing incentives for or requiring private developers to set aside a portion of their developments for lower income housing. Which, if either, of these devices will be necessary in any particular municipality to assure compliance with the constitutional mandate will be initially up to the municipality itself. Where necessary, the trial court overseeing compliance may require their use. We note again that least-cost housing will not ordinarily satisfy a municipality's fair share obligation to provide low and moderate income housing unless and until it has attempted the inclusionary devices outlined below or otherwise has proven the futility of the attempt.

* * *

E.   Judicial Remedies

If a trial court determines that a municipality has not met its *Mount Laurel* obligation, it shall order the municipality to revise its zoning ordinance within a set time period to comply with the constitutional mandate; if the municipality fails adequately to revise its ordinance within that time, the court shall implement the remedies for noncompliance outlined below; and if plaintiff is a developer, the court shall determine whether a builder's remedy should be granted.

1.   Builder's Remedy

Builder's remedies have been one of many controversial aspects of the *Mount Laurel* doctrine. Plaintiffs, particularly plaintiff-developers, maintain that these remedies are (i) essential to maintain a significant level of *Mount Laurel* litigation, and the only effective method to date of enforcing compliance; (ii) required by principles of fairness to compensate developers who have invested substantial time and resources in pursuing such litigation; and (iii) the most likely means of ensuring that lower income housing is actually built. Defendant municipalities contend that even if a plaintiff-developer obtains a judgment that a particular municipality has not complied with *Mount Laurel*, that municipality, and not the developer, should be allowed to determine how and where its fair share obligation will be met.

In [Oakwood at Madison, Inc. v. Township of] *Madison*, this Court, while granting a builder's remedy to the plaintiff appeared to discourage such remedies in the future by stating that "such relief will ordinarily be rare." 72 *N.J.* at 551–52 n. 50, 371 *A.2d* 1192. Experience since *Madison*, however, has demonstrated to us that builder's remedies must be made more readily available to achieve compliance with *Mount Laurel*. We hold that where a developer succeeds in *Mount Laurel* litigation and proposes a project providing a substantial amount of lower income housing, a builder's remedy should be granted unless the municipality establishes that because of environmental or other substantial planning concerns, the plaintiff's proposed project is clearly contrary to sound land use planning. We emphasize that the builder's remedy should not be denied solely because the municipality prefers some other location for lower income housing, even if it is in fact a better site. Nor is it essential that considerable funds be invested or that the litigation be intensive.

Other problems concerning builder's remedies require discussion. Care must be taken to make certain that *Mount Laurel* is not used as an unintended bargaining chip in a builder's negotiations with the municipality, and that the courts not be used as the enforcer for the builder's threat to bring *Mount Laurel* litigation if municipal approvals for projects containing no lower income housing are not forthcoming. Proof of such threats shall be sufficient to defeat *Mount Laurel* litigation by that developer.

* * *

Notes and Questions

1. The *Mount Laurel* litigation became famous as the most vigorous judicial response to the phenomenon of "fiscal zoning"—zoning to attract activities such as commercial and light industrial uses that would increase the tax base, and to keep out people who would drain the tax base through increased pressure on public schools, local welfare agencies, public transit systems and the like. This practice also has been called "exclusionary zoning" because its effect is to increase the cost of housing, thereby reducing the ability of low-and moderate income persons to live in the community. See generally, M. Danielson, The Politics of Exclusion (1976); L. Rubinowitz, Low-income Housing: Suburban Strategies (1974); Branfman, Cohen and Trubeck, Measuring the Invisible Wall: Land Use Controls and the Residential Patterns of the Poor, 82 Yale L.J. 483 (1973); Williams and Norman, Exclusionary Land Use Controls: The Case of North–Eastern New Jersey, 22 Syracuse L.Rev. 475 (1971); Sager, Tight Little Islands: Exclusionary Zoning, Equal Protection and the Indigent, 21 Stanford L.Rev. 767 (1969).

An amicus curiae brief of the American Planning Association argued that:

> "Exclusionary zoning is particularly pernicious because lower income individuals are unable to find affordable housing near suburban places of work, necessitating lengthy commuting trips. As these areas typically have limited, if any, mass transit, the journey to work must be by automobile, creating additional economic hardship for lower income individuals."

Brief of American Planning Association, Wayne Britton v. Town of Chester, 595 A.2d 492 (N.H.1991), citing R. Babcock and F. Bosselman, Exclusionary Zoning: Land Use Regulation and Housing in the 1970s, 114–115 (1973).

2. Does the jurisprudence of *Mount Laurel* strike you as unusual, with its use of the state constitution and the "general welfare" principle? In cases we have studied, "general welfare" was used as a basis to keep out activities and people deemed harmful or undesirable. Here, is "general welfare" being used to allow people in? How can this be accomplished? Is general welfare being read not only as a limit on what government can do when it wants to act, but also as a substantive requirement for what it must do when it acts? When government decides to regulate the development of residential property, must it do so in a way that everyone in the community shares in the good in the same way—everyone in the community has an opportunity to obtain affordable and decent housing? Does this approach not assume a definition of what the community is? Does the court define the community? Should it, or should that be left to the legislative process? In the court's view, is the group to be considered limited to persons who own property in the jurisdiction, or does the group include all those who might choose to live there if regulatory barriers to affordable housing were removed?

3. Is it necessary to be concerned about standing to sue under the *Mount Laurel* court's approach? Persons challenging zoning decisions must be able to show that they have been affected by the zoning decision in some special way different from the general impact all zoning decisions may have on residents and taxpayers. This usually has been held to mean that the challenger must own property and be able to show that the zoning decision at issue harmed that property interest. One of the reasons that *Mount Laurel* was litigated in state courts is that federal courts have taken a very narrow view of the standing required to raise exclusionary zoning issues under the federal Constitution, refusing to consider complaints of persons who did not live or own property in the community whose regulations were being challenged. Warth v. Seldin, 422 U.S. 490, 95 S.Ct. 2197, 45 L.Ed.2d 343 (1975). See Housing for All Under Law 98–104 (R. Fishman ed. 1977) (Report of the American Bar Ass'n Advisory Comm'n on Housing and Urban Growth). See also D. Mandelker, Land Use Law 285, 287, 291–292 (2d Ed.1988).

Some state courts have taken a more relaxed view of standing issues in exclusionary zoning cases, primarily because of the fact that zoning is a delegation of the state's police power to be used to promote the general welfare of the citizens of the state. See, e.g., Britton v. Town of Chester, 595 A.2d 492 (1991) (low income residents who did not own property, along with nonprofit housing corporation, resident taxpayers and person who claimed he had to leave town to find housing had standing to challenge zoning as exclusionary), quoting the Supreme Court's recognition in *Euclid* of "the possibility of cases where the general public interest would so far outweigh the interest of the municipality that the municipality would not be allowed to stand in the way." 272 U.S. at 390. See also Home Builders League v. Township of Berlin, 81 N.J. 127, 405 A.2d 381 (1979) ("inherently fluid" standing rules in cases involving a "substantial public interest," along with state statute granting standing in zoning cases to nonresidents, held sufficient to grant standing to builders trade associations, nonprofit housing organizations and the "public" through the New Jersey Public Advocate). See generally D. Mandelker, Land Use Law 291–92, 316–322 (2d Ed.1988).

4. Why does the *Mount Laurel* court require a local government to look beyond its borders when implementing land use regulations? Is it because the police power is a state power, with the local authority acting only as a delegate of that power and being restricted in the same manner as is the state? Thus when a regulation has a substantial external effect, the welfare of the state's citizens beyond the borders of the particular municipality must be recognized and served? Are there any limits to this view? Must Mount Laurel, New Jersey consider the interests of residents of Philadelphia? Kansas City, Kansas the interests of Kansas City, Missouri? The governmental doctrine of home rule and the moral principal of subsidiary assume that the most effective use of governmental authority is at the level closest to the people directly affected. Is *Mount Laurel* consistent or inconsistent with this assumption? Planners and economists often talk of achieving "economies of scale" that come from operating on a larger rather than a smaller scale. Does *Mount Laurel* push in this direction?

5. What happens under the *Mount Laurel* doctrine when concerns about protecting the tax base or the environment clash with affordable housing needs? Does *Mount Laurel* favor affordable housing over the environment? Over lower tax rates? Or does it hold merely that environmental and tax-base arguments cannot be used to disguise efforts to exclude lower-income persons?

6. Suppose a municipality adopts an affordable housing plan in which it permits higher density, lower cost housing in certain areas of the community. May it adopt higher floor area and lot size requirements in the remaining residential areas, thereby increasing the cost of housing and keeping the rich and the poor separate? Does the "general welfare" require different economic classes to live together, as is the effect of federal law on segregation according to race, religion, sex, age, and family status?

In Builders Service Corp. Inc. v. Planning & Zoning Com'n., 208 Conn. 267, 545 A.2d 530 (1988), the Supreme Court of Connecticut held that local governments had authority to impose minimum floor-area requirements for dwelling units, but invalidated a 1300–square foot requirement that was higher than floor-area requirements in other residential districts in the municipality. The effect of the higher floor-area requirement was to increase the construction cost of a proposed three-bedroom ranch-style modular home with 1026 square feet of living space from $59,000 to $70,000 (over 18 percent). Experts agreed that minimum floor-area requirements that are not linked to the number of occupants can not be justified as promoting public health. Occupancy-based floor-area requirements assume each person needs about 150 square feet, so a three-bedroom house serving a family of six could be as small as 900 square feet before health questions would be raised. The municipality raised two main points in defense of the 1300–square foot requirement: 1) it has the beneficial effect of conserving property values; and 2) an affordable housing plan was in effect in other parts of the municipality. In rejecting the arguments, the Court said:

A regulation that may have some beneficial effect will not, ipso facto, be considered valid and consonant with the general welfare but, rather, inquiry must also be directed toward whatever detrimental effects a particular regulation has. A regulation that has some relationship to promoting the general welfare or some subset of that concept, such as public health, safety, property values or any of the declared purposes set out in the enabling act in § 8–2 would be valid if it does not at the same time promote or generate results that are contrary to the general welfare. "Where, however, a zoning [regulation], in addition to promoting legitimate zoning goals, also has effects contrary to the general welfare, closer scrutiny of the [regulation] and its effects must be undertaken. The fact that a [regulation] may have some adverse effect is not determinative." Home Builders League of South Jersey, Inc. v. Township of Berlin, 81 N.J. 127, 139, 405 A.2d 381, 387 (1979). Such a view is not unlike saying, as this court has: "The limit of the exercise of the police power is necessarily flexible, because it has to be considered in the light of the times and the prevailing conditions. State v. Hillman [supra, 110 Conn. at 105, 147 A. 294]." State v. Gordon, 143 Conn. 698, 703, 125 A.2d 477 (1956).

* * *

We recognize that an essential purpose of zoning regulation is to stabilize property uses. Nevertheless, "[t]he justification for zoning. * * * in any municipality is that it serves to promote the public health, safety, welfare and prosperity of the community." Devaney v. Board of Zoning Appeals, 132 Conn. 537, 539, 45 A.2d 828, 829 (1946). Conserving the value of buildings is only one facet of this archetypical justification for zoning * * *. Not only is the minimum floor area requirement in the plaintiffs' zone higher than in other residential zones of the town, but also we note that the plaintiffs put into evidence documents which demonstrated that the minimum floor area requirements for one-story, single-family detached houses in East Hampton are among the highest among all Connecticut towns and cities. That statistical evidence demonstrates that over 100 other towns and cities have lower minimum floor area requirements for one-story, single-family detached houses than East Hampton. In addition, we note that fifty other towns have no minimum floor area requirements at all.

* * *

In addressing the justification of this regulation because it conserves the value of buildings, we are bound by the trial court's conclusion that the expert testimony of Rowlson was "unconvincing," even though it is not entirely clear that that statement went to all of Rowlson's testimony or solely to his "multiple regression analysis." We observe that, in upholding this regulation, the trial court stressed that minimum floor requirements do indeed bear a direct relation to the cost of a house. The larger the house, the more likely its cost will be greater, the court said, and living in a more spacious home "will be more expensive due to higher taxes, mortgage payment and expenses. * * *" These are realistic observations which, however, raise serious questions in evaluating this regulation. The trial court has already, in effect, conceded that this minimum floor area regulation without reference to occupancy cannot pass rational relation muster on the ground of the promotion of public health, but suggests that what is bigger and costlier is compatible under the circumstances with conserving the value of buildings in this district. That, in turn, implicitly suggests two justifications for this regulation, both of which are questionable. First, most expensive single-family houses are more desirable and, second, more such houses generate more taxes from persons better able to pay more taxes with perhaps less demand upon municipal services.

* * *

* * * Despite the implications of the dissent, there is no reference by the trial court or the dissent itself to any evidence that the house intended to be built by the plaintiffs is "significantly undersized" as compared to any other house in the neighborhood or that it is akin to a mobile home or that it is aesthetically incompatible with other houses in the neighborhood.

Moreover, the trial court made no finding that smaller houses, and specifically this proposed house, would decrease or destabilize the value of buildings in this zone. To "conserve," ordinarily understood, means "to preserve." Webster's Third New International Dictionary. Here again, there is no finding by the trial court of what the value of buildings in the area of the zones subject to § 5.15 were so as to make a reasonable comparison with the plaintiffs' proposed house upon which to premise a conclusion that requiring that house to have a minimum floor area of 1300 square feet would not conserve the value of such buildings. * * *

* * *

Under all the circumstances, the trial court's determination in this case that the challenged "varying minima" regulation without reference to occupancy promotes a legitimate purpose of zoning in that it conserves the value of buildings cannot stand. That determination cannot be supported even giving the commission that deference to which it is due on such matters, which includes our obligation not to substitute our judgment for that of the local zoning authority. The absence of satisfying a proper objective of zoning raises serious concerns that the only possible justification for such varying minima is an intent to discriminate against those with moderate and lower incomes in that district. This form of denial of access to certain residential districts is unequivocally not a purpose authorized by § 8–2. That this is a realistic concern is also underscored by the testimony of defense witness Steven Tuckerman, the town planner for East Hampton from 1979 to 1985, who asserted that the "only justification" for the 1300 square foot minimum "would be to allow for a range of housing choice * * * [w]ithin the entire town." Forcing home buyers in one part of town to have bigger and more costly houses does not provide a choice of housing but rather prevents home buyers from exercising a choice as to the most appropriate housing for their individual means and needs.

* * *

We now reach the trial court's conclusion that "affordable housing" also served as a basis to sustain this regulation. It is evident from the trial court's memorandum of decision that, in finding that the regulation involved was valid, it rested its decision in part upon its determination that East Hampton, "through its zoning and other activities, provided for affordable housing." In this context, it said that there are "other" areas in the town which require less floor area for single-family houses and the floor area for multiple-family houses is "appreciably lower." * * *

The trial court's reliance on its "affordable housing" ground is not proper as a matter of law. Its reference to actions that the town has taken in other areas of East Hampton does not address the rationality and legality of the regulation under attack. * * *

* * *

* * * The trial court erred here because whether there is affordable housing in zones other than those impacted by this regulation is not legally significant. * * *

7. While the *Mount Laurel* cases have generated an enormous amount of discussion and have influenced courts and legislatures in a number of other states, particularly with respect to consideration of the extraterritorial effect of zoning decisions, the fact that the decisions were based on the New Jersey Constitution has limited the transferability of the doctrine to other states. See, e.g. Berenson v. Town of New Castle, 38 N.Y.2d 102, 378 N.Y.S.2d 672, 341 N.E.2d 236 (1975); Township of Williston v. Chesterdale Farms, 462 Pa. 445, 341 A.2d 466 (1975); Associated Home Builders v. City of Livermore, 18 Cal.3d 582, 135 Cal.Rptr. 41, 557 P.2d 473 (1976). Developments in New York and Pennsylvania, as well as other states are discussed in O. Browder, R. Cunningham, G. Nelson, W. Stoebuck & D. Whitman, Basic Property Law 1293–98 (5th Ed.1989). See also D. Mandelker, Land Use Law 292–304 (2d Ed.1988).

In a case with potential national impact, the Supreme Court of New Hampshire applied the *Mount Laurel* principles to the state's zoning enabling act and concluded that the zoning ordinance of a small suburban "bedroom" municipality which effectively limited residential development to single family homes on two-acre lots or duplexes on three acre lots exceeded the municipality's authority under the zoning enabling statute. Britton v. Town of Chester, 595 A.2d 492 (N.H.1991). The statute, based on the Standard State Zoning Enabling Act discussed in *Euclid* from which virtually all state enabling acts initially were drawn, authorized municipalities to zone property "to promote the health, safety, and general welfare of the community." The court's key decision was its conclusion that the term "community" was not equated with the territorial boundaries of the town.

RSA 674:16 authorizes the local legislative body of any city or town to adopt or amend a zoning ordinance "[f]or the purpose of promoting the health, safety, or the general welfare of the community." (Emphasis added.) The defendant asserts that the term "community" as used in the statute refers only to the municipality itself and not to some broader region in which the municipality is situated. We disagree.

The possibility that a municipality might be obligated to consider the needs of the region outside its boundaries was addressed early on in our land use jurisprudence by the United States Supreme Court, paving the way for the term "community" to be used in the broader sense. In Village of Euclid v. Ambler Realty Co., 272 U.S. 365, 47 S.Ct. 114, 71 L.Ed. 303 (1926), the Court recognized "the possibility of cases where the general public interest would so far outweigh the interest of the municipality that the municipality would not be allowed to stand in the way." Id. at 390. When an ordinance will have an impact beyond the boundaries of the municipality, the welfare of the entire affected region must be considered in determining the ordinance's validity.   * * *

Municipalities are not isolated enclaves, far removed from the concerns of the area in which they are situated. As subdivisions of the State, they do not exist solely to serve their own residents, and their regulations should promote the general welfare, both within and without their boundaries. Therefore, we interpret the general welfare provision of the zoning enabling statute [   ] to include the welfare of the "community", as defined in this case, in which a municipality is located and of which it forms a part. Britton v. Town of Chester, 595 A.2d 492 (N.H.1991).

Finding the exclusionary aspects of the town's land use regulations to be incompatible with the housing needs of low and moderate income persons in the "community" affected by the town's decisions, the court invalidated the town's zoning ordinance "in that it flies in the face of the general welfare provision" of the statute and "is, therefore, at odds with the statute upon which it is grounded." The Court did not reach constitutional questions raised by the plaintiffs.

8. As noted earlier, important remedy questions are raised in exclusionary zoning cases. What should a court do if it concludes that a zoning ordinance is invalid as exclusionary? Would an award of monetary damages be sufficient? How would it be calculated? To whom would it be paid? If persons who were excluded by the zoning ordinance do not own property in the community, what have they lost for which they can receive compensation? If the court invalidates the ordinance, does that mean the municipality becomes "unzoned" and loses its ability to regulate land? If not, can the municipality simply amend its ordinance in a minor way, say by reducing a two acre lot minimum to a one acre minimum and still effectively keep out affordable housing?

Courts generally do not order specific changes in a zoning ordinance because of concerns that such action would constitute judicial legislation in violation of constitutional separation of powers principles. See, e.g., Britton v. Town of Chester, 595 A.2d 492 (N.H.1991) "[I]t is not * * * within the power of this court to act as a super zoning board"). However, as discussed in Mount Laurel II, courts have been willing to grant a "builder's remedy" to enable a particular development plan to go forward so long as it complies with other valid local regulations. In Britton v. Town of Chester, 595 A.2d 492 (N.H.1991), the court concluded that the "builder's remedy" was "appropriate in this case, both to compensate the developer who has invested substantial time and resources in pursuing the litigation, and as the most likely means of insuring that low and moderate-income housing is actually built." In awarding the "builder's remedy," the court rejected the *Mount Laurel* approach that it characterized as requiring "the calculation of arbitrary mathematical quotes" in favor of an approach developed by the Illinois courts and adopted in Michigan, Ohio, Pennsylvania and Virginia. Under the Illinois approach, relief is awarded

> if development is found to be reasonable, i.e., providing a realistic opportunity for the construction of low and moderate-income housing and consistent with sound zoning concepts and environmental concerns. Once an existing zoning ordinance is found invalid in whole or in part, whether on constitutional grounds or, as here, on grounds of statutory construction and application, the court may provide relief in the form of a declaration that the plaintiff builder's proposed use is reasonable, and the municipality may not interfere with it. [ ] The plaintiff must bear the burden of proving reasonable use by a preponderance of the evidence. [ ] Once the plaintiff's burden has been met, he will be permitted to proceed with the proposed development, provided he complies with all other applicable regulations. [ ]

Britton v. Town of Chester, 595 A.2d 492 (N.H.1991). For additional discussion of remedies, see D. Mandelker, Land Use Law 332–335 (2d Ed.1988).

G. NON ADVERSARIAL RESOLUTION OF LAND USE DISPUTES

P. SALSICH, LAND USE REGULATION: PLANNING, ZONING, SUBDIVISION REGULATION, AND ENVIRONMENTAL CONTROL

414–416, 541–543 (1991).

§ 6.17 Resolution of Zoning Disputes Through Arbitration or Mediation

A number of jurisdictions are experimenting with various "early warning" techniques to resolve zoning disputes before they escalate into major litigation over whether a particular regulatory decision has "taken" property in a constitutional sense. Examples of such techniques include the use of negotiation between landowners and landmarks preservation boards to seek agreement on appropriate "controls and incentives" to preserve property receiving landmark designation while allowing the owner a reasonable return on investment, and the use of a two-step mediation/arbitration process to resolve disputes regarding appropriate rental increases under rent control ordinances.

The New Jersey Fair Housing Act, enacted in response to the *Mount Laurel* cases, establishes a mediation process for the resolution of disputes regarding certain decisions of the Council on Affordable Housing, a state agency established to determine housing regions, estimate housing need, and establish criteria for determining municipal fair share requirements under the *Mount Laurel* principles. The council is required to engage in mediation in the following situations:

(1) when timely objections are filed to a municipality's proposed substantive certification that its fair share plan and housing element meet the requirements of the Act; or

(2) whenever exclusionary zoning litigation has been instituted against a municipality that has filed a fair share plan and housing element, or has filed a timely resolution of intent to participate in the fair share determination process. NJ Stat Ann § 52:27D–315 (West 1986).

In the latter case, the statute treats the mediation process as an administrative remedy that must be exhausted before a trial on the complaint may be obtained. If objections cannot be resolved through the mediation process, the case is referred to an administrative law judge, who hears it in an expedited manner as a contested matter. The administrative law judge makes an initial decision and forwards that initial decision to the council, which make the final administrative decision on the matter. If the review and mediation process is not completed within six months of receipt of a request for mediation from a party who has instituted litigation, the party may be relieved of the obligation to exhaust administrative remedies upon motion to a court of competent jurisdiction.

The Supreme Court of New Jersey upheld the constitutionality of the Act in *Hills Development Co. v. Bernards Township*, 103 NJ 1, 510 A2d 621 (1986) (*Mount Laurel III*). With respect to the use of mediation prior to litigation when cities have filed fair share plans, the Court made the following observation:

In any lawsuit attacking a municipality's ordinances that have received substantive certification as not in compliance with the Mount Laurel constitutional obligation, the plaintiff will be required to prove such noncompliance by clear and convincing evidence, and the Council shall be made a party to any such lawsuit. § 17a. The difficulties facing any plaintiff attempting to meet such a burden of proof are best understood by noting the variety of methodologies that can be used legitimately to determine regional need and fair share as well as the many different ways in which a realistic opportunity to achieve that fair share may be provided. If the Council conscientiously performs its duties, including determining regional need and evaluating whether the proposed adjustments and ordinances provide the requisite fair share opportunity, a successful Mount Laurel lawsuit should be a rarity. There is therefore a broad range of municipal action that will withstand challenge, given this burden of proof. 510 A2d 621, 639 (1986).

Mediation as an approach to resolution of zoning disputes has been suggested as part of a governmental "accommodation power" which can serve as a "middle ground" between use of eminent domain (taking with compensation) and police power regulation (no compensation).

The accommodation power would be triggered whenever governmental control denied a landowner "reasonable beneficial use" or "adequate return," giving rise to options such as a variance, payment for the difference in value between the controlled value and the reasonable beneficial use value, or payment in non-dollar values such as transfer of development rights. Mediation and the accommodation power may offer "a flexibility [to some forms of land use dispute] which can ease the conflict between the public and the private owner." Proponents of accommodation argue that it has potential in cases involving particular buildings, such as landmarks preservation, but doubt its ability to achieve much in disputes over environmental protection or resource preservation. They stress that the essential balancing process of "public benefit versus private detriment" cannot be reduced to "metric measure," but argue that the public can expect that "the process be open, that it be fair, that whenever possible it seek to accommodate." Berger, *The Accommodation Power in Land Use: A Reply to Professor Costonis*, 76 Colum.L.Rev. 799, 800–01, 817, 821–23 (1976) (commenting on Costonis, *"Fair" Compensation and the Accommodation Power: Antidotes for the Takings Impasse in Land Use Controversies*, 75 Colum.L.Rev. 1021 (1975)).

* * *

§ 9.08—Zoning Override Legislation

One of the first states to respond legislatively to the exclusionary zoning phenomenon was Massachusetts when it enacted its celebrated *anti-snob* law in 1969. Mass Gen Laws Ann ch 40B, §§ 20–23 (Law Co-op 1983 & Supp 1991). For reviews of the operation of the Massachusetts statute, see Resnick, *Mediating Affordable Housing Disputes in Massachusetts: Optimal Intervention Points*, 45 Arb J No 2, at 15 (June 1990); Taub, *The Future of Affordable Housing*, 22 Urb Law 659, 664 (1990). Rather than mandating affordable housing set-asides or authorizing density bonuses, the anti-snob law established a housing appeals committee in the state department of community affairs with authority to override local zoning decisions blocking low- or moderate-income housing developments, defined as housing subsidized by any federal or state housing production program.

Under the act, public agencies and private organizations proposing to build low- and moderate-income housing may by-pass local regulatory agencies by submitting a single application to the local zoning board of appeals, which is responsible for coordinating an analysis of the application by interested regulatory agencies, conducting a public hearing, and making a decision regarding the application. Comprehensive permits or approvals may be issued by the board of appeals, which must act within 40 days after termination of the public hearing.

If the application is denied or approved with conditions that make the project uneconomic, the developer may appeal to the state housing appeals committee, with the issue being whether the decision is reasonable and consistent with local needs. The statute provides that requirements or regulations are consistent with local needs if they are imposed after a comprehensive hearing in one of the following two situations: (1) more than 10 per cent of the housing units, or at least 1.5 per cent of the total land area zoned for residential, commercial, or industrial use in the municipality is low- or moderate-income housing; or (2) the proposal would result in low- or moderate-income housing construction starts on more than .3 per cent of the land area, or 10 acres, whichever is larger, in a calendar year.

If the state housing appeals committee concludes that the local zoning decision was not consistent with local needs, it vacates the decision and orders a comprehensive permit or approval to be issued, provided that the proposed housing would not violate safety standards contained in federal or state building and site plan requirements.

Housing advocates report that the state housing appeals committee has been aggressive in enforcing the spirit as well as the text of the law. As of January 1, 1989, more than 35,000 units of affordable housing had been proposed and 17,000 units built since the enactment of the statute. Resnick, *Mediating Affordable Housing Disputes in Massachusetts: Optimal Intervention Points,* 45 Arb J No 2, 15, 20 (June 1990). Mediation services offered by the Massachusetts Mediation Service, a state agency, have been instrumental in resolving about 25 per cent of cases appealed to the state housing appeals committee.

PROBLEM

Northfield Partnership announced plans to develop a 23–acre tract at the intersection of two thoroughfares in a rapidly growing suburban community into a 460–unit apartment complex for moderate and middle-income persons. The apartments were expected to appeal to young married couples, "empty nesters" and "on the go" persons and couples between the ages of 50 and 65. Rents were to be in the $450—$600/month range. Thirteen acres were zoned for multi-family use, while the remaining ten acres were zoned for light commercial and office use. Northfield filed an application to rezone the commercial acreage to multi-family use.

A group of homeowners who live adjacent to the site in $100,000–$150,000 homes have filed petitions opposing the rezoning and have persuaded the local council member to introduce an ordinance rezoning the entire tract to single-family use except for a five-acre commercial strip at the intersection. The homeowners are concerned about the size of the development, its impact on badly overcrowded streets in the area, the obvious difference in economic status between the homeowners and the expected apartment residents, the project plans which called for rows of "boxy" townhouses encircling a common area, and the lack of effective buffers between the existing houses and the proposed development.

The controversy has begun to heat up in the press. A newly elected councilwoman has consulted you for advice concerning the possibility of seeking a mediated settlement "before the controversy gets out of hand." What advice can you give her?

H. DOES ZONING SERVE A USEFUL PURPOSE?

From the beginning, zoning has had its share of critics. One of the most vocal has been Professor Bernard Siegan:

> "I submit that zoning is not entitled to constitutional protection. It is not necessary; it is not desirable, it is detrimental. It has no relationship to public health, safety, and welfare, except, on the whole, an adverse one. * * *" Siegan, Land Use Without Zoning 221 (1972), quoted in Wolf, The Prescience and Centrality of Euclid v. Ambler, Zoning and the American Dream 267 (C. Haar & J. Kayden eds. 1989).

What do you think your community would be like today without zoning? Houston, the last big-city holdout against zoning, succumbed in January, 1991 to a ground-swell of dissatisfaction with a private, market-based regulatory system and enacted an ordinance changing the name of the Houston Planning Commission to the Houston Planning and Zoning Commission, and directing the Commission to prepare a zoning plan for consideration by the City Council "to undo, or at least freeze, the effects of decades of laissez-faire building." Belkin, Now That City's Grown, They Plan, New York Times, February 10, 1991, at p. 14, col. 6.

Relatively affluent residential areas in Houston are regulated by private land use covenants and deed restrictions of the type discussed in Chapter Six supra. In other areas, though, single-family homes, garden apartments, high-rise condominiums, office towers and manufacturing plans exist side-by-side or in relative proximity. In an interesting land use regulatory wrinkle, Houston has followed the unusual practice of publicly enforcing private restrictions. The practice was upheld as serving a proper public purpose in Young v. City of Houston, 756 S.W.2d 813, 814 (Tex.App.1988).

Most local governments with comprehensive zoning and public subdivision regulation ordinances have not been willing to spend public money to enforce private residential covenants and deed restrictions, although zoning administrators often are requested to do so. Should they? Would a system of public enforcement of privately negotiated covenants and restrictions likely be more or less efficient, and more or less susceptible to political pressure, than the separate public and private systems?

Index

References are to Pages

†